IPv6 Core Protocols Implementation

The Morgan Kaufmann Series in Networking

Series Editor: David Clark, M.I.T.

IPv6 Core Protocols Implementation
Qing Li, Tatuya Jinmei, and Keiichi Shima

Smart Phone and Next-Generation Mobile Computing
Pei Zheng and Lionel Ni

GMPLS: Architecture and Applications
Adrian Farrel and Igor Bryskin

Network Security: A Practical Approach
Jan L. Harrington

Content Networking: Architecture, Protocols, and Practice
Markus Hofmann and Leland R. Beaumont

Network Algorithmics: An Interdisciplinary Approach to Designing Fast Networked Devices
George Varghese

Network Recovery: Protection and Restoration of Optical, SONET-SDH, IP, and MPLS
Jean Philippe Vasseur, Mario Pickavet, and Piet Demeester

Routing, Flow, and Capacity Design in Communication and Computer Networks
Michał Pióro and Deepankar Medhi

Wireless Sensor Networks: An Information Processing Approach
Feng Zhao and Leonidas Guibas

Communication Networking: An Analytical Approach
Anurag Kumar, D. Manjunath, and Joy Kuri

The Internet and Its Protocols: A Comparative Approach
Adrian Farrel

Modern Cable Television Technology: Video, Voice, and Data Communications, 2e
Walter Ciciora, James Farmer, David Large, and Michael Adams

Bluetooth Application Programming with the Java APIs
C Bala Kumar, Paul J. Kline, and Timothy J. Thompson

Policy-Based Network Management: Solutions for the Next Generation
John Strassner

Computer Networks: A Systems Approach, 3e
Larry L. Peterson and Bruce S. Davie

Network Architecture, Analysis, and Design, 2e
James D. McCabe

MPLS Network Management: MIBs, Tools, and Techniques
Thomas D. Nadeau

Developing IP-Based Services: Solutions for Service Providers and Vendors
Monique Morrow and Kateel Vijayananda

Telecommunications Law in the Internet Age
Sharon K. Black

Optical Networks: A Practical Perspective, 2e
Rajiv Ramaswami and Kumar N. Sivarajan

Internet QoS: Architectures and Mechanisms
Zheng Wang

TCP/IP Sockets in Java: Practical Guide for Programmers
Michael J. Donahoo and Kenneth L. Calvert

TCP/IP Sockets in C: Practical Guide for Programmers
Kenneth L. Calvert and Michael J. Donahoo

Multicast Communication: Protocols, Programming, and Applications
Ralph Wittmann and Martina Zitterbart

MPLS: Technology and Applications
Bruce Davie and Yakov Rekhter

High-Performance Communication Networks, 2e
Jean Walrand and Pravin Varaiya

Internetworking Multimedia
Jon Crowcroft, Mark Handley, and Ian Wakeman

Understanding Networked Applications: A First Course
David G. Messerschmitt

Integrated Management of Networked Systems: Concepts, Architectures, and their Operational Application
Heinz-Gerd Hegering, Sebastian Abeck, and Bernhard Neumair

Virtual Private Networks: Making the Right Connection
Dennis Fowler

Networked Applications: A Guide to the New Computing Infrastructure
David G. Messerschmitt

Wide Area Network Design: Concepts and Tools for Optimization
Robert S. Cahn

For further information on these books and for a list of forthcoming titles, please visit our Web site at http://www.mkp.com.

IPv6 Core Protocols Implementation

Qing Li
Blue Coat Systems, Inc.

Tatuya Jinmei
Toshiba Corporation

Keiichi Shima
Internet Initiative Japan, Inc.

AMSTERDAM • BOSTON • HEIDELBERG • LONDON
NEW YORK • OXFORD • PARIS • SAN DIEGO
SAN FRANCISCO • SINGAPORE • SYDNEY • TOKYO

Morgan Kaufmann Publishers is an imprint of Elsevier

Acquisitions Editor Rick Adams
Publishing Services Manager George Morrison
Production Editor Dawnmarie Simpson
Associate Acquisitions Editor Rachel Roumeliotis
Cover Design Eric DeCicco
Cover Image Side-by-Side Design
Cover Illustration Side-by-Side Design
Composition diacriTech
Technical Illustration diacriTech
Copyeditor JC Publishing
Proofreader Janet Cocker
Indexer Joan Green
Interior printer The Maple-Vail Book Manufacturing Group
Cover printer Phoenix Color Corporation

Morgan Kaufmann Publishers is an imprint of Elsevier.
500 Sansome Street, Suite 400, San Francisco, CA 94111

This book is printed on acid-free paper.

Library of Congress Cataloging-in-Publication Data
Li, Qing, 1971-
  IPv6 core protocols implementation/Qing Li, Tatuya Jinmei, Keiichi Shima
       p. cm.
  Includes bibliographical references and index.
  ISBN-13: 978-0-12-447751-3 (hardcover : alk. paper)
  ISBN-10: 0-12-447751-8 (hardcover : alk. paper) 1. TCP/IP (Computer network protocol) I.
Jinmei, Tatuya, 1971- II. Shima, Keiichi, 1970- III. Title.
  TK5105.585.L536 2007
  004.6'2–dc22

2006012796

ISBN 13: 978-0-12-447751-3
ISBN 10: 0-12-447751-8

For information on all Morgan Kaufmann publications,
visit our Web site at *www.mkp.com* or *www.books.elsevier.com*

Printed and bound by CPI Group (UK) Ltd, Croydon, CR0 4YY
Transferred to Digital Print 2012

To Huaying, Jane and Adalia
in Him
—Qing Li

To all those who have been involved in and supported the KAME project: sponsors, supervisors,
developers, contributors, and users.
—Tatuya Jinmei

To all KAME developers, all people who developed the Internet, and all people who will develop
the future Internet.
—Keiichi Shima

Contents

Foreword xix

Preface xxi

About the Authors xxix

Introduction 1

1.1 Introduction 1

1.2 A Brief History of IPv6 and KAME 1

    1.2.1 Commercial Success of KAME 6

1.3 Overview of the KAME Distribution 6

    1.3.1 Source Tree Structure 7

    1.3.2 Build Procedure 7

1.4 Overview of BSD Network Implementation 11

1.5 Source Code Narrations 14

    1.5.1 Typographical Conventions 14

    1.5.2 Sample Source Code Description 15

    1.5.3 Preprocessor Variables 16

    1.5.4 Networking Device and Architecture Assumptions 17

1.6 Mbufs and IPv6 17

    1.6.1 Common Mbuf Manipulation Macros and Functions 20

    1.6.2 Mbuf Tagging 20

    1.6.3 Mbuf Requirement for IPv6 24

    1.6.4 Diagnosing Mbuf Chain 26

2   IPv6 Addressing Architecture   29

2.1   Introduction   29

2.2   IPv6 Addresses   30

2.3   Textual Representation of IPv6 Addresses   31

2.4   Address Scopes   33

   2.4.1   Scope Zones   34

   2.4.2   Zone Indices   36

   2.4.3   Textual Representation of Scoped Addresses   38

   2.4.4   Deprecation of Unicast Site-local Addresses   39

2.5   IPv6 Address Format   40

   2.5.1   Interface Identifier Generation   42

   2.5.2   Notes about Address Format   43

   2.5.3   Multicast Address Format   44

2.6   Node Address Requirements   46

2.7   IPv6 Address Space Management   47

2.8   Code Introduction   47

   2.8.1   IPv6 Address Structures—`in6_addr{}` and
            `sockaddr_in6{}`   48

   2.8.2   Macros and Variables   49

2.9   Handling Scope Zones   51

   2.9.1   Initialization of Scope Zones   52

   2.9.2   Scope Zone IDs   53

   2.9.3   Zone IDs in Address Structures   54

   2.9.4   Scope-Related Utility Functions   57

2.10   Interface Address Structures   64

   2.10.1   `ifaddr{}` and `in6_ifaddr{}` Structures   64

   2.10.2   `in6_ifreq{}` and `in6_aliasreq{}` Structures   67

   2.10.3   Multicast Address Structures   68

2.11   IPv6 Prefix Structure   70

2.12   Overview of Address Manipulation Routines   73

2.13   Interface Initialization for IPv6   76

   2.13.1   `in6_if_up()` Function   76

   2.13.2   `in6_ifattach()` Function   78

   2.13.3   `in6_ifattach_loopback()` Function   81

   2.13.4   `in6_ifattach_linklocal()` Function   82

   2.13.5   `get_ifid()` Function   87

   2.13.6   `get_hw_ifid()` Function   89

   2.13.7   `get_rand_ifid()` Function   93

   2.13.8   `in6if_do_dad()` Function   94

2.14   IPv6 Interface Address Configuration   95
    2.14.1   `in6_control()` Function   95
    2.14.2   `in6_update_ifa()` Function   101
    2.14.3   `in6_joingroup()` and `in6_leavegroup()`
          Functions   115
    2.14.4   `in6_addmulti()` and `in6_delmulti()`
          Functions   116
    2.14.5   `in6_ifinit()` Function   118
    2.14.6   `in6_ifaddloop()` and `in6_ifloop_request()`
          Functions   120
2.15   Deleting an IPv6 Address   122
    2.15.1   `in6_purgeaddr()` Function   123
    2.15.2   `in6_ifremloop()` Function   124
    2.15.3   `in6_unlink_ifa()` Function   125
2.16   Operation with Address Configuration Utility   127

Internet Protocol version 6   131
3.1   Introduction   131
3.2   IPv6 Header Format   132
    3.2.1   Comparison to the IPv4 Header   133
3.3   IPv6 Extension Headers   134
    3.3.1   Order of Extension Headers   135
    3.3.2   Hop-by-Hop Options Header   136
    3.3.3   Destination Options Header   137
    3.3.4   Routing Header   137
    3.3.5   Fragment Header   140
    3.3.6   IPv6 Options   142
3.4   Source Address Selection   144
    3.4.1   Default Address Selection   144
    3.4.2   Source Address Selection   146
    3.4.3   Destination Address Selection   148
3.5   Code Introduction   149
    3.5.1   Statistics   151
    3.5.2   Header Structures   151
    3.5.3   `ip6protosw{}` Structure   157
3.6   IPv6 Packet Address Information in Mbuf   160
    3.6.1   `ip6_setdstifaddr()` Function   162
    3.6.2   `ip6_getdstifaddr()` Function   162

3.6.3   `ip6_setpktaddrs()` Function   163

3.6.4   `ip6_getpktaddrs()` Function   164

3.7   Input Processing: `ip6_input()` Function   164

3.8   Processing Hop-by-Hop Options Header: `ip6_hopopts_input()` Function   179

3.8.1   Processing Each Option: `ip6_process_hopopts()` Function   180

3.8.2   Processing Unknown Option: `ip6_unknown_opt()` Function   184

3.9   Processing Destination Options Header: `dest6_input()` Function   185

3.10   Reassembling Fragmented Packets   187

3.10.1   Structures for Packet Reassembly   187

3.10.2   `frag6_input()` Function   190

3.11   Processing Routing Header: `route6_input()` Function   204

3.12   Forwarding: `ip6_forward()` Function   209

3.13   Output Processing   219

3.13.1   Source Address Selection—`in6_selectsrc()` Function   219

3.13.2   Route Selection: `ip6_selectroute()` Function   234

3.13.3   `ip6_output()` Function   242

3.13.4   Make Extension Headers: `ip6_copyexthdr()` Function   276

3.13.5   Split Headers: `ip6_splithdr()` Function   277

3.13.6   Insert Jumbo Payload Option: `ip6_insert_jumboopt()` Function   278

3.13.7   Fragmentation: `ip6_insertfraghdr()` Function   281

3.13.8   Path MTU Determination: `ip6_getpmtu()` Function   282

3.13.9   Multicast Loopback: `ip6_mloopback()` Function   285

Internet Control Message Protocol for IPv6   287

4.1   Introduction   287

4.2   ICMPv6 Message   288

4.2.1   Destination Unreachable Message   289

4.2.2   Packet Too Big Message   291

4.2.3   Time Exceeded Message   292

4.2.4   Parameter Problem Message   293

4.2.5   Echo Request Message   294

4.2.6 Echo Reply Message 294

4.2.7 ICMPv6 Message Processing Rules 295

4.3 Path MTU Discovery Mechanism 296

4.4 Node Information Query 297

4.4.1 Node Information Message Format 299

4.4.2 NOOP Query 301

4.4.3 Supported Qtypes Query 301

4.4.4 Node Name Query 301

4.4.5 Node Addresses Query 303

4.4.6 IPv4 Addresses Query 304

4.5 Code Introduction 304

4.5.1 Statistics 304

4.5.2 ICMPv6 Header 308

4.6 ICMPv6 Input Processing 308

4.6.1 `icmp6_input()` Function 310

4.6.2 Notifying Errors: `icmp6_notify_error()` Function 320

4.7 Path MTU Discovery Implementation 329

4.7.1 `icmp6_mtudisc_update()` Function 329

4.8 ICMPv6 Output Processing 332

4.8.1 Sending Error: `icmp6_error()` Function 333

4.8.2 Error Rate Limitation: `icmp6_ratelimit()` Function 341

4.8.3 `icmp6_reflect()` Function 342

4.9 Node Information Query Implementation 348

4.9.1 Types and Variables 348

4.9.2 **ping6** Command: Send Queries 350

4.9.3 **ping6** Command: Receive Replies 355

4.9.4 **ping6** Command: Print Supported Qtypes 362

4.9.5 **ping6** Command: Print Node Addresses 365

4.9.6 Query Processing: `ni6_input()` Function 367

4.9.7 Node Name Manipulation 376

4.9.8 Create Node Addresses Reply: `ni6_store_addrs()` Function 383

4.10 Node Information Operation 387

Neighbor Discovery and Stateless Address Autoconfiguration 389

5.1 Introduction 389

5.2 Neighbor Discovery Protocol Overview 390

5.3   Stateless Address Autoconfiguration Overview   391

5.4   ND Protocol Messages   392

5.5   Example Exchanges of ND Protocol Messages   393

5.6   ND Protocol Packet Types and Formats   395

    5.6.1   Router Solicitation Message   396

    5.6.2   Router Advertisement Message   397

    5.6.3   Neighbor Solicitation Message   401

    5.6.4   Neighbor Advertisement Message   402

    5.6.5   Redirect Message   403

5.7   Neighbor Discovery Option Types and Formats   405

    5.7.1   Link-Layer Address Options   405

    5.7.2   Prefix Information Option   406

    5.7.3   Redirected Header Option   407

    5.7.4   MTU Option   407

    5.7.5   Route Information Option   408

5.8   Next-Hop Determination and Address Resolution   410

5.9   Neighbor Unreachability Detection Algorithm   411

5.10   Stateless Address Autoconfiguration   412

    5.10.1   Address Formation and Address States   413

    5.10.2   Duplicate Address Detection Algorithm   415

    5.10.3   Processing Router Advertisement   416

    5.10.4   Privacy Extensions   417

5.11   Router Specific Operation   419

    5.11.1   Sending Unsolicited Router Advertisements   422

    5.11.2   Processing Router Solicitations   422

    5.11.3   Processing Router Advertisements   423

5.12   Host Specific Operation   423

    5.12.1   Sending Router Solicitations   423

    5.12.2   Processing Router Advertisements   425

    5.12.3   Default Router Selection   426

5.13   Code Introduction   426

    5.13.1   ND Message Definitions   427

    5.13.2   Neighbor Cache—`llinfo_nd6{}` Structure   429

    5.13.3   Operational Variables—`nd_ifinfo{}` Structure   432

    5.13.4   Default Router—`nd_defrouter{}` Structure   433

    5.13.5   Prefix—`nd_prefix{}` Structure   434

    5.13.6   Prefix Control—`nd_prefixctl{}` Structure   436

    5.13.7   ND Message Options—`nd_opts{}` Structure   436

    5.13.8   DAD Queue Entry—`dadq{}` Structure   437

5.13.9 IPv6 Address—in6_ifaddr{} Structure 438

5.13.10 Destination Cache 438

5.13.11 Operation Constants 438

5.14 Initialization Functions 439

5.14.1 nd6_init() Function 439

5.14.2 nd6_ifattach() Function 440

5.15 Neighbor Cache Management Functions 441

5.15.1 nd6_rtrequest() Function 441

5.15.2 nd6_cache_lladdr() Function 452

5.15.3 nd6_lookup() Function 463

5.15.4 nd6_free() Function 467

5.15.5 nd6_timer() Function 470

5.16 ND Protocol Messages Processing Functions 478

5.16.1 nd6_ns_output() Function 478

5.16.2 nd6_ns_input() Function 484

5.16.3 nd6_na_input() Function 493

5.16.4 nd6_na_output() Function 504

5.16.5 nd6_rs_input() Function 510

5.16.6 nd6_ra_input() Function 513

5.16.7 icmp6_redirect_input() Function 521

5.16.8 icmp6_redirect_output() Function 528

5.17 ND Protocol Message Options Processing Functions 536

5.17.1 nd6_option_init() Function 536

5.17.2 nd6_option() Function 536

5.17.3 nd6_options() Function 538

5.18 Default Router Management Functions 540

5.18.1 defrouter_addreq() Function 540

5.18.2 defrouter_delreq() Function 541

5.18.3 defrouter_addifreq() Function 542

5.18.4 defrouter_delifreq() Function 544

5.18.5 defrouter_lookup() Function 545

5.18.6 defrouter_select() Function 546

5.18.7 defrtrlist_del() Function 550

5.18.8 defrtrlist_update() Function 553

5.19 Prefix Management Functions 555

5.19.1 nd6_prelist_add() Function 555

5.19.2 prelist_remove() Function 557

5.19.3 prelist_update() Function 558

5.19.4 `find_pfxlist_reachable_router()` Function 568

5.19.5 Prefix and Address State about On-link Condition 568

5.19.6 `pfxlist_onlink_check()` Function 571

5.19.7 `nd6_prefix_onlink()` Function 575

5.19.8 `nd6_prefix_offlink()` Function 578

5.20 Stateless Address Autoconfiguration Functions 580

5.20.1 `in6_ifadd()` Function 580

5.20.2 `in6_tmpifadd()` Function 584

5.20.3 `regen_tmpaddr()` Function 588

5.21 Duplicate Address Detection Functions 590

5.21.1 `nd6_dad_find()` Function 590

5.21.2 `nd6_dad_starttimer()` Function 590

5.21.3 `nd6_dad_stoptimer()` Function 590

5.21.4 `nd6_dad_start()` Function 591

5.21.5 `nd6_dad_stop()` Function 594

5.21.6 `nd6_dad_timer()` Function 594

5.21.7 `nd6_dad_duplicated()` Function 598

5.21.8 `nd6_dad_ns_output()` Function 599

5.21.9 `nd6_dad_ns_input()` Function 600

5.21.10 `nd6_dad_na_input()` Function 601

5.22 Miscellaneous Functions 602

5.22.1 `nd6_is_addr_neighbor()` Function 602

5.22.2 `nd6_output()` Function 604

5.22.3 `rt6_flush()` Function 611

5.22.4 `nd6_rtmsg()` Function 612

Transport Layer Implications 615

6.1 Introduction 615

6.2 TCP and UDP over IPv6 616

6.3 Pseudo Header for IPv6 616

6.4 Checksum Difference between IPv4 and IPv6 617

6.5 IPv4-mapped IPv6 Address Usage 618

6.6 Code Introduction 618

6.6.1 Protocol Control Blocks for IPv6 618

6.7 General Operations on PCBs and Sockets 627

6.7.1 IPv6 PCB Allocation—`in_pcballoc()` Function 627

6.7.2 Bind Local Address—`in6_pcbbind()` Function 630

6.7.3 Fix Remote Address—`in6_pcbconnect()` Function 639

6.7.4   Function `in6_pcbladdr()` 642

6.7.5   Search for a PCB Entry—`in6_pcblookup_local()`
         Function 644

6.7.6   Search for IPv4-mapped PCB—`in_pcblookup_local()`
         Function 647

6.7.7   Search for a PCB Entry—`in6_pcblookup_hash()`
         Function 650

6.7.8   Search for IPv4-mapped PCB—`in_pcblookup_hash()`
         Function 651

6.7.9   Detach an IPv6 PCB—`in6_pcbdetach()` Function 653

6.7.10   Control Message Signaling—`in6_pcbnotify()`
         Function 655

6.7.11   Flush PCB Cached Route—`in6_rtchange()`
         Function 659

6.7.12   Retrieve Peer Address—`in6_setpeeraddr()`
         Function 660

6.7.13   Retrieve Local Address—`in6_setsockaddr()`
         Function 662

6.8   TCP-over-IPv6 663

6.8.1   TCP-over-IPv6 Instance of `ip6protosw{}` 663

6.8.2   TCP Output 663

6.8.3   Initializing Headers—`tcp_fillheaders()` Function 669

6.8.4   TCP Input—`tcp6_input()` and `tcp_input()`
         Functions 670

6.8.5   TCP Control Input—`tcp6_ctlinput()` Function 675

6.8.6   TCP User Requests 678

6.9   UDP-over-IPv6 685

6.9.1   UDP-over-IPv6 Instance of `ip6protosw{}` 685

6.9.2   UDP Output—`udp6_output()` Function 685

6.9.3   UDP Input—`udp6_input()` Function 692

6.9.4   UDP Control Input—`udp6_ctlinput()` Function 699

6.9.5   UDP User Requests Handling 702

6.10   Raw IPv6 709

6.10.1   Raw IPv6 Statistics 709

6.10.2   Raw IPv6 Output—`rip6_output()` Function 710

6.10.3   Raw IPv6 Input—`rip6_input()` Function 715

6.10.4   ICMPv6 Input—`icmp6_rip6_input()` Function 719

6.10.5   Raw IPv6 Control Input—`rip6_ctlinput()`
         Function 724

6.10.6   Raw IPv6 Control Output—`rip6_ctloutput()`
            Function   725

6.10.7   Raw IPv6 User Requests Handling   730

6.11   Summary of Operation with IPv4-mapped IPv6 Addresses   738

6.12   Viewing IPv6 Connections with **netstat**   743

6.13   Configuring IPv4-mapped IPv6 Address Support   745

Socket API Extensions   747

7.1   Introduction   747

7.2   The Basic Socket API—[RFC3493]   748

7.2.1   Basic Definitions   748

7.2.2   Interface Identification   749

7.2.3   IPv4 Communication over `AF_INET6` Socket   750

7.2.4   Address and Name Conversion Functions   752

7.2.5   Basic Socket Options   760

7.3   The Advanced Socket API—[RFC3542]   764

7.3.1   Advanced Definitions   764

7.3.2   IPv6 Raw Sockets   766

7.3.3   Introduction to Ancillary Data   768

7.3.4   IPv6 Packet Information   770

7.3.5   Manipulation of IPv6 Extension Headers   773

7.3.6   Path MTU APIs   778

7.3.7   Socket Extensions for the "r" Commands   778

7.3.8   Summary Tables of Socket Options   780

7.4   Kernel Implementation of IPv6 Socket APIs   783

7.4.1   Code Introduction   783

7.4.2   `ip6_pktopts{}` Structure   786

7.4.3   IPv6 Socket Option Processing—`ip6_ctloutput()`
            Function   790

7.4.4   Getting Socket Options—`ip6_getpcbopt()`
            Function   805

7.4.5   Setting Socket Options and Ancillary Data   807

7.4.6   Cleaning Up—`ip6_freepcbopts()` Function   823

7.4.7   IPv6 Multicast Socket Options   824

7.4.8   IPv6 Raw Socket Options—`ip6_raw_ctloutput()`
            Function   835

7.4.9   ICMPv6 Socket Options—`icmp6_ctloutput()`
            Function   838

7.4.10 Delivering Incoming Information—`ip6_savecontrol()`
Function   840

7.5   Socket Options and Ancillary Data Examples   848

7.5.1   Example of the Send Path   848

7.5.2   Example of the Receive Path   850

7.6   Implementation of Library Functions—`libinet6`   853

7.6.1   `inet_pton()` and `inet_pton6()` Functions   853

7.6.2   `inet_ntop()` and `inet_ntop6()` Functions   859

7.6.3   `getaddrinfo()` Function   863

7.6.4   Address Ordering Examples   888

7.6.5   `freeaddrinfo()` Function   895

7.6.6   `gai_strerror()` Function   897

7.6.7   `getnameinfo()` Function   898

7.6.8   Other Library Functions   906

References   909

Index   915

Foreword

Back in 1994, when the IETF accepted the proposal that is known as IPv6 today, I was convinced from that moment, such a new fundamental protocol would be difficult if not impossible to be accepted, adopted and deployed by the networking community without a high-quality open-source reference implementation that is freely available.

This conviction stems from my close involvement with the original TCP/IPv4 protocols and UC Berkeley's BSD implementation of these protocols. I have seen first-hand how the BSD implementation has made enormous contribution to the success of TCP/IPv4, commonly known as the Internet protocols. We needed a new effort that played the same role for IPv6.

It was our turn to make a contribution to the world of the Internet from a developer's point of view, but at that time the economic impact of the Internet boom already made my colleagues at Berkeley too busy. I understood that we had a mission and so the IPv6 working group was born in the WIDE project for this purpose, which eventually evolved into the KAME project.

One of the requirements demanded of the software to be developed by the KAME project, was to demonstrate how the IPv6 protocols work and how well the protocols operate in real environments—a difficult and challenging task. With the long and very patient help from all the supporters, the KAME project members fulfilled this goal with their diligence and perseverance. The KAME implementation was adopted by all major BSD variants as the de-facto IPv6 implementation. And KAME is often referred to during IPv6 discussions at IETF meetings. I strongly believe the success of the KAME project played a significant role in the wide acceptance and the continued adoption of the IPv6 technology.

Part of my focus now shifts to the knowledge transfer aspect of technology adoption. Experience and wisdom must be shared with the new generation of engineers who will follow the foot steps of KAME and who will be the main users of KAME. While it is true that an established engineer can learn directly from the source code, a good "how-to" book with expert "know-how" would provide insights and guidance far beyond what the standards documents and the source code could ever offer.

Even though there are good learning materials about IPv6 widely available today, these are generally more readable versions of the protocol specifications. I have been longing for something different, one which facilitates a creative landscape for the next generation networking "hackers" to accomplish more in this new technology arena. And this book fills that void.

This book reveals all of the details of the KAME IPv6 protocol stack, explains every line of code about what exactly it does and why it was designed that way. By reading this book, you will gain profound understanding on the implementation as well as on IPv6 in general.

This book is the authoritative reference text on KAME and on IPv6, which fulfills many of the missing pieces not found in other books. I hope this book will become your primary and your only reference on IPv6.

Migration towards the eventual ubiquitous deployment of IPv6 is taking place, and I'm confident this book will be the "Internet Protocols" textbook of today.

Jun Murai, PhD
WIDE Project
Vice President of KEIO University

Preface

The KAME IPv6 implementation has been recognized as the de facto reference IPv6 implementation in academia as well as in the commercial world. Numerous researchers around the world base their IPv6 and next generation Internet research on KAME-enabled systems. The acceptance of KAME, however, transcends mere academic research and has become an integral part of many commercial products.

Our series of books detail the IPv6 and related protocols through the KAME implementation. Our books take the same approach as the *TCP/IP Illustrated* books written by W. Richard Stevens and Gary R. Wright, which bestowed invaluable insights into the internals of TCP/IPv4 networking upon the developer community in the 1990s. We aim to share with you our insights and development experience in KAME and on IPv6 in our series of books to help you jump start your endeavor into this brave new world of ubiquitous connectivity.

Today there are many books about IPv6; a search on Amazon resulted in dozens of books that contained IPv6 in their titles at the time of this writing. But our books are not just another set of books on IPv6. To the best of our knowledge, our series of books are the first and the only books of their kind, which delves into an actual IPv6 implementation that has been adopted by many open source as well as commercial operating systems, and dissects both the code and its design to illustrate how IPv6 and its related protocols have been interpreted and implemented from the standards. Our books will shed light on those ambiguous areas in the standards, which are open to interpretation, problematic in deployment, and subsequently present implementation challenges. Readers will gain an intrinsic understanding of how early implementation experiences help develop and mature a technology.

Book Organization

This book is the first of a two book series on IPv6 and related protocols. It covers core IPv6 protocols from specification to operation by means of thorough code narrations and illustrations on the internals of KAME.

This book discusses the fundamentals of the IPv6 protocol and features, the ICMPv6 protocol, considerations on transport layer issues such as TCP or UDP over IPv6, and socket extensions for developing IPv6-capable applications. The following list is a brief explanation of each chapter in this book.

- Chapter 1 (Introduction) offers a brief history of the KAME project; describes the components of the KAME distribution; explains the steps involved in building a KAME-enabled BSD system; and introduces the basics of the BSD networking system and KAME-derived enhancements to the base system.

- Chapter 2 (IPv6 Addressing Architecture) discusses the format and structure of various types of IPv6 addresses followed by code narration related to address configuration and manipulation.

- Chapter 3 (Internet Protocol version 6) discusses the protocol architecture of IPv6, extension headers, and the KAME implementation of handling IPv6 packet input and output at the IPv6 layer. It also introduces the default address selection algorithms for transmitting an IPv6 packet.

- Chapter 4 (Internet Control Message Protocol for IPv6) discusses the protocol architecture of ICMPv6, which is an integral part of the IPv6 operation. It describes the input and output functions for the basic ICMPv6 operation in the KAME implementation. As an interesting application of ICMPv6, this chapter also details the node information query protocol.

- Chapter 5 (Neighbor Discovery and Stateless Address Autoconfiguration) describes the Neighbor Discovery (ND) protocol. ND operates over ICMPv6 and offers various fundamental services such as link-layer address resolution, router discovery, and route redirection. Automatic address configuration services are also provided using the ND packets. This chapter explains the ND protocol and the Stateless Address Autoconfiguration procedure in great detail. It describes all major KAME kernel functions that relate to the operation of the ND protocol.

- Chapter 6 (Transport Layer Implications) describes modifications that have been made to TCP and UDP in order for the transport layer protocols to operate over IPv6. This chapter also illustrates the modifications to the BSD kernel implementation at the transport layer so that it can be dual-stack.

- Chapter 7 (Socket API Extensions) discusses the IPv6 extensions and enhancements that have been made to the socket APIs. This chapter also describes several standard user libraries that have been extended or created to support IPv6. It offers examples to illustrate how to write portable applications that can run on either IPv4 or IPv6 networks.

The second book of this series is titled *IPv6 Advanced Protocols Implementation* and offers the following list of topics.

- Chapter 1—IPv6 Unicast Routing Protocols
- Chapter 2—IPv6 Multicasting
- Chapter 3—DNS for IPv6
- Chapter 4—Dynamic Host Configuration Protocol for IPv6 (DHCPv6)

- Chapter 5—Mobile IPv6

- Chapter 6—IPv6 and IP Security

The figure below graphically depicts the coverage of the various aspects of IPv6 by these two books. We call this book "Book I" and the *Advanced Protocols* book "Book II."

These two books cover a number of protocol specifications, which are mainly published as Request for Comments (RFCs) and are mutually inter-related. The figure on the next page summarizes the relationship among the major RFCs covered in this book series and the chapters that describe the particular specification. The arrows show reference dependency between two particular specifications. For example, the arrow from RFC3041 to RFC2461 indicates the former refers to the latter.

Each chapter contains two main parts, each of which consists of one or two consecutive sections. The first part provides a digest of the main protocol specifications published as RFCs that are covered in that chapter. For a protocol chapter such as Chapters 3, 4, and 5, the first part describes the basic operations of specific protocols. The first part defines the various protocol packets, explains the meaning and the purpose of each field in each packet, and describes how the related protocol works with the packets. This part also tries to clarify ambiguous text in the RFCs where necessary.

The second part of each chapter concentrates on describing data structures and functions of KAME which implement the RFCs. Diagrams are provided to illustrate graphically the relationships among the various data structures. Function call graphs are provided to show code paths.

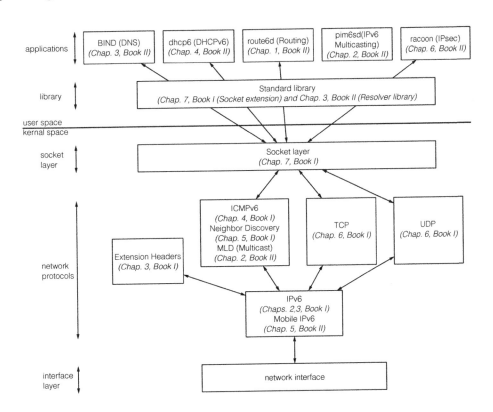

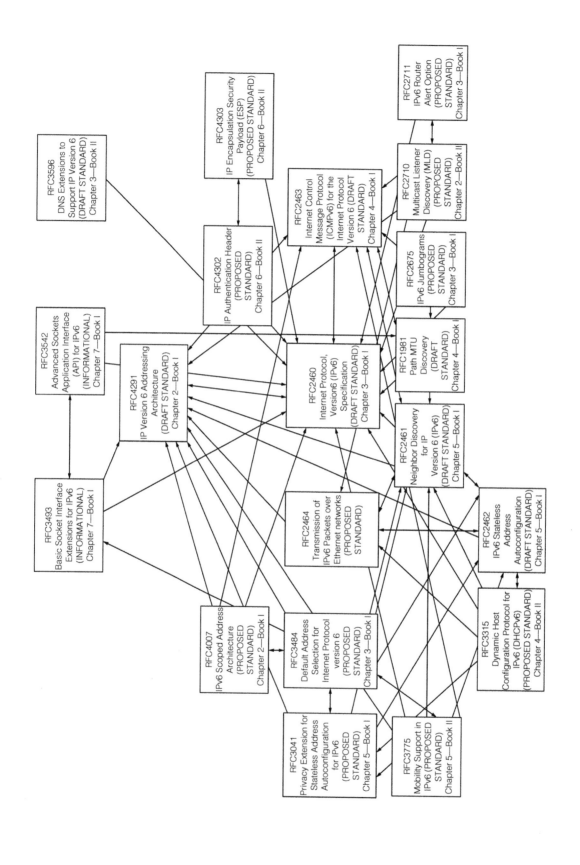

In this part, code narrations may also clarify the ambiguities that exist in the specifications, and also identify areas in the RFCs that are difficult to implement.

Some chapters have an additional trailing part. It describes useful utilities and demonstrates their usages, thereby highlighting how the implementation works in actual operation.

Intended Audience and How to Use this Book

This book can be used as a first book on IPv6 for those developers who are new to either IPv6 or KAME. This book will serve as a reference text for those developers who must either port or maintain KAME-based systems. This is the case for those BSD developers who must assume adoption of the KAME code and maintain and enhance KAME on different variants of BSD.

This book is also suitable as a textbook for an undergraduate senior level computing science course on IPv6 and related protocols. This book can also serve as a reference text of a project-based course on IPv6 for first-year graduate students. Instructors must set as prerequisites the fundamental computing science courses on computer networks, network programming, and a course on TCP/IP (optional). The students are also assumed to be fluent with the C programming language.

Readers are generally encouraged to follow the chapters in sequence, but extensive cross references throughout the book enable a reader to jump directly to the subject of interest from chapter to chapter without the concern of being lost in code mazes. For those readers who are familiar with the existing TCP/IP technologies, Chapters 6 and 7 will provide a useful transition guide on how to port existing applications to IPv6 and how to write IPv6-enabled applications.

The detailed descriptions on the various design decisions reveal the deficiencies that exist in either the specification or the implementation. These insights will enable a researcher to seek out new research topics. The knowledge gained in KAME allows a researcher to establish KAME as a platform on which to build experimental solutions.

Companion Website

This book has a companion website at http://www.elsevierdirect.com/companion.jsp?ISBN=9780124477513. The website hosts two CD images. The first is an ISO image of FreeBSD4.8-RELEASE, which is the base operating system discussed in this book. The image includes installation files. Burn the ISO onto a CD; the installation procedure will start by turning on the computer with the CD. The detailed installation procedure can be found in the INSTALL.TXT file located in the root directory of the burned CD.

The second CD image contains source files of FreeBSD4.8-RELEASE and the KAME snapshot release that are referred to in this book. There are two subdirectories in the root directory of the image.

- FreeBSD4.8-RELEASE—contains the entire source tree of FreeBSD4.8-RELEASE
- kame-snap-20030421—contains the source tree of the KAME snapshot created on April 21, 2003

All source files described throughout this book can be found in the second CD image. Readers can find the complete source code in the CD image as they read this book. It is also possible to install the KAME implementation using the source tree under the kame-snap-20030421 directory to check the actual behavior of the KAME stack. The installation procedure of the KAME snapshot is shown in Section 1.3.2.

Source Code Copyright

This book presents many parts of the source code developed by KAME and also refers to other source code distributed as part of the FreeBSD systems. All of the source code has copyright notices, which are available in the copy of the source code contained in the second CD image.

Reporting Errors and Errata Page

Although we tried hard to identify and fix errors in the review and update phase of this book, it is inevitable to miss some of the errors in this size of material. The authors are happy to receive error reports on the content of this book, and plan to provide an error correction page on the Internet. It will be available at the following web page address: http://books.elsevier.com/companions/0124477518.

Acknowledgments

Personal Acknowledgment from Li, Qing

In January of 2003, having just completed a three-year embedded IPv6 project at Wind River, I was collecting my notes and papers in response to a call-for-paper in ACM SIGCOMM on new communication protocols.

While reading through my thick notebook containing code paths, descriptions on various data structures and code fragments, numerous diagrams, and countless notes-to-self on the KAME implementation, I thought to myself how nice it would have been if there were a book on KAME. Then the idea struck me: I could put all of these notes into a book, which would help others gain understanding of IPv6 and jump start their projects. This thought took a life of its own and grew to an ambitious attempt to cover the entire KAME implementation.

I presented this book idea to Jinmei-san, a Core KAME developer in March of 2003, and invited him to join me in this endeavor. Jinmei-san is a well-known and respected researcher in IPv6 and various important Internet technologies, such as Multicast Routing, DHCPv6, and DNS. He gladly accepted my offer.

Shima-san, another Core KAME developer joined us at the end of March. Shima-san is a well-known and respected researcher in both IPv6 and Mobility.

We agreed on a plan of action by May of 2003 and the book is complete nearly three years later.

Jinmei-san provided technical leadership throughout the entire book. His insightful and meticulous attention to content, detail, and technical accuracy ensured the quality of this book. He helped me with content and has always been responsive to my technical questions and queries even with his busy 24-hour work schedule.

Shima-san helped me with both content and revision. Especially toward the end of the project when I was inundated by both my job and personal life, Shima-san and Jinmei-san carried me through to the finish line. Shima-san has certainly contributed more than his share of responsibility.

It has been a wonderful learning experience working with my co-authors. Their professional excellence, diligence, and work ethics have set a new standard for me to follow.

I would like to thank Rick Adams for sharing my vision of a book and then investing his patience and time over the past three years. I have always appreciated during our many conversations the fact that his frustrations were expressed in such a controlled manner, since the majority of times we spoke I was explaining why the schedule had slipped yet again.

I want to thank my wife Huaying Cheng for her understanding and support of my many late nights and long weekends spent in front of the computer.

Personal Acknowledgment from Jinmei, Tatuya

In addition to the contributors acknowledged below, I personally would like to thank the managers of Toshiba who have supported my activity in the KAME project and authorized this derivative work: Yukio Kamatani, Toshio Murai, Yasuhiro Katsube, and Atsushi Inoue. I would not have been a KAME developer without their understanding and support to begin with, much less written a book on KAME.

Similarly, I would not be what I am without Jun Murai and Hiroshi Esaki. They have always encouraged me in WIDE and KAME, provided new opportunities, and taught me the spirit of global contribution. Murai-san also kindly accepted our request of writing a foreword to this book.

Finally, I would like to thank my co-authors. Clearly, if Qing had not invited me, I would never have imagined writing a book on KAME. He has always generously accepted my delay in writing drafts, and kept the publishing contract valid while I was tweaking every detail of the book, causing another half a year of delay. Shima-san helped me when I desperately updated the draft chapters toward the deadline—far beyond the call of duty.

Personal Acknowledgment from Shima, Keiichi

First of all, I would like to thank all the other KAME developers who had created the high-quality IPv6 reference code. This book would not exist without the code, that is, without their continuous effort to polish the code and their firm minds to deploy IPv6 technology with their code. Fortunately, I could join the project, which was an honor to me, and I could contribute to this great project. It was a precious time and an irreplaceable experience for me. I was a student when I started IPv6-related work. Murai Jun-san and Yamamoto Kazuhiko-san gave me the chance to work on it at the WIDE project. I cannot imagine what I would be if I never met them. Utashiro Kazumasa-san and Wada Eiiti-san supported my activity in the KAME project. All of my work could not have been done without the Internet technology. I thank all of the people who are making a continuous effort to operate the Internet.

Group Acknowledgment

The authors are indebted to all the KAME developers. This is also "their book" in that they wrote the KAME code, which is half of this book. In particular, Shinsuke Suzuki read every chapter and provided valuable comments and suggestions. Kenjiro Cho, Tsuyoshi Momose, and Ryuji Wakikawa carefully reviewed selected chapters, and helped us improve the book through their numerous detailed comments. We would also like to thank external reviewers, specifically, Rob Austein, George Neville-Neil, Andre Oppermann, Shawn Routhier, Randall Stewart, Shinta Sugimoto, and Kazumasa Utashiro. They voluntarily spent a large amount of their private time. The cover image of this book was based on the well-known KAME image, which was used as a symbol of the KAME project designed by Manabu Higashida and Chizuru Higashida (atelier momonga).

We would also like to thank Gary R. Wright and W. Richard Stevens whose book established our basic knowledge of TCP/IP. Their model for describing the BSD's networking code is so effective that we decided to borrow that model for describing KAME's IPv6 implementation in our books. Part of our dedication goes to them for their contribution to the networking engineering community. We hope to make the same level of contribution for the next generation of engineers in the IPv6 technology.

Finally, our sincere gratitude goes to our editors Rick Adams, Rachel Roumeliotis, Dawn-marie Simpson, and the editorial staff at Morgan Kaufmann/Elsevier for their diligent efforts that materialized our manuscript into a professional book.

About the Authors

Li, Qing is a senior architect at Blue Coat Systems, Inc. leading the design and development efforts of the next-generation IPv6 enabled secure proxy appliances. Prior to joining Blue Coat Systems, Qing spent 8 years at Wind River Systems, Inc. as a senior architect in the Networks Business Unit, where he was the lead architect of Wind River's embedded IPv6 products since the IPv6 program inception at the beginning of 2000. Qing holds multiple U.S. patents. Qing is a contributing author of the book titled *Handbook of Networked and Embedded Control Systems* published in June of 2005 by Springer-Verlag. He is also the author of the embedded systems development book titled *Real-Time Concepts for Embedded Systems* published in April of 2003 by CMP Books. Qing participates in open source development projects and is an active FreeBSD src committer.

Jinmei, Tatuya, PhD, is a research scientist at Corporate Research & Development Center, Toshiba Corporation (Jinmei is his family name, which he prefers is presented first according to the Japanese convention). He had been a core developer of the KAME project since the launch of the project through its conclusion. In 2003, he received the PhD degree from Keio University, Japan, based on his work at KAME. He also coauthored three RFCs on IPv6 through his activity in KAME. His research interests spread over various fields of the Internet and IPv6, including routing, DNS, and multicasting.

Shima, Keiichi is a senior researcher at Internet Initiative Japan Inc. His research area is IPv6 and IPv6 mobility. He was a core developer of the KAME project from 2001 to the end of the project and developed Mobile IPv6/NEMO Basic Support protocol stack. He is now working on the new mobility stack (the SHISA stack) for BSD operating systems that is a completely restructured mobility stack.

Introduction

1.1 Introduction

The KAME network software has been regarded as a rock-solid, working reference to Internet Protocol Version 6 (IPv6) by network engineers. As the Internet Protocol Version 4 (IPv4) source code of the BSD (Berkeley Software Distribution) operating systems greatly helped people understand how the Internet protocol works, and as [Ste94] greatly helped people understand the BSD's networking implementation, we aim in this book to describe IPv6, from its specification to operation, using the KAME software implementation.

In this chapter, we present general background information and set the context for subsequent chapters. We begin with a brief history of IPv6 and the KAME project. We then introduce the general network layer architecture of the BSD operating systems on which KAME is built, for the benefit of those readers who are not familiar with these systems. An overview of the entire KAME implementation follows, on top of the base knowledge. Finally, we describe a BSD specific data structure called *mbuf*, with additional notes on KAME extensions made to mbuf, which is frequently referenced in code narrations throughout this book.

1.2 A Brief History of IPv6 and KAME

The rapid growth of the Internet significantly amplified the IPv4 address exhaustion problem in many regions around the world(*). The continued expansion of the Internet as a result of the desire for ubiquitous connectivity, from countless small handheld devices such as network sensors, cell phones, PDAs and laptop computers, to home appliances or automobiles, has led to the demand for unique addresses, which has far exceeded what IPv4 can adequately offer.

(*)Geoff Huston's analysis at the ARIN meeting held in October 2005 shows that the IPv4 address pool will be exhausted around 2012 to 2013 based on some moderate consumption model. The presentation file can be found at *http://www.potaroo.net/presentations/2005-10-27-V4-Projections.pdf*

Network Address Translator (NAT) was developed as a temporary solution to alleviate the address shortage problem while new technologies were being developed to address the root cause. NAT enables multiple network nodes that belong to a region of the network that is situated behind a NAT device to be able to connect to the outside world using a single global IP address. The ability to connect and to communicate, however, came with a price. NAT complicates network management in terms of increased complexity in network configuration and firewall rules that are more prone to errors, but, more importantly, NAT breaks many applications and makes the use of IP security protocols difficult or even impossible.

NAT means Network "Address" Translator. That is, mapping multiple global addresses to the same number of private addresses is the original meaning of NAT. In this case, one private address can use one global address exclusively. If we need to use one or a smaller number of global addresses with a lot of private addresses, we have to re-locate port numbers. Because multiple private addresses using the same port number may be mapped to one global address, that kind of address mapping is called NAPT (Network Address and Port Translator). However, in most cases, NAT boxes usually act as NAPT boxes. We use the word "NAT" as "NAPT" in this book.

In addition, NAT sacrifices the end-to-end communication model, for which the Internet was designed. The end-to-end communication model implies the ability to initiate communication from either end of the communication, which is no longer true when NAT is deployed between the end nodes. Many existing applications cannot function without a special program called an Application Layer Gateway. NAT not only obstructs the deployment of applications such as Voice-over-IP and other types of peer-to-peer applications, but also hinders the development of new and creative applications to meet the expanded use of the Internet.

To recover the end-to-end communication model was the main motivation of the Internet Engineering Task Force (IETF) in 1992 for developing a successor to IPv4. The model builds the intelligence and flexibility in each end node and localizes application complexity that results in the simplification of the core network. At that time, several proposals were submitted for the Next Generation IP (IPng), but one was chosen in 1994 and was termed IP version 6 (IPv6). IPv6 provides 128-bit address space, which allows, for instance, each individual on earth to have several billions of subnets, and allows a trillion end devices in each subnet. The huge address space eliminates the need for NAT devices and restores the secure end-to-end communication model back in the Internet.

Since then, the IETF has been working on standardizing the protocol proposal vigorously. The first base protocol specification was published as [RFC1883] in late 1995. The base specification was then revised in [RFC2460] in 1998 based on implementation and operational experiences on the initial RFC document. At the time of this writing, [RFC2460], with its affiliated documents, are considered as mature standards. Table 1-1 shows such core IPv6 protocol specifications.

TABLE 1-1

[RFC2460]	Internet Protocol, Version 6 (IPv6) Specification
[RFC2461]	Neighbor Discovery for IP Version 6 (IPv6)
[RFC2462]	IPv6 Stateless Address Autoconfiguration
[RFC4443]	Internet Control Message Protocol (ICMPv6) for the Internet Protocol Version 6 (IPv6) Specification

IPv6 core protocol specifications.

Meanwhile, the Widely Integrated Distributed Environment (WIDE) project,[1] which is the largest research community on the Internet in Japan, organized the IPv6 working group in 1995 and has been intensely immersed in the development of IPv6.

The IPv6 working group in the WIDE project concluded triumphantly in 2002 because by then IPv6 had become a part of their common infrastructure. Subsequent IPv6-oriented research activities under the WIDE project umbrella shifted into individual, focused groups such as KAME, the DNS working group, or the backbone-operators working group.

In 1998, WIDE launched the KAME project both to accelerate IPv6 deployment and to heighten the promotion of IPv6. Eight core developers from seven companies, who were also leading members of the WIDE IPv6 working group, came together to develop a reference implementation for IPv6.

The word KAME is not an acronym. Kame is a Japanese word for "turtle." KAME is pronounced as [k'ame] (or kah-meh), not [keim] (like "came") or [k'eimi] (or cam-ē). The KAME project Web page features a turtle that dances when you access the Web page through IPv6. Many IPv6 users visit the Web site to view the famous "dancing turtle" as a way of verifying they have IPv6 connectivity. The reason the turtle was chosen as the project's mascot is simple: It was derived from a lovely stuffed turtle found in an IPv6 workshop where most of the future KAME developers attended. There is even a rumor that the turtle helped a developer debug his code.

The KAME project selected BSD variants as its platform operating system. BSD variants are indeed a good base for developing a reference implementation in the networking area. The BSD variants helped the deployment of TCP/IPv4 networking since its first widely distributed networking code of 4.2BSD. KAME aimed to achieve the same set of goals for IPv6.

KAME's software was released as a "patch" to the base BSD variants (e.g., FreeBSD 2.2.8-RELEASE), which was called KAME "snapshots" during the early stage of the project. While releasing the snapshots independently, the KAME core developers had been collaborating with other BSD developers on methods of incorporating the output from the KAME project directly into the base BSD systems. The KAME developers also collaborated with other early implementors of IPv6 on BSD, such as the NRL (Naval Research Laboratory) in the United States and INRIA (Institut National de Recherche en Informatique et Automatique) in France.

---

1. *http://www.wide.ad.jp/*

By 2000, the KAME IPv6 protocol stack had been successfully merged into the four major variants of BSD: BSD/OS, FreeBSD, NetBSD, and OpenBSD. The integration of KAME into these popular BSD systems is a testimonial to its high quality and its acceptance as the authoritative implementation on IPv6. The KAME snapshots released independently are considered cutting-edge experimental releases, which implement the latest draft and standards documents and can change significantly between releases. On the other hand, the KAME snapshots that have been integrated into the base BSD systems are considered stable releases.

The KAME project was originally formed as a two-year project that would end in March 2000. However, the project produced a tremendous amount of results in its first two years, and with its gradual acceptance by the wider community and its hope to secure the leadership role in IPv6 adoption and deployment, the KAME project has been extended three times. During the project period, KAME as a whole has made enormous contributions to the standardization of the IPv6 specifications as well as to the realization of those specifications in tangible software.

At the time of this writing, IPv4 is still the dominant protocol in deployment, and the vast majority of users access the Internet over the IPv4 networks. Yet the evolution to IPv6 is taking place, slowly but steadily. All major operating systems today, including Microsoft Windows XP, support IPv6, as do network equipment such as routers and switches. The majority of today's network applications such as Mail, FTP, or WWW browser are now IPv6-capable; and new applications such as home appliances with IPv6 are being developed today. In Japan, some of the largest Internet Service Providers (ISPs) have announced or are already offering native IPv6 services. European countries are equally serious about the deployment of IPv6. The United States and China have announced plans to build nationwide IPv6 backbones as short-term projects. Only IPv6 can accommodate the ever-growing demand for address space (currently approximately 54.6 million) with which to access the Internet.

In November 2005, KAME made a significant decision to conclude the project. The project thought it accomplished its missions declared at the beginning of the project. In fact, the IETF concluded that the core IPv6 protocols had been matured enough and that the IPv6 working group meeting in November 2005 would be the last face-to-face meeting. The only remaining work in the protocol standardization would be to make the core protocols advance to the full standard. Also, many IPv6 products other than BSD systems, including various kinds of commercial products and services, were ready in the commercial market at that time. On top of these observations, the WIDE and KAME members decided that this was the best time to complete the original development project targeting the core protocols and to emphasize the maturity of the implementation.

As of this writing, the KAME project is approaching its last stage. Each KAME developer will lead new research and development activities associated with the IPv6 technology in the WIDE project thereafter. The new activities will cover large areas of Internet applications, including mobility, security enhancements, new transport protocols, and evolving fundamental Internet applications such as DNS and Mail. Their next mission is to tighten the deployment of IPv6 in these fields with their own expertise, and to train the next generation of developers with their leadership.

The KAME snapshots will be used for a workplace for the other research activities of the WIDE project after the conclusion of the KAME project. Some advanced features such as Mobile IPv6 will be incorporated from the code base to the BSD variants in the future.

Figure 1-1 summarizes the chronological events of IPv6, the KAME project, the BSD systems, and the relationship between KAME and the BSD projects. The highlighted boxes in the figure

FIGURE 1-1

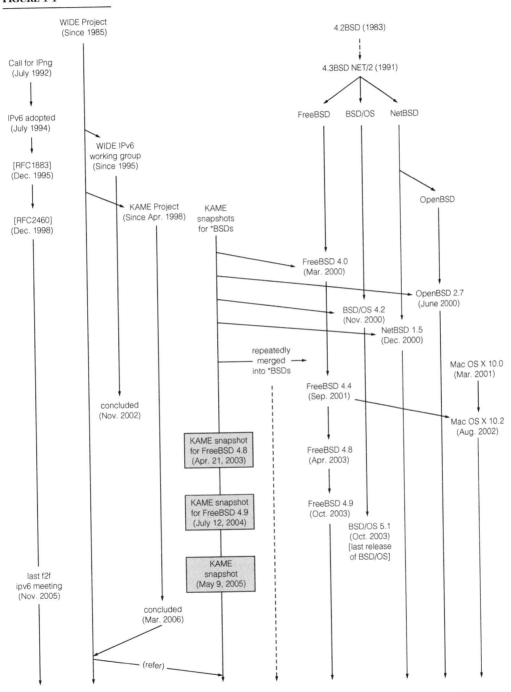

Chronology of IPv6, KAME, and BSD systems. The shaded boxes identify the snapshot releases that this series of books targets (see Section 1.3).

represent the version we discuss in our series of IPv6 books. The code based on May 9, 2005 is used for the DHCPv6 chapter, the code of July 12, 2004 is used for the Mobile IPv6 chapter and the remaining chapters refer the code based on April 21, 2003. The DHCPv6 and the Mobile IPv6 chapters are part of *IPv6 Advanced Protocols Implementation*.

1.2.1   Commercial Success of KAME

The fact of life is that engineers almost always prefer to build their own solutions. This approach in the corporate world often results in delayed product release, lack of features and functionalities, and years to perfect a product. Instead of reinventing the wheel, building a product by utilizing what others have already perfected is the optimal and productive approach to accomplishing greater goals.

Indeed, many open source or commercial products have been built or developed on KAME. The primary "customer" is, of course, the sponsor companies of the project which the core developers are with, such as IIJ, Hitachi, and Fujitsu. The most famous user in the open source field is Internet Software Consortium (ISC, now renamed Internet Systems Consortium). They referred to the KAME IPv6 implementation when they added the support for IPv6 in their latest DNS server implementation commonly known as BIND9. Apple Computer's Mac OS X, code-named Darwin, is based on FreeBSD and, in consequence, uses the KAME IPv6 protocol stack. Other examples include Juniper Networks and Wind River Systems.

In addition to the commercial quality of its design and implementation, KAME carries a license similar to the BSD license, which makes KAME an extremely attractive alternative to commercial in-house development. The open source approach allows any company to build a capable networking product using the open source implementations, for example, from the variants of BSD systems such as FreeBSD. Furthermore, the generous BSD license allows a company to use the software without requiring any counter contribution, even though such contribution is always welcome and respected. In a nutshell, a company is not obligated to release its source code as long as they acknowledge the origin of the source code. Many commercial companies do prefer the BSD-style licenses over other open source licenses for this reason.

This should prove that KAME's choice of BSD variants as its base platforms was a good decision, especially since the primary goal of the project was to promote the wider acceptance and adoption of the new technology.

1.3   Overview of the KAME Distribution

FreeBSD, NetBSD, and OpenBSD have an IPv6 protocol stack that was originally developed by the KAME project. Each BSD system had imported the KAME source based on its own development policy and schedule. As a result, the IPv6 implementation that is provided for each BSD system is slightly different from the others. In general, however, any system that runs an aforementioned BSD variant provides sufficient functionality for acting both as an IPv6 host and as an IPv6 router.

The official integrated distribution prefers stability over functionality. In the majority of the cases, only standardized protocols and technologies are incorporated in the official integrated releases.

On the other hand, the stand-alone KAME distribution, that is, KAME snapshots, is considered the cutting-edge development that implements the latest RFCs and draft documents developed at the IETF. In fact, one of the main objectives of KAME is to gain both implementation experience and to gain deployment experience in real live environments. By implementing the latest specifications, KAME can discover the inconsistencies that may exist in the specification, examine the practicality of the specification, investigate the utility of certain features, and improve the overall quality of the specification. Therefore, when KAME develops these new specifications, these "advanced" features are first distributed as KAME snapshots, which will become a part of the official distribution when these features have been standardized by the IETF.

In this book, we will discuss the IPv6 source code from the KAME snapshot that was generated on April 21, 2003 for FreeBSD 4.8-RELEASE. We have chosen the KAME snapshot because many interesting features such as Mobile IPv6, which is one of the major topics that is covered in *IPv6 Advanced Protocols Implementation*, only exists in the KAME snapshot as of this writing. There are exceptions to the code coverage, however, because either the specification or the implementation was incomplete in April 2003:

- The DHCPv6 implementation, which is covered in Chapter 4 of *IPv6 Advanced Protocols Implementation*, is based on the snapshot of May 9, 2005. The DHCPv6 implementation is independent of the BSD systems.

- The Mobile IPv6 implementation, which is covered in Chapter 5 of *IPv6 Advanced Protocols Implementation*, is based on the snapshot that was created on July 12, 2004, for FreeBSD 4.9-RELEASE.

1.3.1 Source Tree Structure

All of the source codes described in this book are available on the companion website at http://www.elsevierdirect.com/companion.jsp?ISBN=9780124477513. The source code should be built on FreeBSD 4.8-RELEASE. The source code will not work or even be built on any other version of the FreeBSD system.

As mentioned above, the DHCPv6 and the Mobile IPv6 implementations are based on different KAME snapshots that were generated for different versions of FreeBSD. Consult the corresponding chapters for instructions on installation and other details for these implementations. The rest of this section applies to all other codes.

Once the archive file of the KAME distribution is extracted, the snapshot distribution is located under the "kame" directory, which we refer to as "the KAME tree." We use the "${KAME}" notation to denote the absolute file system path to the location where the KAME distribution was extracted, for example, "/usr/local/src/kame". Figure 1-2 illustrates the layout of the KAME source tree.

The top level directory, ${KAME}, contains several informational files, one of which is the "INSTALL" file that contains the general installation instructions. FreeBSD specific files that cannot be shared with other BSDs reside under the "freebsd4" directory. The "kame" directory contains all of the KAME specific source files that are shared among FreeBSD and other operating systems that KAME supports.

1.3.2 Build Procedure

The first step is to install the base FreeBSD system, which is, in our case, FreeBSD 4.8-RELEASE system. The KAME source code can compile without the need for the source code of the original FreeBSD distribution. We omit the details on installing and running FreeBSD.

FIGURE 1-2

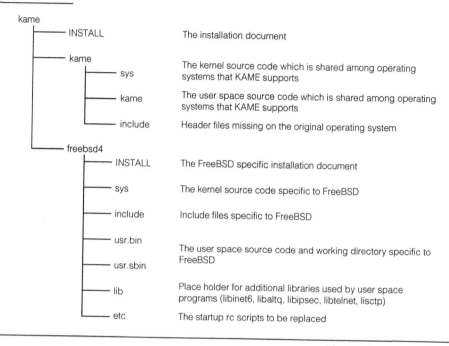

kame		
	INSTALL	The installation document
	kame	
	sys	The kernel source code which is shared among operating systems that KAME supports
	kame	The user space source code which is shared among operating systems that KAME supports
	include	Header files missing on the original operating system
	freebsd4	
	INSTALL	The FreeBSD specific installation document
	sys	The kernel source code specific to FreeBSD
	include	Include files specific to FreeBSD
	usr.bin	The user space source code and working directory specific to FreeBSD
	usr.sbin	
	lib	Place holder for additional libraries used by user space programs (libinet6, libaltq, libipsec, libtelnet, lisctp)
	etc	The startup rc scripts to be replaced

The KAME source tree for FreeBSD4.

For those readers who are not familiar with FreeBSD, consult the FreeBSD documentation at *http://www.freebsd.org/*.

FreeBSD 4.8-RELEASE contains several security flaws and is no longer supported by the FreeBSD project. Therefore, the FreeBSD 4.8-RELEASE system should only be used for reference for learning the KAME implementation as part of reading this book. This version of FreeBSD should not be used in a production environment.

Backup

Once the KAME system has been built, installing the KAME system will replace the original kernel and the kernel modules. The KAME installation will also update the system header files that are located under the "/usr/include" directory. Therefore, it is recommended a backup be made of these files in case the system needs to be restored to its original form. The following commands will back up these files:

```
# cp /kernel /kernel.original
# cp -pr /modules /modules.original
# cd /usr
# mkdir include.original
# cd include.original
# (cd ../include; tar Bpcf - . ) | tar Bpxf -
```

Prepare the Source Tree

We need to construct the correct source tree by creating necessary symbolic links in the `${KAME}/freebsd4/sys` directory, which refers to files under the `${KAME}/kame/sys` directory. The following commands will prepare the source tree:

```
# cd ${KAME}
# make TARGET=freebsd4 prepare
```

Build Kernel and Kernel Modules

The procedure for building a KAME-enabled kernel is the same as the procedure for building the original FreeBSD kernel. The kernel configuration file is located in the "`${KAME}/freebsd4/sys/i386/conf`" directory. The template base configuration file is "`GENERIC.KAME`". Table 1-2 shows some KAME-specific kernel options used in this book.

Similar to the FreeBSD build procedure, the next step is to create a compilation directory by running the **/usr/sbin/config** command. The sequence of commands is:

```
# cd ${KAME}/freebsd4/sys/i386/conf
# cp GENERIC.KAME ${YOURCONFIGFILE}
    (modify ${YOURCONFIGFILE})
# /usr/sbin/config ${YOURCONFIGFILE}
```

The compilation directory is created under the "`${KAME}/freebsd4/sys/compile/`" directory with the name of your configuration file. The following sequence of commands will compile the kernel:

```
# cd ${KAME}/freebsd4/sys/compile/${YOURCONFIGFILE}
# make depend
# make
```

If the build process completes successfully, the following commands need to be executed to install the newly built kernel files.

```
# cd ${KAME}/freebsd4/sys/compile/${YOURCONFIGFILE}
# make install
```

TABLE 1-2

Option name	Function
INET6	Include the IPv6 protocol implementation.
RTPREF	Include the default router preferences support defined in [RFC4191]. The code is discussed in Chapter 5.
MIP6	Include the Mobile IPv6 correspondent node support. Mobile IPv6 will be discussed in Chapter 5 of *IPv6 Advanced Protocols Implementation*.
pseudo-device hif	Include the pseudo device driver `hif` used by Mobile IPv6.
MIP6_MOBILE_NODE	Include the Mobile IPv6 mobile node support.
MIP6_HOME_AGENT	Include the Mobile IPv6 home agent support.

KAME-specific kernel options used in this book.

The installed kernel will take effect after rebooting. The system needs to be rebooted after finishing installation of startup scripts.

Building User Space Programs

The KAME distribution provides several enhanced versions of user space utility programs such as **ndp** and **ifconfig**. Additional new commands are also installed as part of installing the KAME distribution.

The KAME distribution updates many of the system header files, which the KAME versions of the user space programs depend on for building the executable binaries. Therefore, the KAME versions of the system header files must be installed first by running the following commands:

```
# cd ${KAME}/freebsd4
# make includes
# make install-includes
```

Once the new header files are in place, executing the following commands will build all necessary user space programs for the FreeBSD operating system and will install these new programs under the "/usr/local/v6/" directory. Some of the programs installed in this directory do not have compatibility with the original FreeBSD kernel. It is recommended that the programs in this directory be used once the KAME kernel is activated.

```
# cd ${KAME}/freebsd4
# make
# make install
```

Figure 1-3 shows the layout of the /usr/local/v6/ directory.

FIGURE 1-3

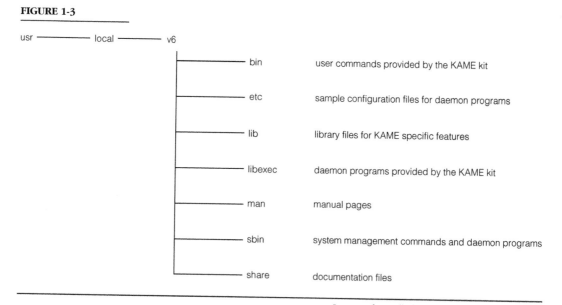

Layout of installed KAME distribution directory.

TABLE 1-3

Script name	Function
`rc`	A replacement of the "`/etc/rc`" that takes into account a new script file, `rc.mobileip6`.
`rc.network6`	A replacement of "`/etc/rc.network6`" that can handle policy-based configuration of the source address selection and privacy-enhanced addresses.
`rc.mobileip6`	A startup script for Mobile IPv6.

KAME specific startup scripts.

Install Startup Scripts

The KAME distribution comes with three startup scripts that are described in Table 1-3.

The KAME specific startup scripts may use special functions which are accessible only from the programs modified for the KAME kernel. To ensure the scripts use the KAME-provided programs, the "`/etc/rc.conf`" file needs to be modified so that it will include `/usr/local/v6` in the search path.

```
PATH=/usr/local/v6/sbin:/usr/local/v6/bin:${PATH}
```

Once all of the above installation procedures are completed, the KAME distribution will become fully functional after system reboot.

1.4 Overview of BSD Network Implementation

Figure 1-4 provides an overview of the structure of the BSD networking stack, in which IPv6 is one of the network layer protocols and is located at the same level as IPv4. Since transport layer protocols such as TCP and UDP operate over both IPv4 and IPv6, the majority of the code is shared between IPv4 and IPv6.

The level of code sharing at the transport layer for IPv4 and IPv6 differs among the BSD variants. For example, NetBSD has a separate UDP module for IPv6.

New modules were introduced for IPv6. An IPv6 packet does not have an option field but adopted a more flexible mechanism called *extension headers* (see Chapter 3 for more details). New extension headers can be created to add more functions or features to IPv6. Extension headers are placed between the IPv6 header and the upper layer protocol header. These headers are processed sequentially based on their order in the packet. Each header has its own protocol number. Every header, except the last header (e.g., upper layer headers like TCP or UDP), has a header field which stores the protocol number of the following header to make a chain of headers. Each header is processed by the input function corresponding to the protocol number. The header processing may involve some special processing, for example, fragmentation or host routing.

An interesting point is the role of Internet Control Message Protocol (ICMP) in IPv6. The general protocol packet format of ICMPv6 is similar to that of ICMPv4. However, while ICMPv4 is

FIGURE 1-4

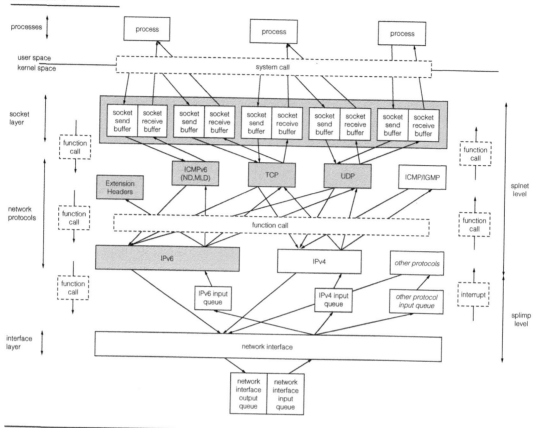

Structure of BSD networking stack.

mainly used for purposes of error notification and simple network diagnostics, ICMPv6 provides the mechanisms for a set of signaling protocols that are an integral part of IPv6 operation. For example, the Neighbor Discovery (ND) Protocol operates over ICMPv6 to perform link layer address resolutions that are similar to Address Resolution Protocol in IPv4; the Multicast Listener Discovery (MLD) Protocol operates over ICMPv6 to perform group membership management functions that are similar to Internet Group Management Protocol (IGMP) in IPv4.

The network interface device will generate a hardware interrupt when a packet arrives at the interface. The network interface device driver transfers the received packets from the interface packet queue to the protocol input queue as part of the interrupt handling procedure. For example, a device driver for an Ethernet interface will dispatch an incoming packet into the corresponding protocol input queue according to the Ethernet frame type. The frame type of 0x86DD is assigned to IPv6 packets, and thus an Ethernet driver will dispatch incoming packets that have that frame type into the IPv6 protocol input queue. Unlike IPv4, which uses two Ethernet frame types (0x0800 for IPv4 and 0x0806 for ARP), IPv6 only uses 0x86DD for all

IPv6-related packets. The device driver will generate a software interrupt after the driver inserts a packet into the protocol input queue.

The handling of packet transmission is different from that for packet reception. An application invokes a library function that is provided by the operating system when that application wants to send a message to a remote process on a different node. Each library function is an interface to a kernel service. The kernel services, such as network services, are available in the kernel space. Since the application resides in the user space, the invoked library function converts the application request into a kernel service request, and invokes the kernel service via a *system call*.

Within the kernel space, each layer obtains the services of the next layer by means of direct function calls. The protocol within each layer of the "network protocols" block of Figure 1-4 inserts a header before the application message as the message travels downward through kernel space. For example, if the application sends a message over a TCP socket, the TCP layer will insert a TCP header before the message. Then the IPv6 layer will insert an IPv6 header after the TCP layer hands that message to the IPv6 layer. The Ethernet layer will insert an Ethernet header when it receives that message from the IPv6 layer. As shown on the left side of Figure 1-4, a message generated by an application will reach the output queue of the network interface through a series of function calls after the message enters the kernel space.

Since there are numerous data structures that are shared between the device driver and the protocol stacks, and since there are numerous data structures that are shared among the protocol modules, access to these data structures must be synchronized to ensure data integrity. In the FreeBSD kernel, data access can take place at multiple interrupt levels, including the device interrupt and the software interrupt for the network layer. These are called the `imp` and `net` levels, respectively. In order to gain synchronization, the FreeBSD kernel offers `splimp()`, `splnet()` and other similar functions to tasks. For example, the `splimp()` function allows a task to disable the network device interrupt, and a task that copies an IPv6 packet from the network device queue calls this function before retrieving the packet from its device input queue. The `splnet()` function allows a task that executes at the `net` level to block other tasks that also run at the same level from executing.

The `imp` level has higher priority than the `net` level. For example, when an Ethernet frame arrives at the device input queue, an ongoing IP packet processing, which is running under the `net` level, is suspended. After the frame has been received, the suspended IP packet processing is resumed. This priority mechanism will reduce the possibility of data loss at the network device level, which usually has a small buffering space for input frames.

The latest FreeBSD system does not use `splxxx()` anymore. The system now uses a more sophisticated data synchronization scheme called the "Fine Grained Locking" system. The Fine Grained Locking system utilizes mutexes to protect data structures. With this mechanism, multiple tasks can access to the same data structure without confliction. While `splxxx()` provides a macro level locking scheme (e.g., locking an entire function), mutexes can provide a locking mechanism for even one small data structure. This mechanism is necessary to gain better performance when the system supports multiple processors which potentially access the same data structure in parallel.

The incoming packet will eventually reach the application data input queue, also known as the *socket queue* or *socket buffer*. The application can be notified of the packet arrival if so desired via the return from a system call.

1.5   Source Code Narrations

We will focus on the KAME implementation and assume FreeBSD 4.8-RELEASE as the underlying operating system. The distribution can be found on the companion website. We assume the source code distributed from KAME is extracted in the `${KAME}` directory. While most of the files mentioned in this book reside in the directory, we may also refer to the original files distributed by the FreeBSD project, which are usually located in the `/usr/src/` directory and the `/usr/include/` directory. All source files referred to in a chapter are listed at the beginning of the code introduction section. For example, Table 1-4 shows the location of three files, `ip6_output.c`, `in_pcb.c` and `inet_ntop.c`.

1.5.1   Typographical Conventions

Global and local variable names, function names, and structure fields are in constant-width fonts when referred to in the code descriptions. For example, `nd6_delay` refers to a global variable. Function names are in constant-width fonts followed by parentheses; `ip6_input()` refers to the IPv6 input function.

The names of the utility programs are in bold font as in **ifconfig**. The command line input and the output of a utility program is displayed in constant-width font. For example, an output of the **ifconfig** command is shown as follows:

```
% ifconfig
lo0: flags=8049<UP,LOOPBACK,RUNNING,MULTICAST> mtu 16384
        inet 127.0.0.1 netmask 0xff000000
        inet6 ::1 prefixlen 128
        inet6 fe80::1%lo0 prefixlen 64 scopeid 0x1
ne0: flags=8843<UP,BROADCAST,RUNNING,SIMPLEX,MULTICAST> mtu 1500
        inet 192.0.2.127 netmask 0xffffff00 broadcast 192.0.2.255
        inet6 fe80::20c:29ff:fef1:1a8b%ne0 prefixlen 64 scopeid 0x2
        ether 00:0c:29:f1:1a:8b
```

Structure names are in constant-width font followed by braces. For example, `llinfo_nd6{}` refers to the `llinfo_nd6` data structure.

TABLE 1-4

File	Description
`${KAME}/kame/sys/netinet6/ip6_output.c`	Processing code of the output operation of IPv6 packets.
`${KAME}/freebsd4/sys/netinet/in_pcb.c`	Functions related to the protocol control block (PCB) operation.
`/usr/lib/libc/net/inet_ntop.c`	Functions which convert an IP address to a printable format.

Sample table which lists source file location.

Names of the source files are in constant-width font, for example, `/usr/include/sys/mbuf.h` represents the `mbuf.h` file that resides under the `/usr/include/sys/` directory.

The programming language keywords are in constant-width font (e.g., `if`, `while`, `for`, `case`).

1.5.2 Sample Source Code Description

We cover a huge amount of source code throughout the book. Each fragment of source code is presented in the following format:

Listing 1-1 _____ in6.c

```
3617    int
3618    in6_leavegroup(imm)
3619            struct in6_multi_mship *imm;
3620    {
        ....
3629            if (imm->i6mm_maddr) {
        ....
3646                    in6_delmulti(imm->i6mm_maddr);
        ....
3648            }
3649            free(imm, M_IPMADDR);
3650            return 0;
3651    }
```
_____ in6.c

Line numbers appear on the left hand side of each line of code in the listing. Code descriptions use the line numbers to indicate which line or block of code the text refers to. For example, the above code is described in the following fashion:

3618–3651 The `in6_leavegroup()` function calls the `in6_delmulti()` function to remove the membership from the list and frees the storage space that holds the membership information.

The ellipsis that appears in the listing indicates code omission due to either the omitted part does not apply to the discussion within the current context, or an assumption of specific values for the preprocessor variables that would eliminate the code from the discussion.

The name of the file in which the function resides appears on the right hand side of the separator lines. In this example, the listing shows that function `in6_leavegroup()` is defined in file `in6.c`. We have not made any modification to the original source code on the CD image on the companion website; you can easily and quickly find the referenced file and line of code as shown in the text.

Note that the code is presented as an exact copy of the implementation. Even if it contains editorial errors such as a misspelling in a comment line, they are purposely not corrected so that readers can easily match the description with the source code included on the companion site.

TABLE 1-5

Macro name	Notes
__FreeBSD__	We assume __FreeBSD__ is always defined and the value is greater than 4, because FreeBSD4 is our base platform.
__NetBSD__	We assume these macros are NOT defined. All source code enclosed by these macros are removed from the code listings.
__OpenBSD__	
__bsdi__	
NEW_STRUCT_ROUTE	We assume this macro is defined.
PULLDOWN_TEST	We assume this macro is NOT defined.
SCOPEDROUTING	We assume this macro is NOT defined.
DIAGNOSTIC	We assume this macro is NOT defined.

Assumed preprocessor values.

1.5.3   Preprocessor Variables

Table 1-5 lists the preprocessor variables for which we have assumed specific values in the context of this book.

We also assume the following kernel options (see Table 1-2) are defined.

- INET6

- RTPREF

- MIP6, MIP6_MOBILE_NODE, MIP6_HOME_AGENT are assumed to be defined in Chapter 5 of *IPv6 Advanced Protocols Implementation*

It is worth mentioning the __P() macro definition because the readers of this book will see the macro frequently in the code listing parts. The following listing is an example of the usage of the macro.

Listing 1-2

```
                                                               in6_var.h
728     int     in6_leavegroup __P((struct in6_multi_mship *));
                                                               in6_var.h
```

The __P() macro is used to provide compatibility to non-ANSI C compilers that do not support prototype declaration. The macro is defined as follows when using non-ANSI C compilers.

```
#define __P((a)) ()
```

The function argument part will be removed when the compiler is not ANSI compliant that does not accept prototype declaration. The above listing will be expanded as follows.

```
int in6_leavegroup ();
```

When using ANSI C compiler, the macro is defined as follows.

```
#define __P((a)) (a)
```

In this case, the function argument leaves as is and used as a part of function declaration. The expanded code looks as follows.

```
int in6_leavegroup (struct in6_multi_mship *);
```

1.5.4 Networking Device and Architecture Assumptions

Throughout the book, we assume the underlying network interface device is Ethernet unless we explicitly refer to other networking devices. The machine architecture is assumed to be Intel-32-bit (aka "i386").

1.6   Mbufs and IPv6

The BSD kernel implementation stores various types of networking-related data, such as socket options, network addresses, and packet data, in a special data structure, called *memory buffers*, commonly referred to as *mbuf*s. Each mbuf contains a small amount of data, typically ranging from 212 to 236 bytes in recent versions of FreeBSD. Larger amounts of data are stored in one of the following two ways:

- The data is divided into multiple blocks, each of which is stored in a single mbuf, and these mbuf structures are chained into a linked list. This linked list is often called an *mbuf chain*.

- A separate large buffer, called an *mbuf cluster*, is allocated and referenced from the mbuf, and the packet data is stored in the cluster. If a single cluster is not large enough to hold the entire packet data, additional mbuf can be created, with or without clusters, and these mbufs are chained to store the entire packet. Multiple mbufs can reference the same cluster block.

The mbuf framework is specifically designed for networking such that networking-related routines that reside at different protocol layers can transfer incoming or outgoing packets efficiently. By using the mbuf framework, each protocol layer can insert its protocol header for an outgoing packet without the need to copy the packet transferred from the layer above. As such, an outgoing packet is typically referenced by an mbuf chain due to multiple protocol headers added by each protocol layer.

For example, when an application sends a datagram over a UDP socket, the kernel socket layer copies the data into a single mbuf. The UDP output function (described in Section 6.9.2) allocates a separate mbuf for the UDP and IPv6 headers, and inserts this header mbuf onto the data mbuf as shown in Figure 1-5. The IPv6 layer may allocate extension headers for the outgoing UDP packet. Each extension header resides in a separate mbuf and the IPv6 layer inserts these extension headers between the IPv6 header and the UDP header. Section 3.13.3 illustrates the extension header allocation and placement for an outgoing packet in detail.

FIGURE 1-5

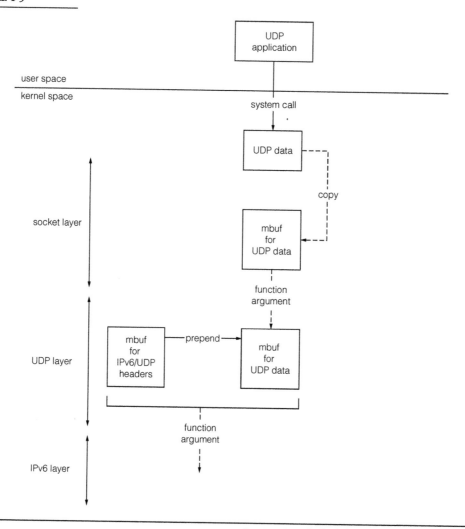

Construction of mbuf chain for a UDP-over-IPv6 packet.

The definition of the mbuf structure is given in the ${KAME}/freebsd4/sys/sys/mbuf.h
as shown in Listing 1-3.

Listing 1-3

```
                                                                        mbuf.h
70 struct m_hdr {
71         struct   mbuf *mh_next;           /* next buffer in chain */
72         struct   mbuf *mh_nextpkt;        /* next chain in queue/record */
73         caddr_t  mh_data;                 /* location of data */
74         int      mh_len;                  /* amount of data in this mbuf */
75         short    mh_type;                 /* type of data in this mbuf */
76         short    mh_flags;                /* flags; see below */
77 };
   ....
```

```
 92 struct pkthdr {
 93         struct    ifnet *rcvif;            /* rcv interface */
 94         int       len;                    /* total packet length */
 95         /* variables for ip and tcp reassembly */
 96         void      *header;                /* pointer to packet header */
 97         /* variables for hardware checksum */
 98         int       csum_flags;             /* flags regarding checksum */
 99         int       csum_data;              /* data field used by csum routines */
100         SLIST_HEAD(packet_tags, m_tag) tags; /* list of packet tags */
101 };
    ....
119 struct mbuf {
120         struct    m_hdr m_hdr;
121         union {
122                 struct {
123                         struct    pkthdr MH_pkthdr;        /* M_PKTHDR set */
124                         union {
125                                 struct    m_ext MH_ext;    /* M_EXT set */
126                                 char      MH_databuf[MHLEN];
127                         } MH_dat;
128                 } MH;
129                 char      M_databuf[MLEN];                  /* !M_PKTHDR, !M_EXT */
130         } M_dat;
131 };
132 #define   m_next        m_hdr.mh_next
133 #define   m_len         m_hdr.mh_len
134 #define   m_data        m_hdr.mh_data
135 #define   m_type        m_hdr.mh_type
136 #define   m_flags       m_hdr.mh_flags
137 #define   m_nextpkt     m_hdr.mh_nextpkt
138 #define   m_act         m_nextpkt
139 #define   m_pkthdr      M_dat.MH.MH_pkthdr
140 #define   m_ext         M_dat.MH.MH_dat.MH_ext
141 #define   m_pktdat      M_dat.MH.MH_dat.MH_databuf
142 #define   m_dat         M_dat.M_databuf
```
                                                                    ————mbuf.h

The m_hdr member, which is an instance of the m_hdr{} structure, is the control structure for managing the mbuf{}. The individual fields of m_hdr{} are accessed via macros defined on lines 132–137. A large packet may be contained in an mbuf chain and the m_next member points to the next mbuf of the same mbuf chain. m_next is NULL when the current mbuf is either the only mbuf or the last mbuf of the chain. The m_len field specifies the amount of data that an mbuf holds or references. The m_data field points to the beginning of the data that is either carried in or referenced by an mbuf.

The m_flags field provides attributes of an mbuf{}. The flags that are most relevant to our discussion are M_EXT, M_PKTHDR and M_LOOP. The M_EXT flag indicates that an mbuf cluster buffer is mapped in the mbuf{} and is accessible via the m_ext macro. The M_PKTHDR flag indicates the mbuf{} contains pkthdr{} and is accessible via the m_pkthdr macro. The packet header holds information about the entire packet; in the pkthdr{} structure, recvif points to the packet arrival interface, and len is the total packet length. The M_LOOP flag indicates the packet originated from a loopback interface. The M_LOOP flag is specific to the KAME implementation and it indicates the mbuf contains a packet that comes from a loopback interface.

The simple example of transmitting a UDP packet over IPv6 given in Figure 1-5 is detailed using the mbuf{}-related structures as shown in Figure 1-6. The first mbuf contains 48 bytes of the IPv6 and UDP headers, and the second mbuf of the chain stores 100 bytes of data.

FIGURE 1-6

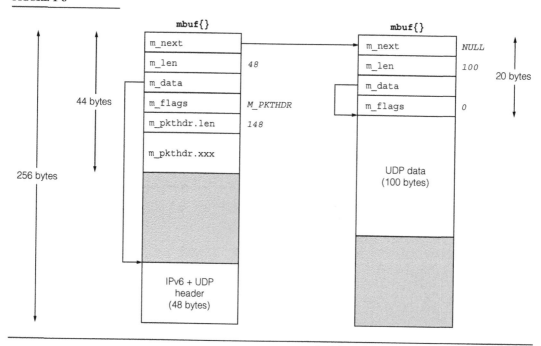

mbuf chain for an outgoing UDP-over-IPv6 packet.

Unlike outgoing packets, incoming packets are often stored in a single mbuf{}, having a single cluster buffer if necessary. Figure 1-7 shows a typical example of an incoming TCP/IPv6 packet with 1024 bytes of TCP data passed to the IPv6 input function. Since the available storage in the mbuf{} is not large enough to store the packet, that is, the available free space in either m_pktdat or m_dat (depending on the value of m_flags) is too small to hold the packet, a cluster buffer is allocated and mapped into the mbuf{}. As shown in Figure 1-7, each mbuf cluster is 2048 bytes on the Intel i386 architecture. Note that since Ethernet has a link MTU of 1500 bytes, the maximum sized Ethernet packet will fit in a single cluster buffer.

1.6.1   Common Mbuf Manipulation Macros and Functions

The kernel provides various macros and functions to operate on the mbuf structure. Table 1-6 (*see page 22*) summarizes a subset of these mbuf-related macros and functions that are often referred to in this book.

1.6.2   Mbuf Tagging

The mbuf tagging mechanism allows any packet processing module, such as protocol modules, pseudo interfaces or any kernel module to create and attach module-specific auxiliary information and meta-data to a particular packet. A module typically uses *mbuf tags* (*mtags*) to keep track of the operations that have been performed on a packet or to schedule operations to

FIGURE 1-7

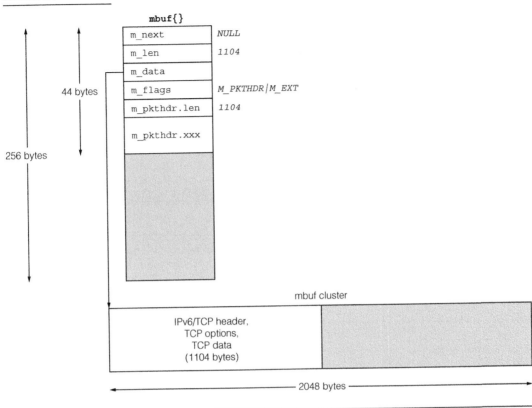

Mbuf containing an incoming TCP-over-IPv6 packet.

be performed at a later time when the processing module reaches a certain operational state. Mbuf tags are maintained across various mbuf operations. The mbuf tags are freed when the associated mbuf is freed. The definition of m_tag{}, the structure of the mbuf tag, is given in Listing 1-4.

Listing 1-4   _mbuf.h

```
82 struct m_tag {
83         SLIST_ENTRY(m_tag)      m_tag_link;     /* List of packet tags */
84         u_int16_t               m_tag_id;       /* Tag ID */
85         u_int16_t               m_tag_len;      /* Length of data */
86         u_int32_t               m_tag_cookie;   /* ABI/Module ID */
87 };
```
                                                                                         _mbuf.h

The pkthdr{} structure shown in Listing 1-3 contains the tags field, whose definition is given by the SLIST_HEAD (singly linked list) macro and translates to the following form:

```
struct packet_tags {
        struct m_tag *slh_first;
} mtags;
```

If the how argument to those macros is M_WAIT, the call to the macro will be blocked until necessary memory is available. In other words, the call always succeeds. On the other hand, if the argument is M_DONTWAIT and necessary memory is not available, the call immediately terminates; for MGET() and MGETHDR(), m will be NULL; for MCLGET(), M_EXT will not be set.

Within m_tag{}, the m_tag_link field chains the m_tag{} structures as shown in Figure 1-8. The m_tag_id holds the packet tag ID, together with m_tag_cookie, identifying the creator of the mbuf tag.

TABLE 1-6

Mbuf Allocation Macros

Function name	*Description*
MGET(struct mbuf *m, int how, int type)	This macro allocates and initializes an mbuf. m will point to the newly allocated mbuf.
MGETHDR(struct mbuf *m, int how, int type)	This macro allocates an mbuf and initializes it for containing a packet header. m will point to the newly allocated mbuf. The M_PKTHDR flag will be set in m_flags on success.
MCLGET(struct mbuf *m, int how)	This macro allocates an mbuf cluster, and attaches it to the mbuf m. On success, the M_EXT flag will be set in m_flags.

Mbuf Adjustment Macros

Function name	*Description*
M_PREPEND(struct mbuf *m, int plen, int how)	This macro adjusts the m_data pointer to reserve plen amount of space if m has enough free leading space, and m_len is updated accordingly. Otherwise, a new mbuf is allocated and is inserted onto m, and m is reinitialized to point to the newly allocated mbuf. Note that this macro assumes plen is less than either MLEN or MHLEN depending on whether the M_PKTHDR flag is set in the m_flags field of m. The how parameter has the semantics described above. This macro frees the original mbuf m and sets it to NULL if a new mbuf allocation is required but fails.
struct mbuf * m_pullup(struct mbuf *m, int len)	This function manipulates the mbuf chain starting at m such that the first len bytes of the chain are contiguous in memory. If necessary, this function allocates a separate mbuf, copies len bytes from the original chain to the newly allocated mbuf, and prepends the new mbuf onto the old chain. This function returns the head of the new mbuf chain on success. If a new mbuf is required but this allocation fails, this function returns NULL. In this case, the original mbuf is freed. Note that this function does not allocate a cluster buffer; len is assumed to be less than or equal to MHLEN bytes.

TABLE 1-6 (*Continued*)

Mbuf Release Functions

Function name	Description
`void m_freem(struct mbuf *m)`	This function frees the entire mbuf chain referenced by m. If any of the mbuf in the chain contains a cluster, that cluster is also freed.
`struct mbuf * m_free(struct mbuf *m)`	This function frees a single mbuf referenced by m. If m has a cluster, it is also freed. The next mbuf pointed to by m_next of m is returned to the caller, but the return value is often ignored.

Common mbuf-related macros.

FIGURE 1-8

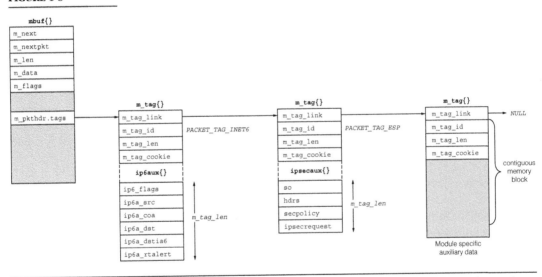

m_tag{} structure and mtag chain.

The FreeBSD kernel provides a set of mtag manipulation functions in `uipc_mbuf2.c`. Table 1-7 lists a subset of these mtag functions.

Figure 1-8 shows sample usage of mbuf tags. In the example, the IPv6 module utilizes the mbuf tag whose tag identifier is PACKET_TAG_INET6, and the IPsec ESP module utilizes the mbuf tag whose identifier is PACKET_TAG_ESP. m_tag_len specifies the length of the module specific data that is carried in the tag.

The ip6aux{} structure is used to keep additional packet information. The structure will be discussed in Section 3.6. The ipsecaux{} structure is used by IPsec stack. We will not provide more information about ipsecaux{} since we do not discuss the detailed implementation of IPsec in this series of books.

TABLE 1-7

Function name	Description

`m_tag_find(struct mbuf *m,`
`            int type,`
`            struct m_tag *t)`
	This function traverses the mtag chain and returns the `m_tag{}` instance that has a matching `m_tag_id` against a given mtag ID specified as `type`. The search will start from the `m_tag()` instance if `t` is specified. Otherwise, the search will start from the head of the mtag chain of the mbuf specified as `m`.

`m_tag_get(int type,`
`           int len,`
`           int wait)`
	This function allocates an `m_tag{}` structure and initializes the `m_tag_id` and the `m_tag_len` fields with values specified as `type` and `len`, respectively. `wait` is either `M_WAITOK` or `M_NOWAIT` to specify if the caller can be blocked or not when the function allocates memory.

`m_tag_delete(struct mbuf *m,` `              struct m_tag *t)`	This function removes a given `m_tag{}` instance `t` from the mtag chain of the mbuf specified as `m` and frees the memory occupied by the `m_tag{}`.

m_tag{} manipulation functions.

1.6.3   Mbuf Requirement for IPv6

The network code of BSD variants generally expects the network layer header and the upper layer protocol headers in a received packet to be stored in a contiguous memory space. This assumption is assured in most cases, since an incoming packet is typically stored in a single mbuf, and therefore in a contiguous space as was explained in Section 1.6.

Some device drivers choose to hold a large incoming packet in an mbuf chain, where each mbuf does not have a cluster buffer. With such drivers, the protocol layer headers may reside in multiple mbuf blocks and do not lie in contiguous memory. Typically, this does not cause trouble, since the mbuf design in newer BSD variants has more than 200 bytes of free space to store both the network and the transport layer headers. However, since the free space was typically about 100 bytes in size in older versions of BSD systems, the situation where the network and the transport layer headers may be stored in multiple mbuf structures was a more likely occurrence. The traditional IPv4 network code calls the `m_pullup()` function in such cases to ensure a particular protocol header is contained in one contiguous block of memory.

Unfortunately, the pullup operation is not suitable for IPv6. If an incoming packet contains extension headers, the protocol stack must retain all of them until the input operation terminates. This is because if a protocol error is found during the processing of the packet and the stack has to return an ICMPv6 error message, it must include as much of the offending packet as will fit as specified in [RFC4443] (see also Section 4.8.1). Due to the nature of `m_pullup()` (see Table 1-6), however, a caller may need to remove some or all of the extension headers before calling `m_pullup()` in order for the operation to succeed, thereby breaking the requirement for the possible generation of an ICMPv6 error message.

As such, the KAME implementation requires that all data from the IPv6 header up to the transport layer header in an incoming packet be referenced by the first `mbuf{}`. In fact, the majority of the network drivers developed today meet this requirement, but IPv6-related input routines cannot trust that assumption unconditionally. Therefore, each input packet processing routine first determines if the header continuity requirement is satisfied, and, if not, the routine discards the packet. Otherwise, it gets access to the beginning of the header by the head of the incoming packet and the offset to the header. Then the routine can process the header and, if necessary, the data following the header without any copies or deletions of other headers.

> Recent versions of the KAME implementation for NetBSD and OpenBSD loosened the requirement, and can deal with the situation where different headers are in different mbufs [Hag00]. Unfortunately, the target system described in this book does not support the new feature and still relies on the requirement.

The `IP6_EXTHDR_CHECK()` macro, which is defined in the `${KAME}/kame/sys/netinet/ip6.h` file as shown in Listing 1-5, performs the header continuity requirement verification. Specifically, the `IP6_EXTHDR_CHECK()` macro ensures that the first `mbuf{}` contain at least `off + hlen` bytes of data on success. Otherwise, this macro triggers the current function to return to its caller, often with an error code (see, for example, Section 3.7 for the IPv6 header processing).

Listing 1-5
_____ ip6.h

```
471    #define IP6_EXTHDR_CHECK(m, off, hlen, ret)                          \
472    do {                                                                 \
473        if ((m)->m_next != NULL) {                                       \
474            if ((m)->m_flags & M_EXT) {                                  \
475                if ((m)->m_len < (off) + (hlen)) {                       \
476                    ip6stat.ip6s_exthdrtoolong++;                        \
477                    m_freem(m);                                          \
478                    return ret;                                          \
479                }                                                        \
480            } else {                                                     \
481                if ((m)->m_len < (off) + (hlen)) {                       \
482                    ip6stat.ip6s_exthdrtoolong++;                        \
483                    m_freem(m);                                          \
484                    return ret;                                          \
485                }                                                        \
486            }                                                            \
487        } else {                                                         \
488            if ((m)->m_len < (off) + (hlen)) {                           \
489                ip6stat.ip6s_tooshort++;                                 \
490                in6_ifstat_inc(m->m_pkthdr.rcvif, ifs6_in_truncated); \
491                m_freem(m);                                              \
492                return ret;                                              \
493            }                                                            \
494        }                                                                \
495    } while (/*CONSTCOND*/ 0)
```
_____ ip6.h

> The first part of this macro is actually redundant. The check is the same whether or not the M_EXT flag is set.

In some cases, drivers need to be modified to meet the header continuity requirement. The loopback interface is a good example of such a driver. As shown in Figure 1-5, an outgoing packet typically consists of an mbuf chain. If the packet is looped back within the transmitting node, that mbuf chain is passed to the `looutput()` function and is appended to the packet input queue of the loopback interface. If the packet were simply passed to the IPv6 input routine, the input routine would encounter an mbuf chain for an incoming packet and the call to the `IP6_EXTHDR_CHECK()` macro may result in the packet being discarded.

Thus, the `looutput()` function in the KAME implementation (defined in the `${KAME}/freebsd4/sys/net/if_loop.h` file) is modified so that packets passed through a loopback interface contain as much of the packet as possible in the first mbuf. Listing 1-6 shows the relevant part of this function.

Listing 1-6

```
                                                                        if_loop.c
152     /*
153      * KAME requires that the packet to be contiguous on the
154      * mbuf.  We need to make that sure.
155      * this kind of code should be avoided.
156      * XXX  fails to join if interface MTU > MCLBYTES.  jumbogram?
157      */
158     if (m && m->m_next != NULL && m->m_pkthdr.len < MCLBYTES) {
159             struct mbuf *n;
160
161             MGETHDR(n, M_DONTWAIT, MT_HEADER);
162             if (!n)
163                     goto contiguousfail;
164             M_MOVE_PKTHDR(n, m);
165             MCLGET(n, M_DONTWAIT);
166             if (! (n->m_flags & M_EXT)) {
167                     m_freem(n);
168                     goto contiguousfail;
169             }
170
171             m_copydata(m, 0, n->m_pkthdr.len, mtod(n, caddr_t));
172             n->m_len = n->m_pkthdr.len;
173             m_freem(m);
174             m = n;
175     }
                                                                        if_loop.c
```

158–175 If the packet being looped back consists of more than one `mbuf{}` and the total packet length is shorter than the predefined cluster buffer size MCLBYTES, which is 2048 bytes for the i386 architecture, the entire packet can be stored in a cluster that is referenced by one `mbuf{}`. A new mbuf and a cluster are allocated. Then the entire packet is copied into the newly allocated cluster. The original mbuf chain is no longer needed and is freed.

Note: The same trick is added in the `ip6_input()` function (Listing 3-16), and this code is redundant.

1.6.4   Diagnosing Mbuf Chain

The KAME kernel collects statistics about the organization of `mbuf{}` blocks for input packets to help diagnose those drivers that do not meet the header continuity requirement. The collected statistics result can be viewed by using the **netstat** command.

Executing "netstat -s -p ip6" would produce the following output:

```
ip6:
        10143006 total packets received
        0 with size smaller than minimum
...
        Mbuf statistics:
                34988 one mbuf
                two or more mbuf:
                        ne0= 13027
                10094991 one ext mbuf
                0 two or more ext mbuf
        0 packets whose headers are not continuous
...
```

The output shows that 13027 packets received on interface "ne0" out of 10143006 total incoming packets were stored in two or more mbuf{} structures, and did not meet the requirement. If the IP6_EXTHDR_CHECK() macro had dropped some of the packets, the next to last line would show positive numbers, which corresponds to the statistics variable ip6s_exthdrtoolong that appears in lines 476 and 482 of Listing 1-5. Such a result indicates that the network driver for interface "ne" should be fixed, if possible, so that the requirement can be met for the KAME implementation.

IPv6 Addressing Architecture

2.1 Introduction

The most well-known and important enhancement introduced by IPv6 is the expansion of the address space as the result of increased bit allocation for an IPv6 address, that is, from 32 bits in IPv4 to 128 bits in IPv6. The IPv6 address architecture also introduces several remarkable characteristics along with the enlarged address space, mainly from operational experience with IPv4.

First, IPv6 has an explicit notion of address scopes, with which the uniqueness and usage of an address is limited to some area of the entire Internet. Whereas limited scoped addresses are used in IPv4 multicasting as an operational technique and IPv4 private addresses used with Network Address Translators can be regarded as having an address scope, these were introduced with hindsight to meet newer requirements and were ad hoc. In IPv6, scoping is a built-in notion of the base specification so that it will be available in every implementation and meet various operational requirements.

Also, an IPv6 address is more structured than an IPv4 address. In particular, an IPv6 address explicitly separates the unique identifier of an address within a single link, called the *interface identifier*. An interface identifier can typically be created autonomously based on the network interface's hardware address. It then allows a node to create a unique IPv6 address whose scope is link-local without relying on any external node such as a DHCP server. Such "plug-and-play" is in fact one of the most useful features of IPv6.

Multicasting is more extensively used in IPv6. For example, IPv6-level broadcasting is realized by multicasting with a group that all IPv6 nodes join, thereby avoiding expensive link-level broadcasting. IPv6 multicasting also takes a fundamental role in other base protocols such as Neighbor Discovery and Stateless Address Autoconfiguration as we will see in Chapter 5. Multicast scopes in IPv6 are more flexible and layered.

29

In this chapter, we will discuss the specification details regarding IPv6 address architecture and show how KAME implements the specification in the BSD kernel. We will then provide operational examples of configuring and managing IPv6 addresses on a BSD system. It will help understand the implementation in a more solid way.

The primary reference in this chapter is [RFC3513], which defines the protocol specification about IPv6 addresses. In fact, the IETF has updated the specification to [RFC4291], but we mainly refer to the previous version because the implementation described in this chapter is generally based on that version. Yet we try to follow the latest standardization status with explicit notes when the implementation is different from the latest specifications. Significant changes include the deprecation of one type of limited-scope unicast addresses and updates to address format of multicast addresses.

2.2   IPv6 Addresses

An IPv6 address is formally a 128-bit unsigned integer, which identifies one or more network interfaces. IPv6 addresses are classified into the following three types:

Unicast A unicast IPv6 address identifies a single network interface. Packets destined to a unicast address are delivered to a single network interface.

Anycast An anycast IPv6 address identifies a group of network interfaces but the packets destined to an anycast address are delivered to only a single interface of that group. The receiving interface is perceived as the closest to the source according to the routing protocols.

Multicast An IPv6 multicast address identifies a group of network interfaces. These interfaces may belong to different nodes. Packets destined to a multicast address are delivered to all members of that group.

Note that IPv6 does not define broadcast addresses, unlike IPv4. One of the reasons for this design decision is because broadcast addresses in the network layer often cause link-level broadcasting, which can disturb all devices in the attached link, including the ones that do not even support the particular network protocol. In IPv6, "broadcasting" in the network layer is realized using multicasting as will soon be described.

IPv6 multicast addresses are identified by their first 8 bits: an address with the first 8 bits being all-one is a multicast address; all other addresses are either unicast or anycast addresses.

An IPv6 anycast address is syntactically the same as a unicast IPv6 address but with different semantics. Due to the lack of enough operational experience with anycast addresses in the global Internet, [RFC3513] imposes the following usage restrictions:

- An anycast address must not be used as the source address for any packet.

- An anycast address can only be assigned to routers, not hosts.

Note: Since [RFC3513], a certain amount of operational experience using anycast addresses has been accumulated, particularly in the DNS operation. Based on this observation, the current trend in the IETF is to remove the restrictions as proposed in [V6-ACAST]. In fact, a revised version of the IPv6 address architecture specification [RFC4291] has removed these restrictions.

Despite the restrictions, many technical discussions regarding unicast and anycast addresses are common. In the rest of this chapter, we will thus call unicast and anycast addresses just "unicast addresses" unless the discussion is specific to anycast addresses.

2.3 Textual Representation of IPv6 Addresses

The conventional textual representation of an IPv6 address is written in hexadecimal values of eight 16-bit pieces separated by ":" as in x0:x1:x2:x3:x4:x5:x6:x7. A typical example is as follows:

```
2001:0DB8:0123:4567:89AB:CDEF:0123:4567
 x0   x1   x2   x3   x4   x5   x6   x7
```

Each hexadecimal value is case-insensitive. Thus, this address is equivalent to:

```
2001:0db8:0123:4567:89ab:cdef:0123:4567
 x0   x1   x2   x3   x4   x5   x6   x7
```

We will use both upper- and lower-case to represent the hexadecimal values of an IPv6 address throughout the book.

At least one hexadecimal digit must be present in each of the 16-bit fields, x0–x7. It is not necessary to write out the leading 0's in a field. An IPv6 address may contain contiguous zero-valued fields as follows:

```
2001 : db8 : 123 : 1 : 0 : 0 : 0 : 1
 x0    x1    x2   x3  x4  x5  x6  x7
```

The leading zeros in fields x1 through x7 are not written. Fields x4, x5, and x6 are all zeros. In general, contiguous all-zero fields can be merged and written in the compressed "::" form. The compressed "::" field can appear only once in order to avoid ambiguity. The compressed "::" field may be used for both leading and trailing all-zero fields in an address. This leads to another way to write the previous IPv6 address by compressing fields x4, x5, and x6:

```
2001:db8:123:1::1
```

The textual representation of an IPv6 network prefix is IPv6-address/prefix-length. The prefix length is a decimal value that is the length of the leading bits identifying the prefix. For example, the network prefix represented with the above address and a prefix length of 64 is written as follows:

```
2001:db8:123:1::1/64
```

The portion of the IPv6 address after the prefix length is insignificant. The same prefix can therefore be equally represented as follows:

```
2001:db8:1:2::/64
```

Unlike IPv4, the IPv6 address architecture does not allow a network to be represented using a noncontiguous mask. Thus, a single number specifying the leading effective bits suffices, and there is no notion of network masks in the IPv6 address architecture.

Two special unicast addresses exist in IPv6: the *loopback address* and the *unspecified address*. The loopback address is defined as

```
0:0:0:0:0:0:0:1     or     ::1
```

A special pseudo-interface, called the *loopback interface*, exists in many systems. The loopback address is assigned to this loopback interface. Packets sent to the loopback address never leave the node and will not be transmitted onto the physical network. Instead, the packets will be redirected as input packets to the transmitting node itself.

The unspecified address is defined as

```
0:0:0:0:0:0:0:0     or     ::
```

The unspecified address is a marker value that indicates the absence of an address for an interface. For example, it is set as the source address for packets exchanged during the IPv6 address autoconfiguration phase. Its usage is discussed in more detail in Chapter 5. The unspecified address must not be set as the destination address of any packets. Routers will not forward packets that have the unspecified address as the source or destination address.

Both IPv4 and IPv6 nodes can coexist in a mixed network environment during the transition from IPv4 to IPv6. Special IPv6 addressees are defined to help the transition. Such special IPv6 addresses are constructed by setting the lower 32 bits of the IPv6 address with an IPv4 address. The remaining 96 bits are filled with a preallocated IPv6 prefix. In such cases it is convenient and may serve to emphasize the transitional nature of the address by using the format x0:x1:x2:x3:x4:x5:a.b.c.d where a.b.c.d is the defined textual representation of an IPv4 address. For example, one type of transitional address prepends `0:0:0:0:0:ffff::/96` to the IPv4 address as in

```
0:0:0:0:0:ffff:192.0.2.1
```

or

```
::ffff:192.0.2.1
```

in compressed form.

These are called *IPv4-mapped IPv6 addresses*. An IPv4-mapped IPv6 address represents an IPv4 node in the form of an IPv6 address. The notable usage of IPv4-mapped IPv6 addresses is a socket API extension that enables IPv4 communication on an IPv6 socket. We will discuss the details and issues of this usage in Sections 7.2.3 and 7.2.5. Another expected use of this type of address is an address translation mechanism between IPv4 and IPv6 as defined in [RFC2765], but it is out of scope of this book.

The other type of transitional address prepends 96 zero bits (i.e., ::/96) to an IPv4 address as in

```
0:0:0:0:0:0:192.0.2.2
```

or

```
::192.0.2.2
```

in compressed form.

These are called *IPv4-compatible IPv6 addresses*. An IPv4-compatible IPv6 address represents an IPv4 node that does not have IPv6 connectivity and is expected to be used in an automatic tunneling mechanism as described in [RFC2893]. However, such a technique turned out to be a bad idea especially due to security concerns, and the IETF deprecated the use of this type of address in a revised version of the specification [RFC4291]. We will not discuss these addresses further in this book.

2.4 Address Scopes

The notion of address scopes is a remarkable characteristic of the IPv6 addressing design. An address scope specifies the span where that address is "valid," that is, it can be used as a unique identifier of an interface or a group of interfaces.

For unicast addresses, [RFC3513] defines three types of scopes: link-local, site-local, and global. Unicast link-local and site-local addresses are designated by dedicated prefixes of `fe80::/10` and `fec0::/10`, respectively. The address scope of all the other unicast addresses is defined as global. In addition, [RFC4007] clarifies that the loopback address (`::1`) is categorized as a special link-local address and that the unspecified address (`::`) does not have any scope.

A link-local address is valid only within the network link to which the interface assigned the address is attached. [RFC3513] requires that every IPv6-capable interface have at least one link-local address (see Section 2.6).

Similarly, a site-local address is valid only within a conceptual span of "site" to which the interface assigned the address belongs. Unlike a link, the span of a site is not determined by the physical property of the network. In other words, a site-border can only be determined by manual configuration.

A global address is valid in the entire Internet.

Multicast addresses have a 4-bit "scope" field in their address format, which identifies the address scope (see Section 2.5.3). Currently defined scopes corresponding to that field are as follows:

```
0   reserved
1   interface-local
2   link-local
3   reserved
4   admin-local
5   site-local
6   unassigned
7   unassigned
8   organization-local
9   unassigned
A   unassigned
B   unassigned
C   unassigned
D   unassigned
E   global
F   reserved
```

The interface-local multicast scope is limited to the interface and is used for loopback transmission of multicast packets within the node in which the interface belongs(*). A typical usage of the interface-local multicast address is for one-to-many inter-process communication, where one process multicasts packets to other processes of the same node. The link-local, site-local, and global multicast addresses have the same semantics as the corresponding scopes of unicast addresses. The admin-local scope defines the minimum scope that involves nonautomatic administrative configuration. The organization-local scope covers multiple sites belonging to the same organization. The unassigned scopes are undefined and may be used by administrators to define additional topological multicast regions.

(*)An old version of the address architecture specification [RFC2373] uses the term "node-local" instead of "interface-local." It was then deprecated and replaced with "interface-local," which is more appropriate based on the semantics of the scope architecture.

All scopes "larger" than link-local and "smaller" than global are logical ones, and the specific topological spans are up to the administrator's decision. One natural interpretation of a site and an organization would be realized in a large company network where the entire company is an "organization" and each division network in the company is a separate "site."

Even though every IPv6 address except the unspecified address belongs to one particular scope, including the global scope, addresses that belong to a nonglobal scope are often called *scoped addresses*, thereby emphasizing the nature of the limited span.

2.4.1   Scope Zones

A particular instance of a given scope, that is, a connected region of topology of that scope, is called a *scope zone* or simply a *zone*. Every IPv6 address belongs to one and only one zone corresponding to the address's scope. For example, a link-local zone (or link zone) consists of one particular network link and the interfaces attached to that link, and a link-local address assigned to an interface belongs to one particular link-local zone.

Scope zones have several properties, notably:

- The uniqueness of an address is ensured only within its scope zone.

- The boundary of multiple zones of a scope resides in a node, not on a link.

- An IPv6 packet with a scoped source or destination address is never forwarded to different zones from the corresponding zone where the packet is originated.

- Multiple zones of different scopes that share some interfaces are strongly ordered according to the range of the topological spans. That is, when $x < y$ where x and y are the scope values corresponding to the "scope" field above, if an interface belongs to zone X whose scope type is represented as x, then any zone Y with scope type y containing the interface also contains all interfaces that belong to zone X. This is a formal description of "a site is equal to or larger than a link, and an organization is equal to or larger than a site, and so on."

Considering a site-border configuration will help understand the second point (Figure 2-1). In the configurations shown in Figure 2-1, a user site is connected to a service provider site with two border routers: one at the user's side and the other at the provider's side.

Now assume both the user and the provider want to configure their own site zones. Which configurations in Figure 2-1 are allowed? Whereas configuration (X) may look reasonable, this is not allowed according to the property described above, because the zone boundary would cut through the intermediate link. The rest of the configurations are all valid. In configurations (A) and (B), one of the routers acts as a site border, while in configuration (C) both the routers are a site border with the third "neutral" site zone.

The third point is confusing and is often misunderstood or implemented incorrectly. Consider three hosts *A*, *B*, and *C*, whose addresses are `fe80::a`, `2001:db8::b`, and `fe80::c`. *A* and *C* are in the same link while *B* is in a different link connected via a router. Figure 2-2 shows two cases where host *A* sends a packet to be forwarded by the router with the source address being its link-local address. On the left side, the destination address is *B*'s global address. Thus, the router must discard the packet; otherwise the packet would be forwarded to a different link zone from the one that the source link-local address belongs to.

FIGURE 2-1

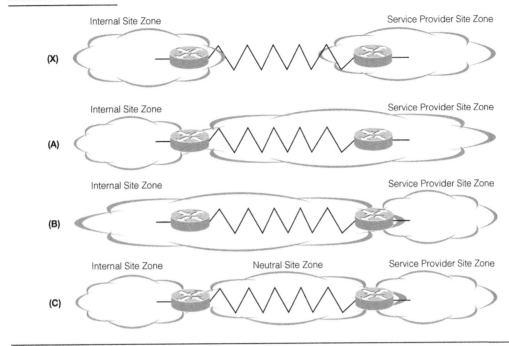

Site border configurations.

FIGURE 2-2

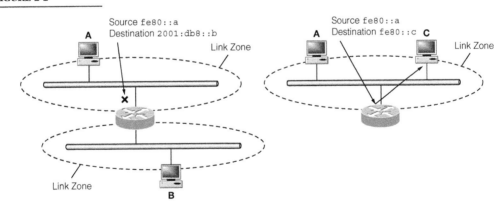

Forwarding a packet using a link-local address.

On the other hand, when host *A* sends a packet with the destination address being *C*'s link-local address, the router must forward the packet back to the incoming link toward host *C*, since the packet stays in the same link zone. Even though this is an unlikely path, it is still completely valid.

Some router implementations are known to behave differently: One implementation would simply forward the packet toward *B* in the left side of Figure 2-2. Another implementation does not handle the right side; it discards the packet unconditionally. While it is less likely to cause trouble in practice, such behavior does not fully conform to the specification.

On the other hand, KAME's implementation can handle both the cases correctly as we will see in Section 3.12.

2.4.2   Zone Indices

A scoped address is inherently ambiguous at its scope zone boundary, since the uniqueness of the address is guaranteed only within the corresponding zone. Consider a router X that connects two links (a multi-link node connecting two link zones in terms of the scope architecture; Figure 2-3). Due to the property of address uniqueness, there can be a node for each link that has the same link-local address, fe80::1 (*A* or *B*). Furthermore, even the two interfaces of *X* can have the same link-local address fe80::2, since these interfaces belong to different link zones.

Thus, it is not sufficient for X to provide the address fe80::1 in order to communicate with either *A* or *B*. Similarly, it does not suffice to provide the address fe80::2 for specifying one particular address of *X*. The corresponding zone must also be given in these cases.

For this purpose, [RFC4007] introduces the notion of *zone indices* or *zone IDs*. A zone index uniquely specifies one particular zone within a single node. It is only meaningful for that node, and its representation can be implementation specific. For example, the zone ID of the upper link in Figure 2-3 for X can be 1 and it can be 2 for *A*.

A zone ID for a particular scope type is sometimes called a "scope-type zone ID" such as "a link zone ID." We also use an abbreviated form of "scope-type ID" like a "link ID" when it obviously means a zone ID from the context.

FIGURE 2-3

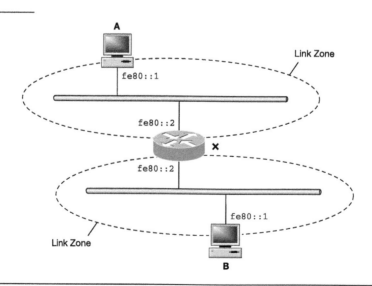

Ambiguity of scoped addresses.

Each interface of a node belongs to one particular zone of each scope type, and has a corresponding zone ID. Each interface belongs to a separate interface zone by definition, and thus has a different interface zone ID. For scopes larger than the interface scope, the zone and zone ID configuration depends on the physical network configuration or administrative settings. [RFC4007] defines the default initial assignment of zone IDs on a node in order to avoid manual configuration in typical cases as follows:

- Each interface has a separate interface zone ID.

- Each interface has a separate link zone ID.

- For scopes larger than link, every interface has a common zone ID.

Figure 2-4 represents the initial assignment on a node that has four interfaces: a loopback (logical) interface, two Ethernet interfaces, and a PPP interface. Each interface belongs to a different link, and has a different link ID.

Figure 2-5 shows a more complex example. In this configuration, the two Ethernet interfaces are connected to the same Ethernet link. This means these interfaces belong to the same link zone, and thus have the same link ID. Even though this is an atypical configuration, this is a valid scenario. Another atypical point of this configuration is that the node is connected to two sites.

FIGURE 2-4

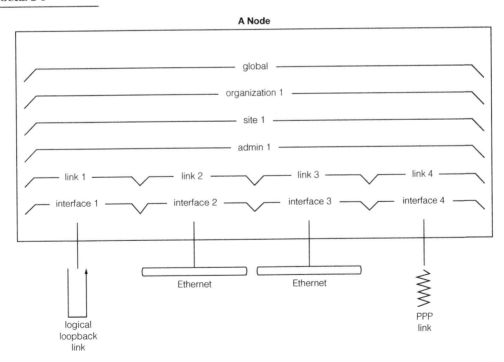

The default assignment of zone IDs.

FIGURE 2-5

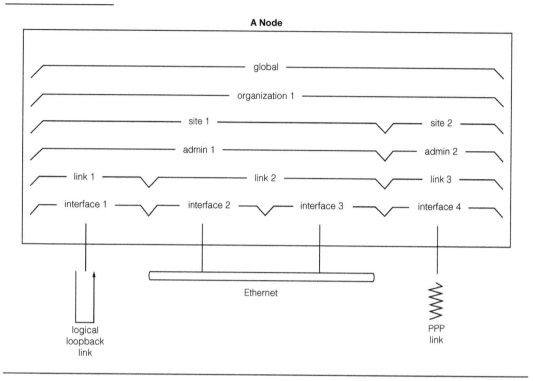

A complex zone ID assignment.

The loopback interface and the Ethernet interfaces belong to the first site while the PPP interface is connected to the second site. These two sites have different zone IDs accordingly. Note that the site configuration automatically requires that the admin-local zone on the PPP interface be different from the admin-local zone(s) on the other interfaces due to the relationship property among multiple scopes explained in the previous section.

[RFC4007] requires that a zone ID contain the type of scope (e.g., link or site) so that all IDs of all scopes are unique within the node. In the actual implementations, however, zone IDs are often defined on a per scope basis. This is at least the case for the KAME implementation. This does not cause a problem in practice, since a zone ID typically accompanies a particular address, which contains the scope type, as will soon be seen in the next subsection.

2.4.3 Textual Representation of Scoped Addresses

It is sometimes convenient if a scoped address can be specified along with its scope zone ID. For example, if an administrator of router X in Figure 2-2 can specify the link-local address of host A with the zone ID of the left side link, the administrator can establish a connection to host A without any ambiguity about the address with host B.

For such purposes, [RFC4007] defines an extension to the basic textual representation of IPv6 addresses described in Section 2.3 as follows:

```
<address>%<zone id>
```

where

- <address> is a literal IPv6 address.

- <zone id> is a string identifying the zone of the address. [RFC4007] requires at least decimal string be supported for this part.

- "%" is a delimiter character that distinguishes between <address> and <zone id>.

Using this extension, the above scenario of connecting from X to A can be realized with the following command:

```
% ssh fe80::1%1
```

where we assume the zone ID for X of the upper link is 1 and the application run over the connection is Secure Shell (SSH).

[RFC4007] also allows an implementation to have implementation-specific representation of the <zone id> part. As can be seen from the default assignment described in Figure 2-4, one natural and useful representation would be interface names for some scope types. In fact, since interface names should provide a one-to-one mapping with interfaces, they are a reasonable representation as an interface zone ID. In addition, it can typically be used as a link zone ID because there is also a one-to-one mapping between links and interfaces in the default assignment, or in other words, an interface is connected to one and only one link by default.

Assuming the default assignment of zone IDs and interface names being used as link IDs, the above example of SSH could also be as follows:

```
% ssh fe80::1%ne0
```

where we assume the interface name of node X on the upper Ethernet link is ne0.

It is sometimes convenient to represent an IPv6 prefix with the corresponding zone. [RFC4007] defines the following notation for this purpose:

```
<IPv6 address>%<zone id>/prefix-length
```

This means an IPv6 prefix "IPv6 address/prefix-length" that corresponds to the zone identified by "zone id." Thus, for example, a link-local subnet prefix for a link zone 1 with the prefix length of 64 bits is represented as:

```
fe80::%1/64
```

2.4.4 Deprecation of Unicast Site-local Addresses

There was a heated discussion in the IETF about the usability of unicast site-local addresses in 2003, and they finally decided to deprecate the syntax and usage of unicast site-local addresses. This decision is documented in [RFC3879].

The main argument for the deprecation was that complexity of unicast site-local addresses due to its inherent ambiguity outweighed their possible benefits. Even though the same point applies to link-local addresses as well, unicast site-local addresses were expected to be used more widely in ordinary applications or in routing protocols, thereby possibly causing much more trouble. Although not everyone was convinced with this argument, the discussion was over by declaring the deprecation of unicast site-local addresses.

The IETF then standardized a replacement of unicast site-local addresses for local communications in [RFC4193]. These addresses are called *Unique Local IPv6 Unicast Addresses* (ULAs). Technically, however, the uniqueness is not 100% guaranteed. Each "site" chooses a 40-bit random value as a pseudo-unique identifier of the "site," and embeds that identifier in the ULAs used in that site.

ULAs have a fixed prefix of `fd00::/8`, followed by a 40-bit random identifier called a *global ID*.

From the scope architecture's point of view, ULAs have the global scope since they are generally assumed to be unique in the entire Internet.

There was another proposal of an alternative to unicast site-local addresses, which is identified by prefix `fc00::/8`, as described in a preliminary draft version of [RFC4193] [ULA-08]. This type of address also has a 40-bit "global ID" field, but it is assumed to be centrally assigned by some authority. It would have assured complete uniqueness and is better than ULAs in this sense, but the IETF decided not to standardize this type of address then due to the lack of consensus about who assigns the IDs and who owns the cost of the assignment.

In the rest of this book, we will generally use the deprecated site-local unicast addresses instead of ULAs. This is because ULAs are relatively new as of this writing and KAME's implementation (described in this book) was written before the deprecation of unicast site-local addresses. However, most of the discussions will not rely on the subtle ambiguity of unicast site-local addresses and should easily apply to ULAs, too.

It should be noted that multicast site-local addresses are not deprecated. The decision only applies to unicast site-local addresses. Thus, examples using a notion of site or site zones in this book such as in Figures 2-1 and 2-5 are still valid regardless of the deprecation of unicast site-local addresses.

2.5 IPv6 Address Format

An IPv6 address is more structured than an IPv4 address. At the high level, the structure of an IPv6 address is similar in concept to the structure of an IPv4 address that is assigned using the Classless Inter-Domain Routing assignment rule as specified in [RFC1519]. Figure 2-6 shows the general format of an IPv6 unicast address.

FIGURE 2-6

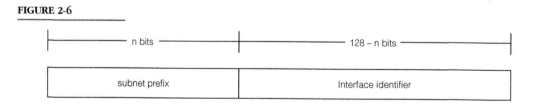

IPv6 unicast address structure.

FIGURE 2-7

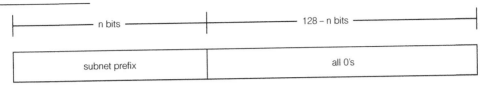

Subnet-router anycast address.

The *subnet prefix* part identifies a specific network link. The subnet prefix typically contains a hierarchical structure. The *interface identifier* identifies a specific interface on the link determined by the subnet prefix. From the pure architectural point of view, an interface index is similar to the host identifier in an IPv4 address; it is just an identifier that uniquely specifies a particular interface (or a set of interfaces in case of anycast address) within a single link. In practice, however, the interface identifier of an IPv6 address often relates to the physical interface of a node on some network types such as Ethernet via an automatic address configuration mechanism, as will be seen in the following subsection.

Associated with this format, there is a predefined anycast address called the *subnet-router anycast address* (Figure 2-7). Packets sent to this address is delivered to a single router on the link identified by the subnet prefix. The receiving router is closest in distance to the source according to some criteria, such as routing protocols. All routers are required to support subnet-router anycast addresses.

[RFC3513] specifies that the length of the interface identifier be 64 bits for all unicast addresses except those starting with binary bits 000. This leads to the following format:

Link-local address format

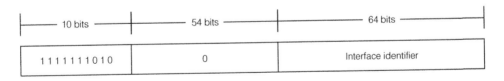

Site-local address format

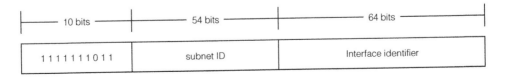

Ordinary global address format

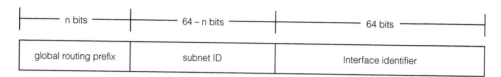

The *global routing prefix* identifies a site or an organization (e.g., a company network) while the *subnet ID* identifies a specific subnet within that site or organization.

2.5.1   Interface Identifier Generation

The interface identifier portion of an IPv6 address can be configured either manually or automatically. The interface identifier must be unique within the link to which the interface is attached regardless of the configuration method.

[RFC3513] requires that all unicast addresses except those starting with binary bits 000 be constructed using the modified IEEE EUI-64 format.

We first describe the original EUI-64 identifier format as in Figure 2-8. The EUI-64 identifier contains a 24-bit Organizationally Unique Identifier (OUI), or company-id, and a 40-bit extension identifier. Within the company-id the universal/local bit indicates whether the 64-bit identifier is globally administered or locally administered (this bit is set if it is local). The group/individual bit indicates whether the identifier identifies a single hardware instance or a group of hardware instances (this bit is set for a group).

The IEEE MAC-48 hardware interface address has a similar format except MAC-48 has a 24-bit extension identifier. Using EUI-64 format the MAC-48 hardware interface address can be converted into a 64-bit interface identifier when IPv6 operates over IEEE 802-based networks. The conversion method inserts 0xFFFE into the MAC-48 address expanding it to 64 bits, and then inverts the universal/local bit. For example, if a MAC-48 address is 00-60-97-8F-6A-4E, then after conversion the final interface identifier is 02-60-97-FF-FE-8F-6A-4E as shown in Figure 2-9.

FIGURE 2-8

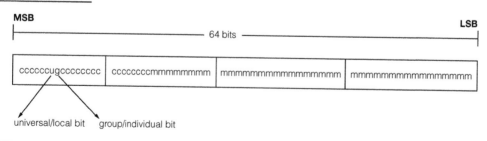

IEEE EUI-64 identifier format.

FIGURE 2-9

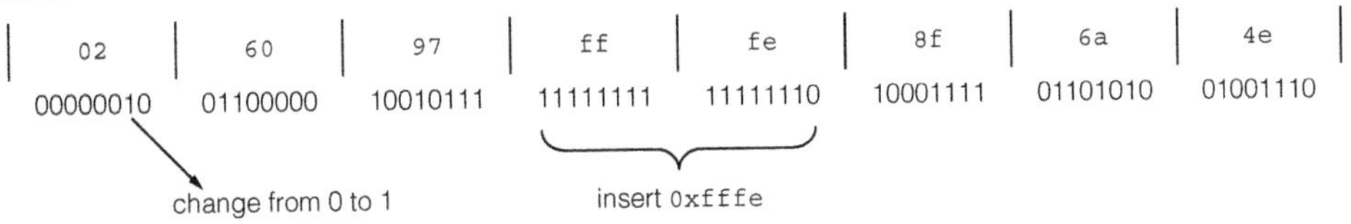

02	60	97	ff	fe	8f	6a	4e
00000010	01100000	10010111	11111111	11111110	10001111	01101010	01001110

change from 0 to 1   insert 0xfffe

MAC-48 to 64-bit interface identifier conversion.

The "modified" format is different from the IEEE's standard extension from a MAC-48 address to the EUI-64 identifier in the following two points:

- The universal/local bit is inverted.

- The inserted 16-bit value is 0xFFFE while 0xFFFF should be used for the standard extension.

The first difference is an intentional modification. If we followed the standard format, an IPv6 interface identifier manually assigned by an administrator would have this bit being 1, since such an identifier is not globally administered. The resulting IPv6 address would then be something like `2001:db8::200:0:0:1`, while the administrators would like to assign a more "readable" address such as `2001:db8::1`. The desired identifier is actually achieved by inverting the universal/local bit.

The second difference is in fact an error in the specification. This was made due to confusion about the standard extension for MAC-48 and EUI-48 identifiers to the EUI-64 identifiers (the extension for EUI-48 identifiers uses 0xFFFE). The error effectively does not matter, though, because the IEEE has obsoleted MAC-48 and it is unlikely that an EUI-48 identifier conflicts with an existing MAC-48 identifier. There should be no worry about conflicting among interface identifiers using the modified EUI-64 format regardless of the inserted 16-bit value. [RFC4291] clarifies this point and states that the "erroneous" value will continue to be used for IPv6 interface identifiers.

On non-802 networks, specific recommendations will be provided in "IPv6 over some-link-type" RFC. Manual configuration or other selection methods are available on network types that do not have built-in identifiers as long as the resulting identifier is unique within the corresponding link.

2.5.2 Notes about Address Format

It should be noted that some parts of the IPv6 address format described so far are not a hard requirement. In particular, a manually configured address may have a different prefix length than 64 or may not be generated using the modified EUI-64 format described in Section 2.5.1. This also means an implementation should not assume a particular format when it handles an IPv6 address. For example, an implementation should not assume the "MAC-48 address" embedded in the interface identifier portion as the link-layer address of the corresponding IPv6 address. Also, an implementation should not discard a packet containing an IPv6 address that is seemingly not "compliant" to the described format.

It is also noteworthy that there are several documents that specify the format of IPv6 addresses seemingly independently. For instance, some "IPv6 over some-link-type" RFCs such as [RFC2464] define the prefix length and the way of generating interface identifiers for IPv6 addresses assigned on an interface of particular link types. While the description is currently consistent, there could be conflicts among these documents in theory. A revised version of the address autoconfiguration protocol document [RFC2462BIS] clarifies that the consistency should be ensured through the IETF's standardization procedure.

2.5.3   Multicast Address Format

The format of IPv6 multicast addresses, which was originally defined in [RFC3513] but then extended in [RFC3306], is shown in Figure 2-10.

FIGURE 2-10

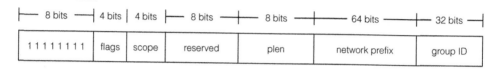

Multicast address format.

The *flags* field identifies the assignment property of the group. The *scope* field indicates the type of address scope as explained in Section 2.4. The *plen* and *network prefix* fields are effective for some type of multicast addresses and identify the IPv6 unicast subnet that owns this multicast address (see below). The *group ID* identifies a specific multicast group. The *reserved* field must be zero.

The flags field is formatted as follows:

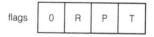

The highest flag is reserved and must be zero.

The T flag indicates whether the multicast group is assigned permanently (T = 0) or dynamically (T = 1). A permanently assigned address is assigned by the Internet Assigned Number Authority (IANA).

The P flag indicates whether the multicast address is assigned based on the network prefix belonging to the subnet that corresponds to some domain owning the multicast address. In this case, the network prefix and plen fields identify the prefix with the prefix being at most 64 bits of the address part and plen being the prefix length. If P is 1, the multicast address is assigned based on the network prefix, in which case the T flag must also be set, thereby indicating this is a dynamically assigned multicast address. This technique ensures unique multicast addresses are easily defined per domain basis.

The R flag further extends multicast addresses based on network prefixes [RFC3956]. If R is 1, it indicates the multicast address embeds the address of the Rendezvous Point (see Chapter 2 of *IPv6 Advanced Protocols Implementation*) for the multicast routing protocol used in the network. In this case, P must also be 1, which then also requires T to be 0 as described above. Thus, this type of multicast address is identified as the common prefix of FF70::/12.

Further details of multicast addresses based on network prefixes are beyond the scope of this book. We will generally focus on the case where both R and P are 0 in the rest of this chapter with a few minor exceptions.

The group ID field was originally a large 112-bit field, but then shrank to a 32-bit field as shown in Figure 2-10. This is advantageous because some major link-layer protocols, such as Ethernet, map an IPv6 multicast address to a link-layer multicast address by taking the lower 32 bits of the network layer address (see Chapter 2 of *IPv6 Advanced Protocols Implementation*); allocating group IDs in the 32-bit field thus ensures the IDs will also be unique at the link-layer level, thereby avoiding collisions.

[RFC3307] sets a guideline of the allocation of the 32-bit group IDs with categorization of this field into the following three ranges:

0x000000001 to 0x3FFFFFFF group IDs for permanent IPv6 multicast addresses. Permanent IPv6 multicast addresses are "well-known" addresses for standard protocol operations (e.g., identifying all IPv6 routers) or correspond to known IPv4 multicast addresses (e.g., identifying a group of Network Time Protocol (NTP) servers [RFC2375]). These IDs are managed and allocated by IANA as part of the entire multicast address.

0x400000000 to 0x7FFFFFFF permanent group IDs. These IDs are also "well-known," managed and allocated by IANA. But they are supposed to be used in multicast addresses based on network prefixes. A particular group ID has the same semantics regardless of the upper 96 bits. For example, if a 32-bit value 0x40404040 is allocated for a group of NTP servers, this can be used for various networks using the prefix-based format as a group of NTP servers in the corresponding networks. More specifically, two organizations that have global unicast subnets 2001:db8:1111::/64 and 2001:db8:aaaa::/64, respectively, can separately define site-local multicast addresses ff35:40:2001:db8:1111:0:4040:4040 and ff35:40:2001:db8:aaaa:0:4040:4040 that specify a group of local NTP servers in their own "sites."

0x800000000 to 0xFFFFFFFF group IDs for dynamic IPv6 multicast addresses. Dynamic IPv6 multicast addresses are allocated by some automatic multicast address allocation mechanism such as the MADCAP protocol [RFC2730] or by hand. The T flag must be set to 1 for dynamic IPv6 multicast addresses.

The group ID of a permanent multicast address or a permanent group ID is independent of the overall scope of the multicast address. For example, ff0X::101 is permanently assigned for a group of Network Time Protocol (NTP) servers [RFC2375]. Thus,

    ff02:0:0:0:0:0:0:101

identifies all NTP servers in a particular link. Similarly, multicast addresses

    ff05:0:0:0:0:0:0:101

and

    ff08:0:0:0:0:0:0:101

identify all NTP servers in a particular site or organization, respectively.

There are some common restrictions on the usage of multicast addresses. A multicast router will not forward any packets beyond the scope zone identified in the destination multicast address (see Section 2.4.1). A multicast address must not be the source address of any packet. A multicast address must not appear in the Type 0 Routing header (Section 3.3.4). All IPv6 nodes will discard packets not meeting these conditions.

The IPv6 address architecture specification defines some special multicast addresses: *all-nodes multicast addresses, all-routers multicast addresses*, and *solicited-node multicast addresses*.

The all-nodes multicast addresses are:

```
ff01:0:0:0:0:0:0:1    interface-local scope
ff02:0:0:0:0:0:0:1    link-local scope
```

The all-routers multicast addresses are:

```
ff01:0:0:0:0:0:0:2    interface-local scope
ff02:0:0:0:0:0:0:2    link-local scope
ff05:0:0:0:0:0:0:2    site-local scope
```

The solicited-node multicast addresses have the prefix `ff02:0:0:0:0:1:ff00::/104`. A solicited-node multicast address is constructed by taking the low-order 24 bits of a unicast or anycast address and prepending it to the solicited-node multicast address prefix. For example, if a unicast address is

```
2001:db8:7654:3210:fedc:ba98:7654:3210
```

then the corresponding solicited-node multicast address is

```
ff02:0:0:0:0:1:ff54:3210.
```

A node is required to join the solicited-node multicast address group for Neighbor Discovery and Duplicate Address Detection. This is discussed in more detail in Chapter 5. When a node has multiple addresses with the same interface-identifier, it has to join only one solicited-node multicast group because their solicited-node multicast address is the same. This contributes to the reduction of the number of multicast groups that a host must join.

2.6   Node Address Requirements

An IPv6-capable node must

- Configure a link-local address for each attached interface. For a logical "loopback" interface, the loopback address is regarded as the required link-local address.

- Join the solicited-node multicast group for each configured unicast and anycast address on the associated interface.

- Join the all-nodes multicast group of the interface-local and link-local scopes.

- Support the loopback address.

- Recognize all of its configured unicast and anycast addresses for each of its attached interfaces.

- Recognize all of the multicast address groups it belongs to.

In addition, an IPv6 router must

- Join the subnet-router anycast address on each interface that is configured as a router.

- Join the all-routers multicast addresses of the interface-local, link-local and site-local scopes.

- Recognize all its configured anycast addresses.

2.7   IPv6 Address Space Management

Global unicast IPv6 addresses are generally allocated via Regional Internet Registries (RIRs) with a few exceptions for special-purpose addresses. There are five RIRs in the world today that provide address allocation and registration services to support the operation of the global Internet. These RIRs are

- African Network Information Center (AfriNIC)

- American Registry for Internet Numbers (ARIN)

- Asia Pacific Network Information Center (APNIC)

- Latin American and Caribbean IP address Regional Registry (LACNIC)

- Reseaux IP Européens Network Co-ordination Centre (RIPE-NCC)

The current IPv6 address allocation space to the RIRs can be seen at a Web page of IANA: http://www.iana.org/assignments/ipv6-unicast-address-assignments.

2.8   Code Introduction

In the following sections we will introduce IPv6 address-related data structures and functions. We will refer to the following files throughout the discussion.

TABLE 2-1

File	Description
${KAME}/freebsd4/sys/net/if_var.h	Interface address structures
${KAME}/kame/sys/netinet6/in6_var.h	Internal address structure for IPv6
${KAME}/kame/sys/netinet6/scope6_var.h	Definitions related to address scopes
${KAME}/kame/sys/netinet6/in6.c	IPv6 address configuration and modification functions
${KAME}/Kame/sys/netinet6/in6.h	IPv6 address structures
${KAME}/kame/sys/netinet6/in6_ifattach.c	Functions relating to enabling IPv6 support on an interface
${KAME}/kame/sys/netinet6/scope6.c	Functions relating to address scopes
${KAME}/kame/sys/netinet6/in6_src.c	Subroutines for handling scope zone IDs

2.8.1   IPv6 Address Structures—`in6_addr{}` and `sockaddr_in6{}`

The `in6_addr{}` and the `sockaddr_in6{}` structures are defined in `in6.h`. The `in6_addr{}` structure represents an IPv6 address. The definition of the `in6_addr{}` structure is as follows.

Listing 2-1

```
                                                                        in6.h
121     struct in6_addr {
122             union {
123                     u_int8_t    __u6_addr8[16];
124                     u_int16_t   __u6_addr16[8];
125                     u_int32_t   __u6_addr32[4];
126             } __u6_addr;                        /* 128-bit IP6 address */
127     };
128
129     #define s6_addr     __u6_addr.__u6_addr8
130     #ifdef _KERNEL  /* XXX nonstandard */
131     #define s6_addr8    __u6_addr.__u6_addr8
132     #define s6_addr16   __u6_addr.__u6_addr16
133     #define s6_addr32   __u6_addr.__u6_addr32
134     #endif
                                                                        in6.h
```

The `in6_addr{}` structure is defined as the union structure of sixteen 8-bit, eight 16-bit, and four 32-bit arrays to make it easy to access various parts of an IPv6 address. There are four macros defined for accessing these arrays. We can access each byte in an IPv6 address by using either the `s6_addr` or the `s6_addr8` macro. The `s6_addr16` and `s6_addr32` macros make it possible to access an IPv6 address in units of 16 bits and 32 bits respectively. For example, `s6_addr16` can be visualized as follows:

```
        2001 : db8 :  1  :  2  :  0  :  0  :  A  :  B

s6_addr16  [0]   [1]   [2]   [3]   [4]   [5]   [6]   [7]
```

The `s6_addr` macro is the only macro defined in [RFC3493]—Basic Socket Extensions for IPv6 (see Chapter 7). Application programs can use this macro to store and retrieve IPv6 addresses. The other address macros are KAME-specific extensions; applications should not use them.

The `sockaddr_in6{}` structure is the IPv6 socket type interpretation of the generic `sockaddr{}` structure. The definition of `sockaddr_in6{}` is as follows:

Listing 2-2

```
                                                                        in6.h
144     struct sockaddr_in6 {
145             u_int8_t        sin6_len;       /* length of this struct(sa_family_t)*/
146             u_int8_t        sin6_family;    /* AF_INET6 (sa_family_t) */
147             u_int16_t       sin6_port;      /* Transport layer port # (in_port_t)*/
148             u_int32_t       sin6_flowinfo;  /* IP6 flow information */
149             struct in6_addr sin6_addr;      /* IP6 address */
150             u_int32_t       sin6_scope_id;  /* scope zone index */
151     };
                                                                        in6.h
```

The `sockaddr_in6{}` structure is used to store the address family information, the port number of the transport layer, the IPv6 flow label information (see Section 3.2), the 128-bit IPv6 address, and its scope zone index. This structure corresponds to the `sockaddr_in{}` structure for IPv4, but KAME's IPv6 kernel implementation uses this socket address structure more aggressively than the IPv4 kernel code in order to deal with scope zones (see Section 2.9 for more details).

The structure member name of sin6_scope_id is confusing in that the corresponding notion in the scoping architecture is "(scope) zone index." Unfortunately, this structure had been defined much earlier than the scoping architecture was clarified when there had been no notion of "zones."

2.8.2 Macros and Variables

The following table describes some of the macros used for masking an IPv6 address.

TABLE 2-2

Address mask macros	Description
IN6MASK0	128 0 bits
IN6MASK32	32 1 bits and 96 0 bits
IN6MASK64	64 1 bits and 64 0 bits
IN6MASK96	96 1 bits and 32 0 bits
IN6MASK128	128 1 bits
IPV6_ADDR_INT32_ONE	The value 1
IPV6_ADDR_INT32_TWO	The value 2
IPV6_ADDR_INT32_MNL	The mask 0xFF010000, which is the interface-local multicast prefix
IPV6_ADDR_INT32_MLL	The mask 0xFF020000, which represents link-local multicast prefix
IPV6_ADDR_INT32_SMP	The mask 0x0000FFFF, used for checking IPv4-compatible IPv6 addresses
IPV6_ADDR_INT16_ULL	The value 0xFE80, which represents the link-local unicast prefix
IPV6_ADDR_INT16_USL	The value 0xFEC0, which represents the site-local unicast prefix
IPV6_ADDR_INT16_MLL	The value 0xFF02, which represents the link-local multicast prefix

Some of the above macros are used for initializing the following variables.

TABLE 2-3

Address mask macros	Description
struct sockaddr_in6 sa6_any	This variable has all of the protocol fields, i.e., sin6_port, sin6_flowinfo, sin6_addr, sin6_scope_id fields set to zero.
const struct in6_addr in6mask0	Initialized using IN6MASK0
const struct in6_addr in6mask32	Initialized using IN6MASK32
const struct in6_addr in6mask64	Initialized using IN6MASK64
const struct in6_addr in6mask96	Initialized using IN6MASK96
const struct in6_addr in6mask128	Initialized using IN6MASK128

The following table describes some of the macro definitions for predefined IPv6 addresses.

TABLE 2-4

Predefined address macros	Description
IN6ADDR_ANY_INIT	Represents the unspecified address.
IN6ADDR_LOOPBACK_INIT	Represents the loopback address.
IN6ADDR_INTFACELOCAL_ALLNODES_INIT	Represents the all-nodes interface-local multicast address.
IN6ADDR_NODELOCAL_ALLNODES_INIT	The same as IN6ADDR_INTERFACELOCAL_ALLNODES_INIT except the name "node-local" has been deprecated.
IN6ADDR_LINKLOCAL_ALLNODES_INIT	Represents all-nodes link-local multicast address.
IN6ADDR_LINKLOCAL_ALLROUTERS_INIT	Represents all-routers link-local multicast address.

The above macros are used for initializing the variables listed in Table 2-5. These macros and variables are frequently used during packet processing.

TABLE 2-5

Predefined address variables	Description
const struct in6_addr in6addr_any	Initialized using IN6ADDR_ANY_INIT
const struct in6_addr in6addr_loopback	Initialized using IN6ADDR_LOOPBACK_INIT
const struct in6_addr in6addr_nodelocal_allnodes	Initialized using IN6ADDR_NODELOCAL_ALLNODES_INIT
const struct in6_addr in6addr_linklocal_allnodes	Initialized using IN6ADDR_LINKLOCAL_ALLNODES_INIT
const struct in6_addr in6addr_linklocal_allrouters	Initialized using IN6ADDR_LINKLOCAL_ALLROUTERS_INIT

Some macros and variables are defined for testing IPv6 address structures, and are frequently used in the kernel implementation. Table 2-6 lists these address comparison macros. The first seven macros are included in the standard API definitions [RFC3493] [RFC3542] and can be used by applications. The last four are kernel-specific macros.

[RFC3493] defines IN6_IS_ADDR_MC_NODELOCAL(), which is internally identical to IN6_IS_ADDR_MC_INTFACELOCAL(), but the kernel implementation does not use the standard macro since it is based on the old terminology of multicast scope (see the note in Section 2.4).

TABLE 2-6

Macro	Description
IN6_ARE_ADDR_EQUAL(a,b)	Checks if two instances of the in6_addr{} structure are equal.
SA6_ARE_ADDR_EQUAL(a,b)	Checks if two instances of the sockaddr_in6{} structure are equal. This macro checks for sin6_scope_id equality in addition to sin6_addr equality. Other fields are not taken into account.
IN6_IS_ADDR_UNSPECIFIED(a)	Checks if the given instance of in6_addr{} structure is the unspecified address.
SA6_IS_ADDR_UNSPECIFIED(a)	Checks if the given instance of sockaddr_in6{} structure is the unspecified address. This macro also confirms that the sin6_scope_id field is set to zero.
IN6_IS_ADDR_LOOPBACK(a)	Checks if the given instance of in6_addr{} structure is the loopback address.
IN6_IS_ADDR_V4COMPAT(a)	Checks if the given instance of in6_addr{} structure is an IPv4-compatible IPv6 address.
IN6_IS_ADDR_V4MAPPED(a)	Checks if the given instance of in6_addr{} structure is an IPv4-mapped IPv6 address.

The following are macro names representing IPv6 scope types. The macro values correspond to the value of the "scope" field of an IPv6 address multicast address (see Section 2.4).

TABLE 2-7

Macro	Value	Description
IPV6_ADDR_SCOPE_INTFACELOCAL	0x01	Interface-local scope
IPV6_ADDR_SCOPE_LINKLOCAL	0x02	Link-local scope
IPV6_ADDR_SCOPE_SITELOCAL	0x05	Site-local scope
IPV6_ADDR_SCOPE_ORGLOCAL	0x08	Organization-local scope
IPV6_ADDR_SCOPE_GLOBAL	0x0e	Global scope

A macro name for the admin-local scope is not defined, since this is not used in the code.

2.9 Handling Scope Zones

In this section, we describe how the KAME kernel manages IPv6 address scopes and scope zones.

2.9.1 Initialization of Scope Zones

As explained in Section 2.4.2, each IPv6 interface is assigned a scope zone ID for each scope type from interface-local to global. KAME's implementation stores the zone IDs of an interface in an IPv6-specific structure called the `in6_ifextra{}` structure attached to the `ifnet{}` structure, the general structure containing link-layer information.

The zone IDs on an interface are represented as a `scope6_id{}` structure as follows:

Listing 2-3

```
                                                                  scope6_var.h
  6    struct scope6_id {
  7            /*
  8             * 16 is correspondent to 4bit multicast scope field.
  9             * i.e. from node-local to global with some reserved/unassigned types.
 10             */
 11            u_int32_t s6id_list[16];
 12    };
                                                                  scope6_var.h
```

This is effectively an array of 32-bit unsigned integers, each of which represents a single zone ID. This array has 16 entries, which corresponds to the number of scope types represented in the 4-bit "scope" field of an IPv6 multicast address.

This structure is initialized when the corresponding interface is attached to the system. It typically happens during the system boot procedure, but can also take place later for removable interfaces such as a PCMCIA Ethernet adaptor. The initialization timing ensures that the IPv6 protocol operation can always assume valid IDs are stored in the `scope6_id{}` structure.

The `scope6_ifattach()` function performs the initialization, which is shown below:

Listing 2-4

```
                                                                      scope6.c
 34    struct scope6_id *
 35    scope6_ifattach(ifp)
 36            struct ifnet *ifp;
 37    {
 41            int s = splnet();
 43            struct scope6_id *sid;
 44
 45            sid = (struct scope6_id *)malloc(sizeof(*sid), M_IFADDR, M_WAITOK);
 46            bzero(sid, sizeof(*sid));
 47
 48            /*
 49             * XXX: IPV6_ADDR_SCOPE_xxx macros are not standard.
 50             * Should we rather hardcode here?
 51             */
 52            sid->s6id_list[IPV6_ADDR_SCOPE_INTFACELOCAL] = ifp->if_index;
 53            sid->s6id_list[IPV6_ADDR_SCOPE_LINKLOCAL] = ifp->if_index;
 54    #ifdef MULTI_SCOPE
 55            /* by default, we don't care about scope boundary for these scopes. */
 56            sid->s6id_list[IPV6_ADDR_SCOPE_SITELOCAL] = 1;
 57            sid->s6id_list[IPV6_ADDR_SCOPE_ORGLOCAL] = 1;
 58    #endif
 59
 60            splx(s);
 61            return sid;
 62    }
                                                                      scope6.c
```

As can be seen from the code, this implementation uses the interface index as interface and link zone IDs by default. Technically, this does not fully conform to the protocol specification, since the IDs do not include the scope type and are not unique among IDs of all the scopes within the system (see Section 2.4.2). Yet this is a natural representation of the default assignment shown in Figure 2-4.

Whereas the KAME kernel provides the most general form of the scope zone IDs for all the defined scopes, it is not yet expected to work on a scope zone boundary for larger than link-local scopes. Therefore, the rest of the s6id_list array is just filled with 0 and is effectively unused. The MULTI_SCOPE preprocessor macro is provided simply for showing the possible default initialization when the kernel can act as a site or organization boundary.

Likewise, the current implementation is not expected to work if the zone ID assignment is dynamically changed during protocol operation. This implicitly means the implementation basically assumes a one-to-one mapping between interfaces and links while technically that is only the case for the default assignment of zone IDs (Figure 2-4). Although an API is provided for a user to reconfigure the assignment, we do not describe that part of the implementation.

2.9.2 Scope Zone IDs

The KAME implementation has the notion of default zone ID for each scope type as specified in [RFC4007]. The default zone ID is used if an IPv6 address given in some context (e.g., passed by a user application) is ambiguous about the scope zone.

In the kernel, the default zone IDs are stored in a statically allocated scope6_id{} structure named sid_default. For example, sid_default.s6id_list[2] contains the default link zone ID.

Although the default zone IDs could be useful in some cases, it may also be rather confusing particularly for novice users. For this reason, the use of the default zone IDs are disabled by default in the following two points:

- Default zone IDs are initialized as "unspecified" by default.

- A system configuration variable for enabling the use of the default IDs is turned off by default.

The first point means a user should manually specify the default IDs. This can be done by the **ndp** program with the -I option specifying an interface. Then the zone IDs of the specified interface will be used as the default. Note that this operation affects all the scope types at once. The current implementation does not allow a user to specify the default zone IDs per scope type basis.

The system configuration variable mentioned in the second point is represented as a global variable named ip6_use_defzone. Its value can be changed by the net.inet6.ip6.use_defaultzone sysctl variable. When this variable is set to non-0, the default zone IDs (if configured) will be respected.

Recall the SSH example shown in Section 2.4.3. Using the default link zone ID, node *X* can also make an SSH connection to host *A* by the following steps:

```
# sysctl -w net.inet6.ip6.use_defaultzone=1
net.inet6.ip6.use_defaultzone: 0 -> 1
```

```
# ndp -I ne0
ND default interface = ne0

# ssh fe80::1
```

2.9.3   Zone IDs in Address Structures

As explained in the example with Figure 2-3, scoped addresses shown as a 128-bit IPv6 address can be ambiguous even within a single node. Thus the IPv6 protocol stack in the kernel must have the ability to identify the appropriate scope zone when it handles an IPv6 address.

This can be done by using the sockaddr_in6{} structure (Listing 2-2), which has a dedicated field for storing the zone ID: the sin6_scope_id field. In fact, the KAME kernel tries to keep an IPv6 address in the form of the sockaddr_in6{} structure with the zone ID whenever possible.

Confusingly, however, there is another form of zone ID representation used in the kernel, mainly for interface-local and link-local addresses. This form embeds the zone ID in the second 16-bit of the 128-bit IPv6 address structure (i.e., in the in6_addr{} structure). Figure 2-11 shows an example of this form for link-local unicast address fe80::a:b:c:d.

> *Note*: Recall that an interface index, which is a 16-bit identifier, is used as the zone ID for interface-local and link-local addresses as explained in Section 2.9.1. Thus one 16-bit field is enough in practice for storing the zone ID, although sin6_scope_id is a 32-bit field.

Since the 16-bit field embedding the zone ID should be 0 on the wire according to the address format shown in Section 2.5, using this field for implementation-specific purposes may be justified as long as it is restricted inside the kernel. Still, you may wonder why we need to be bothered with the strange form while the sockaddr_in6{} structure can contain complete information in a cleaner way.

This is primarily for historical and compatibility reasons. At the time the KAME project started, the sockaddr_in6{} structure did not have the sin6_scope_id field (see [RFC2133]), and link-local addresses had to be disambiguated in an implementation-dependent manner. The embedded form was a KAME-specific workaround to this problem. It was used everywhere in the kernel for representing IPv6 addresses, including some protocol-independent parts of the kernel like the routing table or the routing socket API.

FIGURE 2-11

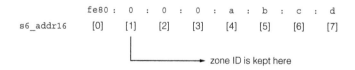

Embedding zone ID in address.

Since then, several applications have been developed, and some of those had to care about the embedded form directly. Among those were routing tools such as **route6d**, a RIPng daemon (which will be described in Chapter 1 of *IPv6 Advanced Protocols Implementation*). Such programs had to deal with the embedded form of IPv6 link-local addresses through the routing socket. Another example is system administration tools that directly refer to the kernel memory, such as the **netstat** program. These applications needed to clear the embedded ID and set the sin6_scope_id correctly before showing the address to the user.

In 1999, [RFC2553] solved the ambiguity issue by adding the sin6_scope_id field to the sockaddr_in6{} structure. The KAME and BSD implementations supported the new API, and updated most IPv6-related interfaces accordingly, including input and output system calls on an AF_INET6 socket. Unfortunately, however, it seemed too late to update the routing table structure and the routing socket interface: routing tools were so tightly associated with the embedded form. On the other hand, the routing interface is generally protocol-independent and the KAME developers did not think it was acceptable for the BSD community to introduce IPv6-specific changes to such a general interface.

Therefore, the current kernel implementation adopts a "hybrid" approach as shown in Figure 2-12. The IPv6 protocol stack in the kernel generally maintains IPv6 addresses in the sockaddr_in6{} structure with the zone ID being both embedded in the sin6_addr field and specified in the sin6_scope_id field. In the protocol independent routing table, the zone ID is only embedded within the sin6_addr field. The IPv6 protocol stack is responsible for clearing or restoring the sin6_scope_id field when it deals with the routing table. The same relationship applies to the protocol independent interface address structures (see Section 2.10), since these are tightly related to the routing table and can often be exchanged with the routing table transparently.

Ordinary applications do not have to care about address scopes; they can and should only be aware of the sin6_scope_id field. They must not directly refer to or set the second 16-bit of an IPv6 address assuming the embedded form. When an application passes an IPv6 address through a standard AF_INET6 socket (e.g., as the packet's destination address), the IPv6 protocol stack will convert the structure into its internal "hybrid" form. Similarly, when the kernel passes an IPv6 address to an application, the protocol stack will make sure that the embedded part is cleared and the sin6_scope_id field is set appropriately.

Finally, applications that need to interact with the kernel part maintaining the embedded form need special handling. They should directly interpret the embedded form, and, when necessary, convert the address in the nonembedded form using the standard sin6_scope_id field to the embedded form before passing the address to the kernel through the AF_INET6 socket interface. Some management tools that directly access the kernel memory image via the kvm interface or IPv6 routing daemons using the routing socket belong to this category.

Another effect of the embedded form is that network masks can be contiguous. For example, we can apply the natural 64-bit contiguous mask for fe80:1:: to represent "fe80::%1/64". On the other hand, if the link identifier were in fact stored in the sin6_scope_id field, we would need a noncontiguous mask for the separate field. This is not a big deal, though, since BSD's routing routines can naturally handle noncontiguous masks.

FIGURE 2-12

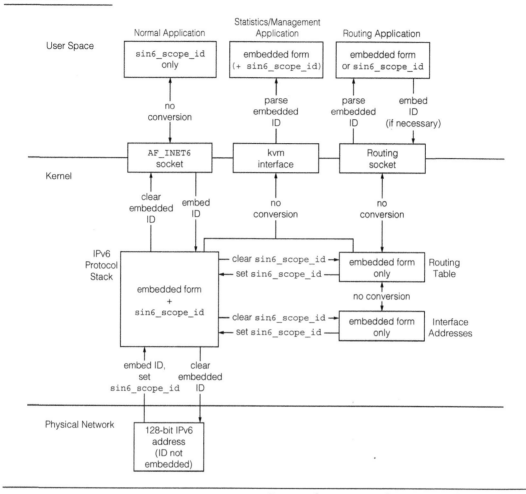

Entire implementation architecture regarding scope zones.

In any event, applications should generally avoid relying on the kernel-specific details whenever possible. Indeed, the applications should not even be aware of such details. There are plenty of reasons for this:

- The first obvious reason is portability. Since the embedded form is specific to the KAME and BSD kernel implementations, applications that take an action relying on that particular form will not work on other operating systems.

- Second, address ambiguity is not specific to link-local or interface-local addresses; any nonglobal, multicast addresses are inherently ambiguous. Thus, an ad hoc check specific to interface-local or link-local scopes assuming the embedded form can be the source of a bug in the future. It should also be noted that we cannot embed the zone ID for unicast prefix-based multicast addresses (see Figure 2-10). It does not have enough space in the address format.

- Third, it is vulnerable to future changes of the embedded form in the kernel. For example, the embedded position may change or the zone ID may not actually be the interface index, even though such a drastic change will unlikely be made due to compatibility concerns.

- Fourth, we may not always be able to assume the embedded field is zero for a packet received from the wire. In fact, there is a new standard format of link-local multicast addresses that requires the second 16-bit of the address be a non-0 value [RFC4489].

- Fifth, while it is moot whether other link-local addresses with the second 16-bit field being non-0 is valid or not in terms of the address architecture specification, it would at least make the validation procedure more complex with the embedded internal form.

- Finally, the embedded field is a 16-bit integer, while the standard `sin6_scope_id` field is 32-bit. This mismatch may cause an annoying corner case or error handling.

2.9.4 Scope-Related Utility Functions

In this subsection, we introduce several kernel utility functions regarding address scope that are often called from other parts of the kernel implementation.

in6_addrscope() Function

The first function is `in6_addrscope()`, which returns the scope type of a given IPv6 address in the `in6_addr{}` type. The return value is one of the `IPV6_ADDR_SCOPE_xxx` macros described in Table 2-7.

The implementation of the `in6_addrscope()` function is shown below.

Listing 2-5

scope6.c

```
157   int
158   in6_addrscope(addr)
159          struct in6_addr *addr;
160   {
161          int scope;
162
163          if (addr->s6_addr[0] == 0xfe) {
164                  scope = addr->s6_addr[1] & 0xc0;
165
166                  switch (scope) {
167                  case 0x80:
168                          return IPV6_ADDR_SCOPE_LINKLOCAL;
169                          break;
170                  case 0xc0:
171                          return IPV6_ADDR_SCOPE_SITELOCAL;
172                          break;
173                  default:
174                          return IPV6_ADDR_SCOPE_GLOBAL; /* just in case */
175                          break;
176                  }
```

```
177                      }
178
179
180                      if (addr->s6_addr[0] == 0xff) {
181                              scope = addr->s6_addr[1] & 0x0f;
182
183                              /*
184                               * due to other scope such as reserved,
185                               * return scope doesn't work.
186                               */
187                              switch (scope) {
188                              case IPV6_ADDR_SCOPE_INTFACELOCAL:
189                                      return IPV6_ADDR_SCOPE_INTFACELOCAL;
190                                      break;
191                              case IPV6_ADDR_SCOPE_LINKLOCAL:
192                                      return IPV6_ADDR_SCOPE_LINKLOCAL;
193                                      break;
194                              case IPV6_ADDR_SCOPE_SITELOCAL:
195                                      return IPV6_ADDR_SCOPE_SITELOCAL;
196                                      break;
197                              default:
198                                      return IPV6_ADDR_SCOPE_GLOBAL;
199                                      break;
200                              }
201                      }
202
203                      /*
204                       * Regard loopback and unspecified addresses as global, since
205                       * they have no ambiguity.
206                       */
207                      if (bcmp(&in6addr_loopback, addr, sizeof(*addr) - 1) == 0) {
208                              if (addr->s6_addr[15] == 1) /* loopback */
209                                      return IPV6_ADDR_SCOPE_LINKLOCAL;
210                              if (addr->s6_addr[15] == 0) /* unspecified */
211                                      return IPV6_ADDR_SCOPE_GLOBAL; /* XXX: correct? */
212                      }
213
214                      return IPV6_ADDR_SCOPE_GLOBAL;
215              }
```
——— scope6.c

163–177 If the given address matches the prefix of a unicast link-local or site-local address, the corresponding scope type is returned. (Note that this implementation does not yet reflect the deprecation of unicast site-local addresses.) Other addresses beginning with prefix `fe00::/8` are simply treated as a global address.

180–201 For multicast addresses, the pre-defined scope type is returned. If the scope type is reserved, it is treated as global.

Note: This part of the code is not really accurate in the following points:

1. This `switch` clause should actually cover the admin-local scope.

2. Since administrators can use the unassigned types for their convenience (Section 2.4), it is probably better to return the value of the "scope" field as an opaque value, rather than treating those as global.

203–212 The loopback address has the link-local scope as specified in [RFC4007]. (Note: The comment is old and does not match the actual implementation.) This implementation treats

the unspecified address as global. While it may be controversial from the architecture
point of view, it does not actually matter in this implementation in the context where this
function is used.

214 All other addresses are simply regarded as global.

in6_addr2zoneid() *Function*

The in6_addr2zoneid() function provides the zone ID of a given address in the context
of a given interface. This function is used to identify the zone of the address contained in an
incoming packet based on the arrival interface. It is also used for performing zone boundary
checks on outgoing packets. The implementation is shown below.

Listing 2-6

scope6.c

```
222    int
223    in6_addr2zoneid(ifp, addr, ret_id)
224            struct ifnet *ifp;          /* must not be NULL */
225            struct in6_addr *addr;      /* must not be NULL */
226            u_int32_t *ret_id;          /* must not be NULL */
227    {
228            int scope;
229            u_int32_t zoneid = 0;
230            struct scope6_id *sid = SID(ifp);
242
243            /*
244             * special case: the loopback address can only belong to a loopback
245             * interface.
246             */
247            if (IN6_IS_ADDR_LOOPBACK(addr)) {
248                    if (!(ifp->if_flags & IFF_LOOPBACK))
249                            return (-1);
250                    else {
251                            *ret_id = 0; /* there's no ambiguity */
252                            return (0);
253                    }
254            }
255
256            scope = in6_addrscope(addr);
257
258            switch (scope) {
259            case IPV6_ADDR_SCOPE_INTFACELOCAL: /* should be interface index */
260                    zoneid = sid->s6id_list[IPV6_ADDR_SCOPE_INTFACELOCAL];
261                    break;
262
263            case IPV6_ADDR_SCOPE_LINKLOCAL:
264                    zoneid = sid->s6id_list[IPV6_ADDR_SCOPE_LINKLOCAL];
265                    break;
266
267            case IPV6_ADDR_SCOPE_SITELOCAL:
268                    zoneid = sid->s6id_list[IPV6_ADDR_SCOPE_SITELOCAL];
269                    break;
270
271            case IPV6_ADDR_SCOPE_ORGLOCAL:
272                    zoneid = sid->s6id_list[IPV6_ADDR_SCOPE_ORGLOCAL];
273                    break;
274
275            default:
276                    zoneid = 0;             /* XXX: treat as global. */
277                    break;
278            }
279
```

```
280            *ret_id = zoneid;
281            return (0);
282    }
```
─── scope6.c

243–254 The loopback address requires special consideration. Whereas it is categorized as having a link-local scope in the scope architecture based on [RFC4007], providing the link ID for a loopback interface will be rather confusing. In fact, since the loopback address is only meaningful within a single node and it is not ambiguous within a node unlike other link-local addresses, there is no need for an application to specify the zone ID of the loopback address. For instance, in the SSH example we have seen so far, executing ssh::1 suffices and is reasonable, rather than ssh::1%lo0. Thus, this function just provides 0 as the zone ID, meaning "unspecified."

258 Other general cases are handled based on the scope type returned by the in6_addrscope() function.

259–278 Variable sid points to the scope6_id{} structure corresponding to the given interface. For known scope types such as interface-local or link-local, the zone ID stored in the structure will be provided. For other scopes, 0 will be used, meaning "unspecified" just like the global scope. Again, this switch clause should cover the admin-local scope. Also, treating "unassigned" multicast scopes as global is controversial and probably incorrect.

280 If the zone ID is successfully determined, it is stored in the address pointed by variable ret_id, which will be implicitly returned to the caller.

Zone ID Conversion Functions

A set of utility functions are provided in order to convert between the kernel-internal representation of zone IDs described in the previous section and the standard form using the sin6_scope_id field of the sockaddr_in6{} structure. These functions are mainly used in the conversions shown in Figure 2-12. Whereas the appropriate source file for these functions should be scope6.c, some of those are actually defined in in6_src.c because they were first implemented as a subroutine for the source address selection algorithm when the notion of address scopes was not fully clarified.

in6_embedscope() Function

The in6_embedscope() function converts a sockaddr_in6{} structure with a proper sin6_scope_id value into the internal format for the IPv6 protocol stack. It is mainly used at the transport or higher layer where an IPv6 address given by an application is examined.

Listing 2-7
─── in6_src.c

```
1168   int
1169   in6_embedscope(in6, sin6)
1170          struct in6_addr *in6;
1171          const struct sockaddr_in6 *sin6;
```

```
1172   {
1180           struct ifnet *ifp;
1181           u_int32_t zoneid = sin6->sin6_scope_id;
1182
1183           *in6 = sin6->sin6_addr;
1184
1185           /*
1186            * don't try to read sin6->sin6_addr beyond here, since the caller may
1187            * ask us to overwrite existing sockaddr_in6
1188            */
1189
1190           if (IN6_IS_SCOPE_LINKLOCAL(in6) || IN6_IS_ADDR_MC_INTFACELOCAL(in6)) {
1191                   /* KAME assumption: link id == interface id */
1192                   if (zoneid) {
1193                           if (if_index < zoneid)
1194                                   return (ENXIO);   /* XXX EINVAL? */
1198                           ifp = ifindex2ifnet[zoneid];
1200                           if (ifp == NULL) /* XXX: this can happen for some OS */
1201                                   return (ENXIO);
1202
1203                           /* XXX assignment to 16bit from 32bit variable */
1204                           in6->s6_addr16[1] = htons(zoneid & 0xffff);
1205                   }
1206           }
1207
1208           return 0;
1210   }
```
                                                                                          _____in6_src.c

1169–1183 Variable `sin6` is the input argument for this function. The address stored in the `sin6_addr` field is converted so that it will have the zone ID embedded (when necessary), and is set in the `in6` argument. In fact, `in6` often points to the address of the `sin6_addr` field of argument `sin6`, in which case `sin6` will be modified in this function as a result.

1190–1201 This function only considers the link-local and interface-local scopes. If the `sin6_scope_id` field of argument `sin6` has a non-0 ID, it should be a valid interface index according to the default assignment shown in Section 2.9.1. This can be confirmed by checking whether the given ID is in the valid range of interface indices and the corresponding entry in the `ifindex2ifnet` array points to a valid `ifnet{}` structure. Note that the given zone ID is not validated against the primary source of zone IDs stored in a `scope6_id{}` structure. Even though these should be consistent based on the default assignment, the actual zone ID may have been changed by hand, and thus this implementation is not really accurate.

1204 A valid zone ID is stored in the second 16-bit field of variable `in6`. At this point it is ensured that `zoneid` has a 16-bit integer value, and so the logical-and operation with value 0xffff is actually redundant.

in6_recoverscope() Function

The `in6_recoverscope()` function, shown below, is a sort of reverse function of `in6_embedscope()`. It converts a given IPv6 address with the zone ID embedded in its 128-bit address field into the standard `sockaddr_in6{}` structure with the `sin6_scope_id` field set correctly. The main purpose of this function is to prepare the standard `sockaddr_in6{}` structure to be returned to an application through the `AF_INET6` socket API.

Listing 2-8

in6_src.c

```
1219    int
1220    in6_recoverscope(sin6, in6, ifp)
1221            struct sockaddr_in6 *sin6;
1222            const struct in6_addr *in6;
1223            struct ifnet *ifp;
1224    {
1225            u_int32_t zoneid;
1226
1227            sin6->sin6_addr = *in6;
1228
1229            /*
1230             * don't try to read *in6 beyond here, since the caller may
1231             * ask us to overwrite existing sockaddr_in6
1232             */
1233
1234            sin6->sin6_scope_id = 0;
1235            if (IN6_IS_SCOPE_LINKLOCAL(in6) || IN6_IS_ADDR_MC_INTFACELOCAL(in6)) {
1236                    /*
1237                     * KAME assumption: link id == interface id
1238                     */
1239                    zoneid = ntohs(sin6->sin6_addr.s6_addr16[1]);
1240                    if (zoneid) {
1241                            /* sanity check */
1242                            if (zoneid < 0 || if_index < zoneid)
1243                                    return ENXIO;
1244                            if (ifp && ifp->if_index != zoneid)
1245                                    return ENXIO;
1246                            sin6->sin6_addr.s6_addr16[1] = 0;
1247                            sin6->sin6_scope_id = zoneid;
1248                    }
1249            }
1250
1251            return 0;
1252    }
```

in6_src.c

1219–1223 Argument in6 is an input address to in6_recoverscope(). This function sets the sin6_addr and sin6_scope_id fields of argument sin6 based on argument in6. If an optional argument ifp is given, it is used as a hint for verifying the embedded zone ID.

1227–1234 The two fields of sin6 are initialized with in6 and a constant of 0 ID.

1235–1239 Like in6_embedscope(), this function only considers the link-local and interface-local cases. In these cases, it assumes the zone ID is embedded in the second 16-bit field of the given address, and extracts the value.

1240–1249 The embedded zone ID must be a valid interface index. It is confirmed by checking that the value is in the appropriate range and, if ifp is specified, it is actually the interface index of ifp. A valid zone ID is then set in the sin6_scope_id field, and the embedded ID is cleared. Again, this function is not really accurate in that it does not check the consistency with the scope6_id{} structure.

in6_clearscope() *Function*

The in6_clearscope() function, shown below, simply zero-clears the second 16-bit of a link-local or interface-local address, assuming a zone ID is embedded there. This function is used just before sending a packet to the network in case a zone ID is embedded in some address field of the outgoing packet.

Listing 2-9

_____ in6_src.c

```
1257    void
1258    in6_clearscope(addr)
1259            struct in6_addr *addr;
1260    {
1261            if (IN6_IS_SCOPE_LINKLOCAL(addr) || IN6_IS_ADDR_MC_INTFACELOCAL(addr))
1262                    addr->s6_addr16[1] = 0;
1263    }
```
_____ in6_src.c

scope6_check_id() *Function*

The scope6_check_id() function, shown below, is intended to be used in the highest layer
of the IPv6 protocol stack where IPv6 addresses given by an application are validated. It also
sets the sin6_scope_id field to the default zone ID for the scope of the given address if that
field is unspecified by the application.

After validating the zone ID, scope6_check_id() calls the in6_embedscope() function in order to convert the standard sockaddr_in6{} structure into the kernel-internal form
with an embedded zone ID. As commented in the code, most of the processing is duplicated
with in6_embedscope(), and these two functions should actually be unified.

Listing 2-10

_____ in6_src.c

```
369    int
370    scope6_check_id(sin6, defaultok)
371            struct sockaddr_in6 *sin6;
372            int defaultok;
373    {
374            u_int32_t zoneid;
375            struct in6_addr *in6 = &sin6->sin6_addr;
376            struct ifnet *ifp;
377
378            if ((zoneid = sin6->sin6_scope_id) != 0) {
379                    /*
380                     * At this moment, we only check interface-local and
381                     * link-local scope IDs, and use interface indices as the
382                     * zone IDs assuming a one-to-one mapping between interfaces
383                     * and links.
384                     * XXX: in6_embedscope() below does the same check (in case
385                     * of !SCOPEDROUTING).  We should eventually centralize the
386                     * check in this function.
387                     */
388                    if (IN6_IS_SCOPE_LINKLOCAL(in6) ||
389                        IN6_IS_ADDR_MC_INTFACELOCAL(in6)) {
390                            if (if_index < zoneid)
391                                    return (ENXIO);
395                            ifp = ifindex2ifnet[zoneid];
397                            if (ifp == NULL) /* XXX: this can happen for some OS */
398                                    return (ENXIO);
399                    }
400            } else if (defaultok)
401                    sin6->sin6_scope_id = scope6_addr2default(in6);
402
403            /* KAME hack: embed scopeid */
404            if (in6_embedscope(in6, sin6) != 0)
405                    return (EINVAL);
406
407            return (0);
408    }
```
_____ in6_src.c

2.10   Interface Address Structures

IPv6 addresses assigned to network interfaces are maintained as a linked list in the kernel. There
are two types of address lists. One address list keeps all of the addresses for one particular
protocol family assigned to all available interfaces in the system. The other address list keeps
track of all of the addresses assigned to a specific interface. For example, the former keeps
track of all IPv6 addresses in the system, and the latter keeps track of all addresses assigned to
a specific interface regardless of the protocol family. The `ifaddr{}` structure contains these
address lists.

2.10.1   `ifaddr{}` and `in6_ifaddr{}` Structures

The `ifaddr{}` structure is used to hold protocol-independent address information. The main
purpose of the `ifaddr{}` structure is a placeholder for keeping pointers to the protocol-specific
information such as an address, a netmask, a link-layer routing management function, etc. The
`ifaddr{}` structure is often used as a part of a larger structure that stores protocol-specific
address information. The `in6_ifaddr{}` structure is the larger structure for IPv6.

Listing 2-11

```
                                                                        if_var.h
446    /*
447     * The ifaddr structure contains information about one address
448     * of an interface.  They are maintained by the different address families,
449     * are allocated and attached when an address is set, and are linked
450     * together so all addresses for an interface can be located.
451     */
452    struct ifaddr {
453            struct  sockaddr *ifa_addr;       /* address of interface */
454            struct  sockaddr *ifa_dstaddr;    /* other end of p-to-p link */
455    #define ifa_broadaddr    ifa_dstaddr      /* broadcast address interface */
456            struct  sockaddr *ifa_netmask;    /* used to determine subnet */
457            struct  if_data if_data;          /* not all members are meaningful */
458            struct  ifnet *ifa_ifp;           /* back-pointer to interface */
459            TAILQ_ENTRY(ifaddr) ifa_link;     /* queue macro glue */
460            void    (*ifa_rtrequest)          /* check or clean routes (+ or -)'d */
461                    (int, struct rtentry *, struct rt_addrinfo *);
462            u_short ifa_flags;                /* mostly rt_flags for cloning */
463            u_int   ifa_refcnt;               /* references to this structure */
464            int     ifa_metric;               /* cost of going out this interface */

468            int (*ifa_claim_addr)             /* check if an addr goes to this if */
469                    (struct ifaddr *, struct sockaddr *);
470
471    };
                                                                        if_var.h
```

The `in6_ifaddr{}` structure is a superset of the `ifaddr{}` structure. It allocates the
space to store an IPv6 address, the IPv6 prefix information, and the link-layer routing function
for IPv6, etc.

Listing 2-12

```
                                                                        in6_var.h
101    struct  in6_ifaddr {
102            struct  ifaddr ia_ifa;            /* protocol-independent info */
103    #define ia_ifp           ia_ifa.ifa_ifp
```

```
104     #define ia_flags            ia_ifa.ifa_flags
105             struct  sockaddr_in6 ia_addr;    /* interface address */
106             struct  sockaddr_in6 ia_net;     /* network number of interface */
107             struct  sockaddr_in6 ia_dstaddr; /* space for destination addr */
108             struct  sockaddr_in6 ia_prefixmask; /* prefix mask */
109             u_int32_t ia_plen;               /* prefix length */
110             struct  in6_ifaddr *ia_next;     /* next in6 list of IP6 addresses */
    ...
115             int     ia6_flags;
116
117             struct in6_addrlifetime ia6_lifetime;
118             time_t  ia6_createtime; /* the creation time of this address, which is
119                                      * currently used for temporary addresses only.
120                                      */
121             time_t  ia6_updatetime;
122
123             /* back pointer to the ND prefix (for autoconfigured addresses only) */
124             struct nd_prefix *ia6_ndpr;
125
126             /* multicast addresses joined from the kernel */
127             LIST_HEAD(, in6_multi_mship) ia6_memberships;
128     };
                                                              _____in6_var.h
```

The relationship between the members of the ifaddr{} and in6_ifaddr{} structures is shown in Figure 2-13.

The first three members of the ifaddr{} structure, namely ifa_addr, ifa_dstaddr, and ifa_netmask, are pointers to the real storage defined in the in6_ifaddr{} structure. These storage fields are ia_addr, ia_dstaddr, and ia_prefixmask of sockaddr_in6{} type. The ia_addr field stores the IPv6 address of the interface; the ia_dstaddr field stores the destination IPv6 address if the interface is a point-to-point interface; and the ia_prefixmask field stores the IPv6 prefix mask that identifies the subnet the interface is attached to.

FIGURE 2-13

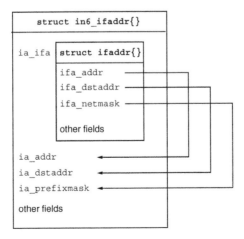

Relationship between ifaddr{} *and* in6_ifaddr{}.

In the `ifaddr{}` structure, `ifa_ifp` points to an instance of the `ifnet{}` structure for the interface on which the address is configured. The `ifa_link` field links all of the addresses that are assigned to the interface regardless of the protocol family so that we can scan every interface address through `ifa_link` pointer.

The `ifa_rtrequest` member is a function pointer for link-layer routing entry management. It is set to a protocol-specific link-layer address resolution function. In the case of IPv6, the `ifa_rtrequest` member is set to the `nd6_rtrequest()` function (see Listing 2-102 later in this chapter). This function will be discussed in Section 5.15.1.

Since IPv6 addressing architecture does not have the notion of noncontiguous netmask (see Section 2.3), the `ia_prefixmask` field could be replaced with a simple prefix length. However, this field is used as a protocol-independent part of the kernel system as shown in Figure 2-13, and thus the seemingly redundant netmask information is still necessary. In fact, `ia_plen` was introduced as a possible replacement of `ia_prefixmask`, but is actually not used in the kernel implementation.

The `ia_net` member was derived from the `in_ifaddr{}` structure, the interface address structure for IPv4, but is not used in the IPv6 implementation.

In KAME, every IPv6 address has associated prefix information. The `ia6_ndpr` member is a pointer to prefix information entry. Addresses and prefixes are closely related to each other but are managed separately. The prefix information and the relationship with addresses are discussed in Section 2.11.

The `ia6_memberships` member keeps pointers to multicast membership structures derived from this address. It will be described in more detail in Section 2.10.3.

The `ia_next` member links all IPv6 interface address structures in the kernel. The `in6_ifaddr` global variable is set to the head of the list. We can scan all IPv6 addresses in the kernel by traversing the `ia_next` pointers.

The `ia6_flags` member stores IPv6 address specific flags as shown in Table 2-8. Note that the only difference between a unicast address and an anycast address in the KAME implementation in terms of address configuration is whether or not the `IN6_IFF_ANYCAST` flag is set in the `ia6_flags` field. We will see in Section 2.16 how to configure an IPv6 anycast address by the **ifconfig** command with the `IN6_IFF_ANYCAST` flag.

The `ia6_lifetime` member keeps lifetime information of the address. The definition of the `in6_addrlifetime{}` structure, type of `ia6_lifetime`, is shown, in Listing 2-13.

Listing 2-13

―――――――――――――――――――――――――――――――――――――in6_var.h
```
85      struct in6_addrlifetime {
86              time_t ia6t_expire;       /* valid lifetime expiration time */
87              time_t ia6t_preferred;    /* preferred lifetime expiration time */
88              u_int32_t ia6t_vltime;    /* valid lifetime */
89              u_int32_t ia6t_pltime;    /* prefix lifetime */
90      };
```
―――――――――――――――――――――――――――――――――――――in6_var.h

An IPv6 address has two kinds of lifetime. One is the *preferred lifetime* and the other is the *valid lifetime*. An address is called a *deprecated address* if its preferred lifetime has expired. The specification generally prohibits the use of a deprecated address for initiating new connections. However, this address may still continue to be used for an existing connection and incoming connections until its valid lifetime has expired. Further details of the address lifetime calculation and management are discussed in Section 5.10.1.

TABLE 2-8

Address flags	Description
IN6_IFF_ANYCAST	The address is an anycast address.
IN6_IFF_TENTATIVE	Duplicate Address Detection (DAD) is in progress for this address.
IN6_IFF_DUPLICATED	DAD detects this address as being duplicated.
IN6_IFF_DETACHED	This address is detached likely due to the relocation of the node to another link (see Section 5.19.5).
IN6_IFF_DEPRECATED	The preferred lifetime of this address has expired (see below).
IN6_IFF_NODAD	DAD is not necessary for this address.
IN6_IFF_AUTOCONF	This address was automatically configured.
IN6_IFF_TEMPORARY	This is a temporary address generated according to the privacy extension mechanism as defined in [RFC3041] (see Section 5.10.4).
IN6_IFF_NOTREADY	A shortcut of (IN6_IFF_TENTATIVE|IN6_IFF_DUPLICATED). This indicates the address cannot be used for communication.
IN6_IFF_READONLY	A shortcut of (IN6_IFF_DUPLICATED|IN6_IFF_DETACHED| IN6_IFF_NODAD|IN6_IFF_TEMPORARY). This indicates the address flags cannot be modified by hand.

The `ia6_createtime` member represents the creation time of the address, which is used for [RFC3041]-style temporary addresses. The usage will be described in more detail in Section 5.10.4. The `ia6_updatetime` member represents the last time the address lifetimes are updated by a Router Advertisement for the lifetime management. This will be discussed in Section 5.19.3.

2.10.2 `in6_ifreq{}` and `in6_aliasreq{}` Structures

The `in6_ifreq{}` and `in6_aliasreq{}` structures are an argument of `ioctl` commands when an application such as the **ifconfig** utility configures an interface with a particular IPv6 address. These `ioctl` commands add or remove an IPv6 address on an interface or change some parameters of an already configured address.

The `in6_ifreq{}` structure is defined as follows.

Listing 2-14

——— in6_var.h
```
258   struct  in6_ifreq {
259           char    ifr_name[IFNAMSIZ];
260           union {
261                   struct    sockaddr_in6 ifru_addr;
262                   struct    sockaddr_in6 ifru_dstaddr;
263                   short     ifru_flags;
264                   int       ifru_flags6;
265                   int       ifru_metric;
266                   caddr_t   ifru_data;
267                   struct in6_addrlifetime ifru_lifetime;
```

```
268                    struct in6_ifstat ifru_stat;
269                    struct icmp6_ifstat ifru_icmp6stat;
270                    u_int32_t ifru_scope_id[16];
271            } ifr_ifru;
272      };
```
_____ in6_var.h

The `ifr_name` member is the textual name of the network interface to which an address is configured. For example, "fxp0" indicates that the interface is an Intel EtherExpress Pro 100 MB PCI device and if multiple cards exist in the system it is the first instance of that device.

The `ifr_ifru{}` union contains various `ioctl` arguments depending on the command type. The `ifru_addr` member is used for the `SIOCDIFADDR_IN6` command for removing the specified IPv6 address from the interface. This member is often referenced by the following shortcut macro defined in `${KAME}/freebsd4/sys/net/if.h`:

```
#define ifr_addr        ifr_ifru.ifru_addr
```

The `in6_aliasreq{}` structure is used as the `ioctl` argument of the `SIOCAIFADDR_IN6` command for adding a new IPv6 address or modifying parameters of an existing address. It is defined as follows.

Listing 2-15
_____ in6_var.h

```
274      struct  in6_aliasreq {
275              char    ifra_name[IFNAMSIZ];
276              struct  sockaddr_in6 ifra_addr;
277              struct  sockaddr_in6 ifra_dstaddr;
278              struct  sockaddr_in6 ifra_prefixmask;
279              int     ifra_flags;
280              struct  in6_addrlifetime ifra_lifetime;
281      };
```
_____ in6_var.h

The `ifra_name` member is the same as `ifr_name` of the `in6_ifreq{}` structure. The `ifra_addr` member is the IPv6 address being configured. The `ifra_dstaddr` member is set to the destination address by choice for a point-to-point interface. The `ifra_prefixmask` member is a mask that defines the subnet prefix of the address contained in `ifra_addr`. As noted in Section 2.10.1, this could simply be an integer that specifies the corresponding prefix length. In fact, it would be better in order to avoid erroneous input of a noncontiguous mask passed by an application. In the actual implementation, however, this structure was defined so that it can directly be mapped to the `ia_prefixmask` member of the `in6_ifaddr{}` structure. The `ifra_flags` member is initialized to a combination of flags if necessary (see Table 2-8). The `ifra_lifetime` member specifies the preferred and valid lifetimes for the address.

2.10.3 Multicast Address Structures

The KAME kernel uses two data structures to keep track of multicast group membership information: `in6_multi{}` and `in6_multi_mship{}`. The `in6_multi{}` structure holds information for group membership of a specific multicast address.

Listing 2-16
─── in6_var.h

```
560    struct  in6_multi {
561            LIST_ENTRY(in6_multi) in6m_entry; /* list glue */
562            struct  sockaddr_in6 in6m_sa;     /* IP6 multicast address */
563            struct  ifnet *in6m_ifp;          /* back pointer to ifnet */

567            struct  ifmultiaddr *in6m_ifma; /* back pointer to ifmultiaddr */

569            u_int   in6m_refcount;            /* # membership claims by sockets */
570            u_int   in6m_state;               /* state of the membership */
571            u_int   in6m_timer;               /* MLD6 listener report timer */
572            struct  router6_info *in6m_rti; /* router info */
573            struct  in6_multi_source *in6m_source;  /* filtered source list */
574    };
```
─── in6_var.h

The `in6m_sa` member contains the multicast address. The `in6m_ifp` member is a pointer to the interface on which the multicast group is joined. The `in6m_ifma` member is a pointer to a protocol-independent list of multicast addresses configured on the interface (see below). The `in6m_refcount` member is not used in the FreeBSD implementation. The `in6m_state` and `in6m_timer` members are related to the Multicast Listener Discovery protocol version 1 (MLDv1), while `in6m_rti` and `in6m_source` are related to version 2 of MLD (MLDv2). We will discuss MLDv1 in Chapter 2 of *IPv6 Advanced Protocols Implementation*. Details of MLDv2 are not covered in this series.

The `ifmultiaddr{}` structure, the instance of the `in6m_ifma` member of the `in6_multi{}` structure, is defined as follows.

Listing 2-17
─── in6_Var.h

```
483    struct ifmultiaddr {
484            LIST_ENTRY(ifmultiaddr) ifma_link; /* queue macro glue */
485            struct  sockaddr *ifma_addr;     /* address this membership is for */
486            struct  sockaddr *ifma_lladdr;   /* link-layer translation, if any */
487            struct  ifnet *ifma_ifp;         /* back-pointer to interface */
488            u_int   ifma_refcount;           /* reference count */
489            void    *ifma_protospec;         /* protocol-specific state, if any */
490    };
```
─── in6_Var.h

This structure is a protocol-independent object that lists all multicast groups of all network protocols used on a particular interface. Each instance of this structure relates to a corresponding protocol-specific structure via the `ifma_protospec` member, which points to an `in6_multi{}` structure in IPv6. The `ifma_addr` member points to a socket address structure whose instance is protocol dependent and is a `sockaddr_in6{}` structure in IPv6. The content of this instance is copied from the `in6m_sa` member of the corresponding `in6_multi{}` structure. The `ifma_refcount` member is a reference counter to this multicast group. In FreeBSD, this member is used instead of the `in6m_refcount` member of the `in6_multi{}` structure.

The `in6_multi_mship{}` structure, shown below, is a referential copy of an `in6_multi{}` structure and maintained by an object, such as an interface address, that joins the corresponding group.

Listing 2-18

_____in6_var.h

```
539    struct in6_multi_mship {
540           struct  in6_multi *i6mm_maddr;   /* Multicast address pointer */
541           struct  sock_msf *i6mm_msf;      /* Multicast source filters */
542           LIST_ENTRY(in6_multi_mship) i6mm_chain;  /* multicast options chain */
543    };
```

_____in6_var.h

The i6mm_maddr member is a pointer to an instance of the in6_multi{} structure that holds the membership information. The in6_multi_mship{} structure is an entry of the ia6_memberships linked list built in either the in6_ifaddr{} structure (Listing 2-12) or the in6p_moptions member of the inpcb{} structure (see Section 7.4.7). The i6mm_msf member is used for MLDv2.

Figure 2-14 depicts the relationship among the various data structures introduced so far in this section (some structures are omitted for brevity).

We consider a node on which two IPv6 addresses are assigned: fe80::203:47ff:fea5:3058 (link-local) and 2001:db8::203:47ff:fea5:3058 (global). In addition, we assume a Dynamic Host Configuration Protocol for IPv6 (DHCPv6) server that joins the well-known site-local multicast group for DHCPv6 servers, ff05::1:3. We also assume for demonstration that this server application happens to join all-nodes link-local multicast group (ff02::1) explicitly.

As explained in Section 2.6, every IPv6 node joins the all-nodes link-local multicast group. The node also joins the multicast group represented by the solicited-node multicast address of each configured unicast address. In this case, the two addresses share the same solicited-node multicast address, ff02::1:ffa5:3085.

The in6_ifaddr{} structure for each unicast address maintains a list of in6_multi_mship{} structures for the required multicast groups. Each entry of the list points to the corresponding in6_multi{} structure.

Similarly, the DHCPv6 server maintains a list of in6_multi_mship{} structures for the multicast groups it joins. But in this case the list is kept in the ip6_moptions{} structure pointed from the PCB for the server's socket.

It should be noted that all link-local unicast and multicast addresses shown in Figure 2-14 are represented in the kernel-internal form as explained in Section 2.9.3, assuming the corresponding link ID is 1. For example, the all-nodes multicast address is represented as ff02:1::1 instead of ff02::1. The sin6_scope_id field of sockaddr_in6{} stored in the in6_multi{} structure has the valid zone ID as shown in Figure 2-12. On the other hand, the sin6_scope_id field of sockaddr_in6{} stored in the in6_ifaddr{} structure for the link-local unicast address is 0-cleared, since this is a part of an interface address structure.

2.11 IPv6 Prefix Structure

In BSD's traditional networking code, the notion of network prefix is implicitly implemented with a corresponding address and a subnet mask. For example, when IPv4 address 192.0.2.1 is assigned to an Ethernet interface with the subnet mask of 0xffffff00, the BSD kernel will automatically install a direct route through the interface for the corresponding prefix of the

FIGURE 2-14

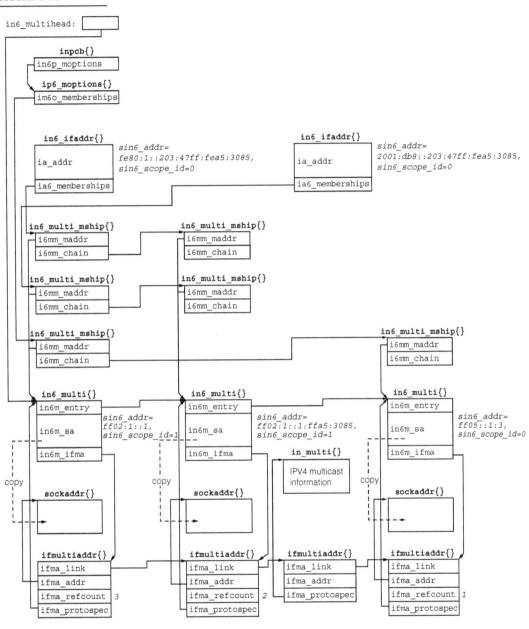

Relationship among multicast related structures.

subnet, `192.0.2.0/24`. When the address is deleted from the interface, the direct route for the subnet prefix is also removed.

This implementation model is not really suitable for IPv6 for the following reasons:

- Multiple addresses may share a single prefix. For example, an IPv6 router typically has a global unicast address and the corresponding subnet-router anycast address on an interface. In this case, the unicast and anycast addresses share the same subnet prefix. Also, a host that assigns a global address via stateless address autoconfiguration may also create temporary addresses for the privacy extension (see Section 5.10.4). Then the "public" (nontemporary) and temporary addresses share the same subnet prefix. In these cases it is not convenient to manage the prefix as if it were owned by one particular address. For instance, deleting the address that "owns" the prefix would require additional processing, such as transferring the ownership to a remaining address. Additionally, the related direct route cannot be removed simply because one of the addresses sharing the prefix is deleted.

- The notion of network prefix identifying on-link destinations is more independent from an interface address, from the protocol architecture point of view. In fact, a host is informed via the Neighbor Discovery protocol of an on-link prefix (see Section 5.7.2), which is not always related to configuring an address that belongs to the prefix. Such a case is not unusual if the host configures its addresses via DHCPv6 as we will see in Chapter 4 of *IPv6 Advanced Protocols Implementation*.

Therefore, KAME's IPv6 implementation introduces a novel model of network prefixes. Each subnet (or on-link in general) prefix in the kernel is represented in a separate data structure named `nd_prefix{}`. Details of this structure will be discussed in Section 5.13.5. For now, it is sufficient to understand the following points:

- A prefix is identified by an IPv6 prefix (address and the prefix length) and the associated interface.

- Each prefix has its own lifetime, which is managed separately from the lifetimes of addresses.

- The `nd_prefix{}` structure has a reference counter field which specifies the number of addresses that share the prefix. This counter can be 0 (see below).

Now recall that the `in6_ifaddr{}` structure has a member pointing to an `nd_prefix{}` structure (the `ia6_ndpr` field in Listing 2-12). Thus, for example, if a host has public and temporary IPv6 addresses `2001:db8:1:2:203:47ff:fea5:3085` and `2001:db8:1:2:1155:bdf5:e87b:b190`, whose subnet prefix is `2001:db8:1:2::/64`, then the kernel should maintain the structures as depicted in Figure 2-15.

In general, the direct route through the interface for the subnet prefix `2001:db8:1:2::/64` is installed or removed along with the corresponding `nd_prefix{}` structure independently from the creation or deletion of addresses. In particular, deleting one of the two addresses in Figure 2-15 simply means the decrement of the reference counter by 1, and the direct route is not affected by this processing since the reference counter is positive and the prefix is still active.

There can be even an active `nd_prefix{}` structure whose reference counter is 0. This can happen if the host is informed of an on-link prefix without creating any associated address. The direct route for the prefix is installed in this case as well, and will remain until the prefix's lifetime expires.

FIGURE 2-15

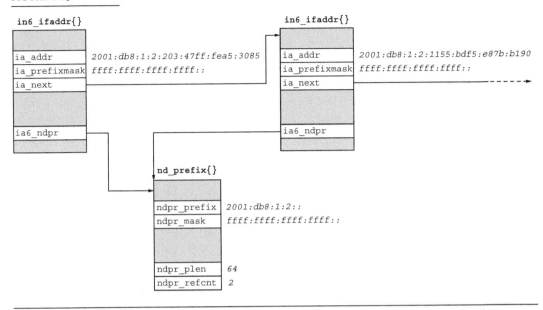

Relationship between interface and prefix structures.

2.12 Overview of Address Manipulation Routines

We will describe the kernel implementation of manipulating IPv6 addresses in the succeeding sections. This processing involves many kernel functions, some of which are covered in other chapters. Figures 2-16 and 2-17 give an overview of the relationship among the related routines through function call graphs. Functions that appear in shaded nodes will be discussed in later sections of this chapter.

Unlike the IPv4 protocol stack in the BSD kernel, KAME's IPv6 stack configures IPv6 addresses in various contexts. These can be categorized into the following three cases:

- As a result of automatic link-local configuration when an interface becomes up.

- By some `ioctl` commands, typically via a configuration utility.

- As a result of stateless address autoconfiguration. This can be done by either receiving a Router Advertisement message or a timer expiration event.

The `in6_update_ifa()` function is the main routine for the configuration procedure, which is commonly called in all the cases. This function will be discussed in Section 2.14.2.

The first path typically takes place during the system bootup procedure by enabling a network interface with the **ifconfig** command. The KAME kernel generates the appropriate interface identifier for the link-local address as described in Section 2.5.1. If the enabled interface is a loopback interface, the kernel also creates the loopback address. These will be discussed in Section 2.13.

The second path is similar to the address configuration processing in the IPv4 protocol stack, where the `in6_control()` function is called as the `ioctl` handler for the `SIOCAIFADDR_IN6`

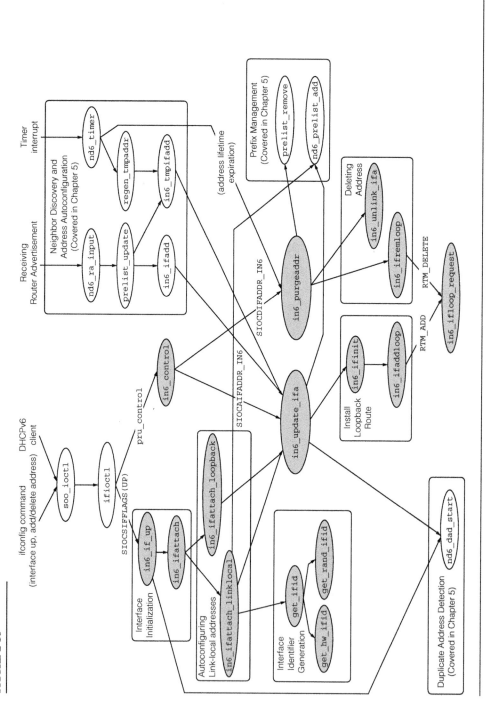

Address configuration call graph.

FIGURE 2-16

FIGURE 2-17

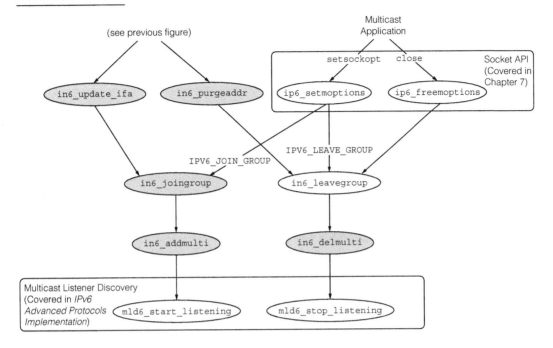

Multicast address configuration call graph.

command. This will be discussed in Section 2.14.1. Note that address configuration by DHCPv6 is performed by a user-space program (see Chapter 4 of *IPv6 Advanced Protocols Implementation*), and this is a kind of "manual configuration" in this context. The third path will be discussed in Chapter 5.

When configuring a new IPv6 address, the in6_update_ifa() function creates a loop-back route for the configured address. This process will be discussed in Sections 2.14.5 and 2.14.6.

Like the configuration procedure, deleting an address can happen in multiple contexts. One is the "traditional" path by the SIOCDIFADDR_IN6 ioctl command, typically through a configuration utility such as **ifconfig**. The other is a result of the expiration of address lifetime, which will be discussed in Section 5.15.5. The main routine for deletion is the in6_purgeaddr() function. It involves a couple of sub-routines for releasing resources created for the address. This process will be discussed in Section 2.15.

Adding or deleting an address may affect the corresponding direct route on the interface. Typically, adding a new address requires the addition of the corresponding direct route, which will then be removed when the address is deleted. As explained in Section 2.11, these procedures are handled in a separate framework for prefixes that is implemented as a part of the Neighbor Discovery processing. These will thus be discussed in Section 5.19.

Finally, the uniqueness of a newly configured address must be confirmed by the DAD mechanism. The DAD procedure is invoked either by the in6_update_ifa() function as a result of adding a new address or by the `in6_if_up()` function when a temporarily disabled interface with several configured addresses is enabled by hand. DAD is defined as a part of stateless address autoconfiguration, which will be discussed in Chapter 5.

Manipulating unicast addresses also causes configuration of multicast addresses. For example, adding a new unicast address will require joining the corresponding solicited-node multicast group (see Section 2.6). On the other hand, applications can join or leave an arbitrary multicast group via some socket options.

The `in6_joingroup()` and `in6_leavegroup()` functions are commonly used for joining and leaving a multicast group, as shown in Figure 2-17. These can then cause related MLDv1 operations via intermediate subroutines. Sections 2.14.3 and 2.14.4 will describe details of these procedures. Details of socket option handling will be described in Chapter 7, while Chapter 2 of *IPv6 Advanced Protocols Implementation* will concentrate on the MLDv1 operations.

2.13 Interface Initialization for IPv6

An interface must be properly initialized before address configuration can take place. The standard interface configuration utility is the **ifconfig** command. For example, issuing the following command

```
#  ifconfig fxp0 up
```

will enable the fxp0 network interface. The execution of the **ifconfig** command invokes the `if_ioctl()` function in the kernel. The `in6_if_up()` function is invoked by the `if_ioctl()` function, which performs the IPv6 specific setup for the interface. As will be seen shortly, this command initiates the automatic address configuration on this interface.

2.13.1 `in6_if_up()` Function

The `in6_if_up()` function processes an IPv6 specific interface setup code.

Listing 2-19
── in6.c
```
3966    /*
3967     * perform DAD when interface becomes IFF_UP.
3968     */
3969    void
3970    in6_if_up(ifp)
3971            struct ifnet *ifp;
3972    {
```
── in6.c

3969–3971 This function has one argument which indicates the network interface to be enabled.

Listing 2-20
── in6.c
```
3973            struct ifaddr *ifa;
3974            struct in6_ifaddr *ia;
3975            int dad_delay;         /* delay ticks before DAD output */
3976
```

```
3977              /*
3978               * special cases, like 6to4, are handled in in6_ifattach
3979               */
3980              in6_ifattach(ifp, NULL);
                                                                          ___in6.c
```

3980 The `in6_ifattach()` function, discussed later, generates a link-local address for the specified network interface. In addition, if the interface is a loopback interface, it assigns the loopback address to the interface.

Listing 2-21
___in6.c
```
3982              dad_delay = 0;

3986              TAILQ_FOREACH(ifa, &ifp->if_addrlist, ifa_list)

3990              {
3991                      if (ifa->ifa_addr->sa_family != AF_INET6)
3992                              continue;
3993                      ia = (struct in6_ifaddr *)ifa;
3994                      if (ia->ia6_flags & IN6_IFF_TENTATIVE)
3995                              nd6_dad_start(ifa, &dad_delay);
3996              }
3997      }
                                                                          ___in6.c
```

3982–3994 For each IPv6 address that is already assigned to the interface, if the address has the `IN6_IFF_TENTATIVE` flag set, then the DAD procedure is started for this address. This typically occurs when we enable an interface for the first time. The implementation illustrates DAD can also be performed for an already configured address by the following steps:

- Disable the interface by `ifconfig` *ifname* `down`.

- Set the "TENTATIVE" flag for the address by `ifconfig` *ifname* `address tentative`.

- Enable the interface again by `ifconfig` `ifname` `up`.

The intended scenario is that a node temporarily detached from a network is reconnected to the previous or new link and the uniqueness of previously assigned addresses needs to be confirmed by hand.

3995 The actual DAD procedure delays by a random number if the second parameter (`dad_delay`) to the `nd6_dad_start()` function is non-NULL. The parameter is 0 at the first iteration of the `FOREACH` loop, in which case `nd6_dad_start()` just computes a random delay based on the DAD specification. Variable `dad_delay` is reset to the latest random delay, and in the succeeding calls to `nd6_dad_start()`, the random delay is ensured to be larger than the previous one. These random delays are required by the DAD specification when the DAD-related packets are the initial transmission from this interface. Note that the fact that this function is called with addresses having the "TENTATIVE" flag does not necessarily mean these packets are the initial transmissions, in which sense the code is an overkill. However, it is generally difficult to identify the condition correctly, so this implementation relaxes the rule. Section 5.10.2 explains the random delay in more detail. The `nd6_dad_start()` function is described in Section 5.21.4.

2.13.2 `in6_ifattach()` Function

The `in6_ifattach()` function first performs some sanity checks for enabling the interface. It then assigns a link-local address to the interface, and, if the enabled interface is a loopback interface, it also assigns the loopback address.

Listing 2-22

in6_ifattach.c
```
853     /*
854      * XXX multiple loopback interface needs more care.  for instance,
855      * nodelocal address needs to be configured onto only one of them.
856      * XXX multiple link-local address case
857      */
858     void
859     in6_ifattach(ifp, altifp)
860             struct ifnet *ifp;
861             struct ifnet *altifp;   /* secondary EUI64 source */
862     {
```
in6_ifattach.c

The `in6_ifattach()` function has two arguments. The first argument is the network interface to be enabled. The second argument is another network interface, which was originally intended to be applied in interface identifier generation when the network interface specified by the first argument does not have an EUI-64 based interface identifier. This was used in an older kernel version for a logical interface of an ATM-PVC (Asynchronous Transfer Mode, Permanent Virtual Circuit) based on the physical ATM interface. This argument is not used anymore, and is always NULL in the version we describe.

Listing 2-23

in6_ifattach.c
```
863             struct in6_ifaddr *ia;
864             struct in6_addr in6;

890             /*
891              * if link mtu is too small, don't try to configure IPv6.
892              * remember there could be some link-layer that has special
893              * fragmentation logic.
894              */
895             if (ifp->if_mtu < IPV6_MMTU) {
896                     nd6log((LOG_INFO, "in6_ifattach: "
897                         "%s has too small MTU, IPv6 not enabled\n",
898                         if_name(ifp)));
899                     return;
900             }
```
in6_ifattach.c

895–900 [RFC2460] requires that every link that is IPv6 capable must be able to carry IPv6 packets up to 1280 bytes in length without IP-level fragmentation. This size is often called the *minimum MTU (size)*. An interface is ignored for IPv6 communication if its MTU is smaller than the minimum MTU size. As commented in the code, simply ignoring such an interface might be an overkill because it may support link-level fragmentation. In practice, however, there is no known network interface that supports such link-level fragmentation with the link MTU smaller than the IPv6 minimum MTU.

Listing 2-24

in6_ifattach.c

```
907             /*
908              * quirks based on interface type
909              */
910             switch (ifp->if_type) {

915     #ifdef IFT_STF
916             case IFT_STF:
917                     /*
918                      * 6to4 interface is a very special kind of beast.
919                      * no multicast, no linklocal.  RFC2529 specifies how to make
920                      * linklocals for 6to4 interface, but there's no use and
921                      * it is rather harmful to have one.
922                      */
923                     if (STF_IS_6TO4(ifp))
924                             return;
925     #endif
926             default:
927                     break;
928             }
```

in6_ifattach.c

910–928 A 6-to-4 (STF) pseudo interface is used for automatic IPv6 over IPv4 tunneling based on the 6to4 technique [RFC3056]. 6to4 uses a special type of global address that encodes the IPv4 address of a tunnel endpoint, by which a remote node can automatically identify the destination IPv4 address of the encapsulating packet. A link-local address is useless with this mechanism, since the fixed format of link-local addresses does not allow the endpoint IPv4 address to be encoded. Thus, the IPv6-level interface initialization for an STF interface stops here. Further details of 6to4 is beyond the scope of this book.

Listing 2-25

in6_ifattach.c

```
930             /*
931              * usually, we require multicast capability to the interface
932              */
933             if ((ifp->if_flags & IFF_MULTICAST) == 0) {
934                     nd6log((LOG_INFO, "in6_ifattach: "
935                         "%s is not multicast capable, IPv6 not enabled\n",
936                         if_name(ifp)));
937                     return;
938             }
```

in6_ifattach.c

933–938 IPv6 utilizes multicasting for its basic operation such as processing of the Neighbor Discovery protocol. Thus, an interface is rejected for IPv6 communication if it is incapable of link-layer multicasting.

Listing 2-26

in6_ifattach.c

```
940             /*
941              * assign loopback address for loopback interface.
942              * XXX multiple loopback interface case.
943              */
```

```
944                     if ((ifp->if_flags & IFF_LOOPBACK) != 0) {
945                             in6 = in6addr_loopback;
946                             if (in6ifa_ifpwithaddr(ifp, &in6) == NULL) {
947                                     if (in6_ifattach_loopback(ifp) != 0)
948                                             return;
949                             }
950                     }
```
———in6_ifattach.c

944–950 If the interface is a loopback interface and the loopback address is not
assigned yet, then the loopback address is assigned to the interface by calling
function `in6_ifattach_loopback()`, which is discussed shortly. Function
`in6ifa_ifpwithaddr()` traverses the interface address list and checks if the loopback address has been assigned to the interface. It returns a pointer to the instance of the
`in6_ifaddr{}` structure containing the loopback address, if one exists.

Technically, just checking the `IFF_LOOPBACK` flag is not sufficient as commented on
in the code. If, while atypical, two loopback interfaces such as `lo0` and `lo1` are configured
and enabled, we will see two instances of the loopback address, one for each loopback
interface. Such a configuration does not match assumptions in other parts of the kernel
and will cause operational mishaps.

Listing 2-27

———in6_ifattach.c
```
952             /*
953              * assign a link-local address, if there's none.
954              */
955             if (ip6_auto_linklocal) {
956                     ia = in6ifa_ifpforlinklocal(ifp, 0);
957                     if (ia == NULL) {
958                             if (in6_ifattach_linklocal(ifp, altifp) == 0) {
959                                     /* linklocal address assigned */
960                             } else {
961                                     /* failed to assign linklocal address. bark? */
962                             }
963                     }
964             }
965     }
```
———in6_ifattach.c

955–959 A network interface must have at least one link-local address. The kernel assigns
the interface a link-local address at this point if the configurable global parameter
`ip6_auto_linklocal` is set to non-0. Otherwise the user is responsible for the link-
local address assignment. This parameter is dynamically configurable by the `sysctl` variable named `net.inet6.ip6.auto_linklocal`, whose default value is 1.

The `in6ifa_ifpforlinklocal()` function returns a pointer to the instance of the
`in6_ifaddr{}` structure containing the link-local address assigned to the network interface specified by the first function argument. The second argument to
`in6ifa_ifpforlinklocal()` specifies the search filter flags. In this case 0 is specified,
which means searching all addresses regardless of the associated address flags. For example, even a link-local address with the `IN6_IFF_TENTATIVE` is searched and returned
as the result if one exists. The actual link-local address assignment takes place inside the
`in6_ifattach_linklocal()` function, discussed shortly.

Note: This code illustrates that a loopback interface has an "ordinary" link-local address in addition to the loopback address. The former is actually redundant according to the requirement shown in Section 2.6. This redundancy simply comes from a historical reason: the scoping architecture was not fully clarified when this code was written, and it was unclear whether the loopback address can be regarded as the required link-local address on a loopback interface. In any case, the specification at least does not prohibit a loopback interface from having an "ordinary" link-local address as well.

960–962 The `in6_ifattach_linklocal()` function should usually succeed, but it may still fail in creating a link-local address due to lack of memory or other unexpected reasons. Even though it is an unusual and unexpected result, it would probably be better to make a kernel log message here as commented in the code. Otherwise, the user enabling the interface will not notice the event since this function does not return a result code.

2.13.3 `in6_ifattach_loopback()` Function

The `in6_ifattach_loopback()` function assigns a loopback address to an interface.

Listing 2-28
_____ in6_ifattach.c
```
743     static int
744     in6_ifattach_loopback(ifp)
745             struct ifnet *ifp;          /* must be IFT_LOOP */
746     {
```
_____ in6_ifattach.c

744–746 `in6_ifattach_loopback()` has one function argument which specifies the loopback interface for loopback address assignment.

Listing 2-29
_____ in6_ifattach.c
```
747             struct in6_aliasreq ifra;
748             int error;
749
750             bzero(&ifra, sizeof(ifra));
751
752             /*
753              * in6_update_ifa() does not use ifra_name, but we accurately set it
754              * for safety.
755              */
756             strncpy(ifra.ifra_name, if_name(ifp), sizeof(ifra.ifra_name));
757
758             ifra.ifra_prefixmask.sin6_len = sizeof(struct sockaddr_in6);
759             ifra.ifra_prefixmask.sin6_family = AF_INET6;
760             ifra.ifra_prefixmask.sin6_addr = in6mask128;
761
762             /*
763              * Always initialize ia_dstaddr (= broadcast address) to loopback
764              * address.  Follows IPv4 practice - see in_ifinit().
765              */
766             ifra.ifra_dstaddr.sin6_len = sizeof(struct sockaddr_in6);
767             ifra.ifra_dstaddr.sin6_family = AF_INET6;
768             ifra.ifra_dstaddr.sin6_addr = in6addr_loopback;
769
```

```
770              ifra.ifra_addr.sin6_len = sizeof(struct sockaddr_in6);
771              ifra.ifra_addr.sin6_family = AF_INET6;
772              ifra.ifra_addr.sin6_addr = in6addr_loopback;
```
—— in6_ifattach.c

747–772 This function first constructs an instance of the `in6_alisareq{}` structure containing the loopback address. It may look strange to set `ifra_dstaddr` in the loopback case. As the comment says, this is copied from the IPv4 code and has no meaning in the current KAME implementation.

Listing 2-30
—— in6_ifattach.c

```
774              /* the loopback  address should NEVER expire. */
775              ifra.ifra_lifetime.ia6t_vltime = ND6_INFINITE_LIFETIME;
776              ifra.ifra_lifetime.ia6t_pltime = ND6_INFINITE_LIFETIME;
777
778              /* we don't need to perform DAD on loopback interfaces. */
779              ifra.ifra_flags |= IN6_IFF_NODAD;
```
—— in6_ifattach.c

774–779 The loopback address has an infinite lifetime. Also, since it is guaranteed to be unique within the link, we do not need to do DAD on it. `IN6_IFF_NODAD` indicates that the address does not require DAD processing.

Listing 2-31
—— in6_ifattach.c

```
781              /*
782               * We are sure that this is a newly assigned address, so we can set
783               * NULL to the 3rd arg.
784               */
785              if ((error = in6_update_ifa(ifp, &ifra, NULL)) != 0) {
786                      nd6log((LOG_ERR, "in6_ifattach_loopback: failed to configure "
787                          "the loopback address on %s (errno=%d)\n",
788                          if_name(ifp), error));
789                      return (-1);
790              }
791
792              return 0;
793      }
```
—— in6_ifattach.c

785–792 Function `in6_update_ifa()` is a general routine that either adds or updates an IPv6 address on an interface. The third argument is used when updating an existing address. The third argument can be NULL because we are assigning the loopback address and this address is guaranteed to be the first one on an interface. The `in6_update_ifa()` function is discussed in Section 2.14.2.

2.13.4 `in6_ifattach_linklocal()` **Function**

The `in6_ifattach_linklocal()` function assigns a link-local address to a specified interface.

Listing 2-32

in6_ifattach.c

```
590     static int
591     in6_ifattach_linklocal(ifp, altifp)
592             struct ifnet *ifp;
593             struct ifnet *altifp;   /* secondary EUI64 source */
594     {
```

in6_ifattach.c

590–593 This function has two arguments. The first argument is the network interface on which a link-local address is assigned. The second argument is always NULL and effectively unused as explained in Listing 2-22.

Listing 2-33

in6_ifattach.c

```
595             struct in6_ifaddr *ia;
596             struct in6_aliasreq ifra;
597             struct nd_prefixctl pr0;
598             int i, error;
599
600             /*
601              * configure link-local address.
602              */
603             bzero(&ifra, sizeof(ifra));
604
605             /*
606              * in6_update_ifa() does not use ifra_name, but we accurately set it
607              * for safety.
608              */
609             strncpy(ifra.ifra_name, if_name(ifp), sizeof(ifra.ifra_name));
610
611             ifra.ifra_addr.sin6_family = AF_INET6;
612             ifra.ifra_addr.sin6_len = sizeof(struct sockaddr_in6);
613             ifra.ifra_addr.sin6_addr.s6_addr32[0] = htonl(0xfe800000);
614             ifra.ifra_addr.sin6_addr.s6_addr32[1] = 0;
615             if ((ifp->if_flags & IFF_LOOPBACK) != 0) {
616                     ifra.ifra_addr.sin6_addr.s6_addr32[2] = 0;
617                     ifra.ifra_addr.sin6_addr.s6_addr32[3] = htonl(1);
618             } else if (ifp->if_type == IFT_STF) {
619                     if (!STF_IS_ISATAP(ifp)) {
620                             nd6log((LOG_ERR,
621                                 "%s: 6to4 I/F cannot have linklocal address\n",
622                                 if_name(ifp)));
623                             return (-1);
624                     }
625
626                     /* ToDo: automatically fetches an IPv4 address for ISATAP */
627                     nd6log((LOG_ERR,
628                         "%s: ISATAP I/F needs static linklocal addressing\n",
629                         if_name(ifp)));
630                     return (0);
631             } else {
632                     if (get_ifid(ifp, altifp, &ifra.ifra_addr.sin6_addr) != 0) {
633                             nd6log((LOG_ERR,
634                                 "%s: no ifid available\n", if_name(ifp)));
635                             return (-1);
636                     }
637             }
```

in6_ifattach.c

609–637 An instance of the `in6_aliasreq{}` structure must be initialized for configuring an address. Since the link-local address has the fixed prefix of `fe80::/10`, this value is set directly in `s6_addr32[0]` of the `ifra_addr` member. The interface identifier portion of the address varies depending on the type of network interface. The interface identifier is set to 1 for a loopback interface. An error would be returned when an STF interface for 6to4 were encountered, but this case was avoided in the `in6_ifattach()` function and should actually not happen. The `get_ifid()` function is called to obtain an interface identifier in other normal cases.

Listing 2-34

in6_ifattach.c

```
638            if (in6_addr2zoneid(ifp, &ifra.ifra_addr.sin6_addr,
639                            &ifra.ifra_addr.sin6_scope_id)) {
640                return (-1);
641            }
642            in6_embedscope(&ifra.ifra_addr.sin6_addr, &ifra.ifra_addr); /* XXX */

644            ifra.ifra_addr.sin6_scope_id = 0; /* XXX */
```

in6_ifattach.c

638–644 A link-local address is generally ambiguous and must be accompanied by a proper zone ID. The `in6_addr2zoneid()` function first identifies the zone ID and sets the `sin6_scope_id` field to that ID. Function `in6_embedscope()` then embeds the ID in the `sin6_addr` member, and the `sin6_scope_id` field is finally 0-cleared. This procedure makes the format used in an interface address structure as shown in Figure 2-12. Since this address is actually the source of a new interface address structure, it must be initialized accordingly.

Listing 2-35

in6_ifattach.c

```
647            ifra.ifra_prefixmask.sin6_len = sizeof(struct sockaddr_in6);
648            ifra.ifra_prefixmask.sin6_family = AF_INET6;
649            ifra.ifra_prefixmask.sin6_addr = in6mask64;
```

in6_ifattach.c

647–649 Since a link-local address has a 64-bit prefix (see Section 2.5), `ifra_prefixmask` is initialized with `in6mask64`, which represents a 64-bit mask.

Listing 2-36

in6_ifattach.c

```
654            /* link-local addresses should NEVER expire. */
655            ifra.ifra_lifetime.ia6t_vltime = ND6_INFINITE_LIFETIME;
656            ifra.ifra_lifetime.ia6t_pltime = ND6_INFINITE_LIFETIME;
```

in6_ifattach.c

655–656 A link-local address also has an infinite lifetime similar to the loopback address.

Listing 2-37

in6_ifattach.c

```
658            /*
659             * Do not let in6_update_ifa() do DAD, since we need a random delay
660             * before sending an NS at the first time the interface becomes up.
```

```
661              * Instead, in6_if_up() will start DAD with a proper random delay.
662              */
663             ifra.ifra_flags |= IN6_IFF_NODAD;
```
                                                                          in6_ifattach.c

663 The `IN6_IFF_NODAD` flag is set on the address to prevent `in6_update_ifa()` from
doing the DAD processing. Without this flag, `in6_update_ifa()` would start DAD
immediately. Since this is likely the first address assigned on the interface, however, it
should be safe to impose a random delay to avoid network congestion (see Section 5.10.2
for the random delay in more detail). Thus, we bypass DAD in `in6_update_ifa()` for
now. Instead, the DAD processing is invoked when this function returns (recall the code
shown in Section 2.13.1).

Listing 2-38
                                                                          in6_ifattach.c

```
665             /*
666              * Now call in6_update_ifa() to do a bunch of procedures to configure
667              * a link-local address. We can set NULL to the 3rd argument, because
668              * we know there's no other link-local address on the interface
669              * and therefore we are adding one (instead of updating one).
670              */
671             if ((error = in6_update_ifa(ifp, &ifra, NULL)) != 0) {
672                     /*
673                      * XXX: When the interface does not support IPv6, this call
674                      * would fail in the SIOCSIFADDR ioctl.  I believe the
675                      * notification is rather confusing in this case, so just
676                      * suppress it.  (jinmei@kame.net 20010130)
677                      */
678                     if (error != EAFNOSUPPORT)
679                             nd6log((LOG_NOTICE, "in6_ifattach_linklocal: failed to "
680                                 "configure a link-local address on %s "
681                                 "(errno=%d)\n",
682                                 if_name(ifp), error));
683                     return (-1);
684             }
```
                                                                          in6_ifattach.c

671–684 Function `in6_update_ifa()` is called to assign the link-local address similar to the
code in `in6_ifattach_loopback()`.

Listing 2-39
                                                                          in6_ifattach.c

```
686             /*
687              * Adjust ia6_flags so that in6_if_up will perform DAD.
688              * XXX: Some P2P interfaces seem not to send packets just after
689              * becoming up, so we skip p2p interfaces for safety.
690              */
691             ia = in6ifa_ifpforlinklocal(ifp, 0); /* ia must not be NULL */
692     #ifdef DIAGNOSTIC
693             if (!ia) {
694                     panic("ia == NULL in in6_ifattach_linklocal");
695                     /* NOTREACHED */
696             }
697     #endif
698             if (in6if_do_dad(ifp) && (ifp->if_flags & IFF_POINTOPOINT) == 0) {
699                     ia->ia6_flags &= ~IN6_IFF_NODAD;
700                     ia->ia6_flags |= IN6_IFF_TENTATIVE;
701             }
```
                                                                          in6_ifattach.c

691 Function `in6ifa_ifpforlinklocal()` should return a valid pointer to the interface address structure for the link-local address just created because the call to `in6_update_ifa()` succeeded.

698–701 Now it is time to perform DAD on the newly assigned address because it was bypassed in `in6_update_ifa()`. Function `in6if_do_dad()` returns true if the interface requires DAD when assigning an address. If DAD is required, the `IN6_IFF_NODAD` flag that was set earlier is now cleared and the `IN6_IFF_TENTATIVE` flag is set, so that DAD will be performed by the `in6_if_up()` function, an implicit caller of the current function, as explained in Section 2.13.1.

Listing 2-40

```
                                                                    in6_ifattach.c
703          /*
704           * Make the link-local prefix (fe80::%link/64) as on-link.
705           * Since we'd like to manage prefixes separately from addresses,
706           * we make an ND6 prefix structure for the link-local prefix,
707           * and add it to the prefix list as a never-expire prefix.
708           * XXX: this change might affect some existing code base...
709           */
710          bzero(&pr0, sizeof(pr0));
711          pr0.ndpr_ifp = ifp;
712          /* this should be 64 at this moment. */
713          pr0.ndpr_plen = in6_mask2len(&ifra.ifra_prefixmask.sin6_addr, NULL);
714          pr0.ndpr_prefix = ifra.ifra_addr;
715          /* apply the mask for safety. (nd6_prelist_add will apply it again) */
716          for (i = 0; i < 4; i++) {
717                  pr0.ndpr_prefix.sin6_addr.s6_addr32[i] &=
718                      in6mask64.s6_addr32[i];
719          }
720          /*
721           * Initialize parameters.  The link-local prefix must always be
722           * on-link, and its lifetimes never expire.
723           */
724          pr0.ndpr_raf_onlink = 1;
725          pr0.ndpr_raf_auto = 1;    /* probably meaningless */
726          pr0.ndpr_vltime = ND6_INFINITE_LIFETIME;
727          pr0.ndpr_pltime = ND6_INFINITE_LIFETIME;
                                                                    in6_ifattach.c
```

710–719 For each IPv6 address its associated prefix information is maintained in the KAME implementation in an instance of the `nd_prefix{}` structure (see Section 2.11). Variable `pr0` is an `nd_prefixctl{}` structure, which is a kernel-internal control structure for managing the `nd_prefix{}` structure. This part of the code first builds the key for the corresponding prefix, which is a combination of the interface and the prefix.

724–727 Other parameters are then set, which will be used for initialization of a new prefix. We can basically ignore the semantics of these parameters for now.

Listing 2-41

```
                                                                    in6_ifattach.c
728 ·        /*
729           * Since there is no other link-local addresses, nd6_prefix_lookup()
730           * probably returns NULL.  However, we cannot always expect the result.
731           * For example, if we first remove the (only) existing link-local
732           * address, and then reconfigure another one, the prefix is still
733           * valid with referring to the old link-local address.
734           */
```

```
735         if (nd6_prefix_lookup(&pr0) == NULL) {
736                 if ((error = nd6_prelist_add(&pr0, NULL, NULL)) != 0)
737                         return (error);
738         }
739
740         return 0;
741     }
```
——— in6_ifattach.c

735–738 The nd6_prefix_lookup() function searches through the system-maintained pre-fixes and determines if the new prefix already exists. If the prefix is new then the nd6_prelist_add() function is called to insert it into the global Prefix List.

2.13.5 get_ifid() Function

The get_ifid() function calculates the 64-bit interface identifier from the given function arguments.

Listing 2-42
——— in6_ifattach.c

```
514     static int

516     get_ifid(ifp0, altifp, in6)
517             struct ifnet *ifp0;
518             struct ifnet *altifp;    /* secondary EUI64 source */
519             struct in6_addr *in6;
520     {
```
——— in6_ifattach.c

516–519 The get_ifid() function has three arguments. The first argument is a pointer to the network interface to which an address is being assigned. The second argument is always NULL and effectively unused, as explained earlier. The third argument will store the result of the interface identifier calculation.

Listing 2-43
——— in6_ifattach.c

```
521             struct ifnet *ifp;
522
523             /* first, try to get it from the interface itself */
524             if (get_hw_ifid(ifp0, in6) == 0) {
525                     nd6log((LOG_DEBUG, "%s: got interface identifier from itself\n",
526                         if_name(ifp0)));
527                     goto success;
528             }
```
——— in6_ifattach.c

524–528 Function get_hw_ifid(), discussed shortly, tries to retrieve an interface identi-fier from the network interface specified by the first argument. The process completes if get_hw_ifid() succeeds.

Listing 2-44
——— in6_ifattach.c

```
530             /* try secondary EUI64 source. this basically is for ATM PVC */
531             if (altifp && get_hw_ifid(altifp, in6) == 0) {
```

```
532                        nd6log((LOG_DEBUG, "%s: got interface identifier from %s\n",
533                            if_name(ifp0), if_name(altifp)));
534                        goto success;
535                }
```
――― in6_ifattach.c

531–535 This part is never executed since `altifp` is always NULL.

Listing 2-45

――― in6_ifattach.c
```
537                /* next, try to get it from some other hardware interface */

541                for (ifp = ifnet.tqh_first; ifp; ifp = ifp->if_list.tqe_next)

543                {
544                        if (ifp == ifp0)
545                                continue;
546                        if (get_hw_ifid(ifp, in6) != 0)
547                                continue;
549                        /*
550                         * to borrow ifid from other interface, ifid needs to be
551                         * globally unique
552                         */
553                        if (IFID_UNIVERSAL(in6)) {
554                                nd6log((LOG_DEBUG,
555                                    "%s: borrow interface identifier from %s\n",
556                                    if_name(ifp0), if_name(ifp)));
557                                goto success;
558                        }
559                }
```
――― in6_ifattach.c

541–559 If `get_hw_ifid()` fails then all other network interfaces that exist in the system are
tried in turn in the attempt to calculate an interface identifier for the new address. If an
alternative interface identifier is found in one of the network interfaces, then its global
uniqueness is verified by the `IFID_UNIVERSAL()` macro, which checks the global/local
bit of an interface identifier. The function returns successfully if the interface identifier is
unique.

Listing 2-46

――― in6_ifattach.c
```
571                /* last resort: get from random number source */
572                if (get_rand_ifid(ifp, in6) == 0) {
573                        nd6log((LOG_DEBUG,
574                            "%s: interface identifier generated by random number\n",
575                            if_name(ifp0)));
576                        goto success;
577                }
578
579                printf("%s: failed to get interface identifier\n", if_name(ifp0));
580                return -1;
581
582        success:
583                nd6log((LOG_INFO, "%s: ifid: 02x:%02x:%02x:%02x:%02x:%02x:%02x:%02x\n",
584                    if_name(ifp0), in6->s6_addr[8], in6->s6_addr[9], in6->s6_addr[10],
585                    in6->s6_addr[11], in6->s6_addr[12], in6->s6_addr[13],
586                    in6->s6_addr[14], in6->s6_addr[15]));
587                return 0;
588        }
```
――― in6_ifattach.c

572–577 If no good source has been found so far, a pseudo "random" value based on the node's hostname is used as a last resort. This is done by the `get_rand_ifid()` function, which is discussed later in Section 2.13.7, where we find that the chosen identifier is actually not a random number but a predictable digest based on the hostname.

2.13.6 `get_hw_ifid()` Function

The `get_hw_ifid()` function creates an interface identifier from the hardware address of the given network interface.

Listing 2-47
_____ in6_ifattach.c

```
365     static int
366     get_hw_ifid(ifp, in6)
367             struct ifnet *ifp;
368             struct in6_addr *in6;    /* upper 64bits are preserved */
369     {
```
_____ in6_ifattach.c

366–368 The first argument of this function is the network interface from which the hardware address will be retrieved. The second argument is the storage into which this function will put the result of the interface identifier calculation.

Listing 2-48
_____ in6_ifattach.c

```
370             struct ifaddr *ifa;
371             struct sockaddr_dl *sdl;
372             char *addr;
373             size_t addrlen;
374             static u_int8_t allzero[8] = { 0, 0, 0, 0, 0, 0, 0, 0 };
375             static u_int8_t allone[8] =
376                     { 0xff, 0xff, 0xff, 0xff, 0xff, 0xff, 0xff, 0xff };
377

381             for (ifa = ifp->if_addrlist.tqh_first;
382                  ifa;
383                  ifa = ifa->ifa_list.tqe_next)

385             {
386                     if (ifa->ifa_addr->sa_family != AF_LINK)
387                             continue;
388                     sdl = (struct sockaddr_dl *)ifa->ifa_addr;
389                     if (sdl == NULL)
390                             continue;
391                     if (sdl->sdl_alen == 0)
392                             continue;
393
394                     goto found;
395             }
396
397             return -1;
```
_____ in6_ifattach.c

381–397 The `if_addrlist` member of `ifp` keeps track of all addresses assigned to an interface regardless of the address family. This means that the link-layer address is also maintained in this list. The address with `AF_LINK` protocol family is searched during the traversal. If the search fails then the interface does not have a hardware address, in which case this function returns an error.

Listing 2-49

```
                                                              in6_ifattach.c
399    found:
400            addr = LLADDR(sdl);
401            addrlen = sdl->sdl_alen;
402
403            switch (ifp->if_type) {
                                                              in6_ifattach.c
```

399–403 If an address of family type AF_LINK is found, interface identifier is calculated according to the network interface type.

Listing 2-50

```
                                                              in6_ifattach.c
404            case IFT_IEEE1394:
405    #ifdef IFT_IEEE80211
406            case IFT_IEEE80211:
407    #endif
408                    /* IEEE1394 uses 16byte length address starting with EUI64 */
409                    if (addrlen > 8)
410                            addrlen = 8;
411            break;
412        default:
413            break;
414        }
                                                              in6_ifattach.c
```

404–414 In the FreeBSD's IEEE1394 implementation, the "hardware address" pointed by addr is a structure that encodes the specific format for Address Resolution Protocol (ARP) for IEEE1394 as defined in [RFC2734]. It begins with the 8-byte EUI-64 identifier, which we need for generating the IPv6 interface identifier. This code fragment adjusts the length of the hardware address so that only the EUI-64 part will be used in the processing below. The additional case for IEEE 802.11 is due to misspelling and is incorrect. Fortunately, however, it does no actual harm because addrlen should not be larger than 8 in this case.

Listing 2-51

```
                                                              in6_ifattach.c
416            /* get EUI64 */
417            switch (ifp->if_type) {
418            /* IEEE802/EUI64 cases - what others? */
419            case IFT_ETHER:
420            case IFT_FDDI:
421            case IFT_ATM:
422            case IFT_IEEE1394:
423    #ifdef IFT_IEEE80211
424            case IFT_IEEE80211:
425    #endif
426                    /* look at IEEE802/EUI64 only */
427                    if (addrlen != 8 && addrlen != 6)
428                            return -1;
429
430                    /*
431                     * check for invalid MAC address - on bsdi, we see it a lot
432                     * since wildboar configures all-zero MAC on pccard before
433                     * card insertion.
434                     */
435                    if (bcmp(addr, allzero, addrlen) == 0)
436                            return -1;
437                    if (bcmp(addr, allone, addrlen) == 0)
```

```
438                              return -1;
439
440                      /* make EUI64 address */
441                      if (addrlen == 8)
442                              bcopy(addr, &in6->s6_addr[8], 8);
443                      else if (addrlen == 6) {
444                              in6->s6_addr[8] = addr[0];
445                              in6->s6_addr[9] = addr[1];
446                              in6->s6_addr[10] = addr[2];
447                              in6->s6_addr[11] = 0xff;
448                              in6->s6_addr[12] = 0xfe;
449                              in6->s6_addr[13] = addr[3];
450                              in6->s6_addr[14] = addr[4];
451                              in6->s6_addr[15] = addr[5];
452                      }
453                      break;
                                                                        in6_ifattach.c
```

419–453 If the network interface has an EUI-64 identifier, that identifier is simply copied to the
in6 variable. If the network interface has a 48-bit MAC address, the identifier is converted
to the modified EUI-64 format according to [RFC3513] (see Section 2.5.1).

Listing 2-52
                                                                        in6_ifattach.c

```
455              case IFT_ARCNET:
456                      if (addrlen != 1)
457                              return -1;
458                      if (!addr[0])
459                              return -1;
460
461                      bzero(&in6->s6_addr[8], 8);
462                      in6->s6_addr[15] = addr[0];
463
464                      /*
465                       * due to insufficient bitwidth, we mark it local.
466                       */
467                      in6->s6_addr[8] &= ~EUI64_GBIT; /* g bit to "individual" */
468                      in6->s6_addr[8] |= EUI64_UBIT;          /* u bit to "local" */
469                      break;
                                                                        in6_ifattach.c
```

455–469 This block of the code converts the hardware ID (1 byte) of an ARCnet interface to
the EUI-64 format according to [RFC2497]. EUI64_GBIT represents the group bit of the
EUI-64 format. Since the interface identifier is not a group address, the group bit is turned
off. EUI64_UBIT represents the global/local bit of the EUI-64 format. We set the interface
identifier as a local ID (not globally unique identifier) because ARCnet allocates only 8
bits for interface identifier, which is too small to guarantee the uniqueness in the world.

Listing 2-53
                                                                        in6_ifattach.c

```
471              case IFT_GIF:
472      #ifdef IFT_STF
473              case IFT_STF:
474      #endif
475                      /*
476                       * RFC2893 says: "SHOULD use IPv4 address as ifid source".
477                       * however, IPv4 address is not very suitable as unique
478                       * identifier source (can be renumbered).
```

```
479                         * we don't do this.
480                         */
481                        return -1;
482
483            default:
484                        return -1;
485            }
```
_____ in6_ifattach.c

471–485 While [RFC4213] mentions the possibility of using the IPv4 address as the interface identifier for a tunneling pseudo interfaces (GIF), the KAME implementation does not adopt the approach. This is because IPv4 addresses are unstable due to conditions such as network renumbering. In fact, the description in the RFC was weakened compared to its predecessor, [RFC2893], due to this reason. Instead, the interface identifier from another network interface is used in the case of GIF. This mechanism for borrowing the interface identifier applies to other types of network interfaces as well. The same argument applies to the STF interface (see Listing 2-24) for non-6to4 purposes.

Listing 2-54
_____ in6_ifattach.c
```
487            /* sanity check: g bit must not indicate "group" */
488            if (EUI64_GROUP(in6))
489                        return -1;
```
_____ in6_ifattach.c

488–489 The interface identifier must have the group bit off. Otherwise it is an error.

Listing 2-55
_____ in6_ifattach.c
```
491            /* convert EUI64 into IPv6 interface identifier */
492            EUI64_TO_IFID(in6);
```
_____ in6_ifattach.c

492 The EUI64_TO_IFID() macro inverts the global/local bit and makes the interface identifier from the original EUI-64 identifier.

Listing 2-56
_____ in6_ifattach.c
```
494            /*
495             * sanity check: ifid must not be all zero, avoid conflict with
496             * subnet router anycast
497             */
498            if ((in6->s6_addr[8] & ~(EUI64_GBIT | EUI64_UBIT)) == 0x00 &&
499                bcmp(&in6->s6_addr[9], allzero, 7) == 0) {
500                        return -1;
501            }
502
503            return 0;
504    }
```
_____ in6_ifattach.c

498–503 The final interface identifier validation consists of checking the individual bit and the local bit is set in the address. In addition, the interface identifier must not contain all 0 bits because that ID is reserved for subnet-router anycast addresses.

2.13.7 `get_rand_ifid()` **Function**

The `get_rand_ifid()` function generates an interface identifier based on the node's hostname. Usually, we can get an interface identifier from some kind of network interface using its hardware address, but this function is used as the last resort for generating an interface identifier.

Despite its name, `get_rand_ifid()` does not generate a random number. However, since the essential requirement for an interface identifier is to be unique in the corresponding link, and the hostname is generally supposed to be unique near the node, it would be a reasonable source as a last resort.

Listing 2-57
_____ in6_ifattach.c

```
180     static int
181     get_rand_ifid(ifp, in6)
182             struct ifnet *ifp;
183             struct in6_addr *in6;    /* upper 64bits are preserved */
184     {
```
_____ in6_ifattach.c

181–183 The first argument to `get_rand_ifid()` points to the network interface that is being assigned an address. The second argument stores the result from the identifier calculation.

Listing 2-58
_____ in6_ifattach.c

```
185             MD5_CTX ctxt;
186             u_int8_t digest[16];

188             int hostnamelen = strlen(hostname);

197             /* generate 8 bytes of pseudo-random value. */
198             bzero(&ctxt, sizeof(ctxt));
199             MD5Init(&ctxt);
200             MD5Update(&ctxt, hostname, hostnamelen);
201             MD5Final(digest, &ctxt);
```
_____ in6_ifattach.c

185–201 The interface identifier is generated by calculating the MD5 hash value over the node's hostname.

Listing 2-59
_____ in6_ifattach.c

```
203             /* assumes sizeof(digest) > sizeof(ifid) */
204             bcopy(digest, &in6->s6_addr[8], 8);
205
206             /* make sure to set "u" bit to local, and "g" bit to individual. */
207             in6->s6_addr[8] &= ~EUI64_GBIT; /* g bit to "individual" */
208             in6->s6_addr[8] |= EUI64_UBIT;  /* u bit to "local" */
```
_____ in6_ifattach.c

204–208 The global/local bit is set to local because there is no guarantee of the global uniqueness of this generated interface identifier.

Listing 2-60

———in6_ifattach.c
```
210              /* convert EUI64 into IPv6 interface identifier */
211              EUI64_TO_IFID(in6);
212
213              return 0;
214      }
```
———in6_ifattach.c

211 The `EUI64_TO_IFID()` macro is performed for obtaining the final interface identifier.

2.13.8 `in6if_do_dad()` Function

The `in6if_do_dad()` function indicates whether DAD processing is necessary for a particular type of interface on which an address is being configured.

Listing 2-61

———in6.c
```
3999    int
4000    in6if_do_dad(ifp)
4001            struct ifnet *ifp;
4002    {
4003            if ((ifp->if_flags & IFF_LOOPBACK) != 0)
4004                    return (0);
```
———in6.c

4003–4004 DAD is not required on a loopback interface because addresses configured on a loopback interface are only used within a single node.

Listing 2-62

———in6.c
```
4006            switch (ifp->if_type) {
4007    #ifdef IFT_DUMMY
4008            case IFT_DUMMY:
4009    #endif

4013            case IFT_FAITH:
4014                    /*
4015                     * These interfaces do not have the IFF_LOOPBACK flag,
4016                     * but loop packets back.  We do not have to do DAD on such
4017                     * interfaces.  We should even omit it, because loop-backed
4018                     * NS would confuse the DAD procedure.
4019                     */
4020                    return (0);
4021            default:
4022                    /*
4023                     * Our DAD routine requires the interface up and running.
4024                     * However, some interfaces can be up before the RUNNING
4025                     * status.  Additionaly, users may try to assign addresses
4026                     * before the interface becomes up (or running).
4027                     * We simply skip DAD in such a case as a work around.
4028                     * XXX: we should rather mark "tentative" on such addresses,
4029                     * and do DAD after the interface becomes ready.
4030                     */
4031                    if ((ifp->if_flags & (IFF_UP|IFF_RUNNING)) !=
4032                        (IFF_UP|IFF_RUNNING))
4033                            return (0);

4035                    return (1);
4036            }
4037    }
```
———in6.c

4006–4037 DAD is not required for pseudo interfaces such as the FAITH pseudo interface, which is used for kernel internal purposes in the implementation of transport layer translation between IPv4 and IPv6 [RFC3142]. For other normal interfaces, DAD is performed on the interface that is in the up and running state, in which case a result value of 1 is returned. Otherwise, this function returns 0, indicating DAD is not necessary.

2.14 IPv6 Interface Address Configuration

We saw in Figure 2-16 that there are several ways of configuring IPv6 addresses on a node and that the `in6_update_ifa()` function is commonly used as the main routine of the configuration procedure.

In this section, we describe the main procedure with additional subroutines. We begin with the entry point of manual configuration via `ioctl` commands handled by the `in6_control()` function.

2.14.1 `in6_control()` Function

The `in6_control()` function is the `ioctl` handler at the IPv6 level. It deals with various `ioctl` commands, but one major purpose among those is to configure a network interface with an IPv6 address. In this subsection, we concentrate on the `SIOCAIFADDR_IN6` command for adding or updating an IPv6 address and the `SIOCDIFADDR_IN6` command for deleting an IPv6 address.

These commands take arguments of the `in6_aliasreq{}` and `in6_ifreq{}` structures described in Section 2.10.2. It should be noted that both structures contain a field for specifying a particular IPv6 address. Unlike IPv4, IPv6 explicitly allows an interface to have multiple IPv6 addresses, and, in fact, an interface usually has at least one link-local and one global IPv6 address. Thus, it is necessary for an application to specify which address of the interface should be updated when it tries to modify or delete an existing address.

Initial Checks

Listing 2-63

─── in6.c
```
418    in6_control(so, cmd, data, ifp)
419            struct          socket *so;
420            u_long cmd;
421            caddr_t         data;
422            struct ifnet *ifp;
424    {
425            struct in6_ifreq *ifr = (struct in6_ifreq *)data;
426            struct in6_ifaddr *ia = NULL;
427            struct in6_aliasreq *ifra = (struct in6_aliasreq *)data;
428            struct sockaddr_in6 *sa6;
432            int privileged;
433
434            privileged = 0;
439            if (p == NULL || !suser(p))
440                    privileged++;
        ....
484            if (ifp == NULL)
485                    return (EOPNOTSUPP);
```
─── in6.c

434–485 Configuring an address typically requires a super user privilege. Variable `privileged` is set to 1 when the caller has the necessary privilege (note that function `suser()` returns 0 if the process is run by a super user). This function must be called with a valid network interface. Otherwise, an error of EOPNOTSUPP would be returned, although this check should have been done in `ifioctl()`, the caller of this function.

Identify and Convert the Address

Listing 2-64

```
                                                                              in6.c
546              /*
547               * Find address for this interface, if it exists.
548               *
549               * In netinet code, we have checked ifra_addr in SIOCSIF*ADDR operation
550               * only, and used the first interface address as the target of other
551               * operations (without checking ifra_addr).  This was because netinet
552               * code/API assumed at most 1 interface address per interface.
553               * Since IPv6 allows a node to assign multiple addresses
554               * on a single interface, we almost always look and check the
555               * presence of ifra_addr, and reject invalid ones here.
556               * It also decreases duplicated code among SIOC*_IN6 operations.
557               */
558              switch (cmd) {
559              case SIOCAIFADDR_IN6:
...
561                      sa6 = &ifra->ifra_addr;
562                      break;
...
569              case SIOCDIFADDR_IN6:
...
580                      sa6 = &ifr->ifr_addr;
581                      break;
582              default:
583                      sa6 = NULL;
584                      break;
585              }
586              if (sa6 && sa6->sin6_family == AF_INET6) {
587                      if (IN6_IS_ADDR_LINKLOCAL(&sa6->sin6_addr)) {
588                              if (sa6->sin6_addr.s6_addr16[1] == 0) {
589                                      /* link ID is not embedded by the user */
590                                      sa6->sin6_addr.s6_addr16[1] =
591                                              htons(ifp->if_index);
592                              } else if (sa6->sin6_addr.s6_addr16[1] !=
593                                      htons(ifp->if_index)) {
594                                      return (EINVAL);        /* link ID contradicts */
595                              }
596                              if (sa6->sin6_scope_id) {
597                                      if (sa6->sin6_scope_id !=
598                                          (u_int32_t)ifp->if_index)
599                                              return (EINVAL);
600                                      sa6->sin6_scope_id = 0; /* XXX: good way? */
601                              }
602                      }
603                      ia = in6ifa_ifpwithaddr(ifp, &sa6->sin6_addr);
604              } else
605                      ia = NULL;
                                                                              in6.c
```

558–585 Variable `sa6` points to the address field of the `ioctl` argument, depending on the argument type.

586–602 If a unicast link-local address is specified, it must first be converted into the kernel internal form with a proper link zone ID (see Section 2.9.3). If the given address is not in the internal form (it actually should not be as explained in Section 2.9.3), the index of the given interface is set in the second 16-bit field of the 128-bit IPv6 address field. On the other hand, if the application specifies a non-0 value in the second 16-bit field (again, the application should not do that), it must be the index of the given interface; otherwise, an EINVAL error is returned. In either case, if the sin6_scope_id field has a non-0 value, it must be the valid link ID, that is, the interface index of ifp; otherwise, an EINVAL error is returned. Then the sin6_scope_id field is cleared, since this structure will soon be used in the context of interface address structures, where only the embedded zone IDs are used as depicted in Figure 2-12.

603 Function in6ifa_ifpwithaddr() traverses the list of IPv6 addresses configured on the interface to see whether the specified address is contained in the list. Variable ia points to the corresponding in6_ifaddr{} structure if it is; otherwise, the variable is set to NULL.

Further Validation

Listing 2-65
_____in6.c

```
607             switch (cmd) {
...
617             case SIOCDIFADDR_IN6:
618                     /*
619                      * for IPv4, we look for existing in_ifaddr here to allow
620                      * "ifconfig if0 delete" to remove the first IPv4 address on
621                      * the interface.  For IPv6, as the spec allows multiple
622                      * interface address from the day one, we consider "remove the
623                      * first one" semantics to be not preferable.
624                      */
625                     if (ia == NULL)
626                             return (EADDRNOTAVAIL);
627                     /* FALLTHROUGH */
628             case SIOCAIFADDR_IN6:
629                     /*
630                      * We always require users to specify a valid IPv6 address for
631                      * the corresponding operation.
632                      */
633                     if (ifra->ifra_addr.sin6_family != AF_INET6 ||
634                         ifra->ifra_addr.sin6_len != sizeof(struct sockaddr_in6))
635                             return (EAFNOSUPPORT);
636                     if (!privileged)
637                             return (EPERM);
638
639                     break;
...
672             }
```
_____in6.c

617–627 For deleting an address from an interface, the address must be specified and exist. Otherwise, an error of EADDRNOTAVAIL is returned. As commented in the code and explained at the beginning of this section, this requirement is one major difference from IPv4 for deleting an address.

628–635 The address specified by the application must be a valid sockaddr_in6{} structure with the family and length fields set correctly. This check is performed here in order to avoid an unexpected failure due to broken input. Note that ifra, which is the ioctl argument specific to the `SIOCAIFADDR_IN6` command, is referenced here while this part of the code is shared with the case of `SIOCDIFADDR_IN6`. This is safe, however, since the referred field commonly points to the address field for both the structures.

636–637 Adding, updating, or deleting an address must be performed by a privileged user. Otherwise, an error of `EPERM` will be returned.

Add or Update Address

Listing 2-66

```
                                                                    in6.c
674          switch (cmd) {
       ...
770
771          case SIOCAIFADDR_IN6:
772          {
773                  int i, error = 0;
774                  struct nd_prefixctl pr0;
775                  struct nd_prefix *pr;
776
777                  /* reject read-only flags */
778                  if ((ifra->ifra_flags & IN6_IFF_READONLY))
779                          return (EINVAL);
780
781                  /*
782                   * when trying to change flags on an existing interface
783                   * address, make sure to preserve old read-only ones.
784                   */
785                  if (ia)
786                          ifra->ifra_flags |= (ia->ia6_flags & IN6_IFF_READONLY);
787
788                  /*
789                   * first, make or update the interface address structure,
790                   * and link it to the list.
791                   */
792                  if ((error = in6_update_ifa(ifp, ifra, ia)) != 0)
793                          return (error);
794                  if ((ia = in6ifa_ifpwithaddr(ifp, &ifra->ifra_addr.sin6_addr))
795                      == NULL) {
796                                  /*
797                                   * this can happen when the user specify the 0 valid
798                                   * lifetime.
799                                   */
800                                  break;
801                  }
                                                                    in6.c
```

674–779 This `switch-case` statement completes the `ioctl` operation by actually taking the specified action. When adding or updating an address, read-only flags must not be specified in the argument structure. Otherwise, an error of `EINVAL` will be returned.

781–786 If this operation updates an existing address, the read-only flags in the existing structure are copied so that these flags will be kept in the updated structure.

788–793 The `in6_update_ifa()` function performs many operations for adding or updating the specified address. This function will be described in the next subsection.

794–801 Normally, a return value of 0 from `in6_update_ifa()` means the specified address is newly created or still exists with the updated parameters. As discussed in the code, however, the address can be removed in the operation when the valid lifetime of the address in the argument is set to 0, probably due to an application bug or erroneous operation. In this case, the process is terminated successfully at this point.

The next part of the code relates to the created address with the corresponding prefix structure as shown in Figure 2-15.

Listing 2-67

```
                                                                        in6.c
803              /*
804               * then, make the prefix on-link on the interface.
805               * XXX: we'd rather create the prefix before the address, but
806               * we need at least one address to install the corresponding
807               * interface route, so we configure the address first.
808               */
809
810              /*
811               * convert mask to prefix length (prefixmask has already
812               * been validated in in6_update_ifa().
813               */
814              bzero(&pr0, sizeof(pr0));
815              pr0.ndpr_ifp = ifp;
816              pr0.ndpr_plen = in6_mask2len(&ifra->ifra_prefixmask.sin6_addr,
817                  NULL);
818              if (pr0.ndpr_plen == 128) {
828                      break;            /* we don't need to install a host route. */
829              }
830              pr0.ndpr_prefix = ifra->ifra_addr;
831              /* apply the mask for safety. */
832              for (i = 0; i < 4; i++) {
833                      pr0.ndpr_prefix.sin6_addr.s6_addr32[i] &=
834                          ifra->ifra_prefixmask.sin6_addr.s6_addr32[i];
835              }
836              /*
837               * XXX: since we don't have an API to set prefix (not address)
838               * lifetimes, we just use the same lifetimes as addresses.
839               * The (temporarily) installed lifetimes can be overridden by
840               * later advertised RAs (when accept_rtadv is non 0), which is
841               * an intended behavior.
842               */
843              pr0.ndpr_raf_onlink = 1; /* should be configurable? */
844              pr0.ndpr_raf_auto =
845                  ((ifra->ifra_flags & IN6_IFF_AUTOCONF) != 0);
846              pr0.ndpr_vltime = ifra->ifra_lifetime.ia6t_vltime;
847              pr0.ndpr_pltime = ifra->ifra_lifetime.ia6t_pltime;
848
849              /* add the prefix if not yet. */
850              if ((pr = nd6_prefix_lookup(&pr0)) == NULL) {
851                      /*
852                       * nd6_prelist_add will install the corresponding
853                       * interface route.
854                       */
855                      if ((error = nd6_prelist_add(&pr0, NULL, &pr)) != 0)
856                              return (error);
857                      if (pr == NULL) {
858                              log(LOG_ERR, "nd6_prelist_add succeeded but "
859                                  "no prefix\n");
860                              return (EINVAL); /* XXX panic here? */
861                      }
862              }
863
864              /* relate the address to the prefix */
865              if (ia->ia6_ndpr == NULL) {
866                      ia->ia6_ndpr = pr;
867                      pr->ndpr_refcnt++;
868
```

```
869                          /*
870                           * If this is the first autoconf address from the
871                           * prefix, create a temporary address as well
872                           * (when required).
873                           */
874                          if ((ia->ia6_flags & IN6_IFF_AUTOCONF) &&
875                              ip6_use_tempaddr && pr->ndpr_refcnt == 1) {
876                                  int e;
877                                  if ((e = in6_tmpifadd(ia, 1)) != 0) {
878                                          log(LOG_NOTICE, "in6_control: failed "
879                                              "to create a temporary address, "
880                                              "errno=%d\n", e);
881                                  }
882                          }
883                  }
884
885                  /*
886                   * this might affect the status of autoconfigured addresses,
887                   * that is, this address might make other addresses detached.
888                   */
889                  pfxlist_onlink_check();
890
891                  break;
892          }
```
                                                                                    ___ in6.c

814–847 This part of the code is similar to Listing 2-40 in Section 2.13.4. The difference is the consideration for the case where the prefix length is 128. The prefix is then identical to the address itself, so the rest of the processing is skipped.

850–862 Function nd6_prefix_lookup() looks for the nd_prefix{} structure in the kernel internal list, and returns a pointer to the structure if one exists. This can happen, for example, if another address that shares the same prefix has already been configured, as in Figure 2-15. If the search fails, nd6_prelist_add() creates a new nd_prefix{} structure with the specified parameters.

865–867 If the in6_ifaddr{} structure has not yet been associated with the prefix, which is the case when the address is just created, the ia6_ndpr member is set to the returned pointer above, and the reference counter to the prefix is incremented.

874–882 If the "autoconf" flag is set in the created address by hand, temporary addresses per [RFC3041] are to be created, and the address is the only owner of the prefix, then a new temporary address is created. This is an atypical operation and is beyond the scope of this chapter.

889 The creation or change of the address and prefix may affect the status of other addresses or prefixes in the kernel. The pfxlist_onlink_check() function checks the ramification. The details of this function is beyond the scope of this chapter and will be discussed in Section 5.19.6.

Delete Address

Listing 2-68
                                                                                    ___ in6.c

```
894          case SIOCDIFADDR_IN6:
895          {
896                  struct nd_prefix *pr;
```

```
897
898                     /*
899                      * If the address being deleted is the only one that owns
900                      * the corresponding prefix, expire the prefix as well.
901                      * XXX: theoretically, we don't have to worry about such
902                      * relationship, since we separate the address management
903                      * and the prefix management.  We do this, however, to provide
904                      * as much backward compatibility as possible in terms of
905                      * the ioctl operation.
906                      * Note that in6_purgeaddr() will decrement ndpr_refcnt.
907                      */
908                     pr = ia->ia6_ndpr;
909                     in6_purgeaddr(&ia->ia_ifa);
910                     if (pr && pr->ndpr_refcnt == 0)
911                             prelist_remove(pr);
912                     break;
913             }
    ...
919             }
920
921             return (0);
922     }
```
                                                                              _____ in6.c

894–909 The `in6_purgeaddr()` function deletes the specified address from the interface.
This function will be described later in Section 2.15.1.

910–911 If the deleted address is the only address that matches the corresponding prefix,
the `prelist_remove()` function also removes the prefix and deletes the associated
direct route as a result. As commented on in the code, we could keep the prefix since
the KAME kernel manages addresses and prefixes separately with separate lifetimes. But
this implementation tries to provide behavior compatible with the traditional IPv4 operation, where deleting an address causes the deletion of the associated direct route. The
`prelist_remove()` function is discussed later in Section 5.19.2.

2.14.2 `in6_update_ifa()` Function

The `in6_update_ifa()` function is called to either add or update an address on an interface.
As shown in Figure 2-16, this function is the most important routine for address configuration
in the KAME implementation. We will see the details of this large function below by examining
its major chunks one by one.

Listing 2-69
                                                                              _____ in6.c

```
924     /*
925      * Update parameters of an IPv6 interface address.
926      * If necessary, a new entry is created and linked into address chains.
927      * This function is separated from in6_control().
928      * XXX: should this be performed under splnet()?
929      */
930     int
931     in6_update_ifa(ifp, ifra, ia)
932             struct ifnet *ifp;
933             struct in6_aliasreq *ifra;
934             struct in6_ifaddr *ia;
935     {
```
                                                                              _____ in6.c

924–935 The first function argument `ifp` is a pointer to the network interface on which we are configuring an address. The second parameter `ifra` contains the address information. The third parameter `ia` is used only when we are updating an existing address. In that case `ia` is a pointer to an existing instance of the `in6_ifaddr{}` structure that contains the address to be updated. Parameter `ia` is set to NULL for new address assignment.

Validate Parameters

Listing 2-70

```
                                                                                in6.c
936              int error = 0, hostIsNew = 0, plen = -1;
937              struct in6_ifaddr *oia;

941              struct sockaddr_in6 dst6;
942              struct in6_addrlifetime *lt;
943              struct in6_multi_mship *imm;

947              struct rtentry *rt;
948
949              /* Validate parameters */
950              if (ifp == NULL || ifra == NULL) /* this maybe redundant */
951                      return (EINVAL);
952
953              /*
954               * The destination address for a p2p link must have a family
955               * of AF_UNSPEC or AF_INET6.
956               */
957              if ((ifp->if_flags & IFF_POINTOPOINT) != 0 &&
958                  ifra->ifra_dstaddr.sin6_family != AF_INET6 &&
959                  ifra->ifra_dstaddr.sin6_family != AF_UNSPEC)
960                      return (EAFNOSUPPORT);
                                                                                in6.c
```

950–951 Neither `ifp` nor `ifra` can be NULL. The caller of this function should ensure that condition, but it is checked explicitly for safety.

957–960 The `ifra_dstaddr` member must be specified for a point-to-point interface. The destination address must be of the `AF_INET6` address family when given or be of the `AF_UNSPEC` address family for an unnumbered point-to-point interface. All other address families are invalid.

Listing 2-71

```
                                                                                in6.c
961              /*
962               * validate ifra_prefixmask.  don't check sin6_family, netmask
963               * does not carry fields other than sin6_len.
964               */
965              if (ifra->ifra_prefixmask.sin6_len > sizeof(struct sockaddr_in6))
966                      return (EINVAL);
967              /*
968               * Because the IPv6 address architecture is classless, we require
969               * users to specify a (non 0) prefix length (mask) for a new address.
970               * We also require the prefix (when specified) mask is valid, and thus
971               * reject a non-consecutive mask.
972               */
973              if (ia == NULL && ifra->ifra_prefixmask.sin6_len == 0)
974                      return (EINVAL);
975              if (ifra->ifra_prefixmask.sin6_len != 0) {
```

```
976                         plen = in6_mask2len(&ifra->ifra_prefixmask.sin6_addr,
977                             (u_char *)&ifra->ifra_prefixmask +
978                             ifra->ifra_prefixmask.sin6_len);
979                         if (plen <= 0)
980                             return (EINVAL);
981                 } else {
982                         /*
983                          * In this case, ia must not be NULL.  We just use its prefix
984                          * length.
985                          */
986                         plen = in6_mask2len(&ia->ia_prefixmask.sin6_addr, NULL);
987                 }
```
                                                                                              in6.c

961–966 `ifra_prefixmask.sin6_len` must not be greater than the size of the
`sockaddr_in6{}` structure. We do not check to see if it is exactly the same size as
the `sockaddr_in6{}` structure because it may be filled with zeros when there is no
need for prefix mask information.

973–987 We need to calculate the prefix length from the prefix mask `ifra_prefixmask`
if given because the `in6_aliasreq{}` structure does not contain such information.
Function `in6_mask2len()` returns the number of contiguous 1 bits starting from the
most significant bit position. The second argument is a stop marker. By default the stop
marker is set at the seventeenth byte. The `ifra_prefixmask` member may not be set
when an existing address is updated, in which case the prefix length is determined from
the existing address given as the third argument to this function.

Listing 2-72
                                                                                              in6.c

```
988                 /*
989                  * If the destination address on a p2p interface is specified,
990                  * and the address is a scoped one, validate/set the scope
991                  * zone identifier.
992                  */
993                 dst6 = ifra->ifra_dstaddr;
994                 if ((ifp->if_flags & (IFF_POINTOPOINT|IFF_LOOPBACK)) != 0 &&
995                     (dst6.sin6_family == AF_INET6)) {
996                         u_int32_t zoneid;
997
999                         if ((error = in6_recoverscope(&dst6,
1000                             &ifra->ifra_dstaddr.sin6_addr, ifp)) != 0)
1001                             return (error);
1003                         if (in6_addr2zoneid(ifp, &dst6.sin6_addr, &zoneid))
1004                             return (EINVAL);
1005                         if (dst6.sin6_scope_id == 0) /* user omit to specify the ID. */
1006                             dst6.sin6_scope_id = zoneid;
1007                         else if (dst6.sin6_scope_id != zoneid)
1008                             return (EINVAL); /* scope ID mismatch. */
1009                         if ((error = in6_embedscope(&dst6.sin6_addr, &dst6)) != 0)
1010                             return (error);
1012                         dst6.sin6_scope_id = 0; /* XXX */
1014                 }
```
                                                                                              in6.c

993–995 For a point-to-point interface we need to check whether the destination address
belongs to the appropriate scope zone corresponding to the local address and the interface.

999–1004 The `in6_recoverscope()` function extracts the scope value from the embedded address form given in the second argument and sets the `sin6_scope_id` field of the first argument. Since the caller may specify the zone ID either in the embedded form or through the `sin6_scope_id` field, it is necessary for us to retrieve the zone ID here again (from the `sockaddr_in6{}` structure that was just rearranged by `in6_recoverscope()`) to make the processing code generic.

1005–1012 We will fill in the `sin6_scope_id` field if the user did not specify one. It is an error condition if the `sin6_scope_id` value supplied by the user does not match the value extracted from the interface scope zone list. The zone ID is embedded into the address by calling `in6_embedscope()`. The `sin6_scope_id` field is then cleared. At this point, `dst6` is in the appropriate form in terms of Figure 2-12.

Listing 2-73

```
──────────────────────────────────────────────────────────────────── in6.c
1015            /*
1016             * The destination address can be specified only for a p2p or a
1017             * loopback interface.  If specified, the corresponding prefix length
1018             * must be 128.
1019             */
1020            if (ifra->ifra_dstaddr.sin6_family == AF_INET6) {

1024
1025                    if ((ifp->if_flags & (IFF_POINTOPOINT|IFF_LOOPBACK)) == 0) {
1026                            /* XXX: noisy message */
1027                            nd6log((LOG_INFO, "in6_update_ifa: a destination can "
1028                                "be specified for a p2p or a loopback IF only\n"));
1029                            return (EINVAL);
1030                    }
1031                    if (plen != 128) {
1032                            nd6log((LOG_INFO, "in6_update_ifa: prefixlen should "
1033                                "be 128 when dstaddr is specified\n"));

1048                            return (EINVAL);

1050                    }
1051            }
──────────────────────────────────────────────────────────────────── in6.c
```

1020–1051 The destination address is specified only for either a point-to-point or a loopback interface. The prefix length must be 128. It is an error if either condition is not met.

Note: This restriction is not based on the protocol specification, but an implementation-specific behavior. Since the **ifconfig** command uses the default prefix length of 64 bits when configuring an IPv6 address, the following execution would implicitly specify a subnet prefix with the length of 64 bits (`2001:db8::/64`) as well as the peer address of a point-to-point interface (tun0):

```
ifconfig tun0 inet6 2001:db8::1 2001:db8::2
```

It would then cause other side effects such as Neighbor Discovery for addresses that match the subnet prefix on the point-to-point link. This is unlikely the result that the user wants, and thus KAME developers chose to throw an error in this case, rather than ignoring the probably erroneous configuration. Due to this restriction, the user should actually specify the prefix length explicitly:

```
ifconfig tun0 inet6 2001:db8::1 2001:db8::2 prefixlen 128
```

Alternatively, the user can also assign the same address with a subnet prefix that covers the destination address:

```
ifconfig tun0 inet6 2001:db8::1 prefixlen 64
```

The major difference in this configuration is that Neighbor Unreachability Detection (Section 5.9) will take place for the destination address, while the user will not notice the underlying behavior.

Listing 2-74
                                                                                                    ___in6.c

```
1052            /* lifetime consistency check */
1053            lt = &ifra->ifra_lifetime;
1054            if (lt->ia6t_pltime > lt->ia6t_vltime)
1055                    return (EINVAL);
1056            if (lt->ia6t_vltime == 0) {
1057                    /*
1058                     * the following log might be noisy, but this is a typical
1059                     * configuration mistake or a tool's bug.
1060                     */
1061                    nd6log((LOG_INFO,
1062                        "in6_update_ifa: valid lifetime is 0 for %s\n",
1063                        ip6_sprintf(&ifra->ifra_addr.sin6_addr)));
1064
1065                    if (ia == NULL)
1066                            return (0); /* there's nothing to do */
1067            }
```
                                                                                                    ___in6.c

1052–1067 The preferred lifetime for an IPv6 address must not be greater than its valid lifetime. The valid lifetime could be zero, but the result would probably be different from what the user wants. If the address is being newly assigned with a zero valid lifetime, it effectively causes nothing without any error; if an existing address is updated with a zero valid lifetime, the address will immediately be deleted. This actually happened with previous versions of the implementation. An explicit log message was issued in this case even if the operation itself was valid. Such an unexpected side effect has been less common in later versions, and the log message is now disabled by default with the nd6log() wrapper function.

Insert a New Address

Listing 2-75
                                                                                                    ___in6.c

```
1069            /*
1070             * If this is a new address, allocate a new ifaddr and link it
1071             * into chains.
1072             */
1073            if (ia == NULL) {
1074                    hostIsNew = 1;
1075                    /*
1076                     * When in6_update_ifa() is called in a process of a received
1077                     * RA, it is called under an interrupt context.  So, we should
1078                     * call malloc with M_NOWAIT.
```

```
1079                         */
1080                    ia = (struct in6_ifaddr *) malloc(sizeof(*ia), M_IFADDR,
1081                        M_NOWAIT);
1082                    if (ia == NULL)
1083                            return (ENOBUFS);
1084                    bzero((caddr_t)ia, sizeof(*ia));
1085                    LIST_INIT(&ia->ia6_memberships);
1086                    /* Initialize the address and masks, and put time stamp */
1087                    ia->ia_ifa.ifa_addr = (struct sockaddr *)&ia->ia_addr;
1088                    ia->ia_addr.sin6_family = AF_INET6;
1089                    ia->ia_addr.sin6_len = sizeof(ia->ia_addr);
1090                    ia->ia6_createtime = ia->ia6_updatetime = time_second;
1091                    if ((ifp->if_flags & (IFF_POINTOPOINT | IFF_LOOPBACK)) != 0) {
1092                            /*
1093                             * XXX: some functions expect that ifa_dstaddr is not
1094                             * NULL for p2p interfaces.
1095                             */
1096                            ia->ia_ifa.ifa_dstaddr =
1097                                (struct sockaddr *)&ia->ia_dstaddr;
1098                    } else {
1099                            ia->ia_ifa.ifa_dstaddr = NULL;
1100                    }
1101                    ia->ia_ifa.ifa_netmask =
1102                        (struct sockaddr *)&ia->ia_prefixmask;
1103
1104                    ia->ia_ifp = ifp;
1105                    if ((oia = in6_ifaddr) != NULL) {
1106                            for ( ; oia->ia_next; oia = oia->ia_next)
1107                                    continue;
1108                            oia->ia_next = ia;
1109                    } else
1110                            in6_ifaddr = ia;

1124                    TAILQ_INSERT_TAIL(&ifp->if_addrlist, &ia->ia_ifa,
1125                                    ifa_list);

1131            }
```
——— in6.c

1073–1083 If the third argument to `in6_update_ifa()` is NULL, a new address will be created.

1080–1104 A new `in6_ifaddr{}` structure is allocated and initialized to store the new address. The pointer fields in the `ifaddr{}` structure are initialized to the `in6_ifaddr` field as explained for Listings 2-11 and 2-12. The address creation and modification times are recorded.

Note: The address modification time must also be updated when an existing address is updated via the `SIOCAIFADDR_IN6` `ioctl`. However, this version of the implementation records the modification time only on creation, and so an application cannot update lifetimes of an existing address. We will see this causes a problem with a DHCPv6 client in Chapter 4 of *IPv6 Advanced Protocols Implementation*.

1105–1124 The new address is linked into the global IPv6 address list (one per protocol family) maintained in the global variable `in6_ifaddr`. This new address is also linked into the per-interface address list maintained in the `if_addrlist` field in the `ifnet{}` structure. Variable `ia` is now a valid pointer to the new address.

Listing 2-76
_____in6.c

```
1133          /* set prefix mask */
1134          if (ifra->ifra_prefixmask.sin6_len) {
1135                  /*
1136                   * We prohibit changing the prefix length of an existing
1137                   * address, because
1138                   * + such an operation should be rare in IPv6, and
1139                   * + the operation would confuse prefix management.
1140                   */
1141                  if (ia->ia_prefixmask.sin6_len &&
1142                      in6_mask2len(&ia->ia_prefixmask.sin6_addr, NULL) != plen) {
1143                          nd6log((LOG_INFO, "in6_update_ifa: the prefix length of an"
1144                              " existing (%s) address should not be changed\n",
1145                              ip6_sprintf(&ia->ia_addr.sin6_addr)));
1146                          error = EINVAL;
1147                          goto unlink;
1148                  }
1149                  ia->ia_prefixmask = ifra->ifra_prefixmask;
1150          }
```
_____in6.c

1141–1149 This implementation does not allow an application to change the prefix length of an existing address. The `in6_update_ifa()` function returns an error when there is a mismatch in the prefix length between the specified address and the existing address being updated.

Listing 2-77
_____in6.c

```
1152          /*
1153           * If a new destination address is specified, scrub the old one and
1154           * install the new destination.  Note that the interface must be
1155           * p2p or loopback (see the check above.)
1156           */
1157          if (dst6.sin6_family == AF_INET6 &&
1158              !IN6_ARE_ADDR_EQUAL(&dst6.sin6_addr, &ia->ia_dstaddr.sin6_addr)) {
1159                  int e;
1160
1161                  if ((ia->ia_flags & IFA_ROUTE) != 0 &&
1162                      (e = rtinit(&(ia->ia_ifa), (int)RTM_DELETE, RTF_HOST)) != 0) {
1163                          nd6log((LOG_ERR, "in6_update_ifa: failed to remove "
1164                              "a route to the old destination: %s\n",
1165                              ip6_sprintf(&ia->ia_addr.sin6_addr)));
1166                          /* proceed anyway... */
1167                  } else
1168                          ia->ia_flags &= ~IFA_ROUTE;
1169                  ia->ia_dstaddr = dst6;
1170          }
```
_____in6.c

1157–1170 The KAME kernel maintains a host routing entry for the destination end of a point-to-point link. The `IFA_ROUTE` flag indicates that a route entry was created for this address. This host route entry is removed from the routing table when the destination address is changed. The `IFA_ROUTE` flag is cleared once the `rtinit()` function removes the previous routing entry successfully.

Listing 2-78
_____in6.c

```
1172          /*
1173           * Set lifetimes.  We do not refer to ia6t_expire and ia6t_preferred
```

```
1174            * to see if the address is deprecated or invalidated, but initialize
1175            * these members for applications.
1176            */
1177           ia->ia6_lifetime = ifra->ifra_lifetime;
1178           if (ia->ia6_lifetime.ia6t_vltime != ND6_INFINITE_LIFETIME) {
1179                   ia->ia6_lifetime.ia6t_expire =
1180                       time_second + ia->ia6_lifetime.ia6t_vltime;
1181           } else
1182                   ia->ia6_lifetime.ia6t_expire = 0;
1183           if (ia->ia6_lifetime.ia6t_pltime != ND6_INFINITE_LIFETIME) {
1184                   ia->ia6_lifetime.ia6t_preferred =
1185                       time_second + ia->ia6_lifetime.ia6t_pltime;
1186           } else
1187                   ia->ia6_lifetime.ia6t_preferred = 0;
```
── in6.c

1177–1187 The address lifetimes are initialized to the given values by the caller. The address expiration times are calculated for noninfinite lifetimes. The `time_second` global variable holds the number of seconds elapsed since epoch. Setting the expiration times to zero implies infinite lifetimes.

Listing 2-79
── in6.c
```
1189           /* reset the interface and routing table appropriately. */
1190           if ((error = in6_ifinit(ifp, ia, &ifra->ifra_addr, hostIsNew)) != 0)
1191                   goto unlink;
```
── in6.c

1190 The `in6_ifinit()` function initializes the interface and installs the necessary routing entries. This function is discussed later in Section 2.14.5.

Listing 2-80
── in6.c
```
1193           /*
1194            * configure address flags.
1195            */
1196           ia->ia6_flags = ifra->ifra_flags;
1197           /*
1198            * backward compatibility - if IN6_IFF_DEPRECATED is set from the
1199            * userland, make it deprecated.
1200            */
1201           if ((ifra->ifra_flags & IN6_IFF_DEPRECATED) != 0) {
1202                   ia->ia6_lifetime.ia6t_pltime = 0;
1203                   ia->ia6_lifetime.ia6t_preferred = time_second;
1204           }
```
── in6.c

1196–1204 If the address provided by the caller contains the `IN6_IFF_DEPRECATED` address flag, the preferred lifetime is set to 0 and the expiration time is set to the current time so it is deprecated immediately. As commented in the code, this is for backward compatibility with older applications. Now that the `SIOCAIFADDR_IN6` API provides a more flexible way of updating the lifetimes, an application that wants to make a particular address deprecated should specify the 0 preferred lifetime for the address. Note, however, that changing lifetimes of an existing address does not work as expected in this version of the kernel implementation as noted in Listing 2-75.

Listing 2-81
_____in6.c

```
1205        /*
1206         * Make the address tentative before joining multicast addresses,
1207         * so that corresponding MLD responses would not have a tentative
1208         * source address.
1209         */
1210        ia->ia6_flags &= ~IN6_IFF_DUPLICATED;    /* safety */

1214        if (hostIsNew && in6if_do_dad(ifp))

1216                ia->ia6_flags |= IN6_IFF_TENTATIVE;
```
_____in6.c

1210–1216 A newly configured address must be unique on the link under a specific prefix, which is going to be confirmed through the DAD procedure. The `IN6_IFF_DUPLICATED` flag, meaning DAD detects it is a duplicate address, is cleared in case the caller sets it accidentally. The `IN6_IFF_TENTATIVE` address flag is set so that the address is not used in any communication while DAD is in progress.

Joining Multicast Groups

An IPv6 node is required to join the all-nodes multicast group and the solicited-node multicast group for each unicast and anycast address configured on the node (Section 2.6). The next part of the `in6_update_ifa()` function performs this process.

Listing 2-82
_____in6.c

```
1218        /*
1219         * Beyond this point, we should call in6_purgeaddr upon an error,
1220         * not just go to unlink.
1221         */
1222
1223        if ((ifp->if_flags & IFF_MULTICAST) != 0) {
1224                struct sockaddr_in6 mltaddr, mltmask;

1226                u_int32_t zoneid = 0;

1228
1229                if (hostIsNew) {
1230                        /* join solicited multicast addr for new host id */
1231                        struct sockaddr_in6 llsol;

1233                        bzero(&llsol, sizeof(llsol));
1234                        llsol.sin6_family = AF_INET6;
1235                        llsol.sin6_len = sizeof(llsol);
1236                        llsol.sin6_addr.s6_addr32[0] = htonl(0xff020000);
1237                        llsol.sin6_addr.s6_addr32[1] = 0;
1238                        llsol.sin6_addr.s6_addr32[2] = htonl(1);
1239                        llsol.sin6_addr.s6_addr32[3] =
1240                                ifra->ifra_addr.sin6_addr.s6_addr32[3];
1241                        llsol.sin6_addr.s6_addr8[12] = 0xff;
1242                        if (in6_addr2zoneid(ifp, &llsol.sin6_addr,
1243                            &llsol.sin6_scope_id)) {
1244                                /* XXX: should not happen */
1245                                log(LOG_ERR, "in6_update_ifa: "
1246                                    "in6_addr2zoneid failed\n");
1247                                goto cleanup;
1248                        }
1249                        in6_embedscope(&llsol.sin6_addr, &llsol); /* XXX */
1250                        imm = in6_joingroup(ifp, &llsol, &error);
```

```
1251                          if (imm) {
1252                                  LIST_INSERT_HEAD(&ia->ia6_memberships, imm,
1253                                          i6mm_chain);
1254                          } else {
1255                                  nd6log((LOG_ERR, "in6_update_ifa: addmulti "
1256                                          "failed for %s on %s (errno=%d)\n",
1257                                          ip6_sprintf(&llsol.sin6_addr),
1258                                          if_name(ifp), error));
1259                                  goto cleanup;
1260                          }
1261                  }
```
_____ in6.c

1229–1248 The solicited-node multicast address is calculated from the newly added address. The prefix is ff02::/16 for the link-local scope multicast address. Function in6_addr2zoneid() is invoked to retrieve the link zone ID for the interface, and then the zone ID is embedded into the address by the in6_embedscope() function. This conversion process makes the variable llsol have the proper zone ID in the sin6_scope_id field as well as embedded in the sin6_addr field. This form is generally expected in the IPv6 protocol stack in the kernel as depicted in Figure 2-12.

1249–1260 After initializing the llsol variable with the solicited-node multicast address, in6_joingroup() adds the multicast membership. On success it returns a pointer to an instance of the in6_multi_mship{} structure containing the multicast membership information. The KAME kernel maintains the multicast memberships globally as shown in Figure 2-14. It is possible for multiple addresses with the same interface identifier but different prefixes to map into the same multicast group. In such cases the node has already joined the multicast group on that interface. The KAME code simply increments the reference counter of the existing membership structure. This new multicast membership is inserted into the list maintained in the ia6_memberships field of the in6_ifaddr{} structure.

Listing 2-83

_____ in6.c
```
1263                  bzero(&mltmask, sizeof(mltmask));
1264                  mltmask.sin6_len = sizeof(struct sockaddr_in6);
1265                  mltmask.sin6_family = AF_INET6;
1266                  mltmask.sin6_addr = in6mask32;
```
_____ in6.c

1263–1266 The node next joins the link-local all-nodes multicast group on the interface. mltmask contains the subnet mask required for adding an associated route entry. Variable mltmask is set to ffff:ffff::/32 instead of ffff::/16 even though the multicast prefix is ff02::/16. This is because the routing table entry is in the embedded address form with the second 16-bit word containing the link zone ID, thereby taking into account the zone ID during the routing table lookup.

Listing 2-84

_____ in6.c
```
1268                  /*
1269                   * join link-local all-nodes address
1270                   */
```

```
1271                    bzero(&mltaddr, sizeof(mltaddr));
1272                    mltaddr.sin6_len = sizeof(struct sockaddr_in6);
1273                    mltaddr.sin6_family = AF_INET6;
1274                    mltaddr.sin6_addr = in6addr_linklocal_allnodes;
1275                    if (in6_addr2zoneid(ifp, &mltaddr.sin6_addr,
1276                        &mltaddr.sin6_scope_id)) {
1277                            goto cleanup; /* XXX: should not fail */
1278                    }
1279                    in6_embedscope(&mltaddr.sin6_addr, &mltaddr); /* XXX */
....
1281                    zoneid = mltaddr.sin6_scope_id;
1282                    mltaddr.sin6_scope_id = 0;
```
——— in6.c

1271–1282 Variable `mltaddr` is initialized with the link-local all-nodes multicast address
of `ff02::1`. The appropriate link zone ID is embedded into the address and the
`sin6_scope_id` field is cleared temporarily before being passed to the `rtalloc1()`
function below.

Listing 2-85
——— in6.c

```
1285                    /*
1286                     * XXX: do we really need this automatic routes?
1287                     * We should probably reconsider this stuff.  Most applications
1288                     * actually do not need the routes, since they usually specify
1289                     * the outgoing interface.
1290                     */

1292                    rt = rtalloc1((struct sockaddr *)&mltaddr, 0, 0UL);

1296                    if (rt) {
1297                            /*
1298                             * 32bit came from "mltmask"
1299                             * XXX: only works in !SCOPEDROUTING case.
1300                             */
1301                            if (memcmp(&mltaddr.sin6_addr,
1302                                &((struct sockaddr_in6 *)rt_key(rt))->sin6_addr,
1303                                32 / 8)) {
1304                                    RTFREE(rt);
1305                                    rt = NULL;
1306                            }
1307                    }
```
——— in6.c

1292–1307 Function `rtalloc1()` searches for a routing entry for the link-local all-nodes
multicast address and returns a pointer to the entry if it exists. If the destination address
for the entry does not match the prefix `ff02:xxxx::/32`, where xxxx is the embedded
link zone ID, the entry is ignored. This is typically the case with the IPv6 default route.

Listing 2-86
——— in6.c

```
1308                    if (!rt) {

1324                            error = rtrequest(RTM_ADD, (struct sockaddr *)&mltaddr,
1325                                (struct sockaddr *)&ia->ia_addr,
1326                                (struct sockaddr *)&mltmask, RTF_UP | RTF_CLONING,
1327                                (struct rtentry **)0);
```

```
1329                          if (error)
1330                                  goto cleanup;
1331                  } else {
1332                          RTFREE(rt);
1333                  }
```
_____ in6.c

1308–1333 Function `rtrequest()` creates a new entry if no matching entry exists in the routing table or an existing one was different from what we expected. The `rtalloc1()` function increments the reference counter on the route entry before returning it to the caller, while `rtrequest()` does not increment the counter if its last argument is NULL. The latter case is the correct behavior here, because the route entry is no longer held for any purpose. Thus, if an existing entry is found by `rtalloc1()`, the reference counter to the entry is explicitly decremented by the `RTFREE()` macro.

Listing 2-87

_____ in6.c

```
1335                  mltaddr.sin6_scope_id = zoneid; /* XXX */

1337                  imm = in6_joingroup(ifp, &mltaddr, &error);
1338                  if (imm) {
1339                          LIST_INSERT_HEAD(&ia->ia6_memberships, imm,
1340                                  i6mm_chain);
1341                  } else {
1342                          nd6log((LOG_WARNING,
1343                              "in6_update_ifa: addmulti failed for "
1344                              "%s on %s (errno=%d)\n",
1345                              ip6_sprintf(&mltaddr.sin6_addr),
1346                              if_name(ifp), error));
1347                          goto cleanup;
1348                  }
```
_____ in6.c

1335–1348 The `sin6_scope_id` field is recovered, and then this multicast address is added to the membership list.

Listing 2-88

_____ in6.c

```
1350                  /*
1351                   * join node information group address
1352                   */
1354  #define hostnamelen          strlen(hostname)
1356                  if (in6_nigroup(ifp, hostname, hostnamelen, &mltaddr) == 0) {
1357                          imm = in6_joingroup(ifp, &mltaddr, &error);
1358                          if (imm) {
1359                                  LIST_INSERT_HEAD(&ia->ia6_memberships, imm,
1360                                          i6mm_chain);
1361                          } else {
1362                                  nd6log((LOG_WARNING, "in6_update_ifa: "
1363                                      "addmulti failed for %s on %s (errno=%d)\n",
1364                                      ip6_sprintf(&mltaddr.sin6_addr),
1365                                      if_name(ifp), error));
1366                                  /* XXX not very fatal, go on... */
1367                          }
1368                  }
1370  #undef hostnamelen
```
_____ in6.c

1356–1368 The next part joins the Node Information Group corresponding to the node's hostname (see Section 4.4). The `in6_nigroup()` function creates a multicast address for this group based on the hostname, and `in6_joingroup()` joins the group as we have seen so far.

Listing 2-89

```
                                                              in6.c
1373                    /*
1374                     * join interface-local all-nodes address.
1375                     * (ff01::1%ifN, and ff01::%ifN/32)
1376                     */
1377                    mltaddr.sin6_addr = in6addr_nodelocal_allnodes;
1378                    if (in6_addr2zoneid(ifp, &mltaddr.sin6_addr,
1379                        &mltaddr.sin6_scope_id)) {
1380                            goto cleanup; /* XXX: should not fail */
1381                    }
1382                    in6_embedscope(&mltaddr.sin6_addr, &mltaddr); /* XXX */
  ...
1384                    zoneid = mltaddr.sin6_scope_id;
1385                    mltaddr.sin6_scope_id = 0;
  ...
1387
1388                    /* XXX: again, do we really need the route? */

1390                    rt = rtalloc1((struct sockaddr *)&mltaddr, 0, 0UL);

1394                    if (rt) {
1395                            /* 32bit came from "mltmask" */
1396                            if (memcmp(&mltaddr.sin6_addr,
1397                                &((struct sockaddr_in6 *)rt_key(rt))->sin6_addr,
1398                                32 / 8)) {
1399                                    RTFREE(rt);
1400                                    rt = NULL;
1401                            }
1402                    }
1403                    if (!rt) {
  ...
1418                            error = rtrequest(RTM_ADD, (struct sockaddr *)&mltaddr,
1419                                (struct sockaddr *)&ia->ia_addr,
1420                                (struct sockaddr *)&mltmask, RTF_UP | RTF_CLONING,
1421                                (struct rtentry **)0);
1422
1423                            if (error)
1424                                    goto cleanup;
1425                    } else {
1426                            RTFREE(rt);
1427                    }
1428
1429                    mltaddr.sin6_scope_id = zoneid; /* XXX */
  ...
1431                    imm = in6_joingroup(ifp, &mltaddr, &error);
1432                    if (imm) {
1433                            LIST_INSERT_HEAD(&ia->ia6_memberships, imm,
1434                                i6mm_chain);
1435                    } else {
1436                            nd6log((LOG_WARNING, "in6_update_ifa: "
1437                                "addmulti failed for %s on %s "
1438                                "(errno=%d)\n",
1439                                ip6_sprintf(&mltaddr.sin6_addr),
1440                                if_name(ifp), error));
1441                            goto cleanup;
1442                    }
1443            }
                                                              in6.c
```

1337–1442 Similar membership processing is performed for the interface-local all-nodes multicast address.

Start Duplicate Address Detection

Listing 2-90
```
                                                                          ___in6.c
1445            /*
1446             * Perform DAD, if needed.
1447             * XXX It may be of use, if we can administratively
1448             * disable DAD.
1449             */

1454            if (hostIsNew && in6if_do_dad(ifp) &&
1455                (ifra->ifra_flags & IN6_IFF_NODAD) == 0)

1457            {
1458                    nd6_dad_start((struct ifaddr *)ia, NULL);
1459            }
1460
1461            return (error);
                                                                          ___in6.c
```

1454–1461 DAD is performed on the new address by calling `nd6_dad_start()` if the interface allows DAD and the `IN6_IFF_NODAD` address flag is not set.

Cleanup on Error

The rest of the `in6_update_ifa()` function cleans up intermediate data structures in case some error occurred during the configuration procedure.

Listing 2-91
```
                                                                          ___in6.c
1463    unlink:
1464            /*
1465             * XXX: if a change of an existing address failed, keep the entry
1466             * anyway.
1467             */
1468            if (hostIsNew)
1469                    in6_unlink_ifa(ia, ifp);
1470            return (error);
1471
1472    cleanup:
1473            in6_purgeaddr(&ia->ia_ifa);
1474            return error;
1475    }
                                                                          ___in6.c
```

1463–1470 If an error occurred during configuration of a new address, it is removed from the various address lists. The `in6_unlink_ifa()` function is discussed later in Section 2.15.3.

1472–1474 Function `in6_purgeaddr()` performs the cleanup process of leaving the multicast groups, removing the routing entries, and removing the new address from the address lists, if an error has occurred while joining the various multicast groups.

2.14.3 `in6_joingroup()` and `in6_leavegroup()` Functions

The `in6_joingroup()` and the `in6_leavegroup()` functions are the top-level interface of
joining and leaving a multicast group as shown in Figure 2-17.

Listing 2-92

```
                                                                          in6.c
3574    struct in6_multi_mship *
3575    in6_joingroup(ifp, addr, errorp)
3576            struct ifnet *ifp;
3577            struct sockaddr_in6 *addr;
3578            int *errorp;
3579    {
3580            struct in6_multi_mship *imm;

3584
3585            imm = malloc(sizeof(*imm), M_IPMADDR, M_NOWAIT);
3586            if (!imm) {
3587                    *errorp = ENOBUFS;
3588                    return NULL;
3589            }
3590
3591            bzero(imm, sizeof(*imm));
        ...
3607            imm->i6mm_maddr = in6_addmulti(addr, ifp, errorp);
3608            if (!imm->i6mm_maddr) {
3609                    /* *errorp is alrady set */
3610                    free(imm, M_IPMADDR);
3611                    return NULL;
3612            }

3614            return imm;
3615    }
                                                                          in6.c
```

3574–3577 The `in6_joingroup()` function has three arguments. The first argument is a
pointer to the network interface on which the multicast group membership is to be added.
The second argument is the multicast address to add. The third argument will store the
function error code upon return.

3580–3591 A new `in6_multi_mship{}` structure is allocated and initialized.

3607–3614 The `in6_addmulti()` function adds the multicast membership on the interface
if it is not yet installed, and returns the pointer to the `in6_multi{}` structure that holds
the multicast address.

Listing 2-93

```
                                                                          in6.c
3617    int
3618    in6_leavegroup(imm)
3619            struct in6_multi_mship *imm;
3620    {

3629            if (imm->i6mm_maddr) {

3646                    in6_delmulti(imm->i6mm_maddr);
3648            }
3649            free(imm, M_IPMADDR);
3650            return 0;
3651    }
                                                                          in6.c
```

3618–3651 The in6_leavegroup() function calls the in6_delmulti() function to remove the membership from the list and frees the storage space that holds the membership information.

2.14.4 in6_addmulti() and in6_delmulti() Functions

The in6_addmulti() and in6_delmulti() functions manipulate the membership list of the joined multicast groups.

Listing 2-94

─── in6.c

```
2896    struct  in6_multi *

2900    in6_addmulti(maddr6, ifp, errorp)

2902            struct sockaddr_in6 *maddr6;
2903            struct ifnet *ifp;
2904            int *errorp;

2911    {
2912            struct  in6_multi *in6m;
2913            struct ifmultiaddr *ifma;

2926            int     s = splnet();
2927
2928            *errorp = 0;

2940            /*
2941             * Call generic routine to add membership or increment
2942             * refcount.  It wants addresses in the form of a sockaddr,
2943             * so we build one here (being careful to zero the unused bytes).
2944             */
2945            *errorp = if_addmulti(ifp, (struct sockaddr *)maddr6, &ifma);
2946            if (*errorp) {
2947                    splx(s);
2948                    return 0;
2949            }
        ...
2951            /*
2952             * If ifma->ifma_protospec is null, then if_addmulti() created
2953             * a new record.  Otherwise, we are done.
2954             */
2955            if (ifma->ifma_protospec != 0) {
        ...
3054                    splx(s);
3055                    return ifma->ifma_protospec;
3056            }
```

─── in6.c

2926 Since this function can be called at the network interrupt level (see Figures 2-16 and 2-17), splnet() is necessary in order to keep other tasks at this level from running.

2945–3056 The if_addmulti() function searches through the list of multicast addresses maintained per interface and determines whether the given multicast address already exists in the list. If so, the existing entry is returned in the third argument ifma. In this case the ifma_protospec field points to an in6_multi{} structure that contains the address. If an error occurred in if_addmulti(), the in6_addmulti() function returns without taking any more action.

Listing 2-95 _____ in6.c

```
3058            /* XXX - if_addmulti uses M_WAITOK.  Can this really be called
3059               at interrupt time?  If so, need to fix if_addmulti. XXX */
3060            in6m = (struct in6_multi *)malloc(sizeof(*in6m), M_IPMADDR, M_NOWAIT);
3061            if (in6m == NULL) {
3062                    splx(s);
3063                    return (NULL);
3064            }
3065
3066            bzero(in6m, sizeof *in6m);
3067            in6m->in6m_sa = *maddr6;
3068            in6m->in6m_ifp = ifp;
3069            in6m->in6m_ifma = ifma;
3070            ifma->ifma_protospec = in6m;
3071            LIST_INSERT_HEAD(&in6_multihead, in6m, in6m_entry);
```
_____ in6.c

3060–3071 If this multicast address is not found in the list, an `in6_multi{}` structure is allocated and initialized with the address and the interface pointer. Note that the `ifma_protospec` field is set to point to the newly created structure. This pointer is assured to be NULL at this point by the check on line 2955. The new multicast address is inserted into the multicast address list kept in the `in6_multihead` global variable.

Listing 2-96 _____ in6.c

```
3073            /*
3074             * Let MLD6 know that we have joined a new IPv6 multicast
3075             * group.
3076             */

3141            mld6_start_listening(in6m);

3149            splx(s);
3150            return (in6m);
3151    }
```
_____ in6.c

3141 The `mld6_start_listening()` function performs the joining process based on MLDv1. This function will be discussed in Chapter 2 of *IPv6 Advanced Protocols Implementation*.

Listing 2-97 _____ in6.c

```
3156    void

3160    in6_delmulti(in6m)
3162            struct in6_multi *in6m;

3170    {
        ...
3182            struct ifmultiaddr *ifma = in6m->in6m_ifma;
3183            int     s = splnet();
3184

3294            if (ifma->ifma_refcount == 1) {
```

```
3295                         /*
3296                          * No remaining claims to this record; let MLD6 know
3297                          * that we are leaving the multicast group.
3298                          */
3299                         mld6_stop_listening(in6m);
3300                         ifma->ifma_protospec = 0;
3301                         LIST_REMOVE(in6m, in6m_entry);
3302                         free(in6m, M_IPMADDR);
3303                 }
3304                 /* XXX - should be separate API for when we have an ifma? */
3305                 if_delmulti(ifma->ifma_ifp, ifma->ifma_addr);

3307                 splx(s);
3308         }
```
——— in6.c

3160–3161 The `in6_delmulti()` function has one argument containing the multicast address for removal.

3294–3303 If no other parts of the kernel refer to this multicast address, the `mld6_stop_listening()` function is called to perform the leaving process based on MLDv1. The address is then removed from the multicast address list and its storage space is returned to the system.

3305 The `if_delmulti()` function is the group membership deletion function in the link-layer which is independent from network-layer protocols. It is called to remove the link-layer group address from the link-layer multicast reception filter so that the link-layer will not capture packets destined for the deleted group address.

2.14.5 `in6_ifinit()` Function

The `in6_ifinit()` function either installs or updates an address on a given interface, and installs necessary routing entries. It is a subroutine of the `in6_update_ifa()` function.

Listing 2-98

——— in6.c
```
1960    /*
1961     * Initialize an interface's intetnet6 address
1962     * and routing table entry.
1963     */
1964    static int
1965    in6_ifinit(ifp, ia, sin6, newhost)
1966            struct ifnet *ifp;
1967            struct in6_ifaddr *ia;
1968            struct sockaddr_in6 *sin6;
1969            int newhost;
1970    {
```
——— in6.c

1964–1970 This function has four arguments. The first argument is a pointer to the interface which will have the address given as the third argument. The second argument is an `in6_ifaddr{}` structure initialized in `in6_update_ifa()`. The fourth argument is a flag that indicates if the given address is a new address or an existing address to be updated.

Listing 2-99

_____ in6.c

```
1971            int     error = 0, plen, ifacount = 0;

1975            int     s = splimp();

1977            struct ifaddr *ifa;
1978
1979            /*
1980             * Give the interface a chance to initialize
1981             * if this is its first address,
1982             * and to validate the address if necessary.
1983             */

1987            TAILQ_FOREACH(ifa, &ifp->if_addrlist, ifa_list)
     ...
1992            {
1993                    if (ifa->ifa_addr == NULL)
1994                            continue;        /* just for safety */
1995                    if (ifa->ifa_addr->sa_family != AF_INET6)
1996                            continue;
1997                    ifacount++;
1998            }
```
_____ in6.c

1987–1998 The `if_addrlist` member of `ifp` is a list of all the addresses assigned to the interface. This list is traversed for counting the number of IPv6 addresses.

Listing 2-100

_____ in6.c

```
2000            ia->ia_addr = *sin6;
2001
2002            if (ifacount <= 1 && ifp->if_ioctl &&
2003                (error = (*ifp->if_ioctl)(ifp, SIOCSIFADDR, (caddr_t)ia))) {
2004                    splx(s);
2005                    return (error);
2006            }
2007            splx(s);
2008
2009            ia->ia_ifa.ifa_metric = ifp->if_metric;
```
_____ in6.c

2002–2005 If the interface has no IPv6 address except the one just being configured, the interface-specific `ioctl` function is called for link-level initialization.

2009 Each interface defines a cost as `ifp->if_metric` for sending packets and this metric value is copied into the `in6_ifaddr{}` structure.

Listing 2-101

_____ in6.c

```
2011            /* we could do in(6)_socktrim here, but just omit it at this moment. */
2012
2013            /*
2014             * Special case:
2015             * If the destination address is specified for a point-to-point
2016             * interface, install a route to the destination as an interface
2017             * direct route.
2018             */
2019            plen = in6_mask2len(&ia->ia_prefixmask.sin6_addr, NULL); /* XXX */
```

```
2020                    if (plen == 128 && ia->ia_dstaddr.sin6_family == AF_INET6) {
2021                            if ((error = rtinit(&(ia->ia_ifa), (int)RTM_ADD,
2022                                              RTF_UP | RTF_HOST)) != 0)
2023                                    return (error);
2024                            ia->ia_flags |= IFA_ROUTE;
2025                    }
```
—— in6.c

2019–2025 An interface direct host route for a point-to-point interface is installed if the destination address is set and has a 128-bit prefix length. The IFA_ROUTE flag is set in the ia_flags field to indicate a route entry has been installed for this address. This flag will be checked when the destination address is changed (Listing 2-77) or the local address on the interface is removed (Listing 2-108). If the ifa_rtrequest field were initialized (see Listing 2-102), the nd6_rtrequest() function would be called during the processing of rtinit(), but this is actually not the case.

Listing 2-102

—— in6.c
```
2027                    /* Add ownaddr as loopback rtentry, if necessary (ex. on p2p link). */
2028                    if (newhost) {
2029                            /* set the rtrequest function to create llinfo */
2030                            ia->ia_ifa.ifa_rtrequest = nd6_rtrequest;
2031                            in6_ifaddloop(&(ia->ia_ifa));
2032                    }
2033
2038
2039                    return (error);
2040            }
```
—— in6.c

2028–2032 The link-layer address resolution function, nd6_rtrequest(), is set for a newly installed address. Also, a routing entry for the address is installed via the in6_ifaddloop() function so that self-destined packets will be looped back through the loopback interface.

2.14.6 in6_ifaddloop() and in6_ifloop_request() Functions

The in6_ifaddloop() function, called from in6_ifinit(), is shown below.

Listing 2-103

—— in6.c
```
287    static void
288    in6_ifaddloop(struct ifaddr *ifa)
289    {
290            struct rtentry *rt;
291
292            /* If there is no loopback entry, allocate one. */
293            rt = rtalloc1(ifa->ifa_addr, 0

295                            , 0

297                            );
298            if (rt == NULL || (rt->rt_flags & RTF_HOST) == 0 ||
299                    (rt->rt_ifp->if_flags & IFF_LOOPBACK) == 0)
```

```
300                    in6_ifloop_request(RTM_ADD, ifa);
301            if (rt)
302                    rt->rt_refcnt--;
303    }
```
—— in6.c

287–303 The function argument points to an installed interface address. The `in6_ifloop_request()` function, described below, installs a routing entry into kernel's routing table with the loopback interface as the outgoing interface.

Listing 2-104
—— in6.c

```
215    static void
216    in6_ifloop_request(int cmd, struct ifaddr *ifa)
217    {
```
—— in6.c

216 The first argument to `in6_ifloop_request()` is a command which indicates route installation or deletion. `RTM_ADD` means route installation, and `RTM_DELETE` means route deletion. The second argument is the interface address to be handled in this function.

Listing 2-105
—— in6.c

```
218            struct sockaddr_in6 all1_sa;
219            struct rtentry *nrt = NULL;
220            int e;
221
222            bzero(&all1_sa, sizeof(all1_sa));
223            all1_sa.sin6_family = AF_INET6;
224            all1_sa.sin6_len = sizeof(struct sockaddr_in6);
225            all1_sa.sin6_addr = in6mask128;
226
227            /*
228             * We specify the address itself as the gateway, and set the
229             * RTF_LLINFO flag, so that the corresponding host route would have
230             * the flag, and thus applications that assume traditional behavior
231             * would be happy.  Note that we assume the caller of the function
232             * (probably implicitly) set nd6_rtrequest() to ifa->ifa_rtrequest,
233             * which changes the outgoing interface to the loopback interface.
234             */
235            e = rtrequest(cmd, ifa->ifa_addr, ifa->ifa_addr,
236                (struct sockaddr *)&all1_sa, RTF_UP|RTF_HOST|RTF_LLINFO, &nrt);
237            if (e != 0) {
238                    /* XXX need more descriptive message */
239                    log(LOG_ERR, "in6_ifloop_request: "
240                        "%s operation failed for %s (errno=%d)\n",
241                        cmd == RTM_ADD ? "ADD" : "DELETE",
242                        ip6_sprintf(&((struct in6_ifaddr *)ifa)->ia_addr.sin6_addr),
243                        e);
244            }
```
—— in6.c

235–244 The `rtrequest()` function is called with both the destination and the gateway having the same value. These values will propagate into the `nd6_rtrequest()` call where the loopback interface is set for the new routing entry. Function `nd6_rtrequest()` is discussed in detail in Section 5.15.1.

Listing 2-106

in6.c

```
246                 /*
247                  * Make sure rt_ifa be equal to IFA, the second argument of the
248                  * function.
249                  * We need this because when we refer to rt_ifa->ia6_flags in
250                  * ip6_input, we assume that the rt_ifa points to the address instead
251                  * of the loopback address.
252                  */
253                 if (cmd == RTM_ADD && nrt && ifa != nrt->rt_ifa) {
254                         IFAFREE(nrt->rt_ifa);
255                         IFAREF(ifa);
256                         nrt->rt_ifa = ifa;
257                 }
```

in6.c

252–257 KAME assumes that the routing entry to an interface's own address has that address as the associated address of the route, that is, the `rt_ifa` member, and that the loopback interface is the outgoing interface. These assumptions are used in the input processing of an IPv6 packet as we will see in Listing 3-25. If the destination address of the routing entry specified by `rt_ifa` is not equal to the interface address given as the second argument, it is reinitialized to that interface address.

Listing 2-107

in6.c

```
259                 /*
260                  * Report the addition/removal of the address to the routing socket.
261                  * XXX: since we called rtinit for a p2p interface with a destination,
262                  *      we end up reporting twice in such a case.  Should we rather
263                  *      omit the second report?
264                  */
265                 if (nrt) {
266                         rt_newaddrmsg(cmd, ifa, e, nrt);
267                         if (cmd == RTM_DELETE) {
268                                 if (nrt->rt_refcnt <= 0) {
269                                         /* XXX: we should free the entry ourselves. */
270                                         nrt->rt_refcnt++;
271                                         rtfree(nrt);
272                                 }
273                         } else {
274                                 /* the cmd must be RTM_ADD here */
275                                 nrt->rt_refcnt--;
276                         }
277                 }
278         }
```

in6.c

265–277 A routing table change notification message is sent upward over the routing socket to applications that monitor the routing table update.

2.15   Deleting an IPv6 Address

An IPv6 address can be removed from an interface either by the **ifconfig** command or by the KAME kernel automatically when the valid lifetime of address expires. In either case the actual work is done in the `in6_purgeaddr()` function as shown in Figure 2-16.

2.15.1 `in6_purgeaddr()` Function

The `in6_purgeaddr()` function is shown below.

Listing 2-108

in6.c

```
1477    void
1478    in6_purgeaddr(ifa)
1479            struct ifaddr *ifa;
1480    {
1481            struct ifnet *ifp = ifa->ifa_ifp;
1482            struct in6_ifaddr *ia = (struct in6_ifaddr *) ifa;
1483            struct in6_multi_mship *imm;
1484
1485            /* stop DAD processing */
1486            nd6_dad_stop(ifa);
1488            /*
1489             * delete route to the destination of the address being purged.
1490             * The interface must be p2p or loopback in this case.
1491             */
1492            if ((ia->ia_flags & IFA_ROUTE) != 0 && ia->ia_dstaddr.sin6_len != 0) {
1493                    int e;
1494
1495                    if ((e = rtinit(&(ia->ia_ifa), (int)RTM_DELETE, RTF_HOST))
1496                        != 0) {
1497                            log(LOG_ERR, "in6_purgeaddr: failed to remove "
1498                                "a route to the p2p destination: %s on %s, "
1499                                "errno=%d\n",
1500                                ip6_sprintf(&ia->ia_addr.sin6_addr), if_name(ifp),
1501                                e);
1502                            /* proceed anyway... */
1503                    } else
1504                            ia->ia_flags &= ~IFA_ROUTE;
1505            }
1507            /* Remove ownaddr's loopback rtentry, if it exists. */
1508            in6_ifremloop(&(ia->ia_ifa));
```

in6.c

1478–1486 Function `in6_purgeaddr()` has one function argument containing the address to be removed from the interface. DAD processing may still be in progress, in which case it is canceled.

1492–1505 If a host route was installed for the destination of a point-to-point link then that routing entry is removed here.

1508 Function `in6_ifremloop()` removes the loopback routing entry that was installed by `in6_ifaddloop()` for this address.

Listing 2-109

in6.c

```
1510            /*
1511             * leave from multicast groups we have joined for the interface
1512             */
1513            while ((imm = ia->ia6_memberships.lh_first) != NULL) {
1514                    LIST_REMOVE(imm, i6mm_chain);
1515                    in6_leavegroup(imm);
1516            }
1517
1518            in6_unlink_ifa(ia, ifp);
1519    }
```

in6.c

1513–1516 Recall that the interface joined the associated multicast groups during an address installation. Conversely, `in6_leavegroup()` (Section 2.14.3) forces the interface to leave those multicast groups before removing the address through its subroutine, `in6_delmulti()`. The membership structures are freed in `in6_leavegroup()`, and the associated `in6_multi{}` structures are also freed when the reference counter on a multicast membership goes down to 0.

1518 The `in6_unlink_ifa()` function removes the instance of the `in6_ifaddr{}` structure from the address lists.

2.15.2 `in6_ifremloop()` Function

The `in6_ifremloop()` function, called from `in6_purgeaddr()`, removes the loopback route for the address being removed from the kernel routing table. It works as a "destructor" function corresponding to the `in6_ifaddloop()` function we described above.

Listing 2-110

```
                                                                    ___in6.c
309    static void
310    in6_ifremloop(struct ifaddr *ifa)
311    {
312            struct in6_ifaddr *ia;
313            struct rtentry *rt;
314            int ia_count = 0;
315
316            /*
317             * Some of BSD variants do not remove cloned routes
318             * from an interface direct route, when removing the direct route
319             * (see comments in net/net_osdep.h).  Even for variants that do remove
320             * cloned routes, they could fail to remove the cloned routes when
321             * we handle multple addresses that share a common prefix.
322             * So, we should remove the route corresponding to the deleted address.
323             */
324
325            /*
326             * Delete the entry only if exact one ifa exists.  More than one ifa
327             * can exist if we assign a same single address to multiple
328             * (probably p2p) interfaces.
329             * XXX: we should avoid such a configuration in IPv6...
330             */
331            for (ia = in6_ifaddr; ia; ia = ia->ia_next) {
332                    if (IN6_ARE_ADDR_EQUAL(IFA_IN6(ifa), &ia->ia_addr.sin6_addr)) {
333                            ia_count++;
334                            if (ia_count > 1)
335                                    break;
336                    }
337            }
338
339            if (ia_count == 1) {
340                    /*
341                     * Before deleting, check if a corresponding loopbacked host
342                     * route surely exists.  With this check, we can avoid to
343                     * delete an interface direct route whose destination is same
344                     * as the address being removed.  This can happen when removing
345                     * a subnet-router anycast address on an interface attahced
346                     * to a shared medium.
347                     */
348                    rt = rtalloc1(ifa->ifa_addr, 0
350                                  , 0
352                                  );
```

```
353                         if (rt != NULL && (rt->rt_flags & RTF_HOST) != 0 &&
354                             (rt->rt_ifp->if_flags & IFF_LOOPBACK) != 0) {
355                                 rt->rt_refcnt--;
356                                 in6_ifloop_request(RTM_DELETE, ifa);
357                         }
358                 }
359         }
```
                                                                                            _____ in6.c

316–323 The comments at the beginning of this function are based on older versions of the implementation which do not apply to the code we are describing in this book. These can be ignored.

331–337 The `for` loop counts the number of instances of the `in6_ifaddr{}` structure containing the address being removed in the entire system. This is usually 1, but in the "unnumbered" link operation of IPv4 some point-to-point interfaces may borrow an IPv4 address from another interface, and the system may have multiple copies of the same address assigned to different interfaces. In such a case, removing the loopback route entry would cause trouble and should be avoided (this is actually a problem in the unnumbered operation in IPv4). As commented, however, this should not happen in IPv6 in the first place because there is no reason for borrowing an address from another interface thanks to the existence of the required link-local address.

339–357 If there is a host route that goes to a loopback interface for the address being removed, it is removed via the `in6_ifloop_request()` function (see Section 2.14.6). The code comment probably intends that we should avoid removing the interface direct route such as `2001:db8::/64` when we remove a subnet-router anycast address `2001:db8::`. However, checking the existence of the route beforehand is meaningless for that purpose, since `in6_ifloop_request()` specifies the netmask for a host route. Thus, we could actually call `in6_ifloop_request()` without any prior tests.

2.15.3 `in6_unlink_ifa()` Function

The `in6_unlink_ifa()` function frees various structures related to an address being removed.

Listing 2-111
                                                                                            _____ in6.c

```
1521    static void
1522    in6_unlink_ifa(ia, ifp)
1523            struct in6_ifaddr *ia;
1524            struct ifnet *ifp;
1525    {
1526            struct in6_ifaddr *oia;

1530            int     s = splnet();
    ...
1551            TAILQ_REMOVE(&ifp->if_addrlist, &ia->ia_ifa, ifa_list);
    ...
1558            oia = ia;
1559            if (oia == (ia = in6_ifaddr))
1560                    in6_ifaddr = ia->ia_next;
1561            else {
1562                    while (ia->ia_next && (ia->ia_next != oia))
1563                            ia = ia->ia_next;
```

```
1564                     if (ia->ia_next)
1565                             ia->ia_next = oia->ia_next;
1566                     else {
1567                             /* search failed */
1568                             printf("Couldn't unlink in6_ifaddr from in6_ifaddr\n");
1569                     }
1570             }
```
─── in6.c

1521–1570 The first argument to in6_unlink_ifa() points to an in6_ifaddr{} structure
that holds the address to be removed. The second argument points to the interface. This
address will be removed from the per interface if_addrlist address list and the global
in6_ifaddr list, containing IPv6 addresses. The address lists are updated appropriately.

Listing 2-112
─── in6.c

```
1599             /*
1600              * Release the reference to the base prefix.  There should be a
1601              * positive reference.
1602              */
1603             if (oia->ia6_ndpr == NULL) {
1604                     nd6log((LOG_NOTICE,
1605                         "in6_unlink_ifa: autoconf'ed address "
1606                         "%p has no prefix\n", oia));
1607             } else {
1608                     oia->ia6_ndpr->ndpr_refcnt--;
1609                     oia->ia6_ndpr = NULL;
1610             }
1612             /*
1613              * Also, if the address being removed is autoconf'ed, call
1614              * pfxlist_onlink_check() since the release might affect the status of
1615              * other (detached) addresses.
1616              */
1617             if ((oia->ia6_flags & IN6_IFF_AUTOCONF))
1618                     pfxlist_onlink_check();
      ...
1620             /*
1621              * release another refcnt for the link from in6_ifaddr.
1622              * Note that we should decrement the refcnt at least once for all *BSD.
1623              */
1624             IFAFREE(&oia->ia_ifa);
1625
1626             splx(s);
1627     }
```
─── in6.c

1603–1610 Each IPv6 address stored in the in6_ifaddr{} structure has the corresponding
prefix information structure referenced by the ia6_ndpr member variable. When an
address is removed, the reference counter on the prefix information is decremented
to reflect one less dependency. As we saw in Section 2.14.1, if this address is being
deleted by the SIOCDIFADDR_IN6 ioctl command and the reference decrements to
0 as a result, the in6_control() function will then remove this prefix by calling the
prelist_remove() function.

1617–1618 If the address being removed is marked as an autoconfigured address, the
pfxlist_onlink_check() function is called to check the effect of the deletion. Details
of the pfxlist_onlink_check() function are discussed in Section 5.19.6.

1624 At last we decrement the reference counter on the `in6_ifaddr{}` structure itself by the `IFAFREE()` macro, which then frees the structure if the reference counter goes down to 0.

2.16 Operation with Address Configuration Utility

We conclude this chapter by illustrating how the kernel implementation described so far works through operational examples. The main tool is the **ifconfig** command, which is a utility for both configuring and displaying network interface parameters including addresses. We do not provide comprehensive usage of the utility commands used in this section. Consult the corresponding manual pages for details.

For example, the following command displays the current interface information.

```
# ifconfig -a
```

A sample output is shown below:

```
lnc0: flags=8843<UP,BROADCAST,RUNNING,SIMPLEX,MULTICAST> mtu 1500
      inet 192.0.2.127 netmask 0xffffff00 broadcast 192.0.2.255 inet6
      fe80::20c:29ff:fef1:1a8b%lnc0 prefixlen 64 scopeid 0x1
      ether 00:0c:29:f1:1a:8b
```

Note that the interface identifier of the link-local address is in the modified EUI-64 format based on the 48-bit Ethernet address as described in Section 2.5.1. It should also be noted that the link-local address is represented in the extended format for IPv6 scoped addresses explained in Section 2.4.3 using the interface name as the link zone ID. This output also shows that the decimal zone ID of this link is 1.

We can manually delete this link-local address by the **ifconfig** command:

```
# ifconfig lnc0 inet6 fe80::20c:29ff:fef1:1a8b%lnc0 -alias
```

As we saw in Section 2.14.1, the same effect can be achieved by:

```
# ifconfig lnc0 inet6 fe80::20c:29ff:fef1:1a8b -alias
```

That is, the link zone ID can be omitted in the address field. The kernel automatically identifies the link zone by the interface (Listing 2-64). Furthermore, even the following causes the same result:

```
# ifconfig lnc0 inet6 fe80:1::20c:29ff:fef1:1a8b -alias
```

Since the embedded link zone ID (1) is the correct one, the kernel regards it as a valid address. As emphasized in Section 2.9.3, however, the operator should never use this form in the application.

The recommended usage is the first one. It is generally advisable to disambiguate a possibly ambiguous address whenever possible, rather than relying on some automatic mechanism of zone identification, so that misconfiguration or an operation error can easily be found.

Now consider reassigning the same address by hand. We show the procedure as well as illustrating how DAD takes place for the newly assigned address:

```
# ifconfig lnc0 inet6 fe80::20c:29ff:fef1:1a8b%lnc0;\
  ifconfig lnc0 inet6;\
  sleep 1;\
  ifconfig lnc0 inet6;
```

Then the output will be as follows:

```
lnc0: flags=8843<UP,BROADCAST,RUNNING,SIMPLEX,MULTICAST> mtu 1500
      inet6 fe80::20c:29ff:fef1:1a8b%lnc0 prefixlen 64 tentative scopeid 0x1
lnc0: flags=8843<UP,BROADCAST,RUNNING,SIMPLEX,MULTICAST> mtu 1500
      inet6 fe80::20c:29ff:fef1:1a8b%lnc0 prefixlen 64 scopeid 0x1
```

That is, the output from the second execution of the **ifconfig** command indicates that the address has the `IN6_IFF_TENTATIVE` flag, which is set in Listing 2-81. While we slept for 1 second, DAD has been completed, and the last line of the output shows the `IN6_IFF_TENTATIVE` flag is cleared. This process will be described in Section 5.21.6.

It should also be noted in the above output that the prefix length of the address is assumed to be 64 bits by default as we explained in Listing 2-73.

If, while atypical, there is another node on the same link already using the same link-local address, DAD will detect it and the last output of the previous example will be as follows:

```
inet6 fe80::20c:29ff:fef1:1a8b%lnc0 prefixlen 64 duplicated scopeid 0x1
```

And the kernel should have dumped the following log message:

```
lnc0: DAD complete for fe80:1::20c:29ff:fef1:1a8b - duplicate found
```

(It is a bad practice that the kernel log message does not convert the internal embedded form of the zone ID.) This case will be described in Section 5.21.7.

Note that the data structure for the duplicate address still exists in the kernel even though it will not be used for any communication. The operator is expected to delete this address by hand.

A global address can be assigned in a similar operation:

```
# ifconfig lnc0 inet6 2001:db8:1:2::1
```

Assuming this node is acting as a router, we can also assign the subnet-router anycast address corresponding to this address:

```
# ifconfig lnc0 inet6 2001:db8:1:2:: anycast
```

Then we have three IPv6 addresses on interface `lnc0`:

```
# ifconfig lnc0 inet6
lnc0: flags=8843<UP,BROADCAST,RUNNING,SIMPLEX,MULTICAST> mtu 1500
      inet6 fe80::20c:29ff:fef1:1a8b%lnc0 prefixlen 64 scopeid 0x1
      inet6 2001:db8:1:2::1 prefixlen 64
      inet6 2001:db8:1:2:: prefixlen 64 anycast
```

At this point, the kernel maintains the addresses and the corresponding prefixes as shown in Figure 2-15. It can be checked by the **ndp** command:

```
# ndp -p 2001:db8:1:2::/64 if=lnc0
flags=LO vltime=infinity, pltime=infinity, expire=Never, ref=2
No advertising router
(...)
```

The notable point in this chapter is that the reference counter is 2, which means this prefix is referenced by the two addresses.

Configuring an address involves automatic installation of some route entries. This can be confirmed by the **netstat** command:

```
# netstat -rn -f inet6
Routing tables

Internet6:
Destination              Gateway                    Flags      Netif
(...)
2001:db8:1:2::           00:0c:29:f1:1a:8b          UHL        lo0 =>
2001:db8:1:2::/64        link#1                     UC         lnc0
2001:db8:1:2::1          00:0c:29:f1:1a:8b          UHL        lo0
```

The first and third lines of the shown entries are the loopback route entries for the anycast and unicast addresses created in the `in6_ifaddloop()` function (Section 2.14.6).

The second entry, which has the same destination key as the loopback entry for the anycast address with a different prefix, is the direct route to the interface. This is associated with the prefix structure and created via the `nd6_prelist_add()` function (Section 5.19.1).

Recall that configuring an address also involves joining multicast groups. The **ifmcstat** command can be used to list the multicast group addresses configured on an interface:

```
# ifmcstat -f inet6 -i lnc0
lnc0:
        inet6 fe80::20c:29ff:fef1:1a8b%lnc0
        inet6 2001:db8:1:2::1
        inet6 2001:db8:1:2::
        group ff02::1:ff00:0%lnc0 refcnt 1
            mcast-macaddr 33:33:ff:00:00:00 multicnt 1
        group ff02::1:ff00:1%lnc0 refcnt 1
            mcast-macaddr 33:33:ff:00:00:01 multicnt 1
        group ff01::1%lnc0 refcnt 1
            mcast-macaddr 33:33:00:00:00:01 multicnt 3
        group ff02::2:d7f6:91a7%lnc0 refcnt 0
            mcast-macaddr 33:33:d7:f6:91:a7 multicnt 3
        group ff02::1%lnc0 refcnt 1
            mcast-macaddr 33:33:00:00:00:01 multicnt 3
        group ff02::1:fff1:1a8b%lnc0 refcnt 1
            mcast-macaddr 33:33:ff:f1:1a:8b multicnt 1
```

The "group" rows show the multicast addresses, which are (from top to bottom):

- The solicited-node multicast address for the anycast address.

- The solicited-node multicast address for the global unicast address.

- The interface-local all-nodes multicast address.

- The node information group address for the hostname (in this example, the hostname is "orange.kame.net").

- The link-local all-nodes multicast address.

- The solicited-node multicast address for the link-local unicast address.

The **ifmcstat** command uses the `kvm` interface and directly gets access to the kernel memory image for the list of `in6_multi{}` structures as shown in Figure 2-14. Note that the shown multicast addresses do not embed link or interface zone IDs in the address field while the IDs are in fact embedded in the kernel. This is because the **ifmcstat** command internally converts the embedded form before printing the addresses as we saw in Figure 2-12. We should emphasize that this only applies to a very special type of application such as **ifmcstat**, and normal applications do not have to, and should actually never, deal with the embedded form directly.

Finally, assume we want to delete the anycast address. It can be done as follows:

```
# ifconfig lnc0 inet6 2001:db8:1:2:: -alias
```

This removes the loopback route entry for the anycast address via the `in6_ifremloop()` function (Section 2.15.2), but the direct route to the interface still remains because the unicast address has a reference to the prefix. It can be checked by the **ndp** and **netstat** commands:

```
# ndp -p
2001:db8:1:2::/64 if=lnc0
flags=LO vltime=infinity, pltime=infinity, expire=Never, ref=1
No advertising router
(...)

# netstat -rn -f inet6
Routing tables

Internet6:
Destination              Gateway                         Flags    Netif
(...)
2001:db8:1:2::/64        link#1                          UC       lnc0
2001:db8:1:2::1          00:0c:29:f1:1a:8b               UHL      lo0
```

Note that this time the reference counter to the prefix is decremented to 1.

Internet Protocol version 6

3.1 Introduction

The basic operational principles are not different between IPv4 and IPv6. From operational experiences of IPv4, however, IPv6 introduces some remarkable changes. One major revision is the introduction of extension headers. Unlike the IPv4 options, each extension header is realized as if it were a separate upper layer protocol, thereby enlarging the possible number and size of options.

Other types of optional information are also implemented using the framework of extension headers. For example, packet fragmentation and source routing are implemented with dedicated extension headers. As a result of the introduction of extension headers, the base IPv6 header has been simplified and only contains essential information for common operation.

Another important change with IPv6 is the source address selection of outgoing IPv6 packets. As explained in Chapter 2, IPv6 provides various types of addresses with different properties: addresses of different scopes or different lifetimes. Selecting a reasonable source address for a given destination is not a matter of preference or optimization; it sometimes affects interoperability.

In this chapter, we discuss such IPv6 specific issues regarding the network layer operations in detail. We first provide an overview of IPv6 extension headers based on [RFC2460]. We then discuss the default address selection algorithm defined in [RFC3484]. While main interest of this chapter is source address selection, we also describe the destination address selection algorithm, since these algorithms share the same basic principle.

A detailed description of KAME's IPv6 implementation of these specifications follow. This part is roughly separated into two sets of sections: input processing (Sections 3.7–3.12) and output processing (Section 3.13). In the former, we describe how the KAME implementation handles the IPv6 header and extension headers and how to deal with scoped addresses stored in an incoming IPv6 packet. The latter part discusses the details of source address selection implementation followed by discussions about general output issues including insertion of extension headers or packet fragmentation.

3.2   IPv6 Header Format

Any IPv6 packet contains a fixed-size header, called the *IPv6 header*. The IPv6 header is 40 bytes in size and consists of a minimum number of fields that are necessary for delivering the packet.
    Figure 3-1 shows the structure of the IPv6 header.

Version The 4-bit version field contains the value 6 for Internet Protocol version 6.

Traffic Class The 8-bit traffic class is meant for end nodes to generate traffic of varying classes and priorities and for intermediate nodes to forward the packets according to the traffic class of each packet. By default the traffic class field is set to zero by the originating node; this field may be changed en route to the destination, whether or not it is originally set to zero. [RFC2474] and [RFC3168] define detailed usage of this field, which is beyond the scope of this book.

Flow Label The 20-bit flow label provides a means to differentiate different traffic flows. [RFC3697] sets some guidelines for nodes that handle this field: the packet's source node identifies a separate "flow," for example, a specific application data stream, as a non-0

FIGURE 3-1

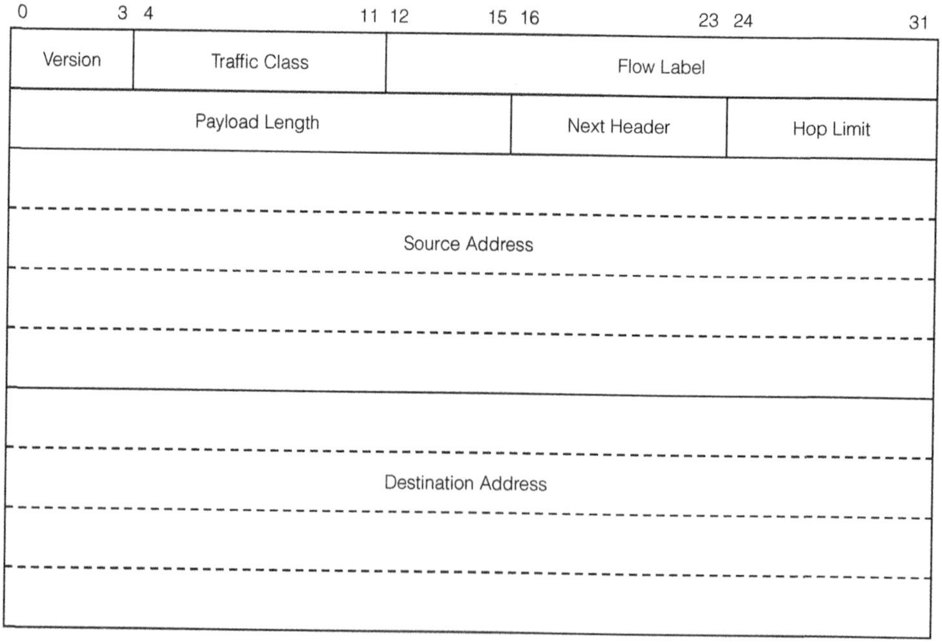

IPv6 header.

flow label; the source node must set this field to zero if it does not associate originating traffic with flows; the flow label field must not be changed en route to the destination. The RFC does not define detailed use of this field, though. In particular, an open issue is how to establish a flow state from the source node to the destination, including routers on the path.

Payload Length The payload length is a 16-bit unsigned integer specifying the size of the IPv6 packet following the IPv6 header, that is, the length includes the size of the extension headers, if any, and the size of the upper layer protocol payload.

Next Header This 8-bit field contains the number that identifies the protocol or extension header that immediately follows the IPv6 header.

Hop Limit This 8-bit field specifies the number of times a given packet can be forwarded by a router toward the destination. Each router that forwards the packet decrements this value by one. Discard the packet if it reaches 0.

Source Address This 128-bit field holds the IPv6 address of the packet originator.

Destination Address This 128-bit field holds the IPv6 address of the packet destination. The destination can be an intermediate node if a Routing header is present (Section 3.3.4). Otherwise the destination is the ultimate packet destination.

3.2.1   Comparison to the IPv4 Header

The differences between the IPv6 and the IPv4 headers can be observed in Figure 3-2 in which the highlighted fields represent those IPv4 header fields that are missing in the IPv6 header.

The *Header Length* (IHL) field is missing in IPv6 because the IPv6 header is a 40-byte fixed size header. Unlike IPv4, IPv6 does not have IP header options; instead, the Internet layer options can be constructed using the IPv6 extension headers. For example, the IPv4 Loose

FIGURE 3-2

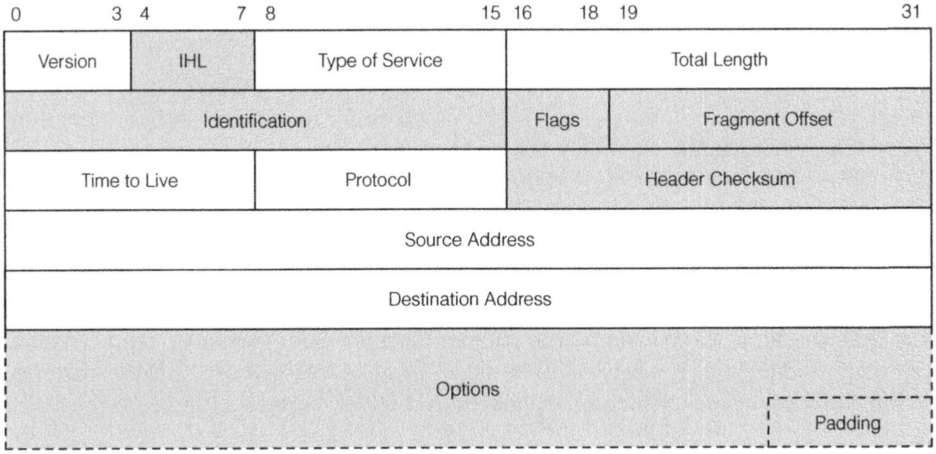

0	3	4	7	8	15	16	18	19	31
Version		IHL		Type of Service		Total Length			
Identification						Flags		Fragment Offset	
Time to Live			Protocol			Header Checksum			
Source Address									
Destination Address									
Options								Padding	

IPv4 header.

Source and Record Route option is covered by the IPv6 Routing header. Therefore, the variable length Options field is no longer necessary in IPv6. IPv6 extension headers are discussed in Section 3.3.

Fields related to fragmentation and reassembly are the *Identification* field, the *Flags* field and the *Fragment Offset* field. The Identification field is set by the sender, which allows the receiver to identify fragments that belong to the same original packet. The Fragment offset field specifies the relative location of the current fragment with respect to the original packet. The Flags field indicates whether a packet is allowed to be fragmented en route to the destination, and whether a fragment is the last fragment. In IPv6, a dedicated extension header is provided for fragmentation and reassembly (see Section 3.3.5), thereby eliminating the associated fields from the IPv6 header.

The *Header Checksum* field is eliminated from the IPv6 header. The design assumptions are that the network layer technology is increasing in reliability, which reduces the error rates. The original IPv4 header checksum covers only the IPv4 header. The upper layer protocols such as TCP and UDP also perform checksum computation that provides protection for both the header and the payload, thus diminishing the benefit of IP layer checksum. The elimination of IP layer checksum combined with the addition of extension headers can increase the router efficiency when forwarding IPv6 packets.

The *Type of Service* field has been replaced by the Traffic Class field. The Protocol field has been replaced by the Next Header field. The Time to Live field has been replaced by the Hop Limit field. Unlike IPv4, the Payload Length in the IPv6 header does not include the size of the IPv6 header.

As can be seen, the IPv6 header has a more efficient design than the IPv4 header. To summarize the points: the 4-byte fields dedicated to fragmentation was removed, which carry no useful information in a packet that does not require fragmentation; the 2-byte header checksum field has become less important and is eliminated from the IPv6 header.

3.3   IPv6 Extension Headers

As explained in Section 3.2.1, the notion of IPv4 options are expanded to the idea of extension headers in IPv6. Each extension header implements some optional feature and partially works like an upper layer protocol. Since routers do not have to process extension headers unless it is explicitly required to do so, IPv6 forwarding with end-to-end optional features can be more lightweight. Also, the extension headers can be much larger than the maximum length of IPv4 options, which provide better flexibility for future new options.

[RFC2460] defines the following extension headers: the Hop-by-Hop options header, the Routing header, the Fragment header, and the Destination options header. In addition, the IP security (IPsec) protocol defines two additional extension headers: the Authentication header and the Encapsulating Security Payload header [RFC4302] [RFC4303]. The extension headers exist between the IPv6 header and upper layer protocol headers. Extension headers are processed in the order that was set in the packet by the source. Usually one upper layer protocol terminates the chain of the extension headers. If there is no upper layer protocol header included in a packet, the No Next header, which is an imaginary header, is used to indicate the end of the header chain.

Each extension header's size is a multiple of 8 bytes (except the Authentication header, which is a multiple of 4 bytes). The size does not include the first 8 bytes since no extension

TABLE 3-1

Name	Next header value in preceding header
Hop-by-Hop options header	0
Destination options header	60
Routing header	43
Fragment header	44
Authentication header (discussed in Chapter 6 of *IPv6 Advanced Protocols Implementation*)	51
Encapsulating Security Payload (discussed in Chapter 6 of *IPv6 Advanced Protocols Implementation*)	50
No Next header	59

TABLE 3-2

Order	Extension header
1	IPv6 header
2	Hop-by-Hop options header
3	Destination options header
4	Routing header
5	Fragment header
6	IPsec headers (AH, ESP)
7	Destination options header
8	Upper-layer header

header's size is less than 8 bytes. Each field within the extension header is aligned on the natural boundary of its data width. Padding is inserted where necessary.

Table 3-1 lists all extension headers defined in the basic specification. Each header will be discussed in the following sections.

Other specifications which extend IPv6 functions may define other extension headers. For example, Mobile IPv6 has its own extension header, which will be discussed in *IPv6 Advanced Protocols Implementation*.

3.3.1 Order of Extension Headers

There is a recommended ordering and number of occurrences of extension headers in one packet. Table 3-2 shows the recommended ordering. Note that this is not a mandatory requirement; the sender node should follow the recommendation, but the receiver node should not assume that the extension headers of the incoming packets are ordered by the recommended ordering. The only exception is the Hop-by-Hop options header. It must be placed just after the IPv6 header and must be present no more than once.

The recommendation states that there should exist no more than one occurrence of each extension header type except for the Destination options header. The Destination options header can appear twice—once before the Routing header and once following the Routing header. The Destination options header that appears before the Routing header is processed by all of the intermediate nodes that are listed in the Routing header. The Destination options header that appears after the Routing header is processed only by the final packet destination. Also, Mobile IPv6 specifies another location of the Destination options header. The option used by Mobile IPv6 will be placed between the Routing header and the Fragment header. Mobile IPv6 will be discussed in Chapter 5 of *IPv6 Advanced Protocols Implementation*.

The ordering of extension headers is a recommendation, which implies that any IPv6 implementation should attempt to process as many of the extension headers as possible that are arranged in any order (possibly with multiple occurrences for each extension header type).

3.3.2 Hop-by-Hop Options Header

The Hop-by-Hop options header is examined and is processed by every intermediate node, for example, the intermediate routers, along the packet delivery path toward the destination. Both the source node and the destination node also process the Hop-by-Hop options header. The value of the Next Header field in the preceding header is 0 for the Hop-by-Hop options header. The Hop-by-Hop options header is required to appear immediately following the IPv6 header. Figure 3-3 shows the format of the Hop-by-Hop options header.

Next Header This 8-bit field contains the protocol number that identifies the protocol header that immediately follows the Hop-by-Hop options header.

Hdr Ext Len This 8-bit field specifies the length of the header in 8-byte units (not including the first 8 bytes).

Options The Options field is variable in length but must have a length such that the overall Hop-by-Hop options header is a multiple of 8 bytes. The format of options will be discussed in Section 3.3.6.

FIGURE 3-3

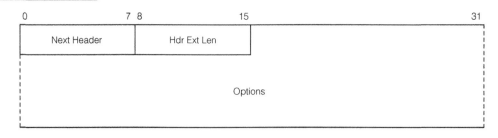

Hop-by-Hop options header.

3.3.3 Destination Options Header

The Destination options header is processed by the final packet destination. However, if the Destination options header appears before the Routing header, that Destination options header is processed by all of the nodes that are listed in the Routing header that follows the Destination options header. The value of the Next Header field in the preceding header is 60 for the Destination options header. Figure 3-4 shows the format of the Destination options header.

Next Header This 8-bit field contains the protocol number that identifies the protocol header that immediately follows the Destination options header.

Hdr Ext Len This 8-bit field specifies the length of the header in 8-byte units (not including the first 8 bytes).

Options The Options field is variable in length but must have a length such that the overall Destination options header is a multiple of 8 bytes. The format of options will be discussed in Section 3.3.6.

3.3.4 Routing Header

A source node performing source routing uses the Routing header to list intermediate nodes (called *route segments*) to be traversed on a packet delivery path. The value of the Next Header field in the preceding header is 43 for the Routing header. Figure 3-5 illustrates the general format of the Routing header.

FIGURE 3-4

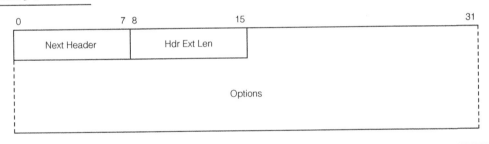

Destination options header.

FIGURE 3-5

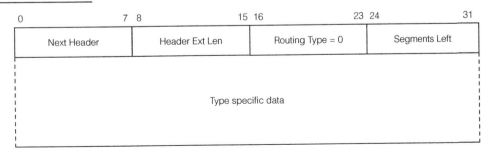

Routing header.

Next Header This 8-bit field contains the protocol number that identifies the protocol header that immediately follows the Routing header.

Header Ext Len This 8-bit field specifies the length of the Routing header in 8-byte units (but not including the first 8 bytes).

Routing Type This 8-bit field has the type number of the Routing header. IPv6 can have several types of Routing header. [RFC2460] defines the type 0 Routing header, which is discussed below.

Segments Left This 8-bit field specifies the number of route segments, that is, the number of intermediate nodes that still need to be visited en route to the ultimate destination.

Type specific data This field contains the data specific to the type value specified in the Routing Type field.

A receiving node will ignore an unrecognized Routing header (that is, an unknown Routing header type) if the Segment Left field is zero. In this case the node will continue to process the packet starting with the header that immediately follows the unrecognized Routing header. On the other hand, if the Segment Left field has a non-0 value, the node will discard the packet and then generate an ICMPv6 error message to the packet source indicating the "parameter problem" condition. This error message will be discussed in Section 4.2.4.

[RFC2460] defines the Type 0 Routing header, shown in Figure 3-6.

Routing Type This 8-bit field has the fixed value 0 that indicates the Routing header is a Type 0 Routing header.

Reserved This 32-bit field is reserved. This field is set to 0 by the packet originator and is ignored by the receivers.

Address 1...N These 128-bit fields hold the addresses of the intermediate nodes to be traversed en route to the destination.

A packet carrying a type 0 Routing header must not have a multicast destination address or a multicast address in the address fields.

Figure 3-7 illustrates the processing at nodes involved in source routing using a Type 0 Routing header. The source node S specifies three intermediate nodes, R1, R2, and R3 in this order. The destination address field of the IPv6 header is set to the address of the first intermediate node, R1, and the Segment Left field of the Routing header is set to 3, the number of intermediate nodes.

R1 decrements the value of the Segment Left field by one, and swaps the destination address with the address in the Routing header whose index is given by subtracting the new Segment Left value from the total number of addresses, which is 1. R1 then forwards the packet toward the next intermediate node, R2.

R2 and R3 repeat the same procedure, and then the packet arrives at the final destination, D, with the Segment Left field being 0. Since the Segment Left value indicates D is the final recipient, it accepts the packet.

Note that an intermediate node that processes a Routing header and forwards the packet to the next route segment does not have to be a router. A host that otherwise does not forward

FIGURE 3-6

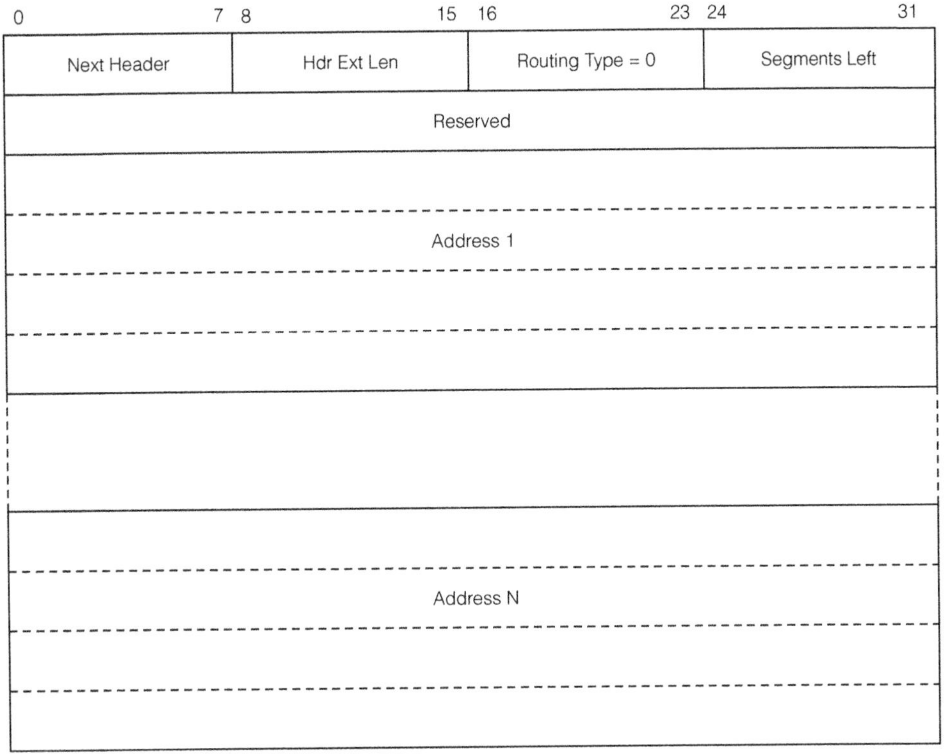

0
7
8
15
16
23
24
31
Next Header
Hdr Ext Len
Routing Type = 0
Segments Left
Reserved
Address 1
Address N

Routing header—Type 0.

FIGURE 3-7

S
R1
R2
R3
D
IPv6 header
Routing header
Source = S
Destination = R1
Segment Left = 3
Address1 = R2
Address2 = R3
Address3 = D
Source = S
Destination = R2
Segment Left = 2
Address1 = R1
Address2 = R3
Address3 = D
Source = S
Destination = R3
Segment Left = 1
Address1 = R1
Address2 = R2
Address3 = D
Source = S
Destination = D
Segment Left = 0
Address1 = R1
Address2 = R2
Address3 = R3

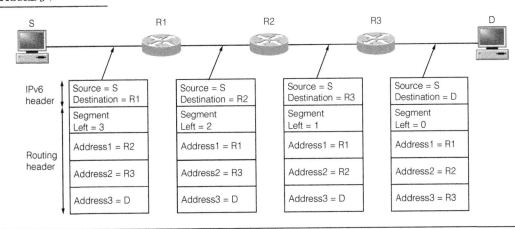

Processing routing header.

packets not destined to it can also be specified as an intermediate route segment, and the host should be able to perform the processing as described above. We intentionally use the term of an "intermediate node" hereafter instead of a "router" when the node can be a host that handles a Routing header as an intermediate route segment.

3.3.5 Fragment Header

Experiments with IPv4 fragmentation have proved that packet fragmentation at the network layer is rather harmful [Ken87]. Fragmentation increases network bandwidth and processing overhead at routers that perform fragmentation and the destination node that performs reassembly. Also, loss of some fragments for a single original packet can greatly reduce the total performance.

The design of IPv6 has incorporated this lesson, and packet fragmentation in IPv6 is discouraged. Instead, IPv6 provides and recommends a mechanism to discover the smallest link MTU between two nodes communicating with each other, in order to determine the correct packet size on the source node. The mechanism is called *Path MTU discovery* and is discussed in Section 4.3.

Yet fragmentation may still be necessary in some cases (e.g., when sending a large UDP or ICMPv6 packet), in which case the Fragment header is used for packet fragmentation and reassembly. In IPv6 only the packet source performs fragmentation; unlike IPv4, IPv6 routers do not fragment packets, thereby reducing work required for routers. Instead, the router will generate an ICMPv6 error message back to the packet source indicating the "packet too big" condition (see Section 4.2.2).

The value of the Next Header field in the preceding header is 44 for the Fragment header. Figure 3-8 shows the format of the Fragment header.

Next Header This 8-bit field contains the protocol number that identifies the protocol of the first header of the fragmentable part (see below) of the original packet.

Reserved This 8-bit reserved field is set to 0 by the sender and is ignored by the receiver.

Fragment Offset The 13-bit offset field specifies the offset of the data that immediately follows the Fragment header relative to the start of the fragmentable part of the original packet (see below) in 8-byte units.

Res This 2-bit reserved field is set to 0 by the sender and is ignored by the receiver.

M This 1-bit Boolean value field specifies whether there are more fragments to follow. There are more fragments to follow if the M bit is set to 1; otherwise the current fragment is the last of the fragments.

FIGURE 3-8

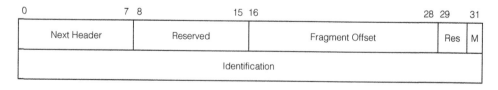

Fragment header.

Identification This 32-bit field holds a value that allows the receiver to identify fragments that belong to the same packet. The packet source generates a different identification value for each packet that requires fragmentation. Note that this field is enlarged compared to the Identification field of the IPv4 header (Figure 3-2). The larger ID space reduces the possibility of Identification collisions [FRAG-HARMFUL].

Each packet that requires fragmentation consists of two parts: the *unfragmentable part* and the *fragmentable part*. Referring to Table 3-2, the unfragmentable part of the original packet is comprised of the IPv6 header and the extension headers up to and including the Routing header. These extension headers can be processed by intermediate nodes along the packet delivery path: the Hop-by-Hop options header is processed by every intermediate node; others are processed by each intermediate destination specified in the Routing header. Thus, this part must not be fragmented during transmission. The unfragmentable part consists only of the Hop-by-Hop options header, if any, if the Routing header is not present. If neither the Hop-by-Hop options header nor the Routing header is present, the unfragmentable part is the IPv6 header. The fragmentable part of the original packet refers to the rest of the extensions headers, the upper layer protocol header and the upper layer data.

Figure 3-9 shows an example of packet fragmentation with the Fragment header. The unfragmentable part is copied to each fragment packet, and the fragmentable part is divided into multiple fragments. Each fragment is a multiple of 8 bytes in size except for the last fragment, whose size may or may not be a multiple of 8 bytes. A Fragment header is inserted between the unfragmentable and fragmentable parts of each fragment packet. The Payload Length field of each fragment packet is adjusted accordingly. The Next Header field of the last header of the unfragmentable part of each fragment packet is set to 44. The Next Header field of the Fragment header of the first fragment packet is set to the Next Header field value of the last header of the unfragmentable part of the original packet.

FIGURE 3-9

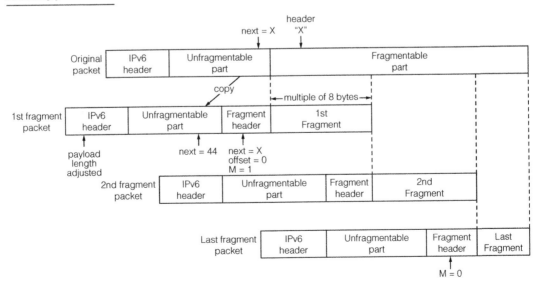

IPv6 fragmentation procedure.

FIGURE 3-10

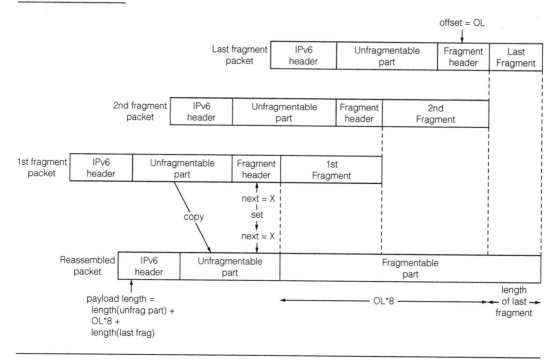

IPv6 reassembly procedure.

The destination node of the fragment packets reassembles the fragments as follows (Figure 3-10). The fragments are concatenated into a single fragmentable part. The unfragmentable part is copied from the first fragment (that is, the fragment packet whose offset is 0). The Next Header field of the last header of the unfragmentable part is set to the Next Header value of the Fragment header contained in the first fragment packet. The payload length field of the IPv6 header is calculated based on the length of the unfragmentable part, the offset and the length of the last fragment. Note that the reassembly procedure does not refer to the unfragmentable part and the Next Header field of the Fragment header for the fragment packets other than the first fragment packet. It is assumed these are the same in all the packets, but the protocol specification does not mandate it and the receiving node does not have to check the consistency.

3.3.6　IPv6 Options

The Hop-by-Hop options header and the Destination options header carry a variable number of option values that are encoded in the type-length-value format, shown in Figure 3-11.

Option Type　The option type field is an 8-bit field that identifies the type of option. [RFC2460] only defines padding options: the Pad1 and PadN options. [RFC2675] defines the Jumbo Payload option, and [RFC2711] defines the Router Alert option, which will be described in Section 3.5.2. There are other options defined, but we will not discuss those in this chapter.

FIGURE 3-11

Option data.

TABLE 3-3

Value	Action
00	Skip the unrecognized option and continue packet processing.
01	Discard the packet.
10	Discard the packet and send an ICMPv6 error message to the packet source indicating the unrecognized option.
11	Discard the packet. Send an ICMPv6 error message to the packet source only if the packet destination is a unicast destination.

FIGURE 3-12

Pad1 option.

Option Data Length This 8-bit field specifies the size of the option data in bytes.

Option Data This is a variable length field that carries the option-specific data.

The upper two bits (bit 0 and bit 1) of the Option Type field specify the action to be taken by a node that is processing the option but does not recognize that option type. Table 3-3 lists the bit values and the associated actions taken by the processing node.

Bit position 2 of the Option Type field specifies whether the option data may be modified by intermediate nodes en route to the final destination of the packet. The option data may change en route if bit 2 is 1. Otherwise, the option data is static. This bit is used when the packet is protected by the Authentication header: when a node is verifying the validity of the packet, it can ignore the IPv6 options which are marked as *modifiable* by overriding the data field with zeros, even if the receiving node does not have any knowledge of the options.

The Pad1 option is used to insert one byte of padding into the options of a particular header. The Pad1 option is a special option. It is a single byte in size and does not have the option length and option value fields. Figure 3-12 shows the format of the Pad1 option.

The PadN option is used to insert two or more bytes of padding into the options of a particular header. The PadN option is encoded in the type-length-value format, impling that the value of the option data length can be 0. Figure 3-13 shows the format of the PadN option.

FIGURE 3-13

PadN option.

The need for option padding implies that a header option has an alignment requirement. The alignment requirement is necessary to ensure each field within the option data area is aligned on its natural boundary (e.g., a 4-byte field is aligned on a 4-byte boundary). The option alignment specification is given in the $x * n + y$ format. The interpretation is that the Option Type field is integer n multiples of x bytes plus y bytes from the start of the options header.

3.4 Source Address Selection

A variety of address types that IPv6 offers cause a new challenge of choosing a reasonable pair of source and destination addresses among multiple candidates for successful communication. This section discusses the standard default algorithm to select such a pair in a deterministic way.

3.4.1 Default Address Selection

The transport or network layer may sometimes need to find an appropriate source address for an outgoing packet. For example, when an application operating over a socket does not explicitly bind an address to that socket, the system must select an appropriate one from addresses available within the node. Since an IPv6 node may have multiple IPv6 addresses on varying address scopes even on a single interface, the selection is not always trivial.

The default source address selection algorithm, as defined in [RFC3484], applies a set of selection rules to a list of node addresses that may potentially serve as the source address to determine an address to be used as the source address. The selection algorithm sorts the potential source addresses by applying the matching rules in a pair-wise fashion, that is, the rules are applied to two potential addresses at a time until the most preferable one is determined. The selection algorithm applies a succeeding rule if the current rule cannot decide which of the two addresses is more preferable. The most preferable address chosen will be used as the source address.

Meanwhile, an application often needs to resolve the destination addresses for a hostname before initiating communication. Assuming the Domain Name System (DNS) is used for this purpose, which is today's most typical case, multiple addresses for a given destination name may be returned by the DNS resolver. The application typically tries each address in turn until either successfully establishing the communication with that peer, or all of the addresses have been attempted (see Section 7.2.4 for an example).

The default destination address selection algorithm, also defined in [RFC3484], applies a set of selection rules to the list of addresses returned from the DNS resolver in a pair-wise fashion similar to the source address selection algorithm. Unlike the source address selection, the algorithm fully sorts these potential destination addresses in decreasing magnitude of preference level, since all of them may need to be tried for establishing communication with a remote host.

The selection algorithms must consider nodes with dual stack deployment where a node may have both IPv4 and IPv6 addresses. The selection algorithms prefer the pair of addresses as the source and the destination addresses, which have matching type and scope; prefer native addresses over transitional addresses; prefer non-deprecated (preferred) addresses over deprecated addresses (see Section 5.10.1); prefer public addresses over temporary addresses (see Section 5.10.4); and finally prefer the pair of addresses that share the longest matching prefix when everything else is equal.

The selection algorithms must also take into account locally defined default address preference policies. These default policies are stored in a table called the *policy table*. On KAME-enabled FreeBSD systems, an administrator can add or remove entries of the policy table through the **ip6addrctl** utility. Each entry in the policy table comprises an address prefix, the *precedence* value of that prefix, and a *label* value.

For a given candidate of source or destination address, the policy entry that has the longest prefix that matches the address is applied. The precedence of a policy table entry is only used for destination address selection and specifies the preference level of the address candidate in the set. The label of an entry identifies a type of address that matches the entry. It is used for matching particular pairs of source and destination addresses in the selection algorithms. Neither precedence nor label values have to be unique in the table, that is, two different entries can have the same precedence or label value.

[RFC3484] defines the default entries of the policy table as shown in Table 3-4.

The ::1/128 prefix identifies the loopback address. This entry is treated separately and has the highest precedence because communication using this address should be closed within the node and thus should be regarded as stable and preferred.

The ::/0 prefix is the "default" entry and is discussed below.

The 2002::/16 prefix is a permanently assigned prefix by IANA for the 6to4 transition scheme [RFC3056]. The ::/96 prefix identifies IPv4-compatible IPv6 addresses, which is used for now-deprecated automatic tunneling (see Section 2.3).

The ::ffff:0:0/96 prefix identifies IPv4-mapped IPv6 addresses. In the address selection algorithms, it is just a convenient form for representing IPv4 addresses in the comparison of IPv4 and IPv6 destination addresses. This entry is effectively meaningless in the source address selection algorithm.

TABLE 3-4

Prefix	Precedence	Label
::1/128	50	0
::/0	40	1
2002::/16	30	2
::/96	20	3
::ffff:0:0/96	10	4

The default policy table for source and destination address selection.

The ::/0 prefix identifies all of the remaining unicast address space. Since this entry has a higher precedence than those for 6to4, IPv4-compatible, and IPv4-mapped addresses, the default behavior of the destination address selection algorithm prefers native IPv6 addresses over the transitional addresses, and IPv6 addresses over IPv4 addresses.

Given a destination address and a set of potential source addresses, the source address selection algorithm prefers the source address that has the matching label value as the destination address. Given a list of destination addresses along with the preferred source addresses, the destination address selection algorithm prefers the destination address with a matching label value as the source address, and prefers the destination address with a higher precedence value.

An administrator can install the default policy entries using the **ip6addrctl** command, commonly at the system startup time, which is executed as part of the system startup scripts. On FreeBSD versions 5.2 and later, the **ip6addrctl** script file residing under the /etc/rc.d directory installs these default policies when configuration variable ip6addrctl_enable is set to "YES" in the /etc/rc.conf file.

The following example illustrates the basic syntax of **ip6addrctl**.

```
# ip6addrctl add ::1/128 50 0
```

This adds a new policy table entry for the prefix ::1/128 with the precedence and the label of 50 and 0 (i.e., the first entry in Table 3-4).

If this command is executed without any argument, it will display the current table entries:

```
% ip6addrctl
Prefix                  Prec    Label    Use
::1/128                 50      0        0
::/0                    40      1        10975
2002::/16               30      2        0
::/96                   20      3        0
::ffff:0.0.0.0/96       10      4        0
```

where the "Use" column shows how many times this entry is used in the kernel for source address selection. As explained above, this field should always be 0 for ::ffff:0.0.0.0/96.

3.4.2   Source Address Selection

[RFC3484] defines the following notions for describing comparison rules for address selection.

Scope(A) Given an address A, Scope(A) refers to the scope of address A. For example, if A is fe80::2 then Scope(A) is the link-local scope; if B is 2001:db8::2, then Scope(B) is the global scope. We also use binary operator < to compare the size of two scopes. In the above example, we denote Scope(A) < Scope(B).

Label(A) Given an address A, Label(A) refers to the label value of the policy table entry that matches address A. For example, if A is 2001:db8::2, then Label(A) is 1 with the default policy table (Table 3-4).

Given a destination address D and two potential source addresses SA and SB, the following rules apply in the order shown for selecting the most preferable source address.

Rule 1 Prefer the same address.
> If SA and D are the same address, then prefer SA. Similarly, if SB and D are the same address, then prefer SB.

Rule 2 Prefer appropriate scope.

> If Scope(SA) < Scope(SB):
>
> > if Scope(SA) < Scope(D), then prefer SB; otherwise, prefer SA.
>
> If Scope(SB) < Scope(SA):
>
> > if Scope(SB) < Scope(D), then prefer SA; otherwise, prefer SB.

For example, given the destination address `2001:db8:1111::1` and the possible source addresses `fe80::1` and `2001:db8:ffff::a`, Rule 2 prefers the latter because Scope(`fe80::1`) < Scope(`2001:db8:ffff::a`) and Scope(`fe80::1`) < Scope(`2001:db8:1111::1`).

In general, this rule prefers addresses that have a larger scope. This is because it will then be more likely that the packet will be delivered to the destination without breaking the source zone.

Rule 3 Avoid deprecated addresses.

Now Scope(SA) is the same as Scope(SB). If SA is deprecated and SB is preferred, then prefer SB. Otherwise, if SB is deprecated and SA is preferred, then prefer SA.

Rule 4 Prefer home addresses.

If SA is simultaneously a Mobile IPv6 home address and care-of address and SB is not, then prefer SA. Similarly, if SB is simultaneously a home and care-of address, and SA is not, then prefer SB.

Home address and care-of address are concepts of Mobile IPv6, which will be discussed in Chapter 5 of *IPv6 Advanced Protocols Implementation*.

Rule 5 Prefer outgoing interface.

If SA is assigned to the interface that will be used to reach D, and SB is assigned to a different interface, then prefer SA. Similarly, if SB is assigned to the interface that will be used to reach D, and SA is assigned to a different interface, then prefer SB.

Rule 6 Prefer matching label.

If Label(SA) is the same as Label(D), and Label(SB) is different from Label(D), then prefer SA. Similarly, if Label(SB) is the same as Label(D), and Label(SA) is different from Label(D), then prefer SB.

In general, Rule 6 implies that preference is given to an address of matching address type as the destination address. For example, if the destination address is a transitional address (i.e., addresses used for transition technologies), then preference is given to a transitional address instead of a native IPv6 address.

Rule 7 Prefer public addresses.

If SA is a public address and SB is a temporary address generated according to [RFC3041], then prefer SA, and vice versa.

This rule may be controversial in that a privacy-conscious user may prefer temporary addresses. In fact, an older draft version of [RFC3484] preferred temporary addresses. There were heated discussions about the preference then, and the IETF finally reversed the preference based on the view that the smaller lifetimes of temporary addresses may potentially cause more trouble and should be less preferred.

Rule 8 Prefer longest prefix matching.
　　　　　If the length of the common prefix shared between SA and D is longer than the length of the common prefix shared between SB and D, then SA is preferred, and vice versa.

As indicated earlier, the selection algorithm terminates at a rule when that rule can clearly identify a more preferable address. For example, given the destination address `2001:db8::2` and the possible source address `2001:db8::2` and `2002:c000:202::2`, assume `2001:db8::2` is deprecated. The selection algorithm terminates at Rule 1 and prefers `2001:db8::2`. Rule 3 is not applied.

3.4.3   Destination Address Selection

Consider a set of potential destination addresses. For each pair of addresses in the set, denoted by DA and DB, the destination address selection algorithm provides a preference between them by applying the following comparison rules in the order shown. The result will sort the entire list in decreasing magnitude of preference level.

In addition to the supplemental definitions used in the previous subsection, we use the following notations:

Source(D) For a given destination address D, Source(D) is the address that would be used as the source address to send packets to D. Source(D) is called *undefined* when the source address for destination D cannot be determined.

Precedence(D) Given an address D, Precedence(D) refers to the precedence value of the policy table entry that matches address D.

As noted above, the destination address selection algorithm considers IPv4 addresses as well as IPv6 addresses, and IPv4 addresses are conceptually represented in the form of IPv4-mapped IPv6 addresses. Also, this algorithm introduces the notion of scopes for IPv4 addresses, too. Specifically, IPv4 private addresses are considered to be site-local; IPv4 auto-configured link-local addresses (i.e., addresses that match `169.254.0.0/16`) [RFC3927] and loopback addresses are considered to be link-local. All other IPv4 prefixes are treated as having the global scope. The notation of Scope(A) is then naturally extended to IPv4 addresses. For example, Scope(`::ffff:192.168.54.10`) is the site-local scope.

Rule 1 Avoid unusable destinations.
　　　　　If DB is known to be unreachable or if Source(DB) is undefined, then prefer DA. Similarly, if DA is known to be unreachable or if Source(DA) is undefined, then prefer DB.

Rule 2 Prefer matching scope.
　　　　　If Scope(DA) equals Scope(Source(DA)) and Scope(DB) is different from Scope(Source(DB)), then prefer DA. Similarly, if Scope(DB) equals Scope(Source(DB)) and Scope(DA) is different from Scope(Source(DA)), then prefer DB.

Rule 3 Avoid deprecated addresses.
　　　　　If Source(DA) is deprecated and Source(DB) is not, then prefer DB. Similarly, if Source(DB) is deprecated and Source(DA) is not, then prefer DA.

Rule 4 Prefer home addresses.

If Source(DA) is simultaneously a Mobile IPv6 home address and care-of address and Source(DB) is not, then prefer DA. Similarly, if Source(DB) is simultaneously a home and care-of address, and Source(DA) is not, then prefer DB.

Rule 5 Prefer matching label.

If Label(Source(DA)) equals Label(DA) and Label(Source(DB)) is different from Label(DB), then prefer DA. Similarly, if Label(Source(DB)) equals Label(DB) and Label(Source(DA)) is different from Label(DA), then prefer DB.

Rule 6 Prefer higher precedence.

If Precedence(DA) is larger than Precedence(DB), then prefer DA. Similarly, if Precedence(DB) is larger than Precedence(DA), then prefer DB.

Rule 7 Prefer native transport.

If DA is reached via an encapsulating transition mechanism and DB is not, then prefer DB. Similarly, if DB is reached via encapsulation and DA is not, then prefer DA.

In general, it is difficult to detect whether a destination address is reached via a transition mechanism. While it is syntactically clear that a 6to4 address [RFC3056] would belong to this category, this case is actually covered by the policy table entry for the prefix of 2002::/16 (see Table 3-4).

Rule 8 Prefer smaller scope.

If Scope(DA) < Scope(DB), then prefer DA. Similarly, if Scope(DA) > Scope(DB), then prefer DB.

This rule may be controversial, but it is based on the view that a destination of a smaller scope should be less troubling in terms of routing. For example, sending a packet to a link-local address usually does not require layer-3 routing.

Rule 9 Use longest matching prefix.

This rule only applies when DA and DB belong to the same address family, that is, both are IPv6 or both are IPv4. If the length of the common prefix shared between DA and Source(DA) is larger than the length of the common prefix shared between DB and Source(DB), then prefer DA. Similarly, if the length of the common prefix shared between DB and Source(DB) is larger than the length of the common prefix shared between DA and Source(DA), then prefer DB.

If none of the rules provides a preference, the preference between DA and DB is unchanged.

As indicated by the case of DNS resolution mentioned above, the destination address selection is typically a matter of application program or of the name resolution library. This is actually the case for the KAME implementation, and we will discuss implementation details of the destination address selection in Section 7.6.3. Examples will be given in Section 7.6.4.

3.5 Code Introduction

The rest of this chapter describes data structures and functions that are related to packet processing at the IPv6 layer. Table 3-5 lists the source files that are covered in this chapter.

TABLE 3-5

File	Description
`${KAME}/kame/sys/netinet6/in6_var.h`	Address selection policy table definition
`${KAME}/kame/sys/netinet6/ip6_var.h`	Kernel internal structures for the IPv6 processing
`${KAME}/kame/sys/netinet/ip6.h`	Kernel internal structures for the various extension headers
`${KAME}/kame/sys/netinet/ip6protosw.h`	Protocol switch structure for IPv6
`${KAME}/kame/sys/netinet6/ip6_output.c`	Packet transmission at the IPv6 layer
`${KAME}/kame/sys/netinet6/ip6_input.c`	Packet reception at the IPv6 layer, and handling the Hop-by-Hop options header
`${KAME}/kame/sys/netinet6/ip6_forward.c`	Forwarding IPv6 packets
`${KAME}/kame/sys/netinet6/frag6.c`	Handling the Fragment header on packet input
`${KAME}/kame/sys/netinet6/route6.c`	Handling the Routing header on packet input
`${KAME}/kame/sys/netinet6/dest6.c`	Handling the Destination options header on packet input
`${KAME}/kame/sys/netinet6/in6_src.c`	Implementation of the source address selection rules

Figure 3-14 illustrates an overview of the processing flow of IPv6 packets. All IPv6 packets are received by each network interface driver and passed to the `ip6intr()` function by using the `netisr` software interrupt mechanism. A packet retrieved from the interface driver queue is passed to the `ip6_input()` function, which performs the actual processing of IPv6 packets. The input packet will be processed based on the protocol number stored in the Next Header field of each header. The proper function for each protocol is chosen by the protocol switch mechanism described in Section 3.5.3. Functions `dest6_input()`, `frag6_input()`, and `route6_input()` process the Destination options header, Fragment header and Routing header, respectively. An IPv6 packet may be forwarded to another node if the packet has a Routing header, in which case the `route6_input()` function subsequently calls the `ip6_forward()` function. The processing of Hop-by-Hop options header is special, because the header has to be processed at all intermediate nodes on the path. The header is processed by the `ip6_hopopts_input()` function before any following header is processed. The actual option processing is done by the `ip6_process_hopopts()` function. The function is also called in the output path, since the header must also be processed at an originating node. The IPv6 packets passed from upper layer protocol output routines are passed to the `ip6_output()` function. If the packet is too large to be sent at once and fragmentation is permitted, the packet is divided and the `ip6_insertfraghdr()` function is called to insert a Fragment header to each divided packet. `ip6_output()` finally calls the `nd6_output()` function to pass the packet to the interface layer output functions.

FIGURE 3-14

Callback functions are chosen based on the next hop variable and `inet6sw[ ]` array

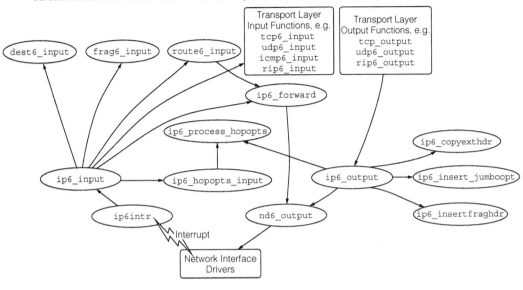

IPv6 packet input/output flow.

3.5.1 Statistics

The statistics of IPv6 node are stored in the `in6_ifstat{}` structure which is kept per network interface. Table 3-6 shows the statistics variables and corresponding Management Information Base (MIB) objects name defined in [RFC2465]. The IPv6 MIB objects are collected per interface, not per node, which is one characteristic of the IPv6 MIB definition. Table 3-7 shows a sample output of the `netstat -I`*ifname*`-s` command, which prints the current statistics values.

3.5.2 Header Structures

This section introduces data structures for various protocol headers discussed in this chapter.

ip6_hdr{} Structure

The `ip6_hdr{}` structure closely maps to the IPv6 header illustrated in Figure 3-1.

Listing 3-1

_____ ip6.h

```
75  struct ip6_hdr {
76      union {
77          struct ip6_hdrctl {
78              u_int32_t ip6_un1_flow; /* 20 bits of flow-ID */
79              u_int16_t ip6_un1_plen; /* payload length */
80              u_int8_t  ip6_un1_nxt;  /* next header */
81              u_int8_t  ip6_un1_hlim; /* hop limit */
82          } ip6_un1;
83          u_int8_t ip6_un2_vfc;        /* 4 bits version, top 4 bits class */
```

```
84                } ip6_ctlun;
85                struct in6_addr ip6_src;        /* source address */
86                struct in6_addr ip6_dst;        /* destination address */
87      } __attribute__((__packed__));
88
89      #define ip6_vfc          ip6_ctlun.ip6_un2_vfc
90      #define ip6_flow         ip6_ctlun.ip6_un1.ip6_un1_flow
91      #define ip6_plen         ip6_ctlun.ip6_un1.ip6_un1_plen
92      #define ip6_nxt          ip6_ctlun.ip6_un1.ip6_un1_nxt
93      #define ip6_hlim         ip6_ctlun.ip6_un1.ip6_un1_hlim
94      #define ip6_hops         ip6_ctlun.ip6_un1.ip6_un1_hlim
```
——— ip6.h

The top 4 bits of ip6_un2_vfc hold the version number and the lower 4 bits belong to the Traffic Class. The ip6_vfc macro is a convenient way of accessing the version field. The upper 4 bits of ip6_un1_flow belong to the Traffic Class and the lower 20 bits hold the flow label. The ip6_flow macro is a convenient way of accessing the flow label. ip6_un1_plen holds the payload length and is accessible via ip6_plen. ip6_un1_nxt holds the next header and is accessible via ip6_nxt. ip6_un1_hlim holds the hop limit and is accessible via either ip6_hlim or ip6_hops.

TABLE 3-6

in6_ifstat member	*SNMP variable*	*Description*
ifs6_in_receive	ipv6IfStatsInReceives	# of total input datagrams
ips6_in_hdrerr	ipv6IfStatsInHdrErrors	# of datagrams with invalid hdr
ifs6_in_toobig	ipv6IfStatsInTooBigErrors	# of datagrams exceeded MTU
ifs6_in_noroute	ipv6IfStatsInNoRoutes	# of datagrams with no route
ifs6_in_addrerr	ipv6IfStatsInAddrErrors	# of datagrams with invalid dst
ifs6_in_protounknown	ipv6IfStatsInUnknownProtos	# of datagrams with unknown proto
ifs6_in_truncated	ipv6IfStatsInTruncatedPkts	# of truncated datagrams
ifs6_in_discard	ipv6IfStatsInDiscards	# of discarded datagrams
ifs6_in_deliver	ipv6IfStatsInDelivers	# of datagrams delivered to ULP
ifs6_out_forward	ipv6IfStatsOutForwDatagrams	# of datagrams forwarded
ifs6_out_request	ipv6IfStatsOutRequests	# of outgoing datagrams from ULP
ifs6_out_discard	ipv6IfStatsOutDiscards	# of discarded datagrams
ifs6_out_fragok	ipv6IfStatsOutFragOKs	# of datagrams fragmented
ifs6_out_fragfail	ipv6IfStatsOutFragFails	# of datagrams failed on fragment
ifs6_out_fragcreat	ipv6IfStatsOutFragCreates	# of fragment datagrams
ifs6_reass_reqd	ipv6IfStatsReasmReqds	# of incoming fragmented packets
ifs6_reass_ok	ipv6IfStatsReasmOKs	# of reassembled packets
ifs6_reass_fail	ipv6IfStatsReasmFails	# of reassembled failures
ifs6_in_mcast	ipv6IfStatsInMcastPkts	# of inbound multicast datagrams
ifs6_out_mcast	ipv6IfStatsOutMcastPkts	# of outbound multicast datagrams

Statistics of IPv6.

TABLE 3-7

in6_ifstat member	netstat -I ifname -s output
ifs6_in_receive	1751398 total input datagrams
ips6_in_hdrerr	0 datagrams with invalid header received
ifs6_in_toobig	0 datagrams exceeded MTU received
ifs6_in_noroute	0 datagrams with no route received
ifs6_in_addrerr	0 datagrams with invalid dst received
ifs6_in_protounknown	0 datagrams with unknown proto received
ifs6_in_truncated	0 truncated datagrams received
ifs6_in_discard	1995 input datagrams discarded
ifs6_in_deliver	1675968 datagrams delivered to an upper layer protocol
ifs6_out_forward	0 datagrams forwarded to this interface
ifs6_out_request	2025473 datagrams sent from an upper layer protocol
ifs6_out_discard	0 total discarded output datagrams
ifs6_out_fragok	9063 output datagrams fragmented
ifs6_out_fragfail	0 output datagrams failed on fragment
ifs6_out_fragcreat	31196 output datagrams succeeded on fragment
ifs6_reass_reqd	27572 incoming datagrams fragmented
ifs6_reass_ok	8466 datagrams reassembled
ifs6_reass_fail	0 datagrams failed on reassembling
ifs6_in_mcast	5256 multicast datagrams received
ifs6_out_mcast	4001 multicast datagrams sent

Statistics printed by netstat -s.

ip6_hbh{} and ip6_dest{} Structures

The ip6_hbh{} and ip6_dest{} structures closely map to the Hop-by-Hop options header and the Destination options header depicted in Figures 3-3 and 3-4 respectively. The ip6_ext{} structure is a template structure of extension headers defined for convenience. When an extension header is processed, the memory space of the header is first mapped to ip6_ext{} structure and the length field is checked to verify the received data has enough bytes to be processed based on the type of extension header. Note that ip6_ext{} structure is not defined in the Advanced Socket API for IPv6 [RFC3542]: It is a KAME implementation specific structure.

Listing 3-2

ip6.h

```
114    /*
115     * Extension Headers
116     */
117
118    struct  ip6_ext {
```

```
119            u_int8_t ip6e_nxt;
120            u_int8_t ip6e_len;
121     } __attribute__((__packed__))
122
123     /* Hop-by-Hop options header */
124     /* XXX should we pad it to force alignment on an 8-byte boundary? */
125     struct ip6_hbh {
126            u_int8_t ip6h_nxt;          /* next header */
127            u_int8_t ip6h_len;          /* length in units of 8 octets */
128            /* followed by options */
129     } __attribute__((__packed__));
130
131     /* Destination options header */
132     /* XXX should we pad it to force alignment on an 8-byte boundary? */
133     struct ip6_dest {
134            u_int8_t ip6d_nxt;          /* next header */
135            u_int8_t ip6d_len;          /* length in units of 8 octets */
136            /* followed by options */
137     } __attribute__((__packed__));
```
——ip6.h

Each structure contains one 8-bit field for holding the next header value and another 8-bit field for holding the header length.

ip6_opt_jumbo{} *Structure*

[RFC2675] discusses the Jumbo Payload option. The option type has the value 0xC2. Its first two bits are 11_b, which indicates that if the processing node does not know how to process the option it must discard the packet, and, if the packet destination is a unicast address it must return an ICMPv6 error message. The third bit is 0, which means the option data cannot be modified en route. The option length is set to 4. The Payload Length must specify a value that is greater than 65535. The alignment requirement of this option is $4n + 2$. Figure 3-15 shows the format of the Jumbo Payload option.

The ip6_opt_jumbo{} structure defines the Jumbo Payload option.

Listing 3-3
——ip6.h

```
172     struct ip6_opt_jumbo {
173            u_int8_t ip6oj_type;
174            u_int8_t ip6oj_len;
175            u_int8_t ip6oj_jumbo_len[4];
176     } __attribute__((__packed__));
```
——ip6.h

FIGURE 3-15

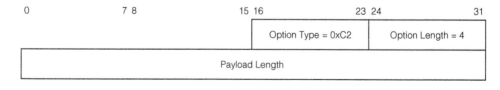

Jumbo Payload option.

The `ip6oj_type` field holds the value 0xC2, which represents bits 16 to 23 as shown in Figure 3-15. The `ip6oj_len` field holds the value 4, which represents bits 24 to 31 as shown in Figure 3-15. The `ip6oj_jumbo_len` field holds the payload length.

ip6_opt_router{} Structure

[RFC2711] defines the Router Alert option to notify intermediate routers that there are some special contents which need to be processed on routers. Figure 3-16 shows the format of the Router Alert option.

The `ip6_opt_router{}` structure defines the Router Alert option.

Listing 3-4
ip6.h

```
196     /* Router Alert Option */
197     struct ip6_opt_router {
198             u_int8_t ip6or_type;
199             u_int8_t ip6or_len;
200             u_int8_t ip6or_value[2];
201     } __attribute__((__packed__));
```
ip6.h

`ip6or_type` field holds 0x05, which represents bits 0 to 7 as shown in Figure 3-16. Its first two bits are both 0, indicating that the option can be skipped if the processing node does not know how to process the option as described in Table 3-3. The third bit of the option type is 0, which means the option data cannot be modified en route. `ip6or_len` field holds 2, which represents bits 8 to 15 as shown in Figure 3-16. `ip6or_value` is a 16-bit field that indicates the content of the input packet. The alignment requirement of this option is $2n + 0$. The available option values are shown in Table 3-8.

FIGURE 3-16

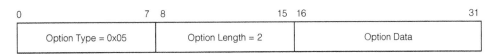

IPv6 Router Alert option.

TABLE 3-8

Name	Value	Description
IP6_ALERT_MLD	0	Packet contains Multicast Listener Discovery (MLD) message.
IP6_ALERT_RSVP	1	Packet contains Resource Reservation Protocol (RSVP) message.
IP6_ALERT_AN	2	Packet contains Active Network message.
	Others	Reserved to IANA for future use.

Router Alert values.

ip6_rthdr{} Structure

The `ip6_rthdr{}` structure is the most generic structure of the various types of Routing header. The structure is depicted in Figure 3-5.

Listing 3-5

_____ip6.h

```
224    struct ip6_rthdr {
225            u_int8_t  ip6r_nxt;      /* next header */
226            u_int8_t  ip6r_len;      /* length in units of 8 octets */
227            u_int8_t  ip6r_type;     /* routing type */
228            u_int8_t  ip6r_segleft;  /* segments left */
229            /* followed by routing type specific data */
230    } __attribute__((__packed__));
```

_____ip6.h

`ip6r_nxt` holds the value of the Next Header field. `ip6r_len` contains the header length in 8-byte units excluding the first 8 bytes of the header. `ip6r_type` specifies the type value of the actual Routing header. Each Routing header type has its own structure. The basic specification defines only the Type 0 Routing header, which is described in Listing 3-6. `ip6r_segleft` contains the number of segments left in the header that still need to be processed.

This structure is used to process the general part of every Routing header regardless of the type value. When the specific type of the Routing header is processed, a separate structure corresponding to that type is used.

ip6_rthdr0{} Structure

The `ip6_rthdr0{}` structure closely corresponds to the Type 0 Routing header depicted in Figure 3-6. The semantics of all the fields except `ip6r0_reserved` is the same as that of the `ip6_rthdr{}` structure. The `ip6r0_reserved` field corresponds to the reserved field of the Type 0 Routing header and is effectively unused.

Listing 3-6

_____ip6.h

```
233    struct ip6_rthdr0 {
234            u_int8_t  ip6r0_nxt;        /* next header */
235            u_int8_t  ip6r0_len;        /* length in units of 8 octets */
236            u_int8_t  ip6r0_type;       /* always zero */
237            u_int8_t  ip6r0_segleft;    /* segments left */
238            u_int32_t ip6r0_reserved;   /* reserved field */
239            /* followed by up to 127 struct in6_addr */
240    } __attribute__((__packed__));
```

_____ip6.h

ip6_frag{} Structure

The `ip6_frag{}` structure closely corresponds to the Fragment header depicted in Figure 3-8.

Listing 3-7

```
253    struct ip6_frag {
254            u_int8_t   ip6f_nxt;           /* next header */
255            u_int8_t   ip6f_reserved;      /* reserved field */
256            u_int16_t  ip6f_offlg;         /* offset, reserved, and flag */
257            u_int32_t  ip6f_ident;         /* identification */
258    } __attribute__((__packed__));
```

ip6f_nxt contains the value of the Next Header field. ip6f_reserved refers to bits 8 to 15 as shown in Figure 3-8 and its value is set to 0 by the sender and ignored by the receiver. ip6f_offlg comprises the fragment offset, the reserved field of bits 28 and 29, and the M bit. ip6f_ident holds the identification value for the original packet.

3.5.3 ip6protosw{} Structure

A protocol switch table is a data structure that contains a set of handler functions to allow the IP layer to deliver incoming packets to the appropriate upper layer protocols, and to allow applications to transmit data using the desired transport protocol. For IPv6, the protocol switch table is the ip6protosw{} structure as defined below.

Listing 3-8

```
117    struct ip6protosw {
....
121            short    pr_type;               /* socket type used for */
....
123            struct   domain *pr_domain;     /* domain protocol a member of */
124            short    pr_protocol;           /* protocol number */
125            short    pr_flags;              /* see below */
126
127    /* protocol-protocol hooks */
128            int      (*pr_input)            /* input to protocol (from below) */
129                         __P((struct mbuf **, int *, int));
....
133            int      (*pr_output)           /* output to protocol (from above) */
134                         __P((struct mbuf *, ...));
....
136            void     (*pr_ctlinput)         /* control input (from below) */
137                         __P((int, struct sockaddr *, void *));
....
139            int      (*pr_ctloutput)        /* control output (from above) */
140                         __P((struct socket *, struct sockopt *));
....
146    /* user-protocol hook */
....
152            int      (*pr_usrreq)           /* user request: see list below */
153                         __P((struct socket *, int, struct mbuf *,
154                              struct mbuf *, struct mbuf *));
....
157    /* utility hooks */
158            void     (*pr_init)             /* initialization hook */
159                         __P((void));
160
161            void     (*pr_fasttimo)         /* fast timeout (200ms) */
162                         __P((void));
163            void     (*pr_slowtimo)         /* slow timeout (500ms) */
```

```
164                      __P((void));
165          void    (*pr_drain)              /* flush any excess space possible */
166                      __P((void));
 ....
168          struct  pr_usrreqs *pr_usrreqs; /* supersedes pr_usrreq() */
 ....
176     };
```
                                                                    _____ip6protosw.h

pr_type specifies the communication type. The KAME implementation supports the types of communication given in Table 3-9. SOCK_STREAM is used with TCP, SOCK_DGRAM is used with UDP, and SOCK_RAW is used with other protocols such as ICMPv6. Recently, the SCTP (Stream Control Transmission Protocol [RFC3286]) implementation defined SOCK_SEQPACKET (sequential packet delivery) as a communication type for the new transport protocol.

The FreeBSD system implements two different protocol switch structures. One is the protosw{} structure defined in ${KAME}/freebsd4/sys/sys/protosw.h. The other is the ip6protosw{} structure described above. Other BSD variants such as NetBSD and OpenBSD have only one protocol switch structure (namely the protosw{} structure) that is shared between IPv4 and IPv6. The implementations differ in the definition of pr_input function: In the FreeBSD system, the pr_input member of the protosw{} structure takes two input parameters while the same member of the ip6protosw{} structure takes three parameters in other BSD variants. The difference between these definitions is the last parameter which specifies the protocol number to be processed by the input function. Historically, pr_input was defined to take a variable number of parameters so that this function can be adapted for future use. However, FreeBSD changed that function definition to a definition that takes a fixed number of parameters.

pr_domain specifies the protocol family and points to the inet6domain domain for IPv6. pr_protocol holds the protocol number (e.g., 6 for TCP and 17 for UDP). pr_flags defines the behavior of the socket operations. The KAME implementation supports the flags listed in Table 3-10.

pr_input is a pointer to the packet input processing function for each protocol. pr_output is not used by the IPv6 domain although some protocols set this member variable. pr_ctlinput is a pointer to the notification function for arriving control messages that are originated from the lower protocol layers. This function is used as an interface for delivering an ICMPv6 error to the corresponding application process (Section 4.6.2). pr_ctloutput is a pointer to the control function that operates on socket options (Figure 7-5). pr_usrreq is not used in FreeBSD. Instead, pr_usrreqs is used to dispatch request messages from the user process to the corresponding internal kernel modules. pr_init is a pointer to the protocol

TABLE 3-9

Communication type	Description
SOCK_STREAM	A reliable byte stream type
SOCK_DGRAM	A best effort packet delivery on transport layer
SOCK_RAW	A best effort packet delivery on network layer

Protocol type.

TABLE 3-10

pr_flags	Description
PR_ATOMIC	Specify that an operation request from the application will map into a single protocol operation request.
PR_ADDR	Specify that addresses are kept with data.
PR_CONNREQUIRED	Specify the protocol associated with a socket is connection oriented.
PR_WANTRECVD	Specify the socket requires notification upon data delivery.
PR_LASTHDR	Indicate the protocol is an upper layer protocol and has no following headers.

Operation behavior.

TABLE 3-11

SOCK_	IPPROTO_	pr_input	pr_ctlinput	pr_ctloutput
DGRAM	UDP	udp6_input()	udp6_ctlinput()	ip6_ctloutput()
STREAM	TCP	tcp6_input()	tcp6_ctlinput()	tcp_ctloutput()
RAW	RAW	rip6_input()	rip6_ctlinput()	rip6_ctloutput()
RAW	ICMPV6	icmp6_input()	rip6_ctlinput()	rip6_ctloutput()
RAW	DSTOPTS	dest6_input()	NULL	NULL
RAW	ROUTING	route6_input()	NULL	NULL
RAW	FRAGMENT	frag6_input()	NULL	NULL
RAW	AH	ah6_input()	NULL	NULL
RAW	ESP	esp6_input()	esp6_ctlinput()	NULL
RAW	IPV4	encap6_input()	encap6_ctlinput()	rip6_ctloutput()
RAW	IPV6	encap6_input()	encap6_ctlinput()	rip6_ctloutput()

A major part of the inet6sw *array.*

initialization function. pr_fasttimo and pr_slowtimo are pointers to the timer functions used for fast timeout processing (called every 200 ms) and slow timeout processing (called every 500 ms), respectively. pr_drain is a pointer to the function to be called by the kernel when the system is running out of mbuf blocks. pr_drain tries to release mbufs from each protocol stack which are less important under memory exhaustion.

The global variable named inet6sw is an array of the ip6protosw{} structures for the supported protocols in the system. Table 3-11 shows the content of this array for some major entries and structure members.

In the body of the table, the first two rows correspond to the major transport protocols, UDP and TCP. The entry for IPPROTO_RAW is the default entry for all unknown protocols. In particular, all incoming packets that have an unknown Next Header value are handled in the `rip6_input()` function. The fourth row corresponds to ICMPv6. It requires a separate array entry because it has a dedicated input function, `icmp6_input()`.

The rows for protocols `IPPROTO_DSTOPTS` through `IPPROTO_ESP` are defined to handle extension headers. These are not a "protocol" in an ordinary sense, and an application normally does not send or receive packets of these "protocols." The main purpose of having these in the `ip6protosw` framework is to handle incoming packets containing these headers through the general `pr_input` functions. Note that there is no entry for `IPPROTO_HOPOPTS`. This is due to the restriction of the location of a Hop-by-Hop options header (Section 3.3.1). A Hop-by-Hop options header is handled as a special case in the IPv6 input routine.

The rows for `IPPROTO_IPV4` and `IPPROTO_IPV6` handle tunneled packets over IPv6; the former is for IPv4 over IPv6 tunneling, and the latter is for IPv6 over IPv6 tunneling.

Input processing often requires a search for the appropriate `ip6protosw{}` structure in the `inet6sw` array corresponding to a particular Next Header value (`IPPROTO_xxx`). In order to make the search efficient, a shortcut array, `ip6_protox`, is generated at the system startup time. It consists of 255 integer entries, each of which contains the index of the `inet6sw` array for the protocol identified by the `ip6_protox` entry index. For example, `inet6sw[ip6_protox[IPPROTO_TCP]]` points to the `ip6protosw{}` structure corresponding to the second row of Table 3-11.

3.6   IPv6 Packet Address Information in Mbuf

We saw in Chapter 2 that IPv6 supports different types of addresses of various scopes and various properties. Whereas such characteristics affect packet processing, an incoming packet may not always carry enough information about the addresses contained in the packet. For example, the source and destination address fields of the IPv6 header only carry the 128-bit IPv6 addresses, and the scope zone IDs of these addresses can be only identified in context with other information such as the receiving interface. Also, the receiving node may behave differently depending on whether the destination address is a unicast address or an anycast address (see, e.g., Section 4.2.7), but it is difficult to tell the address type only from the packet since unicast and anycast addresses cannot be syntactically differentiated.

In order to ease the handling of the address properties of incoming packets, the KAME implementation uses the mbuf tagging framework (Section 1.6.2). For each incoming packet, the IPv6 input processing routine allocates a new `m_tag{}` structure, stores address-related information there, and attaches the tag to the packet. The stored information will be referenced as the incoming packet is processed in various routines in the kernel.

Figure 3-17 illustrates an example of the relationship between an incoming IPv6 packet, the `m_tag{}` structure, and the address-related information. We use link-local addresses to highlight implication with scope zone IDs: the source and destination addresses are `fe80::1234` and `fe80::abcd`, respectively, and we assume the corresponding link zone ID is 1.

The source and destination addresses are extracted from the packet, and converted in the form of the `sockaddr_in6{}` structure containing the proper link zone ID. Note that the zone ID is embedded in the `sin6_addr` field as well as set in the `sin6_scope_id` field. This is the general form used in the IPv6 protocol stack in the kernel as explained in Section 2.9.3. These `sockaddr_in6{}` structures are copied into the `m_tag{}` structure of this packet by the `ip6_setpktaddrs()` function. Other kernel

FIGURE 3-17

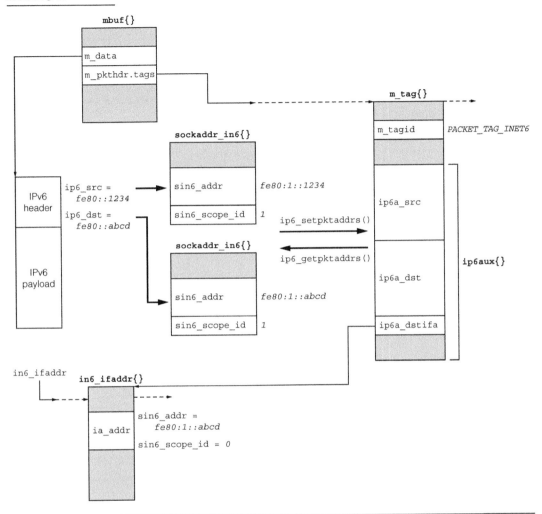

Relationship between mbuf and address-related information stored in m_tag{}.

routines retrieve this information by calling ip6_getpktaddrs(). These functions will be described later in this section.

If the destination address is a unicast or an anycast address destined for the receiving node, the IPv6 input routine identifies the corresponding in6_ifaddr{} structure (Section 2.10.1) through the routing table lookup as will be seen in Section 3.6. A pointer to this structure is also stored in the m_tag{} structure and will be used for checking properties of the address (such as whether it is an anycast address). Storing and retrieving the pointer in m_tag{} are performed by the ip6_setdstifaddr() and ip6_getdstifaddr() functions, respectively (Sections 3.6.1 and 3.6.2).

3.6.1 `ip6_setdstifaddr()` Function

The `ip6_addaux()` function either finds or allocates an IPv6 specific `m_tag{}` structure for the given mbuf. Specifically, it internally calls the `m_tag_find()` function, specifying `PACKET_TAG_INET6` to find a tag and then calls `m_tag_get()` to allocate a new tag. If it succeeds, then the given interface address structure, which typically corresponds to the destination address of the mbuf, is stored in the tag. The `ip6_addaux()` function can fail if that function cannot allocate the required resource, in which case `ip6_setdstifaddr()` simply returns a NULL pointer.

Listing 3-9

—— ip6_input.c

```
1242    /*
1243     * set/grab in6_ifaddr correspond to IPv6 destination address.
1244     * XXX backward compatibility wrapper
1245     */
1246    static struct m_tag *
1247    ip6_setdstifaddr(m, ia6)
1248            struct mbuf *m;
1249            struct in6_ifaddr *ia6;
1250    {
1251            struct m_tag *mtag;
1252
1253            mtag = ip6_addaux(m);
1254            if (mtag)
1255                    ((struct ip6aux *)(mtag + 1))->ip6a_dstia6 = ia6;
1256            return mtag;            /* NULL if failed to set */
1257    }
1258
```

—— ip6_input.c

3.6.2 `ip6_getdstifaddr()` Function

`ip6_getdstifaddr()` first checks whether the `m_tag{}` structure specific to IPv6 is attached to the given mbuf. If it is, the interface address contained in the tag structure is returned to the caller.

Listing 3-10

—— ip6_input.c

```
1259    struct in6_ifaddr *
1260    ip6_getdstifaddr(m)
1261            struct mbuf *m;
1262    {
1263            struct m_tag *mtag;
1264
1265            mtag = ip6_findaux(m);
1266            if (mtag)
1267                    return ((struct ip6aux *)(mtag + 1))->ip6a_dstia6;
1268            else
1269                    return NULL;
1270    }
```

—— ip6_input.c

3.6.3 `ip6_setpktaddrs()` Function

The `ip6_setpktaddrs()` function, shown below, gives source and destination addresses in the form of socket address structure as an mbuf tag.

Listing 3-11

—— ip6_input.c

```
1272    struct m_tag *
1273    ip6_setpktaddrs(m, src, dst)
1274            struct mbuf *m;
1275            struct sockaddr_in6 *src, *dst;
1276    {
1277            struct m_tag *mtag;
1278            struct sockaddr_in6 *sin6;
1279
1280            mtag = ip6_addaux(m);
1281            if (mtag) {
1282                    if (src) {
1283                            if (src->sin6_family != AF_INET6 ||
1284                                src->sin6_len != sizeof(*src)) {
1285                                    printf("ip6_setpktaddrs: illegal src: "
1286                                            "family=%d, len=%d\n",
1287                                            src->sin6_family, src->sin6_len);
1288                                    return (NULL);
1289                            }
1290                            /*
1291                             * we only copy the "address" part to avoid misuse
1292                             * the port, flow info, etc.
1293                             */
1294                            sin6 = &((struct ip6aux *)(mtag + 1))->ip6a_src;
1295                            bzero(sin6, sizeof(*sin6));
1296                            sin6->sin6_family = AF_INET6;
1297                            sin6->sin6_len = sizeof(*sin6);
1298                            sa6_copy_addr(src, sin6);
1299                    }
1300                    if (dst) {
1301                            if (dst->sin6_family != AF_INET6 ||
1302                                dst->sin6_len != sizeof(*dst)) {
1303                                    printf("ip6_setpktaddrs: illegal dst: "
1304                                            "family=%d, len=%d\n",
1305                                            dst->sin6_family, dst->sin6_len);
1306                                    return (NULL);
1307                            }
1308                            sin6 = &((struct ip6aux *)(mtag + 1))->ip6a_dst;
1309                            bzero(sin6, sizeof(*sin6));
1310                            sin6->sin6_family = AF_INET6;
1311                            sin6->sin6_len = sizeof(*sin6);
1312                            sa6_copy_addr(dst, sin6);
1313                    }
1314            }
1315
1316            return (mtag);
1317    }
```

—— ip6_input.c

`ip6_setpktaddr()` first tries to allocate or find an `m_tag{}` structure specific to IPv6 for the given mbuf. If it succeeds, the function then attaches the address structures that correspond to the source and destination addresses of the packet in the tag. As commented, only the address and zone index are copied because the address structures are only intended to be used to designate a layer 3 end point. This function always expects IPv6 addresses to be passed from the caller. Otherwise this function explicitly creates a log message to indicate an internal bug.

3.6.4 `ip6_getpktaddrs()` Function

Listing 3-12

_____ip6_input.c
```
1319    int
1320    ip6_getpktaddrs(m, src, dst)
1321            struct mbuf *m;
1322            struct sockaddr_in6 *src, *dst;
1323    {
1324            struct m_tag *mtag;
1325
1326            if (src == NULL && dst == NULL)
1327                    return (-1);
1328
1329            if ((mtag = ip6_findaux(m)) == NULL) {
1330                    struct ip6_hdr *ip6 = mtod(m, struct ip6_hdr *);
1331
1332                    printf("ip6_getpktaddrs no aux: src=%s, dst=%s, nxt=%d\n",
1333                            ip6_sprintf(&ip6->ip6_src), ip6_sprintf(&ip6->ip6_dst),
1334                            ip6->ip6_nxt);
1335                    return (-1);
1336            }
1337
1338            if (((struct ip6aux *)(mtag + 1))->ip6a_src.sin6_family != AF_INET6 ||
1339                ((struct ip6aux *)(mtag + 1))->ip6a_dst.sin6_family != AF_INET6) {
1340                    printf("ip6_getpktaddrs: src or dst are invalid\n");
1341            }
1342
1343            if (src)
1344                    *src = ((struct ip6aux *)(mtag + 1))->ip6a_src;
1345            if (dst)
1346                    *dst = ((struct ip6aux *)(mtag + 1))->ip6a_dst;
1347
1348            return (0);
1349    }
```
_____ip6_input.c

1326–1327 The `ip6_getpktaddrs()` function returns the address structures that are attached to the given mbuf back to the caller. The caller has the responsibility to pass in valid pointers to store the retrieved addresses.

1329–1340 When called, `ip6_getpktaddrs()` assumes the mbuf has a valid `m_tag{}` containing valid source and destination address structures. Otherwise, this function explicitly prints a log as an internal error.

1343–1346 If all of the necessary validations are complete, this function copies the addresses to the given pointers.

3.7   Input Processing: `ip6_input()` Function

The incoming packet processing at the IPv6 layer is essentially the same as that at the IPv4 layer: dequeue the packet from the input packet queue at the link-layer, validate the header, identify whether the packet is destined for the receiving node or to be forwarded, and, in the former case, pass it to the appropriate "upper layer."

Still, the ip6_input() function is different in some areas from the ip_input() function. This is partly due to the protocol differences, and partly due to the implementation design decision. The main differences are summarized as follows:

- In this implementation, IPv6 extension headers are considered "upper layers" in the inet6sw array, and the corresponding processing routines are called via the protosw{} framework as explained in Section 3.5.3. In particular, reassembling fragmented packets and source routing with a Routing header are performed through this framework.

- Since IPv6 addresses contained in the packet may be ambiguous about their scope zones, the appropriate zones must be determined based on the incoming interface and the address scope types for later processing. ip6_input() performs this procedure, and attaches sockaddr_in6{} structures corresponding to the source and destination addresses to the packet, which has the scope zones disambiguated.

- In order to determine whether the incoming packet is destined for the receiving node, ip6_input() uses routing table information as explained below. This is different from the traditional implementation which linearly searches the interface address list or recent versions of ip_input() that use address hash list. The difference does not necessarily come from the difference between IPv4 and IPv6, but one motivation of this approach is to make an efficient determination on a host with a large number of IPv6 addresses such as an IPv6 tunneling server handling many clients.

We begin with the code description of the ip6intr() function, which is a "preprocessor" of ip6_input(). This function is called by the link-layer driver via a software interrupt (see Section 1.4) and starts the processing of incoming IPv6 packets.

Listing 3-13

─── ip6_input.c

```
381     void
382     ip6intr()
383     {
384             int s;
385             struct mbuf *m;
386
387             for (;;) {
391                     s = splimp();
393                     IF_DEQUEUE(&ip6intrq, m);
394                     splx(s);
395                     if (m == 0)
396                             return;
397                     ip6_input(m);
398             }
399     }
```

─── ip6_input.c

The splimp() function prevents the lower layer kernel code from running so that ip6intrq will not be modified during the processing of ip6intr(). The incoming packet is then de-queued, and is set in mbuf m. The ip6_input() function performs actual input processing. The for loop continues until the input queue becomes empty.

The rest of this section concentrates on the ip6_input() function. Whereas this is a public function, it is called only by the ip6intr() function.

Listing 3-14

_____ip6_input.c
```
416     void
417     ip6_input(m)
418             struct mbuf *m;
419     {
420             struct ip6_hdr *ip6;
421             int off = sizeof(struct ip6_hdr), nest;
422             u_int32_t plen;
423             u_int32_t rtalert = ~0;
424             int nxt, ours = 0;
425             struct ifnet *deliverifp = NULL;
426             struct sockaddr_in6 sa6_src, sa6_dst;
427             u_int32_t srczone, dstzone;
440
449
450             /*
451              * make sure we don't have onion peering information into m_tag.
452              */
453             ip6_delaux(m);
```
_____ip6_input.c

The parameter m contains the incoming packet.

450–453 ip6_delaux() clears the mbuf tag with the type of PACKET_TAG_INET6 (see Section 1.6.2) if it was attached.

Check and Fix Mbuf Assumption

Listing 3-15

_____ip6_input.c
```
454
455             /*
456              * mbuf statistics
457              */
458             if (m->m_flags & M_EXT) {
459                     if (m->m_next)
460                             ip6stat.ip6s_mext2m++;
461                     else
462                             ip6stat.ip6s_mext1++;
463             } else {
464     #define M2MMAX          (sizeof(ip6stat.ip6s_m2m)/sizeof(ip6stat.ip6s_m2m[0]))
465                     if (m->m_next) {
466                             if (m->m_flags & M_LOOP) {
472                                     ip6stat.ip6s_m2m[loif[0].if_index]++; /* XXX */
474                             } else if (m->m_pkthdr.rcvif->if_index < M2MMAX)
475                                     ip6stat.ip6s_m2m[m->m_pkthdr.rcvif->if_index]++;
476                             else
477                                     ip6stat.ip6s_m2m[0]++;
478                     } else
479                             ip6stat.ip6s_m1++;
480     #undef M2MMAX
481             }
482
483             in6_ifstat_inc(m->m_pkthdr.rcvif, ifs6_in_receive);
484             ip6stat.ip6s_total++;
```
_____ip6_input.c

454–479 The KAME implementation of the IPv6 protocol handling often requires a certain amount of data to be positioned in a contiguous memory space as explained in Section 1.6.3. Statistics information for the mbuf structure is collected in order to diagnose problems due to this requirement, which can be displayed with the **netstat** command (see Section 1.6.4). When a packet is looped back within the originating node, the incoming interface referenced by `rcvif` may be a different interface from a loopback interface while the packet was actually processed in the loopback input function. Since the interest is in the statistics that reflect the behavior of the lower-layer driver implementation, loopbacked packets, marked by the `M_LOOP` flag, are categorized as if it arrived at a loopback interface.

483–484 Statistics variables, both per receiving interface and per node, indicate reception of an IPv6 packet are incremented. See Section 3.5.1 for the per interface statistics; the per node statistics are not defined in the standard MIB specification and are implementation specific.

Listing 3-16

―――ip6_input.c
```
487             /*
488              * L2 bridge code and some other code can return mbuf chain
489              * that does not conform to KAME requirement.  too bad.
490              * XXX: fails to join if interface MTU > MCLBYTES.  jumbogram?
491              */
492             if (m && m->m_next != NULL && m->m_pkthdr.len < MCLBYTES) {
493                     struct mbuf *n;
494
495                     MGETHDR(n, M_DONTWAIT, MT_HEADER);
496                     if (n != NULL) {
500                             m_dup_pkthdr(n, m, M_DONTWAIT);
504                     }
505                     if (n != NULL && m->m_pkthdr.len > MHLEN) {
506                             MCLGET(n, M_DONTWAIT);
507                             if ((n->m_flags & M_EXT) == 0) {
508                                     m_freem(n);
509                                     n = NULL;
510                             }
511                     }
512                     if (n == NULL) {
513                             m_freem(m);
514                             return; /* ENOBUFS */
515                     }
516
517                     m_copydata(m, 0, m->m_pkthdr.len, mtod(n, caddr_t));
518                     n->m_len = m->m_pkthdr.len;
519                     m_freem(m);
520                     m = n;
521             }
522             IP6_EXTHDR_CHECK(m, 0, sizeof(struct ip6_hdr), /* nothing */);
```
―――ip6_input.c

492 If the incoming packet is divided into more than one mbuf while the packet is smaller than the mbuf cluster size (`MCLBYTES`), it is likely the packet does not meet the requirement described above. Special handling follows in such a case.

495–515 A separate mbuf is allocated with a cluster buffer if necessary. The new mbuf is pointed to by variable n. If something goes wrong in the allocation procedure due to the lack of memory, the incoming packet is discarded.

517–520 The entire packet is copied into the newly allocated mbuf, and the original packet is discarded. As shown in the code, this process can be expensive for a large packet, but it is expected this workaround is rarely needed.

522 The `IP6_EXTHDR_CHECK()` macro (Section 1.6.3) ensures the first mbuf at least contains the IPv6 header. If not, the packet is discarded.

Validate Packet

Listing 3-17

```
                                                                      ip6_input.c
525             if (m->m_len < sizeof(struct ip6_hdr)) {
526                     struct ifnet *inifp;
527                     inifp = m->m_pkthdr.rcvif;
528                     if ((m = m_pullup(m, sizeof(struct ip6_hdr))) == NULL) {
529                             ip6stat.ip6s_toosmall++;
530                             in6_ifstat_inc(inifp, ifs6_in_hdrerr);
531                             return;
532                     }
533             }
534
535             ip6 = mtod(m, struct ip6_hdr *);
                                                                      ip6_input.c
```

525–535 If the first mbuf contained only a partial IPv6 header, `m_pullup()` would ensure that the entire IPv6 header is contained in contiguous memory by allocating a new mbuf and copying the header data when necessary. This condition should actually not hold, though, since the `IP6_EXTHDR_CHECK()` macro has performed the length check above. Variable `ip6` is then set to point to the beginning of the IPv6 header.

Listing 3-18

```
                                                                      ip6_input.c
537             if ((ip6->ip6_vfc & IPV6_VERSION_MASK) != IPV6_VERSION) {
538                     ip6stat.ip6s_badvers++;
539                     in6_ifstat_inc(m->m_pkthdr.rcvif, ifs6_in_hdrerr);
540                     goto bad;
541             }
...
598             ip6stat.ip6s_nxthist[ip6->ip6_nxt]++;
                                                                      ip6_input.c
```

537–541 The packet is silently discarded if the version field mismatches.

598 The `ip6s_nxthist` field of the `ip6stat{}` structure keeps track of the number of times a particular header type has been seen in received packets. The **netstat** command shows this statistics information as follows:

```
% netstat -s -p ip6
ip6:
(...)
      Input histogram:
              hop by hop: 3506
              TCP: 8014258
              UDP: 524
              ESP: 6034
              ICMP6: 15368
              PIM: 1
```

Listing 3-19

```
628            /*
629             * Check against address spoofing/corruption.
630             */
631            if (IN6_IS_ADDR_MULTICAST(&ip6->ip6_src) ||
632                IN6_IS_ADDR_UNSPECIFIED(&ip6->ip6_dst)) {
633                    /*
634                     * XXX: "badscope" is not very suitable for a multicast source.
635                     */
636                    ip6stat.ip6s_badscope++;
637                    in6_ifstat_inc(m->m_pkthdr.rcvif, ifs6_in_addrerr);
638                    goto bad;
639            }
640            if (IN6_IS_ADDR_MC_INTFACELOCAL(&ip6->ip6_dst) &&
641                !(m->m_flags & M_LOOP)) {
642                    /*
643                     * In this case, the packet should come from the loopback
644                     * interface.  However, we cannot just check the if_flags,
645                     * because ip6_mloopback() passes the "actual" interface
646                     * as the outgoing/incoming interface.
647                     */
648                    ip6stat.ip6s_badscope++;
649                    in6_ifstat_inc(m->m_pkthdr.rcvif, ifs6_in_addrerr);
650                    goto bad;
651            }
```

628–650 Packets with invalid source or destination addresses are discarded here. Invalid addresses include a multicast address in the source address field or the unspecified address in the destination address field. Note that the unspecified address can be in the source address field in some cases (see Section 2.3) and should not be treated as invalid.

Packets destined to an interface-local IPv6 multicast address are also discarded unless it is looped back. As commented inline, it is not enough to check that the receiving interface is a loopback interface.

Listing 3-20

```
653            /*
654             * The following check is not documented in specs.  A malicious
655             * party may be able to use IPv4 mapped addr to confuse tcp/udp stack
656             * and bypass security checks (act as if it was from 127.0.0.1 by using
657             * IPv6 src ::ffff:127.0.0.1).  Be cautious.
658             *
659             * This check chokes if we are in an SIIT cloud.  As none of BSDs
660             * support IPv4-less kernel compilation, we cannot support SIIT
661             * environment at all.  So, it makes more sense for us to reject any
662             * malicious packets for non-SIIT environment, than try to do a
663             * partial support for SIIT environment.
664             */
665            if (IN6_IS_ADDR_V4MAPPED(&ip6->ip6_src) ||
666                IN6_IS_ADDR_V4MAPPED(&ip6->ip6_dst)) {
667                    ip6stat.ip6s_badscope++;
668                    in6_ifstat_inc(m->m_pkthdr.rcvif, ifs6_in_addrerr);
669                    goto bad;
670            }
```

653–670 In the KAME implementation, IPv4-mapped IPv6 addresses (see Section 2.3) can only be used as part of API invocation (Section 7.2.3), and should not appear in the IPv6 source or destination address fields. If the kernel accepts such packets, an upper layer protocol or application may misinterpret the packet as being delivered over IPv4. Packets with IPv4-mapped IPv6 addresses in the header are therefore explicitly discarded.

Note: It is still controversial to reject IPv4-mapped IPv6 addresses at this point when this node is simply forwarding the packet either as a router or as an intermediate node specified in a Routing header.

Listing 3-21

```
                                                           ip6_input.c
688            /*
689             * Drop packets if the link ID portion is already filled.
690             * XXX: this is technically not a good behavior.  But, we internally
691             * use the field to disambiguate link-local addresses, so we cannot
692             * be generous against those a bit strange addresses.
693             */
694            if (!(m->m_pkthdr.rcvif->if_flags & IFF_LOOPBACK)) {
695                    if (IN6_IS_SCOPE_LINKLOCAL(&ip6->ip6_src) &&
696                        ip6->ip6_src.s6_addr16[1]) {
697                            ip6stat.ip6s_badscope++;
698                            goto bad;
699                    }
700                    if ((IN6_IS_ADDR_MC_INTFACELOCAL(&ip6->ip6_dst) ||
701                        IN6_IS_SCOPE_LINKLOCAL(&ip6->ip6_dst)) &&
702                        ip6->ip6_dst.s6_addr16[1]) {
703                            ip6stat.ip6s_badscope++;
704                            goto bad;
705                    }
706            }
                                                           ip6_input.c
```

688–706 The KAME kernel uses the second 16-bit field (i.e., bits 16–31) of an IPv6 address that has interface-local or link-local scope for embedding the appropriate zone ID as explained in Section 2.9.3. Thus, if a packet contains a non-0 value for this special field, the packet is discarded in order to avoid confusion by later processing code. This check is only performed for packets arriving at a non-loopback interface because an older version of the kernel did not clear this special field in order to identify the correct zone ID, even if the loopback interface hides the information about the originating zone. However, this check is not necessary in the version we are describing in this book (see Listing 3-171 in Section 3.13.3), and so the `if` condition at line 694 could actually be omitted.

Listing 3-22

```
                                                           ip6_input.c
709            /*
710             * construct source and destination address structures with
711             * disambiguating their scope zones (if there is ambiguity).
712             * XXX: sin6_family and sin6_len will NOT be referred to, but we fill
713             * in these fields just in case.
714             */
715            if (in6_addr2zoneid(m->m_pkthdr.rcvif, &ip6->ip6_src, &srczone) ||
716                in6_addr2zoneid(m->m_pkthdr.rcvif, &ip6->ip6_dst, &dstzone)) {
717                    /*
718                     * Note that these generic checks cover cases that src or
719                     * dst are the loopback address and the receiving interface
```

```
720                              * is not loopback.
721                              */
722                             ip6stat.ip6s_badscope++;
723                             goto bad;
724                     }
725             bzero(&sa6_src, sizeof(sa6_src));
726             bzero(&sa6_dst, sizeof(sa6_dst));
727             sa6_src.sin6_family = sa6_dst.sin6_family = AF_INET6;
728             sa6_src.sin6_len = sa6_dst.sin6_len = sizeof(struct sockaddr_in6);
729             sa6_src.sin6_addr = ip6->ip6_src;
730             sa6_src.sin6_scope_id = srczone;
731             if (in6_embedscope(&sa6_src.sin6_addr, &sa6_src)) {
732                     /* XXX: should not happen */
733                     ip6stat.ip6s_badscope++;
734                     goto bad;
735             }
736             sa6_dst.sin6_addr = ip6->ip6_dst;
737             sa6_dst.sin6_scope_id = dstzone;
738             if (in6_embedscope(&sa6_dst.sin6_addr, &sa6_dst)) { /* XXX */
739                     ip6stat.ip6s_badscope++;
740                     goto bad;
741             }
742
743             /* attach the addresses to the packet for later use */
744             if (!ip6_setpktaddrs(m, &sa6_src, &sa6_dst))
745                     goto bad;
```
—— ip6_input.c

709–724 Function in6_addr2zoneid() retrieves the scope zone index for an IPv6 address according to the given interface. The zone index is returned in the third function parameter. As commented, in6_addr2zoneid() fails when the source or destination address is invalid for the specified interface, in which case the packet is discarded. The failure case includes a situation where the loopback address is specified for either the source or the destination address fields while the packet comes from a physical link.

725–730 Two sockaddr_in6{} variables are initialized for the source and destination addresses with the proper zone indices. These structures unambiguously identify the proper addresses.

731–741 Function in6_embedscope() embeds the zone index into the sin6_addr member of each sockaddr_in6{} structure. The embedded form is the internal kernel representation. Although the function is intended to be used for all types of scopes, the function actually works for link-local and interface-local scopes only.

743–745 Function ip6_setpktaddrs() allocates an mbuf tag to hold the sockaddr_in6{} structures and attaches the tag to the mbuf for later use.

Determine if the Packet Is Ours

Listing 3-23

—— ip6_input.c
```
747             /*
748              * Multicast check
749              */
750             if (IN6_IS_ADDR_MULTICAST(&sa6_dst.sin6_addr)) {
751                     struct          in6_multi *in6m = 0;
756
757                     in6_ifstat_inc(m->m_pkthdr.rcvif, ifs6_in_mcast);
758                     /*
```

```
759                     * See if we belong to the destination multicast group on the
760                     * arrival interface.
761                     */
762                    IN6_LOOKUP_MULTI(&sa6_dst, m->m_pkthdr.rcvif, in6m);
763                    if (!in6m)
764                            goto nomatch;
805                    ours = 1;
806                    goto matched;
807
808         nomatch:
809                    if (!ip6_mrouter) {
810                            ip6stat.ip6s_notmember++;
811                            ip6stat.ip6s_cantforward++;
812                            in6_ifstat_inc(m->m_pkthdr.rcvif, ifs6_in_discard);
813                            goto bad;
814                    }
815         matched:
816                    deliverifp = m->m_pkthdr.rcvif;
817                    goto hbhcheck;
818             }
```
_____ ip6_input.c

747–814 If the packet's destination is a multicast address, the IN6_LOOKUP_MULTI() macro
verifies that the receiving interface has already joined the given multicast group. in6m
points to the group information if the interface is part of the multicast group. Otherwise,
if the node is not acting as a multicast router, the packet is discarded.

815–818 Variable deliverifp is set to the receiving interface if a multicast group information
is found.

Listing 3-24
_____ ip6_input.c

```
820             /*
821              *  Unicast check
822              */
823             if (ip6_forward_rt.ro_rt != NULL &&
824                 (ip6_forward_rt.ro_rt->rt_flags & RTF_UP) != 0 &&
829                 IN6_ARE_ADDR_EQUAL(&sa6_dst.sin6_addr,
830                                 &((struct sockaddr_in6 *)(&ip6_forward_rt.ro_dst))
    ->sin6_addr)
832                 )
833                    ip6stat.ip6s_forward_cachehit++;
834             else {
835                    struct sockaddr_in6 *dst6;
836
837                    if (ip6_forward_rt.ro_rt) {
838                            /* route is down or destination is different */
839                            ip6stat.ip6s_forward_cachemiss++;
840                            RTFREE(ip6_forward_rt.ro_rt);
841                            ip6_forward_rt.ro_rt = 0;
842                    }
843
844                    bzero(&ip6_forward_rt.ro_dst, sizeof(struct sockaddr_in6));
845                    dst6 = (struct sockaddr_in6 *)&ip6_forward_rt.ro_dst;
846                    *dst6 = sa6_dst;
848                    dst6->sin6_scope_id = 0; /* XXX */
850
852                    rtalloc_ign((struct route *)&ip6_forward_rt, RTF_PRCLONING);
856             }
857
```
_____ ip6_input.c

— Line 830 is broken here for layout reasons. However, it is a single line of code.

820–856 `ip6_forward_rt` is a global variable that stores a cached route for the destination address of incoming or forwarded packets. If the cached route is appropriate for this packet (i.e., the route entry is still valid and the destination address matches), the cached route is reused for the input process. Otherwise, `rtalloc_ign()` attempts to retrieve a new route and stores that route in `ip6_forward_rt` as a cache. Specifying the `RTF_PRCLONING` flag when calling function `rtalloc_ign()` prevents the creation of a cloned host route for the particular destination. The `sin6_scope_id` member must be cleared beforehand as explained in Section 2.9.3.

Listing 3-25

── `ip6_input.c`

```
858   #define rt6_key(r) ((struct sockaddr_in6 *)((r)->rt_nodes->rn_key))
859
860           /*
861            * Accept the packet if the forwarding interface to the destination
862            * according to the routing table is the loopback interface,
863            * unless the associated route has a gateway.
864            * Note that this approach causes to accept a packet if there is a
865            * route to the loopback interface for the destination of the packet.
866            * But we think it's even useful in some situations, e.g. when using
867            * a special daemon which wants to intercept the packet.
868            *
869            * XXX: some OSes automatically make a cloned route for the destination
870            * of an outgoing packet.  If the outgoing interface of the packet
871            * is a loopback one, the kernel would consider the packet to be
872            * accepted, even if we have no such address assinged on the interface.
873            * We check the cloned flag of the route entry to reject such cases,
874            * assuming that route entries for our own addresses are not made by
875            * cloning (it should be true because in6_addloop explicitly installs
876            * the host route).  However, we might have to do an explicit check
877            * while it would be less efficient.  Or, should we rather install a
878            * reject route for such a case?
879            */
880           if (ip6_forward_rt.ro_rt &&
881               (ip6_forward_rt.ro_rt->rt_flags &
882               (RTF_HOST|RTF_GATEWAY)) == RTF_HOST &&
887               !(ip6_forward_rt.ro_rt->rt_flags & RTF_CLONED) &&
889               !(ip6_forward_rt.ro_rt->rt_flags & (RTF_REJECT|RTF_BLACKHOLE)) &&
      ....
903               ip6_forward_rt.ro_rt->rt_ifp->if_type == IFT_LOOP) {
```

── `ip6_input.c`

860–903 If the route to the packet's destination is a valid host route and the outgoing interface is a loopback interface, it implies the packet is destined for the receiving node. The route entry flag `RTF_CLONED` is checked to avoid matching a route that is not created as the result of node address assignment. The `RTF_REJECT` and `RTF_BLACKHOLE` flags are checked to ensure packets that are meant to be filtered are not delivered erroneously.

Listing 3-26

── `ip6_input.c`

```
906               struct in6_ifaddr *ia6 =
907                   (struct in6_ifaddr *)ip6_forward_rt.ro_rt->rt_ifa;
931           /*
932            * record address information into m_tag.
933            */
934           (void)ip6_setdstifaddr(m, ia6);
```

```
935
936                     /*
937                      * packets to a tentative, duplicated, or somehow invalid
938                      * address must not be accepted.
939                      */
940                     if (!(ia6->ia6_flags & IN6_IFF_NOTREADY)) {
941                             /* this address is ready */
942                             ours = 1;
943                             deliverifp = ia6->ia_ifp;        /* correct? */
945                             /* Count the packet in the ip address stats */
946                             ia6->ia_ifa.if_ipackets++;
947                             ia6->ia_ifa.if_ibytes += m->m_pkthdr.len;
953                             goto hbhcheck;
954                     } else {
955                             /* address is not ready, so discard the packet. */
956                             nd6log((LOG_INFO,
957                                 "ip6_input: packet to an unready address %s->%s\n",
958                                 ip6_sprintf(&ip6->ip6_src),
959                                 ip6_sprintf(&ip6->ip6_dst)));
960
961                             goto bad;
962                     }
963             }
```
_____ ip6_input.c

906–934 `ia6` points to an interface address structure that corresponds to the destination address. `ip6_setdstifaddr()` records the interface address structure in the mbuf tag allocated in Listing 3-22.

936–961 `IN6_IFF_NOTREADY` is a set of flags indicating that the address is tentative, that is, its uniqueness is being checked by Duplicate Address Detection (DAD, see Section 5.10.2), or that DAD identifies the address as a duplicate. The packet is discarded if the destination address has this property. Otherwise, variable `deliverifp` points to the interface that has the destination address. Note that it may not be equal to the receiving interface.

Listing 3-27
_____ ip6_input.c
```
1022            /*
1023             * Now there is no reason to process the packet if it's not our own
1024             * and we're not a router.
1025             */
1026            if (!ip6_forwarding) {
1027                    ip6stat.ip6s_cantforward++;
1028                    in6_ifstat_inc(m->m_pkthdr.rcvif, ifs6_in_discard);
1029                    goto bad;
1030            }
```
_____ ip6_input.c

1022–1030 At this point, the packet is determined to be not destined for the receiving node. If the receiving node is not acting as a router, the packet is discarded.

Hop-by-Hop Option Processing

Listing 3-28
_____ ip6_input.c
```
1032    hbhcheck:
1033            /*
1034             * record address information into m_tag, if we don't have one yet.
```

```
1035                          * note that we are unable to record it, if the address is not listed
1036                          * as our interface address (e.g. multicast addresses, addresses
1037                          * within FAITH prefixes and such).
1038                          */
1039                         if (deliverifp && !ip6_getdstifaddr(m)) {
1040                                 struct in6_ifaddr *ia6;
1041
1042                                 ia6 = in6_ifawithifp(deliverifp, &sa6_dst.sin6_addr);
1043                                 if (ia6) {
1044                                         if (!ip6_setdstifaddr(m, ia6)) {
1045                                                 /*
1046                                                  * XXX maybe we should drop the packet here,
1047                                                  * as we could not provide enough information
1048                                                  * to the upper layers.
1049                                                  */
1050                                         }
1051                                 }
1052                         }
1053
```
——— `ip6_input.c`

1033–1052 If an interface address structure has not been attached to the mbuf, which happens in some cases such as for a multicast destination, the `in6_ifawithifp()` function searches for an appropriate interface address based on the arrival interface and the destination address. It generally tries to find a valid unicast address that best matches the given address. Function `ip6_setdstifaddr()` stores the interface address in the mbuf tag if one is found.

Listing 3-29
——— `ip6_input.c`

```
1054                 /*
1055                  * Process Hop-by-Hop options header if it's contained.
1056                  * m may be modified in ip6_hopopts_input().
1057                  * If a JumboPayload option is included, plen will also be modified.
1058                  */
1059                 plen = (u_int32_t)ntohs(ip6->ip6_plen);
1060                 if (ip6->ip6_nxt == IPPROTO_HOPOPTS) {
1061                         struct ip6_hbh *hbh;
1062
1063                         if (ip6_hopopts_input(&plen, &rtalert, &m, &off)) {
....
1067                                 return;          /* m have already been freed */
1068                         }
1069
1070                         /* adjust pointer */
1071                         ip6 = mtod(m, struct ip6_hdr *);
1072
```
——— `ip6_input.c`

1059–1068 `ip6_hopopts_input()` is called to process the header if the next header field of the IPv6 header specifies a Hop-by-Hop options header. Related parameters are stored in `plen` and `rtalert`. On return from `ip6_hopopts_input()`, `plen` holds the full packet length if the Jumbo Payload option is present and `rtalert` holds the Router Alert value if a Router Alert option is present.

1071 The `ip6` pointer is reinitialized in case `ip6_hopopts_input()` has modified the mbuf chain, while it should actually not happen as we will see in Section 3.8.

Listing 3-30

_____ip6_input.c
```
1073                        /*
1074                         * if the payload length field is 0 and the next header field
1075                         * indicates Hop-by-Hop Options header, then a Jumbo Payload
1076                         * option MUST be included.
1077                         */
1078                        if (ip6->ip6_plen == 0 && plen == 0) {
1079                                /*
1080                                 * Note that if a valid jumbo payload option is
1081                                 * contained, ip6_hoptops_input() must set a valid
1082                                 * (non-zero) payload length to the variable plen.
1083                                 */
1084                                ip6stat.ip6s_badoptions++;
1085                                in6_ifstat_inc(m->m_pkthdr.rcvif, ifs6_in_discard);
1086                                in6_ifstat_inc(m->m_pkthdr.rcvif, ifs6_in_hdrerr);
1087                                icmp6_error(m, ICMP6_PARAM_PROB,
1088                                            ICMP6_PARAMPROB_HEADER,
1089                                            (caddr_t)&ip6->ip6_plen - (caddr_t)ip6);
1090                                return;
1091                        }
```
_____ip6_input.c

1078–1091 If the Payload Length field of the IPv6 header is 0 and the Next Header field indicates the Hop-by-Hop options header, a Jumbo Payload option must be present as required by [RFC2675]. At this point of the code, the latter condition is met, and if the Hop-by-Hop options header does not contain a Jumbo Payload option, the `ip6_hopopts_input()` function keeps `plen` intact, which is zero in this case. The receiving node must then send an ICMPv6 error message to notify the sending node of this format error.

Listing 3-31

_____ip6_input.c
```
1093                        /* ip6_hopopts_input() ensures that mbuf is contiguous */
1094                        hbh = (struct ip6_hbh *)(ip6 + 1);
1103                        nxt = hbh->ip6h_nxt;
```
_____ip6_input.c

1096–1103 Variable `hbh` is set to point to the beginning of the Hop-by-Hop options header, and `nxt` holds the value of the Next Header field of the Hop-by-Hop options header.

Listing 3-32

_____ip6_input.c
```
1105                /*
1106                 * accept the packet if a router alert option is included
1107                 * and we act as an IPv6 router.
1108                 */
1109                if (rtalert != ~0 && ip6_forwarding)
1110                        ours = 1;
1111        } else
1112                nxt = ip6->ip6_nxt;
1113
1114        /*
1115         * Check that the amount of data in the buffers
1116         * is as at least much as the IPv6 header would have us expect.
1117         * Trim mbufs if longer than we expect.
1118         * Drop packet if shorter than we expect.
1119         */
1120        if (m->m_pkthdr.len - sizeof(struct ip6_hdr) < plen) {
```

```
1121                    ip6stat.ip6s_tooshort++;
1122                    in6_ifstat_inc(m->m_pkthdr.rcvif, ifs6_in_truncated);
1123                    goto bad;
1124          }
1125     if (m->m_pkthdr.len > sizeof(struct ip6_hdr) + plen) {
1126          if (m->m_len == m->m_pkthdr.len) {
1127                    m->m_len = sizeof(struct ip6_hdr) + plen;
1128                    m->m_pkthdr.len = sizeof(struct ip6_hdr) + plen;
1129          } else
1130                    m_adj(m, sizeof(struct ip6_hdr) + plen - m->m_pkthdr.len);
1131     }
```
———`ip6_input.c`

1106–1110 If the receiving node is acting as a router and the Hop-by-Hop options header contains a Router Alert option, the packet should be treated as if it were destined to the node. This logic is particularly necessary to accept Multicast Listener Discovery messages, some of which are sent to an arbitrary multicast group address.

1112 `nxt` holds the value of the Next Header field of the IPv6 header if the packet does not contain a Hop-by-Hop options header.

1120–1124 The packet is discarded if the actual payload is shorter than what is specified in the header. Note that `plen` must be used instead of the `ip6_plen` member because the latter can be 0 when a Jumbo Payload option is present.

1125–1131 If the above check succeeds and if the packet contains a trailing padding that is possibly added in a lower layer, the mbuf is adjusted so that it contains only the actual payload.

Forward if Not Ours

Listing 3-33
———`ip6_input.c`

```
1133          /*
1134           * Forward if desirable.
1135           */
1136     if (IN6_IS_ADDR_MULTICAST(&ip6->ip6_dst)) {
1137               /*
1138                * If we are acting as a multicast router, all
1139                * incoming multicast packets are passed to the
1140                * kernel-level multicast forwarding function.
1141                * The packet is returned (relatively) intact; if
1142                * ip6_mforward() returns a non-zero value, the packet
1143                * must be discarded, else it may be accepted below.
1144                */
1145               if (ip6_mrouter && ip6_mforward(ip6, m->m_pkthdr.rcvif, m)) {
1146                    ip6stat.ip6s_cantforward++;
1147                    m_freem(m);
1148                    return;
1149               }
1150               if (!ours) {
1151                    m_freem(m);
1152                    return;
1153               }
1154     } else if (!ours) {
1155               ip6_forward(m, 0);
1156               return;
1157     }
```
———`ip6_input.c`

1136–1153 ip6_mforward() is called to forward the packet if the destination is a multicast address and the node is acting as a multicast router, which is indicated by a non-NULL ip6_mrouter value. ip6_mforward() returns 0 on success so that the packet can be passed to the upper layer in case the receiving node is a member of the multicast group.

1154–1157 ip6_forward() is called to forward the packet if the destination is a unicast address and that packet is not destined for the receiving node. ip6_input() can simply return without freeing the mbuf because the packet is being forwarded.

Call Upper Layer Routines

Listing 3-34

```
                                                                    ip6_input.c
1159              /*
1160               * Tell launch routine the next header
1161               */
1170              ip6stat.ip6s_delivered++;
1171              in6_ifstat_inc(deliverifp, ifs6_in_deliver);
1172              nest = 0;
1173
1174              while (nxt != IPPROTO_DONE) {
1175                      if (ip6_hdrnestlimit && (++nest > ip6_hdrnestlimit)) {
1176                              ip6stat.ip6s_toomanyhdr++;
1177                              goto bad;
1178                      }
1179
1180                      /*
1181                       * protection against faulty packet - there should be
1182                       * more sanity checks in header chain processing.
1183                       */
1184                      if (m->m_pkthdr.len < off) {
1185                              ip6stat.ip6s_tooshort++;
1186                              in6_ifstat_inc(m->m_pkthdr.rcvif, ifs6_in_truncated);
1187                              goto bad;
1188                      }
1205
1235                      nxt = (*inet6sw[ip6_protox[nxt]].pr_input)(&m, &off, nxt);
1236              }
1237              return;
1238       bad:
1239              m_freem(m);
1240      }
                                                                    ip6_input.c
```

1170–1171 ip6s_delivered and ifs6_in_deliver are incremented to collect statistics. Since ifs6_in_deliver is an interface specific counter (see Section 3.5.1), deliverifp is necessary for in6_ifstat_inc().

1174 The while loop processes intermediate extension headers until the packet is passed to an appropriate transport layer, such as TCP.

1175–1178 nest is incremented for each extension header. The packet is discarded if the extension header limit ip6_hdrnestlimit is set, which defaults to 50, and nest has reached that limit. In theory, there is no need to set a limit on the number of extension headers. In practice, however, a packet rarely has tens of extension headers, which is more likely an attack packet. An explicit check is therefore performed on the number of extension headers that exist in the packet.

1184–1188 Offset `off` was initialized to the size of the `ip6_hdr{}` structure at the beginning of this function. Each time an extension header is examined, `off` is updated to have the total length from the head of the packet to the end of the header just processed. The packet is discarded if the received data is too short against `off`. This type of check is performed by each subroutine that processes a particular extension header, but `ip6_input()` also performs a check here to avoid unintentional failure.

1235 As described in Section 3.5.3, the `ip6protosw{}` structure for the next header (or protocol) value can be retrieved via the `ip6_protox` and `inet6sw` arrays. The packet with appropriate offset is passed to the function pointed by the `pr_input` member, the input routine for that header value. Since the function may have modified the mbuf chain, such as when processing a Fragment header, the address of `m` is passed into the function. `off` is also updated in this function as described. The function returns either the identifier of the next header or `IPPROTO_DONE`, and the return value is set in `nxt` for the iteration. `IPPROTO_DONE` can indicate an error, such as the termination of the input packet processing due to an error in the header processing, or the completion of packet processing by the transport layer.

3.8 Processing Hop-by-Hop Options Header: `ip6_hopopts_input()` Function

The `ip6_hopopts_input()` function, shown below, is a subroutine of `ip6_input()` that processes the Hop-by-Hop options header if it is included in the incoming packet. In fact, this function only performs minimal validation and simply calls the `ip6_process_hopopts()` function described in the succeeding subsection.

Listing 3-35

—— ip6_output.c
```
1352     /*
1353      * Hop-by-Hop options header processing. If a valid jumbo payload option is
1354      * included, the real payload length will be stored in plenp.
1355      */
1356     static int
1357     ip6_hopopts_input(plenp, rtalertp, mp, offp)
1358             u_int32_t *plenp;
1359             u_int32_t *rtalertp;     /* XXX: should be stored more smart way */
1360             struct mbuf **mp;
1361             int *offp;
1362     {
1363             struct mbuf *m = *mp;
1364             int off = *offp, hbhlen;
1365             struct ip6_hbh *hbh;
1366
1367             /* validation of the length of the header */
1369             IP6_EXTHDR_CHECK(m, off, sizeof(*hbh), -1);
1370             hbh = (struct ip6_hbh *)(mtod(m, caddr_t) + off);
1371             hbhlen = (hbh->ip6h_len + 1) << 3;
1372
1373             IP6_EXTHDR_CHECK(m, off, hbhlen, -1);
1374             hbh = (struct ip6_hbh *)(mtod(m, caddr_t) + off);
1390             off += hbhlen;
1391             hbhlen -= sizeof(struct ip6_hbh);
1392
1393             if (ip6_process_hopopts(m, (u_int8_t *)hbh + sizeof(struct ip6_hbh),
1394                                     hbhlen, rtalertp, plenp) < 0)
```

```
1395                            return (-1);
1396
1397                    *offp = off;
1398                    *mp = m;
1399                    return (0);
1400    }
```
─── ip6_output.c

1367–1371 The first call to the IP6_EXTHDR_CHECK() macro ensures that the first mbuf contains enough data to refer to the length field of the Hop-by-Hop options header. Then the head of the header can be accessed simply by adding the offset length from the head of the mbuf. The length of the Hop-by-Hop options header indicates the length of the header in 8-byte units, excluding the first 8 bytes (Section 3.3). In other words, the length in bytes is calculated by incrementing the value of the length field and then tripling the result.

1373–1374 The second call to the IP6_EXTHDR_CHECK() macro ensures that the first mbuf contains both the IPv6 and the entire Hop-by-Hop options headers. This macro actually does not modify the mbuf, and so line 1374 is redundant.

1390–1391 The offset off is incremented to include the length of the options header, and hbhlen is adjusted so that it excludes the first fixed part of the header before processing the options.

1393–1395 Function ip6_process_hopopts() performs the actual options processing. When a Router Alert option or a Jumbo Payload option is present, rtalertp or plenp is set accordingly.

1397–1398 offp is set to the offset from the head of the IPv6 packet to the end of the Hop-by-Hop options header. *mp is adjusted, but this adjustment is actually redundant because this function does not modify the mbuf as we saw above. This code is a relic of the past when IP6_EXTHDR_CHECK() could modify the mbuf to ensure the assumption.

3.8.1 Processing Each Option: ip6_process_hopopts() Function

The ip6_process_hopopts() function takes the essential role of processing a Hop-by-Hop options header. It examines each option in the header and takes an appropriate action.

Listing 3-36
─── ip6_input.c
```
1402    /*
1403     * Search header for all Hop-by-hop options and process each option.
1404     * This function is separate from ip6_hopopts_input() in order to
1405     * handle a case where the sending node itself process its hop-by-hop
1406     * options header. In such a case, the function is called from ip6_output().
1407     *
1408     * The function assumes that hbh header is located right after the IPv6 header
1409     * (RFC2460 p7), opthead is pointer into data content in m, and opthead to
1410     * opthead + hbhlen is located in continuous memory region.
1411     */
1412    int
1413    ip6_process_hopopts(m, opthead, hbhlen, rtalertp, plenp)
1414            struct mbuf *m;
1415            u_int8_t *opthead;
1416            int hbhlen;
```

```
1417                    u_int32_t *rtalertp;
1418                    u_int32_t *plenp;
1419    {
1420                    struct ip6_hdr *ip6;
1421                    int optlen = 0;
1422                    u_int8_t *opt = opthead;
1423                    u_int16_t rtalert_val;
1424                    u_int32_t jumboplen;
1425                    const int erroff = sizeof(struct ip6_hdr) + sizeof(struct ip6_hbh);
```
                                                                            ─── ip6_input.c

1412–1419 There are five arguments in this function. m is a pointer to the target IPv6 packet, opthead and hbhlen are a pointer to the head of the Hop-by-Hop options header and the length of the header. rtalertp and plenp point to the storage in which the contents of the Router Alert option and the Jumbo Payload option are stored if they exist.

Listing 3-37
                                                                            ─── ip6_input.c

```
1427            for (; hbhlen > 0; hbhlen -= optlen, opt += optlen) {
1428                    switch (*opt) {
1429                    case IP6OPT_PAD1:
1430                            optlen = 1;
1431                            break;
1432                    case IP6OPT_PADN:
1433                            if (hbhlen < IP6OPT_MINLEN) {
1434                                    ip6stat.ip6s_toosmall++;
1435                                    goto bad;
1436                            }
1437                            optlen = *(opt + 1) + 2;
1438                            break;
```
                                                                            ─── ip6_input.c

1427–1438 All options are checked one by one based on the option type stored in the first byte of each option. IP6OPT_PAD1 and IP6OPT_PADN are padding options to align other options. The length of the IP6OPT_PAD1 option is 1. Other options have a length field at the second byte of each option. In other words, every option except IP6OPT_PAD1 must have at least IP6OPT_MINLEN (2) bytes for the type and the length fields.

Listing 3-38
                                                                            ─── ip6_input.c

```
1439            case IP6OPT_RTALERT:
1440                    /* XXX may need check for alignment */
1441                    if (hbhlen < IP6OPT_RTALERT_LEN) {
1442                            ip6stat.ip6s_toosmall++;
1443                            goto bad;
1444                    }
1445                    if (*(opt + 1) != IP6OPT_RTALERT_LEN - 2) {
1446                            /* XXX stat */
1447                            icmp6_error(m, ICMP6_PARAM_PROB,
1448                                ICMP6_PARAMPROB_HEADER,
1449                                erroff + opt + 1 - opthead);
1450                            return (-1);
1451                    }
1452                    optlen = IP6OPT_RTALERT_LEN;
1453                    bcopy((caddr_t)(opt + 2), (caddr_t)&rtalert_val, 2);
1454                    *rtalertp = ntohs(rtalert_val);
1455                    break;
```
                                                                            ─── ip6_input.c

1439–1455 IP6OPT_RTALERT indicates the Router Alert option. The length of the Router
Alert option must be IP6OPT_RTALERT_LEN (4). An ICMPv6 Parameter Problem error
is replied pointing to the length field as a problem pointer if the length is invalid. The
content of the option is copied to the rtalert_val variable and stored in rtalertp
in the host byte order. It should be noted that bcopy() is used to copy the value despite
the alignment requirement (Section 3.3.6). [RFC2711] specifies 2n + 0 as the alignment
requirement of this option, which means the Router Alert value field should be aligned at
a 16-bit boundary. Assuming this requirement, line 1453 could also look like this:

```
rtalert_val = *(u_int16_t *)(opt + 2);
```

In reality, however, the processing cannot unconditionally assume the requirement.
In fact, the alignment requirement is just a guideline rather than a strict rule that every
implementation must obey. Also, the option processing code does not check if the alignment requirement is met. The above alternative code could cause a crash in some machine
architectures such as Sparc if the sender does not honor the requirement.

Listing 3-39

```
                                                                            ip6_input.c
1456                    case IP6OPT_JUMBO:
1457                        /* XXX may need check for alignment */
1458                        if (hbhlen < IP6OPT_JUMBO_LEN) {
1459                                ip6stat.ip6s_toosmall++;
1460                                goto bad;
1461                        }
1462                        if (*(opt + 1) != IP6OPT_JUMBO_LEN - 2) {
1463                                /* XXX stat */
1464                                icmp6_error(m, ICMP6_PARAM_PROB,
1465                                    ICMP6_PARAMPROB_HEADER,
1466                                        erroff + opt + 1 - opthead);
1467                                return (-1);
1468                        }
1469                        optlen = IP6OPT_JUMBO_LEN;
1470
1471                        /*
1472                         * IPv6 packets that have non 0 payload length
1473                         * must not contain a jumbo payload option.
1474                         */
1475                        ip6 = mtod(m, struct ip6_hdr *);
1476                        if (ip6->ip6_plen) {
1477                                ip6stat.ip6s_badoptions++;
1478                                icmp6_error(m, ICMP6_PARAM_PROB,
1479                                    ICMP6_PARAMPROB_HEADER,
1480                                        erroff + opt - opthead);
1481                                return (-1);
1482                        }
1483
1484                        /*
1485                         * We may see jumbolen in unaligned location, so
1486                         * we'd need to perform bcopy().
1487                         */
1488                        bcopy(opt + 2, &jumboplen, sizeof(jumboplen));
1489                        jumboplen = (u_int32_t)htonl(jumboplen);
                                                                            ip6_input.c
```

1456–1489 IP6OPT_JUMBO indicates the Jumbo Payload option. The length must be
IP6OPT_JUMBO_LEN (6). An ICMPv6 Parameter Problem error is sent pointing to the
length field as a problem pointer if the length is invalid.

1475–1482 The payload length field of the IPv6 header must be zero when the Jumbo Payload
option is used. An ICMPv6 Parameter problem error is sent pointing to the type field of
the option as a problem pointer if the IPv6 header has non-0 payload length field.

1488–1489 The option value is stored in the `jumboplen` variable in the host byte order. Note
that `bcopy()` must be used to copy the value as in the case of the Router Alert option.

Listing 3-40

```
1492                        /*
1493                         * if there are multiple jumbo payload options,
1494                         * *plenp will be non-zero and the packet will be
1495                         * rejected.
1496                         * the behavior may need some debate in ipngwg -
1497                         * multiple options does not make sense, however,
1498                         * there's no explicit mention in specification.
1499                         */
1500                        if (*plenp != 0) {
1501                                ip6stat.ip6s_badoptions++;
1502                                icmp6_error(m, ICMP6_PARAM_PROB,
1503                                    ICMP6_PARAMPROB_HEADER,
1504                                    erroff + opt + 2 - opthead);
1505                                return (-1);
1506                        }
....
1508
1509                        /*
1510                         * jumbo payload length must be larger than 65535.
1511                         */
1512                        if (jumboplen <= IPV6_MAXPACKET) {
1513                                ip6stat.ip6s_badoptions++;
1514                                icmp6_error(m, ICMP6_PARAM_PROB,
1515                                    ICMP6_PARAMPROB_HEADER,
1516                                    erroff + opt + 2 - opthead);
1517                                return (-1);
1518                        }
1519                        *plenp = jumboplen;
1520
1521                        break;
```

1500–1506 The `plenp` variable is initialized to zero and is set to the option value of the Jumbo
Payload option. If `plenp` is set to a non-0 value, it means this is the second occurrence
of the same option. While the protocol specification does not prohibit such construction,
the KAME implementation rejects accepting the duplicate options as it is likely to indicate
a sender's bug or even an attempt of an attack, and returns an ICMPv6 Parameter Problem
message to notify the sender of the unexpected event.

1513–1519 The Jumbo Payload option must not be used with a packet that does not need the
option. An ICMPv6 Parameter Problem message is sent if the option value is smaller than
or equal to `IPV6_MAXPACKET`, which is 65535.

Listing 3-41

```
1522                default:                    /* unknown option */
1523                        if (hbhlen < IP6OPT_MINLEN) {
1524                                ip6stat.ip6s_toosmall++;
```

```
1525                                    goto bad;
1526                            }
1527                    optlen = ip6_unknown_opt(opt, m,
1528                        erroff + opt - opthead);
1529                    if (optlen == -1)
1530                            return (-1);
1531                    optlen += 2;
1532                    break;
1533                    }
1534            }
1535
1536            return (0);
1537
1538    bad:
1539            m_freem(m);
1540            return (-1);
1541    }
```
                                                        ————————— ip6_input.c

1522–1533 Other unknown options are processed by the `ip6_unknown_opt()` function (described in the next subsection). The packet is dropped if it contains any option that must be processed by every node. In this case, `ip6_unknown_opt()` will return −1. Otherwise, the unknown option is simply ignored and the next option is processed.

3.8.2 Processing Unknown Option: `ip6_unknown_opt()` Function

The option format used in the Hop-by-Hop and Destination options headers is extensible, and a node processing these options may see unknown options. In such a case, the `ip6_unknown_opt()` function is called to decide what to do with the option.

    This function is commonly used for both the Hop-by-Hop and Destination options, and can also be called from the `dest6_input()` function as described in Section 3.9.

Listing 3-42
                                                        ————————— ip6_input.c
```
1543    /*
1544     * Unknown option processing.
1545     * The third argument 'off' is the offset from the IPv6 header to the option,
1546     * which is necessary if the IPv6 header the and option header and IPv6 header
1547     * is not continuous in order to return an ICMPv6 error.
1548     */
1549    int
1550    ip6_unknown_opt(optp, m, off)
1551            u_int8_t *optp;
1552            struct mbuf *m;
1553            int off;
1554    {
1555            struct ip6_hdr *ip6;
1556
1557            switch (IP6OPT_TYPE(*optp)) {
1558            case IP6OPT_TYPE_SKIP: /* ignore the option */
1559                    return ((int)*(optp + 1));
1560            case IP6OPT_TYPE_DISCARD:        /* silently discard */
1561                    m_freem(m);
1562                    return (-1);
1563            case IP6OPT_TYPE_FORCEICMP: /* send ICMP even if multicasted */
1564                    ip6stat.ip6s_badoptions++;
1565                    icmp6_error(m, ICMP6_PARAM_PROB, ICMP6_PARAMPROB_OPTION, off);
1566                    return (-1);
1567            case IP6OPT_TYPE_ICMP: /* send ICMP if not multicasted */
1568                    ip6stat.ip6s_badoptions++;
```

```
1569                          ip6 = mtod(m, struct ip6_hdr *);
1570                          if (IN6_IS_ADDR_MULTICAST(&ip6->ip6_dst) ||
1571                              (m->m_flags & (M_BCAST|M_MCAST)))
1572                                  m_freem(m);
1573                          else
1574                                  icmp6_error(m, ICMP6_PARAM_PROB,
1575                                              ICMP6_PARAMPROB_OPTION, off);
1576                          return (-1);
1577                  }
1578
1579          m_freem(m);                  /* XXX: NOTREACHED */
1580          return (-1);
1581  }
```
                                                                              ___ip6_input.c

1550–1553 This function has three arguments: `optp` is a pointer to the option whose type is unknown; `m` is a pointer to the mbuf which contains the IPv6 packet that has the option; `off` is an offset from the head of the IPv6 header to the option.

1557 The type value of an option contains a hint to the processing rules when the option is unknown to the processing node as described in Section 3.3.6. The `IP6OPT_TYPE()` macro determines how to process the unknown option from the option type.

1558–1562 The option length is returned if the unknown option is classified as `IP6OPT_TYPE_SKIP`, which means it can be simply ignored. If the option is classified as `IP6OPT_TYPE_DISCARD`, the entire packet is dropped and −1 is returned without any notification.

1563–1576 `IP6OPT_TYPE_FORCEICMP` and `IP6OPT_TYPE_ICMP` generate an ICMPv6 error message. The former type requires the error message to be sent even if the destination address is a multicast address. The latter requires the error message only when the destination address is not a multicast address. In both cases, −1 is returned to the caller function.

3.9   Processing Destination Options Header: `dest6_input()` Function

The `dest6_input()` function is called by `ip6_input()` to process the Destination options header if it is present in the packet.

Listing 3-43
                                                                              ___dest6.c

```
85    int
86    dest6_input(mp, offp, proto)
87          struct mbuf **mp;
88          int *offp, proto;
89    {
90          struct mbuf *m = *mp;
91          int off = *offp, dstoptlen, optlen;
92          struct ip6_dest *dstopts;
93          u_int8_t *opt;
```
                                                                              ___dest6.c

On input, the parameter `mp` contains the pointer to the address of the mbuf containing the packet. `offp` holds the offset from the start of the packet to the Destination options header. On return, `offp` is updated to include the length of the Destination options header. Parameter `proto` is not used by this function.

Listing 3-44

```
                                                                      dest6.c
106              /* validation of the length of the header */
108              IP6_EXTHDR_CHECK(m, off, sizeof(*dstopts), IPPROTO_DONE);
109              dstopts = (struct ip6_dest *)(mtod(m, caddr_t) + off);
115              dstoptlen = (dstopts->ip6d_len + 1) << 3;
118              IP6_EXTHDR_CHECK(m, off, dstoptlen, IPPROTO_DONE);
119              dstopts = (struct ip6_dest *)(mtod(m, caddr_t) + off);

125              off += dstoptlen;
126              dstoptlen -= sizeof(struct ip6_dest);
127              opt = (u_int8_t *)dstopts + sizeof(struct ip6_dest);
                                                                      dest6.c
```

106–119 This part of the code performs the same check as that for the Hop-by-Hop options header (Listing 3-35). It ensures the entire data from the IPv6 header to the Destination options header is in one contiguous block of memory.

125–127 `off` is reset to the offset to the first option contained in the header. `dstoptlen` holds the length of the options data. `opt` points to the first option.

Listing 3-45

```
                                                                      dest6.c
129              /* search header for all options. */
130              for (optlen = 0; dstoptlen > 0; dstoptlen -= optlen, opt += optlen) {
131                      if (*opt != IP6OPT_PAD1 &&
132                          (dstoptlen < IP6OPT_MINLEN || *(opt + 1) + 2 > dstoptlen)) {
133                              ip6stat.ip6s_toosmall++;
134                              goto bad;
135                      }
136
137                      switch (*opt) {
138                      case IP6OPT_PAD1:
139                              optlen = 1;
140                              break;
141                      case IP6OPT_PADN:
142                              optlen = *(opt + 1) + 2;
143                              break;
144      #ifdef MIP6

222      #endif /* MIP6 */
223                      default:             /* unknown option */
224                              optlen = ip6_unknown_opt(opt, m,
225                                  opt - mtod(m, u_int8_t *));
226                              if (optlen == -1)
227                                      return (IPPROTO_DONE);
228                              optlen += 2;
229                              break;
230                      }
231              }
232
233      #ifdef MIP6

237      #endif /* MIP6 */
238
239              *offp = off;
240              return (dstopts->ip6d_nxt);
241
242    bad:
243            m_freem(m);
244            return (IPPROTO_DONE);
245    }
                                                                      dest6.c
```

129–245 The reminder of this function is generally the same as the corresponding part of the `ip6_process_hopopts()` function described in the previous section except that `dest6_input()` handles a mobile IPv6 related option, which is not described in this book.

3.10 Reassembling Fragmented Packets

The difference in the procedure of reassembling fragmented IP packets is minimal between IPv4 and IPv6. As a result, KAME's implementation of IPv6 reassembling is derived from BSD's IPv4 reassembling code: both involves two data structures and one processing function called from the IP input routine. This section describes the structures and the function in detail.

3.10.1 Structures for Packet Reassembly

Reassembling fragmented packets involves two dedicated structures in the kernel. One is the `ip6asfrag{}` structure, which corresponds to each fragment packet; the other is the `ip6q{}` structure, which corresponds to a set of fragment packets generated from a single original packet.

The `ip6asfrag{}` structure is defined as follows.

Listing 3-46

---ip6_var.h
```
 94    struct  ip6asfrag {
 95            u_int32_t           ip6af_head;
 96            u_int16_t           ip6af_len;
 97            u_int8_t            ip6af_nxt;
 98            u_int8_t            ip6af_hlim;
 99            /* must not override the above members during reassembling */
100            struct ip6asfrag *ip6af_down;
101            struct ip6asfrag *ip6af_up;
102            struct mbuf      *ip6af_m;
103            int                 ip6af_offset;  /* offset in ip6af_m to next header */
104            int                 ip6af_frglen;  /* fragmentable part length */
105            int                 ip6af_off;     /* fragment offset */
106            u_int16_t           ip6af_mff;     /* more fragment bit in frag off */
107    };
```
---ip6_var.h

In fact, the first four members are effectively unused. As may be seen by the organization, this structure was originally intended to be used as an overlay structure of the IPv6 header so that the data space of the mbuf storing the fragment could also be used for reassembly processing. However, this approach turned out to be ineffective for several reasons. For example, the pointer members would consume 8 bytes for a 64-bit architecture, making the total size of this structure larger than the size of the IPv6 header (40 bytes).

The current implementation allocates a separate memory space for the `ip6asfrag{}` structure. The unnecessary members could have been removed when the implementation changed, but they still remain in the structure. This was probably just due to missing cleanup.

The `ip6af_down` and `ip6af_up` pointers are used for linking the fragments. `ip6af_m` points to the mbuf that stores the fragment. This member is often referenced via a shortcut macro `IP6_REASS_MBUF()` in the reassembly implementation shown below. `ip6af_offset` points to the first byte past the Fragment header. `ip6af_frglen` holds the payload length of the fragment. `ip6af_off` holds the fragment offset, which is relative to the beginning of the fragmentable part of the original packet. `ip6af_mff` has the M flag bit value of the Fragment header.

The `ip6q{}` structure is defined as follows.

Listing 3-47

```
                                                                     ip6_var.h
74    struct   ip6q {
75             u_int32_t       ip6q_head;
76             u_int16_t       ip6q_len;
77             u_int8_t        ip6q_nxt;        /* ip6f_nxt in first fragment */
78             u_int8_t        ip6q_hlim;
79             struct ip6asfrag *ip6q_down;
80             struct ip6asfrag *ip6q_up;
81             u_int32_t       ip6q_ident;
82             u_int8_t        ip6q_arrive;
83             u_int8_t        ip6q_ttl;
84             struct sockaddr_in6 ip6q_src, ip6q_dst;
85             struct ip6q     *ip6q_next;
86             struct ip6q     *ip6q_prev;
87             int             ip6q_unfrglen;  /* len of unfragmentable part */
91             int             ip6q_nfrag;     /* # of fragments */
92    };
                                                                     ip6_var.h
```

Like the `ip6asfrag{}` structure, the first four members, excluding `ip6q_nxt`, are effectively unused (see below for `ip6q_nxt`). It is not even clear why this structure has these members in the first place. According to the development change history, these members have been included in the structure since the very first versions of the code, but it looks like these have never been used. The intent was probably to use these as a temporary placeholder in case the corresponding fields of the IPv6 header were overridden during the reassembly process.

The `ip6q_arrive` member is also effectively unused. Again, the intent is not clear. It may have been expected to indicate whether the first fragment (i.e., the fragment with the offset flag of 0) has arrived.

`ip6q_nxt` holds the Next Header value from the first fragment. `ip6q_down` and `ip6q_up` are the pointers used to link the fragments. The fragment identification value is retrieved from the first fragment and is stored in `ip6q_ident`. At the arrival of each fragment it is compared against `ip6q_ident` to determine the reassembly queue for a packet. The `ip6q_ttl` is initialized to 60 seconds. The fragments of a packet are discarded if the packet cannot be reassembled within 60 seconds as specified in [RFC2460]. `ip6q_src` and `ip6q_dst` hold the packet source and destination addresses, respectively. `ip6q_next` and `ip6q_prev` are the pointers used to link the packets that are currently being reassembled. `ip6q_unfrglen` holds the length of the unfragmentable part of the original packet and this variable is initialized when the first fragment arrives. `ip6q_nfrag` holds the number of received fragments for the original packet identified by this structure.

Figure 3-18 depicts the relationship between the `ip6q{}` and `ip6asfrag{}` structures. In the figure, one UDP packet is kept in the structures. The packet is divided into three fragments

FIGURE 3-18

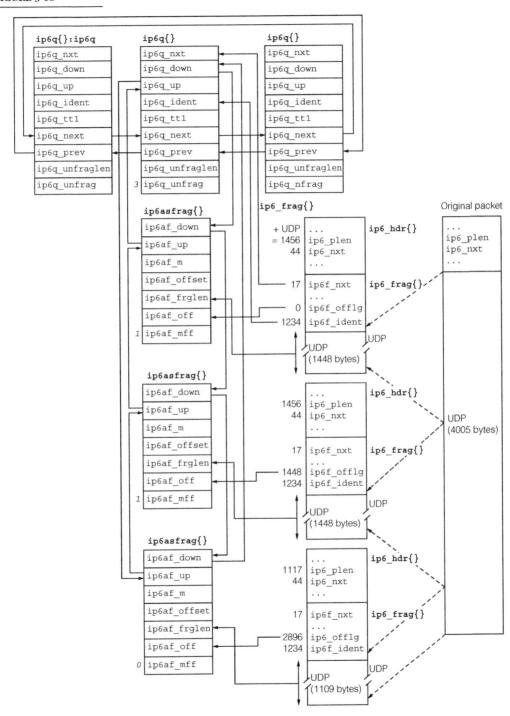

Relationship between ip6q{} *and* ip6asfrag{}.

as described in the lower right section. Each fragmented packet is associated to an instance of the `ip6asfrag{}` structure. Note that the length of the fragmentable part of the last fragment is 1109 bytes, which are not a multiple of 8 bytes. A series of `ip6asfrag{}` represents one original packet and associated to an instance of the `ip6q{}` structure. All instances of the `ip6q{}` structure are linked together and managed as a list structure headed by the global variable `ip6q`.

3.10.2 `frag6_input()` Function

The `frag6_input()` function is called by the `ip6_input()` function to process the Fragment header if it is present in the packet.

Listing 3-48

――― frag6.c
```
224     int
225     frag6_input(mp, offp, proto)
226             struct mbuf **mp;
227             int *offp, proto;
228     {
229             struct mbuf *m = *mp, *t;
230             struct ip6_hdr *ip6;
231             struct ip6_frag *ip6f;
232             struct ip6q *q6;
233             struct ip6asfrag *af6, *ip6af, *af6dwn;
234             struct in6_ifaddr *ia;
235             struct sockaddr_in6 src_sa, dst_sa;
236             int offset = *offp, nxt, i, next;
237             int first_frag = 0;
238             int fragoff, frgpartlen; /* must be larger than u_int16_t */
239             struct ifnet *dstifp;
240             u_int8_t ecn, ecn0;
241
242             ip6 = mtod(m, struct ip6_hdr *);
244             IP6_EXTHDR_CHECK(m, offset, sizeof(struct ip6_frag), IPPROTO_DONE);
245             ip6f = (struct ip6_frag *)((caddr_t)ip6 + offset);
251
252             /* extract full sockaddr structures for the src/dst addresses */
253             if (ip6_getpktaddrs(m, &src_sa, &dst_sa)) {
254                     m_freem(m);
255                     return (IPPROTO_DONE);
256             }
```
――― frag6.c

On input, parameter `mp` contains the pointer to the address of the mbuf holding the fragmented packet. When the function returns and if the packet has been fully reassembled, `mp` will hold the address of the reassembled packet. `offp` holds the offset from the start of the packet to the Fragment header. On return, `offp` is updated if the packet has been fully reassembled. Parameter `proto` is not used by `frag6_input()`.

242–257 The `IP6_EXTHDR_CHECK()` macro ensures that the Fragment header lies in a contiguous memory space in the first mbuf. Pointer `ip6f` is then set to point to the Fragment header. The packet's source and destination addresses with proper zone IDs are retrieved from the `m_tag{}` structure attached to the mbuf for later use.

Listing 3-49
_____frag6.c
```
258              dstifp = NULL;
259     #ifdef IN6_IFSTAT_STRICT
260              /* find the destination interface of the packet. */
261              if ((ia = ip6_getdstifaddr(m)) != NULL)
262                      dstifp = ia->ia_ifp;
263     #else
264              /* we are violating the spec, this is not the destination interface */
265              if ((m->m_flags & M_PKTHDR) != 0)
266                      dstifp = m->m_pkthdr.rcvif;
267     #endif
```
_____frag6.c

258–267 Variable `dstifp` is expected to point to the interface to which the fragment is addressed. It is used for counting per interface statistics regarding the fragment based on [RFC2465]. As the RFC notes, this interface may not necessarily be the receiving interface if the receiving node is multi-homed. In this sense, it is more appropriate to use the interface corresponding to the destination address of the packet, which is available via the `ip6_getdstifaddr()` function. However, this information may not be attached since `ip6_input()` ignored errors from `ip6_setdstifaddr()` (see, for example, Listing 3-26). As a compromise, this implementation lets the user choose the method that determines the interface with the `IN6_IFSTAT_STRICT` kernel compilation flag.

Listing 3-50
_____frag6.c
```
269          /* jumbo payload can't contain a fragment header */
270          if (ip6->ip6_plen == 0) {
271                  icmp6_error(m, ICMP6_PARAM_PROB, ICMP6_PARAMPROB_HEADER, offset);
272                  in6_ifstat_inc(dstifp, ifs6_reass_fail);
273                  return IPPROTO_DONE;
274          }
```
_____frag6.c

269–275 The value of 0 in the Payload Length field indicates a Jumbo Payload (recall Listing 3-39). This is an erroneous case according to [RFC2675], which prohibits the use of a Fragment header in a Jumbo Payload. In fact, the largest fragment offset is 65528 (0xFFFF − 7) according to the definition of the Fragment header (Section 3.3.5), which is far smaller than possible lengths of Jumbo Payloads; if a fragment packet were also a Jumbo Payload, the offset to the next fragment could not be represented in the Fragment header. An ICMPv6 error message is generated and is sent to the packet source in order to indicate the format error.

Listing 3-51
_____frag6.c
```
276      /*
277       * check whether fragment packet's fragment length is
278       * multiple of 8 octets.
279       * sizeof(struct ip6_frag) == 8
280       * sizeof(struct ip6_hdr) = 40
281       */
282      if ((ip6f->ip6f_offlg & IP6F_MORE_FRAG) &&
```

```
283                 (((ntohs(ip6->ip6_plen) - offset) & 0x7) != 0)) {
284                     icmp6_error(m, ICMP6_PARAM_PROB, ICMP6_PARAMPROB_HEADER,
285                         offsetof(struct ip6_hdr, ip6_plen));
286                     in6_ifstat_inc(dstifp, ifs6_reass_fail);
287                     return IPPROTO_DONE;
288             }
```
                                                                        _____ frag6.c

282–288 All fragments except the last must be a multiple of 8 bytes in length. Therefore, if a fragment is not the last fragment and its length is not an integer multiple of 8 bytes, the fragment is erroneous. In this case an ICMPv6 error message is returned to the sender.

Listing 3-52

                                                                        _____ frag6.c
```
290         ip6stat.ip6s_fragments++;
291         in6_ifstat_inc(dstifp, ifs6_reass_reqd);
292
```
                                                                        _____ frag6.c

290–291 The incoming fragment has passed preliminary validation. The arrival of the fragment is then recorded in the statistics variables.

Listing 3-53

                                                                        _____ frag6.c
```
293         /* offset now points to data portion */
294         offset += sizeof(struct ip6_frag);
295
296         IP6Q_LOCK();
297
298         /*
299          * Enforce upper bound on number of fragments.
300          * If maxfrag is 0, never accept fragments.
301          * If maxfrag is -1, accept all fragments without limitation.
302          */
303         if (ip6_maxfrags < 0)
304                 ;
305         else if (frag6_nfrags >= (u_int)ip6_maxfrags)
306                 goto dropfrag;
```
                                                                        _____ frag6.c

294 Variable `offset` holds at a minimum the length of the IPv6 header and the Fragment header.

296 Some data structures used in the `frag6_input()` function can be used in multiple contexts:

- In processing fragmented packets in this function
- In freeing incomplete fragments due to timeout in the `frag6_free()` function (not described in this book)
- In purging fragments being reassembled due to temporary memory shortage via the `frag6_drain()` function (not described in this book)

The consistency of the structure is basically ensured by controlling interrupt levels with the `splxxx()` functions (see Section 1.4), but the `IP6Q_LOCK()` macro is also provided for some exceptional cases of NetBSD and OpenBSD. For FreeBSD, this macro effectively does nothing.

303–306 `ip6_maxfrags` is the maximum allowable number of fragments that can wait for reassembly. `frag6_nfrags` is the current number of fragments that are held, waiting for reassembly. Fragments that exceed the system allowable maximum are discarded. Note that this is not a protocol requirement, but an implementation-specific restriction. These limits were introduced to prevent denial of service attacks intending to consume system memory by sending a massive number of incomplete fragments. It should also be noted that `ip6_maxfrags` is the limit of the total number of fragments regardless of the identity of the original packet. Otherwise, the attacker could mount the attack by sending incomplete fragments with varying source addresses and Fragment identifications. On this version of FreeBSD, `ip6_maxfrags` defaults to 1144 and is configurable via the `net.inet6.ip6.maxfrags` sysctl variable.

Listing 3-54

―――frag6.c
```
308        for (q6 = ip6q.ip6q_next; q6 != &ip6q; q6 = q6->ip6q_next)
309            if (ip6f->ip6f_ident == q6->ip6q_ident &&
310                SA6_ARE_ADDR_EQUAL(&src_sa, &q6->ip6q_src) &&
311                SA6_ARE_ADDR_EQUAL(&dst_sa, &q6->ip6q_dst))
312                    break;
```
―――frag6.c

308–313 The `for` loop traverses the packet reassembly queue to find the entry that holds the fragments belonging to the same original packet as that of the current fragment. The matching reassembly queue has the same fragment identifier, packet destination address and source address as those of the current fragment.

Listing 3-55

―――frag6.c
```
314    if (q6 == &ip6q) {
315            /*
316             * the first fragment to arrive, create a reassembly queue.
317             */
318            first_frag = 1;
319
320            /*
321             * Enforce upper bound on number of fragmented packets
322             * for which we attempt reassembly;
323             * If maxfragpackets is 0, never accept fragments.
324             * If maxfragpackets is -1, accept all fragments without
325             * limitation.
326             */
327            if (ip6_maxfragpackets < 0)
328                    ;
329            else if (frag6_nfragpackets >= (u_int)ip6_maxfragpackets)
330                    goto dropfrag;
331            frag6_nfragpackets++;
332            q6 = (struct ip6q *)malloc(sizeof(struct ip6q), M_FTABLE,
333                M_DONTWAIT);
334            if (q6 == NULL)
335                    goto dropfrag;
336            bzero(q6, sizeof(*q6));
337
338            frag6_insque(q6, &ip6q);
339
340            /* ip6q_nxt will be filled afterwards, from 1st fragment */
```

```
341            q6->ip6q_down   = q6->ip6q_up = (struct ip6asfrag *)q6;
....
345            q6->ip6q_ident  = ip6f->ip6f_ident;
346            q6->ip6q_arrive = 0; /* Is it used anywhere? */
347            q6->ip6q_ttl    = IPV6_FRAGTTL;
348            q6->ip6q_src    = src_sa;
349            q6->ip6q_dst    = dst_sa;
350            q6->ip6q_unfrglen = -1; /* The 1st fragment has not arrived. */
351
352            q6->ip6q_nfrag  = 0;
353     }
```
                                                                    ——— frag6.c

314–318 If this fragment is not found in the queue, variable `first_frag` remembers that fact for later processing.

327–330 `ip6_maxfragpackets` is the maximum allowable number of packets that can wait for reassembly. `frag6_nfragpackets` is the current number of packets that are being reassembled. Fragments of new packets that exceed the system allowable maximum are discarded for the same reason as that explained in Listing 3-53. Note that this limit applies to the number of original packets fragmented and is different from `ip6_maxfrags`. On this version of FreeBSD, `ip6_maxfragpackets` defaults to 1144 and is configurable via the `net.inet6.ip6.maxfragpackets sysctl` variable.

331–353 The `frag6_nfragpackets` counter is incremented for the new packet being reassembled. A new `ip6q{}` structure is allocated for the new packet and inserted into the packet reassembly queue. The fragment identifier `ip6q_ident` is initialized with the identifier value from the packet. The specification requires the node to discard any fragmented packet that cannot be reassembled within 60 seconds after the start of reassembly. `IPV6_FRAGTTL` is set to 120 ticks with each tick occurring every 500 ms. The packet source and destination addresses are stored in `ip6q_src` and `ip6q_dst` respectively.

Listing 3-56
                                                                    ——— frag6.c
```
355     /*
356      * If it's the 1st fragment, record the length of the
357      * unfragmentable part and the next header of the fragment header.
358      */
359     fragoff = ntohs(ip6f->ip6f_offlg & IP6F_OFF_MASK);
360     if (fragoff == 0) {
361            q6->ip6q_unfrglen = offset - sizeof(struct ip6_hdr) -
362                    sizeof(struct ip6_frag);
363            q6->ip6q_nxt = ip6f->ip6f_nxt;
364     }
```
                                                                    ——— frag6.c

359–360 The fragment offset is in 8-byte units. The `IP6F_OFF_MASK` clears the last 3 bits of the offset field, effectively multiplying the fragment offset by 8. The fragment with a fragment offset of zero is called the first fragment per [RFC2460]. Note that the first fragment is not necessarily the fragment that arrives at the node first. In fact, the Internet layer does not ensure the packet arrival order, and there is even an implementation that sends the trailing fragment first.

361–364 The length of the unfragmentable part and the next header value of the fragmentable part are copied from the first fragment into the reassembly queue. [RFC2460] explicitly specifies that the unfragmentable part and the next header value of the first fragment is used for the reassembled packet. Even though the fragmentation rule per the RFC specifies each fragment carry the same content of the unfragmentable part and the same Next Header value, the RFC also indicates these may differ in each fragment. It is therefore necessary to ensure deterministic behavior at the reassembly side.

[RFC2460] requires that the fragmented packet length not exceed the maximum length of 65535 bytes. This is a reasonable requirement, but the implementation is not as trivial as it may sound. The next part of the `frag6_input()` function performs this check.

Listing 3-57

```
                                                                    ─ frag6.c
366     /*
367      * Check that the reassembled packet would not exceed 65535 bytes
368      * in size.
369      * If it would exceed, discard the fragment and return an ICMP error.
370      */
371     frgpartlen = sizeof(struct ip6_hdr) + ntohs(ip6->ip6_plen) - offset;
372     if (q6->ip6q_unfrglen >= 0) {
373             /* The 1st fragment has already arrived. */
374             if (q6->ip6q_unfrglen + fragoff + frgpartlen > IPV6_MAXPACKET) {
375                     icmp6_error(m, ICMP6_PARAM_PROB, ICMP6_PARAMPROB_HEADER,
376                         offset - sizeof(struct ip6_frag) +
377                         offsetof(struct ip6_frag, ip6f_offlg));
378                     IP6Q_UNLOCK();
379                     return (IPPROTO_DONE);
380             }
381     } else if (fragoff + frgpartlen > IPV6_MAXPACKET) {
382             icmp6_error(m, ICMP6_PARAM_PROB, ICMP6_PARAMPROB_HEADER,
383                 offset - sizeof(struct ip6_frag) +
384                     offsetof(struct ip6_frag, ip6f_offlg));
385             IP6Q_UNLOCK();
386             return (IPPROTO_DONE);
387     }
                                                                    ─ frag6.c
```

366–371 `frgpartlen` holds the length of the fragmentable part stored in the current fragment.

372–380 If the first fragment has arrived, the length of the unfragmentable part is fixed, and it is possible to determine whether this fragment causes the length of the reassembled packet to exceed the maximum. If it does, an ICMPv6 error message, pointing to the fragment offset field of the Fragment header, is generated and is sent to the source of the fragment packet.

381–386 Even if the unfragmentable part is currently uncertain, the sum of the fragment offset and the length of the fragmentable part larger than the maximum indicates the resulting packet would break the requirement. An ICMPv6 error message is sent in this case.

Listing 3-58

```
                                                                    ─ frag6.c
388     /*
389      * If it's the first fragment, do the above check for each
390      * fragment already stored in the reassembly queue.
391      */
392     if (fragoff == 0) {
393             for (af6 = q6->ip6q_down; af6 != (struct ip6asfrag *)q6;
394                 af6 = af6dwn) {
395                     af6dwn = af6->ip6af_down;
396
```

```
397                     if (q6->ip6q_unfrglen + af6->ip6af_off + af6->ip6af_frglen >
398                         IPV6_MAXPACKET) {
399                             struct mbuf *merr = IP6_REASS_MBUF(af6);
400                             struct ip6_hdr *ip6err;
401                             int erroff = af6->ip6af_offset;
402
403                             /* dequeue the fragment. */
404                             frag6_deq(af6);
405                             free(af6, M_FTABLE);
406
407                             /* adjust pointer. */
408                             ip6err = mtod(merr, struct ip6_hdr *);
409
410                             /*
411                              * Restore source and destination addresses
412                              * in the erroneous IPv6 header.
413                              */
414                             ip6err->ip6_src = q6->ip6q_src.sin6_addr;
415                             ip6err->ip6_dst = q6->ip6q_dst.sin6_addr;
416
417                             icmp6_error(merr, ICMP6_PARAM_PROB,
418                                 ICMP6_PARAMPROB_HEADER,
419                                 erroff - sizeof(struct ip6_frag) +
420                                 offsetof(struct ip6_frag, ip6f_offlg));
421                     }
422             }
423     }
```
                                                                                    ———— frag6.c

392–423 Due to the reassembly rule the length of the unfragmentable part of the original packet can
be derived only when the first fragment arrives. Therefore, when the first fragment arrives, the
reassembly queue is traversed and the same length validation is performed on each fragment
that was done at line 374. When an error occurs, the mbuf of the fragment is retrieved from
the fragment reassembly data structure and it is then passed to `icmp6_error()` for generating and sending an ICMPv6 error back to the packet originator. The erroneous fragment is
removed from the reassembly queue and its memory is released.

Listing 3-59
                                                                                    ———— frag6.c
```
425     ip6af = (struct ip6asfrag *)malloc(sizeof(struct ip6asfrag), M_FTABLE,
426         M_DONTWAIT);
427     if (ip6af == NULL)
428             goto dropfrag;
429     bzero(ip6af, sizeof(*ip6af));
430     ip6af->ip6af_head = ip6->ip6_flow;
431     ip6af->ip6af_len = ip6->ip6_plen;
432     ip6af->ip6af_nxt = ip6->ip6_nxt;
433     ip6af->ip6af_hlim = ip6->ip6_hlim;
434     ip6af->ip6af_mff = ip6f->ip6f_offlg & IP6F_MORE_FRAG;
435     ip6af->ip6af_off = fragoff;
436     ip6af->ip6af_frglen = frgpartlen;
437     ip6af->ip6af_offset = offset;
438     IP6_REASS_MBUF(ip6af) = m;
```
                                                                                    ———— frag6.c

425–438 A reassembly fragment structure for the arriving fragment is allocated and the fragment
is stored into the newly allocated memory. Some parameters necessary for the reassembly
procedure are copied from the fragment into the structure: the M flag bit, the fragment
offset, the length of the fragmentable part of this fragment, and the mbuf that contains the
actual fragment.

As explained in Section 3.10.1, it is actually meaningless to copy the first four members of the `ip6asfrag{}` structure (lines 430 to 433).

Listing 3-60

```
440     if (first_frag) {
441             af6 = (struct ip6asfrag *)q6;
442             goto insert;
443     }
```

440–443 If the reassembly queue has just been created due to the arrival of this fragment, the fragment can simply be inserted into the queue, and the following checks are bypassed.

Listing 3-61

```
445             /*
446              * Handle ECN by comparing this segment with the first one;
447              * if CE is set, do not lose CE.
448              * drop if CE and not-ECT are mixed for the same packet.
449              */
450             ecn = (ntohl(ip6->ip6_flow) >> 20) & IPTOS_ECN_MASK;
451             ecn0 = (ntohl(q6->ip6q_down->ip6af_head) >> 20) & IPTOS_ECN_MASK;
452             if (ecn == IPTOS_ECN_CE) {
453                     if (ecn0 == IPTOS_ECN_NOTECT) {
454                             free(ip6af, M_FTABLE);
455                             goto dropfrag;
456                     }
457                     if (ecn0 != IPTOS_ECN_CE)
458                             q6->ip6q_down->ip6af_head |= htonl(IPTOS_ECN_CE << 20);
459             }
460             if (ecn == IPTOS_ECN_NOTECT && ecn0 != IPTOS_ECN_NOTECT) {
461                     free(ip6af, M_FTABLE);
462                     goto dropfrag;
463             }
```

450–451 If the sender of the fragments enables the Explicit Congestion Notification (ECN) [RFC3168], a router on the packet delivery path may have marked the ECN field of the IPv6 Traffic Class field with the Congestion Experienced (CE) code point. When the original packet was fragmented, the value of the ECN field may differ among fragments, and [RFC3168] specifies how such a case should be handled. For this processing, variables `ecn` and `ecn0` are set to the value of the ECN field of the current and first fragments, respectively.

452–459 If the CE code point is set in the current fragment, the first fragment should not have the Not-ECT (ECN-Capable Transport) code point; otherwise, the policy on applying ECN among the fragments would be inconsistent at the sender side. The current fragment is dropped in this case. If the first fragment does not have the CE code point, the code point is copied to the first fragment. [RFC3168] requires that if one of the fragments has CE, the reassembled packet must also have that code point.

Note: The CE code point is actually not preserved unless the first fragment has that code point as we will see shortly.

460–462 As in the above case, if the first fragment and the current fragment are inconsistent on the applicability of ECN, the current fragment is dropped.

Listing 3-62

—————————————————————————————————————— frag6.c
```
465     /*
466      * Find a segment which begins after this one does.
467      */
468     for (af6 = q6->ip6q_down; af6 != (struct ip6asfrag *)q6;
469         af6 = af6->ip6af_down)
470             if (af6->ip6af_off > ip6af->ip6af_off)
471                 break;
```
—————————————————————————————————————— frag6.c

468–471 The `for` loop tries to find the fragment that is located in a later position than the current fragment. That is, it tries to find the first fragment that has a larger offset than the offset of the current fragment.

Listing 3-63

—————————————————————————————————————— frag6.c
```
473     #if 0
474             /*
475              * If there is a preceding segment, it may provide some of
476              * our data already.  If so, drop the data from the incoming
477              * segment.  If it provides all of our data, drop us.
478              */
479             if (af6->ip6af_up != (struct ip6asfrag *)q6) {
480                     i = af6->ip6af_up->ip6af_off + af6->ip6af_up->ip6af_frglen
481                         - ip6af->ip6af_off;
482                     if (i > 0) {
483                             if (i >= ip6af->ip6af_frglen)
484                                     goto dropfrag;
485                             m_adj(IP6_REASS_MBUF(ip6af), i);
486                             ip6af->ip6af_off += i;
487                             ip6af->ip6af_frglen -= i;
488                     }
489             }
490
491             /*
492              * While we overlap succeeding segments trim them or,
493              * if they are completely covered, dequeue them.
494              */
495             while (af6 != (struct ip6asfrag *)q6 &&
496                 ip6af->ip6af_off + ip6af->ip6af_frglen > af6->ip6af_off) {
497                     i = (ip6af->ip6af_off + ip6af->ip6af_frglen) - af6->ip6af_off;
498                     if (i < af6->ip6af_frglen) {
499                             af6->ip6af_frglen -= i;
500                             af6->ip6af_off += i;
501                             m_adj(IP6_REASS_MBUF(af6), i);
502                             break;
503                     }
504                     af6 = af6->ip6af_down;
505                     m_freem(IP6_REASS_MBUF(af6->ip6af_up));
506                     frag6_deq(af6->ip6af_up);
507             }
508     #else
```
—————————————————————————————————————— frag6.c

473–508 The disabled code replaces some fragmentable parts of existing fragments with the fragmentable part of the newly received fragments. The code was derived from an old version of the IPv4 reassembly implementation, but this behavior was then known to be vulnerable to a security threat called the *overlapping fragment attack* [RFC1858]. The current recommended practice is to simply drop overlapping fragments as shown below.

Listing 3-64

```
                                                                    frag6.c
509            /*
510             * If the incoming framgent overlaps some existing fragments in
511             * the reassembly queue, drop it, since it is dangerous to override
512             * existing fragments from a security point of view.
513             * We don't know which fragment is the bad guy - here we trust
514             * fragment that came in earlier, with no real reason.
515             */
516            if (af6->ip6af_up != (struct ip6asfrag *)q6) {
517                    i = af6->ip6af_up->ip6af_off + af6->ip6af_up->ip6af_frglen
518                            - ip6af->ip6af_off;
519                    if (i > 0) {
525                            free(ip6af, M_FTABLE);
526                            goto dropfrag;
527                    }
528            }
529            if (af6 != (struct ip6asfrag *)q6) {
530                    i = (ip6af->ip6af_off + ip6af->ip6af_frglen) - af6->ip6af_off;
531                    if (i > 0) {
537                            free(ip6af, M_FTABLE);
538                            goto dropfrag;
539                    }
540            }
541    #endif
                                                                    frag6.c
```

516–528 If the arriving fragment overlaps with the preceding fragment, it is dropped.

529–540 Similarly, the arriving fragment is dropped if it overlaps with the succeeding fragment.

Listing 3-65

```
                                                                    frag6.c
543    insert:
544
545    /*
546     * Stick new segment in its place;
547     * check for complete reassembly.
548     * Move to front of packet queue, as we are
549     * the most recently active fragmented packet.
550     */
551    frag6_enq(ip6af, af6->ip6af_up);
552    frag6_nfrags++;
553    q6->ip6q_nfrag++;
                                                                    frag6.c
```

551–553 The arriving fragment is inserted into the reassembly queue and the corresponding counters are incremented.

Listing 3-66

```
                                                                    frag6.c
560    next = 0;
561    for (af6 = q6->ip6q_down; af6 != (struct ip6asfrag *)q6;
562            af6 = af6->ip6af_down) {
563            if (af6->ip6af_off != next) {
```

```
564                         IP6Q_UNLOCK();
565                         return IPPROTO_DONE;
566                 }
567             next += af6->ip6af_frglen;
568     }
```
_____ frag6.c

560–568 The `for` loop examines the available fragments and determines if a gap exists in
the sequence space, that is, whether more fragments are expected to arrive. Variable
`next` accumulates the length of the fragmentable part of each fragment, which must be
equal to the fragment offset of the examined fragment unless there is a gap. If a gap
is found, the current reassembly process is terminated at this point. The return value
of `IPPROTO_DONE` also terminates the extension header processing in `ip6_input()`
(Listing 3-34).

Listing 3-67
_____ frag6.c

```
569     if (af6->ip6af_up->ip6af_mff) {
570             IP6Q_UNLOCK();
571             return IPPROTO_DONE;
572     }
```
_____ frag6.c

569–572 The above `for` loop has iterated through the entire queue, which means the fragments
are in sequence. If, in addition, the last fragment has the M flag bit cleared, the reassembly
process has completed. Otherwise, the procedure is terminated here.

Figure 3-19 shows the check logic of the reassembly queue implemented in lines 560–572.
In the topmost case, there is a gap between the second and the third fragments, and the check
at line 563 fails. In the middlemost case, all the fragments are contiguous and the `for` loop
successfully terminates. But since the last fragment in the queue has the M flag of the last
fragment being on, the fragments are not complete and the check at line 569 fails. In the
lowermost case, since the fragments are contiguous with the M flag of the last fragment being
off, all the checks succeed and reassembly is now completed.

Listing 3-68
_____ frag6.c

```
574     /*
575      * Reassembly is complete; concatenate fragments.
576      */
577     ip6af = q6->ip6q_down;
578     t = m = IP6_REASS_MBUF(ip6af);
579     af6 = ip6af->ip6af_down;
580     frag6_deq(ip6af);
```
_____ frag6.c

577–580 At this point all of the fragments of the original packets are present. `t` and `m` point to
the mbuf containing the first fragment. `ip6af` holds the first fragment and `af6` points to the
remaining fragment chain. The first fragment block is removed from the reassembly queue.

FIGURE 3-19

The case where the reassembly queue is not contiguous

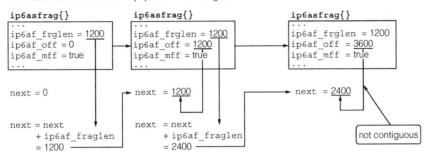

The case where the reassembly queue is contiguous but not completed

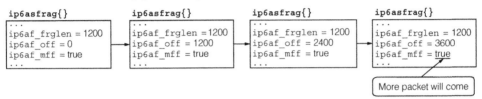

The case where the reassembly queue is contiguous and completed

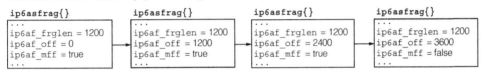

The check logic of the reassembly queue.

Listing 3-69
_____ frag6.c

```
581     while (af6 != (struct ip6asfrag *)q6) {
582             af6dwn = af6->ip6af_down;
583             frag6_deq(af6);
584             while (t->m_next)
585                     t = t->m_next;
586             t->m_next = IP6_REASS_MBUF(af6);
587             m_adj(t->m_next, af6->ip6af_offset);
588             free(af6, M_FTABLE);
589             af6 = af6dwn;
590     }
```
_____ frag6.c

581–590 The `while` loop traverses the fragment chain and concatenates all the mbufs attached
to the reassembly fragment structure. Note that the unfragmentable parts of the fragments
examined in the loop are all removed, since the first fragment must be used for restoring
the unfragmentable part. This is why the first fragment was treated separately before
entering the loop. The reassembly fragment structures are freed.

Listing 3-70
_____ frag6.c
```
592     /* adjust offset to point where the original next header starts */
593     offset = ip6af->ip6af_offset - sizeof(struct ip6_frag);
594     free(ip6af, M_FTABLE);
595     ip6 = mtod(m, struct ip6_hdr *);
596     ip6->ip6_plen = htons(next + offset - sizeof(struct ip6_hdr));
597     /* XXX: ip6q_src, dst may have an embedded zone ID */
598     ip6->ip6_src = q6->ip6q_src.sin6_addr;
599     ip6->ip6_dst = q6->ip6q_dst.sin6_addr;
600     nxt = q6->ip6q_nxt;
```
_____ frag6.c

593–603 Variable offset is set to the length of the unfragmentable part, which is the combined
size of the IPv6 header and the extension headers before the Fragment header contained
in the first fragment. Parameters of the IPv6 header contained in the first fragment are
adjusted: the Payload Length is derived from next and offset, which are the lengths
of the fragmentable (see Listing 3-66) and unfragmentable parts, by subtracting the size
of the IPv6 header. This part of the code should also copy the ECN field from ip6af in
case an intermediate fragment had the CE code point while the first fragment did not. But
this implementation does not copy this field; this is a bug. There is no need for resetting
the source and destination addresses since the content of the mbuf has been intact during
the reassembly procedure (see the note in Section 3.10.1).

Listing 3-71
_____ frag6.c
```
605     /*
606      * Delete frag6 header with as a few cost as possible.
607      */
608     if (offset < m->m_len) {
609             ovbcopy((caddr_t)ip6, (caddr_t)ip6 + sizeof(struct ip6_frag),
610                     offset);
611             m->m_data += sizeof(struct ip6_frag);
612             m->m_len -= sizeof(struct ip6_frag);
613     } else {
614             /* this comes with no copy if the boundary is on cluster */
615             if ((t = m_split(m, offset, M_DONTWAIT)) == NULL) {
616                     frag6_remque(q6);
617                     frag6_nfrags -= q6->ip6q_nfrag;
618                     free(q6, M_FTABLE);
619                     frag6_nfragpackets--;
620                     goto dropfrag;
621             }
622             m_adj(t, sizeof(struct ip6_frag));
623             m_cat(m, t);
624     }
```
_____ frag6.c

608–624 Now the Fragment header should be removed from the packet. The condition of the
if statement always holds, since the IP6_EXTHDR_CHECK() macro ensured that the
first mbuf contains all data from the IPv6 header to the end of the Fragment header. This
if-else branch is a relic of the past when the mbuf was adjusted at the beginning of
this function, and is now meaningless.

Listing 3-72
```
                                                                        frag6.c
626     /*
627      * Store NXT to the original.
628      */
629     {
630             char *prvnxtp = ip6_get_prevhdr(m, offset); /* XXX */
631             *prvnxtp = nxt;
632     }
                                                                        frag6.c
```

630 The `ip6_get_prevhdr()` function returns the address pointing to the Next Header field of the trailing header of the unfragmentable part. The comment means this function can be inefficient when the unfragmentable part contains many extension headers, while this address could have been given by the caller of this function that had actually examined the trailing header.

631 Then the Next Header field is reset to the value stored in the Fragment header of the first fragment.

Listing 3-73
```
                                                                        frag6.c
634     frag6_remque(q6);
635     frag6_nfrags -= q6->ip6q_nfrag;
636     free(q6, M_FTABLE);
637     frag6_nfragpackets--;
638
639     if (m->m_flags & M_PKTHDR) { /* Isn't it always true? */
640             int plen = 0;
641             for (t = m; t; t = t->m_next)
642                     plen += t->m_len;
643             m->m_pkthdr.len = plen;
644     }
645
646     ip6stat.ip6s_reassembled++;
647     in6_ifstat_inc(dstifp, ifs6_reass_ok);
                                                                        frag6.c
```

634–637 The reassembly queue of the current packet is released and the associated counters are updated to reflect the completion of a successful packet reassembly.

639–644 The total packet length of the mbuf containing the reassembled packet is reset to the length of the entire data.

646–647 Statistics counters are incremented to indicate the completion of reassembly.

Listing 3-74
```
                                                                        frag6.c
649     /*
650      * Tell launch routine the next header
651      */
652
653     *mp = m;
654     *offp = offset;
655
656     IP6Q_UNLOCK();
657     return nxt;
                                                                        frag6.c
```

653–657 The reassembled packet, the offset to the byte that immediately follows the unfragmentable part, and the Next Header value are returned to the caller.

Listing 3-75
_____frag6.c
```
659    dropfrag:
660            in6_ifstat_inc(dstifp, ifs6_reass_fail);
661            ip6stat.ip6s_fragdropped++;
662            m_freem(m);
663            IP6Q_UNLOCK();
664            return IPPROTO_DONE;
665    }
```
_____frag6.c

659–664 The above block of code handles any error condition that is encountered during the reassembly process. The current fragment packet is released and the associated counters are updated.

3.11 Processing Routing Header: `route6_input()` Function

The `route6_input()` function, shown below, is called by `ip6_input()` to process a Routing header of various types. Our main interest here is the Type 0 Routing header.

Listing 3-76
_____route6.c
```
71    int
72    route6_input(mp, offp, proto)
73            struct mbuf **mp;
74            int *offp, proto;          /* proto is unused */
75    {
76            struct ip6_hdr *ip6;
77            struct mbuf *m = *mp;
78            struct ip6_rthdr *rh;
79            int off = *offp, rhlen;
```
         (Mobile IPv6 option, omitted;)
```
92
94            IP6_EXTHDR_CHECK(m, off, sizeof(*rh), IPPROTO_DONE);
95            ip6 = mtod(m, struct ip6_hdr *);
96            rh = (struct ip6_rthdr *)((caddr_t)ip6 + off);
105
106           switch (rh->ip6r_type) {
107           case IPV6_RTHDR_TYPE_0:
108                   rhlen = (rh->ip6r_len + 1) << 3;
110                   /*
111                    * note on option length:
112                    * due to IP6_EXTHDR_CHECK assumption, we cannot handle
113                    * very big routing header (max rhlen == 2048).
114                    */
115                   IP6_EXTHDR_CHECK(m, off, rhlen, IPPROTO_DONE);
131                   if (ip6_rthdr0(m, ip6, (struct ip6_rthdr0 *)rh))
132                           return (IPPROTO_DONE);
133                   break;
134   #ifdef MIP6
```
         (Mobile IPv6 option, omitted;)
```
168   #endif /* MIP6 */
169           default:
```

```
170                        /* unknown routing type */
171                        if (rh->ip6r_segleft == 0) {
172                                rhlen = (rh->ip6r_len + 1) << 3;
173                                break;    /* Final dst. Just ignore the header. */
174                        }
175                        ip6stat.ip6s_badoptions++;
176                        icmp6_error(m, ICMP6_PARAM_PROB, ICMP6_PARAMPROB_HEADER,
177                                   (caddr_t)&rh->ip6r_type - (caddr_t)ip6);
178                        return (IPPROTO_DONE);
179                }
180
181                *offp += rhlen;
182                return (rh->ip6r_nxt);
183        }
```
_____ route6.c

94–115 The first call to the `IP6_EXTHDR_CHECK()` macro ensures that the first mbuf contains all the packet data from the IPv6 header to the common header part of the Routing header (Figure 3-5) in a contiguous memory space. If this is a Type 0 Routing header, the second call to the `IP6_EXTHDR_CHECK()` macro ensures that the first mbuf also contains the entire Routing header. As commented in the code, a Type 0 Routing header can be as large as 2048 bytes in length. In this case the first mbuf would not contain all of the data from the IPv6 header, even with a cluster. In practice, however, such a large header should be rare and this restriction would not cause trouble.

131 The `ip6_rthdr0()` function, which will be described shortly, performs the type-specific processing of a Type 0 Routing header.

169–174 If the receiving node does not understand the Routing header type, it first checks the Segment Left field. If it is 0, this node is the final destination, and it must simply accept the packet. Note that the Routing header can be skipped since the length can be calculated even if the node does not understand the further semantics.

174–178 Otherwise, an ICMPv6 error is returned to the sender to indicate the receipt of an unexpected packet.

181–182 If the node accepts the packet, the offset is incremented by the length of the routing header, and the next header value is returned to the caller.

Now we look at the actual processing of the Type 0 Routing header performed in the `ip6_rthdr0()` function.

Listing 3-77
_____ route6.c

```
185   /*
186    * Type0 routing header processing
187    *
188    * RFC2292 backward compatibility warning: no support for strict/loose bitmap,
189    * as it was dropped between RFC1883 and RFC2460.
190    */
191   static int
192   ip6_rthdr0(m, ip6, rh0)
193           struct mbuf *m;
194           struct ip6_hdr *ip6;
195           struct ip6_rthdr0 *rh0;
196   {
197           int addrs, index;
198           struct sockaddr_in6 next_sa;
```

```
199             struct in6_addr *nextaddr, tmpaddr;
200             struct in6_ifaddr *ifa;
201
202             if (rh0->ip6r0_segleft == 0)
203                     return (0);
```
—— route6.c

202–203 If `ip6r0_segleft` is 0, there are no more route segments left to be processed and the function simply returns to the caller.

Listing 3-78

—— route6.c

```
205     if (rh0->ip6r0_len % 2
  ....
209                     ) {
210                     /*
211                      * Type 0 routing header can't contain more than 23 addresses.
212                      * RFC 2462: this limitation was removed since strict/loose
213                      * bitmap field was deleted.
214                      */
215                     ip6stat.ip6s_badoptions++;
216                     icmp6_error(m, ICMP6_PARAM_PROB, ICMP6_PARAMPROB_HEADER,
217                             (caddr_t)&rh0->ip6r0_len - (caddr_t)ip6);
218                     return (-1);
219             }
```
—— route6.c

205–219 The length of the Routing header is specified in 8-byte units and an IPv6 address occupies two 8-byte units. Therefore `ip6r0_len` must be multiples of 2. Otherwise, an ICMPv6 error is generated and sent back to the packet source.

Listing 3-79

—— route6.c

```
221     if ((addrs = rh0->ip6r0_len / 2) < rh0->ip6r0_segleft) {
222             ip6stat.ip6s_badoptions++;
223             icmp6_error(m, ICMP6_PARAM_PROB, ICMP6_PARAMPROB_HEADER,
224                     (caddr_t)&rh0->ip6r0_segleft - (caddr_t)ip6);
225             return (-1);
226     }
```
—— route6.c

221–226 The Segment Left field must contain a valid value with respect to the number of route segments that exist in the Routing header. An invalid value in the Segment Left field will trigger an ICMPv6 error to be sent to the packet source.

Listing 3-80

—— route6.c

```
228     index = addrs - rh0->ip6r0_segleft;
229     rh0->ip6r0_segleft--;
230     nextaddr = ((struct in6_addr *)(rh0 + 1)) + index;
```
—— route6.c

228–230 The value of `index` specifies the index of the next route segment in the Address array of the Routing header. Now that another route segment is being processed, the number of segments left is decremented by one. Variable `nextaddr` is set to point to the next address in the Routing header.

Listing 3-81

── route6.c
```
232     /*
233      * reject invalid addresses.  be proactive about malicious use of
234      * IPv4 mapped/compat address.
235      * XXX need more checks?
236      */
237     if (IN6_IS_ADDR_MULTICAST(nextaddr) ||
238         IN6_IS_ADDR_UNSPECIFIED(nextaddr) ||
239         IN6_IS_ADDR_V4MAPPED(nextaddr) ||
240         IN6_IS_ADDR_V4COMPAT(nextaddr)) {
241             ip6stat.ip6s_badoptions++;
242             m_freem(m);
243             return (-1);
244     }
245     if (IN6_IS_ADDR_MULTICAST(&ip6->ip6_dst) ||
246         IN6_IS_ADDR_UNSPECIFIED(&ip6->ip6_dst) ||
247         IN6_IS_ADDR_V4MAPPED(&ip6->ip6_dst) ||
248         IN6_IS_ADDR_V4COMPAT(&ip6->ip6_dst)) {
249             ip6stat.ip6s_badoptions++;
250             goto bad;
251     }
```
── route6.c

237–251 The packet is discarded if it contains some "invalid" addresses in either the Destination Address field of the IPv6 header or the Next Hop address obtained from the Routing header. [RFC2460] specifies that multicast addresses are invalid in these positions.

It is a KAME-specific behavior to reject other types of addresses. Rejecting the unspecified address should be reasonable as we saw in Section 3.7, while the check for the Destination Address field was done in `ip6_input()` and is redundant. Rejecting IPv4-mapped IPv6 addresses as the Next Hop address is probably controversial as noted in Listing 3-20. In any event, `ip6_input()` already rejects these addresses that appear in the Destination Address field. Likewise, there does not seem to be a reason for rejecting IPv4-compatible IPv6 addresses, particularly as the Next Hop address. However, since these addresses are now effectively deprecated as explained in Section 2.3, rejecting these addresses here would actually not cause trouble.

Listing 3-82

── route6.c
```
253     /*
254      * determine the scope zone of the next hop, based on the interface
255      * of the current hop.
256      * [draft-ietf-ipngwg-scoping-arch, Section 9]
257      */
258     if ((ifa = ip6_getdstifaddr(m)) == NULL)
259             goto bad;
260     /*
261      * construct a sockaddr_in6 for the next hop with the zone ID,
262      * then update the recorded destination address.
263      */
264     bzero(&next_sa, sizeof(next_sa));
265     next_sa.sin6_family = AF_INET6;
266     next_sa.sin6_len = sizeof(next_sa);
267     next_sa.sin6_addr = *nextaddr;
268     if (in6_addr2zoneid(ifa->ia_ifp, nextaddr, &next_sa.sin6_scope_id)) {
269             ip6stat.ip6s_badscope++;
270             goto bad;
271     }
```

```
272        if (in6_embedscope(&next_sa.sin6_addr, &next_sa)) {
273                /* XXX: should not happen */
274                ip6stat.ip6s_badscope++;
275                goto bad;
276        }
277        if (!ip6_setpktaddrs(m, NULL, &next_sa))
278                goto bad;
```
                                                                    _____ route6.c

258–259 Consider, for example, the Next Route Segment's address is a link-local address. While atypical, it is not prohibited by the specification. Then the appropriate link zone for the Next Segment's address must be identified. The problem is that the Next Segment's address itself does not identify the scope zone ID; it must be determined by the forwarding node.

[RFC4007] specifies that it must be determined based on the interface to which the current Destination address belongs. Note that this is not necessarily equal to the incoming interface when the node is multi-homed. The receiving interface can change depending on routing, and cannot ensure the deterministic behavior for a Routing header containing an ambiguous address.

In the KAME implementation, the interface is available via the interface address structure attached to the mbuf, which can be retrieved by the `ip6_getdstifaddr()` function.

264–277 The socket address structure for the Next Segment's address with the proper zone ID is constructed in `next_sa`. It is then converted into the kernel internal format (see Section 2.9.3) by the `in6_embedscope()` function. Function `ip6_setpktaddrs()` replaces the Destination address attached to the mbuf with the one for the Next Segment's address.

Listing 3-83
                                                                    _____ route6.c
```
280        /*
281         * Swap the IPv6 destination address and nextaddr. Forward the packet.
282         */
283        tmpaddr = *nextaddr;
284        *nextaddr = ip6->ip6_dst;
285        ip6->ip6_dst = tmpaddr;
```
                                                                    _____ route6.c

283–285 The current destination address is recorded in the Routing header, and the destination address field of the IPv6 header is reset to the Next Segment's address.

Listing 3-84
                                                                    _____ route6.c
```
293                ip6_forward(m, 1);
295
296                return (-1);                    /* m would be freed in ip6_forward() */
297
298        bad:
299                m_freem(m);
300                return (-1);
301        }
```
                                                                    _____ route6.c

293–296 Processing the Routing header when the segment left field is non-0 implies packet forwarding. Function `ip6_forward()` (Section 3.12) sends the packet out to the Next

Route Segment. The second argument tells the function that this packet is forwarded in the process of a Routing header. The return code when set to -1 indicates the packet buffer has been freed inside this function.

298–300 The packet is freed when the function encounters an error while processing the Routing header.

3.12   Forwarding: `ip6_forward()` Function

When the Destination Address of a received packet is not one of addresses assigned to the receiving node and the node is configured as a router, the packet will be forwarded based on the current routing information. The `ip6_forward()` function is called from `ip6_input()` and performs this procedure. This function is also called from `ip6_rthdr0()` to forward a packet containing a Type 0 Routing header to the next route segment.

Listing 3-85

_____ ip6_forward.c

```
139    void
140    ip6_forward(m, srcrt)
141            struct mbuf *m;
142            int srcrt;
143    {
144            struct ip6_hdr *ip6 = mtod(m, struct ip6_hdr *);
145            struct sockaddr_in6 *dst = NULL;
146            struct rtentry *rt = NULL;
147            int error, type = 0, code = 0;
148            struct mbuf *mcopy = NULL;
149            struct ifnet *origifp;   /* maybe unnecessary */
150            struct sockaddr_in6 sa6_src, sa6_dst;
151            u_int32_t dstzone;
```

_____ ip6_forward.c

139–143 m is a pointer to the mbuf which contains the received packet. `srcrt` indicates that the packet is being forwarded as a result of Routing header processing; `srcrt` is set to 1 when this function is called from `ip6_rthdr0()`.

Listing 3-86

_____ ip6_forward.c

```
163            /* get source and destination addresses with full scope information. */
164            if (ip6_getpktaddrs(m, &sa6_src, &sa6_dst)) {
165                    /*
166                     * we dare to log the fact here because this should be an
167                     * internal bug.
168                     */
169                    log(LOG_ERR, "ip6_forward: can't find src/dst addresses\n");
170                    m_freem(m);
171                    return;
172            }

       .... (IPsec and Mobile IPv6 processing)

205            /*
206             * Do not forward packets to multicast destination (should be handled
207             * by ip6_mforward().
208             * Do not forward packets with unspecified source.  It was discussed
209             * in July 2000, on the ipngwg mailing list.
210             */
```

```
211              if ((m->m_flags & (M_BCAST|M_MCAST)) != 0 ||
212                  IN6_IS_ADDR_MULTICAST(&ip6->ip6_dst) ||
213                  IN6_IS_ADDR_UNSPECIFIED(&ip6->ip6_src)) {
214                      ip6stat.ip6s_cantforward++;
215                      /* XXX in6_ifstat_inc(rt->rt_ifp, ifs6_in_discard) */
216                      if (ip6_log_time + ip6_log_interval < time_second) {
217                          ip6_log_time = time_second;
218                          log(LOG_DEBUG,
219                              "cannot forward "
220                              "from %s to %s nxt %d received on %s\n",
221                              ip6_sprintf(&ip6->ip6_src),
222                              ip6_sprintf(&ip6->ip6_dst),
223                              ip6->ip6_nxt,
224                              if_name(m->m_pkthdr.rcvif));
225                      }
226                      m_freem(m);
227                      return;
228              }
```
                                                                ————————————ip6_forward.c

164–172 The source and destination addresses in the `sockaddr_in6{}` form are retrieved from the mbuf and copied to `sa6_src` and `sa6_dst` for later use.

211–228 Some types of packets should not be forwarded by this function:

- A packet delivered by link-level multicast or broadcast, in which case the mbuf has the `M_MCAST` or `M_BCAST` flag
- A packet whose destination is an IPv6 multicast address
- A packet whose source is the IPv6 unspecified address

These types of packets are checked here and discarded.

In fact, the second case should not happen since the caller of this function should also check and reject this case. This check is performed here just for safety.

Note: The comment about the unspecified source address has been incorporated in the standard specification since [RFC3513] published in April 2003.

Listing 3-87
                                                                ————————————ip6_forward.c

```
230              if (ip6->ip6_hlim <= IPV6_HLIMDEC) {
231                      /* XXX in6_ifstat_inc(rt->rt_ifp, ifs6_in_discard) */
232                      icmp6_error(m, ICMP6_TIME_EXCEEDED,
233                                       ICMP6_TIME_EXCEED_TRANSIT, 0);
234                      return;
235              }
236              ip6->ip6_hlim -= IPV6_HLIMDEC;
237
238              /*
239               * Save at most ICMPV6_PLD_MAXLEN (= the min IPv6 MTU -
240               * size of IPv6 + ICMPv6 headers) bytes of the packet in case
241               * we need to generate an ICMP6 message to the src.
242               * Thanks to M_EXT, in most cases copy will not occur.
243               *
244               * It is important to save it before IPsec processing as IPsec
245               * processing may modify the mbuf.
```

```
246                    */
247                    mcopy = m_copy(m, 0, imin(m->m_pkthdr.len, ICMPV6_PLD_MAXLEN));
```

(IPsec and Mobile IPv6 processing)
—— ip6_forward.c

230–236 An ICMPv6 Time Exceeded error will be returned to the source if the Hop Limit value left is equal to or smaller than 1 (`IPV6_HLIMDEC`). Otherwise, the Hop Limit field of the IPv6 header is decremented by 1 when the packet is forwarded.

247 The packet to be forwarded is copied to `mcopy`. The copied packet is used in case an ICMPv6 error message must be returned later in this process. The copy of the packet has to be kept at this point, since the packet may be processed by the IPsec tunnel function (see Listing 3-92), which may modify the original packet. It is hard or even impossible to recover the original packet on error, once the IPsec processing such as encryption and encapsulation is completed.

Listing 3-88
—— ip6_forward.c

```
464                    dst = (struct sockaddr_in6 *)&ip6_forward_rt.ro_dst;
465                    if (!srcrt) {
466                            /* ip6_forward_rt.ro_dst.sin6_addr is equal to ip6->ip6_dst */
467                            if (ip6_forward_rt.ro_rt == 0 ||
468                                !(ip6_forward_rt.ro_rt->rt_flags & RTF_UP)
469                                ) {
470                                    if (ip6_forward_rt.ro_rt) {
471                                            RTFREE(ip6_forward_rt.ro_rt);
472                                            ip6_forward_rt.ro_rt = 0;
473                                    }
474
475                                    /* this probably fails but give it a try again */
....
477                                    rtalloc_ign((struct route *)&ip6_forward_rt,
478                                            RTF_PRCLONING);
....
482                            }
483
484                            if (ip6_forward_rt.ro_rt == 0) {
485                                    ip6stat.ip6s_noroute++;
486                                    in6_ifstat_inc(m->m_pkthdr.rcvif, ifs6_in_noroute);
487                                    if (mcopy) {
488                                            icmp6_error(mcopy, ICMP6_DST_UNREACH,
489                                                    ICMP6_DST_UNREACH_NOROUTE, 0);
490                                    }
491                                    m_freem(m);
492                                    return;
493                            }
```
—— ip6_forward.c

465 Variable `ip6_forward_rt` holds a route to the destination of the forwarded packet (see Listing 3-24).

466–482 If the packet does not contain a Routing header, the destination address field of this structure should have been set in `ip6_input()` (Listing 3-24). It is also likely that a valid route is already stored for a reachable destination, but it is explicitly checked. If not, `rtalloc_ign()` tries to acquire a valid one, though this attempt cannot be expected to succeed if it did not succeed in `ip6_input()`. The `RTF_PRCLONING` flag indicates that a host route should not be cloned; it is used for maintaining per destination information at an end host, and is useless and a waste of memory for forwarding.

484–493 An ICMPv6 Destination Unreachable error will be sent if there is no route entry for the destination address of the packet.

Listing 3-89

```
                                                         ip6_forward.c
494                } else if ((rt = ip6_forward_rt.ro_rt) == 0 ||
495                        !(ip6_forward_rt.ro_rt->rt_flags & RTF_UP) ||
....
497                        !SA6_ARE_ADDR_EQUAL(&sa6_dst, dst)
....
501                ) {
502                if (ip6_forward_rt.ro_rt) {
503                        RTFREE(ip6_forward_rt.ro_rt);
504                        ip6_forward_rt.ro_rt = 0;
505                }
506                *dst = sa6_dst;
....
508                dst->sin6_scope_id = 0; /* XXX */
....
511                rtalloc_ign((struct route *)&ip6_forward_rt, RTF_PRCLONING);
....
515                if (ip6_forward_rt.ro_rt == 0) {
516                        ip6stat.ip6s_noroute++;
517                        in6_ifstat_inc(m->m_pkthdr.rcvif, ifs6_in_noroute);
518                        if (mcopy) {
519                                icmp6_error(mcopy, ICMP6_DST_UNREACH,
520                                        ICMP6_DST_UNREACH_NOROUTE, 0);
521                        }
522                        m_freem(m);
523                        return;
524                }
525        }
526        rt = ip6_forward_rt.ro_rt;
                                                         ip6_forward.c
```

494–501 When the packet is source routed with a Routing header, the destination address of the received packet (the sa6_dst variable) and the target address stored in ip6_forward_rt typically differ. In this case, a new route for the next route segment should be acquired.

Note: In the rare case of two addresses being the same, it is a route to an address of the node itself and a valid route should be stored. But this implementation checks the validity of the route anyway.

502–511 The previously stored route, if any, is freed, and a new route for the next segment is acquired by the rtalloc_ign() function. Note that the sin6_scope_id field must be cleared beforehand since the routing table routine expects the zone ID, if non-0, is embedded in the sin6_addr field and sin6_scope_id is 0 as explained in Section 2.9.3.

515–524 An ICMPv6 Destination Unreachable error will be sent if a route entry for the next segment address cannot be allocated.

Listing 3-90

ip6_forward.c

```
531              /*
532               * Source scope check: if a packet can't be delivered to its
533               * destination for the reason that the destination is beyond the scope
534               * of the source address, discard the packet and return an icmp6
535               * destination unreachable error with Code 2 (beyond scope of source
536               * address).
537               * [draft-ietf-ipngwg-icmp-v3-02.txt, Section 3.1]
538               */
539              if (in6_addr2zoneid(rt->rt_ifp, &ip6->ip6_src, &dstzone)) {
540                      /* XXX: this should not happen */
541                      ip6stat.ip6s_cantforward++;
542                      ip6stat.ip6s_badscope++;
543                      m_freem(m);
544                      return;
545              }
546              if (sa6_src.sin6_scope_id != dstzone) {
547                      ip6stat.ip6s_cantforward++;
548                      ip6stat.ip6s_badscope++;
549                      in6_ifstat_inc(rt->rt_ifp, ifs6_in_discard);
550
551                      if (ip6_log_time + ip6_log_interval < time_second) {
552                              ip6_log_time = time_second;
553                              log(LOG_DEBUG,
554                                  "cannot forward "
555                                  "src %s, dst %s, nxt %d, rcvif %s, outif %s\n",
556                                  ip6_sprintf(&ip6->ip6_src),
557                                  ip6_sprintf(&ip6->ip6_dst),
558                                  ip6->ip6_nxt,
559                                  if_name(m->m_pkthdr.rcvif), if_name(rt->rt_ifp));
560                      }
561                      if (mcopy)
562                              icmp6_error(mcopy, ICMP6_DST_UNREACH,
563                                      ICMP6_DST_UNREACH_BEYONDSCOPE, 0);
564                      m_freem(m);
565                      return;
566              }
```
ip6_forward.c

539–545 The `in6_addr2zoneid()` function determines the zone ID of the destination scope type for the outgoing interface. `dstzone` is set to the ID.

546–565 An IPv6 packet with a scoped source or destination address cannot be forwarded to different zones from the corresponding zones where the packet is originated (Section 2.4.1). The packet is discarded if the zone containing the incoming interface (`sa6_src.sin6_scope_id`) and the zone containing the outgoing interface (`dstzone`) differ. In addition, an ICMPv6 Destination Unreachable error indicating the packet would break a scope zone boundary will be returned to the source.

Figure 2-2 in Chapter 2 shows an example of this case. In the left side of the figure, a packet from the host A's link-local address is being forwarded to the host B's global address. In this case, dstzone is set to the router's link zone ID for the lower link at line 539. On the other hand, `sa6_src.sin6_scope_id` should be set to the router's zone ID for the upper link in `ip6_input()`. Since these IDs do not match, the packet is discarded with an ICMPv6 error.

Listing 3-91

```
                                                                    ip6_forward.c
568                 /*
569                  * Destination scope check: if a packet is going to break the scope
570                  * zone of packet's destination address, discard it.  This case should
571                  * usually be prevented by appropriately-configured routing table, but
572                  * we need an explicit check because we may mistakenly forward the
573                  * packet to a different zone by (e.g.) a default route.
574                  */
575                 if (in6_addr2zoneid(rt->rt_ifp, &ip6->ip6_dst, &dstzone) ||
576                     sa6_dst.sin6_scope_id != dstzone) {
577                         ip6stat.ip6s_cantforward++;
578                         ip6stat.ip6s_badscope++;
579                         m_freem(m);
580                         return;
581                 }
                                                                    ip6_forward.c
```

575–581 Similarly, the zone index of the destination address of the packet must be checked. The packet is dropped if the zone containing the outgoing interface and the zone containing the incoming interface differ.

Recalling Figure 2-2 again, this check prevents the packet in the right side from being forwarded outside of the originating zone (e.g., to a lower link of the router). As commented, an appropriately configured routing table should not have a route entry that causes this type of invalid forwarding. It should still be checked explicitly, since a misconfigured route, especially created by hand, can cause this.

Listing 3-92

```
                                                                    ip6_forward.c
583                     if (m->m_pkthdr.len > IN6_LINKMTU(rt->rt_ifp)) {
584                             in6_ifstat_inc(rt->rt_ifp, ifs6_in_toobig);
585                             if (mcopy) {
586                                     u_long mtu;
....
592
593                                     mtu = IN6_LINKMTU(rt->rt_ifp);

.... (IPsec processing)

618                                     icmp6_error(mcopy, ICMP6_PACKET_TOO_BIG, 0, mtu);
619                             }
620                             m_freem(m);
621                             return;
622                     }
                                                                    ip6_forward.c
```

583–622 An IPv6 router does not fragment a forwarded packet (Section 3.3.5). An ICMPv6 Packet Too Big error containing the MTU size of the outgoing link will be generated if the size of the packet to be forwarded is larger than the link MTU size.

Listing 3-93

```
                                                                    ip6_forward.c
624                     if (rt->rt_flags & RTF_GATEWAY)
625                             dst = (struct sockaddr_in6 *)rt->rt_gateway;
                                                                    ip6_forward.c
```

624–625 If the next hop toward the destination is another router, `dst` is reset to the address of the next hop.

Listing 3-94
_____ip6_forward.c

```
627             /*
628              * If we are to forward the packet using the same interface
629              * as one we got the packet from, perhaps we should send a redirect
630              * to sender to shortcut a hop.
631              * Only send redirect if source is sending directly to us,
632              * and if packet was not source routed (or has any options).
633              * Also, don't send redirect if forwarding using a route
634              * modified by a redirect.
635              */
636             if (rt->rt_ifp == m->m_pkthdr.rcvif && !srcrt &&
....
643                 (rt->rt_flags & (RTF_DYNAMIC|RTF_MODIFIED)) == 0) {
644                 if ((rt->rt_ifp->if_flags & IFF_POINTOPOINT) &&
645                     nd6_is_addr_neighbor(&sa6_dst, rt->rt_ifp)) {
646                     /*
647                      * If the incoming interface is equal to the outgoing
648                      * one, the link attached to the interface is
649                      * point-to-point, and the IPv6 destination is
650                      * regarded as on-link on the link, then it will be
651                      * highly probable that the destination address does
652                      * not exist on the link and that the packet is going
653                      * to loop.  Thus, we immediately drop the packet and
654                      * send an ICMPv6 error message.
655                      * For other routing loops, we dare to let the packet
656                      * go to the loop, so that a remote diagnosing host
657                      * can detect the loop by traceroute.
658                      * type/code is based on suggestion by Rich Draves.
659                      * not sure if it is the best pick.
660                      */
661                     icmp6_error(mcopy, ICMP6_DST_UNREACH,
662                             ICMP6_DST_UNREACH_ADDR, 0);
663                     m_freem(m);
664                     return;
665                 }
666                 type = ND_REDIRECT;
667             }
```
_____ip6_forward.c

636–667 A router may need to send an ICMPv6 Redirect message, while still forwarding the packet, when `rt->rt_ifp` equals `m_pkthdr.rcvif`, that is, when it forwards a packet back to the incoming interface and the packet is not source routed with a Routing header. Variable `type` records the case. If, however, the interface attaches to a point-to-point link and the destination address of the packet is considered to be a neighbor on the link, the packet is discarded and an ICMPv6 Destination Unreachable error is returned instead of a Redirect message. This behavior was not described in the original specification of ICMPv6 [RFC2463], but has been added to a revised version of the specification [RFC4443] due to the problem described below.

The additional check prevents the following scenario (Figure 3-20): Consider a point-to-point link on which an IPv6 subnet `2001:db8:1:2::/64` is assigned. Two routers, R1 and R2, are located at the ends of the link with IPv6 addresses from the subnet prefix. Now assume R1 receives a packet to `2001:db8:1:2::1`. Since the destination address is not assigned to R1 but matches the subnet prefix on the point-to-point link, R1 forwards the packet toward R2. R2 performs the same thing except the outgoing interface equals the incoming interface. But it is unlikely that the forwarded packet is eventually delivered to the destination, since the next hop should be R1, whichwould then forward the packet

FIGURE 3-20

Forwarding loop on a point-to-point interface.

back to R2. This process continues until the hop limit decreases to 0, wasting the link bandwidth and processing resources of the routers.

Other conditions on whether to send a Redirect message will be checked in the `icmp6_redirect_output()` function (Section 5.16.8).

Note: The check about the `RTF_DYNAMIC` and `RTF_MODIFIED` flags (line 643) was probably simply copied from the corresponding IPv4 code that intends to avoid sending a Redirect message based on a route created by a different Redirect message from a different router. In IPv6, however, this check is almost meaningless, since a router must not change its routing table based on a received Redirect message, and this implementation in fact ignores it (Section 5.16.7). The only possible concern is the case when a host that modified its routing table due to a Redirect message has dynamically become a router via a `sysctl` operation, while the check at line 643 does not seem to intend to address such a rare case.

Listing 3-95
```
                                                                   ip6_forward.c
688            /*
689             * Fake scoped addresses. Note that even link-local source or
690             * destinaion can appear, if the originating node just sends the
691             * packet to us (without address resolution for the destination).
692             * Since both icmp6_error and icmp6_redirect_output fill the embedded
693             * link identifiers, we can do this stuff after making a copy for
694             * returning an error.
695             */
696            if ((rt->rt_ifp->if_flags & IFF_LOOPBACK) != 0) {
697                    /*
698                     * See corresponding comments in ip6_output.
699                     * XXX: but is it possible that ip6_forward() sends a packet
700                     *      to a loopback interface? I don't think so, and thus
701                     *      I bark here. (jinmei@kame.net)
702                     * XXX: it is common to route invalid packets to loopback.
703                     *      also, the codepath will be visited on use of ::1 in
704                     *      rthdr. (itojun)
705                     */
....
719
720                    /* we can just use rcvif in forwarding. */
721                    origifp = m->m_pkthdr.rcvif;
722            }
723            else
```

```
724                         origifp = rt->rt_ifp;
....
726             /*
727              * clear embedded scope identifiers if necessary.
728              * in6_clearscope will touch the addresses only when necessary.
729              */
730             in6_clearscope(&ip6->ip6_src);
731             in6_clearscope(&ip6->ip6_dst);
```
———————————————————————————————————— ip6_forward.c

696–724 The outgoing interface of the searched route (the rt_ifp member of the route entry) may point to a loopback interface if, although atypical, the received packet has a Routing header and the next route segment is the forwarding node itself. In this case, the packet will be looped back and eventually be processed in the ip6_input() function. Since ip6_input() expects the "real" interface to which the address belongs for proper identification of scope zone (see Listing 3-22), it is saved in origifp separately. This variable will be passed to the nd6_output() function below, and then be set in the loopback packet as the "incoming interface."

730–731 The Source and the Destination Address fields of the IPv6 header may contain the corresponding scope zone IDs. These are only meaningful within the node, and must be removed by the in6_clearscope() function before the packet is sent to the interface layer.

Listing 3-96
———————————————————————————————————— ip6_forward.c

```
772             error = nd6_output(rt->rt_ifp, origifp, m, dst, rt);
773             if (error) {
774                     in6_ifstat_inc(rt->rt_ifp, ifs6_out_discard);
775                     ip6stat.ip6s_cantforward++;
776             } else {
777                     ip6stat.ip6s_forward++;
778                     in6_ifstat_inc(rt->rt_ifp, ifs6_out_forward);
779                     if (type)
780                             ip6stat.ip6s_redirectsent++;
781                     else {
782                             if (mcopy)
783                                     goto freecopy;
784                     }
785             }
....
790             if (mcopy == NULL)
791                     return;
792             switch (error) {
793             case 0:
794                     if (type == ND_REDIRECT) {
795                             icmp6_redirect_output(mcopy, rt);
796                             return;
797                     }
798                     goto freecopy;
799
800             case EMSGSIZE:
801                     /* xxx MTU is constant in PPP? */
802                     goto freecopy;
803
804             case ENOBUFS:
805                     /* Tell source to slow down like source quench in IP? */
806                     goto freecopy;
807
808             case ENETUNREACH:       /* shouldn't happen, checked above */
```

```
809            case EHOSTUNREACH:
810            case ENETDOWN:
811            case EHOSTDOWN:
812            default:
813                    type = ICMP6_DST_UNREACH;
814                    code = ICMP6_DST_UNREACH_ADDR;
815                    break;
816            }
817            icmp6_error(mcopy, type, code, 0);
818            return;
819
820    freecopy:
821            m_freem(mcopy);
822            return;
823    }
```
                                                          _____ ip6_forward.c

772–798 The received packet is sent to the outgoing link toward the next hop by the `nd6_output()` function (Section 5.22.2). It should be noted that this function does not have to call `ip6_output()`, unlike the IPv4 implementation where `ip_forward()` calls `ip_output()`, because an IPv6 router does not need to fragment a forwarded packet.

The copied packet which was prepared for an ICMPv6 error message is freed if the packet is forwarded properly and there was no need for a Redirect message; the `icmp6_redirect_output()` function (Section 5.16.8) is called if forwarding was successful but a Redirect message may need to be returned.

Note: Counting the statistics for output Redirect messages at line 780 is actually too early, since `icmp6_redirect_output()` may not send the message as a result of additional checks.

800–822 When `nd6_output()` failed with an error of ENETUNREACH, EHOSTUNREACH, ENETDOWN, or EHOSTDOWN, an ICMPv6 Destination Unreachable message is returned to the source.

Other error codes are not handled and the forwarding procedure just terminates. The explicit case of EMSGSIZE has been in the source code since the very early stages of the KAME implementation. This was probably simply copied from the corresponding IPv4 implementation (`ip_forward()`), which can get a return value of EMSGSIZE from `ip_output()`. In KAME's IPv6 implementation, however, this is not the case and an error of too large packet for the outgoing case is handled explicitly within this function. This EMSGSIZE case should therefore be redundant.

Similarly, the case of ENOBUFS was probably here from an analogy of the IPv4 implementation that caught this error and sent an ICMP Source Quench message to the source under some conditions. However, ICMPv6 does not define a Source Quench message(*), so this case should also be redundant.

(*) In fact, the use of the Source Quench message is discouraged even in IPv4 [RFC1812], and the lack of this message in ICMPv6 is a deliberate decision.

3.13 Output Processing

In the rest of this chapter, we will describe implementation details of output packet processing at the IPv6 layer. The main routine of this processing is the `ip6_output()` function, which is the common interface for outgoing packets from upper layer protocols (see Figure 3-14).

On one hand, the processing of this function is similar to the IPv4 equivalent, `ip_output()`: IP header initialization including option processing, route selection, fragmenting the packet if necessary, and transmitting it to the link-layer. On the other hand, there are some remarkable differences in detail:

- Unlike IPv4 options, inserting extension headers is a more general and complicated operation. `ip6_output()` needs help from some subroutines for this purpose. This is also the case for packet fragmentation.

- As already seen in Section 3.4.2, source address selection for IPv6 is more complex than for IPv4 due to various candidate addresses with different properties. The KAME implementation thus provides a dedicated public function called `in6_selectsrc()` to perform the selection algorithm.

- The address selection algorithm often requires the determination of the outgoing interface, which subsequently often requires route selection. In the KAME implementation, this is also done by a separate function, `in6_selectroute()`, called as an implicit subroutine of `in6_selectsrc()` (see Figure 3-21 on page 220).

- Unlike IPv4, most upper layer protocols over IPv6 have to calculate upper layer checksums including IPv6 source and destination addresses (see Section 6.4). The source address selection algorithm is thus often performed in the upper layer output processing. As a result of this and the previous point, it is less common that `ip6_output()` needs to call `in6_selectroute()`.

Applications can specify extension headers to be included in outgoing IPv6 packets via the standard API (Section 7.3.4). This API also provides means for specifying other parameters of outgoing packets such as the Hop Limit value. Such optional parameters are passed to `ip6_output()` via the `ip6_pktopts{}` structure (Section 7.4.2). We call the information stored in this structure *packet options*.

3.13.1 Source Address Selection—`in6_selectsrc()` Function

As explained above, often the source address selection algorithm is the first phase of IPv6 output processing. We begin with the implementation of the selection algorithm as an introduction to the entire output procedure.

Address Selection Policy Structure

Each address selection policy (see Section 3.4.1) is represented by the `in6_addrpolicy{}` structure as shown below. This is a straightforward representation of a policy table entry with a statistics member.

FIGURE 3-21

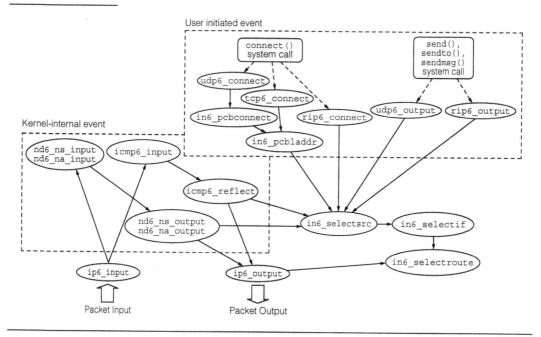

Call graph around `in6_selectsrc()`.

Listing 3-97

—— in6_var.h
```
130     /* control structure to manage address selection policy */
131     struct in6_addrpolicy {
132             struct sockaddr_in6 addr; /* prefix address */
133             struct sockaddr_in6 addrmask; /* prefix mask */
134             int preced;                     /* precedence */
135             int label;                      /* matching label */
136             u_quad_t use;                   /* statistics */
137     };
```
—— in6_var.h

The `addr` member holds the address prefix and `addrmask` is the associated prefix mask.
Members `preced` and `label` contain the precedence and label values. The `use` member is
incremented every time a particular policy entry was selected.

The policy table is implemented as a double linked list and is accessed through the global
variable `addrsel_policytab`. Each table entry is represented by the `addrsel_policyent{}`
structure, shown below.

Listing 3-98

—— in6_src.c
```
1450    /*
1451     * The followings are implementation of the policy table using a
1452     * simple tail queue.
1453     * XXX such details should be hidden.
1454     * XXX implementation using binary tree should be more efficient.
1455     */
```

```
1456    struct addrsel_policyent {
1457            TAILQ_ENTRY(addrsel_policyent) ape_entry;
1458            struct in6_addrpolicy ape_policy;
1459    };
1460
1461    TAILQ_HEAD(addrsel_policyhead, addrsel_policyent);
1462
1463    struct addrsel_policyhead addrsel_policytab;
```
─── in6_src.c

The `ape_entry` member links a table entry to its predecessor and its successor. The `ape_policy` member points to an instance of the `in6_addrpolicy{}` structure containing the policy. As the code comment indicates, the current policy table implementation may be inefficient due to the use of linear search when performing table lookup. Since the policy table search uses the longest prefix matching, a patricia tree implementation would be more efficient and can handle more policy entries. In practice, however, the details of the structure do not matter much because the number of entries is typically expected to be small; in fact, the default policy table (Table 3-4) only contains five entries.

The `ip6addrctl` program utilizes the `in6_addrpolicy{}` structure to install and to remove policy entries from the policy table that is maintained by the kernel. The **ip6addrctl** program opens an `AF_INET6` socket and issues the `SIOCAADDRCTL_POLICY` ioctl command over the socket to install a policy entry into the policy table. The command argument is a pointer to an `in6_addrpolicy{}` structure containing the policy to be added. Similarly, the **ip6addrctl** program issues the `SIODADDRCTL_POLICY` ioctl command over the socket to remove a policy entry from the policy table. The command argument is a pointer to an `in6_addrpolicy{}` structure containing the policy to be deleted.

Listing 3-99

─── in6_src.c
```
1393    SYSCTL_NODE(_net_inet6_ip6, IPV6CTL_ADDRCTLPOLICY, addrctlpolicy,
1394            CTLFLAG_RD, in6_src_sysctl, "");
```
─── in6_src.c

The source address selection module defines a `sysctl` name `IPV6CTL_ADDRCTLPOLICY` under the `net.inet6.ip6` level for accessing the kernel-internal policy table. As shown at line 1394, this `sysctl` name is read-only.

The **ip6addrctl** command, invoked without any argument, translates into a call to `sysctl` call with the `IPV6CTL_ADDRCTLPOLICY` name, which subsequently copies the kernel-internal policy table into the buffer supplied by **ip6addrctl**. The content of this buffer is displayed as the output of **ip6addrctl** as shown in Section 3.4.1.

in6_selectsrc() *Function*

We are now ready to describe the details of the `in6_selectsrc()` function. We begin with the following macros, which are used extensively in this function.

Listing 3-100

─── in6_src.c
```
168     #define REPLACE(r) do {\
169             if ((r) < sizeof(ip6stat.ip6s_sources_rule) / \
170                     sizeof(ip6stat.ip6s_sources_rule[0])) /* check for safety */ \
```

```
171                           ip6stat.ip6s_sources_rule[(r)]++; \
173                goto replace; \
174        } while(0)
175        #define NEXT(r) do {\
176                if ((r) < sizeof(ip6stat.ip6s_sources_rule) / \
177                    sizeof(ip6stat.ip6s_sources_rule[0])) /* check for safety */ \
178                        ip6stat.ip6s_sources_rule[(r)]++; \
180                goto next;         /* XXX: we can't use 'continue' here */ \
181        } while(0)
182        #define BREAK(r) do { \
183                if ((r) < sizeof(ip6stat.ip6s_sources_rule) / \
184                    sizeof(ip6stat.ip6s_sources_rule[0])) /* check for safety */ \
185                        ip6stat.ip6s_sources_rule[(r)]++; \
186                goto out;          /* XXX: we can't use 'break' here */ \
187        } while(0)
```
———————————————————————————————— in6_src.c

168–187 The `ip6stat{}` structure maintains a set of counters that keep track of the number of times each address selection rule is applied. Each of these macros first verifies that the rule number is valid, then the associated counter is updated in the `ip6s_sources_rule` array included in the `ip6stat{}` structure. The `REPLACE()` macro is used when the currently examined address is more preferable to the best candidate found so far; the `NEXT()` macro is used when the known best candidate should still be preferred; the `BREAK()` macro indicates that the selection procedure can terminate with the currently examined address being selected.

Function `in6_selectsrc()` is called from various output functions to choose the source address for an outgoing packet. There are two kinds of events which call `in6_selectsec()`. One is events inside the kernel. For example, an incoming Neighbor Solicitation message and an ICMPv6 Echo Request message, which subsequently cause response packets generated inside the kernel, are categorized into this type. In this case, the output functions implemented in the kernel are directly called via the input processing routines, which calls `in6_selectsrc()` to determine the source address of the response packet. The other kind of events is initiated by a user space program. For example, when a process sends a datagram to a socket with the local address unspecified, `in6_selectsrc()` is called in the output path of the protocol output functions. The other possibility is a result of issuing the `connect()` system call; `in6_selectsrc()` is called when a local address is assigned to a socket before the assignment of the remote address. Figure 3-21 shows a call graph around the `in6_selectsrc()` function, summarizing the various scenarios.

Listing 3-101
———————————————————————————————— in6_src.c

```
189    struct sockaddr_in6 *
190    in6_selectsrc(dstsock, opts, mopts, ro, laddr, ifpp, errorp)
191            struct sockaddr_in6 *dstsock, *laddr;
192            struct ip6_pktopts *opts;
193            struct ip6_moptions *mopts;
....
195            struct route *ro;
....
199            struct ifnet **ifpp;
200            int *errorp;
```
———————————————————————————————— in6_src.c

189 The return value of `in6_selectsrc()` is a pointer to the `sockaddr_in6{}` structure that should be used as the source address for a packet to the given destination. As described below, this structure will typically be a part of the IPv6 interface address structure, `in6_ifaddr{}`, maintained in the system (see Section 2.10.1). This structure may not be really convenient for the caller because it is not in the general format used in the IPv6 protocol stack regarding the scope zone ID as explained in Section 2.9.3. In fact, the calling functions then need to convert the returned address into the general format (see, for example, Sections 4.8.3 and 6.7.4).

190–200 Parameter `dstsock` holds the destination address for which the source address selection will be performed; `opts` holds the packet option that may provide information for overriding address preference and indicating the reachability of the local address; `mopts` holds multicast packet options and is applicable to the address selection process if the destination address is a multicast address; `ro` is routing information provided by the upper layer, which will assist in the selection of the outgoing interface; `laddr` is non-NULL when the packet that triggers source address selection is sent via a socket, and points to the local address space of the corresponding Protocol Control Block (PCB). The outgoing interface that is chosen by the address selection will be saved in `ifpp`. The function return code is saved in `errorp`.

As will soon be shown, the source address selection procedure for a given destination often requires the outgoing interface to which a packet to the destination would be sent. Also, the outgoing interface is often derived from the routing table entry specifying the next hop node to route the packet. As a result, the address selection algorithm can involve the determination of the outgoing interface and route lookups. Since the caller of this function typically needs such information, this function has the two related arguments for efficiency: `ro` and `ifp`. If the caller has a cached route for the destination in `ro`, `in6_selectsrc()` can use it; on the other hand, if the caller has not cached a route, `in6_selectsrc()` acquires one if necessary and returns it to the caller via `ro` so that the caller can use the route for output processing. Similarly, if `in6_selectsrc()` determines the outgoing interface during the selection procedure, it returns the interface to the caller via the `ifpp` pointer for the caller's convenience.

Listing 3-102

```
                                                                    in6_src.c
201     {
202             struct in6_addr *dst;
203             struct ifnet *ifp = NULL;
204             struct in6_ifaddr *ia = NULL, *ia_best = NULL;
205             struct in6_pktinfo *pi = NULL;
206             int dst_scope = -1, best_scope = -1, best_matchlen = -1;
207             struct in6_addrpolicy *dst_policy = NULL, *best_policy = NULL;
208             u_int32_t odstzone;
209             int prefer_tempaddr;
...
215
216             dst = &dstsock->sin6_addr;
217             *errorp = 0;
218             if (ifpp)
219                     *ifpp = NULL;
                                                                    in6_src.c
```

202–209 Local variable `ia_best` stores the current most preferred source address. Variables `best_scope` and `best_matchlen` store the corresponding address scope and the length of matching prefix respectively. These variables can be updated when a better address is encountered in the selection procedure. We will refer to these variables as the *comparison state variables* in the following discussion.

Listing 3-103
_____ in6_src.c

```
221    /*
222     * If the source address is explicitly specified by the caller,
223     * check if the requested source address is indeed a unicast address
224     * assigned to the node, and can be used as the packet's source
225     * address.  If everything is okay, use the address as source.
226     */
227    if (opts && (pi = opts->ip6po_pktinfo) &&
228        !IN6_IS_ADDR_UNSPECIFIED(&pi->ipi6_addr)) {
229            struct sockaddr_in6 srcsock;
230            struct in6_ifaddr *ia6;
231
232            /* get the outgoing interface */
233            if ((*errorp = in6_selectif(dstsock, opts, mopts, ro, &ifp))
234                != 0) {
235                    return (NULL);
236            }
237
238            /*
239             * determine the appropriate zone id of the source based on
240             * the zone of the destination and the outgoing interface.
241             */
242            bzero(&srcsock, sizeof(srcsock));
243            srcsock.sin6_family = AF_INET6;
244            srcsock.sin6_len = sizeof(srcsock);
245            srcsock.sin6_addr = pi->ipi6_addr;
246            if (ifp) {
247                    if (in6_addr2zoneid(ifp, &pi->ipi6_addr,
248                                        &srcsock.sin6_scope_id)) {
249                            *errorp = EINVAL; /* XXX */
250                            return (NULL);
251                    }
252            }
253            if ((*errorp = in6_embedscope(&srcsock.sin6_addr, &srcsock))
254                != 0) {
255                    return (NULL);
256            }
257            srcsock.sin6_scope_id = 0; /* XXX: ifa_ifwithaddr expects 0 */
....
260            ia6 = (struct in6_ifaddr *)ifa_ifwithaddr((struct sockaddr *)(&srcsock));
261            if (ia6 == NULL ||
262                (ia6->ia6_flags & (IN6_IFF_ANYCAST | IN6_IFF_NOTREADY))) {
263                    *errorp = EADDRNOTAVAIL;
264                    return (NULL);
265            }
266            pi->ipi6_addr = srcsock.sin6_addr; /* XXX: this overrides pi */
267            if (ifpp)
268                    *ifpp = ifp;
269            return (&ia6->ia_addr);
270    }
```
_____ in6_src.c

227–230 [RFC3542] allows an application to specify the source address in the `ipi6_addr` member of the `in6_pktinfo{}` structure for an output operation (see Section 7.3.4).

In this case, the kernel is required to verify that the requested source address is a unicast address and has been assigned to the node. The rest of this code block performs the verification.

232–236 Since the specified IPv6 address is represented in the in6_addr{} structure, it may be ambiguous about its scope zone. In order to resolve the possible ambiguity, the in6_selectif() function is called to retrieve the appropriate outgoing interface for the given destination address, taking into account the packet options and the supplied route information.

242–252 Variable srcsock stores the address in the form of a sockaddr_in6{} structure. Based on the outgoing interface, function in6_addr2zoneid() will determine the appropriate scope zone ID for the requested source address. The zone ID is set in the sockaddr_in6{} structure.

253–256 srcsock will be passed to ifa_ifwithaddr() below, which requires the zone ID be embedded in the sin6_addr field and the sin6_scope_id field be 0 (see Section 2.9.3). The in6_embedscope() function embeds the zone ID in the address field.

258–265 Function ifa_ifwithaddr() is called to verify that the requested source address is assigned to one of the interfaces belonging to the node. An anycast address cannot be used as the source address as explained in Section 2.2 and is rejected here. (Note that the implementation follows the restriction described in [RFC3513].) The IN6_IFF_NOTREADY flag set indicates other types of unusable addresses (see Table 2-8), and an address that matches this set is also rejected(*). If any of these checks fail, an error of EADDRNOTAVAIL is returned.

(*) The IN6_IFF_DETACHED flag should also be checked here (see Listing 3-109).

266 The 128-bit IPv6 address stored in srcsock is written back to the in6_pktinfo{} structure. Note that this may be different from the original value if in6_embedscope() embedded the zone ID in the address field above. As commented, this may be a bad practice in that the original value stored in the PCB as a socket option can be modified (when it is set as a socket option).

267–269 If the caller wants to get the outgoing interface as an optional side effect, the retrieved pointer is set in the specified storage. The address selection process terminates by returning a pointer to the sockaddr_in6 structure given by ifa_ifwithaddr() above.

Listing 3-104

in6_src.c
```
272        /*
273         * Otherwise, if the socket has already bound the source, just use it.
274         */
275        if (laddr && !SA6_IS_ADDR_UNSPECIFIED(laddr))
276                return (laddr);
```
in6_src.c

275–276 If a specific address has already been bound to the socket, that address is simply returned. This is the only successful case when the returned address does not come from the `in6_ifaddr{}` structure.

It should also be noted that the selection procedure so far ensures that a source address explicitly specified via the `IPV6_PKTINFO` socket option or an ancillary data item precedes the socket's local address even if the socket is bound. This preference ordering is on purpose and indeed follows the description of [RFC3542].

The rest of this function performs address selection procedure mainly as described in [RFC3484] (see Section 3.4.2). It first acquires some necessary parameters, and then finds the best address assigned to the node as the source address with the given destination address.

Listing 3-105
in6_src.c
```
278                 /*
279                  * If the address is not specified, choose the best one based on
280                  * the outgoing interface and the destination address.
281                  */
282                 /* get the outgoing interface */
283                 if ((*errorp = in6_selectif(dstsock, opts, mopts, ro, &ifp)) != 0)
284                         return (NULL);
```
in6_src.c

283–284 The address selection algorithm often requires the outgoing interface for the destination address. The `in6_selectif()` function determines the interface as shown in Listing 3-103. If it cannot determine the interface, `in6_selectsrc()` also fails and returns the error code from `in6_selectif()` to the caller.

Note: This part of the code indicates that a system call to `connect()` for an unreachable destination fails even if the call does not cause packet output processing (e.g., for a `connect()` call on a UDP socket). This does not match the traditional BSD kernel behavior for IPv4 that allows such a call to an unreachable address. However, it in fact conforms to the POSIX standard that requires that the call shall fail for an unreachable destination. Recent versions of FreeBSD also adopt this behavior for IPv4. Yet the returned error code in this case may not be very accurate in terms of the API standard as will be seen in Section 3.13.2, this implementation generally returns an error of `EHOSTUNREACH` for an unreachable destination while the standard specifies `ENETUNREACH` in this case.

Listing 3-106
in6_src.c
```
317                 if (in6_addr2zoneid(ifp, dst, &odstzone)) { /* impossible */
318                         *errorp = EIO; /* XXX */
319                         return (NULL);
320                 }
```
in6_src.c

317–320 The `in6_addr2zoneid()` function (Section 2.9.4) returns the scope zone ID for the scope type of `dst` on interface `ifp` in `odstzone`. Since the only case where `in6_addr2zoneid()` fails is when the address is the loopback address but `ifp` is not a loopback interface, it should normally not happen here with `in6_selectif()` having succeeded. It can still occur, however, due to a misconfigured routing table or when an application erroneously specifies a non-loopback interface with the loopback address being the destination. An error of `EIO` will be returned in such cases.

Listing 3-107

```
                                                                    in6_src.c
321          for (ia = in6_ifaddr; ia; ia = ia->ia_next) {
322                  int new_scope = -1, new_matchlen = -1;
323                  struct in6_addrpolicy *new_policy = NULL;
324                  u_int32_t srczone, osrczone, dstzone;
325                  struct ifnet *ifp1 = ia->ia_ifp;
                                                                    in6_src.c
```

321–325 The selection algorithm in this implementation treats all of the assigned addresses as potential source addresses. Variable `ia` holds the address to be examined by the selection algorithm and `ifp1` is the interface to which `ia` is assigned.

Listing 3-108

```
                                                                    in6_src.c
327          /*
328           * We'll never take an address that breaks the scope zone
329           * of the destination.  We also skip an address if its zone
330           * does not contain the outgoing interface.
331           * XXX: we should probably use sin6_scope_id here.
332           */
333          if (in6_addr2zoneid(ifp1, dst, &dstzone) ||
334              odstzone != dstzone) {
335                  continue;
336          }
337          if (in6_addr2zoneid(ifp, &ia->ia_addr.sin6_addr, &osrczone) ||
338              in6_addr2zoneid(ifp1, &ia->ia_addr.sin6_addr, &srczone) ||
339              osrczone != srczone) {
340                  continue;
341          }
                                                                    in6_src.c
```

333–336 If the interface of the candidate source address belongs to a different scope zone (`dstzone`) than that of the scope type of the destination (`odstzone`), that candidate source address is ignored.

Note: This check is probably overkilling. Recall the example zone configuration shown in Figure 2-5, and assume the only global address on this node is configured on the loopback interface. If an application sends a packet to site-local multicast address to the PPP interface, the most desirable source address would be the global address since otherwise the packet will not be delivered beyond the direct link. However, the above check rejects this address as a candidate because in this case `odstzone` is 2 and `dstzone` is 1. It should be better to keep this address as a candidate unless it clearly breaks some scope zone boundary.

337–341 If the scope zone of the candidate source address does not contain the outgoing interface, this address is ignored. In particular, this check excludes link-local addresses whose link is different from the outgoing link. Unlike the previous check, this one is necessary in order to ensure the source address does not break its scope zone.

Listing 3-109
_____ in6_src.c

```
343                        /* avoid unusable addresses */
344                        if ((ia->ia6_flags &
345                            (IN6_IFF_NOTREADY | IN6_IFF_ANYCAST | IN6_IFF_DETACHED))) {
346                                    continue;
347                        }
```
_____ in6_src.c

343–347 Unusable addresses are also rejected as we saw in Listing 3-103. The IN6_IFF_DETACHED flag is also checked, since it means the kernel detects that the node has probably moved from the network where this address was assigned and this address is likely unworkable.

Listing 3-110
_____ in6_src.c

```
348                        if (!ip6_use_deprecated && IFA6_IS_DEPRECATED(ia))
349                                    continue;
```
_____ in6_src.c

348–349 ip6_use_deprecated controls whether a "new communication" can be initiated with a deprecated source address (Section 2.10.1) in some cases(*). It defaults to 1, meaning it can, but a deprecated address is rejected here as a candidate if this variable is explicitly set to 0.

(*) The semantics of "new communication" is vague in [RFC2462], but in this chapter we use this term in the context of an outgoing packet whose source address is not yet determined.

Listing 3-111
_____ in6_src.c

```
351                        /* Rule 1: Prefer same address */
352                        if (IN6_ARE_ADDR_EQUAL(dst, &ia->ia_addr.sin6_addr)) {
353                                    ia_best = ia;
354                                    BREAK(1); /* there should be no better candidate */
355                        }
```
_____ in6_src.c

351–355 The code block implements Rule 1 of the source address selection algorithm. In this case, the potential address is the same as the destination address, which is the best address to use as the source address. The selection process terminates here. Rule 1 applies to the case where two processes within a node try to communicate with one another. In this case the source and the destination addresses will be the same.

Listing 3-112

_____in6_src.c
```
357                       if (ia_best == NULL)
358                               REPLACE(0);
```
_____in6_src.c

357–358 If the current address is the first address being examined, variables `ia_best`, `best_matchlen`, and `best_scope` are simply initialized. No comparison is necessary.

Listing 3-113

_____in6_src.c
```
360                       /* Rule 2: Prefer appropriate scope */
361                       if (dst_scope < 0)
362                               dst_scope = in6_addrscope(dst);
363                       new_scope = in6_addrscope(&ia->ia_addr.sin6_addr);
364                       if (IN6_ARE_SCOPE_CMP(best_scope, new_scope) < 0) {
365                               if (IN6_ARE_SCOPE_CMP(best_scope, dst_scope) < 0)
366                                       REPLACE(2);
367                               NEXT(2);
368                       } else if (IN6_ARE_SCOPE_CMP(new_scope, best_scope) < 0) {
369                               if (IN6_ARE_SCOPE_CMP(new_scope, dst_scope) < 0)
370                                       NEXT(2);
371                               REPLACE(2);
372                       }
```
_____in6_src.c

361–372 This code block is a straightforward implementation of Rule 2.

Listing 3-114

_____in6_src.c
```
374                       /*
375                        * Rule 3: Avoid deprecated addresses.  Note that the case of
376                        * !ip6_use_deprecated is already rejected above.
377                        */
378                       if (!IFA6_IS_DEPRECATED(ia_best) && IFA6_IS_DEPRECATED(ia))
379                               NEXT(3);
380                       if (IFA6_IS_DEPRECATED(ia_best) && !IFA6_IS_DEPRECATED(ia))
381                               REPLACE(3);
```
_____in6_src.c

378–381 This code block implements Rule 3. Note that this rule only applies when `ip6_use_deprecated` is set to non-0.

Listing 3-115

_____in6_src.c
```
383                       /* Rule 4: Prefer home addresses */
384                       /*
385                        * XXX: This is a TODO.  We should probably merge the MIP6
386                        * case above.
387                        */
388   #ifdef MIP6
      (omitted)
527   #endif /* MIP6 */
```
_____in6_src.c

383–527 Rule 4 is related to Mobile IPv6. This case is out of scope of this chapter and is omitted.

Listing 3-116

in6_src.c

```
529                     /* Rule 5: Prefer outgoing interface */
530                     if (ia_best->ia_ifp == ifp && ia->ia_ifp != ifp)
531                             NEXT(5);
532                     if (ia_best->ia_ifp != ifp && ia->ia_ifp == ifp)
533                             REPLACE(5);
```

in6_src.c

529–533 This code block is a straightforward implementation of Rule 5. `ifp` points to the outgoing interface acquired in Listing 3-105.

Listing 3-117

in6_src.c

```
535                     /*
536                      * Rule 6: Prefer matching label
537                      * Note that best_policy should be non-NULL here.
538                      */
539                     if (dst_policy == NULL)
540                             dst_policy = lookup_addrsel_policy(dstsock);
541                     if (dst_policy->label != ADDR_LABEL_NOTAPP) {
542                             new_policy = lookup_addrsel_policy(&ia->ia_addr);
543                             if (dst_policy->label == best_policy->label &&
544                                 dst_policy->label != new_policy->label)
545                                     NEXT(6);
546                             if (dst_policy->label != best_policy->label &&
547                                 dst_policy->label == new_policy->label)
548                                     REPLACE(6);
549                     }
```

in6_src.c

539–540 The `lookup_addrsel_policy()` function searches in the policy table for the policy entry that best matches the given address. If the given address does not match any entry, `lookup_addrsel_policy()` returns a dummy entry whose label is `ADDR_LABEL_NOTAPP`. The policy entry for the destination address is stored in `dst_policy`.

541-549 This code block is a straightforward implementation of Rule 6.

Listing 3-118

in6_src.c

```
551                     /*
552                      * Rule 7: Prefer public addresses.
553                      * We allow users to reverse the logic by configuring
554                      * a sysctl variable, so that privacy conscious users can
555                      * always prefer temporary addresses.
556                      */
557                     if (opts == NULL ||
558                         opts->ip6po_prefer_tempaddr == IP6PO_TEMPADDR_SYSTEM) {
559                             prefer_tempaddr = ip6_prefer_tempaddr;
560                     } else if (opts->ip6po_prefer_tempaddr ==
561                         IP6PO_TEMPADDR_NOTPREFER) {
562                             prefer_tempaddr = 0;
563                     } else
564                             prefer_tempaddr = 1;
565                     if (!(ia_best->ia6_flags & IN6_IFF_TEMPORARY) &&
566                         (ia->ia6_flags & IN6_IFF_TEMPORARY)) {
567                             if (prefer_tempaddr)
```

```
568                                          REPLACE(7);
569                           else
570                                          NEXT(7);
571                      }
572                      if ((ia_best->ia6_flags & IN6_IFF_TEMPORARY) &&
573                          !(ia->ia6_flags & IN6_IFF_TEMPORARY)) {
574                              if (prefer_tempaddr)
575                                      NEXT(7);
576                              else
577                                      REPLACE(7);
578                      }
```
_____ in6_src.c

557–564 By default, a public address is preferred over a temporary address (Section 3.4.2). At the same time, [RFC3484] requires the implementation to provide a mechanism for the user to override this behavior. The KAME implementation supports two types of overriding mechanisms: one is per-system variable, `ip6_prefer_tempaddr`, which is configurable via the `sysctl` name of `net.inet6.ip6.prefer_tempaddr`; the other is the `IPV6_PREFER_TEMPADDR` socket option or ancillary data item (see Listing 7-83). The latter is given in the `ip6po_prefer_tempaddr` member of the `ip6_pktopts{}` structure. The possible option values are as follows:

- `IP6PO_TEMPADDR_SYSTEM` use the system default stored in `ip6_prefer_tempaddr`.

- `IP6PO_TEMPADDR_NOTPREFER` prefer public addresses

- `IP6PO_TEMPADDR_PREFER` prefer temporary addresses

If no option is specified or the option value is `IP6PO_TEMPADDR_SYSTEM`, the preference policy is determined by `ip6_prefer_tempaddr`; otherwise, it is based on the value of the `IPV6_PREFER_TEMPADDR` option.

565–578 Depending on the preference policy, this part implements Rule 7, either as specified or using the reversed preference.

Listing 3-119
_____ in6_src.c
```
580                      /*
581                       * Rule 8: prefer addresses on alive interfaces.
582                       * This is a KAME specific rule.
583                       */
584                      if ((ia_best->ia_ifp->if_flags & IFF_UP) &&
585                          !(ia->ia_ifp->if_flags & IFF_UP))
586                              NEXT(8);
587                      if (!(ia_best->ia_ifp->if_flags & IFF_UP) &&
588                          (ia->ia_ifp->if_flags & IFF_UP))
589                              REPLACE(8);
```
_____ in6_src.c

584–589 [RFC3484] recommends using the longest prefix matching as Rule 8 to determine a winner, but this rule may be superseded by an implementation-specific method for choosing the appropriate source address. The KAME implementation gives preference to the address that is assigned to an "alive" interface.

Listing 3-120
$\hspace{8cm}$in6_src.c

```
591                        /*
592                         * Rule 9: prefer addresses on "preferred" interfaces.
593                         * This is a KAME specific rule.
594                         */
595     #define NDI_BEST ND_IFINFO(ia_best->ia_ifp)
596     #define NDI_NEW  ND_IFINFO(ia->ia_ifp)
597                        if ((NDI_BEST->flags & ND6_IFF_PREFER_SOURCE) &&
598                            !(NDI_NEW->flags & ND6_IFF_PREFER_SOURCE))
599                                NEXT(9);
600                        if (!(NDI_BEST->flags & ND6_IFF_PREFER_SOURCE) &&
601                            (NDI_NEW->flags & ND6_IFF_PREFER_SOURCE))
602                                REPLACE(9);
603     #undef NDI_BEST
604     #undef NDI_NEW
```
$\hspace{8cm}$in6_src.c

597–602 The **ndp** utility allows a system administrator to set the ND6_IFF_PREFER_SOURCE flag on a particular interface, which gives all of the addresses of that interface the preferred status. This rule is not in [RFC3484] but is a KAME extension. The **ndp** utility must be built with the ND6_IFF_PREFER_SOURCE flag in order for it to recognize the command option prefer_source. An example of the exact command line syntax is as follows:

```
ndp -i ne0 prefer_source
```

This gives addresses configured on the ne0 interface the preferred status. The successful completion of this command will produce an output similar to the following:

```
# ndp -i ne0 prefer_source
linkmtu=1500, maxmtu=1500, curhlim=64, basereachable=30s0ms,
reachable=39s, retrans=1s0ms
Flags: nud accept_rtadv prefer_source
```

An intended scenario where this implementation specific rule is useful is a router that assigns a "service address" to its loopback address. Then, for example, the source address of an ICMPv6 error message for **traceroute** will be this service address if none of the previous rules shows a clear preference.

Listing 3-121
$\hspace{8cm}$in6_src.c

```
606                        /*
607                         * Rule 14: Use longest matching prefix.
608                         * Note: in the address selection draft, this rule is
609                         * documented as "Rule 8".  However, since it is also
610                         * documented that this rule can be overridden, we assign
611                         * a large number so that it is easy to assign smaller numbers
612                         * to more preferred rules.
613                         */
614     new_matchlen = in6_matchlen(&ia->ia_addr.sin6_addr, dst);
615     if (best_matchlen < new_matchlen)
616             REPLACE(14);
617     if (new_matchlen < best_matchlen)
618             NEXT(14);
```
$\hspace{8cm}$in6_src.c

614–618 This code block implements the original Rule 8 specified in [RFC3484], which prefers the address that shares a longer prefix with the destination.

Function `in6_matchlen()` returns the length of the common prefix between `ia_addr.sin6_addr` and `dst`.

Listing 3-122

```
                                                                    in6_src.c
620                         /* Rule 15 is reserved. */
621
622                         /*
623                          * Last resort: just keep the current candidate.
624                          * Or, do we need more rules?
625                          */
626                         continue;
627
628                 replace:
629                         ia_best = ia;
630                         best_scope = (new_scope >= 0 ? new_scope :
631                                         in6_addrscope(&ia_best->ia_addr.sin6_addr));
632                         best_policy = (new_policy ? new_policy :
633                                         lookup_addrsel_policy(&ia_best->ia_addr));
634                         best_matchlen = (new_matchlen >= 0 ? new_matchlen :
635                                         in6_matchlen(&ia_best->ia_addr.sin6_addr,
636                                                 dst));
637
638                 next:
639                         continue;
640
641                 out:
642                         break;
643                 }
                                                                    in6_src.c
```

628–636 When the `for` loop is executed for the first time or a more preferred address is found, functions `in6_addrscope()`, `lookup_addrsel_policy()` and `in6_matchlen()` are called to initialize or update these state variables.

Listing 3-123

```
                                                                    in6_src.c
645             if ((ia = ia_best) == NULL) {
646                     *errorp = EADDRNOTAVAIL;
647                     return (NULL);
648             }
649
650             if (ifpp)
651                     *ifpp = ifp;
652             return (&ia->ia_addr);
653     }
654     #undef REPLACE
655     #undef BREAK
656     #undef NEXT
                                                                    in6_src.c
```

645–648 An error of `EADDRNOTAVAIL` is returned to the caller if the selection algorithm fails to choose an appropriate source address.

650–652 Otherwise, the selected address is returned to the caller. If the caller also wants to get the outgoing interface, a pointer to the acquired interface is stored in the given address, `ifpp`.

The **netstat** utility can display the number of times each source address selection rule has been applied. For example, issuing the following

```
netstat -s -p ip6
```

will result in the following output (we only show the output specific to the source address selection):

```
ip6:
    Source addresses selection rule applied:
        4633 first candidate
        6392 same address
        4631 appropriate scope
        3923 deprecated address
        4 outgoing interface
        844 public/temporary address
        984 longest match
```

The **netstat** command provides a descriptive string for each selection rule:

Rule 0——first candidate

Rule 1——same address

Rule 2——appropriate scope

Rule 3——deprecated address

Rule 4——home address

Rule 5——outgoing interface

Rule 6——matching label

Rule 7——public/temporary address

Rule 8——alive interface

Rule 9——preferred interface

Rule 10——rule #10

Rule 11——rule #11

Rule 12——rule #12

Rule 13——rule #13

Rule 14——longest match

Rule 15——rule #15

As mentioned in the code description for lines 357–358, the first potential address examined by the selection rules is viewed as the "first candidate."

3.13.2 Route Selection: `ip6_selectroute()` Function

The `in6_selectroute()` function determines either or both of the following for a given destination IPv6 address:

- The outgoing interface to which a packet to the destination address would be transmitted
- A routing table entry that would be used for sending a packet to the address

This function is called from `in6_selectsrc()` via `in6_selectif()` as a part of the source address selection algorithm or from `ip6_output()` for confirming or determining the route to the destination (see Listing 3-157). While this function is named "selectroute," it does not always determine the routing table entry. In fact, the source address selection algorithm only needs the outgoing interface, which can be determined in some cases, especially for a multicast destination address.

Listing 3-124

——— ip6_output.c

```
713    int
714    in6_selectroute(dstsock, opts, mopts, ro, retifp, retrt, clone)
715           struct sockaddr_in6 *dstsock;
716           struct ip6_pktopts *opts;
717           struct ip6_moptions *mopts;
....
719           struct route *ro;
....
723           struct ifnet **retifp;
724           struct rtentry **retrt;
725           int clone;                    /* meaningful only for bsdi and freebsd. */
726    {
727           int error = 0;
728           struct ifnet *ifp = NULL;
729           struct rtentry *rt = NULL;
730           struct sockaddr_in6 *sin6_next;
731           struct in6_pktinfo *pi = NULL;
732           struct in6_addr *dst = &dstsock->sin6_addr;
733
....
746
747           /* If the caller specify the outgoing interface explicitly, use it. */
748           if (opts && (pi = opts->ip6po_pktinfo) != NULL && pi->ipi6_ifindex) {
749                  /* XXX boundary check is assumed to be already done. */
....
751                  ifp = ifnet_byindex(pi->ipi6_ifindex);
....
755                  if (ifp != NULL &&
756                      (retrt == NULL || IN6_IS_ADDR_MULTICAST(dst))) {
757                         /*
758                          * we do not have to check nor get the route for
759                          * multicast.
760                          */
761                         goto done;
762                  } else
763                         goto getroute;
764           }
```

——— ip6_output.c

748–751 An application can specify the outgoing interface through the IPV6_PKTINFO socket option or an ancillary data item of this type (see Section 7.3.4). In this case, a non-0 interface index is passed in the ip6po_pktinfo member of the ip6_pktopts{} structure, and the corresponding interface will be used as the outgoing interface.

755–764 When the outgoing interface is determined above, if a caller does not require to fill in the associated route entry or the packet's destination address is a multicast address, the process in this function terminates here. The function will continue below in other cases.

Listing 3-125

——— ip6_output.c

```
766           /*
767            * If the destination address is a multicast address and the outgoing
768            * interface for the address is specified by the caller, use it.
769            */
770           if (IN6_IS_ADDR_MULTICAST(dst) &&
771               mopts != NULL && (ifp = mopts->im6o_multicast_ifp) != NULL) {
772                  goto done; /* we do not need a route for multicast. */
773           }
```

——— ip6_output.c

770–773 The caller can explicitly specify the outgoing interface for multicast packets through the im6o_multicast_ifp member of the ip6_moptions{} structure. This is typically set as a result of the IPV6_MULTICAST_IF socket option (Section 7.2.5). In this case, the specified interface is used, and the selection procedure terminates.

Listing 3-126
_____ip6_output.c

```
775     getroute:
776             /*
777              * If the next hop address for the packet is specified by the caller,
778              * use it as the gateway.
779              */
780             if (opts && opts->ip6po_nexthop) {
....
782                     struct route *ron;
....
787                     sin6_next = satosin6(opts->ip6po_nexthop);
788
789                     /* at this moment, we only support AF_INET6 next hops */
790                     if (sin6_next->sin6_family != AF_INET6) {
791                             error = EAFNOSUPPORT; /* or should we proceed? */
792                             goto done;
793                     }
794
795                     /*
796                      * If the next hop is an IPv6 address, then the node identified
797                      * by that address must be a neighbor of the sending host.
798                      */
799                     ron = &opts->ip6po_nextroute;
800                     if ((ron->ro_rt &&
801                         (ron->ro_rt->rt_flags & (RTF_UP | RTF_LLINFO)) !=
802                         (RTF_UP | RTF_LLINFO)) ||
803                         !SA6_ARE_ADDR_EQUAL(satosin6(&ron->ro_dst), sin6_next)) {
804                             if (ron->ro_rt) {
805                                     RTFREE(ron->ro_rt);
806                                     ron->ro_rt = NULL;
807                             }
808                             *satosin6(&ron->ro_dst) = *sin6_next;
809                     }
810                     if (ron->ro_rt == NULL) {
811                             rtalloc((struct route *)ron); /* multi path case? */
812                             if (ron->ro_rt == NULL ||
813                                 !(ron->ro_rt->rt_flags & RTF_LLINFO)) {
814                                     if (ron->ro_rt) {
815                                             RTFREE(ron->ro_rt);
816                                             ron->ro_rt = NULL;
817                                     }
818                                     error = EHOSTUNREACH;
819                                     goto done;
820                             }
821                     }
822                     rt = ron->ro_rt;
823                     ifp = rt->rt_ifp;
824
825                     /*
826                      * When cloning is required, try to allocate a route to the
827                      * destination so that the caller can store path MTU
828                      * information.
829                      */
830                     if (!clone)
831                             goto done;
832             }
```
_____ip6_output.c

780–793 An application can explicitly specify the next hop IPv6 address with the IPV6_NEXTHOP socket option or ancillary data item (see Section 7.3.4). When the application uses this API, the next hop address is stored in the ip6po_nexthop member of the ip6_pktopts{} structure.

As commented, this implementation only allows an AF_INET6 socket address, that is, an IPv6 address, as the next hop, while the ip6po_nexthop member points to a general socket address structure. Indeed, this behavior follows the API specification, [RFC3542]. The address family check in this function is actually redundant, since the unsupported families should have been rejected in the kernel API implementation (see Listing 7-76).

799–809 [RFC3542] requires that the node identified by the next hop address must be an on-link neighbor. Whereas the definition of "neighbor" is not very clear here, this implementation regards an address as neighbor in terms of the Neighbor Discovery protocol. This also means the kernel route entry for this address must have the RTF_LLINFO flag.

The ip6po_nextroute member of the ip6_pktopts{} structure contains a cached route for the next hop address (see Section 7.4.2). When a route entry is already cached, the validity of the entry is checked. If the entry is not usable, does not indicate a neighbor, or is for a different destination address, the cached route is released.

810–821 If a route for the next hop address is not cached or has just been released, the rtalloc() function tries to cache a new route. If it fails or the route indicates the destination is not a neighbor, an error of EHOSTUNREACH will be returned.

822–823 Upon successful route retrieval or creation, variable rt is set to the cached route entry and ifp is set to the associated interface.

830–831 If the clone Boolean flag is false, the route selection procedure is completed. Otherwise, this function also tries to get a host (cloned) route to the destination that is expected to store the path MTU size.

Listing 3-127

──ip6_output.c

```
834             /*
835              * Use a cached route if it exists and is valid, else try to allocate
836              * a new one.  Note that we should check the address family of the
837              * cached destination, in case of sharing the cache with IPv4.
838              */
839             if (ro) {
840                     if (ro->ro_rt &&
841                         (!(ro->ro_rt->rt_flags & RTF_UP) ||
842                          ro->ro_dst.sa_family != AF_INET6 ||
  ....
846                          !IN6_ARE_ADDR_EQUAL(&satosin6(&ro->ro_dst)->sin6_addr,
847                                          dst)
  ....
849                         )) {
850                             RTFREE(ro->ro_rt);
851                             ro->ro_rt = (struct rtentry *)NULL;
852                     }
```
──ip6_output.c

839–852 If a cached route structure ro is provided by the caller and it contains a route entry, the validity of the entry is checked: the route entry must be usable, the address family of the destination must be AF_INET6, and the cached destination address must be equal to the given destination address. If the cached route is invalid, it is freed and the route entry field is reset to NULL.

Even though this may not be obvious, the check for the address family is necessary for the following reason. The cached route is typically a part of a Protocol Control Block (PCB) entry in a transport layer, for example, TCP. Specifically, it is the inp_route member of the inpcb{} structure (see Section 6.6.1). Since the KAME implementation for FreeBSD allows communication both over IPv4 and over IPv6 on a single PCB entry, using the special semantics of IPv4-mapped IPv6 addresses, the memory space for the cached route can be shared for both types of communication. If the address family check at line 842 were omitted, the following scenario would happen:

- An application opens an AF_INET6 UDP socket.

- The application sends a UDP datagram via the socket to an IPv6 destination, for example, 2001:db8::1234. Then ro->ro_dst is set to a sockaddr_in6{} structure whose sin6_addr member is the IPv6 address (Figure 3-22(A)).

- The application then sends another UDP datagram via the socket to an IPv4 destination, for example, 192.0.2.1. The IPv4 output routine finds that the destination address of the cached route is different from the current destination, and resets the ro->ro_dst member to a sockaddr_in{} structure with the IPv4 destination address (Figure 3-22(B)). Due to the length difference between these two socket address structures, however, the memory space that stored 2001:db8::1234 is intact.

- Now assume the application tries to send one more UDP datagram to the same IPv6 destination, 2001:db8::1234. If the address family check is omitted, the validity check at line 846 succeeds, and the cached route for the IPv4 destination would be used (Figure 3-22(C)).

Listing 3-128

```
                                                              ip6_output.c
853              if (ro->ro_rt == (struct rtentry *)NULL) {
854                      struct sockaddr_in6 *sa6;
855
856                      /* No route yet, so try to acquire one */
857                      bzero(&ro->ro_dst, sizeof(struct sockaddr_in6));
858                      sa6 = (struct sockaddr_in6 *)&ro->ro_dst;
859                      *sa6 = *dstsock;
....
861                      sa6->sin6_scope_id = 0;
....
863                      if (clone) {
....
871                              rtalloc((struct route *)ro);
....
874                      } else {
....
876                              ro->ro_rt = rtalloc1(&((struct route *)ro)
877                                               ->ro_dst, NULL, 0UL);
....
887                      }
888              }
                                                              ip6_output.c
```

FIGURE 3-22

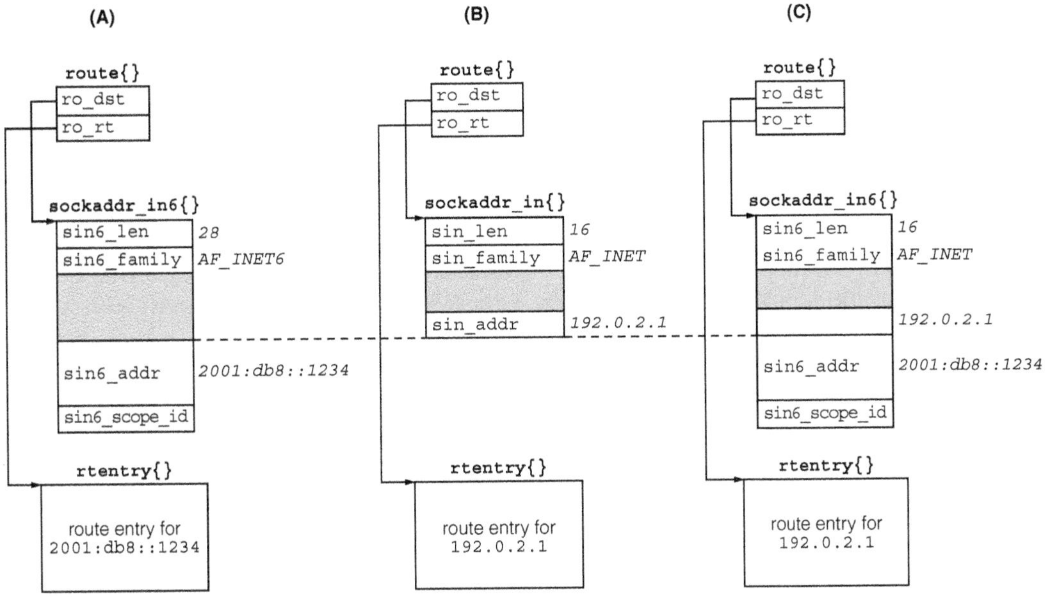

Possible scenario without the address family check for a cached route.

853–861 If a cached route has not yet been stored or has just been freed, a new route should be acquired. The destination address given by the caller is copied to the destination address field of the `route{}` structure.

Note that the `sin6_scope_id` field is reset to 0. This is necessary before an address is used for route lookup as explained in Section 2.9.3. It should also be noted that this field was not cleared in the case of Listing 3-126. This is not a bug because the kernel API code should have already cleared this field as we will see in Listing 7-76.

863–887 Either `rtalloc()` or `rtalloc1()` is called to acquire a valid cached route, depending on the cloning policy. If the variable `clone` is non-0, `rtalloc()` will create a cloned host route for the destination. Otherwise, `rtalloc1()` with the second argument of NULL (0) simply tries to find the best-match route for the destination without making a cloned route.

Note: The latter case is not really correct even though the main purpose of the code happens to be achieved. This should rather be a call to `rtalloc_ign()` with the second argument being RTF_PRCLONING as shown in Listing 3-88.

Listing 3-129

```
                                                                     ip6_output.c
890                     /*
891                      * do not care about the result if we have the nexthop
892                      * explicitly specified.
893                      */
894                     if (opts && opts->ip6po_nexthop)
895                             goto done;
                                                                     ip6_output.c
```

894–895 If the code reaches this point while an explicit next hop is supplied, it is because the caller wanted to make a cached route, if possible. Now that the creation process is completed, this function can terminate regardless of the result. Note that this is not just for optimization, but is actually necessary. Otherwise, the route for the specified next hop (rt) would be overridden below.

Listing 3-130

```
                                                                     ip6_output.c
897                     if (ro->ro_rt) {
898                             ifp = ro->ro_rt->rt_ifp;
899
900                             if (ifp == NULL) { /* can this really happen? */
901                                     RTFREE(ro->ro_rt);
902                                     ro->ro_rt = NULL;
903                             }
904                     }
905                     if (ro->ro_rt == NULL)
906                             error = EHOSTUNREACH;
907                     rt = ro->ro_rt;
                                                                     ip6_output.c
```

897–907 An error of EHOSTUNREACH will be returned to the caller if the kernel cannot find a route to the given destination or if the output interface associated with the returned route is invalid. As indicated by the code comment, the latter case should actually not happen.

   If a valid route is acquired, variable rt remembers the route and ifp is set to the associated interface.

Listing 3-131

```
                                                                     ip6_output.c
909                     /*
910                      * Check if the outgoing interface conflicts with
911                      * the interface specified by ipi6_ifindex (if specified).
912                      * Note that loopback interface is always okay.
913                      * (this may happen when we are sending a packet to one of
914                      * our own addresses.)
915                      */
916                     if (opts && opts->ip6po_pktinfo
917                         && opts->ip6po_pktinfo->ipi6_ifindex) {
918                             if (!(ifp->if_flags & IFF_LOOPBACK) &&
919                                 ifp->if_index !=
920                                 opts->ip6po_pktinfo->ipi6_ifindex) {
921                                     error = EHOSTUNREACH;
922                                     goto done;
923                             }
```

```
924                   }
925              }
```
_____ ip6_output.c

916–925 If an explicit outgoing interface is specified through the IPV6_PKTINFO socket option or ancillary data item, it must be equal to the interface associated with the route to the destination; otherwise, the packet could not be sent to the next hop without breaking the interface specification. A mismatch will result in an error of EHOSTUNREACH.

As commented, if the interface associated with the route is a loopback interface, it cannot be simply rejected because this may be a result of sending a packet to its own address configured on a non-loopback address. Specifically, this can happen with the following execution of the ping6 program:

```
% ping6 -I ne0 fe80::1234%ne0
```

where we assume interface ne0 configures an IPv6 address fe80::1234. This should succeed, but the above check would reject it if it omitted the test for the interface flag.

This relaxation is probably not the best way to implement the check. In fact, this check also allows the following execution:

```
% ping6 -I ne1 fe80::1234%ne0
```

which should actually be rejected explicitly.

Listing 3-132
_____ ip6_output.c

```
927     done:
928          if (ifp == NULL && rt == NULL) {
929               /*
930                * This can happen if the caller did not pass a cached route
931                * nor any other hints.  We treat this case an error.
932                */
933               error = EHOSTUNREACH;
934          }
935          if (error == EHOSTUNREACH)
936               ip6stat.ip6s_noroute++;
```
_____ ip6_output.c

927–934 When this function successfully returns, it must at least determine the outgoing interface. If ifp is NULL, an error of EHOSTUNREACH is explicitly set as the return code. The check for rt is actually redundant, since if ifp is NULL rt should not be NULL at this point.

935–936 If an EHOSTUNREACH error has occurred in this function, the corresponding statistics counter is incremented.

Listing 3-133
_____ ip6_output.c

```
938          if (retifp != NULL)
939               *retifp = ifp;
940          if (retrt != NULL)
941               *retrt = rt;     /* rt may be NULL */
942
943          return (error);
944     }
```
_____ ip6_output.c

938–943 The function returns the references to the interface and the route entry if the caller requested such information.

3.13.3 `ip6_output()` Function

The `ip6_output()` function is the main routine of IPv6 packet transmission. Upper layer protocols call this function to transmit an IPv6 packet, possibly with packet options such as specification of extension headers. Unlike the IPv4 output processing performed in the `ip_output()` function, `ip6_output()` is not called in the forwarding context from `ip6_forward()` as shown in Figure 3-14 (see also Listing 3-96).

The `ip6_output()` function is a large routine. In a nutshell, it performs the following tasks (some of which are optional behavior):

- Building extension headers

- Completing the IPv6 header

- Route and outgoing interface determination

- Processing the Hop-by-Hop options header

- Path MTU determination and packet fragmentation

In the following, we describe this function, generally in this order.

Listing 3-134

```
                                                                    ip6_output.c
251   int
....
253   ip6_output(m0, opt, ro, flags, im6o, ifpp, inp)
....
257           struct mbuf *m0;
258           struct ip6_pktopts *opt;
....
260           struct route *ro;
....
264           int flags;
265           struct ip6_moptions *im6o;
266           struct ifnet **ifpp;             /* XXX: just for statistics */
....
268           struct inpcb *inp;
....
270   {
                                                                    ip6_output.c
```

251–269 Variable `m0` holds the packet to be transmitted. Variable `opt` contains IPv6 extension headers and transmission parameters specified by a user application sending the packet via an API extension (see Section 7.4.2). An upper layer protocol may provide the IP layer with a route entry that is cached in the upper layer Protocol Control Block. The cached route is stored in `ro`. `flags` may take the following values:

- `IPV6_UNSPECSRC` the source address of an IPv6 address must not be the unspecified address except in some limited cases (see Section 2.3). The `ip6_output()` function prevents such packets from being sent unless this flag is specified.

- `IPV6_FORWARDING` the outgoing packet is being sent as a part of multicast forwarding processing. This flag is necessary to avoid infinite calls to `ip6_output()` and the multicast forwarding function.

- `IPV6_MINMTU` send the packet using the minimum MTU value (1280 bytes)

If pointer `im6o` is non-NULL, it points to an instance of the `ip6_moptions{}` structure containing multicast-related transmission options (see Listing 7-85). It typically corresponds to a set of socket options specified by an application, but can also be used as a kernel-internal option for some limited cases (e.g., see Section 5.16.1).

An upper layer protocol may want to know the outgoing interface for updating the statistics, in which case `ifpp` will hold the pointer to the `ifnet{}` structure of the outgoing interface.

Pointer `inp` is actually unused in this implementation.

Listing 3-135
ip6_output.c

```
271             struct ip6_hdr *ip6, *mhip6;
272             struct ifnet *ifp, *origifp = NULL;
273             struct mbuf *m = m0;
274             int hlen, tlen, len, off;
    ....
276             struct route ip6route;
    ....
280             struct rtentry *rt = NULL;
281             struct sockaddr_in6 *dst;
282             struct sockaddr_in6 src_sa, dst_sa, finaldst_sa;
283             int error = 0;
284             struct in6_ifaddr *ia = NULL;
285             u_long mtu;
286             int alwaysfrag, dontfrag;
287             u_int32_t optlen = 0, plen = 0, unfragpartlen = 0;
288             struct ip6_exthdrs exthdrs;
289             int clone = 0;
290             u_int32_t zone;
    ....
292             struct route *ro_pmtu = NULL;
    ....
296             int hdrsplit = 0;
    ....
300             int needipsec = 0;
    ....
333             ip6 = mtod(m, struct ip6_hdr *);
334             bzero(&finaldst_sa, sizeof(finaldst_sa));
```
ip6_output.c

333–334 Variable `ip6` points to the IPv6 header stored in mbuf m and will be accessed to build the IPv6 header. Variable `finaldst_sa` will contain the address of the final destination, which may be different from the destination address contained in the IPv6 header when a Routing header is inserted.

Build Extension Headers

Listing 3-136

```
                                                                    ip6_output.c
336    #define MAKE_EXTHDR(hp, mp)                                              \
337        do {                                                                \
338            if (hp) {                                                       \
339                struct ip6_ext *eh = (struct ip6_ext *)(hp);                \
340                error = ip6_copyexthdr((mp), (caddr_t)(hp),                 \
341                    ((eh)->ip6e_len + 1) << 3);                             \
342                if (error)                                                  \
343                    goto freehdrs;                                          \
344            }                                                               \
345        } while (/*CONSTCOND*/ 0)
346
347        bzero(&exthdrs, sizeof(exthdrs));
348
349        if (opt) {
350            /* Hop-by-Hop options header */
351            MAKE_EXTHDR(opt->ip6po_hbh, &exthdrs.ip6e_hbh);
352            /* Destination options header(1st part) */
353            if (opt->ip6po_rthdr
....
357                ) {
358                    /*
359                     * Destination options header(1st part)
360                     * This only makes sence with a routing header.
361                     * See Section 9.2 of
362                     * draft-ietf-ipngwg-rfc2292bis-02.txt.
363                     * Disabling this part just for MIP6 convenience is
364                     * a bad idea.  We need to think carefully about a
365                     * way to make the advanced API coexist with MIP6
366                     * options, which might automatically be inserted in
367                     * the kernel.
368                     */
369                    MAKE_EXTHDR(opt->ip6po_dest1, &exthdrs.ip6e_dest1);
370            }
371            /* Routing header */
372            MAKE_EXTHDR(opt->ip6po_rthdr, &exthdrs.ip6e_rthdr);
....
377            /* Destination options header(2nd part) */
378            MAKE_EXTHDR(opt->ip6po_dest2, &exthdrs.ip6e_dest2);
....
382        }
                                                                    ip6_output.c
```

349–382 The MAKE_EXTHDR() macro checks for the presence of a given extension header. If it is present, this macro then calls function ip6_copyexthdr() to make a copy of that header and store the copy in a newly allocated mbuf.

The caller may specify extension headers for the outgoing packet. In such a case parameter opt, an instance of the ip6_pktopts{} structure, contains the extension header information. These headers are copied and maintained in the exthdrs variable. Possible extension headers are the Hop-by-Hop options, the Destination options and the Routing headers. The ip6po_dest1 field of the ip6_pktops{} structure is only effective when a Routing header is to be included, too, and refers to Destination options to be processed by each intermediate node specified in the Routing header. In this case the Destination options header is inserted before the Routing header. The ip6po_dest2 field refers to Destination options to be processed only by the final destination, whether a Routing header is present or not.

Listing 3-137

ip6_output.c

```
553            /* get a security policy for this packet */
554            if (so == NULL)
555                    sp = ipsec6_getpolicybyaddr(m, IPSEC_DIR_OUTBOUND, 0, &error);
556            else
557                    sp = ipsec6_getpolicybysock(m, IPSEC_DIR_OUTBOUND, so, &error);
558
559            if (sp == NULL) {
560                    ipsec6stat.out_inval++;
561                    goto freehdrs;
562            }
563
564            error = 0;
565
566            /* check policy */
567            switch (sp->policy) {
568            case IPSEC_POLICY_DISCARD:
569                    /*
570                     * This packet is just discarded.
571                     */
572                    ipsec6stat.out_polvio++;
573                    goto freehdrs;
574
575            case IPSEC_POLICY_BYPASS:
576            case IPSEC_POLICY_NONE:
577                    /* no need to do IPsec. */
578                    needipsec = 0;
579                    break;
580
581            case IPSEC_POLICY_IPSEC:
582                    if (sp->req == NULL) {
583                            /* acquire a policy */
584                            error = key_spdacquire(sp);
585                            goto freehdrs;
586                    }
587                    needipsec = 1;
588                    break;
589
590            case IPSEC_POLICY_ENTRUST:
591            default:
592                    printf("ip6_output: Invalid policy found. %d\n", sp->policy);
593            }
```

ip6_output.c

553–593 The `ipsec6_getpolicybyaddr()` and `ipsec6_getpolicybysock()` functions check the IPsec policy database to see if the outgoing packet requires IPsec. Variable `needipsec` is set to 1 if and only if IPsec processing is required.

Listing 3-138

ip6_output.c

```
597            /*
598             * Calculate the total length of the extension header chain.
599             * Keep the length of the unfragmentable part for fragmentation.
600             */
601            optlen = 0;
602            if (exthdrs.ip6e_hbh) optlen += exthdrs.ip6e_hbh->m_len;
603            if (exthdrs.ip6e_dest1) optlen += exthdrs.ip6e_dest1->m_len;
604            if (exthdrs.ip6e_rthdr) optlen += exthdrs.ip6e_rthdr->m_len;
....
609            unfragpartlen = optlen + sizeof(struct ip6_hdr);
610            /* NOTE: we don't add AH/ESP length here. do that later. */
611            if (exthdrs.ip6e_dest2) optlen += exthdrs.ip6e_dest2->m_len;
```

```
612
613                  /*
614                   * If we need IPsec, or there is at least one extension header,
615                   * separate IP6 header from the payload.
616                   */
....
620                  if ((needipsec || optlen) && !hdrsplit)
....
622                  {
623                          if ((error = ip6_splithdr(m, &exthdrs)) != 0) {
624                                  m = NULL;
625                                  goto freehdrs;
626                          }
627                          m = exthdrs.ip6e_ip6;
628                          hdrsplit++;
629                  }
```
                                                                    ip6_output.c

597–604 Variable `optlen` accumulates the number of bytes of the extension headers that are present in the outgoing packet.

609 The `unfragpartlen` variable stores the length of the unfragmentable part of the packet in case packet fragmentation is necessary. This part consists of the IPv6 header, the Hop-by-Hop options header, the Destination options header appearing before the Routing header, and the Routing header.

620–629 The IPv6 header is split from the rest of the packet into a separate buffer if at least one extension header is present. This header partition is necessary to facilitate the local specific placement of extension headers in a given packet. Variable `hdrsplit` is incremented to reflect that the IPv6 header separation has taken place.

Listing 3-139

                                                                    ip6_output.c
```
631                  /* adjust pointer */
632                  ip6 = mtod(m, struct ip6_hdr *);
```
                                                                    ip6_output.c

632 The `ip6` pointer is reinitialized in case the IPv6 header was detached due to either IPsec or the presence of extension headers. This is necessary because if `ip6_splithdr()` was called previously, the IPv6 header may have been moved to a newly allocated mbuf.

Listing 3-140

                                                                    ip6_output.c
```
634                  /* adjust mbuf packet header length */
635                  m->m_pkthdr.len += optlen;
636                  plen = m->m_pkthdr.len - sizeof(*ip6);
```
                                                                    ip6_output.c

634–637 The original packet length in the mbuf is adjusted to include the length of the extension headers. The Payload Length `plen`, which will be set in the IPv6 header, excludes the standard IPv6 header size.

Listing 3-141

_____ ip6_output.c

```
638                     /* If this is a jumbo payload, insert a jumbo payload option. */
639            if (plen > IPV6_MAXPACKET) {
640                    if (!hdrsplit) {
641                            if ((error = ip6_splithdr(m, &exthdrs)) != 0) {
642                                    m = NULL;
643                                    goto freehdrs;
644                            }
645                            m = exthdrs.ip6e_ip6;
646                            hdrsplit++;
647                    }
648                    /* adjust pointer */
649                    ip6 = mtod(m, struct ip6_hdr *);
650                    if ((error = ip6_insert_jumboopt(&exthdrs, plen)) != 0)
651                            goto freehdrs;
652                    ip6->ip6_plen = 0;
653            } else
654                    ip6->ip6_plen = htons(plen);
```
_____ ip6_output.c

639–652 If the packet's payload (excluding the IPv6 header) is larger than 65535 bytes, the
ip6_insert_jumboopt() function (see Section 3.13.6) is called to insert a Jumbo Payload option in the Hop-by-Hop options header. If the packet does not include a Hop-
by-Hop options header yet, ip6_insert_jumboopt() creates a new one. The IPv6
header payload length is then set to zero as specified in [RFC2460].

653–654 For non-Jumbo Payload the payload length in the IPv6 header is set to plen in the
network byte order.

Listing 3-142

_____ ip6_output.c

```
656            /*
657             * Concatenate headers and fill in next header fields.
658             * Here we have, on "m"
659             *      IPv6 payload
660             * and we insert headers accordingly.  Finally, we should be getting:
661             *      IPv6 hbh dest1 rthdr ah* [esp* dest2 payload]
662             *
663             * during the header composing process, "m" points to IPv6 header.
664             * "mprev" points to an extension header prior to esp.
665             */
666            {
667                    u_char *nexthdrp = &ip6->ip6_nxt;
668                    struct mbuf *mprev = m;
```
_____ ip6_output.c

667–668 Variable nexthdrp points to the Next Header field of the IPv6 header. The usage of
mprev is explained shortly.

Listing 3-143

_____ ip6_output.c

```
670            /*
671             * we treat dest2 specially.  this makes IPsec processing
672             * much easier.  the goal here is to make mprev point the
673             * mbuf prior to dest2.
674             *
675             * result: IPv6 dest2 payload
```

```
676                      * m and mprev will point to IPv6 header.
677                      */
678                     if (exthdrs.ip6e_dest2) {
679                         if (!hdrsplit)
680                             panic("assumption failed: hdr not split");
681                         exthdrs.ip6e_dest2->m_next = m->m_next;
682                         m->m_next = exthdrs.ip6e_dest2;
683                         *mtod(exthdrs.ip6e_dest2, u_char *) = ip6->ip6_nxt;
684                         ip6->ip6_nxt = IPPROTO_DSTOPTS;
685                     }
```
                                                                    ip6_output.c

678–685 In the succeeding code, the mbufs storing the extension headers will be concatenated
to the mbuf containing the IPv6 header and the payload. The processing order is basically
the header ordering, that is, starting with the Hop-by-Hop options header.

   If the Destination options header which only needs to be processed at the final destination is specified, however, this header is linked into the mbuf chain first. As commented,
this is for the convenience of possible IPsec processing later. When any IPsec-related headers are inserted, this Destination options header is the only header placed after the IPsec
headers (see Table 3-2). The special case of the insertion processing ensures that variable
mprev points to the mbuf that should be placed exactly before the IPsec headers.

Listing 3-144

                                                                    ip6_output.c
```
687     #define MAKE_CHAIN(m, mp, p, i)\
688         do {\
689             if (m) {\
690                 if (!hdrsplit) \
691                     panic("assumption failed: hdr not split"); \
692                 *mtod((m), u_char *) = *(p);\
693                 *(p) = (i);\
694                 p = mtod((m), u_char *);\
695                 (m)->m_next = (mp)->m_next;\
696                 (mp)->m_next = (m);\
697                 (mp) = (m);\
698             }\
699         } while (/*CONSTCOND*/ 0)
700                     /*
701                      * result: IPv6 hbh dest1 rthdr dest2 payload
702                      * m will point to IPv6 header.  mprev will point to the
703                      * extension header prior to dest2 (rthdr in the above case).
704                      */
705                     MAKE_CHAIN(exthdrs.ip6e_hbh, mprev, nexthdrp, IPPROTO_HOPOPTS);
```
                                                                    ip6_output.c

687–697 The MAKE_CHAIN() macro inserts a single extension header (stored in m) into the mbuf
chain of the outgoing packet if it is given. Argument mp points to the mbuf to be located
just before the inserted extension header. Argument p points to the Next Header field of the
preceding header, which should actually be the first byte of the data field of mbuf mp. The Next
Header field is set to the value identifying the extension header being inserted, which is
macro argument i. Mbuf m is inserted in the appropriate position, and mp is reset to m.

705 If a Hop-by-Hop options header is set in exthdrs, the MAKE_CHAIN() macro inserts it in
the outgoing packet. Figure 3-23 illustrates a concrete example of the operation performed
at line 705. In this example, a Destination options header is already linked into the mbuf

FIGURE 3-23

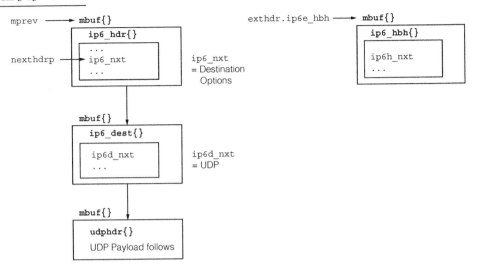

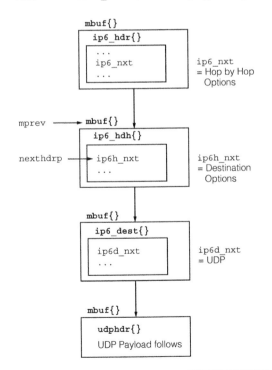

Before	MAKE_CHAIN(exthdrs.ip6e_hbh, mprev, nexthdrp, IPPROTO_HOPOPTS);
After	MAKE_CHAIN(exthdrs.ip6e_hbh, mprev, nexthdrp, IPPROTO_HOPOPTS);

Inserting a Hop-by-Hop options header using the MAKE_CHAIN() macro.

chain as shown in the upper half of Figure 3-23. The MAKE_CHAIN() macro modifies the chain as follows:

- the Next Header field of the Hop-by-Hop options header is copied from the Next Header field of the IPv6 header, which specifies the Destination options header (line 692).

- The Next Header field of the IPv6 header is set to the value specifying the Hop-by-Hop options header (line 693).

- Variable nexthdrp is reset to point to the Next Header field of the Hop-by-Hop options header (line 694).

- The mbuf storing the Hop-by-Hop options header is linked into the chain (lines 695 and 696).

- Variable mprev now points to the Hop-by-Hop options header (line 697).

The resulting mbuf chain is shown in the lower half of Figure 3-21.

Listing 3-145

```
                                                                    ip6_output.c
706                 MAKE_CHAIN(exthdrs.ip6e_dest1, mprev, nexthdrp,
707                     IPPROTO_DSTOPTS);
708                 MAKE_CHAIN(exthdrs.ip6e_rthdr, mprev, nexthdrp,
709                     IPPROTO_ROUTING);
                                                                    ip6_output.c
```

706–709 Similarly, if the Destination options header or the Routing header exist, it will be inserted after the Hop-by-Hop options header. Figure 3-24 depicts the relationship between the mbufs and the ip6_exthdrs{} structure when all possible extension headers are specified and inserted.

Listing 3-146

```
                                                                    ip6_output.c
724    #if defined(IPSEC) && !defined(__OpenBSD__)
725                    if (!needipsec)
726                        goto skip_ipsec2;
       ...
758                    error = ipsec6_output_trans(&state, nexthdrp, mprev, sp, flags,
759                        &needipsectun);
760                    m = state.m;
       ...
792    skip_ipsec2:;
793    #endif
794            }
                                                                    ip6_output.c
```

724–793 If the outgoing packet requires IPsec processing, the ipsec6_output_trans() function inserts necessary IPsec headers corresponding to the security policy. As we explained above, mprev should point to the mbuf which should be located exactly before the IPsec headers. We do not go into further details of the IPsec processing in this chapter.

FIGURE 3-24

IPv6 packet before extension headers are inserted

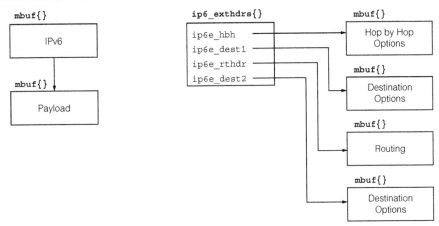

IPv6 packet after extension headers are inserted

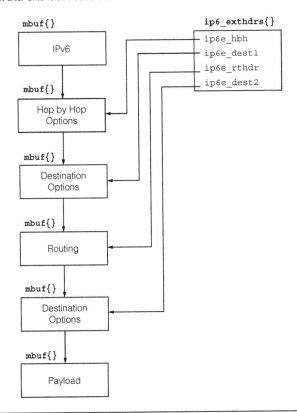

Mbuf chain with extension headers.

Routing Header Processing

Listing 3-147

```
                                                             ip6_output.c
822              /*
823               * If there is a routing header, replace the destination address field
824               * with the first hop of the routing header.
825               */
826              if (exthdrs.ip6e_rthdr
....
830                      ) {
831                      struct ip6_rthdr *rh;
832                      struct ip6_rthdr0 *rh0;
833                      struct in6_addr *addr;
834                      struct sockaddr_in6 sa;
835                      struct in6_addr finaldst;
836
837                      if (exthdrs.ip6e_rthdr)
838                              rh = (struct ip6_rthdr *)(mtod(exthdrs.ip6e_rthdr,
839                                      struct ip6_rthdr *));
....
845
846                      finaldst = ip6->ip6_dst;
847                      switch (rh->ip6r_type) {
....
851                      case IPV6_RTHDR_TYPE_0:
852                              rh0 = (struct ip6_rthdr0 *)rh;
853                              addr = (struct in6_addr *)(rh0 + 1);
                                                             ip6_output.c
```

826–853 Variable `rh0` points to the Type 0 Routing header and `addr` points to the first route segment specified in the Routing header. Variable `finaldst` points to the final destination that will be swapped with the next route segment in the Routing header.

Listing 3-148

```
                                                             ip6_output.c
855                      /* extract the final destination from the packet */
856                      if (ip6_getpktaddrs(m, NULL, &dst_sa))
857                              goto bad; /* XXX: impossible */
858                      finaldst_sa = dst_sa;
                                                             ip6_output.c
```

855–858 The output function of the upper layer protocol such as `udp6_output()` (Section 6.9.2) calls `ip6_setpktaddrs()` to create an mbuf tag attached to the mbuf and stores the packet source and destination addresses there. The `ip6_getpktaddrs()` function retrieves the final destination address from the mbuf tag, which is then copied to variable `finaldst_sa`. The socket address of the ultimate destination will be used in the call to function `ip6_getpmtu()` to obtain the right path MTU information

Listing 3-149

```
                                                             ip6_output.c
860              /*
861               * construct a sockaddr_in6 form of the first hop.
862               * XXX: we may not have enough information about
863               * its scope zone; there is no standard API to pass
864               * the information from the application.
865               */
```

```
866                             bzero(&sa, sizeof(sa));
867                             sa.sin6_family = AF_INET6;
868                             sa.sin6_len = sizeof(sa);
869                             sa.sin6_addr = *addr;
870                             if ((error = scope6_check_id(&sa, ip6_use_defzone))
871                                 != 0) {
872                                     goto bad;
873                             }
874                             if (!ip6_setpktaddrs(m, NULL, &sa)) {
875                                     error = ENOBUFS;
876                                     goto bad;
877                             }
```
——— ip6_output.c

860–873 Since the address of the first route segment specified in the Routing header is given
without its scope zone, it can be ambiguous. For example, if the first route segment
address is a link-local address, it is usually ambiguous about its link zone. This is an
inherent problem of the current API definition (see Section 7.3.5), and the kernel needs to
perform some ad hoc approach to deal with the possible ambiguity. This implementation
uses the scope6_check_id() function (Section 2.9.4) for this purpose, which enforces
the default zone index when ip6_use_defzone is set to non-0. Note that this variable
is set to 0 by default, which means specifying an ambiguous address (like a link-local
address in many cases) as the first route segment address often causes an error.

874–876 Since the packet's current destination is going to be changed to the first route segment,
ip6_setpktaddrs() is called to update the socket address structure attached to the
mbuf.

Listing 3-150
——— ip6_output.c

```
878                             ip6->ip6_dst = sa.sin6_addr;
879                             bcopy((caddr_t)(addr + 1), (caddr_t)addr,
880                                 sizeof(struct in6_addr) * (rh0->ip6r0_segleft - 1));
881                             *(addr + rh0->ip6r0_segleft - 1) = finaldst;
882                             /* XXX */
883                             in6_clearscope(addr + rh0->ip6r0_segleft - 1);
884
885                             break;
886                     default:         /* is it possible? */
887                             error = EINVAL;
888                             goto bad;
889                     }
890             }
```
——— ip6_output.c

878–885 The Destination Address field in the IPv6 header is set to the address of the first
route segment. The route segments from the second segment to the last segment is shifted
in memory by one segment. The last segment of the Routing header is set to the final
destination stored in finaldst. Note that finaldst may contain the embedded zone
index (see Section 2.9.3). It must be cleared before it is sent outside the node by the
in6_clearscope() function. The XXX comment in line 882 indicates why embedding
a zone index in the address is generally a bad idea.

Figure 3-25 summarizes the operation of building the route segments with a Routing
header starting at Listing 3-147.

FIGURE 3-25

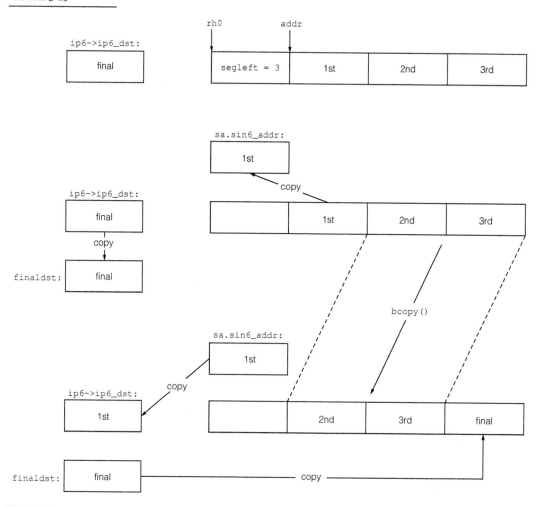

Building route segments with a Routing header.

Listing 3-151

ip6_output.c

```
892              /* Source address validation */
893              if (!(flags & IPV6_UNSPECSRC) &&
894                  IN6_IS_ADDR_UNSPECIFIED(&ip6->ip6_src)) {
895                      /*
896                       * XXX: we can probably assume validation in the caller, but
897                       * we explicitly check the address here for safety.
898                       */
899                      error = EOPNOTSUPP;
900                      ip6stat.ip6s_badscope++;
901                      goto bad;
902              }
903              if (IN6_IS_ADDR_MULTICAST(&ip6->ip6_src)) {
```

```
904                          error = EOPNOTSUPP;
905                          ip6stat.ip6s_badscope++;
906                          goto bad;
907                  }
```
————————————————————————————————————— ip6_output.c

892–901 The unspecified address must not be used as the packet's source address except in some limited cases (see Section 2.3). An outgoing packet with the unspecified source address would be rejected here unless the IPV6_UNSPECSRC flag is specified, which indicates limited special cases. This flag can be set for the Duplicate Address Detection procedure (Section 5.16.1) or for Multicast Listener Discovery (Chapter 2 of *IPv6 Advanced Protocols Implementation*).

Note: This check is probably redundant, since if an application or an upper layer specified the unspecified address, the in6_selectsrc() function (Section 3.13.1) would have replaced it with a valid source address.

903–907 The source address must not be a multicast address, either. Unlike the case of the unspecified address, this check is necessary since a multicast application can bind a socket to a multicast group address for receiving packets to that group. Without this check, packets sent from the socket would have the multicast address in the Source Address field.

Fill in IPv6 Header and Determine Route

Listing 3-152
————————————————————————————————————— ip6_output.c

```
909              ip6stat.ip6s_localout++;
910
911              /*
912               * Route packet.
913               */
914
915              /*
916               * first extract sockaddr_in6 structures for the source and destination
917               * addresses attached to the packet.  when source-routing, the
918               * destination address should specify the first hop.
919               */
920              if (ip6_getpktaddrs(m, &src_sa, &dst_sa)) {
921                      /*
922                       * we dare to dump the fact here because this should be an
923                       * internal bug.
924                       */
925                      printf("ip6_output: can't find src/dst addresses\n");
926                      error = EIO;      /* XXX */
927                      goto bad;
928              }
929              if (finaldst_sa.sin6_family == AF_UNSPEC)
930                      finaldst_sa = dst_sa;
```
————————————————————————————————————— ip6_output.c

909–930 The ip6_getpktaddrs() function retrieves from the mbuf both the source address and the final destination address in the form of the socket address structure. Variable finaldst_sa is set to the final destination address if it is not initialized. Note that it should have been initialized at this point if a Routing header is present.

Listing 3-153

```
                                                                    ip6_output.c
932                /* initialize cached route */
933                if (ro == 0) {
934                        ro = &ip6route;
935                        bzero((caddr_t)ro, sizeof(*ro));
936                }
937                ro_pmtu = ro;
938                if (opt && opt->ip6po_rthdr)
939                        ro = &opt->ip6po_route;

....(Mobile IPv6 code)

947                dst = (struct sockaddr_in6 *)&ro->ro_dst;
                                                                    ip6_output.c
```

932–936 Variable `ro` is an argument to `ip6_output()` and points to a cached route to the destination when non-NULL. If `ro` is NULL, it is set to point to a local variable `ip6route` and is zero-cleared.

937 Variable `ro_pmtu` is a route to the final destination and will be used later for possible packet fragmentation with the path MTU to the destination. It is set to `ro` at this point.

938–939 If a Routing header is present, `ro` is set to the route for the first route segment, which may specify a different gateway or outgoing interface to the final destination.

Listing 3-154

```
                                                                    ip6_output.c
949                /*
950                 * if specified, try to fill in the traffic class field.
951                 * do not override if a non-zero value is already set.
952                 * we check the diffserv field and the ecn field separately.
953                 */
954                if (opt && opt->ip6po_tclass >= 0) {
955                        int mask = 0;
956
957                        if ((ip6->ip6_flow & htonl(0xfc << 20)) == 0)
958                                mask |= 0xfc;
959                        if ((ip6->ip6_flow & htonl(0x03 << 20)) == 0)
960                                mask |= 0x03;
961                        if (mask != 0)
962                                ip6->ip6_flow |= htonl((opt->ip6po_tclass & mask) << 20);
963                }
                                                                    ip6_output.c
```

954–963 The Traffic Class field in the IPv6 header is superseded by the 6-bit differentiated services codepoint (DSCP) defined in [RFC2474], and by the two-bit Explicit Congestion Notification (ECN) field defined in [RFC3168].

If the Traffic Class value is specified by the application, both the DSCP and ECN fields are checked to determine whether these fields have already been set in the IPv6 header. The value of the Traffic Class field in the option will override the associated field in the IPv6 header only if none of these fields are set.

Listing 3-155

```
                                                            ip6_output.c
965              /* fill in or override the hop limit field, if necessary. */
966              if (opt && opt->ip6po_hlim != -1)
967                      ip6->ip6_hlim = opt->ip6po_hlim & 0xff;
968              else if (IN6_IS_ADDR_MULTICAST(&ip6->ip6_dst)) {
969                      if (im6o != NULL)
970                              ip6->ip6_hlim = im6o->im6o_multicast_hlim;
971                      else
972                              ip6->ip6_hlim = ip6_defmcasthlim;
973              }
                                                            ip6_output.c
```

966–967 If a hop limit value for this particular packet is given by the application via the IPV6_HOPLIMIT ancillary data item (see Section 7.3.4), the Hop Limit field in the IPv6 header is overridden with the supplied option value. Note that the application may also specify the hop limit value via a socket option and the upper layer may have set the Hop Limit field to the specified value (see Section 6.9.2). This code indicates that the per packet specification is preferred over the per socket option.

968–972 If the IPV6_HOPLIMIT ancillary data item is absent and the packet is destined to a multicast group, the Hop Limit field is set as follows: If any multicast-related option is specified, the hop limit value stored in the option structure im6o is used; otherwise, the multicast packet is set with the system default for multicast packet hop limit. Note that in the former case the hop limit value may not be explicitly specified (see Listing 7-86), in which case the system default value is also used. Variable ip6_defmcasthlim defaults to 1, and is configurable via the net.inet6.ip6.defmcasthlim sysctl variable.

Listing 3-156

```
                                                            ip6_output.c
1023             if (needipsec && needipsectun
1027                     ) {
...
1046                     error = ipsec6_output_tunnel(&state, sp, flags);
1047
1048                     m = state.m;
1050                     ro = state.ro;
1054                     dst = (struct sockaddr_in6 *)state.dst;
1055                     if (error) {
...
1075                     }
1076                     /*
1077                      * since ipsec6_output_tunnel() may update address
1078                      * information of mbuf, we must update src_sa and
1079                      * dst_sa here.
1080                      */
1081                     if (ip6_getpktaddrs(m, &src_sa, &dst_sa)) {
1082                             printf("ip6_output: can't find src/dst addresses\n");
1083                             error = EIO;      /* XXX */
1084                             goto bad;
1085                     }
1086
1087                     exthdrs.ip6e_ip6 = m;
1088             }
1091
1092             /* adjust pointer */
1093             ip6 = mtod(m, struct ip6_hdr *);
                                                            ip6_output.c
```

1023–1093 If the outgoing packet requires the tunnel mode IPsec, the `ipsec6_output_tunnel()` function encapsulates the packet into a separate IPv6 packet with some IPsec header to a security gateway. The output processing hereafter will be performed for the encapsulating IPv6 packet, and the necessary parameters are updated. We do not go into further details of the IPsec processing in this chapter.

Listing 3-157

_____ ip6_output.c
```
1096                if (ro != &ip6route && !IN6_IS_ADDR_MULTICAST(&ip6->ip6_dst))
1097                    clone = 1;
....
1099
1100                if ((error = in6_selectroute(&dst_sa, opt, im6o, ro,
1101                                    &ifp, &rt, clone)) != 0) {
1102                    switch (error) {
1103                    case EHOSTUNREACH:
1104                            ip6stat.ip6s_noroute++;
1105                            break;
1106                    case EADDRNOTAVAIL:
1107                    default:
1108                            break; /* XXX statistics? */
1109                    }
1110                    if (ifp != NULL)
1111                            in6_ifstat_inc(ifp, ifs6_out_discard);
1112                    goto bad;
1113                }
1114            if (rt == NULL) {
1115                    /*
1116                     * If in6_selectroute() does not return a route entry,
1117                     * dst may not have been updated.
1118                     */
1119                    *dst = dst_sa;  /* XXX */
1120            }
1121
1122            /*
1123             * then rt (for unicast) and ifp must be non-NULL valid values.
1124             */
1125            if ((flags & IPV6_FORWARDING) == 0) {
1126                    /* XXX: the FORWARDING flag can be set for mrouting. */
1127                    in6_ifstat_inc(ifp, ifs6_out_request);
1128            }
1129            if (rt != NULL) {
1130                    ia = (struct in6_ifaddr *)(rt->rt_ifa);
....
1134                    rt->rt_use++;
....
1136            }
```
_____ ip6_output.c

1096–1113 The `in6_selectroute()` function tries to find the best route to the packet's destination address, consulting the kernel routing table and other optional parameters when given. If a cached route is provided for a unicast destination address, the Boolean variable `clone` is set to true, so that `in6_selectroute()` will make a per destination route and cache it in `ro`. On success, this function sets variable `ifp` to the interface structure of the outgoing interface. It also sets variable `rt` to the route entry for the next hop toward the destination if the routing table was used for identifying the outgoing interface.

Note that this call to `in6_selectroute()` often results in just checking the validity of the cached route, since the upper layer often calls this function via `in6_selectsrc()` when it first sends a packet from the corresponding socket. In some cases, however, the cached route may be invalid due to a route change or some unexpected event, and `in6_selectroute()` finds an alternative route in such a case.

1114–1120 There are cases where `in6_selectroute()` will not return a route entry (e.g., if the packet destination is a multicast address and the application has specified the outgoing interface). Since the `ro->ro_dst` field remains empty in such cases, variable `dst`, which points to `ro->rt_dst`, is set to the packet's destination address for later use.

1122–1136 Related statistics counters are incremented. If `in6_selectroute()` returned a route entry, the interface address structure associated with the route is remembered in variable `ia` for later use.

Listing 3-158

```
                                                           ip6_output.c
1138                /*
1139                 * The outgoing interface must be in the zone of source and
1140                 * destination addresses.  We should use ia_ifp to support the
1141                 * case of sending packets to an address of our own.
1142                 */
1143                if (ia != NULL && ia->ia_ifp)
1144                        origifp = ia->ia_ifp;
1145                else
1146                        origifp = ifp;
                                                           ip6_output.c
```

1143–1146 Variable `origifp` points to the "originating interface" associated with the route entry (if given) and will be used later for interface-sensitive checks. This is typically the same as `ifp`, but can be different when the destination address is one of the assigned addresses to the sending node. In this case, the outgoing interface is a loopback interface, but `origifp` points to the interface on which the destination address is assigned. The interface pointer `origifp` is then subsequently passed to functions `looutput()` and `if_simloop()`, where the receiving interface stored in the `m_pkthdr.rcvif` member of the mbuf is set to the originating interface. This is why the scope zone check in the `ip6_input()` function (Listing 3-22) works correctly for a packet looped back.

Listing 3-159

```
                                                           ip6_output.c
1147                if (in6_addr2zoneid(origifp, &src_sa.sin6_addr, &zone) ||
1148                    zone != src_sa.sin6_scope_id) {
 ....
1156                        goto badscope;
1157                }
1158                if (in6_addr2zoneid(origifp, &dst_sa.sin6_addr, &zone) ||
1159                    zone != dst_sa.sin6_scope_id) {
 ....
1165                        goto badscope;
1166                }
1167
1168                /* scope check is done. */
1169                goto routefound;
1170
1171        badscope:
```

```
1172                ip6stat.ip6s_badscope++;
1173                in6_ifstat_inc(origifp, ifs6_out_discard);
1174                if (error == 0)
1175                        error = EHOSTUNREACH; /* XXX */
1176                goto bad;
```
——————————————————————————————————— ip6_output.c

1147–1157 The scope zone of the source address must be equal to the zone of that scope type for the originating interface as specified in [RFC4007]. Function `in6_addr2zoneid()` (Section 2.9.4) stores the latter in `zone`, which is compared to the zone of the source address stored in the `sin6_scope_id` field. If these are different, the packet is discarded and an error of `EHOSTUNREACH` will be returned (line 1175).

Without this check, a packet sent from a socket bound to a narrower scoped address may cause unexpected breakage of the scope zone. For example, consider a socket bound to the loopback address (`::1`). If a packet destined to an external global address is sent on this socket, it would be sent outside the node (with the source address of the loopback address) without the zone check here. This is obviously wrong since the loopback address is only meaningful within the node. Note that the `in6_selectsrc()` function does not reject this case because it simply uses the local address as the source address for a bound socket without any checks.

1158–1166 The zone index of the destination address is validated in a similar fashion. This check normally does not fail since `in6_selectroute()` usually picks up an appropriate outgoing interface for the destination, but this check is still necessary. For example, when the outgoing interface is explicitly specified as a socket option, the scope zone for the scope type of the destination address on that interface may be different from the real scope zone of the destination address. This check rejects such an invalid case.

1171–1176 A mismatch of zone indices between the addresses and the interface will trigger an error of `EHOSTUNREACH` to be returned to the caller. The corresponding statistics are updated accordingly.

Listing 3-160
——————————————————————————————————— ip6_output.c

```
1178        routefound:
1179                if (rt && !IN6_IS_ADDR_MULTICAST(&ip6->ip6_dst)) {
1180                        if (opt && opt->ip6po_nextroute.ro_rt) {
1181                                /*
1182                                 * The nexthop is explicitly specified by the
1183                                 * application.  We assume the next hop is an IPv6
1184                                 * address.
1185                                 */
1186                                dst = (struct sockaddr_in6 *)opt->ip6po_nexthop;
1187                        }
1188                        else if ((rt->rt_flags & RTF_GATEWAY))
1189                                dst = (struct sockaddr_in6 *)rt->rt_gateway;
1190                }
```
——————————————————————————————————— ip6_output.c

1178–1190 Variable `dst` should point the next hop IPv6 address toward the destination, which was originally set to the destination address itself. If an explicit next hop address is specified via the `IPV6_NEXTHOP` socket option or ancillary data item (see Section 7.3.4) and the specified address was confirmed to be a neighbor (see Listing 3-126), dst is replaced with the specified next hop address. Otherwise, for an indirect route, the destination address is set to the gateway address of the route entry.

Multicast Specific Processing

Listing 3-161

```
1192                if (!IN6_IS_ADDR_MULTICAST(&ip6->ip6_dst)) {
1193                    m->m_flags &= ~(M_BCAST | M_MCAST); /* just in case */
```

1192–1193 The broadcast flag M_BCAST and the multicast flag M_MCAST is cleared for a unicast packet.

Listing 3-162

```
1194            } else {
1195                    struct  in6_multi *in6m;
1196
1197                    m->m_flags = (m->m_flags & ~M_BCAST) | M_MCAST;
1198
1199                    in6_ifstat_inc(ifp, ifs6_out_mcast);
1200
```

1195–1199 The multicast flag is set in the mbuf for a multicast packet. A statistics counter for multicast transmission is incremented.

Listing 3-163

```
1201                    /*
1202                     * Confirm that the outgoing interface supports multicast.
1203                     */
1204                    if (!(ifp->if_flags & IFF_MULTICAST)) {
1205                            ip6stat.ip6s_noroute++;
1206                            in6_ifstat_inc(ifp, ifs6_out_discard);
1207                            error = ENETUNREACH;
1208                            goto bad;
1209                    }
```

1201–1209 The outgoing interface must be a multicast-capable interface for a multicast destination. Otherwise, the packet is discarded and an error of ENETUNREACH is returned to the caller.

Listing 3-164

```
1210                    IN6_LOOKUP_MULTI(&dst_sa, ifp, in6m);
1211                    if (in6m != NULL &&
1212                        (im6o == NULL || im6o->im6o_multicast_loop)) {
1213                            /*
```

```
1214                                * If we belong to the destination multicast group
1215                                * on the outgoing interface, and the caller did not
1216                                * forbid loopback, loop back a copy.
1217                                */
1218                               ip6_mloopback(ifp, m, dst);
```
——————————————————————————————————— ip6_output.c

1210–1218 If the transmitting interface belongs to the destination multicast group, the outgoing multicast packet is looped back unless the application prohibits the loopback transmission of multicast packets on the socket. The ip6_mloopback() function will be described later in Section 3.13.9.

Listing 3-165

——————————————————————————————————— ip6_output.c
```
1219                    } else {
1220                            /*
1221                             * If we are acting as a multicast router, perform
1222                             * multicast forwarding as if the packet had just
1223                             * arrived on the interface to which we are about
1224                             * to send.  The multicast forwarding function
1225                             * recursively calls this function, using the
1226                             * IPV6_FORWARDING flag to prevent infinite recursion.
1227                             *
1228                             * Multicasts that are looped back by ip6_mloopback(),
1229                             * above, will be forwarded by the ip6_input() routine,
1230                             * if necessary.
1231                             */
1232                            if (ip6_mrouter && (flags & IPV6_FORWARDING) == 0) {
1233                                    /*
1234                                     * XXX: ip6_mforward expects that rcvif is NULL
1235                                     * when it is called from the originating path.
1236                                     * However, it is not always the case, since
1237                                     * some versions of MGETHDR() does not
1238                                     * initialize the field.
1239                                     */
1240                                    m->m_pkthdr.rcvif = NULL;
1241                                    if (ip6_mforward(ip6, ifp, m) != 0) {
1242                                            m_freem(m);
1243                                            goto done;
1244                                    }
1245                            }
1246                    }
```
——————————————————————————————————— ip6_output.c

1220–1245 If the sending node is configured to act as a multicast router, in which case ip6_mrouter is non-NULL, function ip6_mforward() is invoked to perform the multicast packet-forwarding task.

Since this function can again call ip6_output() with the IPV6_FORWARDING flag, ip6_output() must check for the presence of this flag to avoid infinite packet transmission loop between ip6_output() and ip6_mforward().

The ip6_mforward() function also forwards incoming multicast packets, and it detects whether the packet is from the incoming path or the outgoing path based on the value of the rcvif member of the mbuf's packet header. Since this field may not always be zero-cleared in the outgoing code path, it is explicitly cleared here so that ip6_mforward() will not be confused.

Details of ip6_mforward() will be discussed in Chapter 2 of *IPv6 Advanced Protocols Implementation.*

Listing 3-166

```
1247                    /*
1248                     * Multicasts with a hoplimit of zero may be looped back,
1249                     * above, but must not be transmitted on a network.
1250                     * Also, multicasts addressed to the loopback interface
1251                     * are not sent -- the above call to ip6_mloopback() will
1252                     * loop back a copy if this host actually belongs to the
1253                     * destination group on the loopback interface.
1254                     */
1255                    if (ip6->ip6_hlim == 0 || (ifp->if_flags & IFF_LOOPBACK) ||
1256                        IN6_IS_ADDR_MC_INTFACELOCAL(&ip6->ip6_dst)) {
1257                            m_freem(m);
1258                            goto done;
1259                    }
1260            }
```

1255–1259 The multicast packet is freed and `ip6_output()` returns if one of the following conditions is true:

- The packet has a zero-valued hop limit. This is not required by the protocol specification, but the same code logic as the IPv4 output function applies here.

- The transmitting interface is a loopback interface. This case was covered in Listing 3-164.

- The destination address has the interface-local multicast scope. In this case, the packet can only be looped back within the sending node and must not be sent outside the node.

Save the Outgoing Interface for the Caller

Listing 3-167

```
1262            /*
1263             * Fill the outgoing inteface to tell the upper layer
1264             * to increment per-interface statistics.
1265             */
1266            if (ifpp)
1267                    *ifpp = origifp;
```

1262–1267 The upper layer may provide a placeholder (`ifpp`) for `ip6_output()` to fill in with the outgoing interface pointer (see, for example, Section 4.8.3). The originating interface pointer is stored in `ifpp`.

Reachability Confirmation via API

Listing 3-168

```
1269            /*
1270             * Upper-layer reachability confirmation
1271             */
1272            if (opt && (opt->ip6po_flags & IP6PO_REACHCONF))
1273                    nd6_nud_hint(rt, NULL, 0);
```

1272–1273 The application can provide reachability confirmation for an on-link destination via the IPV6_REACHCONF ancillary data item, thereby skipping Neighbor Unreachability Detection (Section 5.9). Note, however, that this option was not standardized in the official API as will be explained in Listing 7-80.

Determine the Path MTU

Listing 3-169

```
                                                                  ip6_output.c
1275            /* Determine path MTU. */
1276            if ((error = ip6_getpmtu(ro_pmtu, ro, ifp, &finaldst_sa, &mtu,
1277                &alwaysfrag)) != 0)
1278                    goto bad;
                                                                  ip6_output.c
```

1276–1278 The ip6_getpmtu() function (see Section 3.13.8) determines the path MTU to the destination and stores the MTU in variable mtu. [RFC2460] requires every packet be fragmented in some cases regardless of the MTU and packet's length, in which case ip6_getpmtu() sets alwaysfrag to non-0. The special case will be discussed later.

Listing 3-170

```
                                                                  ip6_output.c
1280            /*
1281             * The caller of this function may specify to use the minimum MTU
1282             * in some cases.
1283             * An advanced API option (IPV6_USE_MIN_MTU) can also override MTU
1284             * setting.  The logic is a bit complicated; by default, unicast
1285             * packets will follow path MTU while multicast packets will be sent at
1286             * the minimum MTU.  If IP6PO_MINMTU_ALL is specified, all packets
1287             * including unicast ones will be sent at the minimum MTU.  Multicast
1288             * packets will always be sent at the minimum MTU unless
1289             * IP6PO_MINMTU_DISABLE is explicitly specified.
1290             * See rfc2292bis (07 and later) for more details.
1291             */
1292            if (mtu > IPV6_MMTU) {
1293                    if ((flags & IPV6_MINMTU))
1294                            mtu = IPV6_MMTU;
1295                    else if (opt && opt->ip6po_minmtu == IP6PO_MINMTU_ALL)
1296                            mtu = IPV6_MMTU;
1297                    else if (IN6_IS_ADDR_MULTICAST(&ip6->ip6_dst) &&
1298                        (opt == NULL ||
1299                        opt->ip6po_minmtu != IP6PO_MINMTU_DISABLE)) {
1300                            mtu = IPV6_MMTU;
1301                    }
1302            }
                                                                  ip6_output.c
```

1292–1302 Typically, the outgoing packet is sent without being fragmented as long as it fits the determined path MTU size. If the path MTU discovery is not completed and the packet is too large for some intermediate link, the packet will be discarded, and, when necessary, must be resent with the updated path MTU value.

In some cases, however, it is rather desirable to skip the path MTU discovery procedure and always fragment packets at the minimum MTU size (1280 bytes). For example, it should be better to fragment an ICMPv6 echo reply message whose length is larger than the minimum MTU, rather than trying path MTU discovery for the destination at the risk of the possible loss of the reply packets.

There are several ways to do this:

- The caller of `ip6_output()` can specify this behavior by setting the kernel-internal `IPV6_MINMTU` flag. The scenario of ICMPv6 echo reply described above belongs to this case, and we will see the implementation in Section 4.8.3.

- The application can control the policy using the `IPV6_USE_MIN_MTU` socket option (see Section 7.3.6). If this option is set to `IP6PO_MINMTU_ALL`, any large packets will be fragmented at the minimum MTU size. Otherwise, if the packet's destination is a multicast address, it will be fragmented at the minimum MTU unless this option is explicitly set to `IP6PO_MINMTU_DISABLE`.

In these cases, variable `mtu` is reset to the minimum MTU as if the determined path MTU had that value.

Clear Scope Zone ID

Listing 3-171
——— `ip6_output.c`

```
1305            /*
1306             * clear embedded scope identifiers if necessary.
1307             * in6_clearscope will touch the addresses only when necessary.
1308             */
1309            in6_clearscope(&ip6->ip6_src);
1310            in6_clearscope(&ip6->ip6_dst);
```
——— `ip6_output.c`

1309–1310 The Source and Destination Address fields of the IPv6 header may embed the scope zone IDs (see Section 2.9.3). These must be removed before the packet is sent outside the node, and `in6_clearscope()` performs the cleanup action.

Process Hop-by-Hop Options Header

Listing 3-172
——— `ip6_output.c`

```
1335            /*
1336             * If the outgoing packet contains a hop-by-hop options header,
1337             * it must be examined and processed even by the source node.
1338             * (RFC 2460, section 4.)
1339             */
1340            if (exthdrs.ip6e_hbh) {
1341                    struct ip6_hbh *hbh = mtod(exthdrs.ip6e_hbh, struct ip6_hbh *);
1342                    u_int32_t dummy; /* XXX unused */
1343                    u_int32_t plen = 0; /* XXX: ip6_process will check the value */
....
1349                    /*
1350                     *  XXX: if we have to send an ICMPv6 error to the sender,
1351                     *       we need the M_LOOP flag since icmp6_error() expects
1352                     *       the IPv6 and the hop-by-hop options header are
1353                     *       continuous unless the flag is set.
1354                     */
1355                    m->m_flags |= M_LOOP;
1356                    m->m_pkthdr.rcvif = ifp;
1357                    if (ip6_process_hopopts(m, (u_int8_t *)(hbh + 1),
1358                        ((hbh->ip6h_len + 1) << 3) - sizeof(struct ip6_hbh),
1359                        &dummy, &plen) < 0) {
1360                            /* m was already freed at this point */
```

```
1361                                error = EINVAL;/* better error? */
1362                                goto done;
1363                            }
1364                        m->m_flags &= ~M_LOOP; /* XXX */
1365                        m->m_pkthdr.rcvif = NULL;
1366                    }
```
                                                              ————————ip6_output.c

1340–1363 The Hop-by-Hop options header must be examined by every node en route to the destination, including both the source and the destination nodes as specified by [RFC2460]. If the outgoing packet includes a Hop-by-Hop options header, the ip6_process_hopopts() function (Section 3.8.1) is invoked to process the header by the originating node itself. The dummy arguments correspond to the Router Alert option, which is not used here even if included.

Note that the M_LOOP flag is set before calling ip6_process_hopopts(). As commented, this flag is set in case ip6_process_hopopts() encounters an error and calls icmp6_error(). The icmp6_error() function is usually called for an incoming packet, and expects that a contiguous memory space stores the entire portion of the erroneous packet from the IPv6 header to the point where the error happens (see Sections 1.6.3 and 4.8.1). However, this clearly does not hold in this case as shown in Figure 3-24 (page 251). The IPv6 header and the Hop-by-Hop options header are stored in separate mbufs. The M_LOOP flag is set, expecting the IP6_EXTHDR_CHECK() macro called from icmp6_error() treats the packet as a special case.

Unfortunately, this trick does not work as intended. As shown in Section 1.6.3, the IP6_EXTHDR_CHECK() macro actually does not change the behavior based on the M_LOOP flag in the implementation described in this book. As a result, an ICMPv6 error message will not be sent even if the Hop-by-Hop options header causes an error. It should not matter much in practice, though, since in this case the application that made the erroneous header will be informed of the error by the failure of the transmission system call (e.g., sendto()) with an error of EINVAL.

Similarly, since the icmp6_error() function expects that a valid interface pointer is set in the rcvif member of the packet header, the outgoing interface is temporarily set here. The originating interface, origifp, should be better in this case, though. In any event, it does not actually take effect because icmp6_error() will discard the packet in an early stage, as described above.

1364–1365 The temporarily modified fields for the possible error case are restored.

Whether to Fragment Packet

The next part of the code determines whether the outgoing packet should be fragmented. It is basically decided by the packet length and the path MTU size, but other optional parameters complicate the processing:

- In some cases, a Fragment header must be inserted even if the packet fits in the path MTU size as explained in Listing 3-169. The alwaysfrag variable remembers this condition.

- The `IPV6_DONTFRAG` socket option or an ancillary data item of the same name can be specified by the application to instruct the kernel not to fragment the packet at the known path MTU size so that the application can perform the path MTU discovery procedure by itself (see Section 7.3.6).

Listing 3-173

_____ ip6_output.c

```
1389            /*
1390             * Send the packet to the outgoing interface.
1391             * If necessary, do IPv6 fragmentation before sending.
1392             *
1393             * the logic here is rather complex:
1394             * 1: normal case (dontfrag == 0, alwaysfrag == 0)
1395             * 1-a: send as is if tlen <= path mtu
1396             * 1-b: fragment if tlen > path mtu
1397             *
1398             * 2: if user asks us not to fragment (dontfrag == 1)
1399             * 2-a: send as is if tlen <= interface mtu
1400             * 2-b: error if tlen > interface mtu
1401             *
1402             * 3: if we always need to attach fragment header (alwaysfrag == 1)
1403             *      always fragment
1404             *
1405             * 4: if dontfrag == 1 && alwaysfrag == 1
1406             *      error, as we cannot handle this conflicting request
1407             */
1408            tlen = m->m_pkthdr.len;
1409
1410            if (opt && (opt->ip6po_flags & IP6PO_DONTFRAG))
1411                    dontfrag = 1;
1412            else
1413                    dontfrag = 0;
1414            if (dontfrag && alwaysfrag) {   /* case 4 */
1415                    /* conflicting request - can't transmit */
1416                    error = EMSGSIZE;
1417                    goto bad;
1418            }
1419            if (dontfrag && tlen > IN6_LINKMTU(ifp)) {       /* case 2-b */
1420                    /*
1421                     * Even if the DONTFRAG option is specified, we cannot send the
1422                     * packet when the data length is larger than the MTU of the
1423                     * outgoing interface.
1424                     * Notify the error by sending IPV6_PATHMTU ancillary data as
1425                     * well as returning an error code (the latter is not described
1426                     * in the API spec.)
1427                     */
1428                    u_int32_t mtu32;
1429                    struct ip6ctlparam ip6cp;
1430
1431                    mtu32 = (u_int32_t)mtu;
1432                    bzero(&ip6cp, sizeof(ip6cp));
1433                    ip6cp.ip6c_cmdarg = (void *)&mtu32;
1434                    pfctlinput2(PRC_MSGSIZE, &ro_pmtu->ro_dst, (void *)&ip6cp);
1435
1436                    error = EMSGSIZE;
1437                    goto bad;
1438            }
```

_____ ip6_output.c

1408 Variable `tlen` holds the original packet size.

1410 If the calling application specifies the `IPV6_DONTFRAG` socket option or an equivalent ancillary data item with a non-0 value, `ip6po_flags` of argument `opt` has the

IP6PO_DONTFRAG set. Variable `dontfrag` is set to 1 in this case for later processing; otherwise, it is set to 0.

1414–1417 This implementation prohibits the case where `dontfrag` and `alwaysfrag` are both non-0, and returns an error of `EMSGSIZE` to the caller.

Note: This behavior is controversial, though, since a non-0 `alwaysfrag` value does not necessarily mean the packet is fragmented.

1419–1438 If `dontfrag` is non-0 and the packet is larger than the MTU of the outgoing link, the packet is discarded and an empty message with an `IPV6_PATHMTU` ancillary data item with the known path MTU size (`mtu`) will be delivered to the application by the `ip6_notify_pmtu()` function via `pfctlinput2()` (see Section 6.7.10) as specified in [RFC3542](*). As indicated in the RFC, this implementation also returns an explicit error of `EMSGSIZE` to the application.

(*) It is probably not appropriate to use the known path MTU size here, according to the intended usage of `IPV6_DONTFRAG`. The size of the outgoing link MTU should be better.

Send Packet without Fragmentation

Listing 3-174

```
                                                                    ip6_output.c
1440            /*
1441             * transmit packet without fragmentation
1442             */
1443            if (dontfrag || (!alwaysfrag && tlen <= mtu)) { /* case 1-a and 2-a */
1444                    struct in6_ifaddr *ia6;
1445
1446                    ip6 = mtod(m, struct ip6_hdr *);
1447                    ia6 = in6_ifawithifp(ifp, &ip6->ip6_src);
1448                    if (ia6) {
1449                            /* Record statistics for this interface address. */
    ....
1454                            ia6->ia_ifa.if_opackets++;
1455                            ia6->ia_ifa.if_obytes += m->m_pkthdr.len;
    ....
1460                    }

    ....(IPsec processing)

1465                    error = nd6_output(ifp, origifp, m, dst, rt);
1466                    goto done;
1467            }
                                                                    ip6_output.c
```

1443–1467 If the caller specified `IPV6_DONTFRAG` being on, or if the packet is smaller than the allowable MTU and can be sent without a Fragment header, the packet can be sent to the network at this point. Statistics counters specific to the interface address structure corresponding to the source address are incremented. The nd6_output() function performs the link-level next hop resolution based on the Neighbor Discovery protocol. This function will be discussed in Section 5.22.2.

Fragment Packet
Listing 3-175

```
                                                              ip6_output.c
1469            /*
1470             * try to fragment the packet.  case 1-b and 3
1471             */
1472        if (mtu < IPV6_MMTU) {
1473                /* path MTU cannot be less than IPV6_MMTU */
1474                error = EMSGSIZE;
1475                in6_ifstat_inc(ifp, ifs6_out_fragfail);
1476                goto bad;
1477        } else if (ip6->ip6_plen == 0) {
1478                /* jumbo payload cannot be fragmented */
1479                error = EMSGSIZE;
1480                in6_ifstat_inc(ifp, ifs6_out_fragfail);
1481                goto bad;
                                                              ip6_output.c
```

1472–1476 [RFC2460] requires that every link conveying IPv6 packets must have an minimum MTU of 1280 bytes (IPV6_MMTU). If mtu is smaller than 1280, it means the outgoing link does not meet the requirement, and the packet is discarded with an error of EMSGSIZE.

1477–1481 [RFC2675] specifies that Jumbo Payload option must not be used in a packet containing a Fragment header. If the Payload Length field of the IPv6 header is 0, it commonly means the packet contains a Jumbo Payload option (Listing 3-141). Since the packet that reaches this code point will also contain a Fragment header below, it must be discarded according to the RFC. An error of EMSGSIZE will be returned in this case.

Note: This code has a small bug. The payload length field can also be 0 when the packet does not have any extension header or an upper layer payload, in which case it does not have a Jumbo Payload option. Although such a packet should typically be sent in the previous listing, it can still reach this point when alwaysfrag is non-0. Line 1477 should actually check whether the packet contains a Jumbo Payload option explicitly.

Listing 3-176

```
                                                              ip6_output.c
1482        } else {
1483                struct mbuf **mnext, *m_frgpart;
1484                struct ip6_frag *ip6f;
1485                u_int32_t id = htonl(ip6_id++);
1486                u_char nextproto;
1487                struct ip6ctlparam ip6cp;
1488                u_int32_t mtu32;
1489
1490                /*
1491                 * Too large for the destination or interface;
1492                 * fragment if possible.
1493                 * Must be able to put at least 8 bytes per fragment.
```

```
1494                         */
1495                         hlen = unfragpartlen;
1496                         if (mtu > IPV6_MAXPACKET)
1497                                 mtu = IPV6_MAXPACKET;
1499                         /* Notify a proper path MTU to applications. */
1500                         mtu32 = (u_int32_t)mtu;
1501                         bzero(&ip6cp, sizeof(ip6cp));
1502                         ip6cp.ip6c_cmdarg = (void *)&mtu32;
1503                         pfctlinput2(PRC_MSGSIZE, &ro_pmtu->ro_dst, (void *)&ip6cp);
```
―― ip6_output.c

1485 Variable `id` will be used as the Fragment Identification value. It is monotonically incremented in the system based on global variable `ip6_id`.

1495 Variable `hlen` is set to the length of the unfragmentable part of the original packet, which
must be present in every fragment.

1496–1497 The payload length of each fragment including the Fragment header cannot exceed
`IPV6_MAXPACKET` (65535) bytes, and this restriction enforces an effective upper limit of
the MTU.

> *Note*: This restriction is a bit too restrictive. Since the IPv6 header is not counted as a
> part of the payload, the effective limit of `mtu` can actually be `IPV6_MAXPACKET` +
> size of the IPv6 header, that is, 65575 bytes.

1499–1503 The fact that the packet is fragmented is reported to the application via the
`pfctlinput2()` function the same way we saw in Listing 3-173. This behavior is not
specified in [RFC3542] and can actually be rather harmful: It will deliver an error of
`EMSGSIZE` to sockets connected to the destination address. This happens every time
fragmentation occurs, and it would be just bothersome for an application sending large
datagrams and simply hoping for the necessary fragmentation happening in the kernel.
An NFS client is an example of this type of application. In order to not bother such applications, this part of the code has been disabled in later versions of the kernel code.

Listing 3-177
―― ip6_output.c
```
1505                         len = (mtu - hlen - sizeof(struct ip6_frag)) & ~7;
1506                         if (len < 8) {
1507                                 error = EMSGSIZE;
1508                                 in6_ifstat_inc(ifp, ifs6_out_fragfail);
1509                                 goto bad;
1510                         }
```
―― ip6_output.c

1505–1510 The maximum length of the fragmentable part is the allowable MTU subtracting
the length of the unfragmentable part, then subtracting the length of the Fragment header.
It must then be aligned at a multiple of 8-byte units (note that the size of each packet
fragment must be an integer multiple of 8 bytes except for the last fragment, since fragment
offsets are represented in 8 byte units). If the available space for the fragmentable part is
too short, the packet is discarded and an error of `EMSGSIZE` will be returned.

> *Note*: Technically, this is too restrictive since the original packet itself can be the last fragment when `alwaysfrag` is non-0. This does not actually harm in practice, though, unless the packet has a very long unfragmentable part and a very small fragmentable part.

Listing 3-178

```
                                                                ── ip6_output.c
1512                    mnext = &m->m_nextpkt;
                                                                ── ip6_output.c
```

1512 Variable `mnext` holds the location of the pointer to the next packet for chaining the packet fragments.

Listing 3-179

```
                                                                ── ip6_output.c
1514                    /*
1515                     * Change the next header field of the last header in the
1516                     * unfragmentable part.
1517                     */
...
1528                    if (exthdrs.ip6e_rthdr) {
1529                            nextproto = *mtod(exthdrs.ip6e_rthdr, u_char *);
1530                            *mtod(exthdrs.ip6e_rthdr, u_char *) = IPPROTO_FRAGMENT;
1531                    } else
1532                    if (exthdrs.ip6e_dest1) {
1533                            nextproto = *mtod(exthdrs.ip6e_dest1, u_char *);
1534                            *mtod(exthdrs.ip6e_dest1, u_char *) = IPPROTO_FRAGMENT;
1535                    } else if (exthdrs.ip6e_hbh) {
1536                            nextproto = *mtod(exthdrs.ip6e_hbh, u_char *);
1537                            *mtod(exthdrs.ip6e_hbh, u_char *) = IPPROTO_FRAGMENT;
1538                    } else {
1539                            nextproto = ip6->ip6_nxt;
1540                            ip6->ip6_nxt = IPPROTO_FRAGMENT;
1541                    }
                                                                ── ip6_output.c
```

1528–1541 The Next Header field of the last unfragmentable extension header is reset to the type of Fragment header (`IPPROTO_FRAGMENT`), and the original value of this field is copied to variable `nextproto`.

Listing 3-180

```
                                                                ── ip6_output.c
1543                    /*
1544                     * Loop through length of segment after first fragment,
1545                     * make new header and copy data of each part and link onto
1546                     * chain.
1547                     */
1548                    m0 = m;
1549                    for (off = hlen; off < tlen; off += len) {
                                                                ── ip6_output.c
```

1548–1549 Variable `m0` points to the mbuf containing the original packet. In the `for` loop, the packet is divided into fragments and sent with the Fragment header separately. The loop starts at the length of `hlen` (the length of the unfragmentable part) and continues until the offset reaches the total length of the original packet.

Listing 3-181
_____ip6_output.c
```
1550                        MGETHDR(m, M_DONTWAIT, MT_HEADER);
1551                        if (!m) {
1552                                error = ENOBUFS;
1553                                ip6stat.ip6s_odropped++;
1554                                goto sendorfree;
1555                        }
1556                        m->m_pkthdr.rcvif = NULL;
1557                        m->m_flags = m0->m_flags & M_COPYFLAGS;
1558                        *mnext = m;
1559                        mnext = &m->m_nextpkt;
1560                        m->m_data += max_linkhdr;
1561                        mhip6 = mtod(m, struct ip6_hdr *);
1562                        *mhip6 = *ip6;
1563                        if (!ip6_setpktaddrs(m, &src_sa, &dst_sa)) {
1564                                error = ENOBUFS;
1565                                ip6stat.ip6s_odropped++;
1566                                goto sendorfree;
1567                        }
1568                        m->m_len = sizeof(*mhip6);
```
_____ip6_output.c

1550–1560 A new mbuf is allocated for each fragment, initialized with the parameters stored in the original packet, and linked into the fragment chain. The data pointer is adjusted to reserve space for the link-layer header.

1561–1562 The IPv6 header of the original packet is copied to the fragment packet, and variable `mhip6` is set to point to the new IPv6 header.

1563–1567 The source and destination addresses represented in the socket address structure are attached to the mbuf via an mbuf tag.

1568 The `m_len` field of the newly allocated mbuf is initialized to the IPv6 header size.

Listing 3-182
_____ip6_output.c
```
1569                        error = ip6_insertfraghdr(m0, m, hlen, &ip6f);
1570                        if (error) {
1571                                ip6stat.ip6s_odropped++;
1572                                goto sendorfree;
1573                        }
```
_____ip6_output.c

1569–1573 The `ip6_insertfraghdr()` function (Section 3.13.7) copies the unfragmentable part of the original packet and then creates a Fragment header. The Fragment header is returned in `ip6f` at the successful completion of `ip6_insertfraghdr()`.

Listing 3-183
_____ip6_output.c
```
1574                        ip6f->ip6f_offlg = htons((u_short)((off - hlen) & ~7));
1575                        if (off + len >= tlen)
1576                                len = tlen - off;
```

```
1577                              else
1578                                  ip6f->ip6f_offlg |= IP6F_MORE_FRAG;
1579                         mhip6->ip6_plen = htons((u_short)(len + hlen +
1580                             sizeof(*ip6f) - sizeof(struct ip6_hdr)));
```
―― *ip6_output.c*

1574 The fragment offset (`ip6f_offlg`) is set to the length relative to the start of the fragmentable part of the original packet in 8-byte units.

1575–1578 If the current fragment is the last fragment, `len` is adjusted to the actual length of the fragmentable part; otherwise, the "M" bit flag is set in the Fragment header.

1579–1580 The total length of the fragment is the summation of the following:

- The length of the unfragmentable part including the size of the IPv6 header (`hlen`)

- The length of the fragmentable part contained in this fragment (`len`)

- The size of the Fragment header

The Payload Length field of the IPv6 header of this fragment is set to this length subtracting the size of the IPv6 header.

Listing 3-184
―― *ip6_output.c*
```
1581                         if ((m_frgpart = m_copy(m0, off, len)) == 0) {
1582                                 error = ENOBUFS;
1583                                 ip6stat.ip6s_odropped++;
1584                                 goto sendorfree;
1585                         }
1586                         m_cat(m, m_frgpart);
1587                         m->m_pkthdr.len = len + hlen + sizeof(*ip6f);
1588                         m->m_pkthdr.rcvif = (struct ifnet *)0;
```
―― *ip6_output.c*

1581–1588 The `len` bytes of the original packet starting from offset `off` are copied into a new mbuf chain, `m_frgpart`, to build the current fragment. Function `m_cat()` concatenates the unfragmentable part and the fragmentable part. The overall packet length is initialized to the length of the fragment packet. Line 1588 is actually redundant since this field was initialized to NULL at line 1556.

Listing 3-185
―― *ip6_output.c*
```
1589                             ip6f->ip6f_reserved = 0;
1590                             ip6f->ip6f_ident = id;
1591                             ip6f->ip6f_nxt = nextproto;
1592                             ip6stat.ip6s_ofragments++;
1593                             in6_ifstat_inc(ifp, ifs6_out_fragcreat);
1594                     }

1596                     in6_ifstat_inc(ifp, ifs6_out_fragok);
1597             }
```
―― *ip6_output.c*

1589–1592 The remaining fields in the Fragment header (the Next Header field, the Reserved field, and the Identification field) are initialized (recall `id` was set in Listing 3-176).

1592–1593 Statistics counters for each fragment are incremented which accumulate the number of outgoing fragments created.

1596 On completion of creating all the fragments, a statistics counter is incremented that indicates successful fragmentation of the original IPv6 packet. Note that this line is outside the for loop, and this counter is maintained per original packet.

The process of inserting a Fragment header is depicted in Figure 3-26.

Listing 3-186

```
                                                                    ip6_output.c
1599             /*
1600              * Remove leading garbages.
1601              */
1602     sendorfree:
1603             m = m0->m_nextpkt;
1604             m0->m_nextpkt = 0;
1605             m_freem(m0);
                                                                    ip6_output.c
```

1602–1605 Recall that variable m0 contained the original IPv6 packet header and the unfragmentable extension headers. These headers have been replicated in each fragment packet and can now be freed.

FIGURE 3-26

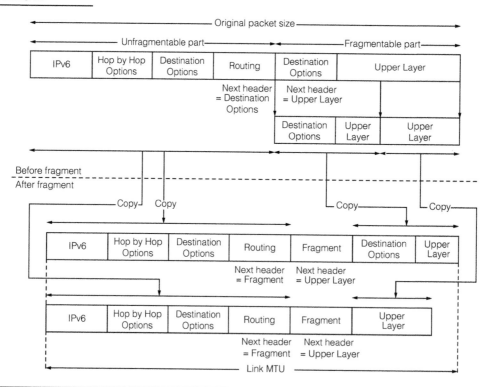

Insertion of the Fragment header.

Listing 3-187
_____ ip6_output.c

```
1606              for (m0 = m; m; m = m0) {
1607                  m0 = m->m_nextpkt;
1608                  m->m_nextpkt = 0;
1609                  if (error == 0) {
1610                      struct in6_ifaddr *ia6;
1611                      ip6 = mtod(m, struct ip6_hdr *);
1612                      ia6 = in6_ifawithifp(ifp, &ip6->ip6_src);
1613                      if (ia6) {
1614                          /*
1615                           * Record statistics for this interface
1616                           * address.
1617                           */
    ....
1622                          ia6->ia_ifa.if_opackets++;
1623                          ia6->ia_ifa.if_obytes += m->m_pkthdr.len;
    ....
1628                      }
```

```
    ....(IPsec processing)
```

```
1633                      error = nd6_output(ifp, origifp, m, dst, rt);
1634                  } else
1635                      m_freem(m);
1636              }
1637
1638              if (error == 0)
1639                  ip6stat.ip6s_fragmented++;
```
_____ ip6_output.c

1606–1639 Each fragment is retrieved from the chain and transmitted by function
nd6_output (). Statistics counters specific to the interface address structure corresponding to the source address are incremented.

> _Note_: If an error occurs during any of the fragment transmission, the remaining fragments
> are freed without being transmitted. It should also be noted that if any error occurred
> during the construction of fragments in the above listings, none of the fragments are
> transmitted here.

Cleanup

Listing 3-188
_____ ip6_output.c

```
1641      done:
1642          if (ro == &ip6route && ro->ro_rt) { /* brace necessary for RTFREE */
1643              RTFREE(ro->ro_rt);
1644          } else if (ro_pmtu == &ip6route && ro_pmtu->ro_rt) {
1645              RTFREE(ro_pmtu->ro_rt);
1646          }
1647
```

```
    ....(IPsec processing)
```

```
1657          return (error);
```
_____ ip6_output.c

1642–1646 If a local `route{}` structure is used in finding a route instead of a cached route passed from the upper layer, the reference must be freed here since no one else uses the route.

1657 Any error code during the output process, which is 0 on success, is returned to the caller.

Listing 3-189

```
                                                                        ip6_output.c
1659    freehdrs:
1660            m_freem(exthdrs.ip6e_hbh);          /* m_freem will check if mbuf is 0 */
1661            m_freem(exthdrs.ip6e_dest1);
1662            m_freem(exthdrs.ip6e_rthdr);
1663            m_freem(exthdrs.ip6e_dest2);
....
1669            /* FALLTHROUGH */
1670    bad:
1671            m_freem(m);
1672            goto done;
1673    }
                                                                        ip6_output.c
```

1659–1663 If an error occurred before completing the creation of the outgoing packet with extension headers, these are freed.

1670–1672 If an error occurred before sending the outgoing packet, including the above cases, the mbuf containing the packet is freed. The code jumps back to the above cleanup process.

3.13.4   Make Extension Headers: `ip6_copyexthdr()` Function

The `ip6_copyexthdr()` function, shown below, is a subroutine of `ip6_output()`. It allocates an instance of mbuf, and, when necessary, an associated cluster buffer that can store the specified length (`hlen`) of an IPv6 extension header (`hdr`).

Note that this function fails if the length is larger than `MCLBYTES`, which is commonly 2048 bytes (line 1683). This is an implementation-specific restriction. While the typical value happens to equal the possible maximum length of most extension headers (see Section 3.3), it does not intend to ensure that the storage has always a sufficient size.

However, this restriction ensures an extension header in this implementation is always stored in a single mbuf and in a contiguous memory space, which simplifies the processing in `ip6_output()`.

Listing 3-190

```
                                                                        ip6_output.c
1675    static int
1676    ip6_copyexthdr(mp, hdr, hlen)
1677            struct mbuf **mp;
1678            caddr_t hdr;
1679            int hlen;
1680    {
1681            struct mbuf *m;
1682
1683            if (hlen > MCLBYTES)
1684                    return (ENOBUFS); /* XXX */
1685
1686            MGET(m, M_DONTWAIT, MT_DATA);
1687            if (!m)
1688                    return (ENOBUFS);
1689
```

```
1690                    if (hlen > MLEN) {
1691                            MCLGET(m, M_DONTWAIT);
1692                            if ((m->m_flags & M_EXT) == 0) {
1693                                    m_free(m);
1694                                    return (ENOBUFS);
1695                            }
1696                    }
1697                    m->m_len = hlen;
1698                    if (hdr)
1699                            bcopy(hdr, mtod(m, caddr_t), hlen);
1700
1701                    *mp = m;
1702                    return (0);
1703            }
```
                                                                    _____ip6_output.c

3.13.5 Split Headers: `ip6_splithdr()` Function

The `ip6_splithdr()` function, shown below, is a subroutine of `ip6_output()` and ensures the first mbuf only contains the IPv6 header as preprocessing of extension header insertion. If the first mbuf contains more data than the IPv6 header, this function allocates a new mbuf, moves the IPv6 header to the allocated space, and prepends the new mbuf to the original mbuf chain. The `ip6e_ip6` member of the given `ip6_exthdrs{}` structure is expected to point to the mbuf containing the IPv6 header. In case the mbuf changed in this function, this member is updated at line 4955.

Listing 3-191
                                                                    _____ip6_output.c

```
4924    /*
4925     * Chop IPv6 header off from the payload.
4926     */
4927    static int
4928    ip6_splithdr(m, exthdrs)
4929            struct mbuf *m;
4930            struct ip6_exthdrs *exthdrs;
4931    {
4932            struct mbuf *mh;
4933            struct ip6_hdr *ip6;
4934
4935            ip6 = mtod(m, struct ip6_hdr *);
4936            if (m->m_len > sizeof(*ip6)) {
4937                    MGETHDR(mh, M_DONTWAIT, MT_HEADER);
4938                    if (mh == 0) {
4939                            m_freem(m);
4940                            return ENOBUFS;
4941                    }
....
4943                    M_MOVE_PKTHDR(mh, m);
....
4947                    MH_ALIGN(mh, sizeof(*ip6));
4948                    m->m_len -= sizeof(*ip6);
4949                    m->m_data += sizeof(*ip6);
4950                    mh->m_next = m;
4951                    m = mh;
4952                    m->m_len = sizeof(*ip6);
4953                    bcopy((caddr_t)ip6, mtod(m, caddr_t), sizeof(*ip6));
4954            }
4955            exthdrs->ip6e_ip6 = m;
4956            return 0;
4957    }
4958
```
                                                                    _____ip6_output.c

3.13.6   Insert Jumbo Payload Option: `ip6_insert_jumboopt()` Function

The `ip6_insert_jumboopt()` function, shown below, is another subroutine of `ip6_output()`, which prepares a Jumbo Payload option for the outgoing packet. When necessary, it also creates a new Hop-by-Hop options header storing the option.

Listing 3-192

```
                                                            ip6_output.c
1705    /*
1706     * Insert jumbo payload option.
1707     */
1708    static int
1709    ip6_insert_jumboopt(exthdrs, plen)
1710            struct ip6_exthdrs *exthdrs;
1711            u_int32_t plen;
1712    {
1713            struct mbuf *mopt;
1714            u_int8_t *optbuf;
1715            u_int32_t v;
1716
1717    #define JUMBOOPTLEN     8       /* length of jumbo payload option and padding */
1718
1719            /*
1720             * If there is no hop-by-hop options header, allocate new one.
1721             * If there is one but it doesn't have enough space to store the
1722             * jumbo payload option, allocate a cluster to store the whole options.
1723             * Otherwise, use it to store the options.
1724             */
1725            if (exthdrs->ip6e_hbh == 0) {
1726                    MGET(mopt, M_DONTWAIT, MT_DATA);
1727                    if (mopt == 0)
1728                            return (ENOBUFS);
1729                    mopt->m_len = JUMBOOPTLEN;
1730                    optbuf = mtod(mopt, u_int8_t *);
1731                    optbuf[1] = 0;  /* = ((JUMBOOPTLEN) >> 3) - 1 */
1732                    exthdrs->ip6e_hbh = mopt;
                                                            ip6_output.c
```

1717 As shown in Figure 3-15, the Jumbo Payload option is a constant length option of 6 bytes. Macro constant `JUMBOOPTLEN` is set to the minimum length that is a multiple of 8 and is long enough to store this option. This is set to this value taking into account possible padding for making the whole header length a multiple of 8 bytes.

1725–1732 If the current set of extension headers for the outgoing packet does not contain a Hop-by-Hop options header, a new mbuf for the header is allocated. The new header is expected to contain the Jumbo Payload option only, and its Length field (`optbuf[1]`) is set to an appropriate size for this purpose. The newly allocated mbuf is stored in the given `ip6_exthdrs{}` structure.

Listing 3-193

```
                                                            ip6_output.c
1733            } else {
1734                    struct ip6_hbh *hbh;
1735
1736                    mopt = exthdrs->ip6e_hbh;
1737                    if (M_TRAILINGSPACE(mopt) < JUMBOOPTLEN) {
1738                            /*
1739                             * XXX assumption:
1740                             * - exthdrs->ip6e_hbh is not referenced from places
```

```
1741                              *    other than exthdrs.
1742                              * - exthdrs->ip6e_hbh is not an mbuf chain.
1743                              */
1744                             int oldoptlen = mopt->m_len;
1745                             struct mbuf *n;
1746
1747                             /*
1748                              * XXX: give up if the whole (new) hbh header does
1749                              * not fit even in an mbuf cluster.
1750                              */
1751                             if (oldoptlen + JUMBOOPTLEN > MCLBYTES)
1752                                     return (ENOBUFS);
1753
1754                             /*
1755                              * As a consequence, we must always prepare a cluster
1756                              * at this point.
1757                              */
1758                             MGET(n, M_DONTWAIT, MT_DATA);
1759                             if (n) {
1760                                     MCLGET(n, M_DONTWAIT);
1761                                     if ((n->m_flags & M_EXT) == 0) {
1762                                             m_freem(n);
1763                                             n = NULL;
1764                                     }
1765                             }
1766                             if (!n)
1767                                     return (ENOBUFS);
1768                             n->m_len = oldoptlen + JUMBOOPTLEN;
1769                             bcopy(mtod(mopt, caddr_t), mtod(n, caddr_t),
1770                                 oldoptlen);
1771                             optbuf = mtod(n, u_int8_t *) + oldoptlen;
1772                             m_freem(mopt);
1773                             mopt = exthdrs->ip6e_hbh = n;
1774                     } else {
1775                             optbuf = mtod(mopt, u_int8_t *) + mopt->m_len;
1776                             mopt->m_len += JUMBOOPTLEN;
1777                     }
```
—— ip6_output.c

1737 If a Hop-by-Hop options header is already present, its length is checked to see whether the Jumbo Payload option can be added at the end. If the existing header does not contain an enough space, a new mbuf to store the entire header with the Jumbo Payload option is allocated as follows.

1751–1773 If the entire buffer with the new option does not fit into an mbuf cluster, the insertion procedure fails(*). Otherwise, a new mbuf with a cluster is allocated with the data space of the original header and the Jumbo Payload option. The content of the original header is copied to the new mbuf. Variable optbuf is set to point to the end of the existing header, where the Jumbo Payload option with padding is expected to be inserted. The original mbuf is freed, and the ip6e_hbh member of the ip6_exthdrs{} structure is replaced with the new mbuf.

(*) Technically, this check is too restrictive. For example, the existing header may end with a large padding option which can be replaced with the jumbo payload length. In practice, however, such an optimization for space will not be worth the complexity, a Hop-by-Hop options header should typically be short enough to have the additional Jumbo Payload option with the padding at the end.

1774–1777 If the free space in the existing mbuf is large enough to contain the Jumbo Payload option as a result of the check at line 1737, the option will be appended at the end of the existing space. Variable `optbuf` is set to the end of the data field of the mbuf, and `m_len` is updated to reflect the new data length.

Listing 3-194

─── ip6_output.c
```
1778                        optbuf[0] = IP6OPT_PADN;
1779                        optbuf[1] = 0;
1780
1781                        /*
1782                         * Adjust the header length according to the pad and
1783                         * the jumbo payload option.
1784                         */
1785                        hbh = mtod(mopt, struct ip6_hbh *);
1786                        hbh->ip6h_len += (JUMBOOPTLEN >> 3);
1787             }
```
─── ip6_output.c

1778–1779 The first two bytes of the 8-byte buffer is filled with a PadN option with empty padding field to meet the alignment requirement of the Jumbo Payload option, which is "4n+2".

1785–1786 The Hdr Ext Len field of the Hop-by-Hop options header is updated according to the 8-byte counting rule.

> *Note*: There is a risk of overflow here. If MCLBYTES is very large and the existing header has the possible maximum size, `ip6h_len` will overflow and reset to 0.

Listing 3-195

─── ip6_output.c
```
1789                /* fill in the option. */
1790                optbuf[2] = IP6OPT_JUMBO;
1791                optbuf[3] = 4;
1792                v = (u_int32_t)htonl(plen + JUMBOOPTLEN);
1793                bcopy(&v, &optbuf[4], sizeof(u_int32_t));
1794
1795                /* finally, adjust the packet header length */
1796                exthdrs->ip6e_ip6->m_pkthdr.len += JUMBOOPTLEN;
1797
1798                return (0);
1799    #undef JUMBOOPTLEN
1800    }
```
─── ip6_output.c

1789–1799 The Jumbo Payload option type is IP6OPT_JUMBO (0xC2) and the option data length is set to 4 bytes. The Jumbo Payload Length field starts at the fourth byte of `optbuf`, which contains the length of the packet. The overall packet size is updated as the final step.

3.13.7 Fragmentation: `ip6_insertfraghdr()` Function

The `ip6_insertfraghdr()` function is also a subroutine of the `ip6_output()` function
(see Listing 3-182). It creates a Fragment header and inserts the header into the outgoing packet.
This function is shown below.

Listing 3-196

ip6_output.c

```
1802      /*
1803       * Insert fragment header and copy unfragmentable header portions.
1804       */
1805      static int
1806      ip6_insertfraghdr(m0, m, hlen, frghdrp)
1807              struct mbuf *m0, *m;
1808              int hlen;
1809              struct ip6_frag **frghdrp;
1810      {
1811              struct mbuf *n, *mlast;
1812
1813              if (hlen > sizeof(struct ip6_hdr)) {
1814                      n = m_copym(m0, sizeof(struct ip6_hdr),
1815                          hlen - sizeof(struct ip6_hdr), M_DONTWAIT);
1816                      if (n == 0)
1817                              return (ENOBUFS);
1818                      m->m_next = n;
1819              } else
1820                      n = m;
```

ip6_output.c

1813–1820 Argument m0 is the original packet to be fragmented, and m is a newly created
mbuf for a separate fragment, which consists of a copied IPv6 header only (see Listing
3-181). Argument hlen includes the length of the unfragmentable part, including the size
of the IPv6 header. If this is larger than the size of the IPv6 header, there are intermediate
extension headers in the unfragmentable part. Function m_copym() allocates a new mbuf
and copies the unfragmentable part there. The new mbuf is concatenated to the head
mbuf, m.

Listing 3-197

ip6_output.c

```
1822          /* Search for the last mbuf of unfragmentable part. */
1823          for (mlast = n; mlast->m_next; mlast = mlast->m_next)
1824                  ;
1825
1826          if ((mlast->m_flags & M_EXT) == 0 &&
1827              M_TRAILINGSPACE(mlast) >= sizeof(struct ip6_frag)) {
1828                  /* use the trailing space of the last mbuf for the fragment hdr */
1829                  *frghdrp = (struct ip6_frag *)(mtod(mlast, caddr_t) +
1830                      mlast->m_len);
1831                  mlast->m_len += sizeof(struct ip6_frag);
1832                  m->m_pkthdr.len += sizeof(struct ip6_frag);
1833          } else {
1834                  /* allocate a new mbuf for the fragment header */
1835                  struct mbuf *mfrg;
1836
1837                  MGET(mfrg, M_DONTWAIT, MT_DATA);
1838                  if (mfrg == 0)
1839                          return (ENOBUFS);
1840                  mfrg->m_len = sizeof(struct ip6_frag);
1841                  *frghdrp = mtod(mfrg, struct ip6_frag *);
```

```
1842                 mlast->m_next = mfrg;
1843         }
1844
1845         return (0);
1846     }
```

1823–1824 The `for` loop iterates through the mbuf chain until it encounters the last mbuf of the chain. Variable `mlast` points to the last mbuf.

1826–1832 If the last mbuf does not have a cluster and it is large enough to hold the Fragment header, the trailing space is used for the Fragment header. Note that the former condition is essential; otherwise, the same mbuf cluster can be shared with other fragments due to the `m_copym()` operation at line 1814, while it actually cannot be shared since each fragment must have a different offset value and possibly a different M bit value.
Parameter `frghdrp` is set to point to the prepared space for the Fragment header.

1837–1842 If the last mbuf cannot be used for the Fragment header, a new mbuf is allocated for the header and is concatenated to the mbuf chain containing the unfragmentable part. Parameter `frghdrp` is set like the above case.

This part of the code is not consistent in that the packet header length (`m_pkthdr.len`) is updated only in the `if` clause. Whereas this is actually harmless since function `ip6_output()`, the caller of this function, soon resets the length field to the correct value at line 1587 (Listing 3-184), it may cause confusion and should be fixed.

3.13.8   Path MTU Determination: `ip6_getpmtu()` Function

The `ip6_output()` function calls `ip6_getpmtu()` to determine the path MTU size when transmitting a packet (see Listing 3-169). This function is also called from `ip6_ctloutput()` to provide an application with the MTU value (see Section 7.4.3).

Listing 3-198

```
1848     static int
1849     ip6_getpmtu(ro_pmtu, ro, ifp, dst, mtup, alwaysfragp)
....
1851             struct route *ro_pmtu, *ro;
....
1855             struct ifnet *ifp;
1856             struct sockaddr_in6 *dst;
1857             u_long *mtup;
1858             int *alwaysfragp;
1859     {
1860             u_int32_t mtu = 0;
1861             int alwaysfrag = 0;
1862             int error = 0;
1863
1864             if (ro_pmtu != ro) {
1865                     /* The first hop and the final destination may differ. */
1866                     struct sockaddr_in6 *sa6_dst =
1867                         (struct sockaddr_in6 *)&ro_pmtu->ro_dst;
1868                     if (ro_pmtu->ro_rt &&
1869                         ((ro_pmtu->ro_rt->rt_flags & RTF_UP) == 0 ||
....
1873                         !IN6_ARE_ADDR_EQUAL(&sa6_dst->sin6_addr, &dst->sin6_addr)
....
```

```
1875                                       )) {
1876                                           RTFREE(ro_pmtu->ro_rt);
1877                                           ro_pmtu->ro_rt = (struct rtentry *)NULL;
1878                                       }
```
—— ip6_output.c

1849–1858 When this function is called by ip6_output(), both arguments ro_pmtu and
ro are non-NULL. Typically, these are identical and expected to store the route to the
packet's destination. When the outgoing packet contains a Routing header, however, ro
is used to store the route to the first route segment in the Routing header while ro_pmtu
is for the final destination (see Listing 3-153).

On the other hand, when this function is called from ip6_ctloutput(), argument
ro is always NULL, since the route to the "first segment" does not matter in that context.

In either case, the route entry stored in ro_pmtu is expected to contain the path
MTU to the corresponding destination. Note that when a Routing header is included, the
path MTU size along with the intermediate route segments may be different from the path
MTU size of the shortest route to the destination. But, this implementation records the
path MTU size per destination address, and the stored size is the smallest MTU among all
the different paths.

1864–1878 If ro_pmtu is different from ro, it may contain a route for a different destination or
the cached route may be stale. (Note that if these two are identical, the validity of ro should
have been checked in the in6_selectroute() function called from ip6_output().)
If a route entry is stored in ro_pmtu but is not valid for the destination, the cached route
is flushed.

Listing 3-199
—— ip6_output.c

```
1879                      if (ro_pmtu->ro_rt == NULL) {
1880                              bzero(sa6_dst, sizeof(*sa6_dst)); /* for safety */
1881                              *sa6_dst = *dst;
....
1883                              sa6_dst->sin6_scope_id = 0; /* XXX */
....
1889                              rtalloc((struct route *)ro_pmtu);
....
1891                      }
1892              }
```
—— ip6_output.c

1879–1891 If ro_pmtu does not have a route entry for the destination, the rtalloc()
function tries to allocate one. This function makes a cloned host route for the specified
destination.

Listing 3-200
—— ip6_output.c

```
1893              if (ro_pmtu->ro_rt) {
1894                      u_int32_t ifmtu;
1895
1896                      if (ifp == NULL)
1897                              ifp = ro_pmtu->ro_rt->rt_ifp;
```

```
1898                    ifmtu = IN6_LINKMTU(ifp);
1899                    mtu = ro_pmtu->ro_rt->rt_rmx.rmx_mtu;
1900                    if (mtu == 0)
1901                            mtu = ifmtu;
1902                    else if (mtu < IPV6_MMTU) {
1903                            /*
1904                             * RFC2460 section 5, last paragraph:
1905                             * if we record ICMPv6 too big message with
1906                             * mtu < IPV6_MMTU, transmit packets sized IPV6_MMTU
1907                             * or smaller, with framgent header attached.
1908                             * (fragment header is needed regardless from the
1909                             * packet size, for translators to identify packets)
1910                             */
1911                            alwaysfrag = 1;
1912                            mtu = IPV6_MMTU;
1913                    } else if (mtu > ifmtu) {
1914                            /*
1915                             * The MTU on the route is larger than the MTU on
1916                             * the interface!  This shouldn't happen, unless the
1917                             * MTU of the interface has been changed after the
1918                             * interface was brought up.  Change the MTU in the
1919                             * route to match the interface MTU (as long as the
1920                             * field isn't locked).
1921                             */
1922                            mtu = ifmtu;
1923                            if (!(ro_pmtu->ro_rt->rt_rmx.rmx_locks & RTV_MTU))
1924                                    ro_pmtu->ro_rt->rt_rmx.rmx_mtu = mtu;
1925                    }
```
—— ip6_output.c

1893–1899 If a route entry is available, ifmtu is set to the link MTU of the possible outgoing interface and mtu is set to the path MTU size stored in the route entry. Note that the interface associated with the route entry may not be the actual outgoing interface when the packet contains a Routing header. It should also be noted that when this function is called from ip6_output(), the outgoing interface is explicitly given, and that interface is used in line 1898.

1900–1901 The link MTU attached to the outgoing interface is used as the initial estimation of the path MTU size when the route entry does not store the path MTU size yet.

1902–1912 An intermediate protocol translator from IPv6 to IPv4 may report a link MTU less than the minimum MTU size—1280 bytes (see also Section 4.7.1). In this case, [RFC2460] requires that the sending node must use the minimum MTU as the path MTU size and attach a Fragment header to the packet regardless of whether the packet is fragmented. Variable alwaysfrag is set to 1 to perform the latter requirement as we saw in Listing 3-174.

1913–1925 The path MTU may be larger than the outgoing link MTU if the link MTU is configurable and it has been modified after the determination of the path MTU. It can also happen when the outgoing link is changed and its link MTU is smaller than the known path MTU. In such a case, the path MTU is reset to the link MTU.

Listing 3-201

—— ip6_output.c
```
1926                    } else if (ifp) {
1927                            mtu = IN6_LINKMTU(ifp);
```
—— ip6_output.c

1926–1927 The outgoing link MTU is used if a route entry is not available (e.g., when the caller explicitly specifies an interface for transmission and `rtalloc()` at line 1889 failed).

Listing 3-202

```
────────────────────────────────────────────────────────────────── ip6_output.c
1928              } else
1929                    error = EHOSTUNREACH; /* XXX */
────────────────────────────────────────────────────────────────── ip6_output.c
```

1929 It is treated as an error when neither the interface nor the route information is available to determine the MTU.

Listing 3-203

```
────────────────────────────────────────────────────────────────── ip6_output.c
1931              *mtup = mtu;
1932              if (alwaysfragp)
1933                    *alwaysfragp = alwaysfrag;
1934              return (error);
1935      }
────────────────────────────────────────────────────────────────── ip6_output.c
```

1931–1934 The determined path MTU value and the flag variable (`alwaysfrag`) instructing the unconditional addition of a Fragment header are returned via the given pointers.

3.13.9 Multicast Loopback: `ip6_mloopback()` Function

The `ip6_mloopback()` function delivers a multicast packet to the sending node itself. This function is called in two cases: (1) The node originates a multicast packet and also joins the destination multicast group on the sending interface (Listing 3-164) and (2) the node is acting as a multicast router and also joins a multicast group. When the node forwards a packet destined to the multicast address, the IPv6 multicast forwarding routine may call `ip6_mloopback()` to deliver a copy of the packet to itself. This will be described in Chapter 2 of *IPv6 Advanced Protocols Implementation*.

Listing 3-204

```
────────────────────────────────────────────────────────────────── ip6_output.c
4859    /*
4860     * Routine called from ip6_output() to loop back a copy of an IP6 multicast
4861     * packet to the input queue of a specified interface.  Note that this
4862     * calls the output routine of the loopback "driver", but with an interface
4863     * pointer that might NOT be &loif -- easier than replicating that code here.
4864     */
4865    void
4866    ip6_mloopback(ifp, m, dst)
4867            struct ifnet *ifp;
4868            struct mbuf *m;
4869            struct sockaddr_in6 *dst;
4870    {
4871            struct mbuf *copym;
4872            struct ip6_hdr *ip6;
4873
4874            if (!(m->m_flags & M_PKTHDR))
4875                    panic("ip6_mloopback: not a M_PKTHDR");
4876
4877            /*
```

```
4878              * Duplicate the packet.
4879              */
4880             copym = m_copy(m, 0, M_COPYALL);
4881             if (copym == NULL)
4882                      return;
```
_____ ip6_output.c

4865–4869 ip6_mloopback() has three arguments. ifp is a pointer to the network interface
to which the packet is delivered; m points to the mbuf storing the multicast packet; dst
holds the destination address of the packet.

4874–4875 Variable m must be an mbuf packet header.

4880–4882 The packet is duplicated for the loopback delivery. The caller of this function will
use the original packet to send it to the real outgoing interface.

Listing 3-205
_____ ip6_output.c
```
4884             /*
4885              * Make sure to deep-copy IPv6 header portion in case the data
4886              * is in an mbuf cluster, so that we can safely override the IPv6
4887              * header portion later.
4888              */
4889             if ((copym->m_flags & M_EXT) != 0 ||
4890                 copym->m_len < sizeof(struct ip6_hdr)) {
4891                     copym = m_pullup(copym, sizeof(struct ip6_hdr));
4892                     if (copym == NULL)
4893                             return;
4894             }
4895

....
4903             ip6 = mtod(copym, struct ip6_hdr *);
....
4905             /*
4906              * clear embedded scope identifiers if necessary.
4907              * in6_clearscope will touch the addresses only when necessary.
4908              */
4909             in6_clearscope(&ip6->ip6_src);
4910             in6_clearscope(&ip6->ip6_dst);
....
4915             (void)if_simloop(ifp, copym, dst->sin6_family, NULL);
....
4922     }
```
_____ ip6_output.c

4889–4894 If the head of the copied mbuf chain has a cluster, the m_pullup() function is
called to ensure that a single mbuf without a cluster holds the whole IPv6 header. When
the packet is stored in an mbuf cluster, m_copy() does not duplicate the data, but makes
the copy share the same cluster buffer with the copy source. As shown below, the IPv6
header can be modified, so a real copy must be created for each packet.

   Similarly, if the head mbuf does not store the entire IPv6 header, m_pullup() ensures
it contains the whole header for later use. (Note: This case should actually not happen in
the context where this function is called.)

4909–4910 The source and the destination address fields of the IPv6 header may contain the
corresponding scope zone IDs, which are removed by the in6_clearscope() function
before the packet is sent to the interface layer (see also Listing 3-171).

4915 Finally, the packet is delivered to the loopback interface.

Internet Control Message Protocol for IPv6

4.1 Introduction

The Internet Control Message Protocol for IPv6 (ICMPv6) is similar to ICMP for IPv4 [RFC792]. [RFC2463] defines the basic ICMPv6 protocol messages. These messages defined in [RFC2463] are for purposes of error reporting and network diagnostics. For example, a node sends ICMPv6 messages to notify a packet source that the node has encountered errors while processing the packet. In addition, a node can utilize the ICMPv6 messages to perform a simple network reachability test.

Different from ICMP for IPv4, ICMPv6 provides a lot of important functions that are necessary for the IPv6 protocol operation. For example, the Neighbor Discovery Protocol, described in the next chapter, operates over ICMPv6, which performs a rich set of functions such as automatic address configuration and link-layer address resolution. Therefore, any node that supports IPv6 must fully implement ICMPv6.

Unlike other upper layer protocols, like TCP or UDP, ICMP for IPv4 and ICMP for IPv6 are completely different protocols. The packet format of TCP or UDP and its algorithms are the same regardless of the IP version. Because of this, IPv4 nodes and IPv6 nodes can communicate with each other to a certain level by using the address translation mechanism. However, it is difficult to provide interoperability for ICMP between IPv4 and IPv6.

In this chapter, we will describe the basic ICMPv6 protocol as defined in [RFC2463]. We will explain ICMPv6-related protocol data structures and the implementation. We will also describe the Path MTU (Maximum Transmission Unit) discovery mechanism, which is performed using an ICMPv6 error message.

The IETF updated [RFC2463] mainly for clarification and error correction and published the new specification as [RFC4443]. The revised specification also introduces several new definitions and behaviors. In some cases, we will also refer to the revised version because some of the changes have been incorporated in the implementation described in this chapter. However, we basically focus on [RFC2463] because the KAME implementation discussed in this book is based on [RFC2463].

At the end of this chapter, we describe the implementation and operation of one interesting application over ICMPv6, called Node Information queries. This is a simple protocol consisting of a single exchange of query and response. The querier part is implemented as a user space program, so the description of this part will provide an example of ICMPv6 application programming.

4.2   ICMPv6 Messages

[RFC2463] defines four error messages and two informational messages. The error messages are reported to the source about the problems encountered during packet processing. The informational messages provide diagnostics functions. The four error messages are

- Destination Unreachable
- Packet Too Big
- Time Exceeded
- Parameter Problem

The two information messages are

- Echo Request
- Echo Reply

Other specifications, such as Neighbor Discovery (ND), Node Information Query, Multicast Listener Discovery, and Mobile IPv6, define additional ICMPv6 messages. For example, Neighbor Discovery packets are carried in ICMPv6 messages. [RFC2461] defines five such ICMPv6 messages for the ND protocol.

IPv6 and the various extension headers can precede an ICMPv6 header. The value of the Next Header field in the preceding header is 58 for the ICMPv6 header. The general format of an ICMPv6 message is shown in Figure 4-1.

Type The 8-bit Type field defines the ICMPv6 message type. An ICMPv6 message is classified as either an error message or an informational message. Types 0–127 are reserved for error messages and types 128–255 are reserved for information messages.

Code The value of the 8-bit Code field depends on the message type, which conveys more information about the specific message.

Checksum The Checksum field holds the 16-bit one's complement of the one's complement sum of the pseudo header plus the entire ICMPv6 message. The pseudo header of upper layer protocols will be discussed in Section 6.3.

The length and content of the message body depends on the message type. Since the ICMPv6 header does not contain a length field, the length of the ICMPv6 message is derived from the total packet length (typically the value of the length field of the IPv6 header) and the size of the extension headers.

FIGURE 4-1

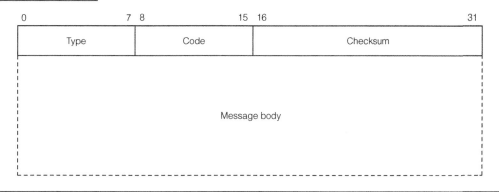

General message format.

FIGURE 4-2

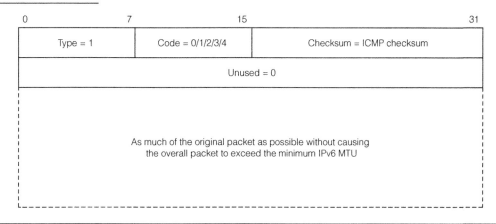

Destination Unreachable message format.

4.2.1 Destination Unreachable Message

The Destination Unreachable message can be generated by the packet-originating node, an intermediate node in the path to the packet's destination, or the final destination node in response to a packet that cannot be delivered due to various reasons. Figure 4-2 shows the format of the Destination Unreachable message.

The Destination Unreachable message has a value of 1 in the Type field. The Code field can take on the values listed in Table 4-1.

The unused field is set to 0 by the sender and is ignored by the receiver. The message body contains as much of the original packet as possible without exceeding the minimum IPv6 MTU size (1280 bytes, see Section 2.13.2). Storing enough bytes from the original packet allows the upper layer protocol at the source node to identify the flow to which the packet that caused

TABLE 4-1

Code	Description
0	No route to destination
	Typically, an intermediate router generates the Code 0 error message to inform the packet source that the router does not have the necessary routing information to forward the packet to the destination. The IPv6 layer at the source node may also generate this error message.
1	Communication with destination administratively prohibited
	Typically, the IPv6 layer at the packet source generates this error message if the source node has some local policies, such as packet filter rules, which prohibit the node from communicating with the destination.
2	Beyond scope of source address
	This is newly defined in the revised specification [RFC4443]. Typically, an intermediate node generates this error message if the source address of the packet is forwarded to a different scope zone from the originating zone.
3	Address unreachable
	This error message is used for other general cases where the packet cannot be delivered to the destination from the reasons listed above. One typical cause of this error is that the source or intermediate node fails in the link-layer address resolution for the Next Hop node toward the destination. Another example is an error indicating a likely forwarding loop on a point-to-point link as explained in Section 3.11.
4	Port unreachable
	Typically, the destination node generates this error message when a packet is destined to a particular upper layer protocol port but there is no end-point associated with the port. For example, when a unicast UDP packet arrives and is destined for a port that does not have a listener, the destination node will generate this error message.

the ICMPv6 error message belongs. For example, TCP needs at least 44 bytes (40 bytes of the IPv6 header and two bytes each of the TCP source and destination port fields) of the original packet in order to identify the flow when TCP operates over IPv6.

It is necessary to limit the maximum size of the original packet because an ICMPv6 error message is not intended to be resent even if it is too big for some intermediate link and is dropped. However, even if the responding node knows the Path MTU (PMTU) size for the destination of the error message, fragmenting the packet should be generally avoided due to its own drawbacks. But at the same time, it is desirable to store the original packet as much as possible since the original packet may contain extension headers and the packet length that is necessary for identifying the flow may be large. It should be noted that in ICMP four IPv4 error messages only store the first 8 bytes of payload in addition to the IP header from the original packet. This is reasonable since IPv4 does not have extension headers that can be arbitrarily large.

The ICMPv6 layer at a node must notify the upper layer process of the unreachability, when receiving a Destination Unreachable error message. Using this information, the upper layer process can take better action to avoid the error. For example, a UDP client application with multiple server candidates can try another server immediately when it is notified by the Port Unreachable error rather than waiting for a timeout.

4.2.2 Packet Too Big Message

The Packet Too Big message is generated by an intermediate node when it cannot forward a packet because the MTU of the outgoing link is smaller than the size of the packet. The PMTU Discovery mechanism [RFC1981] utilizes the Packet Too Big messages to determine the minimum link MTU of all of the segments that exist between two end points. This mechanism helps a transmitting node choose the right packet size so that it can reach the destination without being dropped. Figure 4-3 shows the format of the Packet Too Big message.

The Packet Too Big message has a value of 2 in the Type field and a value of 0 in the Code field. The MTU field stores the MTU value of the Next Hop link. The message body contains as much of the original packet as possible without exceeding the minimum IPv6 MTU like the Destination Unreachable message.

The source node will then fragment packets at the notified MTU size. The ICMPv6 layer at a node must notify the upper layer process when receiving a Packet Too Big message. The upper layer protocol can then optimize its behavior by adjusting TCP segment size to avoid fragmentation.

Note:

- ICMP for IPv4 [RFC792] defines a similar message as a Destination Unreachable message, but there was no MTU field in the original specification. The PMTU discovery mechanism for IPv4 [RFC1191] then revised the message format with a 16-bit "Next Hop MTU" field. The Packet Too Big message of ICMPv6 adopts the latter style of the design to begin with.

- The value stored in the MTU field can be less than the minimum MTU size when a protocol translator between IPv6 and IPv4 [RFC2765] returns this error message.

FIGURE 4-3

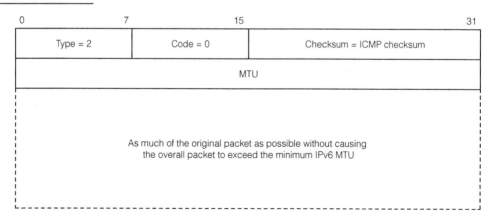

Packet Too Big message format.

It is recommended not to filter out ICMPv6 Destination Unreachable messages at routers or firewalls because the PMTU Discovery mechanism requires the notification of the over-sized packet by such ICMPv6 error messages. Filtering the messages will stop the PMTU discovery mechanism working, that sometimes causes communication disruption. The same problem occurred in IPv4 and should be avoided in IPv6.

4.2.3 Time Exceeded Message

The Time Exceeded message is generated by an intermediate router in response to a packet that has either a 0 value in the Hop Limit field, or the Hop Limit reaches 0 after the router decrements the Hop Limit count. The Time Exceeded message is also generated by the destination node if the node cannot reassemble the packet before the reassembly time (60 seconds, see Section 3.10.1) expires. Figure 4-4 shows the format of the Time Exceeded message.

The Time Exceeded message has a value of 3 in the Type field. The Code field can take the values listed in Table 4-2.

The unused field is set to 0 by the sender and is ignored by the receiver. The message body contains as much of the original packet as possible without exceeding the minimum IPv6 MTU to provide the source node a hint from which it can determine which packet or connection caused the error.

The ICMPv6 layer at a node must notify the upper layer process when receiving the Time Exceeded message.

FIGURE 4-4

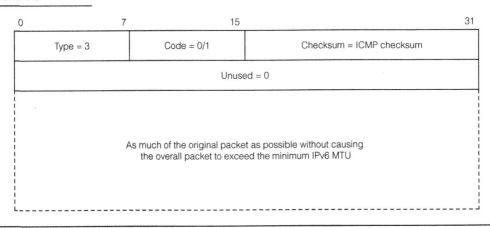

Time Exceeded message format.

TABLE 4-2

Code	Description
0	The Hop Limit has exceeded in transit.
1	The packet reassembly time has exceeded.

4.2.4 Parameter Problem Message

A node will discard a packet and generate a Parameter Problem message when the node processes a packet and encounters a problem in the packet headers. Figure 4-5 shows the format of the Parameter Problem message.

The Parameter Problem message has a value of 4 in the Type field. The Code field can take the values listed in Table 4-3.

The Pointer field is a byte offset within the original packet where the error is encountered which subsequently triggered the ICMPv6 error message. The offset will point past the end of the ICMPv6 packet if the error location is not contained in the message body because of truncation due to the MTU limitation.

The message body contains as much of the original packet as possible without exceeding the minimum IPv6 MTU. From the original packet attached to the ICMPv6 error message and the pointer field, the source node can detect which part of the packet caused the error.

The ICMPv6 layer at a node must notify the upper layer process when receiving the Parameter Problem message.

FIGURE 4-5

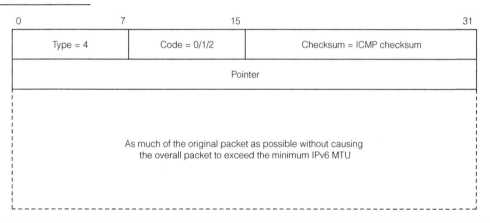

Parameter Problem message format.

TABLE 4-3

Code	Description
0	Erroneous header field encountered
	The node encounters a problem with a field in either the IPv6 header or the extension headers.
1	Unrecognized next header type encountered
	The node retrieves an unrecognizable next header type while processing a header.
2	Unrecognized IPv6 option encountered
	The node encounters an unrecognized IPv6 option while processing a header.

4.2.5   Echo Request Message

A node generates an Echo Request message mainly for diagnostic reasons, for example, to determine the reachability and the round trip delay to a node of interest. Figure 4-6 shows the format of the Echo Request message.

The source node generates the values for the Identifier and the Sequence Number fields. These values help the source match the returning Echo Reply messages. The Data field contains zero or more bytes of arbitrary content.

The ICMPv6 layer at a node may notify the upper layer process when receiving an Echo Request message.

4.2.6   Echo Reply Message

Every IPv6 implementation must respond and generate an Echo Reply message upon receiving an Echo Request message. Figure 4-7 shows the format of the Echo Reply message.

The values of the Identifier and the Sequence Number fields are taken from the Echo Request packet. The content of the Data field is also taken from the Echo Request message.

Note that an Echo Reply packet can be larger than the minimum MTU size, unlike error messages. Since some "**ping**" implementations that send Echo Request and receive Echo Reply

FIGURE 4-6

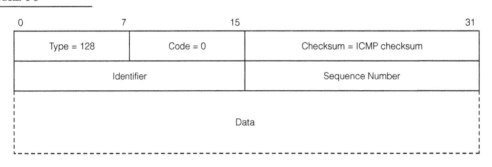

Echo Request message format.

FIGURE 4-7

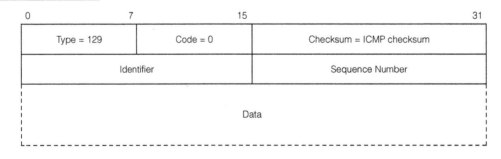

Echo-Reply message format.

messages to perform "integrity" checks about the Data field, truncating the Data field is not appropriate. This requirement implicitly means the responding node has to take care so that the Echo Reply message will not be dropped in an intermediate node due to a "Too Big" error. As will be shown in Section 4.8.3, the KAME implementation simply fragments Echo Reply messages at the minimum MTU size.

The ICMPv6 layer at a source node must notify the upper layer process that originated the Echo Request message to which the Echo Reply message is responding. Other upper layer processes may also be notified of the Echo Reply message, but these notifications are optional.

4.2.7 ICMPv6 Message Processing Rules

A node that generates an ICMPv6 message sets the source address of the resultant IPv6 packet according to the following rules:

- If the ICMPv6 message is generated in response to a packet that was destined for a unicast address assigned to the node, that unicast address is chosen as the source address of the outgoing ICMPv6 message.

- If the ICMPv6 message is generated in response to a packet whose destination address is either a multicast group address, an anycast address, or a unicast address which is not assigned to the node, then the source address of the ICMPv6 message must be one of the unicast addresses assigned to the node. The address should be chosen based on the source address selection rules. However, a node may use another address when this selection may be more informative for the node that receives the message.

With the exception of the Echo Request message, all other types of ICMPv6 messages that have been discussed in the previous sections are destined for the source address of the packet that invoked the ICMPv6 message. The Echo Request message can be destined for any valid IPv6 address.

An ICMPv6 implementation must observe the following rules when processing or generating an ICMPv6 packet:

- The ICMPv6 layer must transfer the packet to the upper layer if either an error or an informational message of an unknown type is received.

- A node must not generate an ICMPv6 error message when receiving an ICMPv6 error message or a Redirect message (Section 5.6.5); this rule prevents the formation of an ICMPv6 error storm between two nodes.

- A node must not generate an ICMPv6 error message if the original packet was destined for a multicast address or with a link-level multicast or broadcast address. The exceptions are that a node can generate a Packet Too Big message and Code 2 Parameter Problem message indicating an error of a Hop-by-Hop or Destinations option. Generating a Packet Too Big message, even if the original packet was destined to a multicast address, facilitates PMTU discovery over multicast channels. [RFC2460] explicitly requests a node to generate an ICMPv6 Code 2 Parameter Problem message regardless of the type of destination address of the original packet if the upper two bits of the option type have a binary value of 10_b (see also Section 3.3.6).

- A node must not generate an ICMPv6 error message if the source address of the original packet does not uniquely identify a single node. Such source addresses include the unspecified address or an address that is known to be an anycast address by the node sending the error message.

- A node must rate limit the generation of ICMPv6 error messages in order to mitigate storms of error messages that can happen when, for example, a broken remote node keeps sending erroneous messages while ignoring the ICMPv6 error messages. The recommended method of rate limitation is that based on a token bucket model, which limits the average number of generated error messages but still allows a burst of error messages for a short period.

Note: The behavior described in this section is generally based on the revised version of the protocol specification [RFC4443] and is different from that described in [RFC2463] in some points. The KAME implementation described later in this chapter basically adopts the new behavior, too.

4.3   Path MTU Discovery Mechanism

The PMTU discovery mechanism utilizes the ICMPv6 Packet Too Big error message to iteratively discover the minimum link MTU of all the links that exist along a given path to a node of interest. We will describe the PMTU discovery mechanism through an example shown in Figure 4-8.

Host A initiates the PMTU discovery process to determine the maximum PMTU value allowable by the intermediate paths between host A and host B. In this example, the link MTU between host A and router R1 is 1500; the link MTU between router R1 and router R2 is 1500; the link MTU between router R2 and router R3 is 1300; and the link MTU between router R3 and host B is 1500.

Host A sends out a packet destined for host B, which is as large as the MTU size of the outgoing link. Router R1 forwards the packet to R2 because the packet fits in the link MTU of

FIGURE 4-8

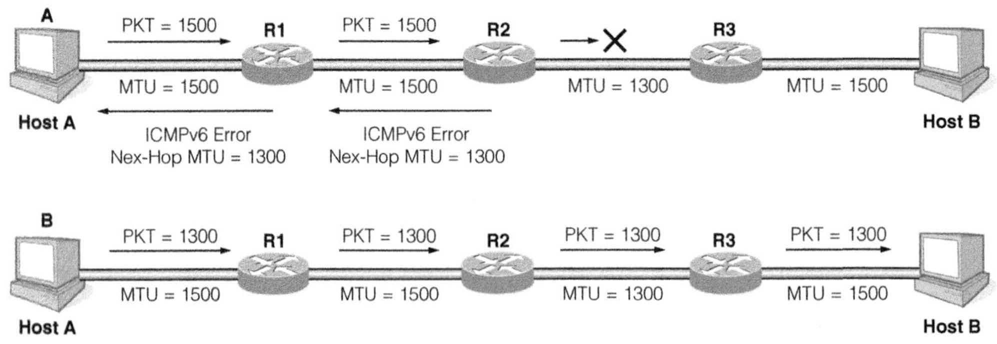

PMTU discovery mechanism.

the network segment between R1 and R2. When R2 is ready to forward the packet toward R3, however, R2 realizes the MTU of the outgoing link is 1300, which is smaller than the packet length. Since IPv6 routers do not perform fragmentation, at this point router R2 sends back an ICMPv6 Packet Too Big error message to host A. Router R2 sets the link MTU of 1300 in the MTU field of the ICMPv6 Too Big error message as shown in Part A of Figure 4-8.

When host A receives the ICMPv6 error message, it retrieves the MTU value from the ICMPv6 error message and updates local information so that future transmissions to host B will utilize this new MTU value. Now host A resends the packet using the new MTU value toward host B as shown in Part B of Figure 4-8. This time the packet successfully reaches host B and host A will assume the PMTU to be 1300 bytes. If there are more intermediate paths between host A and host B, and each path has a different link MTU, then host A may need to repeat the discovery process until no further ICMPv6 Packet Too Big message is returned. For example, assume the link MTU between R3 and host B is 1280 instead of 1500. Then R3 would generate an ICMPv6 Packet Too Big message to host A when R3 receives a packet of 1300 bytes in length, setting the MTU field of the ICMPv6 error message to 1280. Host A would then again reduce the PMTU to 1280 and resend the packet. This time the packet would successfully reach host B. Since no more ICMPv6 error messages are returned, at that point host A will assume the PMTU to be 1280 bytes.

The network is dynamic and the network topology between host A and host B may change. It also means that the path between router R2 and host B may change from R2-to-R3-to-B to a different path of R2-to-R4-to-R5-to-B. The PMTU may change as a result of the topological changes that have taken place. If the PMTU is reduced, then either R4 or R5 will generate ICMPv6 Packet Too Big error messages to host A. However, there is no mechanism that exists for either R4 or R5 to notify host A if there is an expansion in PMTU. Host A should dynamically rediscover the PMTU. For this reason host A sets up a periodic timer and host A will reinitiate the PMTU discover process each time the periodic timer expires.

It is noteworthy that there are some differences in the PMTU discovery mechanism between IPv4 [RFC1191] and IPv6. First, since IPv6 routers do not perform packet fragmentation and the IPv6 header does not have a "Don't Fragment" bit (Section 3.2), the sending node generally needs to be able to perform PMTU discovery. The only alternative for a minimal implementation that does not support this mechanism is to fragment any IPv6 packets at the minimum MTU size. Second, the node performing IPv6 PMTU discovery does not have to guess the appropriate link MTU using the "MTU plateaus" like the IPv4 mechanism because a Packet Too Big message always contains a specific MTU size.

4.4 Node Information Query

The ICMPv6 Node Information (NI) Query provides a simple way to query the name or address of IPv6 nodes. The specification has not been standardized yet. The latest specification at the time of writing can be found as draft-ietf-ipngwg-icmp-name-lookups-15 [NAME-LOOKUPS-15].

The mechanism is quite simple. A node which wants to know some information of author node sends a query message using an ICMPv6 message. In the query message, a sender node, which is called "Querier," specifies what kind of information the querier needs. A querier can send a request to get the name of the IPv6 or IPv4 address of a node. The node which responds to a query message is called "Responder." A responder will reply with an ICMPv6 message which includes corresponding information that was specified in the query message. The target information in a query is called "Subject" name or "Subject" address.

A querier can send a query message to a responder's IPv6 address directly if the address is known to the querier. Also, a querier can send it to the IPv6 multicast address, for example, to the link-local all-node multicast address to get all names on the same link.

When a querier needs to resolve the address of a responder from its node name, the querier has to send its query message to a special IPv6 multicast address. The address is called Node Information Group Address (NI Group Address). The scope of the multicast address is link-local. We cannot query an address of nodes which are located outside of the same link, for example, the same Ethernet segment. The NI Group Address is calculated as follows:

1. The Subject name is converted to the DNS canonical form as defined in DNS Security Extensions [RFC4034].

2. An MD5 hash value is calculated on the canonical name.

3. The NI Group Address is generated by concatenating the IPv6 prefix defined for the NI Group Address (ff02:0:0:0:0:2::/96) and the first 32 bits of the calculated hash value.

Figure 4-9 depicts the algorithm and an example of an NI Group Address calculation for the Subject name "example." The NI Group Address construction algorithm was changed when draft-ietf-ipngwg-icmp-name-lookups-13 [NAME-LOOKUPS-13] was issued. In the latest specification, at the time of writing, the address will be generated by concatenating ff02:0:0:0:0:2:ff00::/104 and the first 24 bits of hashed value. As we discussed in section 2.5.3, the last 32 bits of the multicast address is a group identifier. The range from 0x00000001 to 0x3FFFFFFF is reserved for group IDs for permanent IPv6 multicast addresses; 0x40000000 to 0x7FFFFFFF is reserved for permanent group IDs. When considering the nature

FIGURE 4-9

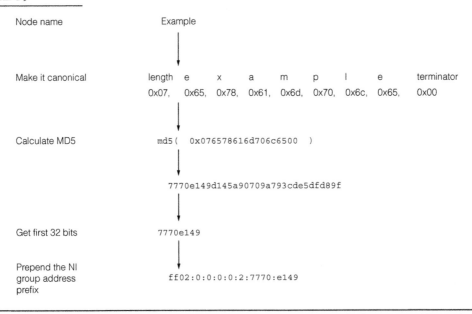

The algorithm and example of NI Group Address calculation.

of the NI Group Address, we have to use group IDs for dynamic IPv6 multicast addresses which range from 0x80000000 to 0xFFFFFFFF. The latest version of the NI specification avoids using IDs from the range associated with permanently assigned multicast groups.

4.4.1   Node Information Message Format

The specification of the Node Information Query specifies two additional message types for a query message and a reply message. The specification also defines several message formats based on the type of message. Figure 4-10 shows the format of the Node Information message.

Type ICMPv6 type number 139 is used for an NI Query message and 140 is used for an NI Reply message.

Code Indicates the detailed message status. Table 4-4 shows the meaning of the value contained in this field.

Checksum The ICMPv6 checksum value.

Qtype The query type. Table 4-5 shows all the type defined in draft-ietf-ipngwg-icmp-name-lookups-12 [NAME-LOOKUPS-12]. Note that the query type "Supported Qtype" is not defined in draft-ietf-ipngwg-icmp-name-lookups-12. It is obsolete type but we list it here since the KAME implementation supports the type.

Flags A flag field which is defined based on the query type. The detailed description of this field is discussed in each query type description.

Nonce A 64-bit random number to avoid spoofing of reply messages and to help matching reply messages received with query messages sent. The Nonce field in a query message must be copied to the Nonce field of the reply message.

Data In a query message, this field contains IP address or node name in query that depends on the ICMPv6 Code field value. Or this field may be empty. In a reply message, this

FIGURE 4-10

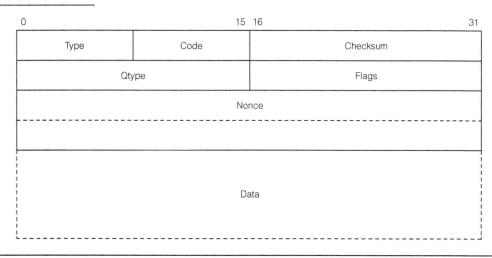

Node Information message format.

TABLE 4-4

Value	Description
In NI Query	
0	The Data field contains an IPv6 address to be resolved to its corresponding node name.
1	The Data field contains a node name to be resolved to its corresponding IPv6 address. Or, the Data field is empty when NOOP or Supported Qtypes Query is specified in the Qtype field.
2	The Data field contains an IPv4 address to be resolved to its corresponding node name.
In NI Reply	
0	Indicates a successful reply. The Data field may contain resolved data.
1	Indicates the responder refused to supply the answer to the querier.
2	Indicates that the value of the Qtype field is unrecognized to the responder.

TABLE 4-5

Name	Value	Description
NOOP	0	No operation.
Supported Qtypes	1	(deprecated) Requests the supported query types.
Node Name	2	Requests a node name corresponding to the IPv6 address in a query message.
Node Addresses	3	Requests node addresses corresponding to the node name in a query message.
IPv4 Addresses	4	Requests IPv4 addresses corresponding to the node name in a query message.

FIGURE 4-11

NOOP format.

field contains information that depends on the Qtype value if the ICMPv6 code field is 0. Otherwise, the field is empty.

4.4.2 NOOP Query

NOOP query is used to check to see if a responder is up and will support the Node Information Query protocol. NOOP query does not have any flags defined or any Data field information. The Code field must be set to 1 in a query message and must be set to 0 in a reply message. On reception, the Code field must be ignored. Figure 4-11 shows the NOOP Query format.

4.4.3   Supported Qtypes Query

Supported Qtypes query is not defined in [NAME-LOOKUPS-12]. This type was removed from the specification when draft-ietf-ipngwg-icmp-name-lookups-12 was published. However, we discuss this obsolete type since KAME partially supports this type .

Figure 4-12 shows the Supported Qtype format.

The C flag is set to 1 in a query message if the querier supports the compressed format of the Data field described below. The C flag in a reply message indicates whether or not the Data field is compressed.

The Data field of a query message of this type is empty. The Data field of a reply message contains bit field information which indicates supported Qtype field values. To reduce the total size of the payload, the bit field can be compressed. Figure 4-13 shows an example of the uncompressed format.

The position of the bit set to 1 is treated as the Qtype value supported. In the example, Qtype 1, 2, 3, and 4 are supported.

Figure 4-14 shows the compressed example.

The compressed bit field consists of a sequence of blocks. Each block consists of three parts. The first part is the number of 32-bit fields which include one or more 1 bits. The second part is the number of 32-bit fields which include no 1 bits. In Figure 4-14, the first two 32-bit fields indicate the lower values of supported Qtype. In the example, Qtype 1, 2, 3, 4, and 60 are supported. The all 0 32-bit field continues after the first two 32-bit fields. The length is 126, which means $126 \times 32 = 4032$ 0 bits. Finally, the 32-bit bit field continues. The bit set to 1 in the last bit field in the example means Qtype 4097.

This Query type disappeared from the specification after its 10th revision.

4.4.4   Node Name Query

Node Name query is used when a querier wants to know the name of a responder. This Qtype does not have any flags as shown in Figure 4-15. A querier may send this query directly to the responder's IP address, or the link-local all-nodes multicast address or an NI Group Address.

A responder will send a reply message containing the Data field as shown in Figure 4-16.
TTL was initially designed to keep the lifetime of the name of the node; however, the

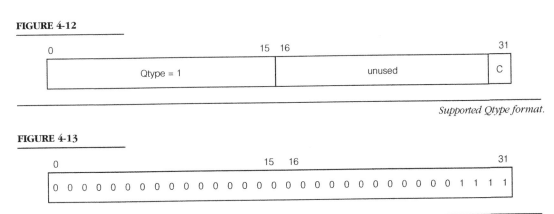

FIGURE 4-12

0	15 16	31
Qtype = 1	unused	C

Supported Qtype format.

FIGURE 4-13

0	15 16	31
0 0 0 0 0 0 0 0 0 0 0 0 0 0 0 0 0 0 0 0 0 0 0 0 0 0 0 0 1 1 1 1		

An example of the uncompressed bit field.

FIGURE 4-14

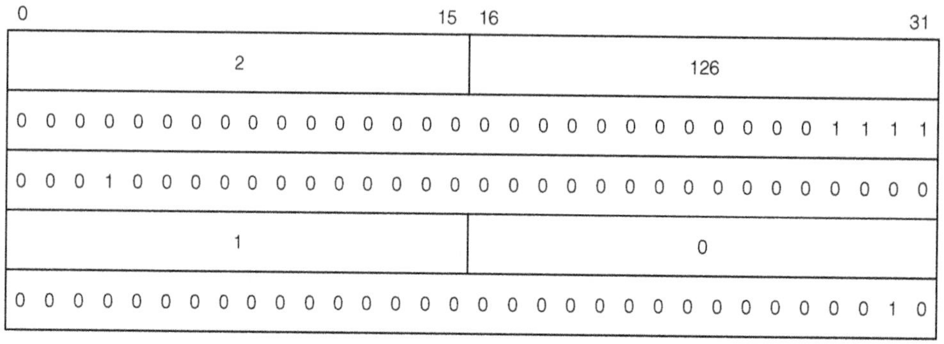

0 15	16 31
2	126

0 0 0 0 0 0 0 0 0 0 0 0 0 0 0 0 0 0 0 0 0 0 0 0 0 0 0 0 1 1 1 1

0 0 0 1 0 0 0 0 0 0 0 0 0 0 0 0 0 0 0 0 0 0 0 0 0 0 0 0 0 0 0 0

1	0

0 0 0 0 0 0 0 0 0 0 0 0 0 0 0 0 0 0 0 0 0 0 0 0 0 0 0 0 0 0 1 0

An example of the compressed bit field.

FIGURE 4-15

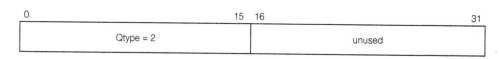

0 15	16 31
Qtype = 2	unused

Node Name format.

FIGURE 4-16

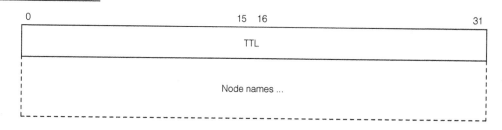

0   15 16   31
TTL
Node names ...

Node Name Data structure.

field now has no meaning and is initialized to 0. The original intention of TTL was to keep a DNS TTL, or DHCP lease time, or prefix lifetime bound to the name, which are all related to the validity of the name. However, retrieving a correct TTL value requires complex procedures, and we cannot always retrieve accurate information. The field is left for backward compatibility.

Node Names field contains a series of names of the node in DNS wire format as defined in [RFC1035]. The name must be a fully qualified domain name if the responder knows the domain suffix, or a single-component domain name following two 0-length labels if it does not.

The Data field may be empty if the responder does not know its name or does not want to reply to its name. In the latter case, the ICMPv6 Code field is set to 1, which indicates refusal of answer.

4.4.5 Node Addresses Query

Node Address query is sent when a querier wants to know IPv6 addresses of a responder. Figure 4-17 shows the format of the query message.

There are 6 flags. Table 4-6 shows the meanings of each flag.

The G, S, L, C, and A flags are copied from a query message to a reply message.

The Data field contains a series of IPv6 addresses as specified in Figure 4-18.

The TTL field is set to 0 for the same reason discussed in Section 4.4.4.

FIGURE 4-17

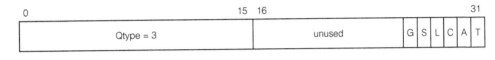

Node Addresses format.

TABLE 4-6

Flag	Description
G	Global: A querier is requesting global addresses of a responder.
S	Site-local: A querier is requesting site-local addresses of a responder. Note that unicast site-local addresses are deprecated (Section 2.4.4).
L	Link-local: A querier is requesting link-local addresses of a responder.
C	Compatible: A querier is requesting IPv4-compatible or IPv4-mapped IPv6 addresses of a responder. Note that IPv4-compatible addresses are deprecated (Section 2.3).
A	All: When set to 1, all addresses assigned to a responder will be returned, otherwise, only addresses assigned to a corresponding interface to the subject information are returned.
T	Truncated: The flag is valid only in a reply message. The flag indicates the Data field will not contain all information because there is not enough space to put all the information.

FIGURE 4-18

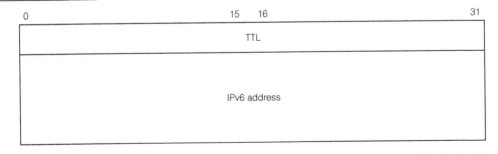

The IPv6 Address Format in a reply message.

FIGURE 4-19

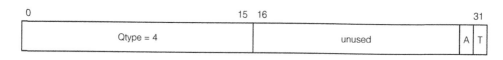

IPv4 Addresses query message.

TABLE 4-7

File	Description
${KAME}/kame/sys/netinet/icmp6.h	Data structure definitions for ICMPv6 and related protocols
${KAME}/kame/sys/netinet6/icmp6.c	Basic ICMPv6 protocol message processing

4.4.6 IPv4 Addresses Query

IPv4 Addresses query is used when a querier needs to know the IPv4 addresses of a responder. Figure 4-19 shows the format of this query message.

The flags used in this query have the same meanings of the flags used for Node Addresses query.

The Data field contains a series of IPv4 addresses as specified in Figure 4-20.

The TTL field is set to 0 for the same reason discussed in Section 4.4.4.

4.5   Code Introduction

We will describe the data structures and functions that relate to ICMPv6 packet processing and generation as defined by [RFC2463]. Table 4-7 lists the source files that are covered in this chapter.

4.5.1 Statistics

The ICMPv6 statistics of the IPv6 node are stored in the `icmp6_ifstat{}` structure which is kept per network interface. Table 4-8 shows the statistics variables and corresponding MIB object name defined in [RFC2466]. Table 4-9 shows the sample output of the `netstat -Iifname -s` command which prints the current statistics values.

FIGURE 4-20

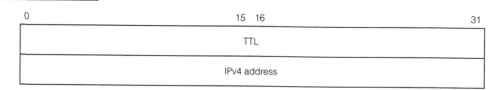

The IPv4 address format in a Reply message.

TABLE 4-8

icmp6_ifstat member	SNMP variable	Description
ifs6_in_msg	ipv6IfIcmpInMsgs	total # of input messages
ifs6_in_error	ipv6IfIcmpInErrors	# of input error messages
ifs6_in_dstunreach	ipv6IfIcmpInDestUnreachs	# of input dest unreach errors
ifs6_in_adminprohib	ipv6IfIcmpInAdminProhib	# of input administratively prohibited errors
ifs6_in_timeexceed	ipv6IfIcmpInTimeExcds	# of input time exceeded errors
ifs6_in_paramprob	ipv6IfIcmpInParmProblems	# of input parameter problem errors
ifs6_in_pkttoobig	ipv6IfIcmpInPktTooBigs	# of input packet too big errors
ifs6_in_echo	ipv6IfIcmpInEchos	# of input echo requests
ifs6_in_echoreply	ipv6IfIcmpInEchoReplies	# of input echo replies
ifs6_in_routersolicit	ipv6IfIcmpInRouterSolicits	# of input router solicitations
ifs6_in_routeradvert	ipv6IfIcmpInRouterAdvertisements	# of input router advertisements
ifs6_in_neighborsolicit	ipv6IfIcmpInNeighborSolicits	# of input neighbor solicitations
ifs6_in_neighboradvert	ipv6IfIcmpInNeighborAdvertisements	# of input neighbor advertisements
ifs6_in_redirect	ipv6IfIcmpInRedirects	# of input redirects
ifs6_in_mldquery	ipv6IfIcmpInGroupMembQueries	# of input MLD queries
ifs6_in_mldreport	ipv6IfIcmpInGroupMembResponses	# of input MLD reports
ifs6_in_mlddone	ipv6IfIcmpInGroupMembReductions	# of input MLD done
ifs6_out_msg	ipv6IfIcmpOutMsgs	total # of output messages
ifs6_out_error	ipv6IfIcmpOutErrors	# of output error messages
ifs6_out_dstunreach	ipv6IfIcmpOutDestUnreachs	# of output dest unreach errors
ifs6_out_adminprohib	ipv6IfIcmpOutAdminProhibs	# of output administratively prohibited errors
ifs6_out_timeexceed	ipv6IfIcmpOutTimeExcds	# of output time exceeded errors

(Continued)

TABLE 4-8 *(Continued)*

icmp6_ifstat member	SNMP variable	Description
ifs6_out_paramprob	ipv6IfIcmpOutParmProblems	# of output parameter problem errors
ifs6_out_pkttoobig	ipv6IfIcmpOutPktTooBigs	# of output packet too big errors
ifs6_out_echo	ipv6IfIcmpOutEchos	# of output echo requests
ifs6_out_echoreply	ipv6IfIcmpOutEchoReplies	# of output echo replies
ifs6_out_routersolicit	ipv6IfIcmpOutRouterSolicits	# of output router solicitations
ifs6_out_routeradvert	ipv6IfIcmpOutRouterAdvertisements	# of output router advertisements
ifs6_out_neighborsolicit	ipv6IfIcmpOutNeighborSolicits	# of output neighbor solicitations
ifs6_out_neighboradvert	ipv6IfIcmpOutNeighborAdvertisements	# of output neighbor advertisements
ifs6_out_redirect	ipv6IfIcmpOutRedirects	# of output redirects
ifs6_out_mldquery	ipv6IfIcmpOutGroupMembQueries	# of output MLD queries
ifs6_out_mldreport	ipv6IfIcmpOutGroupMembResponses	# of output MLD reports
ifs6_out_mlddone	ipv6IfIcmpOutGroupMembReductions	# of output MLD done

Statistics of ICMPv6.

TABLE 4-9

icmp6_ifstat member	*netstat −Iifname −s output*
ifs6_in_msg	4562385 total input messages
ifs6_in_error	51849 total input error messages
ifs6_in_dstunreach	18438 input destination unreachable errors
ifs6_in_adminprohib	181 input administratively prohibited errors
ifs6_in_timeexceed	32876 input time exceeded errors
ifs6_in_paramprob	0 input parameter problem errors
ifs6_in_pkttoobig	535 input packet too big errors
ifs6_in_echo	4387300 input echo requests
ifs6_in_echoreply	9 input echo replies
ifs6_in_routersolicit	0 input router solicitations
ifs6_in_routeradvert	4314 input router advertisements
ifs6_in_neighborsolicit	55659 input neighbor solicitations
ifs6_in_neighboradvert	56429 input neighbor advertisements
ifs6_in_redirect	7 input redirects
ifs6_in_mldquery	6827 input MLD queries
ifs6_in_mldreport	0 input MLD reports
ifs6_in_mlddone	0 input MLD dones
ifs6_out_msg	4526350 total output messages
ifs6_out_error	13309 total output error messages
ifs6_out_dstunreach	2212 output destination unreachable errors
ifs6_out_adminprohib	0 output administratively prohibited errors
ifs6_out_timeexceed	11078 output time exceeded errors
ifs6_out_paramprob	19 output parameter problem errors
ifs6_out_pkttoobig	0 output packet too big errors
ifs6_out_echo	9 output echo requests
ifs6_out_echoreply	4387300 output echo replies
ifs6_out_routersolicit	1 output router solicitations
ifs6_out_routeradvert	0 output router advertisements
ifs6_out_neighborsolicit	56431 output neighbor solicitations
ifs6_out_neighboradvert	55653 output neighbor advertisements
ifs6_out_redirect	0 output redirects
ifs6_out_mldquery	0 output MLD queries
ifs6_out_mldreport	13656 output MLD reports
ifs6_out_mlddone	0 output MLD dones

Statistics printed by netstat −s.

4.5.2   ICMPv6 Header

Listing 4-1

─── icmp6.h

```
110    struct icmp6_hdr {
111            u_int8_t icmp6_type;       /* type field */
112            u_int8_t icmp6_code;       /* code field */
113            u_int16_t icmp6_cksum;     /* checksum field */
114            union {
115                    u_int32_t          icmp6_un_data32[1]; /* type-specific field */
116                    u_int16_t          icmp6_un_data16[2]; /* type-specific field */
117                    u_int8_t icmp6_un_data8[4];  /* type-specific field */
118            } icmp6_dataun;
119    } __attribute__((__packed__));
120
121    #define icmp6_data32       icmp6_dataun.icmp6_un_data32
122    #define icmp6_data16       icmp6_dataun.icmp6_un_data16
123    #define icmp6_data8        icmp6_dataun.icmp6_un_data8
124    #define icmp6_pptr         icmp6_data32[0]          /* parameter prob */
125    #define icmp6_mtu          icmp6_data32[0]          /* packet too big */
126    #define icmp6_id           icmp6_data16[0]          /* echo request/reply */
127    #define icmp6_seq          icmp6_data16[1]          /* echo request/reply */
```

─── icmp6.h

The `icmp6_hdr{}` structure directly maps to the generic ICMPv6 header depicted in Figure 4-1. `icmp6_type`, `icmp6_code`, and `icmp6_cksum` map the Type, Code, and the Checksum fields, respectively. Table 4-10 shows the possible values for the Type and Code fields. The 32-bit `icmp6_dataun` field is interpreted as the Pointer field when the message type is Parameter Problem, and is accessible via `icmp6_pptr`. The 32-bit `icmp6_dataun` field is interpreted as the MTU value when the message type is Packet Too Big, and is accessible via `icmp6_mtu`. The 32-bit `icmp6_dataun` field is interpreted as the identifier and the sequence number fields when the message type is either Echo Request or Echo Reply, and these fields are accessible via `icmp6_id` and `icmp6_seq`, respectively.

4.6   ICMPv6 Input Processing

ICMPv6 messages are processed by the `icmp6_input()` function. It is called from `ip6_input()`. The `icmp6_input()` function processes messages defined in [RFC2463] and other messages that are defined for various protocols operating over ICMPv6, such as the ND or Multicast Listener Discovery (MLD) protocol.

One major role of the `icmp6_input()` function is to handle ICMPv6 error messages. In general, an error message is converted to a protocol independent control command (PRC) defined in `<sys/protosw.h>` depending on the type and code in this function. It will then be passed to control input functions in the transport layer, where the command is further converted to a standard error code which is returned to applications via the `errno` global variable (see Section 6.7.10).

Table 4.11 summarizes the conversion. For example, a Destination Unreachable message (`ICMP6_DST_UNREACH`) with the code of Port unreachable (`ICMP6_DST_UNREACH_NOPORT`) is converted to the `PRC_UNREACH_PORT` command in `icmp6_input()` and then to the `ECONNREFUSED` error in the transport layer. If the error code is delivered to an application, a subsequent receive operation such as a system call to `recvfrom()` will fail due to a "connection refused" error.

TABLE 4-10

Name	Type	Code	Description
ICMP6_DST_UNREACH	1	Following values	Destination node is unreachable.
ICMP6_DST_UNREACH_NOROUTE		0	No route to destination.
ICMP6_DST_UNREACH_ADMIN		1	Administratively prohibited.
ICMP6_DST_UNREACH_BEYONDSCOPE		2	Destination scope is beyond scope of source address.
ICMP6_DST_UNREACH_ADDR		3	Destination address is unreachable.
ICMP6_DST_UNREACH_NOPORT		4	Destination port is unreachable.
ICMP6_PACKET_TOO_BIG	2	0	Packet size exceeds the size of link MTU.
ICMP6_TIME_EXCEEDED	3		Packet did not reach to destination because of timeout.
ICMP6_TIME_EXCEED_TRANSIT		0	Hop limit exceeded.
ICMP6_TIME_EXCEED_REASSEMBLY		1	Fragmented packets cannot be reassembled in 60 seconds.
ICMP6_PARAM_PROB	4	Following values	Destination node is unreachable.
ICMP6_PARAM_PROB_HEADER		0	Error exists in a Header field except next Header field.
ICMP6_PARAM_PROB_NEXTHEADER		1	Error exists in a Next Header field.
ICMP6_PARAM_PROB_OPTION		2	Unknown Hop-by-Hop or Destination option.
ICMP6_ECHO_REQUEST	128	0	Echo message.
ICMP6_ECHO_REPLY	129	0	Echo Reply message.
ICMP6_NI_QUERY	139	Following values	Node Information Query message.
ICMP6_NI_SUBJ_IPV6		0	Query Subject is an IPv6 address.
ICMP6_NI_SUBJ_FQDN		1	Query Subject is a domain name.
ICMP6_NI_SUBJ_IPV4		2	Query Subject is an IPv4 address.
ICMP6_NI_REPLY	140	Following values	Node Information Reply message.
ICMP6_NI_SUCCESS		0	NI Query request succeeded.
ICMP6_NI_REFUSED		1	NI Query request is refused.
ICMP6_NI_UNKNOWN		2	Unknown query type value is specified.

ICMPv6 type and code values.

TABLE 4-11

Type & code (ICMP6_)	Control command (PRC_)	errno
ICMP6_DST_UNREACH		
ICMP6_DST_UNREACH_NOROUTE	PRC_UNREACH_NET	EHOSTUNREACH
ICMP6_DST_UNREACH_ADMIN	PRC_UNREACH_PROTOCOL	ECONNREFUSED
ICMP6_DST_UNREACH_BEYONDSCOPE	PRC_UNREACH_NET	EHOSTUNREACH
ICMP6_DST_UNREACH_ADDR	PRC_HOSTDEAD	EHOSTDOWN
ICMP6_DST_UNREACH_NOPORT	PRC_UNREACH_PORT	ECONNREFUSED
ICMP6_PACKET_TOO_BIG	PRC_MSGSIZE	EMSGSIZE
ICMP6_TIME_EXCEEDED		
ICMP6_TIME_EXCEED_TRANSIT	PRC_TIMXCEED_INTRANS	
ICMP6_TIME_EXCEED_REASSEMBLY	PRC_TIMXCEED_REASS	
ICMP6_PARAM_PROB		
ICMP6_PARAMPROB_NEXTHEADER	PRC_UNREACH_PROTOCOL	ECONNREFUSED
ICMP6_PARAMPROB_HEADER	PRC_PARAMPROB	ENOPROTOOPT
ICMP6_PARAMPROB_OPTION	PRC_PARAMPROB	ENOPROTOOPT

ICMPv6 messages for other protocol such as ND or MLD are generally handled in separate processing routines. In addition, some of the ICMPv6 messages are handled in user space and are sent upward to the socket layer. Figure 4-21 summarizes the general processing flow for incoming ICMPv6 messages.

4.6.1 `icmp6_input()` Function

Listing 4-2

icmp6.c

```
530     /*
531      * Process a received ICMP6 message.
532      */
533     int
534     icmp6_input(mp, offp, proto)
535             struct mbuf **mp;
536             int *offp, proto;
537     {
538             struct mbuf *m = *mp, *n;
539             struct ip6_hdr *ip6, *nip6;
540             struct icmp6_hdr *icmp6, *nicmp6;
541             struct sockaddr_in6 src0, dst0, src, dst;
542             int off = *offp;
543             int icmp6len = m->m_pkthdr.len - *offp;
544             int code, sum, noff;
545
546             icmp6_ifstat_inc(m->m_pkthdr.rcvif, ifs6_in_msg);
```

icmp6.c

FIGURE 4-21

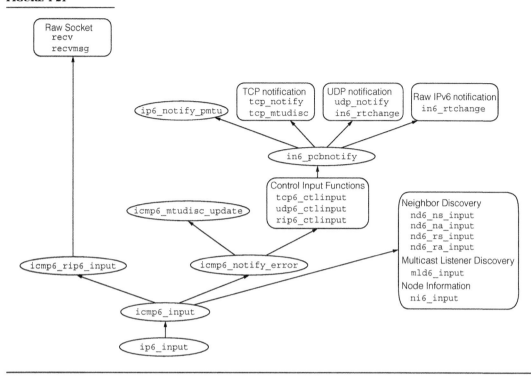

ICMPv6 input processing.

534 mp contains the input packet. offp holds the offset to the start of the ICMPv6 header. proto has the value of IPPROTO_ICMPV6.

Listing 4-3

```
                                                                  icmp6.c
549        IP6_EXTHDR_CHECK(m, off, sizeof(struct icmp6_hdr), IPPROTO_DONE);
550        /* m might change if M_LOOP.  So, call mtod after this */
552
553        /*
554         * Locate icmp6 structure in mbuf, and check
555         * that not corrupted and of at least minimum length
556         */
557
558        ip6 = mtod(m, struct ip6_hdr *);
559        if (icmp6len < sizeof(struct icmp6_hdr)) {
560                icmp6stat.icp6s_tooshort++;
561                icmp6_ifstat_inc(m->m_pkthdr.rcvif, ifs6_in_error);
562                goto freeit;
563        }
564
                                                                  icmp6.c
```

549–563 IP6_EXTHDR_CHECK() ensures the IPv6 header, all extension headers (if any) and the ICMPv6 header are in a contiguous memory space. ip6 is set to point to the beginning of the IPv6 header. The length of the ICMPv6 packet, `icmp6len`, must be at least as large as the common ICMPv6 header.

Note: The comment at line 550 is not correct, since `IP6_EXTHDR_CHECK()` actually does not change the behavior with or without the `M_LOOP` flag (see Section 1.6.3).

Listing 4-4
─── icmp6.c

```
565            /*
566             * calculate the checksum
567             */
569            icmp6 = (struct icmp6_hdr *)((caddr_t)ip6 + off);
578            code = icmp6->icmp6_code;
579
580            if ((sum = in6_cksum(m, IPPROTO_ICMPV6, off, icmp6len)) != 0) {
581                    nd6log((LOG_ERR,
582                        "ICMP6 checksum error(%d|%x) %s\n",
583                        icmp6->icmp6_type, sum, ip6_sprintf(&ip6->ip6_src)));
584                    icmp6stat.icp6s_checksum++;
585                    icmp6_ifstat_inc(m->m_pkthdr.rcvif, ifs6_in_error);
586                    goto freeit;
587            }
588
```
─── icmp6.c

565–578 `icmp6` is set to point to the beginning of the ICMPv6 header. `code` holds the value of the Code field from the ICMPv6 header.

580–587 The checksum calculation is performed on the ICMPv6 packet. The statistics which indicate an invalid checksum value are incremented and the packet is freed if checksum validation fails. The function terminates here.

Listing 4-5
─── icmp6.c

```
612
613            icmp6stat.icp6s_inhist[icmp6->icmp6_type]++;
614
615            /*
616             * extract full sockaddr structures for the src/dst addresses,
617             * and make local copies of the addresses to pass them to applications.
618             */
619            if (ip6_getpktaddrs(m, &src0, &dst0)) {
620                    m_freem(m);
621                    return (IPPROTO_DONE);
622            }
623            src = src0;
624            dst = dst0;
```
─── icmp6.c

612–624 The statistics counter that keeps track of the number of received packets for that particular type of message is incremented. The Source and Destination addresses of the packet in the form of the `sockaddr_in6{}` structure are retrieved from the mbuf tag and are copied in `src0` and `dst0`, respectively.

Listing 4-6

_____ icmp6.c

```
632            switch (icmp6->icmp6_type) {
633            case ICMP6_DST_UNREACH:
634                    icmp6_ifstat_inc(m->m_pkthdr.rcvif, ifs6_in_dstunreach);

641                    switch (code) {
642                    case ICMP6_DST_UNREACH_NOROUTE:
643                            code = PRC_UNREACH_NET;
644                            break;
645                    case ICMP6_DST_UNREACH_ADMIN:
646                            icmp6_ifstat_inc(m->m_pkthdr.rcvif, ifs6_in_adminprohib);
647                            code = PRC_UNREACH_PROTOCOL; /* is this a good code? */
648                            break;
649                    case ICMP6_DST_UNREACH_ADDR:
650                            code = PRC_HOSTDEAD;
651                            break;
 ....
657                    case ICMP6_DST_UNREACH_BEYONDSCOPE:
658                            /* I mean "source address was incorrect." */
659                            code = PRC_UNREACH_NET;
660                            break;
 ....
662                    case ICMP6_DST_UNREACH_NOPORT:
663                            code = PRC_UNREACH_PORT;
664                            break;
665                    default:
666                            goto badcode;
667                    }
668                    goto deliver;
```

_____ icmp6.c

633–668 The interface specific ICMPv6 statistics counter for the Destination Unreachable
message is incremented. This implementation supports the five error code values for the
Destination Unreachable error category shown in Table 4-1. Each error code is converted
to the corresponding protocol control command as shown in Table 4-11.

Listing 4-7

_____ icmp6.c

```
670            case ICMP6_PACKET_TOO_BIG:
671                    icmp6_ifstat_inc(m->m_pkthdr.rcvif, ifs6_in_pkttoobig);
672                    if (code != 0)
673                            goto badcode;
674
675                    /* validation is made in icmp6_mtudisc_update */
676
677                    code = PRC_MSGSIZE;
678
679                    /*
680                     * Updating the path MTU will be done after examining
681                     * intermediate extension headers.
682                     */
683                    goto deliver;
```

_____ icmp6.c

670–683 The interface specific ICMPv6 statistics counter for the Packet Too Big message is
incremented. The Packet Too Big message is mapped to the PRC_MSGSIZE protocol
control command and will be delivered to the upper layer protocol.

Listing 4-8

icmp6.c
```
685                     case ICMP6_TIME_EXCEEDED:
686                             icmp6_ifstat_inc(m->m_pkthdr.rcvif, ifs6_in_timeexceed);
687                             switch (code) {
688                             case ICMP6_TIME_EXCEED_TRANSIT:
689                                     code = PRC_TIMXCEED_INTRANS;
690                                     break;
691                             case ICMP6_TIME_EXCEED_REASSEMBLY:
692                                     code = PRC_TIMXCEED_REASS;
693                                     break;
694                             default:
695                                     goto badcode;
696                             }
697                             goto deliver;
```
icmp6.c

685–697 The interface specific ICMPv6 statistics counter for the Time Exceeded message is incremented. There are two type codes for the Time Exceeded error message: ICMP6_TIME_EXCEED_TRANSIT and ICMP6_TIME_EXCEED_REASSEMBLY that are mapped to PRC_TIMXCEED_INTRANS and PRC_TIMXCEED_REASS, respectively.

Listing 4-9

icmp6.c
```
699                     case ICMP6_PARAM_PROB:
700                             icmp6_ifstat_inc(m->m_pkthdr.rcvif, ifs6_in_paramprob);
707                             switch (code) {
708                             case ICMP6_PARAMPROB_NEXTHEADER:
709                                     code = PRC_UNREACH_PROTOCOL;
710                                     break;
711                             case ICMP6_PARAMPROB_HEADER:
712                             case ICMP6_PARAMPROB_OPTION:
713                                     code = PRC_PARAMPROB;
714                                     break;
715                             default:
716                                     goto badcode;
717                             }
718                             goto deliver;
719
```
icmp6.c

699–718 The interface specific ICMPv6 statistics counter for the Parameter Problem message is incremented. Each error code is converted to the corresponding protocol control command as shown in Table 4-11.

Listing 4-10

icmp6.c
```
720                     case ICMP6_ECHO_REQUEST:
721                             icmp6_ifstat_inc(m->m_pkthdr.rcvif, ifs6_in_echo);
722                             if (code != 0)
723                                     goto badcode;
```
icmp6.c

720–723 The interface specific ICMPv6 statistics counter for the Echo Request message is incremented. The Code field must be zero for an Echo Request message; otherwise the packet is treated as invalid.

Listing 4-11

```
724                /*
725                 * Copy mbuf to send to two data paths: userland socket(s),
726                 * and to the querier (echo reply).
727                 * m: a copy for socket, n: a copy for querier
728                 */
729                if ((n = m_copym(m, 0, M_COPYALL, M_DONTWAIT)) == NULL) {
730                        /* Give up local */
731                        n = m;
732                        m = NULL;
733                        goto deliverecho;
734                }
```

728–734 The incoming packet is replicated in case a process waits on a Raw socket to capture the packet. If copying the packet fails, only the ICMPv6 Echo Reply message in response to the Echo Request will be generated and local node delivery of the received Echo Request message is bypassed.

Listing 4-12

```
735                /*
736                 * If the first mbuf is shared, or the first mbuf is too short,
737                 * copy the first part of the data into a fresh mbuf.
738                 * Otherwise, we will wrongly overwrite both copies.
739                 */
740                if ((n->m_flags & M_EXT) != 0 ||
741                    n->m_len < off + sizeof(struct icmp6_hdr)) {
742                        struct mbuf *n0 = n;
743                        const int maxlen = sizeof(*nip6) + sizeof(*nicmp6);
744
745                        /*
746                         * Prepare an internal mbuf.  m_pullup() doesn't
747                         * always copy the length we specified.
748                         */
749                        if (maxlen >= MCLBYTES) {
750                                /* Give up remote */
751                                m_freem(n0);
752                                break;
753                        }
754                        MGETHDR(n, M_DONTWAIT, n0->m_type);
755                        if (n && maxlen >= MHLEN) {
756                                MCLGET(n, M_DONTWAIT);
757                                if ((n->m_flags & M_EXT) == 0) {
758                                        m_free(n);
759                                        n = NULL;
760                                }
761                        }
```

740–741 If the copied mbuf has an mbuf cluster(*), a separate new mbuf needs to be allocated to hold the IPv6 and ICMPv6 headers. When the data is stored in a cluster, it is shared by the copy source and destination with multiple references. This effectively makes the data read-only. In our case, however, the icmp6_reflect() function will soon modify the copied packet to generate an ICMPv6 Echo Reply message in response to the Echo Request, so the data cannot be shared.

(*) The condition at line 741 is always false for the implementation described in this book, since the first mbuf of the original packet contains all the data to the ICMPv6 header (see Listing 4-3) and `m_copym()` preserves this property.

744–748 The typical operation is to use the `m_pullup()` function, but it is not suitable here; the packet may contain intermediate extension headers, which can be large, and `m_pullup()` fails if the copy length requires an allocation of the mbuf cluster.

749–760 A separate mbuf is allocated with additional space for the packet header. Even though some exceptional cases are considered, a simple, small mbuf without a cluster should actually suffice here, since `maxlen` is small enough.

Listing 4-13

icmp6.c

```
762                               if (n == NULL) {
763                                       /* Give up local */
764                                       m_freem(n0);
765                                       n = m;
766                                       m = NULL;
767                                       goto deliverecho;
768                               }
```

icmp6.c

762–768 The duplicated mbuf chain is freed if the new mbuf for the header cannot be allocated. The local node delivery of the received packet is bypassed in this case.

Listing 4-14

icmp6.c

```
770                               M_MOVE_PKTHDR(n, n0);
774                               /*
775                                * Copy IPv6 and ICMPv6 only.
776                                */
777                               nip6 = mtod(n, struct ip6_hdr *);
778                               bcopy(ip6, nip6, sizeof(struct ip6_hdr));
779                               nicmp6 = (struct icmp6_hdr *)(nip6 + 1);
780                               bcopy(icmp6, nicmp6, sizeof(struct icmp6_hdr));
781                               noff = sizeof(struct ip6_hdr);
782                               n->m_len = noff + sizeof(struct icmp6_hdr);
783                               /*
784                                * Adjust mbuf.  ip6_plen will be adjusted in
785                                * ip6_output().
786                                * n->m_pkthdr.len == n0->m_pkthdr.len at this point.
787                                */
788                               n->m_pkthdr.len += noff + sizeof(struct icmp6_hdr);
789                               n->m_pkthdr.len -= (off + sizeof(struct icmp6_hdr));
790                               m_adj(n0, off + sizeof(struct icmp6_hdr));
791                               n->m_next = n0;
```

icmp6.c

770 The newly allocated packet header of mbuf `n` is initialized with the content of the packet header of mbuf `n0`.

774–791 The IPv6 and ICMPv6 headers are copied into the new buffer. The packet length is adjusted to account for only the IPv6 and ICMPv6 headers and all other headers are

FIGURE 4-22

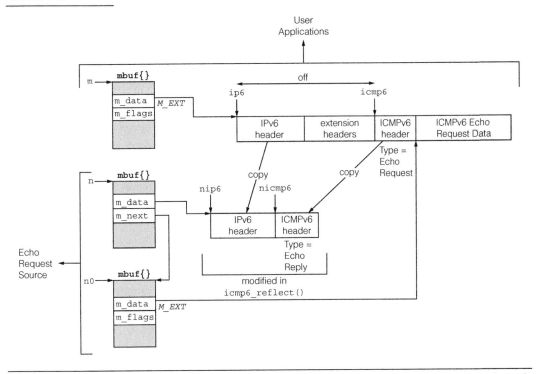

Copying an ICMPv6 Echo Request packet for local delivery and for sending Echo Reply.

removed by adjusting the original packet buffer. The new header buffer and the original buffer packet are linked to create the full packet.

Figure 4-22 summarizes the above procedure. The original packet stored in an mbuf cluster is shared by two mbufs m and n0. The shared data (Echo Request data) will not be modified after the copy and this sharing is safe.

Listing 4-15
_____ icmp6.c
```
792                    } else {
793          deliverecho:
794                         nip6 = mtod(n, struct ip6_hdr *);
795                         nicmp6 = (struct icmp6_hdr *)((caddr_t)nip6 + off);
796                         noff = off;
797                    }
```
_____ icmp6.c

792–797 In the case of the first mbuf of the packet not requiring replication, nip6 and nicmp6 are simply set to point to the IPv6 and ICMPv6 headers of the copied mbuf. noff holds the offset to the beginning of the ICMPv6 header. Note that intermediate extension headers, if any, are not yet stripped off at this point.

Listing 4-16

——icmp6.c
```
798                          nicmp6->icmp6_type = ICMP6_ECHO_REPLY;
799                          nicmp6->icmp6_code = 0;
800                          if (n) {
801                                  icmp6stat.icp6s_reflect++;
802                                  icmp6stat.icp6s_outhist[ICMP6_ECHO_REPLY]++;
803                                  icmp6_reflect(n, noff);
804                          }
805                          if (!m)
806                                  goto freeit;
807                          break;
808
```
——icmp6.c

798–807 The ICMPv6 type is set to `ICMP6_ECHO_REPLY` and the code is set to 0 as specified in [RFC2463]. The statistics counters for the number of reflected packets and for the number of transmitted Echo Reply messages are incremented. `icmp6_reflect()` is called to transmit the packet.

Listing 4-17

——icmp6.c
```
809              case ICMP6_ECHO_REPLY:
810                      icmp6_ifstat_inc(m->m_pkthdr.rcvif, ifs6_in_echoreply);
811                      if (code != 0)
812                              goto badcode;
813                      break;
```
——icmp6.c

809–813 The interface specific ICMPv6 statistics counter for the Echo Reply message is incremented. Again, the Code field must be zero.

Listing 4-18

——icmp6.c
```
815  #ifdef MIP6
```

(Mobile IPv6-related messages)

```
851  #endif /* MIP6 */
852
853          case MLD_LISTENER_QUERY:
854          case MLD_LISTENER_REPORT:
871          case MLD_LISTENER_DONE:
877          case MLD_MTRACE_RESP:
878          case MLD_MTRACE:
```

(Multicast Listener Discovery messages: covered in Chapter 2 of *IPv6 Advanced Protocols Implementation*)

```
883  #ifdef MLDV2
```

(Multicast Listener Discovery version 2 messages: not covered in this series)

```
890  #endif
891
892          case ICMP6_WRUREQUEST:    /* ICMP6_FQDN_QUERY */
```

(ICMPv6 Node Information Query: Section 4.9.6)

```
 982            case ICMP6_WRUREPLY:
```

(ICMPv6 Node Information Reply)

```
 987            case ND_ROUTER_SOLICIT:
1003            case ND_ROUTER_ADVERT:
1019            case ND_NEIGHBOR_SOLICIT:
1035            case ND_NEIGHBOR_ADVERT:
1051            case ND_REDIRECT:
```

(Neighbor Discovery Messages)

```
1067            case ICMP6_ROUTER_RENUMBERING:
```

(Router Renumbering Messages: not covered in this series)

```
1073            break;
```
—— icmp6.c

815–1073 This block of code handles other various types of ICMPv6 messages. These are used
for their own protocol operations, and some of those are described later in this section or
in other chapters of this book series. In general, this part of the code performs a minimal
check for the packet length and calls the relevant processing routine for each specific
message type. We do not go into further details of these cases in this chapter.

Listing 4-19
—— icmp6.c

```
1075        default:
1076            nd6log((LOG_DEBUG,
1077                "icmp6_input: unknown type %d(src=%s, dst=%s, ifid=%d)\n",
1078                icmp6->icmp6_type, ip6_sprintf(&ip6->ip6_src),
1079                ip6_sprintf(&ip6->ip6_dst),
1080                m->m_pkthdr.rcvif ? m->m_pkthdr.rcvif->if_index : 0));
1081            if (icmp6->icmp6_type < ICMP6_ECHO_REQUEST) {
1082                /* ICMPv6 error: MUST deliver it by spec... */
1083                code = PRC_NCMDS;
1084                /* deliver */
1085            } else {
1086                /* ICMPv6 informational: MUST not deliver */
1087                break;
1088            }
1089        deliver:
1090            if (icmp6_notify_error(m, off, icmp6len, code)) {
1091                /* In this case, m should've been freed. */
1092                return (IPPROTO_DONE);
1093            }
1094            break;
1095
1096        badcode:
1097            icmp6stat.icp6s_badcode++;
1098            break;
1099
1100        badlen:
1101            icmp6stat.icp6s_badlen++;
1102            break;
1103        }
1104
1105        /* deliver the packet to appropriate sockets */
1106        icmp6_rip6_input(&m, *offp, &src, &dst);
1107
1108        return IPPROTO_DONE;
1109
1110    freeit:
```

```
1111             m_freem(m);
1112             return IPPROTO_DONE;
1113     }
```
_____ icmp6.c

1075–1080 Any unrecognized message types are logged through function `nd6log()`.

Note: Despite its name, `nd6log()` is widely used in the KAME kernel implementation to suppress informational log messages that can be too noisy. By default, `nd6log()` does not make the specified log message; this can be changed by setting a sysctl variable `net.inet6.icmp6.nd6_debug` to non-0.

1081–1088 The ICMPv6 protocol specification requires that any error message be passed to the relevant upper layer process. An unknown error message will thus be delivered to the upper layer with the code of `PRC_NCMDS`. On the other hand, the specification requires that any unknown information messages be silently discarded.

Note: `PRC_NCMDS` is actually a trailing marker of the possible error codes, and cannot be used as an individual error code. In fact, the transport layer routines that handle this code will simply ignore the delivered message with this code (see Sections 6.8.5 and 6.9.4). Instead of using the unusable code, a new valid code indicating an "other general error" should be defined and used.

1089–1094 Error messages are delivered to the upper layer process that caused the error through function `icmp6_notify_error()` (Section 4.6.2). Note that this part of code is performed for both known and unknown error messages.

1096–1102 The statistics counters for the unrecognized message code and messages that have incorrect length are updated.

1106–1108 The known ICMPv6 message is also delivered to other upper layer processes that are interested in explicitly receiving these types of packets.

1110–1112 The received ICMPv6 message is freed when the function encounters an error while processing the packet.

4.6.2   Notifying Errors: `icmp6_notify_error()` Function

The `icmp6_notify_error()` function is called by `icmp6_input()` to notify the upper layer protocols of received ICMPv6 error messages. The processing is complicated compared to IPv4 due to existence of intermediate extension headers, and is thus provided as a separate function.

Listing 4-20
_____ icmp6.c
```
1115    static int
1116    icmp6_notify_error(m, off, icmp6len, code)
1117            struct mbuf *m;
```

```
1118                int off, icmp6len;
1119        {
1120                struct icmp6_hdr *icmp6;
1121                struct ip6_hdr *eip6;
1122                u_int32_t notifymtu;
1123                struct sockaddr_in6 icmp6src, icmp6dst;
```
─── icmp6.c

1116 m points to the packet buffer. off points to the ICMPv6 header, counted from the beginning of the packet buffer. icmp6len holds the length of the ICMPv6 message counting from the start of the ICMPv6 header. code holds the protocol control command corresponding to the ICMPv6 type and code (see Table 4-11).

Listing 4-21
─── icmp6.c

```
1125                if (icmp6len < sizeof(struct icmp6_hdr) + sizeof(struct ip6_hdr)) {
1126                        icmp6stat.icp6s_tooshort++;
1127                        goto freeit;
1128                }
```
─── icmp6.c

1125–1128 The ICMPv6 error messages should contain as much of the original packet as would fit in the minimum IPv6 MTU. Upper layer protocols cannot retrieve meaningful information from the original packet if the data contained in the ICMPv6 error message is less than a complete IPv6 header. In that case the packet is freed and the function terminates.

Listing 4-22
─── icmp6.c

```
1130                IP6_EXTHDR_CHECK(m, off,
1131                        sizeof(struct icmp6_hdr) + sizeof(struct ip6_hdr),
1132                        -1);
1133                icmp6 = (struct icmp6_hdr *)(mtod(m, caddr_t) + off);
1142                eip6 = (struct ip6_hdr *)(icmp6 + 1);
```
─── icmp6.c

1130–1142 The IP6_EXTHDR_CHECK() macro verifies that both the ICMPv6 and the (inner) IPv6 headers fit in a contiguous memory space. icmp6 is set to point to the beginning of the ICMPv6 header. eip6 is set to point to the beginning of the IPv6 header of the original packet, which is located starting at the ninth byte of the ICMPv6 message.

Listing 4-23
─── icmp6.c

```
1144                /* Detect the upper level protocol */
1145                {
1146                        void (*ctlfunc) __P((int, struct sockaddr *, void *));
1147                        u_int8_t nxt = eip6->ip6_nxt;
1148                        int eoff = off + sizeof(struct icmp6_hdr) +
1149                                sizeof(struct ip6_hdr);
1150                        struct ip6ctlparam ip6cp;
1151                        struct in6_addr *finaldst = NULL;
1152                        int icmp6type = icmp6->icmp6_type;
1153                        struct ip6_frag *fh;
1154                        struct ip6_rthdr *rth;
```

```
1155                     struct ip6_rthdr0 *rth0;
1156                     int rthlen;
1157
1158                     while (1) { /* XXX: should avoid infinite loop explicitly? */
1159                             struct ip6_ext *eh;
```
——icmp6.c

1144–1160 nxt holds the next header identifier retrieved from the original packet that triggered the ICMPv6 error message. eoff holds the offset to the start of the header that immediately follows the IPv6 header in the original packet. The purpose of this while loop is to determine the appropriate upper layer protocol to send the notification to.

Listing 4-24
——icmp6.c

```
1161                     switch (nxt) {
1162                     case IPPROTO_HOPOPTS:
1163                     case IPPROTO_DSTOPTS:
1164                     case IPPROTO_AH:
1166                             IP6_EXTHDR_CHECK(m, 0, eoff +
1167                                                     sizeof(struct ip6_ext),
1168                                                     -1);
1169                             eh = (struct ip6_ext *)(mtod(m, caddr_t)
1170                                                     + eoff);
1179
1180                             if (nxt == IPPROTO_AH)
1181                                     eoff += (eh->ip6e_len + 2) << 2;
1182                             else
1183                                     eoff += (eh->ip6e_len + 1) << 3;
1184                             nxt = eh->ip6e_nxt;
1185                             break;
```
——icmp6.c

1161–1185 For any instance of the Hop-by-Hop options header, the Destination options header, and the Authentication header, the original packet included in the ICMPv6 message must be large enough to contain the common fields, that is, of the extension headers (i.e., the header length and the next header fields); otherwise, the processing terminates here. The next header value is retried and reset in nxt, and the offset eoff is updated according to the length of the extension header.

Listing 4-25
——icmp6.c

```
1186             case IPPROTO_ROUTING:
1187                     /*
1188                      * When the erroneous packet contains a
1189                      * routing header, we should examine the
1190                      * header to determine the final destination.
1191                      * Otherwise, we can't properly update
1192                      * information that depends on the final
1193                      * destination (e.g. path MTU).
1194                      */
1196                     IP6_EXTHDR_CHECK(m, 0, eoff + sizeof(*rth),
1197                                     -1);
1198                     rth = (struct ip6_rthdr *)(mtod(m, caddr_t)
1199                                     + eoff);
1208                     rthlen = (rth->ip6r_len + 1) << 3;
1209                     /*
1210                      * XXX: currently there is no
```

```
1211                    * officially defined type other
1212                    * than type-0.
1213                    * Note that if the segment left field
1214                    * is 0, all intermediate hops must
1215                    * have been passed.
1216                    */
1217                   if (rth->ip6r_segleft &&
1218                       rth->ip6r_type == IPV6_RTHDR_TYPE_0) {
1219                           int hops;
1220
1222                           IP6_EXTHDR_CHECK(m, 0, eoff + rthlen,
1223                                                   -1);
1224                           rth0 = (struct ip6_rthdr0 *)(mtod(m, caddr_t) + eoff);
1234                           /* just ignore a bogus header */
1235                           if ((rth0->ip6r0_len % 2) == 0 &&
1236                               (hops = rth0->ip6r0_len/2))
1237                                   finaldst = (struct in6_addr *)(rth0 + 1) + (hops - 1);
1238                   }
1239                   eoff += rthlen;
1240                   nxt = rth->ip6r_nxt;
1241                   break;
```
                                                                                    ⎯⎯ icmp6.c

1186–1208 Likewise, if a Routing header is present in the original header, the original packet included in the ICMPv6 message must be large enough to contain the minimum part of the Routing header (the `ip6_rthdr{}` structure).

1217–1241 If the Segments Left field of the Routing header is 0, the packet must have arrived at the final destination contained in the Routing header. When the packet that caused the error contained a Routing header, the error may be returned from an intermediate node specified in the header and the Destination Address field of the inner IPv6 packet may not be the final destination. If this is the case, the final destination address must be retrieved from the Routing header in order to identify the corresponding process and update the path MTU information (in case of a Packet Too Big message). The latter processing is only applied for a Type-0 Routing header; this implementation does not support other types and cannot identify the real final destination(*). For a Type-0 Routing header, the packet length and the header parameters are validated, and the final destination address stored in the header is copied to `finaldst`.

(*) If the Segments Left field is non-0 and this is an unsupported type of Routing header, the processing should probably terminate here because the destination address would not help identify the appropriate process. It may even be a security attack, because it is unlikely that the receiving node has sent a packet containing an unsupported type of Routing header.

Listing 4-26
                                                                                    ⎯⎯ icmp6.c
```
1242                           case IPPROTO_FRAGMENT:
1244                                   IP6_EXTHDR_CHECK(m, 0, eoff +
1245                                                   sizeof(struct ip6_frag),
1246                                                   -1);
1247                                   fh = (struct ip6_frag *)(mtod(m, caddr_t)
1248                                                   + eoff);
1257                                   /*
```

```
1258                                    * Data after a fragment header is meaningless
1259                                    * unless it is the first fragment, but
1260                                    * we'll go to the notify label for path MTU
1261                                    * discovery.
1262                                    */
1263                                   if (fh->ip6f_offlg & IP6F_OFF_MASK)
1264                                           goto notify;
1265
1266                                   eoff += sizeof(struct ip6_frag);
1267                                   nxt = fh->ip6f_nxt;
1268                                   break;
```
─── icmp6.c

1242–1268 If the original packet contains a Fragment header, it is unlikely that the original packet has the information for the upper layer process unless it is the first fragment (i.e., with the offset of zero). For all other fragments the loop terminates here and the processing continues to the notification phase in case the error is "Packet Too Big," which may update the PMTU size for the destination address. It can be done without knowing the information about the upper layer process.

Note: It is possible that a non-first fragment contains the information about the upper layer process when the original packet contains a very large Destination Options header. In order to handle such a case, the processing would need to reassemble the fragments in multiple ICMPv6 error messages, but the expected benefit would not be worth the complexity.

Listing 4-27
─── icmp6.c
```
1269                      default:
1270                              /*
1271                               * This case includes ESP and the No Next
1272                               * Header.  In such cases going to the notify,
1273                               * label does not have any meaning
1274                               * (i.e. ctlfunc will be NULL), but we go
1275                               * anyway since we might have to update
1276                               * path MTU information.
1277                               */
1278                              goto notify;
1279                      }
1280              }
```
─── icmp6.c

1269–1280 The while loop terminates and the processing continues to the notification phase for all other types of extension headers. Again, it is mainly for the case of PMTU discovery.

Listing 4-28
─── icmp6.c
```
1281              notify:
1283                  icmp6 = (struct icmp6_hdr *)(mtod(m, caddr_t) + off);
1292
1293                  /*
```

```
1294                              * retrieve parameters from the inner IPv6 header, and convert
1295                              * them into sockaddr structures.
1296                              * XXX: there is no guarante that the source or destination
1297                              * addresses of the inner packet are in the same scope as
1298                              * the addresses of the icmp packet.  But there is no other
1299                              * way to determine the zone.
1300                              */
1301                             eip6 = (struct ip6_hdr *)(icmp6 + 1);
1302
1303                             bzero(&icmp6dst, sizeof(icmp6dst));
1304                             icmp6dst.sin6_len = sizeof(struct sockaddr_in6);
1305                             icmp6dst.sin6_family = AF_INET6;
1306                             if (finaldst == NULL)
1307                                     icmp6dst.sin6_addr = eip6->ip6_dst;
1308                             else
1309                                     icmp6dst.sin6_addr = *finaldst;
1310                             if (in6_addr2zoneid(m->m_pkthdr.rcvif, &icmp6dst.sin6_addr,
1311                                             &icmp6dst.sin6_scope_id))
1312                                     goto freeit;
1313                             if (in6_embedscope(&icmp6dst.sin6_addr, &icmp6dst)) {
1314                                     /* should be impossbile */
1315                                     nd6log((LOG_DEBUG,
1316                                         "icmp6_notify_error: in6_embedscope failed\n"));
1317                                     goto freeit;
1318                             }
```
                                                                                    —— icmp6.c

1281–1301 The block of code is redundant because `icmp6` and `eip6` have not been modified. This was probably intended to deal with a special case of an older version of `IP6_EXTHDR_CHECK()` that can modify the mbuf chain in it.

1301–1309 The Destination address of the original packet in the form of the socket address structure is set to `icmp6dst`. If this error message is returned from an intermediate node specified in a Routing header, in which case `finaldst` is non-NULL (Listing 4-25), the final destination address is retrieved from the Routing header.

1310–1318 Since the retrieved address does not necessarily have information of its scope zone, the receiving node may need to guess the appropriate zone. This code determines the zone based on the receiving interface of the ICMPv6 message and the scope type of the original destination address.

While this may look reasonable, it can actually be different from the correct zone. Figure 4-23 illustrates an example of a problematic case. A site-border node sends a multicast packet with a global source address (`2001:db8::1`) and a site-local multicast destination address (`ff05::ffff`). The multicast receiver identifies an error of the packet and sends an ICMPv6 error message to the source address of the original packet. The source address of the ICMPv6 message is a global address (`2001:db8:ffff::2`), so the packet can be routed along an arbitrary path in the global Internet. If the error message is received at a different side of site, the site zone identifier for the site-local multicast address of the original packet is misinterpreted as if it belonged to Site B.

Unfortunately, there is no reliable way to avoid the problem. Whereas the heuristics of this implementation should work correctly in many cases, it may be better to ignore the error message if the receiving node cannot identify the correct zone in a reliable way.

FIGURE 4-23

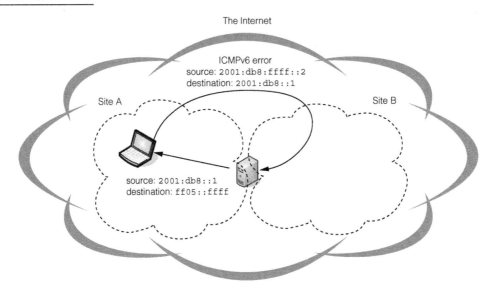

The Internet

ICMPv6 error
source: `2001:db8:ffff::2`
destination: `2001:db8::1`

Site A   Site B

source: `2001:db8::1`
destination: `ff05::ffff`

A problematic case where a site-border node cannot identify the correct scope zone of the erroneous packet in an ICMPv6 message.

Listing 4-29

icmp6.c

```
1320                    bzero(&icmp6src, sizeof(icmp6src));
1321                    icmp6src.sin6_len = sizeof(struct sockaddr_in6);
1322                    icmp6src.sin6_family = AF_INET6;
1323                    icmp6src.sin6_addr = eip6->ip6_src;
1324                    if (in6_addr2zoneid(m->m_pkthdr.rcvif, &icmp6src.sin6_addr,
1325                            &icmp6src.sin6_scope_id)) {
1326                        goto freeit;
1327                    }
1328                    if (in6_embedscope(&icmp6src.sin6_addr, &icmp6src)) {
1329                        /* should be impossible */
1330                        nd6log((LOG_DEBUG,
1331                            "icmp6_notify_error: in6_embedscope failed\n"));
1332                        goto freeit;
1333                    }
1334                    icmp6src.sin6_flowinfo =
1335                        (eip6->ip6_flow & IPV6_FLOWLABEL_MASK);
```

icmp6.c

1320–1333 Similarly, the source address of the original packet is stored in `icmp6src` in the form of a socket address structure with an inferred scope zone ID based on the receiving interface. The determination of the zone ID has the same problem that we described above. But it is actually less problematic for the source address; with the deprecation of site-local unicast addresses (Section 2.4.4), the only troubling case is that the source address is a link-local address, in which case both the source and destination addresses of the ICMPv6 message are likely link-local addresses and the message is not routed outside the original zone. It could perform some stricter checks here, though (e.g., to determine whether the address is really assigned to the receiving node).

1334–1335 The flow label of the original packet is copied to `icmp6src`. This may be used later as a hint to identify the appropriate upper layer process when the returned packet is encrypted and the upper layer header cannot be retrieved (note that the `while` loop of this function terminates if it encounters an ESP header as shown in Listing 4-27). Section 6.6.10 will describe how this value can be used.

Listing 4-30

———icmp6.c

```
1337                     if (finaldst == NULL)
1338                             finaldst = &eip6->ip6_dst;
1339                     ip6cp.ip6c_m = m;
1340                     ip6cp.ip6c_icmp6 = icmp6;
1341                     ip6cp.ip6c_ip6 = (struct ip6_hdr *)(icmp6 + 1);
1342                     ip6cp.ip6c_off = eoff;
1343                     ip6cp.ip6c_src = &icmp6src;
1344                     ip6cp.ip6c_nxt = nxt;
```

———icmp6.c

1337–1338 This code is only effective in an older version of the kernel; it does effectively nothing in this version and should have been cleaned up.

1339–1344 An instance of the `ip6ctlparam{}` structure, `ip6cp`, is initialized with parameters of the error message. This structure is used as an argument to protocol control input functions to identify the corresponding upper layer process. The definition of the structure is shown in Listing 4-31. The initialization sequence well describes the semantics of the structure fields. Figure 4-24 summarizes relationship of the ICMPv6 message and the corresponding `ip6ctlparam{}` structure. In this figure, the ICMPv6 error message contains a TCP over IPv6 packet with a Hop-by-Hop options header and a Destination options header.

FIGURE 4-24

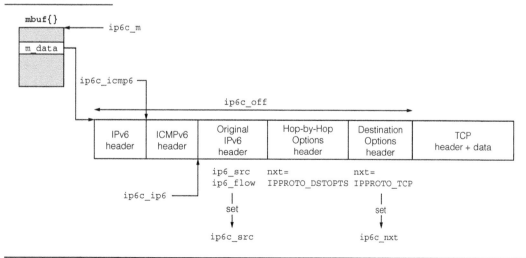

Relationship between an incoming ICMPv6 error message and `ip6ctlparam{}` *structure members.*

Listing 4-31

_____ ip6protosw.h

```
107    struct ip6ctlparam {
108            struct mbuf *ip6c_m;              /* start of mbuf chain */
109            struct icmp6_hdr *ip6c_icmp6;    /* icmp6 header of target packet */
110            struct ip6_hdr *ip6c_ip6;        /* ip6 header of target packet */
111            int ip6c_off;                    /* offset of the target proto header */
112            struct sockaddr_in6 *ip6c_src;   /* srcaddr w/ additional info */
113            void *ip6c_cmdarg;               /* control command dependent data */
114            u_int8_t ip6c_nxt;               /* final next header field */
115    };
```

_____ ip6protosw.h

Listing 4-32

_____ icmp6.c

```
1346                    if (icmp6type == ICMP6_PACKET_TOO_BIG) {
1347                            notifymtu = ntohl(icmp6->icmp6_mtu);
1348                            ip6cp.ip6c_cmdarg = (void *)&notifymtu;
1350                            icmp6_mtudisc_update(&ip6cp, &icmp6dst, 1); /* XXX */
1352                    }
```

_____ icmp6.c

1346–1352 If the type of the ICMPv6 error message is Packet Too Big, the notified MTU value
in the error message is copied to `notifymtu`, and is set in the `ip6ctlparam{}` structure
as an optional argument. Function `icmp6_mtudisc_update()` is then called to update
the PMTU for the destination with the notified MTU.

Listing 4-33

_____ icmp6.c

```
1354                    ctlfunc = (void (*) __P((int, struct sockaddr *, void *)))
1355                            (inet6sw[ip6_protox[nxt]].pr_ctlinput);
1356                    if (ctlfunc) {
1357                            (void) (*ctlfunc)(code, (struct sockaddr *)&icmp6dst,
1358                                              &ip6cp);
1359                    }
1360            }
1361            return (0);
1362
1363    freeit:
1364            m_freem(m);
1365            return (-1);
1366    }
```

_____ icmp6.c

1354–1359 The `pr_ctlinput` member of the `ip6protosw{}` structure corresponding to
the upper layer protocol identified by `nxt` specifies the protocol-dependent function that
notifies upper layer processes of an error (see Section 3.4.3). If this function is specified,
that is, the pointer is non-NULL, it is called with the protocol control command (`code`), the
destination address, and the error parameters stored in the `ip6ctlparam{}` structure.
Note that the `pr_ctlinput` member can be NULL (see Table 3-9), which is the case
when the `while` loop of this function terminates at a Fragment header for a non-first
fragment, and in such a case no protocol specific processing is performed.

   It should also be noted that the comment about the case of ESP and No Next header
in Listing 4-27 is incorrect: These have the control input function as shown in Table 3-9
(the No Next header matches the default raw entry, whose ctlinput function is
`rip6_ctlinput()`).

1363–1365 The `freeit` label is reached when the function encounters an error. In this case the packet containing the ICMPv6 message is freed. Note that it means the packet is not sent to ICMPv6 applications via the `icmp6_rip6_input()` function (see Listing 4-19).

4.7 Path MTU Discovery Implementation

In most BSD variant systems including the one described in this book, the PMTU size of a packet delivery path is maintained in a cached host route entry for the final destination. Technically, the PMTU size for a particular destination can be different if the node uses several different paths with explicit intermediate nodes specified in a Routing header (or the IPv4 Source Route option). In practice, however, it should suffice to maintain the PMTU size per destination basis, since the use of source routing is rare and the maintenance per real route would make the implementation more complicated.

In this section, we describe how the KAME implementation maintains PMTU information for IPv6 destinations.

4.7.1 `icmp6_mtudisc_update()` Function

The `icmp6_mtudisc_update()` function is called by `icmp6_notify_error()` to update the PMTU size for a given destination (Listing 4-32).

It can also be called during the processing of control input functions corresponding to some extension headers. The additional call path is intended to avoid unconditional creation of host route entries for PMTU size that may be a result of an attack attempting to overconsume the kernel memory. The validity of the relevant path is confirmed with other information in the kernel such as IPsec security association. In KAME snapshots for FreeBSD, however, this processing is effectively meaningless because the call from `icmp6_mtudisc_update()` always creates or updates the corresponding PMTU size. Instead, this implementation manages the maximum number of such routes as a part of the general framework controlling dynamically created route entries.

We will look at the details of the `icmp6_mtudisc_update()` function below.

Listing 4-34
```
                                                                   icmp6.c
1372    void
1373    icmp6_mtudisc_update(ip6cp, dst, validated)
1374            struct ip6ctlparam *ip6cp;
1375            struct sockaddr_in6 *dst;
1376            int validated;
1377    {
1384            struct icmp6_hdr *icmp6 = ip6cp->ip6c_icmp6;
1385            u_int mtu = ntohl(icmp6->icmp6_mtu);
1386            struct rtentry *rt = NULL;
1388            struct sockaddr_in6 dst_tmp;
                                                                   icmp6.c
```

1373 `ip6cp` contains various pieces of information about the ICMPv6 message and the original packet. `dst` points to the destination address of the original packet.

`validated` indicates whether the caller has verified the information contained in the original packet that is carried in the ICMPv6 message. As noted above, this variable is always true in the implementation described in this book.

Listing 4-35

_____ icmp6.c
```
1398     #if 0
1399             /*
1400              * RFC2460 section 5, last paragraph.
1401              * even though minimum link MTU for IPv6 is IPV6_MMTU,
1402              * we may see ICMPv6 too big with mtu < IPV6_MMTU
1403              * due to packet translator in the middle.
1404              * see ip6_output() and ip6_getpmtu() "alwaysfrag" case for
1405              * special handling.
1406              */
1407             if (mtu < IPV6_MMTU)
1408                     return;
1409     #endif
1410
1411             /*
1412              * we reject ICMPv6 too big with abnormally small value.
1413              * XXX what is the good definition of "abnormally small"?
1414              */
1415             if (mtu < sizeof(struct ip6_hdr) + sizeof(struct ip6_frag) + 8)
1416                     return;
```
_____ icmp6.c

1407–1417 This code block tries to reject too small a size as the reported MTU because it may indicate some security attack, even though the protocol specification does not require any such validation. While rejecting a size less than the minimum MTU size (1280 bytes) may look reasonable, it is actually incorrect since a certain type of protocol translator between IPv4 and IPv6 may validly send an ICMPv6 Packet Too Big error message reporting such a small MTU size. This check is thus explicitly disabled with comments so that it will not be "reinvented." The check at line 1415 is based on some ad hoc heuristics. While it is probably harmless, it is also meaningless; the effect of the "too small" MTU size is to make the IPv6 output routine fragment packets at the minimum MTU size with a Fragment header (see Section 3.13.8), and the exact MTU value reported in the ICMPv6 message is not used.

Listing 4-36

_____ icmp6.c
```
1441            if (!validated)
1442                    return;
```
_____ icmp6.c

1441–1442 The function terminates here if the upper layer protocol could not validate the information from the original packet that is carried in the ICMPv6 message.

Listing 4-37

_____ icmp6.c
```
1446            dst_tmp = *dst;
1447            dst_tmp.sin6_scope_id = 0;
1448            dst = &dst_tmp;
      ....
1456            rt = rtalloc1((struct sockaddr *)dst, 0,
1457                    RTF_CLONING | RTF_PRCLONING);
```
_____ icmp6.c

1446–1457 The `rtalloc1()` function tries to find a cached host route for the destination. The `RTF_CLONING` and `RTF_PRCLONING` flags avoid creation of a newly cloned route for the destination; `icmp6_mtudisc_update()` only updates an existing route entry. Note also that the `sin6_scope_id` field must be cleared before the route allocation as explained in Section 2.9.3.

Listing 4-38

——*icmp6.c*

```
1471                if (rt && (rt->rt_flags & RTF_HOST) &&
1472                    !(rt->rt_rmx.rmx_locks & RTV_MTU) &&
1473                    (rt->rt_rmx.rmx_mtu > mtu || rt->rt_rmx.rmx_mtu == 0)) {
1474                        if (mtu < IN6_LINKMTU(rt->rt_ifp)) {
1475                                icmp6stat.icp6s_pmtuchg++;
1476                                rt->rt_rmx.rmx_mtu = mtu;
1477
1479                                /*
1480                                 * We intentionally ignore the error case of
1481                                 * rt_timer_add(), because the only bad effect is that
1482                                 * we won't be able to re-increase the path MTU.
1483                                 */
1484                                if (pmtu_expire) {
1485                                        rt_timer_add(rt, icmp6_mtudisc_timeout,
1486                                                     icmp6_mtudisc_timeout_q);
1487                                }
....
1494                        }
1495                }
1496                if (rt) { /* XXX: need braces to avoid conflict with else in RTFREE. */
1497                        RTFREE(rt);
1498                }
```

——*icmp6.c*

1471–1476 If a host route for the destination exists and the reported MTU size is smaller than the currently recorded one(*), the path MTU size is updated with the new value.

(*) The check for the `RTV_MTU` flag is meaningless for the IPv6 implementation; in fact, this flag is never set in IPv6 PMTU discovery. For IPv4, this flag is set when the implementation decides the reported MTU is too small, indicating it should fragment packets with the "don't fragment" bit of the IP header being on. Clearly, this does not work for IPv6 since there is no "don't fragment" bit. Besides, since the minimum MTU size is pretty large for IPv6, it does not make much sense to be sensitive about the reported MTU size.

In the FreeBSD implementation, `rmx_mtu` is effectively always positive, since it is set to the link MTU for the outgoing interface on creation. It is therefore meaningless to see whether `rmx_mtu` is 0.

1484–1487 `pmtu_expire` specifies the timer duration for probing a larger path MTU size again. It defaults to 600 seconds (10 minutes). When this timer expires, the `icmp6_mtudisc_timeout()` function is called with route entry `rt` and resets the recorded path MTU size. The PMTU discovery process beginning with the link MTU for the outgoing interface will take place again.

1496–1498 Once the PMTU size is updated, this routine does not have a reason for retaining the route entry. The reference to the entry gained in `rtalloc1()` is thus released.

Path MTU Discovery Example

A user can see how the PMTU Discovery procedure works using the **ping6** command with the −m and −v command line options. By default, **ping6** tells the kernel to fragment Echo Request messages at the minimum MTU size, but the −m option disables this feature and asks the kernel to deliver any received ICMPv6 Too Big messages to the application via the ICMPv6 socket. The −v option shows the notifications.

Now consider the scenario depicted in Figure 4-25. The **ping6** "client" (the laptop computer at the lefthand side) executes the following command:

```
% ping6 -v -m -s 1300 2001:db8:ffff::1
```

which causes an IPv6 packet of 1348 bytes in length. It fits in the outgoing link, whose MTU is 1500 bytes, but the First Hop Router finds that it is too large for the second link, whose MTU is 1280 bytes, and returns an ICMPv6 Packet Too Big error message containing the MTU size of the second link. Note that some trailing part of the Echo Request data is truncated since the total length of the ICMPv6 error message must not exceed the IPv6 minimum MTU size (1280 bytes).

Execution of the above example on specific version of FreeBSD (at the time of writing, FreeBSD-6.1 and later) will cause a kernel panic. A fix to this problem will be incorporated into a future version of the kernel, but the release note should be consulted for safety.

Then the user at the client host will see the following output from the **ping6** command:

```
new path MTU (1280) is notified
1240 bytes from 2001:db8:1111::2: Packet too big mtu = 1280
Vr TC  Flow Plen Nxt Hlim
  6 00 00000 051c  3a   3f
```

The first line shown corresponds to the control message created in the `icmp6_notify_error()` function and delivered to the application. The rest of the output corresponds to the ICMPv6 error message (with the −v option **ping6** accepts any ICMPv6 messages sent to the host, not only the expected Echo Reply messages).

Then the client host will fragment the succeeding packets at the notified MTU size as shown in the lower half of Figure 4-25.

4.8   ICMPv6 Output Processing

ICMPv6 messages are generated in two ways. One is by user-initiated operation; for example, sending an ICMPv6 Echo message or an ICMPv6 Node Information query message using the **ping6** command. The other way is kernel-internal operation. The response procedure of an ICMPv6 Echo message and generating an ICMPv6 Echo Reply message are implemented in the kernel. Similarly, the input and response processing of Node Information messages are implemented in the kernel also. Also, an ICMPv6 error message may be generated during packet processing.

FIGURE 4-25

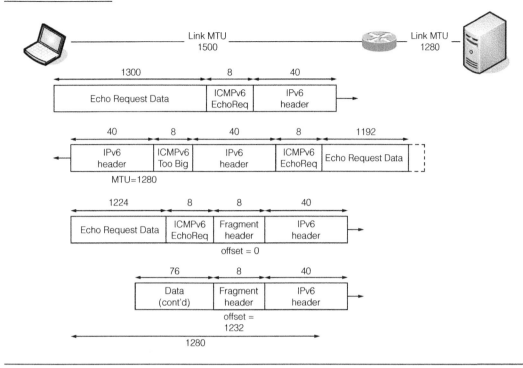

Path MTU discovery procedure for Echo Request messages.

Figure 4-26 shows an overview of the ICMPv6 output path. User space programs can send ICMPv6 messages using the Raw IPv6 socket, which is described in Chapter 6. ICMPv6 messages will be sent via the `rip6_send()` and `rip6_output()` functions. ICMPv6 messages are also generated in response to ICMPv6 message input events. The `icmp6_reflect()` function is called by the `icmp6_input()` function to generate reply messages to the input messages. As discussed in the previous paragraph, receiving ICMPv6 Echo messages or NI messages, and reply procedures to those messages belong to this case. `icmp6_reflect()` will be discussed in Section 4.8.3. The NI message processing will be discussed in Section 4.9. The `icmp6_error()` function also generates ICMPv6 messages. The function is called from various locations in kernel. `icmp6_error()` will be discussed in Section 4.8.1.

4.8.1 Sending Error: `icmp6_error()` Function

The `icmp6_error()` function is invoked from numerous packet processing functions at the Internet layer to generate an ICMPv6 error message. This function can also be called in a packet generating path. Figure 4-27 shows major function call paths to `icmp6_error()` along with possible error types and codes (note that the type and code names are derived from `ICMP6_xxx` macro constants).

FIGURE 4-26

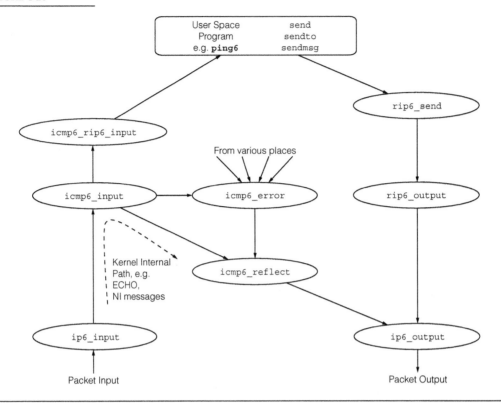

ICMPv6 output path.

Listing 4-39
                                                                                    icmp6.c

```
334     void
335     icmp6_error(m, type, code, param)
336             struct mbuf *m;
337             int type, code, param;
338     {
339             struct ip6_hdr *oip6, *nip6;
340             struct icmp6_hdr *icmp6;
341             struct m_tag *mtag;
342             struct ip6aux *ip6a;
343             struct sockaddr_in6 src_sa, dst_sa;
344             u_int preplen;
345             int off;
346             int nxt;
```
                                                                                    icmp6.c

335–346 On input m points to the packet that triggered the ICMPv6 error message. `type` is the type of error message. `code` is the type-specific error code. If the ICMPv6 error message indicates a parameter problem, then `param` holds the byte offset within the packet m where the parameter problem was encountered. Otherwise `param` is 0.

FIGURE 4-27

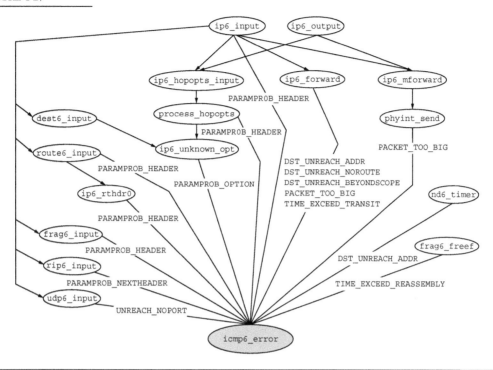

Function call paths to `icmp6_error()`.

Listing 4-40

icmp6.c

```
348             icmp6stat.icp6s_error++;
349
350             /* count per-type-code statistics */
351             icmp6_errcount(&icmp6stat.icp6s_outerrhist, type, code);
```

icmp6.c

348–351 The number of calls made to `icmp6_error()` is updated in the `icp6s_error` field. The statistics counter specific to the message type and code are updated through function `icmp6_errcount()` (not described in this book).

Listing 4-41

icmp6.c

```
354             if (m->m_flags & M_DECRYPTED) {
355                     icmp6stat.icp6s_canterror++;
356                     goto freeit;
357             }
359
361             IP6_EXTHDR_CHECK(m, 0, sizeof(struct ip6_hdr), );
369             oip6 = mtod(m, struct ip6_hdr *);
370             if (ip6_getpktaddrs(m, &src_sa, &dst_sa)) {
371                     goto freeit;
372             }
```

icmp6.c

354–357 If the erroneous packet was originally encrypted in ESP and was decrypted during the input processing, the mbuf is marked with the `M_DECRYPTED` flag. In this case, an error message is not generated and the processing terminates here.

This behavior is not described in the protocol specification but is specific to the KAME implementation. In fact, this situation is difficult to deal with. Clearly, the error message must not contain the decrypted packet since it would disclose the confidential data. The implementation may keep the very original packet before decryption and include that packet in the error message, but it would make the decryption processing more complicated and less efficient. Also, such an error message would probably annoy the recipient, which may not be able to decrypt the possibly shortened packet or may not identify the erroneous point from, for example, the pointer field of a Parameter Problem message. The current implementation is a result of these tradeoff considerations.

359–372 The `IP6_EXTHDR_CHECK()` macro ensures that the IPv6 header is in contiguous memory, and then `oip6` is set to point to the beginning of the IPv6 header. The packet source and destination addresses in the socket address form are retrieved through `ip6_getpktaddrs()` and copied in `src_sa` and `dst_sa`, respectively.

Note: As noted in Listing 3-172, `IP6_EXTHDR_CHECK()` effectively disables the call path to this function from `ip6_output()` via `process_hopopts()`.

Whether to Generate Error

The next part of this function determines whether an ICMPv6 error message should really be sent based on the rules described in Section 3.7.2.

Listing 4-42

```
                                                                    icmp6.c
374            /*
375             * If the destination address of the erroneous packet is a multicast
376             * address, or the packet was sent using link-layer multicast,
377             * we should basically suppress sending an error (RFC 2463, Section
378             * 2.4).
379             * We have two exceptions (the item e.2 in that section):
380             * - the Pakcet Too Big message can be sent for path MTU discovery.
381             * - the Parameter Problem Message that can be allowed an icmp6 error
382             *   in the option type field.  This check has been done in
383             *   ip6_unknown_opt(), so we can just check the type and code.
384             */
385            if ((m->m_flags & (M_BCAST|M_MCAST) ||
386                IN6_IS_ADDR_MULTICAST(&oip6->ip6_dst)) &&
387                (type != ICMP6_PACKET_TOO_BIG &&
388                (type != ICMP6_PARAM_PROB ||
389                code != ICMP6_PARAMPROB_OPTION)))
390                  goto freeit;
                                                                    icmp6.c
```

374–391 In general, a node will not generate an ICMPv6 error message if the original packet was sent either to an IPv6 multicast address or with a link-level multicast or broadcast address (Section 4.2.7). One exception is the Packet Too Big error message, which is allowed in order to support PMTU discovery for multicast traffic. The other exception is the Code 2 Parameter Problem message indicating an unrecognized IPv6 option that has a binary value of 10_b in the upper two bits of the option type. The IPv6 specification explicitly requests a node to generate an ICMPv6 Code 2 Parameter Problem message regardless of the type of the destination address of the original packet, if the upper two bits of the option type has 10_b.

Note that in the case of Code 2 Parameter Problem `ip6_unknown_opt()`, the caller of this function, ensures the option bits. Thus, `icmp6_error()` does not have to check the bits here.

The error generation process terminates if the requirements are not met.

Listing 4-43

_____ icmp6.c

```
392                 /*
393                  * RFC 2463, 2.4 (e.5): source address check.
394                  * XXX: the case of anycast source?
395                  */
396                 if (SA6_IS_ADDR_UNSPECIFIED(&src_sa) ||
397                     IN6_IS_ADDR_MULTICAST(&src_sa.sin6_addr))
398                         goto freeit;
```
_____ icmp6.c

392–398 The packet is silently discarded if the source address of the original packet is either the unspecified address or a multicast address. The current code does not check the source address against the anycast address even though the specification requests such validation. In fact, there is no reliable way to distinguish an anycast address from unicast addresses.

Listing 4-44

_____ icmp6.c

```
400                 /*
401                  * If we are about to send ICMPv6 against ICMPv6 error/redirect,
402                  * don't do it.
403                  */
404                 nxt = -1;
405                 off = ip6_lasthdr(m, 0, IPPROTO_IPV6, &nxt);
406                 if (off >= 0 && nxt == IPPROTO_ICMPV6) {
407                         struct icmp6_hdr *icp;
408
410                         IP6_EXTHDR_CHECK(m, 0, off + sizeof(struct icmp6_hdr), );
411                         icp = (struct icmp6_hdr *)(mtod(m, caddr_t) + off);
420                         if (icp->icmp6_type < ICMP6_ECHO_REQUEST ||
421                             icp->icmp6_type == ND_REDIRECT) {
422                                 /*
423                                  * ICMPv6 error
424                                  * Special case: for redirect (which is
425                                  * informational) we must not send icmp6 error.
426                                  */
427                                 icmp6stat.icp6s_canterror++;
428                                 goto freeit;
429                         } else {
430                                 /* ICMPv6 informational - send the error */
431                         }
432                 }
```
_____ icmp6.c

404–405 A node must not generate an ICMPv6 error message in response to an ICMPv6 error message or a Redirect message. To check this rule, function `ip6_lasthdr()` returns the offset from the head of the packet to the first byte of the upper layer header, skipping any extension headers. It also sets `nxt` to hold the value of the Next Header field of the preceding header, that is, the protocol identifier of the upper layer.

406–428 If the next header is the ICMPv6 header, the second call to `IP6_EXTHDR_CHECK()` ensures that the data from the IPv6 header to the ICMPv6 header is in a contiguous memory space, and the ICMPv6 message type is examined. The processing terminates if the type indicates an error message or a Redirect message.

Listing 4-45

_____icmp6.c
```
447              oip6 = mtod(m, struct ip6_hdr *); /* adjust pointer */
448              if (ip6_getpktaddrs(m, &src_sa, &dst_sa)) {
449                      goto freeit;
450              }
451
452              /* Finally, do rate limitation check. */
453              if (icmp6_ratelimit(&src_sa.sin6_addr, type, code)) {
454                      icmp6stat.icp6s_toofreq++;
455                      goto freeit;
456              }
```
_____icmp6.c

448 There is actually no need to update the pointer for this implementation because m is not updated.

453–456 A node must conduct rate-limiting for ICMPv6 error messages. Function `icmp6_ratelimit()` performs rate limiting on the outbound ICMPv6 error messages and returns 1 if the message should not be generated due to rate limitation. In this case, the corresponding statistics counter is incremented and the processing terminates. The next section discusses `icmp6_ratelimit()` in more detail.

Build and Send Error

At this point, there is no reason for not sending the error message. The last stage of `icmp6_error()` builds the ICMPv6 message containing the original packet and passes it to `icmp6_reflect()` for transmission.

Listing 4-46

_____icmp6.c
```
458              /*
459               * OK, ICMP6 can be generated.
460               */
461
....
484
485              if (m->m_pkthdr.len >= ICMPV6_PLD_MAXLEN)
486                      m_adj(m, ICMPV6_PLD_MAXLEN - m->m_pkthdr.len);
```
_____icmp6.c

485–486 The error message including the original packet must not exceed the IPv6 minimum MTU (1280 bytes). The original packet is trimmed from the tail to meet this requirement if necessary. The `ICMPV6_PLD_MAXLEN` constant is defined in the `netinet/icmp6.h` header file as follows:

```
#define ICMPV6_PLD_MAXLEN  1232    /* IPV6_MMTU - sizeof(struct ip6_hdr)
                                      - sizeof(struct icmp6_hdr) */
```

The meaning of the value should be clear from the comment lines.

Listing 4-47

———icmp6.c
```
488               preplen = sizeof(struct ip6_hdr) + sizeof(struct icmp6_hdr);
489               M_PREPEND(m, preplen, M_DONTWAIT);
490               if (m && m->m_len < preplen)
491                       m = m_pullup(m, preplen);
492               if (m == NULL) {
493                       nd6log((LOG_DEBUG, "ENOBUFS in icmp6_error %d\n", __LINE__));
494                       return;
495               }
```
———icmp6.c

488–496 M_PREPEND() typically creates a new mbuf for the IPv6 header and the ICMPv6 header of the outgoing message. The check at line 490 is actually unnecessary since M_PREPEND() ensures the condition.

Listing 4-48

———icmp6.c
```
497               nip6 = mtod(m, struct ip6_hdr *);
498               nip6->ip6_src  = src_sa.sin6_addr;
499               nip6->ip6_dst  = dst_sa.sin6_addr;
500
501               in6_clearscope(&oip6->ip6_src);
502               in6_clearscope(&oip6->ip6_dst);
```
———icmp6.c

497–499 The Source and Destination address fields of the new IPv6 headers are set to those addresses of the erroneous original packet. icmp6_reflect() will swap or modify these fields (see Section 4.8.3).

501–502 The Address fields of the IPv6 header of the original packet may contain scope zone identifiers, which must be cleared before being transmitted outside the node. The scope zone identifiers of the new packet are inherited from the original Source and Destination addresses.

Listing 4-49

———icmp6.c
```
504               icmp6 = (struct icmp6_hdr *)(nip6 + 1);
505               icmp6->icmp6_type = type;
506               icmp6->icmp6_code = code;
507               icmp6->icmp6_pptr = htonl((u_int32_t)param);
```
———icmp6.c

504–507 The Type and Code fields of the ICMPv6 header are set based on the function parameters. The icmp6_pptr field is set to the value of function parameter param. Note that this is set to 0 for message types other than Parameter Problem.

Figure 4-28 shows the conceptual relationship between the original erroneous packet and the ICMPv6 error message containing the original packet. In this example, the original packet is truncated so that the total ICMPv6 message will fit in the IPv6 minimum MTU size.

FIGURE 4-28

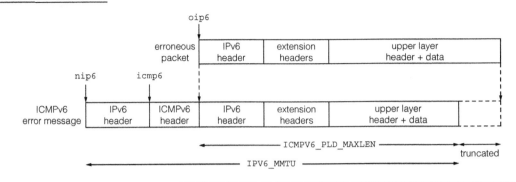

Creation of an ICMPv6 error message containing the error packet.

Listing 4-50

_____ icmp6.c

```
509         /*
510          * icmp6_reflect() is designed to be in the input path.
511          * icmp6_error() can be called from both input and outut path,
512          * and if we are in output path rcvif could contain bogus value.
513          * clear m->m_pkthdr.rcvif for safety, we should have enough scope
514          * information in ip header (nip6).
515          */
516         m->m_pkthdr.rcvif = NULL;
517
518         icmp6stat.icp6s_outhist[type]++;
519         icmp6_reflect(m, sizeof(struct ip6_hdr)); /* header order: IPv6 - ICMPv6 */
520
521         return;
522
523 freeit:
524         /*
525          * If we can't tell wheter or not we can generate ICMP6, free it.
526          */
527         m_freem(m);
528 }
```

_____ icmp6.c

516 `icmp6_reflect()` assumes that the `rcvif` member of the mbuf packet header points to a valid interface structure if it is non-NULL. As commented in the code, however, it is not entirely ensured if the mbuf was created for an outgoing packet, and `icmp6_error()` can be called in an output processing path (see Figure 4-27). It is therefore set to NULL explicitly for safety.

518–519 The statistics counter that keeps track of the number of transmitted packets for that particular type of ICMPv6 message is incremented. The `icmp6_reflect()` function is then called to transmit the packet.

523–527 The `freeit` label is reached when the function encounters an error. In this case the packet is freed and the function terminates.

4.8.2   Error Rate Limitation: `icmp6_ratelimit()` Function

ICMPv6 error messages must be rate limited as specified in [RFC2463] (see also Section 4.2.7). The KAME implementation performs the rate-limiting of error message generation based on the number of packets sent per second.

Listing 4-51

```
                                                                        icmp6.c
3395    static int
3396    icmp6_ratelimit(dst, type, code)
3397            const struct in6_addr *dst;      /* not used at this moment */
3398            const int type;                  /* not used at this moment */
3399            const int code;                  /* not used at this moment */
3400    {
3401            int ret;
3402
3403            ret = 0;         /* okay to send */
3404
3405            /* PPS limit */
3406            if (!ppsratecheck(&icmp6errppslim_last, &icmp6errpps_count,
3407                icmp6errppslim)) {
3408                    /* The packet is subject to rate limit */
3409                    ret++;
3410            }
3411
3412            return ret;
3413    }
                                                                        icmp6.c
```

3396–3400 Parameter `dst` is the destination address of the error message to be sent; `type` and `code` are the ICMPv6 type and code of the error message. The original intention of passing these parameters is to provide more fine-grained rate-limiting mechanisms (e.g., rate-limiting based on the destination nodes or type numbers). However, these variables are not used at this moment.

3406–3412 The `ppsratecheck()` function takes the essential role of rate limitation. It is controlled by three global variables: `icmp6errppslim_last`, `icmp6errpps_count`, and `icmp6errppslim`. When the system starts counting consecutive ICMPv6 errors generated after some calm period, the start time of counting is recorded in `icmp6errppslim_last`. This variable is updated about every second while the counting continues. `icmp6errpps_count` is incremented by one every time `ppsratecheck()` is called, and is reset to zero when `icmp6errppslim_last` is updated. The `ppsratecheck()` function returns false if `icmp6errpps_count` reaches `icmp6errppslim`; otherwise, it returns true.

　　`icmp6errppslim` defaults to 100 and is configurable with the **sysctl** command for the name of `net.inet6.icmp6.errppslimit`.

　　`icmp6_ratelimit()` returns true if this error message is not generated due to a high rate; otherwise, it returns false.

　　This implementation thus effectively limits the maximum number of consecutive ICMPv6 error messages to 100 in any 1-second period while allowing a burst of error generation for a short period.

Figure 4-29 shows an example of rate-limiting ICMPv6 error messages. Assume erroneous events happen at a burst and continue for a while. The `icmp6_ratelimit()` function is

FIGURE 4-29

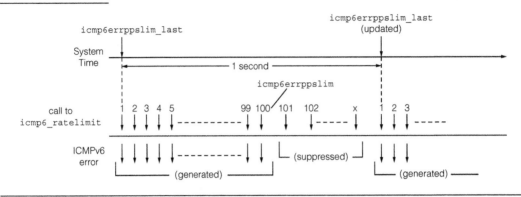

Rate-limiting ICMPv6 error messages.

called for every such event, and `icmp6errppslim_last` remembers the system time when this series of events happens. Since then, `icmp6errpps_count` is incremented for each event until it reaches `icmp6errppslim` (100). All the events that occur in this period generate corresponding ICMPv6 messages. Once `icmp6errpps_count` reaches the limit, succeeding events are simply ignored until 1 second past the time recorded in `icmp6errppslim_last`. The next event after this period will reset `icmp6errppslim_last` and `icmp6errpps_count`, and corresponding ICMPv6 error messages will be generated again.

4.8.3 `icmp6_reflect()` Function

The `icmp6_reflect()` function is called either by `icmp6_input()` or by `icmp6_error()` in response to either a query packet or erroneous packet.

Listing 4-52

── icmp6.c

```
2482    void
2483    icmp6_reflect(m, off)
2484            struct  mbuf *m;
2485            size_t off;
2486    {
2487            struct ip6_hdr *ip6;
2488            struct icmp6_hdr *icmp6;
2489            struct in6_ifaddr *ia;
2490            int plen;
2491            int type, code;
2492            struct ifnet *outif = NULL;
2493            struct sockaddr_in6 *src = NULL, dst, osrc, odst;
2495            struct sockaddr_in6 src_storage;
....
2497            /* too short to reflect */
2498            if (off < sizeof(struct ip6_hdr)) {
2499                    nd6log((LOG_DEBUG,
2500                        "sanity fail: off=%lx, sizeof(ip6)=%lx in %s:%d\n",
2501                        (u_long)off, (u_long)sizeof(struct ip6_hdr),
2502                        __FILE__, __LINE__));
2503                    goto bad;
2504            }
```

── icmp6.c

2483–2504 m points to the ICMPv6 packet to be reflected. On replying to a query or request message, this is the incoming ICMPv6 message; on error generation, this is the ICMPv6 message constructed in `icmp6_error()`. The offset `off` must be at least as large as the size of the IPv6 header.

Initialize Buffer and Headers

Listing 4-53

icmp6.c

```
2506                /*
2507                 * If there are extra headers between IPv6 and ICMPv6, strip
2508                 * off that header first.
2509                 */
2510        #ifdef DIAGNOSTIC
2511                if (sizeof(struct ip6_hdr) + sizeof(struct icmp6_hdr) > MHLEN)
2512                        panic("assumption failed in icmp6_reflect");
2513        #endif
2514                if (off > sizeof(struct ip6_hdr)) {
2515                        size_t l;
2516                        struct ip6_hdr nip6;
2517
2518                        l = off - sizeof(struct ip6_hdr);
2519                        m_copydata(m, 0, sizeof(nip6), (caddr_t)&nip6);
2520                        m_adj(m, l);
2521                        l = sizeof(struct ip6_hdr) + sizeof(struct icmp6_hdr);
2522                        if (m->m_len < l) {
2523                                if ((m = m_pullup(m, l)) == NULL)
2524                                        return;
2525                        }
2526                        bcopy((caddr_t)&nip6, mtod(m, caddr_t), sizeof(nip6));
```

icmp6.c

2506–2526 Extension headers exist if `off` is larger than the size of the IPv6 header. In this case, these headers should be stripped before constructing the response packet. Note that this is only the case for a message responding to a request or a query. First, the IPv6 header is copied into a temporary buffer, nip6; m_adj() is then called to remove the extra headers of length l; when necessary, m_pullup() is called to ensure the first mbuf is large enough to hold both the IPv6 and the ICMPv6 headers in one block; then the IPv6 header is copied back into the adjusted mbuf m from the temporary storage.

Listing 4-54

icmp6.c

```
2527                } else /* off == sizeof(struct ip6_hdr) */ {
2528                        size_t l;
2529                        l = sizeof(struct ip6_hdr) + sizeof(struct icmp6_hdr);
2530                        if (m->m_len < l) {
2531                                if ((m = m_pullup(m, l)) == NULL)
2532                                        return;
2533                        }
2534                }
```

icmp6.c

2527–2534 If the given packet does not contain an extension header and the first mbuf does not contain both the IPv6 and the ICMPv6 headers, m_pullup() makes sure that these headers are in the same single mbuf.

Listing 4-55

```
2535              if (ip6_getpktaddrs(m, &osrc, &odst))
2536                  goto bad;
2537          plen = m->m_pkthdr.len - sizeof(struct ip6_hdr);
2538          ip6 = mtod(m, struct ip6_hdr *);
2539          ip6->ip6_nxt = IPPROTO_ICMPV6;
2540          icmp6 = (struct icmp6_hdr *)(ip6 + 1);
2541          type = icmp6->icmp6_type; /* keep type for statistics */
2542          code = icmp6->icmp6_code; /* ditto. */
```

2535–2536 The source and destination addresses in the form of the socket address structure are extracted from the mbuf tag, and copied to `osrc` and `odst`. For error messages, these are the source and destination addresses of the erroneous packet; otherwise, these are the addresses of the corresponding inbound ICMPv6 message.

2537–2542 `plen` is initialized to the payload length. `ip6` is set to point to the start of the IPv6 header. The Next Header field of the IPv6 header is set to the value identifying ICMPv6. `icmp6` is set to point to the start of the ICMPv6 header. The values of the Type and Code fields are retrieved and save in `type` and `code` respectively.

Source Address Selection

Listing 4-56

```
2544          /*
2545           * If the incoming packet was addressed directly to us (i.e. unicast),
2546           * use dst as the src for the reply.
2547           * The IN6_IFF_NOTREADY case should be VERY rare, but is possible
2548           * (for example) when we encounter an error while forwarding procedure
2549           * destined to a duplicated address of ours.
2550           * Note that ip6_getdstifaddr() may fail if we are in an error handling
2551           * procedure of an outgoing packet of our own, in which case we need
2552           * to search in the ifaddr list.
2553           */
2554          if (!IN6_IS_ADDR_MULTICAST(&odst.sin6_addr)) {
2555                  if ((ia = ip6_getdstifaddr(m))) {
2556                          if (!(ia->ia6_flags &
2557                              (IN6_IFF_ANYCAST|IN6_IFF_NOTREADY)))
2558                                  src = &ia->ia_addr;
2559                  } else {
2561                          struct sockaddr_in6 d = odst;
2562
2563                          d.sin6_scope_id = 0;
2564                          ia = (struct in6_ifaddr *)
2565                                  ifa_ifwithaddr((struct sockaddr *)&d);
2570                          if (ia &&
2571                              !(ia->ia6_flags &
2572                              (IN6_IFF_ANYCAST|IN6_IFF_NOTREADY))) {
2573                                  src = &ia->ia_addr;
2574                          }
2575                  }
2576          }
```

2554–2558 If the original packet was addressed to a unicast destination of the responding node, the source address of the outbound packet is set to the unicast address (Section 4.2.7). The mbuf containing such a packet normally stores the corresponding interface address structure (see Listing 3-26), which can be retrieved by the `ip6_getdstifaddr()` function. The address associated with the interface address structure will be used as the source address unless it is an anycast address.

> *Note*: This structure should not have the `IN6_IFF_NOTREADY` flag, since such a case should have been rejected in `ip6_input()`. The code comment was written when `ip6_input()` did not perform this check, and should now be removed.

2559–2575 If `ip6_getdstifaddr()` returns NULL, `ifa_ifwithaddr()` should also return NULL, that is, the address is not assigned on this node. In fact, the call to `ip6_setdstifaddr()` in `ip6_input()` should not fail since `ip6_setpktaddrs()` should have allocated necessary memory for the mbuf tag (Listing 3-22). The other case of the inconsistent result from `ip6_getdstifaddr()` and `ifa_ifwithaddr()` is when the error occurs in an output path, but it is also impossible in this implementation as explained in Listing 4-41.

Listing 4-57

```
                                                                              icmp6.c
2577            if (src == NULL) {
2578                    int e;
2580                    struct route ro;
2584
2585                    /*
2586                     * This case matches to multicasts, our anycast, or unicasts
2587                     * that we do not own.  Select a source address based on the
2588                     * source address of the erroneous packet.
2589                     */
2590                    bzero(&ro, sizeof(ro));
2591                    src = in6_selectsrc(&osrc, NULL, NULL, &ro, NULL, &outif, &e);
2592                    if (ro.ro_rt) { /* XXX: see comments in icmp6_mtudisc_update */
2593                            RTFREE(ro.ro_rt); /* XXX: we could use this */
2594                    }
2595                    if (src == NULL) {
2596                            nd6log((LOG_DEBUG,
2597                                "icmp6_reflect: source can't be determined: "
2598                                "dst=%s, error=%d\n",
2599                                ip6_sprintf(&osrc.sin6_addr), e));
2600                            goto bad;
2601                    }
2602            }
                                                                              icmp6.c
```

2577–2592 If a source address is not determined at this point, `in6_selectsrc()` is called to find an appropriate source address for the original source address `osrc` based on the default address selection algorithm defined in [RFC3484] (see Section 3.3.2).

Note that this may not fully conform to the address selection rule described in [RFC2463]. It says the source address should be the one "that will be most helpful in diagnosing the error." However, this requirement is not really clear, and a revised version of specification removes this part from the selection guidelines as shown in Section 4.2.7. This implementation adopts the simplest form of the revised specification: it just chooses the address as if the sending node is originating a packet destined for a given destination address.

2592–2594 The call to `in6_selectsrc()` above most likely involved a route lookup and stored the result in variable `ro`. If it did, the route entry isfreed, but there seems to be no reason for not using this route for Next Hop determination in `ip6_output()` as commented in the code. The current implementation causes duplicate route lookups.

2595–2600 If no source address is found, there is no way of sending this message and the processing terminates here.

Listing 4-58

```
                                                              icmp6.c
2604            /*
2605             * XXX: src may not have a valid sin6_scope_id in
2606             * the non-SCOPEDROUTING case.
2607             */
2608            bzero(&src_storage, sizeof(src_storage));
2609            src_storage.sin6_family = AF_INET6;
2610            src_storage.sin6_len = sizeof(src_storage);
2611            if ((in6_recoverscope(&src_storage,
2612                            &src->sin6_addr, NULL)) != 0) {
2613                goto bad;
2614            }
2615            src_storage.sin6_addr = src->sin6_addr; /* XXX */
2616            src = &src_storage;
                                                              icmp6.c
```

2608–2616 As explained in Listing 3-101, the returned address from `in6_selectsrc()` typically is not in the general form used in the IPv6 protocol stack regarding its scope zone (see Section 2.9.3). `in6_recoverscope()` fixes the format issue by setting the `sin6_scope_id` field appropriately. Note that a local copy variable `src_storage` is necessary since the returned address likely points to a part of the interface address structure and should not be modified. `src` is then replaced to point to the socket address structure in the general form.

Complete and Send Message

Listing 4-59

```
                                                              icmp6.c
2619            /*
2620             * ip6_input() drops a packet if its src is multicast.
2621             * So, the src is never multicast and can be used as the destination
2622             * of the returned packet.
2623             * We should make a copy of osrc because we're going to update
2624             * the content of the pointer in ip6_setpktaddrs().
2625             */
2626            dst = osrc;
2627            ip6->ip6_src = src->sin6_addr;
2628            ip6->ip6_dst = dst.sin6_addr;
2629
2630            /* update the record address information */
2631            if (!ip6_setpktaddrs(m, src, &dst))
2632                goto bad;
                                                              icmp6.c
```

2619–2628 The destination address of the outbound reflected packet is the same as the source address of the original packet, which is stored in `osrc`. The source address of the outbound packet is what was selected in the code above. These addresses are then set in the corresponding address fields of the IPv6 header.

2630–2631 The `ip6_setpktaddrs()` updates the source and destination addresses in the socket address form stored in the mbuf tag for the outgoing packet.

Note: The code comment was based on an older version of the `ip6_setpktaddrs()` interface and does not make sense for this version. Since `osrc` itself is a local copy, it should be safely passed to `ip6_setpktaddrs()`.

Listing 4-60

```
                                                                       ──icmp6.c
2634              ip6->ip6_flow = 0;
2635              ip6->ip6_vfc &= ~IPV6_VERSION_MASK;
2636              ip6->ip6_vfc |= IPV6_VERSION;
2637              ip6->ip6_nxt = IPPROTO_ICMPV6;
2638              if (outif)
2639                      ip6->ip6_hlim = ND_IFINFO(outif)->chlim;
2640              else if (m->m_pkthdr.rcvif) {
2641                      /* XXX: This may not be the outgoing interface */
2642                      ip6->ip6_hlim = ND_IFINFO(m->m_pkthdr.rcvif)->chlim;
2643              } else
2644                      ip6->ip6_hlim = ip6_defhlim;
2645
2646              icmp6->icmp6_cksum = 0;
2647              icmp6->icmp6_cksum = in6_cksum(m, IPPROTO_ICMPV6,
2648                  sizeof(struct ip6_hdr), plen);
                                                                       ──icmp6.c
```

2634–2648 The code clears the flow label and the Traffic Class fields in the IPv6 header. The version field is set to 6. The Next Header field is set to the value identifying ICMPv6. The Hop Limit field is set to the default value for the outgoing interface or the receiving interface of the original packet (see Section 5.6.2). If neither of the interfaces is known, the system's default hop limit value stored in `ip6_defhlim` will be used. The Checksum field must be set to zero before calculating the checksum. `in6_cksum()` computes the checksum for the given packet and the return value is stored in the Checksum field of the ICMPv6 header.

Listing 4-61

```
                                                                       ──icmp6.c
2650              /*
2651               * XXX option handling
2652               */
2653
2654              m->m_flags &= ~(M_BCAST|M_MCAST);
                                                                       ──icmp6.c
```

2654 The destination address must be a unicast address regardless of whether `icmp6_reflect()` was called from `icmp6_error()` or `icmp6_input()`. The mbuf flags indicating link-level multicast or anycast are thus cleared for safety.

Listing 4-62

```
                                                                       ──icmp6.c
2656              /* Don't lookup socket */
2657              (void)ipsec_setsocket(m, NULL);
2659
2660              /*
2661               * To avoid a "too big" situation at an intermediate router
2662               * and the path MTU discovery process, specify the IPV6_MINMTU flag.
2663               * Note that only echo and node information replies are affected,
2664               * since the length of ICMP6 errors is limited to the minimum MTU.
2665               */
2666              if (ip6_output(m, NULL, NULL, IPV6_MINMTU, NULL, &outif
2668                              , NULL
2670                              ) != 0 && outif)
```

```
2671                        icmp6_ifstat_inc(outif, ifs6_out_error);
2672
2673             if (outif)
2674                        icmp6_ifoutstat_inc(outif, type, code);
2675
2676             return;
2677
2678     bad:
2679             m_freem(m);
2680             return;
2681     }
```
——— icmp6.c

2657 The `ipsec_setsocket()` function makes sure that the mbuf tag does not store a pointer to an upper layer socket, which may confuse the outbound IPsec processing in `ip6_output()`.

2666–2670 Finally, the `ip6_output()` function is called to transmit the packet. The `IPV6_MINMTU` flag indicates the packet must be fragmented at the minimum MTU size so that the transmitted packet will not be dropped at an intermediate router due to a narrow link (see Listing 3-170). In fact, since this routine does not keep the packet for retransmission and an ICMPv6 "session" should be pretty ephemeral, it does not make sense to perform PMTU discovery for the destination. It should be noted that this flag should not have any effect on an ICMPv6 error message because it is adjusted not to exceed the minimum MTU size (Listing 4-46).

2671–2674 On success, `ip6_output()` stores a pointer to the outgoing interface in `outif`. The corresponding statistics counters per interface are incremented.

2678–2680 On error, the packet is freed and the function terminates.

4.9   Node Information Query Implementation

In this section, we describe implementation details of Node Information query processing, both for requesting and replying. The former is implemented as part of a user program, **ping6**, while the latter is coded in the kernel.

4.9.1   Types and Variables

Table 4-12 shows the global variable used by Node Information (NI) processing. One can change the variable using **sysctl** command to tune the behavior of a node.

Tables 4-13–4-16 show the constants used by Node Information processing.

TABLE 4-12

Name	Description
`icmp6_nodeinfo`	A bit field which indicates the behavior of the responder.
	0x01—reply node names
	0x02—reply IPv6 and IPv4 addresses
	0x04—respond query messages sent to IPv6 temporary addresses

Global variable for NI processing.

TABLE 4-13

ICMPv6 type	Value	Description
ICMP6_NI_QUERY (ICMP6_FQDN_QUERY) (ICMP6_WRUREQUEST)	139	Indicates the message is an NI qeury. ICMP6_FQDN_QUERY and ICMP6_WRUREQUEST are old macro names which are kept for backward source compatibility.
ICMP6_NI_REPLY (ICMP6_FQDN_REPLY) (ICMP6_WRUREPLY)	140	Indicates the message is a NI reply. ICMP6_FQDN_REPLY and ICMP6_WRUREPLY are old macro names, which are kept for backward source compatibility.

ICMPv6 type values for NI messages.

TABLE 4-14

ICMPv6 code	Value	Description
For a query message		
ICMP6_NI_SUBJ_IPV6	0	Query subject is IPv6 addresses.
ICMP6_NI_SUBJ_FQDN	1	Query subject is node names.
ICMP6_NI_SUBJ_IPV4	2	Query subject is IPv4 addresses.
For a reply message		
ICMP6_NI_SUCCESS	0	NI operation succeeded.
ICMP6_NI_REFUSED	1	NI operation is refused.
ICMP6_NI_UNKNOWN	2	Unknown Qtype value.

ICMPv6 code values for NI messages.

TABLE 4-15

Qtype	Value	Description
NI_QTYPE_NOOP	0	No operation query.
NI_QTYPE_SUPTYPES	1	Supported Types query. This type is deprecated from revision 10 [NAME-LOOKUPS-10].
NI_QTYPE_NODENAME (NI_QTYPE_DNSNAME) (NI_QTYPE_FQDN)	2	Node Name query. NI_QTYPE_DNSNAME and NI_QTYPE_FQDN are old macro names, which are kept for backward source compatibility.
NI_QTYPE_NODEADDR	3	Node Addresses query.
NI_QTYPE_IPV4ADDR	4	IPv4 Addresses query.

Qtype values.

TABLE 4-16

Flags	Value	Description
NI_NODEADDR_FLAG_TRUNCATE	0x1	The T flag, which means the Data field is truncated.
NI_NODEADDR_FLAG_ALL	0x2	The A flag, which requests all addresses assigned to a responder.
NI_NODEADDR_FLAG_COMPAT	0x4	The C flag, which requests IPv4-compatible or IPv4-mapped IPv4 addresses.
NI_NODEADDR_FLAG_LINKLOCAL	0x8	The L flag, which requests link-local addresses.
NI_NODEADDR_FLAG_SITE_LOCAL	0x10	The S flag, which requests site-local addresses.
NI_NODEADDR_FLAG_GLOBAL	0x20	The G flag, which requests global addresses.
NI_NODEADDR_FLAG_ANYCAST	0x40	KAME extension, which indicates to include anycast addresses in addition to unicast addresses in a reply message.

Qtype flags.

TABLE 4-17

Flag	Description
-a *X*	Sends a Node Addresses query. X can be the following character.
	a—Specifies the A flag in a query.
	c—Specifies the C flag in a query.
	g—Specifies the G flag in a query.
	s—Specifies the S flag in a query.
	l—Specifies the L flag in a query.
	A—Specifies the KAME extended anycast flag in a query.
-N	Sends a query message to an NI Group Address. When specifying this option flag, the argument of the **ping6** command must be a host name.
-t	Sends a Supported Qtypes query.
-w	Sends a Node Name query.

*Option flags of **ping6** command related to NI operation.*

4.9.2 ping6 Command: Send Queries

The **ping6** command supports sending of NI query messages. Table 4-17 shows the option flags related to Node Information.

Listing 4-63

```
                                                                ping6.c
294    int
295    main(argc, argv)
296          int argc;
297          char *argv[];
```

```
298     {
....
356                while ((ch = getopt(argc, argv,
357                    "a:b:c:dfHg:h:I:i:l:mnNp:qRS:s:tvwW" ADDOPTS)) != -1) {
....
359                    switch (ch) {
360                    case 'a':
361                    {
362                        char *cp;
363
364                        options &= ~F_NOUSERDATA;
365                        options |= F_NODEADDR;
366                        for (cp = optarg; *cp != '\0'; cp++) {
367                            switch (*cp) {
368                            case 'a':
369                                naflags |= NI_NODEADDR_FLAG_ALL;
370                                break;
371                            case 'c':
372                            case 'C':
373                                naflags |= NI_NODEADDR_FLAG_COMPAT;
374                                break;
375                            case 'l':
376                            case 'L':
377                                naflags |= NI_NODEADDR_FLAG_LINKLOCAL;
378                                break;
379                            case 's':
380                            case 'S':
381                                naflags |= NI_NODEADDR_FLAG_SITELOCAL;
382                                break;
383                            case 'g':
384                            case 'G':
385                                naflags |= NI_NODEADDR_FLAG_GLOBAL;
386                                break;
387                            case 'A': /* experimental. not in the spec */
....
389                                naflags |= NI_NODEADDR_FLAG_ANYCAST;
390                                break;
....
396                            default:
397                                usage();
398                                /*NOTREACHED*/
399                            }
400                        }
401                        break;
```
――_ping6.c

360–401 When the −a option switch is specified, the following characters are parsed to get what kind of flags are used in a Name Addresses query message. Based on the flag specified by the −a switch, corresponding flags are set to the `naflags` variable as well as the internal flag F_NODEADDR, which indicates that a user is requesting to send an NI Node Addresses query. Internal flags are listed in Table 4-18.

TABLE 4-18

Flag	Description
F_NODEADDR	Node Addresses query is specified.
F_FQDN	Node Name query is specified.
F_NIGROUP	A user requests to use an NI Group Address for a query message.
F_SUPTYPES	Supported Qtypes query is specified.
F_NOUSERDATA	(F_NODEADDR|F_FQDN|F_SUPTYPES)

Internal flags.

Listing 4-64

———ping6.c
```
495                          case 'N':
496                                  options |= F_NIGROUP;
497                                  break;
     ....
543                          case 't':
544                                  options &= ~F_NOUSERDATA;
545                                  options |= F_SUPTYPES;
546                                  break;
     ....
550                          case 'w':
551                                  options &= ~F_NOUSERDATA;
552                                  options |= F_FQDN;
553                                  break;
```
———ping6.c

495–553 When −N, −t, or −w switches are specified, F_NIGROUP, F_SUPTYPES, or F_FQDN internal flags are set, respectively. F_NIGROUP indicates that the user is requesting to send an NI message to an NI Group Address. F_FQDN indicates the user is requesting to send an NI Node Name query.

Listing 4-65

———ping6.c
```
608                  if (options & F_NIGROUP) {
609                          target = nigroup(argv[argc - 1]);
610                          if (target == NULL) {
611                                  usage();
612                                  /*NOTREACHED*/
613                          }
614                  } else
615                          target = argv[argc - 1];
```
———ping6.c

608–615 nigroup() function calculates an NI Group Address from its argument which is a node name in query. The calculated IPv6 address is returned as a printable form. nigroup() is discussed in the next section. Otherwise, the argument passed to **ping6** command is treated as a Destination address.

Calculate an NI Group Address

nigroup() function calculates an NI Group Address from a node name and returns the calculated IPv6 address in a printable format.

Listing 4-66

———ping6.c
```
2699   char *
2700   nigroup(name)
2701          char *name;
2702   {
2703          char *p;
2704          char *q;
2705          MD5_CTX ctxt;
2706          u_int8_t digest[16];
2707          u_int8_t c;
2708          size_t l;
2709          char hbuf[NI_MAXHOST];
```

```
2710                 struct in6_addr in6;
2711
2712                 p = strchr(name, '.');
2713                 if (!p)
2714                         p = name + strlen(name);
2715                 l = p - name;
2716                 if (l > 63 || l > sizeof(hbuf) - 1)
2717                         return NULL;    /*label too long*/
2718                 strncpy(hbuf, name, l);
2719                 hbuf[(int)l] = '\0';
2720
2721                 for (q = name; *q; q++) {
2722                         if (isupper(*(unsigned char *)q))
2723                                 *q = tolower(*(unsigned char *)q);
2724                 }
2725
2726                 /* generate 8 bytes of pseudo-random value. */
2727                 memset(&ctxt, 0, sizeof(ctxt));
2728                 MD5Init(&ctxt);
2729                 c = l & 0xff;
2730                 MD5Update(&ctxt, &c, sizeof(c));
2731                 MD5Update(&ctxt, (unsigned char *)name, l);
2732                 MD5Final(digest, &ctxt);
2733
2734                 if (inet_pton(AF_INET6, "ff02::2:0000:0000", &in6) != 1)
2735                         return NULL;    /*XXX*/
2736                 bcopy(digest, &in6.s6_addr[12], 4);
2737
2738                 if (inet_ntop(AF_INET6, &in6, hbuf, sizeof(hbuf)) == NULL)
2739                         return NULL;
2740
2741                 return strdup(hbuf);
2742         }
```
——ping6.c

2700–2702 The `nigroup()` function has one argument which indicates the node name used as a seed for the calculation.

2712–2724 The node name is copied to the `hbuf` buffer. If the name is a fully qualified domain name, the first element of the node name is copied. The first element must not be longer than 63 bytes which is defined in the DNS specification. The characters of the name must be all lower case characters.

2727–2732 The hash value is calculated over the name including the preceding byte which indicates the length of the name. The result is stored in the `digest` variable.

2734–2741 The lower 4 bytes of the calculated hash are copied to the LSB side of the NI Group Address. To return the calculated NI Group Address in printable form, `inet_ntop()` function is called to get the printable form and the result is returned.

Calculate Packet Size for Query

The `pingerlen()` function calculates the size of the payload of the ICMPv6 message including the ICMPv6 header part.

Listing 4-67
——ping6.c
```
1254    /*
1255     * pinger --
1256     *      Compose and transmit an ICMP ECHO REQUEST packet.  The IP packet
1257     * will be added on by the kernel.  The ID field is our UNIX process ID,
```

```
1258        * and the sequence number is an ascending integer.  The first 8 bytes
1259        * of the data portion are used to hold a UNIX "timeval" struct in VAX
1260        * byte-order, to compute the round-trip time.
1261        */
1262       size_t
1263       pingerlen()
1264       {
1265               size_t l;
1266
1267               if (options & F_FQDN)
1268                       l = ICMP6_NIQLEN + sizeof(dst.sin6_addr);
....
1271               else if (options & F_NODEADDR)
1272                       l = ICMP6_NIQLEN + sizeof(dst.sin6_addr);
1273               else if (options & F_SUPTYPES)
1274                       l = ICMP6_NIQLEN;
1275               else
1276                       l = ICMP6ECHOLEN + datalen;
1277
1278               return l;
1279       }
```
───ping6.c

1267–1274 Node Name query and Node Addresses query will have the target node address in
the Data field in a query message. ICMP6_NIQLEN is the size of an NI message from the
head of the ICMPv6 header to the flag field. The Supported Qtypes query does not have
any data in the Data field.

Sending a NI Query

Listing 4-68
───ping6.c
```
1281       int
1282       pinger()
1283       {
....
1300               if (options & F_FQDN) {
1301                       icp->icmp6_type = ICMP6_NI_QUERY;
1302                       icp->icmp6_code = ICMP6_NI_SUBJ_IPV6;
1303                       nip->ni_qtype = htons(NI_QTYPE_FQDN);
1304                       nip->ni_flags = htons(0);
1305
1306                       memcpy(nip->icmp6_ni_nonce, nonce,
1307                           sizeof(nip->icmp6_ni_nonce));
1308                       *(u_int16_t *)nip->icmp6_ni_nonce = ntohs(seq);
1309
1310                       memcpy(&outpack[ICMP6_NIQLEN], &dst.sin6_addr,
1311                           sizeof(dst.sin6_addr));
1312                       cc = ICMP6_NIQLEN + sizeof(dst.sin6_addr);
1313                       datalen = 0;
....
1327               } else if (options & F_NODEADDR) {
1328                       icp->icmp6_type = ICMP6_NI_QUERY;
1329                       icp->icmp6_code = ICMP6_NI_SUBJ_IPV6;
1330                       nip->ni_qtype = htons(NI_QTYPE_NODEADDR);
1331                       nip->ni_flags = naflags;
1332
1333                       memcpy(nip->icmp6_ni_nonce, nonce,
1334                           sizeof(nip->icmp6_ni_nonce));
1335                       *(u_int16_t *)nip->icmp6_ni_nonce = ntohs(seq);
1336
1337                       memcpy(&outpack[ICMP6_NIQLEN], &dst.sin6_addr,
1338                           sizeof(dst.sin6_addr));
```

```
1339                    cc = ICMP6_NIQLEN + sizeof(dst.sin6_addr);
1340                    datalen = 0;
1341            } else if (options & F_SUPTYPES) {
1342                    icp->icmp6_type = ICMP6_NI_QUERY;
1343                    icp->icmp6_code = ICMP6_NI_SUBJ_FQDN;   /*empty*/
1344                    nip->ni_qtype = htons(NI_QTYPE_SUPTYPES);
1345                    /* we support compressed bitmap */
1346                    nip->ni_flags = NI_SUPTYPE_FLAG_COMPRESS;
1347
1348                    memcpy(nip->icmp6_ni_nonce, nonce,
1349                        sizeof(nip->icmp6_ni_nonce));
1350                    *(u_int16_t *)nip->icmp6_ni_nonce = ntohs(seq);
1351                    cc = ICMP6_NIQLEN;
1352                    datalen = 0;
1353            } else {
```
                                                                        ———ping6.c

1300–1313 The `F_FQDN` flag indicates that the user is requesting Node Name query message. ICMPv6 code field is set to `ICMPV6_NI_SUBJ_IPV6` and the Qtype field is set to `NI_QTYPE_FQDN`. The nonce field is filled with the random value and the value stored in the `seq` variable, which counts the number of ICMPv6 messages sent in one **ping6** operation. The `seq` value is stored in the first 16 bits and the rest is filled with random numbers. The `dst` variable keeps the Destination address of the query. The address may be a unicast address of the responder or a link-local multicast address or an NI Group Address. The address is copied to the Data field.

1327–1340 The `F_NODEADDR` flag indicates that the user is requesting Node Addresses query message. The difference from the processing code of `F_FQDN` is the value stored in the Qtype field and the Flag field. The flags specified by -a switch are stored in the Flag field.

1342–1352 `F_SUPTYPES` indicates the Supported Qtypes query, which is deprecated in the latest specification. The ICMPv6 code field is set to `ICMP6_NI_SUBJ_FQDN` and the Qtype field is set to `NI_QTYPE_SUPTYPES` as the older specification indicates. The **ping6** command also specifies `NI_SUPTYPE_FLAG_COMPRESS` to notify that the querier supports the compressed format described in Section 4.4.3.

Listing 4-69
                                                                        ———ping6.c
```
1374            smsghdr.msg_name = (caddr_t)&dst;
1375            smsghdr.msg_namelen = sizeof(dst);
1376            memset(&iov, 0, sizeof(iov));
1377            iov[0].iov_base = (caddr_t)outpack;
1378            iov[0].iov_len = cc;
1379            smsghdr.msg_iov = iov;
1380            smsghdr.msg_iovlen = 1;
1381
1382            i = sendmsg(s, &smsghdr, 0);
```
                                                                        ———ping6.c

1374–1382 The NI query message is sent as an ICMPv6 message in the same manner with the other ICMPv6 messages generated by **ping6** command.

4.9.3   ping6 Command: Receive Replies

The kernel does not process NI reply messages. It performs a common ICMPv6 processing for the received NI reply messages and passes them to the application program, usually **ping6**.

The received NI messages by the **ping6** program are passed to `pr_pack()` function to be printed.

Listing 4-70

_____ping6.c
```
1488    void
1489    pr_pack(buf, cc, mhdr)
1490            u_char *buf;
1491            int cc;
1492            struct msghdr *mhdr;
1493    {
```
_____ping6.c

1488–1493 `pr_pack()` has three arguments. `buf` is a pointer to the received ICMPv6 message. `cc` is the size of the received message. `mhdr` is a pointer to the instance of `msghdr{}` structure to get additional information of the message, such as the Destination address or Hop Limit of the packet, although `mhdr` is not used in the NI message processing.

Listing 4-71

_____ping6.c
```
1608            } else if (icp->icmp6_type == ICMP6_NI_REPLY && mynireply(ni)) {
1609                    seq = ntohs(*(u_int16_t *)ni->icmp6_ni_nonce);
1610                    ++nreceived;
1611                    if (TST(seq % mx_dup_ck)) {
1612                            ++nrepeats;
1613                            --nreceived;
1614                            dupflag = 1;
1615                    } else {
1616                            SET(seq % mx_dup_ck);
1617                            dupflag = 0;
1618                    }
```
_____ping6.c

1609–1618 The **ping6** command remembers the sequence numbers at most `mx_dup_ck`. `mx_dup_ck` is set to 8192 at the moment of this writing. The sequence numbers are recorded in an array as a bit field. The `TST()` macro checks if the corresponding bit is set, and the `SET()` macro sets the bit corresponding to the specified sequence number. If **ping6** command receives the same sequence number again which it has received before, the `nrepeats` variable (the number of duplicated packets) is incremented and the number of received packets (the `nreceived` variable) is decremented. Also, the `dupflag` is set to true. Otherwise, the corresponding bit is set to check future duplication of received packets. Note that the check is not perfect, since NI messages must be identified by the nonce value. As we discussed in the sending part, the sequence number is just a part of the nonce value of messages.

Listing 4-72

_____ping6.c
```
1625                    switch (ntohs(ni->ni_code)) {
1626                    case ICMP6_NI_SUCCESS:
1627                            break;
1628                    case ICMP6_NI_REFUSED:
1629                            printf("refused, type 0x%x", ntohs(ni->ni_type));
1630                            goto fqdnend;
1631                    case ICMP6_NI_UNKNOWN:
1632                            printf("unknown, type 0x%x", ntohs(ni->ni_type));
```

```
1633                                  goto fqdnend;
1634                     default:
1635                             printf("unknown code 0x%x, type 0x%x",
1636                                 ntohs(ni->ni_code), ntohs(ni->ni_type));
1637                             goto fqdnend;
1638                     }
                                                                    ping6.c
```

1625–1638 If the ICMPv6 code value is not `ICMP6_NI_SUCCESS`, the command terminates.

Listing 4-73
ping6.c

```
1640                     switch (ntohs(ni->ni_qtype)) {
1641                     case NI_QTYPE_NOOP:
1642                             printf("NodeInfo NOOP");
1643                             break;
1644                     case NI_QTYPE_SUPTYPES:
1645                             pr_suptypes(ni, end - (u_char *)ni);
1646                             break;
1647                     case NI_QTYPE_NODEADDR:
1648                             pr_nodeaddr(ni, end - (u_char *)ni);
1649                             break;
                                                                    ping6.c
```

1640–1649 The reply messages of the Supported Qtypes and the Node Addresses query are processed by `pr_suptypes()` and `pr_nodeaddr()` functions, respectively. These functions are discussed later.

Listing 4-74
ping6.c

```
1650                     case NI_QTYPE_FQDN:
1651                     default:         /* XXX: for backward compatibility */
1652                             cp = (u_char *)ni + ICMP6_NIRLEN;
1653                             if (buf[off + ICMP6_NIRLEN] ==
1654                                 cc - off - ICMP6_NIRLEN - 1)
1655                                     oldfqdn = 1;
1656                             else
1657                                     oldfqdn = 0;
1658                             if (oldfqdn) {
1659                                     cp++;    /* skip length */
1660                                     while (cp < end) {
1661                                             safeputc(*cp & 0xff);
1662                                             cp++;
1663                                     }
                                                                    ping6.c
```

1650–1663 The old specification has a shorter format for the NI messages. We do not discuss the old format in detail in this book. This part of the code tries to support the old Node Name reply, where a node name is stored in the 0 terminated string preceded by the length of the name, not in the DNS wire format.

Listing 4-75
ping6.c

```
1664                             } else {
1665                                     i = 0;
1666                                     while (cp < end) {
1667                                             if (dnsdecode((const u_char **)&cp, end,
1668                                                 (const u_char *)(ni + 1), dnsname,
```

```
1669                              sizeof(dnsname)) == NULL) {
1670                                  printf("???");
1671                                  break;
1672                              }
1673                              /*
1674                               * name-lookup special handling for
1675                               * truncated name
1676                               */
1677                              if (cp + 1 <= end && !*cp &&
1678                                  strlen(dnsname) > 0) {
1679                                      dnsname[strlen(dnsname) - 1] = '\0';
1680                                      cp++;
1681                              }
1682                              printf("%s%s", i > 0 ? "," : "",
1683                                  dnsname);
1684                      }
1685              }
```
                                                                _____ping6.c

1667–1672 If the Data field contains any data, which should be the name of the responder, the name is decoded to the printable format from the DNS wire format by dnsdecode() function. The result is stored to the dnsname variable.

1677–1681 If the zero-length label is put at the end of the node name, the name is stored in the single-component domain name form. The zero-length label is skipped and the function continues to process the next name if it exists.

Listing 4-76

                                                                _____ping6.c
```
1686                  if (options & F_VERBOSE) {
1687                          int32_t ttl;
1688                          int comma = 0;
1689
1690                          (void)printf(" (");      /*)*/
1691
1692                          switch (ni->ni_code) {
1693                          case ICMP6_NI_REFUSED:
1694                                  (void)printf("refused");
1695                                  comma++;
1696                                  break;
1697                          case ICMP6_NI_UNKNOWN:
1698                                  (void)printf("unknown qtype");
1699                                  comma++;
1700                                  break;
1701                          }
```
                                                                _____ping6.c

1686–1701 The F_VERBOSE flag is set if a user specifies the −v flag in the **ping6** arguments. In this case, more detailed information is printed. Lines 1692–1701 try to print the code information; however, the code does not have any effect since messages which have a failure code are discarded on lines 1640–1649, in Listing 4-73.

Listing 4-77

                                                                _____ping6.c
```
1703                  if ((end - (u_char *)ni) < ICMP6_NIRLEN) {
1704                          /* case of refusion, unknown */
1705                          /*(*/
1706                          putchar(')');
```

```
1707                                        goto fqdnend;
1708                                    }
1709                            ttl = (int32_t)ntohl(*(u_long *)&buf
                                [off+ICMP6ECHOLEN+8]);
1710                            if (comma)
1711                                    printf(",");
1712                            if (!(ni->ni_flags & NI_FQDN_FLAG_VALIDTTL)) {
1713                                    (void)printf("TTL=%d:meaningless",
1714                                        (int)ttl);
1715                            } else {
1716                                    if (ttl < 0) {
1717                                            (void)printf("TTL=%d:invalid",
1718                                                ttl);
1719                                    } else
1720                                            (void)printf("TTL=%d", ttl);
1721                            }
1722                            comma++;
```
——ping6.c

1703–1708 If the length of the NI reply message is shorter than the minimum length, no information can be reported.

1709–1721 In the latest specification, at the time of writing the TTL value in a reply message
is kept just for backward compatibility of the format of the message. The
NI_FQDN_FLAG_VALIDTTL flag specifies that the TTL field has a correct value. This
flag existed in the older specification. If the flag is specified, the TTL value is printed
unless it is negative. Otherwise, the message which indicates that the TTL field is not used
anymore is printed.

Listing 4-78
——ping6.c
```
1724                    if (oldfqdn) {
1725                            if (comma)
1726                                    printf(",");
1727                            printf("03 draft");
1728                            comma++;
1729                    } else {
1730                            cp = (u_char *)ni + ICMP6_NIRLEN;
1731                            if (cp == end) {
1732                                    if (comma)
1733                                            printf(",");
1734                                    printf("no name");
1735                                    comma++;
1736                            }
1737                    }
```
——ping6.c

1730–1736 If the Data field contains no data, then the reply message has no name information.

Listing 4-79
——ping6.c
```
1739                    if (buf[off + ICMP6_NIRLEN] !=
1740                        cc - off - ICMP6_NIRLEN - 1 && oldfqdn) {
1741                            if (comma)
1742                                    printf(",");
1743                            (void)printf("invalid namelen:%d/%lu",
1744                                buf[off + ICMP6_NIRLEN],
1745                                (u_long)cc - off - ICMP6_NIRLEN - 1);
1746                            comma++;
1747                    }
1748                    /*(*/
1749                    putchar(')');
```

```
1750                               }
1751             fqdnend:
1752                    ;
1753             }
```

1739–1747 The code is effective only when processing a reply message formatted using the old specification. If the length of the Data field and the length of the node name which is specified in the Data field does not match, the message is printed indicating the mismatch.

Listing 4-80

```
1418    char *
1419    dnsdecode(sp, ep, base, buf, bufsiz)
1420            const u_char **sp;
1421            const u_char *ep;
1422            const u_char *base;      /*base for compressed name*/
1423            char *buf;
1424            size_t bufsiz;
1425    {
1426            int i;
1427            const u_char *cp;
1428            char cresult[MAXDNAME + 1];
1429            const u_char *comp;
1430            int l;
```

1418–1425 dnsdecode() function decodes a node name formatted by the DNS wire format to the 0 terminated string. sp is a pointer to the target name decoded. The pointer will be gained to the next name when this function returns. ep is a pointer to the end of the received NI reply message. base is a pointer to the head of the Data field of the received message. buf and bufsiz are pointers to the storage to store the converted name and its length, respectively.

Listing 4-81

```
1432            cp = *sp;
1433            *buf = '\0';
1434
1435            if (cp >= ep)
1436                    return NULL;
1437            while (cp < ep) {
1438                    i = *cp;
1439                    if (i == 0 || cp != *sp) {
1440                            if (strlcat((char *)buf, ".", bufsiz) >= bufsiz)
1441                                    return NULL;    /*result overrun*/
1442                    }
1443                    if (i == 0)
1444                            break;
1445                    cp++;
```

1437–1444 If the length of the label is 0 or one label has already been processed in this while loop, the label is terminated by the dot character. The function returns if the function sees the zero-length label, which means the end of the node name.

Listing 4-82

```
                                                              ping6.c
1447              if ((i & 0xc0) == 0xc0 && cp - base > (i & 0x3f)) {
1448                      /* DNS compression */
1449                      if (!base)
1450                              return NULL;
1451
1452                      comp = base + (i & 0x3f);
1453                      if (dnsdecode(&comp, cp, base, cresult,
1454                          sizeof(cresult)) == NULL)
1455                              return NULL;
1456                      if (strlcat(buf, cresult, bufsiz) >= bufsiz)
1457                              return NULL;    /*result overrun*/
1458                      break;
                                                              ping6.c
```

1447–1458 If the DNS compression mechanism is used, that is, the 2 most significant bits are set, the rest of the node name is decoded by recursively calling `dnsdecode()` function. The result is concatenated to the already decoded name.

Listing 4-83

```
                                                              ping6.c
1459                  } else if ((i & 0x3f) == i) {
1460                      if (i > ep - cp)
1461                              return NULL;    /*source overrun*/
1462                      while (i-- > 0 && cp < ep) {
1463                              l = snprintf(cresult, sizeof(cresult),
1464                                  isprint(*cp) ? "%c" : "\\%03o", *cp & 0xff);
1465                              if (l >= sizeof(cresult) || l < 0)
1466                                      return NULL;
1467                              if (strlcat(buf, cresult, bufsiz) >= bufsiz)
1468                                      return NULL;    /*result overrun*/
1469                              cp++;
1470                      }
1471                  } else
1472                      return NULL;    /*invalid label*/
1473          }
1474          if (i != 0)
1475                  return NULL;    /*not terminated*/
1476          cp++;
1477          *sp = cp;
1478          return buf;
1479  }
                                                              ping6.c
```

1459–1470 Otherwise, the label pointed by the `cp` pointer variable is copied to the `buf` variable. If the character used in the node name is not a printable character, the character is printed in the octal format. Note that printing an unprintable character in the octal format is not the way that the DNS encoding rules function. In DNS, the three digits with a backslash character means the decimal format. Users of the **ping6** command have to be careful when reading the output string.

1474–1478 An error is returned if the source data finished before terminated by the zero-length label. Otherwise, the `sp` pointer variable is set to the address of the next node name and the function returns the converted node name.

4.9.4   ping6 Command: Print Supported Qtypes

The contents of the Supported Qtypes reply is printed by `pr_suptypes()` function.

Listing 4-84

```
───────────────────────────────────────────────────────────ping6.c
1956   void
1957   pr_suptypes(ni, nilen)
1958           struct icmp6_nodeinfo *ni; /* ni->qtype must be SUPTYPES */
1959           size_t nilen;
1960   {
1961           size_t clen;
1962           u_int32_t v;
1963           const u_char *cp, *end;
1964           u_int16_t cur;
1965           struct cbit {
1966                   u_int16_t words;            /*32bit count*/
1967                   u_int16_t skip;
1968           } cbit;
1969   #define MAXQTYPES         (1 << 16)
1970           size_t off;
1971           int b;
───────────────────────────────────────────────────────────ping6.c
```

1956–1960 `pr_suptypes()` has two arguments. `ni` is a pointer to the received NI reply message and `nilen` is the length of the NI message.

Listing 4-85

```
───────────────────────────────────────────────────────────ping6.c
1973           cp = (u_char *)(ni + 1);
1974           end = ((u_char *)ni) + nilen;
1975           cur = 0;
1976           b = 0;
1977
1978           printf("NodeInfo Supported Qtypes");
1979           if (options & F_VERBOSE) {
1980                   if (ni->ni_flags & NI_SUPTYPE_FLAG_COMPRESS)
1981                           printf(", compressed bitmap");
1982                   else
1983                           printf(", raw bitmap");
1984           }
───────────────────────────────────────────────────────────ping6.c
```

1979–1984 If the verbose switch (-v) is specified in the **ping6** argument, the flag information of the Reply message is displayed.

Listing 4-86

```
───────────────────────────────────────────────────────────ping6.c
1986           while (cp < end) {
1987                   clen = (size_t)(end - cp);
1988                   if ((ni->ni_flags & NI_SUPTYPE_FLAG_COMPRESS) == 0) {
1989                           if (clen == 0 || clen > MAXQTYPES / 8 ||
1990                               clen % sizeof(v)) {
1991                                   printf("???");
1992                                   return;
1993                           }
1994                   } else {
1995                           if (clen < sizeof(cbit) || clen % sizeof(v))
```

```
1996                                    return;
1997                        memcpy(&cbit, cp, sizeof(cbit));
1998                        if (sizeof(cbit) + ntohs(cbit.words) * sizeof(v) >
1999                            clen)
2000                                    return;
2001                        cp += sizeof(cbit);
2002                        clen = ntohs(cbit.words) * sizeof(v);
2003                        if (cur + clen * 8 + (u_long)ntohs(cbit.skip) * 32 >
2004                            MAXQTYPES)
2005                                    return;
2006                    }
```
── ping6.c

1987–1993 The Supported Qtypes implementation of the KAME **ping6** supports up to MAXQTYPES (=65535) Qtypes in the uncompressed format. The message is dropped when the number of bits in the Data field exceeds MAXQTYPES or the Data field is not 32 bits aligned.

1995–2005 If the data is compressed, the length of the bits included in the Data field is calculated based on the format shown in Section 4.4.3. The message is discarded if the Data field is shorter than the base format for the compressed data or the Data field is not aligned to 32 bits.

Listing 4-87
── ping6.c

```
2008                        for (off = 0; off < clen; off += sizeof(v)) {
2009                                memcpy(&v, cp + off, sizeof(v));
2010                                v = (u_int32_t)ntohl(v);
2011                                b = pr_bitrange(v, (int)(cur + off * 8), b);
2012                        }
2013                        /* flush the remaining bits */
2014                        b = pr_bitrange(0, (int)(cur + off * 8), b);
2015
2016                        cp += clen;
2017                        cur += clen * 8;
2018                        if ((ni->ni_flags & NI_SUPTYPE_FLAG_COMPRESS) != 0)
2019                                cur += ntohs(cbit.skip) * 32;
2020                    }
2021            }
```
── ping6.c

2008–2014 At this point, the cp value points the head of the bit field whether the field is compressed or not. The cur variable holds the number of bits already processed. The contents of the bit field is displayed by pr_bitrage() function.

2016–2019 The cp pointer, which specifies the address to be processed in the while loop next time, is gained and the number of processed bits (the cur variable) is updated. If the bit field is compressed, the number of bits in the following logical zero field is added to the cur variable.

Listing 4-88
── ping6.c

```
1907    int
1908    pr_bitrange(v, soff, ii)
1909            u_int32_t v;
1910            int soff;
```

```
1911                    int ii;
1912        {
1913                    int off;
1914                    int i;
```

1907–1912 `pr_bitrange()` has three arguments. `v` is a 32-bit bit field to be processed. `soff` is the number of bits which are processed already. `ii` is the number of contiguous bits set to 1, counted by the previous execution of `pr_bitrange()` function.

Listing 4-89

```
1916                off = 0;
1917                while (off < 32) {
1918                        /* shift till we have 0x01 */
1919                        if ((v & 0x01) == 0) {
1920                                if (ii > 1)
1921                                        printf("-%u", soff + off - 1);
1922                                ii = 0;
1923                                switch (v & 0x0f) {
1924                                case 0x00:
1925                                        v >>= 4;
1926                                        off += 4;
1927                                        continue;
1928                                case 0x08:
1929                                        v >>= 3;
1930                                        off += 3;
1931                                        continue;
1932                                case 0x04: case 0x0c:
1933                                        v >>= 2;
1934                                        off += 2;
1935                                        continue;
1936                                default:
1937                                        v >>= 1;
1938                                        off += 1;
1939                                        continue;
1940                                }
1941                        }
```

1917 The `while` loop checks the bits in the bit field and displays the position of bits which are set to 1.

1919–1941 The bits which are set to 0 are skipped. The `ii` variable counts the number of contiguous bits set to 1. If the `ii` variable is positive, then it means the end of the series of bits set to 1. The `printf()` function on line 1921 displays the end position of the bit sequence set to 1.

Listing 4-90

```
1943                        /* we have 0x01 with us */
1944                        for (i = 0; i < 32 - off; i++) {
1945                                if ((v & (0x01 << i)) == 0)
1946                                        break;
1947                        }
1948                        if (!ii)
1949                                printf(" %u", soff + off);
1950                        ii += i;
```

```
1951                    v >>= i; off += i;
1952            }
1953            return ii;
1954    }
```

1944–1953 If the function finds the bit set to 1, it counts how many bits are set to 1 contiguously. The function prints the start position of the bit sequence set to 1 on line 1949 and updates the ii variable, which is the number of contiguous 1 bits. The bit field (the v variable) and the number of processed bits (the off variable) are also updated accordingly.

If the sequence of 1 bit continues, the value of the ii variable is returned for the next call.

4.9.5 ping6 Command: Print Node Addresses

pr_nodeaddr() function displays the node name returned in an NI Node Name reply message.

Listing 4-91

```
2023    void
2024    pr_nodeaddr(ni, nilen)
2025            struct icmp6_nodeinfo *ni; /* ni->qtype must be NODEADDR */
2026            int nilen;
2027    {
2028            u_char *cp = (u_char *)(ni + 1);
2029            char ntop_buf[INET6_ADDRSTRLEN];
2030            int withttl = 0;
```

2023–2027 pr_nodeaddr() function has two arguments. ni is a pointer to the received Node Address reply message and nilen is the length of the message.

Listing 4-92

```
2032            nilen -= sizeof(struct icmp6_nodeinfo);
2033
2034            if (options & F_VERBOSE) {
2035                    switch (ni->ni_code) {
2036                    case ICMP6_NI_REFUSED:
2037                            (void)printf("refused");
2038                            break;
2039                    case ICMP6_NI_UNKNOWN:
2040                            (void)printf("unknown qtype");
2041                            break;
2042                    }
2043                    if (ni->ni_flags & NI_NODEADDR_FLAG_TRUNCATE)
2044                            (void)printf(" truncated");
2045            }
2046            putchar('\n');
2047            if (nilen <= 0)
2048                    printf("  no address\n");
```

2034–2044 If the verbose switch (-v) is specified in the **ping6** arguments, the information of the ICMPv6 code value and the Flags field are displayed.

2047–2048 The 0-length Data field means there is no address information in the reply message.

Listing 4-93

```
                                                                          ping6.c
2050            /*
2051             * In icmp-name-lookups 05 and later, TTL of each returned address
2052             * is contained in the resposne. We try to detect the version
2053             * by the length of the data, but note that the detection algorithm
2054             * is incomplete. We assume the latest draft by default.
2055             */
2056            if (nilen % (sizeof(u_int32_t) + sizeof(struct in6_addr)) == 0)
2057                    withttl = 1;
2058            while (nilen > 0) {
2059                    u_int32_t ttl;
2060
2061                    if (withttl) {
2062                            /* XXX: alignment? */
2063                            ttl = (u_int32_t)ntohl(*(u_int32_t *)cp);
2064                        cp += sizeof(u_int32_t);
2065                            nilen -= sizeof(u_int32_t);
2066                    }
                                                                          ping6.c
```

2056–2066 The old specification does not have the TTL field in the IPv6 data format of the Node Addresses reply message. The KAME implementation tries to guess if the reply message is the old format or not by checking the size of the Data field. If the size is a multiple of the size of the TTL field plus the IPv6 address field, the reply message is considered to be the new format. Apparently, this guess is not always correct, but provides some compatibility to old messages.

Listing 4-94

```
                                                                          ping6.c
2068                    if (inet_ntop(AF_INET6, cp, ntop_buf, sizeof(ntop_buf)) ==
2069                        NULL)
2070                            strlcpy(ntop_buf, "?", sizeof(ntop_buf));
2071                    printf(" %s", ntop_buf);
2072                    if (withttl) {
2073                            if (ttl == 0xffffffff) {
2074                                    /*
2075                                     * XXX: can this convention be applied to all
2076                                     * type of TTL (i.e. non-ND TTL)?
2077                                     */
2078                                    printf("(TTL=infty)");
2079                            }
2080                            else
2081                                    printf("(TTL=%u)", ttl);
2082                    }
2083                    putchar('\n');
2084
2085                    nilen -= sizeof(struct in6_addr);
2086                    cp += sizeof(struct in6_addr);
2087            }
2088    }
                                                                          ping6.c
```

2068–2082 The address part is converted to the printable form by inet_ntop() function and displayed. If the TTL field exists, the value is also displayed. The value 0xffffffff means infinite TTL.

4.9.6 Query Processing: `ni6_input()` Function

The NI messages are designed as an ICMPv6 message. The packets received by a node are passed to `icmp6_input()` function. After finishing the common ICMPv6 message processing, the messages are processed based on the ICMPv6 type value.

Listing 4-95

—— `icmp6.c`

```
892                case ICMP6_WRUREQUEST:  /* ICMP6_FQDN_QUERY */
893                    {
894                        enum { WRU, FQDN } mode;
895
896                        if (!icmp6_nodeinfo)
897                            break;
898
899                        if (icmp6len == sizeof(struct icmp6_hdr) + 4)
900                            mode = WRU;
901                        else if (icmp6len >= sizeof(struct icmp6_nodeinfo))
902                            mode = FQDN;
903                        else
904                            goto badlen;
....
909                        if (mode == FQDN) {
....
914                            n = m_copym(m, 0, M_COPYALL, M_DONTWAIT);
915                            if (n)
916                                n = ni6_input(n, off);
917                            /* XXX meaningless if n == NULL */
918                            noff = sizeof(struct ip6_hdr);
919                        } else {
.... (process the older message format)
972                        }
```

—— `icmp6.c`

892–897 The macro `ICMP6_WRUREQUEST` has the same value as `ICMP6_FQDN_QUERY` and `ICMP6_NI_QUERY` as shown in Table 4-13, which indicates the message is an NI query message.

The `icmp6_nodeinfo` variable determines that a node should reply to NI query messages. A node never sends reply messages unless corresponding bits of `icmp6_nodeinfo` are set as shown in Table 4-12.

899–904 The mode variable determines the operation mode of the name lookup procedure. The message whose length is shorter than the size of `icmp6_nodeinfo{}` structure is considered an old non-standard message for name lookup. We do not discuss the older message format in this book.

909–919 The received packet is copied to the mbuf n and passed to the `ni6_input()` function for further processing. The copied packet will be passed to the application programs which are waiting for the copy of ICMPv6 messages by opening IPv6 Raw sockets for ICMPv6.

Listing 4-96

—— `icmp6.c`

```
1511    /*
1512     * Process a Node Information Query packet, based on
1513     * draft-ietf-ipngwg-icmp-name-lookups-07.
1514     *
1515     * Spec incompatibilities:
```

```
1516      * - IPv6 Subject address handling
1517      * - IPv4 Subject address handling support missing
1518      * - Proxy reply (answer even if it's not for me)
1519      * - joins NI group address at in6_ifattach() time only, does not cope
1520      *   with hostname changes by sethostname(3)
1521      */
....
1523    #define hostnamelen      strlen(hostname)
....
1528    static struct mbuf *
1529    ni6_input(m, off)
1530            struct mbuf *m;
1531            int off;
1532    {
1533            struct icmp6_nodeinfo *ni6, *nni6;
1534            struct mbuf *n = NULL;
1535            u_int16_t qtype;
1536            int subjlen;
1537            int replylen = sizeof(struct ip6_hdr) + sizeof(struct icmp6_nodeinfo);
1538            struct ni_reply_fqdn *fqdn;
1539            int addrs;              /* for NI_QTYPE_NODEADDR */
1540            struct ifnet *ifp = NULL; /* for NI_QTYPE_NODEADDR */
1541            struct sockaddr_in6 sin6_sbj; /* subject address */
1542            struct sockaddr_in6 sin6_d;
1543            struct ip6_hdr *ip6;
1544            int oldfqdn = 0;        /* if 1, return pascal string (03 draft) */
1545            char *subj = NULL;
1546            struct in6_ifaddr *ia6 = NULL;
1547
1548            ip6 = mtod(m, struct ip6_hdr *);
....
1550            ni6 = (struct icmp6_nodeinfo *)(mtod(m, caddr_t) + off);
....
1558
1559            if (ip6_getpktaddrs(m, NULL, &sin6_d))
1560                    goto bad;
```
                                                                    _____ icmp6.c

1528–1532 ni6_input() has two arguments. m is a pointer to the mbuf which includes the received NI query message. off is an offset from the IPv6 header to the head of the NI message.

1552–1560 In a later step, we have to access the internal member variables of the NI message. IP6_EXTHDR_CHECK() will check that the ICMPv6 header is placed in a contiguous memory space which enables direct pointer access to its internal members.

The Destination address with the scope information recovered during the IPv6 input process is copied to the sin6_d variable by calling ip6_getpktaddrs().

Listing 4-97
                                                                    _____ icmp6.c

```
1562            /*
1563             * Validate IPv6 destination address.
1564             *
1565             * The Responder must discard the Query without further processing
1566             * unless it is one of the Responder's unicast or anycast addresses, or
1567             * a link-local scope multicast address which the Responder has joined.
1568             * [icmp-name-lookups-08, Section 4.]
1569             */
1570            if (IN6_IS_ADDR_MULTICAST(&ip6->ip6_dst)) {
1571                    if (!IN6_IS_ADDR_MC_LINKLOCAL(&ip6->ip6_dst))
1572                            goto bad;
1573                    /* else it's a link-local multicast, fine */
1574            } else {                /* unicast or anycast */
```

```
1575                          if ((ia6 = ip6_getdstifaddr(m)) == NULL)
1576                                  goto bad; /* XXX impossible */
1577
1578                          if ((ia6->ia6_flags & IN6_IFF_TEMPORARY) &&
1579                              !(icmp6_nodeinfo & 4)) {
1580                                  nd6log((LOG_DEBUG, "ni6_input: ignore node info to "
1581                                      "a temporary address in %s:%d",
1582                                      __FILE__, __LINE__));
1583                                  goto bad;
1584                          }
1585                  }
```
                                                                                                _icmp6.c

1570–1585 The Destination address of an NI query message must be one of the following
addresses.

- A unicast address of the responder

- An anycast address of the responder

- A link-local multicast address

The query is dropped if the destination address does not satisfy the requirement.
In the KAME implementation, a query message sent to a temporary address defined
in the Privacy Extension specification [RFC3041] can be ignored to avoid providing the
mapping information between the temporary address and the name of the node. The
responder will not reply to the message if 0x04 is set to the `icmp6_nodeinfo` global
variable.

Listing 4-98
                                                                                                _icmp6.c

```
1587                  /* validate query Subject field. */
1588                  qtype = ntohs(ni6->ni_qtype);
1589                  subjlen = m->m_pkthdr.len - off - sizeof(struct icmp6_nodeinfo);
1590                  switch (qtype) {
1591                  case NI_QTYPE_NOOP:
1592                  case NI_QTYPE_SUPTYPES:
1593                          /* 07 draft */
1594                          if (ni6->ni_code == ICMP6_NI_SUBJ_FQDN && subjlen == 0)
1595                                  break;
1596                          /* FALLTHROUGH */
1597                  case NI_QTYPE_FQDN:
1598                  case NI_QTYPE_NODEADDR:
1599                  case NI_QTYPE_IPV4ADDR:
```
                                                                                                _icmp6.c

1587–1599 The `qtype` variable and the `subjlen` variable will contain the value of the Qtype
field and the length of the Data field. Further validation based on the value of the Qtype
field will be performed.

As we have mentioned before, `NI_QTYPE_SUPTYPES` is obsoleted; however, the
KAME implementation tries to support it. For NOOP and Supported Qtypes queries, the subject information will be empty if the ICMPv6 code value is set to `ICMP6_NI_SUBJ_FQDN`
as discussed in Section 4.4.1.

Listing 4-99

_____ icmp6.c

```
1600                        switch (ni6->ni_code) {
1601                        case ICMP6_NI_SUBJ_IPV6:
1602    #if ICMP6_NI_SUBJ_IPV6 != 0
1603                        case 0:
1604    #endif
1605                                /*
1606                                 * backward compatibility - try to accept 03 draft
1607                                 * format, where no Subject is present.
1608                                 */
1609                                if (qtype == NI_QTYPE_FQDN && ni6->ni_code == 0 &&
1610                                    subjlen == 0) {
1611                                        oldfqdn++;
1612                                        break;
1613                                }
1614    #if ICMP6_NI_SUBJ_IPV6 != 0
1615                                if (ni6->ni_code != ICMP6_NI_SUBJ_IPV6)
1616                                        goto bad;
1617    #endif
1618
1619                                if (subjlen != sizeof(struct in6_addr))
1620                                        goto bad;
```
_____ icmp6.c

1601 When `ICMP6_NI_SUBJ_IPV6` is specified in the ICMPv6 code field, the message will contain an IPv6 address in the Data field, except when the packet is formatted based on the older specification described below.

1602–1620 The `if` clauses try to provide backward compatibility to the older specification, where the definition of the ICMPv6 code values are different. In the old specifications, the code value in a query message is always defined as 0.

When the Qtype field is set to `NI_QTYPE_FQDN` and the ICMPv6 code field is set to 0, indicating the Data field contains subject information, but the Data field is empty, the message is considered as formatted based on the old specification.

Otherwise, the Data field must contain one IPv6 address.

Listing 4-100

_____ icmp6.c

```
1622                        /*
1623                         * Validate Subject address.
1624                         *
1625                         * Not sure what exactly "address belongs to the node"
1626                         * means in the spec, is it just unicast, or what?
1627                         *
1628                         * At this moment we consider Subject address as
1629                         * "belong to the node" if the Subject address equals
1630                         * to the IPv6 destination address; validation for
1631                         * IPv6 destination address should have done enough
1632                         * check for us.
1633                         *
1634                         * We do not do proxy at this moment.
1635                         */
1636                        /* m_pulldown instead of copy? */
1637                        bzero(&sin6_sbj, sizeof(sin6_sbj));
1638                        sin6_sbj.sin6_family = AF_INET6;
1639                        sin6_sbj.sin6_len = sizeof(sin6_sbj);
1640                        m_copydata(m, off + sizeof(struct icmp6_nodeinfo),
1641                            subjlen, (caddr_t)&sin6_sbj.sin6_addr);
1642                        if (in6_addr2zoneid(m->m_pkthdr.rcvif,
1643                                    &sin6_sbj.sin6_addr,
```
_____ icmp6.c

```
1644                                              &sin6_sbj.sin6_scope_id)) {
1645                                     goto bad;
1646                             }
1647                             if (in6_embedscope(&sin6_sbj.sin6_addr, &sin6_sbj))
1648                                     goto bad; /* XXX should not happen */
1649
1650                             subj = (char *)&sin6_sbj;
1651                             if (SA6_ARE_ADDR_EQUAL(&sin6_sbj, &sin6_d))
1652                                     break;
1653
1654                             /*
1655                              * XXX if we are to allow other cases, we should really
1656                              * be careful about scope here.
1657                              * basically, we should disallow queries toward IPv6
1658                              * destination X with subject Y,
1659                              * if scope(X) > scope(Y).
1660                              * if we allow scope(X) > scope(Y), it will result in
1661                              * information leakage across scope boundary.
1662                              */
1663                             goto bad;
```
——— icmp6.c

1637–1663 The subject address must belong to the responder. As the comment says, the subject address is treated as belonging to the responder when it is equal to the destination address of the IPv6 packet.

The scope zone ID of the subject address is recovered since the subject address is stored as `in6_addr{}` structure. The query packet is dropped when the IPv6 Destination address and the Subject address differ.

The XXX comment indicates the following: in the general case, the implementation may need to make a decision on whether to respond to the query based on the condition whether the querier is in the same scope zone as the subject address in order to avoid unexpected leakage of information about narrower-scope addresses; but it is not currently implemented.

Listing 4-101

——— icmp6.c
```
1665                     case ICMP6_NI_SUBJ_FQDN:
1666                             /*
1667                              * Validate Subject name with gethostname(3).
1668                              *
1669                              * The behavior may need some debate, since:
1670                              * - we are not sure if the node has FQDN as
1671                              *   hostname (returned by gethostname(3)).
1672                              * - the code does wildcard match for truncated names.
1673                              *   however, we are not sure if we want to perform
1674                              *   wildcard match, if gethostname(3) side has
1675                              *   truncated hostname.
1676                              */
1677                             n = ni6_nametodns(hostname, hostnamelen, 0);
1678                             if (!n || n->m_next || n->m_len == 0)
1679                                     goto bad;
1680                             IP6_EXTHDR_GET(subj, char *, m,
1681                                 off + sizeof(struct icmp6_nodeinfo), subjlen);
1682                             if (subj == NULL)
1683                                     goto bad;
1684                             if (!ni6_dnsmatch(subj, subjlen, mtod(n, const char *),
1685                                             n->m_len)) {
1686                                     goto bad;
1687                             }
1688                             m_freem(n);
```

```
1689                         n = NULL;
1690                     break;
1691
1692             case ICMP6_NI_SUBJ_IPV4:        /* XXX: to be implemented? */
1693             default:
1694                     goto bad;
1695             }
1696             break;
1697         }
```
_icmp6.c

1665–1690 When `ICMP6_NI_SUBJ_FQDN` is specified in the ICMPv6 type field, the Data field will contain the subject name of the target node in the DNS wire format. `ni6_nametodns()` converts the string of the host name set on the node to the name in the DNS wire format. The subject name must exist in the Data field, otherwise the packet is dropped. The `ni6_dnsmatch()` function compares the local name and the name specified as a subject name. The packet will be dropped if those names differ. `ni6_nametodns()` and `ni6_dnsmatch()` are discussed later.

1692–1695 The KAME implementation does not support `ICMP6_NI_SUBJ_IPV4`. Also, the received packet will be dropped when any other unsupported ICMPv6 code values are received.

Listing 4-102

_icmp6.c

```
1699             /* refuse based on configuration.  XXX ICMP6_NI_REFUSED? */
1700             switch (qtype) {
1701             case NI_QTYPE_FQDN:
1702                     if ((icmp6_nodeinfo & 1) == 0)
1703                             goto bad;
1704                     break;
1705             case NI_QTYPE_NODEADDR:
1706             case NI_QTYPE_IPV4ADDR:
1707                     if ((icmp6_nodeinfo & 2) == 0)
1708                             goto bad;
1709                     break;
1710             }
```
_icmp6.c

1700–1710 Based on the node behavior configuration, the query packet is dropped if the node is configured not to respond to a specific query type. The meaning of the `icmp6_nodeinfo` global variable is described in Table 4-12.

Listing 4-103

_icmp6.c

```
1712             /* guess reply length */
1713             switch (qtype) {
1714             case NI_QTYPE_NOOP:
1715                     break;                /* no reply data */
1716             case NI_QTYPE_SUPTYPES:
1717                     replylen += sizeof(u_int32_t);
1718                     break;
1719             case NI_QTYPE_FQDN:
1720                     /* XXX will append an mbuf */
1721                     replylen += offsetof(struct ni_reply_fqdn, ni_fqdn_namelen);
1722                     break;
```

```
1723                     case NI_QTYPE_NODEADDR:
1724                             addrs = ni6_addrs(ni6, m, &ifp, subj);
1725                             if ((replylen += addrs * (sizeof(struct in6_addr) +
1726                                                     sizeof(u_int32_t))) > MCLBYTES)
1727                                     replylen = MCLBYTES; /* XXX: will truncate pkt later */
1728                             break;
1729                     case NI_QTYPE_IPV4ADDR:
1730                             /* unsupported - should respond with unknown Qtype? */
1731                             goto bad;
1732                     default:
1733                             /*
1734                              * XXX: We must return a reply with the ICMP6 code
1735                              * 'unknown Qtype' in this case.  However we regard the case
1736                              * as an FQDN query for backward compatibility.
1737                              * Older versions set a random value to this field,
1738                              * so it rarely varies in the defined qtypes.
1739                              * But the mechanism is not reliable...
1740                              * maybe we should obsolete older versions.
1741                              */
1742                             qtype = NI_QTYPE_FQDN;
1743                             /* XXX will append an mbuf */
1744                             replylen += offsetof(struct ni_reply_fqdn, ni_fqdn_namelen);
1745                             oldfqdn++;
1746                             break;
1747                     }
```
_____ icmp6.c

1713 Based on the Qtype value, the size of the NI reply message is calculated.

1714–1715 The NOOP reply does not have any additional data.

1716–1718 The Supported Qtypes reply will have a 32-bit bit field. No more space is needed because only the lowest 4 bits are set in the bit field. The KAME implementation only supports NOOP, Supported Qtypes, Node Name, and Node Address queries.

1719–1722 The Node Name reply will contain a node name of the responder. At this point, only the length of the TTL field is considered. The length of the rest of the data is appended later.

1723–1728 The Node Address reply will include a series of IPv6 addresses preceded by the 32-bit TTL value. ni6_addrs() returns the number of addresses to be included in a reply message. As many addresses can be replied as long as the maximum mbuf size is not exceeded.

1729–1731 KAME does not support the IPv4 Address query.

1732–1746 The latest specification does not define other Qtype values and theoretically we should send a reply with the unknown Qtype code. However, the KAME implementation tries to support the older specification, which does not have the Qtype field in a query message. The KAME implementation blindly assumes the received packet is a Node Name query message and tries to respond, hoping that the assumption is correct.

Listing 4-104
_____ icmp6.c

```
1749                    /* allocate an mbuf to reply. */
1750                    MGETHDR(n, M_DONTWAIT, m->m_type);
1751                    if (n == NULL) {
1752                            m_freem(m);
1753                            return (NULL);
1754                    }
```

```
        ....
1758            m_dup_pkthdr(n, m, M_DONTWAIT);
        ....
1762            if (replylen > MHLEN) {
1763                    if (replylen > MCLBYTES) {
1764                            /*
1765                             * XXX: should we try to allocate more? But MCLBYTES
1766                             * is probably much larger than IPV6_MMTU...
1767                             */
1768                            goto bad;
1769                    }
1770                    MCLGET(n, M_DONTWAIT);
1771                    if ((n->m_flags & M_EXT) == 0) {
1772                            goto bad;
1773                    }
1774            }
1775            n->m_pkthdr.len = n->m_len = replylen;
1776
1777            /* copy mbuf header and IPv6 + Node Information base headers */
1778            bcopy(mtod(m, caddr_t), mtod(n, caddr_t), sizeof(struct ip6_hdr));
1779            nni6 = (struct icmp6_nodeinfo *)(mtod(n, struct ip6_hdr *) + 1);
1780            bcopy((caddr_t)ni6, (caddr_t)nni6, sizeof(struct icmp6_nodeinfo));
```
                                                                    ——————— icmp6.c

1750–1775 A new mbuf is allocated based on the message length of a reply message. As discussed before, the length may be shorter than the final message when a node name or addresses have to be inserted in the Data field. The total packet size will be adjusted later when the required data is appended.

1778–1780 The IPv6 header and the NI message header are copied to the newly allocated mbuf. Extension headers will not be copied even if they exist in a query message.

Listing 4-105

                                                                    ——————— icmp6.c
```
1782            /* qtype dependent procedure */
1783            switch (qtype) {
1784            case NI_QTYPE_NOOP:
1785                    nni6->ni_code = ICMP6_NI_SUCCESS;
1786                    nni6->ni_flags = 0;
1787                    break;
1788            case NI_QTYPE_SUPTYPES:
1789            {
1790                    u_int32_t v;
1791                    nni6->ni_code = ICMP6_NI_SUCCESS;
1792                    nni6->ni_flags = htons(0x0000); /* raw bitmap */
1793                    /* supports NOOP, SUPTYPES, FQDN, and NODEADDR */
1794                    v = (u_int32_t)htonl(0x0000000f);
1795                    bcopy(&v, nni6 + 1, sizeof(u_int32_t));
1796                    break;
1797            }
1798            case NI_QTYPE_FQDN:
1799                    nni6->ni_code = ICMP6_NI_SUCCESS;
1800                    fqdn = (struct ni_reply_fqdn *)(mtod(n, caddr_t) +
1801                                            sizeof(struct ip6_hdr) +
1802                                            sizeof(struct icmp6_nodeinfo));
1803                    nni6->ni_flags = 0; /* XXX: meaningless TTL */
1804                    fqdn->ni_fqdn_ttl = 0;  /* ditto. */
1805                    /*
1806                     * XXX do we really have FQDN in variable "hostname"?
1807                     */
1808                    n->m_next = ni6_nametodns(hostname, hostnamelen, oldfqdn);
1809                    if (n->m_next == NULL)
1810                            goto bad;
```

```
1811                    /* XXX we assume that n->m_next is not a chain */
1812                    if (n->m_next->m_next != NULL)
1813                            goto bad;
1814                    n->m_pkthdr.len += n->m_next->m_len;
1815                    break;
1816            case NI_QTYPE_NODEADDR:
1817            {
1818                    int lenlim, copied;
1819
1820                    nni6->ni_code = ICMP6_NI_SUCCESS;
1821                    n->m_pkthdr.len = n->m_len =
1822                        sizeof(struct ip6_hdr) + sizeof(struct icmp6_nodeinfo);
1823                    lenlim = M_TRAILINGSPACE(n);
1824                    copied = ni6_store_addrs(ni6, nni6, ifp, lenlim);
1825                    /* XXX: reset mbuf length */
1826                    n->m_pkthdr.len = n->m_len = sizeof(struct ip6_hdr) +
1827                            sizeof(struct icmp6_nodeinfo) + copied;
1828                    break;
1829            }
1830            default:
1831                    break;          /* XXX impossible! */
1832            }
1833
1834            nni6->ni_type = ICMP6_NI_REPLY;
1835            m_freem(m);
1836            return (n);
1837
1838      bad:
1839            m_freem(m);
1840            if (n)
1841                    m_freem(n);
1842            return (NULL);
1843    }
```
——— *icmp6.c*

1783 The Header fields of a reply message are filled based on the Qtype value. All message types have `ICMP6_NI_SUCCESS` as the ICMPv6 code value, because at this point the processing of the input message has been completed successfully.

1784–1787 The NOOP reply does not have any defined flag information.

1788–1797 The Supported Qtypes reply will have a 32-bit bit field which indicates that the KAME implementation supports NOOP, Supported Qtypes, Node Name and Node Address queries, which result in 0x0000000f. The C flag of the Flags field will be cleared since the bit field of the reply message is not compressed.

1798–1815 The Node Name query will contain the name of the responder in the Data field. A new mbuf which contains the name in the DNS wire format is allocated by `ni6_nametodns()` function and appended to the end of the NI reply message.

1816–1829 The Node Addresses query will contain a series of addresses of the responder. `ni6_store_addrs()` function will construct the Data field of the reply message. The function will be discussed later.

1830–1831 Other Qtypes which are not supported have already been dropped at this point.

1834–1836 The ICMPv6 type value is replaced with `ICMP6_NI_REPLY` to indicate that the message is a reply message to the received NI query message and the newly created mbuf which contains the reply message is returned. The reply message will be sent by the `icmp6_reflect()` function.

4.9.7   Node Name Manipulation

A node name has to be treated in the DNS wire format in many places when processing NI messages. The KAME implementation provides two support functions.

- ni6_nametodns() converts the provided node name to the form in the DNS wire format.

- ni6_dnsmatch() compares node names specified in the DNS wire format.

Listing 4-106
_____ icmp6.c

```
1851   /*
1852    * make a mbuf with DNS-encoded string.  no compression support.
1853    *
1854    * XXX names with less than 2 dots (like "foo" or "foo.section") will be
1855    * treated as truncated name (two \0 at the end).  this is a wild guess.
1856    */
1857   static struct mbuf *
1858   ni6_nametodns(name, namelen, old)
1859           const char *name;
1860           int namelen;
1861           int old;         /* return pascal string if non-zero */
1862   {
1863           struct mbuf *m;
1864           char *cp, *ep;
1865           const char *p, *q;
1866           int i, len, nterm;
1867
1868           if (old)
1869                   len = namelen + 1;
1870           else
1871                   len = MCLBYTES;
1872
1873           /* because MAXHOSTNAMELEN is usually 256, we use cluster mbuf */
1874           MGET(m, M_DONTWAIT, MT_DATA);
1875           if (m && len > MLEN) {
1876                   MCLGET(m, M_DONTWAIT);
1877                   if ((m->m_flags & M_EXT) == 0)
1878                           goto fail;
1879           }
1880           if (!m)
1881                   goto fail;
1882           m->m_next = NULL;
```
_____ icmp6.c

1857–1862 ni6_nametodns() has three arguments. name and namelen are the name of the node and the length of the string stored in the system. old indicates that the received query message is based on the old specification or the recent specification.

1868–1882 A new mbuf is allocated to store the converted node name. The old specification requires the name to be stored as a form of length value pair. The size of the name plus 1 byte for storing the length is enough. For the new specification, the possible maximum size for an mbuf is reserved as a working space.

Listing 4-107
_____ icmp6.c

```
1884           if (old) {
1885                   m->m_len = len;
1886                   *mtod(m, char *) = namelen;
```

```
1887                          bcopy(name, mtod(m, char *) + 1, namelen);
1888                          return m;
1889               } else {
```
_____ icmp6.c

1884–1888 The length of the node name is stored at the head of the mbuf and the name itself follows the length. The result is returned to the caller. No further processing is required for the old format.

Listing 4-108
_____ icmp6.c

```
1890                     m->m_len = 0;
1891                     cp = mtod(m, char *);
1892                     ep = mtod(m, char *) + M_TRAILINGSPACE(m);
1893
1894                     /* if not certain about my name, return empty buffer */
1895                     if (namelen == 0)
1896                             return m;
1897
1898                     /*
1899                      * guess if it looks like shortened hostname, or FQDN.
1900                      * shortened hostname needs two trailing "\0".
1901                      */
1902                     i = 0;
1903                     for (p = name; p < name + namelen; p++) {
1904                             if (*p && *p == '.')
1905                                     i++;
1906                     }
1907                     if (i < 2)
1908                             nterm = 2;
1909                     else
1910                             nterm = 1;
```
_____ icmp6.c

1895–1896 When the system does not have a node name, an empty data is returned.

1902–1910 The specification says that we need to append two zero-length labels if the node name in a reply message is not a fully qualified domain name. The KAME implementation assumes that the node name is not fully qualified if it contains two dots or less. The `nterm` value indicates the number of required zero-length labels which are appended after the name.

This kind of guess sometimes causes an interoperability problem. The more strict rules to create a node name for the NI queries and replies have to be defined when the specification is revised.

Listing 4-109
_____ icmp6.c

```
1912                     p = name;
1913                     while (cp < ep && p < name + namelen) {
1914                             i = 0;
1915                             for (q = p; q < name + namelen && *q && *q != '.'; q++)
1916                                     i++;
1917                             /* result does not fit into mbuf */
1918                             if (cp + i + 1 >= ep)
1919                                     goto fail;
1920                             /*
1921                              * DNS label length restriction, RFC1035 page 8.
```

```
1922                           * "i == 0" case is included here to avoid returning
1923                           * 0-length label on "foo..bar".
1924                           */
1925                          if (i <= 0 || i >= 64)
1926                                  goto fail;
1927                          *cp++ = i;
1928                          if (!isalpha(p[0]) || !isalnum(p[i - 1]))
1929                                  goto fail;
1930                          while (i > 0) {
1931                                  if (!isalnum(*p) && *p != '-')
1932                                          goto fail;
1933                                  if (isupper(*p)) {
1934                                          *cp++ = tolower(*p);
1935                                          p++;
1936                                  } else
1937                                          *cp++ = *p++;
1938                                  i--;
1939                          }
1940                          p = q;
1941                          if (p < name + namelen && *p == '.')
1942                                  p++;
1943                  }
```
—— icmp6.c

1914–1919 The length of one label (between dots) of the node name is counted. If the total length of the converted result is larger than the size of the allocated mbuf, the function returns as failure.

1925–1929 The length of each label must not exceed 63, nor is an empty label accepted. The label must start with an alphabet character. If the label does not satisfy these conditions, the function returns an error. As specified in the DNS wire format, the length of the label is preceded by the label string.

1930–1939 The label string is copied to the newly allocated mbuf. Any label which contains characters other than alphabet, numbers, or a dash is considered an error. The characters are converted to lowercase during the copy.

1940–1942 The copying procedure continues as long as there are unprocessed labels in the node name.

Listing 4-110
—— icmp6.c

```
1944                          /* termination */
1945                          if (cp + nterm >= ep)
1946                                  goto fail;
1947                          while (nterm-- > 0)
1948                                  *cp++ = '\0';
1949                          m->m_len = cp - mtod(m, char *);
1950                          return m;
1951                  }
1952
1953          panic("should not reach here");
1954          /* NOTREACHED */
1955
1956  fail:
1957          if (m)
1958                  m_freem(m);
1959          return NULL;
1960  }
```
—— icmp6.c

1945–1950 Two zero-length labels are appended if the node name is not considered to be a fully qualified domain name. Otherwise, one zero-length label is appended. The calculated DNS wire format node name is returned as an mbuf to the caller.

Listing 4-111
                                                                    ————icmp6.c

```
1962    /*
1963     * check if two DNS-encoded string matches.  takes care of truncated
1964     * form (with \0\0 at the end).  no compression support.
1965     * XXX upper/lowercase match (see RFC2065)
1966     */
1967    static int
1968    ni6_dnsmatch(a, alen, b, blen)
1969            const char *a;
1970            int alen;
1971            const char *b;
1972            int blen;
1973    {
1974            const char *a0, *b0;
1975            int l;
1976
1977            /* simplest case - need validation? */
1978            if (alen == blen && bcmp(a, b, alen) == 0)
1979                    return 1;
```
                                                                    ————icmp6.c

1967–1973 `ni6_dnsmatch()` compares two node names in the context of the DNS wire format. It returns 1 if the names are identical; otherwise it returns 0. `a` and `b` are pointers to the names, and `alen` and `blen` are the length of the names, respectively.

1978–1979 If the length is equal and the names are equal in a binary form, those two names are considered identical.

Listing 4-112
                                                                    ————icmp6.c

```
1981            a0 = a;
1982            b0 = b;
1983
1984            /* termination is mandatory */
1985            if (alen < 2 || blen < 2)
1986                    return 0;
1987            if (a0[alen - 1] != '\0' || b0[blen - 1] != '\0')
1988                    return 0;
1989            alen--;
1990            blen--;
1991
1992            while (a - a0 < alen && b - b0 < blen) {
1993                    if (a - a0 + 1 > alen || b - b0 + 1 > blen)
1994                            return 0;
1995
1996                    if ((signed char)a[0] < 0 || (signed char)b[0] < 0)
1997                            return 0;
1998                    /* we don't support compression yet */
1999                    if (a[0] >= 64 || b[0] >= 64)
2000                            return 0;
2001
2002                    /* truncated case */
2003                    if (a[0] == 0 && a - a0 == alen - 1)
2004                            return 1;
2005                    if (b[0] == 0 && b - b0 == blen - 1)
2006                            return 1;
```

```
2007                    if (a[0] == 0 || b[0] == 0)
2008                            return 0;
2009
2010                    if (a[0] != b[0])
2011                            return 0;
2012                    l = a[0];
2013                    if (a - a0 + 1 + l > alen || b - b0 + 1 + l > blen)
2014                            return 0;
2015                    if (bcmp(a + 1, b + 1, l) != 0)
2016                            return 0;
2017
2018                    a += 1 + l;
2019                    b += 1 + l;
2020            }
2021
2022            if (a - a0 == alen && b - b0 == blen)
2023                    return 1;
2024        else
2025                    return 0;
2026    }
```
——icmp6.c

1985–1988 Invalid names are checked and an error is returned. The name cannot be less than 2 bytes, because we need two zero-length labels at least, even when the node name is empty. The name which does not have the zero-length label at the end of its name is also considered an error as specified in the NI specification.

1993–1994 If the pointer to the next label exceeds the length of the name, then such a name is considered invalid.

1996–2000 The name is considered invalid if the length (the first byte of each label) is negative. The length of each label name must be shorter than 64, because the current implementation does not support the compressed format. The function returns 0 if the input name is stored in the compressed format.

2003–2006 If the name is not a fully qualified domain name, it is terminated with two single zero-length labels. If the current label is a zero-length label (e.g., `a[0]` `==` 0) and the length after the current label is 1 (a-a0 `==` `alen` `-` 1), that means the last label is also a zero-length label, and the name is considered as truncated. In this case, the two names are considered identical. For example, the two names "foo.bar.example.net" and "foo", where the former is a fully qualified and the latter is truncated, are considered identical.

2007 Otherwise, the zero-length label means the end of the name. This means one of the names reached to the end of its name, while the other did not. The two names passed to this function are not identical.

2010–2016 The length of each label must be the same value to be identical. If the end of the label exceeds the specified length of the name, the name is invalid. Otherwise, two labels are compared by `bcmp()` function. If the labels differ, the names are not identical.

2018–2019 The pointers which specify the head of each label are moved to the next labels.

2022–2025 The function returns 1 if all characters stored in the names are the same. However, this comparison has already been done on line 1978 so this part could be removed.

Note that as the comment of the function says, this comparison function assumes that the names are stored in uncompressed format. Also the function does not take care of the case of each character. This may cause interoperability issues.

Calculate the Number of Addresses

We need to know the number of addresses when replying to an NI Node Addresses query to decide the length of the reply packet.

Listing 4-113
_____ icmp6.c

```
2028    /*
2029     * calculate the number of addresses to be returned in the node info reply.
2030     */
2031    static int
2032    ni6_addrs(ni6, m, ifpp, subj)
2033            struct icmp6_nodeinfo *ni6;
2034            struct mbuf *m;
2035            struct ifnet **ifpp;
2036            char *subj;
2037    {
2038            struct ifnet *ifp;
2039            struct in6_ifaddr *ifa6;
2040            struct ifaddr *ifa;
2041            struct sockaddr_in6 *subj_ip6 = NULL; /* XXX pedant */
2042            int addrs = 0, addrsofif, iffound = 0;
2043            int niflags = ni6->ni_flags;
```
_____ icmp6.c

2031–2036 ni6_addrs() calculates the number of addresses to be included in a reply message. ni6 is a pointer to the received NI query message. m is a pointer to the mbuf which includes the received packet. ifpp is a pointer to the space which will be filled by the network interface to which the subject address belongs in this function. subj is a pointer to the subject information of the query.

Listing 4-114
_____ icmp6.c

```
2045            if ((niflags & NI_NODEADDR_FLAG_ALL) == 0) {
2046                    switch (ni6->ni_code) {
2047                    case ICMP6_NI_SUBJ_IPV6:
2048                            if (subj == NULL) /* must be impossible... */
2049                                    return (0);
2050                            subj_ip6 = (struct sockaddr_in6 *)subj;
2051                            break;
2052                    default:
2053                            /*
2054                             * XXX: we only support IPv6 subject address for
2055                             * this Qtype.
2056                             */
2057                            return (0);
2058                    }
2059            }
```
_____ icmp6.c

2045–2059 KAME does not support a Node Addresses query message, which includes a subject name in the Data field, when NI_NODEADDR_FLAG_ALL is not specified. There is no way to determine the corresponding interface from the node name specified.

Listing 4-115

```
                                                                    icmp6.c
2064            for (ifp = TAILQ_FIRST(&ifnet); ifp; ifp = TAILQ_NEXT(ifp, if_list))
....
2066            {
2067                    addrsofif = 0;
....
2071                    TAILQ_FOREACH(ifa, &ifp->if_addrlist, ifa_list)
....
2076                    {
2077                            if (ifa->ifa_addr->sa_family != AF_INET6)
2078                                    continue;
2079                            ifa6 = (struct in6_ifaddr *)ifa;
2080
2081                            if ((niflags & NI_NODEADDR_FLAG_ALL) == 0 &&
2082                                IN6_ARE_ADDR_EQUAL(&subj_ip6->sin6_addr,
2083                                                   &ifa6->ia_addr.sin6_addr))
2084                                    iffound = 1;
                                                                    icmp6.c
```

2064–2076 All addresses assigned to the responder node will be checked to see if the address should be included in a reply message.

2081–2084 The interface whose address is the same as the address specified as a subject name is considered as a target interface when NI_NODE_ADDR_FLAG_ALL is not specified.

Listing 4-116

```
                                                                    icmp6.c
2086                    /*
2087                     * IPv4-mapped addresses can only be returned by a
2088                     * Node Information proxy, since they represent
2089                     * addresses of IPv4-only nodes, which perforce do
2090                     * not implement this protocol.
2091                     * [icmp-name-lookups-07, Section 5.4]
2092                     * So we don't support NI_NODEADDR_FLAG_COMPAT in
2093                     * this function at this moment.
2094                     */
2095
2096                    /* What do we have to do about ::1? */
2097                    switch (in6_addrscope(&ifa6->ia_addr.sin6_addr)) {
2098                    case IPV6_ADDR_SCOPE_LINKLOCAL:
2099                            if ((niflags & NI_NODEADDR_FLAG_LINKLOCAL) == 0)
2100                                    continue;
2101                        break;
2102                    case IPV6_ADDR_SCOPE_SITELOCAL:
2103                            if ((niflags & NI_NODEADDR_FLAG_SITELOCAL) == 0)
2104                                    continue;
2105                        break;
2106                    case IPV6_ADDR_SCOPE_GLOBAL:
2107                            if ((niflags & NI_NODEADDR_FLAG_GLOBAL) == 0)
2108                                    continue;
2109                        break;
2110                    default:
2111                            continue;
2112                    }
                                                                    icmp6.c
```

2097–2112 The scope of the requested address is specified in the Flags field of the received query message. If the responder has an address which matches the specified scope requirements from the querier, the address is counted as the one to be included in a reply message.

As the comment says, IPv4-mapped IPv6 addresses can be replied only by NI proxy nodes. KAME does not support the function. Also IPv4-compatible IPv6 addresses are not considered, since KAME does not implement this feature.

Listing 4-117

```
                                                                    icmp6.c
2114                          /*
2115                           * check if anycast is okay.
2116                           * XXX: just experimental.  not in the spec.
2117                           */
2118                          if ((ifa6->ia6_flags & IN6_IFF_ANYCAST) != 0 &&
2119                              (niflags & NI_NODEADDR_FLAG_ANYCAST) == 0)
2120                                  continue; /* we need only unicast addresses */
2121                          if ((ifa6->ia6_flags & IN6_IFF_TEMPORARY) != 0 &&
2122                              (icmp6_nodeinfo & 4) == 0) {
2123                                  continue;
2124                          }
2125                          addrsofif++; /* count the address */
2126                  }
2127                  if (iffound) {
2128                          *ifpp = ifp;
2129                          return (addrsofif);
2130                  }
2131
2132                  addrs += addrsofif;
2133          }
2134
2135          return (addrs);
2136  }
                                                                    icmp6.c
```

2118–2120 NI_NODEADDR_FLAG_ANYCAST is a KAME extension which indicates that a querier requests to include anycast addresses in a reply message. Anycast addresses are counted if the flag is specified in a query message.

2121–2124 The responder can control whether it includes temporary addresses defined in the privacy extension specification to a reply message by setting the icmp6_nodeinfo global variable. Table 4-12 describes the meaning of each bit of the variable.

2127–2135 The number of addresses counted only on the interface related to the subject address is returned if NI_NODEADDR_FLAG_ALL is not set. Otherwise, the number of all addresses to be returned is provided.

4.9.8 Create Node Addresses Reply: `ni6_store_addrs()` Function

ni6_store_addrs() creates the Data field for the reply message to the NI Node Addresses query.

Listing 4-118

```
                                                                    icmp6.c
2138    static int
2139    ni6_store_addrs(ni6, nni6, ifp0, resid)
2140            struct icmp6_nodeinfo *ni6, *nni6;
2141            struct ifnet *ifp0;
2142            int resid;
2143    {
```

```
....
2147          struct ifnet *ifp = ifp0 ? ifp0 : TAILQ_FIRST(&ifnet);
....
2149          struct in6_ifaddr *ifa6;
2150          struct ifaddr *ifa;
2151          struct ifnet *ifp_dep = NULL;
2152          int copied = 0, allow_deprecated = 0;
2153          u_char *cp = (u_char *)(nni6 + 1);
2154          int niflags = ni6->ni_flags;
2155          u_int32_t ltime;
....
2160          if (ifp0 == NULL && !(niflags & NI_NODEADDR_FLAG_ALL))
2161                  return (0);    /* needless to copy */
```
_____ icmp6.c

2138–2143 ni6_store_addrs() has four arguments. ni6 and nni6 are pointers to the received NI query message and newly allocated NI reply message, respectively. ifp0 is a pointer to the network interface which has the address specified as a subject address in the received NI Addresses query message. resid is the size of payload which can be used to store addresses.

2160–2161 The function terminates if ifp0 is not specified, even if the querier requested to receive addresses which belong to the interface specified in the query message.

Listing 4-119

_____ icmp6.c

```
2163    again:
2164
....
2168          for (; ifp; ifp = TAILQ_NEXT(ifp, if_list))
....
2170          {
....
2174                  for (ifa = ifp->if_addrlist.tqh_first; ifa;
2175                       ifa = ifa->ifa_list.tqe_next)
....
2177                  {
2178                          if (ifa->ifa_addr->sa_family != AF_INET6)
2179                                  continue;
2180                          ifa6 = (struct in6_ifaddr *)ifa;
2181
2182                          if (IFA6_IS_DEPRECATED(ifa6) &&
2183                              allow_deprecated == 0) {
2184                                  /*
2185                                   * prefererred address should be put before
2186                                   * deprecated addresses.
2187                                   */
2188
2189                                  /* record the interface for later search */
2190                                  if (ifp_dep == NULL)
2191                                          ifp_dep = ifp;
2192
2193                                  continue;
2194                          }
2195                          else if (!IFA6_IS_DEPRECATED(ifa6) &&
2196                              allow_deprecated != 0)
2197                                  continue; /* we now collect deprecated addrs */
```
_____ icmp6.c

2168–2180 All IPv6 addresses assigned to the responder are checked to see if the address should be included in the reply or not. The processing procedure is similar to ni6_addrs() function.

2182–2197 There are no rules for the order of the addresses included in the reply message, except one. Deprecated addresses must be listed after preferred addresses. If the address currently under check is deprecated, the address is skipped and collected later. To collect deprecated addresses later, the `ifp_dep` variable stores the pointer of the first found interface which has a deprecated address.

Listing 4-120

```
                                                                          icmp6.c
2199                         /* What do we have to do about ::1? */
2200                         switch (in6_addrscope(&ifa6->ia_addr.sin6_addr)) {
2201                         case IPV6_ADDR_SCOPE_LINKLOCAL:
2202                                 if ((niflags & NI_NODEADDR_FLAG_LINKLOCAL) == 0)
2203                                         continue;
2204                                 break;
2205                         case IPV6_ADDR_SCOPE_SITELOCAL:
2206                                 if ((niflags & NI_NODEADDR_FLAG_SITELOCAL) == 0)
2207                                         continue;
2208                                 break;
2209                         case IPV6_ADDR_SCOPE_GLOBAL:
2210                                 if ((niflags & NI_NODEADDR_FLAG_GLOBAL) == 0)
2211                                         continue;
2212                                 break;
2213                         default:
2214                                 continue;
2215                         }
2216
2217                         /*
2218                          * check if anycast is okay.
2219                          * XXX: just experimental.  not in the spec.
2220                          */
2221                         if ((ifa6->ia6_flags & IN6_IFF_ANYCAST) != 0 &&
2222                             (niflags & NI_NODEADDR_FLAG_ANYCAST) == 0)
2223                                 continue;
2224                         if ((ifa6->ia6_flags & IN6_IFF_TEMPORARY) != 0 &&
2225                             (icmp6_nodeinfo & 4) == 0) {
2226                                 continue;
2227                         }
                                                                          icmp6.c
```

2199–2227 If the address need not be included in a reply message, it is skipped. Almost the same code exists in the `ni6_addrs()` function as shown in Listing 4-117.

Listing 4-121

```
                                                                          icmp6.c
2229                         /* now we can copy the address */
2230                         if (resid < sizeof(struct in6_addr) +
2231                             sizeof(u_int32_t)) {
2232                                 /*
2233                                  * We give up much more copy.
2234                                  * Set the truncate flag and return.
2235                                  */
2236                                 nni6->ni_flags |=
2237                                         NI_NODEADDR_FLAG_TRUNCATE;
2238                                 return (copied);
2239                         }
                                                                          icmp6.c
```

2230–2239 If the space left to include the next address is smaller than the size of IPv6 address information, `NI_NODEADDR_FLAG_TRUNCATE` flag is set to the reply message to indicate that the address data is not complete.

Listing 4-122

_____ icmp6.c
```
2241                             /*
2242                              * Set the TTL of the address.
2243                              * The TTL value should be one of the following
2244                              * according to the specification:
2245                              *
2246                              * 1. The remaining lifetime of a DHCP lease on the
2247                              *    address, or
2248                              * 2. The remaining Valid Lifetime of a prefix from
2249                              *    which the address was derived through Stateless
2250                              *    Autoconfiguration.
2251                              *
2252                              * Note that we currently do not support stateful
2253                              * address configuration by DHCPv6, so the former
2254                              * case can't happen.
2255                              *
2256                              * TTL must be 2^31 > TTL >= 0.
2257                              */
2258                             if (ifa6->ia6_lifetime.ia6t_expire == 0)
2259                                     ltime = ND6_INFINITE_LIFETIME;
2260                             else {
2261                                     if (ifa6->ia6_lifetime.ia6t_expire >
2262                                         time_second) {
2263                                             ltime = ifa6->ia6_lifetime.ia6t_expire
2264                                                 - time_second;
2265                                     } else
2266                                             ltime = 0;
2267                             }
2268                             if (ltime > 0x7fffffff)
2269                                     ltime = 0x7fffffff;
2270                             ltime = htonl(ltime);
2271
2272                             bcopy(&ltime, cp, sizeof(u_int32_t));
2273                             cp += sizeof(u_int32_t);
2274
2275                             /* copy the address itself */
2276                             bcopy(&ifa6->ia_addr.sin6_addr, cp,
2277                                 sizeof(struct in6_addr));
2278                             in6_clearscope((struct in6_addr *)cp); /* XXX */
2279                             cp += sizeof(struct in6_addr);
2280
2281                             resid -= (sizeof(struct in6_addr) + sizeof(u_int32_t));
2282                             copied += (sizeof(struct in6_addr) +
2283                                         sizeof(u_int32_t));
2284                     }
```
_____ icmp6.c

2258–2273 A TTL value for the address is calculated. In this implementation, the lifetime of the address is considered as its TTL. It is almost precise as long as only the static address assignment or the IPv6 stateless address autoconfiguration mechanism are performed. KAME implemented DHCPv6, which is a stateful address autoconfiguration mechanism, after the NI processing had been implemented. Because of this, the code needs to be updated to interact with the DHCPv6 mechanism.

2276–2283 The IPv6 address is copied after the 32-bit TTL value. The address information taken from `in6_ifaddr{}` structure may contain an embedded scope zone ID, if the address is a scoped one. `in6_clearscope()` will clear the embedded zone ID.

   The `resid` variable is decremented by the IPv6 address information including the TTL field and the copied variable is incremented by the same amount.

Listing 4-123

```
                                                                            icmp6.c
2285                    if (ifp0)        /* we need search only on the specified IF */
2286                          break;
2287          }
2288
2289          if (allow_deprecated == 0 && ifp_dep != NULL) {
2290                  ifp = ifp_dep;
2291                  allow_deprecated = 1;
2292
2293                  goto again;
2294          }
2295
2296          return (copied);
2297    }
                                                                            icmp6.c
```

2285–2286 If ifp0 is specified, the reply message only contains the addresses assigned to ifp0.

2289–2294 If there are deprecated addresses in the first pass, ifp_dep is set to the network interface which has the deprecated addresses. To collect all deprecated addresses, the ifp variable is initialized with the ifp_dep variable and the address collection loop is performed again with the allow_deprecated variable set to true.

2296 The function returns the number of bytes stored in the Data field.

4.10   Node Information Operation

The following requests global and link-local addresses of all link-local nodes attached to the ne0 interface of the querier.

```
% ping6 -aagl ff02::1%ne0
PING6(72=40+8+24 bytes) fe80::202:b3ff:fe3a:8a6f%fxp0 --> ff02::1%ne0
96 bytes from fe80::202:b3ff:fe3a:8a6f%ne0:
  fe80::202:b3ff:fe3a:8a6f(TTL=2147483647)
  2001:db8:0:1000:202:b3ff:fe3a:8a6f(TTL=2591485)
  ::1(TTL=2147483647)
  fe80::1(TTL=2147483647)
136 bytes from fe80::202:b3ff:fe3a:87d9%ne0:
  fe80::202:b3ff:fe3a:87d9(TTL=2147483647)
  2001:db8:0:1000:202:b3ff:fe3a:87d9(TTL=2147483647)
  2001:db8:0:2000::1(TTL=2147483647)
  fe80::202:b3ff:fe3a:84ac(TTL=2147483647)::1(TTL=2147483647)
  fe80::202:b3ff:fe3a:87d9(TTL=2147483647)
76 bytes from fe80::290:27ff:fe8a:b941%ne0:
  fe80::290:27ff:fe8a:b941(TTL=infty) ::1(TTL=infty) fe80::1(TTL=infty)

^C--- ff02::1%ne0 ping6 statistics ---
1 packets transmitted, 1 packets received, +2 duplicates, 0.0% packet loss
```

In the above example, three nodes replied to the querier. The first node has one global address, two link-local addresses, and the loopback address. The second node has two global addresses, three link-local addresses, and the loopback address. The last node does not have a global address. It only has two link-local addresses and a loopback address.

The following is an example of sending the Supported Qtypes query.

```
% ping6 -c 1 -t 2001:db8:0:1000:202:b3ff:fe3a:8a6f
PING6(56=40+8+8 bytes) 2001:db8:0:1000:202:b3ff:fe3a:8a6f --> 2001:db8:0:1000:202:b3ff:fe3a:8a6f
20 bytes from 2001:db8:0:1000:202:b3ff:fe3a:8a6f: NodeInfo Supported Qtypes 0-3

--- 2001:db8:0:1000:202:b3ff:fe3a:8a6f ping6 statistics ---
1 packets transmitted, 1 packets received, 0.0% packet loss
```

From the example, we can see the node 2001:db8:0:1000:202:b3ff:fe3a:8a6f supports 0 to 3 Qtype values, which are NOOP, Supported Qtypes, Node Name and Node Addresses queries.

The following is an example of the Node Name query.

```
% ping6 -c 1 -w 2001:db8:0:1000:202:b3ff:fe3a:8a6f
PING6(56=40+8+8 bytes) 2001:db8:0:1000:202:b3ff:fe3a:8a6f --> 2001:db8:0:1000:202:b3ff:fe3a:8a6f
38 bytes from 2001:db8:0:1000:202:b3ff:fe3a:8a6f: desktop.example.com

--- 2001:db8:0:1000:202:b3ff:fe3a:8a6f ping6 statistics ---
1 packets transmitted, 1 packets received, 0.0% packet loss
```

We can see the name of the node 2001:db8:0:1000:202:b3ff:fe3a:8a6f is desktop. example.com.

Neighbor Discovery and Stateless Address Autoconfiguration

5.1   Introduction

A network layer protocol often needs to access link-layer information when communication takes place at the network layer among different nodes. For example, a node connected to an Ethernet link needs to know the Ethernet address of a remote node when it communicates with that remote node at the network layer. IPv4 uses the Address Resolution Protocol (ARP) for this purpose. While ARP works quite well, several drawbacks have been pointed out from operational experiences, such as the dependency on expensive link-level broadcasting.

The internet user base has grown dramatically over the past decade and so has the network complexity. Configuring network and networked devices has become even more of a challenge, despite the existence of mechanisms such as the Dynamic Host Configuration Protocol (DHCP) for automating the configuration procedure. It is unrealistic to expect users of new Internet applications and network appliances to have enough networking knowledge to perform such tasks.

One of the design goals of IPv6 was to meet these challenges. The IETF developed the Neighbor Discovery Protocol (ND) and the Stateless Address Autoconfiguration mechanism to automate the configuration process and to ease user intervention. ND handles various types of information needed for communication within a single link, including link-layer address resolution, Router Discovery, and route Redirection. While similar mechanisms exist in IPv4, ND was designed based on operational experiences to work better than the IPv4 counterparts. For example, link-layer address resolution utilizes link-level multicasting and is less disturbing than ARP; Router Discovery is a base part of the protocol and is available in any IPv6 host implementation.

The stateless address autoconfiguration mechanism is a remarkable advantage over IPv4. With the help of the larger address space, this mechanism allows a host to configure its addresses that are highly likely unique without an external aid such as a DHCP server. The combination of this mechanism and Router Discovery enables full "plug and play" networking.

389

In this chapter, we will discuss the ND protocol and describe the Stateless Address Autoconfiguration mechanism in full detail. We first provide a general overview of these protocols with formal definitions. We will then describe in detail the KAME kernel implementation of the protocols, which will provide a more profound understanding of the mechanisms than can be seen from just reading the specification documents.

Due to the ND protocol operational differences between hosts and routers, we will use the terms "host" and "router" to mean an IPv6 host and an IPv6 router unless indicated otherwise. We use the term "node" to mean an IPv6-capable device that may be either a host or a router.

The primary references for this chapter are [RFC2461] and [RFC2462], which describe the ND protocol and the Stateless Address Autoconfiguration mechanism, respectively. These are already mature standards but are still under minor revision to include clarifications and improvements gained from implementation and operational experiences. The revised specifications are currently only published as Internet Drafts and require more operational experiences, but we also refer to the new specifications when necessary, mainly because the KAME implementation already supports some parts of the newer specifications. We will also discuss some of the latest extensions to the base protocols, such as privacy extensions to [RFC2462].

5.2   Neighbor Discovery Protocol Overview

The IPv6 Neighbor Discovery (ND) Protocol provides a set of solutions to resolve the various communication-related issues facing the nodes.

The ND protocol enables address resolution, that is, it resolves an IPv6 address to its corresponding link-layer address of an interface in the IPv6 node. During operation a node may change its link-layer address. Neighboring nodes that are on the same link can detect this link-layer address change through specific ND protocol packets. The ND protocol for address resolution is independent of the link type because the protocol operates at the ICMPv6 layer.

The ND protocol enables router discovery. Through the ND protocol a host can detect the presence of routers and determine the identity of those that are willing to forward packets. Therefore, the ND protocol eliminates the need for a host to snoop on routing protocol messages, such as RIPng messages, in order to determine the availability of active routers that are present on its attached links. A host can determine the presence of routers through active queries or through the passive reception of Router Advertisements.

The ND protocol enables prefix discovery. A router can distribute prefix information onto its directly attached links with the ND protocol. The prefix information enables hosts on those links to determine which addresses are on-link, and which addresses are reachable via a router. This operation is known as on-link determination. A node considers an address to be on-link if that address satisfies one of the following conditions: the address is covered by one of the on-link prefixes assigned to the link; the address is the target address of a Redirect message sent by a router; the address is the target address of a Neighbor Advertisement message; the address is the source address of any Neighbor Discovery message received by the node.

The ND protocol also supports parameter discovery: It facilitates centralized administration of configuration parameters on the routers and ensures the proper distribution of this information to every attached host. These configuration parameters can be the link MTU value and IPv6 protocol parameters such as the hop limit value placed in outgoing packets by the sending nodes.

The ND protocol enables Neighbor Unreachability Detection (NUD). A node can determine the two-way reachability state of its communicating peer through the ND protocol. For any two nodes A and B, node A performs NUD to verify both the path from node A to node B, and the path from node B to node A. A host will try alternate routers if the host detects the current default router or routers are unreachable.

The ND protocol allows a router to inform a host of a better first hop. In some cases the first hop is in fact the destination.

5.3 Stateless Address Autoconfiguration Overview

The stateless address autoconfiguration procedure defines the processes necessary for a host to configure addresses of various scopes using both locally available information and information distributed by routers. This configuration process requires no manual intervention at the host, minimal configuration at the router, and does not require any type of server other than the routers. Part of the procedure defines the Duplicate Address Detection (DAD) algorithm that is executed for each configured address on a given link. For each configured address a node will operate the DAD algorithm over the ND protocol messages to verify the uniqueness of that address on the associated link.

The stateless address autoconfiguration process begins with the generation of a link-local address followed by address uniqueness validation through DAD. This part of the process is completely autonomous, that is, it does not require any external aid such as a router or a server. A host can begin communication with neighbors that are attached to the same link as soon as the link-local address validation completes.

A global scope address is required to communicate with off-link (i.e., not on-link) nodes. A host uses the prefix information distributed through Router Advertisement messages for the autonomous generation of global scope addresses. This part of autoconfiguration requires help from a router, but it is still stateless in that the router does not have to manage the information about which hosts configure which addresses.

IPv6 also supports DHCP for host configuration (DHCPv6, see Chapter 4 of *IPv6 Advanced Protocols Implementation*). With DHCPv6, hosts can acquire nonaddress configuration information (e.g., recursive DNS server addresses), or both addresses and additional configuration information from a DHCPv6 server. Figure 5-1 illustrates an example in which a host performs both DHCPv6 and Stateless Address Autoconfiguration. As a first step in configuring itself, host A begins Stateless Address Autoconfiguration and generates an IPv6 link-local address `fe80::205:5eff:fe15:ec32`. Host A performs DAD on this address and verifies that the address is unique on the attached link. Host A then receives a Router Advertisement that contains a global prefix. In step 3, host A generates another address `2001:db8:1:1:205:5eff:fe15:ec32` using the advertised prefix in step 2. Again, host A successfully verifies that this newly generated address is unique on the given link. The Router Advertisement also indicates DHCPv6 service is available. Host A subsequently queries the DHCPv6 server and obtains the DNS server address `2001:db8:1:2:20c:29ff:fe33:fdb3` in step 4.

Address autoconfiguration by DHCPv6 is deployed in sites where administrative control over address assignments is important. Stateless Address Autoconfiguration is appropriate both when the administrative control is unnecessary, and when hosts are not concerned with the

FIGURE 5-1

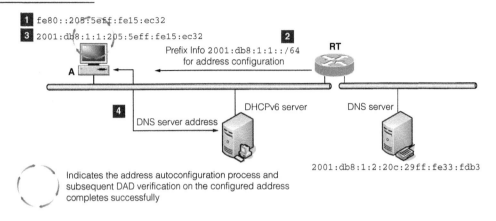

An example of concurrent use of DHCPv6 and Stateless Address Autoconfiguration.

exact addresses that are used in communication as long as these addresses are unique and are routable within the address scope. The uniqueness of every address is verified through DAD on a given link regardless of whether the address is obtained through DHCPv6 or stateless configuration.

Hosts and routers apply the Stateless Address Autoconfiguration procedure to configure link-local addresses on each of their interfaces. Hosts may also use this procedure to acquire global addresses while, in general, routers obtain their non link-local addresses through manual configuration. A router performs the DAD algorithm on all of its addresses before use.

Note: [RFC2461] and [RFC2462] use the term "stateful configuration" or "stateful protocol" as the counterpart of Stateless Address Autoconfiguration, partly because DHCPv6 was not standardized at the time the RFCs were written. The terminology has now turned out to be confusing, since DHCPv6 has its own "stateless" subset [RFC3736]. To avoid the confusion we do not use the term "stateful" in this chapter. We consistently say DHCPv6 instead.

5.4   ND Protocol Messages

The ND protocol packets are carried inside ICMPv6 packets. The ND protocol defines five ICMPv6 packet types for its operation. These packet types are Router Solicitation message, Router Advertisement message, Neighbor Solicitation message, Neighbor Advertisement message, and the Redirect message.

A router sends out Router Advertisement (RA) packets periodically. Router Advertisement messages are also sent in response to Router Solicitation messages received from hosts. Each Router Advertisement message may contain prefix information, link configuration and IPv6 protocol parameters. The Router Advertisement messages indicate the presence of a router and the router's willingness to forward packets. As such, Router Advertisement messages contain information about the transmitting router itself. This information allows a host to perform next-hop determination for outgoing packets. Section 5.8 describes next-hop determination. A host relies on Router Advertisement messages to discover router availability and to build a list of discovered routers called the *Default Router List*. With the Default Router List the host can continue its communication with off-link peers if the host detects a router failure through NUD. When the host detects a router failure, it will prefer as the next-hop any other reachable router in the list over the unreachable router.

A host sends out Router Solicitation (RS) packets to actively query routers for configuration information as well as for information about the routers. Each router is configured with a time interval for sending out successive Router Advertisement messages. These intervals can range from seconds to minutes. A host may send out Router Solicitation packets as part of its startup sequence in order to avoid potentially long waiting periods before obtaining configuration information and beginning communication.

A node sends out Neighbor Solicitation (NS) packets to resolve the link-layer address of another node, to verify the reachability state of another node, and to verify address uniqueness on a particular link.

A node sends out Neighbor Advertisement (NA) packets in response to Neighbor Solicitation packets. It also sends out unsolicited Neighbor Advertisement packets to notify other nodes of its link-layer address change.

A router sends out Redirect packets to inform a host about a better first hop when that host transmits packets to certain destinations. Some destinations may be on the same link as the sending host but have addresses that are not covered by any of the advertised on-link prefixes. This may be true in a non-broadcast and multiple-access link. In such a case the router will inform the sending host that a particular destination is on-link and is in fact a neighbor of the sending host.

5.5   Example Exchanges of ND Protocol Messages

This section illustrates how the ND protocol messages are used to perform the various functions necessary to facilitate communication among different nodes.

In Figure 5-2, host A generates a Router Solicitation message as part of its initial configuration process. Router RT responds with a Router Advertisement message containing two prefixes, one for address autoconfiguration and one for on-link determination. Host A configures an address `2001:db8:1:1:205:5eff:fe15:ec32` using the advertised prefix and verifies the uniqueness of this address through DAD.

In Figure 5-3, router RT sends out Router Advertisement messages periodically. The Router Advertisement message advertises the prefix `2001:db8:1:1::/64` for address configuration. The Router Advertisement message also advertises the prefix `2001:db8:1:2::/64` as an on-link prefix. Host A and host C each generates an address using prefix `2001::db8:1:1::/64` upon receiving the Router Advertisement message. The DAD algorithm verifies the uniqueness of these generated addresses.

FIGURE 5-2

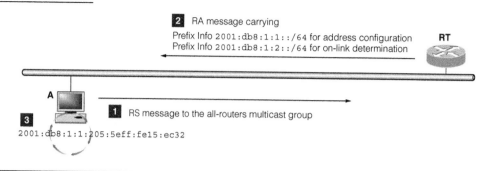

An example of Router Solicitation and Router Advertisement exchange.

FIGURE 5-3

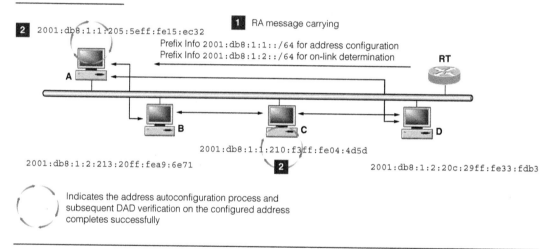

An example of Router Advertisement message advertising on-link prefix.

When host A and host C want to communicate with host B or host D, on-link determination at host A and host C will indicate that both host B and host D are in fact on-link, which means these hosts can communicate with each other directly. In this example, we assume host B and host D are configured to ignore the Router Advertisement message, and these hosts will not generate addresses based on prefix `2001:db8:1:1::/64` as a result.

In Figure 5-4, host A initiates communication to host B for the first time. Host A sends out a Neighbor Solicitation message asking for the linker-layer address of host B. The Neighbor Solicitation message contains the link-layer address of host A. Host B replies with a Neighbor Advertisement message providing its link-layer address in the message. Address resolution completes and normal communication begins once host A processes the Neighbor Advertisement response from host B.

FIGURE 5-4

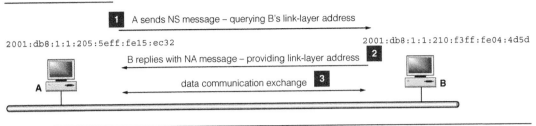

An example of address resolution.

FIGURE 5-5

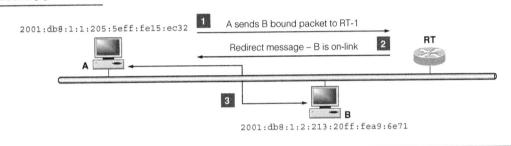

An example of Redirect scenario.

In Figure 5-5, on-link determination at host A indicates that host B is an off-link node. Host A sends the packet destined for host B to router RT. Router RT is aware that host B is on-link, and it sends a Redirect message to host A indicating that host B is in fact a neighbor. Host A will attempt to communicate with host B directly upon receiving the Redirect message.

5.6 ND Protocol Packet Types and Formats

The ND protocol packets use the general ICMPv6 message format. Each message begins with the ICMPv6 message type, the message code, the Checksum field, and is followed by the message body as illustrated in Figure 5-6. ICMPv6 is discussed in detail in Chapter 4.

In the explanation to follow, source address refers to the *Source Address* field in the IPv6 packet header, and destination address refers to the *Destination Address* field in the IPv6 header as shown in Figure 5-6. The message body is composed of various fields depending on the packet type. Each ND packet may contain a number of option fields.

The propagation of ND protocol packets is limited within a single link. This is enforced by using the hop limit value of 255 for all ND packets. Since ND packets that originate from off-link nodes have hop limit values less than 255, the receiving node can reject such packets by checking the Hop Limit field.

FIGURE 5-6

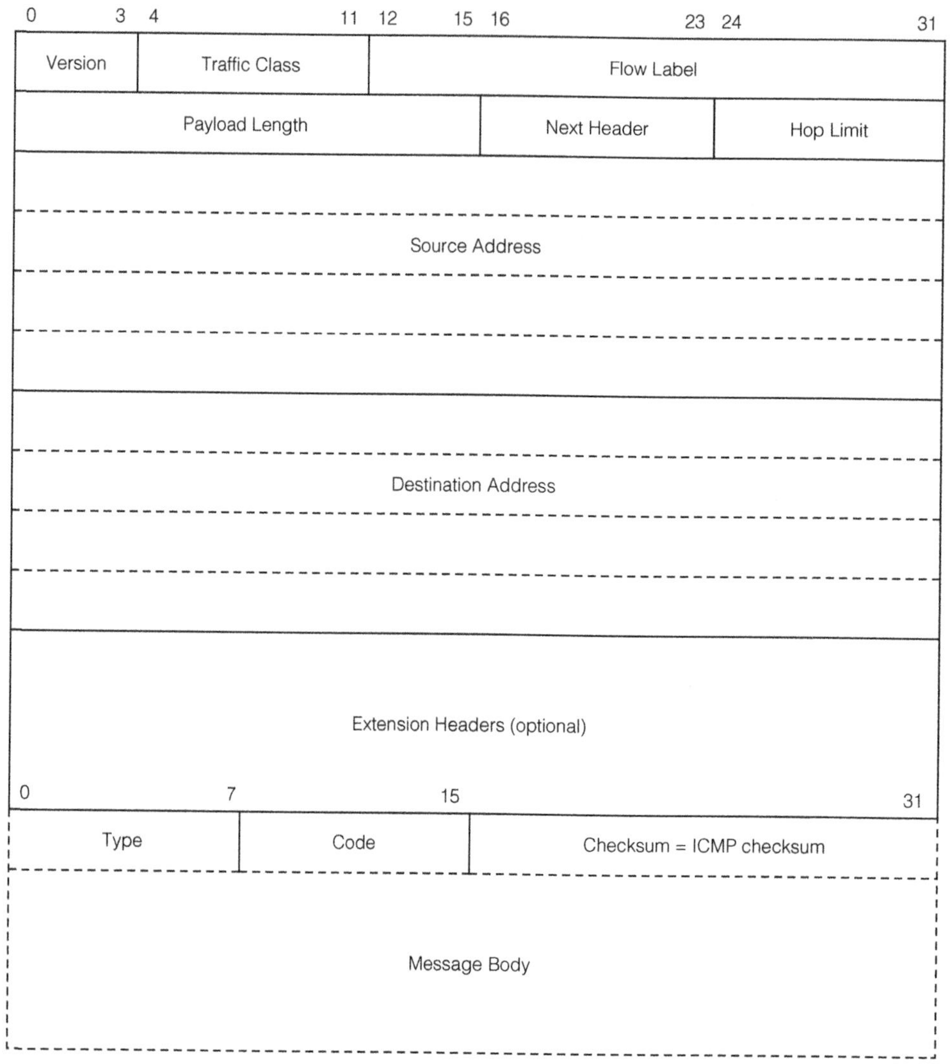

General Neighbor Discovery Protocol packet format.

5.6.1   Router Solicitation Message

A host sends Router Solicitation messages to the all-routers multicast address ff02::2 (Section 2.5.3). Figure 5-7 details the message format. The source address can be either one of the addresses of the sending interface or the unspecified address if the transmitting interface has not been given any addresses.

The Type field has the value 133. The Code field has the value 0. The checksum field contains the ICMPv6 checksum value. The Reserved field must be set to 0 by the sender and is ignored by the receiver.

FIGURE 5-7

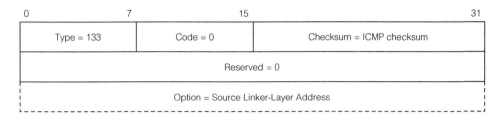

Router Solicitation Message format.

The Source Link-Layer Address option is the only currently defined option for Router Solicitation messages. If the sender knows its link-layer address, it will include a Source Link-Layer Address option with that information in the Router Solicitation message. The Source Link-Layer Address option must be omitted if the source address is the unspecified address. The receiver must ignore both unrecognized and other recognized options silently, that is, without generating any ICMPv6 error messages, and continue processing the message.

5.6.2 Router Advertisement Message

Routers send unsolicited Router Advertisement packets periodically to the all-nodes multicast address ff02::1 (Section 2.5.3). A router usually sends solicited (that is, in response to a Router Solicitation) Router Advertisement packets to the all-nodes multicast address, but the router may choose to unicast the Router Advertisement message to the originator of the Router Solicitation packets. A router inserts the link-local address of the sending interface in the source address field of the IPv6 packet header when transmitting Router Advertisement messages. Doing so allows a host to maintain router association using the router's link-local address. A host can thereby maintain the router association even when the router's non-link-local addresses change due to events such as site renumbering.

Router Advertisement Message Format

Figure 5-8 details the message format as defined in [RFC2461]. The Type field has the value 134. The Code field has the value 0. The Checksum field contains the ICMPv6 checksum value. The Reserved field must be set to 0 by the sender and is ignored by the receiver.

The Current Hop Limit field contains the default value to be placed in the Hop Limit field of the IPv6 header of all outgoing packets. The value 0 in the Current Hop Limit field indicates the router does not specify the Hop Limit configuration.

The M bit field is called the "Managed Address Configuration" flag. The M bit, when set to TRUE, indicates that Dynamic Host Configuration Protocol (DHCPv6) is available for address configuration.

The O bit field is called the "Other Stateful Configuration" flag. The O bit, when set to TRUE, indicates that the stateless subset of DHCPv6 [RFC3736] is available for obtaining non-address-related configuration information, such as the IPv6 addresses of DNS recursive name servers.

FIGURE 5-8

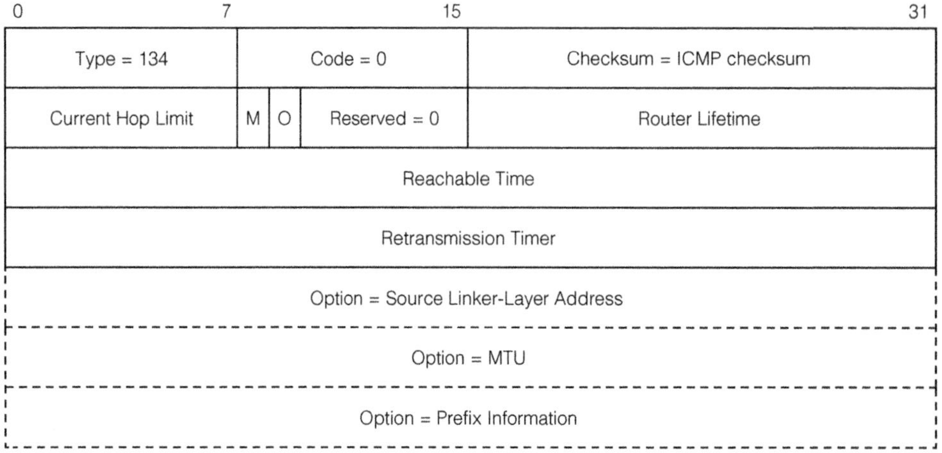

| 0 | 7 | 15 | 31 |

Router Advertisement Message format.

Note: The precise use of the M and O bits is still being discussed at the IETF as of this writing. At this time, it is generally advisable to not rely on the use of these bits in actual operations.

The Router Lifetime field is a 16-bit unsigned integer specifying how long a router will act as the default router. The value is measured in seconds and has a maximum value of 18.2 hours. A value of 0 indicates the transmitting router is not a default router. In this case the router will not be selected as a next-hop candidate to send packets to off-link destinations.

The Reachable Time field is a 32-bit unsigned integer specifying how long a node considers its communicating neighbor reachable after receiving a reachability confirmation from that neighbor. The value is in units of milliseconds. A node begins NUD when Reachable Time elapses without a positive reachable confirmation from its neighbor. A value of 0 indicates the advertising router does not specify this parameter.

The Retransmission Timer field is a 32-bit unsigned integer that specifies the interval in milliseconds between packet transmissions for both the NUD and the address resolution algorithms. A value of 0 indicates the advertising router does not specify this parameter.

[RFC2461] defines three options for the Router Advertisement messages. These options are the Source Link-Layer Address option, the MTU option and the Prefix Information option. In addition, [RFC4191] defines a new option for fine-grained router selection, called the Route Information option.

The router can set the link-layer address of the sending interface in the Source Link-Layer Address option if applicable, so that the receiving host does not have to perform link-layer address resolution when sending packets via the router. The router may choose to omit this option for purposes of inbound load balancing. A router may have multiple interfaces attached to the same link. By omitting the Source Link-Layer Address option a router forces its neighbors to perform address resolution, thereby giving the router the opportunity to choose an inbound interface per neighbor or other division.

Through the MTU option a router can provide a uniform MTU value on links that lack well-defined MTU sizes. A well-defined MTU value is necessary to ensure correct multicast operations. Since a multicast source cannot know the MTU values of every member of the multicast group, it must choose the packet size based on the well-defined MTU value so that all of the members can properly receive the complete multicast packets.

Extensions to Router Advertisement

Each host builds and maintains the Default Router List from received Router Advertisement messages. Each host also builds and maintains a list of on-link prefixes, called the *Prefix List* from received Router Advertisement messages. A host consults the Prefix List to determine whether a node is on-link or off-link. The host consults the Default Router List when it wants to communicate with an off-link node. When multiple default routers are present on a single link and the host forwards the packet destined for an off-link node to a default router, that default router can send a Redirect packet to the host if there is a better default router for that particular destination prefix. Router redirect can redirect a host to another router that is on the same link as the router which originated the redirect packet.

The redirect mechanism generally works well, but it is sometimes desirable to avoid triggering Redirect messages depending on the network topology. Consider the example given in Figure 5-9.

Both routers RT-1 and RT-2 advertise themselves as a default router, but only RT-1 is directly connected to the Internet; RT-2 is a router connecting a leaf link (where Host B resides) and the link shared with RT-1. Assuming Host A usually wants to communicate with nodes in the Internet rather than with Host B, it is better for Host A to send packets to RT-1; however, since the two routers send Router Advertisement, there is no deterministic way for Host A to prefer RT-1 by default. But RT-2 cannot stop sending Router Advertisement because Host A would then not be able to communicate with Host B. (The communication between Host A and Host B must succeed through router RT-2 even though such communication may be rare.)

In order to optimize the use of Redirect messages in such a situation, [RFC4191] provides an extension to the Router Advertisement message that allows the Router Advertisement message

FIGURE 5-9

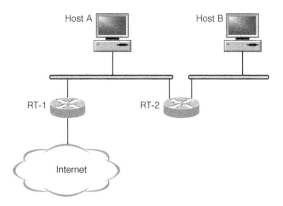

Selection among multiple routers.

to convey router preferences to hosts so that the hosts can make better decisions on which routers to use when communicating with off-link nodes. The modified Router Advertisement message format is shown in Figure 5-10.

The H bit field is called the "Home Agent" flag. This flag is defined in [RFC3775] for the Mobility Support in IPv6. Mobility Support is discussed in Chapter 5 of *IPv6 Advanced Protocols Implementation*.

The Prf field is the 2-bit router preference field that encodes the router preference as a signed integer. The preference field indicates whether the advertising default router should be preferred over other default routers. The encoded values and associated definitions are listed in Table 5-1.

The medium preference level is encoded to be backward compatible with those hosts that do not understand the extended Router Advertisement message format. Receivers treat the reserved value 10_b as 00_b when processing Router Advertisement messages. A router must set the preference field to 0 when sending Router Advertisement messages with zero Router Lifetime. Receivers ignore the preference field when the received Router Advertisement message has a zero Router Lifetime.

The Rsvd field is the 3-bit reserved field. This field is set to zero by the sender and is ignored by the receiver.

Returning to the example shown in Figure 5-9, the network administrator can configure router RT-1 to advertise a high preference by using Router Preference. Doing so would allow

FIGURE 5-10

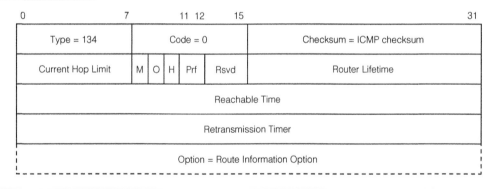

Modified Router Advertisement Message format.

TABLE 5-1

Encoding	Preference level
01	High
00	Medium
11	Low
10	Reserved

Router preference encoding.

Host A to send packets through RT-1 by default, which is the desired routing effect. Host A will still trigger Redirect from RT-1 when it sends packets to Host B, but such Redirect packets have little impact due to the fact that communication between Host A and Host B rarely takes place.

[RFC4191] also introduces a more fine-grained control mechanism: A new Router Advertisement message option, called Route Information option, is defined for advertising router preference for specific prefixes. This option is described in Section 5.7.5.

5.6.3 Neighbor Solicitation Message

A node sends the Neighbor Solicitation messages to the solicited-node multicast address (Section 2.5.3) of the target IPv6 address when the sender performs address resolution requesting the link-layer address of the target node. A node sends the Neighbor Solicitation messages to the IPv6 address of the target node when the sender performs the NUD algorithm. The source address is one of the addresses assigned to the transmitting interface when the sender is performing address resolution or running the NUD algorithm. The source address is the unspecified address if the sender is performing DAD during an address configuration. Figure 5-11 details the message format.

The Type field has the value 135. The Code field has the value 0. The Checksum field contains the ICMPv6 checksum value. The Reserved field must be set to 0 by the sender and is ignored by the receiver.

The Target Address field contains the address of the target of the solicitation. This field must not contain a multicast address.

The Source Link-Layer Address option is the only currently defined option for Neighbor Solicitation messages. The sender must include its linker-layer address when multicasting the Neighbor Solicitation message. The Source Link-Layer Address option must be omitted if the source address is the unspecified address. The receiver must ignore both unrecognized and other recognized options silently.

FIGURE 5-11

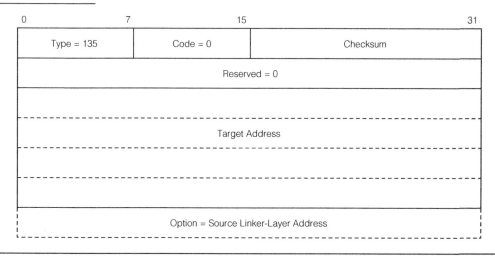

Neighbor Solicitation message format.

5.6.4 Neighbor Advertisement Message

A node sends an unsolicited Neighbor Advertisement message to notify other nodes about its information change, such as a change in the link-layer address of the transmitting interface. The unsolicited Neighbor Advertisement messages are sent to the all-nodes multicast address. A node sends solicited Neighbor Advertisement messages to the address of the originator of the Neighbor Solicitation packets. The source address is one of the addresses assigned to the transmitting interface. The Neighbor Advertisement message format is detailed in Figure 5-12.

The Type field has the value 136. The Code field has the value 0. The Checksum field contains the ICMPv6 checksum value. The Reserved field must be set to 0 by the sender and is ignored by the receiver.

The R-bit field is called the "IsRouter" flag. This flag indicates that the sender is a router if the R-bit is set in the received Neighbor Advertisement messages. Hosts need to perform corrective procedures to ensure proper operation when a node transits from a router to a host. For example, a host needs to remove those route entries that have the node as the next-hop, and also needs to remove that node from its Default Router List.

The S-bit field is called the "Solicited" flag. This flag indicates whether the received Neighbor Advertisement message was sent in response to a solicitation from the node specified by the destination address of the advertisement. The S-bit must be cleared in Neighbor Advertisement messages with a multicast destination address.

The O-bit field is called the "Override" flag. When the O-bit is set in the Neighbor Advertisement message, the receiver will update the cached link-layer address of the sender Neighbor Advertisement message if such a cache entry exists. If the cache entry does not exist, the receiver will create the entry containing the link-layer address of the sender.

The O-bit must not be set for anycast addresses. Consider the example shown in Figure 5-13. In this figure, servers SA and SB are configured with the anycast address `2001:db8:1:1:205:5eff:fe15:ec32`. When SA and SB receive a Neighbor Solicitation message for that anycast address, each server delays the transmission of the corresponding

FIGURE 5-12

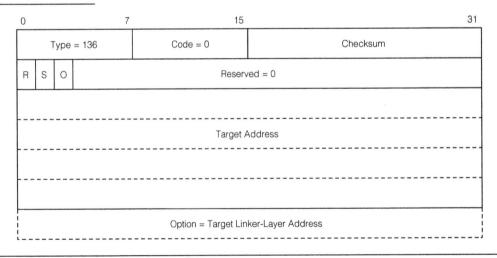

Neighbor Advertisement message format.

FIGURE 5-13

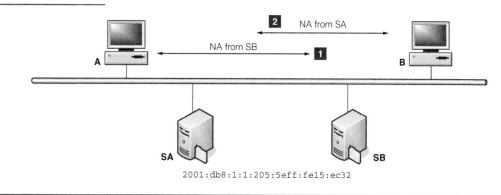

2001:db8:1:1:205:5eff:fe15:ec32

No override in Neighbor Advertisement message for anycast address.

Neighbor Advertisement message by a random time between 0 and 1 second. Assume host A sends out a Neighbor Solicitation message, and assume SA has a random delay of 750 ms and SB has a random delay of 250 ms for this Neighbor Solicitation message. In this case, SB responds first. Since the Neighbor Advertisement message from SA does not have the *Override* flag bit set, host A will send its service requests to SB. Similarly, when host B sends out a Neighbor Solicitation message for the 2001:db8:1:1:205:5eff:fe15:ec32 anycast address, SA may respond first due to a shorter delay. The end result is that SA services requests from host B while SB services requests from host A. In this example, setting the *Override* flag in the message from SB would result in SB servicing requests from both host A and host B.

> *Note*: While [RFC3513] only allows a router to configure an anycast address, we assume in this example the less restrictive usage described in Section 2.2.

The Target Address field contains the value of the target address field from the Neighbor Solicitation message for a solicited Neighbor Advertisement message. A node may send unsolicited Neighbor Advertisement messages to inform its neighbor about a new link-layer address. For an unsolicited Neighbor Advertisement message the Target Address field contains the address whose associated link-layer address has changed. This field must not contain a multicast address. The receiver must ignore both unrecognized and other recognized options silently.

The Target Link-Layer Address option is the only currently defined option for Neighbor Advertisement messages. The sender must include its linker-layer address when multicasting the Neighbor Advertisement message. The receiver must ignore both unrecognized and other recognized options silently.

5.6.5 Redirect Message

A router sends the Redirect message to the source of the packets that triggered the Redirect. The source address of the Redirect messages must be a link-local address assigned to the transmitting interface. The source address requirement allows hosts to continue to uniquely identify on-link routers in case of site renumbering. The Redirect message format is detailed in Figure 5-14.

FIGURE 5-14

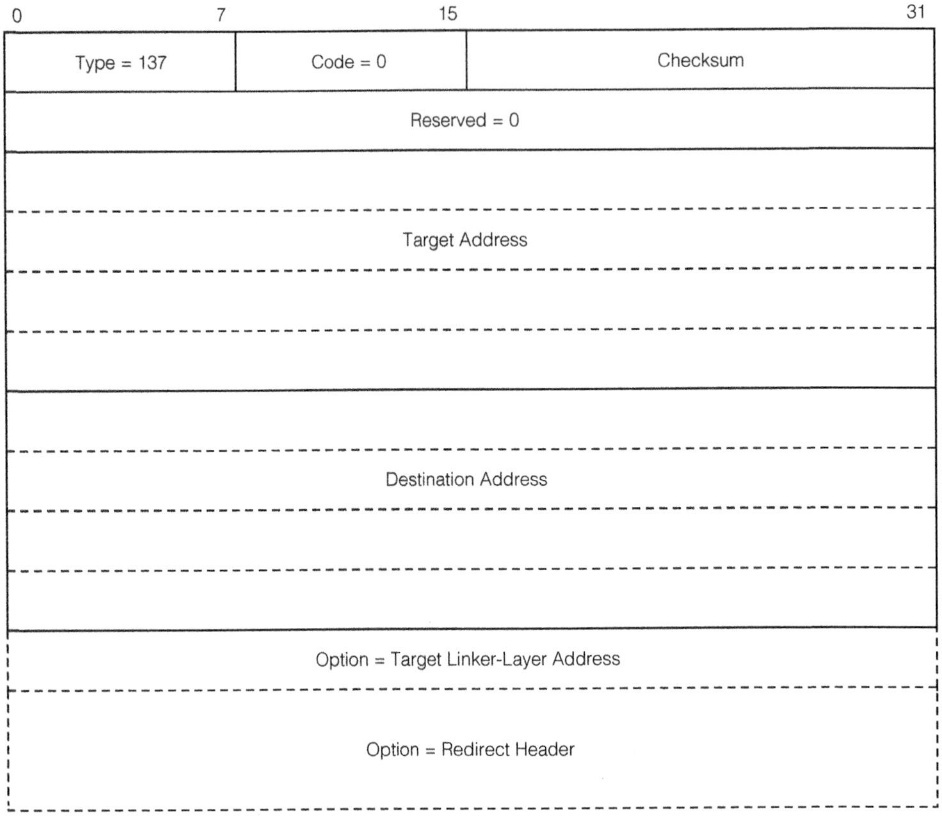

Redirect message format.

The Type field has the value 137. The Code field has the value 0. The Checksum field contains the ICMPv6 checksum value. The Reserved field must be set to 0 by the sender and is ignored by the receiver.

A router sends the Redirect message if there is a better first-hop router, or if the destination is an on-link neighbor. In the first case the Target Address field contains the link-local address of the better first-hop router. In the second case the Target Address field has the same value as the Destination Address field.

The Destination Address field contains the address of the ultimate packet destination.

There are two possible options for the Redirect messages. These two options are the Target Link-Layer Address option and the Redirected Header option. The Target Link-Layer Address option contains the link-layer address of the Target Address. The Redirected Header option contains as much of the original IPv6 packet that triggered the Redirect as possible without causing the total Redirect packet to exceed the minimum link MTU, which is currently 1280 bytes (see Section 2.13.2).

5.7 Neighbor Discovery Option Types and Formats

Each ND protocol message includes zero or more options. Some options may appear multiple times in a single message. Of the options defined in [RFC2461] the Prefix Information option may appear multiple times in a single Router Advertisement message.

The message options have the general Type-Length-Value (TLV) format as illustrated in Figure 5-15. The Type field specifies the type of option. The Length field specifies the size of the option in 8-byte units, including the size of the Type and the Length fields.

Table 5-2 summarizes the possible option or options that have been defined for each message type.

5.7.1 Link-Layer Address Options

The Link-Layer Address option can be either the Source Link-Layer Address option or the Target Link-Layer Address option. As shown in Table 5-2 the Source Link-Layer Address option containing the link-layer address of the sender is included in the Router Solicitation messages, the Router Advertisement messages, and the Neighbor Solicitation messages. The Target

FIGURE 5-15

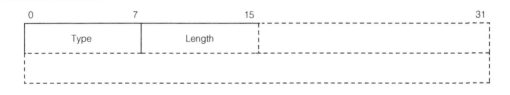

General option format.

TABLE 5-2

Message type	Possible option(s)
Router Solicitation	Source Link-Layer Address
Router Advertisement	Source Link-Layer Address
	MTU
	Prefix Information
	Route Information
Neighbor Solicitation	Source Link-Layer Address
Neighbor Advertisement	Target Link-Layer Address
Redirect	Target Link-Layer Address
	Redirected Header

Possible options per message type.

Link-Layer Address option containing the link-layer address of the target address is included in the Neighbor Advertisement messages and the Redirect messages. The option format is detailed in Figure 5-16.

For Source Link-Layer Address option, the value of the Type field is 1. For Target Link-Layer Address option, the value of the Type field is 2. The size, content, and format of the link-layer address depend on the properties of the physical network on which IPv6 operates. For example, on Ethernet the size of the link-layer address is 6 bytes. The Length field is set to 1 because Link-Layer Address option is 8 bytes in size.

5.7.2   Prefix Information Option

The Prefix Information option is part of the Router Advertisement messages. Prefix information advertised by routers indicates which prefixes are on-link, that is, reachable via the directly connected link, and which prefixes can be used for autonomous address configuration. This option format is detailed in Figure 5-17.

FIGURE 5-16

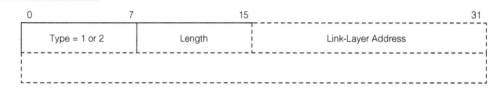

Link-Layer Address option format.

FIGURE 5-17

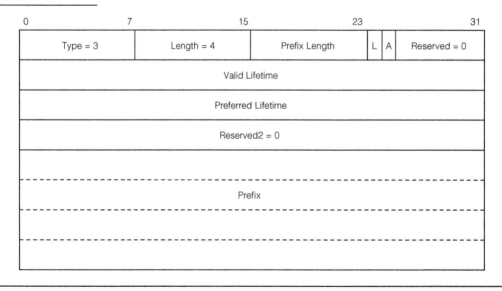

Prefix Information option format.

The Type field has the value 3. The Length field has the value 4, indicating this option is 32 bytes long. The Reserved and the Reserved2 fields must be set to 0 by the sender and are ignored by the receiver.

The Prefix Length is an 8-bit integer specifying the number of leading bits of the prefix that are valid.

The A-bit field is called the "Autonomous Address Configuration" flag. The supplied prefix can be used for autonomous (stateless) address configuration when the A-bit is set in the option.

The L-bit field is called the "On-Link" flag. The supplied prefix is considered on-link when the L-bit is set in the option. When the L-bit is not set, whether the prefix is on-link or off-link is unknown and the prefix cannot be used for on-link determination. For example, a prefix information option may have the L-bit cleared and the A-bit set. In this case, the prefix is only used for address configuration.

The Valid Lifetime field is a 32-bit unsigned integer. Its value is in units of seconds. The special value 0xFFFFFFFF represents an infinite time. When the Prefix Information option specifies an on-link prefix, the Valid Lifetime field specifies the length of time in seconds during which the prefix can be used for on-link determination. When the Prefix Information option specifies a prefix that can be used for address configuration, the Valid Lifetime field specifies the length of time an address generated from that prefix remains valid. In IPv6, addresses are considered as being leased to interfaces. The Valid Lifetime field specifies the address lease time in seconds. Once the Valid Lifetime expires, the address to interface binding becomes invalid and the same address may be reassigned to another interface. An invalid address cannot be used as the source address in any outgoing communication.

The Preferred Lifetime field is a 32-bit unsigned integer. Its value is in units of seconds. The special value 0xFFFFFFFF represents an infinite time. The Preferred Lifetime field specifies a length of time within the Valid Lifetime when a configured address from the advertised prefix may be used in *new communication*. The definition of new communication is application specific, and the feasibility of using a non-deprecated address in new communication is determined by each application. Existing communication will continue with the address that has expired Preferred Lifetime until the Valid Lifetime expires.

5.7.3 Redirected Header Option

The Redirected Header option contains a portion of the original packet that triggered the Redirect message. This option format is detailed in Figure 5-18.

The Type field has the value 4. The Length field specifies the size of the option in 8-byte units including the size of the Type and the Length fields. The Reserved field must be set to 0 by the sender and is ignored by the receiver.

The IPv6 Header and Data portion of the option contains the original packet header and data. All or part of the original packet can be included as long as the overall Redirect message does not exceed the IPv6 minimum MTU.

5.7.4 MTU Option

A router can be configured to distribute link MTU to hosts on a network without a well-defined MTU value. Consider the situation where the IPv6 network is a logical network that comprises multiple physical segments of varying properties and technologies. These segments are

FIGURE 5-18

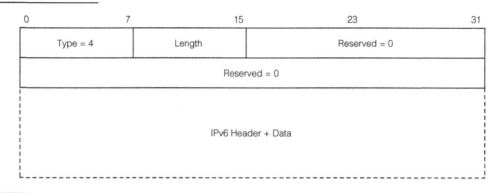

Redirected Header option format.

FIGURE 5-19

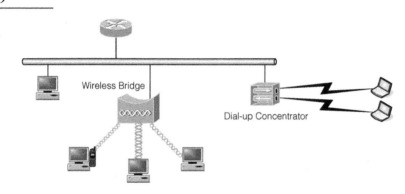

Bridged network of heterogeneous segments.

bridged through various hardware equipments from different vendors. Figure 5-19 illustrates this scenario.

As shown in Figure 5-19 the IPv6 logical network comprises three segments: the Ethernet segment, the wireless segment, and the dial-up segment, each of which may have a different MTU value. In the case of each bridge not generating ICMPv6 Too-Big message, it becomes difficult if not impossible for a node on one segment to know the proper MTU value to use when communicating with another node on a different segment.

The option format is detailed in Figure 5-20. The Type field has the value 5. The Length field has the value 1 indicating this option is 8 bytes long. The Reserved field must be set to 0 by the sender and is ignored by the receiver. The MTU field is a 32-bit integer containing the MTU value to be used by all hosts on the network.

5.7.5   Route Information Option

Route Information option advertises router preference for specific prefixes. This option format is detailed in Figure 5-21.

FIGURE 5-20

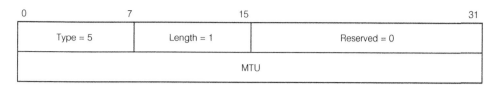

MTU option format.

FIGURE 5-21

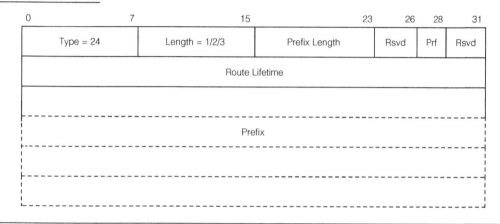

Route Information option format.

The Type field has the value 24. The Length field is an 8-bit integer specifying the size of the option, in 8-byte units, including the size of the Type and the Length fields. The value of this field can be 1, 2, or 3, depending on the prefix length. The Length field has the value 1 for the default route : : / 0 because the prefix length is 0. The Length field has the value 2 if the prefix length is less than or equal to 64 bits. The Length field has the value 3 if the prefix length is larger than 64 bits.

The Prefix Length field is an 8-bit integer specifying the number of leading bits of the prefix that are valid.

The Prf field is the 2-bit router preference field that encodes the router preference as a signed integer. The preference encoding is given in Table 5-1 (page 400). The preference indicates whether the advertising router associated with this particular prefix should be preferred over other routers that advertise the same prefix. The Route Information option is ignored if the Prf field contains the reserved value 10_b.

The Rsvd field is the 3-bit reserved field. This field is set to zero by the sender and is ignored by the receiver.

The Route Lifetime field is a 32-bit value that specifies the length of time in seconds that the prefix is valid for route determination. The value 0xFFFFFFFF represents an infinite lifetime.

The Prefix field is a variable length field that contains either the IPv6 address or the prefix of an IPv6 address. The size of this field is determined by the value of Prefix Length. If the Prefix field contains a prefix, the bits after the Prefix Length must be set to zero by the sender and ignored by the receiver.

If the Route Information option advertises the default route, then the router preference and the lifetime in the Route Information option overwrites the router preference and the lifetime values carried in the Router Advertisement message.

5.8   Next-Hop Determination and Address Resolution

One of the main functions of the ND protocol is address resolution, that is, determining the link-layer address of a given IPv6 address. The IPv6 address must be a unicast address and considered on-link.

When a node has packets to send to a destination, the node must determine whether the destination is on-link or off-link and subsequently how to reach the destination. This process is known as next-hop determination, which works as follows. The sending node first decides whether the destination is on-link based on the definitions described in Section 5.2. If it is, the next-hop address is the same as the destination address. For an off-link destination, a router is selected from the Default Router List. In this case the next-hop address is the same as the address of the default router. Next-hop determination completes at this point.

The next step is to resolve the link-layer address of the next-hop address. The node begins the resolution procedure by sending out a Neighbor Solicitation packet destined for the solicited-node multicast address of the next-hop address. The source address of the Neighbor Solicitation packet is set to the source address of the packet that prompted the address resolution(*). The node must include the link-layer address that corresponds to the source address in the Source Link-Layer Address option when sending a multicast Neighbor Solicitation packet. A node may already have the link-layer address of the destination but the information may be stale. In this case the node may send a unicast solicitation, and including its link-layer address is optional.

(*) A router also sends a Neighbor Solicitation message when forwarding a packet to determine the link-layer address of the next-hop, but in this case the source address of the Neighbor Solicitation message is one of the router's addresses configured on the outgoing interface, rather than the source address of the forwarded packet.

Before sending the first Neighbor Solicitation message, the node that is performing address resolution will create a cache entry, called the *Neighbor Cache* entry, for the next-hop address if one does not already exist. Each Neighbor Cache entry maintains information about a neighbor, which can be either the destination or a default router to which traffic has been sent recently. This information includes:

- The neighbor's on-link unicast address and its associated link-layer address.

- The type of neighbor, that is, whether the neighbor is a host or a router. The type is often identified by a flag variable called the *IsRouter* flag, which is set to true if the neighbor is a router.

- The operating parameters for the NUD algorithm such as the neighbor's reachability state, the number of unanswered probes sent, and a timer set for triggering the next NUD algorithm event.

- A packet queue maintaining outgoing packets transmitted by the upper layers or being forwarded while address resolution is in progress.

Once the corresponding Neighbor Advertisement packet is received, the resolved link-layer address is saved into the Neighbor Cache. The reason for using the source address of the packet that prompted the address resolution as the source address of the Neighbor Solicitation packet is to allow the recipient of the packet to install a Neighbor Cache entry that most likely will be used for future traffic between the two nodes.

Associated with Neighbor Cache is a conceptual data structure called the *Destination Cache*. Each Destination Cache entry contains information about a destination to which traffic has been sent recently. In other words, each destination cache entry contains the result of next-hop determination for a destination address (i.e., each entry maps a destination IPv6 address to a next-hop address). The next-hop address for a particular destination may be changed by Redirect messages. Other information such as the Path MTU value and packet round trip time may also be maintained in the Destination Cache entry.

5.9 Neighbor Unreachability Detection Algorithm

The reachability state of the neighbor is an important piece of information that is part of each Neighbor Cache entry. The reachability state of a neighbor can be one of five values: INCOMPLETE, REACHABLE, STALE, DELAY, or PROBE.

The reachability state of the neighbor is in the INCOMPLETE state when the cache entry is newly created. The INCOMPLETE state represents address resolution for the link-layer address of the neighbor being in progress. Packets destined to the neighbor are queued while the reachability state of the neighbor is INCOMPLETE.

The neighbor becomes REACHABLE when the address resolution completes successfully. At this state queued packets are transmitted immediately.

The STALE state indicates the neighbor is not known to be reachable. The state remains STALE until traffic is generated to the neighbor and at that point probe packets are sent to verify the reachability of that neighbor.

A node begins reachability probe when traffic is generated to a neighbor in the STALE state. The node will delay probe packet transmission for a short period to give upper layer protocols a chance to provide neighbor reachability information. This delay causes the neighbor reachability state to transit to the DELAY state. The neighbor in the DELAY state is considered no longer known to be reachable.

Probe packets are sent to neighbor once the delay period expires. Subsequently the neighbor reachability state transits into the PROBE state. The probe packets are unicast Neighbor Solicitation packets. The neighbor in the PROBE state is considered no longer known to be reachable.

State transition from any of STALE, DELAY, and PROBE states to the REACHABLE state takes place once reachability confirmation arrives either from the neighbor or from upper layer protocols.

The NUD algorithm verifies the bidirectional connectivity between two communicating peers. The NUD algorithm effectively detects the case where a node sends unicast packets to a peer and the path between them is broken.

A node sends NUD-triggered Neighbor Solicitation packets using the cached link-layer address of the neighbor. A node considers a peer reachable after receiving a valid solicited Neighbor Advertisement response. A node also considers a peer reachable after receiving reachability confirmation from upper layer protocols. Upper layer protocols such as TCP that provide reliable service can extrapolate reachability confirmation from its protocol exchanges, such as receiving an acknowledgment packet for previously sent data, and convey this reachability information to the entity running the NUD. We call this confirmation the positive reachability confirmation. Note well that upper layer protocol indication can be considered a positive reachability confirmation only if the local node has a cached link-layer address of the neighbor. In other words, the Neighbor Cache entry has a neighbor reachability state other than the INCOMPLETE state. Receiving a valid solicited Neighbor Advertisement response is a positive indication that the neighbor is reachable because the Neighbor Solicitation must have reached the neighbor to prompt the neighbor to respond with a Neighbor Advertisement.

Including the Source Link-Layer address option with the Neighbor Solicitation packets is optional when performing NUD. Since the Neighbor Solicitation receiver may need to perform address resolution before responding with the Neighbor Advertisement packets if this option is missing, the recommendation is for the Neighbor Solicitation sender to include this option whenever possible.

Packet transmissions continue using the cached link-local address while the NUD algorithm operates in parallel to confirm the neighbor's reachability.

5.10   Stateless Address Autoconfiguration

Stateless address autoconfiguration is performed only on multicast-capable networks. The network interface must also have the ability to transmit and receive multicast packets. A node must join both the all-nodes multicast group and the solicited-node multicast group of the tentative address before performing DAD on that address. The definition of tentative address is given in the next section.

Stateless address autoconfiguration mainly applies to hosts, but each router uses the same mechanism to generate and validate link-local addresses for all its interfaces.

A host begins stateless address autoconfiguration by first generating a link-local address for each of its interfaces. In the following discussions we will focus on the case where a host has a single network interface though the discussions apply to multi-homed hosts. For multi-homed hosts, stateless address autoconfiguration is performed independently on each interface for each address. A host then probes the routers that are present to gather additional information for further configuration of non-link-local addresses, and the configuration of other nonaddress-related operating parameters. A host may send a Router Solicitation message before configuring any address. In that case the source address of the Router Solicitation is the unspecified address.

5.10.1 Address Formation and Address States

Combining the prefix `fe80::/10` with the interface identifier forms a link-local address as illustrated in Figure 5-22. In the majority of cases the interface identifier is 64 bits long.

Similarly, hosts can generate additional non-link-local addresses from advertised prefixes when a router is present. See Figure 5-23.

Each address is associated with a state attribute that can transit and take on different values. At any one time an address may be in one of the following states: *tentative, preferred, deprecated,* and *invalid*. Both the preferred and deprecated states are considered as the *valid* state. In addition, the KAME implementation supports an additional state called *duplicated* for its convenience.

There are two kinds of lifetimes for each valid address: the *preferred lifetime* and the *valid lifetime*. The valid lifetime of an address must be larger than or equal to the preferred lifetime. A valid address is in the preferred state until its preferred lifetime expires when the state transits to deprecated. The address becomes invalid when its valid lifetime expires.

Figure 5-24 depicts the address state transition diagram along with the expiration events of address lifetimes.

A newly formed address is considered a tentative address and is not assigned to an interface. The address remains a tentative address while DAD is performed on it. A tentative address is not yet bound to an interface, and thus cannot be used in any communication. With the tentative address, however, an interface can send and receive ND packets for the execution of the DAD algorithm while all other types of packets are discarded.

A tentative address becomes valid (that is, either preferred or deprecated) once DAD completes and verifies that the address is unique on the attached link. A valid address is bound to an interface and can be used in any communication. For a link-local address its binding to the interface is permanent, that is, the address has infinite preferred and valid lifetimes. A tentative address with a non-link-local prefix must also have a non-0 valid lifetime before becoming a valid address. If the preferred lifetime is also non-0, the address has the preferred state, and it

FIGURE 5-22

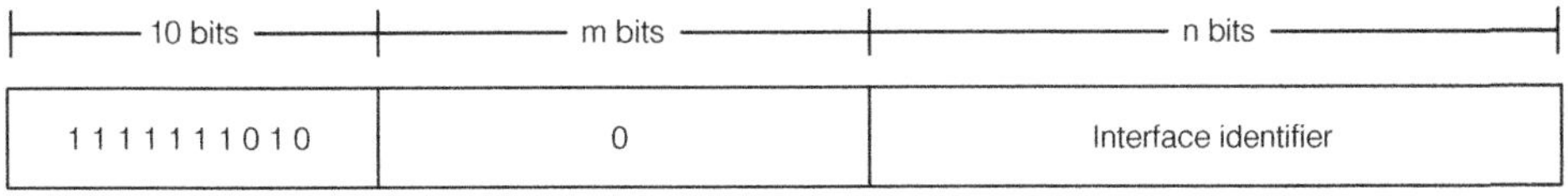

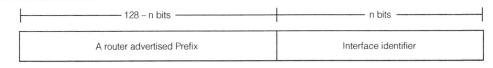

10 bits	m bits	n bits
1 1 1 1 1 1 1 0 1 0	0	Interface identifier

Link-local address formation.

FIGURE 5-23

128 – n bits	n bits
A router advertised Prefix	Interface identifier

Non-link-local address formation.

FIGURE 5-24

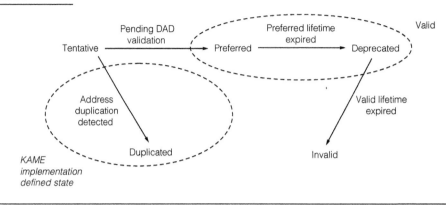

Address state transition.

can be used in any type of communication without any restrictions by the upper layer protocols such as TCP and UDP.

A tentative address becomes a duplicated address if DAD detects that another node is already using that address on the attached link. A duplicated address may be a valid address that is in use by another node. Two nodes performing DAD on the same address may detect the address as being a duplicate at about the same time. In this case neither node will be able to use the address.

A preferred address becomes a deprecated address when its preferred lifetime expires. The initial state of a valid address can also be deprecated when its preferred lifetime is zero. A deprecated address is still a valid address: Existing communications can continue using the deprecated address if switching to a different address will disrupt the current communications. In particular, an existing TCP communication with a deprecated address should be able to continue. New communications, however, should not be established with the deprecated address if the applications consider the communication feasible using a non-deprecated address. Address scopes of non-deprecated addresses must be taken into account when considering whether to continue the use of a deprecated address in new communications (see Section 3.4 for the source address selection rules for this consideration). Packets sent to a deprecated address are delivered in the usual manner.

A deprecated address becomes an invalid address when the valid lifetime of the address prefix expires. Packets addressed to an invalid address cannot be delivered because an invalid address is not bound to any interface.

Using the two types of lifetimes helps network renumbering. When a site renumbers its network addresses, the administrator will first advertise the new prefix as well as the old one, and then decrease the preferred lifetime of the old prefix toward zero, making addresses based on the old prefix deprecated. By definition of deprecated address, newer communication in the site will eventually use the new addresses. The site administrator will be able to stop the use of the old prefix and addresses once the communication with the new address is stabilized.

5.10.2   Duplicate Address Detection Algorithm

A host performs DAD on all addresses independent of whether an address was obtained through stateless autoconfiguration, DHCPv6, or manual configuration. A router also performs DAD on all of its addresses.

The DAD algorithm operates over the Neighbor Solicitation and Neighbor Advertisement messages on a directly attached link. For a given interface, basically, a node that is performing DAD on a tentative address transmits a number of Neighbor Solicitation packets having that tentative address set as the Target address. The sending node will receive a corresponding Neighbor Advertisement packet if that tentative address is already in use by another node. Otherwise the sending node can complete the DAD process and claim that address once that node transmits a number of Neighbor Solicitation packets without receiving any Neighbor Advertisement packet in response. The number of Neighbor Solicitation packet transmissions is a configurable parameter for each interface. The interval between consecutive Neighbor Solicitation packets is another configurable parameter. The Neighbor Solicitation packets for DAD have the packet properties listed in Table 5-3.

In situations where no prior packet transmissions of any type took place on a given interface, for example, when a system is just starting up, the first Neighbor Solicitation packet transmission must be delayed by a random time between 0 and 1 second. Each consecutive packet transmission is separated by a constant time delay. After the final Neighbor Solicitation packet transmission, a node waits for the same amount of time delay for a response before claiming the address. For example, if the number of Neighbor Solicitation packet transmissions is configured at 5 packets and the inter-packet delay is 1 second, assuming the initial random delay is 1 second, then a node can claim a tentative address after 6 seconds if no response is received within this period. Otherwise, another node has already claimed the address. In this case the sending node requires manual configuration of either a different interface identifier or the entire address for that interface.

In the case where two nodes are performing DAD on the same address simultaneously, each node will detect it by receiving the Neighbor Solicitation from the other node and treat the address as a duplicate address. In other words, none of the nodes will claim the address for interface assignment.

A given interface should be disabled if the link-local address is generated from an interface identifier based on the hardware address which is supposed to be uniquely assigned and if DAD indicates the tentative link-local address is a duplicate. This failure is likely an indication that the link-layer address is duplicated. Instead of regenerating another address and attempting further

TABLE 5-3

Packet field	Value
Source Address	Unspecified address (::)
Destination Address	Solicited-node multicast address
Target Address	Tentative address under verification

Packet properties in DAD packet.

communication using that interface, the node should disable the interface so that no traffic will originate on that interface and traffic received on that interface is discarded. Disabling the interface prevents disruption of existing communications that are destined to the node with the duplicate link-layer address, and prevents a node from initiating communication that will have intermittent packet reception.

Note: In [RFC2462], the meaning of "disabling interface" was not clear. A successor version of the specification [RFC2462BIS] clarifies that it means no IPv6 operation should be performed on that interface.

During the period when DAD is verifying an address, the information displayed from the **ifconfig** utility will show the address as a tentative address. An example output is shown below.

```
ne0: flags=8843<UP,BROADCAST,RUNNING,SIMPLEX,MULTICAST> mtu 1500
        inet 192.0.2.127 netmask 0xffffff00 broadcast 192.0.2.255
        inet6 fe80::20c:29ff:fef1:1a8b%ne0 prefixlen 64 tentative scopeid 0x1
        ether 00:0c:29:f1a:8b
```

The current recommendation is to perform DAD on any address regardless of how it is configured; whether it is configured via Stateless Address Autoconfiguration, allocated via DHCPv6, or manually configured. [RFC2462] presented a DAD "optimization," which allows a node to omit DAD for addresses that were generated from an interface identifier that has already been verified as unique by DAD on another generated address. Since then, different types of addresses have been introduced, such as temporary addresses for privacy extensions (Section 5.10.4), which invalidates the assumption. The successor version of the specification thus discourages the aforementioned optimization and strongly recommends performing DAD without exceptions.

It is worth noting that DAD is not 100% reliable. For example, a network may be segmented temporarily due to link failure. Two hosts on two different segments may be verifying the same address during the failure period. Each host cannot receive packets transmitted by the other host due to link segmentation resulting in these two hosts using the same address but on different segments. Once the link is restored, multiple nodes end up using the duplicate address in the same link.

5.10.3   Processing Router Advertisement

Prefix information options of a Router Advertisement contain prefixes that allow a host to automatically generate and configure non-link-local addresses.

A host will form a new address using an advertised prefix on an interface if that prefix has a non-0 valid lifetime, and no address has been configured with that prefix previously on that interface. The host will record the valid lifetime of this address. If a later Router Advertisement contains the same prefix information, then the valid lifetime may require modification according to the following rules:

- If the newly received valid lifetime is greater than 2 hours or greater than the remaining valid lifetime of the address, then the valid lifetime is updated to the newly received valid lifetime.

- If the remaining lifetime is less than or equal to 2 hours, then the valid lifetime is left unchanged unless the Router Advertisement is authenticated such as via Secure

ND protocol (SEND) [RFC3971]; if the Router Advertisement is authenticated, the valid lifetime is updated to the received lifetime.

• Otherwise, the valid lifetime is reset to 2 hours.

The "two-hour rule" prevents a type of denial of service attacks where forged Router Advertisements advertise prefixes that have short valid lifetimes, triggering hosts to prematurely invalidate addresses that were generated from those prefixes. The premature address invalidation may then terminate upper layer communication (e.g., terminating active TCP connections).

Note that hosts also use the Prefix Information options that are carried in a Router Advertisement to make on-link determination of addresses. The two-hour rule does not apply to prefixes that are advertised for on-link determination because such attacks do not result in catastrophic effects. Prematurely removing prefixes from the on-link prefix list will result in a host sending packets to a neighbor through a default router, but the router will immediately send Redirect to the host.

The preferred lifetime is always updated to the received value regardless of whether the valid lifetime is updated or ignored. Preferred lifetime provides a hint to upper layers that an address may soon become invalid. An address transits from being a preferred address to a deprecated address, but a deprecated address is still a valid address. The two-hour rule that guards the valid lifetime is sufficient in protecting an address without introducing additional mechanisms for updating the preferred lifetime.

5.10.4 Privacy Extensions

A common practice in Stateless Address Autoconfiguration is to derive the 64-bit interface identifier portion of an IPv6 address from an IEEE identifier. By design, the IEEE interface identifiers are globally unique and static. IPv6 addresses that are formed from the embedded IEEE identifiers are also likely to be globally unique. Such types of addresses are commonly known as *public addresses*, which allow extraction of information that can be used in correlating traffic and making inferences about the communication activities and behaviors of a particular node. With embedded IEEE identifier, the interface identifier portion of the address does not change even when the node obtains a different prefix.

An IPv6 node that supports the privacy extension for stateless address autoconfiguration [RFC3041] will generate global scope addresses from randomized interface identifiers that change over time. These addresses are termed *temporary addresses* and are used when initiating outbound communication. These temporary addresses have short lifetimes that range from hours to a few days. With the privacy extension, a temporary address is generated for each global prefix that has a valid address installed through Stateless Address Autoconfiguration.

The lifetimes of a temporary address are derived from the lifetimes of a public address in the following manner.

The valid lifetime of a temporary address is the smaller of the valid lifetime of the public address and TEMP_VALID_LIFETIME. The default value for TEMP_VALID_LIFETIME is 1 week.

The preferred lifetime of a temporary address is the smaller of the preferred lifetime of the public address and (TEMP_PREFERRED_LIFETIME - DESYNC_FACTOR). The default value for `TEMP_PREFERRED_LIFETIME` is 1 day. `DESYNC_FACTOR` is a random value for avoiding the situation where hosts are synchronized in regenerating new temporary addresses exactly at the same time (see below). Its value is randomly chosen in the range between 0 and `MAX_DESYNC_FACTOR` where `MAX_DESYNC_FACTOR` is 10 minutes. If this calculated preferred lifetime is less than `REGEN_ADVANCE`, the temporary address is not generated. `REGEN_ADVANCE` is a constant value of 5 seconds.

The lifetimes of a temporary address typically only decrements due to its nature of limited period of use, even if the host keeps receiving valid Router Advertisement messages with the prefix information. When a temporary address is deprecated, a new temporary address is created with a new randomized identifier.

The privacy extension document recommends that an implementation generate a new randomized interface identifier periodically. The recommended interval is (`TEMP_PREFERRED_LIFETIME` - `REGEN_ADVANCE` - `DESYNC_FACTOR`) so that the new interface identifier will be ready when a new temporary address needs to be created due to the deprecation of the old one.

DAD is performed for each temporary address. If a temporary address is duplicated, a new randomized interface identifier is generated followed by the generation of a new temporary address.

Figure 5-25 illustrates the procedure of generating randomized interface identifiers and temporary addresses with the default lifetime values (1 day and 1 week) and `DESYNC_FACTOR` being 0. This figure shows that in a stable state there are always 7 temporary addresses based on a single public address, and there is at most 1 preferred temporary address at any point of time.

The extended mechanism was first introduced in [RFC3041]. The IETF has since slightly modified the protocol specification based on early experiences. The current specification is

FIGURE 5-25

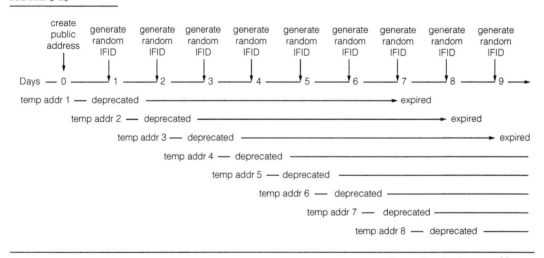

Generating temporary addresses.

[PRIVACY-ADDRS2]. While our primary reference to specification is [RFC3041] in this chapter, we also refer to the successor version since the KAME implementation has partly incorporated the new specification.

5.11 Router Specific Operation

A router maintains a set of configuration variables for each multicast capable interface. Table 5-4 describes these variables that are specific to router operations defined in [RFC2461]. The names of these variables are for illustration purposes only and are taken from the RFC verbatim. Implementations are free to choose any names for these variables as long as the external behaviors of these variables conform to the specification. A node that functions as a router must allow these variables to be configurable by the system administrative entity. Some of these default values may be overridden by specific documents that describe how IPv6 operates over different media link layers.

A router transmits Router Advertisement packets on interfaces that are configured as advertising interfaces. An interface becomes an advertising interface when it is enabled and its

TABLE 5-4

Variable	Default	Description
AdvSendAdvertisements	FALSE	This variable controls whether a router will transmit periodic router advertisements on an interface. This variable also controls whether a router will respond to router solicitation messages on that interface. The default value prevents a node from acting as a router unless specifically configured to do so.
MaxRtrAdvInterval	600 s	The maximum interval, in seconds, which is allowed between consecutive unsolicited multicast Router Advertisement messages. A configured value must fall between 4 and 1800 seconds inclusive.
MinRtrAdvInterval	$0.33 \times$ *MaxRtrAdvInterval*	The minimum interval, in seconds, which is required between consecutive unsolicited multicast Router Advertisement messages. A configured value must fall between 3 seconds and $0.75 \times$ *MaxRtrAdv Interval*.
AdvManagedFlag	FALSE	The value to be set for the M-bit in the outgoing Router Advertisement messages.
AdvOtherConfigFlag	FALSE	The value to be set for the O-bit in the outgoing Router Advertisement messages.

(Continued on page 420)

TABLE 5-4 (*Continued from page 419*)

Variable	Default	Description
AdvLinkMTU	0	The MTU value to be placed in the MTU option of Router Advertisement messages. A default value of 0 indicates the advertising router does not specify an MTU value for the link.
AdvReachableTime	0	The value, in milliseconds, to be placed in the Reachable Time field of the outing Router Advertisement messages. A value of 0 indicates the advertising router does not specify this parameter. The maximum allowable value is 36,000,000 ms or 1 hour.
AdvRetransTimer	0	The value, in milliseconds, to be placed in the Retransmission Timer field of the outgoing Router Advertisement messages. A value of 0 indicates the advertising router does not specify this parameter.
AdvCurHopLimit	As recommended by IANA (KAME code sets the default to 64)	The value to be placed in the Current Hop Limit field of the outgoing Router Advertisement messages. A value of 0 indicates the advertising router does not specify this parameter.
AdvDefaultLifetime	3 × MaxRtrAdvInterval	The value, in seconds, to be placed in the Router Lifetime field of the outgoing Router Advertisement messages. A value of 0 indicates the advertising router must not be used as a default router by the receiving nodes. Otherwise a configured value must fall between MaxRtrAdvInterval and 9000 seconds inclusive.

Router configuration variables.

configuration variable *AdvSendAdvertisements* is set to TRUE. An interface ceases being an advertising interface either when it is disabled or when *AdvSendAdvertisements* is set to FALSE. None of the interfaces of a node are advertising interfaces when the node stops being a router. A router must join the all-routers multicast group on each advertising interface.

A router may send Router Advertisement messages with information that allows automatic address configuration at hosts; however, it may choose to not offer packet-forwarding service. In this case the router will send out Router Advertisement messages that have value 0 in the Router Lifetime field.

A router maintains a set of configuration variables for each prefix that the router advertises. Table 5-5 describes these variables. The names of these variables are for illustration purposes only and are taken from the RFC verbatim. Implementations are free to choose any names for these variables as long as the external behaviors of these variables conform to the specification. A node that functions as a router must allow these variables to be configurable by the system administrative entity. Constants that are applicable to router operations are listed in Table 5-6.

TABLE 5-5

Variable	Default	Description
AdvPrefixList	Prefixes that are considered on-link according to the active routing protocols	This is a list of prefixes to be advertised through the Prefix Information options by the router. There exists a set of configurable parameters for each prefix in the list. The link-local prefix must not be part of this list and must not be advertised by any router.
AdvValidLifetime	2,592,000 s or 30 days (fixed)	The value, in seconds, to be placed in the Valid Lifetime field of the Prefix Information option of the outgoing Router Advertisement messages. The value 0xFFFFFFFF represents infinity. The advertised valid lifetime can be decremented in real-time and each subsequent advertisement will contain a smaller value. Alternatively the advertised valid lifetime can be a fixed value (i.e., each subsequent advertisement carries the same value).
AdvOnLinkFlag	TRUE	The value to be placed in the L-bit field of the Prefix Information option of the outgoing Router Advertisement messages.
AdvPreferredLifetime	604,800 s or 7 days (fixed)	The value, in seconds, to be placed in the Preferred Lifetime field of the Prefix Information option of the outgoing Router Advertisement messages. The value 0xFFFFFFFF represents infinity. The Preferred Lifetime can be advertised either as a value that decrements in real-time, or as a fixed value similar to the advertisement of the Valid Lifetime field.
AdvAutonomousFlag	TRUE	The value to be placed in the A-bit field of the Prefix Information option of the outgoing Router Advertisement messages.

Per-prefix configuration variables.

TABLE 5-6

Variable	Value
MAX_INITIAL_RTR_ADVERT_INTERVAL	16 s
MAX_INITIAL_RTR_ADVERTISEMENTS	3 transmissions
MAX_FINAL_RTR_ADVERTISEMENTS	3 transmissions
MIN_DELAY_BETWEEN_RAS	3 s
MAX_RA_DELAY_TIME	0.5 s

Router constants.

5.11.1   Sending Unsolicited Router Advertisements

Routers send periodic unsolicited Router Advertisement messages in addition to solicited Router Advertisement messages on each advertising interface to allow hosts to discover both default routers and on-link prefixes (see Section 5.6.2). Since unsolicited Router Advertisement messages are sent to the all-nodes multicast address on each of its advertising interfaces, a router sets the interval to the next unsolicited Router Advertisement transmission to a randomized value in the range of *MinRtrAdvInterval* and *MaxRtrAdvInterval* seconds. This randomized interval helps a router avoid synchronized Router Advertisement transmissions with other routers on the link associated with the advertising interface.

For the first `MAX_INITIAL_RTR_ADVERTISEMENTS` advertisements on an interface that just became an advertising interface, if the generated interval is larger than `MAX_INITIAL_RTR_ADVERT_INTERVAL` seconds then `MAX_INITIAL_RTR_ADVERT_INTERVAL` will be set as the inter-packet delay. The purpose of these rapid transmissions is to allow hosts to discover the router quickly when it becomes available. The same rule applies when the system management entity has changed the configuration variables, which subsequently change the values in the associated fields of the Router Advertisement messages.

A router may transmit up to `MAX_FINAL_RTR_ADVERTISEMENTS` advertisements when an interface ceases being an advertising interface. The Router Lifetime field must be set to 0 indicating the router is no longer a default router on that link. The same rule applies to each advertising interface when a router stops being a router and begins to function as a host. In this case the router should leave the all-router multicast group on each advertising interface. Once the node becomes a host it must ensure that Neighbor Advertisement messages will have the "Is Router" flag bit set to 0.

Router Advertisement messages have the source address set to the link-local address of the advertising interface. Hosts cache this address as the first-hop router address if the Router Advertisement messages contain non-0 router lifetime. This link-local address rarely changes for a router, but in the case where the address is changed, the router must multicast a number of Router Advertisement messages with 0 Router Lifetime using the old link-local address. Then the router multicasts a number of Router Advertisement messages with non-0 Router Lifetime using the new link-local address. The number of advertisements to be sent with either the old or the new link-local address is implementation-dependent. However, this number should be chosen such that nodes have a good chance of receiving both types of advertisements and recognizing the address change.

A router should include all message options when sending unsolicited Router Advertisement messages. A router should transmit multiple Router Advertisement messages, each with a different option, if including all options in a single message results in the size of the advertisement exceeding the link MTU.

5.11.2   Processing Router Solicitations

For each valid Router Solicitation message the router has the choice as to where to send the response. A router may send the unicast response directly to the soliciting host, provided the source address of the Router Solicitation message is not the unspecified address. However, it is more common for the router to multicast the response to the all-nodes multicast group. The idea is to reduce network traffic if other hosts are also in the router discovery and on-link prefix discovery process.

A router must delay sending the solicited Router Advertisement message by a random time between 0 and MAX_RA_DELAY_TIME seconds for a unicast response. For a multicast response the delay must be MIN_DELAY_BETWEEN_RAS seconds plus the random value with respect to the last multicast Router Advertisement transmission. If the next scheduled unsolicited Router Advertisement transmission takes place sooner than the randomized delay then the already scheduled time is used for the solicited Router Advertisement transmission. Solicited multicast Router Advertisement messages are sent more frequently than unsolicited Router Advertisement messages.

5.11.3 Processing Router Advertisements

A router processes received Router Advertisement messages to inspect the content and detect the case where there are routers advertising inconsistent information. A router that discovers advertisement inconsistencies should log the condition and notify the system management entity accordingly. A router should inspect the following information in received Router Advertisement messages for inconsistencies:

- Current Hop-Limit field
- M-bit flag and O-bit flag
- Reachable Time field
- Retransmission Timer field
- MTU value from the MTU option
- Preferred Lifetime and Valid Lifetime fields of the Prefix Information option for each prefix known to the receiving router

It is not considered an error, for example, if one router advertises a value for the link MTU while another router does not specify such a value in its advertisement.

5.12 Host Specific Operation

A host does not have any ND protocol-related configuration parameters, but for each active interface a host maintains a set of variables for ND-related operations. These variables are described in Table 5-7. The names of these variables are for illustration purposes only and are taken from the RFC verbatim. Implementations are free to choose any names for these variables as long as the external behaviors of these variables conform to the specification.

A host uses the default values if there are no routers on a link, or if no received Router Advertisement messages advertise a value for a particular variable. Some of these default values may be overridden by specific documents that describe how IPv6 operates over different media link layers.

Constants that are applicable to host operations are listed in Table 5-8.

5.12.1 Sending Router Solicitations

The interval between unsolicited Router Advertisement messages is a configurable value specific to an advertising router. This interval may be on the order of tens of minutes. When a host is

TABLE 5-7

Variable	*Default*	*Description*
LinkMTU	The MTU value defined by the link layer over which IPv6 operates.	The MTU value chosen when transmitting packets.
CurHopLimit	As recommended by IANA (KAME code sets the default to 64)	The value to be placed in the Hop-Limit field of the IPv6 header of the outgoing unicast packets.
BaseReachableTime	REACHABLE_TIME ms	The base value used in computing *Reachable-Time*.
ReachableTime	N/A	The time during which a neighbor is considered reachable after receiving a response qualified as a reachability confirmation. The value is randomly generated and must fall between MIN_RANDOM_FACTOR and MAX_RANDOM_FACTOR times BaseReachable-TIme inclusive. The value of *ReachableTime* must be refreshed every time the *BaseReachableTime* changes, or every few hours when no Router Advertisement messages are received.
RetransTimer	RETRANS_TIMER ms	The interval between transmissions of Neighbor Solicitation messages for either address resolution or neighbor unreachability detection.

Host operational variables.

TABLE 5-8

Variable	*Value*
MAX_RTR_SOLICITATION_DELAY	1 s
RTR_SOLICITATION_INTERVAL	4 s
MAX_RTR_SOLICITATIONS	3 transmissions

Host constants.

unwilling to wait for an undetermined amount of time before completing its configuration and beginning normal operations, the host sends out Router Solicitations. The conditions that trigger Router Solicitation transmissions on an interface are when the interface is attached to the link and becomes enabled by the system management entity, or when the interface was disabled and then re-enabled by system management, or when a node changes from being a router to being a host.

A host should delay the initial Router Solicitation packet transmission by a random time between 0 and MAX_RTR_SOLICITATION_DELAY seconds. This delay helps to alleviate the problem of synchronized Router Solicitation packet transmissions from hosts that are starting up at about the same time. A host may transmit up to MAX_RTR_SOLICITATIONS number of solicitations with each successive transmission delayed by at least

`RTR_SOLICITATION_INTERVAL` seconds. The source address of the Router Solicitation messages can be one of the unicast addresses of the sending interface. In this case the Source Link-Layer Address option of the associated unicast address should be provided along with each Router Solicitation message. The source address can also be the unspecified address if the host does not have a valid address. The destination address of the Router Solicitation packets is the all-routers multicast address.

A host that has sent out the last Router Solicitation packet and waited `MAX_RTR_SOLICITATION_DELAY` seconds without receiving any Router Advertisement messages assumes that there are no routers present on that link. On the other hand, if a host receives a valid Router Advertisement with a non-0 router lifetime then the host will stop sending additional Router Solicitation packets on that interface until the interface condition changes.

5.12.2 Processing Router Advertisements

A host must join the all-nodes multicast group on each of its active multicast-capable interfaces when it attaches to a link via the interface. A host combines and maintains the information retrieved from the advertisements originated from different routers. A host that receives an advertisement in which a parameter is unspecified must not override a previously saved value for the same parameter advertised by a different router. In the case where a host receives different values for the same parameter from Router Advertisement messages originated from different routers, the most recently received value takes precedence.

Upon receiving a valid Router Advertisement message, the host creates a new entry in the Default Router List if the host has not seen this advertising router, and provided the Router Lifetime field is non-0. The host then starts an invalidation timer for this newly created entry using the value given in the Router Lifetime field. The host is not required to cache all known default routers, but a host must retain at least two default routers even when it has resource limitations.

For a known router already in the Default Router List the host will reset the invalidation timer of the existing entry to the newly received non-0 router lifetime value. If the newly received router lifetime value is 0, the host will timeout the existing entry and remove it from the list immediately.

Upon receiving a valid Router Advertisement message, the host will initialize its operational variables by extracting the necessary information from the corresponding fields of the Router Advertisement message. The *CurHopLimit* variable is set with the non-0 value of the Current Hop-Limit field of the Router Advertisement message. The *BaseReachableTimer* variable is set with the non-0 value of the Reachable Time field of the Router Advertisement message. The *ReachableTime* variable is calculated each time the value of *BaseReachableTimer* changes. In general the value of *BaseReachableTimer* seldom changes and thus the value of *ReachableTime* should be randomized every few hours. The *RetransTimer* variable is set with the non-0 value of the Retransmission Timer field of the Router Advertisement message.

A host processes valid Router Advertisement message options if these are present. The *LinkMTU* variable is set with the value of the MTU field of the MTU option if the advertised value is at least as large as the minimum value required by the IPv6 specification. The advertised value must not be larger than the default link MTU as specified by the documents that describe how IPv6 operates over a specific media link layer.

Upon receiving a valid Router Advertisement message, the host creates a new entry in the Prefix List for each Prefix Information option, provided that the host has not seen this prefix, given the prefix is not a link-local prefix, and provided that the Valid Lifetime of the prefix is non-0. The host then starts an invalidation timer for this newly created entry using the value retrieved from the Valid Lifetime field of the Prefix Information option. For a known prefix that is already in the Prefix List the host will update the invalidation timer of the existing entry.

The host also configures or updates addresses based on the received Prefix Information options as described in Section 5.10.3.

5.12.3   Default Router Selection

A router that is reachable or has been known to be reachable or probably reachable (that is, in any state other than INCOMPLETE) is preferred over a router that is in the INCOMPLETE state, and is preferred over a router that does not have a Neighbor Cache entry. Router preference is used as the tie breaker to select a router when multiple routers have the same reachability state (see Sections 5.6.2 and 5.7.5).

When all routers on the Default Router List are neither known to be reachable nor probably reachable, router selection returns the router in a round-robin fashion. This selection process causes the NUD algorithm to be run for each router.

5.13   Code Introduction

In this section we introduce ND-related data structures and functions. We will cover the files listed in Table 5-9 throughout the discussion.

TABLE 5-9

File	Description
${KAME}/kame/sys/netinet6/icmp6.h	Definition of ND message types and headers.
${KAME}/kame/sys/netinet6/icmp6.c	Redirect message handling functions.
${KAME}/kame/sys/netinet6/nd6.h	Data structures and constant definitions that correspond to those that are specified in the RFC.
${KAME}/kame/sys/netinet6/nd6.c	The timer function, utility functions that interact with upper layers and the kernel, and general initialization functions.
${KAME}/kame/sys/netinet6/nd6_rtr.c	Default router and prefix management functions.
${KAME}/kame/sys/netinet6/nd6_nbr.c	Processing functions for ND messages that are applicable to both hosts and routers.

Files referenced in Chapter 5.

5.13.1 ND Message Definitions

This section summarizes standard definitions of ND messages and option types, and data structures of ND-related messages that are often referred to in the subsequent description.

Tables 5-10 and 5-11 show standard macro names for ND message types and option types defined in [RFC3542].

Listing 5-1 shows the standard definition of data structures for ND message headers. Since every ND message is an ICMPv6 message, all the data structures begin with a member of the `icmp6_hdr{}` structure (Section 4.5.2). For ND messages that have a larger fixed header than the ICMPv6 header, specific members are defined within the corresponding structure. One example is the Reachable Time field of the Router Advertisement message, which is identified by the `nd_ra_reachable` member. ND-specific message fields encoded in the common ICMPv6 header part are often accessed via shortcut macros. For example, the `nd_ra_curhoplimit` member of the `nd_router_advert{}` structure specifies the Current Hop Limit field of the Router Advertisement header.

Some protocol flag values are also provided as macro names. [RFC3542] defines the values of these macros while taking into account the byte ordering specific to the machine architecture, but in the code listing we only show the definitions for "little endian" machines, which provide the natural representation of the network byte order.

The definitions are generally straightforward representation of the message structures shown in Section 5.6, and we do not explain each of them in detail.

TABLE 5-10

Name	Type	Description
ND_ROUTER_SOLICIT	133	Router Solicitation
ND_ROUTER_ADVERT	134	Router Advertisement
ND_NEIGHBOR_SOLICIT	135	Neighbor Solicitation
ND_NEIGHBOR_ADVERT	136	Neighbor Advertisement
ND_REDIRECT	137	Redirect

ND type names.

TABLE 5-11

Name	Type	Description
ND_OPT_SOURCE_LINKADDR	1	Source Link-Layer Address option
ND_OPT_TARGET_LINKADDR	2	Target Link-Layer Address option
ND_OPT_PREFIX_INFORMATION	3	Prefix Information option
ND_OPT_REDIRECTED_HEADER	4	Redirected Header option
ND_OPT_MTU	5	MTU option

ND option names.

Listing 5-1

```
313    struct nd_router_solicit {        /* router solicitation */
314            struct icmp6_hdr          nd_rs_hdr;
315            /* could be followed by options */
316    } __attribute__((__packed__));
317
318    #define nd_rs_type           nd_rs_hdr.icmp6_type
319    #define nd_rs_code           nd_rs_hdr.icmp6_code
320    #define nd_rs_cksum          nd_rs_hdr.icmp6_cksum
321    #define nd_rs_reserved       nd_rs_hdr.icmp6_data32[0]
322
323    struct nd_router_advert {         /* router advertisement */
324            struct icmp6_hdr          nd_ra_hdr;
325            u_int32_t                 nd_ra_reachable;         /* reachable time */
326            u_int32_t                 nd_ra_retransmit;        /* retransmit timer */
327            /* could be followed by options */
328    } __attribute__((__packed__));
329
330    #define nd_ra_type              nd_ra_hdr.icmp6_type
331    #define nd_ra_code              nd_ra_hdr.icmp6_code
332    #define nd_ra_cksum             nd_ra_hdr.icmp6_cksum
333    #define nd_ra_curhoplimit       nd_ra_hdr.icmp6_data8[0]
334    #define nd_ra_flags_reserved    nd_ra_hdr.icmp6_data8[1]
...
352    struct nd_neighbor_solicit {      /* neighbor solicitation */
353            struct icmp6_hdr          nd_ns_hdr;
354            struct in6_addr           nd_ns_target;   /*target address */
355            /* could be followed by options */
356    } __attribute__((__packed__));
357
358    #define nd_ns_type              nd_ns_hdr.icmp6_type
359    #define nd_ns_code              nd_ns_hdr.icmp6_code
360    #define nd_ns_cksum             nd_ns_hdr.icmp6_cksum
361    #define nd_ns_reserved          nd_ns_hdr.icmp6_data32[0]
362
363    struct nd_neighbor_advert {       /* neighbor advertisement */
364            struct icmp6_hdr          nd_na_hdr;
365            struct in6_addr           nd_na_target;   /* target address */
366            /* could be followed by options */
367    } __attribute__((__packed__));
368
369    #define nd_na_type              nd_na_hdr.icmp6_type
370    #define nd_na_code              nd_na_hdr.icmp6_code
371    #define nd_na_cksum             nd_na_hdr.icmp6_cksum
372    #define nd_na_flags_reserved    nd_na_hdr.icmp6_data32[0]

374    #define ND_NA_FLAG_ROUTER            0x80000000
375    #define ND_NA_FLAG_SOLICITED         0x40000000
376    #define ND_NA_FLAG_OVERRIDE          0x20000000

385    struct nd_redirect {              /* redirect */
386            struct icmp6_hdr          nd_rd_hdr;
387            struct in6_addr           nd_rd_target;   /* target address */
388            struct in6_addr           nd_rd_dst;      /* destination address */
389            /* could be followed by options */
390    } __attribute__((__packed__));
391
392    #define nd_rd_type              nd_rd_hdr.icmp6_type
393    #define nd_rd_code              nd_rd_hdr.icmp6_code
394    #define nd_rd_cksum             nd_rd_hdr.icmp6_cksum
395    #define nd_rd_reserved          nd_rd_hdr.icmp6_data32[0]
```

Listing 5-2 shows the standard definition of data structures for ND option headers. Again, the definitions are straightforward translation of the option format shown in Section 5.7.

Listing 5-2
——— icmp6.h

```
462   struct nd_opt_hdr {                /* Neighbor discovery option header */
463           u_int8_t        nd_opt_type;
464           u_int8_t        nd_opt_len;
465           /* followed by option specific data*/
466   } __attribute__((__packed__));
 ....
480   struct nd_opt_prefix_info {      /* prefix information */
481           u_int8_t        nd_opt_pi_type;
482           u_int8_t        nd_opt_pi_len;
483           u_int8_t        nd_opt_pi_prefix_len;
484           u_int8_t        nd_opt_pi_flags_reserved;
485           u_int32_t       nd_opt_pi_valid_time;
486           u_int32_t       nd_opt_pi_preferred_time;
487           u_int32_t       nd_opt_pi_reserved2;
488           struct in6_addr nd_opt_pi_prefix;
489   } __attribute__((__packed__));
490
491   #define ND_OPT_PI_FLAG_ONLINK          0x80
492   #define ND_OPT_PI_FLAG_AUTO            0x40
494
495   struct nd_opt_rd_hdr {            /* redirected header */
496           u_int8_t        nd_opt_rh_type;
497           u_int8_t        nd_opt_rh_len;
498           u_int16_t       nd_opt_rh_reserved1;
499           u_int32_t       nd_opt_rh_reserved2;
500           /* followed by IP header and data */
501   } __attribute__((__packed__));
502
503   struct nd_opt_mtu {               /* MTU option */
504           u_int8_t        nd_opt_mtu_type;
505           u_int8_t        nd_opt_mtu_len;
506           u_int16_t       nd_opt_mtu_reserved;
507           u_int32_t       nd_opt_mtu_mtu;
508   } __attribute__((__packed__));
```
——— icmp6.h

5.13.2   Neighbor Cache—`llinfo_nd6{}` Structure

The `llinfo_nd6{}` structure is referred to as the Neighbor Cache entry introduced in Section 5.8.

Listing 5-3
——— nd6.h

```
47  struct llinfo_nd6 {
48          struct  llinfo_nd6 *ln_next;
49          struct  llinfo_nd6 *ln_prev;
50          struct  rtentry *ln_rt;
51          struct  mbuf *ln_hold;  /* last packet until resolved/timeout */
52          long    ln_asked;       /* number of queries already sent for this addr */
53          u_long  ln_expire;      /* lifetime for NDP state transition */
54          short   ln_state;       /* reachability state */
55          short   ln_router;      /* 2^0: ND6 router bit */
56          int     ln_byhint;      /* # of times we made it reachable by UL hint */
57  };
```
——— nd6.h

The Neighbor Cache entries for this interface are doubly linked through the `ln_next` and `ln_prev` fields. `ln_hold` holds the outgoing packet while address resolution takes place. The `ln_rt` route entry (`rtentry{}`) contains the next-hop information. A route entry with the `RTF_LLINFO` flag set refers to a route entry containing the link-layer address of either the next-hop router or the final destination. A route entry with the `RTF_GATEWAY` flag set refers to an indirect destination through the gateway identified by `rt_gateway` field of the route entry. The route entry flag bits are defined in `<net/route.h>`. `ln_asked` maintains the number of Neighbor Solicitations that have been sent to this neighbor. The `ln_expire` field holds the expiration time when the state of the Neighbor Cache will change. The `ln_router` flag is the *IsRouter* flag, which indicates whether the neighbor is a router. The `ln_byhint` field tracks the number of times this neighbor is marked as reachable as a result of input from upper layer protocols.

The `ln_state` member identifies the state of the cache entry (see Section 5.9). Table 5-12 shows possible values of `ln_state`. These are straightforward representation of the protocol states except for `ND6_LLINFO_NOSTATE`. `ND6_LLINFO_NOSTATE` is an implementation-specific temporary state for a Neighbor Cache entry that is not yet used in the ND protocol operation (see Listing 5-43).

The ordering of the integer state values shown in the table gives a simple way to test whether the neighbor is "probably reachable," that is, its state is not INCOMPLETE (or NOSTATE) (see Section 5.12.3). The following macro is defined for this test and will be often used in the code described in this chapter:

```
#define ND6_IS_LLINFO_PROBREACH(n) ((n)->ln_state > ND6_LLINFO_INCOMPLETE)
```

Figure 5-26 illustrates the relation between structure `rtentry{}` and structure `llinfo_nd6{}`. Since this is a complex relationship involving various structures, the fields of the structures are simplified and some structure values are omitted. The neighbor cache state value is represented by its first letter (for example, "S" means `ND6_LLINFO_STALE`).

Figure 5-26 represents a node that assigns an IPv6 link-local address `fe80::205:5eff:fe15:ec32` on interface fxp0. There are two other neighbors identified by link-local addresses: `fe80::202:b3ff:fe07:a545` and `fe80::20c:29ff:fe33:fdb3`. The latter announces itself as a Router in Neighbor Advertisement messages.

TABLE 5-12

Name	*Value*	*Description*
ND6_LLINFO_INCOMPLETE	0	INCOMPLETE
ND6_LLINFO_REACHABLE	1	REACHABLE
ND6_LLINFO_STALE	2	STALE
ND6_LLINFO_DELAY	3	DELAY
ND6_LLINFO_PROBE	4	PROBE
ND6_LLINFO_NOSTATE	−1	Not in operation

Neighbor Cache State values.

FIGURE 5-26

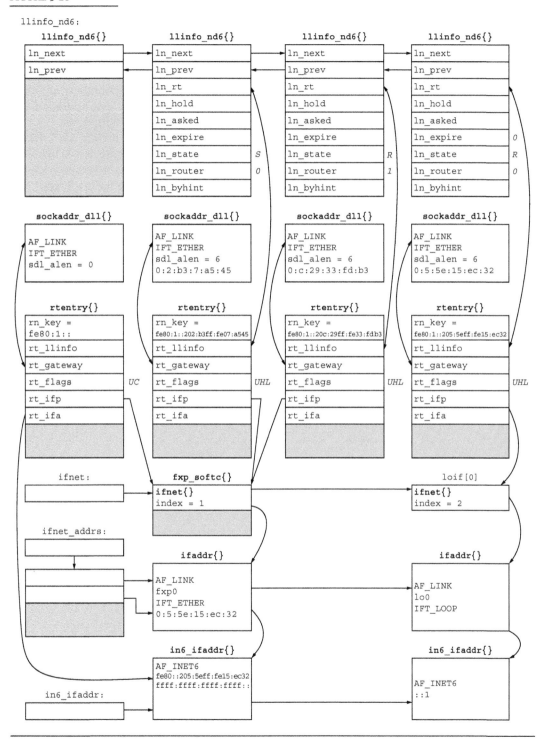

rtentry{} and llinfo_nd6{}.

Every Neighbor Cache entry is associated with an `rtentry{}` structure containing its link-layer address. The route entries have the "L" (RTF_LLINFO) flag set since they have the associated link-layer information.

The third entry is for the node's own address. It is special in that it has zero expiration time, meaning the entry is permanent, that is, never expires (see Listing 5-23). Another important point is that the outgoing interface (`rt_ifp`) for sending packets toward this address is the loopback interface because the packets must be looped back to the originating node.

It should also be noted that all link-local addresses in the figure embed the link zone IDs in the IPv6 addresses. As explained in Section 2.9.3, IPv6 scoped addresses that are stored in kernel data structures, such as in the routing table and the interface address list need to be represented this way. In this example the embedded link IDs are 1, which is the interface index of fxp0. This is not a coincidence, since the KAME implementation assumes a one-to-one mapping between links and interfaces and uses interface indices as link IDs.

The **ndp** command with the `-a` command line option displaces Neighbor Cache entries. Its output, that corresponds to Figure 5-26, would be as follows:

```
% ndp -an
Neighbor                          Linklayer Address  Netif Expire      St Flgs Prbs
fe80::202:b3ff:fe07:a545%fxp0     0:2:b3:7:a5:45     fxp0  23h44m53s S
fe80::20c:29ff:fe33:fdb3%fxp0     0:c:29:33:fd:b3    fxp0  3s           R  R
fe80::205:5eff:fe15:ec32%fxp0     0:5:5e:15:ec:32    fxp0  permanent  R
...
```

Note that link-local addresses are represented in the extended format for scoped addresses (Section 2.4.3) rather than embedding link IDs within the address. This is because the **ndp** program converts the address so that the `sin6_scope_id` field of the corresponding `sockaddr_in6{}` structure is set properly (see Figure 2.12).

5.13.3   Operational Variables—`nd_ifinfo{}` Structure

The `nd_ifinfo{}` structure is allocated in the domain-specific processing code for each interface as illustrated in Figure 5-27.

Listing 5-4
                                                                                                    ———nd6.h
```
82      struct nd_ifinfo{
83              u_int32_t linkmtu;                /* LinkMTU */
84              u_int32_t maxmtu;                 /* Upper bound of LinkMTU */
85              u_int32_t basereachable;          /* BaseReachableTime */
86              u_int32_t reachable;              /* Reachable Time */
87              u_int32_t retrans;                /* Retrans Timer */
88              u_int32_t flags;                  /* Flags */
89              int recalctm;                     /* BaseReacable re-calculation timer */
90              u_int8_t chlim;                   /* CurHopLimit */
91              u_int8_t initialized; /* Flag to see the entry is initialized */
92              /* the following 3 members are for privacy extension for addrconf */
93              u_int8_t randomseed0[8]; /* upper 64 bits of MD5 digest */
94              u_int8_t randomseed1[8]; /* lower 64 bits (usually the EUI64 IFID) */
95              u_int8_t randomid[8];    /* current random ID */
96      };
```
                                                                                                    ———nd6.h

FIGURE 5-27

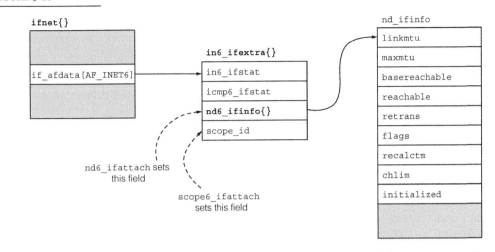

Per interface nd_ifonfo{} structure.

The fields linkmtu, basereachable, reachable, retrans, and chlim correspond to the Host operational variables presented in Table 5-7. Even though these variables are called host specific in Section 5.12, these variables also apply to routers for ND-related operations in practice because applications that run on routers can originate traffic.

The recalctm timer ensures the reachable time is refreshed when there are no Router Advertisement packets (i.e., there are no routers on the link) or received Router Advertisement packets have not changed basereachable. The next fields are related to generating randomized interface identifiers for the privacy extensions to Stateless Address Autoconfiguration. We do not discuss details of these fields.

5.13.4   Default Router—nd_defrouter{} Structure

The Default Router List maintains a list of routers to which packets may be directed to off-link destinations. The Default Router List is constructed from information extracted from Router Advertisement messages. Each entry maintains per-router information and is represented by the nd_defrouter{} structure.

Listing 5-5
_____nd6.h

```
251    TAILQ_HEAD(nd_drhead, nd_defrouter);
252    struct  nd_defrouter {
253            TAILQ_ENTRY(nd_defrouter) dr_entry;
254            struct  sockaddr_in6 rtaddr;
255            u_char  flags;          /* flags on RA message */
256            u_short rtlifetime;
257            u_long  expire;
258            u_long  advint;         /* Mobile IPv6 addition (milliseconds) */
259            u_long  advint_expire;  /* Mobile IPv6 addition */
260            int     advints_lost;   /* Mobile IPv6 addition */
261            struct  ifnet *ifp;
```

```
262              int       installed;        /* is installed into kernel routing table */
263     };
264
```

The default routers are linked by `dr_entry` as a tail queue. `rtaddr` contains the router address. `flags` contains the flags field from the Router Advertisement message. `rtlifetime` is the router lifetime. The `expire` field is a counter down timer. When this value reaches zero the router is removed from the Default Router List. The `ifp` field points to the interface on which the default router is learned. The `installed` field indicates the default router has been installed into the kernel routing table. This field is necessary since most BSD variants can hold only a single default in the routing table.

5.13.5 Prefix—`nd_prefix{}` Structure

The Prefix List contains on-link prefixes or prefixes that can be used for address configuration. Each Prefix list entry contains per-prefix information such as the prefix, and the (valid) lifetime of the prefix. This information is extracted from the Prefix Information option of a Router Advertisement message. The link-local prefix is an entry in this list with an infinite (valid) lifetime. The Prefix List may also contain manually configured prefixes. Each entry in the Prefix List is represented by the `nd_prefix{}` structure.

Listing 5-6

```
278     struct nd_prefix {
279             struct ifnet *ndpr_ifp;
280             LIST_ENTRY(nd_prefix) ndpr_entry;
281             struct sockaddr_in6 ndpr_prefix;        /* prefix */
282             struct in6_addr ndpr_mask; /* netmask derived from the prefix */
283
284             u_int32_t ndpr_vltime;   /* advertised valid lifetime */
285             u_int32_t ndpr_pltime;   /* advertised preferred lifetime */
286
287             time_t ndpr_expire;      /* expiration time of the prefix */
288             time_t ndpr_preferred;   /* preferred time of the prefix */
289             time_t ndpr_lastupdate; /* reception time of last advertisement */
290
291             struct prf_ra ndpr_flags;
292             u_int32_t ndpr_stateflags; /* actual state flags */
293             /* list of routers that advertise the prefix: */
294             LIST_HEAD(pr_rtrhead, nd_pfxrouter) ndpr_advtrs;
295             u_char  ndpr_plen;
296             int     ndpr_refcnt;     /* reference couter from addresses */
297     };
```

The `nd_prefix{}` structures are linked together by `ndpr_entry` as a singly-linked list. `ndpr_ifp` points to the associated interface. `ndpr_prefix` contains the prefix and `ndpr_mask` is the prefix mask derived from the prefix and the prefix length. For an advertised prefix the field `ndpr_vltime` is set with advertised valid lifetime and the field `ndpr_pltime` is set with the advertised preferred lifetime, although `ndpr_pltime` is meaningless, since a prefix does not have a notion of preferred lifetime. `ndpr_expire` and `ndpr_preferred` were only meaningful in older versions of the implementation and are effectively unused in this code. `ndpr_lastupdate` is set to the time when the Router Advertisement containing the Prefix Information option is processed. The `ndpr_flags` field contains the flag bits from the Prefix Information option. The `ndpr_stateflags` contains the current state of the prefix which can be one of the states listed in Table 5-13.

Multiple routers may have advertised the same prefix and these advertising routers are maintained in the `ndpr_advrtrs` field. `ndpr_plen` specifies the prefix length. `ndpr_refcnt` indicates the number of references held on this structure. This structure cannot be deleted until the reference count is zero.

Figure 5-28 depicts the relation between the `nd_prefix{}` and the `nd_defrouter{}` structures.

TABLE 5-13

State	Description
NDPRF_ONLINK	The prefix is on-link.
NDPRF_DETACHED	The router that advertised this prefix is off-link (see Section 5.19.5).
NDPRF_HOME	For older Mobile IPv6 code and is not used any more.

State of `nd_prefix{}`.

FIGURE 5-28

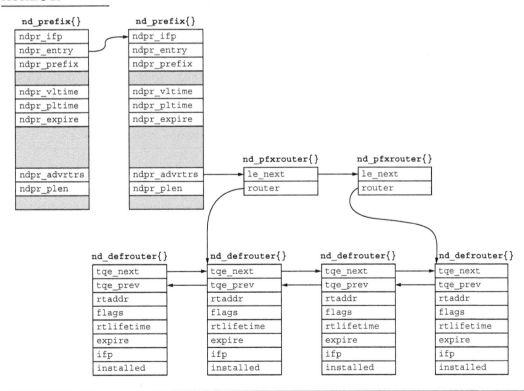

nd_prefix{} (prefix) and `nd_defrouter{}` *(advertising routers).*

The operational relations among these data structures can be best described through next-hop determination and address resolution. When performing address resolution, the Neighbor Cache is searched for the link-layer address of the next-hop address once next-hop determination completes. A Neighbor Cache entry is created for a next-hop address that does not yet exist in the Neighbor Cache. As an optimization, the result of next-hop determination is saved in the Destination Cache if an entry does not exist. Next-hop determination is unnecessary if the Destination Cache contains an entry covering the destination. When transmitting packets a node will consult its Destination Cache first before performing next-hop determination.

5.13.6 Prefix Control—`nd_prefixctl{}` Structure

The `nd_prefixctl{}` structure is used by prefix management functions. This structure is used for both input and output, that is, this structure is used by the management functions to install prefixes into the kernel; this structure is also used by the kernel to return prefix information that was retrieved from the Prefix Information option (discussed in Section 5.7.2) to the management functions.

Listing 5-7
——nd6.h
```
265     struct nd_prefixctl {
266             struct ifnet *ndpr_ifp;
267
268             /* prefix */
269             struct sockaddr_in6 ndpr_prefix;
270             u_char  ndpr_plen;
271
272             u_int32_t ndpr_vltime;   /* advertised valid lifetime */
273             u_int32_t ndpr_pltime;   /* advertised preferred lifetime */
274
275             struct prf_ra ndpr_flags;
276     };
```
——nd6.h

The `ndpr_ifp` member points to the network interface associated with the prefix. In case the prefix is configured via a Router Advertisement message, this interface is the receiving interface of the message. The `ndpr_prefix` and `ndpr_plen` members hold the prefix value and the prefix length, which correspond to the Prefix field and the Prefix Length field as shown in Figure 5-17, respectively. The `ndpr_vltime` and `ndpr_pltime` members indicate the valid lifetime and the preferred lifetime, which are the Valid Lifetime and the Preferred Lifetime fields, respectively. The `ndpr_pltime` member is actually meaningless since a prefix does not have the notion of preferred lifetime (see also the description about the `ndpr_pltime` member in Listing 5-6). `ndpr_flags` corresponds to the flags fields and keeps the value of the L flags and the A flag.

5.13.7 ND Message Options—`nd_opts{}` Structure

The `nd_opt{}` structure is used to store option values received as a part of ND messages. The received ND message is parsed by the ND option parsing functions. The parsing functions are discussed in Section 5.17.

Listing 5-8

```
368     union nd_opts {
369             struct nd_opt_hdr *nd_opt_array[13];     /* max = target address list */
370             struct {
371                     struct nd_opt_hdr *zero;
372                     struct nd_opt_hdr *src_lladdr;
373                     struct nd_opt_hdr *tgt_lladdr;
374                     struct nd_opt_prefix_info *pi_beg; /* multiple opts, start */
375                     struct nd_opt_rd_hdr *rh;
376                     struct nd_opt_mtu *mtu;
377                     struct nd_opt_hdr *six;
378                     struct nd_opt_advinterval *adv;
379                     struct nd_opt_homeagent_info *hai;
380                     struct nd_opt_hdr *src_addrlist;
381                     struct nd_opt_hdr *tgt_addrlist;
382                     struct nd_opt_hdr *search;          /* multiple opts */
383                     struct nd_opt_hdr *last;            /* multiple opts */
384                     int done;
385                     struct nd_opt_prefix_info *pi_end;/* multiple opts, end */
386             } nd_opt_each;
387     };
```

Each ND option is stored in the structure defined on lines 370–386. These options are also accessible through the nd_opt_array[] array using the options type number, since the two structures have overlapping memory space.

The zero and six members are placeholders for option types 0 and 6 and are not used. The option types begin at value 1 and option type 6 is currently undefined. Members src_lladdr and tgt_lladdr point to the Source Link-Layer Address option and the Target Link-Layer Address option discussed in Section 5.7.1. Members pi_beg points to the beginning of the Prefix Information option (Section 5.7.2). If there are multiple Prefix Information options in a single ND message, the pi_end member points to the last Prefix Information option (if there is only one Prefix Information option pi_beg and pi_end will point to the same address). Member rh points to the Redirected Header option (Section 5.7.3). Members adv and hai are Advertisement Interval option and Home Agent Information option which are used by Mobile IPv6. Mobile IPv6 is discussed in Chapter 5 of *IPv6 Advanced Protocols Implementation*. src_addrlist and tgt_addrlist are the Source/Target Address List options used by the Inverse Neighbor Discovery Protocol [RFC3122]. The Inverse Neighbor Discovery Protocol is outside the scope of this book. search is used to point to the next option when function nd6_option() picks options sequentially. last points to the last option in the structure and is used to check that option processing has been completed. Member done is set when all options have been parsed and the instance of nd6_opts{} has been constructed correctly.

5.13.8   DAD Queue Entry—dadq{} Structure

The DAD procedure keeps track of its progress on each address that is being verified by DAD via a set of processing parameters. These Parameters are maintained in a dadq{} structure for each address.

Listing 5-9

```
1224    TAILQ_HEAD(dadq_head, dadq);
1225    struct dadq {
1226            TAILQ_ENTRY(dadq) dad_list;
```

```
1227            struct ifaddr *dad_ifa;
1228            int dad_count;          /* max NS to send */
1229            int dad_ns_tcount;      /* # of trials to send NS */
1230            int dad_ns_ocount;      /* NS sent so far */
1231            int dad_ns_icount;
1232            int dad_na_icount;
    ....
1234            struct callout dad_timer_ch;
    ....
1238    };
```
                                                            ──────────nd6_nbr.c

dad_list links the list of instances of the dadq{} structure. dad_ifa points to the interface address structure that is tentatively assigned to the interface. dad_count is the number of Neighbor Solicitation messages to be sent by DAD before the address is confirmed for normal use. The value of dad_count is initialized by the ip6_dad_count global variable, whose default value is 1. This global variable is configurable via the **sysctl** variable net.inet6.ip6.dad_count. dad_tcount and dad_ocount are the number of attempts to send Neighbor Solicitation messages and the number of messages sent successfully. dad_ns_icount and dad_na_icount are the number of received Neighbor Solicitation messages and Neighbor Advertisement messages in response to the Neighbor Solicitation messages. The DAD procedure is discussed in Section 5.10.2; its implementation will be described in Section 5.21.

The system-wide DAD queue is comprised of all the dadq{} structures and is accessible through the global variable dadq.

5.13.9   IPv6 Address—`in6_ifaddr{}` Structure

Each IPv6 address has its state and is associated with valid and preferred lifetimes (Section 5.10.1). Section 2.10.1 showed the in6_ifaddr{} structure encoding the state and lifetime information in the IPv6 interface address structure.

5.13.10   Destination Cache

In the KAME implementation, an IPv6 destination cache entry is implemented implicitly as a host route entry, which is an instance of the rtentry{} structure. In fact, a host route entry stores the link-layer address of the next-hop address for a given destination address, which is exactly what a destination cache entry is expected to contain.

Another good reason for using a route entry as destination cache is that it can contain a path MTU for the destination. KAME's implementation indeed stores the path MTU information in a route entry as explained in Section 4.7.1.

Since rtentry{} is not a specially designed data structure for the KAME implementation but is provided in BSD derived systems in general, we do not describe the details of the structure in this chapter.

5.13.11   Operation Constants

The ND protocol specification defines a set of constants that apply to both host and router operations. The uses of these constants are discussed throughout the remaining sections of this chapter. These constants are listed in Table 5-14 as a reference for later discussions.

TABLE 5-14

Variable	Value
MAX_MULTICAST_SOLICIT	3 transmissions
MAX_UNICAST_SOLICIT	3 transmissions
MAX_ANYCAST_DELAY_TIME	1 s
MAX_NEIGHBOR_ADVERTISEMENT	3 transmissions
REACHABLE_TIME	30,000 ms
RETRANS_TIMER	1000 ms
DELAY_FIRST_PROBE_TIME	5 s
MIN_RANDOM_FACTOR	0.5
MAX_RANDOM_FACTOR	1.5

Operation constants.

5.14 Initialization Functions

5.14.1 nd6_init() Function

The nd6_init() function is called when the system boots up and is called only once to initialize the system-wide global variables that are essential to the ND protocol operation.

Listing 5-10

nd6.c

```
185     void
186     nd6_init()
187     {
188             static int nd6_init_done = 0;
189             int i;
190
191             if (nd6_init_done) {
192                     log(LOG_NOTICE, "nd6_init called more than once(ignored)\n");
193                     return;
194             }
195
196             all1_sa.sin6_family = AF_INET6;
197             all1_sa.sin6_len = sizeof(struct sockaddr_in6);
198             for (i = 0; i < sizeof(all1_sa.sin6_addr); i++)
199                     all1_sa.sin6_addr.s6_addr[i] = 0xff;
200
201             /* initialization of the default router list */
202             TAILQ_INIT(&nd_defrouter);
```

nd6.c

191–202 The static variable all1_sa is initialized to all one bits and serves as the mask argument when calling rtrequest() to install host routes. The Default Router List nd_defrouter is a double-linked list and is initialized here. The TAILQ-related definitions are provided in the header file <sys/queue.h>. In theory each interface maintains a Default Router List, but the KAME implementation uses this global variable to maintain all of the known default routers from all of the interfaces in one place.

Listing 5-11

```
                                                                    nd6.c
204             nd6_init_done = 1;
205
206             /* start timer */
208             callout_reset(&nd6_slowtimo_ch, ND6_SLOWTIMER_INTERVAL * hz,
209                 nd6_slowtimo, NULL);
    ....
216      }
                                                                    nd6.c
```

204–216 The "slow" timer for ND protocol operation is initialized. It expires every hour with a
call to the callback function nd6_slowtimo(), which recomputes *BaseReachableTime*
for each interface if necessary. Variable nd6_init_done is set to indicate the successful
initialization of the ND module and to guard against multiple invocations (which would
be a bug) of this function.

5.14.2 nd6_ifattach() Function

The nd6_ifattach() function is called when the AF_INET6 protocol domain is initialized for
an interface. The nd6_ifattach() function allocates a per interface nd_ifinfo{} structure
and attaches this structure to the interface.

Listing 5-12

```
                                                                    nd6.c
218     struct nd_ifinfo *
219     nd6_ifattach(ifp)
220             struct ifnet *ifp;
221     {
222             struct nd_ifinfo *nd;
223
224             nd = (struct nd_ifinfo *)malloc(sizeof(*nd), M_IP6NDP, M_WAITOK);
225             bzero(nd, sizeof(*nd));
226
227             nd->initialized = 1;
228
229             nd->chlim = IPV6_DEFHLIM;
230             nd->basereachable = REACHABLE_TIME;
231             nd->reachable = ND_COMPUTE_RTIME(nd->basereachable);
232             nd->retrans = RETRANS_TIMER;
233             /*
234              * Note that the default value of ip6_accept_rtadv is 0, which means
235              * we won't accept RAs by default even if we set ND6_IFF_ACCEPT_RTADV
236              * here.
237              */
238             nd->flags = (ND6_IFF_PERFORMNUD | ND6_IFF_ACCEPT_RTADV);
239
240             /* XXX: we cannot call nd6_setmtu since ifp is not fully initialized */
241             nd6_setmtu0(ifp, nd);
242
243             return nd;
244     }
                                                                    nd6.c
```

218–244 nd6_ifattach() allocates an nd_ifinfo{} structure, which is assigned to the
nd_ifinfo field of the in6_ifextra{} structure. The newly allocated nd_ifinfo{}
structure maintains a set of ND operational variables for that given interface, which are
described in Table 5-7. These per interface ND variables are initialized to the default values
that are defined in the specification.

By initializing the `flags` field to (`ND6_IFF_PERFORMNUD |
ND6_IFF_ACCEPT_RTADV`), the default policy is set to perform NUD algorithm on the
interface and allow the interface to accept Router Advertisement packets. The global
variable `ip6_accept_rtadv` is checked first upon receiving a Router Advertisement
packet. The packet is discarded if `ip6_accept_rtadv` is set to 0 regardless of whether
`ND6_IFF_ACCEPT_RTADV` is set on the receiving interface.

The inter data structure relations are depicted in Figure 5-27. `in6_ifextra` is allocated in `if_attachdomain1()` function.

`nd6_setmtu0()` initializes the `maxmtu` field of the `nd_info{}` structure to the
interface MTU for some types of interfaces including Ethernet.

5.15 Neighbor Cache Management Functions

A node maintains the information about its neighbor in the Neighbor Cache. This section
describes a set of utilities functions that perform the tasks of maintaining the Neighbor Cache in
an IPv6 node. These functions are called to create, delete, and update a Neighbor Cache entry.

5.15.1 `nd6_rtrequest()` Function

Function `nd6_rtrequest()` is considered the back-end function that handles the requests to
create and delete Neighbor Cache entries. The implementation of `nd6_rtrquest()` is derived
from the IPv4 function `arp_rtrequest()` that handles requests to create and delete ARP
entries. This function is set in the `ifa_rtrequest` field of the `ifaddr{}` structure, which is
created for each IPv6 address that is assigned to an interface. `nd6_rtrequest()` is invoked
in function `rtrequest1()`.

The Neighbor Cache is maintained as part of the kernel routing table. It could be implemented as a separate data structure, but KAME adopted the same design as the IPv4 ARP
implementation. In fact, since BSD's routing table architecture has protocol-independent framework to handle link-layer information in the routing table such as route cloning (see below),
it is advantageous to use the existing general framework rather than designing a dedicated
implementation architecture separately.

Implementing the cache in the routing table also means the creation of a Neighbor Cache
entry is part of a route entry creation. There are many situations that can trigger the creation of
a Neighbor Cache entry. For example, assigning a new IPv6 address to an interface creates a
loopback route containing the link-layer address of that interface; generating traffic to on-link
neighbors; and creating a Neighbor Cache for a neighbor as the result of receiving a router
Redirect message. Also, system management entity can create static Neighbor Cache entries
using the **ndp** program.

The FreeBSD network implementation has a route cloning concept that creates more specific routes from a less specific route. The `RTF_CLONING` flag is designed specifically for this
purpose. Normally an interface route is created for a prefix when an address of that prefix
is assigned to an interface. Consider the following example, where a network administrator
assigns an IPv6 address to an interface:

```
# ifconfig ne0 inet6 2001:db8:1111::1234 prefixlen 64
```

Figure 5-29 depicts the call-graph triggered by the above **ifconfig** command.

FIGURE 5-29

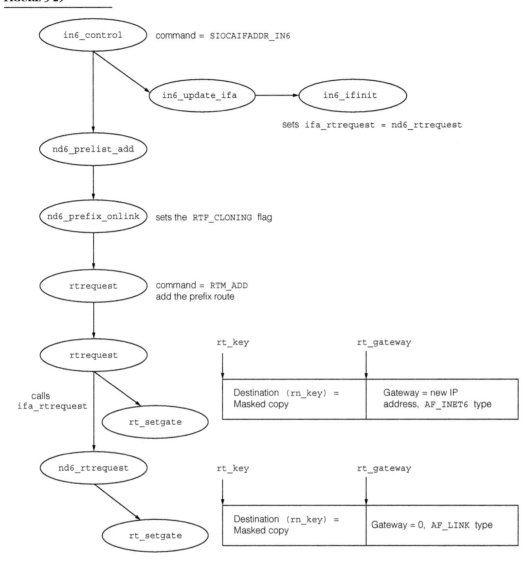

IPv6 interface route creation call-graph.

The **ifconfig** command translates into a call into in6_control() with the SIOCAIFADDR_IN6 command. As part of the SIOCAIFADDR_IN6 command processing, function in6_update_ifa() is called to create a new in6_ifaddr{} structure for the address (see Section 2.14.2). The ifa_rtrequest field of the ifaddr{} structure within in6_ifaddr{} is set to the function nd6_rtrequest(). Once the new address structure has been created and attached to the interface, nd6_prelist_add() is called to add the associated prefix into the system. nd6_prelist_add() subsequently calls nd6_prefix_onlink() to add the interface direct route for the prefix into the kernel routing table.

When nd6_prefix_onlink() calls rtrequest(), the gateway parameter is set to the newly added interface address. The flags parameter has the RTF_CLONING flag set for the prefix route. When traffic is sent to an on-link destination of that prefix, the interface direct route will be chosen from the routing table. The RTF_CLONING flag will trigger route cloning, which will create a host route for the given destination using information retrieved from the interface direct route. The interface direct route is also set as the rt_parent of the newly created host route.

When rtrequest1() calls rt_setgate(), storage is allocated for the destination and gateway in one contiguous block of memory, which are referenced by rt_key and rt_gateway, respectively. The size of the gateway is set to the size of sockaddr_in6{}. The nd6_rtrequest() is called just before rtrequest1() finishes processing. nd6_rtrequest() calls rt_setgate() to change the storage for rt_gateway from sockaddr_in6{} to sockaddr_dl{} of the AF_LINK address family type. The remaining content of sockaddr_dl{} is zero. This data structure replacement enables the proper storage allocation for the link-layer address of the on-link destination when creating cloned routes, as we will show shortly.

Returning to the example, once the address 2001:db8:1111::1234 is configured on the interface ne0, issuing the **ping6** command will result in the RTF_RESOLVE command being sent to function rtrequest1().

```
% ping6 2001:db8:1111::abcd
```

A host route with destination 2001:db8:111::abcd is created. The gateway address is a blank sockaddr_dl{} when rtrequest1() calls rt_setgate(). The blank sockaddr_dl{} structure serves as a placeholder for memory allocation when performing route cloning. The ND address resolution process stores the link-layer address of the destination into the rt_gateway field that is of the AF_LINK type as shown in Figure 5-30.

This newly added host route also has the RTF_LLINFO flag set indicating it is a Neighbor Cache entry.

We now describe the nd6_rtrequest() function next.

FIGURE 5-30 ⎯⎯⎯⎯

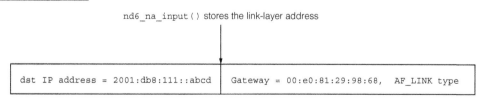

Neighbor cache entry as a host route.

Listing 5-13

───nd6.c
```
1212     void
....
1214     nd6_rtrequest(req, rt, info)
1215             int     req;
1216             struct rtentry *rt;
1217             struct rt_addrinfo *info; /* xxx unused */
....
1224     {
1225             struct sockaddr *gate = rt->rt_gateway;
1226             struct llinfo_nd6 *ln = (struct llinfo_nd6 *)rt->rt_llinfo;
1227             static struct sockaddr_dl null_sdl = {sizeof(null_sdl), AF_LINK};
1228             struct ifnet *ifp = rt->rt_ifp;
1229             struct ifaddr *ifa;
....
1233             int mine = 0;
```
───nd6.c

1214 Function parameter `req` contains the route command that was issued to `rtrequest1()`. Parameter `rt` points to the route entry associated with that command. For example, `rt` points to the newly created entry if `req` is the RTM_ADD or RTM_RESOLVE command. `rt` points to an existing entry in the routing table if `req` is the RTM_DELETE command.

Listing 5-14

───nd6.c
```
1235             if ((rt->rt_flags & RTF_GATEWAY) != 0)
1236                     return;
```
───nd6.c

1235–1236 `nd6_rtrequest()` returns without performing any action for indirect routes (i.e., route entry with the RTF_GATEWAY flag set). The reason is simple: Neighbor Cache applies only to directly connected neighbors and `nd6_rtrequest()` handles Neighbor Cache-related requests.

Listing 5-15

───nd6.c
```
1238             if (nd6_need_cache(ifp) == 0 && (rt->rt_flags & RTF_HOST) == 0) {
1239                     /*
1240                      * This is probably an interface direct route for a link
1241                      * which does not need neighbor caches (e.g. fe80::%lo0/64).
1242                      * We do not need special treatment below for such a route.
1243                      * Moreover, the RTF_LLINFO flag which would be set below
1244                      * would annoy the ndp(8) command.
1245                      */
1246                     return;
1247             }
```
───nd6.c

1238–1246 This function returns without performing any actions for interface direct routes that do not have link-layer addresses. The condition `(nd6_need_cache(ifp) == 0)` implies Neighbor Cache entries are not created on such an interface. The condition `((rt->rt_flags & RTF_HOST) == 0)` implies the route is an interface direct route.

Neighbor Caches do not exist over these types of interfaces. For example, the link-local prefix configured on the loopback interface has the following output when displayed using the **netstat -r** command.

```
fe80::%lo0/64          fe80::1%lo0              Uc              lo0
```

In other words, such types of interface routes do not to have to have storage allocated for the link-layer address. The processing is thus terminated here.

Listing 5-16

———nd6.c
```
1249            if (req == RTM_RESOLVE &&
1250                (nd6_need_cache(ifp) == 0 || /* stf case */
1251                 !nd6_is_addr_neighbor((struct sockaddr_in6 *)rt_key(rt), ifp))) {
1252                    /*
1253                     * FreeBSD and BSD/OS often make a cloned host route based
1254                     * on a less-specific route (e.g. the default route).
1255                     * If the less specific route does not have a "gateway"
1256                     * (this is the case when the route just goes to a p2p or an
1257                     * stf interface), we'll mistakenly make a neighbor cache for
1258                     * the host route, and will see strange neighbor solicitation
1259                     * for the corresponding destination.  In order to avoid the
1260                     * confusion, we check if the destination of the route is
1261                     * a neighbor in terms of neighbor discovery, and stop the
1262                     * process if not.  Additionally, we remove the LLINFO flag
1263                     * so that ndp(8) will not try to get the neighbor information
1264                     * of the destination.
1265                     */
1266                    rt->rt_flags &= ~RTF_LLINFO;
1267                    return;
1268            }
```
———nd6.c

1249–1268 As commented, FreeBSD makes cloned host routes more aggressively than other systems due to the mechanism called "cloning required by the protocol." If the parent route of such a host route is simply directed to an interface (which is typically a point-to-point interface) without any layer-3 gateway address, the destination of the route may not be a neighbor and should not have a Neighbor Cache entry. This code block prevents this scenario. In this case the RTF_LLINFO flag is cleared from the route entry so that the **ndp** command will not be confused. The function returns without further processing.

Listing 5-17

———nd6.c
```
1270            switch (req) {
1271            case RTM_ADD:
1272                    /*
1273                     * There is no backward compatibility :)
1274                     *
1275                     * if ((rt->rt_flags & RTF_HOST) == 0 &&
1276                     *     SIN(rt_mask(rt))->sin_addr.s_addr != 0xffffffff)
1277                     *         rt->rt_flags |= RTF_CLONING;
1278                     */
1279                    if (rt->rt_flags & (RTF_CLONING | RTF_LLINFO)) {
1280                            /*
1281                             * Case 1: This route should come from
```

```
1282                              * a route to interface.  RTF_LLINFO flag is set
1283                              * for a host route whose destination should be
1284                              * treated as on-link.
1285                              */
1286                             rt_setgate(rt, rt_key(rt),
1287                                         (struct sockaddr *)&null_sdl);
1288                             gate = rt->rt_gateway;
1289                             SDL(gate)->sdl_type = ifp->if_type;
1290                             SDL(gate)->sdl_index = ifp->if_index;
1291                             if (ln)
1292                                     ln->ln_expire = time_second;
1293     #if 1
1294                             if (ln && ln->ln_expire == 0) {
1295                                     /* kludge for desktops */
      ....
1300                                     ln->ln_expire = 1;
1301                             }
1302     #endif
1303                             if ((rt->rt_flags & RTF_CLONING) != 0)
1304                                     break;
1305                     }
```
                                                                 ————nd6.c

1279 The condition of the `if` statement at line 1279 holds when this route is an interface direct route (Figure 5-29), where the `RTF_CLONING` flag is set, or the destination should be treated as a neighbor by the protocol specification, where the `RTF_LLINFO` flag is set. The latter case happens, for example, upon receiving a Redirect message indicating the destination is a neighbor or when the node receives an ND packet whose source is not considered as on-link at this point. The `nd6_lookup()` function creates such a route (see Listing 5-43).

1280–1292 The call to function `rt_setgate()` with the gateway being a `sockaddr_dl{}` structure effectively allocates a new `sockaddr_dl{}` structure for a cloned route.

1294–1301 If the route entry happens to have the link-layer information `ln` (which should be rare), the expiration time (`ln_expire`) of the entry is initialized to the current system time. If it is 0, it means the interface is being configured even if the system time is not yet initialized. Since a value of 0 has the special semantics of non expiry, it is reset to 1 as an ad hoc workaround.

1303–1304 No further processing is necessary if the `RTF_CLONING` flag is set, since it means this entry is an interface-direct route and does not need processing specific to Neighbor Cache entries.

Listing 5-18
                                                                 ————nd6.c
```
1306                     /*
1307                      * In IPv4 code, we try to annonuce new RTF_ANNOUNCE entry here.
1308                      * We don't do that here since llinfo is not ready yet.
1309                      *
1310                      * There are also couple of other things to be discussed:
1311                      * - unsolicited NA code needs improvement beforehand
1312                      * - RFC2461 says we MAY send multicast unsolicited NA
1313                      *   (7.2.6 paragraph 4), however, it also says that we
1314                      *   SHOULD provide a mechanism to prevent multicast NA storm.
1315                      *   we don't have anything like it right now.
1316                      *   note that the mechanism needs a mutual agreement
1317                      *   between proxies, which means that we need to implement
```

```
1318                         *    a new protocol, or a new kludge.
1319                         * - from RFC2461 6.2.4, host MUST NOT send an unsolicited NA.
1320                         *   we need to check ip6forwarding before sending it.
1321                         *   (or should we allow proxy ND configuration only for
1322                         *   routers?  there's no mention about proxy ND from hosts)
1323                         */
1324     #if 0
1325                         /* XXX it does not work */
1326                         if (rt->rt_flags & RTF_ANNOUNCE)
1327                                 nd6_na_output(ifp,
1328                                     &SIN6(rt_key(rt))->sin6_addr,
1329                                     &SIN6(rt_key(rt))->sin6_addr,
1330                                     ip6_forwarding ? ND_NA_FLAG_ROUTER : 0,
1331                                     1, NULL);
1332     #endif
```
── nd6.c

1324–1332 This part of the code was derived from the IPv4 ARP proxy implementation (in the
`arp_rtrequest()` function) and was intended to send an unsolicited Neighbor Advertisement when a Neighbor Cache entry for the proxy target is manually configured with
the `RTF_ANNOUNCE` flag. The code was later disabled as shown in the listing (for reasons
unknown to the authors). The code comment seems to indicate the reason: Even though
the `llinfo_nd6{}` structure has not been allocated for the route, but `nd6_output()`
actually does not need this structure (see Section 5.22.2). Yet it should be valid to not
send the Neighbor Advertisement immediately at this point since [RFC2461] requires a
small delay if multiple unsolicited Neighbor Advertisements are going to be sent. The
current code does not implement the requirement. Note that the unsolicited Neighbor
Advertisement messages are optional, which means disabling this block of code does not
necessarily affect specification conformance.

> *Note*: The last bullet of the code comment is misleading: Section 6.2.4 of [RFC2461] defines
> the behavior of unsolicited Router Advertisements, not Neighbor Advertisements. The original
> developer was probably confused here.

Listing 5-19
── nd6.c

```
1333                     /* FALLTHROUGH */
1334             case RTM_RESOLVE:
1335                     if ((ifp->if_flags & (IFF_POINTOPOINT | IFF_LOOPBACK)) == 0) {
1336                             /*
1337                              * Address resolution isn't necessary for a point to
1338                              * point link, so we can skip this test for a p2p link.
1339                              */
1340                             if (gate->sa_family != AF_LINK ||
1341                                 gate->sa_len < sizeof(null_sdl)) {
1342                                     log(LOG_DEBUG,
1343                                         "nd6_rtrequest: bad gateway value: %s\n",
1344                                         if_name(ifp));
1345                                     break;
1346                             }
1347                             SDL(gate)->sdl_type = ifp->if_type;
1348                             SDL(gate)->sdl_index = ifp->if_index;
1349                     }
1350                     if (ln != NULL)
1351                             break;  /* This happens on a route change */
```

```
1352                        /*
1353                         * Case 2: This route may come from cloning, or a manual route
1354                         * add with a LL address.
1355                         */
1356                        R_Malloc(ln, struct llinfo_nd6 *, sizeof(*ln));
1357                        rt->rt_llinfo = (caddr_t)ln;
1358                        if (!ln) {
1359                                log(LOG_DEBUG, "nd6_rtrequest: malloc failed\n");
1360                                break;
1361                        }
```
                                                                        _____nd6.c

1335–1349 If this interface type requires link-layer address resolution (i.e., not point-to-point or loopback), the rt_gateway field of the newly created host route entry must be a link-layer socket address structure where the result of address resolution is stored. Otherwise, something went wrong and processing terminates. If the gateway is valid, its type and index are initialized based on the given interface.

1350 If this route entry already has link-layer information, the processing is completed. This condition is not typical at this point but can happen if a system administrator explicitly tries to modify an existing entry by issuing the RTM_CHANGE command via a routing socket. This code was simply derived from an old version of the IPv4 ARP implementation, and it is not clear if this operation has any meaningful effect.

1356 Memory is allocated for the Neighbor Cache entry and it is attached to the route entry through the rt_llinfo field.

Listing 5-20
                                                                        _____nd6.c
```
1362                        nd6_inuse++;
1363                        nd6_allocated++;
```
                                                                        _____nd6.c

1362–1363 ND-related global counters are updated: the total number of Neighbor Cache entries that are active and the total number of Neighbor Cache entries allocated in the system.

Listing 5-21
                                                                        _____nd6.c
```
1364                        Bzero(ln, sizeof(*ln));
1365                        ln->ln_rt = rt;
```
                                                                        _____nd6.c

1364–1365 The content of the newly allocated Neighbor Cache entry is cleared. The back pointer from the Neighbor Cache entry to the corresponding route entry is also initialized here.

Listing 5-22
                                                                        _____nd6.c
```
1366                        /* this is required for "ndp" command. - shin */
1367                        if (req == RTM_ADD) {
1368                                /*
1369                                 * gate should have some valid AF_LINK entry,
1370                                 * and ln->ln_expire should have some lifetime
```

```
1371                              * which is specified by ndp command.
1372                              */
1373                             ln->ln_state = ND6_LLINFO_REACHABLE;
1374                             ln->ln_byhint = 0;
1375                     } else {
1376                             /*
1377                              * When req == RTM_RESOLVE, rt is created and
1378                              * initialized in rtrequest(), so rt_expire is 0.
1379                              */
1380                             ln->ln_state = ND6_LLINFO_NOSTATE;
1381                             ln->ln_expire = time_second;
1382                     }
1383                     rt->rt_flags |= RTF_LLINFO;
1384                     ln->ln_next = llinfo_nd6.ln_next;
1385                     llinfo_nd6.ln_next = ln;
1386                     ln->ln_prev = &llinfo_nd6;
1387                     ln->ln_next->ln_prev = ln;
```
——nd6.c

1366–1374 If the command is RTM_ADD, the newly created Neighbor Cache state is initialized
to REACHABLE in case this entry is manually configured (e.g., by the **ndp** command).
The state may soon be reset to a more appropriate value depending on the context (see,
for example, Section 5.15.2).

1375–1381 If the command is RTM_RESOLVE, the route entry is typically newly cloned from
an interface direct route. The corresponding cache state is unknown at this stage, and is
initialized to NOSTATE. Again, this can soon be overridden by an appropriate state.

Note: The comment about rt_expire is for an older version where this field of the route
entry was used as the expiration timer of the Neighbor Cache entry. Since the current code
has a separate timer in the llinfo_nd6 structure, the comment is no longer applicable.

1383 The newly created Neighbor Cache entry is inserted into the front of the Neighbor Cache
table, which is referenced by the global variable llinfo_nd6. It is important to set
the RTF_LLINFO flag to indicate that this route entry is related to Neighbor Cache (or,
generally, some link-layer protocol).

Listing 5-23
——nd6.c

```
1389                     /*
1390                      * check if rt_key(rt) is one of my address assigned
1391                      * to the interface.
1392                      */
1393                     ifa = (struct ifaddr *)in6ifa_ifpwithaddr(rt->rt_ifp,
1394                         &SIN6(rt_key(rt))->sin6_addr);
1395                     if (ifa) {
1396                             caddr_t macp = nd6_ifptomac(ifp);
1397                             ln->ln_expire = 0;
1398                             ln->ln_state = ND6_LLINFO_REACHABLE;
1399                             ln->ln_byhint = 0;
1400                             mine = 1;
1401                             if (macp) {
1402                                     Bcopy(macp, LLADDR(SDL(gate)), ifp->if_addrlen);
1403                                     SDL(gate)->sdl_alen = ifp->if_addrlen;
1404                             }
```
——nd6.c

1393–1404 If the destination address (`rt_key(rt)`) is one of the addresses assigned to the interface, the Neighbor Cache becomes a permanent entry, and the state is set to REACHABLE. If the link-layer has an address, it is copied from the interface into the storage allocated for the `sockaddr_dl{}` structure. `nd6_ifptomac()` is a simple subroutine that returns a pointer to the link-layer address, if any, of the given interface.

Listing 5-24

```
                                                                  nd6.c
1405                    if (nd6_useloopback) {
....
1417                            rt->rt_ifp = &loif[0];  /* XXX */
....
1419                            /*
1420                             * Make sure rt_ifa be equal to the ifaddr
1421                             * corresponding to the address.
1422                             * We need this because when we refer
1423                             * rt_ifa->ia6_flags in ip6_input, we assume
1424                             * that the rt_ifa points to the address instead
1425                             * of the loopback address.
1426                             */
1427                            if (ifa != rt->rt_ifa) {
1428                                    IFAFREE(rt->rt_ifa);
1429                                    IFAREF(ifa);
1430                                    rt->rt_ifa = ifa;
1431                            }
1432                    }
                                                                  nd6.c
```

1405–1417 By default, traffic that is internal within the node goes through a loopback interface. The outgoing interface of the route entry is reset to the loopback interface here. This is why the **netstat** command shows `lo0` as the outgoing interface for the route to a node's own address configured on a non-loopback interface.

1427–1431 As commented, this part of the code tries to make sure that the loopback route to a node's own address should have that address as the associated interface address (`rt_ifa`) rather than an arbitrary address assigned on the interface. This check was for an older version of the kernel code and is now unnecessary; the loopback route for each configured address is now explicitly created at the time when the address is assigned to the interface, and the associated interface address is set to the configured address (see Section 2.14.6).

Listing 5-25

```
                                                                  nd6.c
1433                    } else if (rt->rt_flags & RTF_ANNOUNCE) {
1434                            ln->ln_expire = 0;
1435                            ln->ln_state = ND6_LLINFO_REACHABLE;
1436                            ln->ln_byhint = 0;
1437
1438                            /* join solicited node multicast for proxy ND */
1439                            if (ifp->if_flags & IFF_MULTICAST) {
1440                                    struct sockaddr_in6 llsol;
1441                                    int error;
1442
1443                                    llsol = *SIN6(rt_key(rt));
1444                                    llsol.sin6_addr.s6_addr32[0] =
```

```
1445                                            htonl(0xff020000);
1446                           llsol.sin6_addr.s6_addr32[1] = 0;
1447                           llsol.sin6_addr.s6_addr32[2] = htonl(1);
1448                           llsol.sin6_addr.s6_addr8[12] = 0xff;
1449                           error = in6_addr2zoneid(ifp, &llsol.sin6_addr,
1450                                   &llsol.sin6_scope_id);
1451                           if (error)
1452                                   break;
1453                           in6_embedscope(&llsol.sin6_addr,
1454                                   &llsol); /* XXX */
....
1458                           if (in6_addmulti(&llsol, ifp, &error) == NULL)
....
1460                           {
1461                                   nd6log((LOG_ERR, "%s: failed to join "
1462                                       "%s (errno=%d)\n", if_name(ifp),
1463                                       ip6_sprintf(&llsol.sin6_addr),
1464                                       error));
1465                           }
1466                   }
1467           }
```
―― nd6.c

1433–1437 The **ndp** command allows a node to respond to ND address resolution related packets for an address that is not its own. In this case a route entry is created for this foreign address and the route entry carries the RTF_ANNOUNCE flag. The Neighbor Cache state is set to REACHABLE because the link-layer address is known and is manually configured. The RTF_ANNOUNCE flag is an alias of the RTF_PROTO2 flag defined in the header file <netinet6/nd6.h>.

1439–1465 For a multicast capable interface, the node will join the solicited-node multicast address of the proxied address and add this multicast address into the interface filter.

Listing 5-26
―― nd6.c

```
1469                   /*
1470                    * if this is a cached route, which is very likely,
1471                    * put it in the timer queue.
1472                    */
....
1474                   if (!(rt->rt_flags & (RTF_STATIC | RTF_ANNOUNCE)) && !mine)
1475                           rt_add_cache(rt, nd6_rtdrain);
....
1477                   break;
```
―― nd6.c

1473–1476 Each cloned route is added into the route timeout cache list to be examined by the garbage collection process. For example, the garbage collection process will call the nd6_rtdrain() function, which is not described in this book, to remove a cloned entry that has remained long enough in the STALE state.

Listing 5-27
―― nd6.c

```
1479           case RTM_DELETE:
1480                   if (!ln)
1481                           break;
1482                   /* leave from solicited node multicast for proxy ND */
```

```
1483                     if ((rt->rt_flags & RTF_ANNOUNCE) != 0 &&
1484                         (ifp->if_flags & IFF_MULTICAST) != 0) {
1485                         struct sockaddr_in6 llsol;
1486                         struct in6_multi *in6m;
1487
1488                         llsol = *SIN6(rt_key(rt));
1489                         llsol.sin6_addr.s6_addr32[0] = htonl(0xff020000);
1490                         llsol.sin6_addr.s6_addr32[1] = 0;
1491                         llsol.sin6_addr.s6_addr32[2] = htonl(1);
1492                         llsol.sin6_addr.s6_addr8[12] = 0xff;
1493                         if (in6_addr2zoneid(ifp, &llsol.sin6_addr,
1494                             &llsol.sin6_scope_id) == 0) {
1495                                 in6_embedscope(&llsol.sin6_addr,
1496                                                &llsol); /* XXX */
1497                                 IN6_LOOKUP_MULTI(&llsol, ifp, in6m);
1498                                 if (in6m) {
....
1503                                         in6_delmulti(in6m);
....
1505                                 }
1506                         } else {
1507                                 /* XXX: this should not fail.  bark here? */
1508                         }
1509                     }
1510                     nd6_inuse--;
1511                     ln->ln_next->ln_prev = ln->ln_prev;
1512                     ln->ln_prev->ln_next = ln->ln_next;
1513                     ln->ln_prev = NULL;
1514                     rt->rt_llinfo = 0;
1515                     rt->rt_flags &= ~RTF_LLINFO;
1516                     if (ln->ln_hold)
1517                             m_freem(ln->ln_hold);
1518                     Free((caddr_t)ln);
1519             }
1520     }
```
——*nd6.c*

1483–1509 When deleting a Neighbor Cache entry, if the local node is responding to ND address resolution related packets on behalf of a foreign address, then it is time for the node to leave the solicited node multicast group of the proxied address and remove the multicast address from the interface filter if that multicast address was added previously.

1510–1518 The Neighbor Cache entry is removed from the cache list. The reference to the cache in the route entry is cleared so that there is no dangling pointer reference. Any queued packet is freed and then the Neighbor Cache entry is freed.

5.15.2 `nd6_cache_lladdr()` Function

The `nd6_cache_lladdr()` function is called by the ND packet processing functions to create a Neighbor Cache entry for a given neighbor, which will store the neighbor's link-layer address. The neighbor can be either a router, or a destination to which communication will take place. A call graph of `nd6_cache_lladdr()` is shown in Figure 5-31.

An important task performed by `nd6_cache_lladdr()` is to update the reachability state of a neighbor. Each Neighbor Cache entry contains a state that directly maps to the reachability state of the neighbor. As mentioned in Section 5.9, a Neighbor Cache entry can be in one of five states: INCOMPLETE, STALE, DELAY, PROBE, and REACHABLE.

A Neighbor Cache entry is created when packets are sent to a neighbor for the first time. A Neighbor Cache entry is in the INCOMPLETE state when address resolution is in progress.

FIGURE 5-31

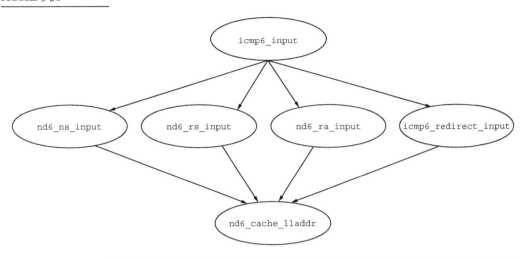

nd6_cache_lladdr{} call graph.

The local node is yet to receive a Neighbor Advertisement packet in response to the Neighbor Solicitation packets that were sent to the solicited-node multicast address. Address resolution fails after a node has sent MAX_MULTICAST_SOLICIT number of Neighbor Solicitation packets, each separated by RetransTimer ms, without receiving any solicited Neighbor Advertisement responses. The Neighbor Cache entry is then deleted.

A Neighbor Cache entry changes to the REACHABLE state when a valid solicited Neighbor Advertisement response has arrived, or when the upper layer protocols have provided positive reachability confirmation. A node does not perform any action for an entry in the REACHABLE state. The Neighbor Cache entry remains in the REACHABLE state for ReachableTime ms and then transits to the STALE state if no positive reachability confirmation arrives within that period.

A Neighbor Cache entry transits to the STALE state when ReachableTime ms have elapsed since the node received the last positive reachability confirmation. The STALE state can also be reached when a node receives an unsolicited Neighbor Advertisement packet that updates the cached link-layer address. A node does not perform any action for an entry in the STALE state until packets are sent to the neighbor. Since the Neighbor Solicitation, Router Solicitation, Router Advertisement, and Redirect packet types carry the link-layer address of either the sender or the redirected target, a Neighbor Cache entry may be created upon receiving one of these types of packets.

A Neighbor Cache entry enters the DELAY state when a packet is sent to a neighbor in the STALE state. The DELAY state gives upper layer protocols an opportunity to provide positive reachability confirmation before sending out NUD probes. The Neighbor Cache entry remains in the DELAY state for at most DELAY_FIRST_PROBE_TIME seconds waiting for positive reachability confirmation. The local node sends out the first Neighbor Solicitation packet once DELAY_FIRST_PROBE_TIME seconds elapse while the cache entry state is still in the DELAY state. The Neighbor Cache entry state then transits to the PROBE state.

While a Neighbor Cache entry is in the PROBE state a node uses the cached link-layer address to transmit a Neighbor Solicitation packet every RetransTime ms until positive reachability confirmation arrives or when the maximum number of retransmissions MAX_UNICAST_SOLICIT is exhausted. The Neighbor Cache entry is deleted after sending MAX_UNICAST_SOLICIT Neighbor Solicitation packets without any response in return.

Below we describe the nd6_cache_lladdr() function in detail.

Listing 5-28

_____nd6.c
```
1795    /*
1796     * Create neighbor cache entry and cache link-layer address,
1797     * on reception of inbound ND6 packets.  (RS/RA/NS/redirect)
1798     */
1799    struct rtentry *
1800    nd6_cache_lladdr(ifp, from, lladdr, lladdrlen, type, code)
1801            struct ifnet *ifp;
1802            struct sockaddr_in6 *from;
1803            char *lladdr;
1804            int lladdrlen;
1805            int type;           /* ICMP6 type */
1806            int code;           /* type dependent information */
1807    {
1808            struct rtentry *rt = NULL;
1809            struct llinfo_nd6 *ln = NULL;
1810            int is_newentry;
1811            struct sockaddr_dl *sdl = NULL;
1812            int do_update;
1813            int olladdr;
1814            int llchange;
1815            int newstate = 0;
```
_____nd6.c

1800 The processing of inbound ND messages of Router Solicitation, Router Advertisement, Neighbor Solicitation, or Redirect may invoke nd6_cache_lladdr() to save the link-layer address of the transmitting neighbor.

ifp points to the interface on which the packet arrived. from holds the source address of the packet. lladdr points to the link-layer address within the ND option, and lladdrlen is the corresponding link-layer address length. type identifies the ND packet type, which can be one of Router Solicitation, Router Advertisement, Neighbor Solicitation, or Redirect packet. code holds information specific to a packet type. Currently only the Redirect message uses this parameter, which can be either ND_REDIRECT_ONLINK or ND_REDIRECT_ROUTER.

Listing 5-29

_____nd6.c
```
1820            if (!ifp)
1821                    panic("ifp == NULL in nd6_cache_lladdr");
1822            if (!from)
1823                    panic("from == NULL in nd6_cache_lladdr");
1824
1825            /* nothing must be updated for unspecified address */
1826            if (IN6_IS_ADDR_UNSPECIFIED(&from->sin6_addr))
1827                    return NULL;
```
_____nd6.c

1820–1827 The Link-Layer address option must be ignored if the source address is the unspecified address, and the function terminates here.

Listing 5-30
_____nd6.c
```
1829            /*
1830             * Validation about ifp->if_addrlen and lladdrlen must be done in
1831             * the caller.
1832             *
1833             * XXX If the link does not have link-layer address, what should
1834             * we do? (ifp->if_addrlen == 0)
1835             * Spec says nothing in sections for RA, RS and NA.  There's small
1836             * description on it in NS section (RFC 2461 7.2.3).
1837             */
1838
1839            rt = nd6_lookup(from, 0, ifp);
1840            if (!rt) {
....
1846
1847                    rt = nd6_lookup(from, 1, ifp);
1848                    is_newentry = 1;
```
_____nd6.c

1839–1848 Function `nd6_lookup()` is called here to search into the Neighbor Cache to see
if an entry exists for the packet source. A new Neighbor Cache entry is created by the
second call to function `nd6_lookup()` if the neighbor is seen for the first time. The
second function parameter of `nd6_lookup()` indicates whether a new Neighbor Cache
entry should be created if the search fails. `nd6_lookup()` is described in Section 5.15.3.
The `is_newentry` flag is set accordingly as an indicator for later processing code.

The condition used here for creating a Neighbor Cache entry is not entirely correct.
On a link type that does not have a link-layer address, a packet containing a Link-
Layer address option is likely invalid, or at least the information contained in the
option does not apply to the link. Since the specification does not explicitly discuss
such a scenario but briefly touches on this subject for only the Neighbor Solicitation
packet, the KAME implementation chose to stick with a simple decision for the time
being until the specification is updated.

Listing 5-31
_____nd6.c
```
1849            } else {
1850                    /* do nothing if static ndp is set */
1851                    if (rt->rt_flags & RTF_STATIC)
1852                            return NULL;
1853                    is_newentry = 0;
1854            }
```
_____nd6.c

1849–1854 No further processing is necessary if an entry is found but it is statically configured.
Otherwise the `is_newentry` flag is set accordingly as an indicator for later processing
code.

Listing 5-32
_____nd6.c
```
1856            if (!rt)
1857                    return NULL;
```
_____nd6.c

1856–1857 This function returns a NULL pointer if a new Neighbor Cache entry cannot be created.

Listing 5-33

```
1858                    if ((rt->rt_flags & (RTF_GATEWAY | RTF_LLINFO)) != RTF_LLINFO) {
1859     fail:
1860                            (void)nd6_free(rt, 0);
1861                            return NULL;
1862                    }
1863                    ln = (struct llinfo_nd6 *)rt->rt_llinfo;
1864                    if (!ln)
1865                            goto fail;
1866                    if (!rt->rt_gateway)
1867                            goto fail;
1868                    if (rt->rt_gateway->sa_family != AF_LINK)
1869                            goto fail;
```

1858–1869 Since the Neighbor Cache is maintained as part of the routing table, it is important to verify that the route entry carries the `RTF_LLINFO` flag, which indicates the route entry was created for caching the link-layer address. Otherwise the entry is deleted and the function terminates and returns NULL to the caller. The storage for the Neighbor Cache entry must have been allocated, which is referenced by `rt_gateway`, and must be of the right storage type (i.e., the address family must be `AF_LINK`).

   Note that the above validations are redundant because these validations have already been performed by `nd6_lookup()`.

Listing 5-34

```
1870                    sdl = SDL(rt->rt_gateway);
1871
1872                    olladdr = (sdl->sdl_alen) ? 1 : 0;
1873                    if (olladdr && lladdr) {
1874                            if (bcmp(lladdr, LLADDR(sdl), ifp->if_addrlen))
1875                                    llchange = 1;
1876                            else
1877                                    llchange = 0;
1878                    } else
1879                            llchange = 0;
```

1870–1872 The `rt_gateway` field is cast from a generic `sockaddr{}` structure into a `sockaddr_dl{}` structure. A non-0 `sdl_alen` indicates there is a cached link-layer address and the `olladdr` flag is set accordingly.

1873–1879 If a link-layer address was cached, the cached value is compared with the received value and the `llchange` flag is set to indicate whether there is a change in value.

   The `olladdr` and the `llchange` flags are used to determine the new state of the cache below.

Listing 5-35

nd6.c

```
1881                /*
1882                 * newentry olladdr   lladdr   llchange   (*=record)
1883                 *    0        n        n        --       (1)
1884                 *    0        y        n        --       (2)
1885                 *    0        n        y        --       (3) * STALE
1886                 *    0        y        y        n        (4) *
1887                 *    0        y        y        y        (5) * STALE
1888                 *    1       --        n        --       (6)   NOSTATE(= PASSIVE)
1889                 *    1       --        y        --       (7) * STALE
1890                . */
1891
1892                if (lladdr) {              /* (3-5) and (7) */
1893                        /*
1894                         * Record source link-layer address
1895                         * XXX is it dependent to ifp->if_type?
1896                         */
1897                        sdl->sdl_alen = ifp->if_addrlen;
1898                        bcopy(lladdr, LLADDR(sdl), ifp->if_addrlen);
1899                }
1900
1901                if (!is_newentry) {
1902                        if ((!olladdr && lladdr) ||              /* (3) */
1903                            (olladdr && lladdr && llchange)) {   /* (5) */
1904                                do_update = 1;
1905                                newstate = ND6_LLINFO_STALE;
1906                        } else                                   /* (1-2,4) */
1907                                do_update = 0;
1908                } else {
1909                        do_update = 1;
1910                        if (!lladdr)                             /* (6) */
1911                                newstate = ND6_LLINFO_NOSTATE;
1912                        else                                     /* (7) */
1913                                newstate = ND6_LLINFO_STALE;
1914                }
```

nd6.c

1881–1914 nd6_cache_lladdr() is called from Router Solicitation, Router Advertisement, Neighbor Solicitation, and Redirect messages. The matrix given in the code comment represents the following situations:

Case (1) represents the situation where a Link-Layer address option is not present and the neighbor has been seen by the local node before.

Case (2) represents the situation where a cache entry for the neighbor is present but the Link-Layer address option is missing from the message. No conclusion can be drawn as to whether the reachability state of the neighbor has changed.

Case (3) represents the situation where a Link-Layer address option is present and a cache entry for the neighbor exists without the link-layer address. Neighbor Cache state is set to STALE in this case.

Case (4) represents the situation where the Link-Layer address option carries the same link-layer address as the cached value.

Case (5) represents the situation where the Link-Layer address option carries a different link-layer address than the cached value. For example, a router changes its link-layer address and it sends out an unsolicited Router Advertisement message to update its link-layer address cached by its neighbors.

Case (6) represents the situation where the local node sees the neighbor for the first time, but the message does not carry a Link-Layer address option. For example, communication has taken place between two nodes. At some point later one node might send a unicast Neighbor Solicitation message using its cached value to another node as part of executing the NUD algorithm (see Listing 5-88).

Case (7) represents the situation where the local node sees the neighbor for the first time, and the Link-Layer address option is present in the message (e.g., a Router Advertisement message).

Upon receiving a valid Neighbor Solicitation message, a node either creates a new ND entry or modifies an existing one according to the following rules, which are best described in pseudo code.

Pseudo Code Listing 5-1

```
IF (Source Address != Unspecified Address)
    IF (Source Link-Layer Address option is Present)
        IF (Neighbor Cache entry DOES NOT exist)
            1. Create a new cache entry
            2. Save the received link-layer address
            3. Set the neighbor reachability state to STALE
            4. Set the IsRouter flag to FALSE
        ELSE
            IF (Received link-layer address != Cached link-layer address)
                1. Update the cache value to the received value
                2. Set the neighbor reachability state to STALE
                3. The IsRouter flag must not be modified
            END-IF
        END-IF
    END-IF
END-IF
```

Upon receiving a valid Router Solicitation message, a router either creates a new ND entry or modifies an existing one according to the following rules, which are best described in pseudo code.

Pseudo Code Listing 5-2

```
IF  (the Source Address == Unspecified address)
    DO NOT Update or Create a Neighbor Cache entry
ELSE
    IF (Source Link-Layer Address option is Present)
        IF (Neighbor Cache entry exists) AND
          (Received link-layer address != Cached link-layer address)
            1. Update the cache value to the received value
            2. Set the neighbor reachability state to STALE
        END-IF
        IF (Neighbor Cache entry DOES NOT exist)
            1. Create a new cache entry
            2. Save the received link-layer address
            3. Set the neighbor reachability state to STALE
        END-IF
    ELSE
        The router may responds with either a unicast or multicast RA message.
    END-IF
    Set the entry's IsRouter flag to FALSE
END-IF
```

Upon receiving a valid Router Advertisement message, a host either creates a new ND entry or modifies an existing one according to the following rules, which are best described in pseudo code.

Pseudo Code Listing 5-3

```
IF (Source Link-Layer Address option is Present)
    IF (Neighbor Cache entry exists) AND
       (Received link-layer address != Cached link-layer address)
          1. Update the cache value to the received value
          2. Set the neighbor reachability state to STALE
    END-IF
    IF (Neighbor Cache entry DOES NOT exist)
          2. Create a new cache entry
          3. Save the received link-layer address
          4. Set the neighbor reachability state to STALE
    END-IF
    Set the entry's IsRouter flag to TRUE
ELSE
    IF (Neighbor Cache entry exists)
          Set the entry's IsRouter flag to TRUE
    END-IF
END-IF
```

Upon receiving a valid Redirect message, a host either creates or updates its Neighbor Cache for the Destination Address according to the following rules, which are best described in the following pseudo code.

Pseudo Code Listing 5-4

```
IF (Neighbor Cache not available)
    1. Create a cache entry for Destination Address and store the link-layer address
    2. Set the cache state to STALE
ELSE
    IF (Received Target link-layer address  !=  Cached link-layer address)
        1. Set the cache state to STALE
        2. Store the Target link-layer address into the cache entry
    END-IF
END-IF
```

A host receiving the Redirect message sets the value of the *IsRouter* flag according to the following logic.

Pseudo Code Listing 5-5

```
IF (Destination Address != Target Address)
    Set the IsRouter flag to TRUE for the Target address
ELSE
    IF (Neighbor Cache entry DOES NOT exist)
        Set the IsRouter flag to FALSE
    ELSE
        Leave the IsRouter flag unmodified
    END-IF
END-IF
```

The Redirect message informs the receiving node of a better first-hop router when the target address is different from the destination address. Since the target address contains a router address, the *IsRouter* flag must be set to true.

The code block of lines 1881–1914 updates the state of the Neighbor Cache according to the rules that are shown in the pseudo code listings. do_update is set to 1 if the state of the Neighbor Cache needs update.

Figure 5-32 details the state transitions among the various ND states after receiving a valid ND packet that is one of the following types: Neighbor Solicitation, Router Solicitation, Router Advertisement, or Redirect. The diagram has the following notation: events that trigger the state transition are enclosed in angled brackets, and the corresponding actions to perform are enclosed in curly brackets.

For example, an event <NS / RS / RA / REDIR, DIFF> means the received ND packet is one of Neighbor Solicitation, Router Solicitation, Router Advertisement, or Redirect. The link-layer address is included in a packet option and is different from the cached value.

FIGURE 5-32

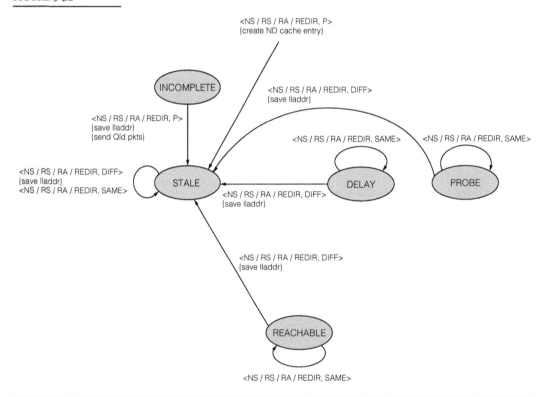

Neighbor Cache state transition diagram for any valid non-Neighbor Advertisement packet.

Listing 5-36

———nd6.c
```
1916                 if (do_update) {
1917                         /*
1918                          * Update the state of the neighbor cache.
1919                          */
1920                         ln->ln_state = newstate;
1921
1922                         if (ln->ln_state == ND6_LLINFO_STALE) {
1923                                 /*
1924                                  * XXX: since nd6_output() below will cause
1925                                  * state transition to DELAY and reset the timer,
1926                                  * we must set the timer now, although it is actually
1927                                  * meaningless.
1928                                  */
1929                                 ln->ln_expire = time_second + nd6_gctimer;
1930
1931                                 if (ln->ln_hold) {
1932                                         /*
1933                                          * we assume ifp is not a p2p here, so just
1934                                          * set the 2nd argument as the 1st one.
1935                                          */
1936                                         nd6_output(ifp, ifp, ln->ln_hold,
1937                                             (struct sockaddr_in6 *)rt_key(rt), rt);
1938                                         ln->ln_hold = NULL;
1939                                 }
1940                         } else if (ln->ln_state == ND6_LLINFO_INCOMPLETE) {
1941                                 /* probe right away */
1942                                 ln->ln_expire = time_second;
1943                         }
1944                 }
```
———nd6.c

1916–1939 do_update indicates that the Neighbor Cache state has changed. The Neighbor
Cache entry is then updated with the new state. If the new state is STALE, it may be a
result of the link-layer address of the neighbor provided in a way other than receiving a
solicited Neighbor Advertisement (as shown in Figure 5-32). In this case, the cache entry
may contain a packet pending transmission to the neighbor, and if so, it is now transmitted
even though there is only unidirectional reachability confirmation.

1940–1943 For an INCOMPLETE entry the local node will send Neighbor Solicitation packet
to probe the neighbor's reachability immediately.

Listing 5-37

———nd6.c
```
1946                 /*
1947                  * ICMP6 type dependent behavior.
1948                  *
1949                  * NS: clear IsRouter if new entry
1950                  * RS: clear IsRouter
1951                  * RA: set IsRouter if there's lladdr
1952                  * redir: clear IsRouter if new entry
1953                  *
1954                  * RA case, (1):
1955                  * The spec says that we must set IsRouter in the following cases:
1956                  * - If lladdr exist, set IsRouter.  This means (1-5).
1957                  * - If it is old entry (!newentry), set IsRouter.  This means (7).
1958                  * So, based on the spec, in (1-5) and (7) cases we must set IsRouter.
1959                  * A quetion arises for (1) case.  (1) case has no lladdr in the
1960                  * neighbor cache, this is similar to (6).
1961                  * This case is rare but we figured that we MUST NOT set IsRouter.
```

```
1962          *
1963          * newentry olladdr  lladdr  llchange        NS  RS  RA  redir
1964          *                                                       D R
1965          *       0       n       n       --      (1)     c   ?     s
1966          *       0       y       n       --      (2)     c   s     s
1967          *       0       n       y       --      (3)     c   s     s
1968          *       0       y       y       n       (4)     c   s     s
1969          *       0       y       y       y       (5)     c   s     s
1970          *       1       --      n       --      (6) c   c       c s
1971          *       1       --      y       --      (7) c   c   s   c s
1972          *
1973          *                                       (c=clear s=set)
1974          */
1975          switch (type & 0xff) {
1976          case ND_NEIGHBOR_SOLICIT:
1977                  /*
1978                   * New entry must have is_router flag cleared.
1979                   */
1980                  if (is_newentry)            /* (6-7) */
1981                          ln->ln_router = 0;
1982                  break;
```
——nd6.c

1949–1973 The matrix given in the code comment summarizes the conditions and the value to set for the `ln_router` (*IsRouter* flag) variable, based on the logics that are given in pseudo code Listings 5-1 to 5-5.

1976–1982 Since a Neighbor Solicitation message does not convey whether the sender is a router or not, a newly created Neighbor Cache entry sets the `ln_router` flag to FALSE; otherwise `ln_router` is left unmodified in an existing cache entry. Refer to pseudo code Listing 5-1 for more detail.

Listing 5-38
——nd6.c

```
1983          case ND_REDIRECT:
1984                  /*
1985                   * If the icmp is a redirect to a better router, always set the
1986                   * is_router flag.  Otherwise, if the entry is newly created,
1987                   * clear the flag.  [RFC 2461, sec 8.3]
1988                   */
1989                  if (code == ND_REDIRECT_ROUTER)
1990                          ln->ln_router = 1;
1991                  else if (is_newentry) /* (6-7) */
1992                          ln->ln_router = 0;
1993                  break;
```
——nd6.c

1983–1993 For a Redirect message `ln_router` flag is set to 1 if the Destination Address field and the Target Address field contain different values, which means the Redirect is providing a better next-hop router. Refer to pseudo code Listing 5-4 for more detail. `ND_REDIRECT_ROUTER` is given by `icmp6_redirect_input()` when that function calls `nd6_cache_lladdr()` (see Listing 5-28).

Listing 5-39
——nd6.c

```
1994          case ND_ROUTER_SOLICIT:
1995                  /*
1996                   * is_router flag must always be cleared.
```

```
1997                        */
1998                      ln->ln_router = 0;
1999                      break;
2000              case ND_ROUTER_ADVERT:
2001                      /*
2002                       * Mark an entry with lladdr as a router.
2003                       */
2004                      if ((!is_newentry && (olladdr || lladdr)) ||    /* (2-5) */
2005                          (is_newentry && lladdr)) {                  /* (7) */
2006                              ln->ln_router = 1;
2007                      }
2008                      break;
2009              }
```
─── nd6.c

1994–1998 Since only hosts send Router Solicitation packets, the *IsRouter* flag is set to 0 when processing a Router Solicitation packet. Refer to pseudo code listing 5-2 for more detail.

2000–2008 [RFC2461] specifies that on receipt of a valid Router Advertisement packet, *IsRouter* flag must be set if a Neighbor Cache entry already exists for the advertising router regardless of the state of that cache entry. Refer to pseudo code Listing 5-3.

Listing 5-40
─── nd6.c

```
2011              /*
2012               * When the link-layer address of a router changes, select the
2013               * best router again.  In particular, when the neighbor entry is newly
2014               * created, it might affect the selection policy.
2015               * Question: can we restrict the first condition to the "is_newentry"
2016               * case?
2017               * XXX: when we hear an RA from a new router with the link-layer
2018               * address option, defrouter_select() is called twice, since
2019               * defrtrlist_update called the function as well.  However, I believe
2020               * we can compromise the overhead, since it only happens the first
2021               * time.
2022               * XXX: although defrouter_select() should not have a bad effect
2023               * for those are not autoconfigured hosts, we explicitly avoid such
2024               * cases for safety.
2025               */
2026              if (do_update && ln->ln_router && !ip6_forwarding && ip6_accept_rtadv)
2027                      defrouter_select();
2028
2029              return rt;
2030      }
```
─── nd6.c

2026–2027 The bidirectional reachability state of a router is not confirmed when the link-layer address of a router has changed. A new router may become known to the local node as result of the ND message processing. In either case the local host must perform the default router selection algorithm due to changing conditions concerning default routers.

5.15.3 `nd6_lookup()` **Function**

The `nd6_lookup()` function is called frequently to search for the Neighbor Cache entry of a neighbor. The caller may instruct this function to create a new entry for a given neighbor if it does not exist in the Neighbor Cache. Figure 5-33 shows the callers of `nd6_lookup()` and the purpose of calling `nd6_lookup()` from the context of a specific caller.

FIGURE 5-33

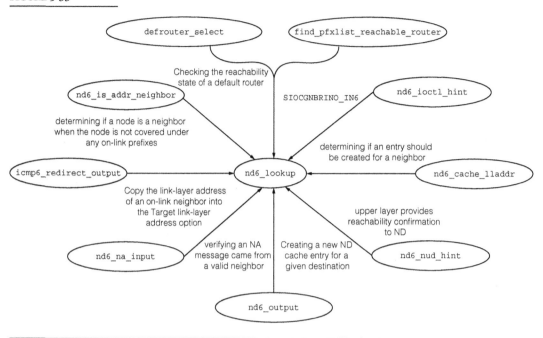

nd6_lookup() call graph.

Listing 5-41

```
                                                                    nd6.c
868     struct rtentry *
869     nd6_lookup(addr6, create, ifp)
870             struct sockaddr_in6 *addr6;
871             int create;
872             struct ifnet *ifp;
873     {
874             struct rtentry *rt;
....
876             struct sockaddr_in6 addr6_tmp; /* XXX */
....
878
....
880             addr6_tmp = *addr6;
881             addr6_tmp.sin6_scope_id = 0;
882             addr6 = &addr6_tmp;
....
884
885             rt = rtalloc1((struct sockaddr *)addr6, create
....
887                             , 0UL
....
889                             );
                                                                    nd6.c
```

869 The parameter addr6 contains the address of a node. The create flag indicates whether a new entry should be created if the search fails. The ifp parameter points to a valid interface to the link on which the neighbor resides. This interface is either the interface on which a packet arrived or the output interface depending on the caller of this function.

885 A search is made into the Neighbor Cache to determine if the given address already exists. Specifically, functions `nd6_cache_lladdr()` and `nd6_output()` (Section 5.22.2) call `nd6_lookup()` with the `create` flag set to TRUE. `rtalloc1()` will create a host route entry if the search fails and the `create` flag is set to TRUE. In function `nd6_output()`, the destination is first verified to be an on-link neighboring node before `nd6_output()` invokes `nd6_lookup()` with the creation flag set.

Listing 5-42

_____nd6.c
```
890             if (rt && (rt->rt_flags & RTF_LLINFO) == 0) {
891                     /*
892                      * This is the case for the default route.
893                      * If we want to create a neighbor cache for the address, we
894                      * should free the route for the destination and allocate an
895                      * interface route.
896                      */
897                     if (create) {
898                             RTFREE(rt);
899                             rt = 0;
900                     }
901             }
```
_____nd6.c

890–901 The check here represents the situation where the local node had just received a packet from an on-link neighbor who is not covered by any of the prefixes. `rtalloc1()` will find the default route and create an indirect route for the neighboring node. This route entry, being an indirect route, will not have the `RTF_LLINFO` flag set. Since this route does not correspond to a Neighbor Cache entry, it is freed here so that an interface host route will be created by the next block of code.

Listing 5-43

_____nd6.c
```
902         if (!rt) {
903                 if (create && ifp) {
904                         int e;
905
906                         /*
907                          * If no route is available and create is set,
908                          * we allocate a host route for the destination
909                          * and treat it like an interface route.
910                          * This hack is necessary for a neighbor which can't
911                          * be covered by our own prefix.
912                          */
913                         struct ifaddr *ifa =
914                             ifaof_ifpforaddr((struct sockaddr *)addr6, ifp);
915                         if (ifa == NULL)
916                                 return (NULL);
917
918                         /*
919                          * Create a new route.  RTF_LLINFO is necessary
920                          * to create a Neighbor Cache entry for the
921                          * destination in nd6_rtrequest which will be
922                          * called in rtrequest via ifa->ifa_rtrequest.
923                          * We also specify RTF_CACHE so that the entry
924                          * will be subject to cached route management.
925                          */
926                         if ((e = rtrequest(RTM_ADD, (struct sockaddr *)addr6,
```

```
927                             ifa->ifa_addr, (struct sockaddr *)&all1_sa,
928                             (ifa->ifa_flags | RTF_HOST | RTF_LLINFO | RTF_CACHE) &
929                             ~RTF_CLONING, &rt)) != 0) {
936                                 return (NULL);
937                     }
938                     if (rt == NULL)
939                             return (NULL);
940                     if (rt->rt_llinfo) {
941                             struct llinfo_nd6 *ln =
942                                 (struct llinfo_nd6 *)rt->rt_llinfo;
943                             ln->ln_state = ND6_LLINFO_NOSTATE;
944                     }
945             } else
946                     return (NULL);
947     }
```
——nd6.c

902–947 The condition in which the route search fails, the `create` flag is true, and the interface
pointer is given, calls for the creation of an interface route to an on-link neighbor whose
address prefix is not covered by the local node as explained earlier. The newly created
interface route is a host route that will contain the link-layer address of the neighbor, and
this new entry is subject to cached route management.

   The state of the new entry is set to NOSTATE, which is not yet functional in terms of
the ND protocol. Note that this state is not part of the protocol specification: KAME uses
this pseudo state so that it can create the placeholder (e.g., at an early stage of processing
incoming packets).

Note: RTF_CACHE is a KAME-specific flag in order to manage resource consumption for route
entries that are considered as "cache" in a finer way. This is not directly related to the ND
protocol, and we do not describe details of the management mechanism in this book.

Listing 5-44

——nd6.c
```
948             rt->rt_refcnt--;
949             /*
950              * Validation for the entry.
951              * Note that the check for rt_llinfo is necessary because a cloned
952              * route from a parent route that has the L flag (e.g. the default
953              * route to a p2p interface) may have the flag, too, while the
954              * destination is not actually a neighbor.
955              * XXX: we can't use rt->rt_ifp to check for the interface, since
956              *      it might be the loopback interface if the entry is for our
957              *      own address on a non-loopback interface. Instead, we should
958              *      use rt->rt_ifa->ifa_ifp, which would specify the REAL
959              *      interface.
960              * Note also that ifa_ifp and ifp may differ when we connect two
961              * interfaces to a same link, install a link prefix to an interface,
962              * and try to install a neighbor cache on an interface that does not
963              * have a route to the prefix.
964              */
965             if ((rt->rt_flags & RTF_GATEWAY) || (rt->rt_flags & RTF_LLINFO) == 0 ||
966                 rt->rt_gateway->sa_family != AF_LINK || rt->rt_llinfo == NULL ||
967                 (ifp && rt->rt_ifa->ifa_ifp != ifp)) {
968                     if (create) {
969                             nd6log((LOG_DEBUG,
```

```
970                                         "nd6_lookup: failed to lookup %s (if = %s)\n",
971                                         ip6_sprintf(&addr6->sin6_addr),
972                                         ifp ? if_name(ifp) : "unspec"));
973                              }
974                      return (NULL);
975                  }
976          return (rt);
977      }
```
                                                                                    ____ nd6.c

948–978 Function `nd6_lookup()`, when invoked without the creation flag, is intended to
verify the existence of the Neighbor Cache for a neighboring node, and `nd6_lookup()`
returns this entry if it is present. A route entry with the `RTF_GATEWAY` flag or without
the `RTF_LLINFO` flag indicates `addr6` belongs to an off-link node. The check for the
`rt_llinfo` member is also necessary to avoid confusion with an indirect host route that
has the `RTF_LLINFO` flag. Such a route can be cloned from a less specific indirect route(*)
to a particular interface due to cloning by the protocol (see Listing 5-18). In these cases
`nd6_lookup()` will return a failure to its caller.

> (*) For example, this type of less specific route can be created by the following command:
>
> route add -inet6 2001:db8:1111::/48 -interface gif0

967 As the code comment explains, the interface comparison on line 967 is necessary for
a multihoming configuration where multiple interfaces are connected to the same link.
Since only a single prefix route associated with one of these interfaces can be installed, an
incoming packet may be received by the interface that is not associated with the installed
interface direct route. In this case a failure is returned to the caller to avoid the creation
of a cache entry on the wrong interface. Another case is the entry that was created for an
interface address, which has `rt_ifp` pointing to the loopback interface. The comparison
with `ifa_ifp` should perform the correct validation and helps the **ndp** command display
such entries correctly.

5.15.4 `nd6_free()` Function

The `nd6_free()` function is called to remove an unreachable entry from the Neighbor Cache
if it is unused anywhere.

Listing 5-45
                                                                                    ____ nd6.c

```
1038     /*
1039      * Free an nd6 llinfo entry.
1040      * Since the function would cause significant changes in the kernel, DO NOT
1041      * make it global, unless you have a strong reason for the change, and are sure
1042      * that the change is safe.
1043      */
1044     static struct llinfo_nd6 *
1045     nd6_free(rt, gc)
1046          struct rtentry *rt;
1047          int gc;
1048     {
1049          struct llinfo_nd6 *ln = (struct llinfo_nd6 *)rt->rt_llinfo, *next;
```

```
1050                 struct nd_defrouter *dr;
1051
1052                 /*
1053                  * we used to have pfctlinput(PRC_HOSTDEAD) here.
1054                  * even though it is not harmful, it was not really necessary.
1055                  */
1056
1057                 if (!ip6_forwarding && ip6_accept_rtadv) { /* XXX: too restrictive? */
1058                         int s;
....
1062                         s = splnet();
....
1064                         dr = defrouter_lookup((struct sockaddr_in6 *)rt_key(rt),
1065                             rt->rt_ifp);
1066
1067                         if (dr != NULL && dr->expire &&
1068                             ln->ln_state == ND6_LLINFO_STALE && gc) {
1069                                 /*
1070                                  * If the reason for the deletion is just garbage
1071                                  * collection, and the neighbor is an active default
1072                                  * router, do not delete it.  Instead, reset the GC
1073                                  * timer using the router's lifetime.
1074                                  * Simply deleting the entry would affect default
1075                                  * router selection, which is not necessarily a good
1076                                  * thing, especially when we're using router preference
1077                                  * values.
1078                                  * XXX: the check for ln_state would be redundant,
1079                                  *     but we intentionally keep it just in case.
1080                                  */
1081                                 ln->ln_expire = dr->expire;
1082                                 splx(s);
1083                                 return (ln->ln_next);
1084                         }
```
——— nd6.c

1045 The parameter `rt` points to the Neighbor Cache entry to be freed. The parameter `gc` indicates whether the caller is the garbage collection function, `nd6_rtdrain()` (see Listing 5-26).

1057 When the local node is a host and is configured to accept incoming Router Advertisement messages, removing a Neighbor Cache entry which specifies a router may affect router selection. The following part of code handles the processing.

1064–1083 `defrouter_lookup()` (Section 5.18.5) is called to determine whether the entry that is being deleted belongs to a default router. Removing the Neighbor Cache entry of an active default router simply because the garbage collection interval is shorter than the router lifetime will result in subsequent default router selection making suboptimal choices. The entry expiration time is thus reset to the router lifetime.

Listing 5-46

——— nd6.c
```
1086                 if (ln->ln_router || dr) {
1087                         struct sockaddr_in6 sin6;
1088                         int e = 0; /* XXX */
1089
1090                         sin6 = *((struct sockaddr_in6 *)rt_key(rt));
1091                         /*
1092                          * rt6_flush must be called whether or not the neighbor
1093                          * is in the Default Router List.
1094                          * See a corresponding comment in nd6_na_input().
1095                          */
....
```

```
1097                              /* sin6 may not have a valid sin6_scope_id */
1098                              e = in6_recoverscope(&sin6, &sin6.sin6_addr, NULL);
1099                              if (e == 0) { /* XXX */
1100                                      sin6.sin6_addr = ((struct sockaddr_in6 *)
      rt_key(rt))->sin6_addr;
1101                              }
    ....
1103                              if (e == 0)
1104                                      rt6_flush(&sin6, rt->rt_ifp);
1105                      }
```
———nd6.c

— Line 1100 is broken here for layout reasons. However, it is a single line of code.

1086–1105 If the Neighbor Cache entry being deleted was created for a neighboring router,
`rt6_flush()` is invoked to remove all of the route entries that utilize this router as the
next-hop. For example, the NUD algorithm might have determined that a router is no
longer reachable and decide to remove the entry (see Listing 5-58).

Listing 5-47
———nd6.c

```
1107                      if (dr) {
1108                              /*
1109                               * Unreachablity of a router might affect the default
1110                               * router selection and on-link detection of advertised
1111                               * prefixes.
1112                               */
1113
1114                              /*
1115                               * Temporarily fake the state to choose a new default
1116                               * router and to perform on-link determination of
1117                               * prefixes correctly.
1118                               * Below the state will be set correctly,
1119                               * or the entry itself will be deleted.
1120                               */
1121                              ln->ln_state = ND6_LLINFO_INCOMPLETE;
1122
1123                              /*
1124                               * Since defrouter_select() does not affect the
1125                               * on-link determination and MIP6 needs the check
1126                               * before the default router selection, we perform
1127                               * the check now.
1128                               */
1129                              pfxlist_onlink_check();
1130
1131                              /*
1132                               * refresh default router list
1133                               */
1134                              defrouter_select();
1135                      }
1136                      splx(s);
1137              }
```
———nd6.c

1107–1137 Removing the Neighbor Cache entry of a default router can affect default router
selection and the on-link status of some prefixes. Function `pfxlist_onlink_check()`
is called to check the on-link status of each prefix and updates the state of each prefix
accordingly. `defrouter_select()` (Section 5.18.6) will choose a new default router if
necessary.

The state of the Neighbor Cache is set to INCOMPLETE first before calling
`pfxlist_onlink_check()` and `defrouter_select()`, so that these functions can
ignore this router when performing the corresponding selection and update algorithms.

If a change in default router took place, defrouter_select() will delete the currently installed default router from the kernel routing table and install the new selected entry.

Listing 5-48

```
                                                                    nd6.c
1139              /*
1140               * Before deleting the entry, remember the next entry as the
1141               * return value.  We need this because pfxlist_onlink_check() above
1142               * might have freed other entries (particularly the old next entry) as
1143               * a side effect (XXX).
1144               */
1145              next = ln->ln_next;
1146
1147              /*
1148               * Detach the route from the routing tree and the list of neighbor
1149               * caches, and disable the route entry not to be used in already
1150               * cached routes.
1151               */
1152              rtrequest(RTM_DELETE, rt_key(rt), (struct sockaddr *)0,
1153                  rt_mask(rt), 0, (struct rtentry **)0);
1154
1155              return (next);
1156      }
                                                                    nd6.c
```

1145–1155 The next entry in the Neighbor Cache list is returned to the caller and is saved into next before calling rtrequest(). rtrequest() invalidates the route entry corresponding to the given Neighbor Cache in the kernel routing table. next is returned to the caller.

As commented, it is important to update next and return it to the caller, because the call to pfxlist_onlink_check() above may have freed some Neighbor Cache entries as a side effect, and the next cache entry that the caller retains may be invalid when this function returns.

5.15.5 nd6_timer() Function

The nd6_timer() function processes the various timers specified by the ND protocol. These timers are:

- A valid lifetime timer for each advertised prefix that is used for on-link determination
- Valid and preferred lifetime timers for each configured address
- The router lifetime timer for each router in the Default Router List
- A timer for retransmitting a Neighbor Solicitation message for address resolution or NUD
- Delay timer for transition of a Neighbor Cache entry to the PROBE state

Whereas the nd6_timer() function handles structures other than Neighbor Cache entries, we discuss this function here because the management of the cache entries is one major duty of the function.

Listing 5-49

──nd6.c
```
473     /*
474      * ND6 timer routine to expire default route list and prefix list
475      */
476     void
477     nd6_timer(ignored_arg)
478             void    *ignored_arg;
479     {
480             int s;
481             struct llinfo_nd6 *ln;
482             struct nd_defrouter *dr;
483             struct nd_prefix *pr;
....
487             struct ifnet *ifp;
488             struct in6_ifaddr *ia6, *nia6;
489             struct in6_addrlifetime *lt6;
490
....
494             s = splnet();
....
497             callout_reset(&nd6_timer_ch, nd6_prune * hz,
498                     nd6_timer, NULL);
```
──nd6.c

497–498 `callout_reset()` is called to re-arm the timer so that the `nd6_timer()` function runs every `nd6_prune` seconds. By default `nd6_prune` is set to 1. `nd6_prune` can be modified through the **sysctl** command. The corresponding **sysctl** variable is `net.inet6.icmp6.nd6_prune`. The function argument `ignored_arg` is not used by this function.

Note: The timer granularity is not really appropriate. In fact, it is too coarse for retransmission of Neighbor Solicitations because the retransmission timer is in the order of milliseconds; it is too fine for prefix or address lifetime expirations because the lifetime values typically have an order of hours or days. The origin of the timer granularity is the IPv4 ARP timer implementation where a timer with an interval of 1 second made sense. But a more fundamental issue was that the traditional BSD kernel did not support fine-grained and scalable kernel timers when this code was first written. Since then, all BSD variants have supported a more scalable timer framework in the kernel, which is deployed by later versions of the KAME kernel for managing various timers including those related to Neighbor Cache entries.

Listing 5-50

──nd6.c
```
506             ln = llinfo_nd6.ln_next;
507             while (ln && ln != &llinfo_nd6) {
508                     struct rtentry *rt;
509                     struct sockaddr_in6 *dst;
510                     struct llinfo_nd6 *next = ln->ln_next;
511                     /* XXX: used for the DELAY case only: */
512                     struct nd_ifinfo *ndi = NULL;
513
514                     if ((rt = ln->ln_rt) == NULL) {
515                             ln = next;
516                             continue;
517                     }
```

```
518                     if ((ifp = rt->rt_ifp) == NULL) {
519                             ln = next;
520                             continue;
521                     }
522                     ndi = ND_IFINFO(ifp);
523                     dst = (struct sockaddr_in6 *)rt_key(rt);
```
――nd6.c

506–521 The timer process traverses the entire Neighbor Cache List. Partially initialized Neighbor Cache entries are skipped because timers are not yet initialized for these entries. A fully initialized Neighbor Cache entry should have an association to a valid route entry (i.e., the `ln_rt` pointer is non-NULL). The route entry should have a valid outgoing interface (i.e., the `rt_ifp` pointer is non-NULL) and this pointer is stored in the local variable `ifp`.

522–523 The per interface data structure that contains the ND protocol operating parameters is retrieved from `ifp` and stored in variable `ndi`. The address of the neighbor is stored in `dst`.

Listing 5-51

――nd6.c
```
525                     if (ln->ln_expire > time_second) {
526                             ln = next;
527                             continue;
528                     }
```
――nd6.c

525–528 The pruning process skips an entry that has not expired yet.

Listing 5-52

――nd6.c
```
530                     /* sanity check */
531                     if (!rt)
532                             panic("rt=0 in nd6_timer(ln=%p)", ln);
533                     if (rt->rt_llinfo && (struct llinfo_nd6 *)rt->rt_llinfo != ln)
534                             panic("rt_llinfo(%p) is not equal to ln(%p)",
535                                     rt->rt_llinfo, ln);
536                     if (!dst)
537                             panic("dst=0 in nd6_timer(ln=%p)", ln);
```
――nd6.c

530–537 This code block performs sanity checks. The link-layer information (i.e., the Neighbor Cache contents) must be present, and `rt_llinfo` must refer to the same storage as that referenced by the Neighbor Cache entry `ln`. The neighbor address `dst` must exist.

Listing 5-53

――nd6.c
```
539                     switch (ln->ln_state) {
540                     case ND6_LLINFO_INCOMPLETE:
541                             if (ln->ln_asked < nd6_mmaxtries) {
542                                     ln->ln_asked++;
543                                     ln->ln_expire = time_second +
544                                         ND6_RETRANS_SEC(ND_IFINFO(ifp)->retrans);
545                                     nd6_ns_output(ifp, NULL, dst, ln, 0);
546                             } else {
547                                     struct mbuf *m = ln->ln_hold;
548                                     if (m) {
```

```
549                                        ln->ln_hold = NULL;
550                                        /*
551                                         * Fake rcvif to make the ICMP error
552                                         * more helpful in diagnosing for the
553                                         * receiver.
554                                         * XXX: should we consider
555                                         * older rcvif?
556                                         */
557                                        m->m_pkthdr.rcvif = rt->rt_ifp;
558
559                                        icmp6_error(m, ICMP6_DST_UNREACH,
560                                                    ICMP6_DST_UNREACH_ADDR, 0);
561                               }
562                               next = nd6_free(rt, 0);
563                        }
564                 break;
```
──nd6.c

541–545 If the Neighbor Cache entry has the INCOMPLETE state, then address resolution is being performed on the given neighbor and the process is not yet complete. When performing address resolution, by default, a node may transmit up to 3 Neighbor Solicitation packets, each separated by 1 second. nd6_mmaxtries is initialized to 3 transmissions. nd6_mmaxtries can be modified through the **sysctl** command using the variable net.inet6.icmp6.nd6_mmaxtries. The retrans field of the nd_ifinfo{} structure holds the retransmission time.

546–564 A node concludes that the neighbor is unreachable once the node has transmitted the maximum allowable number of Neighbor Solicitation packets without receiving any Neighbor Advertisement response in return. An ICMPv6 Destination Unreachable error with error code Address Unreachable (code 3) is returned to the source of the queued packet. The incomplete cache entry is then deleted by nd6_free().

Listing 5-54
──nd6.c
```
565                 case ND6_LLINFO_REACHABLE:
566                         if (ln->ln_expire) {
567                                 ln->ln_state = ND6_LLINFO_STALE;
568                                 ln->ln_expire = time_second + nd6_gctimer;
569                         }
570                 break;
```
──nd6.c

565–570 ReachableTime ms have passed since the last reachability confirmation. The state of this cache entry is changed to STALE. The NUD algorithm will begin neighbor reachability verification the next time packets are sent to this neighbor. The expiration time for this entry is set to the garbage collection timeout value.

Listing 5-55
──nd6.c
```
572                 case ND6_LLINFO_STALE:
573                         /* Garbage Collection(RFC 2461 5.3) */
574                         if (ln->ln_expire)
575                                 next = nd6_free(rt, 1);
576                 break;
```
──nd6.c

572–576 The NUD algorithm determines if and when a node needs to purge a stale Neighbor Cache entry and perform next-hop determination again. This ensures a new path is chosen for the traffic when the previous path has failed. A Neighbor Cache entry has remained in the STALE state long enough that the garbage collection process finally decides to delete the entry.

Listing 5-56

_____nd6.c
```
578                         case ND6_LLINFO_DELAY:
579                                 if (ndi && (ndi->flags & ND6_IFF_PERFORMNUD) != 0) {
580                                         /* We need NUD */
581                                         ln->ln_asked = 1;
582                                         ln->ln_state = ND6_LLINFO_PROBE;
583                                         ln->ln_expire = time_second +
584                                                 ND6_RETRANS_SEC(ndi->retrans);
585                                         nd6_ns_output(ifp, dst, dst, ln, 0);
```
_____nd6.c

578–585 The local node has not received any type of positive reachability confirmation from the neighbor. The Neighbor Cache entry for that neighbor has remained in the DELAY state long enough that the DELAY state timer has expired. For an interface that allows the NUD algorithm to run, the state of this cache entry is changed to the PROBE state and the NUD algorithm begins sending the Neighbor Solicitation probe packets to that neighbor by calling `nd6_ns_output()`.

Listing 5-57

_____nd6.c
```
586                                 } else {
587                                         ln->ln_state = ND6_LLINFO_STALE; /* XXX */
588                                         ln->ln_expire = time_second + nd6_gctimer;
589                                 }
590                         break;
```
_____nd6.c

586–590 For an interface that does not allow the NUD algorithm to run, the state of the Neighbor Cache entry is changed to the STALE state. The expiration time of the entry is set to garbage collection timeout value.

Listing 5-58

_____nd6.c
```
591                         case ND6_LLINFO_PROBE:
592                                 if (ln->ln_asked < nd6_umaxtries) {
593                                         ln->ln_asked++;
594                                         ln->ln_expire = time_second +
595                                                 ND6_RETRANS_SEC(ND_IFINFO(ifp)->retrans);
596                                         nd6_ns_output(ifp, dst, dst, ln, 0);
597                                 } else {
598                                         next = nd6_free(rt, 0);
599                                 }
600                         break;
601                 }
602         ln = next;
603 }
```
_____nd6.c

591–596 If the Neighbor Cache entry has the PROBE state, then NUD is being performed on the given neighbor and the process is not yet complete. When performing NUD, by default, a node may transmit up to 3 Neighbor Solicitation packets, each separated by 1 second. `nd6_umaxtries` is initialized to 3 transmissions. `nd6_umaxtries` can be modified through the **sysctl** command using the variable `net.inet6.icmp6.nd6_umaxtries`. The `retrans` field of the `nd_ifinfo{}` structure holds the retransmission time.

598 A node concludes that the neighbor is unreachable once the node has transmitted the maximum allowable number of Neighbor Solicitation packets without receiving any Neighbor Advertisement response in return. The cache entry is deleted by `nd6_free()`.

602 `ln` is the loop variable for stepping through the Neighbor Cache list. Now `ln` iterates to the next entry.

Listing 5-59

--nd6.c
```
605             /* expire default router list */
606             dr = TAILQ_FIRST(&nd_defrouter);
607             while (dr) {
608                     if (dr->expire && dr->expire < time_second) {
609                             struct nd_defrouter *t;
610                             t = TAILQ_NEXT(dr, dr_entry);
611                             defrtrlist_del(dr);
612                             dr = t;
613                     } else {
614                             dr = TAILQ_NEXT(dr, dr_entry);
615                     }
616             }
```
--nd6.c

605–616 Every router that advertises itself as a default router is kept in the Default Router List. Each router has a lifetime indicating how long it is willing to be a default router. A router is removed from the Default Router List by `defrtrlist_del()` when its lifetime expires. When the removal occurs, any dynamic routes or cloned routes that go through that particular router as the next hop router will be removed from the kernel routing table (see Section 5.18.7).

Listing 5-60

--nd6.c
```
618             /*
619              * expire interface addresses.
620              * in the past the loop was inside prefix expiry processing.
621              * However, from a stricter speci-confrmance standpoint, we should
622              * rather separate address lifetimes and prefix lifetimes.
623              */
624     addrloop:
625             for (ia6 = in6_ifaddr; ia6; ia6 = nia6) {
626                     nia6 = ia6->ia_next;
627                     /* check address lifetime */
628                     lt6 = &ia6->ia6_lifetime;
629                     if (IFA6_IS_INVALID(ia6)) {
630                             int regen = 0;
631
632                             /*
633                              * If the expiring address is temporary, try
634                              * regenerating a new one.  This would be useful when
635                              * we suspended a laptop PC, then turned it on after a
```

```
636                             * period that could invalidate all temporary
637                             * addresses.  Although we may have to restart the
638                             * loop (see below), it must be after purging the
639                             * address.  Otherwise, we'd see an infinite loop of
640                             * regeneration.
641                             */
642                            if (ip6_use_tempaddr &&
643                                (ia6->ia6_flags & IN6_IFF_TEMPORARY) != 0) {
644                                    if (regen_tmpaddr(ia6) == 0)
645                                            regen = 1;
646                            }
647
648                            in6_purgeaddr(&ia6->ia_ifa);
649
650                            if (regen)
651                                    goto addrloop; /* XXX: see below */
652                    }
```
── nd6.c

618–628 All addresses assigned to the node, which are accessible through the global variable
in6_ifaddr, are traversed to determine which addresses have expired, and corresponding actions are performed on those expired addresses.

629 The IFA6_IS_INVALID() macro returns true if the valid lifetime of the given address
has expired. The definition of this macro is as follows:

```
#define IFA6_IS_INVALID(a) \
        ((a)->ia6_lifetime.ia6t_vltime != ND6_INFINITE_LIFETIME && \
        (u_int32_t)((time_second - (a)->ia6_updatetime)) > \
        (a)->ia6_lifetime.ia6t_vltime)
```

That is, it returns true if the valid lifetime is not infinity and the specified lifetime has passed
since the last time the address lifetimes were updated. The ia6_updatetime member is
reset when an appropriate Router Advertisement message is received, effectively extending
the valid lifetime (Listing 5-217). Note that this macro does not try to calculate the "expiration
time" and compare it to the current time. Since the lifetime can be a very large number, a
naive calculation of the expiration time would cause integer overflow (consider the case
where it is 0xFFFFFFFF − 1). This implementation proactively avoids such a programming
error.

642–645 Variable ip6_use_tempaddr indicates whether temporary addresses are used for
privacy extensions (Section 5.10.4) in the system. If the address that has expired is a
temporary address, then regen_tmpaddr() generates a new temporary address. The
value of ip6_use_tempaddr can be modified through the **sysctl** command using the
variable net.inet6.ip6.ip6_use_tempaddr.

648 Function in6_purgeaddr() removes the expired address from the interface and performs the necessary cleanup.

650 A newly generated temporary address is added into the interface address list by the
regen_tmpaddr() function, which subsequently modifies the list. In this case, the pruning process starts over from the beginning of the address list for safety.

Listing 5-61
── nd6.c
```
653                    if (IFA6_IS_DEPRECATED(ia6)) {
654                            int oldflags = ia6->ia6_flags;
655
```

```
656                            ia6->ia6_flags |= IN6_IFF_DEPRECATED;
657
658                            /*
659                             * If a temporary address has just become deprecated,
660                             * regenerate a new one if possible.
661                             */
662                            if (ip6_use_tempaddr &&
663                                (ia6->ia6_flags & IN6_IFF_TEMPORARY) != 0 &&
664                                (oldflags & IN6_IFF_DEPRECATED) == 0) {
665
666                                    if (regen_tmpaddr(ia6) == 0) {
667                                            /*
668                                             * A new temporary address is
669                                             * generated.
670                                             * XXX: this means the address chain
671                                             * has changed while we are still in
672                                             * the loop.  Although the change
673                                             * would not cause disaster (because
674                                             * it's not a deletion, but an
675                                             * addition,) we'd rather restart the
676                                             * loop just for safety.  Or does this
677                                             * significantly reduce performance??
678                                             */
679                                            goto addrloop;
680                                    }
681                            }
682                    } else {
683                            /*
684                             * A new RA might have made a deprecated address
685                             * preferred.
686                             */
687                            ia6->ia6_flags &= ~IN6_IFF_DEPRECATED;
688                    }
689            }
```
                                                                                              ____nd6.c

653–656 An address becomes deprecated when its preferred lifetime expires, in which case
IFA6_IS_DEPRECATED() returns true. The deprecated address is marked with the
IN6_IFF_DEPRECATED flag. The definition of the IFA6_IS_DEPRECATED() macro
is as follows, which is similar to IFA6_IS_INVALID() shown above:

```
#define IFA6_IS_DEPRECATED(a) \
        ((a)->ia6_lifetime.ia6t_pltime != ND6_INFINITE_LIFETIME && \
        (u_int32_t)((time_second - (a)->ia6_updatetime)) > \
        (a)->ia6_lifetime.ia6t_pltime)
```

Note: This code has a bug. Since an invalid address is also deprecated by definition (recall
the valid lifetime of an address must be equal or greater than its preferred lifetime), this code
block is performed for an invalid address, too. But the interface address structure should
have been freed at line 648 in Listing 5-60, and this code touches an invalid memory space.
This bug has been fixed in later versions of the kernel.

662–681 A new temporary address is generated if the deprecated address is a temporary
address. The pruning process will start from the beginning of the address chain but should
in fact be safe to continue to the next entry in this case as commented.

682–687 An address may have been marked as IN6_IFF_DEPRECATED. But a new Router
Advertisement may then have updated the address prefix and subsequently reset the

lifetime of the address, thereby making the address transition out of the deprecated state. The `IN6_IFF_DEPRECATED` flag is therefore cleared from the address flags.

Listing 5-62

——nd6.c
```
691              /* expire prefix list */
692              pr = nd_prefix.lh_first;
693              while (pr) {
694                      /*
695                       * check prefix lifetime.
696                       * since pltime is just for autoconf, pltime processing for
697                       * prefix is not necessary.
698                       */
699                      if (pr->ndpr_vltime != ND6_INFINITE_LIFETIME &&
700                          time_second - pr->ndpr_lastupdate > pr->ndpr_vltime) {
701                              struct nd_prefix *t;
702                              t = pr->ndpr_next;
703
704                              /*
705                               * address expiration and prefix expiration are
706                               * separate.  NEVER perform in6_purgeaddr here.
707                               */
708
709                              prelist_remove(pr);
710                              pr = t;
711                      } else
712                              pr = pr->ndpr_next;
713              }
714              splx(s);
715      }
```
——nd6.c

682–687 The prefix list is traversed and prefixes with expired (valid) lifetimes are deleted by calling function `prelist_remove()` (see Section 5.19.2). Note that `ndpr_pltime` is not used in this processing, which proves this member is meaningless for prefix management (see Listing 5-6).

5.16   ND Protocol Messages Processing Functions

5.16.1   `nd6_ns_output()` Function

The `nd6_ns_output()` function is responsible for constructing and transmitting Neighbor Solicitation packets.

Listing 5-63

——nd6_nbr.c
```
372      /*
373       * Output a Neighbor Solicitation Message. Caller specifies:
374       *      - ICMP6 header source IP6 address
375       *      - ND6 header target IP6 address
376       *      - ND6 header source datalink address
377       *
378       * Based on RFC 2461
379       * Based on RFC 2462 (duplicated address detection)
380       */
381      void
382      nd6_ns_output(ifp, daddr0, taddr0, ln, dad)
```

```
383                 struct ifnet *ifp;
384                 const struct sockaddr_in6 *daddr0, *taddr0;
385                 struct llinfo_nd6 *ln;   /* for source address determination */
386                 int dad;          /* duplicated address detection */
387     {
388                 struct mbuf *m;
389                 struct ip6_hdr *ip6;
390                 struct nd_neighbor_solicit *nd_ns;
391                 struct sockaddr_in6 *daddr6, *taddr6, src_sa, dst_sa;
....
393                 struct sockaddr_in6 daddr6_storage, taddr6_storage;
....
395                 struct ip6_moptions im6o;
396                 int icmp6len;
397                 int maxlen;
398                 caddr_t mac;
....
403                 struct route ro;
....
407
408                 bzero(&ro, sizeof(ro));
```
——— nd6_nbr.c

382–386 Function parameter `ifp` points to the outgoing interface. `daddr0` specifies the packet's destination address: `daddr0` contains the unicast address of the neighbor when the local node is performing NUD; if the local node is performing DAD or address resolution, `daddr0` is NULL, in which case the destination address is determined by the target address. `taddr0` is the target address of the solicitation. The `ln` parameter holds the Neighbor Cache for the destination of the Neighbor Solicitation packet if the local node is performing either NUD or address resolution. `ln` is NULL when the local node is performing DAD. The `dad` variable indicates whether the caller is performing DAD and is set by the caller `nd6_dad_ns_output()`.

Listing 5-64
——— nd6_nbr.c
```
411                 /*
412                  * XXX: since the daddr and taddr may come from the routing table
413                  * entries, sin6_scope_id fields may not be filled in this case.
414                  */
415                 daddr6 = &daddr6_storage;
416                 taddr6 = &taddr6_storage;
417                 if (daddr0) {
418                         *daddr6 = *daddr0;
419                         if (in6_addr2zoneid(ifp, &daddr6->sin6_addr,
420                                             &daddr6->sin6_scope_id)) {
421                                 /* XXX impossible */
422                                 return;
423                         }
424                 } else
425                         daddr6 = NULL;
426                 *taddr6 = *taddr0;
427                 if (in6_addr2zoneid(ifp, &taddr6->sin6_addr, &taddr6->sin6_scope_id)) {
428                         /* XXX: impossible */
429                         return;
430                 }
....
435
436                 if (IN6_IS_ADDR_MULTICAST(&taddr6->sin6_addr))
437                         return;
```
——— nd6_nbr.c

415–437 daddr0 is non-NULL if the local node is performing NUD. In this case a local copy is made in daddr6_storage and function in6_addr2zoneid() is called to retrieve the scope zone ID of the destination address. The scope zone ID is stored into the sin6_scope_id field.

A local copy of taddr0 is made in taddr6_storage and its scope zone ID is also retrieved by in6_addr2zoneid().

Listing 5-65

_____ nd6_nbr.c
```
439             /* estimate the size of message */
440             maxlen = sizeof(*ip6) + sizeof(*nd_ns);
441             maxlen += (sizeof(struct nd_opt_hdr) + ifp->if_addrlen + 7) & ~7;
....
450
451             MGETHDR(m, M_DONTWAIT, MT_DATA);
452             if (m && max_linkhdr + maxlen >= MHLEN) {
453                     MCLGET(m, M_DONTWAIT);
454                     if ((m->m_flags & M_EXT) == 0) {
455                             m_free(m);
456                             m = NULL;
457                     }
458             }
459             if (m == NULL)
460                     return;
461             m->m_pkthdr.rcvif = NULL;
```
_____ nd6_nbr.c

440–461 The estimated packet length includes the IPv6 header, the ICMPv6 header, and the length of the Link-Layer address option.

MGETHDR() will allocate an mbuf{} for the Neighbor Solicitation packet and MCLGET() will allocate a cluster buffer for the outgoing packet.

Listing 5-66

_____ nd6_nbr.c
```
494             if (daddr6 == NULL || IN6_IS_ADDR_MULTICAST(&daddr6->sin6_addr)) {
495                     m->m_flags |= M_MCAST;
496                     im6o.im6o_multicast_ifp = ifp;
497                     im6o.im6o_multicast_hlim = 255;
498                     im6o.im6o_multicast_loop = 0;
499             }
```
_____ nd6_nbr.c

494–499 The M_MCAST bit is set in the buffer flag for a multicast destination. Recall that daddr6 is NULL when this Neighbor Solicitation is for DAD or address resolution, in which case the destination is a multicast address. A multicast packet option structure im6o (see Listing 7-85) is initialized for transmission. It should be particularly noted that im6o_multicast_loop is set to 0 to prohibit local loopback of this packet, which is important to prevent the local node confusing the packet with a Neighbor Solicitation packet sent from other nodes.

Listing 5-67

_____ nd6_nbr.c
```
501             icmp6len = sizeof(*nd_ns);
502             m->m_pkthdr.len = m->m_len = sizeof(*ip6) + icmp6len;
```

```
503                 m->m_data += max_linkhdr;          /* or MH_ALIGN() equivalent? */
504
505                 /* fill neighbor solicitation packet */
506                 ip6 = mtod(m, struct ip6_hdr *);
507                 ip6->ip6_flow = 0;
508                 ip6->ip6_vfc &= ~IPV6_VERSION_MASK;
509                 ip6->ip6_vfc |= IPV6_VERSION;
510                 /* ip6->ip6_plen will be set later */
511                 ip6->ip6_nxt = IPPROTO_ICMPV6;
512                 ip6->ip6_hlim = 255;
```
——— nd6_nbr.c

501–512 The packet data pointer m_data is adjusted to reserve space for the link-layer header.
The 4-bit version field is set to IPV6_VERSION. The packet hop limit is set to 255 and
the next header field is set to ICMPv6.

Listing 5-68
——— nd6_nbr.c
```
513                 /* determine the source and destination addresses */
514                 bzero(&src_sa, sizeof(src_sa));
515                 bzero(&dst_sa, sizeof(dst_sa));
516                 src_sa.sin6_family = dst_sa.sin6_family = AF_INET6;
517                 src_sa.sin6_len = dst_sa.sin6_len = sizeof(struct sockaddr_in6);
518                 if (daddr6)
519                         dst_sa = *daddr6;
....
524                 else {
525                         dst_sa.sin6_addr.s6_addr16[0] = IPV6_ADDR_INT16_MLL;
526                         dst_sa.sin6_addr.s6_addr16[1] = 0;
527                         dst_sa.sin6_addr.s6_addr32[1] = 0;
528                         dst_sa.sin6_addr.s6_addr32[2] = IPV6_ADDR_INT32_ONE;
529                         dst_sa.sin6_addr.s6_addr32[3] = taddr6->sin6_addr.s6_addr32[3];
530                         dst_sa.sin6_addr.s6_addr8[12] = 0xff;
531                         if (in6_addr2zoneid(ifp, &dst_sa.sin6_addr,
532                                             &dst_sa.sin6_scope_id)) {
533                                 goto bad; /* XXX */
534                         }
535                         in6_embedscope(&dst_sa.sin6_addr, &dst_sa); /* XXX */
536                 }
537                 ip6->ip6_dst = dst_sa.sin6_addr;
```
——— nd6_nbr.c

513–537 The destination address is set to the solicited-node multicast address of the target
address if the caller is performing address resolution or DAD. The destination address is
the target address when the caller is performing NUD.

Listing 5-69
——— nd6_nbr.c
```
538                 if (!dad) {
539                         /*
540                          * RFC2461 7.2.2:
541                          * "If the source address of the packet prompting the
542                          * solicitation is the same as one of the addresses assigned
543                          * to the outgoing interface, that address SHOULD be placed
544                          * in the IP Source Address of the outgoing solicitation.
545                          * Otherwise, any one of the addresses assigned to the
546                          * interface should be used."
547                          *
548                          * We use the source address for the prompting packet
549                          * (saddr6), if:
550                          * - saddr6 is given from the caller (by giving "ln"), and
551                          * - saddr6 belongs to the outgoing interface.
```

```
552                            * Otherwise, we perform the source address selection as usual.
553                            */
554                     struct ip6_hdr *hip6;          /* hold ip6 */
555                     struct sockaddr_in6 hsrc0, *hsrc = NULL;
556
557                     if (ln && ln->ln_hold) {
558                             hip6 = mtod(ln->ln_hold, struct ip6_hdr *);
559                             if (ip6_getpktaddrs(ln->ln_hold, &hsrc0, NULL))
560                                     goto bad; /* XXX: impossible */
561                             hsrc = &hsrc0;
562                     }
563                     if (hsrc && in6ifa_ifpwithaddr(ifp, &hsrc->sin6_addr))
564                             src_sa = *hsrc;
565                     else {
566                             struct sockaddr_in6 *src0;
567                             int error;
....
576                             bcopy(&dst_sa, &ro.ro_dst, sizeof(dst_sa));
577                             src0 = in6_selectsrc(&dst_sa,
....
581                                             NULL,
....
583                                             NULL, &ro, NULL, NULL, &error);
584                             if (src0 == NULL) {
585                                     nd6log((LOG_DEBUG,
586                                         "nd6_ns_output: source can't be "
587                                         "determined: dst=%s, error=%d\n",
588                                         ip6_sprintf(&dst_sa.sin6_addr), error));
589                                     goto bad;
590                             }
591                             src_sa = *src0;
....
593                             if (in6_addr2zoneid(ifp, &src_sa.sin6_addr,
594                                             &src_sa.sin6_scope_id)) {
595                                     /* XXX: impossible*/
596                                     goto bad;
597                             }
....
599                     }
600             } else {
601                     /*
602                      * Source address for DAD packet must always be IPv6
603                      * unspecified address. (0::0)
604                      * We actually don't have to 0-clear the address (we did it
605                      * above), but we do so here explicitly to make the intention
606                      * clearer.
607                      */
608                     bzero(&src_sa.sin6_addr, sizeof(src_sa.sin6_addr));
609             }
```
── nd6_nbr.c

538–564 When performing address resolution or NUD, if the source address of the packet that triggered the generation of this Neighbor Solicitation is one of the node's own addresses configured on the outgoing interface, the source address of the Neighbor Solicitation should be the source address of the triggering packet. The packet that triggered the Neighbor Solicitation is held in `ln_hold` when the caller provided `ln` (see Listing 5-291). In this case, `ip6_getpktaddrs()` is called to retrieve the packet source address and stores it in `hsrc0`. If `hsrc0` matches one of the interface addresses, `hsrc0` is set as the source address of the outgoing Neighbor Solicitation packet.

565–599 If the caller did not specify `ln`, or if `hsrc0` does not match any interface address, then `in6_selectsrc()` is called to perform source selection. The source address selection algorithm and `in6_selectsrc()` is explained in detail in Section 3.13.1.

600–608 The source address must be the unspecified address when the caller is performing
DAD.

Listing 5-70

———nd6_nbr.c
```
610             ip6->ip6_src = src_sa.sin6_addr;
611             /* attach the full sockaddr_in6 addresses to the packet */
612             if (!ip6_setpktaddrs(m, &src_sa, &dst_sa))
613                     goto bad;
614             nd_ns = (struct nd_neighbor_solicit *)(ip6 + 1);
615             nd_ns->nd_ns_type = ND_NEIGHBOR_SOLICIT;
616             nd_ns->nd_ns_code = 0;
617             nd_ns->nd_ns_reserved = 0;
618             nd_ns->nd_ns_target = taddr6->sin6_addr;
619             in6_clearscope(&nd_ns->nd_ns_target); /* XXX */
620
621             /*
622              * Add source link-layer address option.
623              *
624              *                                 spec            implementation
625              *                                 ---             ---
626              * DAD packet              MUST NOT        do not add the option
627              * there's no link layer address:
628              *                                 impossible      do not add the option
629              * there's link layer address:
630              *      Multicast NS             MUST add one     add the option
631              *      Unicast NS               SHOULD add one   add the option
632              */
633             if (!dad && (mac = nd6_ifptomac(ifp))) {
634                     int optlen = sizeof(struct nd_opt_hdr) + ifp->if_addrlen;
635                     struct nd_opt_hdr *nd_opt = (struct nd_opt_hdr *)(nd_ns + 1);
636                     /* 8 byte alignments... */
637                     optlen = (optlen + 7) & ~7;
638
639                     m->m_pkthdr.len += optlen;
640                     m->m_len += optlen;
641                     icmp6len += optlen;
642                     bzero((caddr_t)nd_opt, optlen);
643                     nd_opt->nd_opt_type = ND_OPT_SOURCE_LINKADDR;
644                     nd_opt->nd_opt_len = optlen >> 3;
645                     bcopy(mac, (caddr_t)(nd_opt + 1), ifp->if_addrlen);
646             }
```
———nd6_nbr.c

610–619 An mbuf tag is created and the source and destination addresses are copied into the
tag. The fields in the Neighbor Solicitation packet header are initialized with the corresponding values. The Target Address field of the Neighbor Solicitation packet, copied from
`taddr6`, may embed a scope zone ID in its address field, which must be zero-cleared by
`in6_clearscope()` before the packet is sent to the network.

633–645 Since the source IP address is the unspecified address when the caller is performing
DAD, the Source Link-Layer address option is not applicable in that case. The Source
Link-Layer address option must be present for a multicast Neighbor Solicitation; the
option may be omitted for a unicast Neighbor Solicitation. The assumption in the
unicast case is that the local node has the Neighbor Cache for the neighbor due to
prior communication between the two nodes. It is highly likely the neighbor also has a
Neighbor Cache for the sending node and thus omitting the Link-Layer address option
is permissible. When the option is included, its header is initialized and the link-layer
address is copied into the option.

Listing 5-71

_____nd6_nbr.c

```
648              ip6->ip6_plen = htons((u_short)icmp6len);
649              nd_ns->nd_ns_cksum = 0;
650              nd_ns->nd_ns_cksum =
651                  in6_cksum(m, IPPROTO_ICMPV6, sizeof(*ip6), icmp6len);
652
     ....
657              ip6_output(m, NULL, &ro, dad ? IPV6_UNSPECSRC : 0, &im6o, NULL
     ....
659                      ,NULL
     ....
661                  );
662              icmp6_ifstat_inc(ifp, ifs6_out_msg);
663              icmp6_ifstat_inc(ifp, ifs6_out_neighborsolicit);
664              icmp6stat.icp6s_outhist[ND_NEIGHBOR_SOLICIT]++;
665
666              if (ro.ro_rt) {          /* we don't cache this route. */
667                      RTFREE(ro.ro_rt);
668              }
669              return;
```
_____nd6_nbr.c

648–669 in6_cksum() computes the checksum for the final ICMPv6 packet and the computed checksum is inserted into the ICMPv6 header. ip6_output() is called to transmit the packet. Since the source address is the unspecified address in the case of DAD, the IPV6_UNSPECSRC flag is specified to disable the validation check in ip6_output() that disallows the unspecified source address (see Listing 3-151).

662–669 The ICMPv6 statistics are updated. The ro variable holds the reference to the interface route if in6_selectsrc() was called to select a source address for the Neighbor Solicitation packet. In that case RTFREE() is called to release the reference held on that route entry.

5.16.2 nd6_ns_input() **Function**

icmp6_input() calls nd6_ns_input() function to process incoming Neighbor Solicitation packets. A node must perform the following validations on received Neighbor Solicitation messages. The node must discard Neighbor Solicitation messages that fail any of the following validity checks. Some of the checks are performed in icmp6_input(). This is the case for other input functions described in the succeeding subsections.

- The Hop Limit field of the IPv6 header has the value 255 (i.e., a router has not forwarded this Neighbor Solicitation message).

- The message authenticates correctly if an Authentication Header is included.

- The ICMPv6 checksum field is valid.

- The ICMPv6 code is 0.

- The ICMPv6 portion of the packet is at least 24 bytes large.

- The Target Address is not a multicast address.

- Each included option has non-0 length.

- The IPv6 destination address must be the solicited-node multicast address if the source address is the unspecified address.

- The Neighbor Solicitation message does not contain the Source Link-Layer address option if the source address is the unspecified address.

The receiving node must ignore the reserved field and any unrecognized message options. Any options other than the Source Link-Layer address option must be ignored and packet processing continues as normal.

Listing 5-72

```
                                                                   nd6_nbr.c
109     /*
110      * Input a Neighbor Solicitation Message.
111      *
112      * Based on RFC 2461
113      * Based on RFC 2462 (duplicated address detection)
114      */
115     void
116     nd6_ns_input(m, off, icmp6len)
117             struct mbuf *m;
118             int off, icmp6len;
119     {
120             struct ifnet *ifp = m->m_pkthdr.rcvif;
121             struct ip6_hdr *ip6 = mtod(m, struct ip6_hdr *);
122             struct nd_neighbor_solicit *nd_ns;
123             struct sockaddr_in6 saddr6, daddr6, taddr6;
124             char *lladdr = NULL;
125             struct ifaddr *ifa;
126             int lladdrlen = 0;
127             int anycast = 0, proxy = 0, tentative = 0;
128             int router = ip6_forwarding;
129             int tlladdr;
130             union nd_opts ndopts;
131             struct sockaddr_dl *proxydl = NULL;
132
   ....
134             IP6_EXTHDR_CHECK(m, off, icmp6len,);
135             nd_ns = (struct nd_neighbor_solicit *)((caddr_t)ip6 + off);
                                                                   nd6_nbr.c
```

116–118 On input, m contains the received Neighbor Solicitation packet. off is the offset from the start of the packet to the beginning of the Neighbor Solicitation packet header. icmp6len holds the length of the packet excluding the bytes that precede the Neighbor Solicitation packet header.

134–140 Variable nd_ns is set to point to the beginning of the Neighbor Solicitation message. The IP6_EXTHDR_CHECK() macro (Section 1.6.3) verifies that the entire IPv6 packet is contained within a single contiguous block of memory.

Listing 5-73

```
                                                                   nd6_nbr.c
144             if (ip6_getpktaddrs(m, &saddr6, &daddr6))
145                     goto bad;        /* should be impossible */
                                                                   nd6_nbr.c
```

144–145 The packet source and destination addresses are tagged in m during `ip6_input()` processing. `ip6_getpktaddrs()` retrieves the packet source and destination addresses from the buffer tag and stores these addresses into `saddr6` and `daddr6`, respectively.

Listing 5-74

nd6_nbr.c
```
147            ip6 = mtod(m, struct ip6_hdr *); /* adjust pointer for safety */
148            bzero(&taddr6, sizeof(taddr6));
149            taddr6.sin6_family = AF_INET6;
150            taddr6.sin6_len = sizeof(struct sockaddr_in6);
151            taddr6.sin6_addr = nd_ns->nd_ns_target;
```
nd6_nbr.c

147–151 The target address is retrieved from the Neighbor Solicitation message and is saved in `taddr`.

Listing 5-75

nd6_nbr.c
```
152            if (in6_addr2zoneid(ifp, &taddr6.sin6_addr, &taddr6.sin6_scope_id))
153                    goto bad;        /* XXX: impossible */
154            in6_embedscope(&taddr6.sin6_addr, &taddr6); /* XXX */
155
156            if (ip6->ip6_hlim != 255) {
157                    nd6log((LOG_ERR,
158                        "nd6_ns_input: invalid hlim (%d) from %s to %s on %s\n",
159                        ip6->ip6_hlim, ip6_sprintf(&ip6->ip6_src),
160                        ip6_sprintf(&ip6->ip6_dst), if_name(ifp)));
161                    goto bad;
162            }
```
nd6_nbr.c

152–154 `in6_addr2zoneid()` retrieves the scope zone index of the target address, then `in6_embedscope()` converts the address with the zone index into an internal representation by embedding the index into the address.

156–162 A valid Neighbor Solicitation packet must have a hop limit of 255, which indicates the Neighbor Solicitation packet is not forwarded by a router, a strong proof that the packet originated from an on-link neighbor.

Listing 5-76

nd6_nbr.c
```
164            if (SA6_IS_ADDR_UNSPECIFIED(&saddr6)) {
165                    /* dst has to be a solicited node multicast address. */
166                    if (daddr6.sin6_addr.s6_addr16[0] == IPV6_ADDR_INT16_MLL &&
167                        daddr6.sin6_addr.s6_addr32[1] == 0 &&
168                        daddr6.sin6_addr.s6_addr32[2] == IPV6_ADDR_INT32_ONE &&
169                        daddr6.sin6_addr.s6_addr8[12] == 0xff) {
170                            ; /* good */
171                    } else {
172                            nd6log((LOG_INFO, "nd6_ns_input: bad DAD packet "
173                                "(wrong ip6 dst)\n"));
174                            goto bad;
175                    }
176            }
```
nd6_nbr.c

164–176 The destination address must be the solicited-node multicast address if the source address is the unspecified address, which indicates the source is performing DAD on the target address as part of address configuration. If the destination address is not a solicited-node multicast address while the source is the unspecified address, the packet is dropped.

Listing 5-77

```
                                                                           nd6_nbr.c
178            if (IN6_IS_ADDR_MULTICAST(&taddr6.sin6_addr)) {
179                    nd6log((LOG_INFO, "nd6_ns_input: bad NS target (multicast)\n"));
180                    goto bad;
181            }
                                                                           nd6_nbr.c
```

178–180 The target address of the solicitation must not be a multicast address.

Listing 5-78

```
                                                                           nd6_nbr.c
183            icmp6len -= sizeof(*nd_ns);
184            nd6_option_init(nd_ns + 1, icmp6len, &ndopts);
185            if (nd6_options(&ndopts) < 0) {
186                    nd6log((LOG_INFO,
187                            "nd6_ns_input: invalid ND option, ignored\n"));
188                    /* nd6_options have incremented stats */
189                    goto freeit;
190            }
                                                                           nd6_nbr.c
```

183–190 The Neighbor Solicitation packet header processing is complete so `icmp6len` is updated to exclude the header length. `nd6_option_init()` prepares the `ndopts` data structure for processing any possible ND options (Section 5.17.1). If ND options are present, `nd6_options()` will parse these options and store the byte locations of these options in the various fields of `nd_opts{}`. The Source Link-Layer address option is the only allowed message option for the Neighbor Solicitation packet.

Listing 5-79

```
                                                                           nd6_nbr.c
192            if (ndopts.nd_opts_src_lladdr) {
193                    lladdr = (char *)(ndopts.nd_opts_src_lladdr + 1);
194                    lladdrlen = ndopts.nd_opts_src_lladdr->nd_opt_len << 3;
195            }
196
197            if (IN6_IS_ADDR_UNSPECIFIED(&ip6->ip6_src) && lladdr) {
198                    nd6log((LOG_INFO, "nd6_ns_input: bad DAD packet "
199                            "(link-layer address option)\n"));
200                    goto bad;
201            }
                                                                           nd6_nbr.c
```

192–201 When the Source Link-Layer address option is present, `lladdr` is set to point to the start of the source link-layer address, and `lladdrlen` is initialized to contain the length of the Link-Layer address option. Since the option length `nd_opt_len` is specified in 8-byte units, multiplying `nd_opt_len` by 8 gives the option length. The Source Link-Layer address option must not be present if the source address is the unspecified address.

Listing 5-80

```
203              /*
204               * Attaching target link-layer address to the NA?
205               * (RFC 2461 7.2.4)
206               *
207               * NS IP dst is unicast/anycast              MUST NOT add
208               * NS IP dst is solicited-node multicast     MUST add
209               *
210               * In implementation, we add target link-layer address by default.
211               * We do not add one in MUST NOT cases.
212               */
    ....
219              if (!IN6_IS_ADDR_MULTICAST(&daddr6.sin6_addr))
220                      tlladdr = 0;
221              else
222                      tlladdr = 1;
```

219–222 The code here determines whether the corresponding Neighbor Advertisement message should include the Target Link-Layer address option. According to Section 7.2.4 of [RFC2461], if the destination address of the Neighbor Solicitation packet is a unicast or anycast address, which implies the Neighbor Solicitation source already has a cached link-layer address of the receiving node, then the Target Link-Layer address option may be omitted from the Neighbor Advertisement message. However, the Target Link-Layer address option must be included if Neighbor Solicitation packet was addressed to a multicast address. The flag variable tlladdr is set according to the forementioned rule, which will be checked again when the resulting Neighbor Advertisement is sent.

Listing 5-81

```
224              /*
225               * Target address (taddr6) must be either:
226               * (1) Valid unicast/anycast address for my receiving interface,
227               * (2) Unicast address for which I'm offering proxy service, or
228               * (3) "tentative" address on which DAD is being performed.
229               */
230              /* (1) and (3) check. */
231              ifa = (struct ifaddr *)in6ifa_ifpwithaddr(ifp, &taddr6.sin6_addr);
```

224–232 A node receiving a Neighbor Solicitation packet must validate the target address. The target address is considered valid if one of the following criterias is true:

- The address is assigned to the receiving interface as either a unicast or anycast address.

- The address is one of the addresses for which the receiving node is acting as a proxy.

- The address is a tentative address on which the receiving node is currently performing DAD.

Function in6ifa_ifpwithaddr() returns the interface address structure associated with the target address if the target address meets either the first or the third criteria listed above.

Listing 5-82

nd6_nbr.c

```
233                    /* (2) check. */
234                    if (!ifa) {
235                            struct rtentry *rt;
236                            struct sockaddr_in6 tsin6;
237
238                            tsin6 = taddr6;
....
240                            tsin6.sin6_scope_id = 0; /* XXX */
....
242
243                            rt = rtalloc1((struct sockaddr *)&tsin6, 0
....
245                                            , 0
....
247                                            );
248                            if (rt && (rt->rt_flags & RTF_ANNOUNCE) != 0 &&
249                                rt->rt_gateway->sa_family == AF_LINK) {
250                                    /*
251                                     * proxy NDP for single entry
252                                     */
253                                    ifa = (struct ifaddr *)in6ifa_ifpforlinklocal(ifp,
254                                            IN6_IFF_NOTREADY|IN6_IFF_ANYCAST);
255                                    if (ifa) {
256                                            proxy = 1;
257                                            proxydl = SDL(rt->rt_gateway);
258                                            router = 0;       /* XXX */
259                                    }
260                            }
261                            if (rt)
262                                    rtfree(rt);
263                    }
```

nd6_nbr.c

233–262 If the target address is an address for which the local node is providing proxy service, then a search in the interface address list will fail because the target address is not assigned to the receiving interface. However, performing a search into the kernel routing table should yield a route entry. This entry must have the `RTF_ANNOUNCE` flag set, which indicates it is an entry allocated for proxying for another node. `rt_gateway` must have the address family `AF_LINK`, which indicates the entry is allocated for storing a link-layer address.

Function `in6ifa_ifpforlinklocal()` is called to retrieve a link-local address that will be used as the source address of the corresponding Neighbor Advertisement reply packet. The variable `proxy` is set to indicate that the local node will be sending the Neighbor Advertisement on behalf of the proxied node. The variable `proxydl` points to the link-layer address that is assigned to the proxied address.

Listing 5-83

nd6_nbr.c

```
269                    if (!ifa) {
270                            /*
271                             * We've got an NS packet, and we don't have that addddress
272                             * assigned for us.  We MUST silently ignore it.
273                             * See RFC2461 7.2.3.
274                             */
275                            goto freeit;
276                    }
```

nd6_nbr.c

269–275 The Neighbor Solicitation packet is discarded and the function is terminated here if the Neighbor Solicitation packet is querying for an address that is not assigned on the receiving interface.

Listing 5-84

———nd6_nbr.c
```
277             anycast = ((struct in6_ifaddr *)ifa)->ia6_flags & IN6_IFF_ANYCAST;
278             tentative = ((struct in6_ifaddr *)ifa)->ia6_flags & IN6_IFF_TENTATIVE;
279             if (((struct in6_ifaddr *)ifa)->ia6_flags & IN6_IFF_DUPLICATED)
280                     goto freeit;
```
———nd6_nbr.c

277–278 Variable `anycast` is set if the address is an anycast address. `anycast` will be used to determine whether the *Override* flag bit should be set in the corresponding Neighbor Advertisement packet.

Variable `tentative` is set if the address is a tentative address. `tentative` will be used to determine whether the address is a duplicated address.

279–280 If the local node was performing DAD on an address and DAD determined that address was already in use, then that address would be marked with the `IN6_IFF_DUPLICATED` flag to prevent further use of that address. Since the duplicated address may be in use by another node, the local node will discard the Neighbor Solicitation packet.

Listing 5-85

———nd6_nbr.c
```
282             if (lladdr && ((ifp->if_addrlen + 2 + 7) & ~7) != lladdrlen) {
283                     nd6log((LOG_INFO, "nd6_ns_input: lladdrlen mismatch for %s "
284                         "(if %d, NS packet %d)\n",
285                         ip6_sprintf(&taddr6.sin6_addr),
286                         ifp->if_addrlen, lladdrlen - 2));
287                     goto bad;
288             }
289
290             if (SA6_ARE_ADDR_EQUAL(&((struct in6_ifaddr *)ifa)->ia_addr,
291                 &saddr6)) {
292                     nd6log((LOG_INFO, "nd6_ns_input: duplicate IP6 address %s\n",
293                         ip6_sprintf(&saddr6.sin6_addr)));
294                     goto freeit;
295             }
```
———nd6_nbr.c

282–287 The length of the link-layer address is aligned on the 8-byte boundary. This length must match the length of the link-layer address of the receiving interface. Since `lladdrlen` accounts for the Type and Length fields of the option, the interface link-layer address length must also account for these two bytes when comparing the two length values.

290–295 The sender of the Neighbor Solicitation packet is using a duplicated address if the source address of the packet matches an address configured on the receiving interface. In this case an error message is logged via `nd6log()` and the incoming packet is released.

Note: In fact, `nd6log()` suppresses log messages by default to avoid a flood.

Listing 5-86

```
297            /*
298             * We have neighbor solicitation packet, with target address equals to
299             * one of my tentative address.
300             *
301             * src addr      how to process?
302             * ---           ---
303             * multicast     of course, invalid (rejected in ip6_input)
304             * unicast       somebody is doing address resolution -> ignore
305             * unspec        dup address detection
306             *
307             * The processing is defined in RFC 2462.
308             */
309            if (tentative) {
310                    /*
311                     * If source address is unspecified address, it is for
312                     * duplicated address detection.
313                     *
314                     * If not, the packet is for addess resolution;
315                     * silently ignore it.
316                     */
317                    if (SA6_IS_ADDR_UNSPECIFIED(&saddr6))
318                            nd6_dad_ns_input(ifa);
319
320                    goto freeit;
321            }
```

309–320 If the target address is tentative and the source address is the unspecified address,
that indicates the sender is performing DAD. The target address may be a duplicated
address either in the local node or in the originator of the Neighbor Solicitation packet, or
both. Function nd6_dad_ns_input() (Section 5.21.9) performs the necessary address
duplication checks and will update information relating to the address appropriately.

The input packet is released and the function is terminated because a tentative address
may not be in use for normal communication.

Listing 5-87

```
323            /*
324             * If the source address is unspecified address, entries must not
325             * be created or updated.
326             * It looks that sender is performing DAD.  Output NA toward
327             * all-node multicast address, to tell the sender that I'm using
328             * the address.
329             * S bit ("solicited") must be zero.
330             */
331            if (SA6_IS_ADDR_UNSPECIFIED(&saddr6)) {
332                    struct sockaddr_in6 sa6_all;
333
334                    bzero(&sa6_all, sizeof(sa6_all));
335                    sa6_all.sin6_family = AF_INET6;
336                    sa6_all.sin6_len = sizeof(struct sockaddr_in6);
337                    sa6_all.sin6_addr = in6addr_linklocal_allnodes;
338                    if (in6_addr2zoneid(ifp, &sa6_all.sin6_addr,
339                                        &sa6_all.sin6_scope_id)) {
340                            goto bad; /* XXX impossible */
341                    }
342                    in6_embedscope(&sa6_all.sin6_addr, &sa6_all);
343                    nd6_na_output(ifp, &sa6_all, &taddr6,
344                        ((anycast || proxy || !tlladdr) ? 0 : ND_NA_FLAG_OVERRIDE) |
345                        (router ? ND_NA_FLAG_ROUTER : 0),
```

```
346                         tlladdr, (struct sockaddr *)proxydl);
347                  goto freeit;
348             }
```
—— nd6_nbr.c

331–347 A packet with the unspecified source address is an indication that the packet originator
is performing DAD on an address that is already claimed by the local node. The local node
responds with a Neighbor Advertisement packet sent to the all-nodes multicast address as
specified in [RFC2461].

The solicited bit must be set to zero because the Neighbor Advertisement response is
not generated due to address resolution. The *Override* flag must be set to zero if the target
address is an anycast address, or if the target address is a proxied address. The *IsRouter*
flag is set if packet forwarding is enabled.

Listing 5-88
—— nd6_nbr.c
```
350             nd6_cache_lladdr(ifp, &saddr6, lladdr, lladdrlen,
351                  ND_NEIGHBOR_SOLICIT, 0);
```
—— nd6_nbr.c

350 Function nd6_cache_lladdr() is called to create a Neighbor Cache entry for the packet
source and its link-layer address is saved into the new cache entry.

Listing 5-89
—— nd6_nbr.c
```
353             nd6_na_output(ifp, &saddr6, &taddr6,
354                  ((anycast || proxy || !tlladdr) ? 0 : ND_NA_FLAG_OVERRIDE) |
355                  (router ? ND_NA_FLAG_ROUTER : 0) | ND_NA_FLAG_SOLICITED,
356                  tlladdr, (struct sockaddr *)proxydl);
```
—— nd6_nbr.c

353 Function nd6_na_output() is called to respond with a unicast Neighbor Advertisement
packet. The *Solicited* flag bit must be set. The *Override* flag bit is not set if one of the
following conditions is true: the Neighbor Advertisement source address is an anycast
address, the target address is a proxied address, or the Target Link-Layer address option is
omitted from the Neighbor Advertisement packet. The first condition clears the *Override*
flag to avoid overriding an earlier response from another node that has the anycast address.
The second condition clears the *Override* flag so that if the proxied node is actually on-link,
then the Neighbor Advertisement response from the proxied node will take precedence.
The third condition clears the *Override* flag because the Neighbor Solicitation packet was
sent as a unicast packet, which implies the originator has a valid cached link-layer address
of the local node. As such the *Override* flag is not necessary.

The *IsRouter* bit is set only if ip6_forwarding is enabled on the local node. The
link-layer address of the proxied node is supplied to nd6_na_output() if the source
address is a proxied address.

Listing 5-90
—— nd6_nbr.c
```
357     freeit:
358             m_freem(m);
359             return;
```

```
360
361    bad:
362            nd6log((LOG_ERR, "nd6_ns_input: src=%s\n",
363                ip6_sprintf(&saddr6.sin6_addr)));
364            nd6log((LOG_ERR, "nd6_ns_input: dst=%s\n",
365                ip6_sprintf(&daddr6.sin6_addr)));
366            nd6log((LOG_ERR, "nd6_ns_input: tgt=%s\n",
367                ip6_sprintf(&taddr6.sin6_addr)));
368            icmp6stat.icp6s_badns++;
369            m_freem(m);
370    }
```
─── nd6_nbr.c

361–369 If any error occurs, it will trigger a system log message. Then the corresponding
ICMPv6 statistics counter is incremented and the packet is freed.

5.16.3 `nd6_na_input()` Function

`icmp6_input()` calls `nd6_na_input()` to process incoming Neighbor Advertisement packets. A node must perform the following validations on received Neighbor Advertisement messages. The node must discard Neighbor Advertisement messages that fail any of the validity
checks.

- The Hop Limit field of the IPv6 header has the value 255 (i.e., a router has not forwarded this Neighbor Advertisement message).

- The message authenticates correctly if an Authentication Header is included.

- The ICMPv6 checksum field is valid.

- The ICMPv6 code is 0.

- The ICMPv6 portion of the packet is at least 24 bytes large.

- The Target Address is not a multicast address.

- The *Solicited* flag is 0 for Neighbor Advertisement message with the multicast destination.

- Each included option has non-0 length.

The receiving node must ignore the reserved field and any unrecognized message options.
Any options other than the Target Link-Layer address option must be ignored and packet processing continues as normal.

Listing 5-91
─── nd6_nbr.c
```
679    /*
680     * Neighbor advertisement input handling.
681     *
682     * Based on RFC 2461
683     * Based on RFC 2462 (duplicated address detection)
684     *
685     * the following items are not implemented yet:
686     * - proxy advertisement delay rule (RFC2461 7.2.8, last paragraph, SHOULD)
687     * - anycast advertisement delay rule (RFC2461 7.2.7, SHOULD)
688     */
689    void
690    nd6_na_input(m, off, icmp6len)
691            struct mbuf *m;
692            int off, icmp6len;
```

```
693     {
694             struct ifnet *ifp = m->m_pkthdr.rcvif;
695             struct ip6_hdr *ip6 = mtod(m, struct ip6_hdr *);
696             struct nd_neighbor_advert *nd_na;
697             struct sockaddr_in6 saddr6, taddr6;
698             int flags;
699             int is_router;
700             int is_solicited;
701             int is_override;
702             char *lladdr = NULL;
703             int lladdrlen = 0;
704             struct ifaddr *ifa;
705             struct llinfo_nd6 *ln;
706             struct rtentry *rt;
707             struct sockaddr_dl *sdl;
708             union nd_opts ndopts;
....
712
713             if (ip6->ip6_hlim != 255) {
714                     nd6log((LOG_ERR,
715                         "nd6_na_input: invalid hlim (%d) from %s to %s on %s\n",
716                         ip6->ip6_hlim, ip6_sprintf(&ip6->ip6_src),
717                         ip6_sprintf(&ip6->ip6_dst), if_name(ifp)));
718                     goto bad;
719             }
```
——— nd6_nbr.c

690–692 On input, m contains the received Neighbor Advertisement packet. off is the offset
from the start of the packet to the beginning of the Neighbor Advertisement packet header.
icmp6len holds the length of the packet excluding the bytes that precede the Neighbor
Advertisement packet header.

713–718 A valid Neighbor Advertisement packet must have a hop limit of 255, which indicates
the Neighbor Advertisement packet is not forwarded by a router.

Listing 5-92

——— nd6_nbr.c
```
722             IP6_EXTHDR_CHECK(m, off, icmp6len,);
723             nd_na = (struct nd_neighbor_advert *)((caddr_t)ip6 + off);
....
731
732             if (ip6_getpktaddrs(m, &saddr6, NULL))
733                     goto bad;          /* should be impossible */
```
——— nd6_nbr.c

721–733 Variable nd_na is set to point to the beginning of the Neighbor Advertisement message. The IP6_EXTHDR_CHECK() macro verifies that the entire IPv6 packet is contained
within a single contiguous block of memory.

   The packet source and destination addresses are tagged in m during ip6_input()
processing. ip6_getpktaddrs() is called here to retrieve the packet source address
from the mbuf tag and stores the address in saddr6.

Listing 5-93

——— nd6_nbr.c
```
735             flags = nd_na->nd_na_flags_reserved;
736             is_router = ((flags & ND_NA_FLAG_ROUTER) != 0);
737             is_solicited = ((flags & ND_NA_FLAG_SOLICITED) != 0);
738             is_override = ((flags & ND_NA_FLAG_OVERRIDE) != 0);
```
——— nd6_nbr.c

735–738 The *IsRouter*, *Solicited*, and the *Override* flags are retrieved from the Neighbor Advertisement packet header and are stored in `is_router`, `is_solicited`, and `is_override` respectively. These flags are important in deciding how a Neighbor Cache would be updated, which is explained shortly.

Listing 5-94

nd6_nbr.c

```
740             bzero(&taddr6, sizeof(taddr6));
741             taddr6.sin6_family = AF_INET6;
742             taddr6.sin6_len = sizeof(taddr6);
743             taddr6.sin6_addr = nd_na->nd_na_target;
```

nd6_nbr.c

740–743 The target address is retrieved from the Neighbor Advertisement message and is saved in `taddr6`.

Listing 5-95

nd6_nbr.c

```
744             if (in6_addr2zoneid(ifp, &taddr6.sin6_addr, &taddr6.sin6_scope_id))
745                     return;            /* XXX: impossible */
746             if (in6_embedscope(&taddr6.sin6_addr, &taddr6))
747                     return;
```

nd6_nbr.c

744–747 `in6_addr2zoneid()` retrieves the scope zone index of the target address, then `in6_embedscope()` converts the address with the zone index into an internal representation by embedding the index into the address.

Listing 5-96

nd6_nbr.c

```
749             if (IN6_IS_ADDR_MULTICAST(&taddr6.sin6_addr)) {
750                     nd6log((LOG_ERR,
751                         "nd6_na_input: invalid target address %s\n",
752                         ip6_sprintf(&taddr6.sin6_addr)));
753                     goto bad;
754             }
```

nd6_nbr.c

749–754 The target address of the advertisement can be either a unicast or an anycast address, but multicast address is invalid.

Listing 5-97

nd6_nbr.c

```
755             if (is_solicited && IN6_IS_ADDR_MULTICAST(&ip6->ip6_dst)) {
756                     nd6log((LOG_ERR,
757                         "nd6_na_input: a solicited adv is multicasted\n"));
758                     goto bad;
759             }
```

nd6_nbr.c

755–759 The IPv6 packet must have a unicast destination address if the Neighbor Advertisement packet is a response to a previous Neighbor Solicitation query. Otherwise the packet is invalid.

Listing 5-98

———nd6_nbr.c
```
761                icmp6len -= sizeof(*nd_na);
762                nd6_option_init(nd_na + 1, icmp6len, &ndopts);
763                if (nd6_options(&ndopts) < 0) {
764                    nd6log((LOG_INFO,
765                        "nd6_na_input: invalid ND option, ignored\n"));
766                    /* nd6_options have incremented stats */
767                    goto freeit;
768                }
```
———nd6_nbr.c

762–768 The Neighbor Advertisement packet header processing is complete so icmp6len is updated to exclude the header length. nd6_option_init() prepares the nd_opts{} data structure for processing any possible options. If ND options are present, nd6_options() will parse these options and store the byte locations of these options in the various fields of nd_opts{}. The Target Link-Layer address option is the only ND option allowed for a Neighbor Advertisement packet.

Listing 5-99

———nd6_nbr.c
```
770            if (ndopts.nd_opts_tgt_lladdr) {
771                lladdr = (char *)(ndopts.nd_opts_tgt_lladdr + 1);
772                lladdrlen = ndopts.nd_opts_tgt_lladdr->nd_opt_len << 3;
773            }
```
———nd6_nbr.c

770–773 When the Target Link-Layer address option is present, lladdr is set to point to the start of the target link-layer address, and lladdrlen is initialized to contain the length of the Link-Layer address option. Since the option length nd_opt_len is specified in 8-byte units, multiplying nd_opt_len by 8 gives the option length.

Listing 5-100

———nd6_nbr.c
```
775            ifa = (struct ifaddr *)in6ifa_ifpwithaddr(ifp, &taddr6.sin6_addr);
```
———nd6_nbr.c

775 Function in6ifa_ifpwithaddr() returns an interface address structure if the target address is assigned to the interface, or if the target address is a tentative address on which the receiving node is currently performing DAD.

Listing 5-101

———nd6_nbr.c
```
782        /*
783         * Target address matches one of my interface address.
784         *
785         * If my address is tentative, this means that there's somebody
786         * already using the same address as mine.  This indicates DAD failure.
787         * This is defined in RFC 2462.
788         *
789         * Otherwise, process as defined in RFC 2461.
790         */
791        if (ifa
792            && (((struct in6_ifaddr *)ifa)->ia6_flags & IN6_IFF_TENTATIVE)) {
```

```
793                         nd6_dad_na_input(ifa);
794                         goto freeit;
795                 }
796
797                 /* Just for safety, maybe unnecessary. */
798                 if (ifa) {
799                         log(LOG_ERR,
800                             "nd6_na_input: duplicate IP6 address %s\n",
801                             ip6_sprintf(&taddr6.sin6_addr));
802                         goto freeit;
803                 }
```
—— nd6_nbr.c

791–795 If `in6ifa_ifpwithaddr()` returns a valid interface address structure, then the target address matches a tentative address that the local node is performing DAD on. This match is an indication that there is an address assignment conflict, that is, the local node is trying to assign an address that is already in use by the originating node of the Neighbor Advertisement packet. In this case, function `nd6_dad_na_input()` is called to mark this address as a duplicated address so that the local node will refrain from using it.

798–803 The condition of the `if` statement holds when the target address of this Neighbor Advertisement is a valid address assigned to the receiving interface. [RFC2461] does not seem to describe the reasonable behavior for this case. It states in Section 5.4.4:

> On receipt of a valid Neighbor Advertisement message on an interface, node behavior depends on whether the target address is tentative or matches a unicast or anycast address assigned to the interface. If the target address is assigned to the receiving interface, the solicitation is processed as described in [DISCOVERY].

It is clearly incorrect to mention "solicitation" while the discussion focal point is on processing a Neighbor Advertisement message. Applying the trivial fix of replacing the word "solicitation" with "advertisement," does not resolve the semantic error in the specification because the node behavior is not described in [DISCOVERY] (which is [RFC2461]). In fact, such a situation is an abnormal case where some neighboring node sends a Neighbor Advertisement targeting a valid address that has been assigned to the receiving node, which has been verified as unique.

The BSD/KAME implementation thus simply discards the Neighbor Advertisement in such a case. It may be a reasonable behavior, but may still be controversial: if this scenario could ever happen, it would probably mean the address is actually a duplicate and the responding node (that has the authority for the address) just reacted too slowly. In any case, the specification should be corrected.

Listing 5-102
—— nd6_nbr.c

```
805         if (lladdr && ((ifp->if_addrlen + 2 + 7) & ~7) != lladdrlen) {
806                 nd6log((LOG_INFO, "nd6_na_input: lladdrlen mismatch for %s "
807                     "(if %d, NA packet %d)\n", ip6_sprintf(&taddr6.sin6_addr),
808                     ifp->if_addrlen, lladdrlen - 2));
809                 goto bad;
810         }
```
—— nd6_nbr.c

805–810 The length of the link-layer address is aligned on the 8-byte boundary. This length must match the length of the link-layer address of the receiving interface. Since `lladdrlen` accounts for the Type and Length fields of the option, the interface link-layer address length must also account for these two bytes when comparing the two length values.

Listing 5-103

———nd6_nbr.c
```
812             /*
813              * If no neighbor cache entry is found, NA SHOULD silently be
814              * discarded.
815              */
816             rt = nd6_lookup(&taddr6, 0, ifp);
817             if ((rt == NULL) ||
818                 ((ln = (struct llinfo_nd6 *)rt->rt_llinfo) == NULL) ||
819                 ((sdl = SDL(rt->rt_gateway)) == NULL))
820                     goto freeit;
```
———nd6_nbr.c

812–820 `nd6_lookup()` is called to find the Neighbor Cache for the target address. A missing entry implies that the local node did not trigger the Neighbor Advertisement packet and is not interested in this advertisement, or that the local node had abandoned the previous attempt. The Neighbor Advertisement packet is dropped in either case.

Note: The check at lines 818 and 819 is actually redundant, since `nd6_lookup()` ensures that a non-NULL return value also passes these checks (see Listing 5-44):

Listing 5-104

———nd6_nbr.c
```
822             if (ln->ln_state == ND6_LLINFO_INCOMPLETE) {
823                 /*
824                  * If the link-layer has address, and no lladdr option came,
825                  * discard the packet.
826                  */
827                 if (ifp->if_addrlen && !lladdr)
828                         goto freeit;
```
———nd6_nbr.c

822–828 The Neighbor Advertisement packet is dropped if the local node is performing address resolution on the target address but the Target Link-Layer Address option is not present for a link that has link-layer address (see pseudo code Listing 5-6 on pages 500–501).

Listing 5-105

———nd6_nbr.c
```
830                 /*
831                  * Record link-layer address, and update the state.
832                  */
833                 sdl->sdl_alen = ifp->if_addrlen;
834                 bcopy(lladdr, LLADDR(sdl), ifp->if_addrlen);
835                 if (is_solicited) {
836                         ln->ln_state = ND6_LLINFO_REACHABLE;
837                         ln->ln_byhint = 0;
838                         if (ln->ln_expire)
839                                 ln->ln_expire = time_second +
```

```
840                                      ND_IFINFO(rt->rt_ifp)->reachable;
841                    } else {
842                            ln->ln_state = ND6_LLINFO_STALE;
843                            ln->ln_expire = time_second + nd6_gctimer;
844                    }
845                    if ((ln->ln_router = is_router) != 0) {
846                            /*
847                             * This means a router's state has changed from
848                             * non-reachable to probably reachable, and might
849                             * affect the status of associated prefixes..
850                             */
851                            pfxlist_onlink_check();
852                    }
```
—— nd6_nbr.c

830 The link-layer address of the target address is stored in the Neighbor Cache entry. The state of the cache entry is set to REACHABLE if the received Neighbor Advertisement is a response to a previously sent Neighbor Solicitation packet. The expiration timer for this entry is set to the reachable time configured for the link. Since the update to the cache entry state is due to a Neighbor Advertisement packet, not by hints from upper layers, the ln_byhint field is set to 0.

841 The state of the cache entry is set to STALE if the Neighbor Advertisement is not a response to a previously sent Neighbor Solicitation packet. The expiration is set to the garbage collection time.

845 If the originator of the Neighbor Advertisement packet is a router then the reachability state of the router can affect the on-link state of the prefixes. Function pfxlist_onlink_check() (Section 5.19.6) is called to check the on-link state of each prefix and updates the state of each prefix accordingly.

Listing 5-106

—— nd6_nbr.c
```
853        } else {
854                int llchange;
855
856                /*
857                 * Check if the link-layer address has changed or not.
858                 */
859                if (!lladdr)
860                        llchange = 0;
861                else {
862                        if (sdl->sdl_alen) {
863                                if (bcmp(lladdr, LLADDR(sdl), ifp->if_addrlen))
864                                        llchange = 1;
865                                else
866                                        llchange = 0;
867                        } else
868                                llchange = 1;
869                }
870
871                /*
872                 * This is VERY complex.  Look at it with care.
873                 *
874                 * override solicit lladdr llchange      action
875                 *                                       (L: record lladdr)
876                 *
877                 *    0       0      n        --         (2c)
878                 *    0       0      y        n          (2b) L
879                 *    0       0      y        y          (1)    REACHABLE->STALE
```

```
880                    *        0        1        n        --       (2c)   *->REACHABLE
881                    *        0        1        y        n        (2b) L *->REACHABLE
882                    *        0        1        y        y        (1)    REACHABLE->STALE
883                    *        1        0        n        --       (2a)
884                    *        1        0        y        n        (2a) L
885                    *        1        0        y        y        (2a) L *->STALE
886                    *        1        1        n        --       (2a)   *->REACHABLE
887                    *        1        1        y        n        (2a) L *->REACHABLE
888                    *        1        1        y        y        (2a) L *->REACHABLE
889                    */
890                    if (!is_override && (lladdr && llchange)) {          /* (1) */
891                            /*
892                             * If state is REACHABLE, make it STALE.
893                             * no other updates should be done.
894                             */
895                            if (ln->ln_state == ND6_LLINFO_REACHABLE) {
896                                    ln->ln_state = ND6_LLINFO_STALE;
897                                    ln->ln_expire = time_second + nd6_gctimer;
898                            }
899                            goto freeit;
900                    } else if (is_override                              /* (2a) */
901                            || (!is_override && (lladdr && !llchange)) /* (2b) */
902                            || !lladdr) {                               /* (2c) */
903                            /*
904                             * Update link-local address, if any.
905                             */
906                            if (lladdr) {
907                                    sdl->sdl_alen = ifp->if_addrlen;
908                                    bcopy(lladdr, LLADDR(sdl), ifp->if_addrlen);
909                            }
910
911                            /*
912                             * If solicited, make the state REACHABLE.
913                             * If not solicited and the link-layer address was
914                             * changed, make it STALE.
915                             */
916                            if (is_solicited) {
917                                    ln->ln_state = ND6_LLINFO_REACHABLE;
918                                    ln->ln_byhint = 0;
919                                    if (ln->ln_expire) {
920                                            ln->ln_expire = time_second +
921                                                    ND_IFINFO(ifp)->reachable;
922                                    }
923                            } else {
924                                    if (lladdr && llchange) {
925                                            ln->ln_state = ND6_LLINFO_STALE;
926                                            ln->ln_expire = time_second + nd6_gctimer;
927                                    }
928                            }
929                    }
```
—— nd6_nbr.c

859–929 For a complete Neighbor Cache entry containing the source of the Neighbor Advertisement packet, how the cache state is updated depends on its current state, the flag bits of the Neighbor Advertisement packet and whether the Target Link-Layer Address option contains a value that is different from the cached value. The update logic is best described by part of the following pseudo code.

Pseudo Code Listing 5-6

```
IF (ND reachability state == INCOMPLETE)
    IF (Target Link-Layer Address option is NOT Present)
        Discard the packet
```

```
         ELSE
             1. Record the link-layer address in the cache entry
             2. IF (Solicited flag == TRUE)
                     Set ND reachability state to REACHABLE
                ELSE
                     Set ND reachability state to STALE
                END-IF
             3. Set the IsRouter flag based on the R-bit value of the message
             4. Send the queued packets
         END-IF
             NOTE: the Override flag is ignored in the INCOMPLETE state
    ELSE
         IF (Override flag is CLEAR) AND (*)
            (Received link-layer address != Cached link-layer address)
             IF (Neighbor Cache reachability state == REACHABLE)
                 1. Set ND reachability state to STALE
                 2. DO NOT update the Neighbor Cache entry in any other way
             ELSE
                 Discard the packet and no update to the Neighbor Cache entry
             END-IF
         ELSE
             IF (Override flag is SET)
                < OR >
                (Received link-layer address == Cached link-layer address)
                < OR >
                (Target Link-Layer Address option is NOT Present)
                 IF (Target Link-Layer Address option IS Present) AND
                    (Received link-layer address != Cached link-layer address)
                     Update the link-layer address in the Neighbor Cache entry
                 END-IF
                 IF (Solicited Flag == TRUE)
                     Set ND reachability state to REACHABLE
                    ELSE
                     IF (Cached link-layer address was updated)
                         Set Neighbor Cache reachability state to STALE
                     ELSE
                         No Change to ND reachability state
                     END-IF
                 END-IF
                 Set the IsRouter flag according to the S-bit value of the message
             END-IF
         END-IF
    END-IF
END-IF
```

(*) The condition about the *Override* flag is actually redundant, but is kept so that it matches the specification described in [RFC2461]. A successor version of the specification [RFC2461BIS] has removed the redundant condition.

Figure 5-34 details the state transitions among the various ND states after receiving a valid Neighbor Advertisement packet. The diagram has the following notation: Events that trigger the state transition are enclosed in angled brackets, and the corresponding actions to perform are enclosed in curly brackets.

For example, an event <0, 1, DIFF> means the received Neighbor Advertisement packet has the following properties:

- *Solicited* flag = 0
- *Override* flag = 1
- The received link-layer address is different from the cached value.

FIGURE 5-34

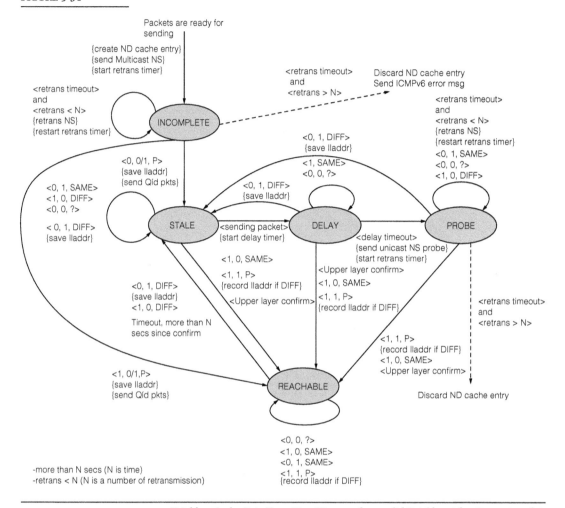

Neighbor Cache State Transition Diagram for a valid Neighbor Advertisement packet.

An event <0, 0/1, P> means

- *Solicited* flag = 0
- *Override* flag can be either 0 or 1
- The Target Link-Layer address option is present

P = "Present." NP = "Not Present." "?" represents the don't-care condition.

A Neighbor Advertisement packet with the *Solicited* flag bit set indicates that the cached link-layer address in the local node is valid, and the neighbor has the link-layer address of the local node. Thus the bidirectional connectivity is working.

A Neighbor Advertisement message with the *Override* flag bit set and the *Solicited* flag cleared indicates the neighbor is announcing updated information proactively, such as a change in its link-layer address.

Listing 5-107

```
_____nd6_nbr.c
931                     if (ln->ln_router && !is_router) {
932                             /*
933                              * The peer dropped the router flag.
934                              * Remove the sender from the Default Router List and
935                              * update the Destination Cache entries.
936                              */
937                             struct nd_defrouter *dr;
938                             int s;
939
940                             /*
941                              * Lock to protect the default router list.
942                              * XXX: this might be unnecessary, since this function
943                              * is only called under the network software interrupt
944                              * context.  However, we keep it just for safety.
945                              */
....
949                             s = splnet();
....
951                             dr = defrouter_lookup((struct sockaddr_in6 *)rt_key(rt),
952                                 rt->rt_ifp);
953                             if (dr)
954                                     defrtrlist_del(dr);
955                             else if (!ip6_forwarding && ip6_accept_rtadv) {
956                                     /*
957                                      * Even if the neighbor is not in the default
958                                      * router list, the neighbor may be used
959                                      * as a next hop for some destinations
960                                      * (e.g. redirect case). So we must
961                                      * call rt6_flush explicitly.
962                                      */
963                                     rt6_flush(&saddr6, rt->rt_ifp);
964                             }
965                             splx(s);
966                     }
967                     ln->ln_router = is_router;
968             }
_____nd6_nbr.c
```

931–968 The originator of the Neighbor Advertisement message may be a default router. A Neighbor Advertisement message that indicates its originator has stopped being a router will cause that router to be removed from the Default Router List. All of the Destination Cache entries (represented as host route entries) that utilize the removed router are also removed by rt6_flush().

Listing 5-108

```
_____nd6_nbr.c
969             rt->rt_flags &= ~RTF_REJECT;
970             ln->ln_asked = 0;
971             if (ln->ln_hold) {
972                     /*
973                      * we assume ifp is not a loopback here, so just set the 2nd
974                      * argument as the 1st one.
975                      */
```

```
976                        nd6_output(ifp, ifp, ln->ln_hold,
977                                (struct sockaddr_in6 *)rt_key(rt), rt);
978                        ln->ln_hold = NULL;
979          }
```
—— nd6_nbr.c

969–979 The `ln_asked` counter is reset to 0 because the address resolution process is now complete. If there was a queued packet waiting for the resolution, that packet is transmitted.

> *Note*: Clearing the `RTF_REJECT` flag is probably meaningless. In fact, ND-related code never sets this flag. This line is likely a mere copy of the similar part of the IPv4 ARP implementation, where this flag is used for an ARP target that is probably unreachable. Since ND has the finer unreachable detection algorithm, the implementation does not need the flag.

5.16.4 `nd6_na_output()` Function

The `nd6_na_output()` function is responsible for constructing and transmitting Neighbor Advertisement messages.

A node sends a Neighbor Advertisement message in response to Neighbor Solicitation messages. The node copies the value of the Target Address field of the Neighbor Solicitation packet and sets it in the same field of the outgoing Neighbor Advertisement packet. The Target Link-Layer address option must be included if the destination address of the Neighbor Solicitation packet is a multicast address. Otherwise the option may be omitted because the soliciting node sent the Neighbor Solicitation using a cached link-layer address of the solicited node and that cached value is still valid.

A node must set the *IsRouter* flag bit in the outgoing Neighbor Advertisement packet if it is a router. Otherwise the node sets the *IsRouter* flag to 0.

The *Override* flag bit is set to 0 if the Target Address is an anycast address, or a unicast address for which the node is acting as a proxy. A node that provides proxy service for an address does not set the *Override* flag bit in case the proxied node responds with its own Neighbor Advertisement directly. In the case where the proxied node is present on the link, its Neighbor Advertisement will take precedence over other Neighbor Advertisement messages sent by the node that is providing the proxy service. The *Override* flag bit is set to 0 when the Target Link-Layer address option is omitted. Otherwise the *Override* flag is set to 1. A node should delay transmitting the Neighbor Advertisement response between 0 and `MAX_ANYCAST_DELAY_TIME` seconds if the Target Address is either an anycast address or an address under proxy service.

The *Solicited* flag bit is set to 1 if the source address of the Neighbor Solicitation is a unicast address. The *Solicited* flag bit is set to 0 if the source address of the Neighbor Solicitation packet is the unspecified address, and the Neighbor Advertisement will be multicast to the all-nodes multicast address.

A node may send unsolicited Neighbor Advertisement messages on an interface when the node detects a change in the interface link-layer address. Sending unsolicited Neighbor Advertisement messages to the all-nodes multicast address allows a node to quickly convey updated information to its neighboring nodes. A node may transmit up to

MAX_NEIGHBOR_ADVERTISEMENT number of unsolicited Neighbor Advertisement messages
with each separated by at least *RetransTimer* milliseconds. The Target Link-Layer address option
contains the new link-layer address, and the Target Address contains the corresponding IPv6
address. The *Solicited* flag is set to 0. The *Override* flag may be set to either 0 or 1. Setting the
Override flag to 1 prompts the receiver to update the cached link-layer address upon receiving
the Neighbor Advertisement message. The receiver ignores the new link-layer address if the
Override flag is set to 0. In either case the state of the Neighbor Cache entry is set to STALE
prompting the receiver to perform NUD to verify bidirectional reachability.

Sending unsolicited Neighbor Advertisement messages is an unreliable optimization to
update the stale information in neighbors about the transmitting node. The NUD algorithm
ensures a node will obtain a reachable link-layer address of its communicating peer reliably.

Listing 5-109

nd6_nbr.c

```
990     /*
991      * Neighbor advertisement output handling.
992      *
993      * Based on RFC 2461
994      *
995      * the following items are not implemented yet:
996      * - proxy advertisement delay rule (RFC2461 7.2.8, last paragraph, SHOULD)
997      * - anycast advertisement delay rule (RFC2461 7.2.7, SHOULD)
998      */
999     void
1000    nd6_na_output(ifp, daddr6, taddr6, flags, tlladdr, sdl0)
1001            struct ifnet *ifp;
1002            const struct sockaddr_in6 *daddr6, *taddr6;
1003            u_long flags;
1004            int tlladdr;            /* 1 if include target link-layer address */
1005            struct sockaddr *sdl0;  /* sockaddr_dl (= proxy NA) or NULL */
1006    {
1007            struct mbuf *m;
1008            struct ip6_hdr *ip6;
1009            struct nd_neighbor_advert *nd_na;
1010            struct ip6_moptions im6o;
1011            struct sockaddr_in6 src_sa, dst_sa, *src0;
1012            int icmp6len, maxlen, error;
1013            caddr_t mac;
....
1015            struct route ro;
....
1022
1023            mac = NULL;
1024            bzero(&ro, sizeof(ro));
1025
1026            /* estimate the size of message */
1027            maxlen = sizeof(*ip6) + sizeof(*nd_na);
1028            maxlen += (sizeof(struct nd_opt_hdr) + ifp->if_addrlen + 7) & ~7;
```

nd6_nbr.c

1000 The parameter ifp holds the outgoing interface. daddr6 holds the destination address of
the Neighbor Advertisement packet. daddr6 contains the unicast address of the neighbor
when the local node is responding to a directly addressed Neighbor Solicitation packet. The
taddr6 parameter is the target address of the advertisement. The flags parameter maps to
the flag bits in the Neighbor Advertisement packet. tlladdr specifies whether the Neighbor Advertisement packet should include the Target Link-Layer address option. The sdl0
variable indicates whether the caller is providing proxy service for the given target address.

1027–1028 `maxlen` is calculated as the sum of the IPv6 header size, the size of the Neighbor Advertisement message, and the size of the Target Link-Layer address option aligned on the 8-byte boundary.

Listing 5-110

```
                                                                    nd6_nbr.c
1038            MGETHDR(m, M_DONTWAIT, MT_DATA);
1039            if (m && max_linkhdr + maxlen >= MHLEN) {
1040                    MCLGET(m, M_DONTWAIT);
1041                    if ((m->m_flags & M_EXT) == 0) {
1042                            m_free(m);
1043                            m = NULL;
1044                    }
1045            }
1046            if (m == NULL)
1047                    return;
1048            m->m_pkthdr.rcvif = NULL;
                                                                    nd6_nbr.c
```

1038–1048 An `mbuf{}` is allocated and saved in variable `m` for the outgoing Neighbor Advertisement packet. A cluster buffer is allocated by `MCLGET()` if the space in the `mbuf{}` is insufficient to hold the entire Neighbor Advertisement packet including the link-layer header. This function returns if memory allocation fails.

The global variable `max_linkhdr` is configurable through the **sysctl** command using the variable `kern.ipc.max_linkhdr`. By default `max_linkhdr` is set to 16 bytes at a minimum. `MHLEN` is defined in `<sys/mbuf.h>` with related definitions given in `<sys/param.h>`.

Listing 5-111

```
                                                                    nd6_nbr.c
1050            if (IN6_IS_ADDR_MULTICAST(&daddr6->sin6_addr)) {
1051                    m->m_flags |= M_MCAST;
1052                    im6o.im6o_multicast_ifp = ifp;
1053                    im6o.im6o_multicast_hlim = 255;
1054                    im6o.im6o_multicast_loop = 0;
1055            }
                                                                    nd6_nbr.c
```

1050–1055 If the destination address is a multicast addresss, the `M_MCAST` flag is set in the `m_flags` of `m` to indicate that the packet will be transmitted as link-level multicast. The interface and packet hop limit fields of the multicast option `im6o` (see Listing 7-85) are initialized, respectively.

Listing 5-112

```
                                                                    nd6_nbr.c
1057            icmp6len = sizeof(*nd_na);
1058            m->m_pkthdr.len = m->m_len = sizeof(struct ip6_hdr) + icmp6len;
1059            m->m_data += max_linkhdr;         /* or MH_ALIGN() equivalent? */
                                                                    nd6_nbr.c
```

1057–1059 `icmp6len` is the size of the Neighbor Advertisement message without any message option. The packet length is the size of the IPv6 header plus the size of the Neighbor Advertisement message. The packet data pointer points to the beginning of the IPv6 header and space is reserved for the link-layer header.

Listing 5-113

nd6_nbr.c

```
1061              /* fill neighbor advertisement packet */
1062              ip6 = mtod(m, struct ip6_hdr *);
1063              ip6->ip6_flow = 0;
1064              ip6->ip6_vfc &= ~IPV6_VERSION_MASK;
1065              ip6->ip6_vfc |= IPV6_VERSION;
1066              ip6->ip6_nxt = IPPROTO_ICMPV6;
1067              ip6->ip6_hlim = 255;
```

nd6_nbr.c

1061–1067 The 4-bit version field is set to `IPV6_VERSION`. The packet hop limit is set to 255 and the next header field is set to ICMPv6.

Listing 5-114

nd6_nbr.c

```
1068              dst_sa = *daddr6;
1069              if (SA6_IS_ADDR_UNSPECIFIED(daddr6)) {
1070                      /* reply to DAD */
1071                      dst_sa.sin6_addr.s6_addr16[0] = IPV6_ADDR_INT16_MLL;
1072                      dst_sa.sin6_addr.s6_addr16[1] = 0;
1073                      dst_sa.sin6_addr.s6_addr32[1] = 0;
1074                      dst_sa.sin6_addr.s6_addr32[2] = 0;
1075                      dst_sa.sin6_addr.s6_addr32[3] = IPV6_ADDR_INT32_ONE;
1076                      if (in6_addr2zoneid(ifp, &dst_sa.sin6_addr,
1077                                          &dst_sa.sin6_scope_id)) {
1078                              goto bad;
1079                      }
1080                      in6_embedscope(&dst_sa.sin6_addr, &dst_sa); /* XXX */
1081
1082                      flags &= ~ND_NA_FLAG_SOLICITED;
1083              }
1084              ip6->ip6_dst = dst_sa.sin6_addr;
```

nd6_nbr.c

1068–1084 The destination address of the Neighbor Advertisement message is set to the link-local all-nodes multicast address if the given function parameter `daddr6` contains the unspecified address. In other words, the source of the Neighbor Solicitation is performing DAD. In this case the Neighbor Advertisement is an unsolicited Neighbor Advertisement, and so the *Solicited* flag bit is cleared. `in6_addr2zoneid()` retrieves the scope zone index of the destination address, then `in6_embedscope()` converts the address with the index into the internal representation by embedding the index into the address.

The IPv6 packet destination is set to the given address `daddr6` for the outgoing Neighbor Advertisement if it is generated in response to address resolution or NUD.

The destination address is then copied into the corresponding IPv6 header field.

Listing 5-115

nd6_nbr.c

```
1086              /*
1087               * Select a source whose scope is the same as that of the dest.
1088               */
....
1093              bcopy(&dst_sa, &ro.ro_dst, sizeof(dst_sa));
1094              src0 = in6_selectsrc(&dst_sa,
....
1098                              NULL,
....
1100                              NULL, &ro, NULL, NULL, &error);
```

```
1101                if (src0 == NULL) {
1102                        nd6log((LOG_DEBUG, "nd6_na_output: source can't be "
1103                            "determined: dst=%s, error=%d\n",
1104                            ip6_sprintf(&dst_sa.sin6_addr), error));
1105                        goto bad;
1106                }
1107                src_sa = *src0;
....
1109                if (in6_addr2zoneid(ifp, &src_sa.sin6_addr, &src_sa.sin6_scope_id))
1110                        goto bad;        /* XXX: impossible*/
....
1112                ip6->ip6_src = src_sa.sin6_addr;
```
—— nd6_nbr.c

1101–1112 Function `in6_selectsrc()` is called to select the source address for the outgoing Neighbor Advertisement packet, and if successful, the source address is copied into the IPv6 header.

Note: The code comment at line 1087 is out of date; `in6_selectsrc()` does not only consider the address scope (see Section 3.13.1).

Listing 5-116
—— nd6_nbr.c
```
1113                /* attach the full sockaddr_in6 addresses to the packet */
1114                if (!ip6_setpktaddrs(m, &src_sa, &dst_sa))
1115                        goto bad;
1116                nd_na = (struct nd_neighbor_advert *)(ip6 + 1);
1117                nd_na->nd_na_type = ND_NEIGHBOR_ADVERT;
1118                nd_na->nd_na_code = 0;
1119                nd_na->nd_na_target = taddr6->sin6_addr;
1120                in6_clearscope(&nd_na->nd_na_target); /* XXX */
```
—— nd6_nbr.c

1116–1120 An mbuf tag is created and the source and destination addresses are copied into the tag. The fields in the Neighbor Advertisement packet header are initialized with the corresponding values. The scope zone ID is stored inside the address in the internal kernel representation. `in6_clearscope()` is called to remove the ID from the target address that will appear on the wire.

Listing 5-117
—— nd6_nbr.c
```
1122                /*
1123                 * "tlladdr" indicates NS's condition for adding tlladdr or not.
1124                 * see nd6_ns_input() for details.
1125                 * Basically, if NS packet is sent to unicast/anycast addr,
1126                 * target lladdr option SHOULD NOT be included.
1127                 */
1128                if (tlladdr) {
1129                        /*
1130                         * sdl0 != NULL indicates proxy NA.  If we do proxy, use
1131                         * lladdr in sdl0.  If we are not proxying (sending NA for
1132                         * my address) use lladdr configured for the interface.
1133                         */
1134                        if (sdl0 == NULL)
1135                                mac = nd6_ifptomac(ifp);
1136                        else if (sdl0->sa_family == AF_LINK) {
```

```
1137                          struct sockaddr_dl *sdl;
1138                          sdl = (struct sockaddr_dl *)sdl0;
1139                          if (sdl->sdl_alen == ifp->if_addrlen)
1140                              mac = LLADDR(sdl);
1141                      }
1142                  }
```
—— nd6_nbr.c

1128–1142 Variable `tlladdr` determines whether to include the Target Link-Layer address option in the Neighbor Advertisement packet. In general, the Link-Layer address option is omitted if the destination of the Neighbor Solicitation packet that triggered this Neighbor Advertisement is a unicast or anycast address (see Listing 5-80).

If the Neighbor Advertisement packet is to include the Link-Layer address option, the caller may provide the link-layer address for the Neighbor Advertisement that is generated on behalf of a proxied node. In that case the given link-layer address is set in the option. Otherwise the link-layer address of the transmitting interface is used in the option.

Listing 5-118
—— nd6_nbr.c

```
1143          if (tlladdr && mac) {
1144              int optlen = sizeof(struct nd_opt_hdr) + ifp->if_addrlen;
1145              struct nd_opt_hdr *nd_opt = (struct nd_opt_hdr *)(nd_na + 1);
1146
1147              /* roundup to 8 bytes alignment! */
1148              optlen = (optlen + 7) & ~7;
1149
1150              m->m_pkthdr.len += optlen;
1151              m->m_len += optlen;
1152              icmp6len += optlen;
1153              bzero((caddr_t)nd_opt, optlen);
1154              nd_opt->nd_opt_type = ND_OPT_TARGET_LINKADDR;
1155              nd_opt->nd_opt_len = optlen >> 3;
1156              bcopy(mac, (caddr_t)(nd_opt + 1), ifp->if_addrlen);
1157          } else
1158              flags &= ~ND_NA_FLAG_OVERRIDE;
```
—— nd6_nbr.c

1143–1156 The Target Link-Layer address option has an 8-byte alignment requirement. The packet length and the length of the option are updated accordingly. The option header fields are initialized and then the link-layer address is copied into the address field of the option.

1158 As explained earlier, the *Override* flag must be cleared if the Link-Layer address option is missing.

Listing 5-119
—— nd6_nbr.c

```
1160          ip6->ip6_plen = htons((u_short)icmp6len);
1161          nd_na->nd_na_flags_reserved = flags;
1162          nd_na->nd_na_cksum = 0;
1163          nd_na->nd_na_cksum =
1164              in6_cksum(m, IPPROTO_ICMPV6, sizeof(struct ip6_hdr), icmp6len);
1165
      ....
1170          ip6_output(m, NULL, &ro, 0, &im6o, NULL
      ....
1172                      ,NULL
      ....
```

```
1174                        );
1175
1176                icmp6_ifstat_inc(ifp, ifs6_out_msg);
1177                icmp6_ifstat_inc(ifp, ifs6_out_neighboradvert);
1178                icmp6stat.icp6s_outhist[ND_NEIGHBOR_ADVERT]++;
1179
1180                if (ro.ro_rt) {           /* we don't cache this route. */
1181                        RTFREE(ro.ro_rt);
1182                }
1183                return;
```
───nd6_nbr.c

1160–1183 `in6_cksum()` computes the checksum for the final ICMPv6 packet and the computed checksum is inserted into the ICMPv6 header. `ip6_output()` is called to transmit the Neighbor Advertisement packet. The ICMPv6 statistics are updated. The `ro` variable may hold the reference to the interface route because `in6_selectsrc()` was called to select a source address for the Neighbor Advertisement packet. `RTFREE()` is called to release the reference held on that route entry.

5.16.5 `nd6_rs_input()` Function

The `nd6_rs_input()` function is called by `icmp6_input()` to process incoming Router Solicitation packets. The main task performed by `nd6_rs_input()` is to process the Source Link-Layer address option if it is present in the Router Solicitation packet. The userland program **rtadvd**, if it is running, will process a copy of the same Router Solicitation packet and will respond with a Router Advertisement packet that advertises system configured parameters.

A router must perform the following validations on received Router Solicitation messages. The router must discard Router Solicitation messages that fail any of the validity checks.

- The Hop Limit field of the IPv6 header has the value 255 (i.e., a router has not forwarded this Router Solicitation message).

- The message authenticates correctly if an Authentication Header is included.

- The ICMPv6 checksum field is valid.

- The ICMPv6 code is 0.

- The ICMPv6 portion of the packet is at least 8 bytes large.

- Each included option has non-0 length.

- The Router Solicitation message does not contain the Source Link-Layer address option if the source address is the unspecified address.

The router must ignore the reserved field and any unrecognized message options. Any options other than the Source Link-Layer address option must be ignored and packet processing continues as normal.

Listing 5-120
───nd6_rtr.c
```
126     /*
127      * Receive Router Solicitation Message - just for routers.
128      * Router solicitation/advertisement is mostly managed by userland program
129      * (rtadvd) so here we have no function like nd6_ra_output().
```

```
130        *
131        * Based on RFC 2461
132        */
133       void
134       nd6_rs_input(m, off, icmp6len)
135              struct mbuf *m;
136              int off, icmp6len;
137       {
138              struct ifnet *ifp = m->m_pkthdr.rcvif;
139              struct ip6_hdr *ip6 = mtod(m, struct ip6_hdr *);
140              struct nd_router_solicit *nd_rs;
141              struct sockaddr_in6 src_sa6;
142              char *lladdr = NULL;
143              int lladdrlen = 0;
....
150              union nd_opts ndopts;
151
152              /* If I'm not a router, ignore it. */
153              if (ip6_accept_rtadv != 0 || ip6_forwarding != 1)
154                      goto freeit;
```
── nd6_rtr.c

134–136 On input, m contains the received Router Solicitation packet. off is the offset from the start of the packet to the beginning of the Router Solicitation packet header. icmp6len holds the length of the packet excluding the bytes that precede the Router Solicitation packet header.

153–154 Hosts must ignore an incoming Router Solicitation packet. This implementation regards a node as a host if it is configured to accept Router Advertisements or it does not enable IPv6 packet forwarding. It is not clear whether the first condition is reasonable from the specification point of view, but it should not matter in practice since a router is not supposed to set ip6_accept_rtadv to non-0.

Listing 5-121
── nd6_rtr.c
```
156              /* Sanity checks */
157              if (ip6->ip6_hlim != 255) {
158                      nd6log((LOG_ERR,
159                          "nd6_rs_input: invalid hlim (%d) from %s to %s on %s\n",
160                          ip6->ip6_hlim, ip6_sprintf(&ip6->ip6_src),
161                          ip6_sprintf(&ip6->ip6_dst), if_name(ifp)));
162                      goto bad;
163              }
```
── nd6_rtr.c

157–162 A valid Router Solicitation packet must have a hop limit of 255, which indicates the Router Solicitation packet is not forwarded by a router.

Listing 5-122
── nd6_rtr.c
```
165              /*
166               * Don't update the neighbor cache, if src = ::.
167               * This indicates that the src has no IP address assigned yet.
168               */
169              if (IN6_IS_ADDR_UNSPECIFIED(&ip6->ip6_src))
170                      goto freeit;
```
── nd6_rtr.c

169–170 A Router Solicitation packet with an unspecified source address indicates the packet source is yet to acquire an address and Source Link-Layer address option is missing. Since the main purpose of nd6_rs_input() is to process the Source Link-Layer address option, the packet is discarded and the function terminates here.

Listing 5-123

```
                                                                    nd6_rtr.c
173             IP6_EXTHDR_CHECK(m, off, icmp6len,);
174             nd_rs = (struct nd_router_solicit *)((caddr_t)ip6 + off);
                                                                    nd6_rtr.c
```

172–180 The IP6_EXTHDR_CHECK() macro verifies that the entire IPv6 packet is contained within a single contiguous block of memory. The function terminates here if the verification fails. Variable nd_rs is set to point to the beginning of the Router Solicitation message.

Listing 5-124

```
                                                                    nd6_rtr.c
183             if (ip6_getpktaddrs(m, &src_sa6, NULL))
184                     goto freeit;
                                                                    nd6_rtr.c
```

183–184 The packet source and destination addresses are tagged in m during ip6_input() processing (see Listing 3-22). ip6_getpktaddrs() retrieves the packet source address and stores it into src_sa6.

Listing 5-125

```
                                                                    nd6_rtr.c
186             icmp6len -= sizeof(*nd_rs);
187             nd6_option_init(nd_rs + 1, icmp6len, &ndopts);
188             if (nd6_options(&ndopts) < 0) {
189                     nd6log((LOG_INFO,
190                         "nd6_rs_input: invalid ND option, ignored\n"));
191                     /* nd6_options have incremented stats */
192                     goto freeit;
193             }
                                                                    nd6_rtr.c
```

186–193 The Router Solicitation packet header processing is complete so icmp6len is updated to exclude the header length. nd6_option_init() prepares the ndopts data structure for processing any possible options. If message options are present, nd6_options() will parse these options and store the byte locations of these options in the various fields of ndopts{}. The Source Link-Layer address option is the only allowed message option for the Router Solicitation packet.

Listing 5-126

```
                                                                    nd6_rtr.c
195             if (ndopts.nd_opts_src_lladdr) {
196                     lladdr = (char *)(ndopts.nd_opts_src_lladdr + 1);
197                     lladdrlen = ndopts.nd_opts_src_lladdr->nd_opt_len << 3;
198             }
199
200             if (lladdr && ((ifp->if_addrlen + 2 + 7) & ~7) != lladdrlen) {
```

```
201                         nd6log((LOG_INFO,
202                             "nd6_rs_input: lladdrlen mismatch for %s "
203                             "(if %d, RS packet %d)\n",
204                             ip6_sprintf(&src_sa6.sin6_addr),
205                             ifp->if_addrlen, lladdrlen - 2));
206                         goto bad;
207             }
```
                                                                              _____nd6_rtr.c

195–206 When the Source Link-Layer address option is present, `lladdr` is set to point to the
start of the source link-layer address, and `lladdrlen` is initialized to contain the length of
the option. Since the option length `nd_opt_len` is specified in 8-byte units, multiplying
`nd_opt_len` by 8 gives the option length.

The length of the link-layer address is aligned on the 8-byte boundary. This length
must match the length of the link-layer address of the receiving interface. Since `lladdrlen`
accounts for the Type and Length fields of the option, the interface link-layer address
length must also account for these two bytes when comparing the two length values. The
packet is discarded if there is mismatch between the two values.

Listing 5-127
                                                                              _____nd6_rtr.c
```
209             nd6_cache_lladdr(ifp, &src_sa6, lladdr, lladdrlen, ND_ROUTER_SOLICIT, 0);
```
                                                                              _____nd6_rtr.c

209 Function `nd6_cache_lladdr()` is called to create a Neighbor Cache entry for the packet
source and its link-layer address is saved into the new cache entry.

Listing 5-128
                                                                              _____nd6_rtr.c
```
211     freeit:
212             m_freem(m);
213             return;
214
215     bad:
216             icmp6stat.icp6s_badrs++;
217             m_freem(m);
218     }
```
                                                                              _____nd6_rtr.c

211–218 Any error condition will trigger a system log message, depending on the behavior
of `nd6log()`. Then the corresponding ICMPv6 statistics counter is incremented and the
packet is freed.

5.16.6   `nd6_ra_input()` Function

The `nd6_ra_input()` function processes incoming Router Advertisement packets. A node
must perform the following validations on received Router Advertisement messages. The node
must discard Router Advertisement messages that fail any of the validity checks.

- The IPv6 source address is a link-local address.
- The Hop Limit field of the IPv6 header has the value 255 (i.e., a router has not forwarded
  this Router Advertisement message).

- The message authenticates correctly if an Authentication header is included.

- The ICMPv6 checksum field is valid.

- The ICMPv6 code is 0.

- The ICMPv6 portion of the packet is at least 16 bytes large.

- Each included option has non-0 length.

The source address must be the link-local address of the sending interface of the advertising router. The source address requirement allows hosts to continue to uniquely identify on-link routers in case of site renumbering.

The receiving node must ignore the reserved field and any unrecognized message options. Any options other than those that are defined to be used with the Router Advertisement messages must be ignored and packet processing continues as normal.

Listing 5-129

―――nd6_rtr.c
```
220     /*
221      * Receive Router Advertisement Message.
222      *
223      * Based on RFC 2461
224      * TODO: on-link bit on prefix information
225      * TODO: ND_RA_FLAG_{OTHER,MANAGED} processing
226      */
227     void
228     nd6_ra_input(m, off, icmp6len)
229             struct  mbuf *m;
230             int off, icmp6len;
231     {
232             struct ifnet *ifp = m->m_pkthdr.rcvif;
233             struct nd_ifinfo *ndi = ND_IFINFO(ifp);
234             struct ip6_hdr *ip6 = mtod(m, struct ip6_hdr *);
235             struct nd_router_advert *nd_ra;
236             struct sockaddr_in6 src_sa6;
237             struct nd_defrouter dr0;
....
243             union nd_opts ndopts;
244             struct nd_defrouter *dr;
....
248             char *lladdr = NULL;
249             int lladdrlen = 0;
250
251             /*
252              * We only accept RAs only when
253              * the system-wide variable allows the acceptance, and
254              * per-interface variable allows RAs on the receiving interface.
255              */
256             if (ip6_accept_rtadv == 0)
257                     goto freeit;
258             if (!(ndi->flags & ND6_IFF_ACCEPT_RTADV))
259                     goto freeit;
```
―――nd6_rtr.c

228–230 On input, `m` contains the received Router Advertisement packet. `off` is the offset from the start of the packet to the beginning of the Router Advertisement packet header. `icmp6len` holds the length of the packet excluding the bytes that precede the Router Advertisement packet header.

256–259 A node that rejects Router Advertisement messages will discard the packet. The acceptance of Router Advertisement messages is controlled by the system-wide variable `ip6_accept_rtadv` and by the per interface flag `ND6_IFF_ACCEPT_RTADV`. `ip6_accept_rtadv` can be modified through the **sysctl** command using the variable `net.inet6.ip6.accept_rtadv`. The per interface `ND6_IFF_ACCEPT_RTADV` flag can be modified through the **ndp** command. For example, the following command line execution will disable accepting Router Advertisements on interface `ne0`.

```
# ndp -i ne0 -- -accept_rtadv
```

Listing 5-130

————————————————————————————————— nd6_rtr.c

```
261             if (ip6->ip6_hlim != 255) {
262                     nd6log((LOG_ERR,
263                         "nd6_ra_input: invalid hlim (%d) from %s to %s on %s\n",
264                         ip6->ip6_hlim, ip6_sprintf(&ip6->ip6_src),
265                         ip6_sprintf(&ip6->ip6_dst), if_name(ifp)));
266                     goto bad;
267             }
```
————————————————————————————————— nd6_rtr.c

261–266 A valid Router Advertisement packet must have a hop limit of 255, which indicates the Router Advertisement packet is not forwarded by a router.

Listing 5-131

————————————————————————————————— nd6_rtr.c

```
269             if (!IN6_IS_ADDR_LINKLOCAL(&ip6->ip6_src)) {
270                     nd6log((LOG_ERR,
271                         "nd6_ra_input: src %s is not link-local\n",
272                         ip6_sprintf(&ip6->ip6_src)));
273                     goto bad;
274             }
```
————————————————————————————————— nd6_rtr.c

269–274 The source address of a Router Advertisement must be a link-local address (Section 5.6.2); otherwise, the packet is erroneous and is discarded by the receiver.

Listing 5-132

————————————————————————————————— nd6_rtr.c

```
277             IP6_EXTHDR_CHECK(m, off, icmp6len,);
278             nd_ra = (struct nd_router_advert *)((caddr_t)ip6 + off);
```
————————————————————————————————— nd6_rtr.c

277–278 The `IP6_EXTHDR_CHECK()` macro verifies that the entire IPv6 packet is contained within a single contiguous block of memory. The function terminates here if the verification fails. Variable `nd_ra` is set to point to the beginning of the Router Advertisement message.

Listing 5-133

————————————————————————————————— nd6_rtr.c

```
287             if (ip6_getpktaddrs(m, &src_sa6, NULL))
288                     goto freeit;
```
————————————————————————————————— nd6_rtr.c

287–288 The packet source and destination addresses are tagged in m during `ip6_input()` processing. `ip6_getpktaddrs()` retrieves the packet source address and stores it into `src_sa6`.

Listing 5-134

```
                                                         __nd6_rtr.c
290              icmp6len -= sizeof(*nd_ra);
291              nd6_option_init(nd_ra + 1, icmp6len, &ndopts);
292              if (nd6_options(&ndopts) < 0) {
293                      nd6log((LOG_INFO,
294                          "nd6_ra_input: invalid ND option, ignored\n"));
295                      /* nd6_options have incremented stats */
296                      goto freeit;
297              }
                                                         __nd6_rtr.c
```

290–296 The minimal validation of the Router Advertisement packet is complete, and `icmp6len` is updated to exclude the header length. `nd6_option_init()` prepares the `ndopts` data structure for processing any possible options. If message options are present, `nd6_options()` will parse these options and store the byte locations of these options in the various fields of `nd_opts{}`.

Listing 5-135

```
                                                         __nd6_rtr.c
299              /*
300               * Default Router Information
301               */
    ....
305              Bzero(&dr0, sizeof(dr0));
306              dr0.rtaddr = src_sa6;
307              dr0.flags  = nd_ra->nd_ra_flags_reserved;
308              if (rtpref(&dr0) == RTPREF_RESERVED) {
309                      /*
310                       * "reserved" router preference should be treated as
311                       * 0-lifetime.  Note that rtpref() covers the case that the
312                       * kernel is not configured to support the preference
313                       * extension.
314                       */
315                      dr0.rtlifetime = 0;
316              } else
317                      dr0.rtlifetime = ntohs(nd_ra->nd_ra_router_lifetime);
318              dr0.expire = time_second + dr0.rtlifetime;
319              dr0.ifp = ifp;
320              dr0.advint = 0;          /* Mobile IPv6 */
321              dr0.advint_expire = 0;   /* Mobile IPv6 */
322              dr0.advints_lost = 0;    /* Mobile IPv6 */
                                                         __nd6_rtr.c
```

305–317 The `nd_defrouter{}` structure `dr0` records the router address, router lifetime, and the associated interface on which the router is seen. The function `rtpref()` retrieves the router preference from the Router Advertisement packet if the router supports the default router preferences according to [RFC4191]. The router lifetime is treated as 0 valued lifetime if the router preference is the reserved preference value(*). Otherwise, the router lifetime from the Router Advertisement packet is saved.

(*) This behavior was based on an older version of the specification and does not really conform to [RFC4191]. This case should be treated as if the Medium preference is specified.

Listing 5-136

```
                                                                        nd6_rtr.c
323                 /* unspecified or not? (RFC 2461 6.3.4) */
324                 if (nd_ra->nd_ra_reachable) {
325                         u_int32_t advreachable = nd_ra->nd_ra_reachable;
326
327                         NTOHL(advreachable);
328                         if (advreachable <= MAX_REACHABLE_TIME &&
329                             ndi->basereachable != advreachable) {
330                                 ndi->basereachable = advreachable;
331                                 ndi->reachable = ND_COMPUTE_RTIME(ndi->basereachable);
332                                 ndi->recalctm = nd6_recalc_reachtm_interval; /* reset */
333                         }
334                 }
                                                                        nd6_rtr.c
```

323–334 The receiving host updates its *BaseReachableTime* and recomputes the *ReachableTime* as shown in Table 5-7 when a router advertises a valid *ReachableTime*. The *ReachableTime* is scheduled to be recalculated in nd6_recalc_reachtm_interval, which is 2 hours by default.

Listing 5-137

```
                                                                        nd6_rtr.c
335                 if (nd_ra->nd_ra_retransmit)
336                         ndi->retrans = ntohl(nd_ra->nd_ra_retransmit);
337                 if (nd_ra->nd_ra_curhoplimit)
338                         ndi->chlim = nd_ra->nd_ra_curhoplimit;
                                                                        nd6_rtr.c
```

335–338 The receiving host updates its *RetransTimer* if the router advertises a valid value for it. The host also updates the default hop limit for outgoing packets if the router advertises such a value.

Listing 5-138

```
                                                                        nd6_rtr.c
339                 dr = defrtrlist_update(&dr0);
                                                                        nd6_rtr.c
```

339 The state change in a known router may require adjustment in the Default Router List. A newly discovered router should be added to the Default Router List. defrtrlist_update() is called to perform the necessary tasks with respect to the given router.

Listing 5-139

```
                                                                        nd6_rtr.c
352                 /*
353                  * prefix
354                  */
355                 if (ndopts.nd_opts_pi) {
```

```
356                    struct nd_opt_hdr *pt;
357                    struct nd_opt_prefix_info *pi = NULL;
358                    struct nd_prefixctl pr;
359
    ....
363                    for (pt = (struct nd_opt_hdr *)ndopts.nd_opts_pi;
364                        pt <= (struct nd_opt_hdr *)ndopts.nd_opts_pi_end;
365                        pt = (struct nd_opt_hdr *)((caddr_t)pt +
366                                            (pt->nd_opt_len << 3))) {
367                        if (pt->nd_opt_type != ND_OPT_PREFIX_INFORMATION)
368                            continue;
369                        pi = (struct nd_opt_prefix_info *)pt;
370
371                        if (pi->nd_opt_pi_len != 4) {
372                            nd6log((LOG_INFO,
373                                "nd6_ra_input: invalid option "
374                                "len %d for prefix information option, "
375                                "ignored\n", pi->nd_opt_pi_len));
376                            continue;
377                        }
378
379                        if (128 < pi->nd_opt_pi_prefix_len) {
380                            nd6log((LOG_INFO,
381                                "nd6_ra_input: invalid prefix "
382                                "len %d for prefix information option, "
383                                "ignored\n", pi->nd_opt_pi_prefix_len));
384                            continue;
385                        }
386
387                        if (IN6_IS_ADDR_MULTICAST(&pi->nd_opt_pi_prefix)
388                            || IN6_IS_ADDR_LINKLOCAL(&pi->nd_opt_pi_prefix)) {
389                            nd6log((LOG_INFO,
390                                "nd6_ra_input: invalid prefix "
391                                "%s, ignored\n",
392                                ip6_sprintf(&pi->nd_opt_pi_prefix)));
393                            continue;
394                        }
395
396                        /* aggregatable unicast address, rfc2374 */
397                        if ((pi->nd_opt_pi_prefix.s6_addr8[0] & 0xe0) == 0x20
398                            && pi->nd_opt_pi_prefix_len != 64) {
399                            nd6log((LOG_INFO,
400                                "nd6_ra_input: invalid prefixlen "
401                                "%d for rfc2374 prefix %s, ignored\n",
402                                pi->nd_opt_pi_prefix_len,
403                                ip6_sprintf(&pi->nd_opt_pi_prefix)));
404                            continue;
405                        }
406
407                        bzero(&pr, sizeof(pr));
408                        pr.ndpr_prefix.sin6_family = AF_INET6;
409                        pr.ndpr_prefix.sin6_len = sizeof(pr.ndpr_prefix);
410                        pr.ndpr_prefix.sin6_addr = pi->nd_opt_pi_prefix;
411                        pr.ndpr_ifp = (struct ifnet *)m->m_pkthdr.rcvif;
412
413                        pr.ndpr_raf_onlink = (pi->nd_opt_pi_flags_reserved &
414                            ND_OPT_PI_FLAG_ONLINK) ? 1 : 0;
415                        pr.ndpr_raf_auto = (pi->nd_opt_pi_flags_reserved &
416                            ND_OPT_PI_FLAG_AUTO) ? 1 : 0;
    ....
421                        pr.ndpr_plen = pi->nd_opt_pi_prefix_len;
422                        pr.ndpr_vltime = ntohl(pi->nd_opt_pi_valid_time);
423                        pr.ndpr_pltime = ntohl(pi->nd_opt_pi_preferred_time);
    ....
429                        (void)prelist_update(&pr, dr, m);
430                    }
431            }
```
_____nd6_rtr.c

355–394 The Router Advertisement message may carry the Prefix Information option. The Prefix Information option must be 32 bytes long, the prefix length cannot excceed 128 bits, the prefix must not have a link-local scope and must not be a multicast address prefix.

397–405 This block of code rejects a prefix length other than 64 bits if the corresponding prefix matches a certain type of unicast addresses. This check is actually too strict and is incorrect or inappropriate for several reasons. First, this option may simply provide an on-link prefix, in which case any length of prefix should be allowed. Secondly, even though many IPv6-related protocols use the magic number of 64, it is generally inadvisable to assume a constant length of prefix in general processing such as this case, as discussed in [RFC2462BIS]. Later versions of this code remove this check, and check the prefix length only when it is really necessary in configuring an address.

407–429 A valid Prefix Information option is stored in an `nd_prefixctl{}` structure and is passed to `prelist_update()` (Section 5.19.3) for further processing, for example, generating new addresses based on this prefix.

Listing 5-140

```
                                                                      nd6_rtr.c
463              /*
464               * MTU
465               */
466              if (ndopts.nd_opts_mtu && ndopts.nd_opts_mtu->nd_opt_mtu_len == 1) {
467                      u_long mtu;
468                      u_long maxmtu;
469
470                      mtu = (u_long)ntohl(ndopts.nd_opts_mtu->nd_opt_mtu_mtu);
471
472                      /* lower bound */
473                      if (mtu < IPV6_MMTU) {
474                              nd6log((LOG_INFO, "nd6_ra_input: bogus mtu option "
475                                  "mtu=%lu sent from %s, ignoring\n",
476                                  mtu, ip6_sprintf(&ip6->ip6_src)));
477                              goto skip;
478                      }
479
480                      /* upper bound */
481                      maxmtu = (ndi->maxmtu && ndi->maxmtu < ifp->if_mtu)
482                          ? ndi->maxmtu : ifp->if_mtu;
483                      if (mtu <= maxmtu) {
484                              int change = (ndi->linkmtu != mtu);
485
486                              ndi->linkmtu = mtu;
487                              if (change) /* in6_maxmtu may change */
488                                      in6_setmaxmtu();
489                      } else {
490                              nd6log((LOG_INFO, "nd6_ra_input: bogus mtu "
491                                  "mtu=%lu sent from %s; "
492                                  "exceeds maxmtu %lu, ignoring\n",
493                                  mtu, ip6_sprintf(&ip6->ip6_src), maxmtu));
494                      }
495              }
                                                                      nd6_rtr.c
```

466–495 The Router Advertisement message may carry the MTU option. The MTU option must be 8 bytes long and its value must be at least the minimum required value of 1280. The advertised value must not exceed the physical limit as defined by the link type. A new valid MTU value will trigger an update to the global variable in6_maxmtu, which stores the largest link MTU used for IPv6 communication in this node.

Listing 5-141

─── nd6_rtr.c

```
497     skip:
498
499             /*
500              * Source linklayer address
501              */
502             if (ndopts.nd_opts_src_lladdr) {
503                     lladdr = (char *)(ndopts.nd_opts_src_lladdr + 1);
504                     lladdrlen = ndopts.nd_opts_src_lladdr->nd_opt_len << 3;
505             }
506
507             if (lladdr && ((ifp->if_addrlen + 2 + 7) & ~7) != lladdrlen) {
508                     nd6log((LOG_INFO,
509                         "nd6_ra_input: lladdrlen mismatch for %s "
510                         "(if %d, RA packet %d)\n", ip6_sprintf(&src_sa6.sin6_addr),
511                         ifp->if_addrlen, lladdrlen - 2));
512                     goto bad;
513             }
514
515             nd6_cache_lladdr(ifp, &src_sa6, lladdr,
516                 lladdrlen, ND_ROUTER_ADVERT, 0);
517
518             /*
519              * Installing a link-layer address might change the state of the
520              * router's neighbor cache, which might also affect our on-link
521              * detection of advertised prefixes.
522              */
523             pfxlist_onlink_check();
```

─── nd6_rtr.c

502–523 When the Source Link-Layer address option is present, lladdr is set to point to the start of the source link-layer address, and lladdrlen is initialized to contain the length of the option.

The length of the link-layer address is aligned on the 8-byte boundary. This length must match the length of the link-layer address of the receiving interface. Since lladdrlen accounts for the Type and Length fields of the option, the interface link-layer address length must also account for these two bytes when comparing the two length values.

Function nd6_cache_lladdr() is called to create a Neighbor Cache entry for the packet source and its link-layer address is saved into the new cache entry.

Since the reachability state of a router may have changed and can subsequently affect the receiver's perception of which prefixes are on-link, function pfxlist_onlink_check() is called to check the on-link status of each prefix and updates the state of each prefix accordingly.

Listing 5-142

─── nd6_rtr.c

```
525     freeit:
526             m_freem(m);
527             return;
528
529     bad:
```

```
530             icmp6stat.icp6s_badra++;
531             m_freem(m);
532      }
```
nd6_rtr.c

526–532 The packet is discarded at the completion of Router Advertisement processing. The
ICMPv6 statistics counter is updated in case of an erroneous Router Advertisement packet.

5.16.7 `icmp6_redirect_input()` Function

The ICMPv6 Redirect mechanism allows a router to direct a host to send traffic to a more
appropriate first-hop router. A host may send packets to a router for forwarding to an on-link
neighbor when the address prefix of that neighbor is unknown to the transmitting host. In such
a situation the receiving router will generate a Redirect message to inform the packet source
that the destination is in fact a neighboring node on the same link. See Figure 5-5 as an example
exchange of a Redirect message.

The `icmp6_redirect_input()` function processes incoming Redirect packets. A host
must perform the following validations on received Redirect messages. The host must discard
Redirect messages that fail any of the following validity checks.

- The source address of the Redirect message must be a link-local address.

- The Hop Limit field of the IPv6 header has the value 255 (i.e., a router has not forwarded
  this Redirect message).

- The message authenticates correctly if an Authentication header is included.

- The ICMPv6 checksum field is valid.

- The ICMPv6 code is 0.

- The ICMPv6 portion of the packet is at least 40 bytes large.

- The Destination address field of the Redirect message is not a multicast address.

- The target address is a link-local address when being redirected to a router, or is the
  same as the destination address of the Redirect message when told about an on-link
  neighbor.

- Each included option has non-0 length.

The receiving node must ignore the reserved field and any unrecognized message options.
Any options other than the Source Link-Layer address option must be ignored and packet
processing continues as normal.

Listing 5-143
icmp6.c

```
2716     void
2717     icmp6_redirect_input(m, off)
2718            struct mbuf *m;
2719            int off;
2720     {
2721            struct ifnet *ifp = m->m_pkthdr.rcvif;
2722            struct ip6_hdr *ip6 = mtod(m, struct ip6_hdr *);
2723            struct nd_redirect *nd_rd;
```

```
2724            int icmp6len = ntohs(ip6->ip6_plen);
2725            char *lladdr = NULL;
2726            int lladdrlen = 0;
2727            u_char *redirhdr = NULL;
2728            int redirhdrlen = 0;
2729            struct rtentry *rt = NULL;
2730            int is_router;
2731            int is_onlink;
2732            struct sockaddr_in6 src_sa, reddst6, redtgt6, rodst;
2733            union nd_opts ndopts;
2734
2735            if (!ifp)
2736                    return;
```
——— icmp6.c

2717–2736 On input, m refers to the received packet. off holds the offset from the start of
the packet to the beginning of the Redirect header. The receiving interface is stored in
the m_pkthdr.rcvif field of the packet mbuf{}. This interface pointer is set in ifp
and must not be NULL because information will be retrieved from the interface structure
ifnet{}.

Note that variable icmp6len is initialized with the value of the payload length field
of the IPv6 header, but it includes the size of the extension headers if extension headers
are present. This is a bug of this code.

Listing 5-144
——— icmp6.c

```
2738            /* XXX if we are router, we don't update route by icmp6 redirect */
2739            if (ip6_forwarding)
2740                    goto freeit;
```
——— icmp6.c

2739–2740 The global flag ip6_forwarding serves as an indicator as to whether a node is
acting as a router or as a host. The node is acting as a router if ip6_forwarding is set
to a non-0 value. Since a Redirect message is sent by a router to redirect a host to a better
first-hop or to inform the host the destination is in fact an on-link neighbor, the Redirect
message does not apply to a router and the router must not modify its routing table upon
receiving a Redirect message. A router simply discards the Redirect packet.

Listing 5-145
——— icmp6.c

```
2741            if (!icmp6_rediraccept)
2742                    goto freeit;
```
——— icmp6.c

2741–2742 A Redirect message is only accepted when the configuration variable
icmp6_rediraccept is non-0. Its default value is 1 (accept) and can be configured
through the **sysctl** command using the variable net.inet6.icmp6.rediraccept.

Listing 5-146
——— icmp6.c

```
2745            IP6_EXTHDR_CHECK(m, off, icmp6len,);
2746            nd_rd = (struct nd_redirect *)((caddr_t)ip6 + off);
```
——— icmp6.c

2745–2746 As explained in Section 1.6.3, the KAME implementation generally expects the entire portion of an incoming packet starting from the IPv6 header to the transport layer header to be in contiguous memory. The `IP6_EXTHDR_CHECK()` macro checks for this condition and the function terminates here if the verification fails. Variable `nd_rd` is set to point to the beginning of the Redirect message.

Listing 5-147

———————————————————————————————————————icmp6.c
```
2755                 /*
2756                  * extract address parameters from the packet and convert them to a
2757                  * sockaddr_in6 form.
2758                  */
2759                 if (ip6_getpktaddrs(m, &src_sa, NULL))
2760                         goto freeit;
```
———————————————————————————————————————icmp6.c

2759–2760 `ip6_input()` creates an mbuf tag that contains the source and destination addresses of the packet. `ip6_getpktaddrs()` is called here to retrieve the packet source address.

Listing 5-148

———————————————————————————————————————icmp6.c
```
2761                 bzero(&redtgt, sizeof(redtgt6));
2762                 bzero(&reddst, sizeof(reddst6));
2763                 redtgt6.sin6_family = reddst6.sin6_family = AF_INET6;
2764                 redtgt6.sin6_len = reddst6.sin6_len = sizeof(struct sockaddr_in6);
2765                 redtgt6.sin6_addr = nd_rd->nd_rd_target;
2766                 reddst6.sin6_addr = nd_rd->nd_rd_dst;
2767                 if (in6_addr2zoneid(m->m_pkthdr.rcvif, &redtgt6.sin6_addr,
2768                                     &redtgt6.sin6_scope_id) ||
2769                     in6_addr2zoneid(m->m_pkthdr.rcvif, &reddst6.sin6_addr,
2770                                     &reddst6.sin6_scope_id)) {
2771                         goto freeit;    /* XXX impossible */
2772                 }
2773                 if (in6_embedscope(&redtgt6.sin6_addr, &redtgt6) ||
2774                     in6_embedscope(&reddst6.sin6_addr, &reddst6) ||
2775                         goto freeit;    /* XXX impossible */
2776                 }
```
———————————————————————————————————————icmp6.c

2761–2776 The target address and the destination address are copied out of the packet and stored into `redtgt6` and `reddst6` in `sockaddr_in6{}` format, respectively. `in6_addr2zoneid()` is called to retrieve the zone ID of each address and `in6_embedscope()` converts each address along with its zone ID into an internal representation. Many functions in the KAME implementation operate on addresses of this internal representation.

Listing 5-149

———————————————————————————————————————icmp6.c
```
2778                 /* validation */
2779                 if (!IN6_IS_ADDR_LINKLOCAL(&src_sa.sin6_addr)) {
2780                         nd6log((LOG_ERR,
2781                                 "ICMP6 redirect sent from %s rejected; "
```

```
2782                         "must be from linklocal\n",
2783                         ip6_sprintf(&src_sa.sin6_addr)));
2784                 goto bad;
2785         }
```
—— icmp6.c

2779–2784 A router is required to use its link-local address as the source address when sending Redirect messages. The source of the Redirect message must be a link-local address that uniquely identifies the router.

Listing 5-150
—— icmp6.c

```
2786         if (ip6->ip6_hlim != 255) {
2787                 nd6log((LOG_ERR,
2788                         "ICMP6 redirect sent from %s rejected; "
2789                         "hlim=%d (must be 255)\n",
2790                         ip6_sprintf(&src_sa.sin6_addr), ip6->ip6_hlim));
2791                 goto bad;
2792         }
```
—— icmp6.c

2786–2791 The hop limit of the Redirect packet must be 255, which indicates the Redirect message is not forwarded by a router; otherwise, the packet is discarded.

Listing 5-151
—— icmp6.c

```
2794         if (IN6_IS_ADDR_MULTICAST(&reddst6.sin6_addr)) {
2795                 nd6log((LOG_ERR,
2796                         "ICMP6 redirect rejected; "
2797                         "redirect dst must be unicast: %s\n",
2798                         icmp6_redirect_diag(&src_sa, &reddst6, &redtgt6)));
2799                 goto bad;
2800         }
```
—— icmp6.c

2794–2799 The Destination address field in the Redirect message must not be a multicast address. Otherwise, the packet is discarded and a message is written to the log (depending on the behavior of nd6log()).

Listing 5-152
—— icmp6.c

```
2802         /* ip6->ip6_src must be equal to gw for icmp6->icmp6_reddst */
2803         rodst = reddst6; /* XXX: we don't need rodst if SCOPEDROUTING */
....
2805         rodst.sin6_scope_id = 0;
....
2807         rt = rtalloc1((struct sockaddr *)&rodst, 0
....
2809                         , 0UL
....
2811                         );
2812         if (rt) {
2813                 struct sockaddr_in6 *gw6;
2814
2815                 if (rt->rt_gateway == NULL ||
```

```
2816                         rt->rt_gateway->sa_family != AF_INET6) {
2817                             nd6log((LOG_ERR,
2818                                 "ICMP6 redirect rejected; no route "
2819                                 "with inet6 gateway found for redirect dst: %s\n",
2820                                 icmp6_redirect_diag(&src_sa, &reddst6, &redtgt6)));
2821                             RTFREE(rt);
2822                             goto bad;
2823                         }
2824
2825                         gw6 = (struct sockaddr_in6 *)rt->rt_gateway;
2826                         if (
....
2830                             !IN6_ARE_ADDR_EQUAL(&gw6->sin6_addr,
2831                                             &src_sa.sin6_addr)
....
2833                             ) {
2834                             nd6log((LOG_ERR,
2835                                 "ICMP6 redirect rejected; "
2836                                 "not equal to gw-for-src=%s (must be same): "
2837                                 "%s\n",
2838                                 ip6_sprintf(&gw6->sin6_addr),
2839                                 icmp6_redirect_diag(&src_sa, &reddst6,
2840                                             &redtgt6)));
2841                             RTFREE(rt);
2842                             goto bad;
2843                         }
2844             } else {
2845                 nd6log((LOG_ERR,
2846                     "ICMP6 redirect rejected; "
2847                     "no route found for redirect dst: %s\n",
2848                     icmp6_redirect_diag(&src_sa, &reddst6, &redtgt6)));
2849                 goto bad;
2850             }
2851         RTFREE(rt);
2852         rt = NULL;
```
──── icmp6.c

2803–2842 A host receives Redirect messages from routers which are known to the host, and to which the host has actively sent packets for forwarding. Therefore, if the Redirect message came from a known router, performing a search on the redirected destination should find a route entry that uses that router as the gateway.

The code here calls `rtalloc1()` to perform a search into the kernel routing table for the redirected destination. If a route entry is found, this entry must be an indirect route with a valid gateway address. The source address of the Redirect packet belongs to the router, so the source address must match the gateway address.

The packet is discarded and a log message is written if there is no route to the destination. The packet is discarded if a valid route is found but reaching that destination does not require a gateway. The packet is also discarded if there is a mismatch between the source address and the gateway address obtained from the route entry.

Listing 5-153
──── icmp6.c

```
2854         is_router = is_onlink = 0;
2855         if (IN6_IS_ADDR_LINKLOCAL(&redtgt6.sin6_addr))
2856             is_router = 1;  /* router case */
2857         if (SA6_ARE_ADDR_EQUAL(&redtgt6, &reddst6))
2858             is_onlink = 1;  /* on-link destination case */
2859         if (!is_router && !is_onlink) {
2860             nd6log((LOG_ERR,
```

```
2861                        "ICMP6 redirect rejected; "
2862                        "neither router case nor onlink case: %s\n",
2863                        icmp6_redirect_diag(&src_sa, &reddst6, &redtgt6)));
2864                goto bad;
2865        }
2866        /* validation passed */
```
_____ icmp6.c

2854–2865 The Target address must be a link-local address if the Redirect message provides
a better next-hop router. In this case the `is_router` flag is set to true. The Redirect
message indicates the destination is an on-link neighbor if the target address is the same
as the destination address. In this case the `is_onlink` flag is set to true. Any other
condition indicates the packet is erroneous and the packet is discarded.

Listing 5-154

_____ icmp6.c
```
2868            icmp6len -= sizeof(*nd_rd);
2869            nd6_option_init(nd_rd + 1, icmp6len, &ndopts);
2870            if (nd6_options(&ndopts) < 0) {
2871                    nd6log((LOG_INFO, "icmp6_redirect_input:"
2872                        "invalid ND option, rejected: %s\n",
2873                        icmp6_redirect_diag(&src_sa, &reddst6, &redtgt6)));
2874                    /* nd6_options have incremented stats */
2875                    goto freeit;
2876            }
2877
2878            if (ndopts.nd_opts_tgt_lladdr) {
2879                    lladdr = (char *)(ndopts.nd_opts_tgt_lladdr + );
2880                    lladdrlen = ndopts.nd_opts_tgt_lladdr->nd_opt_len << 3;
2881            }
2882
2883            if (ndopts.nd_opts_rh) {
2884                    redirhdrlen = ndopts.nd_opts_rh->nd_opt_rh_len;
2885                    redirhdr = (u_char *)(ndopts.nd_opts_rh + 1); /* XXX */
2886            }
```
_____ icmp6.c

2868–2885 `icmp6len` is updated to reflect that the processing of the fixed part of the Redirect
message is now complete. `nd6_option_init()` prepares the `ndopts` data structure
for processing possible options. Two options are allowed for the Redirect message: the
Target Link-Layer Address option and the Redirected Header option. `nd6_options()`
parses the options and returns the results in `ndopts`. If the Target Link-Layer address
option is present, `lladdr` is set to point to the first byte of the link-layer address field,
and `lladdrlen` is set to 8 multiplying the value of the Length field from the option. In the
case of Ethernet, the value of `lladdrlen` is 8. If the Redirected Header option is present,
`redirhdrlen` is set to the value of the Length field from the option, and `redirhdr` is
set to point to the first byte of the original packet header.

Listing 5-155

_____ icmp6.c
```
2888            if (lladdr && ((ifp->if_addrlen + 2 + 7) & ~7) != lladdrlen) {
2889                    nd6log((LOG_INFO,
2890                        "icmp6_redirect_input: lladdrlen mismatch for %s "
2891                        "(if %d, icmp6 packet %d): %s\n",
2892                        ip6_sprintf(&redtgt6.sin6_addr),
2893                        ifp->if_addrlen, lladdrlen - 2,
2894                        icmp6_redirect_diag(&src_sa, &reddst6, &redtgt6)));
```

```
2895                    goto bad;
2896            }
```
——— *icmp6.c*

2888–2895 The length of the link-layer address is aligned on the 8-byte boundary. This length must match the length of the link-layer address of the receiving interface. Since `lladdrlen` accounts for the Type and Length fields of the option, the interface link-layer address length must also account for these two bytes when comparing the two length values.

Listing 5-156
——— *icmp6.c*
```
2898            /* RFC 2461 8.3 */
2899            nd6_cache_lladdr(ifp, &redtgt6, lladdr, lladdrlen, ND_REDIRECT,
2900                    is_onlink ? ND_REDIRECT_ONLINK : ND_REDIRECT_ROUTER);
```
——— *icmp6.c*

2899 `nd6_cache_lladdr()` is called to create either a new Neighbor Cache entry for the destination if that destination is an on-link neighbor, or a new entry for the router if a better next-hop is present.

Listing 5-157
——— *icmp6.c*
```
2902            if (!is_onlink) {        /* better router case.  perform rtredirect. */
2903                    /* perform rtredirect */
2904                    struct sockaddr_in6 sdst;
2905                    struct sockaddr_in6 sgw;
2906                    struct sockaddr_in6 ssrc;
....
2935                    sgw = redtgt6;
2936                    sdst = reddst6;
2937                    ssrc = src_sa;
....
2939                    sgw.sin6_scope_id = sdst.sin6_scope_id =
2940                            ssrc.sin6_scope_id = 0;
....
2942
2943                    rtredirect((struct sockaddr *)&sdst, (struct sockaddr *)&sgw,
2944                            (struct sockaddr *)NULL, RTF_GATEWAY | RTF_HOST,
2945                            (struct sockaddr *)&ssrc,
....
2953                            );
....
2962            }
2963            /* finally update cached route in each socket via pfctlinput */
2964            pfctlinput(PRC_REDIRECT_HOST, (struct sockaddr *)&reddst6);
```
——— *icmp6.c*

2902–2964 `rtredirect()` is called here to create or modify an indirect host route for the destination if the Redirect message is informing the host about a better next-hop router. `redtgt6` contains the link-local address of the better next-hop router. `reddst6` contains the destination address. `src_sa` contains the address of the router that originated the Redirect message. `rtredirect()` will perform a similar gateway validation as that done at lines 2830–2831 in Listing 5-152.

`pfctlinput()` sends the `PRC_REDIRECT_HOST` to upper layer protocols informing them about the route change. This notification allows protocols such as TCP that caches a route reference in the protocol control block to flush the cache entry and obtain a new route reference (see Section 6.7.10).

Listing 5-158

```
                                                                    icmp6.c
2969    freeit:
2970            m_freem(m);
2971            return;
2972
2973    bad:
2974            icmp6stat.icp6s_badredirect++;
2975            m_freem(m);
2976    }
                                                                    icmp6.c
```

2969–2975 The `freeit` label is reached if the Redirect packet is silently ignored, or if normal processing completes. The packet is freed and this function returns to caller. On error, the ICMPv6 `icp6s_badredirect` statistics counter is incremented and the packet is freed.

5.16.8 `icmp6_redirect_output()` Function

When a router receives a packet for forwarding, if the packet destination is in fact on-link in the incoming link, or if there is a better next-hop router, the receiving router will forward the packet as well as generating Redirect packet to the source. In the KAME implementation, this is done by `ip6_forward()` calling `icmp6_redirect_output()`. In a nutshell, `ip6_forward()` decides that a Redirect message is necessary when the outgoing interface used for forwarding the packet is the same as the interface on which the packet arrived. See Section 3.12 for more details about the processing of the `ip6_forward()` function.

The router sets the Target address field to the link-local address of a neighboring router if the router is redirecting the source to a better first-hop router. The router sets the Target address to the same value as the Destination address field when the router is informing the source about the on-link destination. The Redirect message may contain the Target Link-Layer address option if the link-layer address of the target is known to the transmitting router; the Redirected header option contains as much of the forwarded packet as possible without exceeding the IPv6 minimum link MTU for the overall Redirect packet. The Redirect packets must not exceed the rate-limit policy that may be configured on the router.

Listing 5-159

```
                                                                    icmp6.c
2978    void
2979    icmp6_redirect_output(m0, rt)
2980            struct mbuf *m0;
2981            struct rtentry *rt;
2982    {
2983            struct ifnet *ifp;        /* my outgoing interface */
2984            struct sockaddr_in6 src_sa, dst_sa, *nexthop, *ifp_ll6;
....
2986            struct sockaddr_in6 ifp_ll6_storage;
....
2988            struct ip6_hdr *sip6;     /* m0 as struct ip6_hdr */
2989            struct mbuf *m = NULL;    /* newly allocated one */
2990            struct ip6_hdr *ip6;      /* m as struct ip6_hdr */
2991            struct nd_redirect *nd_rd;
2992            size_t maxlen;
```

```
2993            u_char *p;
2994            struct in6_ifaddr *ia;
```
_____icmp6.c

2979–2981 The first parameter m0 references the original packet. The referenced amount is
ICMPV6_PLD_MAXLEN bytes. rt points to the route entry to use when transmitting the
Redirect packet.

Listing 5-160
_____icmp6.c

```
2996            icmp6_errcount(&icmp6stat.icp6s_outerrhist, ND_REDIRECT, 0);
2997
2998            /* if we are not router, we don't send icmp6 redirect */
2999            if (!ip6_forwarding || ip6_accept_rtadv)
3000                goto fail;
```
_____icmp6.c

2996 The ICMPv6 statistics counter icp6s_outerrhist is incremented through function
icmp6_errcount().

2999–3000 A host must not send a Redirect message. The logic is the same as Listing 5-120.

Listing 5-161
_____icmp6.c

```
3002            /* sanity check */
3003            if (!m0 || !rt || !(rt->rt_flags & RTF_UP) || !(ifp = rt->rt_ifp))
3004                goto fail;
```
_____icmp6.c

3003 The code here performs sanity checks: The Redirect packet must be present, the referenced route is active, and the outgoing interface is available. Otherwise the function
terminates here.

Listing 5-162
_____icmp6.c

```
3006            /*
3007             * Address check:
3008             *  the source address must identify a neighbor, and
3009             *  the destination address must not be a multicast address
3010             *  [RFC 2461, sec 8.2]
3011             */
3012            sip6 = mtod(m0, struct ip6_hdr *);
3013            if (ip6_getpktaddrs(m0, &src_sa, &dst_sa))
3014                goto fail;
3015            if (nd6_is_addr_neighbor(&src_sa, ifp) == 0)
3016                goto fail;
3017            if (IN6_IS_ADDR_MULTICAST(&dst_sa.sin6_addr))
3018                goto fail;
```
_____icmp6.c

3012–3018 The protocol specification imposes some requirements about the source and destination addresses of a packet that can trigger a Redirect message: The packet source must
be on-link because a Redirect message can only be sent to an on-link host; the destination address must not be a multicast address. ip6_getpktaddrs() is called to retrieve
the packet source and destination addresses and store these addresses in src_sa and
dst_sa, respectively, and the required checks are performed on these variables.

Note: The check about the destination address is actually redundant since this function is only called from `ip6_forward()`, which does not handle a multicast packet.

Listing 5-163

```
                                                                        icmp6.c
3020            /* rate limit */
3021            if (icmp6_ratelimit(&src_sa.sin6_addr, ND_REDIRECT, 0))
3022                    goto fail;
                                                                        icmp6.c
```

3021–3022 The Redirect messages should be subject to rate limiting if the packet source does not correctly react to Redirect messages, or if the packet source chooses to ignore the Redirect packets. The rate limitation is done by the `icmp6_ratelimit()` function as described in Section 4.8.2. Note that a host that runs the KAME implementation can choose to ignore the Redirect messages by setting the global variable `icmp6_rediraccept` to zero (Listing 5-145). If a host keeps sending packets that cause Redirect messages at a high rate and ignores the Redirect messages, this function can be called very frequently.

Listing 5-164

```
                                                                        icmp6.c
3024            /*
3025             * Since we are going to append up to 1280 bytes (= IPV6_MMTU),
3026             * we almost always ask for an mbuf cluster for simplicity.
3027             * (MHLEN < IPV6_MMTU is almost always true)
3028             */
3029    #if IPV6_MMTU >= MCLBYTES
3030    # error assumption failed about IPV6_MMTU and MCLBYTES
3031    #endif
3032            MGETHDR(m, M_DONTWAIT, MT_HEADER);
3033            if (m && IPV6_MMTU >= MHLEN)
3034                    MCLGET(m, M_DONTWAIT);
3035            if (!m)
3036                    goto fail;
3037            m->m_pkthdr.rcvif = NULL;
3038            m->m_len = 0;
3039            maxlen = M_TRAILINGSPACE(m);
3040            maxlen = min(IPV6_MMTU, maxlen);
3041            /* just for safety */
3042            if (maxlen < sizeof(struct ip6_hdr) + sizeof(struct icmp6_hdr) +
3043                ((sizeof(struct nd_opt_hdr) + ifp->if_addrlen + 7) & ~7)) {
3044                    goto fail;
3045            }
                                                                        icmp6.c
```

3029–3045 An `mbuf{}` is allocated for the outgoing Redirect packet. A cluster block is allocated if the free space in the `mbuf{}` is not larger than the minimum MTU. The system configured cluster block size must be at least as large as the minimum MTU value required by IPv6, which is 1280 bytes. The Target Link-Layer Address option may be included in the Redirect message, which is why an option header and the size of the interface link-layer address is included in the memory requirement calculation. The packet is discarded and the function terminates here if the allocated memory is insufficient.

Listing 5-165

```
                                                                    icmp6.c
3047            /* get ip6 linklocal address for ifp (my outgoing interface). */
3048            if ((ia = in6ifa_ifpforlinklocal(ifp,
3049                                        IN6_IFF_NOTREADY | IN6_IFF_ANYCAST))
3050                == NULL) {
3051                goto fail;
3052            }
3053            ifp_ll6 = &ia->ia_addr;
....
3055            /*
3056             * XXX: ifp_ll6 may not have a valid sin6_scope_id in
3057             * the non-SCOPEDROUTING case.
3058             */
3059            ifp_ll6_storage = *ifp_ll6;
3060            if (in6_addr2zoneid(ifp, &ifp_ll6_storage.sin6_addr,
3061                            &ifp_ll6_storage.sin6_scope_id)) {
3062                    goto fail;
3063            }
3064            ifp_ll6 = &ifp_ll6_storage;
                                                                    icmp6.c
```

3048–3064 A router must use its link-local address as the source address of the Redirect packet. `in6ifa_ifpforlinklocal()` retrieves a link-local address from the outgoing interface and uses this address as the packet source. `in6_addr2zoneid()` determines the appropriate link zone ID for the link-local address and embeds the ID into the address.

Note that since the interface address structure does not generally set its `sin6_scope_id` field correctly as discussed in Section 2.9.3, a local copy of `ifp_ll6_storage` must be used for work space. Otherwise, the interface address structure would be modified by `in6_addr2zoneid()`.

Listing 5-166

```
                                                                    icmp6.c
3067            /* get ip6 linklocal address for the router. */
3068            if (rt->rt_gateway && (rt->rt_flags & RTF_GATEWAY)) {
3069                    nexthop = (struct sockaddr_in6 *)rt->rt_gateway;
3070                    if (!IN6_IS_ADDR_LINKLOCAL(&nexthop->sin6_addr))
3071                            nexthop = NULL;
3072            } else
3073                    nexthop = NULL;
                                                                    icmp6.c
```

3067–3073 If the route is a gateway route that contains a valid router address, then the local node is forwarding the packet to a better next-hop. The better next-hop router must be referenced by a link-local address.

Listing 5-167

```
                                                                    icmp6.c
3075            /* ip6 */
3076            ip6 = mtod(m, struct ip6_hdr *);
3077            ip6->ip6_flow = 0;
3078            ip6->ip6_vfc &= ~IPV6_VERSION_MASK;
3079            ip6->ip6_vfc |= IPV6_VERSION;
3080            /* ip6->ip6_plen will be set later */
3081            ip6->ip6_nxt = IPPROTO_ICMPV6;
3082            ip6->ip6_hlim = 255;
```

```
3083              /* ip6->ip6_src must be linklocal addr for my outgoing if. */
3084              bcopy(&ifp_ll6->sin6_addr, &ip6->ip6_src, sizeof(struct in6_addr));
3085              bcopy(&src_sa.sin6_addr, &ip6->ip6_dst, sizeof(struct in6_addr));
3086              /* set the packet addresses in a sockaddr_in6 form */
3087              if (!ip6_setpktaddrs(m, ifp_ll6, &src_sa))
3088                    goto fail;
```
_____ icmp6.c

3076–3088 The code here builds the IPv6 header of the outgoing Redirect packet. The 4-bit version field is set to `IPV6_VERSION`. The Hop Limit must be set to 255 as required by the specification. The Next Header field is set to ICMPv6. The Source Address is a link-local address of the outgoing interface. The Destination Address is the source address of the original packet.

An mbuf tag is created and the source and destination addresses are copied into the tag.

Listing 5-168
_____ icmp6.c

```
3090              /* ND Redirect */
3091              nd_rd = (struct nd_redirect *)(ip6 + 1);
3092              nd_rd->nd_rd_type = ND_REDIRECT;
3093              nd_rd->nd_rd_code = 0;
3094              nd_rd->nd_rd_reserved = 0;
3095              if (rt->rt_flags & RTF_GATEWAY) {
3096                    /*
3097                     * nd_rd->nd_rd_target must be a link-local address in
3098                     * better router cases.
3099                     */
3100                    if (!nexthop)
3101                          goto fail;
3102                    bcopy(&nexthop->sin6_addr, &nd_rd->nd_rd_target,
3103                          sizeof(nd_rd->nd_rd_target));
3104                    bcopy(&dst_sa.sin6_addr, &nd_rd->nd_rd_dst,
3105                          sizeof(nd_rd->nd_rd_dst));
3106              } else {
3107                    /* make sure redtgt == reddst */
3108                    nexthop = &dst_sa;
3109                    bcopy(&dst_sa.sin6_addr, &nd_rd->nd_rd_target,
3110                          sizeof(nd_rd->nd_rd_target));
3111                    bcopy(&dst_sa.sin6_addr, &nd_rd->nd_rd_dst,
3112                          sizeof(nd_rd->nd_rd_dst));
3113              }
```
_____ icmp6.c

3090–3112 The code here builds the Redirect packet header. The Target Address field has the same value as the Destination Address field if the destination is on-link. Otherwise the Target Address field is set to the link-local address of the better next-hop router. The Destination Address field contains the destination address of the original packet that triggered the Redirect message.

Listing 5-169
_____ icmp6.c

```
3115              p = (u_char *)(nd_rd + 1);
3116
3117              {
3118                    /* target lladdr option */
```

```
3119                        struct rtentry *rt_nexthop = NULL;
3120                        int len;
3121                        struct sockaddr_dl *sdl;
3122                        struct nd_opt_hdr *nd_opt;
3123                        char *lladdr;
3124
3125                        rt_nexthop = nd6_lookup(nexthop, 0, ifp);
3126                        if (!rt_nexthop)
3127                                goto nolladdropt;
3128                        len = sizeof(*nd_opt) + ifp->if_addrlen;
3129                        len = (len + 7) & ~7;    /* round by 8 */
3130                        /* safety check */
3131                        if (len + (p - (u_char *)ip6) > maxlen)
3132                                goto nolladdropt;
3133                        if (!(rt_nexthop->rt_flags & RTF_GATEWAY) &&
3134                            (rt_nexthop->rt_flags & RTF_LLINFO) &&
3135                            (rt_nexthop->rt_gateway->sa_family == AF_LINK) &&
3136                            (sdl = (struct sockaddr_dl *)rt_nexthop->rt_gateway) &&
3137                            sdl->sdl_alen) {
3138                                nd_opt = (struct nd_opt_hdr *)p;
3139                                nd_opt->nd_opt_type = ND_OPT_TARGET_LINKADDR;
3140                                nd_opt->nd_opt_len = len >> 3;
3141                                lladdr = (char *)(nd_opt + 1);
3142                                bcopy(LLADDR(sdl), lladdr, ifp->if_addrlen);
3143                                p += len;
3144                        }
3145                }
3146        nolladdropt:
```
_____ icmp6.c

3115–3145 nexthop holds either the gateway address or the address of the destination. nd6_lookup() is called to search into the local Neighbor Cache and determines if the link-layer address of nexthop is known to the local node. If a Neighbor Cache entry is found, it must contain link-layer information, that is, the RTF_LLINFO flag is set for the route entry and rt_gateway has the address family AF_LINK. A Target Link-Layer address option is created and is included with the Redirect message if the Neighbor Cache validation completes successfully.

Listing 5-170
_____ icmp6.c

```
3148            m->m_pkthdr.len = m->m_len = p - (u_char *)ip6;
```
_____ icmp6.c

3148 The overall packet length is updated to include the length of the Target Link-Layer address option.

Listing 5-171
_____ icmp6.c

```
3150            /* just to be safe */
....
3155            if (p - (u_char *)ip6 > maxlen)
3156                    goto noredhdropt;
3157
3158            {
3159                    /* redirected header option */
3160                    int len;
3161                    struct nd_opt_rd_hdr *nd_opt_rh;
```
_____ icmp6.c

3155 A Redirected header option is included if there is sufficient space left in the allocated buffer.

Listing 5-172

___icmp6.c

```
3163                      /*
3164                       * compute the maximum size for icmp6 redirect header option.
3165                       * XXX room for auth header?
3166                       */
3167                      len = maxlen - (p - (u_char *)ip6);
3168                      len &= ~7;
3169
3170                      /*
3171                       * Redirected header option spec (RFC2461 4.6.3) talks nothing
3172                       * about padding/truncate rule for the original IP packet.
3173                       * From the discussion on IPv6imp in Feb 1999,
3174                       * the consensus was:
3175                       * - "attach as much as possible" is the goal
3176                       * - pad if not aligned (original size can be guessed by
3177                       *   original ip6 header)
3178                       * Following code adds the padding if it is simple enough,
3179                       * and truncates if not.
3180                       */
3181                      if (len - sizeof(*nd_opt_rh) < m0->m_pkthdr.len) {
3182                              /* not enough room, truncate */
3183                              m_adj(m0, (len - sizeof(*nd_opt_rh)) -
3184                                  m0->m_pkthdr.len);
3185                      } else {
3186                              /*
3187                               * enough room, truncate if not aligned.
3188                               * we don't pad here for simplicity.
3189                               */
3190                              size_t extra;
3191
3192                              extra = m0->m_pkthdr.len % 8;
3193                              if (extra) {
3194                                      /* truncate */
3195                                      m_adj(m0, -extra);
3196                              }
3197                      }
```

___icmp6.c

3170–3180 As the code comment indicates, the specification does not discuss padding issues with respect to how much of the original packet is to be included. The consensus that was reached by the implementors at the time is to include as much of the original packet as possible and to pad the data on the 8-byte boundary.

3181–3196 The packet is truncated if there is not sufficient space to hold the entire original packet or if the space is sufficient but the length of the entire original packet is not aligned. The latter part does not match the "consensus" mentioned above. An older version of the code actually implemented padding, but it was then overwritten to simplify the code.

Listing 5-173

___icmp6.c

```
3199                      nd_opt_rh = (struct nd_opt_rd_hdr *)p;
3200                      bzero(nd_opt_rh, sizeof(*nd_opt_rh));
3201                      nd_opt_rh->nd_opt_rh_type = ND_OPT_REDIRECTED_HEADER;
3202                      nd_opt_rh->nd_opt_rh_len = len >> 3;
```

```
3203                         p += sizeof(*nd_opt_rh);
3204                         m->m_pkthdr.len = m->m_len = p - (u_char *)ip6;
3205
3206                         /* connect m0 to m */
3207                         m_cat(m, m0);
3208                         m->m_pkthdr.len += m0->m_pkthdr.len;
3209                         m0 = NULL;
3210                 }
```
─── icmp6.c

3199–3204 The Redirected header option is initialized and the packet length is set to the option length.

3207–3209 The original packet m0 is appended to m, which contains the Redirect message. The packet length is updated accordingly.

Listing 5-174
─── icmp6.c
```
3211    noredhdropt:
3212            if (m0) {
3213                    m_freem(m0);
3214                    m0 = NULL;
3215            }
3216
3217            /* XXX: clear embedded link IDs in the inner header */
3218            in6_clearscope(&sip6->ip6_src);
3219            in6_clearscope(&sip6->ip6_dst);
3220            in6_clearscope(&nd_rd->nd_rd_target);
3221            in6_clearscope(&nd_rd->nd_rd_dst);
3222
3223            ip6->ip6_plen = htons(m->m_pkthdr.len - sizeof(struct ip6_hdr));
3224
3225            nd_rd->nd_rd_cksum = 0;
3226            nd_rd->nd_rd_cksum = in6_cksum(m, IPPROTO_ICMPV6,
3227                                    sizeof(*ip6), ntohs(ip6->ip6_plen));
3228
3229            /* send the packet to outside... */
....
3234            if (ip6_output(m, NULL, NULL, 0, NULL, NULL
....
3236                            , NULL
....
3238                            ) != 0)
3239                    icmp6_ifstat_inc(ifp, ifs6_out_error);
3240
3241            icmp6_ifstat_inc(ifp, ifs6_out_msg);
3242            icmp6_ifstat_inc(ifp, ifs6_out_redirect);
3243            icmp6stat.icp6s_outhist[ND_REDIRECT]++;
3244
3245            return;
```
─── icmp6.c

3218–3243 The scope zone ID is embedded inside the address in the internal kernel representation. `in6_clearscope()` is called to remove the ID from the Source and Destination addresses in the IPv6 header, and the Target Address and the Destination Address from the Redirect message. All of these addresses will appear on the wire and must not contain the embedded zone IDs.

`in6_cksum()` computes the checksum for the final ICMPv6 packet and the computed checksum is inserted into the ICMPv6 header. `ip6_output()` is called to transmit the packet. The ICMPv6 statistics are updated.

Listing 5-175

_____ icmp6.c
```
3247    fail:
3248            if (m)
3249                    m_freem(m);
3250            if (m0)
3251                    m_freem(m0);
3252    }
```
_____ icmp6.c

3247–3251 The packet buffers are released on error and the function returns.

5.17 ND Protocol Message Options Processing Functions

5.17.1 nd6_option_init() Function

The nd6_option_init() function marks the start and end positions of the ICMPv6 options in a given packet.

Listing 5-176

_____ nd6.c
```
318     void
319     nd6_option_init(opt, icmp6len, ndopts)
320             void *opt;
321             int icmp6len;
322             union nd_opts *ndopts;
323     {
324
325             bzero(ndopts, sizeof(*ndopts));
326             ndopts->nd_opts_search = (struct nd_opt_hdr *)opt;
327             ndopts->nd_opts_last
328                     = (struct nd_opt_hdr *)(((u_char *)opt) + icmp6len);
329
330             if (icmp6len == 0) {
331                     ndopts->nd_opts_done = 1;
332                     ndopts->nd_opts_search = NULL;
333             }
334     }
```
_____ nd6.c

325–333 Function parameter opt points to the ICMPv6 packet; specifically it points to the byte immediately following the ND packet header. icmp6len specifies the length of the packet excluding the bytes that precede the first option if it exists. ndopts is a nd_opts{} structure given by the caller for storing the option processing results.

  nd_opts_search field points to the beginning of the options, and nd_opts_last points to the end of the options. nd_opts_search is updated each time an option is processed by the nd6_option() function.

  icmp6len is zero if the ND packet does not contain any option. In this case nd_opts_done is set to 1 and nd_opts_search is set to NULL to indicate option processing is complete.

5.17.2 nd6_option() Function

The nd6_option() function returns a single option back to the caller.

Listing 5-177

```
336     /*
337      * Take one ND option.
338      */
339     struct nd_opt_hdr *
340     nd6_option(ndopts)
341             union nd_opts *ndopts;
342     {
343             struct nd_opt_hdr *nd_opt;
344             int olen;
345
346             if (!ndopts)
347                     panic("ndopts == NULL in nd6_option");
348             if (!ndopts->nd_opts_last)
349                     panic("uninitialized ndopts in nd6_option");
350             if (!ndopts->nd_opts_search)
351                     return NULL;
352             if (ndopts->nd_opts_done)
353                     return NULL;
```

346–353 `nd_opts_search` points to the option to be processed next. `nd_opts_last` points to the end of the options and must never be NULL even when there are no options present. The `nd_opts_done` is set to 1 if option processing is complete.

Listing 5-178

```
355             nd_opt = ndopts->nd_opts_search;
356
357             /* make sure nd_opt_len is inside the buffer */
358             if ((caddr_t)&nd_opt->nd_opt_len >= (caddr_t)ndopts->nd_opts_last) {
359                     bzero(ndopts, sizeof(*ndopts));
360                     return NULL;
361             }
362
363             olen = nd_opt->nd_opt_len << 3;
364             if (olen == 0) {
365                     /*
366                      * Message validation requires that all included
367                      * options have a length that is greater than zero.
368                      */
369                     bzero(ndopts, sizeof(*ndopts));
370                     return NULL;
371             }
```

355–371 Each option begins with the Type and Length fields. First, the option length field is validated to be within the packet range. The option length is given in 8-byte units and is saved in `olen`. The option length must not be zero or the condition is treated as an error.

Listing 5-179

```
373             ndopts->nd_opts_search = (struct nd_opt_hdr *)((caddr_t)nd_opt + olen);
374             if (ndopts->nd_opts_search > ndopts->nd_opts_last) {
375                     /* option overruns the end of buffer, invalid */
376                     bzero(ndopts, sizeof(*ndopts));
377                     return NULL;
378             } else if (ndopts->nd_opts_search == ndopts->nd_opts_last) {
379                     /* reached the end of options chain */
```

```
380                        ndopts->nd_opts_done = 1;
381                        ndopts->nd_opts_search = NULL;
382                }
383            return nd_opt;
384    }
```
nd6.c

373–383 The `nd_opts_search` field is updated to point to the next ND option. `nd_opts_done` is set to 1 and `nd_opts_search` is set to NULL if processing has reached the end of the ND options.

5.17.3   `nd6_options()` Function

The `nd6_options()` function parses all of the ND options that are present in a given packet and stores these options in the corresponding fields of the `nd_opts{}` structure discussed in Section 5.13.7.

Listing 5-180

nd6.c

```
386    /*
387     * Parse multiple ND options.
388     * This function is much easier to use, for ND routines that do not need
389     * multiple options of the same type.
390     */
391    int
392    nd6_options(ndopts)
393            union nd_opts *ndopts;
394    {
395            struct nd_opt_hdr *nd_opt;
396            int i = 0;
397
398            if (!ndopts)
399                    panic("ndopts == NULL in nd6_options");
400            if (!ndopts->nd_opts_last)
401                    panic("uninitialized ndopts in nd6_options");
402            if (!ndopts->nd_opts_search)
403                    return 0;
404
405            while (1) {
406                    nd_opt = nd6_option(ndopts);
407                    if (!nd_opt && !ndopts->nd_opts_last) {
408                            /*
409                             * Message validation requires that all included
410                             * options have a length that is greater than zero.
411                             */
412                            icmp6stat.icp6s_nd_badopt++;
413                            bzero(ndopts, sizeof(*ndopts));
414                            return -1;
415                    }
416
417                    if (!nd_opt)
418                            goto skip1;
419
420                    switch (nd_opt->nd_opt_type) {
421                    case ND_OPT_SOURCE_LINKADDR:
422                    case ND_OPT_TARGET_LINKADDR:
423                    case ND_OPT_MTU:
424                    case ND_OPT_REDIRECTED_HEADER:
425                    case ND_OPT_ADVINTERVAL:
426                    case ND_OPT_SOURCE_ADDRLIST:
427                    case ND_OPT_TARGET_ADDRLIST:
428                            if (ndopts->nd_opt_array[nd_opt->nd_opt_type]) {
```

```
429                                    nd6log((LOG_INFO,
430                                        "duplicated ND6 option found (type=%d)\n",
431                                        nd_opt->nd_opt_type));
432                                    /* XXX bark? */
433                                } else {
434                                    ndopts->nd_opt_array[nd_opt->nd_opt_type]
435                                        = nd_opt;
436                                }
437                                break;
                                                                    ───nd6.c
```

405–437 ndopts is the option structure nd_opts{} that has been initialized by function nd_option_init().

Function nd6_option() is called to retrieve a single option into nd_opt. A bad option is encountered if options are present but nd6_option() returns NULL. In this case the function updates the ICMPv6 icp6s_nd_badopt counter and terminates here.

Some of the ND options can be present only once in the message. Table 5-15 shows such options that are considered in this implementation. [RFC2461] does not indicate what to do when a duplicated option is encountered. The KAME implementation chose to skip the duplicated option and continue processing. Otherwise, the starting address of the option is saved in the corresponding nd_opt_array location.

Listing 5-181
```
                                                                    ───nd6.c
438                        case ND_OPT_PREFIX_INFORMATION:
439                            if (ndopts->nd_opt_array[nd_opt->nd_opt_type] == 0) {
440                                ndopts->nd_opt_array[nd_opt->nd_opt_type]
441                                    = nd_opt;
442                            }
443                            ndopts->nd_opts_pi_end =
444                                (struct nd_opt_prefix_info *)nd_opt;
445                            break;
                                                                    ───nd6.c
```

438–445 Multiple Prefix Information options can be present in a single Router Advertisement message. The starting address of the first Prefix Information option is stored into the corresponding location in nd_opt_array. The address of the last Prefix Information

TABLE 5-15

Option name	Description
ND_OPT_SOURCE_LINKADDR	Source Link-Layer address option
ND_OPT_TARGET_LINKADDR	Target Link-Layer address option
ND_OPT_MTU	MTU option
ND_OPT_REDIRECTED_HEADER	Redirected Header option
ND_OPT_ADVINTERVAL	Advertisement Interval option for Mobile IPv6
ND_OPT_SOURCE_ADDRLIST	Source Address List option for Inverse Discovery
ND_OPT_TARGET_ADDRLIST	Target Address List option for Inverse Discovery

ND options that can appear only once in one ND message.

option is saved in `nd_opts_pi_end`. The `nd_opts_pi_end` pointer is updated each time an additional Prefix Information option is processed.

Listing 5-182

——nd6.c
```
458    skip1:
459                    i++;
460                    if (i > nd6_maxndopt) {
461                            icmp6stat.icp6s_nd_toomanyopt++;
462                            nd6log((LOG_INFO, "too many loop in nd opt\n"));
463                            break;
464                    }
465
466                    if (ndopts->nd_opts_done)
467                            break;
468            }
469
470            return 0;
471    }
```
——nd6.c

459–471 The maximum number of ND options that can be processed is limited to `nd6_maxndopt` options. The KAME implementation restricts the maximum allowable options to prevent the possible attack attempting to make the receiving node consume its computation resource with a large number of options. `nd6_maxndopt` is set to 10 and is not changeable. This is not part of the protocol specification, but is based on an implementation decision. The constant maximum number may be too restrictive, though, especially because new Router Advertisement options have been introduced.

5.18   Default Router Management Functions

5.18.1   `defrouter_addreq()` Function

Function `defrouter_addreq()` is called by `defrouter_select()` to install a new default route into the kernel routing table.

Listing 5-183

——nd6_rtr.c
```
565    void
566    defrouter_addreq(new)
567            struct nd_defrouter *new;
568    {
569            struct sockaddr_in6 def, mask, gate;
570            struct rtentry *newrt = NULL;
571            int s;
572            int error;
573
574            Bzero(&def, sizeof(def));
575            Bzero(&mask, sizeof(mask));
576            Bzero(&gate, sizeof(gate)); /* for safety */
577
578            def.sin6_len = mask.sin6_len = sizeof(struct sockaddr_in6);
579            def.sin6_family = mask.sin6_family = AF_INET6;
580            gate = new->rtaddr;
....
582            gate.sin6_scope_id = 0; /* XXX */
```

```
      ....
584
      ....
588            s = splnet();
      ....
590            error = rtrequest(RTM_ADD, (struct sockaddr *)&def,
591                (struct sockaddr *)&gate, (struct sockaddr *)&mask,
592                RTF_GATEWAY, &newrt);
593            if (newrt) {
594                    nd6_rtmsg(RTM_ADD, newrt); /* tell user process */
595                    newrt->rt_refcnt--;
596            }
597            if (error == 0)
598                    new->installed = 1;
599            splx(s);
600            return;
601    }
                                                                    nd6_rtr.c
```

574–601 A default route has the prefix `::/0` (i.e., the unspecified address as the destination with the zero-length mask). The `RTF_GATEWAY` flag is set because the default route is an indirect route. A successful installation will trigger a call to function `nd6_rtmsg()` (Section 5.22.4), which will generate a message on routing sockets to notify the listeners of the newly installed route entry. The new default router is marked to indicate that it has been installed into the kernel routing table.

5.18.2 `defrouter_delreq()` Function

Function `defrouter_delreq()` is called to remove a default route going through the given router from the kernel routing table.

Listing 5-184
                                                                    nd6_rtr.c
```
774    /*
775     * Remove the default route for a given router.
776     * This is just a subroutine function for defrouter_select(), and should
777     * not be called from anywhere else.
778     */
779    static void
780    defrouter_delreq(dr)
781            struct nd_defrouter *dr;
782    {
783            struct sockaddr_in6 def, mask, gw;
784            struct rtentry *oldrt = NULL;
785
      ....
790
791            Bzero(&def, sizeof(def));
792            Bzero(&mask, sizeof(mask));
793            Bzero(&gw, sizeof(gw)); /* for safety */
794
795            def.sin6_len = mask.sin6_len = sizeof(struct sockaddr_in6);
796            def.sin6_family = mask.sin6_family = AF_INET6;
797            gw = dr->rtaddr;
      ....
801
802            rtrequest(RTM_DELETE, (struct sockaddr *)&def,
803                (struct sockaddr *)&gw,
804                (struct sockaddr *)&mask, RTF_GATEWAY, &oldrt);
805            if (oldrt) {
```

```
806                         nd6_rtmsg(RTM_DELETE, oldrt);
807                         if (oldrt->rt_refcnt <= 0) {
808                                 /*
809                                  * XXX: borrowed from the RTM_DELETE case of
810                                  * rtrequest().
811                                  */
812                                 oldrt->rt_refcnt++;
813                                 rtfree(oldrt);
814                         }
815                 }
816
817             dr->installed = 0;
818     }
```
——nd6_rtr.c

774–818 A default route has the prefix `::/0`. The gateway address is set to the address of
the given router `dr`, and then function `rtrequest()` is called to delete the route entry.
A successful route deletion will trigger a call to `nd6_rtmsg()` to inform the listeners
about the deleted route entry. The router is marked to indicate it is not installed in the
kernel routing table.

5.18.3 `defrouter_addifreq()` Function

Function `defrouter_addifreq()` is called to install a default route through a given interface,
which is known as the *default interface*. The concept of *default interface* is a KAME extension
for implementing, in a multihomed host that all destinations are treated as on-link when there
are no default routers available.

> *Note*: This behavior for the case of no routers is based on the specification defined in
> [RFC2461], but the recommendation from current practices is that treating all destinations
> as on-link is rather harmful. Indeed, this on-link assumption in the original algorithm poses a
> number of problems. First, the destination address selection algorithm as defined in [RFC3484]
> could prefer unreachable IPv6 addresses over reachable IPv4 addresses because this rule
> effectively makes any destination (possibly) reachable. Second, performing address resolu-
> tion on each unreachable IPv6 address causes delay: An application may need to try each
> unreachable address in turn, thus extending the delay to an unacceptable level from the
> application user perspective. Third, multihomed nodes complicate the implementation of this
> on-link assumption: A multihomed node needs to attempt the communication to an address
> on multiple interfaces. The on-link assumption also introduces security vulnerability in that
> a malicious attacker can disable the default router and because all destinations are assumed
> on-link, the malicious attacker can spoof off-link nodes. Subsequently text describing this
> on-link assumption was removed from a successor version of the ND protocol specification
> [RFC2461BIS].
>
>   The KAME developers also noticed some of the problems, and disabled this feature by
> not specifying the default interface by default.

A user can specify the default interface with the `-I` command line option for the **ndp**
command. For example, executing the following command sets the default interface to `ne0`:

```
# ndp -I ne0
ND default interface = ne0
```

When no default routers are available with this configuration, the **netstat** command will show the following routing table entry:

```
% netstat -rn -f inet6
Routing tables

Internet6:
Destination          Gateway         Flags      Netif Expire
   ...
default              link#1          UC         ne0
```

Note that the cloning (C) flag is set for the default route, which means any unknown destination matches this entry and a separate cloned route entry with Neighbor Cache information will be created.

Listing 5-185

──nd6_rtr.c

```
603    /* Add a route to a given interface as default */
604    static void
605    defrouter_addifreq(ifp)
606            struct ifnet *ifp;
607    {
608            struct sockaddr_in6 def, mask;
609            struct ifaddr *ifa;
610            struct rtentry *newrt = NULL;
611            int error, flags;
```

──nd6_rtr.c

605 On input, the parameter `ifp` specifies the designated default interface.

Listing 5-186

──nd6_rtr.c

```
616            /* remove one if we have already installed one */
617            if (nd6_defif_installed)
618                    defrouter_delifreq();
```

──nd6_rtr.c

616–618 The global variable `nd6_defif_installed` points to an address of the default interface if such a route has been installed previously. In this case, since only one such route is allowed for the system, any current default interface route is deleted before adding a new one. The route is deleted by function `defrouter_delifreq()` (see Section 5.18.4).

Listing 5-187

──nd6_rtr.c

```
620            bzero(&def, sizeof(def));
621            bzero(&mask, sizeof(mask));
622
623            def.sin6_len = mask.sin6_len = sizeof(struct sockaddr_in6);
624            def.sin6_family = mask.sin6_family = AF_INET6;
625
626            /*
627             * Search for an ifaddr belonging to the specified interface.
628             * XXX: An IPv6 address is required to be assigned on the interface.
629             */
630            if ((ifa = ifaof_ifpforaddr((struct sockaddr *)&def, ifp)) == NULL) {
631                    nd6log((LOG_ERR,            /* better error? */
632                        "defrouter_addifreq: failed to find an ifaddr "
```

```
633                          "to install a route to interface %s\n",
634                          if_name(ifp)));
635                     return;
636              }
637
638              /* RTF_CLONING is necessary to make sure to perform ND */
639              flags = ifa->ifa_flags | RTF_CLONING;
```
─── nd6_rtr.c

630–639 The default route generally has the prefix `::/0`. Function `ifaof_ifpforaddr()` is called to retrieve an interface address, which will serve as the default gateway when adding the route. Using the interface address as the gateway is similar to creating an interface route when assigning an address to an interface. This interface route has the `RTF_CLONING` flag set to allow for the creation of Neighbor Cache entries for the destinations that are assumed to be reachable over this interface.

Listing 5-188
─── nd6_rtr.c
```
649              error = rtrequest(RTM_ADD, (struct sockaddr *)&def, ifa->ifa_addr,
650                  (struct sockaddr *)&mask, flags, &newrt);
....
652              if (error != 0) {
653                     nd6log((LOG_ERR,
654                         "defrouter_addifreq: failed to install a route to "
655                         "interface %s (errno = %d)\n",
656                         if_name(ifp), error));
657
658                     if (newrt)     /* maybe unnecessary, but do it for safety */
659                            newrt->rt_refcnt--;
660              } else {
661                     if (newrt) {
662                            nd6_rtmsg(RTM_ADD, newrt);
663                            newrt->rt_refcnt--;
664                     }
665              }
666
667              nd6_defif_installed = ifa;
668              IFAREF(ifa);
669      }
```
─── nd6_rtr.c

649 `rtrequest()` is called to install the default interface route into the kernel routing table. Note that this entry is created without the `RTF_GATEWAY` flag. With the presence of the `RTF_CLONING` flag, the end effect is identical to creating an interface direct route for the prefix when an address is assigned to the interface. The newly created entry is returned by `rtrequest()` and a reference is held on that entry.

652–668 A log message is generated and the reference that is held on the route entry is released when an error is encountered. Otherwise, `nd6_defif_installed` is initialized to the address of the newly chosen interface to indicate the presence of a default interface. A reference is held on the address so that it cannot be freed while the route is active. A routing socket message is generated to notify the listeners of the new route.

5.18.4 `defrouter_delifreq()` Function

Function `defrouter_delifreq()` is called to remove the default interface route from the kernel routing table.

Listing 5-189

```
                                                                ──nd6_rtr.c
671     /* Remove a default route points to interface */
672     static void
673     defrouter_delifreq()
674     {
675             struct sockaddr_in6 def, mask;
676             struct rtentry *oldrt = NULL;
677
678             if (!nd6_defif_installed)
679                     return;
680
681             Bzero(&def, sizeof(def));
682             Bzero(&mask, sizeof(mask));
683
684             def.sin6_len = mask.sin6_len = sizeof(struct sockaddr_in6);
685             def.sin6_family = mask.sin6_family = AF_INET6;
686
687             rtrequest(RTM_DELETE, (struct sockaddr *)&def,
688                 (struct sockaddr *)nd6_defif_installed->ifa_addr,
689                 (struct sockaddr *)&mask, RTF_GATEWAY, &oldrt);
690             if (oldrt) {
691                     nd6_rtmsg(RTM_DELETE, oldrt);
692                     if (oldrt->rt_refcnt <= 0) {
693                             /*
694                              * XXX: borrowed from the RTM_DELETE case of
695                              * rtrequest().
696                              */
697                             oldrt->rt_refcnt++;
698                             rtfree(oldrt);
699                     }
700             }
701
702             IFAFREE(nd6_defif_installed);
703             nd6_defif_installed = NULL;
704     }
                                                                ──nd6_rtr.c
```

671–689 rtrequest() is called to delete the current default interface route from the kernel routing table. While the corresponding interface address stored in nd6_defif_installed is passed to rtrequest(), this actually does not matter much because rtrequest() works based on the destination address and the prefix mask. nd6_defif_installed takes an effective role when a KAME-specific extension called *multi-path routing* is enabled, which allows the routing table to have multiple route entries for the same destination. But this feature is not discussed in this book.

690–703 A routing socket message is generated to notify the listeners of the deleted route. The interface address reference is released and the global variable nd6_defif_installed is set to NULL to reflect the absence of the default interface.

5.18.5 defrouter_lookup() Function

Function defrouter_lookup() searches through the Default Router List to determine if a given pair of address and interface is found in the list. There are several scenarios where this function is called:

- This function is called by nd6_free() to determine if the ND garbage collection process should remove a particular Neighbor Cache entry (Listing 5-45).

- `defrtrlist_update()` calls `defrouter_lookup()` upon receiving a Router Advertisement message to update the default router information if the router is present in the list (Listing 5-199).

- `nd6_na_input()` calls `defrouter_lookup()` when a Neighbor Advertisement message indicates that a node has ceased to act as a router (Listing 5-107). In this case the entry returned by `defrouter_lookup()` will then be removed from the system.

Listing 5-190

——nd6.c
```
706     struct nd_defrouter *
707     defrouter_lookup(addr, ifp)
708             struct sockaddr_in6 *addr;
709             struct ifnet *ifp;
710     {
711             struct nd_defrouter *dr;
712
713             for (dr = TAILQ_FIRST(&nd_defrouter); dr;
714                  dr = TAILQ_NEXT(dr, dr_entry)) {
715                     if (dr->ifp == ifp &&
....
719                             /*
720                              * XXX: when addr comes from the routing table, it does
721                              * not have a valid scope zone ID.
722                              */
723                             IN6_ARE_ADDR_EQUAL(&addr->sin6_addr, &dr->rtaddr.sin6_addr)
....
725                             ) {
726                             return (dr);
727                     }
728             }
729
730             return (NULL);          /* search failed */
731     }
```
——nd6.c

713–730 Parameter `addr` holds the address of the router. Since the same default router may be learned over multiple interfaces for a multihomed host (recall that routers are identified by their link-local addresses), a specific interface is given and must match the interface associated with a given default router. Note that this effectively means the Default Router List is maintained on a per-interface basis, even though this is represented as a single global list structure. Either the matching entry or a NULL entry is returned to the caller.

5.18.6 `defrouter_select()` Function

Function `defrouter_select()` chooses one router from the Default Router List and installs the default route entry into the kernel routing table. The function is called when one of the following events occurs.

- The Default Router List is changed by addition or deletion of a default router. For example, when a host receives a Router Advertisement message from a new router, or a host receives a Router Advertisement message with its lifetime set to 0, the most appropriate router may change in the list, in which case the host has to select the most appropriate one from the list.

- The Neighbor Cache status of a router is changed. For example, if the currently chosen router becomes unreachable, a host may have to choose another router as the most appropriate one from its Default Router List.

There are three different cases in which to choose a default router.

1. When a host has a non-empty Default Router List, then a "probably reachable" router is chosen. If the host has multiple probably reachable routers, then a router that has the highest preference value is chosen (see Listing 5-193 below).

   The term "probably reachable" is derived from [RFC2461], whose definition is that the router as a neighbor has a valid Neighbor Cache with a non-INCOMPLETE (state or NOSTATE in the KAME implementation).

2. If a host does not have any (probably) reachable router, one of routers in the Default Router List is chosen using the round-robin algorithm (see Listing 5-194).

3. If the Default Router List is empty, a host removes the default route entry from the kernel routing table unless the default interface is specified; if the default interface is specified, that interface is chosen as the default direct route, assuming that all nodes are on the same link (see Listing 5-192).

Note, however, that this behavior based on the "on-link assumption" is now discouraged and is almost deprecated as explained in Section 5.18.3.

Listing 5-191

───nd6_rtr.c
```
860     void
861     defrouter_select()
862     {
....
866             int s = splnet();
....
868             struct nd_defrouter *dr, *selected_dr = NULL, *installed_dr = NULL;
869             struct rtentry *rt = NULL;
870             struct llinfo_nd6 *ln = NULL;
871
872             /*
873              * This function should be called only when acting as an autoconfigured
874              * host.  Although the remaining part of this function is not effective
875              * if the node is not an autoconfigured host, we explicitly exclude
876              * such cases here for safety.
877              */
878             if (ip6_forwarding || !ip6_accept_rtadv) {
879                     nd6log((LOG_WARNING,
880                         "defrouter_select: called unexpectedly (forwarding=%d, "
881                         "accept_rtadv=%d)\n", ip6_forwarding, ip6_accept_rtadv));
882                     splx(s);
883                     return;
884             }
```
───nd6_rtr.c

878–884 The `defrouter_select()` function is designed for hosts performing autoconfiguration; the default router must not be installed if the node is acting as a router (`ip6_forwarding` is set to true). Also, if the node is not configured to perform autoconfiguration via Router Advertisement messages (ip6_accept_rtadv is set to false), the function returns without doing anything.

Listing 5-192

```
                                                                      nd6_rtr.c
886            /*
887             * Let's handle easy case (3) first:
888             * If default router list is empty, we should probably install
889             * an interface route and assume that all destinations are on-link.
890             */
891            if (!TAILQ_FIRST(&nd_defrouter)) {
892                    /*
893                     * XXX: The specification does not say this mechanism should
894                     * be restricted to hosts, but this would be not useful
895                     * (even harmful) for routers.
896                     * This test is meaningless due to a test at the beginning of
897                     * the function, but we intentionally keep it to make the note
898                     * clear.
899                     */
900                    if (!ip6_forwarding) {
901                            if (nd6_defifp) {
902                                    /*
903                                     * Install a route to the default interface
904                                     * as default route.
905                                     */
906                                    defrouter_addifreq(nd6_defifp);
907                            } else {
908                                    /*
909                                     * purge the existing route.
910                                     * XXX: is this really correct?
911                                     */
912                                    defrouter_delifreq();
913                                    nd6log((LOG_INFO, "defrouter_select: "
914                                        "there's no default router and no default"
915                                        " interface\n"));
916                            }
917                    }
918                    splx(s);
919                    return;
920            }
                                                                      nd6_rtr.c
```

900–920 This part handles case 3. The nd6_defifp variable provides the default interface of the node. If the default interface is specified, the defrouter_addifreq() function is called to install the default route over that interface. Otherwise, the defrouter_delifreq() is called to remove the existing default route entry.

Listing 5-193

```
                                                                      nd6_rtr.c
922            /*
923             * If we have a default route for the default interface, delete it.
924             * Note that the existence of the route is checked in the delete
925             * function.
926             */
927            defrouter_delifreq();
928
929            /*
930             * Search for a (probably) reachable router from the list.
931             * We just pick up the first reachable one (if any), assuming that
932             * the ordering rule of the list described in defrtrlist_update().
933             */
```

```
934            for (dr = TAILQ_FIRST(&nd_defrouter); dr;
935                 dr = TAILQ_NEXT(dr, dr_entry)) {
936                    if (!selected_dr &&
937                        (rt = nd6_lookup(&dr->rtaddr, 0, dr->ifp)) &&
938                        (ln = (struct llinfo_nd6 *)rt->rt_llinfo) &&
939                        ND6_IS_LLINFO_PROBREACH(ln)) {
940                            selected_dr = dr;
941                    }
942
943                    if (dr->installed && !installed_dr)
944                            installed_dr = dr;
945                    else if (dr->installed && installed_dr) {
946                            /* this should not happen.  warn for diagnosis. */
947                            log(LOG_ERR, "defrouter_select: more than one router"
948                                " is installed\n");
949                    }
950            }
```
--*nd6_rtr.c*

927 Now that there is at least one default router in the list, the default route to the default interface, if installed, is removed from the routing table by `defrouter_delifreq()` (Section 5.18.4). It is safe to call this function unconditionally because it checks to see if the route is actually installed.

934–950 The `for` loop checks all default routers stored in the Default Router List, `nd_defrouter`. Variable `installed_dr` is set to the first probably reachable router if no router is installed yet. The `installed` member variable of the `nd_defrouter{}` structure indicates whether the entry is installed as a default route. If an entry whose `installed` member variable is set to true is found after another router has been set to the `installed_dr` variable, a warning message is printed since this kernel implementation never installs multiple default route entries.

At this point `selected_dr` remembers the first probably reachable router in the list as a candidate of the router to be chosen, and `installed_dr` keeps the router currently installed for the default route.

Listing 5-194
--*nd6_rtr.c*
```
951            /*
952             * If none of the default routers was found to be reachable,
953             * round-robin the list regardless of preference.
954             * Otherwise, if we have an installed router, check if the selected
955             * (reachable) router should really be preferred to the installed one.
956             * We only prefer the new router when the old one is not reachable
957             * or when the new one has a really higher preference value.
958             */
959            if (!selected_dr) {
960                    if (!installed_dr || !TAILQ_NEXT(installed_dr, dr_entry))
961                            selected_dr = TAILQ_FIRST(&nd_defrouter);
962                    else
963                            selected_dr = TAILQ_NEXT(installed_dr, dr_entry);
964            } else if (installed_dr &&
965                (rt = nd6_lookup(&installed_dr->rtaddr, 0, installed_dr->ifp)) &&
966                (ln = (struct llinfo_nd6 *)rt->rt_llinfo) &&
967                ND6_IS_LLINFO_PROBREACH(ln) &&
968                rtpref(selected_dr) <= rtpref(installed_dr)) {
969                    selected_dr = installed_dr;
970            }
971
```

```
972          /*
973           * If the selected router is different than the installed one,
974           * remove the installed router and install the selected one.
975           * Note that the selected router is never NULL here.
976           */
977          if (installed_dr != selected_dr) {
978                  if (installed_dr)
979                          defrouter_delreq(installed_dr);
980                  defrouter_addreq(selected_dr);
981          }
982
983          splx(s);
984          return;
985      }
```
── nd6_rtr.c

959–963 This part handles case 2. If there are no (probably) reachable routers, the next entry to the currently installed router is chosen at line 963, thereby implementing the round-robin selection algorithm. If no router is installed at this point, the first router in the list is chosen.

964–970 If there is a reachable router in the list and a router is installed for the default route, those two entries are compared to choose the more appropriate one. The entry which is probably reachable and has higher preference value is chosen. If both routers are reachable and have the same preference value, the current router is kept.

977–981 If the selected router (selected_dr) is different from the currently installed router (installed_dr), the current router is removed by calling function defrouter_delreq() and the selected router is installed by the defrouter_addreq() function.

Figure 5-35 illustrates three different cases of router selection performed by the defrouter_select() function. We assume four routers with different preferences: X, Y, Z, and W. Router Z is currently installed in the routing table. Routers that are (probably) reachable are represented as thicker rectangles. Note that the routers are listed in the order of preference as explained in Section 5.18.8. This figure also shows which router selected_dr points to after the search in Listing 5-193.

In case (A), selected_dr points to router Y, the first reachable router in the list. Since selected_dr is different from installed_dr, router Y will be the next installed router. Note that a router that has a higher preference is chosen.

In case (B), selected_dr points to router Z. Even though router W is also reachable, it is not selected because it has a lower preference. Then the currently installed router will keep working.

In case (C), since no routers are reachable, the search in Listing 5-193 fails and selected_dr is NULL. Then router W will be the next installed router, as a result of the round-robin selection algorithm even if it has the lowest preference.

5.18.7 `defrtrlist_del()` Function

Function defrtrlist_del() removes the given router from the Default Router List. If the removed router is installed in the kernel routing table, the route entry is also deleted.

FIGURE 5-35

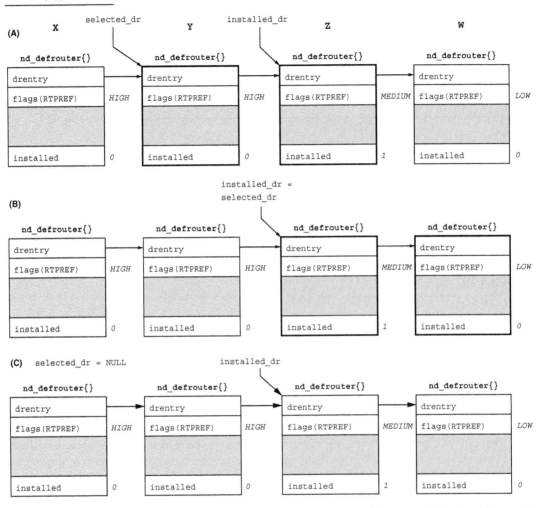

Default router selection examples.

Listing 5-195

```
733     void
734     defrtrlist_del(dr)
735            struct nd_defrouter *dr;
736     {
737            struct nd_defrouter *deldr = NULL;
738            struct nd_prefix *pr;
739
740            /*
741             * Flush all the routing table entries that use the router
742             * as a next hop.
743             */
744            if (!ip6_forwarding && ip6_accept_rtadv) /* XXX: better condition? */
745                    rt6_flush(&dr->rtaddr, dr->ifp);
```

744–745 The `rt6_flush()` function will remove all dynamic routes that use the default router `dr` as the next-hop router from the kernel routing table. This function will be executed only when acting as a host node, that is, with `ip6_forwarding` off and accepting Router Advertisement messages (i.e., with `ip6_accept_rtadv` being true) in order to avoid unnecessarily traversing the entire routing table as a side effect of `rt6_flush()`.

Listing 5-196
_____ nd6_rtr.c
```
747             if (dr->installed) {
748                     deldr = dr;
749                     defrouter_delreq(dr);
750             }
751             TAILQ_REMOVE(&nd_defrouter, dr, dr_entry);
```
_____ nd6_rtr.c

747–751 The default route entry going through gateway `dr` is removed from the kernel routing table by calling function `defrouter_delreq()` if it has been installed as indicated by the `installed` field. Router `dr` is also removed from the Default Router List.

Listing 5-197
_____ nd6_rtr.c
```
753             /*
754              * Also delete all the pointers to the router in each prefix list.
755              */
756             for (pr = nd_prefix.lh_first; pr; pr = pr->ndpr_next) {
757                     struct nd_pfxrouter *pfxrtr;
758                     if ((pfxrtr = pfxrtr_lookup(pr, dr)) != NULL)
759                             pfxrtr_del(pfxrtr);
760             }
761             pfxlist_onlink_check();
```
_____ nd6_rtr.c

756–761 Each prefix in the Prefix List is examined. If router `dr` has advertised that prefix, it is removed from the advertising routers list of that prefix. Since the change in the advertising routers list may affect on-link state of the prefixes, `pfxlist_onlink_check()` (Section 5.19.6) is called to update the state of the prefixes if necessary.

Listing 5-198
_____ nd6_rtr.c
```
763             /*
764              * If the router is the primary one, choose a new one.
765              * Note that defrouter_select() will remove the current gateway
766              * from the routing table.
767              */
768             if (deldr)
769                     defrouter_select();
770
771             free(dr, M_IP6NDP);
772     }
```
_____ nd6_rtr.c

768–771 If the deleted default router is installed in the kernel, the route entry must be deleted and a different router must be chosen instead. The `defrouter_select()` function performs this process. Finally, the memory allocated for this router is released.

5.18.8   `defrtrlist_update()` Function

The `defrtrlist_update()` function is called to update a router's attributes using the information received from the latest Router Advertisement message.

Listing 5-199

nd6_rtr.c

```
1019    static struct nd_defrouter *
1020    defrtrlist_update(new)
1021            struct nd_defrouter *new;
1022    {
1023            struct nd_defrouter *dr, *n;
....
1027            int s = splnet();
....
1029
1030            if ((dr = defrouter_lookup(&new->rtaddr, new->ifp)) != NULL) {
1031                    /* entry exists */
1032                    if (new->rtlifetime == 0) {
1033                            defrtrlist_del(dr);
1034                            dr = NULL;
```

nd6_rtr.c

1030–1034 The current Default Router List is examined to determine if the router given in `new` is already present. If the router exists in the current Default Router List and its advertised lifetime is zero, this indicates the router has ceased to be a default router, and the router is removed from the list. Function `defrtrlist_del()` updates the advertising routers lists of prefixes and would select another primary default router if necessary.

Listing 5-200

nd6_rtr.c

```
1035            } else {
1036                    int oldpref = rtpref(dr);
1037
1038                    /* override */
1039                    dr->flags = new->flags; /* xxx flag check */
1040                    dr->rtlifetime = new->rtlifetime;
1041                    dr->expire = new->expire;
```

nd6_rtr.c

1035–1041 The given router is present in the Default Router List and is still valid. The current router preference must be retrieved and stored in `oldpref` because the `flags` field is about to be reinitialized. The router flags, lifetime, and the new expiration time are updated in the current entry with the values given by `new`.

Listing 5-201

nd6_rtr.c

```
1043                    /*
1044                     * If the preference does not change, there's no need
1045                     * to sort the entries.
1046                     */
1047                    if (rtpref(new) == oldpref) {
1048                            splx(s);
1049                            return (dr);
```

```
1050                                }
1051
1052                                /*
1053                                 * preferred router may be changed, so relocate
1054                                 * this router.
1055                                 * XXX: calling TAILQ_REMOVE directly is a bad manner.
1056                                 * However, since defrtrlist_del() has many side
1057                                 * effects, we intentionally do so here.
1058                                 * defrouter_select() below will handle routing
1059                                 * changes later.
1060                                 */
1061                                TAILQ_REMOVE(&nd_defrouter, dr, dr_entry);
1062                                n = dr;
1063                                goto insert;
1064                        }
1065                        splx(s);
1066                        return (dr);
1067                }
```
── nd6_rtr.c

1047–1063 The router preference value is used for determining where in the Default Router List
to insert the given router, provided the given host supports the default router preferences.
If the router preference does not change, the work preformed by this function is complete
and the function returns; otherwise, the router may need to be relocated in the list. In the
latter case the current router is temporarily removed from the list and will be reinserted
into the appropriate position within the list below.

1065–1066 This part can only be reached when the new router lifetime is 0. dr is thus NULL,
which will be returned to the caller.

Listing 5-202

── nd6_rtr.c
```
1069                /* entry does not exist */
1070                if (new->rtlifetime == 0) {
1071                        splx(s);
1072                        return (NULL);
1073                }
1074
1075                n = (struct nd_defrouter *)malloc(sizeof(*n), M_IP6NDP, M_NOWAIT);
1076                if (n == NULL) {
1077                        splx(s);
1078                        return (NULL);
1079                }
1080                bzero(n, sizeof(*n));
1081                *n = *new;
```
── nd6_rtr.c

1069–1081 This router is currently not in the Default Router List. If the advertised router lifetime
is 0, the process terminates here, effectively ignoring this router. Otherwise, a new default
router entry, n, is allocated and parameters are copied from new.

Listing 5-203

── nd6_rtr.c
```
1083        insert:
1084                        /*
1085                         * Insert the new router in the Default Router List;
1086                         * The Default Router List should be in the descending order
1087                         * of router-preferece.  Routers with the same preference are
1088                         * sorted in the arriving time order.
```

```
1089              */
1090
1091              /* insert at the end of the group */
1092              for (dr = TAILQ_FIRST(&nd_defrouter); dr;
1093                   dr = TAILQ_NEXT(dr, dr_entry)) {
1094                      if (rtpref(n) > rtpref(dr))
1095                              break;
1096              }
1097              if (dr)
1098                      TAILQ_INSERT_BEFORE(dr, n, dr_entry);
1099              else
1100                      TAILQ_INSERT_TAIL(&nd_defrouter, n, dr_entry);
1101
1102              defrouter_select();
1103
1104              splx(s);
1105
1106              return (n);
1107      }
```
── nd6_rtr.c

1083–1106 Routers are maintained in the Default Router List in the descending order of router preferences. Since the new router may be the most preferred one, `defrouter_select()` is called to perform the router selection again.

5.19 Prefix Management Functions

5.19.1 `nd6_prelist_add()` Function

Function `nd6_prelist_add()` is called to add a new prefix structure (`nd_prefix{}`) to the Prefix List.

Listing 5-204
── nd6_rtr.c

```
1168      int
1169      nd6_prelist_add(pr, dr, newp)
1170              struct nd_prefixctl *pr;
1171              struct nd_prefix **newp;
1172              struct nd_defrouter *dr;
1173      {
1174              struct nd_prefix *new = NULL;
1175              int error = 0;
1176              int i, s;
1177
1178              new = (struct nd_prefix *)malloc(sizeof(*new), M_IP6NDP, M_NOWAIT);
1179              if (new == NULL)
1180                      return(ENOMEM);
1181              bzero(new, sizeof(*new));
1182              new->ndpr_ifp = pr->ndpr_ifp;
1183              new->ndpr_prefix = pr->ndpr_prefix;
1184              new->ndpr_plen = pr->ndpr_plen;
1185              new->ndpr_vltime = pr->ndpr_vltime;
1186              new->ndpr_pltime = pr->ndpr_pltime;
1187              new->ndpr_flags = pr->ndpr_flags;
1188              if ((error = in6_init_prefix_ltimes(new)) != 0) {
1189                      free(new, M_IP6NDP);
1190                      return(error);
1191              }
      ...
1195              new->ndpr_lastupdate = time_second;
```
── nd6_rtr.c

1168–1172 The `pr` parameter points to the instance of the `nd_prefixctl{}` structure that holds the parameters of the prefix to be added. The `dr` parameter points to the instance of the `nd_defrouter{}` structure of the router that sent the Prefix Information option when the prefix comes from a Router Advertisement message; `dr` is NULL if this prefix is configured manually, typically as part of manual address configuration. The information will be stored as an instance of the `nd_prefix{}` structure and the pointer is returned as parameter `newp`.

1178–1195 A memory space to keep the instance of the `nd_prefix{}` structure is allocated and all members of the `nd_prefixctl{}` structure are copied to the corresponding member variables of the `nd_prefix{}` structure.

Function `in6_init_prefix_ltimes()` calculates the expiration time of the valid lifetime and the preferred lifetime of the prefix from the values of the `ndpr_vltime` and the `ndpr_pltime` variables. The calculated times are stored in `ndpr_expire` and `ndpr_preferred` variables respectively.

Note: As noted in Listing 5-4, `ndpr_expire` and `ndpr_preferred` are meaningless in the current implementation.

Listing 5-205

——nd6_rtr.c
```
1197            if (newp != NULL)
1198                    *newp = new;
1199
1200            /* initialization */
1201            LIST_INIT(&new->ndpr_advrtrs);
1202            in6_prefixlen2mask(&new->ndpr_mask, new->ndpr_plen);
1203            /* make prefix in the canonical form */
1204            for (i = 0; i < 4; i++)
1205                    new->ndpr_prefix.sin6_addr.s6_addr32[i] &=
1206                            new->ndpr_mask.s6_addr32[i];
1207
....
1211            s = splnet();
....
1213            /* link ndpr_entry to nd_prefix list */
1214            LIST_INSERT_HEAD(&nd_prefix, new, ndpr_entry);
1215            splx(s);
1216
1217            /* ND_OPT_PI_FLAG_ONLINK processing */
1218            if (new->ndpr_raf_onlink) {
1219                    int e;
1220
1221                    if ((e = nd6_prefix_onlink(new)) != 0) {
1222                            nd6log((LOG_ERR, "nd6_prelist_add: failed to make "
1223                                "the prefix %s/%d on-link on %s (errno=%d)\n",
1224                                ip6_sprintf(&pr->ndpr_prefix.sin6_addr),
1225                                pr->ndpr_plen, if_name(pr->ndpr_ifp), e));
1226                            /* proceed anyway. XXX: is it correct? */
1227                    }
1228            }
1229
1230            if (dr)
1231                    pfxrtr_add(new, dr);
1232
1233            return 0;
1234    }
```
——nd6_rtr.c

1201–1206 `ndpr_advrtrs` is a list that holds pointers to the router entries which have advertised this prefix information. The prefix value is masked by the mask pattern created from the prefix length to keep only the prefix part and strip the interface identifier part.

1213 The newly created prefix information is inserted into the global Prefix List `nd_prefix`.

1218–1228 If the prefix is to be regarded as on-link, the `nd6_prefix_onlink()` function is called to install the interface direct route related to that prefix. `nd6_prefix_onlink()` is discussed in Section 5.19.7.

1230–1231 If the prefix comes from a Router Advertisement message, the router that has advertised the prefix information (`dr`) is added to the `ndpr_advrtrs` variable by calling the `pfxrtr_add()` function (this function is trivial and is not described in this book).

5.19.2 `prelist_remove()` Function

Function `prelist_remove()` is called to remove a prefix from the system.

Listing 5-206

```
                                                                        nd6_rtr.c
1236    void
1237    prelist_remove(pr)
1238            struct nd_prefix *pr;
1239    {
1240            struct nd_pfxrouter *pfr, *next;
1241            int e, s;
1242
1243            /* make sure to invalidate the prefix until it is really freed. */
1244            pr->ndpr_vltime = 0;
1245            pr->ndpr_pltime = 0;
....
1254            if ((pr->ndpr_stateflags & NDPRF_ONLINK) != 0 &&
1255                (e = nd6_prefix_offlink(pr)) != 0) {
1256                    nd6log((LOG_ERR, "prelist_remove: failed to make %s/%d offlink "
1257                        "on %s, errno=%d\n",
1258                        ip6_sprintf(&pr->ndpr_prefix.sin6_addr),
1259                        pr->ndpr_plen, if_name(pr->ndpr_ifp), e));
1260                    /* what should we do? */
1261            }
1262
1263            if (pr->ndpr_refcnt > 0)
1264                    return;          /* notice here? */
                                                                        nd6_rtr.c
```

1244–1245 The prefix is invalidated so that it cannot be used while the deletion process is in progress.

1254–1261 For a given prefix, if the prefix is on-link, function `nd6_prefix_offlink()` is called to remove the interface direct route for the prefix from the kernel routing table and then the prefix is marked as off-link.

1263–1264 The prefix reference count is non-0 when addresses that were generated from this prefix still exist in the system. As such the function terminates here. The `nd6_timer()` function will periodically call this function (see Listing 5-62), and the prefix will be eventually removed once all of those associated addresses have also been deleted from the system.

Listing 5-207

```
                                                                  nd6_rtr.c
1269            s = splnet();
....
1271
1272            /* unlink ndpr_entry from nd_prefix list */
1273            LIST_REMOVE(pr, ndpr_entry);
1274
1275            /* free list of routers that adversed the prefix */
1276            for (pfr = pr->ndpr_advrtrs.lh_first; pfr; pfr = next) {
1277                    next = pfr->pfr_next;
1278
1279                    free(pfr, M_IP6NDP);
1280            }
1281            splx(s);
1282
1283            free(pr, M_IP6NDP);
1284
1285            pfxlist_onlink_check();
1286    }
                                                                  nd6_rtr.c
```

1276–1285 The prefix is deleted from the system Prefix List if there are no addresses that are generated from this prefix. The associated memory is freed. Since removing a prefix can affect the reachability state of known routers, function `pfxlist_onlink_check()` is called to perform prefix onlink check and perform necessary actions accordingly.

5.19.3 `prelist_update()` Function

Function `prelist_update()` is called by `nd6_ra_input()` to process each Prefix Information option found in the Router Advertisement message.

Listing 5-208

```
                                                                  nd6_rtr.c
1288    static int
1289    prelist_update(new, dr, m)
1290            struct nd_prefixctl *new;
1291            struct nd_defrouter *dr; /* may be NULL */
1292            struct mbuf *m;
1293    {
1294            struct in6_ifaddr *ia6 = NULL, *ia6_match = NULL;
1295            struct ifaddr *ifa;
1296            struct ifnet *ifp = new->ndpr_ifp;
1297            struct nd_prefix *pr;
....
1301            int s = splnet();
....
1303            int error = 0;
1304            int newprefix = 0;
1305            int auth;
1306            struct in6_addrlifetime lt6_tmp;
                                                                  nd6_rtr.c
```

1289 Parameter new contains the prefix information, dr specifies the router that advertised the prefix, and m is the actual Router Advertisement packet that contains the Prefix Information option.

Listing 5-209

```
                                                                   nd6_rtr.c
1308              auth = 0;
1309              if (m) {
1310                      /*
1311                       * Authenticity for NA consists authentication for
1312                       * both IP header and IP datagrams, doesn't it ?
1313                       */
....
1321                      auth = ((m->m_flags & M_AUTHIPHDR) &&
1322                          (m->m_flags & M_AUTHIPDGM));
....
1324              }
1325
1326              if ((pr = nd6_prefix_lookup(new)) != NULL) {
1327                      /*
1328                       * nd6_prefix_lookup() ensures that pr and new have the same
1329                       * prefix on a same interface.
1330                       */
1331
1332                      /*
1333                       * Update prefix information.  Note that the on-link (L) bit
1334                       * and the autonomous (A) bit should NOT be changed from 1
1335                       * to 0.
1336                       */
1337                      if (new->ndpr_raf_onlink == 1)
1338                              pr->ndpr_raf_onlink = 1;
1339                      if (new->ndpr_raf_auto == 1)
1340                              pr->ndpr_raf_auto = 1;
1341                      if (new->ndpr_raf_onlink) {
1342                              pr->ndpr_vltime = new->ndpr_vltime;
1343                              pr->ndpr_pltime = new->ndpr_pltime;
1344                              (void)in6_init_prefix_ltimes(pr); /* XXX error case? */
....
1348                              pr->ndpr_lastupdate = time_second;
....
1350                      }
1351
1352                      if (new->ndpr_raf_onlink &&
1353                          (pr->ndpr_stateflags & NDPRF_ONLINK) == 0) {
1354                              int e;
1355
1356                              if ((e = nd6_prefix_onlink(pr)) != 0) {
1357                                      nd6log((LOG_ERR,
1358                                          "prelist_update: failed to make "
1359                                          "the prefix %s/%d on-link on %s "
1360                                          "(errno=%d)\n",
1361                                          ip6_sprintf(&pr->ndpr_prefix.sin6_addr),
1362                                          pr->ndpr_plen, if_name(pr->ndpr_ifp), e));
1363                                      /* proceed anyway. XXX: is it correct? */
1364                              }
1365                      }
1366
1367                      if (dr && pfxrtr_lookup(pr, dr) == NULL)
1368                              pfxrtr_add(pr, dr);
                                                                   nd6_rtr.c
```

1308–1322 auth is a Boolean variable that indicates whether the Router Advertisement message carrying this Prefix Information option is authenticated by the IP security protocol (IPsec). It is initialized to 0 (not authenticated), and is then reset to non-0 if the mbuf has the flags M_AUTHIPHDR and M_AUTHIPDGM set. The IPsec authentication routine sets these flags if it successfully authenticates the incoming packet.

1326 Function nd6_prefix_lookup() (shown in Listing 5-210) is called to search for the given prefix on the given interface in the current Prefix List. If the prefix already exists, the prefix information stored in variable `pr` (which points to an `nd_prefix{}` structure—see Listing 5-8) is updated with the latest values.

Listing 5-210

nd6_rtr.c

```
1150    struct nd_prefix *
1151    nd6_prefix_lookup(key)
1152            struct nd_prefixctl *key;
1153    {
1154            struct nd_prefix *search;
1155
1156            for (search = nd_prefix.lh_first; search; search = search->ndpr_next) {
1157                    if (key->ndpr_ifp == search->ndpr_ifp &&
1158                        key->ndpr_plen == search->ndpr_plen &&
1159                        in6_are_prefix_equal(&key->ndpr_prefix.sin6_addr,
1160                        &search->ndpr_prefix.sin6_addr, key->ndpr_plen)) {
1161                            break;
1162                    }
1163            }
1164
1165            return (search);
1166    }
```

nd6_rtr.c

Note: (Going back to Listing 5-209)

1337–1340 The on-link L flag and the autonomous A flag can change from 0 to 1, that is, a prefix can be treated as on-link and a prefix can be used for address configuration if the current Router Advertisement message has the associated flags set. Note that if these flags are cleared in the Router Advertisement message, the prefix must be ignored for the corresponding information in the local prefix information according to the protocol specification; the receiving node must not clear these flags in the local information. In order to cancel the on-link status of the prefix, the administrator must send Router Advertisement messages with a Prefix Information option for this prefix with the (valid) lifetime of 0. The same rule applies to the A flag.

1341–1350 For an on-link prefix its (valid) lifetime is updated in the local prefix information. While the preferred lifetime is also updated in the structure, it does not have any effect since it is not related to the management of the on-link state of a prefix. The `ndpr_lastupdate` field is set to the current time and is used to determine when a prefix has expired (see Listing 5-62).

1352–1365 If a prefix is now advertised as on-link while it has not been regarded as on-link, then `nd6_prefix_onlink()` (Section 5.19.7) is called to install an interface direct route for the prefix into the kernel routing table.

1367–1368 Each `nd_prefix{}` structure maintains a list of routers that advertised that prefix. If the router that sent this Router Advertisement message is not stored in the structure, `pfxrtr_add()` function (not described in this book) inserts it into the list.

Listing 5-211

nd6_rtr.c

```
1369            } else {
1370                    struct nd_prefix *newpr = NULL;
```

```
1371
1372                        newprefix = 1;
1373
1374                if (new->ndpr_vltime == 0)
1375                        goto end;
1376                if (new->ndpr_raf_onlink == 0 && new->ndpr_raf_auto == 0)
1377                        goto end;
1378
1379                error = nd6_prelist_add(new, dr, &newpr);
1380                if (error != 0 || newpr == NULL) {
1381                        nd6log((LOG_NOTICE, "prelist_update: "
1382                                "nd6_prelist_add failed for %s/%d on %s "
1383                                "errno=%d, returnpr=%p\n",
1384                                ip6_sprintf(&new->ndpr_prefix.sin6_addr),
1385                                new->ndpr_plen, if_name(new->ndpr_ifp),
1386                                error, newpr));
1387                        goto end; /* we should just give up in this case. */
1388                }
1389
1390                /*
1391                 * XXX: from the ND point of view, we can ignore a prefix
1392                 * with the on-link bit being zero.  However, we need a
1393                 * prefix structure for references from autoconfigured
1394                 * addresses.  Thus, we explicitly make sure that the prefix
1395                 * itself expires now.
1396                 */
1397                if (newpr->ndpr_raf_onlink == 0) {
1398                        newpr->ndpr_vltime = 0;
1399                        newpr->ndpr_pltime = 0;
1400                        in6_init_prefix_ltimes(newpr);
1401                }
1402
1403                pr = newpr;
1404        }
```
――――――――――――――――――――――――――――――――――――― nd6_rtr.c

1372–1377 This is a new prefix. If the (valid) lifetime of the prefix is 0, the prefix is ignored. Similarly, if the prefix does not indicate it is on-link or cannot be used for address configuration, the prefix is useless and is of no interest to the receiver. The prefix is also ignored in this case.

1379–1388 Function `nd6_prelist_add()` (Section 5.19.1) is called to insert this prefix to the system-wide Prefix List.

1397–1401 If the L flag is cleared in the new prefix, the A flag must be set at this point due to the check at line 1376, and the prefix will be used to autoconfigure an address below. Since the KAME kernel implementation must keep the prefix structure while the corresponding address remains, `newpr` is retained with 0 lifetimes (see the discussion in Section 2.11).

Listing 5-212
――― nd6_rtr.c

```
1406            /*
1407             * Address autoconfiguration based on Section 5.5.3 of RFC 2462.
1408             * Note that pr must be non NULL at this point.
1409             */
1410
1411            /* 5.5.3 (a). Ignore the prefix without the A bit set. */
1412            if (!new->ndpr_raf_auto)
1413                    goto end;
```
――― nd6_rtr.c

1412–1413 The remaining work performed by this function is to generate or update addresses
if the prefix can be used for address autoconfiguration. If the new prefix does not have
the A flag set, this function has completed its work and it returns to the caller.

Listing 5-213

```
                                                                   nd6_rtr.c
1415            /*
1416             * 5.5.3 (b). the link-local prefix should have been ignored in
1417             * nd6_ra_input.
1418             */
1419
1420            /* 5.5.3 (c). Consistency check on lifetimes: pltime <= vltime. */
1421            if (new->ndpr_pltime > new->ndpr_vltime) {
1422                    error = EINVAL; /* XXX: won't be used */
1423                    goto end;
1424            }
                                                                   nd6_rtr.c
```

1415–1423 The code here performs some consistency checks according to [RFC2462]: If the
preferred lifetime is larger than the valid lifetime, the prefix is invalid and ignored.
While the RFC also specifies that a link-local prefix be ignored, this check was done
in the `nd6_ra_input()` (Listing 5-139) as commented in the code, and does not need
to be repeated here.

Listing 5-214

```
                                                                   nd6_rtr.c
1426            /*
1427             * 5.5.3 (d). If the prefix advertised does not match the prefix of an
1428             * address already in the list, and the Valid Lifetime is not 0,
1429             * form an address.  Note that even a manually configured address
1430             * should reject autoconfiguration of a new address.
1431             */
....
1435            TAILQ_FOREACH(ifa, &ifp->if_addrlist, ifa_list)
....
1439            {
1440                    struct in6_ifaddr *ifa6;
1441                    u_int32_t storedlifetime;
....
1445
1446                    if (ifa->ifa_addr->sa_family != AF_INET6)
1447                            continue;
1448
1449                    ifa6 = (struct in6_ifaddr *)ifa;
1450
1451                    /*
1452                     * Spec is not clear here, but I believe we should concentrate
1453                     * on unicast (i.e. not anycast) addresses.
1454                     * XXX: other ia6_flags? detached or duplicated?
1455                     */
1456                    if ((ifa6->ia6_flags & IN6_IFF_ANYCAST) != 0)
1457                            continue;
1458
1459                    /*
1460                     * Ignore the address if it is not associated with a prefix
1461                     * or is associated with a prefix that is different from this
1462                     * one.  (pr is never NULL here)
```

```
1463                         */
1464                 if (ifa6->ia6_ndpr != pr)
1465                         continue;
1466
1467                 if (ia6_match == NULL) /* remember the first one */
1468                         ia6_match = ifa6;
1469
1470                 if ((ifa6->ia6_flags & IN6_IFF_AUTOCONF) == 0)
1471                         continue;
```
── nd6_rtr.c

1432–1457 A search is performed through the interface address list to determine if any address has been configured using the given prefix. The search process ignores anycast addresses. As the code comment indicates, this treatment is a KAME interpretation of the specification because the specification does not explicitly state how anycast addresses should be handled in this processing.

1464–1471 If an address whose prefix matches the given prefix is found, it is recorded in variable ia6_match in order to prevent the additional creation of addresses below. An address that was manually configured (indicated by the IN6_IFF_AUTOCONF flag being cleared) is also regarded as a valid match, as required by the RFC, but the lifetimes of a manually configured address remain unmodified. Only autoconfigured addresses are subject to the following processing of lifetime management.

Listing 5-215
── nd6_rtr.c
```
1473                 /*
1474                  * An already autoconfigured address matched.  Now that we
1475                  * are sure there is at least one matched address, we can
1476                  * proceed to 5.5.3. (e): update the lifetimes according to the
1477                  * "two hours" rule and the privacy extension.
1478                  */
1479     #define TWOHOUR         (120*60)
1480                 /*
1481                  * RFC2462 introduces the notion of StoredLifetime to the
1482                  * "two hours" rule as follows:
1483                  *   the Lifetime associated with the previously autoconfigured
1484                  *   address.
1485                  * Our interpretation of this definition is "the remaining
1486                  * lifetime to expiration at the evaluation time".  One might
1487                  * be wondering if this interpretation is really conform to the
1488                  * RFC, because the text can read that "Lifetimes" are never
1489                  * decreased, and our definition of the "storedlifetime" below
1490                  * essentially reduces the "Valid Lifetime" advertised in the
1491                  * previous RA.  But, this is due to the wording of the text,
1492                  * and our interpretation is the same as an author's intention.
1493                  * See the discussion in the IETF ipngwg ML in August 2001,
1494                  * with the Subject "StoredLifetime in RFC 2462".
1495                  */
1496                 lt6_tmp = ifa6->ia6_lifetime;
1497                 if (lt6_tmp.ia6t_vltime == ND6_INFINITE_LIFETIME)
1498                         storedlifetime = ND6_INFINITE_LIFETIME;
1499                 else if (time_second - ifa6->ia6_updatetime >
1500                         lt6_tmp.ia6t_vltime) {
1501                         /*
1502                          * The case of "invalid" address.  We should usually
1503                          * not see this case.
1504                          */
1505                         storedlifetime = 0;
```

```
1506                    } else
1507                            storedlifetime = lt6_tmp.ia6t_vltime -
1508                                    (time_second - ifa6->ia6_updatetime);
1509
1510                    /* when not updating, keep the current stored lifetime. */
1511                    lt6_tmp.ia6t_vltime = storedlifetime;
1512
1513                    if (TWOHOUR < new->ndpr_vltime ||
1514                        storedlifetime < new->ndpr_vltime) {
1515                            lt6_tmp.ia6t_vltime = new->ndpr_vltime;
1516                    } else if (storedlifetime <= TWOHOUR
....
1525                            ) {
1526                            if (auth) {
1527                                    lt6_tmp.ia6t_vltime = new->ndpr_vltime;
1528                            }
1529                    } else {
1530                            /*
1531                             * new->ndpr_vltime <= TWOHOUR &&
1532                             * TWOHOUR < storedlifetime
1533                             */
1534                            lt6_tmp.ia6t_vltime = TWOHOUR;
1535                    }
1536
1537                    /* The 2 hour rule is not imposed for preferred lifetime. */
1538                    lt6_tmp.ia6t_pltime = new->ndpr_pltime;
1539
1540                    in6_init_address_ltimes(pr, &lt6_tmp);
```
——— nd6_rtr.c

1479–1535 The valid lifetime of the address is updated according to the two-hour rule as described in Section 5.10.3.

Note that `storedlifetime` in the code, which is derived from [RFC2462], represents the "remaining valid lifetime" mentioned in Section 5.10.3; while "stored" may not be an appropriate term to represent the notation, this is the real intent of the RFC author. A successor version of the protocol specification [RFC2462BIS] updates the terminology to "RemainingLifetime," which is probably more intuitive, and a later version of the kernel code has also been adjusted. Note, however, that this is a matter of terminology, and the behavior is the same.

It should also be noted that `auth` specifies whether the corresponding Router Advertisement message was authenticated by IPsec while the description in Section 5.10.3 refers to the SEND protocol. This is simply because the code was written when SEND was not standardized. It was based on [RFC2462], which only mentioned the use of IPsec.

1538 As explained in Section 5.10.3, the two-hour rule is not imposed on the preferred lifetime of the address. The preferred lifetime is always set to that of the newly received Prefix Information option.

Listing 5-216

——— nd6_rtr.c
```
1542                    /*
1543                     * We need to treat lifetimes for temporary addresses
1544                     * differently, according to
1545                     * draft-ietf-ipngwg-temp-addresses-v2-00.txt 3.3 (1);
1546                     * we only update the lifetimes when they are in the maximum
```

```
1547                          * intervals.
1548                          */
1549                         if ((ifa6->ia6_flags & IN6_IFF_TEMPORARY) != 0) {
1550                                 u_int32_t maxvltime, maxpltime;
1551
1552                                 if (ip6_temp_valid_lifetime >
1553                                     (u_int32_t)(time_second - ifa6->ia6_createtime)) {
1554                                         maxvltime = ip6_temp_valid_lifetime -
1555                                                 (time_second - ifa6->ia6_createtime);
1556                                 } else
1557                                         maxvltime = 0;
1558                                 if (ip6_temp_preferred_lifetime >
1559                                     (u_int32_t)((time_second - ifa6->ia6_createtime) +
1560                                     ip6_desync_factor)) {
1561                                         maxpltime = ip6_temp_preferred_lifetime -
1562                                                 (time_second - ifa6->ia6_createtime) -
1563                                                 ip6_desync_factor;
1564                                 } else
1565                                         maxpltime = 0;
1566
1567                                 if (lt6_tmp.ia6t_vltime == ND6_INFINITE_LIFETIME ||
1568                                     lt6_tmp.ia6t_vltime > maxvltime) {
1569                                         lt6_tmp.ia6t_vltime = maxvltime;
1570                                 }
1571                                 if (lt6_tmp.ia6t_pltime == ND6_INFINITE_LIFETIME ||
1572                                     lt6_tmp.ia6t_pltime > maxpltime) {
1573                                         lt6_tmp.ia6t_pltime = maxpltime;
1574                                 }
1575                         }
```
———nd6_rtr.c

1542–1548 The update procedure of the lifetimes of a temporary address is complicated. Typically the lifetimes can only be lowered when they are adjusted by a received Router Advertisement message due to the ephemeral nature of temporary addresses. In order to avoid deprecating or invalidating the address in an unexpectedly short term when advertised lifetimes are short, however, a revised version of the protocol specification [PRIVACY-ADDRS2] allows the lifetimes of a temporary address to be extended as long as the address does not remain valid or preferred for more than TEMP_VALID_LIFETIME seconds or (TEMP_PREFERRED_LIFETIME − DESYNC_FACTOR) seconds, respectively. The additional rule avoids, for example, the scenario where the router keeps advertising a prefix with the valid lifetime of 1 hour and any temporary address is invalidated in 1 hour.

1549–1565 maxvltime and maxpltime are set to the maximum allowable valid and preferred lifetimes that meet the above rules. If the rule should have invalidated or deprecated the address, the corresponding lifetimes are reset to 0. Variables ip6_temp_valid_lifetime and ip6_temp_preferred_lifetime used in this calculation are set to TEMP_VALID_LIFETIME and TEMP_PREFERRED_LIFETIME by default, and can be modified via **sysctl** variables named net.inet6.ip6.tempvltime and net.inet6. ip6.temppltime.

1567–1573 If the advertised lifetime is larger than the allowable maximum value, it is adjusted to the maximum lifetime.

Figure 5-36 summarizes the relationship between the related parameters. It clarifies for each of the valid and preferred lifetimes which value will be used for the new lifetime, the advertised value or the allowable maximum.

FIGURE 5-36

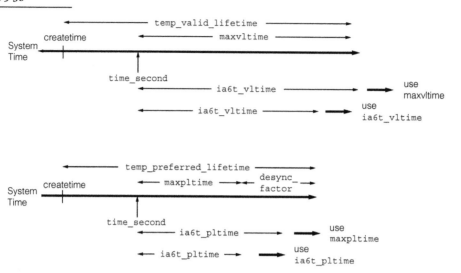

Updating lifetimes of a temporary address.

Note: The above rule and the implementation are slightly different from what is described in the protocol specification [PRIVACY-ADDRS2]: The specification states the address must not remain valid for more than (TEMP_VALID_LIFETIME – DESYNC_FACTOR) seconds. But this is an error of the specification. It does not make sense to include DESYNC_FACTOR for the valid lifetime because the expiration of the lifetime does not cause an action in which synchronized behavior causes trouble. The revised specification will be corrected on this point before the official publication, which will also make the implementation compliant.

Listing 5-217

—— nd6_rtr.c

```
1577                    ifa6->ia6_lifetime = lt6_tmp;
1578                    ifa6->ia6_updatetime = time_second;
1579            }
```

—— nd6_rtr.c

1577–1578 lt6_tmp contains the new valid and preferred lifetimes. These are then copied to the interface address structure. The timestamp of the lifetime update is recorded in the ia6_updatetime member.

Listing 5-218

—— nd6_rtr.c

```
1580            if (ia6_match == NULL && new->ndpr_vltime) {
1581                    /*
1582                     * No address matched and the valid lifetime is non-zero.
1583                     * Create a new address.
1584                     */
```

```
1585                        if ((ia6 = in6_ifadd(new)) != NULL) {
1586                                /*
1587                                 * note that we should use pr (not new) for reference.
1588                                 */
1589                                pr->ndpr_refcnt++;
1590                                ia6->ia6_ndpr = pr;
1591
1592                                /*
1593                                 * draft-ietf-ipngwg-temp-addresses-v2-00 3.3 (2).
1594                                 * When a new public address is created as described
1595                                 * in RFC2462, also create a new temporary address.
1596                                 *
1597                                 * draft-ietf-ipngwg-temp-addresses-v2-00 3.5.
1598                                 * When an interface connects to a new link, a new
1599                                 * randomized interface identifier should be generated
1600                                 * immediately together with a new set of temporary
1601                                 * addresses.  Thus, we specify 1 as the 2nd arg of
1602                                 * in6_tmpifadd().
1603                                 */
1604                                if (ip6_use_tempaddr) {
1605                                        int e;
1606                                        if ((e = in6_tmpifadd(ia6, 1)) != 0) {
1607                                                nd6log((LOG_NOTICE, "prelist_update: "
1608                                                    "failed to create a temporary "
1609                                                    "address, errno=%d\n",
1610                                                    e));
1611                                        }
1612                                }
1613
1614                                /*
1615                                 * A newly added address might affect the status
1616                                 * of other addresses, so we check and update it.
1617                                 * XXX: what if address duplication happens?
1618                                 */
1619                                pfxlist_onlink_check();
1620                        } else {
1621                                /* just set an error. do not bark here. */
1622                                error = EADDRNOTAVAIL; /* XXX: might be unused. */
1623                        }
1624                }
1625
1626    end:
1627            splx(s);
1628            return error;
1629    }
```
── nd6_rtr.c

1580–1624 If no matching address is found in Listing 5-214 and the advertised valid lifetime is non-0, function in6_ifadd() (Section 5.20.1) is called to create a new interface address using the newly acquired prefix. If this function succeeds, the prefix and the created address are associated as shown in Figure 2-15.

1604–1612 A new temporary address is also generated by in6_tmpifadd() (Section 5.20.2) if the system is configured to use the privacy extensions. net.inet6.ip6.use_tempaddr is the **sysctl** variable that controls this policy, and its value is stored in ip6_use_tempaddr.

1619 Since the newly created address may have changed the on-link state of other addresses, pfxlist_onlink_check() is called to update the status of all known prefixes and addresses.

5.19.4 `find_pfxlist_reachable_router()` Function

Function `find_pfxlist_reachable_router()`, shown below, searches through the list of routers that advertised this prefix to find a probably reachable router. This function is used as a subroutine of other prefix-related functions described in succeeding sections and effectively works as a test function to see whether there is any probably reachable router that advertises a given prefix.

Listing 5-219

nd6_rtr.c

```
1631    /*
1632     * A supplement function used in the on-link detection below;
1633     * detect if a given prefix has a (probably) reachable advertising router.
1634     * XXX: lengthy function name...
1635     */
1636    static struct nd_pfxrouter *
1637    find_pfxlist_reachable_router(pr)
1638            struct nd_prefix *pr;
1639    {
1640            struct nd_pfxrouter *pfxrtr;
1641            struct rtentry *rt;
1642            struct llinfo_nd6 *ln;
1643
1644            for (pfxrtr = LIST_FIRST(&pr->ndpr_advrtrs); pfxrtr;
1645                pfxrtr = LIST_NEXT(pfxrtr, pfr_entry)) {
1646                    if ((rt = nd6_lookup(&pfxrtr->router->rtaddr, 0,
1647                        pfxrtr->router->ifp)) &&
1648                        (ln = (struct llinfo_nd6 *)rt->rt_llinfo) &&
1649                        ND6_IS_LLINFO_PROBREACH(ln))
1650                            break;  /* found */
1651            }
1652
1653            return (pfxrtr);
1654    }
```

nd6_rtr.c

5.19.5 Prefix and Address State about On-link Condition

The KAME implementation introduced a custom state for each prefix and addresses associated with the prefix that indicates whether the prefix is regarded as on-link or off-link, specifically for nomadic nodes moving from link to link.

To understand the background of this extension, consider the following scenario in Figure 5-37.

Router RT-1 distributes prefix X for address configuration on network N1. Node A originally resided on N1 and acquired an address X:A. Node A then moved off N1 and reattached onto network N3. Both the prefix X and address X:A are still valid if the movement took place within the lifetimes of the prefix and the address. Since router RT-3 advertises a different prefix Y on network N3 for address configuration, node A will acquire prefix Y and subsequently generate an additional address Y:A.

When node A tries to communicate with node B in a different network, if node A chooses address X:A as the source address for the communication, then the return traffic from node B will not reach node A unless node B has an explicit route to node A on network N3. As shown in Figure 5-37, when node B sends packets to node A, without the host route to node A on

FIGURE 5-37

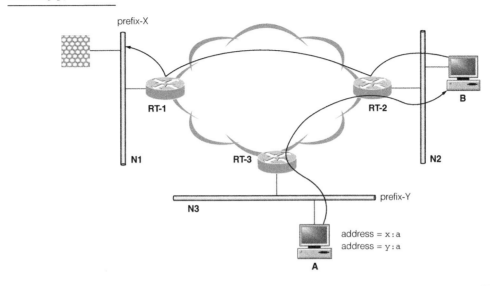

A node moved to a different link and cannot receive packets.

network N3, the return traffic will be routed through RT-2 toward RT-1 to network N1 where prefix X resides.

Another problem occurs if a node D was an on-link neighbor of node A on network N1 (Figure 5-38). After the movement from N1 to N3, if node A tries to communicate with node D using address X:A, it will treat node D as on-link and the communication attempt will fail.

One simple solution to these problems is to force the node to discard the old prefix and the old address after moving. But this approach may cause an unexpected deletion of prefixes and addresses that should remain valid. For instance, suppose that there is a failure of the router on a network while a laptop computer is suspended. When the laptop's operation is resumed, it would have to discard the prefix and the address that were advertised before suspension, since there is a possibility that the laptop has moved from the network. The laptop, however, cannot get a prefix anymore because the router has already stopped; it fails to communicate with any nodes, even with those within the network, unless it relies on the "on-link assumption," which is now discouraged, or on the use of link-local addresses with some autonomous service discovery within the link.

The KAME implementation thus introduces a mechanism that detects whether a prefix or an address is valid (on-link) in the current link. It defines two notions for each prefix, *attached* and *detached*. A prefix is called *attached* if none of its advertising routers are (probably) reachable or no prefixes including that prefix have a reachable advertising router. Note that the second condition deals with the case of no router available in the current link. Otherwise, the prefix is called *detached*.

On top of this, the implementation introduces the following definitions for autoconfigured addresses: an autoconfigured address is called *attached* if its associated prefix is attached or

FIGURE 5-38

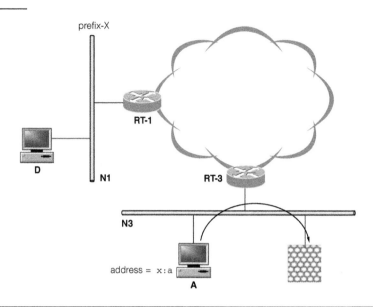

A node treats off-link nodes as on-link.

any prefixes for any addresses are detached. Again, the latter condition corresponds to the case where no router is available. Otherwise, the address is called *detached*.

Note: As we will see in the next subsection, the actual implementation is a bit more complicated to support some other corner cases.

A detached prefix is not regarded as on-link, and addresses that match a detached prefix are not regarded as a neighbor. Similarly, a detached address is not used as a packet's source address.

Going back to the above examples, node A can quickly identify RT-1 (which is the only advertising router in network N1) is unreachable after moving to the new link. This makes address X:A detached in Figure 5-37, thereby avoiding the use of that address as a source address and avoiding the depicted scenario. In Figure 5-38, node A will not try link-layer address resolution for X:D since prefix X is detached for the node.

Regarding the implementation, a detached prefix (an instance of the `nd_prefix{}` structure) is marked in its `ndpr_stateflags` member with the `NDPRF_DETACHED` flag set to on; otherwise, the prefix is regarded as attached. A detached IPv6 address (an instance of the `in6_ifaddr{}` structure—Section 2.10.1), is marked in its `ia6_flags` member with the `IN6_IFF_DETACHED` flag set to on; otherwise, the address is regarded as attached.

5.19.6 `pfxlist_onlink_check()` Function

The `pfxlist_onlink_check()` function examines the on-link status of each known prefix and associated addresses based on the definitions and the mechanism described in the previous section.

Listing 5-220

```
1656    /*
1657     * Check if each prefix in the prefix list has at least one available router
1658     * that advertised the prefix (a router is "available" if its neighbor cache
1659     * entry is reachable or probably reachable).
1660     * If the check fails, the prefix may be off-link, because, for example,
1661     * we have moved from the network but the lifetime of the prefix has not
1662     * expired yet. So we should not use the prefix if there is another prefix
1663     * that has an available router.
1664     * But, if there is no prefix that has an available router, we still regards
1665     * all the prefixes as on-link.  This is because we can't tell if all the
1666     * routers are simply dead or if we really moved from the network and there
1667     * is no router around us.
1668     */
1669    void
1670    pfxlist_onlink_check()
1671    {
1672            struct nd_prefix *pr;
1673            struct in6_ifaddr *ifa;
1674            struct nd_defrouter *dr;
1675            struct nd_pfxrouter *pfxrtr = NULL;
1676
1677            /*
1678             * Check if there is a prefix that has a reachable advertising
1679             * router.
1680             */
1681            for (pr = nd_prefix.lh_first; pr; pr = pr->ndpr_next) {
1682                    if (pr->ndpr_raf_onlink && find_pfxlist_reachable_router(pr))
1683                            break;
1684            }
```

1681–1683 First a search is made for a prefix that is marked as on-link and is advertised by a reachable or probably reachable router.

Listing 5-221

```
1685            /*
1686             * If we have no such prefix, check whether we still have a router
1687             * that does not advertise any prefixes.
1688             */
1689            if (!pr) {
1690                    for (dr = TAILQ_FIRST(&nd_defrouter); dr;
1691                        dr = TAILQ_NEXT(dr, dr_entry)) {
1692                            struct nd_prefix *pr0;
1693
1694                            for (pr0 = nd_prefix.lh_first; pr0;
1695                                pr0 = pr0->ndpr_next) {
1696                                    if ((pfxrtr = pfxrtr_lookup(pr0, dr)) != NULL)
1697                                            break;
1698                            }
1699                            if (pfxrtr)
1700                                    break;
1701                    }
1702            }
```

1689–1702 If the first search failed, the Default Router List is traversed to find a router that advertises any prefix. The first router that is found in the loop, if any, is recorded in `pfxrtr`.

Listing 5-222

--nd6_rtr.c
```
1703              if (pr != NULL || (TAILQ_FIRST(&nd_defrouter) && !pfxrtr)) {
1704                      /*
1705                       * There is at least one prefix that has a reachable router,
1706                       * or at least a router which probably does not advertise
1707                       * any prefixes.  The latter would be the case when we move
1708                       * to a new link where we have a router that does not provide
1709                       * prefixes and we configure an address by hand.
1710                       * Detach prefixes which have no reachable advertising
1711                       * router, and attach other prefixes.
1712                       */
1713                      for (pr = nd_prefix.lh_first; pr; pr = pr->ndpr_next) {
1714                              /* XXX: a link-local prefix should never be detached */
1715                              if (IN6_IS_ADDR_LINKLOCAL(&pr->ndpr_prefix.sin6_addr))
1716                                      continue;
1717
1718                              /*
1719                               * we aren't interested in prefixes without the L bit
1720                               * set.
1721                               */
1722                              if (pr->ndpr_raf_onlink == 0)
1723                                      continue;
1724
1725                              if ((pr->ndpr_stateflags & NDPRF_DETACHED) == 0 &&
1726                                  find_pfxlist_reachable_router(pr) == NULL)
1727                                      pr->ndpr_stateflags |= NDPRF_DETACHED;
1728                              if ((pr->ndpr_stateflags & NDPRF_DETACHED) != 0 &&
1729                                  find_pfxlist_reachable_router(pr) != 0)
1730                                      pr->ndpr_stateflags &= ~NDPRF_DETACHED;
1731                      }
```
--nd6_rtr.c

1703 If the first search succeeded or if the Default Router List is not empty but no router advertises any prefix, some of the prefixes should be treated as attached and some others may have to be regarded as detached. As commented in the code, the latter condition handles a subtle case, for example, where a host manually configures its addresses while configuring the default router via Router Advertisement messages.

1713–1723 The entire Prefix List is examined, ignoring a link-local prefix or a prefix whose L flag is cleared (that is, this prefix is irrelevant to on-link determination in the first place).

1725–1727 A prefix whose `NDPRF_DETACHED` state flag is cleared, namely an attached prefix, becomes detached if it does not have any reachable advertising router.

1727–1729 A detached prefix now becomes attached if it has a reachable advertising router.

Listing 5-223

--nd6_rtr.c
```
1732              } else {
1733                      /* there is no prefix that has a reachable router */
1734                      for (pr = nd_prefix.lh_first; pr; pr = pr->ndpr_next) {
1735                              if (IN6_IS_ADDR_LINKLOCAL(&pr->ndpr_prefix.sin6_addr))
1736                                      continue;
```

```
1737
1738                          if (pr->ndpr_raf_onlink == 0)
1739                                  continue;
1740
1741                          if ((pr->ndpr_stateflags & NDPRF_DETACHED) != 0)
1742                                  pr->ndpr_stateflags &= ~NDPRF_DETACHED;
1743                  }
1744          }
```
── nd6_rtr.c

1732–1744 All prefixes are considered attached if none of the prefixes have a reachable router based on the definition given in the previous subsection.

Listing 5-224
── nd6_rtr.c

```
1746          /*
1747           * Remove each interface route associated with a (just) detached
1748           * prefix, and reinstall the interface route for a (just) attached
1749           * prefix.  Note that all attempt of reinstallation does not
1750           * necessarily success, when a same prefix is shared among multiple
1751           * interfaces.  Such cases will be handled in nd6_prefix_onlink,
1752           * so we don't have to care about them.
1753           */
1754          for (pr = nd_prefix.lh_first; pr; pr = pr->ndpr_next) {
1755                  int e;
1756
1757                  if (IN6_IS_ADDR_LINKLOCAL(&pr->ndpr_prefix.sin6_addr))
1758                          continue;
1759
1760                  if (pr->ndpr_raf_onlink == 0)
1761                          continue;
1762
1763                  if ((pr->ndpr_stateflags & NDPRF_DETACHED) != 0 &&
1764                      (pr->ndpr_stateflags & NDPRF_ONLINK) != 0) {
1765                          if ((e = nd6_prefix_offlink(pr)) != 0) {
1766                                  nd6log((LOG_ERR,
1767                                      "pfxlist_onlink_check: failed to "
1768                                      "make %s/%d offlink, errno=%d\n",
1769                                      ip6_sprintf(&pr->ndpr_prefix.sin6_addr),
1770                                      pr->ndpr_plen, e));
1771                          }
1772                  }
1773                  if ((pr->ndpr_stateflags & NDPRF_DETACHED) == 0 &&
1774                      (pr->ndpr_stateflags & NDPRF_ONLINK) == 0 &&
1775                      pr->ndpr_raf_onlink) {
1776                          if ((e = nd6_prefix_onlink(pr)) != 0) {
1777                                  nd6log((LOG_ERR,
1778                                      "pfxlist_onlink_check: failed to "
1779                                      "make %s/%d onlink, errno=%d\n",
1780                                      ip6_sprintf(&pr->ndpr_prefix.sin6_addr),
1781                                      pr->ndpr_plen, e));
1782                          }
1783                  }
1784          }
```
── nd6_rtr.c

1754–1761 The entire Prefix List is traversed again, to perform processing for possible state changes.

1763–1771 A prefix has just been detached if both the NDPRF_DETACHED flag and the NDPRF_ONLINK flag are set. The nd6_prefix_offlink() function is then called for such prefix to delete interface direct route for the prefix.

1773–1783 Similarly, a prefix is just attached when both the NDPRF_DETACHED flag and the
NDPRF_ONLINK flag are cleared. In this case the interface direct route for the prefix is
installed into the kernel routing table by function nd6_prefx_onlink().

Note: The condition at line 1775 is redundant since this is always true due to the check at
line 1760.

Listing 5-225

_____nd6_rtr.c

```
1786          /*
1787           * Changes on the prefix status might affect address status as well.
1788           * Make sure that all addresses derived from an attached prefix are
1789           * attached, and that all addresses derived from a detached prefix are
1790           * detached.  Note, however, that a manually configured address should
1791           * always be attached.
1792           * The precise detection logic is same as the one for prefixes.
1793           */
1794          for (ifa = in6_ifaddr; ifa; ifa = ifa->ia_next) {
1795                  if (!(ifa->ia6_flags & IN6_IFF_AUTOCONF))
1796                          continue;
1797
1798                  if (ifa->ia6_ndpr == NULL) {
1799                          /*
1800                           * This can happen when we first configure the address
1801                           * (i.e. the address exists, but the prefix does not).
1802                           * XXX: complicated relationships...
1803                           */
1804                          continue;
1805                  }
1806
1807                  if (find_pfxlist_reachable_router(ifa->ia6_ndpr))
1808                          break;
1809          }
1810          if (ifa) {
1811                  for (ifa = in6_ifaddr; ifa; ifa = ifa->ia_next) {
1812                          if ((ifa->ia6_flags & IN6_IFF_AUTOCONF) == 0)
1813                                  continue;
1814
1815                          if (ifa->ia6_ndpr == NULL) /* XXX: see above. */
1816                                  continue;
1817
1818                          if (find_pfxlist_reachable_router(ifa->ia6_ndpr))
1819                                  ifa->ia6_flags &= ~IN6_IFF_DETACHED;
1820                          else
1821                                  ifa->ia6_flags |= IN6_IFF_DETACHED;
1822                  }
1823          }
1824          else {
1825                  for (ifa = in6_ifaddr; ifa; ifa = ifa->ia_next) {
1826                          if ((ifa->ia6_flags & IN6_IFF_AUTOCONF) == 0)
1827                                  continue;
1828
1829                          ifa->ia6_flags &= ~IN6_IFF_DETACHED;
1830                  }
1831          }
....
1842  }
```

_____nd6_rtr.c

Finally, the states of the addresses that are associated with prefixes are synchronized with the state changes of the prefixes.

1794–1796 All IPv6 interface addresses are examined to find an autoconfigured address whose prefix has a reachable advertising router. Addresses that do not have the IN6_IFF_AUTOCONF flag, namely manually configured addresses, are bypassed and are always treated as attached. As we will see in Section 5.20.1, function in6_ifadd() sets this flag for autoconfigured addresses, thereby separating these addresses from manually configured addresses.

1798–1805 This block of code seems to touch an interface address structure that is not fully initialized according to the code comment, but the real intent is not clear. In fact, the ia6_ndpr member should have been initialized even for a newly created address by the time this function is called (see Listings 2-67, 5-218, and 5-248). This is probably a leftover from the time this comment was first written when ia6_ndpr could be NULL in some corner cases. In any case this check should do no harm.

1807–1808 If the associated prefix of this address has a (probably) reachable advertising router, the search completes with the current address.

1810–1831 This block of code updates the on-link state of each address according to the result of the above search and the definition described in the previous subsection. If the search succeeded, it means that address is attached. In this case the other autoconfigured addresses become detached unless they have a (probably) reachable advertising router. On the other hand, if no autoconfigured addresses have a (probably) reachable router, all addresses are regarded as attached.

5.19.7 `nd6_prefix_onlink()` Function

Function nd6_prefix_onlink() installs an interface direct route for the given prefix into the kernel routing table.

Listing 5-226

——nd6_rtr.c
```
1844     int
1845     nd6_prefix_onlink(pr)
1846             struct nd_prefix *pr;
1847     {
1848             struct ifaddr *ifa;
1849             struct ifnet *ifp = pr->ndpr_ifp;
1850             struct sockaddr_in6 mask6;
1851             struct nd_prefix *opr;
1852             u_long rtflags;
1853             int error = 0;
1854             struct rtentry *rt = NULL;
1855
1856             /* sanity check */
1857             if ((pr->ndpr_stateflags & NDPRF_ONLINK) != 0) {
1858                     nd6log((LOG_ERR,
1859                         "nd6_prefix_onlink: %s/%d is already on-link\n",
1860                         ip6_sprintf(&pr->ndpr_prefix.sin6_addr), pr->ndpr_plen);
1861                     return (EEXIST));
1862             }
```
——nd6_rtr.c

1857 This statement checks if an interface direct route for the given prefix is already installed in the kernel routing table. The caller of nd6_prefix_onlink() is generally assumed to call this function only when necessary, and this check should usually fail, that is, the NDPRF_ONLINK flag should not be set.

Listing 5-227

```
                                                                  nd6_rtr.c
1864            /*
1865             * Add the interface route associated with the prefix.  Before
1866             * installing the route, check if there's the same prefix on another
1867             * interface, and the prefix has already installed the interface route.
1868             * Although such a configuration is expected to be rare, we explicitly
1869             * allow it.
1870             */
1871            for (opr = nd_prefix.lh_first; opr; opr = opr->ndpr_next) {
1872                    if (opr == pr)
1873                            continue;
1874
1875                    if ((opr->ndpr_stateflags & NDPRF_ONLINK) == 0)
1876                            continue;
1877
1878                    if (opr->ndpr_plen == pr->ndpr_plen &&
1879                        in6_are_prefix_equal(&pr->ndpr_prefix.sin6_addr,
1880                        &opr->ndpr_prefix.sin6_addr, pr->ndpr_plen))
1881                            return (0);
1882            }
                                                                  nd6_rtr.c
```

1871–1882 The for loop searches for a different instance of nd_prefix{} structure that has the same prefix as the given one and is already marked as on-link on a different interface (note that since nd6_prefix_lookup() compares the interface as well as the prefix, more than one nd_prefix{} structure for the same prefix can coexist in the system). As commented in the code, this should be rare, but can still happen if, for example, two Ethernet interfaces are connected to the same link and the same Router Advertisement messages are accepted on these interfaces. Since the traditional BSD kernel only allows one routing entry for the same destination, only one interface direct route for the prefix can be installed in the routing table. This implementation simply picks the one installed first.

Listing 5-228

```
                                                                  nd6_rtr.c
1884            /*
1885             * We prefer link-local addresses as the associated interface address.
1886             */
1887            /* search for a link-local addr */
1888            ifa = (struct ifaddr *)in6ifa_ifpforlinklocal(ifp,
1889                IN6_IFF_NOTREADY | IN6_IFF_ANYCAST);
1890            if (ifa == NULL) {
1891                    /* XXX: freebsd does not have ifa_ifwithaf */
....
1895                    TAILQ_FOREACH(ifa, &ifp->if_addrlist, ifa_list)
....
1901                    {
1902                            if (ifa->ifa_addr->sa_family == AF_INET6)
1903                                    break;
1904                    }
1905                    /* should we care about ia6_flags? */
1906            }
                                                                  nd6_rtr.c
```

1888 The preference is to use an interface's link-local address as the gateway for installing the interface direct route because it should be more stable than global addresses. If no link-local address is configured, the first IPv6 address from the interface address list is used instead. The `rt_ifa` field of the newly created route will point to the selected interface address.

Listing 5-229

```
                                                                    nd6_rtr.c
1907            if (ifa == NULL) {
1908                    /*
1909                     * This can still happen, when, for example, we receive an RA
1910                     * containing a prefix with the L bit set and the A bit clear,
1911                     * after removing all IPv6 addresses on the receiving
1912                     * interface.  This should, of course, be rare though.
1913                     */
1914                    nd6log((LOG_NOTICE,
1915                        "nd6_prefix_onlink: failed to find any ifaddr"
1916                        " to add route for a prefix(%s/%d) on %s\n",
1917                        ip6_sprintf(&pr->ndpr_prefix.sin6_addr),
1918                        pr->ndpr_plen, if_name(ifp)));
1919                    return (0);
1920            }
                                                                    nd6_rtr.c
```

1907–1919 It is still possible that no IPv6 address is found on the interface as commented in the code. This happens if an administrator has deliberately removed all IPv6 addresses from the interface, including link-local addresses, and then a Router Advertisement message with the A flag off and the L flag on arrives on the interface. This implementation simply stops installing an interface direct route for the prefix in such a special case, while it should be quite rare in practice.

Listing 5-230

```
                                                                    nd6_rtr.c
1922            /*
1923             * in6_ifinit() sets nd6_rtrequest to ifa_rtrequest for all ifaddrs.
1924             * ifa->ifa_rtrequest = nd6_rtrequest;
1925             */
1926            bzero(&mask6, sizeof(mask6));
1927            mask6.sin6_len = sizeof(mask6);
1928            mask6.sin6_addr = pr->ndpr_mask;
1929            /* rtrequest() will probably set RTF_UP, but we're not sure. */
1930            rtflags = ifa->ifa_flags | RTF_UP;
1931            if (nd6_need_cache(ifp)) {
1932                    /* explicitly set in case ifa_flags does not set the flag. */
1933                    rtflags |= RTF_CLONING;
1934            } else {
1935                    /*
1936                     * explicitly clear the cloning bit in case ifa_flags sets it.
1937                     */
1938                    rtflags &= ~RTF_CLONING;
1939            }
                                                                    nd6_rtr.c
```

1926–1939 The route entry has the cloning (`RTF_CLONING`) flag set if and only if the interface needs Neighbor Cache entries. Setting the cloning flag allows the creation of host routes from this interface direct route for destinations covered by the prefix, which is described in detail in Section 5.15.1.

Listing 5-231

nd6_rtr.c

```
1940                    error = rtrequest(RTM_ADD, (struct sockaddr *)&pr->ndpr_prefix,
1941                        ifa->ifa_addr, (struct sockaddr *)&mask6, rtflags, &rt);
1942                if (error == 0) {
1943                        if (rt != NULL) /* this should be non NULL, though */
1944                                nd6_rtmsg(RTM_ADD, rt);
1945                        pr->ndpr_stateflags |= NDPRF_ONLINK;
1946                } else {
1947                        nd6log((LOG_ERR, "nd6_prefix_onlink: failed to add route for a"
1948                            " prefix (%s/%d) on %s, gw=%s, mask=%s, flags=%lx "
1949                            "errno = %d\n",
1950                            ip6_sprintf(&pr->ndpr_prefix.sin6_addr),
1951                            pr->ndpr_plen, if_name(ifp),
1952                            ip6_sprintf(&((struct sockaddr_in6 *)ifa->ifa_addr)
        ->sin6_addr),
1953                            ip6_sprintf(&mask6.sin6_addr), rtflags, error));
1954                }
```

nd6_rtr.c

— *Line 1952 is broken here for layout reasons. However, it is a single line of code.*

1940–1945 The interface direct route is installed into the kernel by calling function `rtrequest()`, which will subsequently invoke `nd6_rtrequest()` in order to set up the template structure for route cloning for on-link neighbors (see Section 5.15.1). The prefix state flag now reflects the successful route installation, that is, the `NDPRF_ONLINK` flag is now set. Also, a message is sent to routing sockets to notify upper layer applications that are interested about this change in the kernel routing table.

5.19.8 `nd6_prefix_offlink()` Function

Function `nd6_prefix_offlink()` removes an interface direct route for the given prefix from the kernel routing table and performs necessary cleanup.

Listing 5-232

nd6_rtr.c

```
1962    int
1963    nd6_prefix_offlink(pr)
1964            struct nd_prefix *pr;
1965    {
1966            int error = 0;
1967            struct ifnet *ifp = pr->ndpr_ifp;
1968            struct nd_prefix *opr;
1969            struct sockaddr_in6 sa6, mask6;
1970            struct rtentry *rt = NULL;
1971
1972            /* sanity check */
1973            if ((pr->ndpr_stateflags & NDPRF_ONLINK) == 0) {
1974                    nd6log((LOG_ERR,
1975                        "nd6_prefix_offlink: %s/%d is already off-link\n",
1976                        ip6_sprintf(&pr->ndpr_prefix.sin6_addr), pr->ndpr_plen));
1977                    return (EEXIST);
1978            }
```

nd6_rtr.c

1973–1978 This statement checks to see if a route for the given prefix is already installed in the kernel routing table. This function simply returns if the route is not present. Similar to `nd6_prefix_onlink()` this check should usually fail, that is, the `NDPRF_ONLINK` flag should be set.

Listing 5-233

---
nd6_rtr.c

```
1980                bzero(&sa6, sizeof(sa6));
1981                sa6.sin6_family = AF_INET6;
1982                sa6.sin6_len = sizeof(sa6);
1983                bcopy(&pr->ndpr_prefix.sin6_addr, &sa6.sin6_addr,
1984                    sizeof(struct in6_addr));
1985                bzero(&mask6, sizeof(mask6));
1986                mask6.sin6_family = AF_INET6;
1987                mask6.sin6_len = sizeof(sa6);
1988                bcopy(&pr->ndpr_mask, &mask6.sin6_addr, sizeof(struct in6_addr));
1989                error = rtrequest(RTM_DELETE, (struct sockaddr *)&sa6, NULL,
1990                    (struct sockaddr *)&mask6, 0, &rt);
```
---
nd6_rtr.c

1980–1990 Function `rtrequest()` is called to remove the interface direct route from the kernel routing table.

Listing 5-234

---
nd6_rtr.c

```
1991                if (error == 0) {
1992                    pr->ndpr_stateflags &= ~NDPRF_ONLINK;
1993
1994                    /* report the route deletion to the routing socket. */
1995                    if (rt != NULL)
1996                        nd6_rtmsg(RTM_DELETE, rt);
```
---
nd6_rtr.c

1991–1996 If the route deletion was successful, the `NDPRF_ONLINK` flag is cleared from the prefix to mark it as off-link. A route message is sent to notify interested applications.

Listing 5-235

---
nd6_rtr.c

```
1998                /*
1999                 * There might be the same prefix on another interface,
2000                 * the prefix which could not be on-link just because we have
2001                 * the interface route (see comments in nd6_prefix_onlink).
2002                 * If there's one, try to make the prefix on-link on the
2003                 * interface.
2004                 */
2005                for (opr = nd_prefix.lh_first; opr; opr = opr->ndpr_next) {
2006                    if (opr == pr)
2007                        continue;
2008
2009                    if ((opr->ndpr_stateflags & NDPRF_ONLINK) != 0)
2010                        continue;
2011
2012                    /*
2013                     * KAME specific: detached prefixes should not be
2014                     * on-link.
2015                     */
2016                    if ((opr->ndpr_stateflags & NDPRF_DETACHED) != 0)
2017                        continue;
2018
2019                    if (opr->ndpr_plen == pr->ndpr_plen &&
2020                        in6_are_prefix_equal(&pr->ndpr_prefix.sin6_addr,
2021                        &opr->ndpr_prefix.sin6_addr, pr->ndpr_plen)) {
2022                        int e;
2023
2024                        if ((e = nd6_prefix_onlink(opr)) != 0) {
```

```
2025                                    nd6log((LOG_ERR,
2026                                        "nd6_prefix_offlink: failed to "
2027                                        "recover a prefix %s/%d from %s "
2028                                        "to %s (errno = %d)\n",
2029                                        ip6_sprintf(&opr->ndpr_prefix.sin6_addr),
2030                                        opr->ndpr_plen, if_name(ifp),
2031                                        if_name(opr->ndpr_ifp), e));
2032                                }
2033                            }
2034                    }
2035        } else {
2036                /* XXX: can we still set the NDPRF_ONLINK flag? */
2037                nd6log((LOG_ERR,
2038                    "nd6_prefix_offlink: failed to delete route: "
2039                    "%s/%d on %s (errno = %d)\n",
2040                    ip6_sprintf(&sa6.sin6_addr), pr->ndpr_plen, if_name(ifp),
2041                    error));
2042        }
```
_____ nd6_rtr.c

2005–2035 As explained in Listing 5-227, there can be multiple instances of the same prefix in the system, which may be going through different interfaces. If the system has another instance of the same prefix, another interface direct route through a different interface may now be installed, which is implemented by this block of code.

Listing 5-236
_____ nd6_rtr.c

```
2044        if (rt != NULL) {
2045                if (rt->rt_refcnt <= 0) {
2046                        /* XXX: we should free the entry ourselves. */
2047                        rt->rt_refcnt++;
2048                        rtfree(rt);
2049                }
2050        }
2051
2052        return (error);
2053    }
```
_____ nd6_rtr.c

2044–2050 The route entry has been removed from the kernel routing table successfully. If this function is the only user of the entry, the entry must be released here (note that `rtrequest()` does not increment the reference counter on the entry in the delete case).

5.20   Stateless Address Autoconfiguration Functions

5.20.1   `in6_ifadd()` Function

Function `in6_ifadd()` creates a new address out of the given prefix.

Listing 5-237
_____ nd6_rtr.c

```
2055    static struct in6_ifaddr *
2056    in6_ifadd(pr)
2057            struct nd_prefixctl *pr;
2058    {
```

```
2059              struct ifnet *ifp = pr->ndpr_ifp;
2060              struct ifaddr *ifa;
2061              struct in6_aliasreq ifra;
2062              struct in6_ifaddr *ia, *ib;
2063              int error, plen0;
2064              struct in6_addr mask;
2065              int prefixlen = pr->ndpr_plen;
2066
2067              in6_prefixlen2mask(&mask, prefixlen);
2068
2069              /*
2070               * find a link-local address (will be interface ID).
2071               * Is it really mandatory? Theoretically, a global or a site-local
2072               * address can be configured without a link-local address, if we
2073               * have a unique interface identifier...
2074               *
2075               * it is not mandatory to have a link-local address, we can generate
2076               * interface identifier on the fly.  we do this because:
2077               * (1) it should be the easiest way to find interface identifier.
2078               * (2) RFC2462 5.4 suggesting the use of the same interface identifier
2079               * for multiple addresses on a single interface, and possible shortcut
2080               * of DAD.  we omitted DAD for this reason in the past.
2081               * (3) a user can prevent autoconfiguration of global address
2082               * by removing link-local address by hand (this is partly because we
2083               * don't have other way to control the use of IPv6 on an interface.
2084               * this has been our design choice - cf. NRL's "ifconfig auto").
2085               * (4) it is easier to manage when an interface has addresses
2086               * with the same interface identifier, than to have multiple addresses
2087               * with different interface identifiers.
2088               */
2089              ifa = (struct ifaddr *)in6ifa_ifpforlinklocal(ifp, 0); /* 0 is OK? */
2090              if (ifa)
2091                      ib = (struct in6_ifaddr *)ifa;
2092              else
2093                      return NULL;
2094
2095      #if 0 /* don't care link local addr state, and always do DAD */
2096              /* if link-local address is not eligible, do not autoconfigure. */
2097              if (((struct in6_ifaddr *)ifa)->ia6_flags & IN6_IFF_NOTREADY) {
2098                      printf("in6_ifadd: link-local address not ready\n");
2099                      return NULL;
2100              }
2101      #endif
2102
2103              /* prefixlen + ifidlen must be equal to 128 */
2104              plen0 = in6_mask2len(&ib->ia_prefixmask.sin6_addr, NULL);
2105              if (prefixlen != plen0) {
2106                      nd6log((LOG_INFO, "in6_ifadd: wrong prefixlen for %s "
2107                          "(prefix=%d ifid=%d)\n",
2108                          if_name(ifp), prefixlen, 128 - plen0));
2109                      return NULL;
2110              }
```
———nd6_rtr.c

2067 Function `in6_prefixlen2mask()` creates a prefix mask based on the given prefix length.

2070–2093 This implementation uses the same interface identifier for both link-local and global addresses. The `in6ifa_ifpforlinklocal()` function first searches for a link-local address configured on the interface for this purpose. This is not a required behavior by the specification, but an implementation's decision as commented in the code.

The decision was made based on an older version of the implementation, and does not seem to be very convincing for the current version.

1. It is not clear what the "easy" means, but it should be pretty easy to generate an interface identifier because this kernel implementation has a dedicated routine for this purpose (see Section 2.13.5). Even though the generation procedure involves overhead, it should not matter much since address generation is a rare event.

2. This part talks about the optimization of skipping DAD described in Section 5.10.2. But since the current practice is to discourage this optimization and this implementation in fact disables the feature, it is now unconvincing.

3. Actually, it is possible to prevent autoconfiguration via the `net.inet6.ip6.accept_rtadv` **sysctl** variable or with the −i option of the **ndp** command (see Listing 5-129). While it is true that "address" configuration can be disabled simply by removing the link-local address, it is dubious whether such operational configuration makes sense; in addition, it is riskier to rely on this assumption for suppressing address configuration because a link-local address may be reconfigured when the interface becomes down and then becomes up.

4. Again, it is not clear what "easier" means here, but the statement about interface having addresses with the same identifier now does not hold in the first place due to the introduction of temporary addresses.

Perhaps one valid justification of this implementation decision that still holds is that the administrator can specify an interface identifier for a global address that is not based on an EUI-64 identifier. In fact, it might be rather desirable to avoid an EUI-64 based interface identifier for a well-known server host that configures itself using the autoconfiguration mechanism, since such an identifier is vulnerable to hardware change (such as replacement of a network interface card).

On a FreeBSD server, this can be done by manually configuring a link-local address in the `/etc/start_if.IFNAME` file where `IFNAME` is the interface name such as `ne0`. For example, if `/etc/start_if.ne0` is set up as follows:

```
ifconfig ne0 inet6 fe80::1%ne0 prefixlen 64
```

then link-local address `fe80::1` will be configured on interface `ne0` on start-up time before accepting inbound Router Advertisement messages, which ensures that global addresses configured via autoconfiguration will also have the non-EUI-64 identifiers such as in `2001:db8:1234::1`.

2104–2110 The prefix length and the length of the interface identifier in bits must add up to 128, which is the size of an IPv6 address.

Listing 5-238

                                                                                     nd6_rtr.c

```
2112            /* make ifaddr */
2113
2114            bzero(&ifra, sizeof(ifra));
2115            /*
2116             * in6_update_ifa() does not use ifra_name, but we accurately set it
2117             * for safety.
2118             */
2119            strncpy(ifra.ifra_name, if_name(ifp), sizeof(ifra.ifra_name));
```

```
2120            ifra.ifra_addr.sin6_family = AF_INET6;
2121            ifra.ifra_addr.sin6_len = sizeof(struct sockaddr_in6);
2122            /* prefix */
2123            bcopy(&pr->ndpr_prefix.sin6_addr, &ifra.ifra_addr.sin6_addr,
2124                sizeof(ifra.ifra_addr.sin6_addr));
2125            ifra.ifra_addr.sin6_addr.s6_addr32[0] &= mask.s6_addr32[0];
2126            ifra.ifra_addr.sin6_addr.s6_addr32[1] &= mask.s6_addr32[1];
2127            ifra.ifra_addr.sin6_addr.s6_addr32[2] &= mask.s6_addr32[2];
2128            ifra.ifra_addr.sin6_addr.s6_addr32[3] &= mask.s6_addr32[3];
```
——— nd6_rtr.c

2112–2128 The in6_aliasreq{} structure (Section 2.10.2) is initialized with the name of the interface. The address field is initialized with the prefix.

Listing 5-239

——— nd6_rtr.c
```
2130            /* interface ID */
2131            ifra.ifra_addr.sin6_addr.s6_addr32[0] |=
2132                (ib->ia_addr.sin6_addr.s6_addr32[0] & ~mask.s6_addr32[0]);
2133            ifra.ifra_addr.sin6_addr.s6_addr32[1] |=
2134                (ib->ia_addr.sin6_addr.s6_addr32[1] & ~mask.s6_addr32[1]);
2135            ifra.ifra_addr.sin6_addr.s6_addr32[2] |=
2136                (ib->ia_addr.sin6_addr.s6_addr32[2] & ~mask.s6_addr32[2]);
2137            ifra.ifra_addr.sin6_addr.s6_addr32[3] |=
2138                (ib->ia_addr.sin6_addr.s6_addr32[3] & ~mask.s6_addr32[3]);
```
——— nd6_rtr.c

2130–2138 The interface identifier is extracted from the existing link-local address and is set into the address field of the in6_aliasreq{} structure. Note that the mask values are inverted here.

Listing 5-240

——— nd6_rtr.c
```
2140            /* new prefix mask. */
2141            ifra.ifra_prefixmask.sin6_len = sizeof(struct sockaddr_in6);
2142            ifra.ifra_prefixmask.sin6_family = AF_INET6;
2143            bcopy(&mask, &ifra.ifra_prefixmask.sin6_addr,
2144                sizeof(ifra.ifra_prefixmask.sin6_addr));
2145
2146            /* lifetimes. */
2147            ifra.ifra_lifetime.ia6t_vltime = pr->ndpr_vltime;
2148            ifra.ifra_lifetime.ia6t_pltime = pr->ndpr_pltime;
2149
2150            /* XXX: scope zone ID? */
2151
2152            ifra.ifra_flags |= IN6_IFF_AUTOCONF; /* obey autoconf */
```
——— nd6_rtr.c

2141–2144 The prefix mask field of in6_aliasreq{} is initialized here.

2147–2149 The preferred and valid lifetimes of the address are initialized according to those values of the advertised prefix.

2152 The new address is marked as an automatically configured address with the IN6_IFF_AUTOCONF flag being set.

Listing 5-241

```
2154                /* allocate ifaddr structure, link into chain, etc. */
2155                if ((error = in6_update_ifa(ifp, &ifra, NULL)) != 0) {
2156                        nd6log((LOG_ERR,
2157                            "in6_ifadd: failed to make ifaddr %s on %s (errno=%d)\n",
2158                            ip6_sprintf(&ifra.ifra_addr.sin6_addr), if_name(ifp),
2159                            error));
2160                        return (NULL);   /* ifaddr must not have been allocated. */
2161                }
2162
2163                ia = in6ifa_ifpwithaddr(ifp, &ifra.ifra_addr.sin6_addr);
2164
2165                return (ia);              /* this is always non-NULL */
2166        }
```

2155–2165 The new address is added into the interface address list through the
`in6_update_ifa()` function (Section 2.14.2). `in6_update_ifa()` will also initiate
the DAD process on the newly generated address. `in6ifa_ifpwithaddr()` is called
to retrieve the newly added address and is returned to the caller.

5.20.2 `in6_tmpifadd()` Function

Function `in6_tmpifadd()` is called from `prelist_update()` (Section 5.19.3) when a new
public address is created and from `regen_tmpaddr()` (Section 5.20.3) when an existing temporary address becomes invalidated or deprecated.

Listing 5-242

```
2168    int
2169    in6_tmpifadd(ia0, forcegen)
2170            const struct in6_ifaddr *ia0; /* corresponding public address */
2171            int forcegen;
2172    {
2173            struct ifnet *ifp = ia0->ia_ifa.ifa_ifp;
2174            struct in6_ifaddr *newia, *ia;
2175            struct in6_aliasreq ifra;
2176            int i, error;
2177            int trylimit = 3;        /* XXX: adhoc value */
2178            u_int32_t randid[2];
2179            u_int32_t vltime0, pltime0;
....
2184            bzero(&ifra, sizeof(ifra));
2185            strncpy(ifra.ifra_name, if_name(ifp), sizeof(ifra.ifra_name));
2186            ifra.ifra_addr = ia0->ia_addr;
2187            /* copy prefix mask */
2188            ifra.ifra_prefixmask = ia0->ia_prefixmask;
2189            /* clear the old IFID */
2190            for (i = 0; i < 4; i++) {
2191                    ifra.ifra_addr.sin6_addr.s6_addr32[i] &=
2192                        ifra.ifra_prefixmask.sin6_addr.s6_addr32[i];
2193            }
```

2169 On input, parameter `ia0` holds the public (nontemporary) address. Parameter `forcegen`
specifies whether to generate the temporary interface identifier. `forcegen` is 1 when this
function is called from `prelist_update()`; it is 0 when this function is called from
`regen_tmpaddr()`.

2184–2193 The temporary address and the public address have the same prefix. The prefix is
extracted from the public address and is copied for the new temporary address.

Listing 5-243

_____nd6_rtr.c
```
2195        again:
2196                if (in6_get_tmpifid(ifp, (u_int8_t *)randid,
2197                        (const u_int8_t *)&ia0->ia_addr.sin6_addr.s6_addr[8], forcegen)) {
2198                        nd6log((LOG_NOTICE, "in6_tmpifadd: failed to find a good "
2199                                "random IFID\n"));
2200                        return (EINVAL);
2201                }
2202                ifra.ifra_addr.sin6_addr.s6_addr32[2] |=
2203                        (randid[0] & ~(ifra.ifra_prefixmask.sin6_addr.s6_addr32[2]));
2204                ifra.ifra_addr.sin6_addr.s6_addr32[3] |=
2205                        (randid[1] & ~(ifra.ifra_prefixmask.sin6_addr.s6_addr32[3]));
```
_____nd6_rtr.c

2196–2205 Function `in6_get_tmpifid()` (not described in this book) returns a randomized temporary interface identifier. The system periodically generates new randomized identifiers as described in the protocol specification, and `in6_get_tmpifid()`
usually just returns a new pregenerated identifier. If `forcegen` is non-0, however,
`in6_get_tmpifid()` generates a new identifier by itself and returns the new one. This
identifier is then combined with the prefix to form a new temporary address.

Listing 5-244

_____nd6_rtr.c
```
2207                /*
2208                 * in6_get_tmpifid() quite likely provided a unique interface ID.
2209                 * However, we may still have a chance to see collision, because
2210                 * there may be a time lag between generation of the ID and generation
2211                 * of the address.  So, we'll do one more sanity check.
2212                 */
2213                for (ia = in6_ifaddr; ia; ia = ia->ia_next) {
2214                        if (SA6_ARE_ADDR_EQUAL(&ia->ia_addr, &ifra.ifra_addr)) {
2215                                if (trylimit-- == 0) {
2216                                        /*
2217                                         * Give up.  Something strange should have
2218                                         * happened.
2219                                         */
2220                                        nd6log((LOG_NOTICE, "in6_tmpifadd: failed to "
2221                                            "find a unique random IFID\n"));
2222                                        return (EEXIST);
2223                                }
2224                                forcegen = 1;
2225                                goto again;
2226                        }
2227                }
```
_____nd6_rtr.c

2213–2227 The `for` loop is executed to verify that the generated temporary address is a unique
interface address within the node. In fact, the pregenerated randomized identifier was
verified to be unique within the node at creation time as specified in the protocol specification, and it is likely to be unique at this point in time, too. Yet there can be an
exception, for example, if a user manually configures an address with a conflicting interface identifier. This check is to catch such minor cases. If it is a duplicate, the generation

process is repeated by calling `in6_get_tmpifid()` again, with `forcegen` reset to 1, specifying that a new interface identifier must be generated. Up to three attempts are made at regenerating a unique address before giving up. The maximum number of attempts, 3, is an arbitrary implementation choice as commented at line 2177 above, although it is identical to the similar upper limit in the periodic generation procedure as defined in [PRIVACY-ADDRS2].

Listing 5-245

```
──────────────────────────────────────────────────nd6_rtr.c
2229            /*
2230             * The Valid Lifetime is the lower of the Valid Lifetime of the
2231             * public address or TEMP_VALID_LIFETIME.
2232             * The Preferred Lifetime is the lower of the Preferred Lifetime
2233             * of the public address or TEMP_PREFERRED_LIFETIME -
2234             * DESYNC_FACTOR.
2235             */
2236            if (ia0->ia6_lifetime.ia6t_vltime != ND6_INFINITE_LIFETIME) {
2237                    vltime0 = IFA6_IS_INVALID(ia0) ? 0 :
2238                        (ia0->ia6_lifetime.ia6t_vltime -
2239                        (time_second - ia0->ia6_updatetime));
2240                    if (vltime0 > ip6_temp_valid_lifetime)
2241                            vltime0 = ip6_temp_valid_lifetime;
2242            } else
2243                    vltime0 = ip6_temp_valid_lifetime;
2244            if (ia0->ia6_lifetime.ia6t_pltime != ND6_INFINITE_LIFETIME) {
2245                    pltime0 = IFA6_IS_DEPRECATED(ia0) ? 0 :
2246                        (ia0->ia6_lifetime.ia6t_pltime -
2247                        (time_second - ia0->ia6_updatetime));
2248                    if (pltime0 > ip6_temp_preferred_lifetime - ip6_desync_factor){
2249                            pltime0 = ip6_temp_preferred_lifetime -
2250                                ip6_desync_factor;
2251                    }
2252            } else
2253                    pltime0 = ip6_temp_preferred_lifetime - ip6_desync_factor;
2254            ifra.ifra_lifetime.ia6t_vltime = vltime0;
2255            ifra.ifra_lifetime.ia6t_pltime = pltime0;
──────────────────────────────────────────────────nd6_rtr.c
```

2236–2255 The valid and preferred lifetimes of the temporary address are specified as described in Section 5.10.4. Note that the valid and preferred lifetimes for the corresponding public address are the remaining lifetimes, rather than the advertised values via the latest Router Advertisement message. While the specification does not clearly specify the former, this interpretation should be the most reasonable. If the corresponding lifetime never expires (`ND6_INFINITE_LIFETIME`), it is always regarded as larger than `TEMP_VALID_LIFETIME` (`TEMP_PREFERRED_LIFETIME` – `DESYNC_FACTOR`). Also, if the public address is already invalidated or deprecated, which should be rare in this function, the corresponding lifetimes of the temporary address are set to 0.

Listing 5-246

```
──────────────────────────────────────────────────nd6_rtr.c
2257            /*
2258             * A temporary address is created only if this calculated Preferred
2259             * Lifetime is greater than REGEN_ADVANCE time units.
2260             */
2261            if (ifra.ifra_lifetime.ia6t_pltime <= ip6_temp_regen_advance)
2262                    return (0);
──────────────────────────────────────────────────nd6_rtr.c
```

2261–2262 [RFC3041] states that a temporary address is created only if the calculated preferred lifetime is larger than the constant REGEN_ADVANCE, which is 5 seconds.

Listing 5-247

```
2264            /* XXX: scope zone ID? */
2265
2266            ifra.ifra_flags |= (IN6_IFF_AUTOCONF|IN6_IFF_TEMPORARY);
```

2266 The newly generated temporary address must have both the IN6_IFF_AUTOCONF and IN6_IFF_TEMPORARY flag bits set. The IN6_IFF_AUTOCONF flag indicates the address is an automatically generated address; the IN6_IFF_TEMPORARY flag indicates the address is a temporary address.

Listing 5-248

```
2268            /* allocate ifaddr structure, link into chain, etc. */
2269            if ((error = in6_update_ifa(ifp, &ifra, NULL)) != 0)
2270                    return (error);
2271
2272            newia = in6ifa_ifpwithaddr(ifp, &ifra.ifra_addr.sin6_addr);
2273            if (newia == NULL) {    /* XXX: can it happen? */
2274                    nd6log((LOG_ERR,
2275                        "in6_tmpifadd: ifa update succeeded, but we got "
2276                        "no ifaddr\n"));
2277                    return (EINVAL); /* XXX */
2278            }
2279            newia->ia6_ndpr = ia0->ia6_ndpr;
2280            newia->ia6_ndpr->ndpr_refcnt++;
2281
2282            /*
2283             * A newly added address might affect the status of other addresses.
2284             * XXX: when the temporary address is generated with a new public
2285             * address, the onlink check is redundant.  However, it would be safe
2286             * to do the check explicitly everywhere a new address is generated,
2287             * and, in fact, we surely need the check when we create a new
2288             * temporary address due to deprecation of an old temporary address.
2289             */
2290            pfxlist_onlink_check();
2291
2292            return (0);
2293    }
```

2269–2279 The new temporary address is added into the interface address list by in6_update_ifa(). Function in6ifa_ifpwithaddr() retrieves the installed address and the ia6_ndpr field is set to reference the given address prefix. A reference is held on the prefix for the new temporary address.

2290 pfxlist_onlink_check() is called to verify and if necessary update the on-link status of the known prefixes and addresses. Note that this call is redundant when this function is called from prelist_update() since the caller also performs the same check (see Listing 5-218). As commented in the code, however, regen_tmpaddr() does not call pfxlist_onlink_check(), and the check must be performed here. While the call to `pfxlist_onlink_check()` could be done selectively depending on the context, this implementation prefers simplicity. At least the multiple invocation does no harm except the additional overhead.

5.20.3   `regen_tmpaddr()` Function

Function `regen_tmpaddr()` attempts to generate a new temporary address. This function is called from `nd6_timer()` when an existing temporary address becomes invalidated or deprecated.

Listing 5-249

```
                                                              ───nd6.c
717     static int
718     regen_tmpaddr(ia6)
719           struct in6_ifaddr *ia6; /* deprecated/invalidated temporary address */
720     {
721           struct ifaddr *ifa;
722           struct ifnet *ifp;
723           struct in6_ifaddr *public_ifa6 = NULL;
                                                              ───nd6.c
```

717–723 The function parameter `ia6` points to the existing temporary address from which the interface information and the prefix information will be retrieved below.

Listing 5-250

```
                                                              ───nd6.c
725           ifp = ia6->ia_ifa.ifa_ifp;
....
729           for (ifa = ifp->if_addrlist.tqh_first; ifa;
730                ifa = ifa->ifa_list.tqe_next)
....
732           {
733                 struct in6_ifaddr *it6;
734
735                 if (ifa->ifa_addr->sa_family != AF_INET6)
736                       continue;
737
738                 it6 = (struct in6_ifaddr *)ifa;
739
740                 /* ignore no autoconf addresses. */
741                 if ((it6->ia6_flags & IN6_IFF_AUTOCONF) == 0)
742                       continue;
743
744                 /* ignore autoconf addresses with different prefixes. */
745                 if (it6->ia6_ndpr == NULL || it6->ia6_ndpr != ia6->ia6_ndpr)
746                       continue;
                                                              ───nd6.c
```

725–747 Each address in the interface address list is examined for finding an automatically generated IPv6 address that has the same prefix as the existing temporary address.

Listing 5-251

```
                                                              ───nd6.c
748                 /*
749                  * Now we are looking at an autoconf address with the same
750                  * prefix as ours.  If the address is temporary and is still
```

```
751                      * preferred, do not create another one.  It would be rare, but
752                      * could happen, for example, when we resume a laptop PC after
753                      * a long period.
754                      */
755                     if ((it6->ia6_flags & IN6_IFF_TEMPORARY) != 0 &&
756                         !IFA6_IS_DEPRECATED(it6)) {
757                             public_ifa6 = NULL;
758                             break;
759                     }
```
——nd6.c

748–759 This function will not generate another temporary address if one already exists and is still preferred. This can happen when this function is called due to invalidation of an existing temporary address; another temporary address created later than the invalidated one may still be preferred.

Listing 5-252
——nd6.c
```
761                     /*
762                      * This is a public autoconf address that has the same prefix
763                      * as ours.  If it is preferred, keep it.  We can't break the
764                      * loop here, because there may be a still-preferred temporary
765                      * address with the prefix.
766                      */
767                     if (!IFA6_IS_DEPRECATED(it6))
768                         public_ifa6 = it6;
769             }
```
——nd6.c

761–768 An active public address with the same address prefix is found and this address may be used to generate the new temporary address. As commented in the code, the loop cannot terminate here because a preferred temporary address may exist in the remaining addresses of the list.

Listing 5-253
——nd6.c
```
771             if (public_ifa6 != NULL) {
772                     int e;
773
774                     if ((e = in6_tmpifadd(public_ifa6, 0)) != 0) {
775                             log(LOG_NOTICE, "regen_tmpaddr: failed to create a new"
776                                 " tmp addr,errno=%d\n", e);
777                             return (-1);
778                     }
779                     return (0);
780             }
781
782             return (-1);
783     }
```
——nd6.c

771–782 At this point it has been verified that another preferred temporary address does not exist, and an active public address is available. The `in6_tmpifadd()` function (Section 5.20.2) is then called to generate a new temporary address. Note that the second argument to `in6_tmpifadd()` is 0, which means a new randomized interface identifier will not be generated; a pregenerated identifier will simply be used.

5.21   Duplicate Address Detection Functions

5.21.1 `nd6_dad_find()` Function

The `nd6_dad_find()` function, shown below, searches into the DAD queue (see Section 5.13.8), and returns the entry if the given address is found.

Listing 5-254

── nd6_nbr.c
```
1243    static struct dadq *
1244    nd6_dad_find(ifa)
1245            struct ifaddr *ifa;
1246    {
1247            struct dadq *dp;
1248
1249            for (dp = dadq.tqh_first; dp; dp = dp->dad_list.tqe_next) {
1250                    if (dp->dad_ifa == ifa)
1251                            return dp;
1252            }
1253            return NULL;
1254    }
```
── nd6_nbr.c

5.21.2 `nd6_dad_starttimer()` Function

The `nd6_dad_starttimer()` function starts the DAD timer for a given DAD queue entry. The timer value is specified by the `ticks` parameter. The `nd6_dad_timer()` function will be called when the timer expires; it is described in detail in Section 5.21.6.

Listing 5-255

── nd6_nbr.c
```
1256    static void
1257    nd6_dad_starttimer(dp, ticks)
1258            struct dadq *dp;
1259            int ticks;
1260    {
1261
    ....
1263            callout_reset(&dp->dad_timer_ch, ticks,
1264                    (void (*) __P((void *)))nd6_dad_timer, (void *)dp->dad_ifa);
    ....
1273    }
```
── nd6_nbr.c

5.21.3 `nd6_dad_stoptimer()` Function

The `nd6_dad_stoptimer()` function, shown below, stops the DAD timer on a given DAD queue entry.

Listing 5-256

```
1275    static void
1276    nd6_dad_stoptimer(dp)
1277            struct dadq *dp;
1278    {
1279
    ....
1281            callout_stop(&dp->dad_timer_ch);
    ....
1287    }
```

5.21.4 `nd6_dad_start()` Function

The `nd6_dad_start()` function initiates the DAD process for a given address. This function is called from `in6_update_ifa()` (Section 2.14.2) when a new address is configured or from `in6_if_up()` (Section 2.13.1) when an interface comes up with tentative addresses.

Listing 5-257

```
1289    /*
1290     * Start Duplicated Address Detection (DAD) for specified interface address.
1291     */
1292    void
1293    nd6_dad_start(ifa, tick)
1294            struct ifaddr *ifa;
1295            int *tick;       /* minimum delay ticks for IFF_UP event */
1296    {
1297            struct in6_ifaddr *ia = (struct in6_ifaddr *)ifa;
1298            struct dadq *dp;
1299
1300            if (!dad_init) {
1301                    TAILQ_INIT(&dadq);
1302                    dad_init++;
1303            }
```

1300–1303 On input, parameter `ifa` holds the address for which the DAD algorithm will be executed, and `tick` specifies the time delay before transmitting the first DAD packet.

The DAD queue, which is used to track the addresses on which DAD is performed, is initialized first if the initialization has not already been done. `dad_init` remembers that the initialization has been completed to avoid multiple initialization attempts.

Listing 5-258

```
1305            /*
1306             * If we don't need DAD, don't do it.
1307             * There are several cases:
1308             * - DAD is disabled (ip6_dad_count == 0)
1309             * - the interface address is anycast
1310             */
1311            if (!(ia->ia6_flags & IN6_IFF_TENTATIVE)) {
1312                    log(LOG_DEBUG,
1313                            "nd6_dad_start: called with non-tentative address "
1314                            "%s(%s)\n",
```

```
1315                             ip6_sprintf(&ia->ia_addr.sin6_addr),
1316                             ifa->ifa_ifp ? if_name(ifa->ifa_ifp) : "???");
1317                     return;
1318             }
1319             if (ia->ia6_flags & IN6_IFF_ANYCAST) {
1320                     ia->ia6_flags &= ~IN6_IFF_TENTATIVE;
1321                     return;
1322             }
1323             if (!ip6_dad_count) {
1324                     ia->ia6_flags &= ~IN6_IFF_TENTATIVE;
....
1328                     return;
1329             }
1330             if (!ifa->ifa_ifp)
1331                     panic("nd6_dad_start: ifa->ifa_ifp == NULL");
1332             if (!(ifa->ifa_ifp->if_flags & IFF_UP)) {
....
1336                     return;
1337             }
```
——— nd6_nbr.c

1311–1318 The absence of the `IN6_IFF_TENTATIVE` flag bit in an address implies DAD does not have to be performed on this address. This test is meaningless in this implementation, though, because the callers of this function always set this flag.

1319–1322 As required by [RFC2462], DAD must not be performed for an anycast address.

1323–1329 If the global variable `ip6_dad_count`, which is configurable through the **sysctl** variable `net.inet6.ip6.dad_count`, is set to 0, it indicates that DAD has been administratively disabled. In this case the address is considered to be valid to the local node and the function returns without further processing.

1330–1337 A valid and operational interface must be present in order to transmit the DAD packets.

Listing 5-259
——— nd6_nbr.c
```
1338             if (nd6_dad_find(ifa) != NULL) {
1339                     /* DAD already in progress */
....
1343                     return;
1344             }
```
——— nd6_nbr.c

1338–1344 This function returns without further processing if DAD is already in progress for the given address.

Listing 5-260
——— nd6_nbr.c
```
1346             dp = malloc(sizeof(*dp), M_IP6NDP, M_NOWAIT);
1347             if (dp == NULL) {
1348                     log(LOG_ERR, "nd6_dad_start: memory allocation failed for "
1349                             "%s(%s)\n",
1350                             ip6_sprintf(&ia->ia_addr.sin6_addr),
1351                             ifa->ifa_ifp ? if_name(ifa->ifa_ifp) : "???");
....
1355                     return;
1356             }
```

```
1357              bzero(dp, sizeof(*dp));
....
1359              callout_init(&dp->dad_timer_ch, 0);
....
1365              TAILQ_INSERT_TAIL(&dadq, (struct dadq *)dp, dad_list);
1366
1367              nd6log((LOG_DEBUG, "%s: starting DAD for %s\n", if_name(ifa->ifa_ifp),
1368                  ip6_sprintf(&ia->ia_addr.sin6_addr)));
```
── nd6_nbr.c

1346–1367 A `dadq{}` structure is allocated to store the given address in the DAD queue.
A DAD timer is also initialized for this entry. The new entry is inserted into the global
queue, `dadq`.

Listing 5-261
── nd6_nbr.c
```
1370      /*
1371       * Send NS packet for DAD, ip6_dad_count times.
1372       * Note that we must delay the first transmission, if this is the
1373       * first packet to be sent from the interface after interface
1374       * (re)initialization.
1375       */
1376      dp->dad_ifa = ifa;
1377      IFAREF(ifa);    /* just for safety */
1378      dp->dad_count = ip6_dad_count;
1379      dp->dad_ns_icount = dp->dad_na_icount = 0;
1380      dp->dad_ns_ocount = dp->dad_ns_tcount = 0;
1381      if (tick == NULL) {
1382              nd6_dad_ns_output(dp, ifa);
1383              nd6_dad_starttimer(dp,
1384                  ND6_RETRANS_SEC(ND_IFINFO(ifa->ifa_ifp)->retrans) * hz);
1385      } else {
1386              int ntick;
1387
....
1391              if (*tick == 0)
1392                      ntick = arc4random() % (MAX_RTR_SOLICITATION_DELAY * hz);
1393              else
1394                      ntick = *tick + arc4random() % (hz / 2);
....
1398              *tick = ntick;
1399              nd6_dad_starttimer(dp, ntick);
1400      }
1401  }
```
── nd6_nbr.c

1376–1380 A reference to the interface address structure is acquired so that this address will not
be freed while the DAD procedure waits on a timer. The global variable `ip6_dad_count`
specifies the number of Neighbor Solicitation packets to send as part of DAD processing
for each address. By default only one Neighbor Solicitation packet is sent. The DAD related
counters are initialized here.

1381–1400 The DAD packet is sent immediately and the DAD timer is started with the retransmission interval if `tick` is unspecified. Otherwise, the timer is set to delay starting the
DAD processing by `tick` plus a random offset. Any DAD transmission is deferred for this
interval.

In the case where a delay is imposed, if the value stored in the pointer
`tick` is 0 it means this is the first invocation of this function in a series of DAD
attempts (see Section 2.13.1). The delay is set to some random value between 0 and

MAX_RTR_SOLICITATION_DELAY seconds. This code intends to implement a requirement described in [RFC2462] that a random delay must be imposed if this Neighbor Solicitation packet is the first packet sent from this system. In practice, however, implementing this requirement is quite difficult because it is hard to tell whether a particular packet is the first packet. This code makes a compromise between specification compliance and practical challenges in the actual implementation.

When tick is non-NULL, the random delay is stored in the pointer and implicitly returned to the caller. The caller is expected to reuse the value for the next call to this function as shown in Section 2.13.1, thereby ensuring that the series of Neighbor Solicitation packets are sent in the order of calls to this function. This is not a protocol requirement, but an implementation choice.

5.21.5 nd6_dad_stop() Function

The nd6_dad_stop() function, shown below, stops the DAD timer and terminates the DAD process for a given address. The address is then removed from the DAD queue.

Listing 5-262

——nd6_nbr.c
```
1403    /*
1404     * terminate DAD unconditionally.  used for address removals.
1405     */
1406    void
1407    nd6_dad_stop(ifa)
1408            struct ifaddr *ifa;
1409    {
1410            struct dadq *dp;
1411
1412            if (!dad_init)
1413                    return;
1414            dp = nd6_dad_find(ifa);
1415            if (!dp) {
1416                    /* DAD wasn't started yet */
1417                    return;
1418            }
1419
1420            nd6_dad_stoptimer(dp);
1421
1422            TAILQ_REMOVE(&dadq, (struct dadq *)dp, dad_list);
1423            free(dp, M_IP6NDP);
1424            dp = NULL;
1425            IFAFREE(ifa);
1426    }
```
——nd6_nbr.c

5.21.6 nd6_dad_timer() Function

The nd6_dad_timer() function processes an expired timer that was set for a given address.

Listing 5-263

——nd6_nbr.c
```
1428    static void
1429    nd6_dad_timer(ifa)
1430            struct ifaddr *ifa;
1431    {
1432            int s;
```

```
1433                struct in6_ifaddr *ia = (struct in6_ifaddr *)ifa;
1434                struct dadq *dp;
1435
....
1439                s = splnet();              /* XXX */
....
1441
1442                /* Sanity check */
1443                if (ia == NULL) {
1444                        log(LOG_ERR, "nd6_dad_timer: called with null parameter\n");
1445                        goto done;
1446                }
1447                dp = nd6_dad_find(ifa);
1448                if (dp == NULL) {
1449                        log(LOG_ERR, "nd6_dad_timer: DAD structure not found\n");
1450                        goto done;
1451                }
```
——————————————————————————————————————— nd6_nbr.c

1443–1451 The DAD timer has expired for an address that is being validated. First
nd6_dad_find() is called to find the given address ifa in the DAD queue. The function
terminates here if the address is not found.

Listing 5-264
——————————————————————————————————————— nd6_nbr.c
```
1452                if (ia->ia6_flags & IN6_IFF_DUPLICATED) {
1453                        log(LOG_ERR, "nd6_dad_timer: called with duplicated address"
1454                                "%s(%s)\n",
1455                                ip6_sprintf(&ia->ia_addr.sin6_addr),
1456                                ifa->ifa_ifp ? if_name(ifa->ifa_ifp) : "???");
1457                        goto done;
1458                }
1459                if ((ia->ia6_flags & IN6_IFF_TENTATIVE) == 0) {
1460                        log(LOG_ERR, "nd6_dad_timer: called with non-tentative address"
1461                                "%s(%s)\n",
1462                                ip6_sprintf(&ia->ia_addr.sin6_addr),
1463                                ifa->ifa_ifp ? if_name(ifa->ifa_ifp) : "???");
1464                        goto done;
1465                }
```
——————————————————————————————————————— nd6_nbr.c

1452–1458 If the address is detected to be a duplicate by the DAD procedure, it is marked with
the IN6_IFF_DUPLICATED flag (see Section 5.21.7). In this case the result is logged and
the processing is completed.

1459–1465 An address should have been marked with the IN6_IFF_TENTATIVE flag when
the DAD operations are being performed on the address. If this flag is missing it likely
means there exists a kernel bug or an unexpected operation. The processing terminates
here with a log message.

Listing 5-265
——————————————————————————————————————— nd6_nbr.c
```
1467                /* timeouted with IFF_{RUNNING,UP} check */
1468                if (dp->dad_ns_tcount > dad_maxtry) {
1469                        nd6log((LOG_INFO, "%s: could not run DAD, driver problem?\n",
1470                            if_name(ifa->ifa_ifp)));
1471
1472                        TAILQ_REMOVE(&dadq, (struct dadq *)dp, dad_list);
1473                        free(dp, M_IP6NDP);
```

```
1474                    dp = NULL;
....
1478                    IFAFREE(ifa);
1479                    goto done;
1480            }
```
── nd6_nbr.c

1468–1480 Since DAD often takes place during the system boot procedure, the network interface may not be fully functional when the process starts. The KAME implementation introduces a workaround for this issue by repeatedly trying to send the Neighbor Solicitation message for DAD while watching the interface status. As shown in Section 5.21.8, the Neighbor Solicitation message is not actually sent until the interface has both the `IFF_UP` and `IFF_RUNNING` flags set.

While the above condition is not met, only `dad_ns_tcount` is incremented. If the unsuccessful attempts repeat `dad_maxtry` times, which is set to 15, it probably means interface failure and the DAD process terminates. Note that the `IN6_IFF_TENTATIVE` flag is kept in the address, which disallows the use of this address.

Listing 5-266

── nd6_nbr.c

```
1482            /* Need more checks? */
1483            if (dp->dad_ns_ocount < dp->dad_count) {
1484                    /*
1485                     * We have more NS to go.  Send NS packet for DAD.
1486                     */
1487                    nd6_dad_ns_output(dp, ifa);
1488                    nd6_dad_starttimer(dp,
1489                        ND6_RETRANS_SEC(ND_IFINFO(ifa->ifa_ifp)->retrans) * hz);
```
── nd6_nbr.c

1482–1489 The DAD process will send additional packets if the configured value requires more transmissions. The DAD timer is reset when more transmissions take place. Note that this is also the case when the DAD procedure was delayed in the `nd6_dad_start()` function (see Listing 5-261).

Listing 5-267

── nd6_nbr.c

```
1490            } else {
1491                    /*
1492                     * We have transmitted sufficient number of DAD packets.
1493                     * See what we've got.
1494                     */
1495                    int duplicate;
1496
1497                    duplicate = 0;
1498
1499                    if (dp->dad_na_icount) {
1500                            /*
1501                             * the check is in nd6_dad_na_input(),
1502                             * but just in case
1503                             */
1504                            duplicate++;
1505                    }
1506
1507                    if (dp->dad_ns_icount) {
```

```
1508    #if 0 /* heuristics */
1509                            /*
1510                             * if
1511                             * - we have sent many(?) DAD NS, and
1512                             * - the number of NS we sent equals to the
1513                             *   number of NS we've got, and
1514                             * - we've got no NA
1515                             * we may have a faulty network card/driver which
1516                             * loops back multicasts to myself.
1517                             */
1518                            if (3 < dp->dad_count
1519                             && dp->dad_ns_icount == dp->dad_count
1520                             && dp->dad_na_icount == 0) {
1521                                    log(LOG_INFO, "DAD questionable for %s(%s): "
1522                                        "network card loops back multicast?\n",
1523                                        ip6_sprintf(&ia->ia_addr.sin6_addr),
1524                                        if_name(ifa->ifa_ifp));
1525                                    /* XXX consider it a duplicate or not? */
1526                                    /* duplicate++; */
1527                            } else {
1528                                    /* We've seen NS, means DAD has failed. */
1529                                    duplicate++;
1530                            }
1531    #else
1532                            /* We've seen NS, means DAD has failed. */
1533                            duplicate++;
1534    #endif
1535                    }
1536
1537                    if (duplicate) {
1538                            /* (*dp) will be freed in nd6_dad_duplicated() */
1539                            dp = NULL;
1540                            nd6_dad_duplicated(ifa);
```
——nd6_nbr.c

1490–1540 A non-0 value for either dad_na_icount or dad_ns_icount indicates another
node has claimed the address. The nd6_dad_duplicated() function is then called to
mark the address as a duplicate.

The disabled code from line 1508 to line 1531 intends to handle odd network interface
cards that unconditionally loop multicast packets back to the local node. As explained in
Listing 5-66, such a loopback packet will be treated as a packet sent from other nodes,
mistakenly making the address a duplicate under the DAD operation. In order to deal
with this case, the disabled code loosens the protocol requirement as follows: If the local
node has sent more than three Neighbor Solicitation packets, the number of incoming
Neighbor Solicitation packets are the same as the number of outgoing packets, and no
Neighbor Advertisement packets have been received, it determines that this is likely due
to multicast loopback and allows the address to be used. Since doing so raises the risk of
missing a duplicate, however, this block of code is explicitly disabled.

Listing 5-268
——nd6_nbr.c
```
1541                    } else {
1542                            /*
1543                             * We are done with DAD.  No NA came, no NS came.
1544                             * duplicated address found.
1545                             */
1546                            ia->ia6_flags &= ~IN6_IFF_TENTATIVE;
1547
1548                            nd6log((LOG_DEBUG,
1549                                "%s: DAD complete for %s - no duplicates found\n",
```

```
1550                              if_name(ifa->ifa_ifp),
1551                              ip6_sprintf(&ia->ia_addr.sin6_addr)));
1552
1553                         TAILQ_REMOVE(&dadq, (struct dadq *)dp, dad_list);
1554                         free(dp, M_IP6NDP);
1555                         dp = NULL;
....
1559                         IFAFREE(ifa);
1560                    }
1561               }
1562
1563    done:
1564          splx(s);
1565    }
```
——— nd6_nbr.c

1541–1561 The local node has not received any Neighbor Advertisement or Neighbor Solicitation packet for the given address and DAD has completed all the necessary transmissions. The local node now claims the address is unique and can be used for normal operation. The `IN6_IFF_TENTATIVE` flag is cleared, and the reference to the interface address structure temporarily gained is released.

5.21.7 `nd6_dad_duplicated()` Function

The `nd6_dad_duplicated()` function processes a tentative local address that is known to be a duplicated address.

Listing 5-269
——— nd6_nbr.c

```
1567    void
1568    nd6_dad_duplicated(ifa)
1569          struct ifaddr *ifa;
1570    {
1571          struct in6_ifaddr *ia = (struct in6_ifaddr *)ifa;
1572          struct dadq *dp;
1573
1574          dp = nd6_dad_find(ifa);
1575          if (dp == NULL) {
1576                log(LOG_ERR, "nd6_dad_duplicated: DAD structure not found\n");
1577                return;
1578          }
```
——— nd6_nbr.c

1574 `nd6_dad_find()` searches for the given address in the DAD queue.

Listing 5-270
——— nd6_nbr.c

```
1580          log(LOG_ERR, "%s: DAD detected duplicate IPv6 address %s: "
1581               "NS in/out=%d/%d, NA in=%d\n",
1582               if_name(ifa->ifa_ifp), ip6_sprintf(&ia->ia_addr.sin6_addr),
1583               dp->dad_ns_icount, dp->dad_ns_ocount, dp->dad_na_icount);
1584
1585          ia->ia6_flags &= ~IN6_IFF_TENTATIVE;
1586          ia->ia6_flags |= IN6_IFF_DUPLICATED;
```
——— nd6_nbr.c

1580–1586 Since this address is determined to be a duplicate, the interface address structure is marked with the `IN6_IFF_DUPLICATED` flag. In addition, the `IN6_IFF_TENTATIVE` flag is cleared now that the DAD procedure has completed.

Listing 5-271

```
                                                              ——nd6_nbr.c
1588              /* We are done with DAD, with duplicated address found. (failure) */
1589              nd6_dad_stoptimer(dp);
1590
1591              log(LOG_ERR, "%s: DAD complete for %s - duplicate found\n",
1592                  if_name(ifa->ifa_ifp), ip6_sprintf(&ia->ia_addr.sin6_addr));
1593              log(LOG_ERR, "%s: manual intervention required\n",
1594                  if_name(ifa->ifa_ifp));
1595
1596              TAILQ_REMOVE(&dadq, (struct dadq *)dp, dad_list);
1597              free(dp, M_IP6NDP);
1598              dp = NULL;
....
1602              IFAFREE(ifa);
1603      }
                                                              ——nd6_nbr.c
```

1588–1602 The DAD timer is stopped for this address. The `dadq{}` structure associated with this address is removed and freed. The reference to the interface address structure is released.

Note that the address still exists in the system with the `IN6_IFF_DUPLICATED` flag (see also the example shown in Section 2.16). Although the kernel code could remove this address, this implementation does not do so because it might simply result in repeating the same procedure of generating the same address and then invalidating it as a duplicate. By retaining the address in an unusable state this implementation explicitly indicates the need for replacement to the system administrator.

5.21.8 `nd6_dad_ns_output()` Function

Listing 5-272

```
                                                              ——nd6_nbr.c
1605      static void
1606      nd6_dad_ns_output(dp, ifa)
1607              struct dadq *dp;
1608              struct ifaddr *ifa;
1609      {
1610              struct in6_ifaddr *ia = (struct in6_ifaddr *)ifa;
1611              struct ifnet *ifp = ifa->ifa_ifp;
1612
1613              dp->dad_ns_tcount++;
1614              if ((ifp->if_flags & IFF_UP) == 0) {
....
1618                      return;
1619              }
1620              if ((ifp->if_flags & IFF_RUNNING) == 0) {
....
1624                      return;
1625              }
1626
1627              dp->dad_ns_ocount++;
1628              nd6_ns_output(ifp, NULL, &ia->ia_addr, NULL, 1);
1629      }
                                                              ——nd6_nbr.c
```

1605–1629 The `nd6_dad_ns_output()` function calls `nd6_ns_output()` function to transmit a Neighbor Solicitation message according to the DAD algorithm. The `dad_ns_tcount` field tracks the number of attempts that have been made to send the Neighbor Solicitation packet. The `dad_ns_ocount` field tracks the number of Neighbor Solicitation packets that have been sent. Note that the Neighbor Solicitation message is not sent and only `dad_ns_tcount` is incremented unless both the `IFF_UP` and `IFF_RUNNING` flags are set (see also Listing 5-265).

5.21.9 `nd6_dad_ns_input()` Function

The `nd6_dad_ns_input()` function processes an incoming Neighbor Solicitation message according to the DAD algorithm.

Listing 5-273

_____ nd6_nbr.c

```
1631    static void
1632    nd6_dad_ns_input(ifa)
1633            struct ifaddr *ifa;
1634    {
1635            struct in6_ifaddr *ia;
1636            struct ifnet *ifp;
1637            const struct in6_addr *taddr6;
1638            struct dadq *dp;
1639            int duplicate;
1640
1641            if (!ifa)
1642                    panic("ifa == NULL in nd6_dad_ns_input");
1643
1644            ia = (struct in6_ifaddr *)ifa;
1645            ifp = ifa->ifa_ifp;
1646            taddr6 = &ia->ia_addr.sin6_addr;
1647            duplicate = 0;
1648            dp = nd6_dad_find(ifa);
```

_____ nd6_nbr.c

1644–1648 Parameter `ifa` points to the interface address structure on which DAD is performed. `nd6_dad_find()` is called to find the given address `ifa` in the DAD queue.

Listing 5-274

_____ nd6_nbr.c

```
1650            /* Quickhack - completely ignore DAD NS packets */
1651            if (dad_ignore_ns) {
1652                    nd6log((LOG_INFO,
1653                        "nd6_dad_ns_input: ignoring DAD NS packet for "
1654                        "address %s(%s)\n", ip6_sprintf(taddr6),
1655                        if_name(ifa->ifa_ifp)));
1656                    return;
1657            }
1658
1659            /*
1660             * if I'm yet to start DAD, someone else started using this address
1661             * first.  I have a duplicate and you win.
1662             */
1663            if (!dp || dp->dad_ns_ocount == 0)
1664                    duplicate++;
```

_____ nd6_nbr.c

1651–1657 This function returns if the system is configured to ignore DAD Neighbor Solicitation packets. This is another form of workaround for network interface cards that loop multicast packets back to the local node (see also Listing 5-267). Being a workaround, this variable is set to 0 by default and cannot be modified via an API such as **sysctl**; the kernel code must be modified by hand and rebuilt to enable this feature.

1663–1664 If the address is not yet in the DAD queue or the number of Neighbor Solicitation packets transmitted for DAD is 0, the received Neighbor Solicitation is clearly from a different node regardless of the loopback behavior of the receiving interface, and the tentative address is determined to be a duplicate.

Listing 5-275

```
                                                              nd6_nbr.c
1666            /* XXX more checks for loopback situation - see nd6_dad_timer too */
1667
1668        if (duplicate) {
1669                dp = NULL;        /* will be freed in nd6_dad_duplicated() */
1670                nd6_dad_duplicated(ifa);
                                                              nd6_nbr.c
```

1668–1670 If the address is considered a duplicate, the nd6_dad_duplicated() function is called to process it accordingly.

Listing 5-276

```
                                                              nd6_nbr.c
1671        } else {
1672                /*
1673                 * not sure if I got a duplicate.
1674                 * increment ns count and see what happens.
1675                 */
1676                if (dp)
1677                        dp->dad_ns_icount++;
1678        }
1679    }
                                                              nd6_nbr.c
```

1676–1677 The received DAD packet count is incremented for this address and the processing is delayed until the DAD timer expires for this entry. The decision is not made immediately because it is not clear whether this packet is from another node, in which case the tentative address is a duplicate, or it is sent from the local node and looped back.

5.21.10   nd6_dad_na_input() Function

As part of Neighbor Advertisement processing, the nd6_dad_na_input() function is called to process a tentative address that is known to be a duplicated address (see Listing 5-101).

Listing 5-277

```
                                                              nd6_nbr.c
1681    static void
1682    nd6_dad_na_input(ifa)
1683            struct ifaddr *ifa;
1684    {
1685            struct dadq *dp;
```

```
1686
1687                 if (!ifa)
1688                         panic("ifa == NULL in nd6_dad_na_input");
1689
1690                 dp = nd6_dad_find(ifa);
1691                 if (dp)
1692                         dp->dad_na_icount++;
1693
1694                 /* remove the address. */
1695                 nd6_dad_duplicated(ifa);
1696         }
```
—— nd6_nbr.c

1681–1696 nd6_dad_find() is called to find the given address, ifa, in the DAD queue.
The dad_na_icount counter is incremented and function nd6_dad_duplicated()
is called to process this duplicate address.

5.22   Miscellaneous Functions

5.22.1   nd6_is_addr_neighbor() Function

Function nd6_is_addr_neighbor() determines whether the given address belongs to an
interface on the link to which the given local interface is attached. This function returns 1 if the
address is regarded as on-link; otherwise, it returns 0.

Listing 5-278

—— nd6.c
```
979      /*
980       * Detect if a given IPv6 address identifies a neighbor on a given link.
981       * XXX: should take care of the destination of a p2p link?
982       */
983      int
984      nd6_is_addr_neighbor(addr, ifp)
985              struct sockaddr_in6 *addr;
986              struct ifnet *ifp;
987      {
988              struct nd_prefix *pr;
989              struct rtentry *rt;
990
991              /*
992               * A link-local address is always a neighbor.
993               * XXX: we should use the sin6_scope_id field rather than the embedded
994               * interface index.
995               * XXX: a link does not necessarily specify a single interface.
996               */
997              if (IN6_IS_ADDR_LINKLOCAL(&addr->sin6_addr) &&
998                  ntohs(*(u_int16_t *)&addr->sin6_addr.s6_addr[2]) == ifp->if_index)
999                      return (1);
```
—— nd6.c

997–999 A link-local address is always regarded as an on-link neighbor. The only necessary
check here is to confirm its link is equal to that of the given interface. This code assumes
the address is in the kernel internal form that embeds the link (zone) ID in the address
for a link-local address as described in Section 2.9.3, and compares the link ID to the
interface index of the given interface. As indicated by the code comment, this works but
is an example of a bad practice for the reasons given in Section 2.9.3. Ideally, this function
should take a sockaddr_in6{} structure and compare its sin6_scope_id field to the
link ID derived from the given interface.

Listing 5-279

———nd6.c
```
1001             /*
1002              * If the address matches one of our on-link prefixes, it should be a
1003              * neighbor.
1004              */
1005             for (pr = nd_prefix.lh_first; pr; pr = pr->ndpr_next) {
1006                     if (pr->ndpr_ifp != ifp)
1007                             continue;
1008
1009                     if (!(pr->ndpr_stateflags & NDPRF_ONLINK))
1010                             continue;
1011
1012                     if (IN6_ARE_MASKED_ADDR_EQUAL(&pr->ndpr_prefix.sin6_addr,
1013                         &addr->sin6_addr, &pr->ndpr_mask))
1014                             return (1);
1015             }
```
———nd6.c

1005–1015 For a non-link-local address, a search is made in the Prefix List to try finding a prefix that covers the address. Prefixes that are not learnt on the given interface or prefixes that are not regarded as on-link are excluded from the comparison. If a match is found, this function returns 1.

Listing 5-280

———nd6.c
```
1017             /*
1018              * If the default router list is empty, all addresses are regarded
1019              * as on-link, and thus, as a neighbor.
1020              * XXX: we restrict the condition to hosts, because routers usually do
1021              * not have the "default router list".
1022              */
1023             if (!ip6_forwarding && TAILQ_FIRST(&nd_defrouter) == NULL &&
1024                 nd6_defifindex == ifp->if_index) {
1025                     return (1);
1026             }
```
———nd6.c

1023–1026 [RFC2461] requires that any destination address must be regarded as on-link for a host whose Default Router List is empty (see Section 5.18.3). This block of code makes a decision based on this assumption: If this node is acting as a host, its Default Router List is empty, and the default interface is configured and equals to the given interface, then the address is regarded as on-link.

As explained in Section 5.18.3, however, this assumption is now considered harmful and is discouraged. This block should eventually be disabled.

Listing 5-281

———nd6.c
```
1028             /*
1029              * Even if the address matches none of our addresses, it might be
1030              * in the neighbor cache.
1031              */
1032             if ((rt = nd6_lookup(addr, 0, ifp)) != NULL)
1033                     return (1);
1034
1035             return (0);
1036     }
```
———nd6.c

1032–1033 The Neighbor Cache may still contain an entry that matches the given address. For example, a Redirect message may have told this node that an address not covered by any prefix in the Prefix List is actually a neighbor. nd6_lookup() is called to search into the Neighbor Cache and see if the address has a Neighbor Cache, and if so, this function returns 1.

1035 If none of the above tests determine the address is on-link, this function returns 0.

5.22.2   nd6_output() Function

Function nd6_output() is called to transmit an IPv6 packet. This function is a common entry point from the IPv6 layer to the link-layer. This is largely derived from the ether_output() and arpresolve() functions for transmitting IPv4 packets over Ethernet, but is provided independently from any particular link types due to the link-independent nature of the ND protocol.

Listing 5-282

————————————————————————————————————nd6.c
```
2075      #define senderr(e) { error = (e); goto bad;}
2076      int
2077      nd6_output(ifp, origifp, m0, dst, rt0)
2078              struct ifnet *ifp;
2079              struct ifnet *origifp;
2080              struct mbuf *m0;
2081              struct sockaddr_in6 *dst;
2082              struct rtentry *rt0;
2083      {
2084              struct mbuf *m = m0;
2085              struct rtentry *rt = rt0;
2086              struct sockaddr_in6 *gw6 = NULL;
2087              struct llinfo_nd6 *ln = NULL;
2088              int error = 0;
    ....
2114              if (IN6_IS_ADDR_MULTICAST(&dst->sin6_addr))
2115                      goto sendpkt;
2116
2117              if (nd6_need_cache(ifp) == 0)
2118                      goto sendpkt;
```
————————————————————————————————————nd6.c

2076–2082 On input, ifp points to the interface on which the packet will be transmitted. origifp refers to the interface to which the source address of this packet belongs. The usage of these two interface pointers will be explained in Listing 5-292 below. m0 holds the outgoing packet. rt0 holds the route entry for reaching the destination dst.

2114–2118 The packet is transmitted without further processing if the destination is a multicast address. The packet is also just transmitted if the link-layer address does not utilize a Neighbor Cache, that is, neither link-layer address resolution nor NUD is performed on the link.

Listing 5-283

————————————————————————————————————nd6.c
```
2120          /*
2121           * next hop determination.  This routine is derived from ether_outpout.
2122           */
```

```
2123               if (rt) {
2124                   if ((rt->rt_flags & RTF_UP) == 0) {
....
2126                       if ((rt0 = rt = rtalloc1((struct sockaddr *)dst,
2127                           1, 0UL)) != NULL)
....
2132                       {
2133                           rt->rt_refcnt--;
2134                           if (rt->rt_ifp != ifp) {
2135                               /* XXX: loop care? */
2136                               return nd6_output(ifp, origifp, m0,
2137                                   dst, rt);
2138                           }
2139                       } else
2140                           senderr(EHOSTUNREACH);
2141                   }
```
                                                              ————nd6.c

2123–2141 If the route given by the caller is down, a search is performed to try to find a valid route. If the outgoing interface of the new route is different from the current one, `nd6_output()` is recursively called with the new interface.

2136 If another route cannot be located for the destination, this function terminates and an error of `EHOSTUNREACH` is returned to the caller.

> *Note*: The intent of this code is not really clear. It is not clear why the RTF_UP was cleared from the route entry in the first place (see the check at line 2124). A typical case where this flag is cleared is when a cached host route is invalidated and needs to be updated, but this check should have been done in the `in6_selectroute()` function called from `ip6_output()` (Listing 3-157) and should not be the case at this point.
>
> According to the code history, this is apparently derived from the `ether_output()` function of BSD/OS, where there might be a scenario that made this check reasonable.

Listing 5-284
                                                              ————nd6.c

```
2143               if (rt->rt_flags & RTF_GATEWAY) {
2144                   gw6 = (struct sockaddr_in6 *)rt->rt_gateway;
2145
2146                   /*
2147                    * We skip link-layer address resolution and NUD
2148                    * if the gateway is not a neighbor from ND point
2149                    * of view, regardless of the value of nd_ifinfo.flags.
2150                    * The second condition is a bit tricky; we skip
2151                    * if the gateway is our own address, which is
2152                    * sometimes used to install a route to a p2p link.
2153                    */
2154                   if (!nd6_is_addr_neighbor(gw6, ifp) ||
2155                       in6ifa_ifpwithaddr(ifp, &gw6->sin6_addr)) {
2156                       /*
2157                        * We allow this kind of tricky route only
2158                        * when the outgoing interface is p2p.
2159                        * XXX: we may need a more generic rule here.
2160                        */
2161                       if ((ifp->if_flags & IFF_POINTOPOINT) == 0)
2162                           senderr(EHOSTUNREACH);
2163
2164                       goto sendpkt;
2165                   }
```

```
2166
2167                              if (rt->rt_gwroute == 0)
2168                                      goto lookup;
2169                              if (((rt = rt->rt_gwroute)->rt_flags & RTF_UP) == 0) {
2170                                      rtfree(rt); rt = rt0;
2171                              lookup:
....
2173                                      rt->rt_gwroute = rtalloc1
     (rt->rt_gateway, 1, 0UL);
....
2177                                      if ((rt = rt->rt_gwroute) == 0)
2178                                              senderr(EHOSTUNREACH);
....
2188                              }
....
2192                      }
2193              }
```
_____nd6.c

— Line 2173 is broken here for layout reasons. However, it is a single line of code.

2143–2144 If the destination is reachable through a gateway, a Neighbor Cache for the gateway must be identified to send the packet on the outgoing link.

2154–2164 If the gateway address is not regarded as on-link or if the address is one of the local node's addresses on the outgoing interface, the packet is simply transmitted by skipping further operations related to the ND protocol. This shortcut is provided to deal with an indirect route toward an interface which does not require link-layer address resolution. A common practice of this case is to install a route toward a point-to-point interface. For example, the following execution of the **route** command will make a route entry that indicates all packets matching 2001:db8:1234::/48 should be sent to interface gif0:

```
# route add -inet6 2001:db8:1234::/48 ::1 -ifp gif0
```

This route entry would be displayed by the **netstat** command as follows:

```
% netstat -rn -f inet6 | head
Routing tables

Internet6:
Destination            Gateway          Flags        Netif Expire
[...]
2001:db8:1234::/48     ::1              UGSc         gif0
```

In such a case the actual gateway address does not matter and the packet should simply be sent to the outgoing interface.

The check at line 2161 prohibits the use of this type of route entry unless the outgoing interface is a point-to-point interface. This is ad hoc heuristics, as commented in the code, but in practice it does not make sense to skip link-layer address resolution for a multiple-access link.

2167–2170 For an indirect route the rt_gwroute field points to the route entry that specifies how to reach the next-hop router, that is, the Neighbor Cache entry for the gateway. If the cache entry is not yet identified, the processing goes to the lookup label to find it. If the cache entry exists but has been invalidated (which should be the rare case), the cache is freed.

2171–2178 rtalloc1() finds or creates (by cloning) a Neighbor Cache entry for the gateway address. If this attempt fails, an error of EHOSTUNREACH is returned to the caller.

Listing 5-285

———nd6.c
```
2195            /*
2196             * Address resolution or Neighbor Unreachability Detection
2197             * for the next hop.
2198             * At this point, the destination of the packet must be a unicast
2199             * or an anycast address(i.e. not a multicast).
2200             */
2201
2202            /* Look up the neighbor cache for the nexthop */
2203            if (rt && (rt->rt_flags & RTF_LLINFO) != 0)
2204                    ln = (struct llinfo_nd6 *)rt->rt_llinfo;
2205            else {
2206                    /*
2207                     * Since nd6_is_addr_neighbor() internally calls nd6_lookup(),
2208                     * the condition below is not very efficient.  But we believe
2209                     * it is tolerable, because this should be a rare case.
2210                     */
2211                    if (nd6_is_addr_neighbor(dst, ifp) &&
2212                        (rt = nd6_lookup(dst, 1, ifp)) != NULL)
2213                            ln = (struct llinfo_nd6 *)rt->rt_llinfo;
2214            }
```
———nd6.c

2203–2204 At this point `rt` should be a neighboring next-hop and contain a valid Neighbor Cache entry. `ln` is set to the link-layer information of this cache.

2205–2214 This block of code is apparently meaningless. According to the code history, this was originally derived from the `arpresolve()` function that attempts to create an IPv4 ARP entry for the next-hop when the entry is not available. This could happen for IPv4 if the application specifies the `SO_DONTROUTE` option and the IPv4 output function bypasses a route lookup; however, this scenario does not occur for the KAME IPv6 implementation because its output routine always provides a route entry for a unicast destination (see the description of `in6_selectroute()` described in Section 3.13.2).

The reason the `nd6_is_addr_neighbor()` function is called is probably to avoid creating an inappropriate Neighbor Cache entry for an off-link destination by accident. But the right fix should actually be to not call `nd6_lookup()` and treat this case as an error.

Listing 5-286

———nd6.c
```
2215            if (!ln || !rt) {
2216                    if ((ifp->if_flags & IFF_POINTOPOINT) == 0 &&
2217                        !(ND_IFINFO(ifp)->flags & ND6_IFF_PERFORMNUD)) {
2218                            log(LOG_DEBUG,
2219                                "nd6_output: can't allocate llinfo for %s "
2220                                "(ln=%p, rt=%p)\n",
2221                                ip6_sprintf(&dst->sin6_addr), ln, rt);
2222                            senderr(EIO);    /* XXX: good error? */
2223                    }
2224
2225                    goto sendpkt;    /* send anyway */
2226            }
```
———nd6.c

2215–2226 In general, a route entry with valid link-layer information for the neighbor must be available at this point. The inner `if` statement tries to loosen the condition for a point-to-point interface configured not to perform NUD. The exceptional code is not correct, however; it would allow an attempt to send a packet to a multiple-access link while bypassing link-layer address resolution when the ND6_IFF_PERFORMNUD is cleared on the outgoing interface, but such an attempt should simply fail.

Listing 5-287
_____nd6.c

```
2228                /* We don't have to do link-layer address resolution on a p2p link. */
2229                if ((ifp->if_flags & IFF_POINTOPOINT) != 0 &&
2230                    ln->ln_state < ND6_LLINFO_REACHABLE) {
2231                        ln->ln_state = ND6_LLINFO_STALE;
2232                        ln->ln_expire = time_second + nd6_gctimer;
2233                }
```
_____nd6.c

2228–2233 Since link-layer address resolution does not have to be performed on a point-to-point link, this part of the code is only executed for NUD on such a link. If this is the first use for the Neighbor Cache entry, its state is changed to STALE with the expiration timer set to the garbage collection period. The state will soon be changed to DELAY below, triggering the NUD procedure.

Listing 5-288
_____nd6.c

```
2235                /*
2236                 * The first time we send a packet to a neighbor whose entry is
2237                 * STALE, we have to change the state to DELAY and a sets a timer to
2238                 * expire in DELAY_FIRST_PROBE_TIME seconds to ensure do
2239                 * neighbor unreachability detection on expiration.
2240                 * (RFC 2461 7.3.3)
2241                 */
2242                if (ln->ln_state == ND6_LLINFO_STALE) {
2243                        ln->ln_asked = 0;
2244                        ln->ln_state = ND6_LLINFO_DELAY;
2245                        ln->ln_expire = time_second + nd6_delay;
2246                }
```
_____nd6.c

2242–2246 According to [RFC2461], the first time a node sends a packet to a neighbor whose cache entry is in the STALE state, the state is changed to DELAY and a timer is started that expires in DELAY_FIRST_PROBE_TIME seconds. The state will be changed to the PROBE state if the cache remains in the DELAY state when the timer expires (Listing 5-56), and then NUD will begin for that neighbor.

Listing 5-289
_____nd6.c

```
2248                /*
2249                 * If the neighbor cache entry has a state other than INCOMPLETE
2250                 * (i.e. its link-layer address is already resolved), just
2251                 * send the packet.
2252                 */
2253                if (ln->ln_state > ND6_LLINFO_INCOMPLETE)
2254                        goto sendpkt;
```
_____nd6.c

2253–2254 Any cache state other than INCOMPLETE (and NOSTATE for the KAME implementation) implies the link-layer address has been resolved and the address can be used for transmission. The packet is transmitted with the known link-layer address.

Listing 5-290

———————————————————————————————————————nd6.c

```
2256            /*
2257             * There is a neighbor cache entry, but no ethernet address
2258             * response yet.  Replace the held mbuf (if any) with this
2259             * latest one.
2260             */
2261            if (ln->ln_state == ND6_LLINFO_NOSTATE)
2262                    ln->ln_state = ND6_LLINFO_INCOMPLETE;
2263            if (ln->ln_hold)
2264                    m_freem(ln->ln_hold);
2265            ln->ln_hold = m;
```

———————————————————————————————————————nd6.c

2261–2262 The state of a newly created Neighbor Cache that does not have any link-layer information was temporarily set to NOSTATE (see Listing 5-35). The state is reset to INCOMPLETE the first time the entry is actually used for an outgoing packet. The "temporary" entry now becomes a Neighbor Cache entry in terms of the ND protocol.

2263–2265 At this point the cache state must be INCOMPLETE. As written in [RFC2461], packets transmitted by upper layer protocols are queued in the Neighbor Cache entry while the address resolution is in progress. This packet queue must hold at least one packet, and packets in the queue should be replaced in a FIFO fashion when the queue overflows. This implementation follows the specification trivially using a single-entry queue.

Listing 5-291

———————————————————————————————————————nd6.c

```
2266            /*
2267             * If there has been no NS for the neighbor after entering the
2268             * INCOMPLETE state, send the first solicitation.
2269             * Technically this can be against the rate-limiting rule described in
2270             * Section 7.2.2 of RFC 2461 because the interval to the next scheduled
2271             * solicitation issued in nd6_timer() may be less than the specified
2272             * retransmission time.  This should not be a problem from a practical
2273             * point of view, because we'll typically see an immediate response
2274             * from the neighbor, which suppresses the succeeding solicitations.
2275             */
2276            if (ln->ln_expire && ln->ln_asked == 0) {
2277                    ln->ln_asked++;
2278                    ln->ln_expire = time_second +
2279                        ND6_RETRANS_SEC(ND_IFINFO(ifp)->retrans);
2280                    nd6_ns_output(ifp, NULL, dst, ln, 0);
2281            }
2282            return (0);
```

———————————————————————————————————————nd6.c

2276–2281 If this cache entry has a valid timer (`ln_expire` is non-0) and address resolution is not yet in progress (`ln_asked` is 0), the address resolution process is now started by sending out the first Neighbor Solicitation packet for the neighbor. The counter for the number of Neighbor Solicitation packets is incremented, and the timer is reset to the Retransmission Timer value.

Note that only the first outgoing packet since the cache entry becoming INCOMPLETE invokes the transmission of the Neighbor Solicitation. Further retransmission is handled by the `nd6_timer()` function (Listing 5-53).

It should also be noted that the first retransmission can take place within the Retransmission Time period due to the timing of starting the timer and of invoking the `nd6_timer()` function. Figure 5-39 depicts the situation with the default transmission interval of 1 second (1,000 ms). As shown in the figure, the interval between the first and second Neighbor Solicitation can be smaller than the expected interval, depending on the relationship between the system time and the invocation timing of `nd6_timer()` (the interval can also be larger than the expected value). Later versions of the kernel implementation avoids this issue by introducing a more fine-grained timer for each Neighbor Cache entry.

Listing 5-292

```
                                                                  nd6.c
2284      sendpkt:
....
2298              if ((ifp->if_flags & IFF_LOOPBACK) != 0) {

2308                      return ((*ifp->if_output)(origifp, m, (struct sockaddr *)dst,
2309                                      rt));
2310              }
....
2320              return ((*ifp->if_output)(ifp, m, (struct sockaddr *)dst, rt));
2321
2322      bad:
2323              if (m)
2324                      m_freem(m);
2325              return (error);
2326      }
2327      #undef senderr
                                                                  nd6.c
```

2298–2310 Care should be taken if the outgoing interface is a loopback interface. In this case `ifp` and `origifp` are often different: `ifp` points to the outgoing loopback interface, while `origifp`, called the *originating interface*, points to the interface to which the destination address belongs (see Listing 3-158). By passing the originating interface

FIGURE 5-39

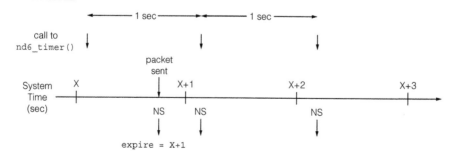

Retransmission timing of Neighbor Solicitation for address resolution.

to the output function for the loopback interface, which is typically `looutput()`, the
`ip6_input()` function will be able to identify the scope zones of the source and destination addresses correctly as explained in Section 3.7.

2320 For interfaces other than loopback, the packet is simply passed to the interface's output
function with its own interface structure (`ifp`) as an argument.

5.22.3 `rt6_flush()` Function

The `rt6_flush()` function is called when a router is known to be not functional. Specifically,
it is called in the following cases:

- From `nd6_free()` when a router is detected to be unreachable

- From `nd6_na_input()` when a known router announces that it ceases to act as a
  router by a Neighbor Advertisement message

- From `defrtrlist_del()` function when a router is removed from the Default Router
  List for some reason (e.g., due to the expiration of router lifetime)

This function disables the next-hop information for every "destination cache entry," which is
realized as a host route entry in the KAME implementation, that uses the non-functional router.

Listing 5-293

_____nd6_rtr.c

```
2347    /*
2348     * Delete all the routing table entries that use the specified gateway.
2349     * XXX: this function causes search through all entries of routing table, so
2350     * it shouldn't be called when acting as a router.
2351     */
2352    void
2353    rt6_flush(gateway, ifp)
2354            struct sockaddr_in6 *gateway;
2355            struct ifnet *ifp;
2356    {
2357            struct radix_node_head *rnh = rt_tables[AF_INET6];
2361            int s = splnet();
2363
2364            /* We'll care only link-local addresses */
2365            if (!IN6_IS_ADDR_LINKLOCAL(&gateway->sin6_addr)) {
2366                    splx(s);
2367                    return;
2368            }
2369
2370            rnh->rnh_walktree(rnh, rt6_deleteroute, (void *)gateway);
2371            splx(s);
2372    }
```
_____nd6_rtr.c

2357–2371 The function is quite trivial: it traverses the entire routing table and calls the
`rt6_deleteroute()` function with the argument of the given gateway.

The `rt6_deleteroute()` function is shown below. It compares the gateway address of
the given route entry (`rt_gateway`) to the given gateway address `arg`. If it matches and the
route is a dynamically created host route, this function invalidates the route entry. The call to

`rtrequest()` function with the `RTM_DELETE` command removes the route entry from the kernel routing table and clears the `RTF_UP` flag.

The next time this entry is used, the output routine will notice that the cached route is now invalid and try to acquire a new one (see Section 3.13.2). Since the invalid entry has already been removed from the table, the next search will find an alternative, possibly a functional gateway.

This processing provides an effective method of dead router detection. When a transport layer application caches a default router in its PCB entry (see Section 6.6.1) and the router becomes non-functional, the NUD algorithm soon detects the router is unreachable, and the cached information is updated.

Listing 5-294

nd6_rtr.c

```
2374    static int
2375    rt6_deleteroute(rn, arg)
2376            struct radix_node *rn;
2377            void *arg;
2378    {
2379    #define SIN6(s)  ((struct sockaddr_in6 *)s)
2380            struct rtentry *rt = (struct rtentry *)rn;
2381            struct sockaddr_in6 *gate = (struct sockaddr_in6 *)arg;
2382
2383            if (rt->rt_gateway == NULL || rt->rt_gateway->sa_family != AF_INET6)
2384                    return (0);
2385
2390            if (!IN6_ARE_ADDR_EQUAL(&gate->sin6_addr,
2391                                    &SIN6(rt->rt_gateway)->sin6_addr)) {
2392                    return (0);
2393            }
2395
2396            /*
2397             * Do not delete a static route.
2398             * XXX: this seems to be a bit ad-hoc. Should we consider the
2399             * 'cloned' bit instead?
2400             */
2401            if ((rt->rt_flags & RTF_STATIC) != 0)
2402                    return (0);
2403
2404            /*
2405             * We delete only host route. This means, in particular, we don't
2406             * delete default route.
2407             */
2408            if ((rt->rt_flags & RTF_HOST) == 0)
2409                    return (0);
2410
2411            return (rtrequest(RTM_DELETE, rt_key(rt), rt->rt_gateway,
2412                    rt_mask(rt), rt->rt_flags, 0));
2413    #undef SIN6
2414    }
```

nd6_rtr.c

5.22.4 `nd6_rtmsg()` Function

Function `nd6_rtmsg()` is called to notify interested application when either a default router or an interface direct route is added or removed from the kernel routing table.

Listing 5-295

                                                                          ___nd6_rtr.c

```
534     /*
535      * default router list proccessing sub routines
536      */
537
538     /* tell the change to user processes watching the routing socket. */
539     static void
540     nd6_rtmsg(cmd, rt)
541             int cmd;
542             struct rtentry *rt;
543     {
544             struct rt_addrinfo info;
545
546             bzero((caddr_t)&info, sizeof(info));
....
551             info.rti_info[RTAX_DST] = rt_key(rt);
552             info.rti_info[RTAX_GATEWAY] = rt->rt_gateway;
553             info.rti_info[RTAX_NETMASK] = rt_mask(rt);
....
557             info.rti_info[RTAX_IFP] =
558                 (struct sockaddr *)TAILQ_FIRST(&rt->rt_ifp->if_addrlist);
....
560             info.rti_info[RTAX_IFA] = rt->rt_ifa->ifa_addr;
561
562             rt_missmsg(cmd, &info, rt->rt_flags, 0);
563     }
```

                                                                          ___nd6_rtr.c

540–563 The `cmd` parameter specifies the route command, which can be either `RTM_ADD` or `RTM_DELETE`. The `rt` parameter is the route entry in question. `rt_missmsg()` generates a routing socket message to inform the listeners of the change that just took place in the kernel routing table.

Transport Layer Implications

6.1 Introduction

The layering model of communication protocols provides a pretty clear boundary between the network layer and the transport layer. In fact, major transport protocols such as UDP and TCP basically work fine over either IPv4 or IPv6. The only major difference is in the endpoint addresses—at least in theory.

Yet we need to consider some nontrivial issues for the operation of the various transport protocols over IPv6. Regarding the protocol, the elimination of IP-layer checksum may impose special consideration on the upper layer checksums. Also, various types of IPv6 properties require specific considerations for the transport layer operation.

Other issues arise with the API usage. [RFC3493] allows an application to make IPv4 communication over an `AF_INET6` socket using IPv4-mapped IPv6 addresses. Despite the seeming simplicity, it makes the implementation in the transport layer very complicated and can introduce operational confusion.

In this chapter, we discuss these miscellaneous issues regarding transport layer protocols. We first provide a summary of these issues, and then focus on the implementation-specific topics. As for the implementation, we begin with the Protocol Control Blocks (PCBs), BSD's traditional data structure representing a transport layer endpoint, by explaining how the PCBs handle IPv4 and IPv6 addresses. Our main focus is implication with IPv4-mapped IPv6 addresses. We describe subtle cases with this usage in order to clarify possible confusion in it. It should be noted, however, that the purpose of the clarification is to highlight the problems of IPv4-mapped IPv6 addresses, rather than recommending the "correct" use of them. We then discuss IPv6 specific implementation topics on UDP, TCP, and Raw sockets. We conclude this chapter with examples of specific operational scenarios with IPv4-mapped IPv6 addresses and of operations with a diagnosing tool.

6.2   TCP and UDP over IPv6

Since the Transmission Control Protocol (TCP) and the User Datagram Protocol (UDP) are transport layer protocols, TCP and UDP are independent of the network layer protocols in theory. In other words, the operations of TCP and UDP should be independent of IPv4 and IPv6. Traditionally TCP and UDP are carried over IPv4 only, and, as such, there exists a dependency between the IP header and the TCP and UDP headers. The operations of these transport protocols remain largely unaffected by the shift in the network protocol. This chapter focuses on the discussions centered on those IPv6-related modifications that are necessary due to the historical design. These modifications include transport layer header checksum, the packet lifetime, and the maximum payload size for upper layer protocols.

TCP and UDP headers contain a checksum field for detecting packet corruption. The TCP checksum covers the entire TCP packet, and the UDP checksum covers the entire UDP packet. Both TCP and UDP checksums include a pseudo header that contains IP header fields such as the source and destination IP addresses. The size of these addresses expands from 32 bits to 128 bits.

In IPv4, the Time-To-Live (TTL) field in the IP header specifies the lifetime of an IP datagram. An upper layer protocol can limit the lifetimes of its packets by setting the TTL value during data transmission. Officially, the TTL value is specified in units of seconds by definition. In practice, however, most routers always decrement the TTL value by one when forwarding a packet, and the packet is discarded when its TTL value reaches zero. Therefore applications treat the TTL value as the number of routers a packet is allowed to traverse before reaching its destination. There exists a similar mechanism in IPv6 to limit the packet lifetime. Each IPv6 header contains a Hop Limit field that accurately defines the number of times a packet may be forwarded by intermediate routers.

The increase in address size means reduction in maximum payload size for upper layer protocols. The minimum IPv4 header length is 20 bytes while the minimum IPv6 header length is 40 bytes. In IPv4, options are part of the IP header, which limits the maximum size for options to 44 bytes. In IPv6, the header length is fixed at 40 bytes; however, options are carried in various extension headers. There the size of the extension headers carried in each packet is limited only by the link MTU. In any case, upper layer protocols must account for the size of IP header including options when packetizing payload for transmission.

6.3   Pseudo Header for IPv6

The IPv6 specification [RFC2460] defines an upper layer pseudo header used in the upper layer checksum calculation. Figure 6-1 depicts the pseudo header format used by TCP, UDP, and ICMPv6. Even though [RFC2460] mentions these three protocols, other major upper layer protocols over IPv6 use the same pseudo header format, including OSPF for IPv6 [RFC2740] and PIM [PIM-SM-V2] (see also Chapter 2 of *IPv6 Advanced Protocols Implementation*).

The TCP, UDP, and ICMPv6 checksum computation includes a pseudo header that is prepended to the transport layer header, which contains the Source address, the Destination address, and the Next Header from the network layer headers. The pseudo header does not include any information from extension headers. Figure 6-1 depicts the pseudo header used for checksum calculation.

FIGURE 6-1

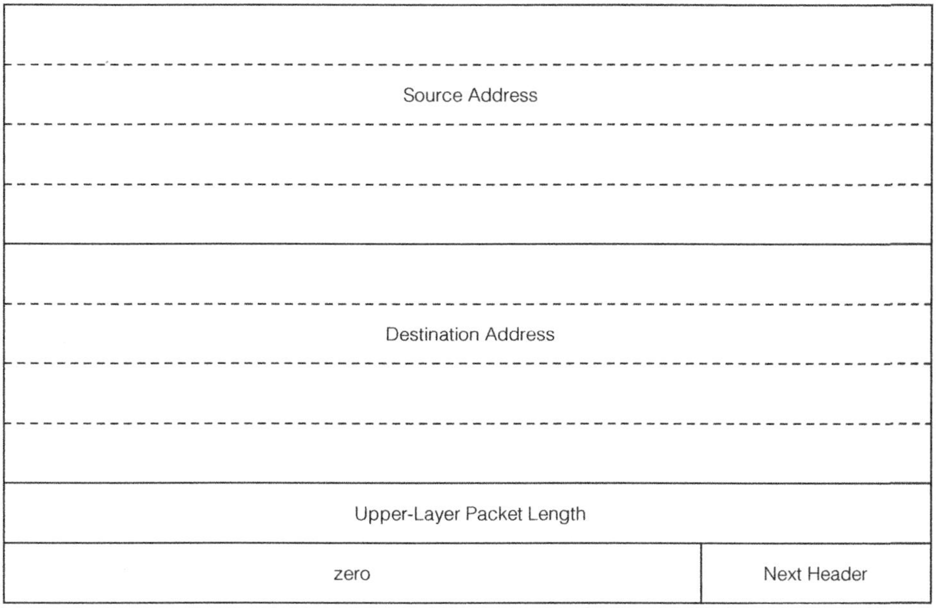

Source Address	
Destination Address	
Upper-Layer Packet Length	
zero	Next Header

TCP/UDP pseudo header for IPv6.

The Source Address and the Destination Address fields contain the same values as those present in the IPv6 header. If the packet contains a Routing header, the Destination Address field contains the final destination address specified in the Routing header.

The Upper-Layer Packet Length field is the size from the start of the upper layer header to the end of the upper layer payload excluding any bytes located between the IPv6 header and the upper layer protocol header.

The Next Header field contains the protocol number of the transport protocol (e.g., 6 for TCP and 17 for UDP). In a real packet, the field contains the protocol number of the header immediately following the IPv6 header, which can be, for example, the IPsec AH and ESP headers rather than TCP or UDP.

The checksum algorithm is the same as that used by IPv4, which is calculated as the 16-bit one's complement of the one's complement sum of the pseudo header and the upper layer data, including zero filled padding bytes if there are odd bytes of data. The checksum value must be replaced with 0xffff if the computed result is 0.

6.4 Checksum Difference between IPv4 and IPv6

The UDP checksum is optional in IPv4. The checksum field contains the zero value if the node did not compute the checksum. On the other hand, the UDP checksum is mandatory in IPv6. A receiving IPv6 node discards any UDP packet containing a zero valued checksum field.

The ICMPv6 checksum covers more information than that of IPv4. The ICMPv4 checksum covers the ICMPv4 header and its payload. The ICMPv6 checksum covers the pseudo header, the ICMPv6 header, and its payload.

The reason for the change in UDP and ICMPv6 checksum requirements is due to the change in the information carried in the IPv6 header. Since the IPv6 layer no longer computes a checksum covering the IP header, UDP checksum becomes mandatory. The UDP and ICMPv6 checksum must include the pseudo header in order to protect against corruption in the IPv6 header, and guarantees that the receiving node is the intended recipient.

6.5 IPv4-mapped IPv6 Address Usage

IPv4-mapped IPv6 addresses (Section 2.3) take a characteristic role in the transport layer along with its API usage [RFC3493]. In short, the standard API allows an application to make IPv4 communication over an IPv6 (AF_INET6) socket using IPv4-mapped IPv6 addresses.

To realize this usage, an implementation of dual-protocol stack for IPv4 and IPv6 needs some special handling for IPv4-mapped IPv6 addresses. The KAME kernel deals with those addresses mainly in the transport layer processing, which will be discussed in the following sections. Further details of the use of IPv4-mapped IPv6 addresses and its implication from the API point of view will be discussed in Section 7.2.3.

The design goal of the IPv4-mapped IPv6 address usage defined in [RFC3493] is to provide application level compatibility especially to legacy programs that cannot be easily modified to support both IPv4 and IPv6 with dedicated sockets. In this design, IPv4-mapped IPv6 addresses are assumed to not appear on the wire. The KAME implementation thus rejects any packets whose Source or Destination address is an IPv4-mapped IPv6 address. The related code is described in Listing 3-20 (Section 3.7).

Note that the purpose of the detailed discussion about the processing of IPv4-mapped IPv6 addresses is **not** to encourage the use of these addresses. It is provided to show how the support for these addresses complicates the kernel implementation through concrete examples. The authors generally agree on the argument against the API usage of IPv4-mapped IPv6 addresses described in [V4MAPPED]. But it simply mentions the complexity of the system software supporting IPv4-mapped IPv6 addresses, and such a general argument is vulnerable to criticism that it is just a matter of sense. The authors thus try to prove that the complexity is real via live code examples.

6.6 Code Introduction

In the following sections, we will describe implementation details about IPv6-specific operations at around the transport layers. Unlike the source code described in other chapters of this book, most parts of the implementation discussed in this chapter are not specific to IPv6. We will thus focus on some remarkable points that particularly matter in the transport layer operations over IPv6.

We will refer to the kernel source files shown in Table 6-1 throughout the discussion.

6.6.1 Protocol Control Blocks for IPv6

The protocol control block (PCB) structure, inpcb{}, is a BSD-specific data structure containing various types of information for an endpoint of a transport layer protocol (e.g., TCP or UDP). In general, an instance of the inpcb{} structure is associated with one and only one socket, which is the top-level interface to user applications.

TABLE 6-1

File	Description
`${KAME}/freebsd4/sys/netinet/in_pcb.h`	Internet Protocol Control Block (PCB)—IPv4
`${KAME}/kame/sys/netinet6/in6_pcb.h`	Internet Protocol Control Block—IPv6
`${KAME}/freebsd4/sys/netinet/in_pcb.c`	PCB processing functions
`${KAME}/kame/sys/netinet6/in6_pcb.c`	PCB processing functions for IPv6
`${KAME}/freebsd4/sys/netinet/tcp_input.c`	TCP input processing
`${KAME}/freebsd4/sys/netinet/tcp_output.c`	TCP output processing
`${KAME}/freebsd4/sys/netinet/tcp_subr.c`	TCP signal handling
`${KAME}/freebsd4/sys/netinet/tcp_usrreq.c`	TCP user request handler functions
`${KAME}/freebsd4/sys/netinet6/udp6_usrreq.c`	UDP input/signal handling/user request handler functions
`${KAME}/kame/sys/netinet6/udp6_output.c`	UDP output processing
`${KAME}/kame/sys/netinet6/raw_ip6.h`	RAW IPv6 definitions
`${KAME}/freebsd4/sys/netinet6/raw_ip6.c`	RAW IPv6 processing

The basic content of PCB is the same as that used in the IPv4 era. In FreeBSD/KAME, the PCB structure is designed as an extended version of the original IPv4 PCB structure to accommodate IPv6, while the NetBSD/KAME and the OpenBSD/KAME implementations have separate PCB structures for each protocol. We only focus on FreeBSD/KAME implementation in this book. The following discussion is based on FreeBSD/KAME, but we also note the implementation of other BSD variants for some important points such as processing of IPv4-mapped IPv6 addresses.

Different upper layer protocols maintain different lists of PCB entries, each of which is represented as the `inpcbinfo{}` structure; TCP and UDP have their own lists; other protocols including ICMPv6 share a common separate list. These are identified by global variables `tcbinfo`, `udbinfo`, and `ripcbinfo`. The `inpcbinfo{}` structure is shown below.

Listing 6-1

```
                                                                    in_pcb.h
250     struct inpcbinfo { /* XXX documentation, prefixes */
251             struct inpcbhead *hashbase;
252             u_long hashmask;
253             struct inpcbporthead *porthashbase;
254             u_long porthashmask;
255             struct inpcbhead *listhead;
256             u_short lastport;
257             u_short lastlow;
258             u_short lasthi;
259             struct vm_zone *ipi_zone; /* zone to allocate pcbs from */
260             u_int ipi_count; /* number of pcbs in this list */
261             u_quad_t ipi_gencnt; /* current generation count */
262     };
                                                                    in_pcb.h
```

250–262 The listhead member of the `inpcbinfo{}` points to a head structure of a doubly
linked list that contains all PCB entries operating over the same upper layer protocol. Each
`inpcb{}` structure is linked in this list via its `inp_list` member (see the next listing).
In addition to the base list, `inpcbinfo{}` contains two types of hash table for efficient
lookup over the entries. The `hashbase` member points to one type of hash table. Each
entry in the hash table is a doubly linked hash list whose entries are hashed by the local
port, foreign address, and foreign port. The `inp_hash` member of the `inpcb{}` structure
builds this type of hash list.

The `porthashbase` member is the other type of hash table. Each entry in the hash table is
a doubly linked hash list whose entries are hashed by the local port. The `inp_portlist` member of the `inpcb{}` structure builds the hash list. Figure 6-2 shows the relationship between
structures `inpcbinfo{}` and `inpcb{}`.

The next listing shows the internal details of the `inpcb{}` structure.

Listing 6-2

_____in_pcb.h

```
137     struct inpcb {
138             LIST_ENTRY(inpcb) inp_hash; /* hash list */
139             LIST_ENTRY(inpcb) inp_list; /* list for all PCBs of this proto */
140             u_int32_t       inp_flow;
141
142             /* local and foreign ports, local and foreign addr */
143             struct  in_conninfo inp_inc;
144
145             caddr_t inp_ppcb;                  /* pointer to per-protocol pcb */
146             struct  inpcbinfo *inp_pcbinfo; /* PCB list info */
147             struct  socket *inp_socket;    /* back pointer to socket */
148                                               /* list for this PCB's local port */
149             int     inp_flags;             /* generic IP/datagram flags */
150
151             struct  inpcbpolicy *inp_sp; /* for IPSEC */
152             u_char  inp_vflag;
153     #define INP_IPV4        0x1
154     #define INP_IPV6        0x2
155             u_char  inp_ip_ttl;               /* time to live proto */
156             u_char  inp_ip_p;                 /* protocol proto */
```
_____in_pcb.h

138–156 `inp_list`, `inp_hash`, and `inp_portlist` members are already explained.

`inp_flow` holds the value used in the flow label field of the IPv6 header for IPv6 packets
originated from this PCB.

The `in_conninfo` structure maintains the information of the endpoints represented by
a given PCB, which include information such as the IP addresses and port numbers of the
endpoints and a place holder of a route cache. The details of this structure will be shown
shortly.

`inp_ppcb` is a pointer to an upper layer protocol control block, for example, `inp_ppcb`
points to a separate structure for a TCP connection called the `tcpcb{}` structure. The upper
layer protocol control block maintains the parameters and state information that are necessary
for the proper protocol operation.

`inp_socket` references the socket structure associated with a given PCB. `inp_flags`
specifies various attributes of this PCB. Most of the flags indicate whether a socket option with

FIGURE 6-2

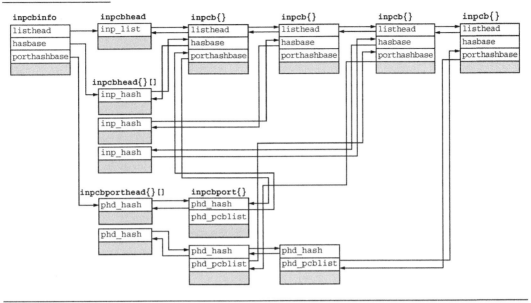

PCB chaining.

TABLE 6-2

Flag	Socket option (`IPV6_PORTRANGE`) value	Description
INP_HIGHPORT	IPV6_PORTRANGE_HIGH	Use the port range of 49152–65535 by default.
INP_LOWPORT	IPV6_PORTRANGE_LOW	Use the port range of 600–1023 by default.
INP_ANONPORT	N/A	Whether the kernel has chosen an ephemeral local port for the application. It does not affect the kernel behavior, but helps management utilities such as **netstat**.

Protocol-independent PCB flag macros.

a Boolean argument is specified or cleared on the corresponding socket. Tables 6-2, 6-3, and 6-4 summarize these flags with the corresponding socket option name. Of these options Chapter 7 discusses IPv6 specific ones in more detail. Section 7.4.3 shows how the kernel correlates the options with the PCB flags.

The KAME IPsec implementation permits the user to define per socket security policy. The `inp_sp` member points to the policy information.

TABLE 6-3

Flag	Socket option	Description
INP_HDRINCL	IP_HDRINCL	The IP header is included in send data.
INP_RECVDSTADDR	IP_RECVDSTADDR	Return the destination IP address.
INP_RECVIF	IP_RECVIF	Return the receiving interface.
INP_RECVOPTS	IP_RECVOPTS	Return receiving IP options(*).
INP_RECVRETOPTS	IP_RECVRETOPTS	Return source route information of incoming packets(*).

IPv4-specific PCB flag macros.

(*) These options have actually no effect since they are disabled in the inbound processing code.

TABLE 6-4

Flag	Socket option	Description
IN6P_IPV6_V6ONLY	IPV6_V6ONLY	Disable IPv4 communication on an AF_INET6 socket using IPv4-mapped IPv6 addresses.
IN6P_MTU	IPV6_RECVPATHMTU	Return updated Path MTU information.
IN6P_PKTINFO	IPV6_RECVPKTINFO	Return the destination IPv6 address and receiving interface.
IN6P_HOPLIMIT	IPV6_RECVHOPLIMIT	Return the Hop Limit value of incoming packets.
IN6P_HOPOPTS	IPV6_RECVHOPOPTS	Return the Hop-by-Hop options of incoming packets, if included.
IN6P_DSTOPTS	IPV6_RECVDSTOPTS	Return Destination options of incoming packets, if included.
IN6P_RTHDR	IPV6_RECVRTHDR	Return Routing headers of incoming packets, if included.
IN6P_TCLASS	IPV6_RECVTCLASS	Return the Traffic Class field value of incoming packets.
IN6P_AUTOFLOWLABEL	IPV6_AUTOFLOWLABEL	Enable automatic generation of flow label for outgoing packets.
IN6P_RFC2292	N/A	Old-style socket options defined in [RFC2292] are specified. This flag is automatically set in the kernel for validation purposes when an old application hardcodes the old options.
IN6P_CONTROLOPTS	N/A	A shortcut definition representing a logical OR of IN6P_PKTINFO, IN6P_HOPLIMIT, IN6P_DSTOPTS, IN6P_RTHDR, IN6P_RTHDRDSTOPTS, and IN6P_TCLASS. In short, this "combination flag" indicates that some packet information needs to be passed to the socket as ancillary data items along with a received packet (see Section 7.3.4).
IN6P_RTHDRDSTOPTS	IPV6_RECVRTHDRDSTOPTS	Obsolete and should not be used.

IPv6-specific PCB flag macros.

inp_vflags specifies the IP version of the PCB. The version flag is necessary because the FreeBSD/KAME code uses the same PCB structure for communication over both IPv4 and IPv6.

inp_ip_ttl represents the Time To Live (TTL) value for IPv4 or the Hop Limit value for IPv6.

inp_ip_p stores the upper layer protocol number over IPv4 or the Next Header value in the context of IPv6.

Listing 6-3

in_pcb.h

```
158            /* protocol dependent part; options */
159            struct {
160                    u_char  inp4_ip_tos;            /* type of service proto */
161                    struct  mbuf *inp4_options;     /* IP options */
162                    struct  ip_moptions *inp4_moptions; /* IP multicast options */
163            } inp_depend4;
164    #define inp_fport       inp_inc.inc_fport
165    #define inp_lport       inp_inc.inc_lport
166    #define inp_faddr       inp_inc.inc_faddr
167    #define inp_laddr       inp_inc.inc_laddr
168    #define inp_route       inp_inc.inc_route
169    #define inp_ip_tos      inp_depend4.inp4_ip_tos
170    #define inp_options     inp_depend4.inp4_options
171    #define inp_moptions    inp_depend4.inp4_moptions
```

in_pcb.h

159–163 The inp_depend4 structure maintains options specific to the IPv4 protocol and protocol operation.

Listing 6-4

in_pcb.h

```
172            struct {
173                    /* IP options */
174                    struct  mbuf *inp6_options;
175                    /*
176                     * IP6 options for incoming packets.
177                     * XXX: currently unused but remained just in case.
178                     */
179                    struct  ip6_recvpktopts *inp6_inputopts;
180                    /* IP6 options for outgoing packets */
181                    struct  ip6_pktopts *inp6_outputopts;
182                    /* IP multicast options */
183                    struct  ip6_moptions *inp6_moptions;
184                    /* ICMPv6 code type filter */
185                    struct  icmp6_filter *inp6_icmp6filt;
186                    /* IPV6_CHECKSUM setsockopt */
187                    int     inp6_cksum;
188                    u_short inp6_ifindex;
189                    short   inp6_hops;
190            } inp_depend6;
```

in_pcb.h

172–190 The inp_depend6 structure maintains options specific to the IPv6 protocol and protocol operation.

inp6_options was used for older specification of the standard API [RFC2292] and is effectively unused in this implementation.

inp6_inputopts keeps packet options for an incoming packet to be passed to the application (see Listing 7-113). inp6_outputopts keeps packet options for outgoing packets from the corresponding socket (see Section 7.4.2).

inp6_moptions references the multicast-related options (see Section 7.4.7).

inp6_icmp6filt stores the filtering information for ICMPv6 packets. The filtering mechanism is discussed later in Section 6.10.4 and the API is discussed in Section 7.3.2. inp6_cksum specifies how to calculate the upper layer checksum for a raw socket. This is set to −1 by default, and can be changed by the IPV6_CHECKSUM socket option (Section 7.3.2). When explicitly set, the raw socket output processing calculates the checksum using the value of this member as the offset from the upper layer header to the checksum field; the raw socket input processing calculates the checksum based on the standard checksum algorithm for UDP and TCP. This member does not have any effect on a socket whose type is not SOCK_RAW or on an ICMPv6 socket.

inp6_ifindex is not currently used by the implementation.

inp6_hops specifies the value to be set in the Hop Limit field of the IPv6 header of the outgoing packet. The default Hop Limit value is used when inp6_hops is set to −1 (default).

Listing 6-5

─── in_pcb.h
```
191          LIST_ENTRY(inpcb) inp_portlist;
192          struct  inpcbport *inp_phd;      /* head of this list */
193          inp_gen_t         inp_gencnt;    /* generation count of this instance */

  (in6p_ macros: see below)

216     };
```
─── in_pcb.h

191–193 inp_portlist constructs a list of PCB entries that have the same hash value of a local port number. inp_phd is the head element of this hash list. inp_gencnt holds the instance number of the generated PCB entry for a particular protocol. This is a sequential serial number of this entry.

Listing 6-6

─── in_pcb.h
```
194   #define in6p_fsa        inp_inc.inc_ie.ie_dependfaddr.ie6_foreign
195   #define in6p_lsa        inp_inc.inc_ie.ie_dependladdr.ie6_local
196   #define in6p_faddr      inp_inc.inc6_fsa.sin6_addr
197   #define in6p_laddr      inp_inc.inc6_lsa.sin6_addr
198   #define in6p_route      inp_inc.inc6_route
199   #define in6p_ip6_hlim   inp_depend6.inp6_hlim
200   #define in6p_hops       inp_depend6.inp6_hops   /* default hop limit */
201   #define in6p_ip6_nxt    inp_ip_p
202   #define in6p_flowinfo   inp_flow
203   #define in6p_vflag      inp_vflag
204   #define in6p_options    inp_depend6.inp6_options
205   #define in6p_inputopts  inp_depend6.inp6_inputopts
206   #define in6p_outputopts inp_depend6.inp6_outputopts
207   #define in6p_moptions   inp_depend6.inp6_moptions
208   #define in6p_icmp6filt  inp_depend6.inp6_icmp6filt
```

```
209    #define in6p_cksum        inp_depend6.inp6_cksum
210    #define inp6_ifindex      inp_depend6.inp6_ifindex
211    #define in6p_flags        inp_flags  /* for KAME src sync over BSD*'s */
212    #define in6p_socket       inp_socket  /* for KAME src sync over BSD*'s */
213    #define in6p_lport        inp_lport  /* for KAME src sync over BSD*'s */
214    #define in6p_fport        inp_fport  /* for KAME src sync over BSD*'s */
215    #define in6p_ppcb         inp_ppcb  /* for KAME src sync over BSD*'s */
```
─── in_pcb.h

194–215 These macro definitions all have the "ip6p_" prefix to replace in6p_prefix for
increased code readability. Unfortunately, the naming convention of some PCB members
for IPv6 varies among BSD variants. Some use in6p_*xxx* and others use inp6_*xxx*.
KAME generally tries to share the same code base for all the BSD variants, and it consistently uses in6p_*xxx* names. This is the case for the code described below.

The in_pcb{} structure contains the in_conninfo{} structure via the inp_inc member. This structure maintains endpoint information of a connection established for the PCB entry.
Its definition is as follows.

Listing 6-7
─── in_pcb.h

```
 97    /*
 98     * XXX
 99     * At some point struct route should possibly change to:
100     *    struct rtentry *rt
101     *    struct in_endpoints *ie;
102     */
103    struct in_conninfo {
104            u_int8_t        inc_flags;
105            u_int8_t        inc_len;
106            u_int16_t       inc_pad;          /* XXX alignment for in_endpoints */
107            /* protocol dependent part; cached route */
108            struct  in_endpoints inc_ie;
109            union {
110                    /* placeholder for routing entry */
111                    struct  route inc4_route;
....
113                    struct  route inc6_route;
....
117            } inc_dependroute;
118    };
119    #define inc_isipv6      inc_flags      /* temp compatibility */
120    #define inc_fport       inc_ie.ie_fport
121    #define inc_lport       inc_ie.ie_lport
122    #define inc_faddr       inc_ie.ie_faddr
123    #define inc_laddr       inc_ie.ie_laddr
124    #define inc_route       inc_dependroute.inc4_route
125    #define inc6_fsa        inc_ie.ie6_fsa
126    #define inc6_lsa        inc_ie.ie6_lsa
127    #define inc6_route      inc_dependroute.inc6_route
```
─── in_pcb.h

104–115 The inc_flags and inc_len members are obsolete. inc_pad is used as a padding
area to align the following member inc_ie at a 32-bit boundary. inc_ie is an instance
of in_endpoints{} structure that holds the endpoint address and port information (see
below). The inc_dependroute{} union references a cached route for the destination
address. Previously, inc_dependroute{} was defined as a union of different structures
of different sizes according to the network layer protocol, route{} and route_in6{}.

However, the `route{}` structure has been extended by KAME statically to be large enough to hold IPv6 route information so that common code can reference the same structure.

119–127 These macro definitions are created for better readability.

Note: The code discussed in this book uses `sockaddr_in6{}` structure to hold the endpoint addresses. However, KAME changed this basic design in February 2004. The current KAME uses the `in6_addr{}` structure instead of `sockaddr_in6{}` so that the maintainer of each BSD can merge the KAME code with the original BSD development trees easily because the BSD variants all use `in6_addr{}` for IPv6 address maintenance.

The `in_endpoints{}` structure included in `in_conninfo{}` is shown below.

Listing 6-8

_____ in_pcb.h

```
73      /*
74       * NOTE: ipv6 addrs should be 64-bit aligned, per RFC 2553.
75       * in_conninfo has some extra padding to accomplish this.
76       */
77      struct in_endpoints {
78              /* protocol dependent part, local and foreign addr */
79              union {
80                      /* foreign host table entry */
81                      struct  sa_4in6 ie46_foreign;
82                      struct  sockaddr_in6 ie6_foreign;
83              } ie_dependfaddr;
84              union {
85                      /* local host table entry */
86                      struct  sa_4in6 ie46_local;
87                      struct  sockaddr_in6 ie6_local;
88              } ie_dependladdr;
89      #define ie_fport        ie_dependfaddr.ie6_foreign.sin6_port
90      #define ie_lport        ie_dependladdr.ie6_local.sin6_port
91      #define ie_faddr        ie_dependfaddr.ie46_foreign.sa46_addr4
92      #define ie_laddr        ie_dependladdr.ie46_local.sa46_addr4
93      #define ie6_fsa         ie_dependfaddr.ie6_foreign
94      #define ie6_lsa         ie_dependladdr.ie6_local
95      };
```

_____ in_pcb.h

77–88 The code comment written on lines 74–75 is wrong. At the time of this writing the IPv6 addresses were not aligned on the 64-bit boundary. When `in_endpoints{}` structure was first defined, there were another two 16-bit members before the `ie_dependfaddr{}` structure which keeps port number information. At some later time, those members were merged into the `ie_dependfaddr{}` and `ie_dependladdr{}` structures that are part of the `sockaddr_in6{}` structure. It appears the programmer forgot to adjust the padding. The `ie_dependfaddr{}` structure keeps track of the address and port information of the remote node while the `ie_dependladdr{}` structure keeps track of the address and port of the local node. The `sa_4in6{}` structure, shown below, basically represents an IPv4 address, but fancy padding is necessary to map the IPv4 address and port number to the lower 32-bit of the IPv6 address and port number defined as `ie6_foreign` and `ie6_local`, respectively.

89–94 These macro definitions are short names for accessing endpoint information such as address and port number.

Listing 6-9

—— in_pcb.h

```
65      #define offsetof(type, member)   ((size_t)(&((type *)0)->member))
66      #endif
67      struct sa_4in6 {
68              u_int8_t sa46_pad1[offsetof(struct sockaddr_in6, sin6_addr)]; /* XXX */
69              u_int32_t sa46_pad2[3];
70              struct in_addr sa46_addr4;
71      }
```

—— in_pcb.h

65–70 The `offsetof()` macro calculates the number of bytes from the top of the structure type to the location of the member variable in the structure. Thus, the size of `sa46_pad1` is the length from the start byte position of the `sockaddr_in6{}` structure to the `sin6_addr` member variable. `sa46_addr4` is stored at the lower 32 bits of the `sin6_addr` member because `sa46_pad2` starts at the byte offset as the `sin6_addr` member variable.

The endpoint address fields of the PCB structure is a bit complicated. The reason for this complex design is to make it possible to keep IPv4-mapped IPv6 addresses in a PCB entry and use the entry both for IPv4 and IPv6 communication. The IPv4-mapped IPv6 address is stored in the same manner with other kinds of IPv6 addresses. At the same time, the lower 32 bits of the address, which represents the IPv4 address, can be accessible from IPv4 PCB manipulation functions, thanks to this design. Figure 6-3 illustrates the relationship of structures. We can see that the IPv4 address part, represented by `sa6_addr4`, is mapped to the lower 32 bit of the `sockaddr_in6{}` structure.

6.7 General Operations on PCBs and Sockets

In this section, we describe various kernel routines that handle PCB-related operations not specific to particular transport protocols such as TCP or UDP.

6.7.1 IPv6 PCB Allocation—`in_pcballoc()` Function

The mechanism for allocating an IPv6 PCB is the same as that for IPv4. A PCB entry is created when a socket is created through the `socket()` system call. The optional `bind()` system call that follows will assign an address and a port number to the local endpoint. The `connect()` system call assigns an address and port number to the remote endpoint. All operations related to a PCB entry is routed to the protocol-dependent PCB manipulation functions. Figure 6-4 illustrates the call flow involved in allocating a PCB for an IPv6 socket.

FIGURE 6-3

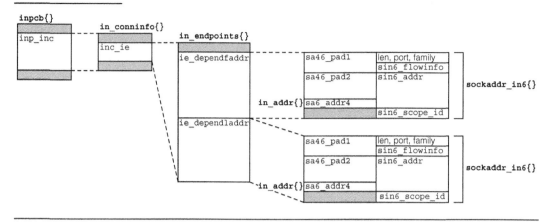

Address field sharing mechanism in the PCB structure.

FIGURE 6-4

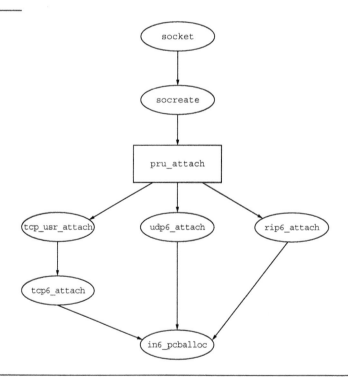

Call flow to `in_pcballoc()`.

Listing 6-10

─── in_pcb.c
```
183     int
184     in_pcballoc(so, pcbinfo, p)
185             struct socket *so;
186             struct inpcbinfo *pcbinfo;
187             struct proc *p;
188     {
189             register struct inpcb *inp;
190     #ifdef IPSEC
191             int error;
192     #endif
193
194             inp = zalloci(pcbinfo->ipi_zone);
195             if (inp == NULL)
196                     return (ENOBUFS);
197             bzero((caddr_t)inp, sizeof(*inp));
198             inp->inp_gencnt = ++pcbinfo->ipi_gencnt;
199             inp->inp_pcbinfo = pcbinfo;
200             inp->inp_socket = so;
 ....
208     #if defined(INET6)
209             if (INP_SOCKAF(so) == AF_INET6) {
210                     if (ip6_v6only)
211                             inp->inp_flags |= IN6P_IPV6_V6ONLY;
212                     inp->in6p_fsa.sin6_family =
213                             inp->in6p_lsa.sin6_family = AF_INET6;
214                     inp->in6p_fsa.sin6_len =
215                             inp->in6p_lsa.sin6_len = sizeof(struct sockaddr_in6);
216             }
217     #endif
218             LIST_INSERT_HEAD(pcbinfo->listhead, inp, inp_list);
219             pcbinfo->ipi_count++;
220             so->so_pcb = (caddr_t)inp;
221     #ifdef INET6
222             if (ip6_auto_flowlabel)
223                     inp->inp_flags |= IN6P_AUTOFLOWLABEL;
224     #endif
225             return (0);
226     }
```
─── in_pcb.c

184–200 The function `in_pcballoc()` takes three parameters: `so` is a pointer to the `socket{}` structure that will contain the PCB entry to be allocated in this function; `pcbinfo` is a structure that holds information specific to the upper layer protocol; `p` is a pointer to the process that owns the socket `so`.

    `zalloci()` is a function that allocates a memory block of the proper size depending on the PCB type. `inp_gencnt` is a monotonically increasing serial number of PCB entries. `inp_socket` is a back pointer to the socket that contains this PCB entry.

209–216 `ip6_v6only` is a global variable that specifies the system's default behavior about whether the IPv6 stack permits IPv4 communication performed over an IPv6 (`AF_INET6`) socket.

    The `ip6_v6only` variable is mapped to the `net.inet6.ip6.v6only` sysctl variable. The value can be changed by the **sysctl** command. When this variable is set to zero (false), an IPv6 socket will accept the connection requests that has an IPv4-mapped IPv6 address as an endpoint address of the connection request. If the value is set to true, an IPv6 socket never accepts connections whose address is an IPv4-mapped IPv6 address.

The corresponding PCB flag, inp_flags, can also be configured via the IPV6_V6ONLY socket option (see Table 6-4). Thus, ip6_v6only effectively gives the default value of this option.

> *Note*: The default value of ip6_v6only is 0 for the FreeBSD version described in this book. However, the FreeBSD developers then changed the policy and the default value to 1 due to various concerns about the usage of IPv4-mapped IPv6 addresses that will be discussed in Section 7.2.3.

218–220 The newly created PCB entry is inserted into the PCB list kept in pcbinfo->listhead. ipi_count counts the number of PCB entries in the list structure. The so_pcb member of the socket structure is set to reference the new PCB.

222–223 The IN6P_AUTOFLOWLABEL flag is set in inp_flags if the global variable ip6_auto_flowlabel is non-0. This variable can be changed by the **sysctl** command. The correspondent sysctl variable name is net.inet6.ip6.auto_flowlabel, whose default value is 1.

6.7.2   Bind Local Address—in6_pcbbind() Function

Assignment of a local address and port number occurs in two major cases. One is a direct result of processing of the bind() system call; the other is in the processing of the connect() system call. Figure 6-5 illustrates the call flow involved in binding address information to the local endpoint represented by a PCB. The address binding takes place in function in6_pcbbind().

Listing 6-11

——— in6_pcb.c
```
122    int
123    in6_pcbbind(inp, nam, p)
124            register struct inpcb *inp;
125            struct sockaddr *nam;
126            struct proc *p;
127    {
128            struct socket *so = inp->inp_socket;
129            struct sockaddr_in6 *sin6 = (struct sockaddr_in6 *)NULL;
130            struct inpcbinfo *pcbinfo = inp->inp_pcbinfo;
131            u_short  lport = 0;
132            int wild = 0, reuseport = (so->so_options & SO_REUSEPORT);
133
134            if (!in6_ifaddr) /* XXX broken! */
135                    return (EADDRNOTAVAIL);
136            if (inp->inp_lport || !SA6_IS_ADDR_UNSPECIFIED(&inp->in6p_lsa))
137                    return(EINVAL);
```
——— in6_pcb.c

123–126 Function in6_pcbbind() takes three parameters: inp is a pointer to the PCB entry that will be bound to a local address; nam is a pointer to the binding address information; p is a pointer to the calling process.

134–137 in6_ifaddr is the head of the address list that contains all IPv6 addresses configured in the local node. An error of EADDRNOTAVAIL is returned if no IPv6 address is configured

FIGURE 6-5

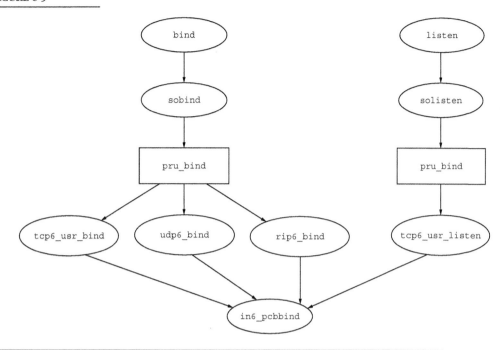

Call flow to in6_pcbbind().

in the system. Since binding local endpoint information to a socket can take place only once, an error is returned if the socket already has an address binding.

Listing 6-12
_____ in6_pcb.c
```
138             if ((so->so_options & (SO_REUSEADDR|SO_REUSEPORT)) == 0)
139                  wild = 1;
```
_____ in6_pcb.c

138–139 The SO_REUSEADDR and SO_REUSEPORT options allow multiple bindings to a specific address and port number under a certain condition. SO_REUSEADDR is typically used by server applications to enable the program to be quickly restarted with a listening TCP socket even if some sockets using the same local port remain in the TIME WAIT state. SO_REUSEPORT is typically used by multicast applications so that multiple processes on the same node can simultaneously listen to the same multicast group and the same port. The wild flag is set to true if neither of these socket options is set.

Parameter Validation

Listing 6-13
_____ in6_pcb.c
```
140             if (nam) {
141                  int error;
```

```
142
143                                 sin6 = (struct sockaddr_in6 *)nam;
144                                 if (nam->sa_len != sizeof(*sin6))
145                                         return(EINVAL);
146                                 if (nam->sa_family != AF_INET6)
147                                         return(EAFNOSUPPORT);
148
149                                 if ((error = scope6_check_id(sin6, ip6_use_defzone)) != 0)
150                                         return(error);
```
── in6_pcb.c

140–147 nam points to an instance of the sockaddr_in6{} structure if the caller wants to bind a specific address to the IPv6 socket. The function returns an EAFNOSUPPORT error if nam is not referencing an IPv6 address. nam can be NULL when the caller is willing to bind to any port number. In this case the kernel will automatically generate a port number and bind that port to the given socket.

149–150 Function scope6_check_id() (Section 2.9.4) checks to see if the sin6_scope_id member of nam has the correct value. ip6_use_defzone informs the kernel to set the default scope zone ID for an address if the ID is not already set. If the sin6_scope_id member is 0, that is, the zone ID is not specified, and if ip6_use_defzone is set to true, then scope6_check_id() sets the default ID for the scope extracted from sin6.

Listing 6-14
── in6_pcb.c
```
152                                 lport = sin6->sin6_port;
153                                 if (IN6_IS_ADDR_MULTICAST(&sin6->sin6_addr)) {
154                                         /*
155                                          * Treat SO_REUSEADDR as SO_REUSEPORT for multicast;
156                                          * allow compete duplication of binding if
157                                          * SO_REUSEPORT is set, or if SO_REUSEADDR is set
158                                          * and a multicast address is bound on both
159                                          * new and duplicated sockets.
160                                          */
161                                         if (so->so_options & SO_REUSEADDR)
162                                                 reuseport = SO_REUSEADDR|SO_REUSEPORT;
```
── in6_pcb.c

153–162 The reuseport variable is set to true when the binding address is a multicast address and either SO_REUSEADDR or SO_REUSEPORT is specified.

Listing 6-15
── in6_pcb.c
```
163                                 } else if (!SA6_IS_ADDR_UNSPECIFIED(sin6)) {
164                                         struct ifaddr *ia = NULL;
....
166                                         u_int32_t lzone;
....
168
169                                         sin6->sin6_port = 0;                /* yech... */
....
171                                         lzone = sin6->sin6_scope_id;
172                                         sin6->sin6_scope_id = 0; /* XXX: for ifa_ifwithaddr */
....
174                                         if ((ia = ifa_ifwithaddr((struct sockaddr *)sin6)) == 0)
```

```
175                                   return(EADDRNOTAVAIL);
....
177                         sin6->sin6_scope_id = lzone;
....
179
180                         /*
181                          * XXX: bind to an anycast address might accidentally
182                          * cause sending a packet with anycast source address.
183                          * We should allow to bind to a deprecated address, since
184                          * the application dares to use it.
185                          */
186                         if (ia &&
187                             ((struct in6_ifaddr *)ia)->ia6_flags &
188                             (IN6_IFF_ANYCAST|IN6_IFF_NOTREADY|IN6_IFF_DETACHED)) {
189                                   return(EADDRNOTAVAIL);
190                         }
191                 }
```
—— in6_pcb.c

163–177 The binding address is validated if it is a unicast address and is not the unspecified address. The address must be one of the addresses assigned to one of the network interfaces of the local node. Function `ifa_ifwithaddr()` searches each interface and its address list for the binding address specified in `sin6`. The function returns an error of `EADDRNOTAVAIL` if the search fails. The `sin6_scope_id` member must be cleared before calling `ifa_ifwithaddr()` because each address that is kept in the interface structure is not in the embedded scope form (see Section 2.9.3).

186–189 An anycast address, a tentative address, a duplicated address and a detached address, are all considered invalid addresses for binding to a socket and an error of `EADDRNOTAVAIL` is returned (see Table 2.8 for the address flags, and note that `IN6_IFF_NOTREADY` is a logical AND of `IN6_IFF_TENTATIVE` and `IN6_IFF_DUPLICATED`).

As commented, the reason why an anycast address is rejected here is because an anycast address bound as a local address might be used as the source address of outgoing packets—a prohibited behavior by the specification (see Section 2.2). This may not be a convincing argument, though, because a multicast address, which has the same restriction, can be used as the local address. The major difference is that multicast addresses are syntactically distinguished from unicast or anycast addresses, and it is easy to detect the illegal use for outgoing packets from the socket (Listing 3-151). Since it is difficult and might be expensive to perform the same check for anycast addresses in `ip6_output()`, this implementation simply prohibits binding an anycast address to a socket as the local address.

It should also be noted that this code implicitly (but as explicitly commented) allows an application to bind a socket to a deprecated IPv6 address (Section 5.10.1). Even though this binding may cause "new communication" using the bound address as the source address, which is generally discouraged by [RFC2462], this implementation purposely respects the application's decision. And, in fact, the revised version of the protocol specification [RFC2462BIS] clarifies that such a case must be allowed.

Listing 6-16

—— in6_pcb.c
```
192                 if (lport) {
193                         struct inpcb *t;
194
```

```
195                         /* GROSS */
196                         if (ntohs(lport) < IPV6PORT_RESERVED && p &&
197                             suser_xxx(0, p, PRISON_ROOT))
198                                 return(EACCES);
```
_____ in6_pcb.c

196–198 The function returns an error of EACCESS if a user other than the super user tries to bind a port from the reserved space to the socket.

Duplicate Binding Check

In the majority of cases, a specific address and port number can be bound to only one socket. The following code segments detect an attempt of duplicate binding and reject it if such an attempt is found. This process is pretty complicated due to security considerations and the possibility of IPv4 communication over an AF_INET6 socket using IPv4-mapped IPv6 addresses.

Listing 6-17

_____ in6_pcb.c
```
199                 if (so->so_cred->cr_uid != 0 &&
200                     !IN6_IS_ADDR_MULTICAST(&sin6->sin6_addr)) {
201                         t = in6_pcblookup_local(pcbinfo, sin6, lport,
202                                             INPLOOKUP_WILDCARD);
203                     if (t &&
204                         (!SA6_IS_ADDR_UNSPECIFIED(sin6) ||
205                          !SA6_IS_ADDR_UNSPECIFIED(&t->in6p_lsa) ||
206                          (t->inp_socket->so_options &
207                          SO_REUSEPORT) == 0) &&
208                         (so->so_cred->cr_uid !=
209                          t->inp_socket->so_cred->cr_uid))
210                             return (EADDRINUSE);
211                     if ((inp->inp_flags & IN6P_IPV6_V6ONLY) == 0 &&
212                         SA6_IS_ADDR_UNSPECIFIED(sin6)) {
213                             struct sockaddr_in sin;
214
215                             in6_sin6_2_sin(&sin, sin6);
216                             t = in_pcblookup_local(pcbinfo,
217                                     sin.sin_addr, lport,
218                                     INPLOOKUP_WILDCARD);
219                             if (t &&
220                                 (so->so_cred->cr_uid !=
221                                  t->inp_socket->so_cred->cr_uid) &&
222                                 (ntohl(t->inp_laddr.s_addr) !=
223                                  INADDR_ANY ||
224                                  INP_SOCKAF(so) ==
225                                  INP_SOCKAF(t->inp_socket)))
226                                     return (EADDRINUSE);
227                     }
228                 }
```
_____ in6_pcb.c

199–200 The first part concentrates on one typical case where the effective user ID of the socket is non-0 (i.e., the application user is not the super user and the address to be bound is not a multicast address).

201–210 in6_pcblookup_local() (to be discussed in Section 6.7.5) is called to check a duplicate binding attempt. This call to this function returns any matching PCB entry for the given local address and local port, including a wildcard matching entry, or returns NULL if it cannot find any matching entry.

This attempt of binding is rejected with an error of EADDRINUSE if the following conditions are met:

- in6_pcblookup_local() returns a valid PCB entry.
- Either the given address or the local address of the found entry is a normal IPv6 address, that is, a non-unspecified address.
- The SO_REUSEPORT option is not set in the matching entry.
- The effective users are different between the found socket (PCB) and the socket for this binding attempt.

This check tries to avoid a security risk called *port theft* performed by the following steps:

1. User A opens a wildcard socket with a specific port, say, 80.
2. A different user B then opens another socket to which a specific local address and the same port are bound.
3. Then succeeding traffic (new TCP connections or UDP packets) that was originally destined for user A's application will be "hijacked" by user B.

The user ID check at lines 208 and 209 rejects such an attempt.

211–227 The introduction of IPv4-mapped IPv6 addresses and the usage of IPv4 communication over an AF_INET6 socket make things even more complicated. If the given address to be bound is the unspecified address while the IN6P_IPV6_V6ONLY flag is cleared in the PCB, the corresponding socket will allow communication over both IPv4 and IPv6. In this case, conflict with an existing AF_INET socket must also be checked, and thus the in_pcblookup_local() function is called with an all-zero IPv4 address (i.e., INADDR_ANY).

As the above case, this attempt of binding is rejected with an error of EADDRINUSE if the following conditions are met:

- in_pcblookup_local() returns a valid PCB entry.
- The effective users are different.
- The local address of the found entry is not INADDR_ANY or the address family of the two sockets is the same.

The first condition of the third bullet detects a conflict similar to the one identified at line 205 above: Someone has already opened a socket bound to a specific IPv4 address and a different user then tries to bind a different socket to the IPv6 unspecified address and the same port number.

The intent of the latter condition of the third bullet is unclear. It can be evaluated to be true only when there is already another socket bound to the IPv6 unspecified address. However, this case will be rejected in a general procedure of conflict detection below, and there is no reason for handling the case here as an exception. This part of the code is probably a result of a thoughtless copy of the general code. In fact, later versions of FreeBSD has revised this block entirely and removed this address family check.

Listing 6-18

in6_pcb.c

```
229                    t = in6_pcblookup_local(pcbinfo, sin6, lport, wild);
230                    if (t && (reuseport & t->inp_socket->so_options) == 0)
231                        return(EADDRINUSE);
232                    if ((inp->inp_flags & IN6P_IPV6_V6ONLY) == 0 &&
233                        SA6_IS_ADDR_UNSPECIFIED(sin6)) {
234                        struct sockaddr_in sin;
235
236                        in6_sin6_2_sin(&sin, sin6);
237                        t = in_pcblookup_local(pcbinfo, sin.sin_addr,
238                                    lport, wild);
239                        if (t &&
240                            (reuseport & t->inp_socket->so_options)
241                            == 0 &&
242                            (ntohl(t->inp_laddr.s_addr)
243                            != INADDR_ANY ||
244                            INP_SOCKAF(so) ==
245                            INP_SOCKAF(t->inp_socket)))
246                                return (EADDRINUSE);
247                    }
248                }
249                sa6_copy_addr(sin6, &inp->in6p_lsa);
250            }
```

in6_pcb.c

229–231 The second part of the duplicate binding detection handles general cases. Like the first part, `in6_pcblookup_local()` is called to find an existing binding that matches this attempt. This time, however, the fourth parameter `wild` varies depending on options specified in the socket to be bound (Listing 6-12). When the `wild` variable is set to true, the socket can be bound to the address or port that is already bound to other sockets, as long as the other sockets permit the duplicate binding.

 If `wild` is false, `in6_pcblookup_local()` only returns an exact-matching entry; otherwise, it returns the best matching entry including a "wildcard" socket bound to the unspecified address. The existence of a matching entry indicates a duplicate binding attempt, and an error of `EADDRINUSE` will be returned unless a "reuseport" option is specified in the matching socket (`SO_REUSEPORT` and optionally `SO_REUSEADDR` for a multicast address).

232–248 Again, the processing cannot be that straightforward due to IPv4-mapped IPv6 addresses. If the `AF_INET6` socket to be bound allows IPv4 communication as well as IPv6 communication, `in_pcblookup_local()` searches for a matching socket that is used for IPv4 communication.

 This binding attempt is rejected with an error of `EADDRINUSE` if the following conditions are met:

- `in_pcblookup_local()` returns a valid PCB entry.
- A "reuseport" option is not set in the found socket.
- The local address of the found entry is not `INADDR_ANY` or the address family of the two sockets is the same.

The first condition of the third bullet detects and rejects a conflicting attempt with a socket bound to a specific IPv4 address when any wildcard matching is prohibited.

The second condition of the third bullet seems unnecessary. This check probably intended to make sure that the following are met:

1. Rejecting duplicate bindings to the IPv6 unspecified addresses for multiple AF_INET6 sockets.

2. Allowing a binding to the unspecified address for an AF_INET6 socket even if a binding to INADDR_ANY for an AF_INET socket exists.

But the first goal is achieved by the check at lines 229–231; the second goal is achieved regardless of the check at lines 244–245. In fact, there is similar code in in_pcbbind() for handling the bind() system call on an AF_INET socket, which is really necessary for achieving the goal similar to point 2 above. Again, the redundant check is likely due to a thoughtless copy from the in_pcbbind() implementation.

249 If no invalid duplicate is detected, the given address is stored in the local address field of the PCB.

Port Number Allocation

Listing 6-19

_____ in6_pcb.c
```
251             if (lport == 0) {
252                     int e;
253                     if ((e = in6_pcbsetport(&inp->in6p_lsa, inp, p)) != 0)
254                             return(e);
255             }
256             else {
257                     inp->inp_lport = lport;
258                     if (in_pcbinshash(inp) != 0) {
259                             sa6_copy_addr(&sa6_any, &inp->in6p_lsa);
260                             inp->inp_lport = 0;
261                             return (EAGAIN);
262                     }
263             }
264             return(0);
265     }
```
_____ in6_pcb.c

251–255 in6_pcbsetport() is called to assign an anonymous local port to the socket if the caller does not specify the port information. This can happen when an application tries to send a packet from a socket without binding it to a particular address or port number.

256–263 Otherwise, the specified local port number is set to the PCB entry. in_pcbinshash() inserts the PCB entry into the PCB hash table according to the hash value calculated from the local and remote addresses and port numbers.

Implication in Binding **AF_INET** *Socket*

As noted above, the special usage of IPv4-mapped IPv6 addresses introduces subtle implication about IPv4 communication over an AF_IENT6 socket; also, It also affects the processing of bind() for an AF_INET socket; also, it may conflict with an existing AF_INET6 socket bound to IPv4-mapped IPv6 addresses or the IPv6 unspecified address allowing IPv4 communication.

Listing 6-20 is a part of the in_pcbbind() function that has the implication. The in_pcblookup_local() function (Section 6.7.6) can identify a matching AF_INET6 socket as well as an AF_INET socket to detect a duplicate binding attempt, so the code basically does not have to care about the cases of conflict with an AF_INET6 socket.

The only subtle case is handled in the two code segments enabled by the INET6 preprocessor macro. The check at lines 306–307 and 323–324 allows a new binding for an AF_INET socket to INADDR_ANY even if there is an AF_INET6 socket bound to the IPv6 unspecified address.

In the general case, this may be reasonable. In the context of avoiding *port theft*, however, this behavior is doubtful. Consider user A opens an AF_INET6 socket bound to the IPv6 unspecified address and a specific port number and allows IPv4 and IPv6 communication via the socket. If a different user B opens an AF_INET socket and tries to bind it to INADDR_ANY and the same port number, this attempt will succeed, since none of the conditions from lines, 303–307 is true: s_addr fields are both INADDR_ANY and the address families are different.

Then user B will successfully "steal" succeeding IPv4 communication which may originally be destined for user A's application, due to the PCB selection algorithm for incoming packets (see Section 6.7.8).

Later versions of FreeBSD have thus disabled this part of the code. The attempt of user B in the above scenario now fails with an error of EADDRINUSE.

Listing 6-20

in6_pcb.c

```
280                 if (lport) {
281                         struct inpcb *t;
282
283                         /* GROSS */
284                         if (ntohs(lport) < IPPORT_RESERVED && p &&
285                             suser_xxx(0, p, PRISON_ROOT))
286                                 return (EACCES);
287                         if (p && p->p_prison)
288                                 prison = 1;
289                         if (so->so_cred->cr_uid != 0 &&
290                             !IN_MULTICAST(ntohl(sin->sin_addr.s_addr))) {
291                                 t = in_pcblookup_local(inp->inp_pcbinfo,
292                                     sin->sin_addr, lport,
293                                     prison ? 0 : INPLOOKUP_WILDCARD);
294                                 if (t &&
295                                     (ntohl(sin->sin_addr.s_addr) != INADDR_ANY ||
296                                     ntohl(t->inp_laddr.s_addr) != INADDR_ANY ||
297                                     (t->inp_socket->so_options &
298                                         SO_REUSEPORT) == 0) &&
299                                     (so->so_cred->cr_uid !=
300                                     t->inp_socket->so_cred->cr_uid)) {
301   #if defined(INET6)
302                                         if (ntohl(sin->sin_addr.s_addr) !=
303                                             INADDR_ANY ||
304                                             ntohl(t->inp_laddr.s_addr) !=
305                                             INADDR_ANY ||
306                                             INP_SOCKAF(so) ==
307                                             INP_SOCKAF(t->inp_socket))
308   #endif /* defined(INET6) */
309                                             return (EADDRINUSE);
310                                 }
311                         }
312                         if (prison &&
313                             prison_ip(p, 0, &sin->sin_addr.s_addr))
314                                 return (EADDRNOTAVAIL);
315                         t = in_pcblookup_local(pcbinfo, sin->sin_addr,
316                             lport, prison ? 0 : wild);
317                         if (t &&
```

```
318                                 (reuseport & t->inp_socket->so_options) == 0) {
319     #if defined(INET6)
320                                     if (ntohl(sin->sin_addr.s_addr) !=
321                                         INADDR_ANY ||
322                                         ntohl(t->inp_laddr.s_addr) !=
323                                         INADDR_ANY ||
324                                         INP_SOCKAF(so) ==
325                                         INP_SOCKAF(t->inp_socket))
326     #endif /* defined(INET) */
327                                         return (EADDRINUSE);
328                             }
329                     }
330                 inp->inp_laddr = sin->sin_addr;
331             }
```
―――in6_pcb.c

6.7.3   Fix Remote Address—`in6_pcbconnect()` Function

Issuing the `connect()` system call specifies a particular remote address to the socket. Also, for a passive TCP connection, the remote address and port number are assigned to a PCB at the socket creation time as part of the incoming TCP SYN packet processing. The `in6_pcbconnect()` function handles the processing in either case. Figure 6-6 illustrates the call flow involved in assigning the remote endpoint information to a socket.

FIGURE 6-6

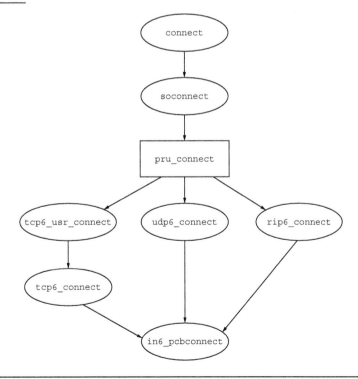

Call flow to `in6_pcbconnect ()`.

Listing 6-21

```
340    int
341    in6_pcbconnect(inp, nam, p)
342            register struct inpcb *inp;
343            struct sockaddr *nam;
344            struct proc *p;
345    {
```

340–344 in6_pcbconnect() has three input parameters: inp is a pointer to the PCB entry to be assigned remote endpoint information; nam specifies the remote endpoint; p is the pointer to the process that owns the given PCB.

Listing 6-22

```
346            struct sockaddr_in6 *addr6;
....
348            struct sockaddr_in6 addr6_storage;
....
350            register struct sockaddr_in6 *sin6 = (struct sockaddr_in6 *)nam;
351            int error;
352
353            /*
354             * Call inner routine, to assign local interface address.
355             * in6_pcbladdr() may automatically fill in sin6_scope_id.
356             */
357            if ((error = in6_pcbladdr(inp, nam, &addr6)) != 0)
358                    return(error);
360            addr6_storage = *addr6;
361            if ((error = in6_recoverscope(&addr6_storage,
362                                      &addr6->sin6_addr, NULL)) != 0) {
363                    return (error);
364            }
365            /* XXX: also recover the embedded zone ID */
366            addr6_storage.sin6_addr = addr6->sin6_addr;
367            addr6 = &addr6_storage;
```

357–358 in6_pcbladdr() looks up the most appropriate local address for the given remote address specified by the nam parameter (Section 6.7.4). addr6 is initialized to reference the chosen local address.

360–367 As shown in Section 6.7.4 in6_pcbladdr() is effectively a front-end of the in6_selectsrc() function. Since the selected source address by in6_selectsrc() often comes from a system's interface address, especially when the socket is not bound to a particular address, and the address is not in the general form regarding the scope zone ID for the IPv6 protocol stack (Section 2.9.3), it may have to be converted to the general form here. A local copy is used for the conversion because addr6 may point to a part of the interface structure and may not be modified, and in6_recoverscope() performs the conversion.

Listing 6-23

——in6_pcb.c

```
370                     if (in6_pcblookup_hash(inp->inp_pcbinfo, sin6, sin6->sin6_port,
371                                 SA6_IS_ADDR_UNSPECIFIED(&inp->in6p_lsa)
372                                 ? addr6 : &inp->in6p_lsa,
373                                 inp->inp_lport, 0, NULL) != NULL) {
374                 return (EADDRINUSE);
375             }
```
——in6_pcb.c

370–375 in6_pcblookup_hash() is called to determine whether binding the socket to the given remote address results in a duplicated connection. An error of EADDRINUSE is returned when a duplicated connection binding is detected. The parameters supplied to in6_pcblookup_hash() are the specific remote address and port number, the local port number assigned to the PCB, and the local address assigned to the PCB or the candidate local address returned by the source address selection process if the PCB has not been assigned a local address.

Listing 6-24

——in6_pcb.c

```
376                     if (SA6_IS_ADDR_UNSPECIFIED(&inp->in6p_lsa)) {
377                         if (inp->inp_lport == 0) {
378                             error = in6_pcbbind(inp, (struct sockaddr *)0, p);
379                             if (error)
380                                 return (error);
381                         }
382                         inp->in6p_lsa.sin6_addr = addr6->sin6_addr;
383                         inp->in6p_lsa.sin6_scope_id = addr6->sin6_scope_id;
384                     }
385                     inp->in6p_faddr = sin6->sin6_addr;
386                     inp->in6p_fsa.sin6_scope_id = sin6->sin6_scope_id;
387                     inp->inp_fport = sin6->sin6_port;
388                     /* update flowinfo - draft-itojun-ipv6-flowlabel-api-00 */
389                     inp->in6p_flowinfo &= ~IPV6_FLOWLABEL_MASK;
390                     if (inp->in6p_flags & IN6P_AUTOFLOWLABEL)
391                         inp->in6p_flowinfo |=
392                             (htonl(ip6_flow_seq++) & IPV6_FLOWLABEL_MASK);
393
394                     in_pcbrehash(inp);
395                     return (0);
396     }
```
——in6_pcb.c

376–383 An application may call connect() without having to call bind() first. In this case the local address is not specified in the PCB. For this situation in6_pcbbind() is called to assign a local port and only the local port to the PCB. Then the selected address with the proper scope zone ID is assigned to the PCB.

385–395 The remote endpoint information is stored in the PCB. The in6p_flowinfo field is set to the value of the global variable ip6_flow_seq if the IN6P_AUTOFLOWLABLE flag is set in the PCB. The value of this field will be used in the flow label field of outgoing packets from this socket (see Listings 6-59, 6-91, and 6-122). Since in_pcbconnect() changes the endpoint information in the PCB, which is used in the computation of the hash value, in_pcbrehash() is called to reinsert the PCB into the hash table.

6.7.4 Function `in6_pcbladdr()`

Function `in6_pcbladdr()` chooses the address for the local endpoint according to the given remote address.

Listing 6-25

_____ in6_pcb.c

```
279    int
280    in6_pcbladdr(inp, nam, plocal_addr6)
281           register struct inpcb *inp;
282           struct sockaddr *nam;
283           struct sockaddr_in6 **plocal_addr6;
284    {
```

_____ in6_pcb.c

279–283 `in6_pcbladdr()` takes three input parameters. `inp` is a pointer to the PCB entry. `nam` contains the remote endpoint information including the remote address. `plocal_addr6` will store the local address that will be chosen by this function.

Listing 6-26

_____ in6_pcb.c

```
285           register struct sockaddr_in6 *sin6 = (struct sockaddr_in6 *)nam;
286           int error = 0;
287
288           if (nam->sa_len != sizeof (*sin6))
289                   return (EINVAL);
290           if (sin6->sin6_family != AF_INET6)
291                   return (EAFNOSUPPORT);
292           if (sin6->sin6_port == 0)
293                   return (EADDRNOTAVAIL);
294
295           if ((error = scope6_check_id(sin6, ip6_use_defzone)) != 0)
296                   return(error);
```

_____ in6_pcb.c

288–293 Error `EINVAL` or `EAFNOSUPPORT` is returned if the given remote address is not a valid IPv6 address. A remote port number of 0 is invalid and error `EADDRNOTAVAIL` is returned accordingly.

295–296 `scope6_check_id()` checks the validity of `sin6_scope_id` of the remote address and will set the scope zone ID when such information is missing and if the system is configured to use the default zone ID.

Listing 6-27

_____ in6_pcb.c

```
298           if (in6_ifaddr) {
299                   /*
300                    * If the destination address is UNSPECIFIED addr,
301                    * use the loopback addr, e.g ::1.
302                    */
303                   if (SA6_IS_ADDR_UNSPECIFIED(sin6))
304                           sin6->sin6_addr = in6addr_loopback;
305           }
```

_____ in6_pcb.c

298–305 `in6_ifaddr` is a head of the list of IPv6 addresses that have been assigned to this node. The remote address is set to the loopback address if the caller did not provide the remote address information.

Listing 6-28

─── `in6_pcb.c`

```
306            {
307                    struct ifnet *ifp = NULL;
308
309                    *plocal_addr6 = in6_selectsrc(sin6, inp->in6p_outputopts,
310                                                  inp->in6p_moptions,
311                                                  &inp->in6p_route,
312                                                  &inp->in6p_lsa, &ifp, &error);
313                    if (ifp && sin6->sin6_scope_id == 0 &&
314                        (error = scope6_setzoneid(ifp, sin6)) != 0) { /* XXX */
315                            return(error);
316                    }
317
318                    if (*plocal_addr6 == NULL) {
319                            if (error == 0)
320                                    error = EADDRNOTAVAIL;
321                            return(error);
322                    }
323                    /*
324                     * Don't do pcblookup call here; return interface in
325                     * plocal_addr6
326                     * and exit to caller, that will do the lookup.
327                     */
328            }
329
330            return(0);
331    }
```

─── `in6_pcb.c`

309–312 `in6_selectsrc()` selects the appropriate source address according to the remote address: the IPv6 packet options specified by `inp->in6p_outputopts`, the multicast packet options specified by `inp->in6p_moptions` and the cached route information. The local address cannot be determined by only the remote address because output packet options may contain information which affects the local address selection. For example, `in6p_outputopts` may contain the next hop router address which may restrict the outgoing interface to be used, and `in6p_moptions` may explicitly specify the multicast outgoing interface. In such cases, the local address must be chosen from the addresses assigned to the outgoing interface. `in6_selectsrc()` returns the best matched local address and sets the outgoing interface and error code, respectively.

313–316 If `in6_selectsrc()` provides the outgoing interface, `ifp`, which is typically the case, and the scope zone ID of the Destination address is not yet determined(*), `scope6_setzoneid()` function is called to determine the appropriate zone ID based on the interface and the scope type of the Destination address, and sets the `sin6_scope_id` member of `sin6` accordingly.

This block of code tries to provide a remedy for a scenario like this: The sending application specifies a link-local address as the destination address without filling in the `sin6_scope_id` member but explicitly provides the outgoing interface with the `IPV6_PKTINFO` socket option or ancillary data item.

In general, this is a bad practice in that the implicit relationship between the outgoing interface specification and the scope zone ID of the destination address may cause unexpected or non-deterministic behavior. It is recommended that the scope zone ID of a Destination address be explicitly specified in its `sin6_scope_id` member, whether or not the outgoing interface is separately specified. However, since there are applications that rely on this implicit binding, the kernel provides the workaround.

Note: For a global address, a value of zero for the `sin6_scope_id` field is normal. But this implementation always calls `scope6_setzoneid()` for simplicity.

318–330 The function returns the `EADDRNOTAVAIL` error if no proper address can be used as the source address. Otherwise, the function returns 0 as a success.

6.7.5   Search for a PCB Entry—`in6_pcblookup_local()` Function

There exist two PCB search functions. One is `in6_pcblookup_local()` that searches for a PCB entry based on a local address and a local port number. The other is `in6_pcblookup_hash()` that searches for a PCB entry based on a local address, a foreign address, and a foreign port number.

Listing 6-29

─── `in6_pcb.c`

```
674      struct inpcb *
675      in6_pcblookup_local(pcbinfo, laddr, lport_arg, wild_okay)
676              struct inpcbinfo *pcbinfo;
677              struct sockaddr_in6 *laddr;
678              u_int lport_arg;
679              int wild_okay;
680      {
681              register struct inpcb *inp;
682              int matchwild = 3, wildcard;
683              u_short lport = lport_arg;
```

─── `in6_pcb.c`

675 `in6_pcblookup_local()` takes four input parameters: `pcbinfo` is a pointer to the `inpcbinfo{}` structure containing the global PCB list for an upper layer protocol; `laddr` and `lport_arg` are the local address and port number, respectively, which are used as the search keys; `wild_okay` specifies whether the search is for the exact match only or for the best match allowing a wildcard matching.

Listing 6-30

─── `in6_pcb.c`

```
685              if (!wild_okay) {
686                      struct inpcbhead *head;
687                      /*
688                       * Look for an unconnected (wildcard foreign addr) PCB that
```

```
689                      * matches the local address and port we're looking for.
690                      */
691                     head = &pcbinfo->hashbase[INP_PCBHASH(INADDR_ANY, lport, 0,
692                                                 pcbinfo->hashmask)];
693                     LIST_FOREACH(inp, head, inp_hash) {
694                             if ((inp->inp_vflag & INP_IPV6) == 0)
695                                     continue;
696                             if (SA6_IS_ADDR_UNSPECIFIED(&inp->in6p_fsa) &&
697                                 SA6_ARE_ADDR_EQUAL(&inp->in6p_lsa, laddr) &&
698                                 inp->inp_lport == lport) {
699                                     /*
700                                      * Found.
701                                      */
702                                     return (inp);
703                             }
704                     }
705                     /*
706                      * Not found.
707                      */
708                     return (NULL);
```
——— *in6_pcb.c*

685–708 As discussed in Section 6.6.1 pcbinfo->hashbase is a hash table of PCB entries
that was constructed using the foreign address, the local port number, and the foreign port
number, as the hash key. When the wildcard matching is allowed, the foreign address is
set to INADDR_ANY and foreign port is set to 0. As a result, the search is narrowed to the
set of unconnected PCB entries that has the same local port number as lport (copied
from lport_arg).

The search skips PCB entries that do not have the INP_IPV6 flag set because
these PCBs cannot be used for IPv6 communication. For the perfect match,
in6_pcblookup_local() returns the PCB entry that has the matching local address,
the matching local port number, and the unspecified foreign address. Otherwise, the function returns NULL as the failure indication.

Listing 6-31
——— *in6_pcb.c*

```
709                 } else {
710                     struct inpcbporthead *porthash;
711                     struct inpcbport *phd;
712                     struct inpcb *match = NULL;
713                     /*
714                      * Best fit PCB lookup.
715                      *
716                      * First see if this local port is in use by looking on the
717                      * port hash list.
718                      */
719                     porthash = &pcbinfo->porthashbase[INP_PCBPORTHASH(lport,
720                         pcbinfo->porthashmask)];
721                     LIST_FOREACH(phd, porthash, phd_hash) {
722                             if (phd->phd_port == lport)
723                                     break;
724                     }
```
——— *in6_pcb.c*

719–724 For the best match, in6_pcblookup_local() returns the PCB entry that has the
most number of suitable components. pcbinfo->porthashbase is a hash table of the

PCB entries that was constructed using the local port number as the hash key. `porthash` is set to the head of the hash table slot hashed on the given port `lport`.

Listing 6-32

_____in6_pcb.c
```
725                        if (phd != NULL) {
726                                /*
727                                 * Port is in use by one or more PCBs. Look for best
728                                 * fit.
729                                 */
730                                LIST_FOREACH(inp, &phd->phd_pcblist, inp_portlist) {
731                                        wildcard = 0;
732                                        if ((inp->inp_vflag & INP_IPV6) == 0)
733                                                continue;
734                                        if (!SA6_IS_ADDR_UNSPECIFIED(&inp->in6p_fsa))
735                                                wildcard++;
736                                        if (!SA6_IS_ADDR_UNSPECIFIED(&inp->in6p_lsa)) {
737                                                if (SA6_IS_ADDR_UNSPECIFIED(laddr))
738                                                        wildcard++;
739                                                else if (!SA6_ARE_ADDR_EQUAL(
740                                                              &inp->in6p_lsa,
741                                                              laddr)) {
742                                                        continue;
743                                                }
744                                        } else {
745                                                if (!SA6_IS_ADDR_UNSPECIFIED(laddr))
746                                                        wildcard++;
747                                        }
748                                        if (wildcard < matchwild) {
749                                                match = inp;
750                                                matchwild = wildcard;
751                                                if (matchwild == 0) {
752                                                        break;
753                                                }
754                                        }
755                                }
756                        }
757                        return (match);
758                }
759        }
```
_____in6_pcb.c

725–735 The search skips non-IPv6 PCB entries. A PCB entry with its foreign address set is less preferred in selection preference by incrementing the variable `wildcard` (note that the foreign address is not given as part of the search key, which effectively means this is a wildcard matching).

736–743 If this PCB entry has an initialized local address and the given local address `laddr` is the unspecified address, then this is a wildcard matching and this PCB is less preferred in relevance; otherwise, if the two addresses are different, the PCB entry is skipped.

745–746 Similarly, if this PCB entry has the unspecified address and the given local address is a specific address, then this PCB is less preferred.

748–757 The value of `wildcard` indicates how relevant a PCB entry is with respect to the search criteria; the smaller the value of `wildcard` the more relevant a PCB entry is. The current PCB will become the new candidate entry if the current PCB has a smaller value of `wildcard` than the previously saved candidate entry. If `wildcard` is 0, it means this entry is the exact match. Since the exact match is known to be the best, the search terminates here and this entry is returned to the caller. Otherwise, the search continues for a better match, and this function eventually returns the most relevant candidate entry.

6.7.6 Search for IPv4-mapped PCB—`in_pcblookup_local()` Function

While the `in6_pcblookup_local()` function is called to find a PCB entry based on a local IPv6 address and port, `in_pcblookup_local()` is used with IPv4 addresses. The function is extended to support IPv4-mapped IPv6 address.

Listing 6-33 is the function definition. We will examine only the IPv6 extended part of the function.

Listing 6-33
_____ in6_pcb.c

```
848     /*
849      * Lookup a PCB based on the local address and port.
850      */
851     /*
852      * we never select the wildcard pcb which has INP_IPV6 flag if we have
853      * INP_IPV4 only wildcard pcb.  INP_LOOKUP_MAPPED_PCB_COST must be
854      * greater than the max value of matchwild (currently 3).
855      */
856     #define INP_LOOKUP_MAPPED_PCB_COST 4
857     struct inpcb *
858     in_pcblookup_local(pcbinfo, laddr, lport_arg, wild_okay)
859             struct inpcbinfo *pcbinfo;
860             struct in_addr laddr;
861             u_int lport_arg;
862             int wild_okay;
863     {
864             register struct inpcb *inp;
865             int matchwild = 3 + INP_LOOKUP_MAPPED_PCB_COST, wildcard;
866             u_short lport = lport_arg;
867
868             if (!wild_okay) {
869                     struct inpcbhead *head;
870                     /*
871                      * Look for an unconnected (wildcard foreign addr) PCB that
872                      * matches the local address and port we're looking for.
873                      */
874                     head = &pcbinfo->hashbase[INP_PCBHASH(INADDR_ANY, lport, 0,
                                         pcbinfo->hashmask)];
875                     LIST_FOREACH(inp, head, inp_hash) {
876     #ifdef INET6
877                             if ((inp->inp_vflag & INP_IPV4) == 0)
878                                     continue;
879     #endif
880                             if (inp->inp_faddr.s_addr == INADDR_ANY &&
881                                 inp->inp_laddr.s_addr == laddr.s_addr &&
882                                 inp->inp_lport == lport) {
883                                     /*
884                                      * Found.
885                                      */
886                                     return (inp);
887                             }
888                     }
889                     /*
890                      * Not found.
891                      */
892                     return (NULL);
```
_____ in6_pcb.c

877–892 This code block searches for a PCB entry whose local IPv4 address and port exactly match the parameters specified as function arguments. PCB entries which do not support IPv4 (the INP_IPV4 is not set) are skipped.

Listing 6-34

_____ in_pcb.c

```
893        } else {
894                struct inpcbporthead *porthash;
895                struct inpcbport *phd;
896                struct inpcb *match = NULL;
897                /*
898                 * Best fit PCB lookup.
899                 *
900                 * First see if this local port is in use by looking on the
901                 * port hash list.
902                 */
903                porthash = &pcbinfo->porthashbase[INP_PCBPORTHASH(lport,
904                    pcbinfo->porthashmask)];
905                LIST_FOREACH(phd, porthash, phd_hash) {
906                        if (phd->phd_port == lport)
907                                break;
908                }
909                if (phd != NULL) {
910                        /*
911                         * Port is in use by one or more PCBs. Look for best
912                         * fit.
913                         */
914                        LIST_FOREACH(inp, &phd->phd_pcblist, inp_portlist) {
915                                wildcard = 0;
916        #ifdef INET6
917                                if ((inp->inp_vflag & INP_IPV4) == 0)
918                                        continue;
919                                if ((inp->inp_vflag & INP_IPV6) != 0)
920                                        wildcard += INP_LOOKUP_MAPPED_PCB_COST;
921        #endif
922                                if (inp->inp_faddr.s_addr != INADDR_ANY)
923                                        wildcard++;
924                                if (inp->inp_laddr.s_addr != INADDR_ANY) {
925                                        if (laddr.s_addr == INADDR_ANY)
926                                                wildcard++;
927                                        else if (inp->inp_laddr.s_addr != laddr.s_addr)
928                                                continue;
929                                } else {
930                                        if (laddr.s_addr != INADDR_ANY)
931                                                wildcard++;
932                                }
933                                if (wildcard < matchwild) {
934                                        match = inp;
935                                        matchwild = wildcard;
936                                        if (matchwild == 0) {
937                                                break;
938                                        }
939                                }
940                        }
941                }
942                return (match);
943        }
944 }
945 #undef INP_LOOKUP_MAPPED_PCB_COST
```

_____ in_pcb.c

894–941 The code of lines 894–941 searches for the best match PCB entry compared to the port number specified as a function argument. In this process, we have to remember that there may be an IPv6 PCB waiting for a connection from IPv4 node, if the system allows IPv4 communication over an AF_INET6 socket.

In FreeBSD, IPv4 and IPv6 use the same PCB structure and every instance is linked in the same list. When we are chasing the list, we can see both IPv4 and IPv6 PCB entries. In this part, what we have to take care of is the wildcard address. With the support for IPv4-mapped IPv6 addresses, we can bind the same IPv4 address 0.0.0.0 for two different sockets: one for IPv4 and the other for IPv6. For example, we can bind 0.0.0.0 on an IPv4 socket, and we can also bind :: on an IPv6 socket later. The IPv6 socket must only accept IPv6 connections even if IPv4-mapped IPv6 addresses is allowed since IPv4 wildcard is assigned to another socket.

The code defines INP_LOOKUP_MAPPED_PCB_COST to add a weight to IPv6 sockets bound to ::. The wildcard variable indicates the cost to be selected as a result: The larger value has less chance to be chosen. The code adds INP_LOOKUP_MAPPED_PCB_COST to all PCB entries that allow IPv6 communication as well as IPv4 communication, so that such PCB entries will have less priority compared to IPv4-only PCB entries. If we find both IPv4 and IPv6 PCB entries bound to the IPv4 and IPv6 wildcard addresses, respectively, the former PCB entry is always chosen.

Figure 6-7 shows sample PCB entries. In the figure, there are three PCB entries in a node. The addresses and port numbers of the first entry are fixed. The local address is bound to 192.0.2.1 port 80 and the remote address is set to 192.0.2.10 port 3000. The second entry is bound to the IPv6 wildcard address with port 80. The last entry is bound to the IPv4 wildcard address with port 80. The #wildcard column indicates the value of the wildcard variable.

When a packet arrives at the local node 192.0.2.1 port 80 from a remote node 192.0.2.10 port 4000, the in_pcblookup_local() function is called to determine the PCB entry to which the packet should be delivered. The first entry does not match because the foreign port number is not equal to the incoming packet. The second entry matches to two columns: One is the local address (::) and the other is the foreign address. Note that the foreign port number is not taken into account until the foreign address matches exactly. The value of wildcard will be 2, but we add INP_LOOKUP_MAPPED_PCB_COST to wildcard if the PCB entry supports IPv6 connection. As a result, wildcard will be 6. The last entry matches two columns, one is the local address (0.0.0.0) and the other is the foreign address. The wildcard variable will be 2. Considering the result, the third PCB entry will be chosen for the incoming packet.

FIGURE 6-7

Local address	Local port	Foreign address	Foreign port	#wildcard
192.0.2.1	80	192.0.2.10	3000	–
::	80	*	*	6
0.0.0.0	80	*	*	2

Wildcard calculation when a packet from 192.0.2.10 *port 4000 arrives to* 192.0.2.1 *port 80.*

6.7.7   Search for a PCB Entry—`in6_pcblookup_hash()` Function

Function `in6_pcblookup_hash()` searches for a PCB entry based on the foreign and local addresses and port numbers. `in6_pcblookup_hash()` will search for the PCB entry that has the same local port number specified by the search key if `wildcard` is set to true.

Listing 6-35

_____in6_pcb.c
```
884     struct inpcb *
885     in6_pcblookup_hash(pcbinfo, faddr, fport_arg, laddr, lport_arg, wildcard, ifp)
886             struct inpcbinfo *pcbinfo;
887             struct sockaddr_in6 *faddr, *laddr;
888             u_int fport_arg, lport_arg;
889             int wildcard;
890             struct ifnet *ifp;
891     {
892             struct inpcbhead *head;
893             register struct inpcb *inp;
894             u_short fport = fport_arg, lport = lport_arg;
895             int faith;
896
897             if (faithprefix_p != NULL)
898                     faith = (*faithprefix_p)(&laddr->sin6_addr);
899             else
900                     faith = 0;
901
902             /*
903              * First look for an exact match.
904              */
905             head = &pcbinfo->hashbase[INP_PCBHASH(faddr->sin6_addr.s6_addr32[3]
    /* XXX */,
906                                                   lport, fport,
907                                                   pcbinfo->hashmask)];
908             LIST_FOREACH(inp, head, inp_hash) {
909                     if ((inp->inp_vflag & INP_IPV6) == 0)
910                             continue;
911                     if (SA6_ARE_ADDR_EQUAL(&inp->in6p_fsa, faddr) &&
912                         SA6_ARE_ADDR_EQUAL(&inp->in6p_lsa, laddr) &&
913                         inp->inp_fport == fport &&
914                         inp->inp_lport == lport) {
915                             /*
916                              * Found.
917                              */
918                             return (inp);
919                     }
920             }
```
_____in6_pcb.c

— *Line 905 is broken here for layout reasons. However, it is a single line of code.*

897–900 If the receiving node is acting as a FAITH translator [RFC3142], a transport relay between IPv4 and IPv6, function pointer `faithprefix_p` is non-NULL and checks whether the packet's destination matches the special prefix for translation. Since the FAITH service requires special packet handling on reception, the given local address is marked if the address is covered by the FAITH prefix.

> *Note*: Further details of the FAITH translator is beyond the scope of this book.

905–920 Variable `head` is set to the head of the hash table slot hashed on the local port `lport`, foreign port `fport`, and the foreign address `faddr`. The search examines every PCB entry stored at this slot. The search bypasses PCB entries that do not have the `INP_IPV6` flag set. The function returns the PCB entry that has the exact match on both the local and foreign endpoint information.

Listing 6-36

_____ in6_pcb.c
```
921             if (wildcard) {
922                     struct inpcb *local_wild = NULL;
923
924                     head = &pcbinfo->hashbase[INP_PCBHASH(INADDR_ANY, lport, 0,
925                                             pcbinfo->hashmask)];
926                     LIST_FOREACH(inp, head, inp_hash) {
927                             if ((inp->inp_vflag & INP_IPV6) == 0)
928                                     continue;
929                             if (SA6_IS_ADDR_UNSPECIFIED(&inp->in6p_fsa) &&
930                                 inp->inp_lport == lport) {
931                                     if (faith && (inp->inp_flags & INP_FAITH) == 0)
932                                             continue;
933                                     if (SA6_ARE_ADDR_EQUAL(&inp->in6p_lsa, laddr))
934                                             return (inp);
935                                     else if (SA6_IS_ADDR_UNSPECIFIED(&inp->in6p_lsa))
936                                             local_wild = inp;
937                             }
938                     }
939                     return (local_wild);
940             }
941
942             /*
943              * Not found.
944              */
945             return (NULL);
946     }
```
_____ in6_pcb.c

921–930 Variable `head` is set to the head of the hash table slot hashed on the local port only if `wildcard` is specified. In this case the search returns the best match entry. The search bypasses PCB entries that do not have the `INP_IPV6` flag set.

931–932 The search excludes PCB entries that are used by the FAITH translation service.

933–934 The function returns the PCB that has the matching local address.

935–936 A PCB entry is marked as a candidate if the local address of the PCB entry is the unspecified address. The candidate PCB entry is returned if there is no PCB that has the exact match on the local address.

945 The search fails if there is neither an exact match nor a candidate PCB entry.

6.7.8 Search for IPv4-mapped PCB—`in_pcblookup_hash()` Function

A socket bound to an IPv4-mapped IPv6 address can accept packets from IPv4 nodes. IPv4 packets are received by the `ip_input()` function and passed to the proper transport-layer input function. To decide the PCB entry to which the received packet should be delivered, a node calls `in_pcblookup_hash()` to find a proper PCB entry that matches the received packet. If the identified PCB is associated with an `AF_INET6` socket that allows IPv4 communication, the data will be delivered to the application on the socket.

The basic procedure of `in_pcblookup_hash()` is the same as the `in6_pcblookup_hash()` function discussed in Section 6.7.7. We will only discuss IPv6-related parts of `in_pcblookup_hash()` in this section.

Listing 6-37

_____in6_pcb.c
```
947    /*
948     * Lookup PCB in hash list.
949     */
950    struct inpcb *
951    in_pcblookup_hash(pcbinfo, faddr, fport_arg, laddr, lport_arg, wildcard,
952                      ifp)
953            struct inpcbinfo *pcbinfo;
954            struct in_addr faddr, laddr;
955            u_int fport_arg, lport_arg;
956            int wildcard;
957            struct ifnet *ifp;
958    {
959            struct inpcbhead *head;
960            register struct inpcb *inp;
961            u_short fport = fport_arg, lport = lport_arg;
962
963            /*
964             * First look for an exact match.
965             */
966            head = &pcbinfo->hashbase[INP_PCBHASH(faddr.s_addr, lport, fport, pcbinfo
       ->hashmask)];
967            LIST_FOREACH(inp, head, inp_hash) {
968    #ifdef INET6
969                    if ((inp->inp_vflag & INP_IPV4) == 0)
970                            continue;
971    #endif
972                    if (inp->inp_faddr.s_addr == faddr.s_addr &&
973                        inp->inp_laddr.s_addr == laddr.s_addr &&
974                        inp->inp_fport == fport &&
975                        inp->inp_lport == lport) {
976                            /*
977                             * Found.
978                             */
979                            return (inp);
980                    }
981            }
```
_____in6_pcb.c
— *Line 966 is broken here for layout reasons. However, it is a single line of code.*

969–981 Lines 969–981 search for the exact-match PCB entry for the specified parameters passed as function arguments. PCB entries with `INP_IPV4` cleared are used only for IPv6 communication and are skipped.

Listing 6-38

_____in6_pcb.c
```
982            if (wildcard) {
983                    struct inpcb *local_wild = NULL;
984    #if defined(INET6)
985                    struct inpcb *local_wild_mapped = NULL;
986    #endif /* defined(INET6) */
987
988                    head = &pcbinfo->hashbase[INP_PCBHASH(INADDR_ANY, lport, 0,
       pcbinfo->hashmask)];
```

```
989                             LIST_FOREACH(inp, head, inp_hash) {
990      #ifdef INET6
991                                     if ((inp->inp_vflag & INP_IPV4) == 0)
992                                             continue;
993      #endif
994                                     if (inp->inp_faddr.s_addr == INADDR_ANY &&
995                                         inp->inp_lport == lport) {
996                                             if (ifp && ifp->if_type == IFT_FAITH &&
997                                                 (inp->inp_flags & INP_FAITH) == 0)
998                                                     continue;
999                                             if (inp->inp_laddr.s_addr == laddr.s_addr)
1000                                                    return (inp);
1001                                            else if (inp->inp_laddr.s_addr == INADDR_ANY) {
1002     #if defined(INET6)
1003                                                    if (INP_CHECK_SOCKAF(inp->inp_socket,
1004                                                                         AF_INET6))
1005                                                            local_wild_mapped = inp;
1006                                                    else
1007     #endif /* defined(INET6) */
1008                                                            local_wild = inp;
1009                                            }
1010                                    }
1011                            }
1012     #if defined(INET6)
1013                    if (local_wild == NULL)
1014                            return (local_wild_mapped);
1015     #endif /* defined(INET6) */
1016                    return (local_wild);
1017            }
1018
1019            /*
1020             * Not found.
1021             */
1022            return (NULL);
1023    }
```

———————————in6_pcb.c

— Line 988 is broken here for layout reasons. However, it is a single line of code.

985 Lines 982–1017 search for the PCB entry whose local port matches the given local port. `local_wild_mapped` will hold the PCB entry which is bound to the wildcard address either for IPv4 or IPv6, if such an entry exists and no other preferable entry is found.

991–992 All PCB entries that are used only for IPv6 connections are skipped.

1003–1005 If the local address of the candidate PCB entry is the wildcard address (`INADDR_ANY`), the address family of the corresponding socket is examined. Either `local_wild_mapped` (in case of `AF_INET6`) or `local_wild` (`AF_INET` case) is set to the matching entry, depending on the address family.

1013–1016 This part of the code ensures that if both `AF_INET` and `AF_INET6` wildcard sockets for the same port exist, the best match for a given port and an IPv4 address is the former, regardless of the ordering of these sockets in the hash list. In other words, an incoming IPv4 packet to this port will be preferably delivered to the `AF_INET` socket.

6.7.9 Detach an IPv6 PCB—`in6_pcbdetach()` Function

A PCB entry is removed from the various PCB-related lists and is then deleted when its associated socket is closed. Figure 6-8 illustrates the call flow involved in the `close()` socket function that reaches `in6_pcbdetach()` function to perform the PCB cleanup work.

FIGURE 6-8

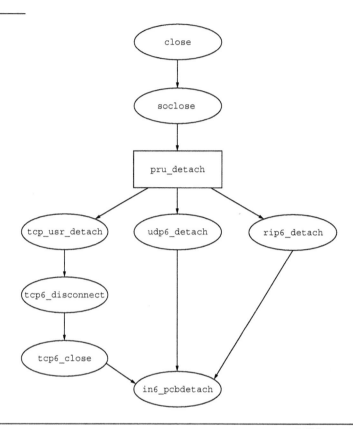

Call flow to `in6_pcbdetach()`.

Listing 6-39

<code>in6_pcb.c</code>

```
412    in6_pcbdetach(inp)
413            struct inpcb *inp;
414    {
415            struct socket *so = inp->inp_socket;
416            struct inpcbinfo *ipi = inp->inp_pcbinfo;
417
....
422            inp->inp_gencnt = ++ipi->ipi_gencnt;
423            in_pcbremlists(inp);
424            sotoinpcb(so) = 0;
425            sofree(so);
426
427            if (inp->in6p_inputopts) /* Free all received options. */
428                    m_freem(inp->in6p_inputopts->head); /* this is safe */
429            ip6_freepcbopts(inp->in6p_outputopts);
430            ip6_freemoptions(inp->in6p_moptions);
431            if (inp->in6p_route.ro_rt)
432                    rtfree(inp->in6p_route.ro_rt);
433            /* Check and free IPv4 related resources in case of mapped addr */
434            if (inp->inp_options)
435                    (void)m_free(inp->inp_options);
436            ip_freemoptions(inp->inp_moptions);
```

```
437
438                 inp->inp_vflag = 0;
439                 zfreei(ipi->ipi_zone, inp);
440         }
```
── in6_pcb.c

422–423 Function `in_pcbremlists()` removes the specified PCB entry from the various PCB lists.

424–425 The `sotoinpcb()` macro retrieves the `so_pcb` pointer that references the given PCB and clears this reference because the `sofree()` function removes the socket from the system and releases the memory occupied by the socket.

427–432 All of the options are freed at this point. `in6p_inputopts` used to keep packet options extracted from a received packet in older versions of the implementation, but it is not used any longer and is always NULL. `ip6_outputopts` may contain extension headers or other packet options associated with outgoing packets sent from the socket. `in6p_moptions` may contain multicast-related packet options. `in6p_route` is a cached route for reaching the foreign endpoint.

434–436 `inp_options` is a placeholder to contain IPv4 options for outgoing IPv4 packets set via the IP_OPTIONS. For an AF_INET6 socket, however, this is always NULL, since it does not allow IPv4-specific socket options even if it allows IPv4 communication using IPv4-mapped IPv6 addresses. The same note applies to the `inp_moptions` member, but the call to `ip_freemoptions()` is safe since it performs nothing if the argument is NULL.

438–439 Function `zfreei()` will release the memory that was allocated by function `zalloci()` (Section 6.7.1).

6.7.10 Control Message Signaling—`in6_pcbnotify()` Function

The local endpoint may receive control messages from its communicating peer or an intermediate node to the peer in the form of ICMPv6 messages. In addition, the local node may sometimes send a control message up to transport layers for some exceptional notifications. In many cases, these messages are delivered to the `in6_pcbnotify()` function via protocol-dependent control functions and then onto the application that owns the PCB.

`in6_pcbnotify()`, shown below, examines the given list of PCB, determines which entries need the control message, and notifies the associated application of the arrival of the message.

Listing 6-40
── in6_pcb.c

```
574    void
575    in6_pcbnotify(head, dst, fport_arg, src, lport_arg, cmd, cmdarg, notify)
576            struct inpcbhead *head;
577            struct sockaddr *dst;
578            const struct sockaddr *src;
579            u_int fport_arg, lport_arg;
580            int cmd;
581            void *cmdarg;
582            void (*notify) __P((struct inpcb *, int));
583    {
584            struct inpcb *inp, *ninp;
585            struct sockaddr_in6 sa6_src, *sa6_dst;
```

```
586              u_short fport = fport_arg, lport = lport_arg;
587              u_int32_t flowinfo;
588              int errno, s;
```
_____ in6_pcb.c

575–582 Function `in6_pcbnotify()` takes eight input parameters: `head` is a pointer to the head element of the PCB list of a specific upper layer protocol; `dst` and `fport_arg` are the remote address and port number to which the packet was destined but triggered this notification; `src` and `lport_arg` are the address and port number of the local endpoint; `cmd` is one of the protocol-independent commands listed in Table 6-5; `cmdarg` carries additional information for the command; `notify` is a function pointer to the command-specific callback function.

Listing 6-41
_____ in6_pcb.c

```
590              if ((unsigned)cmd > PRC_NCMDS || dst->sa_family != AF_INET6)
591                      return;
592
593              sa6_dst = (struct sockaddr_in6 *)dst;
594              if (SA6_IS_ADDR_UNSPECIFIED(sa6_dst))
595                      return;
```
_____ in6_pcb.c

590–595 This function returns without further action if the command is out of range or if the Destination address is not an IPv6 address. An unspecified Destination address is invalid and causes the function to return.

TABLE 6-5
_____

Message type	Description
PRC_MSGSIZE	A packet is too big to be forwarded.
PRC_HOSTDEAD	A destination host is down.
PRC_UNREACH_NET	There is no route for the destination network.
PRC_UNREACH_HOST	There is no route for the destination host.
PRC_UNREACH_PROTOCOL	The upper layer protocol is not supported.
PRC_UNREACH_PORT	There is no process waiting at the port.
PRC_UNREACH_SRCFAIL	Source routing failed.
PRC_REDIRECT_HOST	A better route for the host exists.
PRC_TIMXCEED_INTRANS	A packet Hop limit exceeded.
PRC_TIMXCEED_REASS	A packet cannot be reassembled due to timeout.
PRC_PARAMPROB	An incorrect header field.

Notification commands.

Listing 6-42
                                                                            ——————————in6_pcb.c
```
597                /*
598                 * note that src can be NULL when we get notify by local fragmentation.
599                 */
600                sa6_src = (src == NULL) ? sa6_any : *(const struct sockaddr_in6 *)src;
601                flowinfo = sa6_src.sin6_flowinfo;
```
                                                                            ——————————in6_pcb.c

600–601 A NULL `src` is treated as the unspecified address and `sa6_src` is initialized accordingly; otherwise `sa6_src` is initialized to the value of `src`. Despite the code comment, `src` should not be non-NULL since the caller passes a dummy structure when the source address is unavailable (e.g., see Section 6.8.5).

Listing 6-43
                                                                            ——————————in6_pcb.c
```
603                /*
604                 * Redirects go to all references to the destination,
605                 * and use in6_rtchange to invalidate the route cache.
606                 * Dead host indications: also use in6_rtchange to invalidate
607                 * the cache, and deliver the error to all the sockets.
608                 * Otherwise, if we have knowledge of the local port and address,
609                 * deliver only to that socket.
610                 */
611                if (PRC_IS_REDIRECT(cmd) || cmd == PRC_HOSTDEAD) {
612                        fport = 0;
613                        lport = 0;
614                        bzero((caddr_t)&sa6_src.sin6_addr, sizeof(sa6_src.sin6_addr));
615
616                        if (cmd != PRC_HOSTDEAD)
617                                notify = in6_rtchange;
618                }
```
                                                                            ——————————in6_pcb.c

611–617 The `PRC_IS_REDIRECT()` macro determines whether a given command belongs to a set of redirect commands. For IPv6, however, `PRC_REDIRECT_HOST` is the only possible command, since network Redirect for IPv4 turned out to be ineffective and was not introduced in IPv6. For a redirect command, the callback function is set to `in6_rtchange()` that flushes cached route in PCB entries for the Destination address. Flushing the cached route triggers the IPv6 layer to retrieve the latest routing information on the next packet transmission and restores the updated route into the PCB.

For a redirect command or `PRC_REDIRECT_HOST`, the local port, remote port, and local address information are cleared to enable notification delivery to multiple PCBs. The redirect information will be delivered to all PCB entries that are communicating with the node that has sent the redirect message.

Listing 6-44
                                                                            ——————————in6_pcb.c
```
619                errno = inet6ctlerrmap[cmd];
```
                                                                            ——————————in6_pcb.c

619 The `inet6ctlerrmap[]` array maps protocol-dependent commands to system error codes. Table 6-6 outlines the command to error code mapping. Any command not listed in the table is mapped to 0, which means no error.

TABLE 6-6

Message type	Description
PRC_MSGSIZE	EMSGSIZE
PRC_HOSTDEAD	EHOSTDOWN
PRC_UNREACH_NET	EHOSTUNREACH
PRC_UNREACH_HOST	EHOSTUNREACH
PRC_UNREACH_PROTOCOL	ECONNREFUSED
PRC_UNREACH_PORT	ECONNREFUSED
PRC_UNREACH_SRCFAIL	EHOSTUNREACH
PRC_PARAMPROB	ENOPROOOPT

Notification commands to system error code mapping table.

Listing 6-45

———in6_pcb.c

```
620              s = splnet();
621              for (inp = LIST_FIRST(head); inp != NULL; inp = ninp) {
622                      ninp = LIST_NEXT(inp, inp_list);
623
624                      if ((inp->inp_vflag & INP_IPV6) == 0)
625                              continue;
626
627                      /*
628                       * If the error designates a new path MTU for a destination
629                       * and the application (associated with this socket) wanted to
630                       * know the value, notify. Note that we notify for all
631                       * disconnected sockets if the corresponding application
632                       * wanted. This is because some UDP applications keep sending
633                       * sockets disconnected.
634                       * XXX: should we avoid to notify the value to TCP sockets?
635                       */
636                      if (cmd == PRC_MSGSIZE && (inp->inp_flags & IN6P_MTU) != 0 &&
637                          (SA6_IS_ADDR_UNSPECIFIED(&inp->in6p_fsa) ||
638                           SA6_ARE_ADDR_EQUAL(&inp->in6p_fsa, sa6_dst))) {
639                              ip6_notify_pmtu(inp, (struct sockaddr_in6 *)dst,
640                                              (u_int32_t *)cmdarg);
641                      }
642
643                      /*
644                       * Detect if we should notify the error. If no source and
645                       * destination ports are specifed, but non-zero flowinfo and
646                       * local address match, notify the error. This is the case
647                       * when the error is delivered with an encrypted buffer
648                       * by ESP. Otherwise, just compare addresses and ports
649                       * as usual.
650                       */
651                      if (lport == 0 && fport == 0 && flowinfo &&
652                          inp->inp_socket != NULL &&
653                          flowinfo == (inp->in6p_flowinfo & IPV6_FLOWLABEL_MASK) &&
654                          SA6_ARE_ADDR_EQUAL(&inp->in6p_lsa, &sa6_src))
655                              goto do_notify;
656                      else if (!SA6_ARE_ADDR_EQUAL(&inp->in6p_fsa, sa6_dst) ||
657                          inp->inp_socket == 0 ||
658                          (lport && inp->inp_lport != lport) ||
659                          (!SA6_IS_ADDR_UNSPECIFIED(&sa6_src) &&
```

```
660                             !SA6_ARE_ADDR_EQUAL(&inp->in6p_lsa, &sa6_src)) ||
661                             (fport && inp->inp_fport != fport))
662                             continue;
663
664             do_notify:
665                     if (notify)
666                             (*notify)(inp, errno);
667             }
668         splx(s);
669     }
```
—— *in6_pcb.c*

621–622 The `for` loop checks all the PCB entries and determines whether each entry should receive the notification message.

624–625 A PCB that is not meant for IPv6 communication will not receive any IPv6-related notifications.

636–640 If the command is `PRC_MSGSIZE`, the PCB entry is configured to receive Path MTU messages with the `IPV6_RECVPATHMTU` socket option, and the PCB has the matching remote address against `sa6_dst` (including "wildcard" matching), then function `ip6_notify_pmtu()` is called to notify the corresponding application of this message. It creates a CMSG data block that contains a path MTU information structure (`ip6_mtuinfo{}`) and sends the message to the socket with empty data. As noted in the comment, this message is also delivered to PCBs that do not specify the foreign address. This is different from conventional notification rule in the socket API, but is the deliberate behavior as specified in [RFC3542].

651–655 If `lport` and `fport` are 0, meaning unavailable or unknown, but the flow label matches that stored in the PCB and the local address matches, this message is delivered to the corresponding socket. As commented in the code, this helps when an encrypted packet in ESP is dropped with an ICMPv6 error: Since the ICMPv6 input routine does not try to decrypt the erroneous packet (see Listing 4-27), the upper layer information is not passed to this function. Using the flow label for identifying the corresponding PCB may help detect the error at the application using IPsec.

656–662 A PCB that has a mismatched foreign address, or a mismatched local address or a mismatched port number is not notified of the error message.

654–667 If a notification is necessary and the callback function is available, the function is called and the corresponding error code, if any, is sent to the PCB entry.

6.7.11 Flush PCB Cached Route—`in6_rtchange()` Function

A PCB entry has a cached route for reaching the Destination address. The route to the destination is dynamic and is subject to change due to a change of network topology. This means the route that was cached in the PCB may have stale route information. A packet that was sent to the destination using an invalid route will result in ICMPv6 error messages originated by some node in the network. The ICMPv6 error message is delivered to the `in6_pbnotify()` function and will subsequently reach the `in6_rtchange()` function to flush a cache route from a given PCB entry.

Listing 6-46

_____ in6_pcb.c

```
866     void
867     in6_rtchange(inp, errno)
868             struct inpcb *inp;
869             int errno;
870     {
871             if (inp->in6p_route.ro_rt) {
872                     rtfree(inp->in6p_route.ro_rt);
873                     inp->in6p_route.ro_rt = 0;
874                     /*
875                      * A new route can be allocated the next time
876                      * output is attempted.
877                      */
878             }
879     }
```

_____ in6_pcb.c

867–879 inp is a pointer to a PCB entry that may have a stale cached route. errno is a system error code associated with the received ICMPv6 error message. However, errno is not used in this function.

in6p_route.ro_rt is the cache for a route if it references a non-NULL location. Function rtfree() is called to remove the route reference and delete the route if the reference count is zero. in6p_route.ro_rt is reset to 0 to indicate the PCB does not have a route cache. The IP layer will resolve a new route the next time when a packet is sent to the same destination, which will be stored into the PCB route cache.

6.7.12   Retrieve Peer Address—in6_setpeeraddr() Function

The getpeername() system call will invoke the in6_mapped_peeraddr() function that may subsequently invoke in6_setpeeraddr(). The in6_setpeeraddr() function is an IPv6 equivalent of the in_setpeeraddr() function for IPv4. In IPv6, however, we cannot call in6_setpeeraddr() directly because the peer address may be an IPv4-mapped IPv6 address. We will clarify this point shortly.

Listing 6-47

_____ in6_pcb.c

```
488     int
489     in6_setpeeraddr(so, nam)
490             struct socket *so;
491             struct sockaddr **nam;
492     {
493             int s;
494             struct inpcb *inp;
495             register struct sockaddr_in6 *sin6;
496
497             /*
498              * Do the malloc first in case it blocks.
499              */
500             MALLOC(sin6, struct sockaddr_in6 *, sizeof(*sin6), M_SONAME, M_WAITOK);
501             bzero((caddr_t)sin6, sizeof (*sin6));
502             sin6->sin6_family = AF_INET6;
503             sin6->sin6_len = sizeof(struct sockaddr_in6);
504
505             s = splnet();
506             inp = sotoinpcb(so);
507             if (!inp) {
```

```
508                     splx(s);
509                     free(sin6, M_SONAME);
510                     return EINVAL;
511             }
512             sin6->sin6_port = inp->inp_fport;
513             sa6_copy_addr(&inp->in6p_fsa, sin6);
514             splx(s);
515
....
517             in6_clearscope(&sin6->sin6_addr);
....
519
520             *nam = (struct sockaddr *)sin6;
521             return 0;
522     }
```
_____ in6_pcb.c

500–503 A memory block is allocated to store the peer address.

506–521 The port number and address of the remote peer is copied from the PCB of the socket
to the newly allocated storage. In KAME, each IPv6 address has associated scope zone
ID stored in it, which should not be exposed to applications (see Section 2.9.3). Function
in6_clearscope() is called to remove the embedded zone ID from the address.

The in6_mapped_peeraddr() function returns the address of the remote peer
according to the IP protocol version. The returned peer address is a normal IPv6 address
for an AF_INET6 socket that operates TCP over IPv6. An AF_INET6 TCP listening socket
can also accept a TCP connection request from an IPv4 peer. In that case, the returned peer
address is an IPv4-mapped IPv6 address and the AF_INET6 socket operates TCP over IPv4.

Listing 6-48
_____ in6_pcb.c

```
544     int
545     in6_mapped_peeraddr(struct socket *so, struct sockaddr **nam)
546     {
547             struct  inpcb *inp = sotoinpcb(so);
548             int     error;
549
550             if (inp == NULL)
551                     return EINVAL;
552             if ((inp->inp_vflag & (INP_IPV4 | INP_IPV6)) == INP_IPV4) {
553                     error = in_setpeeraddr(so, nam);
554                     if (error == 0)
555                             in6_sin_2_v4mapsin6_in_sock(nam);
556             } else
557             /* scope issues will be handled in in6_setpeeraddr(). */
558             error = in6_setpeeraddr(so, nam);
559
560             return error;
561     }
```
_____ in6_pcb.c

552–555 The connection operates over IPv4 if the PCB variable inp_vflag has the INP_IPV4
flag set and the INP_IPV6 flag cleared. In this case, the peer address is retrieved
as an IPv4 address by the in_setpeeraddr() function, which is then passed to
in6_sin_2_v4mapsin6_in_sock() to convert the IPv4 address to an IPv4-mapped
IPv6 address.

558 Otherwise, the in6_setpeeraddr() function is called to retrieve peer address, which
is a normal IPv6 address.

6.7.13   Retrieve Local Address—`in6_setsockaddr()` Function

Function `in6_setsockaddr()` and function `in6_mapped_sockaddr()` are called as a result of the `getsockname()` system call on a socket.

`in6_setsockaddr()` is equivalent to `in_setsockaddr()` for IPv4, which is used to retrieve the local address from a PCB entry. Similar to why the `in6_mapped_peeraddr()` function is a wrapper function for the `in6_setpeeraddr()`, `in6_mapped_sockaddr()` is a wrapper function for `in6_setsockaddr()`.

Listing 6-49

```
                                                                         in6_pcb.c
452    int
453    in6_setsockaddr(so, nam)
454            struct socket *so;
455            struct sockaddr **nam;
456    {
457            int s;
458            register struct inpcb *inp;
459            register struct sockaddr_in6 *sin6;
460
461            /*
462             * Do the malloc first in case it blocks.
463             */
464            MALLOC(sin6, struct sockaddr_in6 *, sizeof *sin6, M_SONAME, M_WAITOK);
465            bzero(sin6, sizeof *sin6);
466            sin6->sin6_family = AF_INET6;
467            sin6->sin6_len = sizeof(*sin6);
468
469            s = splnet();
470            inp = sotoinpcb(so);
471            if (!inp) {
472                    splx(s);
473                    free(sin6, M_SONAME);
474                    return EINVAL;
475            }
476            sin6->sin6_port = inp->inp_lport;
477            sa6_copy_addr(&inp->in6p_lsa, sin6);
478            splx(s);
479
....
481            in6_clearscope(&sin6->sin6_addr);
....
483
484            *nam = (struct sockaddr *)sin6;
485            return 0;
486    }
                                                                         in6_pcb.c
```

453 The `in6_setsockaddr()` function has two parameters: `so` is a pointer to the socket from which the local address is being retrieved; `nam` is used to store the retrieved local address for the caller.

464–467 A memory block to store the local address information is allocated.

470–477 The local port number and the local IPv6 address is copied to the newly allocated memory block.

481 In KAME, each IPv6 address has associated scope zone ID stored in it, which should be hidden from applications. Function `in6_clearscope()` is called to remove the embedded zone ID from the address.

Listing 6-50

in6_pcb.c

```
524    int
525    in6_mapped_sockaddr(struct socket *so, struct sockaddr **nam)
526    {
527            struct  inpcb *inp = sotoinpcb(so);
528            int     error;
529
530            if (inp == NULL)
531                    return EINVAL;
532            if ((inp->inp_vflag & (INP_IPV4 | INP_IPV6)) == INP_IPV4) {
533                    error = in_setsockaddr(so, nam);
534                    if (error == 0)
535                            in6_sin_2_v4mapsin6_in_sock(nam);
536            } else {
537                    /* scope issues will be handled in in6_setsockaddr(). */
538                    error = in6_setsockaddr(so, nam);
539            }
540
541            return error;
542    }
```

in6_pcb.c

532–539 If the PCB has only `INP_IPV4` flag set, that is, the socket is used only for communication over IPv4, function `in_setsockaddr()` is called to retrieve the local IPv4 address. Function `in6_sin_2_v4mapsin6_in()` converts the returned IPv4 address to an IPv4-mapped IPv6 address. For a non IPv4-only socket, function `in6_setsockaddr()` is simply called to get the local IPv6 address.

6.8   TCP-over-IPv6

In general, TCP packet processing is the same whether it is over IPv4 or over IPv6. One main difference is in the processing of packets that are either originated from or sent to IPv4-mapped IPv6 addresses. A user can bind an IPv4-mapped IPv6 address on an IPv6 socket to accept IPv4 connections; a user can use an IPv6 socket to connect to an IPv4 address using the IPv4-mapped IPv6 address; in addition, a user can bind an unspecified address to an IPv6 socket to accept both IPv4 and IPv6 incoming connections. Other characteristics of IPv6 addresses, specifically, anycasting or address lifetimes, have also some implications in TCP operation. In this section, we will mainly focus on such differences in TCP processing between IPv6 and IPv4. The basic TCP protocol operation is outside the scope of this book.

6.8.1   TCP-over-IPv6 Instance of `ip6protosw{}`

Table 6-7 shows the values of the various fields in the TCP-over-IPv6 instance of the `ip6protosw{}` structure. `ip6protosw{}` is discussed in Section 3.5.3.

6.8.2   TCP Output

The TCP output routine is shared by IPv4 and IPv6. The majority of the code is the same for both protocols. IPv6 specific processing code is conditionally guarded by the `INET6` preprocessor macro.

TABLE 6-7

ip6protosw{} *fields*	*Value*	*Description*
pr_type	SOCK_STREAM	Reliable byte stream service
pr_domain	&inet6domain	Indicates the IPv6 protocol
pr_protocol	IPPROTO_TCP (6)	Protocol number (6)
pr_flags	PR_CONNREQUIRED|PR_WANTRCVD	Indicates the protocol is connection-oriented and needs data receive notification
pr_input	tcp6_input()	Input function
pr_output	0	Not used
pr_ctlinput	tcp6_ctlinput()	Control messages input processing
pr_ctloutput	tcp_ctloutput()	Control messages output processing
pr_init	0	Not used (shared with TCP over IPv4)
pr_fasttimo	0	Not used (shared with TCP over IPv4)
pr_slowtimo	0	Not used (shared with TCP over IPv4)
pr_drain	0	Not used (shared with TCP over IPv4)
pr_usrreqs	tcp6_usrreqs	User request dispatch functions

TCP instance of the ip6protosw{} *structure.*

Listing 6-51

tcp_output.c

```
114     int
115     tcp_output(tp)
116             register struct tcpcb *tp;
117     {
 ....
142     #ifdef INET6
143             isipv6 = (tp->t_inpcb->inp_vflag & INP_IPV6) != 0;
144     #endif
```

tcp_output.c

143 The isipv6 variable indicates whether the given TCP connection is used for IPv6 communication. tp is a pointer to the TCP protocol control block (TCPCB), which has a back pointer to the Internet PCB. As previously described, the PCB structure contains an IP version flag. The PCB is created for IPv6 communication if the version flag is set to INP_IPV6 (e.g., see Listing 6-76). In this case, isipv6 is set to true.

Listing 6-52

tcp_output.c

```
420             /*
421              * Before ESTABLISHED, force sending of initial options
422              * unless TCP set not to do any options.
423              * NOTE: we assume that the IP/TCP header plus TCP options
424              * always fit in a single mbuf, leaving room for a maximum
425              * link header, i.e.
426              *      max_linkhdr + sizeof (struct tcpiphdr) + optlen <= MCLBYTES
```

```
427                 */
428                 optlen = 0;
429     #ifdef INET6
430             if (isipv6)
431                     hdrlen = sizeof (struct ip6_hdr) + sizeof (struct tcphdr);
432             else
433     #endif
434             hdrlen = sizeof (struct tcpiphdr);
```

(Option length calculation)

──tcp_output.c

429–434 The code performs the default header length computation for the outgoing packet. The TCP header is the same for IPv4 and IPv6. However, the header length must account for the appropriate IP header size. TCP options to be inserted to the outgoing segment are prepared, and the total length of the options is set to optlen.

Listing 6-53

──tcp_output.c

```
550     #ifdef INET6
551             if (isipv6)
552                     ipoptlen = ip6_optlen(tp->t_inpcb);
553             else
554     #endif
555             {
556             if (tp->t_inpcb->inp_options) {
557                     ipoptlen = tp->t_inpcb->inp_options->m_len -
558                                     offsetof(struct ipoption, ipopt_list);
559             } else {
560                     ipoptlen = 0;
561             }
562             }
563     #ifdef IPSEC
564             ipoptlen += ipsec_hdrsiz_tcp(tp);
565     #endif
566
567             /*
568              * Adjust data length if insertion of options will
569              * bump the packet length beyond the t_maxopd length.
570              * Clear the FIN bit because we cut off the tail of
571              * the segment.
572              */
573             if (len + optlen + ipoptlen > tp->t_maxopd) {
574                     /*
575                      * If there is still more to send, don't close the connection.
576                      */
577                     flags &= ~TH_FIN;
578                     len = tp->t_maxopd - optlen - ipoptlen;
579                     sendalot = 1;
580             }
```

──tcp_output.c

550–562 An important issue to consider when operating the same transport protocol over different IP layers is the MTU size. The size of the transport layer payload is derived from the MTU size, the size of the transport layer header options, and the size of the IP layer options or the total size of IPv6 extension headers. ip6_optlen() calculates the total size of extension headers that would be attached to packets sent on the socket so that the TCP output routine can identify an appropriate MTU size that would not cause IP fragmentation.

573–580 tp->t_maxopd stores the possible maximum length of IP-layer options (extension
headers in case of IPv6), TCP options, and TCP data so that the total packet length would
not exceed the path MTU size. This value is adjusted every time the path MTU size for
this connection is updated due to an ICMPv6 Too Big message, considering the fixed size
of the IPv6 and TCP headers (the lower part of Figure 6-9). If the len bytes of given TCP
data with the option length would exceed the value of tp->t_maxopd, some trailing
portion of the data is omitted for this transmission. It will be included in the next TCP
segment. The complete packet for this transmission that should fit the known path to the
peer is shown in the center of Figure 6-9.

Listing 6-54

———tcp_output.c
```
583     #ifdef INET6
584             if (max_linkhdr + hdrlen > MCLBYTES)
585                     panic("tcphdr too big");
586     #else
587             if (max_linkhdr + hdrlen > MHLEN)
588                     panic("tcphdr too big");
589     #endif
```
———tcp_output.c

583–589 The total size for the IPv6 and the TCP headers must not exceed the size of the mbuf
cluster. The IPv4 header is limited to 64 bytes including the IP options due to the 4-bit
Internet Header Length (IHL) field that specifies the size of the IPv4 header in 4-byte units.
The length of TCP header is also limited to 64 bytes due to the 4-bit Data Offset field. As
such, a maximum 128-byte sized buffer is big enough to hold both IPv4 and TCP headers.
MHLEN is defined as follows.

```
#define MLEN (MSIZE - sizeof(struct m_hdr)) /* normal data len */
#define MHLEN (MLEN - sizeof(struct pkthdr)) /* data len w/pkthdr */
```

MSIZE is defined as 256 in FreeBSD system. The sizes of m_hdr{} structure and
pkthdr{} structure are 20 and 24 bytes, respectively. As a result, MHLEN will be 212 and

FIGURE 6-9

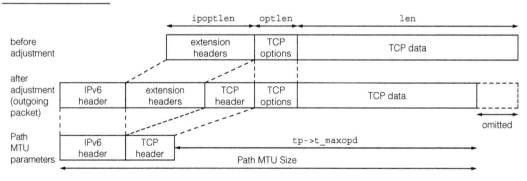

Adjusting TCP data segment for the known path MTU size.

is large enough to hold the IPv4 header, the TCP header, as well as the link-layer header. The situation differs in IPv6. Since the IPv6 header is fixed at 40 bytes, the combined IPv6 and TCP header lengths will be a maximum of 104 bytes. Even with the inclusion of the link-layer header, the length will never exceed MCLBYTES. Therefore, the check has little benefit for validation purposes. In fact, the check is redundant because the output code will allocate an mbuf cluster when sending TCP data if necessary as we will show in the following listing.

Listing 6-55

```
                                                                    tcp_output.c
619                         MGETHDR(m, M_DONTWAIT, MT_HEADER);
620                         if (m == NULL) {
621                                 error = ENOBUFS;
622                                 goto out;
623                         }
624     #ifdef INET6
625                         if (MHLEN < hdrlen + max_linkhdr) {
626                                 MCLGET(m, M_DONTWAIT);
627                                 if ((m->m_flags & M_EXT) == 0) {
628                                         m_freem(m);
629                                         error = ENOBUFS;
630                                         goto out;
631                                 }
632                         }
633     #endif
                                                                    tcp_output.c
```

619–633 A new mbuf cluster is allocated for the packet header if the total size of the IPv6 header, the TCP header, and the link-layer header exceeds MHLEN. tcp_output() frees the allocated mbuf and returns an ENOBUFS error if the memory allocation failed.

Listing 6-56

```
                                                                    tcp_output.c
682     #ifdef INET6
683             if (isipv6) {
684                     ip6 = mtod(m, struct ip6_hdr *);
685                     th = (struct tcphdr *)(ip6 + 1);
686                     tcp_fillheaders(tp, ip6, th);
687             } else
688     #endif /* INET6 */
689             {
690                     ip = mtod(m, struct ip *);
691                     ipov = (struct ipovly *)ip;
692                     th = (struct tcphdr *)(ip + 1);
693                     /* this picks up the pseudo header (w/o the length) */
694                     tcp_fillheaders(tp, ip, th);
695             }
                                                                    tcp_output.c
```

683–686 The pointers are initialized to reference the IPv6 and TCP headers if the mbuf allocation succeeded. Function tcp_fillheaders() fills the contents of the headers, which are necessary for the TCP checksum calculation. tcp_fillheaders() will be discussed in Section 6.8.3.

Listing 6-57

_____tcp_output.c

```
804     #ifdef INET6
805             if (isipv6)
806                     /*
807                      * ip6_plen is not need to be filled now, and will be filled
808                      * in ip6_output.
809                      */
810                     th->th_sum = in6_cksum(m, IPPROTO_TCP, sizeof(struct ip6_hdr),
811                                             sizeof(struct tcphdr) + optlen + len);
812             else
813     #endif /* INET6 */
```

_____tcp_output.c

805–811 `in6_cksum()` is a generic function that calculates checksum for ICMPv6, for TCP
over IPv6 and for UDP over IPv6. As discussed in Section 6.3, TCP checksum computation
includes information from the IPv6 header, which was why `tcp_fillheaders()` was
called on line 694 to fill in the upper layer pseudo header.

Listing 6-58

_____tcp_output.c

```
925     #ifdef INET6
926         if (isipv6) {
927                 /*
928                  * we separately set hoplimit for every segment, since the
929                  * user might want to change the value via setsockopt.
930                  * Also, desired default hop limit might be changed via
931                  * Neighbor Discovery.
932                  */
933                 ip6->ip6_hlim = in6_selecthlim(tp->t_inpcb,
934                                         tp->t_inpcb->in6p_route.ro_rt ?
935                                         tp->t_inpcb->in6p_route.ro_rt->rt_ifp
936                                         : NULL);
937
    ....
949                 if (!ip6_setpktaddrs(m, &tp->t_inpcb->in6p_lsa,
950                                     &tp->t_inpcb->in6p_fsa)) {
951                         m_freem(m);
952                         error = ENOBUFS;
953                         goto out;
954                 }
955                 error = ip6_output(m,
956                         tp->t_inpcb->in6p_outputopts,
957                         &tp->t_inpcb->in6p_route,
958                         (so->so_options & SO_DONTROUTE), NULL, NULL
    ....
960                         , tp->t_inpcb
    ....
962                         );
963         } else
964     #endif /* INET6 */
```

_____tcp_output.c

933–936 The Hop Limit field of the IPv6 header is chosen by one of the following three ways
in the `in6_selecthlim()` function.

- By explicitly specifying the value via the `IPV6_UNICAST_HOPS` socket option
  (Section 7.2.5).

- By using the Hop Limit stored in the per interface data structure (nd_ifinfo{}) if there is no value explicitly specified and the outgoing interface is known(*). Information stored in nd_ifinfo{} is obtained from Router Advertisements (see Section 5.13.3).

- By using the system-wide default value if there is no router advertising Hop Limit.

(*) Technically, this code is not necessarily correct since the interface associated with the cached route may not be the real outgoing interface.

949–954 tp->t_inpcb is a back pointer to the PCB structure associated with the given TCP connection. in6p_lsa and in6p_fsa are the local and remote addresses of this connection, respectively. ip6_setpktaddrs() sets the packet Source and Destination addresses in the form of the sockaddr_in6{} structure that are part of the mbuf tag so that the scope zone ID can be preserved. ip6_output() is called to send the packet once all necessary packet parameters are set.

955–962 The parameters passed to ip6_output() are fields from the PCB structure that is referenced by t_inpcb.

The second parameter is a pointer to the ip6_pktopts{} structure that maintains packet options such as IPv6 extension headers to be inserted in the outgoing packet. An application can specify the packet options via corresponding socket options (see Section 7.4.3).

The third parameter is the cached route for the destination address of this connection. The fourth parameter is effectively always 0, since ip6_output() does not care about the only possible flag, SO_DONTROUTE (see Section 3.13.3).

The fifth parameter is a pointer to the multicast option. Since TCP does not use multicast address, the multicast option is not specified.

If the sixth parameter were non-NULL, ip6_output() would store a pointer to the outgoing interface structure in it so that the caller can update per-interface statistics counter. Since the management information base for TCP [RFC4022] does not have per-interface counters, this parameter can simply be NULL in this call.

6.8.3 Initializing Headers—`tcp_fillheaders()` Function

The tcp_fillheaders() function fills in both the IPv6 and TCP header fields.

Listing 6-59

tcp_subr.c
```
265     void
266     tcp_fillheaders(tp, ip_ptr, tcp_ptr)
267             struct tcpcb *tp;
268             void *ip_ptr;
269             void *tcp_ptr;
270     {
271             struct inpcb *inp = tp->t_inpcb;
272             struct tcphdr *tcp_hdr = (struct tcphdr *)tcp_ptr;
273
274     #ifdef INET6
275             if ((inp->inp_vflag & INP_IPV6) != 0) {
276                     struct ip6_hdr *ip6;
```

```
277
278                             ip6 = (struct ip6_hdr *)ip_ptr;
279                             ip6->ip6_flow = (ip6->ip6_flow & ~IPV6_FLOWINFO_MASK) |
280                                     (inp->in6p_flowinfo & IPV6_FLOWINFO_MASK);
281                             ip6->ip6_vfc = (ip6->ip6_vfc & ~IPV6_VERSION_MASK) |
282                                     (IPV6_VERSION & IPV6_VERSION_MASK);
283                             ip6->ip6_nxt = IPPROTO_TCP;
284                             ip6->ip6_plen = sizeof(struct tcphdr);
285                             ip6->ip6_src = inp->in6p_laddr;
286                             ip6->ip6_dst = inp->in6p_faddr;
287                             tcp_hdr->th_sum = 0;
288                     } else
289     #endif

    (IPv4 processing)

316     }
                                                                      _____tcp_subr.c
```

266–288 `tcp_fillheaders()` takes three input parameters: `tp` is a pointer to the TCPCB of the connection to which the output packets belong; `ip_ptr` points to the beginning of the IPv6 header; `tcp_ptr` points to the start of the TCP header. The pointer to the generic PCB entry can be retrieved from the `t_inpcb` member. For a TCP over IPv6 connection, the `ip_ptr` pointer is cast to a pointer to the `ip6_hdr{}` structure. The flow label and the IPv6 Source and Destination addresses are set using information stored in the PCB. The IP version number is set to `IPV6_VERSION` (6) and the Next Header field is set to `IPPROTO_TCP`. The packet length (`ip6_plen`) is temporarily set to the size of the TCP header and will be updated by the `ip6_output()` function. The checksum value is set to 0 and will be calculated by the `in6_cksum()` function later.

6.8.4 TCP Input—`tcp6_input()` and `tcp_input()` Functions

The TCP input function is defined as `tcp6_input()` that is invoked from `ip6_input()` function via the `inet6sw[]` array defined in `in6_proto.c` (see Section 3.5.3).

Listing 6-60

```
                                                                      _____tcp_input.c
310     #ifdef INET6
311     int
312     tcp6_input(mp, offp, proto)
313             struct mbuf **mp;
314             int *offp, proto;
315     {
316             register struct mbuf *m = *mp;
317             struct in6_ifaddr *ia6;
318
319             IP6_EXTHDR_CHECK(m, *offp, sizeof(struct tcphdr), IPPROTO_DONE);
320
321             /*
322              * draft-itojun-ipv6-tcp-to-anycast
323              * better place to put this in?
324              */
325             ia6 = ip6_getdstifaddr(m);
326             if (ia6 && (ia6->ia6_flags & IN6_IFF_ANYCAST)) {
327                     struct ip6_hdr *ip6;
328
329                     ip6 = mtod(m, struct ip6_hdr *);
330                     icmp6_error(m, ICMP6_DST_UNREACH, ICMP6_DST_UNREACH_ADDR,
331                             (caddr_t)&ip6->ip6_dst - (caddr_t)ip6);
332                     return IPPROTO_DONE;
```

```
333                 }
334
335                 tcp_input(m, *offp);
336                 return IPPROTO_DONE;
337         }
338    #endif
```
——— tcp_input.c

312–314 `tcp6_input()` has three parameters: `mp` is a pointer to the mbuf that contains a
TCP segment to be processed; `offp` is a pointer to an offset from the start of the IPv6
header to the start of the TCP header of this packet; `proto` holds the protocol number,
which is 6 (`IPPROTO_TCP`) in this case.

319 `IP6_EXTHDR_CHECK()` ensures that all incoming data from the IPv6 header to the TCP
header is located in a contiguous memory region. This is important because we will cast
the memory address of the TCP header to a pointer of the `tcphdr{}` structure and access
the structure members directly.

325–333 The `ip6_getdstifaddr()` function retrieves the interface address structure corresponding to the packet's destination address. If it has the `IN6_IFF_ANYCAST` flag,
the packet is destined for an anycast address of the receiving node. The packet cannot
be processed further in the case of TCP, because it would cause a responding packet
whose source address is the anycast address, which is prohibited by the specification
(Section 2.2). This implementation returns a Destination Unreachable ICMPv6 error message to the packet source in this case in order to provide a hint for diagnosing the problem.
This is not part of the standard protocol specification, but was proposed as an individual
Internet Draft by a KAME developer [TCP-TO-ANYCAST].

335–336 Similar to the output processing, the majority of the TCP input packet processing is identical between IPv4 and IPv6. The rest of the processing is performed in the
`tcp_input()` function.

Listing 6-61
——— tcp_input.c
```
340    void
341    tcp_input(m, off0)
342            register struct mbuf *m;
343            int off0;
344    {
```
——— tcp_input.c

340–343 `tcp_input()` takes two parameters. `m` is a pointer to the mbuf that contains the IPv6
packet. `off0` is the offset from the start of the IP header to the start of the TCP header.

Listing 6-62
——— tcp_input.c
```
384    #ifdef INET6
385            isipv6 = (mtod(m, struct ip *)->ip_v == 6) ? 1 : 0;
386    #endif
```
——— tcp_input.c

385 `isipv6` indicates whether the TCP packet is carried over IPv6. The value of `isipv6` is
set according to the IP protocol version retrieved from the IP header.

Listing 6-63

```
                                                                                    tcp_input.c
391                     if (isipv6) {
392                             /* IP6_EXTHDR_CHECK() is already done at tcp6_input() */
393                             ip6 = mtod(m, struct ip6_hdr *);
394                             tlen = sizeof(*ip6) + ntohs(ip6->ip6_plen) - off0;
395     #ifdef TCP_ECN
396                             iptos = (ntohl(ip6->ip6_flow) >> 20) & 0xff;
397     #endif
398                             if (in6_cksum(m, IPPROTO_TCP, off0, tlen)) {
399                                     tcpstat.tcps_rcvbadsum++;
400                                     goto drop;
401                             }
402                             th = (struct tcphdr *)((caddr_t)ip6 + off0);
403
404                             /*
405                              * Be proactive about unspecified IPv6 address in source.
406                              * As we use all-zero to indicate unbounded/unconnected pcb,
407                              * unspecified IPv6 address can be used to confuse us.
408                              *
409                              * Note that packets with unspecified IPv6 destination is
410                              * already dropped in ip6_input.
411                              */
412                             if (IN6_IS_ADDR_UNSPECIFIED(&ip6->ip6_src)) {
413                                     /* XXX stat */
414                                     goto drop;
415                             }
416                     } else {
                                                                                    tcp_input.c
```

391–415 For a TCP packet carried over IPv6, variables `ip6` and `th` point to the IPv6 header and the TCP header, respectively. `tlen` is the length of the TCP segment including the TCP header. A packet is dropped if it fails the checksum validation or if the source address is the unspecified address.

Listing 6-64

```
                                                                                    tcp_input.c
470                     /*
471                      * Check that TCP offset makes sense,
472                      * pull out TCP options and adjust length.            XXX
473                      */
474                     off = th->th_off << 2;
475                     if (off < sizeof(struct tcphdr) || off > tlen) {
476                             tcpstat.tcps_rcvbadoff++;
477                             goto drop;
478                     }
479                     tlen -= off;    /* tlen is used instead of ti->ti_len */
480                     if (off > sizeof(struct tcphdr)) {
481                             if (isipv6) {
482                                     IP6_EXTHDR_CHECK(m, off0, off, );
483                                     ip6 = mtod(m, struct ip6_hdr *);
484                                     th = (struct tcphdr *)((caddr_t)ip6 + off0);
485                             } else {
    .... [processing for IPv4]
496                             }
497                             optlen = off - sizeof(struct tcphdr);
498                             optp = (u_char *)(th + 1);
499                     }
                                                                                    tcp_input.c
```

474–479 A TCP segment may contain TCP options between the header and the actual data segment. The starting address of the data portion is `th_off` set as an offset from the head of the TCP header in 4-byte units. The packet is invalid and is discarded if the offset is smaller than the size of the TCP header or if the offset is larger than the total size of the TCP segment. For a valid packet, `tlen` is updated to discount the size of TCP options.

480–498 The TCP segment contains options if the offset is larger than the size of the TCP header. Macro `IP6_EXTHDR_CHECK()` is called to ensure the options are located in a contiguous memory area of the first mbuf. The pointers `ip6` and `th` are reinitialized afterward.

Note: Pointer adjustment is actually unnecessary, since the `IP6_EXTHDR_CHECK()` we are describing does not modify the mbuf.

Listing 6-65

tcp_input.c

```
540             /*
541              * Locate pcb for segment.
542              */
543     findpcb:
 ....
564     #ifdef INET6
565                 if (isipv6)
566                     inp = in6_pcblookup_hash(&tcbinfo,
567                                         &src_sa6, th->th_sport,
568                                         &dst_sa6, th->th_dport,
569                                         1, m->m_pkthdr.rcvif);
570                 else
571     #endif /* INET6 */

 .... [find IPv4 PCB]
```

tcp_input.c

566–569 The `in6_pcblookup_hash()` function locates the PCB entry that matches the search criteria specified by the function parameters.

Listing 6-66

tcp_input.c

(part of processing block when a TCP connection is LISTEN state)

```
783     #ifdef INET6
784             /*
785              * If deprecated address is forbidden,
786              * we do not accept SYN to deprecated interface
787              * address to prevent any new inbound connection from
788              * getting established.
789              * When we do not accept SYN, we send a TCP RST,
790              * with deprecated source address (instead of dropping
791              * it).  We compromise it as it is much better for peer
792              * to send a RST, and RST will be the final packet
793              * for the exchange.
794              *
795              * If we do not forbid deprecated addresses, we accept
796              * the SYN packet.  RFC2462 does not suggest dropping
797              * SYN in this case.
798              * If we decipher RFC2462 5.5.4, it says like this:
799              * 1. use of deprecated addr with existing
800              *    communication is okay - "SHOULD continue to be
801              *    used"
802              * 2. use of it with new communication:
```

```
803                  *      (2a) "SHOULD NOT be used if alternate address
804                  *           with sufficient scope is available"
805                  *      (2b) nothing mentioned otherwise.
806                  * Here we fall into (2b) case as we have no choice in
807                  * our source address selection - we must obey the peer.
808                  *
809                  * The wording in RFC2462 is confusing, and there are
810                  * multiple description text for deprecated address
811                  * handling - worse, they are not exactly the same.
812                  * I believe 5.5.4 is the best one, so we follow 5.5.4.
813                  */
814                 if (isipv6 && !ip6_use_deprecated) {
815                         struct in6_ifaddr *ia6;
816
817                         if ((ia6 = ip6_getdstifaddr(m)) &&
818                             (ia6->ia6_flags & IN6_IFF_DEPRECATED)) {
819                                 tp = NULL;
820                                 rstreason = BANDLIM_RST_OPENPORT;
821                                 goto dropwithreset;
822                         }
823                 }
824     #endif
                                                                      ─────tcp_input.c
```

814–823 An address becomes a deprecated address and is marked with the
IN6_IFF_DEPRECATED flag when its preferred lifetime expires (see Section 2.10.1). While
[RFC2462] requires that "new communications" should generally not be initiated with a deprecated source address, this implementation accepts (or rejects with RST) an incoming SYN
segment to a deprecated address unless the global variable ip6_use_deprecated is set
to 0 (see also Section 3.12.1). This causes the corresponding ACK segment, with the source
address being the deprecated address. In fact, a revised version of the RFC [RFC2462BIS]
clarifies that responding to a TCP SYN segment is not regarded as initiating a "new communication"; an implementation should respond to such a SYN segment by default.

Listing 6-67

```
                                                                      ─────tcp_input.c
```
(part of processing block when a TCP connection is in the LISTEN state)
```
845                         if (m->m_flags & (M_BCAST|M_MCAST))
846                                 goto drop;
847                         if (isipv6) {
848                                 if (IN6_IS_ADDR_MULTICAST(&ip6->ip6_dst) ||
849                                     IN6_IS_ADDR_MULTICAST(&ip6->ip6_src))
850                                         goto drop;
851                         } else {
```
(processing for IPv4)
```
857                         }
                                                                      ─────tcp_input.c
```

845–850 A multicast address cannot be used for TCP connections. The packet is discarded if
the packet (stored in mbuf) is delivered with a link-level broadcast or multicast address.
The packet is also discarded if either the source or the destination address contains a
multicast address. The check for the source IPv6 address is redundant, though, since it
was done in ip6_input() (Listing 3-19).

The remaining TCP input processing for IPv6 is identical to that for IPv4.

6.8.5 TCP Control Input—`tcp6_ctlinput()` Function

The TCP stack may receive notification messages from the lower layers of the protocol stack due to connection errors, change in the network path, and operation status change in the network interface. Figure 6-10 illustrates the various notification messages that can reach the TCP stack and the call flow of these notifications. The notification handler is the `tcp6_ctlinput()` function when TCP operates over IPv6.

Listing 6-68
——tcp_subr.c
```
1101    void
1102    tcp6_ctlinput(cmd, sa, d)
1103            int cmd;
1104            struct sockaddr *sa;
1105            void *d;
1106    {
```
——tcp_subr.c

FIGURE 6-10

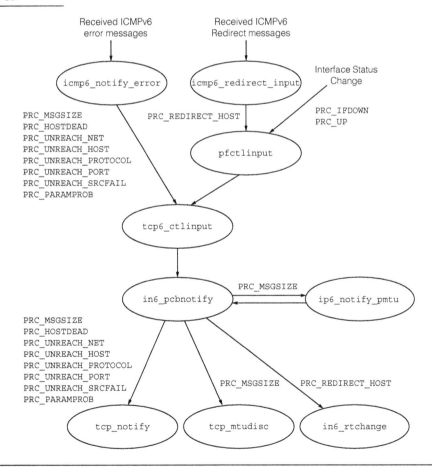

TCP over IPv6 notification call flow.

1102–1105 cmd is a protocol-independent notification code described in Table 6-5. sa is a pointer to the destination address of the packet that caused this notification. d is a pointer to transfer ICMPv6 error information if the notification is generated from ICMPv6.

Listing 6-69
```
                                                                       tcp_subr.c
1107          struct tcphdr th;
1108          void (*notify) __P((struct inpcb *, int)) = tcp_notify;
1109          struct ip6_hdr *ip6;
1110          struct mbuf *m;
1111          struct ip6ctlparam *ip6cp = NULL;
1112          const struct sockaddr_in6 *sa6_src = NULL;
1113          int off;
1114          struct tcp_portonly {
1115                  u_int16_t th_sport;
1116                  u_int16_t th_dport;
1117          } *thp;
1118
1119          if (sa->sa_family != AF_INET6 ||
1120              sa->sa_len != sizeof(struct sockaddr_in6))
1121                  return;
                                                                       tcp_subr.c
```

1119–1121 The function simply returns if either the Destination address is not an IPv6 address or the structure has the wrong size. Normally this would not happen except for a bug.

Listing 6-70
```
                                                                       tcp_subr.c
1123          if (cmd == PRC_QUENCH)
1124                  notify = tcp_quench;
1125          else if (cmd == PRC_MSGSIZE)
1126                  notify = tcp_mtudisc;
1127          else if (!PRC_IS_REDIRECT(cmd) &&
1128                  ((unsigned)cmd > PRC_NCMDS || inet6ctlerrmap[cmd] == 0))
1129                  return;
                                                                       tcp_subr.c
```

1123–1124 The callback function invoked from the in6_pcbnotify() function is set according to the notification command. The PRC_QUENCH notification can only happen on reception of an ICMP Source Quench message, which is impossible for ICMPv6 since it does not define this message (see the note for Listing 3-96).

1125–1126 The PRC_MSGSIZE notification is typically generated on receiving an ICMPv6 Packet Too Big message and informs a TCP endpoint that the Path MTU size has decreased in the path to its peer. In this case, function tcp_mtudisc() will be called to adjust the TCP segment size appropriately. It will adjust the maxopd member of the TCP control block taking into account the notified MTU size (see Figure 6-9).

1127–1129 For other notification commands, only the redirect notification and those that have a corresponding system error code listed in Table 6-5 are handled; the rest of the commands are ignored.

Listing 6-71

———————————————————————————————————*tcp_subr.c*

```
1131                /* if the parameter is from icmp6, decode it. */
1132                if (d != NULL) {
1133                        ip6cp = (struct ip6ctlparam *)d;
1134                        m = ip6cp->ip6c_m;
1135                        ip6 = ip6cp->ip6c_ip6;
1136                        off = ip6cp->ip6c_off;
1137                        sa6_src = ip6cp->ip6c_src;
1138                } else {
1139                        m = NULL;
1140                        ip6 = NULL;
1141                        off = 0;             /* fool gcc */
1142                        sa6_src = &sa6_any;
1143                }
```

———————————————————————————————————*tcp_subr.c*

1132–1137 d should be set to the `ip6ctlparam{}` structure if this notification is generated due to an ICMPv6 error or in `ip6_output()` for transmitting a large packet that does not fit in the outgoing link (Listing 3-173). As for the former case, we saw the relationship between the ICMPv6 error message and the `ip6ctlparam{}` structure in Figure 4-24: `ip6cp->ip6c_m` points to the mbuf that contains the packet that triggered the notification; `ip6cp->ip6c_ip6` points to the starting address of the IPv6 header of the erroneous packet; `ip6cp->ip6c_off` is the offset length from the IPv6 header to the head of the upper layer header (the TCP header of the packet in this case). sa6_src points to `ip6cp->ip6c_src`, the source address of the packet. Note that these values may be NULL when the notification is generated in `ip6_output()`.

1139–1142 d will be NULL if the notification is not due to an ICMPv6 error message. In this case we cannot get any information on the source of the notification, and the unspecified address will be used as an argument to the notification callback.

Listing 6-72

———————————————————————————————————*tcp_subr.c*

```
1145                if (ip6) {
1146                        struct in_conninfo inc;
1147                        /*
1148                         * XXX: We assume that when IPV6 is non NULL,
1149                         * M and OFF are valid.
1150                         */
1151
1152                        /* check if we can safely examine src and dst ports */
1153                        if (m->m_pkthdr.len < off + sizeof(*thp))
1154                                return;
1155
1156                        bzero(&th, sizeof(th));
1157                        m_copydata(m, off, sizeof(*thp), (caddr_t)&th);
1158
1159                        in6_pcbnotify(&tcb, sa, th.th_dport,
1160                            (struct sockaddr *)ip6cp->ip6c_src,
1161                            th.th_sport, cmd, NULL, notify);
```

———————————————————————————————————*tcp_subr.c*

1145–1161 If the original erroneous packet contained in the ICMPv6 packet is large enough to cover the TCP header, the TCP source and destination port numbers are extracted from the original packet. This information is passed to the `in6_pcbnotify()` function to identify the corresponding PCB and perform the necessary PCB-related processing according to the notification command.

Listing 6-73

———tcp_subr.c

```
1163                    bzero(&inc, sizeof(inc));
1164                    inc.inc_fport = th.th_dport;
1165                    inc.inc_lport = th.th_sport;
1166                    inc.inc6_fsa.sin6_family = inc.inc6_lsa.sin6_family = AF_INET6;
1167                    inc.inc6_fsa.sin6_len = inc.inc6_lsa.sin6_len =
1168                            sizeof(struct sockaddr_in6);
1169                    sa6_copy_addr((struct sockaddr_in6 *)sa, &inc.inc6_fsa);
1170                    sa6_copy_addr(ip6cp->ip6c_src, &inc.inc6_lsa);
1171                    inc.inc_isipv6 = 1;
1172                    syncache_unreach(&inc, &th);
```
———tcp_subr.c

1163–1172 Receiving an ICMPv6 error message indicates the erroneous packet was discarded. It may help to purge the corresponding cache entry of syncache [Lem02], a special framework for managing incomplete passive TCP connections, while avoiding the TCP SYN flooding attacks. The `syncache_unreach()` function searches the cache for an entry that matches the dropped packet, and, if found, accumulates the error count for the entry. When the counter exceeds a threshold, the entry is removed from the cache.

Listing 6-74

———tcp_subr.c

```
1173            } else
1174                    in6_pcbnotify(&tcb, sa, 0, (const struct sockaddr *)sa6_src,
1175                            0, cmd, NULL, notify);
1176    }
```
———tcp_subr.c

1174–1175 The notification is sent to the TCP stack with the Destination address and the Source address (which may be the unspecified address if information about the original packet is unavailable).

Table 6-8 summarizes the notification commands that can reach the TCP stack and the associated callback functions for these notifications.

6.8.6   TCP User Requests

Any socket operation related to a TCP connection is dispatched to the corresponding function initialized in the `tcp6_usrreqs` variable. `tcp6_usrreqs` is an instance of the `pr_usrreqs{}` structure, which defines the dispatch functions for handling the varaious socket operations that originate from the user applications. Some of the TCP socket dispatch functions are shared between TCP-over-IPv4 and TCP-over-IPv6. Table 6-9 lists the content of `tcp6_usrreqs`.

Accept TCP Connections—tcp6_usr_accept() Function

A call to the `accept()` system call on a TCP listening socket will reach `tcp6_usr_accept()`, which retrieves from the internal connection queues an established TCP connection

TABLE 6-8

TCP over IPv6	Callback function
PRC_IFDOWN	tcp_notify()
PRC_IFUP	tcp_notify()
PRC_MSGSIZE	tcp_mtudisc()
PRC_HOSTDEAD	tcp_notify()
PRC_UNREACH_NET	tcp_notify()
PRC_UNREACH_HOST	tcp_notify()
PRC_UNREACH_PROTOCOL	tcp_notify()
PRC_UNREACH_PORT	tcp_notify()
PRC_UNREACH_SRCFAIL	tcp_notify()
PRC_REDIRECT_HOST	in6_rtchange()
PRC_PARAMPROB	tcp_notify()

Notifications and TCP callback functions.

TABLE 6-9

pr_usrreqs	tcp6_usrreqs	Shared with IPv4
pru_abort	tcp_usr_abort	Yes
pru_accept	tcp6_usr_accept	No
pru_attach	tcp_usr_attach (calls tcp_attach)	Yes
pru_bind	tcp6_usr_bind	No
pru_connect	tcp6_usr_connect	No
pru_control	in6_control	No
pru_detach	tcp_usr_detach	Yes
pru_disconnect	tcp_usr_disconnect	Yes
pru_listen	tcp6_usr_listen	No
pru_peeraddr	in6_mapped_peeraddr	No
pru_rcvd	tcp_usr_rcvd	Yes
pru_rcvoob	tcp_usr_rcvoob	Yes
pru_send	tcp_usr_send	Yes
pru_shutdown	tcp_usr_shutdown	Yes
pru_sockaddr	in6_mapped_sockaddr	No

TCP instance of the pr_usrreqs{} *structure.*

that was initiated from a peer and returns the associated socket back to the calling application.

Listing 6-75

```
184     #define COMMON_END(req) out: TCPDEBUG2(req); splx(s); return error; goto out
....
440     static int
441     tcp6_usr_accept(struct socket *so, struct sockaddr **nam)
442     {
443             int s = splnet();
444             int error = 0;
445             struct inpcb *inp = sotoinpcb(so);
446             struct tcpcb *tp = NULL;
....
449             if (so->so_state & SS_ISDISCONNECTED) {
450                     error = ECONNABORTED;
451                     goto out;
452             }
453             if (inp == 0) {
454                     splx(s);
455                     return (EINVAL);
456             }
457             tp = intotcpcb(inp);
....
459             in6_mapped_peeraddr(so, nam);
460             COMMON_END(PRU_ACCEPT);
461     }
```

440–460 The `tcp6_usr_accept()` function has two parameters: `so` is a pointer to the socket associated with the TCP connection; `nam` is used to store the peer address for the caller. `tcp6_usr_accept()` returns an error of `ECONNABORTED` if the socket is in the disconnected state. Otherwise, it calls function `in6_mapped_peeraddr()` (Section 6.7.12) to retrieve the peer address. The `COMMON_END()` macro (shown at line 184) defines a general code block for concluding a request handler function.

Attach PCB—tcp_attach() Function

The `tcp_attach()` function allocates a PCB and attaches the PCB to the given TCP socket. This function is called from the `tcp_usr_attach()` function, which is a shared function between TCP-over-IPv4 and TCP-over-IPv6.

Listing 6-76

```
1032    static int
1033    tcp_attach(so, p)
1034            struct socket *so;
1035            struct proc *p;
1036    {
1037            register struct tcpcb *tp;
1038            struct inpcb *inp;
1039            int error;
1040    #ifdef INET6
1041            int isipv6 = INP_CHECK_SOCKAF(so, AF_INET6) != NULL;
1042    #endif
1043
```

```
1044                if (so->so_snd.sb_hiwat == 0 || so->so_rcv.sb_hiwat == 0) {
1045                        error = soreserve(so, tcp_sendspace, tcp_recvspace);
1046                        if (error)
1047                                return (error);
1048                }
1049                error = in_pcballoc(so, &tcbinfo, p);
1050                if (error)
1051                        return (error);
1052                inp = sotoinpcb(so);
1053        #ifdef INET6
1054                if (isipv6) {
1055                        inp->inp_vflag |= INP_IPV6;
1056                        inp->in6p_hops = -1;    /* use kernel default */
1057                }
1058                else
1059        #endif
1060                inp->inp_vflag |= INP_IPV4;
1061                tp = tcp_newtcpcb(inp);
1062                if (tp == 0) {
1063                        int nofd = so->so_state & SS_NOFDREF;    /* XXX */
1064
1065                        so->so_state &= ~SS_NOFDREF;    /* don't free the socket yet */
1066        #ifdef INET6
1067                        if (isipv6)
1068                                in6_pcbdetach(inp);
1069                        else
1070        #endif
1071                                in_pcbdetach(inp);
1072                        so->so_state |= nofd;
1073                        return (ENOBUFS);
1074                }
1075                tp->t_state = TCPS_CLOSED;
1076                return (0);
1077        }
```
——— *tcp_usrreq.c*

1041 INP_CHECK_SOCKAF() checks if the socket is an IPv6 socket (i.e., the address family is AF_INET6) and sets the variable isipv6 accordingly.

1049–1052 The PCB associated with the given socket is allocated by the in_pcballoc() function.

1053–1060 The PCB variable inp_vflag will have the INP_IPV6 flag set if isipv6 is true, which indicates that this PCB can be used for an IPv6 connection. The PCB will also have the INP_IPV4 flag set at line 1060, which means the socket that was created with the AF_INET6 address family can be used for both IPv4 and IPv6 communication by default. The INP_IPV6 flag is cleared when an IPv4-mapped IPv6 address is set as the local address of the socket because such a socket can only communicate with IPv4 nodes. Similarly, the INP_IPV4 flag is cleared when a normal IPv6 address is set as the local address of the socket. In this case, the socket can be used only for IPv6 communication. Setting the local address as the unspecified address allows an IPv6 socket to accept both IPv4 and IPv6 connection requests.

These operations on the flags will be described in the next subsection.

Bind Local Address of—tcp6_usr_bind() Function

The tcp6_usr_bind() function is called as a result of the bind() system call on a TCP socket. tcp6_usr_bind() assigns a local address to a TCP socket.

Listing 6-77

_____tcp_usrreq.c

```
174     #define COMMON_START()    TCPDEBUG0; \
175                               do { \
176                                           if (inp == 0) { \
177                                                   splx(s); \
178                                                   return EINVAL; \
179                                           } \
180                                           tp = intotcpcb(inp); \
181                                           TCPDEBUG1(); \
182                               } while(0)
  ....
219     static int
220     tcp6_usr_bind(struct socket *so, struct sockaddr *nam, struct proc *p)
221     {
222             int s = splnet();
223             int error = 0;
224             struct inpcb *inp = sotoinpcb(so);
225             struct tcpcb *tp;
226             struct sockaddr_in6 *sin6p;
227
228             COMMON_START();
229
230             /*
231              * Must check for multicast addresses and disallow binding
232              * to them.
233              */
234             sin6p = (struct sockaddr_in6 *)nam;
235             if (sin6p->sin6_family == AF_INET6 &&
236                 IN6_IS_ADDR_MULTICAST(&sin6p->sin6_addr)) {
237                     error = EAFNOSUPPORT;
238                     goto out;
239             }
240             inp->inp_vflag &= ~INP_IPV4;
241             inp->inp_vflag |= INP_IPV6;
242             if ((inp->inp_flags & IN6P_IPV6_V6ONLY) == 0) {
243                     if (SA6_IS_ADDR_UNSPECIFIED(sin6p))
244                             inp->inp_vflag |= INP_IPV4;
245                     else if (IN6_IS_ADDR_V4MAPPED(&sin6p->sin6_addr)) {
246                             struct sockaddr_in sin;
247
248                             in6_sin6_2_sin(&sin, sin6p);
249                             inp->inp_vflag |= INP_IPV4;
250                             inp->inp_vflag &= ~INP_IPV6;
251                             error = in_pcbbind(inp, (struct sockaddr *)&sin, p);
252                             goto out;
253                     }
254             }
255             error = in6_pcbbind(inp, nam, p);
256             if (error)
257                     goto out;
258             COMMON_END(PRU_BIND);
259     }
```

_____tcp_usrreq.c

220 The `tcp6_usr_bind()` function has three parameters: `so` is a socket pointer; `nam` contains the address information to be set as the local address of the given socket; `p` is a pointer to the calling process.

228 `COMMON_START()` is a macro containing a common block code for the general initialization of TCP user request functions. As defined in lines 174–182, the `COMMON_START()` macro checks the validity of the PCB pointer (`inp`) and initializes the TCP control block pointer `tp` using the `intotcpcb()` macro.

234–239 A multicast address cannot be set as a local address for a TCP connection. The function returns an error of EAFNOSUPPORT if the nam parameter contains an IPv6 multicast address.

240–255 Which network protocols (IPv4 and/or IPv6) can be used on this socket is determined by the IN6P_IPV6_V6ONLY flag set or cleared on the PCB and the type of addresses given with the bind() system call as follows:

- If the IN6P_IPV6_V6ONLY flag is set, only IPv6 communication is allowed, regardless of the specified address (lines 240–241).

- Otherwise, if the given address is the IPv6 unspecified address, communication over both IPv4 and IPv6 is allowed (lines 243–244).

- If the IN6P_IPV6_V6ONLY flag is not set and the specified address is an IPv4-mapped IPv6 address, only IPv4 communication is allowed (lines 246–253).

The INP_IPV4 and INP_IPV6 flags are set or cleared on the PCB accordingly. In addition, if this socket only allows IPv4 communication, in_pcbbind() is called to set the local IPv4 address. Note that the socket address structure containing the IPv4-mapped IPv6 address is converted in the form of sockaddr_in{} structure by in6_sin6_2_sin() beforehand. For other cases, in6_pcbbind() is called to set the local IPv6 address.

Some server applications wait for connection requests from both IPv4 and IPv6 nodes by binding an unspecified address on the listening socket. This mechanism only requires minimal changes to the existing IPv4 server programs, thereby helping application transition. As will be discussed in Section 7.2.3, however, a node deploying this mechanism must carefully configure security settings such as packet filter rules; otherwise, this transition mechanism may increase security risks.

Note: NetBSD did not allow binding of an IPv4-mapped IPv6 address to an IPv6 socket when IPv6 support was added. At the beginning binding the unspecified address was the only way to use IPv4-mapped IPv6 addresses. The latest version of NetBSD supports binding IPv4-mapped IPv6 addresses to IPv6 sockets. OpenBSD does not support IPv4-mapped IPv6 addresses at all because of the potential security threats.

Initiate TCP Connection—Active Open

The tcp6_usr_connect() function is called as a result of the connect() system call on a TCP socket. tcp6_usr_connect() assigns the remote address for a given socket and initiates the connection request to the peer.

Listing 6-78
```
                                                                    tcp_usrreq.c
340     static int
341     tcp6_usr_connect(struct socket *so, struct sockaddr *nam, struct proc *p)
342     {
```

```
343              int s = splnet();
344              int error = 0;
345              struct inpcb *inp = sotoinpcb(so);
346              struct tcpcb *tp;
347              struct sockaddr_in6 *sin6p;
348
349              COMMON_START();
350
351              /*
352               * Must disallow TCP ``connections'' to multicast addresses.
353               */
354              sin6p = (struct sockaddr_in6 *)nam;
355              if (sin6p->sin6_family == AF_INET6
356                  && IN6_IS_ADDR_MULTICAST(&sin6p->sin6_addr)) {
357                      error = EAFNOSUPPORT;
358                      goto out;
359              }
360
361              if (IN6_IS_ADDR_V4MAPPED(&sin6p->sin6_addr)) {
362                      struct sockaddr_in sin;
363
364                      if ((inp->inp_flags & IN6P_IPV6_V6ONLY) != 0) {
365                              error = EINVAL;
366                              goto out;
367                      }
368
369                      in6_sin6_2_sin(&sin, sin6p);
370                      inp->inp_vflag |= INP_IPV4;
371                      inp->inp_vflag &= ~INP_IPV6;
372                      if ((error = tcp_connect(tp, (struct sockaddr *)&sin, p)) != 0)
373                              goto out;
374                      error = tcp_output(tp);
375                      goto out;
376              }
377              inp->inp_vflag &= ~INP_IPV4;
378              inp->inp_vflag |= INP_IPV6;
379              inp->inp_inc.inc_isipv6 = 1;
380              if ((error = tcp6_connect(tp, nam, p)) != 0)
381                      goto out;
382              error = tcp_output(tp);
383              COMMON_END(PRU_CONNECT);
384      }
```

———tcp_usrreq.c

341 The `tcp6_usr_connect()` function has three parameters: `so` is a socket pointer; `nam` contains the remote address to which connection will be made; `p` is a pointer to the caller process.

354–359 Since TCP cannot connect to a multicast destination, the function returns an error of `EAFNOSUPPORT` if `nam` contains an IPv6 multicast address.

361–376 If the remote address specified by `nam` is an IPv4-mapped IPv6 address and the PCB allows for both IPv4 and IPv6 communication, `tcp6_usr_connect()` sets the `INP_IPV4` flag and clears the `INP_IPV6` flag. The `tcp_connect()` is called to perform TCP state transition followed by the `tcp_output()` function to initiate the connection with a SYN segment.

377–382 If the remote address is a normal IPv6 address, the `tcp6_connect()` function is called instead of `tcp_connect()` followed by `tcp_output()` to initiate the connection. Note that one and only one of `INP_IPV4` and `INP_IPV6` flags is set in the PCB at the end of this function.

Initiate TCP Connection—Passive Open

The `tcp6_usr_listen()` function is called as a result of the `listen()` system call on a TCP socket. `tcp6_usr_listen()` sets the TCP state to the LISTEN state, the passive open state in which the socket waits for incoming connection requests.

Listing 6-79

```
                                                                        tcp_usrreq.c
282     static int
283     tcp6_usr_listen(struct socket *so, struct proc *p)
284     {
285             int s = splnet();
286             int error = 0;
287             struct inpcb *inp = sotoinpcb(so);
288             struct tcpcb *tp;
289
290             COMMON_START();
291             if (inp->inp_lport == 0) {
292                     inp->inp_vflag &= ~INP_IPV4;
293                     if ((inp->inp_flags & IN6P_IPV6_V6ONLY) == 0)
294                             inp->inp_vflag |= INP_IPV4;
295                     error = in6_pcbbind(inp, (struct sockaddr *)0, p);
296             }
297             if (error == 0)
298                     tp->t_state = TCPS_LISTEN;
299             COMMON_END(PRU_LISTEN);
300     }
                                                                        tcp_usrreq.c
```

291–295 If the local port of the socket is not set, function `in6_pcbbind()` is called to assign a local port. As described in Section 6.7.2, `in6_pcbbind()` will automatically choose a free local port if the second function parameter is NULL.

In addition, if the `IN6P_IPV6_V6ONLY` flag is set in the PCB, the `INP_IPV4` flag is cleared at this point so that this socket will not accept a connection request over IPv4.

297–298 The TCP state is set to the LISTEN state if the local port is already bound on the socket or if the `in6_pcbbind()` function returns with success.

6.9   UDP-over-IPv6

Similar to TCP-over-IPv6, there is no significant difference between UDP-over-IPv4 and UDP-over-IPv6. IPv4-mapped IPv6 addresses can be used with UDP-over-IPv6 the same way that the mapped address is used with TCP-over-IPv6.

6.9.1   UDP-over-IPv6 Instance of `ip6protosw{}`

Table 6-10 shows the values of the various fields in the UDP-over-IPv6 instance of the `ip6protofw{}` structure. `ip6protofw{}` is discussed in Section 3.5.3.

6.9.2   UDP Output—`udp6_output()` Function

Unlike in TCP-over-IPv6 where most of the processing code is shared between IPv4 and IPv6, the majority of the code is re-implemented separately for UDP-over-IPv6. The main reason is

TABLE 6-10

ip6protosw{} fields	*Value*	*Description*
pr_type	SOCK_DGRAM	Best effort datagram service
pr_domain	&inet6domain	Indicates the IPv6 protocol
pr_protocol	IPPROTO_UDP (17)	Protocol number (17)
pr_flags	PR_ATOMIC|PR_ADDR	Indicates each process request operation maps a single protocol request operation, and data is passed with its addresses
pr_input	udp6_input	Input function
pr_output	0	Not used
pr_ctlinput	udp6_ctlinput	Control messages input processing
pr_ctloutput	ip6_ctloutput	Control messages output processing
pr_init	0	Not used
pr_fasttimo	0	Not used
pr_slowtimo	0	Not used
pr_drain	0	Not used
pr_usrreqs	udp6_usrreqs	User request dispatch functions

UDP instance of the ip6protosw{} *structure.*

due to the simplicity of UDP, which does not have much network protocol-independent code that can be easily shared between IPv4 and IPv6.

Listing 6-80

```
                                                              ─udp6_output.c
137     int
138     udp6_output(in6p, m, addr6, control, p)
139             struct in6pcb *in6p;
140             struct mbuf *m;
141             struct mbuf *control;
142             struct sockaddr *addr6;
....
146             struct proc *p;
....
162     {
                                                              ─udp6_output.c
```

138 The udp6_output() has five parameters: in6p is a pointer to the PCB associated with a UDP socket on which data is being sent; m is a pointer to the mbuf that contains UDP data to be sent; addr6 is a pointer to the storage containing the peer address; control is a pointer to the mbuf that contains transmit options for the given packet; p is a pointer to the process that owns the socket.

Listing 6-81

_____ udp6_output.c

```
163          u_int32_t plen = sizeof(struct udphdr) + m->m_pkthdr.len;
164          struct ip6_hdr *ip6;
165          struct udphdr *udp6;
166          struct sockaddr_in6 *lsa6 = NULL, *fsa6 = NULL;
167          struct ifnet *oifp = NULL;
....
169          struct sockaddr_in6 lsa6_storage;
....
172          struct sockaddr_in6 lsa6_mapped; /* XXX ugly */
....
174          u_short fport;
175          int error = 0;
176          struct ip6_pktopts opt, *stickyopt = in6p->in6p_outputopts;
177          int priv;
178          int af = AF_INET6, hlen = sizeof(struct ip6_hdr);
....
185          int flags = 0;
186          struct sockaddr_in6 tmp;
....
192
193              priv = 0;
....
198          if (p && !suser(p))
199                  priv = 1;
....
205          if (addr6) {
....
207                  /* addr6 has been validated in udp6_send(). */
208                  fsa6 = (struct sockaddr_in6 *)addr6;
....
218
219                  /* protect *sin6 from overwrites */
220                  tmp = *fsa6;
221                  fsa6 = &tmp;
222
223                  if ((error = scope6_check_id(fsa6, ip6_use_defzone)) != 0)
224                          return (error);
225          }
```

_____ udp6_output.c

205–225 Function `scope6_check_id()` is called to recover scope zone ID if the Destination address is explicitly specified. The address information is copied into the `tmp` variable first because `scope6_check_id()` may modify the content of the address structure inside the function.

Listing 6-82

_____ udp6_output.c

```
227          if (control) {
228                  if ((error = ip6_setpktoptions(control, &opt, stickyopt, priv,
229                                          0, IPPROTO_UDP)) != 0)
230                          goto release;
231                  in6p->in6p_outputopts = &opt;
232          }
```

_____ udp6_output.c

227–232 `control` may contain more than one packet option. Function `ip6_setpktoptions()` extracts these packet options from the control mbuf and stores these options in the `ip6_pktopts{}` structure. The `in6p_outputopts` field of the PCB points to these options while sending a packet.

Listing 6-83

————————————————————————————————————udp6_output.c
```
234              if (fsa6) {
235                      /*
236                       * IPv4 version of udp_output calls in_pcbconnect in this case,
237                       * which needs splnet and affects performance.
238                       * Since we saw no essential reason for calling in_pcbconnect,
239                       * we get rid of such kind of logic, and call in6_selectsrc
240                       * and in6_pcbsetport in order to fill in the local address
241                       * and the local port.
242                       */
243                      if (fsa6->sin6_port == 0) {
244                              error = EADDRNOTAVAIL;
245                              goto release;
246                      }
247
248                      if (!SA6_IS_ADDR_UNSPECIFIED(&in6p->in6p_fsa)) {
249                              /* how about ::ffff:0.0.0.0 case? */
250                              error = EISCONN;
251                              goto release;
252                      }
253
254                      fport = fsa6->sin6_port; /* allow 0 port */
```
————————————————————————————————————udp6_output.c

243–252 This part of the code to validate the Destination address if it is specified. The destination port number must be specified. Otherwise, the packet is dropped with EADDRNOTAVAIL error. If the foreign address of the PCB entry is already set, (i.e., if the socket is already connected to a peer), then the same socket cannot be used to transmit packets to any other destinations. In this case the packet is dropped with the EISCONN error.

Listing 6-84

————————————————————————————————————udp6_output.c
```
256              if (IN6_IS_ADDR_V4MAPPED(&fsa6->sin6_addr)) {

       (The IPv6 mapped IPv6 address processing, which is not used by FreeBSD)

289              }
```
————————————————————————————————————udp6_output.c

256–289 The FreeBSD version of the code does not process IPv4-mapped IPv6 addresses here. Instead the processing is done in the udp6_send() function, which will be discussed in a later section.

Listing 6-85

————————————————————————————————————udp6_output.c
```
291              if (!IN6_IS_ADDR_V4MAPPED(&fsa6->sin6_addr)) {
292                      lsa6 = in6_selectsrc(fsa6, in6p->in6p_outputopts,
293                                           in6p->in6p_moptions,
294                                           &in6p->in6p_route,
295                                           &in6p->in6p_lsa, &oifp, &error);
....
297                      /*
298                       * XXX: sa6 may not have a valid sin6_scope_id in
299                       * the non-SCOPEDROUTING case.
300                       */
301                      if (lsa6) {
```

```
302                                           bzero(&lsa6_storage, sizeof(lsa6_storage));
303                                           lsa6_storage.sin6_family = AF_INET6;
304                                           lsa6_storage.sin6_len = sizeof(lsa6_storage);
305                                           if ((error = in6_recoverscope(&lsa6_storage,
306                                                                          &lsa6->sin6_addr,
307                                                                          NULL)) != 0) {
308                                                   goto release;
309                                           }
310                                           /* XXX */
311                                           lsa6_storage.sin6_addr = lsa6->sin6_addr;
312                                           lsa6 = &lsa6_storage;
313                                   }
....
315                           if (oifp && fsa6->sin6_scope_id == 0 &&
316                               (error = scope6_setzoneid(oifp, fsa6)) != 0) {
317                                   goto release;
318                           }
319                   } else {
....
356                           {
357                                   lsa6 = &in6p->in6p_lsa;
358                           }
359                   }
```
                                                                                    ——— udp6_output.c

291–295 The `in6_selectsrc()` is called to select the appropriate source address when the
specified peer address is not an IPv4-mapped IPv6 address.

301–313 The return value from `in6_selectsrc()` must be copied to a local variable
and converted by `in6_recoverscope()` for the same reason as that described for
Listing 6-22.

315–318 Function `scope6_setzoneid()` is called in case the scope zone ID of the destination address needs to be disambiguated (see Listing 6-28).

357 Encountering an IPv4-mapped IPv6 Destination address will result in IPv4 output packet
processing through function `udp_output()` instead of function `udp6_output()` in the
FreeBSD implementation. The `else` clause is designed for the NetBSD system, which will
select the local address that is also an IPv4-mapped IPv6 address when encountering such
an address for the peer.

Listing 6-86
                                                                                    ——— udp6_output.c

```
360                   if (lsa6 == NULL) {
361                           if (error == 0)
362                                   error = EADDRNOTAVAIL;
363                           goto release;
364                   }
365                   if (in6p->in6p_lport == 0 &&
366                       (error = in6_pcbsetport(lsa6, in6p, p)) != 0)
367                           goto release;
```
                                                                                    ——— udp6_output.c

360–363 The function returns the `EADDRNOTAVAIL` error if the local address of this packet
cannot be determined.

365–367 The `in6_pcbsetport()` is called to assign an available local port if the local port
number is not yet assigned.

Listing 6-87

```
                                                           udp6_output.c
368              } else {
369                      if (SA6_IS_ADDR_UNSPECIFIED(&in6p->in6p_fsa)) {
370                              error = ENOTCONN;
371                              goto release;
372                      }
                                                           udp6_output.c
```

368–372 The function returns the ENOTCONN error if a remote address is not specified by the caller and the PCB has an uninitialized remote address.

Listing 6-88

```
                                                           udp6_output.c
373                      if (IN6_IS_ADDR_V4MAPPED(&in6p->in6p_faddr)) {

    (The IPv4 mapped IPv6 address processing, which is not used by FreeBSD)

393                      }
                                                           udp6_output.c
```

373–393 This block of validation code on the IPv4-mapped IPv6 address does not apply to the FreeBSD implementation.

Note: NetBSD creates UDP over IPv4 packet here whose destination address is an IPv4-mapped IPv6 address. In FreeBSD, sending to an IPv4-mapped IPv6 destination address is processed by the IPv4 specific code. As mentioned earlier, OpenBSD does not support IPv4-mapped IPv6 addresses at all.

Listing 6-89

```
                                                           udp6_output.c
394                      lsa6 = &in6p->in6p_lsa;
395                      fsa6 = &in6p->in6p_fsa;
396                      fport = in6p->in6p_fport;
397              }
                                                           udp6_output.c
```

394–397 The local address, remote addresses, and foreign port number are stored from the PCB into temporary variables for faster access in later code.

Listing 6-90

```
                                                           udp6_output.c
399              if (af == AF_INET)
400                      hlen = sizeof(struct ip);
401
402              /*
403               * Calculate data length and get a mbuf
404               * for UDP and IP6 headers.
405               */
406              M_PREPEND(m, hlen + sizeof(struct udphdr), M_DONTWAIT);
407              if (m == 0) {
408                      error = ENOBUFS;
409                      goto release;
410              }
411
412              /*
```

```
413                     * Stuff checksum and output datagram.
414                     */
415                    udp6 = (struct udphdr *)(mtod(m, caddr_t) + hlen);
416                    udp6->uh_sport = in6p->in6p_lport; /* lport is always set in the PCB */
417                    udp6->uh_dport = fport;
418                    if (plen <= 0xffff)
419                            udp6->uh_ulen = htons((u_short)plen);
420                    else
421                            udp6->uh_ulen = 0;
422                    udp6->uh_sum = 0;
```
——udp6_output.c

406–410 An mbuf for the outgoing packet is allocated. `hlen` is set to the size of the IPv6 header for an IPv6 packet; `hlen` is set to the size of an IPv4 header if the packet is sent to an IPv4-mapped IPv6 Destination address. The address family is always set to `AF_INET6` in this function in the FreeBSD implementation.

415–422 The UDP header fields are initialized. Since the checksum computation depends on the version of IP protocol, the calculation is delayed to later code.

Listing 6-91

——udp6_output.c
```
424                switch (af) {
425                case AF_INET6:
426                        ip6 = mtod(m, struct ip6_hdr *);
427                        ip6->ip6_flow   = in6p->in6p_flowinfo & IPV6_FLOWINFO_MASK;
428                        ip6->ip6_vfc    &= ~IPV6_VERSION_MASK;
429                        ip6->ip6_vfc    |= IPV6_VERSION;
....
433                        ip6->ip6_nxt    = IPPROTO_UDP;
434                        ip6->ip6_hlim   = in6_selecthlim(in6p, oifp);
435                        ip6->ip6_src    = lsa6->sin6_addr;
436                        ip6->ip6_dst    = fsa6->sin6_addr;
437
438                        if ((udp6->uh_sum = in6_cksum(m, IPPROTO_UDP,
439                                        sizeof(struct ip6_hdr), plen)) == 0) {
440                            udp6->uh_sum = 0xffff;
441                        }
442
443                        udp6stat.udp6s_opackets++;
....
450                        /* attach the full sockaddr_in6 addresses to the packet. */
451                        if (!ip6_setpktaddrs(m, lsa6, fsa6)) {
452                                error = ENOBUFS;
453                                goto release;
454                        }
455                        error = ip6_output(m, in6p->in6p_outputopts, &in6p->in6p_route,
456                                        flags, in6p->in6p_moptions, NULL
....
458                                        ,NULL
....
460                                        );
461                        break;
```
——udp6_output.c

425–441 Some of the IPv6 header fields are initialized based on the available information. As explained in Section 6.8.2, the Hop Limit value is chosen from several possible candidates. The UDP checksum field is calculated by the `in6_cksum()` function.

451–460 The KAME implementation stores the Source and Destination address information in the mbuf as `sockaddr_in6{}` structures. Variables `lsa6` and `fsa6` are stored in the outgoing mbuf by the ip6_setpktaddrs() function. Finally, the ip6_output() is called with the packet options given in ip6p_outputopts to send the packet.

Listing 6-92

```
                                                              udp6_output.c
462             case AF_INET:
    ....
546                     error = EAFNOSUPPORT;
547                     goto release;
    ....
549             }
550             goto releaseopt;
551
552     release:
553             m_freem(m);
554
555     releaseopt:
556             if (control) {
557                     ip6_clearpktopts(in6p->in6p_outputopts, -1);
558                     in6p->in6p_outputopts = stickyopt;
559                     m_freem(control);
560             }
561             return (error);
562     }
                                                              udp6_output.c
```

462–547 This block of code does not apply to the FreeBSD implementation.

556–560 Per packet IPv6 options that are specified by the control parameter may have been set in the in6p_outputopts. The ip6_clearpktopts() function removes these per packet options from in6p_outputopts. The static options are restored.

6.9.3 UDP Input—udp6_input() Function

UDP-over-IPv6 input function is defined as the udp6_input() function. The function is called from the ip6_input() function via the inet6sw[] array that is defined in in6_proto.c.

Listing 6-93

```
                                                              udp6_usrreq.c
125     int
126     udp6_input(mp, offp, proto)
127             struct mbuf **mp;
128             int *offp, proto;
129     {
130             struct mbuf *m = *mp;
131             register struct ip6_hdr *ip6;
132             register struct udphdr *uh;
133             register struct inpcb *in6p;
134             struct ip6_recvpktopts opts;
135             int off = *offp;
136             int plen, ulen;
137             struct sockaddr_in6 src, dst, fromsa;
                                                              udp6_usrreq.c
```

126 The udp6_input() has three parameters: mp is a pointer to the mbuf that contains the incoming UDP packet; offp is a pointer to an offset from the start of IPv6 header to the start of the UDP header of the given packet; `proto` is a protocol number retrieved from the packet. In this case `proto` has the value 17 for UDP.

Listing 6-94

```
146             bzero(&opts, sizeof(opts));
147
148             ip6 = mtod(m, struct ip6_hdr *);
149
150             if (faithprefix_p != NULL && (*faithprefix_p)(&ip6->ip6_dst)) {
151                     /* XXX send icmp6 host/port unreach? */
152                     m_freem(m);
153                     return IPPROTO_DONE;
154             }
155
157             IP6_EXTHDR_CHECK(m, off, sizeof(struct udphdr), IPPROTO_DONE);
158             ip6 = mtod(m, struct ip6_hdr *);
159             uh = (struct udphdr *)((caddr_t)ip6 + off);
```

146 `opts` is an instance of the `ip6_recvpktopts{}` structure, which contains the extension headers and other information about the received packet.

150–153 The packet is dropped if the Destination address has a prefix that matches the prefix assigned to the FAITH translator (see Section 6.7.7), because KAME's implementation of the FAITH translator only supports TCP.

157–159 The `IP6_EXTHDR_CHECK()` macro ensures that the first mbuf stores all data from the IPv6 header to the UDP header in a contiguous memory space. With this assumption, `ip6` and `uh` can be safely pointed to the IPv6 and UDP headers.

Listing 6-95

```
166             /*
167              * extract full sockaddr structures for the src/dst addresses,
168              * and make local copies of them.
169              */
170             if (ip6_getpktaddrs(m, &src, &dst)) {
171                     m_freem(m);
172                     goto bad;
173             }
```

170–173 The Source and Destination addresses from the packet are stored with the packet mbuf as `sockaddr_in6{}` structures. Function `ip6_getpktaddrs()` extracts these addresses and stores these addresses in `src` and `dst`, respectively.

Listing 6-96

```
175             /*
176              * XXX: the address may have embedded scope zone ID, which should be
177              * hidden from applications.
178              */
179             fromsa = src;
....
181             in6_clearscope(&fromsa.sin6_addr);
```

179–181 `fromsa` is used when notifying application of the source address of the packet. The `in6_clearscope()` function clears the embedded zone index from the address because the embedded format is the internal-kernel representation and must not be disclosed to the application layer. Applications can get the scope zone ID from `sin6_scope_id` field.

Listing 6-97

_____ udp6_usrreq.c
```
184                  udpstat.udps_ipackets++;
185
186                  plen = ntohs(ip6->ip6_plen) - off + sizeof(*ip6);
187                  ulen = ntohs((u_short)uh->uh_ulen);
188
189                  if (plen != ulen) {
190                          udpstat.udps_badlen++;
191                          goto bad;
192                  }
```
_____ udp6_usrreq.c

186–192 `ip6_plen` specifies the length of the IPv6 payload including the Extension Headers, if any, but excludes the size of the IPv6 header. By subtracting `off` and adding back the size of IPv6 header, `plen` will be set to the length of the UDP header plus its payload. The packet is discarded if there is a mismatch between `plen` and `ulen`.

Listing 6-98

_____ udp6_usrreq.c
```
194                  /*
195                   * Checksum extended UDP header and data.
196                   */
197                  if (uh->uh_sum == 0)
198                          udpstat.udps_nosum++;
199                  else if (in6_cksum(m, IPPROTO_UDP, off, ulen) != 0) {
200                          udpstat.udps_badsum++;
201                          goto bad;
202                  }
```
_____ udp6_usrreq.c

197–202 Note that, unlike IPv4, UDP checksum is mandatory in IPv6. [RFC2460] specifies that a packet must be discarded if the checksum field is set to 0. Apparently, the code does not follow the specification and has been fixed in a later release of the KAME implementation. The packet is discarded if the checksum field contains an incorrect value.

Listing 6-99

_____ udp6_usrreq.c
```
204                  if (IN6_IS_ADDR_MULTICAST(&ip6->ip6_dst)) {
205                          struct  inpcb *last;
206
207                          /*
208                           * Deliver a multicast datagram to all sockets
209                           * for which the local and remote addresses and ports match
210                           * those of the incoming datagram.  This allows more than
211                           * one process to receive multicasts on the same port.
212                           * (This really ought to be done for unicast datagrams as
213                           * well, but that would cause problems with existing
214                           * applications that open both address-specific sockets and
215                           * a wildcard socket listening to the same port -- they would
216                           * end up receiving duplicates of every unicast datagram.
217                           * Those applications open the multiple sockets to overcome an
```

```
218                    * inadequacy of the UDP socket interface, but for backwards
219                    * compatibility we avoid the problem here rather than
220                    * fixing the interface.  Maybe 4.5BSD will remedy this?)
221                    */
222
223                   /*
224                    * In a case that laddr should be set to the link-local
225                    * address (this happens in RIPng), the multicast address
226                    * specified in the received packet does not match with
227                    * laddr. To cure this situation, the matching is relaxed
228                    * if the receiving interface is the same as one specified
229                    * in the socket and if the destination multicast address
230                    * matches one of the multicast groups specified in the socket.
231                    */
```
—— udp6_usrreq.c

204 The packet is delivered to all sockets listening on the same destination port if the packet has a multicast destination address.

Listing 6-100

—— udp6_usrreq.c
```
233                   /*
234                    * Construct sockaddr format source address.
235                    */
236                  fromsa.sin6_port = uh->uh_sport;
237                   /*
238                    * KAME note: traditionally we dropped udpiphdr from mbuf here.
239                    * We need udphdr for IPsec processing so we do that later.
240                    */
241
242                   /*
243                    * Locate pcb(s) for datagram.
244                    * (Algorithm copied from raw_intr().)
245                    */
246                  last = NULL;
247                  LIST_FOREACH(in6p, &udb, inp_list) {
248                          if ((in6p->inp_vflag & INP_IPV6) == 0)
249                                  continue;
250                          if (in6p->in6p_lport != uh->uh_dport)
251                                  continue;
```
—— udp6_usrreq.c

247–251 The loop traverses all of the UDP PCB entries and determines if a PCB should receive the given multicast packet. The search bypasses any non-IPv6 PCBs or PCBs that are not on the right port.

Listing 6-101

—— udp6_usrreq.c
```
252                          if (!SA6_IS_ADDR_UNSPECIFIED(&in6p->in6p_lsa)) {
253                                  if (!SA6_ARE_ADDR_EQUAL(&in6p->in6p_lsa, &dst))
254                                          continue;
255                          }
256                          if (!SA6_IS_ADDR_UNSPECIFIED(&in6p->in6p_fsa)) {
257                                  if (!SA6_ARE_ADDR_EQUAL(&in6p->in6p_fsa,
258                                                  &src) ||
259                                      in6p->in6p_fport != uh->uh_sport) {
260                                          continue;
261                                  }
262                          }
```
—— udp6_usrreq.c

252–255 If a PCB is not mapped to a wildcard address (i.e., the local address is specified), then this address must match the destination address of the incoming packet. Otherwise the PCB is skipped.

256–262 A PCB that is initialized with a specific foreign address must match the source address of the incoming packet. In addition, the foreign port must match the source port of the packet. Otherwise any mismatch will result in the PCB being bypassed.

Listing 6-102

_____udp6_usrreq.c

```
415                     if (last != NULL) {
416                             struct  mbuf *n;
417
  . . . .
435                             if ((n = m_copy(m, 0, M_COPYALL)) != NULL) {
436                                     /*
437                                      * KAME NOTE: do not
438                                      * m_copy(m, offset, ...) above.
439                                      * sbappendaddr() expects M_PKTHDR,
440                                      * and m_copy() will copy M_PKTHDR
441                                      * only if offset is 0.
442                                      */
443                                     if (last->in6p_flags & IN6P_CONTROLOPTS
444                                         || last->in6p_socket->so_options &
                                            SO_TIMESTAMP)
445                                             ip6_savecontrol(last, ip6,
446                                                             n, &opts);
447
448                                     m_adj(n, off + sizeof(struct udphdr));
449                                     if (sbappendaddr(&last->in6p_socket->so_rcv,
450                                                     (struct sockaddr *)&fromsa,
451                                                     n, opts.head) == 0) {
452                                             m_freem(n);
453                                             if (opts.head)
454                                                     m_freem(opts.head);
455                                             udpstat.udps_fullsock++;
456                                     } else
457                                             sorwakeup(last->in6p_socket);
458                                     bzero(&opts, sizeof(opts));
459                             }
460                     }
  . . . .
462                     last = in6p;
463                     /*
464                      * Don't look for additional matches if this one does
465                      * not have either the SO_REUSEPORT or SO_REUSEADDR
466                      * socket options set.  This heuristic avoids searching
467                      * through all pcbs in the common case of a non-shared
468                      * port.  It assumes that an application will never
469                      * clear these options after setting them.
470                      */
471                     if ((last->in6p_socket->so_options &
472                         (SO_REUSEPORT|SO_REUSEADDR)) == 0)
473                             break;
  . . . .
477             }
478
479             if (last == NULL) {
480                     /*
481                      * No matching pcb found; discard datagram.
482                      * (No need to send an ICMP Port Unreachable
483                      * for a broadcast or multicast datgram.)
484                      */
485                     udpstat.udps_noport++;
```

```
486                              udpstat.udps_noportmcast++;
487                              goto bad;
488                      }
....
506                      if (last->in6p_flags & IN6P_CONTROLOPTS
507                          || last->in6p_socket->so_options & SO_TIMESTAMP)
508                              ip6_savecontrol(last, ip6, m, &opts);
509
510                      m_adj(m, off + sizeof(struct udphdr));
511                      if (sbappendaddr(&last->in6p_socket->so_rcv,
512                                      (struct sockaddr *)&fromsa,
513                                      m, opts.head) == 0) {
514                              udpstat.udps_fullsock++;
515                              goto bad;
516                      }
517                      sorwakeup(last->in6p_socket);
518                      return IPPROTO_DONE;
519              }
```
── udp6_usrreq.c

415 last is set to the matched PCB entry on line 462. The packet delivery is delayed by one code loop because the incoming packet must be copied for delivering to multiple sockets. This delay prevents the cost of unnecessary packet copying if there is only one receiver for the given packet.

435 The incoming packet is copied for delivery to a socket. As the comment says, the entire packet is copied instead of only the UDP data part in order to keep the M_PKTHDR flag set in the mbuf.

443–446 If the IN6P_CONTROLOPTS flag is set in the PCB (i.e., some additional information about the packet needs to be passed to the socket (see Table 6-4)), or if the associated socket has the SO_TIMESTAMP option set, the requested information is extracted from the incoming mbuf and stored into the ip6_recvpktopts{} structure by the ip6_savecontrol() function.

448–457 Since the socket buffer maintains only UDP packet payload, the IPv6 header, the Extension Headers and the UDP header are removed from the packet before storing the payload on the socket receive buffer. The sbappendaddr() function delivers the payload to the socket. If the payload delivery is successful then function sorwakeup() is called to notify the upper layer application. Otherwise the replicated packet and additional packet information are released.

458 The contents of opts will be freed by the socket receiving process. The opts variable is reinitialized for the next packet delivery.

471–473 If the matching socket does not have either the SO_REUSEPORT or SO_REUSEADDR option set then we can safely assume that there is no other socket that is waiting on the same address or the same port. The search process can terminate and proceed to complete the input processing.

479–487 The packet is dropped if there is no matching PCB.

506–517 The packet is delivered to the last (or the only) matching socket. The process is almost identical to the code in lines 443–457. The difference is we need not copy the packet because this is the final delivery.

Listing 6-103

```
                                                                    udp6_usrreq.c
520              /*
521               * Locate pcb for datagram.
522               */
523              in6p = in6_pcblookup_hash(&udbinfo, &src, uh->uh_sport,
524                               &dst, uh->uh_dport, 1,
525                               m->m_pkthdr.rcvif);
526              if (in6p == 0) {
527                      if (log_in_vain) {
528                              char buf[INET6_ADDRSTRLEN];
529
530                              strcpy(buf, ip6_sprintf(&ip6->ip6_dst));
531                              log(LOG_INFO,
532                                  "Connection attempt to UDP [%s]:%d from [%s]:%d\n",
533                                  buf, ntohs(uh->uh_dport),
534                                  ip6_sprintf(&ip6->ip6_src), ntohs(uh->uh_sport));
535                      }
536                      udpstat.udps_noport++;
537                      if (m->m_flags & M_MCAST) {
538                              printf("UDP6: M_MCAST is set in a unicast packet.\n");
539                              udpstat.udps_noportmcast++;
540                              goto bad;
541                      }
542                      icmp6_error(m, ICMP6_DST_UNREACH, ICMP6_DST_UNREACH_NOPORT, 0);
543                      return IPPROTO_DONE;
544              }
                                                                    udp6_usrreq.c
```

523–544 Function `in6_pcblookup_hash()` is used to search for the corresponding PCB if the packet is a unicast packet. The correct PCB must match the connection 4-tuple parameters, that is, the Source address, the Destination address, the Source port, and the Destination port of the packet. A failure to find a PCB will trigger an ICMPv6 Destination Unreachable (port unreachable) error.

Listing 6-104

```
                                                                    udp6_usrreq.c
563              /*
564               * Construct sockaddr format source address.
565               * Stuff source address and datagram in user buffer.
566               */
567              fromsa.sin6_port = uh->uh_sport;
568              if (in6p->in6p_flags & IN6P_CONTROLOPTS
569                  || in6p->in6p_socket->so_options & SO_TIMESTAMP)
570                      ip6_savecontrol(in6p, ip6, m, &opts);
571              m_adj(m, off + sizeof(struct udphdr));
572              if (sbappendaddr(&in6p->in6p_socket->so_rcv,
573                          (struct sockaddr *)&fromsa,
574                          m, opts.head) == 0) {
575                      udpstat.udps_fullsock++;
576                      goto bad;
577              }
578              sorwakeup(in6p->in6p_socket);
579              return IPPROTO_DONE;
580      bad:
581              if (m)
582                      m_freem(m);
583              if (opts.head)
584                      m_freem(opts.head);
585              return IPPROTO_DONE;
586      }
                                                                    udp6_usrreq.c
```

567–579 Finally, the incoming UDP packet is delivered to the right socket. The delivery process is identical to the multicast packet delivery process.

581–585 The packet mbuf and any additional memory occupied by the packet options is released if the receiving process encounters any error.

Note: In NetBSD, IPv4 packet is processed by the `udp_input()` function first. If the receiving node is using an IPv4-mapped IPv6 address for the packet, then an IPv4 PCB entry does not exist for that destination. In this case, `udp_input()` tries again to insert the packet to IPv6 UDP input routine as a packet having an IPv4-mapped IPv6 address as a Destination address.

6.9.4 UDP Control Input—`udp6_ctlinput()` Function

The UDP event notification mechanism is similar to that used by TCP. Figure 6-11 illustrates the various notification messages that can reach the UDP stack and the call flow of these

FIGURE 6-11

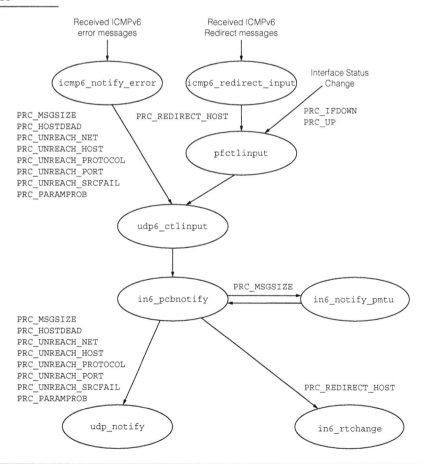

UDP over IPv6 notification call flow.

notifications. The notification handler is the `udp6_ctlinput()` function when UDP operates over IPv6.

There exists a little difference between the notification handling in the `udp6_ctlinput()` and `tcp6_ctlinput()` functions. The main difference is the absence of syncache handling, which is only applicable to TCP. Therefore, the code description about `udp6_ctlinput()` focuses on the process difference that exists between the two protocols.

Listing 6-105

```
                                                                   udp6_usrreq.c
588    void
589    udp6_ctlinput(cmd, sa, d)
590            int cmd;
591            struct sockaddr *sa;
592            void *d;
593    {
594            struct udphdr uh;
595            struct ip6_hdr *ip6;
596            struct mbuf *m;
597            int off = 0;
598            struct ip6ctlparam *ip6cp = NULL;
599            const struct sockaddr_in6 *sa6_src = NULL;
600            void *cmdarg;
601            void (*notify) __P((struct inpcb *, int)) = udp_notify;
602            struct udp_portonly {
603                    u_int16_t uh_sport;
604                    u_int16_t uh_dport;
605            } *uhp;
606
607            if (sa->sa_family != AF_INET6 ||
608                sa->sa_len != sizeof(struct sockaddr_in6))
609                    return;
610
611            if ((unsigned)cmd >= PRC_NCMDS)
612                    return;
613            if (PRC_IS_REDIRECT(cmd))
614                    notify = in6_rtchange, d = NULL;
615            else if (cmd == PRC_HOSTDEAD)
616                    d = NULL;
617            else if (inet6ctlerrmap[cmd] == 0)
618                    return;
```
                                                                   udp6_usrreq.c

613–618 Unlike in function `tcp6_ctlinput()` where special handling of `PRC_MSGSIZE` is required by TCP to dynamically modify the TCP segment size according to the current path MTU, UDP handles the `PRC_MSGSIZE` in the protocol-independent `in6_pcbnotify()` function without any special treatment by the UDP layer. The user of a UDP socket is responsible for setting the appropriate UDP packet size. The UDP layer handles the `PRC_REDIRECT` message through the standard `in6_rtchange()` function that flushes the PCB cached route entry. These two notification messages are not required to be delivered to the UDP layer; these are handled by protocol-independent functions.

If the notification message is `PRC_HOSTDEAD` then the pointer d is cleared. d may point to the information about the packet that caused this notification. Decoding the addresses and port numbers from the packet information allows the delivery of the notification to the appropriate PCBs. However, the `PRC_HOSTDEAD` notification indicates that the destination host is down. In this case, setting the pointer d to NULL enables the delivery

of the notification to all PCB entries that have the same foreign address as the address
carried in the sa parameter.

Listing 6-106
——udp6_usrreq.c
```
620                /* if the parameter is from icmp6, decode it. */
621                if (d != NULL) {
622                        ip6cp = (struct ip6ctlparam *)d;
623                        m = ip6cp->ip6c_m;
624                        ip6 = ip6cp->ip6c_ip6;
625                        off = ip6cp->ip6c_off;
626                        cmdarg = ip6cp->ip6c_cmdarg;
627                        sa6_src = ip6cp->ip6c_src;
628                } else {
629                        m = NULL;
630                        ip6 = NULL;
631                        cmdarg = NULL;
632                        sa6_src = &sa6_any;
633                }
634
635                if (ip6) {
636                        /*
637                         * XXX: We assume that when IPV6 is non NULL,
638                         * M and OFF are valid.
639                         */
640
641                        /* check if we can safely examine src and dst ports */
642                        if (m->m_pkthdr.len < off + sizeof(*uhp))
643                                return;
644
645                        bzero(&uh, sizeof(uh));
646                        m_copydata(m, off, sizeof(*uhp), (caddr_t)&uh);
647
648                        (void) in6_pcbnotify(&udb, (const struct sockaddr *)sa,
649                                        uh.uh_dport,
650                                        (const struct sockaddr *)ip6cp->ip6c_src,
651                                        uh.uh_sport, cmd, cmdarg, notify);
652                } else
653                        (void) in6_pcbnotify(&udb, sa, 0, (struct sockaddr *)sa6_src,
654                                        0, cmd, cmdarg, notify);
655        }
```
——udp6_usrreq.c

621–633 The d variable is set when the function is called from ICMPv6 error input routine or
the pfctlinput2() function called by the ip6_output() function. d is a pointer to
the ip6ctlparam{} structure which keeps the packet information that caused this notification. ip6cp->ip6c_m, ip6c->ip6c_ip6, ip6c->ip6c_off and sa6_src are set
only when the notification is triggered from ICMPv6 error input. Each variable represents
a pointer to the mbuf instance which holds the packet, address of the IPv6 packet that
caused the ICMPv6 error, the offset to the upper layer protocol of the IPv6 packet, and the
source address of the ICMPv6 packet, respectively. cmdarg keeps additional information
based on notification type. Currently, the variable is only used to notify the value of path
MTU size.

sa6_src is set to sa6_any to deliver the notification to all PCB entries whose local
address matches the Destination address of the notification, if d is not specified.

635–651 The source and destination ports are decoded from the upper layer header information, the UDP header in this case, and the notification message is sent to the PCB entry

TABLE 6-11

UDP-over-IPv6	Callback function
PRC_IFDOWN	udp_notify()
PRC_IFUP	udp_notify()
PRC_MSGSIZE	udp_notify()
PRC_HOSTDEAD	udp_notify()
PRC_UNREACH_NET	udp_notify()
PRC_UNREACH_HOST	udp_notify()
PRC_UNREACH_PROTOCOL	udp_notify()
PRC_UNREACH_PORT	udp_notify()
PRC_UNREACH_SRCFAIL	udp_notify()
PRC_REDIRECT_HOST	in6_rtchange()
PRC_PARAMPROB	udp_notify()

Notifications and UDP callback functions.

that matches the addresses and ports information by calling the `ip6_pcbnotify()` function.

653–654 If there is no specific information about where to deliver the notification, then the message is delivered to all PCB entries whose local address matches the Destination address of the notification (`sa`).

Table 6-11 shows each notification message and its corresponding UDP handler function.

6.9.5   UDP User Requests Handling

Any UDP related socket request is dispatched to the corresponding function initialized in `udp6_usrreqs`. `udp6_usrreqs` is another instance of the `pr_usrreqs{}` structure. Table 6-12 lists the content of `udp6_usrreqs`.

Attach PCB—udp6_attach() Function

The `udp6_attach()` function is called as a result of the `socket()` system call issued on a UDP socket. `udp6_attach()` creates a PCB entry for a given socket and establishes the links between the two objects.

Listing 6-107

_____udp6_usrreq.c
```
715     static int
716     udp6_attach(struct socket *so, int proto, struct proc *p)
717     {
718             struct inpcb *inp;
719             int s, error;
720
721             inp = sotoinpcb(so);
```

```
722                  if (inp != 0)
723                          return EINVAL;
724
725                  if (so->so_snd.sb_hiwat == 0 || so->so_rcv.sb_hiwat == 0) {
726                          error = soreserve(so, udp_sendspace, udp_recvspace);
727                          if (error)
728                                  return error;
729                  }
730                  s = splnet();
731                  error = in_pcballoc(so, &udbinfo, p);
732                  splx(s);
733                  if (error)
734                          return error;
735                  inp = (struct inpcb *)so->so_pcb;
736                  inp->inp_vflag |= INP_IPV6;
737                  if (!ip6_v6only)
738                          inp->inp_vflag |= INP_IPV4;
739                  inp->in6p_hops = -1;     /* use kernel default */
740                  inp->in6p_cksum = -1;    /* just to be sure */
741                  /*
742                   * XXX: ugly!!
743                   * IPv4 TTL initialization is necessary for an IPv6 socket as well,
744                   * because the socket may be bound to an IPv6 wildcard address,
745                   * which may match an IPv4-mapped IPv6 address.
746                   */
747                  inp->inp_ip_ttl = ip_defttl;
748                  return 0;
749          }
```
_____udp6_usrreq.c

716 The `udp6_attach()` function has three parameters: `so` is a pointer to the socket that will reference the new PCB; `proto` is an upper layer protocol number; `p` is a pointer to the calling process.

721–723 The `sotoinpcb()` function returns a pointer to the PCB associated with a socket. The function returns the `EINVAL` error if a PCB entry is already allocated for the given socket.

TABLE 6-12

pr_usrreqs	*udp6_usrreqs*	*Shared with IPv4*
pru_abort	udp6_abort	No
pru_attach	udp6_attach	No
pru_bind	udp6_bind	No
pru_connect	udp6_connect	No
pru_control	in6_control	No
pru_detach	udp6_detach	No
pru_disconnect	udp6_disconnect	No
pru_peeraddr	in6_mapped_peeraddr	No
pru_send	udp6_send	No
pru_shutdown	udp_shutdown	Yes
pru_sockaddr	in6_mapped_sockaddr	No

UDP instance of the `pr_usrreqs{}` *structure.*

725–728 The high watermark values for the send and receive buffers of the socket are initialized with the values from the global variables `udp_sendspace` and `udp_recvspace`, respectively, if the high watermark values are not set. Variables `udp_sendspace` and `udp_recvspace` are configurable via the **sysctl** command.

730–735 Function `in_pcballoc()` is called to allocate a PCB entry for the given UDP socket. The new PCB is set in the pointer `so->so_pcb`.

736–738 The `INP_IPV6` flag is set to indicate that the socket is used for IPv6 communication. At the same time, if the system is configured to use an IPv4-mapped IPv6 address, the `INP_IPV4` flag is set so that the socket can also be used for IPv4 communication.

739–747 The Hop Limit fields of the outgoing packets are set with the internal default value if `in6p_hlim` is set to −1. The `in6p_cksum` member is only applicable to raw sockets, and is set to −1, meaning disabled. `inp_ip_ttl` is used to set the TTL value of outgoing IPv4 packets if the PCB is used for IPv4 communication. `inp_ip_ttl` is initialized with the system default value.

Bind Local Address—udp6_bind() Function

The `udp6_bind()` function is called as a result of the `bind()` system call issued on a UDP socket. `udp6_bind()` assigns a local address of a UDP socket.

The function code is shown below. This is essentially the same as `tcp6_usr_bind()` (Listing 6-77) except it allows an IPv6 multicast address to be bound for receiving a multicast stream to that address. See the code description of Listing 6-77 for more details.

Listing 6-108

── udp6_usrreq.c

```
751     static int
752     udp6_bind(struct socket *so, struct sockaddr *nam, struct proc *p)
753     {
754             struct inpcb *inp;
755             int s, error;
756
757             inp = sotoinpcb(so);
758             if (inp == 0)
759                     return EINVAL;
760
761             inp->inp_vflag &= ~INP_IPV4;
762             inp->inp_vflag |= INP_IPV6;
763             if ((inp->inp_flags & IN6P_IPV6_V6ONLY) == 0) {
764                     struct sockaddr_in6 *sin6_p;
765
766                     sin6_p = (struct sockaddr_in6 *)nam;
767
768                     if (SA6_IS_ADDR_UNSPECIFIED(sin6_p))
769                             inp->inp_vflag |= INP_IPV4;
770                     else if (IN6_IS_ADDR_V4MAPPED(&sin6_p->sin6_addr)) {
771                             struct sockaddr_in sin;
772
773                             in6_sin6_2_sin(&sin, sin6_p);
774                             inp->inp_vflag |= INP_IPV4;
775                             inp->inp_vflag &= ~INP_IPV6;
776                             s = splnet();
777                             error = in_pcbbind(inp, (struct sockaddr *)&sin, p);
778                             splx(s);
```

```
779                        return error;
780                }
781           }
782
783      s = splnet();
784      error = in6_pcbbind(inp, nam, p);
785      splx(s);
786      return error;
787  }
```

Fix Remote Address—udp6_connect() Function

The udp6_connect() function is called as a result of the connect() system call issued on a UDP socket. udp6_connect() assigns a remote address on the socket.

Listing 6-109

```
789  static int
790  udp6_connect(struct socket *so, struct sockaddr *nam, struct proc *p)
791  {
792      struct inpcb *inp;
793      int s, error;
794
795      inp = sotoinpcb(so);
796      if (inp == 0)
797            return EINVAL;
798
799      if ((inp->inp_flags & IN6P_IPV6_V6ONLY) == 0) {
800            struct sockaddr_in6 *sin6_p;
801
802            sin6_p = (struct sockaddr_in6 *)nam;
803            if (IN6_IS_ADDR_V4MAPPED(&sin6_p->sin6_addr)) {
804                  struct sockaddr_in sin;
805
806                  if (inp->inp_faddr.s_addr != INADDR_ANY)
807                        return EISCONN;
808                  in6_sin6_2_sin(&sin, sin6_p);
809                  s = splnet();
810                  error = in_pcbconnect(inp, (struct sockaddr *)&sin, p);
811                  splx(s);
812                  if (error == 0) {
813                        inp->inp_vflag |= INP_IPV4;
814                        inp->inp_vflag &= ~INP_IPV6;
815                        soisconnected(so);
816                  }
817                  return error;
818            }
819      }
820      if (!SA6_IS_ADDR_UNSPECIFIED(&inp->in6p_fsa))
821            return EISCONN;
822      s = splnet();
823      error = in6_pcbconnect(inp, nam, p);
824      splx(s);
825      if (error == 0) {
826            if (!ip6_v6only) { /* should be non mapped addr */
827                  inp->inp_vflag &= ~INP_IPV4;
828                  inp->inp_vflag |= INP_IPV6;
829            }
830            soisconnected(so);
831      }
832      return error;
833  }
```

790 Function `udp6_connect()` has three parameters: `so` is a pointer to the socket to which a remote address is being assigned; `nam` points to the remote address to be assigned to the socket; `p` is a pointer to the calling process.

795–797 The function returns the `EINVAL` error if the socket does not have a PCB entry.

799 The remote address is examined and the necessary PCB processing is performed if the PCB is configured to support both IPv4 and IPv6 communication (i.e., the `IN6P_IPV6_V6ONLY` flag is not set).

803–817 Function `in_pcbconnect()` is called to assign the remote IPv4 address if the specified remote address is an IPv4-mapped IPv6 address. The foreign address of the given socket PCB must not have been initialized previously. After successful remote address assignment, the `INP_IPV4` flag is set and the `INP_IPV6` flag is dropped so that the socket can be used only for communicating with IPv4 nodes.

820–832 Function `in6_pcbconnect()` is called to assign the remote address if the specified remote address is a normal IPv6 address. The function returns the `EISCONN` error if the foreign address is already initialized. The socket can be used only for IPv6 communication. The `INP_IPV4` flag is thus dropped and the `INP_IPV6` flag is set. The global variable `ip6_v6only` is a system-wide configurable variable that indicates the default behavior of the socket with respect to treatment of the IPv4-mapped IPv6 address. As discussed previously, the `INP_IPV4` flag is not set in a PCB unless the `ip6_v6only` variable is set to true. Thus there is no need to drop the `INP_IPV4` flag if `ip6_v6only` is set.

Detach PCB—udp6_detach() Function

The `udp6_detach()` function is called as a result of the `close()` system call on a UDP socket. `udp6_detach()` releases the PCB entry related to the socket.

Listing 6-110

```
                                                              ─udp6_usrreq.c
835     static int
836     udp6_detach(struct socket *so)
837     {
838             struct inpcb *inp;
839             int s;
840
841             inp = sotoinpcb(so);
842             if (inp == 0)
843                     return EINVAL;
844             s = splnet();
845             in6_pcbdetach(inp);
846             splx(s);
847             return 0;
848     }
                                                              ─udp6_usrreq.c
```

836 The `udp6_detach()` function has one parameter. `so` is a pointer to be closed.

841–843 If the socket does not have a PCB entry to be released, the function returns the `EINVAL` error.

844–845 The PCB entry is released by function `in6_pcbdetach()`.

Send a Packet—udp6_send() Function

The udp6_send() function is called as a result of the send() call, the sendto() call or the sendmsg() call issued on a UDP socket to send the specified datagram to the peer node specified as the destination of the datagram.

Listing 6-111

——————————————————————————————————udp6_usrreq.c

```
880     static int
881     udp6_send(struct socket *so, int flags, struct mbuf *m, struct sockaddr *addr,
882             struct mbuf *control, struct proc *p)
883     {
884             struct inpcb *inp;
885             int error = 0;
886
887             inp = sotoinpcb(so);
888             if (inp == 0) {
889                     error = EINVAL;
890                     goto bad;
891             }
```
——————————————————————————————————udp6_usrreq.c

881 The udp6_send() function has six input parameters: so is a pointer to the socket on which the data is sent; flags is a set of flags specified by the fourth argument of the send() or the sendto() system call, or by the third argument of the sendmsg() system call; m is a pointer to the mbuf containing the data to be sent; addr contains the packet destination address; control holds the packet options that can affect the behavior of udp6_output(); p points to the calling process.

887–891 The function returns the EINVAL error if the socket does not have a PCB entry.

Listing 6-112

——————————————————————————————————udp6_usrreq.c

```
893             if (addr) {
894                     if (addr->sa_len != sizeof(struct sockaddr_in6)) {
895                             error = EINVAL;
896                             goto bad;
897                     }
898                     if (addr->sa_family != AF_INET6) {
899                             error = EAFNOSUPPORT;
900                             goto bad;
901                     }
902             }
```
——————————————————————————————————udp6_usrreq.c

893–902 The Destination address is validated if it is specified. The address must be an IPv6 address. The foreign address set in the PCB entry will be used as the Destination address if addr is invalid.

Listing 6-113

——————————————————————————————————udp6_usrreq.c

```
904     #ifdef INET
905             if (!ip6_v6only) {
906                     int hasv4addr;
907                     struct sockaddr_in6 *sin6 = 0;
```

```
908
909                    if (addr == 0)
910                            hasv4addr = (inp->inp_vflag & INP_IPV4);
911                    else {
912                            sin6 = (struct sockaddr_in6 *)addr;
913                            hasv4addr = IN6_IS_ADDR_V4MAPPED(&sin6->sin6_addr)
914                                    ? 1 : 0;
915                    }
```
_____udp6_usrreq.c

905–915 The Destination address may be an IPv4-mapped IPv6 address. The Destination
address is checked, when the system is configured to allow IPv6-mapped IPv6 address
(that is, ip6_v6only is false). The packet Destination is assumed to be an IPv4 node if
the Destination address is not supplied by the caller and the PCB has the INP_IPV4 flag
bit set. Variable hasv4addr is set accordingly for later processing.

Listing 6-114

_____udp6_usrreq.c
```
916                    if (hasv4addr) {
917                            struct pr_usrreqs *pru;
918
919                            if ((inp->inp_flags & IN6P_IPV6_V6ONLY)) {
920                                    /*
921                                     * since a user of this socket set the
922                                     * IPV6_V6ONLY flag, we discard this
923                                     * datagram destined to a v4 addr.
924                                     */
925                                    return EINVAL;
926                            }
927                            if (!SA6_IS_ADDR_UNSPECIFIED(&inp->in6p_lsa)
928                                && !IN6_IS_ADDR_V4MAPPED(&inp->in6p_laddr)) {
929                                    /*
930                                     * when remote addr is IPv4-mapped
931                                     * address, local addr should not be
932                                     * an IPv6 address; since you cannot
933                                     * determine how to map IPv6 source
934                                     * address to IPv4.
935                                     */
936                                    return EINVAL;
937                            }
938                            if (sin6)
939                                    in6_sin6_2_sin_in_sock(addr);
940                            pru = inetsw[ip_protox[IPPROTO_UDP]].pr_usrreqs;
941                            error = ((*pru->pru_send)(so, flags, m, addr, control,
942                                    p));
943                            /* addr will just be freed in sendit(). */
944                            return error;
945                    }
946            }
```
_____udp6_usrreq.c

916–926 The function returns the EINVAL error if the packet is sent to an IPv4-mapped IPv6
address as the Destination, but the PCB is configured for IPv6 communication only.

927–937 The function returns an EINVAL error if the local address is specified, but the address
is not an IPv4-mapped IPv6 address because we cannot determine the source IPv4 address
for the outgoing packet.

938–946 The function in6_sin6_2_sin_in_sock() is called to convert the IPv4-mapped
IPv6 address to a normal IPv4 address. Then the udp_send() function, which is mapped
to pru_send, is called to transmit the packet.

Note: NetBSD also supports IPv4-mapped IPv6 addressess. NetBSD processess UDP/IPv4 packets given with IPv4-mapped IPv6 destination addresses in the `udp6_output()` function, while FreeBSD processes this type of packet in `udp_output()` function.

Listing 6-115

_____udp6_usrreq.c
```
949             return udp6_output(inp, m, addr, control, p);
950
951     bad:
952             m_freem(m);
953             return(error);
954     }
```
_____udp6_usrreq.c

949–953 The `udp6_output()` function is called to send the packet if the packet is destined to a normal IPv6 address.

6.10 Raw IPv6

Each upper layer protocol defines its input and output routines. These routines are initialized in each instance of the `ip6protosw{}` structure in `in6_proto.c`. Raw IPv6 is the mechanism for sending and receiving data over protocols other than TCP or UDP. The `ip6protosw{}` instances of these protocols are defined in `in6_proto.c`.

Table 6-13 shows the values of the various fields in the Raw IPv6 instance of the `ip6protosw{}` structure. `ip6protosw{}` is discussed in Section 3.4.3.

ICMPv6 is a special case of Raw IPv6. The most of functions defined in `ip6protosw{}` for ICMPv6 are shared with Raw IPv6. The difference is `pr_input` function that is `icmp6_input()` in ICMPv6. ICMPv6 provides a dedicated function for input processing, since ICMPv6 messages require much processing based on message types and codes.

6.10.1 Raw IPv6 Statistics

The statistics table is shared between IPv4 and IPv6 operations for both TCP and UDP because the statistics are independent of the network layer for these two protocols. However, Raw IPv6 defines a separate structure that implements its own statistics table as shown below.

Listing 6-116

_____raw_ip6.h
```
38      struct rip6stat {
39              u_quad_t rip6s_ipackets;        /* total input packets */
40              u_quad_t rip6s_isum;            /* input checksum computations */
41              u_quad_t rip6s_badsum;          /* of above, checksum error */
42              u_quad_t rip6s_nosock;          /* no matching socket */
43              u_quad_t rip6s_nosockmcast;     /* of above, arrived as multicast */
44              u_quad_t rip6s_fullsock;        /* not delivered, input socket full */
45
46              u_quad_t rip6s_opackets;        /* total output packets */
47      };
```
_____raw_ip6.h

TABLE 6-13

ip6protosw{} fields	*Value*	*Description*
pr_type	SOCK_RAW	Best effort datagram service
pr_domain	&inet6domain	Indicates the IPv6 protocol
pr_protocol	IPPROTO_RAW (255)	Protocol number
pr_flags	PR_ATOMIC|PR_ADDR	Indicates each process request operation maps a single protocol request operation, and data is passed with its addresses
pr_input	rip6_input	Input function
pr_output	rip6_output	Not used actually
pr_ctlinput	rip6_ctlinput	Control messages notification input processing
pr_ctloutput	rip6_ctloutput	Control messages output processing
pr_init	0	Not used
pr_fasttimo	0	Not used
pr_slowtimo	0	Not used
pr_drain	0	Not used
pr_usrreqs	rip6_usrreqs	User request dispatch functions

Raw IPv6 instance of the ip6protosw{} *structure.*

39–46 ip6s_ipackets is the total number of input packets that are neither TCP nor UDP packets.

rip6s_isum is the number of input packets that have checksum values.

rip6s_badsum is the number of input packets that have invalid checksum values.

rip6s_nosock is the number of dropped packets due to no matching PCB entry for the incoming packet.

rip6s_nosockmcast is similar to rip6s_nosock, except the destination address of incoming packets is a multicast address.

rip6s_fullsock is the number of packets dropped because the destination socket is full of unprocessed data.

rip6s_opackets is the number of output packets sent through a raw socket. Note that ICMPv6 has a separate statistics structure although ICMPv6 packets are sent through the Raw IPv6 output routine.

6.10.2 Raw IPv6 Output—rip6_output() Function

The rip6_output() function transmits data that was handed down from an upper layer protocol to the destination as a simple IPv6 datagram. There is no support for inserting upper layer headers. The caller is responsible for creating the necessary upper layer header before sending the packet over the Raw socket.

Listing 6-117

```
334     int
335     rip6_output(m, so, dstsock, control)
336             struct mbuf *m;
337             struct socket *so;
338             struct sockaddr_in6 *dstsock;
339             struct mbuf *control;
340     {
```

335–339 The `rip6_output()` function has four parameters: `m` is a pointer to the data to be sent; `so` is a pointer to the socket; `dstsock` is the destination address to which the datagram is sent; `control` is a pointer to the mbuf that contains packet options to be inserted into the packet.

Listing 6-118

```
341             struct in6_addr *dst;
342             struct ip6_hdr *ip6;
343             struct inpcb *in6p;
344             u_int   plen = m->m_pkthdr.len;
345             int error = 0;
346             struct ip6_pktopts opt, *stickyopt = NULL;
347             struct ifnet *oifp = NULL;
348             int type = 0, code = 0;         /* for ICMPv6 output statistics only */
349             int priv = 0;
350             struct sockaddr_in6 *sa6;
351
352             in6p = sotoin6pcb(so);
353             stickyopt = in6p->in6p_outputopts;
354
355             priv = 0;
356             if (so->so_cred->cr_uid == 0)
357                     priv = 1;
358             dst = &dstsock->sin6_addr;
359             if (control) {
360                     if ((error = ip6_setpktoptions(control, &opt,
361                                             stickyopt, priv, 0,
362                                             so->so_proto->pr_protocol))
363                         != 0) {
364                         goto bad;
365                     }
366                     in6p->in6p_outputopts = &opt;
367             }
```

352–353 The `stickyopt` is initialized to the default output packet options stored in the `in6p_outputopts` field of the PCB. At the completion of this routine the original default options stored in `stickyopt` will be restored back to `in6p_outputopts`. The `ip6_setpktoptions()` function merges two option groups: One is options specified by a caller and the other is options already stored in the PCB related to this socket. If a caller specifies the `control` parameter, `ip6_setpktoptions()` is called to merge those options. The merged options are stored in the `opt` variable.

Listing 6-119

```
369             /*
370              * For an ICMPv6 packet, we should know its type and code
```

```
371                 * to update statistics.
372                 */
373                if (so->so_proto->pr_protocol == IPPROTO_ICMPV6) {
374                        struct icmp6_hdr *icmp6;
375                        if (m->m_len < sizeof(struct icmp6_hdr) &&
376                            (m = m_pullup(m, sizeof(struct icmp6_hdr))) == NULL) {
377                                error = ENOBUFS;
378                                goto bad;
379                        }
380                        icmp6 = mtod(m, struct icmp6_hdr *);
381                        type = icmp6->icmp6_type;
382                        code = icmp6->icmp6_code;
383                }
```
——— raw_ip6.c

373–383 The type and code for an ICMPv6 packet is saved in the `type` and `code` variables respectively for updating the ICMPv6 statistics.

Listing 6-120
——— raw_ip6.c
```
385                M_PREPEND(m, sizeof(*ip6), M_WAIT);
386                ip6 = mtod(m, struct ip6_hdr *);
```
——— raw_ip6.c

385–386 The IPv6 header is prepended to the output data.

Listing 6-121
——— raw_ip6.c
```
388                /* Source address selection. */
389                if ((sa6 = in6_selectsrc(dstsock, in6p->in6p_outputopts,
390                                         in6p->in6p_moptions, &in6p->in6p_route,
391                                         &in6p->in6p_lsa, &oifp, &error)) == NULL) {
392                        if (error == 0)
393                                error = EADDRNOTAVAIL;
394                        goto bad;
395                }
396                ip6->ip6_src = sa6->sin6_addr;
397
398                if (oifp && dstsock->sin6_scope_id == 0 &&
399                    (error = scope6_setzoneid(oifp, dstsock)) != 0) { /* XXX */
400                        goto bad;
401                }
```
——— raw_ip6.c

389–396 Function `in6_selectsrc()` selects the source address of the packet based on the source address selection rules implemented in the function. The output packet is dropped if source address selection fails to yield a valid address.

398–401 Function `scope6_setzoneid()` is called in case the scope zone ID of the destination address needs to be disambiguated (see Listing 6-28).

Listing 6-122
——— raw_ip6.c
```
403                /* fill in the rest of the IPv6 header fields */
404                ip6->ip6_dst = *dst;
```

```
405                    ip6->ip6_flow = (ip6->ip6_flow & ~IPV6_FLOWINFO_MASK) |
406                          (in6p->in6p_flowinfo & IPV6_FLOWINFO_MASK);
407                    ip6->ip6_vfc = (ip6->ip6_vfc & ~IPV6_VERSION_MASK) |
408                          (IPV6_VERSION & IPV6_VERSION_MASK);
409                    /* ip6_plen will be filled in ip6_output, so not fill it here. */
410                    ip6->ip6_nxt = in6p->in6p_ip6_nxt;
411                    ip6->ip6_hlim = in6_selecthlim(in6p, oifp);
```
── raw_ip6.c

403–411 The IPv6 header fields are filled. The `rip6_output()` function is designed to send
data for any type of protocols. The Next Header value of the IPv6 header is set according to the value of `in6p_ip6_nxt` field of the PCB entry, which is initialized in the
`rip6_attach()` function to be described in the later section.

Listing 6-123
── raw_ip6.c

```
413                if (so->so_proto->pr_protocol == IPPROTO_ICMPV6 ||
414                    in6p->in6p_cksum != -1) {
415                        struct mbuf *n;
416                        int off;
417                        u_int16_t *p;
418
419                        /* compute checksum */
420                        if (so->so_proto->pr_protocol == IPPROTO_ICMPV6)
421                                off = offsetof(struct icmp6_hdr, icmp6_cksum);
422                        else
423                                off = in6p->in6p_cksum;
424                        if (plen < off + 1) {
425                                error = EINVAL;
426                                goto bad;
427                        }
428                        off += sizeof(struct ip6_hdr);
429
430                        n = m;
431                        while (n && n->m_len <= off) {
432                                off -= n->m_len;
433                                n = n->m_next;
434                        }
435                        if (!n)
436                                goto bad;
437                        p = (u_int16_t *)(mtod(n, caddr_t) + off);
438                        *p = 0;
439                        *p = in6_cksum(m, ip6->ip6_nxt, sizeof(*ip6), plen);
440                }
```
── raw_ip6.c

413–440 The checksum calculation for the outgoing packet is performed if either the packet
is an ICMPv6 packet or the PCB entry is set to calculate checksum (i.e., `in6p_cksum`
is not −1).

420–423 `off` holds the offset of the checksum field from the start of the packet header. The
offset can be easily derived for ICMPv6. However, the `in6p_cksum` field must hold
the correct offset value for other protocols. The caller can set `in6p_cksum` via the
socket API.

424–426 The checksum is a 2-byte value and must be within the packet data. The packet is
dropped if the packet length (`plen`) is smaller than `off + 1`.

430–439 p points to the beginning of the checksum field. Function `in6_cksum()` calculates the checksum and sets the value through pointer p.

Listing 6-124

_____raw_ip6.c

```
449            /*
450             * attach the full sockaddr_in6 addresses to the packet.
451             * XXX: sa6 may not have a valid sin6_scope_id in the
452             * non-SCOPEDROUTING case.
453             */
....
460            {
461                    struct sockaddr_in6 sa6_src = *sa6;
462
463                    if ((error = in6_recoverscope(&sa6_src, &sa6->sin6_addr,
464                                                  oifp)) != 0) {
465                            goto bad;
466                    }
467                    sa6_src.sin6_addr = sa6->sin6_addr; /* XXX */
468                    if (!ip6_setpktaddrs(m, &sa6_src, dstsock)) {
469                            error = ENOBUFS;
470                            goto bad;
471                    }
472            }
```

_____raw_ip6.c

461–467 The return value from `in6_selectsrc()` (sa6) must be copied to a local variable and converted by `in6_recoverscope()` for the same reason as that described for Listing 6-22.

468–471 Function `ip6_setpktaddrs()` sets the Source and Destination addresses in the form of the socket address structure with appropriate scope zone IDs into the packet pointed to by the mbuf m.

Listing 6-125

_____raw_ip6.c

```
475            oifp = NULL;            /* just in case */
476            error = ip6_output(m, in6p->in6p_outputopts, &in6p->in6p_route, 0,
477                               in6p->in6p_moptions, &oifp
....
479                               , in6p
....
481                               );
482            if (so->so_proto->pr_protocol == IPPROTO_ICMPV6) {
483                    if (oifp)
484                            icmp6_ifoutstat_inc(oifp, type, code);
485                    icmp6stat.icp6s_outhist[type]++;
486            } else
487                    rip6stat.rip6s_opackets++;
488
489            goto freectl;
490
491    bad:
492            if (m)
493                    m_freem(m);
494
495    freectl:
496            if (control) {
497                    ip6_clearpktopts(in6p->in6p_outputopts, -1);
498                    in6p->in6p_outputopts = stickyopt;
499                    m_freem(control);
```

```
500                 }
501                 return(error);
502         }
```
── raw_ip6.c

475–489 The packet is sent via the `ip6_output()` function. `ip6_output()` will set `oifp` to the actual interface from which the packet is sent. The interface statistics are updated if the packet was sent successfully.

491–493 The packet is released if an error occurred during output processing.

495–501 The combined packet options that include default options and caller specified options are released. The original default packet options are restored from `stickyopt`.

6.10.3   Raw IPv6 Input—`rip6_input()` Function

An incoming packet with a Next Header value that does not have an exact matching entry in the `inet6sw[]` array will be sent to the `rip6_input()` function by default (see Section 3.5.3). `rip6_input()` searches for a PCB entry that has the matching local and foreign addresses as the Destination and Source addresses from the packet, respectively. The packet is delivered to the associated socket if a matching PCB is found.

Listing 6-126
── raw_ip6.c
```
129     int
130     rip6_input(mp, offp, proto)
131             struct  mbuf **mp;
132             int     *offp, proto;
133     {
```
── raw_ip6.c

130–132 This function has three input parameters: `mp` is a pointer to the mbuf that contains the incoming packet; `offp` points to the offset value that is from the start of the IPv6 header to the start of the payload; `proto` holds the protocol number of the payload.

Listing 6-127
── raw_ip6.c
```
134             struct mbuf *m = *mp;
135             register struct ip6_hdr *ip6 = mtod(m, struct ip6_hdr *);
136             register struct inpcb *in6p;
137             struct inpcb *last = 0;
138             struct ip6_recvpktopts opts;
139             struct sockaddr_in6 src, dst, fromsa;
140
141             rip6stat.rip6s_ipackets++;
142
143             /*
144              * extract full sockaddr structures for the src/dst addresses,
145              * and make local copies of them.
146              */
147             if (ip6_getpktaddrs(m, &src, &dst)) {
148                     m_freem(m);
149                     return (IPPROTO_DONE);
150             }
```
── raw_ip6.c

147–150 The Source and Destination addresses that include the scope zone indices are retrieved by calling `ip6_getpktaddrs()`.

Listing 6-128

```
                                                                  raw_ip6.c
152            /*
153             * XXX: the address may have embedded scope zone ID, which should be
154             * hidden from applications.
155             */
156            fromsa = src;
  ....
158            in6_clearscope(&fromsa.sin6_addr);
                                                                  raw_ip6.c
```

156–158 `fromsa` holds the Source address of the incoming packet and is used as a return value of the receiving system call for each matching socket. If the address retrieved by `ip6_getpktaddrs()` contains an embedded scope zone ID in the address field, `in6_clearscope()` is called to remove it before returning the address to the application.

Listing 6-129

```
                                                                  raw_ip6.c
161            if (faithprefix_p != NULL && (*faithprefix_p)(&ip6->ip6_dst)) {
162                    /* XXX send icmp6 host/port unreach? */
163                    m_freem(m);
164                    return IPPROTO_DONE;
165            }
                                                                  raw_ip6.c
```

161–165 If the destination matches the FAITH prefix (see Section 6.7.7), the packet is simply discarded here because this type of translator cannot handle arbitrary transport protocols. In fact, KAME's implementation of the FAITH translator only supports TCP.

Listing 6-130

```
                                                                  raw_ip6.c
167            bzero(&opts, sizeof(opts));
168
169            LIST_FOREACH(in6p, &ripcb, inp_list) {
170                    if ((in6p->in6p_vflag & INP_IPV6) == 0)
171                            continue;
172                    if (in6p->in6p_ip6_nxt &&
173                        in6p->in6p_ip6_nxt != proto)
174                            continue;
175                    if (!SA6_IS_ADDR_UNSPECIFIED(&in6p->in6p_lsa) &&
176                        !SA6_ARE_ADDR_EQUAL(&in6p->in6p_lsa, &dst))
177                            continue;
178                    if (!SA6_IS_ADDR_UNSPECIFIED(&in6p->in6p_fsa) &&
179                        !SA6_ARE_ADDR_EQUAL(&in6p->in6p_fsa, &src))
180                            continue;
181                    if (in6p->in6p_cksum != -1) {
182                            rip6stat.rip6s_isum++;
183                            if (in6_cksum(m, ip6->ip6_nxt, *offp,
184                                m->m_pkthdr.len - *offp)) {
185                                    rip6stat.rip6s_badsum++;
186                                    continue;
```

```
187                           }
188                        }
```
_____raw_ip6.c

169–171 `ripcb` maintains a list of PCB entries that do not belong to any well-known transport protocols such as TCP or UDP. The `LIST_FOREACH` block traverses the entire list.

172–174 A PCB entry is bypassed if its protocol (the `in6p_ip6_nxt` member) does not match the protocol `proto` indicated in the packet.

175–180 The PCB entry is skipped if the entry has an initialized local address that does not match the packet destination address or if the entry has an initialized foreign address that does not match the packet source address.

181–188 If the kernel is expected to perform checksum validation for this socket via the `IPV6_CHECKSUM` socket option, the content is passed to `in6_cksum()` for validation. The PCB entry is skipped if the checksum is invalid. However, the loop processing continues because other PCBs may exist that do not require checksum validation in the kernel.

Listing 6-131
_____raw_ip6.c

```
189                    if (last) {
190                            struct mbuf *n = m_copy(m, 0, (int)M_COPYALL);
191
....
211                        if (n) {
212                            if (last->in6p_flags & IN6P_CONTROLOPTS ||
213                                last->in6p_socket->so_options & SO_TIMESTAMP)
214                                    ip6_savecontrol(last, ip6, n, &opts);
215                            /* strip intermediate headers */
216                            m_adj(n, *offp);
217                            if (sbappendaddr(&last->in6p_socket->so_rcv,
218                                    (struct sockaddr *)&fromsa,
219                                    n, opts.head) == 0) {
220                                m_freem(n);
221                                if (opts.head)
222                                        m_freem(opts.head);
223                                rip6stat.rip6s_fullsock++;
224                            } else
225                                    sorwakeup(last->in6p_socket);
226                            bzero(&opts, sizeof(opts));
227                        }
228                    }
229                    last = in6p;
230                }
```
_____raw_ip6.c

189 Variable `last` defaults to NULL and will be set at line 229 if a matching PCB is found. The actual processing of the packet is delayed by one loop time and is identical to the processing logic described in Section 6.9.3 for UDP packets.

212–215 If a PCB is set to receive additional packet information, that is, either the PCB has the `IN6P_CONTROLOPTS` flag set or the associated socket has the `SO_TIMESTAMP` option set, `ip6_savecontrol()` extracts the packet options from the incoming packet or creates a current timestamp and stores these options in `opts`.

216–226 The header part (i.e., the IPv6 header and intermediate extension header), is removed from the copied packet and the payload part of the packet is appended onto the socket buffer by calling `sbappendaddr()`. Note that the behavior is different from the input processing of an IPv4 raw socket, where the IPv4 header and IP options (if any) are passed to the application as well as the payload. This raw socket behavior is an intentional change in the standard API [RFC3542] (see Section 7.3.2), and this part of the code implements the API specification. The packet and the extracted packet options are released if the payload delivery failed. Otherwise, function `sorwakeup()` is called to notify the process associated with the socket that incoming data is available.

Listing 6-132

```
                                                                          raw_ip6.c
252                 if (last) {
253                         if (last->in6p_flags & IN6P_CONTROLOPTS ||
254                             last->in6p_socket->so_options & SO_TIMESTAMP)
255                                 ip6_savecontrol(last, ip6, m, &opts);
256                         /* strip intermediate headers */
257                         m_adj(m, *offp);
258                         if (sbappendaddr(&last->in6p_socket->so_rcv,
259                                         (struct sockaddr *)&fromsa, m,
260                                         opts.head) == 0) {
261                                 m_freem(m);
262                                 if (opts.head)
263                                         m_freem(opts.head);
264                                 rip6stat.rip6s_fullsock++;
265                         } else
266                                 sorwakeup(last->in6p_socket);
                                                                          raw_ip6.c
```

252–266 The packet is delivered to the last matching PCB entry. The code is almost identical to that in lines 212–226 except the packet is not duplicated.

Listing 6-133

```
                                                                          raw_ip6.c
267                 } else {
268                         rip6stat.rip6s_nosock++;
269                         if (m->m_flags & M_MCAST)
270                                 rip6stat.rip6s_nosockmcast++;
271                         if (proto == IPPROTO_NONE)
272                                 m_freem(m);
273                         else {
274                                 char *prvnxtp = ip6_get_prevhdr(m, *offp); /* XXX */
275                                 icmp6_error(m, ICMP6_PARAM_PROB,
276                                             ICMP6_PARAMPROB_NEXTHEADER,
277                                             prvnxtp - mtod(m, char *));
278                         }
279                         ip6stat.ip6s_delivered--;
280                 }
281         return IPPROTO_DONE;
282     }
                                                                          raw_ip6.c
```

267–279 The packet is discarded if no matching PCB entry can be found. If the packet does not contain any upper layer protocol header, the packet is simply released. Otherwise, an ICMPv6 error message is sent with an error code of `ICMP6_PARAMPROB_NEXTHEADER` to indicate to the packet originator that the receiving node encounters an unrecognized Next Header value. This processing covers the case where a Next Header value of zero appears in a header other than the IPv6 header as specified in [RFC2460].

Note: There are some subtle cases around this check. First, the check for the invalid occurrence of a Next Header value of zero does not work when an application opens an `AF_INET6` raw socket with the protocol of `IPPROTO_HOPOPTS`. This clearly violates the protocol specification and should actually be prohibited. Secondly, a packet for a "well-known" protocol may cause the ICMPv6 error. For example, a packet containing OSPF for IPv6 [RFC2740], which is identified by the Next Header value of 89, will trigger an ICMPv6 error unless an OSPF routing daemon runs on the receiving node. This is probably a suboptimal behavior, but this is primarily due to the unclear definition of "unrecognized" header value.

6.10.4   ICMPv6 Input—`icmp6_rip6_input()` Function

An ICMPv6 packet processed by the `icmp6_input()` function is delivered to sockets by the `icmp6_rip6_input()` function. As the function name implies, it is based on the `rip6_input()` function described in the previous section.

The processing performed in this function is almost the same as that of `rip6_input()`. However, the ICMPv6 specific routine is provided in order to implement the message filtering mechanism based on ICMPv6 types as defined in the standard API [RFC3542]. The implementation of this mechanism is described below.

ICMPv6 Message Filtering

Any incoming ICMPv6 messages will be delivered to all raw sockets with the protocol of ICMPv6 (`IPPROTO_ICMPV6`) by default. This can be noisy for the receiving applications, since ICMP is more frequently used in IPv6 than in IPv4. (For example, Neighbor Discovery messages are carried over ICMPv6.)

The standard socket API [RFC3542] defines a mechanism so that an application using an ICMPv6 socket can filter out ICMPv6 messages of specific types and can concentrate on those of interest. Whereas the API is primarily intended for user applications, the KAME kernel also uses the API definitions. We thus describe these definitions in this section.

The filtering policy is encoded in the `icmp6_filter{}` structure through a set of macro functions. [RFC3542] defines this structure as an opaque type: it is discouraged for an application to get access to the internal structure, and an individual implementation can adopt its own internal definition of the structure.

The KAME implementation simply uses the example definition shown in [RFC3542] as follows:

Listing 6-134
                                                                         ──────── icmp6.h
```
706     struct icmp6_filter {
707             u_int32_t icmp6_filt[8];
708     };
```
                                                                         ──────── icmp6.h

706–708 The `icmp6_filter{}` structure holds the specification of the ICMPv6 filter. The structure has an array of 32-bit integers that consist of eight entries. The array is used as a

TABLE 6-14

Name	Description
ICMP6_FILTER_SETPASSALL (*filter*)	Set the filter *filter* to accept all ICMPv6 messages.
ICMP6_FILTER_SETBLOCKALL (*filter*)	Set the filter *filter* to block all ICMPv6 messages.
ICMP6_FILTER_SETPASS (*type, filter*)	Set the filter *filter* to pass the specified type *type*.
ICMP6_FILTER_SETBLOCK (*type, filter*)	Set the filter *filter* to block the specified type *type*.
ICMP6_FILTER_WILLPASS (*type, filter*)	Return true if the filter *filter* is configured to pass the specified type *type*.
ICMP6_FILTER_WILLBLOCK (*type, filter*)	Return true if the filter *filter* is configured to block the specified type *type*.

Macro functions to handle the ICMPv6 filter specification.

bit field to specify the filter (note that the array contains 256 bits, which is necessary and sufficient to represent all possible ICMPv6 types). The position of each bit corresponds to the type number of each ICMPv6 message. When the bit is set, the corresponding ICMPv6 message will be passed to the application; otherwise the message will be dropped in the icmp6_rip6_input() function as shown shortly.

In the kernel, the icmp6_filter{} structure is stored in the PCB entry corresponding to the socket. It is created when a raw socket for ICMPv6 and its PCB entry are allocated, and set in the in6p_icmp6filt member of the inpcb{} structure (Listing 6-151).

Table 6-14 shows a list of function macros defined in [RFC3542] for managing the filter information.

Like the details of the icmp6_filter{} structure, the internal definitions of these macros can be implementation specific. Again, the KAME implementation generally uses the example code shown in [RFC3542] as described in Listing 6-135.

Listing 6-135

```
                                                                        icmp6.h
710    #ifdef _KERNEL
711    #define ICMP6_FILTER_SETPASSALL(filterp) \
712    do {                                                               \
713            int i; u_char *p;                                          \
714            p = (u_char *)filterp;                                     \
715            for (i = 0; i < sizeof(struct icmp6_filter); i++)          \
716                    p[i] = 0xff;                                       \
717    } while (/*CONSTCOND*/ 0)
718    #define ICMP6_FILTER_SETBLOCKALL(filterp) \
719            bzero(filterp, sizeof(struct icmp6_filter))
720    #else /* _KERNEL */
721    #define ICMP6_FILTER_SETPASSALL(filterp) \
722            memset(filterp, 0xff, sizeof(struct icmp6_filter))
723    #define ICMP6_FILTER_SETBLOCKALL(filterp) \
724            memset(filterp, 0x00, sizeof(struct icmp6_filter))
725    #endif /* _KERNEL */
726
727    #define ICMP6_FILTER_SETPASS(type, filterp) \
728            (((filterp)->icmp6_filt[(type) >> 5]) |= (1 << ((type) & 31)))
729    #define ICMP6_FILTER_SETBLOCK(type, filterp) \
730            (((filterp)->icmp6_filt[(type) >> 5]) &= ~(1 << ((type) & 31)))
```

```
731     #define ICMP6_FILTER_WILLPASS(type, filterp) \
732             (((( (filterp)->icmp6_filt[(type) >> 5]) & (1 << ((type) & 31))) != 0)
733     #define ICMP6_FILTER_WILLBLOCK(type, filterp) \
734             (((( (filterp)->icmp6_filt[(type) >> 5]) & (1 << ((type) & 31))) == 0)
```
——— icmp6.h

711–718 The example code of ICMP6_FILTER_SETPASSALL() and ICMP6_FILTER_SETBLOCKALL() shown in [RFC3452] uses the memset() function. The KAME implementation uses this code for user space programs as shown in lines 721–724. For the kernel code, an alternate implementation is used since memset() may not be provided in some systems, while the FreeBSD kernel version described in this book has this function.

722–733 ICMP6_FILTER_SETPASSALL() clears all bits in the icmp6_filter{} structure. ICMP6_FILTER_SETBLOCKALL() sets all bits in the icmp6_filter{} structure. ICMP6_FILTER_SETPASS() and ICMP6_FILTER_SETBLOCK() sets and clears the bit corresponding to the type value respectively. ICMP6_FILTER_WILLPASS() and ICMP6_FILTER_WILLBLOCK() checks if the bit corresponding to the type value is set or cleared respectively.

icmp6_rip6_input() Function

We are now ready to describe the icmp6_rip6_input() function. Below we will mainly focus on characteristic parts of this function.

Listing 6-136

——— icmp6.c
```
2299    /*
2300     * XXX almost dup'ed code with rip6_input.
2301     */
2302    static int
2303    icmp6_rip6_input(mp, off, src, dst)
2304            struct mbuf **mp;
2305            int off;
2306            struct sockaddr_in6 *src, *dst;
2307    {
2308            struct mbuf *m = *mp;
2309            struct ip6_hdr *ip6 = mtod(m, struct ip6_hdr *);
2310            struct in6pcb *in6p;
2311            struct in6pcb *last = NULL;
2312            struct sockaddr_in6 fromsa;
2313            struct icmp6_hdr *icmp6;
2314            struct ip6_recvpktopts opts;
....
2317            /* this is assumed to be safe. */
2318            icmp6 = (struct icmp6_hdr *)((caddr_t)ip6 + off);
```
——— icmp6.c

2302–2306 mp is a pointer to the mbuf which holds the received ICMPv6 packet; off is an offset from the head of the IPv6 header to the head of the ICMPv6 header; src and dst are the source and destination addresses of the packet in the form of the sockaddr_in6{} structure that were retrieved from the mbuf tag.

2318 icmp6 is set to point to the ICMPv6 header. This operation is safe because the memory block for the ICMPv6 packets are confirmed to be in a contiguous space in the first mbuf in the icmp6_input() function (see Section 4.6.1).

Listing 6-137

```
                                                           ___icmp6.c
2327            /*
2328             * XXX: the address may have embedded scope zone ID, which should be
2329             * hidden from applications.
2330             */
2331            fromsa = *src;
....
2333            in6_clearscope(&fromsa.sin6_addr);
                                                           ___icmp6.c
```

2331–2333 The packet's source address is copied to `fromsa`, which will be used as a return value of receiving applications. It may contain the corresponding scope zone ID in the IPv6 address field, and must be cleared before sent to the applications (Section 2.9.3).

Listing 6-138

```
                                                           ___icmp6.c
2336            bzero(&opts, sizeof(opts));
2337
....
2339            LIST_FOREACH(in6p, &ripcb, inp_list)
....
2348            {
....
2350                    if ((in6p->inp_vflag & INP_IPV6) == 0)
2351                            continue;
....
2357                    if (in6p->in6p_ip6_nxt != IPPROTO_ICMPV6)
2358                            continue;
2359                    if (!SA6_IS_ADDR_UNSPECIFIED(&in6p->in6p_lsa) &&
2360                        !SA6_ARE_ADDR_EQUAL(&in6p->in6p_lsa, dst))
2361                            continue;
2362                    if (!SA6_IS_ADDR_UNSPECIFIED(&in6p->in6p_fsa) &&
2363                        !SA6_ARE_ADDR_EQUAL(&in6p->in6p_fsa, src))
2364                            continue;
2365                    if (in6p->in6p_icmp6filt
2366                        && ICMP6_FILTER_WILLBLOCK(icmp6->icmp6_type,
2367                                   in6p->in6p_icmp6filt))
2368                            continue;
                                                           ___icmp6.c
```

2339 This loop goes through all PCB entries corresponding to Raw IPv6 sockets and delivers the input packet to ICMPv6 sockets. Note that the PCB list starting at `ripcb` is shared with the general raw socket processing.

2350–2364 `in6p` is a pointer to a PCB entry. A PCB entry has a flag field that identifies whether the entry is used for IPv4 or IPv6. The incoming ICMPv6 packet is ignored if the PCB entry is not used for IPv6 or if the source or destination address stored in the PCB differs from the packet's address.

2365–2368 If the ICMPv6 filter for this PCB entry indicates this type of messages should be blocked, this packet is ignored. Note that the check at line 2365 is actually meaningless since `in6p_icmp6filt` member is initialized at the PCB creation time and is always non-NULL.

Listing 6-139

```
                                                           ___icmp6.c
2369                    if (last) {
2370                            struct  mbuf *n = NULL;
```

```
2371
2372                                      /*
2373                                       * Recent network drivers tend to allocate a single
2374                                       * mbuf cluster, rather than to make a couple of
2375                                       * mbufs without clusters.  Also, since the IPv6 code
2376                                       * path tries to avoid m_pullup(), it is highly
2377                                       * probable that we still have an mbuf cluster here
2378                                       * even though the necessary length can be stored in an
2379                                       * mbuf's internal buffer.
2380                                       * Meanwhile, the default size of the receive socket
2381                                       * buffer for raw sockets is not so large.  This means
2382                                       * the possibility of packet loss is relatively higher
2383                                       * than before.  To avoid this scenario, we copy the
2384                                       * received data to a separate mbuf that does not use
2385                                       * a cluster, if possible.
2386                                       * XXX: it is better to copy the data after stripping
2387                                       * intermediate headers.
2388                                       */
2389                                      if ((m->m_flags & M_EXT) && m->m_next == NULL &&
2390                                          m->m_len <= MHLEN) {
2391                                              MGET(n, M_DONTWAIT, m->m_type);
2392                                              if (n != NULL) {
....
2397                                                      m_dup_pkthdr(n, m, M_DONTWAIT);
....
2401                                                      bcopy(m->m_data, n->m_data, m->m_len);
2402                                                      n->m_len = m->m_len;
2403                                              }
2404                                      }
2405                                      if (n != NULL ||
2406                                          (n = m_copy(m, 0, (int)M_COPYALL)) != NULL) {
2407                                              if (last->in6p_flags & IN6P_CONTROLOPTS)
2408                                                      ip6_savecontrol(last, ip6, n, &opts);
2409                                              /* strip intermediate headers */
2410                                              m_adj(n, off);
2411                                              if (sbappendaddr(&last->in6p_socket->so_rcv,
2412                                                              (struct sockaddr *)&fromsa,
2413                                                              n, opts.head) == 0) {
2414                                                      /* should notify about lost packet */
2415                                                      m_freem(n);
2416                                                      if (opts.head) {
2417                                                              m_freem(opts.head);
2418                                                      }
2419                                              } else
2420                                                      sorwakeup(last->in6p_socket);
2421                                              bzero(&opts, sizeof(opts));
2422                                      }
2423                              }
2424                      last = in6p;
2425              }
```
                                                                           ____icmp6.c

2369–2425 This part of the code is mostly identical to the corresponding part of the
rip6_input() function. The following is a description of this code block that is specific
to ICMPv6 processing.

Within the loop, the packet must be copied before it is appended to the socket buffer
since other sockets may need it. If the incoming packet is stored in a single mbuf with
a cluster and its packet length is smaller than MHLEN, a new mbuf without a cluster is
allocated and the packet is copied to the new mbuf. Otherwise, m_copy() duplicates
the packet in a separate mbuf. The former condition may look rare, but can actually
happen for some Ethernet driver implementations (such as the fxp driver of this version
of FreeBSD) that always store incoming packets into an mbuf cluster regardless of the
length. m_copy() is not used in this case because the copied packet would also have a

cluster and consume the socket's receive buffer accordingly. It is not negligible compared to the default receive buffer size of a raw socket, 8192 bytes (Section 6.10.7). In fact, the **ping6** command for all-nodes multicast address `ff02::1` could drop some responses with a certain number of responders.

The header part is stripped and the ICMPv6 header and data are delivered to the socket buffer using the `sbappendaddr()` function. The delivery will be notified by the `sorwakeup()` function, if `sbappendaddr()` succeeds.

Listing 6-140
```
                                                                            icmp6.c
2426           if (last) {
2427                   if (last->in6p_flags & IN6P_CONTROLOPTS)
2428                           ip6_savecontrol(last, ip6, m, &opts);
2429                   /* strip intermediate headers */
2430                   m_adj(m, off);
2431
2432                   /* avoid using mbuf clusters if possible (see above) */
2433                   if ((m->m_flags & M_EXT) && m->m_next == NULL &&
2434                       m->m_len <= MHLEN) {
2435                           struct mbuf *n;
2436
2437                           MGET(n, M_DONTWAIT, m->m_type);
2438                           if (n != NULL) {
     ....
2443                                   m_dup_pkthdr(n, m, M_DONTWAIT);
     ....
2447                                   bcopy(m->m_data, n->m_data, m->m_len);
2448                                   n->m_len = m->m_len;
2449
2450                                   m_freem(m);
2451                                   m = n;
2452                           }
2453                   }
2454                   if (sbappendaddr(&last->in6p_socket->so_rcv,
2455                                   (struct sockaddr *)&fromsa,
2456                                   m, opts.head) == 0) {
2457                           m_freem(m);
2458                           if (opts.head)
2459                                   m_freem(opts.head);
2460                   } else
2461                           sorwakeup(last->in6p_socket);
2462           } else {
2463                   m_freem(m);
2464                   ip6stat.ip6s_delivered--;
2465           }
2466           return IPPROTO_DONE;
2467   }
                                                                            icmp6.c
```

2427–2461 Almost the same work with the code done between lines 2407–2422 is performed. The difference is that we do not need to copy the packet before delivering to the socket buffer as we did on line 2406, since this is the last delivery. Note that converting from a cluster mbuf to a non-cluster mbuf is still desirable.

6.10.5   Raw IPv6 Control Input—`rip6_ctlinput()` Function

The Raw IP event notification mechanism is similar to that used by UDP. Figure 6-12 illustrates the call flow of the various notification messages. The Raw IP notification handler is

FIGURE 6-12

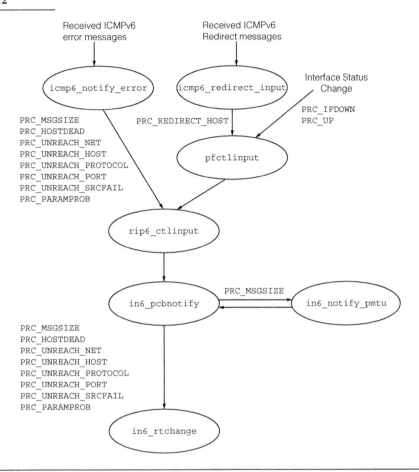

Raw IPv6 notification call flow.

the `rip6_ctlinput()` function. For the most part, the code in `rip6_ctlinput()` is identical to the code in the `udp6_ctlinput()` function. The major difference is that `rip6_ctlinput()` does not decode the upper layer port numbers because the upper layer protocol is unknown to this function.

Table 6-15 shows the each notification message and its corresponding Raw IPv6 handler function.

6.10.6   Raw IPv6 Control Output—`rip6_ctloutput()` Function

Raw IPv6 has its own control output function `rip6_ctloutput()` for handling socket options-related operations. This function is called as a result of the `setsockopt()` or the `getsockopt()` function calls issued on a Raw IPv6 socket.

TABLE 6-15

Raw IPv6	*Callback function*
PRC_IFDOWN	in6_rtchange()
PRC_IFUP	in6_rtchange()
PRC_MSGSIZE	in6_rtchange()
PRC_HOSTDEAD	in6_rtchange()
PRC_UNREACH_NET	in6_rtchange()
PRC_UNREACH_HOST	in6_rtchange()
PRC_UNREACH_PROTOCOL	in6_rtchange()
PRC_UNREACH_PORT	in6_rtchange()
PRC_UNREACH_SRCFAIL	in6_rtchange()
PRC_PARAMPROB	in6_rtchange()

Notifications and Raw IPv6 callback functions.

Listing 6-141

―――raw_ip6.c
```
507     int
508     rip6_ctloutput(so, sopt)
509            struct socket *so;
510            struct sockopt *sopt;
511     {
```
―――raw_ip6.c

508–510 Function `rip6_ctloutput()` has two parameters: `so` is a pointer to the socket; `sopt` is a pointer to the storage that contains the socket option information.

Listing 6-142

―――raw_ip6.c
```
512             int error;
513
514             if (sopt->sopt_level == IPPROTO_ICMPV6)
515                     /*
516                      * XXX: is it better to call icmp6_ctloutput() directly
517                      * from protosw?
518                      */
519                     return(icmp6_ctloutput(so, sopt));
520             else if (sopt->sopt_level != IPPROTO_IPV6)
521                     return (EINVAL);
522
523             error = 0;
```
―――raw_ip6.c

514–519 If the operation is performed on ICMPv6 options, then the call is transfered to the `icmp6_ctloutput()` function.

520–521 The function returns the `EINVAL` error if the socket option does not apply to IPv6.

Listing 6-143

raw_ip6.c

```
525              switch (sopt->sopt_dir) {
526              case SOPT_GET:
527                      switch (sopt->sopt_name) {
528                      case MRT6_INIT:
529                      case MRT6_DONE:
530                      case MRT6_ADD_MIF:
531                      case MRT6_DEL_MIF:
532                      case MRT6_ADD_MFC:
533                      case MRT6_DEL_MFC:
534                      case MRT6_PIM:
535                              error = ip6_mrouter_get(so, sopt);
536                              break;
537                      case IPV6_CHECKSUM:
538                              error = ip6_raw_ctloutput(so, sopt);
539                              break;
540                      default:
541                              error = ip6_ctloutput(so, sopt);
542                              break;
543                      }
544                      break;
545
546              case SOPT_SET:
547                      switch (sopt->sopt_name) {
548                      case MRT6_INIT:
549                      case MRT6_DONE:
550                      case MRT6_ADD_MIF:
551                      case MRT6_DEL_MIF:
552                      case MRT6_ADD_MFC:
553                      case MRT6_DEL_MFC:
554                      case MRT6_PIM:
555                              error = ip6_mrouter_set(so, sopt);
556                              break;
557                      case IPV6_CHECKSUM:
558                              error = ip6_raw_ctloutput(so, sopt);
559                              break;
560                      default:
561                              error = ip6_ctloutput(so, sopt);
562                              break;
563                      }
564                      break;
565              }
566
567              return (error);
568      }
```

raw_ip6.c

528–536 and **548–556** If the operation is performed on multicast routing options then the call
   is transferred to function `ip6_mrouter_set()`.

537–539 and **557–559** If the operation is performed on the IPv6 checksum-offset option then
   the call is transferred to function `ip6_raw_ctloutput()`, which is discussed next.

560–562 The generic socket option handler `ip6_ctloutput()` processes all other options.

Listing 6-144

raw_ip6.c

```
3055    int
3056    ip6_raw_ctloutput(so, sopt)
3057            struct socket *so;
3058            struct sockopt *sopt;
....
3067    {
```

raw_ip6.c

3056–3058 Function `ip6_raw_ctloutput()` has two parameters that are identical to those
of function `rip6_ctloutput()`.

Listing 6-145

```
                                                                      raw_ip6.c
3068            int error = 0, optval, optlen;
3069            const int icmp6off = offsetof(struct icmp6_hdr, icmp6_cksum);
    ....
3073            struct in6pcb *in6p = sotoin6pcb(so);
    ....
3076            int level, op, optname;
    ....
3080            struct proc *p;
                                                                      raw_ip6.c
```

3069 `icmp6off` specifies the offset from the start of the ICMPv6 header to the start of the
ICMPv6 checksum field. This value is used later to prevent a user from modifying the
ICMPv6 checksum calculation behavior.

Listing 6-146

```
                                                                      raw_ip6.c
3087            if (sopt) {
3088                    level = sopt->sopt_level;
3089                    op = sopt->sopt_dir;
3090                    optname = sopt->sopt_name;
3091                    optlen = sopt->sopt_valsize;
    ....
3095                    p = sopt->sopt_p;
    ....
3097            } else {
3098                    panic("ip6_ctloutput: arg soopt is NULL");
3099            }
    ....
3103
3104            if (level != IPPROTO_IPV6) {
    ....
3109                    return (EINVAL);
3110            }
                                                                      raw_ip6.c
```

3087–3110 `level` specifies the protocol. `op` specifies the type of operation, which can be
either the SET or the GET operation. `optname` specifies the option. `optlen` is the length
of option data. `p` points to the calling process.

The system considers a NULL `sopt` pointer as a fatal error and the system will panic.
The function will return the `EINVAL` error if the socket option does not apply to IPv6.

Listing 6-147

```
                                                                      raw_ip6.c
3111
3112            switch (optname) {
3113            case IPV6_CHECKSUM:
3114                    /*
3115                     * For ICMPv6 sockets, no modification allowed for checksum
3116                     * offset, permit "no change" values to help existing apps.
3117                     *
3118                     * XXX 2292bis says: "An attempt to set IPV6_CHECKSUM
3119                     * for an ICMPv6 socket will fail."
```

```
3120                          * The current behavior does not meet 2292bis.
3121                          */
3122                         switch (op) {
....
3124                         case SOPT_SET:
....
3128                                 if (optlen != sizeof(int)) {
3129                                         error = EINVAL;
3130                                         break;
3131                                 }
....
3133                                 error = sooptcopyin(sopt, &optval, sizeof(optval),
3134                                                 sizeof(optval));
3135                                 if (error)
3136                                         break;
....
3140                                 if ((optval % 2) != 0) {
3141                                         /* the API assumes even offset values */
3142                                         error = EINVAL;
3143                                 } else if (so->so_proto->pr_protocol ==
3144                                     IPPROTO_ICMPV6) {
3145                                         if (optval != icmp6off)
3146                                                 error = EINVAL;
3147                                 } else
3148                                         in6p->in6p_cksum = optval;
3149                                 break;
....
3152                         case SOPT_GET:
....
3156                                 if (so->so_proto->pr_protocol == IPPROTO_ICMPV6)
3157                                         optval = icmp6off;
3158                                 else
3159                                         optval = in6p->in6p_cksum;
3160
....
3162                                 error = sooptcopyout(sopt, &optval, sizeof(optval));
....
3168                                 break;
3169
3170                         default:
3171                                 error = EINVAL;
3172                                 break;
3173                         }
3174                         break;
3175
3176                 default:
3177                         error = ENOPROTOOPT;
3178                         break;
3179                 }
....
3186         return (error);
3187 }
```
─── raw_ip6.c

3113 Function `ip6_raw_ctloutput()` handles only the `IPV6_CHECKSUM` socket option, which sets or gets the checksum-offset parameter for the PCB entry. The `IPV6_CHECKSUM` option allows a user application to specify to the kernel the location of the checksum field so that the kernel can calculate the value and insert the checksum value into the correct location within the packet.

3124–3142 For the set operation, the option value must be an integer value. Function `sooptcopyin()` copies the given option value into the supplied buffer optval. The offset to the checksum field must be an even offset because the checksum field is two bytes large. The function returns the `EINVAL` error if an odd offset is supplied.

TABLE 6-16

pr_usrreqs	udp6_usrreqs	Shared with IPv4
pru_abort	rip6_abort	No
pru_attach	rip6_attach	No
pru_bind	rip6_bind	No
pru_connect	rip6_connect	No
pru_control	in6_control	No
pru_detach	rip6_detach	No
pru_disconnect	rip6_disconnect	No
pru_peeraddr	in6_setpeeraddr	No
pru_send	rip6_send	No
pru_shutdown	rip6_shutdown	No
pru_sockaddr	in6_setsockaddr	No

Raw IPv6 instance of the pr_usrreqs{} *structure.*

3143–3148 For the ICMPv6 protocol the application-supplied offset must be equal to the offset value defined by the ICMPv6 header, otherwise the function returns the EINVAL error. As the code comment indicates, the RFC does not allow the modification of the in6p_cksum field of the PCB for the ICMPv6 protocol-based socket, and the implementation is not compliant with the socket API specification as defined by [RFC3542]. The in6p_cksum field is set to optval for all other protocols.

3152–3162 For the GET operation the function returns the fixed offset value if the socket is based on the ICMPv6 protocol. The function returns the value of in6p_cksum for all other protocols. Function sooptcopyout() copies the given option value into the supplied buffer sopt.

6.10.7   Raw IPv6 User Requests Handling

Any Raw IPv6 related socket request is dispatched to the corresponding function initialized in rip6_usrreqs, which is another instance of the pr_usrreqs{} structure. Table 6-16 lists the content of rip6_usrreqs.

In TCP and UDP, pru_peeraddr() and pru_sockaddr() are set to in6_mapped_peeraddr() and in6_mapped_sockaddr() to support IPv4-mapped IPv6 addresses. On the other hand, these types of addresses are not supported in Raw IPv6, and pru_peeraddr() and pru_sockaddr() are directly set to functions in6_setpeeraddr() and in6_setsockaddr().

Attach PCB—rip6_attach() Function

The rip6_attach() function is called as a result of the socket() system call issued on a Raw IPv6 socket. rip6_attach() creates a PCB entry for a Raw IPv6 socket.

Listing 6-148

raw_ip6.c

```
570     static int
571     rip6_attach(struct socket *so, int proto, struct proc *p)
572     {
```

raw_ip6.c

571 Function `rip6_attach()` has three input parameters: `so` is a pointer to the socket for which we will create a PCB entry; `proto` is an upper layer protocol number specified as the third parameter of the `socket()` system call; `p` is a pointer to the calling process.

Listing 6-149

raw_ip6.c

```
573             struct inpcb *inp;
574             int error, s;
575
576             inp = sotoinpcb(so);
577             if (inp)
578                     panic("rip6_attach");
579             if (p && (error = suser(p)) != 0)
580                     return error;
```

raw_ip6.c

576–580 The kernel will panic if the socket already has a PCB entry allocated to it. A Raw IPv6 socket can be created only by a superuser. The function will return an `EPERM` error if `suser()` indicates the calling process has insufficient privilege to perform this operation.

Listing 6-150

raw_ip6.c

```
582             error = soreserve(so, rip_sendspace, rip_recvspace);
583             if (error)
584                     return error;
585             s = splnet();
586             error = in_pcballoc(so, &ripcbinfo, p);
587             splx(s);
588             if (error)
589                     return error;
```

raw_ip6.c

582–584 The sizes of the send and receive buffers of the Raw socket are set to `rip_sendspace` and `rip_recvspace`, respectively. These values are initialized to 8192, and the latter can be modified by the **sysctl** command for the name of `net.inet6.raw.revspace`.

585–589 The memory space for a new PCB entry for the socket is allocated. The newly created PCB entry is inserted into the `ripcb` list that contains all PCB entries created for Raw IPv6 communications.

Listing 6-151

raw_ip6.c

```
590             inp = (struct inpcb *)so->so_pcb;
591             inp->inp_vflag |= INP_IPV6;
592             inp->in6p_ip6_nxt = (long)proto;
593             inp->in6p_hops = -1;     /* use kernel default */
594             inp->in6p_cksum = -1;
```

```
595              MALLOC(inp->in6p_icmp6filt, struct icmp6_filter *,
596                   sizeof(struct icmp6_filter), M_PCB, M_NOWAIT);
597              ICMP6_FILTER_SETPASSALL(inp->in6p_icmp6filt);
598              return 0;
599      }
```
—— raw_ip6.c

590–594 Each member variable of the newly created PCB is initialized. `in6p_ip6_nxt` is set to `proto`. `in6p_cksum` is set to −1, which specifies that the checksum calculation should be performed by the application process.

595–597 A new instance of the `icmp6_filter{}` structure is allocated and set in the `in6p_icmp6filt` member of the PCB. While it is created for any PCB entry for a raw socket, it is only used when `proto` is `IPPROTO_ICMPV6`. The structure is then initialized so that any type of ICMPv6 messages will be passed by default.

Note: This part of the code has a bug that misses the case where `MALLOC()` fails. In this case, initializing the ICMPv6 filters at line 597 will cause a kernel panic.

Bind Local Address—`rip6_bind()` Function

Function `rip6_bind()` is called as a result of the `bind()` system call issued on a Raw IPv6 socket. `rip6_bind()` assigns a local address to the specified Raw IPv6 socket.

Listing 6-152
—— raw_ip6.c
```
638      static int
639      rip6_bind(struct socket *so, struct sockaddr *nam, struct proc *p)
640      {
```
—— raw_ip6.c

639 Function `ip6_bind()` has three input parameters: `so` points to the socket to be assigned the given address; `nam` points to the address for local assignment; `p` points to the calling process.

Listing 6-153
—— raw_ip6.c
```
641              struct inpcb *inp = sotoinpcb(so);
642              struct sockaddr_in6 *addr = (struct sockaddr_in6 *)nam;
643              struct ifaddr *ia = NULL;
644              int error = 0;
....
646              u_int32_t lzone;
....
648
649              if (nam->sa_len != sizeof(*addr))
650                      return EINVAL;
651              if (nam->sa_family != AF_INET6)
652                      return EAFNOSUPPORT;
653              if (TAILQ_EMPTY(&ifnet) || addr->sin6_family != AF_INET6)
654                      return EADDRNOTAVAIL;
```
—— raw_ip6.c

649–652 The function returns the EINVAL error if the given address has an invalid size. The function returns the EAFNOSUPPORT error if the address family is not IPv6.

653–654 ifnet is a list of ifnet{} structures that reference available node interfaces. Local address assignment is impossible if no interface is present in the system. In this case the function returns the EADDRNOTAVAIL error.

Listing 6-154

raw_ip6.c

```
655             if ((error = scope6_check_id(addr, ip6_use_defzone)) != 0)
656                     return(error);
```

raw_ip6.c

655–656 Function scope6_check_id() sets the sin6_scope_id field of the specified address. The default interface is chosen if ambiguity exists when determining the scope zone ID and the ip6_use_defzone flag is set to true.

Listing 6-155

raw_ip6.c

```
658             lzone = addr->sin6_scope_id;
659             addr->sin6_scope_id = 0; /* for ifa_ifwithaddr */
....
661
662             if (!SA6_IS_ADDR_UNSPECIFIED(addr) &&
663                 (ia = ifa_ifwithaddr((struct sockaddr *)addr)) == 0)
664                     return EADDRNOTAVAIL;
665             if (ia &&
666                 ((struct in6_ifaddr *)ia)->ia6_flags &
667                 (IN6_IFF_ANYCAST|IN6_IFF_NOTREADY|
668                  IN6_IFF_DETACHED|IN6_IFF_DEPRECATED)) {
669                     return(EADDRNOTAVAIL);
670             }
```

raw_ip6.c

658–659 The sin6_scope_id is cleared because function ifa_ifwithaddr() expects the embedded scope zone index to be present and it does not expect the sin6_scope_id field to be filled.

662–664 The function returns the EADDRNOTAVAIL error if the specified local address is not assigned to any of the network interfaces in the node.

665–670 The function returns the EADDRNOTAVAIL error if the interface address returned by function ifa_ifwithaddr() is invalid for local address assignment (i.e., the address flag contains any one of the bit values IN6_IFF_ANYCAST, IN6_IFF_NOTREADY, IN6_IFF_DETACHED or IN6_IFF_DEPRECATED).

Listing 6-156

raw_ip6.c

```
672             addr->sin6_scope_id = lzone;
....
674             sa6_copy_addr(addr, &inp->in6p_lsa);
675             return 0;
676     }
```

raw_ip6.c

672–674 The original value of sin6_scope_id which was saved on line 658 is restored and the local address of the PCB entry is initialized based on the address information specified by the caller.

Fix Remote Address—rip6_connect() Function

Function rip6_connect() is called as a result of the connect() system call issued on a Raw IPv6 socket. rip6_connect() assigns an address to the remote node.

Listing 6-157

raw_ip6.c

```
678     static int
679     rip6_connect(struct socket *so, struct sockaddr *nam, struct proc *p)
680     {
```

raw_ip6.c

679 Function rip6_connect() has three parameters: so points to the socket to be assigned to a remote address; nam points to the address to be assigned to the remote endpoint in the PCB; p points to the calling process.

Listing 6-158

raw_ip6.c

```
681             struct inpcb *inp = sotoinpcb(so);
682             struct sockaddr_in6 *addr = (struct sockaddr_in6 *)nam, *sa6;
683             struct ifnet *ifp = NULL;
684             int error = 0;
    ....
686             struct sockaddr_in6 sa6_storage;
    ....
688
689             if (nam->sa_len != sizeof(*addr))
690                     return EINVAL;
691             if (TAILQ_EMPTY(&ifnet))
692                     return EADDRNOTAVAIL;
693             if (addr->sin6_family != AF_INET6)
694                     return EAFNOSUPPORT;
```

raw_ip6.c

689–694 The specified remote address is validated. The function returns the EINVAL error if the size of the address is invalid. The function returns the EADDRNOTAVAIL error if there is no network interface installed in the node. The function returns the EAFNOSUPPORT error if the given remote address is not an IPv6 address.

Listing 6-159

raw_ip6.c

```
695             if ((error = scope6_check_id(addr, ip6_use_defzone)) != 0)
696                     return(error);
697
698             /* Source address selection. XXX: need pcblookup? */
699             sa6 = in6_selectsrc(addr, inp->in6p_outputopts,
700                             inp->in6p_moptions, &inp->in6p_route,
701                             &inp->in6p_lsa, &ifp, &error);
702             if (sa6 == NULL)
703                     return (error ? error : EADDRNOTAVAIL);
```

```
705          /*
706           * XXX: sa6 may not have a valid sin6_scope_id in
707           * the non-SCOPEDROUTING case.
708           */
709          bzero(&sa6_storage, sizeof(sa6_storage));
710          sa6_storage.sin6_family = AF_INET6;
711          sa6_storage.sin6_len = sizeof(sa6_storage);
712          if ((error = in6_recoverscope(&sa6_storage, &sa6->sin6_addr,
713                                        NULL)) != 0) {
714                  return(error);
715          }
716          sa6_storage.sin6_addr = sa6->sin6_addr; /* XXX */
717          sa6 = &sa6_storage;

719
720          /* see above */
721          if (ifp && addr->sin6_scope_id == 0 &&
722              (error = scope6_setzoneid(ifp, addr)) != 0) { /* XXX */
723                  return(error);
724          }
```
———raw_ip6.c

695–723 This block of the code performs similar processing as the source address selection and handling scope zone IDs in the `rip6_output()` function (Section 6.10.2). See the relevant code description of `rip6_output()`.

Listing 6-160
———raw_ip6.c

```
725          sa6_copy_addr(sa6, &inp->in6p_lsa);
726          sa6_copy_addr(addr, &inp->in6p_fsa);
727          soisconnected(so);
728          return 0;
729  }
```
———raw_ip6.c

725–728 Both the remote address and the local address are set in the PCB and the socket status is changed to the connected state.

Detach PCB—*rip6_detach()* Function

Function `rip6_detach()` is called as a result of the `close()` system call issued on a Raw IPv6 socket. `rip6_detach()` disassociates the PCB from the Raw IPv6 socket and releases the memory occupied by the PCB entry.

Listing 6-161
———raw_ip6.c

```
601  static int
602  rip6_detach(struct socket *so)
603  {
604          struct inpcb *inp;
605
606          inp = sotoinpcb(so);
607          if (inp == 0)
608                  panic("rip6_detach");
609          /* xxx: RSVP */
610          if (so == ip6_mrouter)
611                  ip6_mrouter_done();
612          if (inp->in6p_icmp6filt) {
613                  FREE(inp->in6p_icmp6filt, M_PCB);
```

```
614                          inp->in6p_icmp6filt = NULL;
615                  }
616          in6_pcbdetach(inp);
617          return 0;
618  }
```
─── raw_ip6.c

606–608 The kernel panics if the socket does not have a valid PCB.

610–611 The function `ip6_mrouter_done()` is called to perform additional post processing
if the socket belongs to the multicast routing daemon.

612–615 The storage allocated for the ICMPv6 filter is released here.

616 The function `in6_pcbdetach()` is called to remove the PCB from the global list and the
memory allocated for the PCB is released.

Send Packet—rip6_send() Function

Function `rip6_send()` is called as a result of the `send()`, the `sendto()`, or the `sendmsg()`
system call issued on a Raw IPv6 socket.

Listing 6-162
─── raw_ip6.c

```
738  static int
739  rip6_send(struct socket *so, int flags, struct mbuf *m, struct sockaddr *nam,
740          struct mbuf *control, struct proc *p)
741  {
```
─── raw_ip6.c

739–740 Function `rip6_send()` has six input parameters: `so` points to the socket on which
data is sent; `flags` contains the output flag bits but is not used by this function; m is a
pointer to the mbuf that contains the data to be transmitted; `nam` holds the packet destination address; `control` holds the packet options to be constructed into the outgoing
packet in function `ip6_output()`; p points to the calling process.

Listing 6-163
─── raw_ip6.c

```
742          int error = 0;
743          struct inpcb *inp = sotoinpcb(so);
744          struct sockaddr_in6 tmp;
745          struct sockaddr_in6 *dst;
746
747          /* always copy sockaddr to avoid overwrites */
748          if (so->so_state & SS_ISCONNECTED) {
749                  if (nam) {
750                          m_freem(m);
751                          return EISCONN;
752                  }
753                  /* XXX */
754                  bzero(&tmp, sizeof(tmp));
755                  tmp.sin6_family = AF_INET6;
756                  tmp.sin6_len = sizeof(struct sockaddr_in6);
757                  bcopy(&inp->in6p_faddr, &tmp.sin6_addr,
758                          sizeof(struct in6_addr));
759                  dst = &tmp;
```
─── raw_ip6.c

748–752 The socket having the SS_ISCONNECTED bit set implies the socket has a valid remote address configured in its PCB. In this case the function will return the EISCONN error if nam holds a valid address. Otherwise the foreign address stored in the in6p_faddr field is used as the packet destination address.

Listing 6-164

——*raw_ip6.c*
```
760                } else {
761                        if (nam == NULL) {
762                                m_freem(m);
763                                return ENOTCONN;
764                        }
```
——*raw_ip6.c*

760–764 This function returns the ENOTCONN error if the PCB does not have an initialized foreign address and nam does not hold a valid address either.

Listing 6-165

——*raw_ip6.c*
```
765                        if (nam->sa_len != sizeof(struct sockaddr_in6)) {
766                                m_freem(m);
767                                return(EINVAL);
768                        }
769                        tmp = *(struct sockaddr_in6 *)nam;
770                        dst = &tmp;
771                        if (dst->sin6_family == AF_UNSPEC) {
772                                /*
773                                 * XXX: we allow this case for backward
774                                 * compatibility to buggy applications that
775                                 * rely on old (and wrong) kernel behavior.
776                                 */
777                                log(LOG_INFO, "rip6 SEND: address family is "
778                                    "unspec. Assume AF_INET6\n");
779                                dst->sin6_family = AF_INET6;
780                        } else if (dst->sin6_family != AF_INET6) {
781                                m_freem(m);
782                                return(EAFNOSUPPORT);
783                        }
784                        if ((error = scope6_check_id(dst, ip6_use_defzone)) != 0) {
785                                m_freem(m);
786                                return(error);
787                        }
788                }
789        return rip6_output(m, so, dst, control);
790    }
```
——*raw_ip6.c*

765–783 The Destination address is validated. An address with the AF_UNSPEC family type is set to the AF_INET6 address family to maintain backward compatibility. The traditional BSD raw socket code allows a datagram to be sent to a socket whose address family is not specified. To save some applications which assume the behavior, the function treats AF_UNSPEC as AF_INET6.

784–787 The function scope6_check_id() is called to initialize the scope zone ID in the sin6_scope_id member of the Destination address.

789 Finally, the packet is passed to rip6_output() for transmission.

6.11   Summary of Operation with IPv4-mapped IPv6 Addresses

We have seen that the special processing for IPv4-mapped IPv6 addresses complicates the kernel implementation. The complexity may also confuse the user about what exactly happens in operations with IPv4-mapped IPv6 addresses.

In this section, we summarize such major operations with concrete examples, thereby clarifying the possible confusion. Throughout this section, we assume a dual-stack node that has an IPv4 address of 192.0.2.1 and a global IPv6 address of 2001:db8::1. We focus on the usage over UDP in the examples, but the essential points generally apply to other transport protocols.

Note that the purpose of the clarification is not to encourage the use of IPv4–mapped IPv6 addresses. The purpose of this section is to show the complexity of the kernel implementation introduced by supporting for IPv4–mapped IPv6 addresses. The problems caused by IPv4–mapped IPv6 addresses will be discussed in Section 7.2.3.

Bind UDP Sockets

Figure 6-13 summarizes what happens when an application program issues the bind() system call for an AF_INET or AF_INET6 socket with or without specific addresses, and with a fixed port number of 53.

We consider the following seven scenarios:

A   bind an AF_INET socket to the IPv4 wildcard address (INADDR_ANY)

B   bind an AF_INET socket to the specific IPv4 address of 192.0.2.1

C   bind an AF_INET6 socket to the specific IPv4 address of 192.0.2.1 in the form of IPv4-mapped IPv6 address, ::ffff:192.0.2.1

D   bind an AF_INET6 socket with the IPV6_V6ONLY option enabled to the specific IPv4 address of 192.0.2.1 in the form of IPv4-mapped IPv6 address, ::ffff:192.0.2.1

E   bind an AF_INET6 socket to the IPv6 wildcard address (::)

F   bind an AF_INET6 socket with the IPV6_V6ONLY option enabled to the IPv6 wildcard address (::)

G   bind an AF_INET6 socket to the specific IPv6 address of 2001:db8::1

Figure 6-13 shows function call graphs in the kernel with labeled arrows corresponding to the above scenarios, and the content of the resulting PCB entries on success. Remarkable points are as follows:

- In scenario C, udp6_bind() calls in_pcbbind() to make the IPv4-specific binding (Listing 6-108). The resulting PCB entry clears the INP_IPV6 flag since this socket can only be used for IPv4 communication.

- On the other hand, scenario D fails with an error of EADDRNOTAVAIL unless the IPv4-mapped IPv6 address is configured as a normal IPv6 address on a local interface, a very atypical case or misconfiguration.

- Scenarios B and C cannot coexist, since these bindings are identical for in_pcblookup_local(), which only compares the inp_laddr fields (Section 6.7.6).

FIGURE 6-13

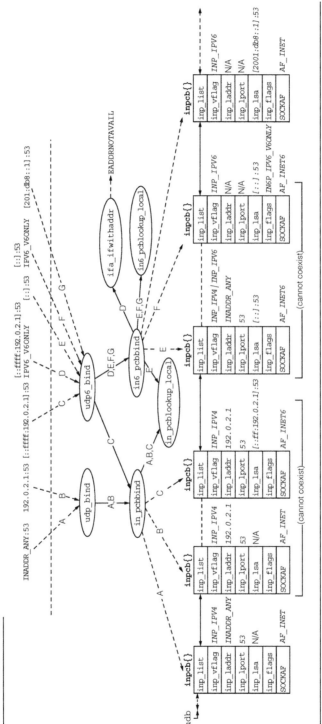

Scenarios of binding UDP sockets.

- On the other hand, scenarios A and D can coexist because the address families of the corresponding sockets are different: If a PCB based on scenario A exists and scenario D follows, in_pcblookup() returns the existing entry, but it does not cause an error in in6_pcbbind() as explained in Listing 6-18. Similarly, if a PCB based on scenario D exists and scenario A follows, in_pcblookup() returns the existing entry, but it does not cause an error in in_pcbbind() due to the difference of address family (Listing 6-20).

- In scenario F, the INP_IPV4 flag is cleared in the inp_vflag field as a result of the bind() operation, and no IPv4 communication will be performed on this socket.

Transmitting UDP Packets

Figure 6-14 shows various scenarios where an application sends UDP packets to IPv4 or IPv6 destinations over AF_INET or AF_INET6 sockets:

A send a packet to the IPv4 destination of 192.0.2.2 over an AF_INET socket

B send a packet to the IPv4 destination of 192.0.2.2 in the form of IPv4-mapped IPv6 address, ::ffff:192.0.2.2 over an AF_INET6 socket

C send a packet to the IPv4 destination of 192.0.2.2 in the form of IPv4-mapped IPv6 address, ::ffff:192.0.2.2 over an AF_INET6 socket with the IPV6_V6ONLY option enabled

D send a packet to the IPv6 destination of 2001:db8::2 over an AF_INET6 socket

FIGURE 6-14

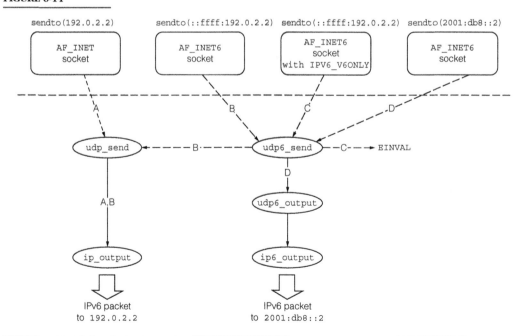

Scenarios of receiving a UDP packet.

In scenario B, the udp6_send() function detects that the destination address is an IPv4-mapped IPv6 address, and calls udp_send() function for packet transmission over IPv4 (Listing 6-114). Scenario C fails since communication over IPv4 on this socket is disabled by the IPV6_V6ONLY option (Listing 6-114).

Receive and Demultiprex a UDP Packet

Figure 6-15 shows various scenarios of receiving a UDP over an IPv4 packet from 192.0.2.2 to 192.0.2.1. This packet is processed at the udp_input() function where inp_pcblookup_hash() function is called to identify the best matching socket for delivering the packet (Section 6.7.8). It first prefers an exact match, that is, an AF_INET socket bound to 192.0.2.1 or an AF_INET6 socket bound to ::ffff:192.0.2.1. Note that only one of these bindings can exist as we explained above.

If no exact match is found, inp_pcblookup_hash() next prefers an AF_INET wildcard socket; if it does not exist, then this function finally chooses an AF_INET6 wildcard socket.

FIGURE 6-15

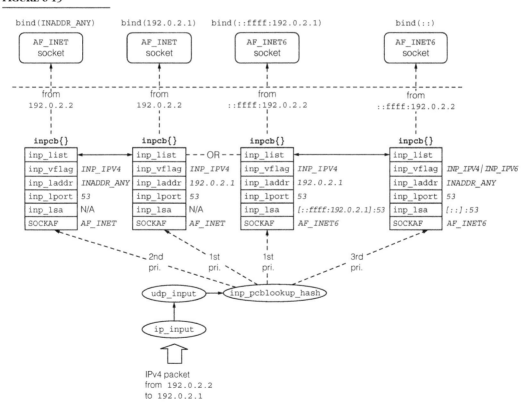

Scenarios of sending UDP packets.

If the packet is delivered to an `AF_INET6` socket, the remote address passed to the receiving system call (e.g., `recvfrom()`) is represented as IPv4-mapped IPv6 address, `::ffff:192.0.2.2`.

Socket Options and Joining a Multicast Group

Finally, Figure 6-16 illustrates what happens if IPv4-related socket options are set on an `AF_INET6` socket, using IPv4-mapped IPv6 addresses implicitly or explicitly.

We consider two cases: One is the `IP_OPTIONS` socket option which specifies IP options for outgoing IPv4 packets; the other is an attempt to join an IPv4 multicast group of `224.0.2.5`. Scenarios A and B are normal operation on an `AF_INET` socket, and should succeed as long as the socket option arguments are valid.

Scenario C fails with an error of `EINVAL`, because the `ip6_ctloutput()` function (the socket option hander in the IPv6 layer), does not accept socket options at the `IPPROTO_IP` level (see Listing 7-60). Unlike the cases in Figure 6-13 or 6-15, there is no detour to the IPv4 specific routines.

In scenario D, the application tries to join the IPv4 multicast group using IPv6 socket option, `IPV6_JOINGROUP`, with the group address in the form of IPv4-mapped IPv6 address. This attempt also fails with an error of `EINVAL` in the `ip6_setmoptions()` function, which handles this socket option, since the specified group address is not an IPv6 multicast address (Listing 7-91).

FIGURE 6-16

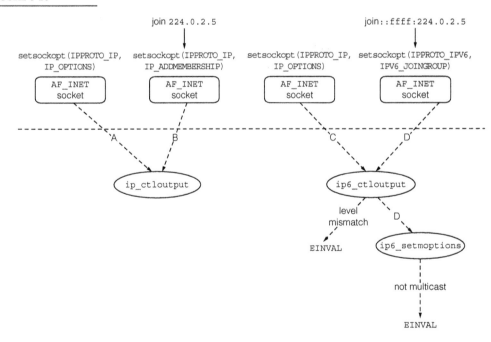

Scenarios of setting socket options and joining a multicast group.

6.12   Viewing IPv6 Connections with netstat

The connection status can be examined by **netstat** command. For example,

```
% netstat -an
Active Internet connections (includig servers)
Proto Recv-Q  Send-Q  Local Address      Foreign Address    (state)
tcp6    0       0      *.22               *.*                LISTEN
tcp4    0       0      *.22               *.*                LISTEN
tcp4    0       0      *.53               *.*                LISTEN
tcp6    0       0      *.53               *.*                LISTEN
tcp6    0       0      *.25               *.*                LISTEN
tcp6    0       0      *.80               *.*                LISTEN
tcp4    0       0      *.25               *.*
udp4    0       0      *.53               *.*
udp6    0       0      *.53               *.*
udp6    0       0      *.*                *.*
udp6    0       0      *.547              *.*
udp4    0       0      *.514              *.*
udp6    0       0      *.514              *.*
udp6    0       0      *.521              *.*
icm6    0       0      *.*                *.*
```

The **netstat** command has been extended to show IPv6 connections. The number after "`tcp`," "`udp`," and "`icm`" keywords refers to the IP version number. The version number corresponds to the `INP_IPV4` and `INP_IPV6` flags set in each PCB entry (i.e., if a PCB has the `INP_IPV4` flag set, then "`4`" will appear in the output; if a PCB has the `INP_IPV6` flag set, then "`6`" will appear in the output). The string "`46`" will appear after the protocol name if a PCB has both flag bits set, (i.e., if the PCB is configured to support IPv4-mapped IPv6 addresses).

The "`Recv-Q`" column shows the data size in the socket receive queue. The "`Send-Q`" column shows the data size in the socket send queue. The "`Local Address`" column shows the address and port number of the local node. Similarly the "`Foreign Address`" column shows the address and port number of the remote node. The dot separates the address and the port. "`(state)`" shows the state of the TCP protocol for each connection.

The previous output of the **netstat** command represents the following running services:

- SSH over TCP over IPv6 (Proto = tcp6, Local Address = *.22)

- SSH over TCP over IPv4 (Proto = tcp4, Local Address = *.22)

- DOMAIN (DNS) over TCP over IPv4 (Proto = tcp4, Local Address = *.53)

- DOMAIN (DNS) over TCP over IPv6 (Proto = tcp6, Local Address = *.53)

- SMTP over TCP over IPv6 (Proto = tcp6, Local Address = *.25)

- HTTP over TCP over IPv6 (Proto = tcp6, Local Address = *.80)

- SMTP over TCP over IPv4 (Proto = tcp4, Local Address = *.25)

- DOMAIN (DNS) over UDP over IPv4 (Proto = udp4, Local Address = *.53)

- DOMAIN (DNS) over UDP over IPv6 (Proto = udp6, Local Address = *.53)

- DHCPv6 over UDP over IPv6 (Proto = udp6, Local Address = *.547)

- SYSLOG over UDP over IPv4 (Proto = udp4, Local Address = *.514)

- SYSLOG over UDP over IPv6 (Proto = udp6, Local Address = *.514)

- RIPNG over UDP over IPv6 (Proto = udp6, Local Address = *.521)

- ICMPv6 (Proto = icm6)

All services bind an unspecified address as their local address so that connection requests that reach at any address of the local node can be accepted by these service processes.

There is a UDP-over-IPv6 socket that is bound to `*.*`. This socket is used by the DHCPv6 server process to send DHCPv6 messages on UDP-over-IPv6. Unfortunately we cannot identify which process uses which socket from the output of the **netstat** command. The FreeBSD system has the **sockstat** command that shows a process name and the status of all of the sockets owned by that process. However, the **sockstat** command does not work on the KAME kernel because of the differences that exist in the PCB structure definition between the original FreeBSD and the KAME kernel. The sample output of **sockstat** came from a FreeBSD system.

```
% sockstat -6
USER    COMMAND    PID    FD   PROTO   LOCAL ADDRESS           FOREIGN ADDRESS
john    sshd      58258   0    tcp6    201:db8:1:200:202:b3    2001:db8:1:200:2002:b3
john    sshd      58258   1    tcp6    201:db8:1:200:202:b3    2001:db8:1:200:2002:b3
john    sshd      58258   2    tcp6    201:db8:1:200:202:b3    2001:db8:1:200:2002:b3
john    sshd      58258   3    tcp6    201:db8:1:200:202:b3    2001:db8:1:200:2002:b3
john    sshd      58258   5    tcp6    201:db8:1:200:202:b3    2001:db8:1:200:2002:b3
john    sshd      58258   6    tcp6    201:db8:1:200:202:b3    2001:db8:1:200:2002:b3
john    sshd      58258   7    tcp6    201:db8:1:200:202:b3    2001:db8:1:200:2002:b3
root    sshd      58184   0    tcp6    201:db8:1:200:202:b3    2001:db8:1:200:2002:b3
root    sshd      58184   1    tcp6    201:db8:1:200:202:b3    2001:db8:1:200:2002:b3
root    sshd      58184   2    tcp6    201:db8:1:200:202:b3    2001:db8:1:200:2002:b3
root    sshd      58184   3    tcp6    201:db8:1:200:202:b3    2001:db8:1:200:2002:b3
root    sshd      58184   5    tcp6    201:db8:1:200:202:b3    2001:db8:1:200:2002:b3
root    sshd      58184   6    tcp6    201:db8:1:200:202:b3    2001:db8:1:200:2002:b3
root    sshd      58184   7    tcp6    201:db8:1:200:202:b3    2001:db8:1:200:2002:b3
root    named       195   4    udp46   *:53                    *.*
root    named       195   5    tcp46   *:53                    *.*
root    dhcp6s      185   5    udp6    *:547                   *.*
root    dhcp6s      182   6    udp46   *:*                     *.*
root    sshd        171   3    tcp46   *:22                    *.*
root    sendmail    169   3    tcp46   *:25                    *.*
root    httpd       161   3    tcp46   *:80                    *.*
root    syslogd     126   4    udp6    *:514                   *.*
root    rtadvd      111   3    icmp6   *:*                     *.*
root    route6d     109   3    udp46   *:521                   *.*
```

`icmp6` indicates the socket was created as a Raw IPv6 socket having ICMPv6 as the protocol. The socket will receive all ICMPv6 packets addressed to any address that belongs to this node. In this case this particular ICMPv6 Raw socket was opened by the **rtadvd** Router Advertisement daemon.

The output of **netstat** for established TCP connections follows:

```
% netstat -an
Active Internet connections (including servers)
Proto Recv-Q send-Q  Local Address        Foreign Address         (state)
tcp6     0      64    2001:db8:1:200:2.22  2001:240:1:200:2.1711   ESTABLISHED
tcp6     0       0    2001:db8:1:200:2.80  2001:240:1:202:2.1055   ESTABLISHED
```

```
tcp6        0        0   2001:db9:1:200:2.80   2001:240:1:202:a.1064   ESTABLISHED
tcp6        0        0   2001:db0:1:200:2.80   2001:240:1:200:c.1058   ESTABLISHED
```

We can see from this output that four TCP-over-IPv6 connections exist. The first one is an SSH connection and the remaining three are HTTP connections. The IPv6 address strings are truncated in the output. Using the "−l" switch will allow full IPv6 address strings to be printed.

6.13   Configuring IPv4-mapped IPv6 Address Support

The kernel checks the `ip6_v6only` flag at the socket creation time. The PCB is set with both the `INP_IPV4` and `INP_IPV6` flags if `ip6_v6only` is set to false. In this case the socket is capable of accepting both IPv4 and IPv6 connection requests when the socket is bound to the wildcard address.

On the other hand if `ip6_v6only` is set to true then a PCB will not have the `INP_IPV4` flag bit set by default. In this case the socket can accept only IPv6 connection requests even if the socket is bound to the wildcard local address.

The `ip6_v6only` variable can be modified through the **sysctl** command. For example, we can issue the following command to set the variable to false:

```
# sysctl net.inet6.ip6.v6only=0
```

Similarly, to set the variable to true, we need to issue the following command:

```
# sysctl net.inet6.ip6.v6only=1
```

The following shows the output of **netstat** when `ip6_v6only` is set to false.

```
% netstat -an
Active Internet connections (includig servers)
Proto  Recv-Q  Send-Q  Local Address      Foreign Address   (state)
tcp46      0       0   *.22               *.*               LISTEN
tcp4       0       0   *.22               *.*               LISTEN
tcp4       0       0   *.53               *.*               LISTEN
tcp46      0       0   *.53               *.*               LISTEN
tcp46      0       0   *.25               *.*               LISTEN
tcp46      0       0   *.80               *.*               LISTEN
tcp4       0       0   *.25               *.*
udp4       0       0   *.53               *.*
udp46      0       0   *.53               *.*
udp46      0       0   *.*                *.*
udp6       0       0   *.547              *.*
udp4       0       0   *.514              *.*
udp6       0       0   *.514              *.*
udp6       0       0   *.521              *.*
icm6       0       0   *.*                *.*
```

The **netstat** output shows that some of the PCB entries have both the `INP_IPV6` and `INP_IPV4` flags set. However, a socket having both flag bits set does not imply that socket will always accept both IPv4 and IPv6 connections. For example, two sockets exist for SSH (port 22) services. One socket is bound to the IPv4 wildcard address and the other is bound to the IPv6 unspecified address that supports IPv4-mapped IPv6 addresses. In this case, an SSH connection request over IPv4 will be accepted by the IPv4 socket because of the algorithm implemented in the PCB search function. On the other hand, only one socket exists for the HTTP (port 80) service, which is bound to the IPv6 unspecified address and the PCB entry has both the INP_IPV6 and INP_IPV4 flag bits set. This socket will accept an HTTP request over IPv4 because there is no specific socket that is waiting for HTTP service requests over the IPv4 protocol.

Another interesting point to note is that the sockets for the DHCPv6 (port 547) and the RIPNG (port 521) services only wait for IPv6 connections even when the ip6_v6only flag is false. These applications explicitly remove the INP_IPV4 flag through the socket API to limit the connection acceptance to only IPv6 connections.

7

Socket API Extensions

7.1 Introduction

Network applications use standard application programming interfaces (APIs) that are provided by the underlying operating system to access the available network services. The BSD socket API is one of the most commonly deployed APIs that is supported by a wide variety of operating systems. Although the socket API has a flexible design that can accommodate various network protocols including IPv6, additional extensions for providing useful and portable interfaces for IPv6 network programming are still necessary.

The IETF standardized two sets of extensions: One is classified as the Basic Socket API Extensions defined in [RFC3493], and the other is classified as the Advanced Socket API Extensions defined in [RFC3542].

The Basic Socket API provides standard definitions which represent IPv6 addresses, name and address conversion functions, and multicast-related interfaces. Most IPv6 network applications can be implemented on top of this API. On the other hand, the Advanced Socket API defines interfaces for accessing special IPv6 packet information such as the IPv6 header and the extension headers. The Advanced Socket API is also used to extend the capability of IPv6 raw sockets. Not all applications need this API, but a wide range of applications such as unicast and multicast routing daemons or network management tools such as traceroute or ping for IPv6 require the services provided by the Advanced Socket API.

In this chapter, we first provide a brief overview of these API specifications along with sample code usage. We will then explain the internal kernel implementation that realizes the services offered by the API sets. Last, we will discuss the implementation of some interesting library functions defined in the Basic Socket API in detail.

Note that both API specifications have their predecessors. [RFC3493] is the latest specification and is the successor to [RFC2133] and [RFC2553]. [RFC3542] is the latest specification and is the successor to [RFC2292]. While we mainly concentrate on the latest specifications, some parts of the described implementation have special consideration for compatibility to the older specifications. Additionally, the latest specifications are often referred to as "2553bis" or "2292bis," particularly in code comment lines of the implementation, because the implementation was written during the revision process. And the actual behavior basically conforms to the latest document, so "2553bis" and "2292bis" should refer to "3493" and "3542," respectively.

7.2 The Basic Socket API—[RFC3493]

7.2.1 Basic Definitions

We have already seen the definitions of the `in6_addr{}` and the `sockaddr_in6{}` structures in Chapter 2. It should be noted, however, that [RFC3493] defines these structures in `<netinet/in.h>`, though the KAME implementation actually defines them in `<netinet6/in6.h>` and has `in.h` include `in6.h`. This was for a historical convenience, and an application should not directly include `in6.h`. We have also seen the IPv6 address family definition `AF_INET6` in many places of the implementation description, which is defined in `<sys/socket.h>` on systems that conform to [RFC3493].

Another important data structure is `sockaddr_storage{}`, which has enough space to contain all possible socket address structures for various address families including `AF_INET6` and `AF_UNIX`. Listing 7-1 shows the definition of the `sockaddr_storage{}` structure defined for the FreeBSD system that this book is targeting.

Listing 7-1

_____ sys/socket.h
```
146    #define _SS_MAXSIZE    128
147    #define _SS_ALIGNSIZE (sizeof(int64_t))
148    #define _SS_PAD1SIZE  (_SS_ALIGNSIZE - sizeof(u_char) - sizeof(sa_family_t))
149    #define _SS_PAD2SIZE  (_SS_MAXSIZE - sizeof(u_char) - sizeof(sa_family_t) - \
150                            _SS_PAD1SIZE - _SS_ALIGNSIZE)
151
152    struct sockaddr_storage {
153            u_char      ss_len;    /* address length */
154            sa_family_t ss_family; /* address family */
155            char        __ss_pad1[_SS_PAD1SIZE];
156            int64_t     __ss_align; /* force desired structure storage alignment */
157            char        __ss_pad2[_SS_PAD2SIZE];
158    };
```
_____ sys/socket.h

As shown in Listing 7-1, the size of the structure is 128 bytes, which is defined by the `_SS_MAXSIZE` macro. A common usage of `sockaddr_storage{}` is as follows:

Listing 7-2

_____ sample code
```
    struct sockaddr_storage ss;
    struct sockaddr_in6 *sin6 = (struct sockaddr_in6 *)&ss;
```
_____ sample code

In other words, the `sockaddr_storage{}` structure is a placeholder structure that can be safely type-casted to any socket address structure of a specific address family type.

The `sockaddr_storage{}` structure is particularly important for IPv6 because the `sockaddr_in6{}` structure is larger than the normal `sockaddr{}` structure on most systems. For such systems, the following bug is very likely to appear:

Listing 7-3

```
struct sockaddr sa;
struct sockaddr_in6 *sin6 = (struct sockaddr *)&sa;

memset(sin6, 0, sizeof(*sin6));
```

In this code, the `memset()` operation will overwrite the memory region immediately following the space that was allocated for the `sockaddr{}` structure. It is therefore important to use `sockaddr_storage{}` as a socket address placeholder throughout the code in order to avoid introducing this kind of programming bug.

7.2.2 Interface Identification

[RFC3493] defines four library functions that manipulate network interface names. The function prototypes and the necessary header file for these functions are shown below.

Listing 7-4

```
#include <net/if.h>

unsigned int  if_nametoindex(const char *ifname);

char * if_indextoname(unsigned int ifindex, char *ifname);

struct if_nameindex *if_nameindex(void);

void if_freenameindex(struct if_nameindex *ptr);
```

`if_nametoindex()` returns the interface index for the given interface name `ifname`.

`if_indextoname()` performs the reverse function of `if_nametoindex()`, that is, it returns the interface name for the given interface index denoted as `ifindex` in the given buffer `ifname`. The return value will be the pointer to the given buffer when the function succeeds.

`if_nameindex()` provides an array of information on all interfaces that are available in the node. The information is stored in the `if_nameindex{}` structure, which is defined in `<net/if.h>` as follows:

Listing 7-5

```
struct if_nameindex {
        u_int   if_index;       /* 1, 2, ... */
        char    *if_name;       /* null terminated name: "le0", ... */
};
```

The `if_nameindex()` function allocates a new array, fills in the array with the `if_nameindex{}` structures, and returns the pointer to the newly allocated array to the caller. Each `if_nameindex{}` structure corresponds to a single interface. The `if_index` member is the interface index. The `if_name` member is a printable string of the interface name, such as "le0" or "fxp0".

Note that `if_nameindex()` does not return the length of the array. Instead, the last entry of the array is indicated by an entry with `if_index` being 0 and `if_name` being a NULL pointer.

Since the array returned from `if_nameindex()` is allocated within that function, a separate "destructor" function is necessary. `if_freenameindex()` is the corresponding destructor function. It takes a pointer to an array of `if_nameindex()` structures and frees all resources allocated by `if_nameindex()`.

7.2.3 IPv4 Communication over `AF_INET6` Socket

[RFC3493] allows an application program to perform IPv4 communication over an IPv6 (`AF_INET6`) socket using IPv4-mapped IPv6 addresses (Section 2.3). For example, when an application binds IPv4-mapped IPv6 address `::ffff:192.0.2.1` to an `AF_INET6` socket, those IPv4 packets with destination address of `192.0.2.1` will be delivered to that application through this `AF_INET6` socket. Similarly, the application can send IPv4 packets through this socket if the destination IPv6 address is represented in the form of an IPv4-mapped IPv6 address such as `::ffff:192.0.2.9`. The application data is then transmitted inside IPv4 frames and is delivered to the node whose IPv4 address is `192.0.2.9`, even though the data was sent through an `AF_INET6` socket.

The main purpose of this feature is to provide an easy way for application programmers to support both IPv6 and IPv4 protcols in one application and to make an IPv4-only application IPv6-aware. For example, consider the following code fragment, which is a common coding style for an IPv4 server application (error cases are omitted for brevity).

Listing 7-6
_____ sample code
```
        int s;
        unsigned short port;
        struct sockaddr_in sin, sin_from;
        socklen_t fromlen = sizeof(sin_from);

        s = socket(AF_INET, SOCK_STREAM, IPPROTO_TCP);
        memset(&sin, 0, sizeof(sin));
        sin.sin_family = AF_INET;
        sin.sin_len = sizeof(sin);
        sin.sin_port = htons(atoi(port));
        bind(s, (struct sockaddr *)&sin, sizeof(sin));
        listen(s, 1);
        accept(s, (struct sockaddr *)&sin_from, &fromlen);
```
_____ sample code

With the usage of IPv4-mapped IPv6 addresses, we can easily convert this code to a dual-stack application as follows:

Listing 7-7
_____ sample code
```
        int s;
        unsigned short port;
        struct sockaddr_in6 sin6, sin6_from;
```

```
        socklen_t fromlen = sizeof(sin6_from);

        s = socket(AF_INET6, SOCK_STREAM, IPPROTO_TCP);
        memset(&sin, 0, sizeof(sin));
        sin6.sin6_family = AF_INET6;
        sin6.sin6_len = sizeof(sin6);
        sin6.sin6_port = htons(atoi(port));
        bind(s, (struct sockaddr *)&sin6, sizeof(sin6));
        listen(s, 1);
        accept(s, (struct sockaddr *)&sin6_from, &fromlen);
```
——— sample code

The transport layer treats the IPv6 unspecified address :: as a special wildcard address bound to the AF_INET6 socket (as a result of memset() initialization), and accepts any IPv6 address including IPv4-mapped IPv6 addresses. This means the AF_INET6 socket can receive both IPv4 and IPv6 packets. As such, this server application can accept both IPv4 and IPv6 connections with a single socket.

It may look useful, but some people recommend avoiding such usage of IPv4-mapped IPv6 addresses due to various technical reasons. Section 6.11 covered some of the issues, which are summarized as follows:

Binding ambiguity For example, when an application binds 192.0.2.1 to an AF_INET socket, and then binds ::ffff:192.0.2.1 to an AF_INET6 socket then it is impossible for the kernel to determine the right socket for delivering the incoming data. A related problem is that when an application binds 0.0.0.0 to an AF_INET and :: to an AF_INET6 socket, the kernel cannot determine the right socket for delivering IPv4 packets. At the time of this writing, there are no standards on the handling of this situation and incompatibility exists among implementations.

Socket options handling Standardized approach on handling socket options issued over an IPv6 socket that is bound to an IPv4-mapped IPv6 address does not exist. Similarly, handling of IPv4 socket options issued on such a socket is undetermined.

Multicast ambiguity There are no standards on the handling of multicast packets delivered over a socket bound to an IPv4-mapped IPv6 multicast address. For example, when an application specifies the outgoing interface using either the IP_MULTICAST_IF or IPV6_MULTICAST_IF option for multicast packet transmission, the kernel behavior on the choice of the outgoing interface is undetermined.

Section 6.11 explained how the KAME kernel implementation on FreeBSD handles these cases. This is completely implementation specific; the user or the application programmer cannot assume the behavior on other systems. It leads to indeterministic behavior and less portability.

The use of IPv4-mapped IPv6 addresses can also cause security issues [V4MAPPED]. Consider a simple subroutine shown on the next page for an example, which is supposed to be used to reject access from a set of addresses specified in the access control list, acl (whose definition should be straightforward and omitted in the code for brevity). The user of this function would specify 192.0.2.1 in the list if access from this IPv4 address should be denied, but it is not sufficient when the system allows IPv4 communication over an AF_INET6 socket; ::ffff:192.0.2.1 should also be specified. The hidden dependency will increase the operational cost and may lead to insecure operation.

_____ sample code

```
int
access_deny(sa)
        struct sockaddr *sa;
{
        struct aclist *acl;
        struct sockaddr_in *sin, *sin_ac;
        struct sockaddr_in6 *sin6, *sin6_ac;

        for (acl = acl_top; acl != NULL; acl = acl->next) {
                if (sa->sa_family != acl->sa->sa_family)
                        continue;
                switch(sa->sa_family) {
                case AF_INET:
                        sin = (struct sockaddr_in *)sa;
                        sin_ac = (struct sockaddr_in *)acl->sa;
                        if (sin->sin_addr.s_addr == sin_ac->sin_addr.s_addr)
                                return(1);
                        break;
                case AF_INET6:
                        sin6 = (struct sockaddr_in6 *)sa;
                        sin6_ac = (struct sockaddr_in6 *)acl->sa;
                        if (IN6_ARE_ADDR_EQUAL(&sin6->sin6_addr,
                                               &sin6_ac->sin6_addr))
                                return(1);
                        break;
                }
        }

        return(0);
}
```

_____ sample code

In order to address these concerns, [RFC3493] defines a specific IPv6 socket option that disables the usage of IPv4-mapped IPv6 addresses. This option will be described in Section 7.2.5.

7.2.4   Address and Name Conversion Functions

One key feature of [RFC3493] is the definition of a set of functions which convert an IPv6 address to a host name.

inet_pton() **and** *inet_ntop()* *Functions*

The following two functions can convert an IPv6 address in binary form to a printable string, and vice versa.

Listing 7-8

_____ arpa/inet.h

```
#include <arpa/inet.h>

int inet_pton(int af, const char *src, void *dst);
const char *inet_ntop(int af, const void *src,
                      char *dst, socklen_t size);
```

_____ arpa/inet.h

inet_pton() takes an address in the printable string format (src) and converts it into a binary format (dst). inet_ntop() performs the reverse transformation of inet_pton().

FIGURE 7-1

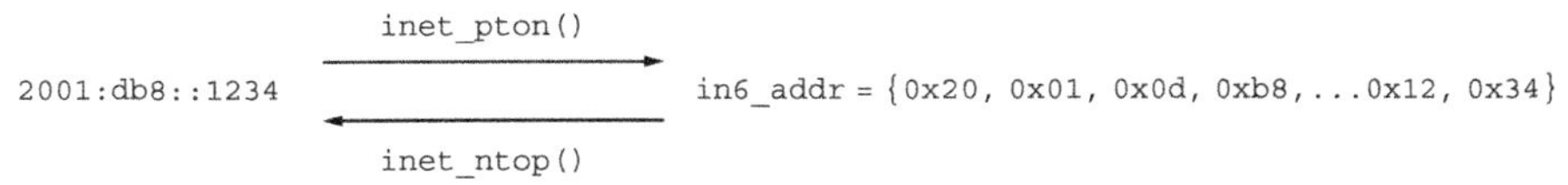

                      `inet_pton()`

   `2001:db8::1234`   ⟶   `in6_addr = {0x20, 0x01, 0x0d, 0xb8,...0x12, 0x34}`

                      `inet_ntop()`

Address conversion by `inet_pton()` and `inet_ntop()`.

As implied by the first argument `af`, rather than just supporting IPv6, these functions are independent of any address family. In theory, these functions can handle any address family type while all implementations known to the authors only support the `AF_INET` and the `AF_INET6` address families.

`inet_pton()` returns 1 on success; it returns 0 if the given address is not parseable; it returns −1 if other system errors occur, in which case an appropriate error code will be set in `errno`.

`inet_ntop()` returns a pointer to variable `dst` on success; it returns `NULL` on failure, in which case an appropriate error code will be set in `errno`.

Figure 7-1 illustrates the transformations performed by `inet_pton()` and `inet_ntop()` between a printable string and the internal representation of an IPv6 address `2001:db8::1234` in the `in6_addr{}` structure.

Another important characteristic of these functions is that they can be thread-safe. These functions can run concurrently on different threads because the caller is responsible for allocating space to store the result. Recall that some of the IPv4-specific library functions such as `inet_ntoa()` cannot be easily thread-safe since those do not take a separate buffer for the output.

getaddrinfo() Function

[RFC3493] provides the `getaddrinfo()` function to convert a fully qualified domain name (FQDN) to IP addresses, described below.

Listing 7-9

                                        `netdb.h`

```
#include <sys/socket.h>
#include <netdb.h>

int getaddrinfo(const char *nodename, const char *servname,
                const struct addrinfo *hints, struct addrinfo **res);
void freeaddrinfo(struct addrinfo *ai);
```

                                        `netdb.h`

`getaddrinfo()` takes a service name like "http" or a numeric port number like "80" as well as an FQDN, and returns a list of addresses along with the corresponding port number. `nodename` and `servname` are strings containing the FQDN and the service name, respectively. `hints` points to a structure specific to `getaddrinfo()`, the `addrinfo{}`

structure, which specifies additional information that guides the conversion process. The definition of the `addrinfo{}` structure is as follows:

Listing 7-10

```
struct addrinfo {
        int     ai_flags;         /* AI_PASSIVE, AI_CANONNAME, AI_NUMERICHOST */
        int     ai_family;        /* PF_xxx */
        int     ai_socktype;      /* SOCK_xxx */
        int     ai_protocol;      /* 0 or IPPROTO_xxx for IPv4 and IPv6 */
        size_t  ai_addrlen;       /* length of ai_addr */
        char    *ai_canonname;    /* canonical name for hostname */
        struct  sockaddr *ai_addr;      /* binary address */
        struct  addrinfo *ai_next;      /* next structure in linked list */
};
```

`ai_flags` specifies particular behavior of `getaddrinfo()`, which can be either zero (if nothing special is required) or the bitwise-inclusive OR of some of the flags shown in Table 7-1.

`ai_family` specifies the address family for `nodename`. This is `AF_UNSPEC` if the caller does not care about the family, but can also be a specific family value (e.g., `AF_INET` or `AF_INET6` when only addresses of a particular family are required).

`ai_socktype` and `ai_protocol` specify the socket type and the transport protocol, and can be used as the second and third arguments to the `socket()` system call, respectively.

TABLE 7-1

Flag	Description
AI_PASSIVE	The caller requires addresses that are suitable for accepting incoming connections. When this flag is specified, `nodename` is usually NULL, and the address field of the `ai_addr` member is filled with the "any" address (e.g., INADDR_ANY for IPv4).
AI_CANONNAME	The caller requires a "canonical" name to be returned in the `ai_canonname` member of the result.
AI_NUMERICHOST	The caller specifies that the `nodename` should be interpreted as a numeric IP address, not a host name. In particular, this flag suppresses DNS name lookups.
AI_NUMERICSERV	The caller specifies that the `servname` should be interpreted as a numeric port number, not a service name.
AI_V4MAPPED	If no IPv6 addresses are matched, IPv4-mapped IPv6 addresses (Section 2.3) for IPv4 addresses that match `nodename` shall be returned. This flag is applicable only when `ai_family` is `AF_INET6` in the `hints` structure.
AI_ALL	When used with the `AI_V4MAPPED` flag, this flag specifies that IPv4 addresses be returned in the form of IPv4-mapped IPv6 addresses with other regular IPv6 addresses.
AI_ADDRCONFIG	When specified, only addresses whose family is supported by the system will be returned.

ai_addrlen is the length of the `ai_addr` member, which is the socket address structure that corresponds to `nodename`. The value of `ai_addrlen` should be equal to the value of the `sa_len` member of `ai_addr` on systems that support the length member in the socket address structure, and thus is not so useful. However, it is important to provide the member in order to ensure portability with systems that do not have the length member in the socket address structure (e.g., Linux or Solaris, or systems derived from the 4.3 BSD socket API in general).

ai_canonname is used to store the "canonical" name of `nodename`. For example, if "www" is given to `getaddrinfo()` as nodename in the "kame.net" domain (and the `AI_CANONNAME` is specified), then `ai_canonname` will store a string "www.kame.net". ai_addr stores one conversion result for `nodename` and `servname`. An address-family-dependent "address" field of the `ai_addr` member stores a binary address for `nodename`.

Similarly, an address-family-dependent "port" field of the `ai_addr` member stores the port number for `servname`. For the `AF_INET6` family, these are the `sin6_addr` and `sin6_port` members, respectively.

The result of `getaddrinfo()` is a list of multiple `addrinfo{}` structures because a single FQDN can often be resolved to multiple addresses of multiple address families. `ai_next` points to the next entry of such a list.

On success, the `getaddrinfo()` function returns 0, providing a list of addresses in the `res` argument. The list is allocated within the function and the pointer to the list is stored in the `res` argument.

The `freeaddrinfo()` function is a freeing function for the dynamically allocated `addrinfo{}` structure list. The function takes a pointer to the `addrinfo{}` structure, which is usually the pointer stored in the `res` argument to `getaddrinfo()`, and frees all of the dynamically allocated resources.

On failure, `getaddrinfo()` returns a non-0 error code, which can be converted to a printable string using the `gai_strerror()` function:

Listing 7-11

―――――――――――――――――――――――――――――――――――――――netdb.h
```
const char *gai_strerror(int ecode);
```
―――――――――――――――――――――――――――――――――――――――netdb.h

gai_strerror() is similar to the standard `strerror()` function, but only handles specific error codes returned from the `getaddrinfo()` function.

The following is a common example of code fragment that actively opens an HTTP connection to a host "www.kame.net."

Listing 7-12

―――――――――――――――――――――――――――――――――――――sample code
```
1         struct addrinfo hints, *res, *res0;
2         int error;
3         int s;
4
5         memset(&hints, 0, sizeof(hints));
6         hints.ai_family = AF_UNSPEC;
7         hints.ai_socktype = SOCK_STREAM;
8         error = getaddrinfo("www.kame.net", "http", &hints, &res0);
9         if (error) {
10                fprintf(stderr, "getaddrinfo failed: %s\n",
11                    gai_strerror(error));
```

```
12                    exit(1);
13            }
14            s = -1;
15            for (res = res0; res; res = res->ai_next) {
16                    s = socket(res->ai_family, res->ai_socktype,
17                      res->ai_protocol);
18                    if (s < 0)
19                            continue;
20
21                    if (connect(s, res->ai_addr, res->ai_addrlen) < 0) {
22                            close(s);
23                            s = -1;
24                            continue;
25                    }
26
27                    break;  /* okay we got one */
28            }
29            if (s < 0) {
30                    fprintf(stderr, "no addresses are reachable\n");
31                    exit(1);
32            }
33
34            freeaddrinfo(res0);
```
_____ sample code

The above example illustrates the usage of getaddrinfo() and how the results from getaddrinfo() are applied in subsequent calls to socket() and to connect().

The following is an example that passively opens listening sockets to accept incoming HTTP connections.

Listing 7-13
_____ sample code
```
1            struct addrinfo hints, *res, *res0;
2            int error;
3            int s[MAXSOCK];
4            int nsock;
5            const char *cause = NULL;
6
7            memset(&hints, 0, sizeof(hints));
8            hints.ai_family = AF_UNSPEC;
9            hints.ai_socktype = SOCK_STREAM;
10           hints.ai_flags = AI_PASSIVE;
11           error = getaddrinfo(NULL, "http", &hints, &res0);
12           if (error) {
13                   fprintf(stderr, "getaddrinfo failed: %s\n",
14                     gai_strerror(error));
15                   exit(1);
16           }
17           nsock = 0;
18           for (res = res0; res && nsock < MAXSOCK; res = res->ai_next) {
19                   s[nsock] = socket(res->ai_family, res->ai_socktype,
20                     res->ai_protocol);
21                   if (s[nsock] < 0)
22                           continue;
23
24   #ifdef IPV6_V6ONLY
25                   if (res->ai_family == AF_INET6) {
26                           int on = 1;
27
28                           if (setsockopt(s[nsock], IPPROTO_IPV6, IPV6_V6ONLY,
29                             &on, sizeof(on))) {
30                                   close(s[nsock]);
31                                   continue;
32                           }
```

```
33                        }
34   #endif
35
36                        if (bind(s[nsock], res->ai_addr, res->ai_addrlen) < 0) {
37                                close(s[nsock]);
38                                continue;
39                        }
40
41                        if (listen(s[nsock], SOMAXCONN) < 0) {
42                                close(s[nsock]);
43                                continue;
44                        }
45
46                        nsock++;
47                }
48          if (nsock == 0) {
49                  fprintf(stderr, "no listening socket is available\n");
50                  exit(1);
51          }
52          freeaddrinfo(res0);
```
_____ sample code

Again, the above example illustrates the usage of getaddrinfo() and how the results from getaddrinfo() are applied in subsequent calls to the socket APIs.

Note that this code explicitly enables the IPV6_V6ONLY option for each socket (lines 24–34). We will describe this option in Section 7.2.5.

getnameinfo() *Function*

The getnameinfo() function is a reverse function of getaddrinfo(), which takes a socket address structure and converts it to printable host and service names. The function prototype is shown below.

Listing 7-14
_____ netdb.h

```
int getnameinfo(const struct sockaddr *sa, socklen_t salen,
                char *node, socklen_t nodelen,
                char *service, socklen_t servicelen, int flags);
```
_____ netdb.h

sa points to the socket address structure to be converted and salen specifies the length of the structure. sa and salen are the main input to the getnameinfo() function. node provides the storage to hold the resulting host name. nodelen specifies the size of the buffer referenced by node. Similarly, service is a buffer for storing the resulting service name. servicelen is the length of the buffer.

flags specifies some optional behavior for getnameinfo(). Available flags defined in [RFC3493] are shown in Table 7-2.

> *Note*: The KAME implementation previously supported a non-standard flag, NI_WITHSCOPEID, but it was then made obsolete. Applications should not use this flag.

getnameinfo() returns 0 on success; node and service will be filled in with the resolved host name and service name, respectively. It is possible that either node or service may be NULL, in which case only the non-NULL buffer will be filled. The function returns

TABLE 7-2

Flag	Description
NI_NOFQDN	When set, only the node name portion of the FQDN shall be returned for local hosts. Though the semantics is not very clear, the expected behavior is to return the first label of an FQDN. For example, if a host name "www.kame.net" is returned by the DNS, only "www" will be returned by getnameinfo().
NI_NUMERICHOST	Specifies that a numeric address string instead of an FQDN should be returned.
NI_NAMEREQD	Specifies that an FQDN-like host name is required; if getnameinfo() fails to get a name, it will return an error.
NI_NUMERICSERV	Specifies that a numeric port string instead of a service name should be returned.
NI_DGRAM	Specifies that the intended service is a datagram service (SOCK_DGRAM). By default, getnameinfo() assumes a stream service (SOCK_STREAM).

a non-0 error code on failure, which can be converted to a printable string by the gai_strerror() function.

The caller is responsible for memory allocation to store the results. Some systems provide the following definitions in <netdb.h> as reasonable default sizes for these buffers.

```
#define NI_MAXHOST  1025
#define NI_MAXSERV    32
```

Note: These constants were officially defined in [RFC2553], but was then removed in [RFC3493]. New portable applications should not assume these constants are always available.

In other words, the default buffer size in bytes for node is NI_MAXHOST and the default buffer size for service is NI_MAXSERV.

The following sample code illustrates the use of getnameinfo() to print out the source address of an incoming packet.

Listing 7-15

_____ sample code

```
struct sockaddr_storage from0;
struct sockaddr *from;
socklen_t fromlen;
char *packet;
size_t packetlen;
char hbuf[NI_MAXHOST], sbuf[NI_MAXSERV];
int error, s;

from = (struct sockaddr *)&from0;
fromlen = sizeof(from0);
recvfrom(s, packet, packetlen, from, &fromlen);
error = getnameinfo(from, fromlen, hbuf, sizeof(hbuf), sbuf,
    sizeof(sbuf), 0);
if (error != 0) {
        fprintf(stderr, "getnameinfo failed: %s\n",
            gai_strerror(error));
} else
        printf("host=%s, serv=%s\n", hbuf, sbuf);
```

_____ sample code

Notice that this code uses a `sockaddr_storage{}` structure, `from0`, so that the `recvfrom()` call can store an address of any address families. Using a `sockaddr{}` structure is not enough because the size of the structure is usually smaller than that of the `sockaddr_in6{}` structure.

The `getnameinfo()` function returns a non-0 error code on failure, which can also be converted to a printable string by `gai_strerror()`. Most of the error codes are shared with `getaddrinfo()`. Table 7-3 summarizes the error codes defined in [RFC3493].

An implementation may define specific error codes. An application should use the codes in an opaque manner through the `gai_strerror()` function.

Important Features of `getaddrinfo()` and `getnameinfo()`

Both `getaddrinfo()` and `getnameinfo()` are designed as address-family-independent functions. In addition, these functions either receive or return the generic socket address structure and never use structures that are specific to a particular family (e.g., `sockaddr_in6{}` or `in6_addr{}`). Consequently, applications using these functions are not concerned about whether the kernel supports a particular address family. Therefore these functions enable portable application design and allow application migration to support future network protocols without the need for source code modification.

Another important property of `getaddrinfo()` and `getnameinfo()` is that these functions are thread safe, that is, these functions can be executed by multiple threads simultaneously. In comparison, most traditional name and address conversion functions were originally not thread safe. Some operating systems provided special thread-safe versions of such traditional conversion functions. In general, however, a portable application cannot assume such special properties exist in the underlying OSes.

TABLE 7-3

Code	Description
`EAI_AGAIN`	The name could not be resolved at this time. Future attempts may succeed.
`EAI_BADFLAGS`	The flags had an invalid value.
`EAI_FAIL`	A non-recoverable error occurred.
`EAI_FAMILY`	The address family was not recognized or the address length was invalid for the specified family.
`EAI_MEMORY`	There was a memory allocation failure.
`EAI_NONAME`	The name does not resolve for the supplied parameters. `NI_NAMEREQD` is set and the host's name cannot be located, or both `nodename` and `servname` were null.
`EAI_OVERFLOW`	An argument buffer overflowed. (`getnameinfo()` only)
`EAI_SERVICE`	The service passed was not recognized for the specified socket type. (`getaddrinfo()` only)
`EAI_SOCKTYPE`	The intended socket type was not recognized. (`getaddrinfo()` only)
`EAI_SYSTEM`	A system error occurred. The error code can be found in `errno`.

Even though by itself each of these functions is implemented in a thread-safe manner, many of the underlying libraries that each of these functions depends on are still not thread safe. As such, the overall execution of these functions is often not thread safe either. In fact, we will show why these functions provided by KAME lack the thread-safe feature in later sections of this chapter (see Sections 7.6.3 and 7.6.7).

7.2.5   Basic Socket Options

RFC3493 defines several new socket options specific to the AF_INET6 sockets. All of these options are specified at the IPPROTO_IPV6 level when the getsockopt() and setsockopt() system calls are called, and are available by including the <netinet/in.h> header file.

Unicast Option

The IPV6_UNICAST_HOPS option specifies the hop limit value of outgoing packets sent from the socket. If a special value of −1 is specified, the system default value will be used.

IPV6_V6ONLY Option and Code Portability

The IPV6_V6ONLY option specifies that when set to non-zero the socket should not send or receive IPv4 packets using IPv4-mapped IPv6 addresses (recall the discussion in Section 7.2.3). This option defaults to zero.

The following sample code illustrates the usage of the IPV6_V6ONLY option. (Note: Error cases are ignored for brevity.)

Listing 7-16
_____ sample code

```
#include <sys/types.h>
#include <sys/socket.h>

#include <netinet/in.h>

#include <stdio.h>
#include <netdb.h>

int
main()
{
        struct sockaddr_in6 sin6, sin6_accept;
        socklen_t sin6_len;
        int s0, s;
        int on;
        char hbuf[NI_MAXHOST];

        memset(&sin6, 0, sizeof(sin6));
        sin6.sin6_family = AF_INET6;
        sin6.sin6_len = sizeof(sin6);
        sin6.sin6_port = htons(5001);

        s0 = socket(AF_INET6, SOCK_STREAM, IPPROTO_TCP);
        on = 1;
        setsockopt(s0, SOL_SOCKET, SO_REUSEADDR, &on, sizeof(on));

#ifdef USE_IPV6_V6ONLY
        on = 1;
```

```
            setsockopt(s0, IPPROTO_IPV6, IPV6_V6ONLY, &on, sizeof(on));
#endif

        bind(s0, (const struct sockaddr *)&sin6, sizeof(sin6));
        listen(s0, 1);
        while (1) {
                sin6_len = sizeof(sin6_accept);
                s = accept(s0, (struct sockaddr *)&sin6_accept, &sin6_len);
                getnameinfo((struct sockaddr *)&sin6_accept, sin6_len,
                    hbuf, sizeof(hbuf), NULL, 0, NI_NUMERICHOST);
                printf("accept a connection from %s\n", hbuf);

                close(s);
        }

        exit(0);
}
```
_____sample code

Suppose that an executable named **accept** is created from the above code and is running on a host system. If the following **telnet** commands are executed on the same host:

```
% telnet ::1 5001
% telnet 127.0.0.1 5001
```

The following output is produced if the code was built without USE_IPV6_V6ONLY and the IPv4-mapped address is supported by the system.

```
accept a connection from ::1
accept a connection from ::ffff:127.0.0.1
```

On the other hand, if the code was built with USE_IPV6_V6ONLY, the following output is produced:

```
        accept a connection from ::1
```

Executing the second **telnet** command produces the following result:

```
% telnet 127.0.0.1 5001
Trying 127.0.0.1...
telnet: connect to address 127.0.0.1: Connection refused
```

As seen from this example, an AF_INET6 socket with the IPV6_V6ONLY socket option being true will only listen to and accept IPv6 connection requests.

The IPV6_V6ONLY socket option is new in [RFC3493] and some systems may not support this option. Some other systems use a different default value than the one defined in the specification. It is thus important to understand this option when attempting to write portable applications.

According to [RFC3493], an IPv6-enabled kernel should be able to send or receive IPv4 packets on an AF_INET6 socket using the IPv4-mapped IPv6 addresses as explained in Section 7.2.3. Real-world implementations, however, do not necessarily conform to this requirement. For example, due to concerns about the mechanism itself, some OSes such as OpenBSD refuse to implement this feature. In such a system, the only way to handle both IPv4 and IPv6 communications in a single application is to create two separate sockets (i.e., one of AF_INET for IPv4 and the other of AF_INET6 for IPv6). On the other hand, some OSes do not allow the creation of both AF_INET and AF_INET6 sockets that are bound to the wildcard address and on the same port.

The most likely approach for portability is thus to use two separate sockets and turn the `IPV6_V6ONLY` option on for the `AF_INET6` socket. In this case, under the common interpretation of this option (even though not officially documented), both the `AF_INET` and `AF_INET6` sockets can coexist and be bound on the same port.

If the "default" behavior described in [RFC3493] is desired for some reason, it is advisable to set this option with the value of 0 explicitly. Even though this is the default, some systems such as NetBSD and recent versions of FreeBSD deliberately adopt a different system default based on their implementation policy (see the note in Section 6.7.1).

In any case, the authors recommend the approach of two separate sockets with the `IPV6_V6ONLY` option set to true for the `AF_INET6` socket. Now that most of the major OSes support this option, this approach will provide the most portable, most deterministic, and safest behavior.

Multicast Socket Options

[RFC3493] defines a set of socket options for multicast-related communication. These IPv6 multicast socket options are similar to those defined in IPv4 with one significant difference: An interface is specified by an interface index in the IPv6 multicast socket options while an interface is specified by an IPv4 address in the IPv4 options. There are two reasons for the difference. First of all, IPv6 explicitly allows the assignment of multiple IPv6 addresses on a single interface and thus there usually exists a one-to-many mapping between the interface and interface addresses. If we choose a particular address as the identifier of an interface, there will be an issue of ensuring consistency among multiple choices. Secondly, and more importantly, IPv6 link-local addresses may not be unique even within a single node, which implies that if an interface only has a link-local address then we may not be able to uniquely identify that interface by the address. Thus, using interface index is a more appropriate identifier of an interface in the IPv6 API. This is one of the reasons that library functions such as `if_nametoindex()` are defined in the API specification.

The `IPV6_JOIN_GROUP` and `IPV6_LEAVE_GROUP` socket options are defined for joining and leaving a multicast group on a specified interface. Both options take the `ipv6_mreq{}` structure as the option argument, which is defined below.

Listing 7-17

netinet/in.h

```
struct ipv6_mreq {
        struct in6_addr        ipv6mr_multiaddr;
        unsigned int           ipv6mr_interface;
};
```

netinet/in.h

The `ipv6mr_multiaddr` field specifies the multicast group to join or to leave. The `ipv6mr_interface` field specifies the interface by its index in the host byte order.

The following code fragment illustrates a common example of joining an IPv6 multicast group. (Note: Error cases are ignored for brevity.) The code opens an IPv6 UDP socket, joins an IPv6 multicast group `ff02::2` on the interface "fxp0", and then waits for multicast packets sent to that group on UDP port 5001.

Listing 7-18
_____ sample code

```
#include <sys/types.h>
#include <sys/socket.h>
#include <netinet/in.h>

...

        struct sockaddr_in6 sin6;
        int s;
        struct ipv6_mreq mreq;

        s = socket(AF_INET6, SOCK_DGRAM, IPPROTO_UDP);

        memset(&mreq, 0, sizeof(mreq));
        inet_pton(AF_INET6, "ff02::2", &mreq.ipv6mr_multiaddr);
        mreq.ipv6mr_interface = if_nametoindex("fxp0");
        setsockopt(s, IPPROTO_IPV6, IPV6_JOIN_GROUP, &mreq, sizeof(mreq));

        memset(&sin6, 0, sizeof(sin6));
        sin6.sin6_family = AF_INET6;
        sin6.sin6_len = sizeof(sin6);
        sin6.sin6_port = htons(5001);
        bind(s, (const struct sockaddr *)&sin6, sizeof(sin6));
```
_____ sample code

The following three socket options are also available.

The `IPV6_MULTICAST_HOPS` option specifies the hop limit value for the outgoing multicast packets on a given socket. If a special value of -1 is specified, the system default value will be used. This option is similar to the IPv4 `IP_MULTICAST_TTL` socket option but takes an integer, not a character like the IPv4 option, for specifying the hop limit. This option defaults to 1 (the minimum hop limit).

The `IPV6_MULTICAST_IF` option specifies the outgoing interface for multicast packets sent on a given socket. This option is similar to the IPv4 `IP_MULTICAST_IF` socket option but takes an interface identifier for identifying the interface.

The `IPV6_MULTICAST_LOOP` option specifies whether outgoing multicast packets on a given socket should be looped back to the sending node if there are listeners on that multicast group. When set to 0, multicast packets should not be looped back; when set to 1, multicast packets should be looped back. This option is similar to the IPv4 `IP_MULTICAST_LOOP` socket option but takes an integer, not a character like the IPv4 option, as the option value. This option defaults to 1.

Note: [RFC3678] defines further extensions to the socket API in order to support source specific multicast. These extensions are beyond the scope of this book.

Address Testing Macros

[RFC3493] provides convenient macros that check a given IPv6 address against a particular type of address. We have already seen some of these macros in Table 2-8. Table 7-4 lists the remaining

TABLE 7-4

Macro	Description
IN6_IS_ADDR_LINKLOCAL	Checks if the given address is a unicast link-local address.
IN6_IS_ADDR_SITELOCAL	Checks if the given address is a unicast site-local address (see Note 1).
IN6_IS_ADDR_MULTICAST	Checks if the given address is a multicast address.
IN6_IS_ADDR_MC_NODELOCAL	Checks if the given address is an interface-local multicast address (see Note 2).
IN6_IS_ADDR_MC_LINKLOCAL	Checks if the given address is a link-local multicast address.
IN6_IS_ADDR_MC_SITELOCAL	Checks if the given address is a site-local multicast address.
IN6_IS_ADDR_MC_ORGLOCAL	Checks if the given address is an organization-local multicast address.
IN6_IS_ADDR_MC_GLOBAL	Checks if the given address is a global multicast address.

Note 1: The IETF has deprecated the syntax and usage of site-local unicast addresses [RFC3879], and is now defining a new address space for local communication [RFC4193] (see also Section 2.4.4). However, the corresponding macro for the new space is not defined.

Note 2: According to the latest address architecture documents since [RFC3513], multicast addresses with the "scope" field being 1 are called "interface-local" multicast addresses. The API macro is based on an old architecture document [RFC2373] that defined this class of addresses as "node-local" multicast addresses.

macros defined by [RFC3493]. All of these macros take a pointer to an `in6_addr{}` structure and return true (non-0) or false (0) based on the test result.

7.3   The Advanced Socket API—[RFC3542]

7.3.1   Advanced Definitions

[RFC3542] defines a large set of new definitions that includes IPv6 and the extension headers. We will show a summary of the major ones rather than showing the complete definitions. This is partly because many of the definitions are also used in the kernel as part of the IPv6 protocol stack implementation and in fact were explained in the appropriate sections in this book. In addition, the majority of applications do not care about the details, because most applications do not use such advanced definitions at all. Even for those applications that need information defined in [RFC3542], the information can be accessed via higher layer functions as explained in Section 7.3.5.

The first set of the advanced definitions includes data structure for IPv6 and the extension headers. These definitions are available by including `<netinet/ip6.h>` and are summarized in Table 7-5.

The next set of definitions includes structure definitions for ICMPv6, Neighbor Discovery (ND) protocol and Multicast Listener Discovery (MLD) protocol headers. These definitions are available by including `<netinet/icmp6.h>` and are summarized in Table 7-6.

[RFC3542] also defines common protocol values. Table 7-7 lists IPv6 specific protocol values defined in the RFC that can appear in the "next header" field of an IPv6 or an extension header (see Section 3.3). These definitions are available by including `<netinet/in.h>`.

Table 7-8 lists the ICMPv6 message type definitions that are defined in [RFC3542] and provided by including `<netinet/icmp6.h>`. Some of the types are already given in

TABLE 7-5

Structure name	Description
ip6_hdr{}	IPv6 header (Section 3.5.2)
ip6_hbh{}	Hop-by-Hop Options header (Section 3.5.2)
ip6_dest{}	Destination Options header (Section 3.5.2)
ip6_rthdr{}	Routing header (in the general form) (Section 3.5.2)
ip6_rthdr0{}	Type-0 Routing header (Section 3.5.2)
ip6_frag{}	Fragment header (Section 3.5.2)

TABLE 7-6

Structure name	Description
icmp6_hdr{}	ICMPv6 header (Section 4.5)
nd_router_solicit{}	Neighbor Solicitation message header (Section 5.13.1)
nd_router_advert{}	Neighbor Advertisement message header (Section 5.13.1)
nd_neighbor_solicit{}	Router Solicitation message header (Section 5.13.1)
nd_neighbor_advert{}	Router Advertisement message header (Section 5.13.1)
nd_redirect{}	Redirect message header (Section 5.13.1)
nd_opt_hdr{}	General header of Neighbor Discovery options (Section 5.13.1)
nd_opt_prefix_info{}	Neighbor Discovery prefix information option (Section 5.13.1)
nd_opt_rd_hdr{}	Neighbor Discovery redirected header option (Section 5.13.1)
nd_opt_mtu{}	Neighbor Discovery MTU option (Section 5.13.1)
mld_hdr{}	Multicast Listener Discovery message header (Chapter 2 of *IPv6 Advanced Protocols Implementation*)
icmp6_router_renum{}	Router Renumbering message header (see Note below)
rr_pco_match{}	Router Renumbering Match-Prefix part
rr_pco_use{}	Router Renumbering Use-Prefix part
rr_result{}	Router Renumbering Result message

Note: The Router Renumbering protocol is defined in [RFC2894]. This book does not cover this protocol; in fact, it is not really deployed.

Sections 4.5.2 and 5.13.1, but are shown here again for convenience. For ICMPv6 error and echo messages, refer to Section 4.2; for Neighbor Discover messages (types 133–137), refer to Section 5.6; for MLD messages, refer to Chapter 2 of *IPv6 Advanced Protocols Implementation*; Router Renumbering is not described in this book.

TABLE 7-7

Name	Value	Description
IPPROTO_HOPOPTS	0	IPv6 Hop-by-Hop Options
IPPROTO_IPV6	41	IPv6 header
IPPROTO_ROUTING	43	IPv6 Routing header
IPPROTO_FRAGMENT	44	IPv6 Fragment header
IPPROTO_ESP	50	Encapsulating security payload
IPPROTO_AH	51	Authentication header
IPPROTO_ICMPV6	58	ICMPv6
IPPROTO_NONE	59	IPv6 No Next header
IPPROTO_DSTOPTS	60	IPv6 Destination Options header

TABLE 7-8

Message type	Value	Description
ICMP6_DST_UNREACH	1	ICMPv6 destination unreachable error
ICMP6_PACKET_TOO_BIG	2	ICMPv6 packet too big error
ICMP6_TIME_EXCEEDED	3	ICMPv6 time exceeded error
ICMP6_PARAM_PROB	4	ICMPv6 parameter problem error
ICMP6_ECHO_REQUEST	128	ICMPv6 echo request
ICMP6_ECHO_REPLY	129	ICMPv6 echo reply
ND_ROUTER_SOLICIT	133	Router Solicitation
ND_ROUTER_ADVERT	134	Router Advertisement
ND_NEIGHBOR_SOLICIT	135	Neighbor Solicitation
ND_NEIGHBOR_ADVERT	136	Neighbor Advertisement
ND_REDIRECT	137	Redirect
MLD_LISTENER_QUERY	130	Multicast Listener Query
MLD_LISTENER_REPORT	131	Multicast Listener Report (version 1)
MLD_LISTENER_REDUCTION	132	Multicast Listener Done (version 1) (see Note below)
ICMP6_ROUTER_RENUMBERING	138	Router Renumbering

Note: This macro name does not match the official type name defined in [RFC2710]. The mismatch is an error in the API specification and [RFC3542] should have corrected it before publication. Unfortunately, the document was published with the confusing name.

7.3.2   IPv6 Raw Sockets

The raw socket is used in general as a mechanism to transmit and to receive data over transport protocols other than the protocols implemented in the kernel by default (e.g., TCP, UDP, or

SCTP when available). Major applications of raw sockets are routing daemons that use transport protocols other than TCP or UDP, including OSPF (unicast) and PIM (multicast) routing daemons. ICMPv6 packets are also handled via a raw socket because ICMPv6 contains various functions that can be implemented in the user space, including some parts of ND and MLD.

The `type` argument to the `socket()` system call is SOCK_RAW when creating an IPv6 raw socket. The `protocol` argument is set to the corresponding transport protocol. For example, the following code fragment illustrates how to open an AF_INET6 socket for ICMPv6 transport.

```
int s;
s = socket(AF_INET6, SOCK_RAW, IPPROTO_ICMPV6);
```

Unlike IPv4 raw sockets, all data sent via IPv6 raw sockets must be in the network byte order and all data received via raw sockets will be in the network byte order.

Another major difference between IPv6 and IPv4 raw sockets is that complete packets, such as IPv6 packets with extension headers, cannot be sent or received on an IPv6 raw socket. In other words, IPv6 socket API does not include an option that is equivalent to the IPv4 IP_HDRINCL socket option.

For outgoing packets, the majority of the header fields in both the IPv6 header and the extension headers can be set either through the *ancillary data* specified in the sendmsg() system call or by corresponding socket options.

For incoming packets, applications can retrieve the majority of the header fields from the IPv6 header and the extension headers through the ancillary data returned from the recvmsg() system call provided that the appropriate socket options have been set before issuing the recvmsg() system call. The details of such ancillary data and socket options will be described in Sections 7.3.3 through 7.3.5.

IPv6 Raw Socket Options

[RFC3542] defines two new socket options specific to IPv6 raw sockets.

The IPV6_CHECKSUM option specifies the offset to the checksum field, if any, in the transport layer header, assuming the use of the 16-bit one's complement of the one's complement sum as the checksum algorithm and that the checksum field is aligned on a 16-bit boundary. The kernel will automatically add the checksum value for outgoing packets and verify the checksum value for incoming packets on the socket if the offset is given by this option. This is a useful functionality because the IPv6 checksum computation includes a pseudo IPv6 header containing the source and destination addresses that may be unknown to an application.

The ICMP6_FILTER option allows an application to set an inbound packet filter on an ICMPv6 socket (i.e., an AF_INET6 raw socket with the IPPROTO_ICMPV6 protocol). The filter is set based on the ICMPv6 message types. The ICMP6_FILTER option enables an application to avoid receiving uninterested ICMPv6 packets and reduces the overhead incurred by unnecessary packet processing; by default, the kernel will pass all incoming ICMPv6 messages to an ICMPv6 socket.

This option takes an icmp6_filter{} structure as the argument, which contains the filter rules configured with a set of macro functions as explained in Section 6.10.4. The structure and the macro functions are available by including <netinet/icmp6.h>.

The following code fragment is extracted from the **rtadvd** implementation, which is a network daemon that sends Router Advertisement messages. The daemon receives Router

Solicitations from hosts as well as Router Advertisements from other routers, which are the only two types of ICMPv6 messages that the daemon wants to see. Therefore, the code first configures the filter with `ICMP6_FILTER_SETBLOCKALL()` so that the socket would block any ICMPv6 messages. It then specifies Router Solicitation messages and Router Advertisement messages to be passed through by calling the `ICMP6_FILTER_SETPASS()` function.

Listing 7-19

rtadvd/rtadvd.c

```
        struct icmp6_filter filt;
        int sock;
...
        ICMP6_FILTER_SETBLOCKALL(&filt);
        ICMP6_FILTER_SETPASS(ND_ROUTER_SOLICIT, &filt);
        ICMP6_FILTER_SETPASS(ND_ROUTER_ADVERT, &filt);
...
        if (setsockopt(sock, IPPROTO_ICMPV6, ICMP6_FILTER, &filt,
                    sizeof(filt)) < 0) {
             syslog(LOG_ERR, "<%s> IICMP6_FILTER: %s",
                    __func__, strerror(errno));
             exit(1);
        }
```

rtadvd/rtadvd.c

7.3.3 Introduction to Ancillary Data

As mentioned in the previous section, the IPv6 advanced socket API employs a general framework called "ancillary data" to exchange "ancillary" information between the kernel and the application. The ancillary data is stored in the `msghdr{}` structure and is passed between the kernel and the application through the `recvmsg()` and `sendmsg()` system calls. The following is the definition of the `msghdr{}` structure:

Listing 7-20

sys/socket.h

```
struct msghdr {
        void        *msg_name;        /* ptr to socket address structure */
        socklen_t   msg_namelen;      /* size of socket address structure */
        struct iovec *msg_iov;        /* scatter/gather array */
        int         msg_iovlen;       /* # elements in msg_iov */
        void        *msg_control;     /* ancillary data */
        socklen_t   msg_controllen;   /* ancillary data buffer length */
        int         msg_flags;        /* flags on received message */
};
```

sys/socket.h

As shown in the comment lines, the `msg_control` member points to a buffer containing the ancillary data, and the `msg_controllen` member specifies the length of the buffer.

The actual ancillary data is a sequence of objects, each of which begins with a header structure called `cmsghdr{}` followed by data specific to the header type. The definition of the `cmsghdr{}` structure is as follows:

Listing 7-21

sys/socket.h

```
struct cmsghdr {
        socklen_t  cmsg_len;   /* #bytes, including this header */
```

```
        int         cmsg_level; /* originating protocol */
        int         cmsg_type;  /* protocol-specific type */
                    /* followed by unsigned char cmsg_data[]; */
};
```
── sys/socket.h

Padding may be necessary between the header and the data, and between the data and the next header to ensure natural pointer alignment. Whether padding is necessary and the length of the padding, when it is necessary, depend on the machine architecture. In this book, we assume the 32-bit architecture where pointers should be aligned at a 32-bit boundary.

The macros CMSG_SPACE() and CMSG_LEN() are defined to help determine the padding needed for an ancillary data object as follows:

Listing 7-22
── sys/socket.h

```
socklen_t CMSG_SPACE(socklen_t length);
socklen_t CMSG_LEN(socklen_t length);
```
── sys/socket.h

Given the length of an ancillary data object, CMSG_SPACE() returns an upper bound on the space required by the object and its cmsghdr{} structure, including any padding needed to satisfy alignment requirements.

Similarly, given the length of an ancillary data object, CMSG_LEN() returns the value to store in the cmsg_len member of the cmsghdr{} structure, taking into account any padding necessary to satisfy alignment requirements.

Figure 7-2 clarifies the relationship between the ancillary data-related structures and these two macros by showing the organization of two ancillary data objects. [RFC3542] defines a set of macros to parse a sequence of ancillary objects similar to the layout illustrated in Figure 7-2.

Listing 7-23
── sys/socket.h

```
    struct cmsghdr *CMSG_FIRSTHDR(const struct msghdr *mhdr);
    struct cmsghdr *CMSG_NXTHDR(const struct msghdr *mhdr,
                               const struct cmsghdr *cmsg);
    unsigned char *CMSG_DATA(const struct cmsghdr *cmsg);
```
── sys/socket.h

CMSG_FIRSTHDR() returns a pointer to the first cmsghdr{} structure in the msghdr{} structure pointed to by mhdr. The macro returns NULL if there is no ancillary data pointed to by the msghdr{} structure (i.e., if msg_control is NULL or msg_controllen is less than the size of a cmsghdr{} structure).

CMSG_NXTHDR() returns a pointer to the cmsghdr{} structure describing the next ancillary data object in the sequence. mhdr is a pointer to an msghdr{} structure and cmsg is a pointer to a cmsghdr{} structure. The return value is NULL if no additional ancillary data object exists in the sequence. A pointer to cmsghdr{} describing the first ancillary data object of the sequence is returned if the value of the cmsg pointer is NULL.

FIGURE 7-2

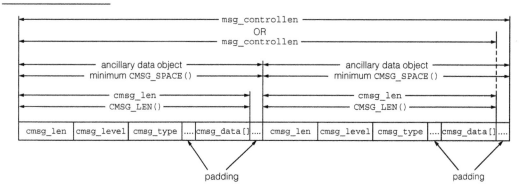

Ancillary data objects.

CMSG_DATA() returns a pointer to the data that immediately follows a cmsghdr{} structure, which is often called the "cmsg_data" member, even though such a member is not explicitly defined in the structure and the application cannot directly refer to it.

The following code fragment illustrates a common way of iterating through a sequence of ancillary data objects and processing each object in turn.

Listing 7-24

_____ sample code

```
struct msghdr   msg;
struct cmsghdr  *cmsgptr;

...

for (cmsgptr = CMSG_FIRSTHDR(&msg); cmsgptr != NULL;
    cmsgptr = CMSG_NXTHDR(&msg, cmsgptr)) {
        if (cmsgptr->cmsg_level == ... &&
            cmsgptr->cmsg_type == ... ) {
                unsigned char  *ptr;

                ptr = CMSG_DATA(cmsgptr);
                /* process data pointed to by ptr */
        }
}
```

_____ sample code

7.3.4 IPv6 Packet Information

As previously explained, an application does not have direct access to the IPv6 header and any extension headers of any packet. Instead, [RFC3542] defines a higher level interface to access this packet information using ancillary data objects, which are

(1) The send and receive interface, the source and destination addresses

(2) The Hop Limit

(3) The Traffic Class

(4) Routing header

(5) Hop-by-Hop options header

(6)   Destination options header

(7)   Next Hop address

Send Information

An application takes one or both of the following approaches when providing information for the outgoing packet:

- Specify the value via a socket option
- Specify the value as an ancillary data object

Packet information specified via the first approach is called the *"sticky options"* because these options affect all outgoing packets sent on the corresponding socket. On the other hand, packet information specified via the ancillary data objects affect only the packet to which the ancillary data objects are attached.

Table 7-9 lists the synopsis of these options and objects corresponding to the information above. Note that the same constant for the cmsg_level member is used as the second argument to the getsockopt() and setsockopt() functions, which is called the socket "option level." Similarly, the same constant for the cmsg_type member is used as the third argument to getsockopt() and setsockopt(), which is called the socket "option name."

It should be noted that two separate options or object types are assigned the same information type 6 (i.e., the Destination options header). This assignment reflects the fact that there are two types of Destination options headers in the standard ordering of extension headers (see Section 3.3.1 for details). IPV6_DSTOPTS refers to the common type of Destination options header that is addressed to the final recipient of the packet, while IPV6_RTHDRDSTOPTS is only effective when the Routing header is also present. The Destination options header specified by IPV6_RTHDRDSTOPTS must be placed before the Routing header.

Another note is that IPV6_HOPLIMIT can be specified only through an ancillary data object because the basic API defines more fine-grained socket options: the IPV6_UNICAST_HOPS and the IPV6_MULTICAST_HOPS options.

TABLE 7-9

Type of information	*optlevel/cmsg_level*	*optname/cmsg_type*	*optval/cmsg_data[]*
1	IPPROTO_IPV6	IPV6_PKTINFO	in6_pktinfo{}
2	IPPROTO_IPV6	IPV6_HOPLIMIT	int
3	IPPROTO_IPV6	IPV6_TCLASS	int
4	IPPROTO_IPV6	IPV6_RTHDR	ip6_rthdr{}
5	IPPROTO_IPV6	IPV6_HOPOPTS	ip6_hbh{}
6	IPPROTO_IPV6	IPV6_DSTOPTS	ip6_dest{}
6	IPPROTO_IPV6	IPV6_RTHDRDSTOPTS	ip6_dest{}
7	IPPROTO_IPV6	IPV6_NEXTHOP	sockaddr{}

A new structure, in6_pktinfo{}, is introduced for specifying or retrieving values of the IPV6_PKTINFO option. in6_pktinfo{} is defined in <netinet/in.h> and its definition is as follows:

Listing 7-25
── netinet/in.h

```
struct in6_pktinfo {
        struct in6_addr      ipi6_addr;      /* src/dst IPv6 address */
        unsigned int         ipi6_ifindex;   /* send/recv interface index */
};
```
── netinet/in.h

The in6_pktinfo{} structure can be used as an option value with the IPV6_PKTINFO socket option or as an ancillary data object. For incoming packets, ipi6_addr and ipi6_ifindex contain the destination address of the packets and the index of the receiving interface, respectively. For outgoing packets, ipi6_addr specifies the source address of the packets and ipi6_ifindex specifies the index of the outgoing interface. In the latter case, the source address is not specified when the ipi6_addr member is the unspecified address; the outgoing interface is not specified if the ipi6_ifindex member is 0.

Receive Information

An application can retrieve the desired information from received packets by indicating to the kernel one or more of the following options:

- IPV6_RECVPKTINFO

- IPV6_RECVHOPLIMIT

- IPV6_RECVTCLASS

- IPV6_RECVRTHDR

- IPV6_RECVHOPOPTS

- IPV6_RECVDSTOPTS

These options generally correspond to the options listed in Table 7-9 except IPV6_RTHDRDSTOPTS and IPV6_NEXTHOP. A receiving application should expect any ordering of extension headers. Thus it is meaningless to try to classify Destination options headers based on a particular ordering. The IPV6_NEXTHOP option is only applicable to packet transmissions.

An application informs the kernel of its interested information by setting the corresponding option to a non-0 value (the default is zero). The kernel automatically creates an ancillary data object and attaches that object to the received data when the kernel receives a packet that contains the desired information. The application can access the information through the msg_control member of the msghdr{} structure when the application calls recvmsg() to receive the packet. For example, the following code fragment is found in an application that wants to retrieve the Hop Limit value from the incoming packets.

Listing 7-26

_____sample code
```
    int on;

    on = 1;
    setsockopt(s, IPPROTO_IPV6, IPV6_RECVHOPLIMIT, &on, sizeof(on));
```
_____sample code

Transport Layer Considerations

An application communicating over either UDP or raw sockets can use the ancillary data objects and the socket options mechanisms described so far to either specify packet information for outgoing packets or receive packet information from incoming packets. However, an application communicating over TCP sockets can only specify the packet information for outgoing packets through socket options. The limitation is due to the fact that the TCP protocol offers data stream service that does not map user data to TCP segment (or packet) boundaries. (Recall that ancillary data objects work per packet basis.)

7.3.5 Manipulation of IPv6 Extension Headers

The advanced socket API provides a set of higher-level interfaces that allows the manipulation of some of the IPv6 extension headers in the application space. Using these interfaces an application can either construct or parse the extension headers without the need to know the detailed header formats.

Manipulation of a Routing Header

The following six library functions are provided to manipulate the IPv6 Routing headers.

Listing 7-27

_____netinet/in.h
```
    #include <netinet/in.h>

    socklen_t inet6_rth_space(int type, int segments);
    void *inet6_rth_init(void *bp, socklen_t bp_len, int type,
                         int segments);
    int inet6_rth_add(void *bp, const struct in6_addr *addr);
    int inet6_rth_reverse(const void *in, void *out);
    int inet6_rth_segments(const void *bp);
    struct in6_addr *inet6_rth_getaddr(const void *bp, int index);
```
_____netinet/in.h

The first three functions are for constructing a Routing header. `inet6_rth_space()` returns the number of bytes required to build a Routing header based on the given information. `inet6_rth_init()` initializes buffer data for a Routing header. `inet6_rth_add()` adds an IPv6 address to the Routing header being constructed.

The next three functions are for examining a received Routing header. `inet6_rth_reverse()` reverses the addresses stored in a Routing header. `inet6_rth_segments()` returns the number of segments that are in a Routing header. `inet6_rth_getaddr()` fetches the address at the given index from a Routing header.

We omit the detailed description of these functions (see [RFC3542] for details).

Manipulation of Hop-by-Hop and Destination Options Headers

A set of library functions are provided to manipulate the Hop-by-Hop and the Destination options headers. These functions are generic and can be used for both types of options. The following four functions are for constructing an options header.

Listing 7-28
_____netinet/in.h

```
#include <netinet/in.h>

int inet6_opt_init(void *extbuf, socklen_t extlen);
int inet6_opt_append(void *extbuf, socklen_t extlen, int offset,
                 uint8_t type, socklen_t len, uint_t align,
                 void **databufp);
int inet6_opt_finish(void *extbuf, socklen_t extlen, int offset);
int inet6_opt_set_val(void *databuf, int offset, void *val,
                 socklen_t vallen);
```
_____netinet/in.h

inet6_opt_init() initializes the buffer data for an options header.
inet6_opt_append() adds one TLV (Type-Length-Value) option to a list of options.
inet6_opt_finish() completes the insertion of a TLV option to a list of options headers.
inet6_opt_set_val() sets the value of an option.

The following three functions are for examining a received options header.

Listing 7-29
_____netinet/in.h

```
#include <netinet/in.h>

int inet6_opt_next(void *extbuf, socklen_t extlen, int offset,
                 uint8_t *typep, socklen_t *lenp,
                 void **databufp);
int inet6_opt_find(void *extbuf, socklen_t extlen, int offset,
                 uint8_t type, socklen_t *lenp,
                 void **databufp);
int inet6_opt_get_val(void *databuf, int offset, void *val,
                 socklen_t vallen);
```
_____netinet/in.h

inet6_opt_next() extracts the next option from the options header pointed by extbuf. inet6_opt_find() extracts an option of a specified type from the header. inet6_opt_get_val() retrieves the value of an option.

We omit the detailed description of these functions. Instead, we will show a usage example using the **pim6sd** daemon, which is the KAME implementation of an IPv6 multicast routing daemon (see Chapter 2 of *IPv6 Advanced Protocols Implementation*). The **pim6sd** daemon needs to send Multicast Listener Discovery (MLD) query packets, which contain a Router Alert Hop-by-Hop option. The **pim6sd** daemon also specifies the source address and the outgoing interface using the IPV6_PKTINFO ancillary data object.

Listing 7-30 illustrates the function make_mld6_msg(), which is the function used in **pim6sd** to construct ancillary data objects including the one for Router Alert option (omitting unnecessary parts for the discussion here).

Listing 7-30

```
440    static void
441    make_mld6_msg(type, code, src, dst, group, ifindex, delay, datalen, alert)
442        int type, code, ifindex, delay, datalen, alert;
443        struct sockaddr_in6 *src, *dst;
444        struct in6_addr *group;
445    {
446        struct mld_hdr *mhp = (struct mld_hdr *)mld6_send_buf;
447        int ctllen, hbhlen = 0;
448
....
478
479        /* estimate total ancillary data length */
480        ctllen = 0;
481        if (ifindex != -1 || src)
482                ctllen += CMSG_SPACE(sizeof(struct in6_pktinfo));
483        if (alert) {
484    #ifdef USE_RFC2292BIS
485            if ((hbhlen = inet6_opt_init(NULL, 0)) == -1)
486                    log(LOG_ERR, 0, "inet6_opt_init(0) failed");
487            if ((hbhlen = inet6_opt_append(NULL, 0, hbhlen, IP6OPT_ROUTER_ALERT, 2,
488                                           2, NULL)) == -1)
489                    log(LOG_ERR, 0, "inet6_opt_append(0) failed");
490            if ((hbhlen = inet6_opt_finish(NULL, 0, hbhlen)) == -1)
491                    log(LOG_ERR, 0, "inet6_opt_finish(0) failed");
492            ctllen += CMSG_SPACE(hbhlen);
493    #else   /* old advanced API */
494            hbhlen = inet6_option_space(sizeof(raopt));
495            ctllen += hbhlen;
496    #endif
497        }
498        /* extend ancillary data space (if necessary) */
499        if (ctlbuflen < ctllen) {
500                if (sndcmsgbuf)
501                        free(sndcmsgbuf);
502                if ((sndcmsgbuf = malloc(ctllen)) == NULL)
503                        log(LOG_ERR, 0, "make_mld6_msg: malloc failed");
                                        /* assert */
504                ctlbuflen = ctllen;
505        }
506        /* store ancillary data */
507        if ((sndmh.msg_controllen = ctllen) > 0) {
508                struct cmsghdr *cmsgp;
509
510                sndmh.msg_control = sndcmsgbuf;
511                cmsgp = CMSG_FIRSTHDR(&sndmh);
512
513                if (ifindex != -1 || src) {
514                        struct in6_pktinfo *pktinfo;
515
516                        cmsgp->cmsg_len = CMSG_LEN(sizeof(struct in6_pktinfo));
517                        cmsgp->cmsg_level = IPPROTO_IPV6;
518                        cmsgp->cmsg_type = IPV6_PKTINFO;
519                        pktinfo = (struct in6_pktinfo *)CMSG_DATA(cmsgp);
520                        memset((caddr_t)pktinfo, 0, sizeof(*pktinfo));
521                        if (ifindex != -1)
522                                pktinfo->ipi6_ifindex = ifindex;
523                        if (src)
524                                pktinfo->ipi6_addr = src->sin6_addr;
525                        cmsgp = CMSG_NXTHDR(&sndmh, cmsgp);
526                }
527                if (alert) {
528    #ifdef USE_RFC2292BIS
529                        int currentlen;
530                        void *hbhbuf, *optp = NULL;
531
532                        cmsgp->cmsg_len = CMSG_LEN(hbhlen);
533                        cmsgp->cmsg_level = IPPROTO_IPV6;
```

```
534                              cmsgp->cmsg_type = IPV6_HOPOPTS;
535                              hbhbuf = CMSG_DATA(cmsgp);
536
537                              if ((currentlen = inet6_opt_init(hbhbuf, hbhlen)) == -1)
538                                      log(LOG_ERR, 0, "inet6_opt_init(len = %d) failed",
539                                          hbhlen);
540                              if ((currentlen = inet6_opt_append(hbhbuf, hbhlen,
541                                                                 currentlen,
542                                                                 IP6OPT_ROUTER_ALERT, 2,
543                                                                 2, &optp)) == -1)
544                                      log(LOG_ERR, 0,
545                                          "inet6_opt_append(len = %d/%d) failed",
546                                          currentlen, hbhlen);
547                              (void)inet6_opt_set_val(optp, 0, &rtalert_code,
548                                                      sizeof(rtalert_code));
549                              if (inet6_opt_finish(hbhbuf, hbhlen, currentlen) == -1)
550                                      log(LOG_ERR, 0, "inet6_opt_finish(buf) failed");
551      #else   /* old advanced API */
552                              if (inet6_option_init((void *)cmsgp, &cmsgp, IPV6_HOPOPTS))
553                                      log(LOG_ERR, 0, /* assert */
554                                          "make_mld6_msg: inet6_option_init failed");
555                              if (inet6_option_append(cmsgp, raopt, 4, 0))
556                                      log(LOG_ERR, 0, /* assert */
557                                          "make_mld6_msg: inet6_option_append failed");
558      #endif
559                              cmsgp = CMSG_NXTHDR(&sndmh, cmsgp);
560                      }
561          }
562          else
563                  sndmh.msg_control = NULL; /* clear for safety */
564      }
```
─── ${KAME}/kame/kame/pim6sd/mld6.c

Buffer size estimation

479–482 For MLD query messages, `ifindex` is always a non-0 positive integer specifying the outgoing interface. `src` specifies an IPv6 link-local address to be used as the packet source address. `CMSG_SPACE()` gives the length of the space necessary for storing the `IPV6_PKTINFO` object including any trailing padding if required.

483–497 Similarly, `alert` is always non-0 for MLD query packets. The `inet6_opt_xxx()` functions are used here just for calculating the length of the required space for storing the information in the context in which they are called (e.g., the base Hop-by-Hop options header, the Router Alert option, or the necessary paddings), when the first argument to these functions is a NULL pointer. `inet6_opt_init()` would return 2 that include the Next Header and the Header Length fields of the Hop-by-Hop options header. `inet6_opt_append()` then calculates the length needed to store the Router Alert option, taking into account paddings when necessary. In this case, this function would return 4, the length of the Router Alert option including its type and length fields. Finally, `inet6_opt_finish()` provides the length of trailing padding bytes or simply 0 if no padding is necessary. In this particular case, the function would return 2 because trailing padding bytes are necessary to make the entire length of the Hop-by-Hop options header a multiple of 8 bytes. As a result, `hbhlen` would be 8. `CMSG_SPACE()` gives the necessary length of the space to store the header, including padding.

Allocate buffer

498–505 `ctlbuflen` is a static variable that remembers the length of an already allocated buffer. If `ctlbuflen` is shorter than the length just calculated, which is always the case when this function is called for the first time, the previously allocated buffer (if any) is freed and a new buffer of the required length is allocated.

Build ancillary data objects

507–511 sndmh is the msghdr{} structure for this packet. Its msg_control member is set to the allocated buffer for the ancillary data objects. CMSG_FIRSTHDR() gives the head of the buffer as a pointer to a cmsghdr{} structure.

513–526 The first ancillary data is an IPV6_PKTINFO object containing the source address and the outgoing interface. cmsg_level and cmsg_type are set to IPPROTO_IPV6 and IPV6_PKTINFO, respectively, as shown in Table 7-9. CMSG_DATA() is an in6_pktinfo{} structure that is pointed to by the variable pktinfo. Both of the ipi6_ifindex and ipi6_addr structure members are initialized with the given parameters. CMSG_NXTHDR() then advances the pointer to the next cmsghdr{}.

527–561 Similarly, the cmsg_level and cmsg_type members for the second ancillary data object are set for the IPV6_HOPOPTS object. This time inet6_opt_init() initializes the Header Length field of the data, assuming it is an ip6_hbh{} structure, as shown in part A of Figure 7-3. inet6_opt_append() sets the option type and length fields for the Router Alert option as shown in part B of Figure 7-3. inet6_opt_set_val() copies the Router Alert code to the data field of the option in part C of Figure 7-3. Finally, inet6_opt_finish() fills in the rest of the buffer with a PadN option that contains only a one byte length field as shown in part D of Figure 7-3.

Figure 7-4 depicts the complete form of the msghdr{} structure and ancillary data objects after the building process. As shown in this figure, there is no need for padding in this example. Therefore, CMSG_SPACE() and CMSG_LEN() give the same length for both objects. In fact, this is the common case because the requirement alignment is a multiple of 4 bytes for the main target architecture of KAME's implementation, and both the cmsghdr{} structure and many ancillary objects are aligned on a 4-byte boundary.

FIGURE 7-3

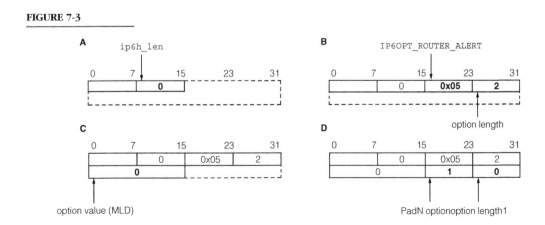

Building a Hop-by-Hop options header containing a Router Alert option.

FIGURE 7-4

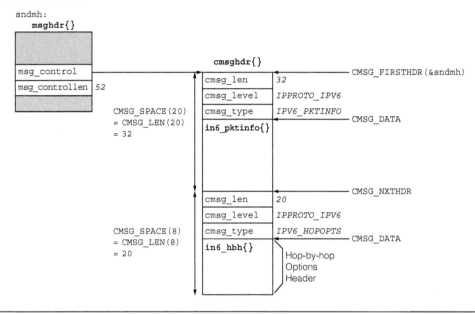

Complete form of the msghdr *and ancillary data objects.*

7.3.6   Path MTU APIs

The advanced API defines a set of interfaces that deal with path MTU information. All of these interfaces work as socket option while some also work as ancillary data objects. The socket option level or the cmsg level is always set to IPPROTO_IPV6.

Table 7-10 summarizes these options.

7.3.7   Socket Extensions for the "r" Commands

[RFC3542] defines the following three functions to support the "r" (remote) commands, for example, **rlogin**.

- rresvport_af() – a multiprotocol version of rresvport()
- rcmd_af()   – a multiprotocol version of rcmd()
- rexec_af()   – a multiprotocol version of rexec()

The reason separate functions are introduced is that the original functions hide details of the underlying socket and the original implementations may not be prepared to handle IPv6 addresses via, for example, the getpeername() system call. Defining new functions while keeping the old ones intact assures backward compatibility for the traditional applications.

Since "r" commands are rarely used these days, we simply list the new function names here and do not go into the details. Consult [RFC3542] for the complete information including function prototypes of these functions.

TABLE 7-10

Option	Description
IPV6_USE_MIN_MTU	This option controls whether path MTU discovery should be performed for outgoing packet(s) or the packet(s) should simply be fragmented at the IPv6 minimum MTU (1280 bytes). Its parameter takes one of the following integer values:
	−1 perform path MTU discovery for unicast destinations but do not perform it for multicast destinations. Packets to multicast destinations are therefore sent with the minimum MTU.
	0 always perform path MTU discovery.
	1 always disable path MTU discovery and send packets at the minimum MTU.
	The default value is −1.
	IPV6_USE_MIN_MTU can also be specified as an ancillary data object.
IPV6_DONTFRAG	This option specifies whether IPv6 fragmentation should be performed for outgoing packet(s). It takes an integer parameter, which if set to a non-0 value indicates that fragmentation should be disabled.
	IPV6_DONTFRAG can also be specified as an ancillary data object. Additionally, it is only expected to work for UDP and raw sockets. Its effect on a TCP socket is undefined.
IPV6_RECVPATHMTU	IPV6_RECVPATHMTU only works as a socket option.
	This option allows an application to inform the kernel that the application wants to be informed when the kernel receives an ICMPv6 Packet Too Big Message as a part of path MTU discovery. In such a case, the kernel will send an ancillary data object to the application with the level set to IPPROTO_IPV6 and the type set to IPV6_PATHMTU.
	The first byte of cmsg_data[] will point to an ip6_mtuinfo{} structure carrying the path MTU value together with the associated IPv6 destination address. The definition of this structure is as follows: ```c\nstruct ip6_mtuinfo {\n /* dst address including zone ID */\n struct sockaddr_in6 ip6m_addr;\n\n /* path MTU in host byte order */\n uint32_t ip6m_mtu;\n};\n``` The ip6m_addr member specifies the destination address of the corresponding path, while the ip6m_mtu member specifies the path MTU value in the host byte order.
IPV6_PATHMTU	IPV6_PATHMTU only works as a socket option and is only applicable to the getsockopt() operation on a connected socket. Its argument is an ip6_mtuinfo{} structure just described above, storing the known path MTU to the destination of the socket.

7.3.8 Summary Tables of Socket Options

Socket options at the IPPROTO_IPV6 level for SOCK_RAW, SOCK_DGRAM, or SOCK_STREAM sockets are summarized in this section. For each option, the kernel function that processes that particular option is specified. These kernel functions will be described in Section 7.4.

Table 7-11 lists multicast-related options. These options are processed by ip6_setmoptions() and ip6_getmoptions().

TABLE 7-11

optname	optval type	Description
IPV6_JOIN_GROUP	struct ipv6_mreq	Join a multicast group on a specified interface (set only)
IPV6_LEAVE_GROUP	struct ipv6_mreq	Leave from a multicast group on a specified interface (set only)
IPV6_MULTICAST_HOPS	int	Set or get the Hop Limit for outgoing multicast packets
IPV6_MULTICAST_IF	u_int	Set or get the outgoing interface for multicast packets
IPV6_MULTICAST_LOOP	u_int	Set or get a Boolean value of whether outgoing multicast packets are looped back to local listeners

Table 7-12 lists other basic API socket options.

TABLE 7-12

optname	optval type	Kernel function	Description
IPV6_UNICAST_HOPS	int	ip6_ctloutput()	Set or get the hop limit for outgoing unicast packets
IPV6_V6ONLY	int	ip6_ctloutput()	Set or get a Boolean value of whether IPv4 packets can be sent to or received on an AF_INET6 socket

Table 7-13 lists socket options related to raw IPv6 sockets.

TABLE 7-13

optname	optval type	Kernel function	Description
IPV6_CHECKSUM	int	ip6_raw_ctloutput()	Set or get the offset to the checksum field
ICMP6_FILTER	struct icmp6_filter	icmp6_ctloutput()	Set or get filter configuration based on ICMPv6 types (ICMPv6 only)

Table 7-14 lists options for retrieving information from incoming packets.

TABLE 7-14

optname	*optval type*	*Kernel function*	*Description*
IPV6_RECVPKTINFO	int	ip6_ctloutput()	Enable or disable receiving inbound packet information (the receiving interface and the packet's destination address)
IPV6_RECVHOPLIMIT	int	ip6_ctloutput()	Enable or disable receiving the hop limit of inbound packets
IPV6_RECVRTHDR	int	ip6_ctloutput()	Enable or disable receiving the Routing header(s) (if any) of inbound packets
IPV6_RECVHOPOPTS	int	ip6_ctloutput()	Enable or disable receiving the Hop-by-Hop options header (if any) of inbound packets (superuser privilege required*)
IPV6_RECVDSTOPTS	int	ip6_ctloutput()	Enable or disable receiving the Destination options header(s) (if any) of inbound packets (superuser privilege required*)
IPV6_RECVTCLASS	int	ip6_ctloutput()	Enable or disable receiving the Traffic Class value of inbound packets
IPV6_RECVRTHDRDSTOPTS	int	ip6_ctloutput()	(obsolete)

* The privilege requirement is not given in the API specification, but is given by KAME specific. See the discussion for Listing 7-38.

Table 7-15 lists options that specify attributes for outbound packets. Most of these options can also be specified as ancillary data types to manipulate a particular behavior for a single output operation. Note that IPV6_HOPLIMIT cannot be used as a socket option.

TABLE 7-15

optname	*optval type*	*Kernel function*	*Description*
IPV6_PKTINFO	struct in6_pktinfo	ip6_setpktoption()	Set or get outgoing packet information (the outgoing interface and the packet's source address)

(Continued)

TABLE 7-15 (*Continued*)

optname	*optval type*	*Kernel function*	*Description*
IPV6_HOPLIMIT	int	ip6_setpktoption()	Set or get the hop limit of outgoing packets (ancillary data only)
IPV6_NEXTHOP	struct sockaddr	ip6_setpktoption()	Set or get the next hop address
IPV6_RTHDR	struct ip6_rthdr	ip6_setpktoption()	Set or get the Routing header included in outgoing packets
IPV6_HOPOPTS	struct ip6_hbh	ip6_setpktoption()	Set or get the Hop-by-Hop options header included in outgoing packets (superuser privilege required*)
IPV6_DSTOPTS	struct ip6_dest	ip6_setpktoption()	Set or get the Destination options header included in outgoing packets (superuser privilege required*)
IPV6_RTHDRDSTOPTS	struct ip6_dest	ip6_setpktoption()	Set or get the Destination options header before a Routing header (when specified) included in outgoing packets (superuser privilege required*)
IPV6_TCLASS	int	ip6_setpktoption()	Set or get the Traffic Class value of outgoing packets
IPV6_PREFER_TEMPADDR	int	ip6_setpktoption()	Enable or disable whether temporary addresses (for privacy extension to address autoconfiguration) should be preferred in source address selection (not defined in standard document)

* *The privilege requirement is not in the API specification, but is KAME specific. See the discussion for Listing 7-38.*

Table 7-16 lists path MTU-related options. The first two options can also be specified as ancillary data types.

TABLE 7-16

optname	*optval type*	*Kernel function*	*Description*
IPV6_USE_MIN_MTU int		ip6_setpktoption()	Set or get the control value to specify whether outgoing packets should be fragmented at the minimum MTU
IPV6_DONTFRAG	int	ip6_setpktoption()	Set or get a Boolean value of whether IPv6 fragmentation should be prohibited
IPV6_RECVPATHMTU int		ip6_ctloutput()	Enable or disable receiving path MTU information for the path of outgoing packets (non TCP socket only)
IPV6_PATHMTU	struct ip6_mtuinfo	ip6_ctloutput()	Get the path MTU information for the current destination (connected socket only)

7.4   Kernel Implementation of IPv6 Socket APIs

In this section, we describe the KAME kernel implementation of the API specifications shown so far. We particularly focus on how the IPv6 socket options and ancillary data objects are specified and work in the kernel implementation.

7.4.1   Code Introduction

Table 7-17 summarizes the source files containing the kernel implementation of the various IPv6 APIs that are described in this chapter.

In general, the kernel implementation is categorized into the following three sections.

The IPv6 socket option processing section handles the `setsockopt()` and `getsockopt()` system calls through the corresponding transport layer. Figure 7-5 shows function call graphs of this section.

TABLE 7-17

File	*Description*
${KAME}/kame/sys/netinet6/ip6_var.h	Kernel internal structures for the API implementation
${KAME}/kame/sys/netinet6/ip6_output.c	Handling socket options and the outgoing path of ancillary data objects
${KAME}/kame/sys/netinet6/icmp6.c	Handling ICMPv6 socket options
${KAME}/kame/sys/netinet6/ip6_input.c	Handling the incoming path of ancillary data objects

The outgoing path of the ancillary data objects section deals with ancillary data objects specified for a particular outgoing packet. Figure 7-6 shows the function call graphs for this part. Notice that some parts of Figure 7-6 are shared with Figure 7-5.

In the inbound path, ancillary data objects that correspond to an incoming packet are constructed in the ip6_savecontrol() function and are handed to the receiving socket. Figure 7-7 shows function call graphs of this part.

FIGURE 7-5

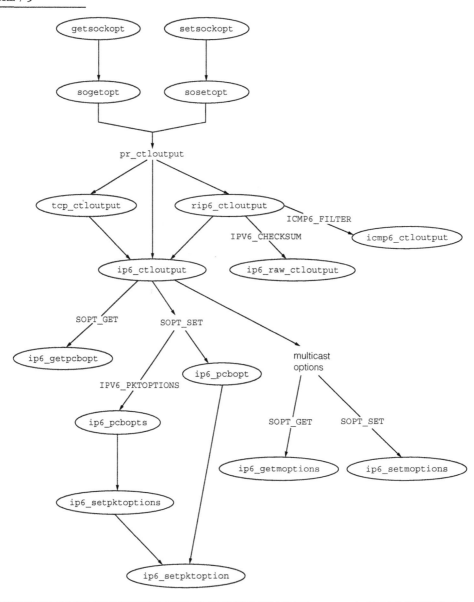

FIGURE 7-6

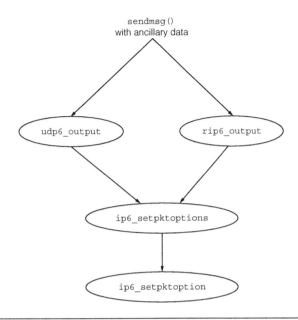

Outgoing path of ancillary data objects.

FIGURE 7-7

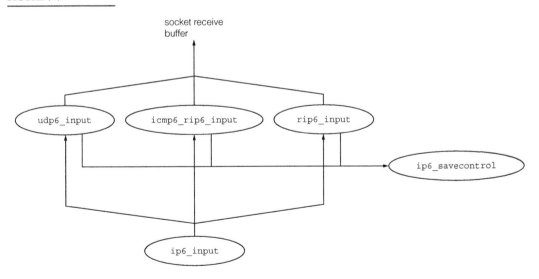

Incoming path of ancillary data objects.

FIGURE 7-8

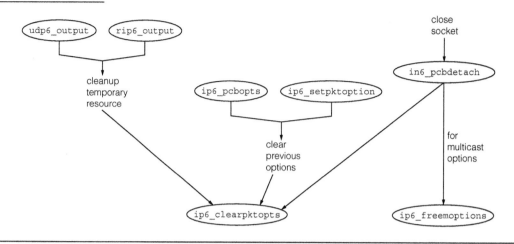

Cleanup process.

In addition to the above three parts, cleanup routines for resources that were temporarily allocated are sometimes necessary as a part of error handling or for closing a socket. Figure 7-8 shows the procedure for such cleanup.

7.4.2 `ip6_pktopts{}` Structure

The `ip6_pktopts{}` structure contains packet option information for outgoing packets. This structure can be specified for an outgoing packet or for a socket to specify the option information that applies to all outgoing packets transmitted over that socket.

Listing 7-31 shows the definition of the `ip6_pktopts{}` structure.

Listing 7-31

_____ ip6_var.h

```
148     struct      ip6_pktopts {
149             int     ip6po_hlim;         /* Hoplimit for outgoing packets */
150
151             /* Outgoing IF/address information */
152             struct  in6_pktinfo *ip6po_pktinfo;
153
154             /* Next-hop address information */
155             struct  ip6po_nhinfo ip6po_nhinfo;
156
157             struct  ip6_hbh *ip6po_hbh; /* Hop-by-Hop options header */
158
159             /* Destination options header (before a routing header) */
160             struct  ip6_dest *ip6po_dest1;
161
162             /* Routing header related info. */
163             struct  ip6po_rhinfo ip6po_rhinfo;
164
165             /* Mobile IPv6 type 2 Routing header. */
166             struct  ip6po_rhinfo ip6po_rhinfo2;
167
168             /* Destination options header (after a routing header) */
169             struct  ip6_dest *ip6po_dest2;
170
```

```
171                  /* Mobility header (just before an upper layer header) */
172                  struct   ip6_mobility *ip6po_mobility;
173
174                  int      ip6po_tclass;        /* traffic class */
175
176                  int      ip6po_minmtu;  /* fragment vs PMTU discovery policy */
177       #define IP6PO_MINMTU_MCASTONLY  -1 /* default; send at min MTU for multicast*/
178       #define IP6PO_MINMTU_DISABLE     0 /* always perform pmtu disc */
179       #define IP6PO_MINMTU_ALL         1 /* always send at min MTU */
180
181                  int      ip6po_prefer_tempaddr;  /* whether temporary addresses are
182                                                     preferred as source address */
183       #define IP6PO_TEMPADDR_SYSTEM   -1 /* follow the system default */
184       #define IP6PO_TEMPADDR_NOTPREFER 0 /* not prefer temporary address */
185       #define IP6PO_TEMPADDR_PREFER    1 /* prefer temporary address */
186
187                  int ip6po_flags;
188       #define IP6PO_REACHCONF 0x01          /* upper-layer reachability confirmation */
192       #define IP6PO_DONTFRAG  0x04          /* disable fragmentation (IPV6_DONTFRAG) */
193       #define IP6PO_USECOA    0x08          /* use care of address */
194
195                  int      needfree;      /* members dynamically allocated */
196       };
```
――――――――――――――――――――――――――――――――――――――― ip6_var.h

148–196 The structure members `ip6po_hlim`, `ip6po_pktinfo`, `ip6po_nhinfo`, and `ip6po_tclass` specify non-default attributes for the outgoing packet(s). `ip6po_hlim` specifies the hop limit to be inserted in the Hop Limit field of the IPv6 header. `ip6po_pktinfo` specifies both the outgoing interface and the packet's source address. `ip6po_tclass` specifies the Traffic Class value. The `ip6po_nhinfo` member specifies a non-default next hop address that is often a router. Listing 7-32 below gives the definition of the `ip6po_nhinfo{}` structure. The `ip6_rhinfo` member stores Routing header-related information. It will be described in Listing 7-33.

The structure members `ip6po_hbh` through `ip6po_dest2` specify IPv6 extension headers that are to be inserted in the outgoing packet(s). Note that there are two types of Destination options header: the one before a Routing header (if any), and the one after a Routing header. `ip6po_dest1` and `ip6po_dest2` correspond to a Destination options header before and after a Routing header, respectively.

`ip6po_rhinfo2` and `ip6po_mobility` are header information related to Mobile IPv6. These are out of scope of this book.

`ip6po_minmtu` controls the policy on how path MTU discovery should be applied for the corresponding outgoing packets.

`ip6po_prefer_tempaddr` is taken into consideration in source address selection for outgoing packets in terms of whether temporary addresses that are generated for privacy extension, which is defined in [RFC3041], should be preferred (see Section 3.13.1).

`ip6po_flags` controls several additional parameters which indicate whether confirmation about a neighbor's reachability provided by an upper layer should be used, whether to disable IPv6 fragmentation (mainly for debugging purposes), and whether a care-of-address should be preferred over a home address for a source address on a mobile node (which will be discussed in Chapter 5 of *IPv6 Advanced Protocols Implementation*).

`needfree` is a member for internal use to control memory management of this structure.

The following two listings show internal structures used in the ip6_pktopts{} structure.

Listing 7-32

```
136    /* Nexthop related info */
137    struct   ip6po_nhinfo {
138            struct      sockaddr *ip6po_nhi_nexthop;
140            struct      route ip6po_nhi_route; /* Route to the nexthop */
144    };
145    #define ip6po_nexthop         ip6po_nhinfo.ip6po_nhi_nexthop
146    #define ip6po_nextroute       ip6po_nhinfo.ip6po_nhi_route
```

136–144 ip6po_nhi_nexthop is a socket address structure that contains the address of the next hop. ip6po_nhi_route stores a cached route for this next hop address.

145–146 Two shortcut macros are defined to get access to the structure members from the ip6_pktopts{} structure.

Listing 7-33

```
122    /* Routing header related info */
123    struct   ip6po_rhinfo {
124            struct  ip6_rthdr *ip6po_rhi_rthdr; /* Routing header */
126            struct  route ip6po_rhi_route; /* Route to the 1st hop */
130    };
131    #define ip6po_rthdr       ip6po_rhinfo.ip6po_rhi_rthdr
132    #define ip6po_route       ip6po_rhinfo.ip6po_rhi_route
```

122–130 ip6po_rhi_rthdr points to the actual routing header. ip6po_rhi_route stores a cached route for the first hop specified in the Routing header. Usage of these members is described in Section 3.13.3.

131–132 Two shortcut macros are defined to get access to the structure members from the ip6_pktopts{} structure.

A couple of utility functions that handle the ip6_pktopts{} structure are defined, which will be described below.

init_ip6pktopts() *Functions*

The init_ip6pktopts() function simply initializes the content of the ip6_pktopts{} structure with system default parameters.

Listing 7-34

```
3269   void
3270   init_ip6pktopts(opt)
3271           struct ip6_pktopts *opt;
3272   {
3273
3274           bzero(opt, sizeof(*opt));
3275           opt->ip6po_hlim = -1;        /* -1 means default hop limit */
3276           opt->ip6po_tclass = -1;          /* -1 means default traffic class */
3277           opt->ip6po_minmtu = IP6PO_MINMTU_MCASTONLY;
```

```
3278                    opt->ip6po_prefer_tempaddr = IP6PO_TEMPADDR_SYSTEM;
3279    }
```
———ip6_output.c

ip6_clearpktopts() Function

The `ip6_clearpktopts()` function initializes the option data freeing the values which were set by a previous operation with the default value if applicable.

Listing 7-35
———ip6_output.c

```
3426    void
3427    ip6_clearpktopts(pktopt, optname)
3428            struct ip6_pktopts *pktopt;
3429            int optname;
3430    {
3431            int needfree;
3432
3433            if (pktopt == NULL)
3434                    return;
3435
3436            needfree = pktopt->needfree;
3437
3438            if (optname == -1 || optname == IPV6_PKTINFO) {
3439                    if (needfree && pktopt->ip6po_pktinfo)
3440                            free(pktopt->ip6po_pktinfo, M_IP6OPT);
3441                    pktopt->ip6po_pktinfo = NULL;
3442            }
3443            if (optname == -1 || optname == IPV6_HOPLIMIT)
3444                    pktopt->ip6po_hlim = -1;
3445            if (optname == -1 || optname == IPV6_TCLASS)
3446                    pktopt->ip6po_tclass = -1;
3447            if (optname == -1 || optname == IPV6_NEXTHOP) {
3448                    if (pktopt->ip6po_nextroute.ro_rt) {
3449                            RTFREE(pktopt->ip6po_nextroute.ro_rt);
3450                            pktopt->ip6po_nextroute.ro_rt = NULL;
3451                    }
3452                    if (needfree && pktopt->ip6po_nexthop)
3453                            free(pktopt->ip6po_nexthop, M_IP6OPT);
3454                    pktopt->ip6po_nexthop = NULL;
3455            }
3456            if (optname == -1 || optname == IPV6_HOPOPTS) {
3457                    if (needfree && pktopt->ip6po_hbh)
3458                            free(pktopt->ip6po_hbh, M_IP6OPT);
3459                    pktopt->ip6po_hbh = NULL;
3460            }
3461            if (optname == -1 || optname == IPV6_RTHDRDSTOPTS) {
3462                    if (needfree && pktopt->ip6po_dest1)
3463                            free(pktopt->ip6po_dest1, M_IP6OPT);
3464                    pktopt->ip6po_dest1 = NULL;
3465            }
3466            if (optname == -1 || optname == IPV6_RTHDR) {
3467                    if (needfree && pktopt->ip6po_rhinfo.ip6po_rhi_rthdr)
3468                            free(pktopt->ip6po_rhinfo.ip6po_rhi_rthdr, M_IP6OPT);
3469                    pktopt->ip6po_rhinfo.ip6po_rhi_rthdr = NULL;
3470                    if (pktopt->ip6po_route.ro_rt) {
3471                            RTFREE(pktopt->ip6po_route.ro_rt);
3472                            pktopt->ip6po_route.ro_rt = NULL;
3473                    }
3474            }
3475            if (optname == -1 || optname == IPV6_DSTOPTS) {
3476                    if (needfree && pktopt->ip6po_dest2)
3477                            free(pktopt->ip6po_dest2, M_IP6OPT);
3478                    pktopt->ip6po_dest2 = NULL;
3479            }
3480    }
```
———ip6_output.c

3426–3434 `optname` specifies the option name for which function `ip6_clearpktopts()` will clear and initialize the data. All options are cleared if optname is −1. `ip6_clearpktopts()` does not perform any action if `pktopt` is NULL.

3436 The `needfree` member of the `pktopt` structure is set if the corresponding options were used as sticky options that are stored in dynamically allocated memory.

3438–3479 The rest of the function just re-initializes the specified field(s) of the `pktopt` structure. The memory space is freed here if the option content was dynamically allocated. In addition, if a routing entry is associated with a particular option, which is the case for the `IPV6_NEXTHOP` and the `IPV6_RTHDR` options, then the `RTFREE()` macro is invoked to release the reference count on that route entry.

7.4.3   IPv6 Socket Option Processing—`ip6_ctloutput()` Function

The `ip6_ctloutput()` function is a common routine for most IPv6-related socket options that is called from upper layer `ctloutput` functions (see Figure 7-5). It is a large function containing more than 1000 lines, but its organization is pretty straightforward. The function essentially consists of one big `switch` statement for the operation types: `SOPT_SET` which corresponds to the `setsockopt()` system call and `SOPT_GET` which corresponds to the `getsockopt()` system call. In the following subsections, we see the function based on this big picture.

Initialization

Listing 7-36

─── ip6_output.c
```
1937    /*
1938     * IP6 socket option processing.
1939     */
1941    int
1942    ip6_ctloutput(so, sopt)
1943            struct socket *so;
1944            struct sockopt *sopt;
1953    {
1954            int privileged, optdatalen, uproto;
1955            void *optdata;
1956            struct ip6_recvpktopts *rcvopts;
1964            struct inpcb *in6p = sotoinpcb(so);
1965            int error, optval;
1966            int level, op, optname;
1967            int optlen;
1971            struct proc *p;
1973
1974            if (sopt) {
1975                    level = sopt->sopt_level;
1976                    op = sopt->sopt_dir;
1977                    optname = sopt->sopt_name;
1978                    optlen = sopt->sopt_valsize;
1982                    p = sopt->sopt_p;
1984            } else {
1985                    panic("ip6_ctloutput: arg soopt is NULL");
1986            }
2007            error = optval = 0;
2008
2012            privileged = (p == 0 || suser(p)) ? 0 : 1;
2016            uproto = (int)so->so_proto->pr_protocol;
2017            rcvopts = in6p->in6p_inputopts;
```
─── ip6_output.c

1974–2007 `sopt` is a generic structure defined in FreeBSD for identifying a particular socket option. The `ip6_ctloutput()` function first decodes some part of the structure. Since the `getsockopt()` and the `setsockopt()` system calls always pass a valid `sopt` structure, and because the `ip6_ctloutput()` function is only called from a socket option context, this function assumes `sopt` is non-NULL.

2012–2017 `privileged` is set to 1 when the superuser calls the operation. `uproto` is the upper layer protocol associated with the socket, such as IPPROTO_TCP or IPPROTO_UDP. `rcvopts` is actually not used in this function.

Set Operations

We then show the `setsockopt()` operations for IPv6 socket options.

Listing 7-37

```
                                                                    ip6_output.c
2019            if (level == IPPROTO_IPV6) {
2020                    switch (op) {
2021
2023                    case SOPT_SET:
2027                            switch (optname) {
2028                            case IPV6_2292PKTOPTIONS:
2029    #ifdef IPV6_PKTOPTIONS
2030                            case IPV6_PKTOPTIONS:
2031    #endif
2032                            {
2034                                    struct mbuf *m;
2035
2036                                    error = soopt_getm(sopt, &m); /* XXX */
2037                                    if (error != NULL)
2038                                            break;
2039                                    error = soopt_mcopyin(sopt, m); /* XXX */
2040                                    if (error != NULL)
2041                                            break;
2042                                    error = ip6_pcbopts(&in6p->in6p_outputopts,
2043                                            m, so, sopt);
2044                                    m_freem(m); /* XXX */
2049                                    break;
2050                            }
                                                                    ip6_output.c
```

2028–2050 The `IPV6_PKTOPTIONS` socket option allows the application to specify a set of option information that applies to outgoing packets transmitted over a particular socket. This feature was once specified in [RFC2292] but was removed from [RFC3542]. The kernel code still keeps the `case` statement just for maintaining binary backward compatibility.

Listing 7-38

```
                                                                    ip6_output.c
2052                            /*
2053                             * Use of some Hop-by-Hop options or some
2054                             * Destination options, might require special
2055                             * privilege.  That is, normal applications
2056                             * (without special privilege) might be forbidden
2057                             * from setting certain options in outgoing packets,
```

```
2058                         * and might never see certain options in received
2059                         * packets. [RFC 2292 Section 6]
2060                         * KAME specific note:
2061                         *  KAME prevents non-privileged users from sending or
2062                         *  receiving ANY hbh/dst options in order to avoid
2063                         *  overhead of parsing options in the kernel.
2064                         */
2065             case IPV6_RECVHOPOPTS:
2066             case IPV6_RECVDSTOPTS:
2067             case IPV6_RECVRTHDRDSTOPTS:
2068                         if (!privileged) {
2069                                 error = EPERM;
2070                                 break;
2071                         }
2072                         /* FALLTHROUGH */
```
                                                                    ip6_output.c

2052–2072 KAME implementation requires the application to have the superuser privilege in order to receive the Hop-by-Hop or the Destination options headers. This is too restrictive since [RFC3542] only states that a non-privileged application may not see some options. However, KAME's restriction is intentional and helps to avoid expensive packet parsing for determining whether or not the incoming options can be passed to the application.

Listing 7-39
                                                                    ip6_output.c
```
2073                     case IPV6_UNICAST_HOPS:
2074                     case IPV6_HOPLIMIT:
2075                     case IPV6_FAITH:
2076
2077                     case IPV6_RECVPKTINFO:
2078                     case IPV6_RECVHOPLIMIT:
2079                     case IPV6_RECVRTHDR:
2080                     case IPV6_RECVPATHMTU:
2081                     case IPV6_RECVTCLASS:
2082                     case IPV6_V6ONLY:
2083                     case IPV6_AUTOFLOWLABEL:
2084                             if (optlen != sizeof(int)) {
2085                                     error = EINVAL;
2086                                     break;
2087                             }
```
                                                                    ip6_output.c

2073–2087 All these options take a fixed size (i.e., an integer) argument. Other data types are rejected here.

Listing 7-40
                                                                    ip6_output.c
```
2089                             error = sooptcopyin(sopt, &optval,
2090                                     sizeof optval, sizeof optval);
2091                             if (error)
2092                                     break;
```
                                                                    ip6_output.c

2089–2092 The `sooptcopyin()` function copies the socket option data passed from the application to a memory space internal to the kernel.

Listing 7-41

ip6_output.c

```
2096                                   switch (optname) {
2097
2098                                   case IPV6_UNICAST_HOPS:
2099                                           if (optval < -1 || optval >= 256)
2100                                                   error = EINVAL;
2101                                           else {
2102                                                   /* -1 = kernel default */
2103                                                   in6p->in6p_hops = optval;
2105                                                   if ((in6p->in6p_vflag &
2106                                                       INP_IPV4) != 0)
2107                                                           in6p->inp_ip_ttl = optval;
2109                                           }
2110                                           break;
```

ip6_output.c

2098–2110 The `IPV6_UNICAST_HOPS` socket option specifies the hop limit of outgoing unicast packets. A valid value is copied into the corresponding PCB entry (recall the PCB structure described in Section 6.6.1.). The given hop limit value is also used as the TTL value in IPv4 packets if the socket is used for both IPv4 and IPv6 communication using IPv4-mapped IPv6 addresses. This behavior is a FreeBSD-specific extension and is not defined in the specification.

Listing 7-42

ip6_output.c

```
2111    #define OPTSET(bit) \
2112    do { \
2113            if (optval) \
2114                    in6p->in6p_flags |= (bit); \
2115            else \
2116                    in6p->in6p_flags &= ~(bit); \
2117    } while (/*CONSTCOND*/ 0)
```

ip6_output.c

2111–2117 Socket options are often used to turn on or off a particular behavior that can be represented by a Boolean value. The `OPTSET()` macro is a shortcut to support the common operation.

Listing 7-43

ip6_output.c

```
2118    #define OPTSET2292(bit) \
2119    do { \
2120            in6p->in6p_flags |= IN6P_RFC2292; \
2121            if (optval) \
2122                    in6p->in6p_flags |= (bit); \
2123            else \
2124                    in6p->in6p_flags &= ~(bit); \
2125    } while (/*CONSTCOND*/ 0)
2126    #define OPTBIT(bit) (in6p->in6p_flags & (bit) ? 1 : 0)
```

ip6_output.c

2118–2125 [RFC2292] and [RFC3542] define incompatible advanced APIs, and the usage when these two specifications are mixed is not defined. For example, if the `IPV6_PKTOPTIONS` socket option (only available in [RFC2292]) specifies a Hop-by-Hop options header to be included in outbound packets while the [RFC3542] version of the `IPV6_HOPOPTS` socket option is specified for the same socket, it is not clear which option should be preferred. While this kernel implementation tries to support both specifications as much as possible, it is inadvisable to mix the different specifications. In order to detect and reject the mixed usage, the `OPTSET2292()` macro is used to turn the `IN6P_RFC2292` flag in the PCB on or off, which controls whether the associated socket will only accept options that are defined in [RFC2292].

2126 The `OPTBIT()` macro is a shortcut for checking if a particular option is turned on.

Listing 7-44
———ip6_output.c
```
2128                        case IPV6_RECVPKTINFO:
2129                                /* cannot mix with RFC2292 */
2130                                if (OPTBIT(IN6P_RFC2292)) {
2131                                        error = EINVAL;
2132                                        break;
2133                                }
2134                                OPTSET(IN6P_PKTINFO);
2135                                break;
2136
2137                        case IPV6_HOPLIMIT:
2138                        {
2139                                struct ip6_pktopts **optp;
2140
2141                                /* cannot mix with RFC2292 */
2142                                if (OPTBIT(IN6P_RFC2292)) {
2143                                        error = EINVAL;
2144                                        break;
2145                                }
2146                                optp = &in6p->in6p_outputopts;
2147                                error = ip6_pcbopt(IPV6_HOPLIMIT,
2148                                                (u_char *)&optval,
2149                                                sizeof(optval),
2150                                                optp,
2151                                                privileged, uproto);
2152                                break;
2153                        }
2154
2155                        case IPV6_RECVHOPLIMIT:
2156                                /* cannot mix with RFC2292 */
2157                                if (OPTBIT(IN6P_RFC2292)) {
2158                                        error = EINVAL;
2159                                        break;
2160                                }
2161                                OPTSET(IN6P_HOPLIMIT);
2162                                break;
2163
2164                        case IPV6_RECVHOPOPTS:
2165                                /* cannot mix with RFC2292 */
2166                                if (OPTBIT(IN6P_RFC2292)) {
2167                                        error = EINVAL;
2168                                        break;
2169                                }
2170                                OPTSET(IN6P_HOPOPTS);
2171                                break;
2172
2173                        case IPV6_RECVDSTOPTS:
2174                                /* cannot mix with RFC2292 */
2175                                if (OPTBIT(IN6P_RFC2292)) {
2176                                        error = EINVAL;
2177                                        break;
2178                                }
```

```
2179                        OPTSET(IN6P_DSTOPTS);
2180                        break;
2181
2182            case IPV6_RECVRTHDRDSTOPTS:
2183                        /* cannot mix with RFC2292 */
2184                        if (OPTBIT(IN6P_RFC2292)) {
2185                                error = EINVAL;
2186                                break;
2187                        }
2188                        OPTSET(IN6P_RTHDRDSTOPTS);
2189                        break;
2190
2191            case IPV6_RECVRTHDR:
2192                        /* cannot mix with RFC2292 */
2193                        if (OPTBIT(IN6P_RFC2292)) {
2194                                error = EINVAL;
2195                                break;
2196                        }
2197                        OPTSET(IN6P_RTHDR);
2198                        break;
2199
2200            case IPV6_FAITH:
2201                        OPTSET(IN6P_FAITH);
2202                        break;
2203
2204            case IPV6_RECVPATHMTU:
2205                        /*
2206                         * We ignore this option for TCP
2207                         * sockets.
2208                         * (rfc2292bis leaves this case
2209                         * unspecified.)
2210                         */
2211                        if (uproto != IPPROTO_TCP)
2212                                OPTSET(IN6P_MTU);
2213                        break;
2214
2215            case IPV6_V6ONLY:
2216                        /*
2217                         * make setsockopt(IPV6_V6ONLY)
2218                         * available only prior to bind(2).
2219                         * see ipng mailing list, Jun 22 2001.
2220                         */
2221                        if (in6p->in6p_lport ||
2222                            !SA6_IS_ADDR_UNSPECIFIED(&in6p->in6p_lsa)) {
2223                                error = EINVAL;
2224                                break;
2225                        }
2234                        OPTSET(IN6P_IPV6_V6ONLY);
2236                        if (optval)
2237                                in6p->in6p_vflag &= ~INP_IPV4;
2238                        else
2239                                in6p->in6p_vflag |= INP_IPV4;
2248                        break;
2249            case IPV6_RECVTCLASS:
2250                        /* cannot mix with RFC2292 XXX */
2251                        if (OPTBIT(IN6P_RFC2292)) {
2252                                error = EINVAL;
2253                                break;
2254                        }
2255                        OPTSET(IN6P_TCLASS);
2256                        break;
2257            case IPV6_AUTOFLOWLABEL:
2258                        OPTSET(IN6P_AUTOFLOWLABEL);
2259                        break;
2260
2261            }
2262            break;
```

—— ip6_output.c

2128–2262 These cases are almost based on the same logic, that is, set or clear the flag bit associated with a particular option in the corresponding socket. An error of `EINVAL` is returned if an [RFC3542] option is being specified while an [RFC2292] option has already been set.

IPV6_HOPLIMIT is an exception. The option value is an actual hop limit value, not a flag bit. The `ip6_pcbopt()` function will handle the actual procedure later.

Since [RFC3542] intentionally leaves it open how the `IPV6_RECVPATHMTU` option can be used for TCP sockets, this option is ignored on TCP sockets.

The `IPV6_V6ONLY` option disables the usage of IPv4-mapped IPv6 addresses on an `AF_INET6` socket for IPv4 communication. This option can be set only when the socket is not bound to any specific address. Otherwise, an error of `EINVAL` is returned.

This restriction was introduced to avoid the following scenario:

- An `AF_INET6` socket is created and the `IPV6_V6ONLY` option is turned on.

- The `AF_INET6` socket is then bound to a specific TCP port (e.g., 80).

- An `AF_INET` socket is created and bound to the same TCP port. This should succeed, since these two sockets do not conflict with each other.

- The `IPV6_V6ONLY` option is then turned off on the `AF_INET6` socket. Without the restriction, this would also succeed.

- Now the two sockets effectively conflict, and it will be unclear which socket accepts incoming TCP/IPv4 connections to port 80.

While this restriction should make sense, it was not incorporated in [RFC3493], unfortunately. Even if it is not prohibited, an application should not set this option on a bound socket.

It should also be noted that the `setsockopt()` operation simply sets the `IN6P_IPV6_V6ONLY` flag in the PCB flags field. It does not yet clear the `INP_IPV4` flag of the `inp_vflag`, and in this sense the socket is not really "IPv6-only" at the moment. The `INP_IPV4` flag will be cleared when other socket operations such as the `bind()` system call are performed as we saw in Section 6.8.6.

Listing 7-45

─── ip6_output.c
```
2264                    case IPV6_OTCLASS:
2265                    {
2266                            struct ip6_pktopts **optp;
2267                            u_int8_t tclass;
2268
2269                            if (optlen != sizeof(tclass)) {
2270                                    error = EINVAL;
2271                                    break;
2272                            }
2274                            error = sooptcopyin(sopt, &tclass,
2275                                    sizeof tclass, sizeof tclass);
2276                            if (error)
2277                                    break;
2281                            optp = &in6p->in6p_outputopts;
2282                            error = ip6_pcbopt(optname,
```

```
2283                                           (u_char *)&tclass,
2284                                           sizeof(tclass),
2285                                           optp,
2286                                           privileged, uproto);
2287                           break;
2288               }
```
———————————————————————————————————— ip6_output.c

2264–2288 This `case` statement handles an old definition of a socket option for specifying the value of the IPv6 Traffic Class field of an outgoing packet. Formerly, the option value was defined as an unsigned 8-bit integer, but it was later changed to a generic integer in [RFC3542]. The `case` statement for `IPV6_OTCLASS` provides binary backward compatibility for old applications that still use the previous definition. For this reason, `IPV6_OTCLASS` is a kernel-only definition and is hidden from applications. We will only describe the new option, `IPV6_TCLASS`, in this chapter.

Listing 7-46

———————————————————————————————————— ip6_output.c
```
2290               case IPV6_TCLASS:
2291               case IPV6_DONTFRAG:
2292               case IPV6_USE_MIN_MTU:
2293               case IPV6_PREFER_TEMPADDR:
2294                       if (optlen != sizeof(optval)) {
2295                               error = EINVAL;
2296                               break;
2297                       }
2299                       error = sooptcopyin(sopt, &optval,
2300                               sizeof optval, sizeof optval);
2301                       if (error)
2302                               break;
2306                       {
2307                               struct ip6_pktopts **optp;
2308                               optp = &in6p->in6p_outputopts;
2309                               error = ip6_pcbopt(optname,
2310                                       (u_char *)&optval,
2311                                       sizeof(optval),
2312                                       optp,
2313                                       privileged, uproto);
2314                               break;
2315                       }
```
———————————————————————————————————— ip6_output.c

2290–2315 These options take integer values and are not subject to compatibility issues that exist between the two versions of the advanced API specification. The `sooptcopyin()` function copies the option value after length validation. The `ip6_pcbopt()` function completes the process.

Listing 7-47

———————————————————————————————————— ip6_output.c
```
2317               case IPV6_2292PKTINFO:
2318               case IPV6_2292HOPLIMIT:
2319               case IPV6_2292HOPOPTS:
2320               case IPV6_2292DSTOPTS:
2321               case IPV6_2292RTHDR:
2322                       /* RFC 2292 */
2323                       if (optlen != sizeof(int)) {
2324                               error = EINVAL;
2325                               break;
```

```
2326                            }
2328                            error = sooptcopyin(sopt, &optval,
2329                                    sizeof optval, sizeof optval);
2330                            if (error)
2331                                    break;
2335                            switch (optname) {
2336                            case IPV6_2292PKTINFO:
2337                                    OPTSET2292(IN6P_PKTINFO);
2338                                    break;
2339                            case IPV6_2292HOPLIMIT:
2340                                    OPTSET2292(IN6P_HOPLIMIT);
2341                                    break;
2342                            case IPV6_2292HOPOPTS:
2343                                    /*
2344                                     * Check super-user privilege.
2345                                     * See comments for IPV6_RECVHOPOPTS.
2346                                     */
2347                                    if (!privileged)
2348                                            return (EPERM);
2349                                    OPTSET2292(IN6P_HOPOPTS);
2350                                    break;
2351                            case IPV6_2292DSTOPTS:
2352                                    if (!privileged)
2353                                            return (EPERM);
2354                                    OPTSET2292(IN6P_DSTOPTS|IN6P_RTHDRDSTOPTS);
      /* XXX */
2355                                    break;
2356                            case IPV6_2292RTHDR:
2357                                    OPTSET2292(IN6P_RTHDR);
2358                                    break;
2359                            }
2360                            break;
```
── ip6_output.c

— *Line 2354 is broken here for layout reasons. However, it is a single line of code.*

2317–2360 These `case` statements provide backward compatibility to [RFC2292]-specific options. The `OPTSET2292()` macro is used to mark the socket so that it processes only [RFC2292] options. For Hop-by-Hop and Destination options headers a superuser privilege is required for the same reason described earlier.

Since [RFC3542] differentiates the two possible positions of Destination options headers and the kernel implementation supports the specification, the code in the `case` statement for `IPV6_2292DSTOPTS` sets two flag bits in the socket: one flag bit for the Destination options header that appears before the Routing header, and one flag bit for the Destination options header that appears after the Routing header (if any Routing header exists).

Listing 7-48

── ip6_output.c

```
2361                    case IPV6_PKTINFO:
2362                    case IPV6_HOPOPTS:
2363                    case IPV6_RTHDR:
2364                    case IPV6_DSTOPTS:
2365                    case IPV6_RTHDRDSTOPTS:
2366                    case IPV6_NEXTHOP:
2367                    {
2368                            /* new advanced API (2292bis) */
2369                            u_char *optbuf;
2370                            int optlen;
2371                            struct ip6_pktopts **optp;
2372
2373                            /* cannot mix with RFC2292 */
2374                            if (OPTBIT(IN6P_RFC2292)) {
2375                                    error = EINVAL;
2376                                    break;
2377                            }
```

```
2378
2380                                     optbuf = sopt->sopt_val;
2381                                     optlen = sopt->sopt_valsize;
2395                                     optp = &in6p->in6p_outputopts;
2396                                     error = ip6_pcbopt(optname,
2397                                                        optbuf, optlen,
2398                                                        optp, privileged, uproto);
2399                                     break;
2400                         }
```

——— ip6_output.c

2361–2400 These option types were defined in [RFC2292] but are currently used only in the context of [RFC3542]. So the case statements first check for the presence of the IN6P_RFC2292 flag to reject a mixed usage, and then call function ip6_pcbopt() for the actual processing.

Note: This code has a bug. Since sopt_val points to an address in the user space, the value must be verified and copied to the kernel space using copyin() via sooptcopyin(). Although the direct reference to sopt_val as is done in this code does not cause a problem for valid values, invalid input can make the kernel panic. This bug has been fixed in later versions of the kernel.

Listing 7-49

——— ip6_output.c

```
2401    #undef OPTSET
2402
2403                         case IPV6_MULTICAST_IF:
2404                         case IPV6_MULTICAST_HOPS:
2405                         case IPV6_MULTICAST_LOOP:
2406                         case IPV6_JOIN_GROUP:
2407                         case IPV6_LEAVE_GROUP:
2409                             {
2410                                 if (sopt->sopt_valsize > MLEN) {
2411                                     error = EMSGSIZE;
2412                                     break;
2413                                 }
2414                                 /* XXX */
2415                             }

2438                                 MGET(m, sopt->sopt_p ? M_WAIT : M_DONTWAIT,
        MT_HEADER);
2440                                 if (m == 0) {
2441                                     error = ENOBUFS;
2442                                     break;
2443                                 }
2456                                 m->m_len = sopt->sopt_valsize;
```

——— ip6_output.c

— *Line 2438 is broken here for layout reasons. However, it is a single line of code.*

2403–2456 Since the ip6_setmoptions() function expects an mbuf to store option value, the value passed from the application should be copied into an mbuf. This allocation is actually redundant but is done here for portability with other BSD variants.

Listing 7-50

——— ip6_output.c

```
2457                                 error = sooptcopyin(sopt, mtod(m, char *),
2458                                                     m->m_len, m->m_len);
2459                                 error = ip6_setmoptions(sopt->sopt_name,
```

```
2460                                           &in6p->in6p_moptions,
2461                                           m);
2462                      (void)m_free(m);
2463                    }
```
```
2473                      break;                                       ip6_output.c
```

2457–2463 The `sooptcopyin()` function copies the option value into the kernel. The `ip6_setmoptions()` function processes the options. (Note: There is a small bug here. An error from `sooptcopyin()` should be handled correctly.) The temporarily allocated `mbuf` is not necessary and is freed.

Listing 7-51
_____ip6_output.c
```
2476                  case IPV6_PORTRANGE:
2478                      error = sooptcopyin(sopt, &optval,
2479                          sizeof optval, sizeof optval);
2480                      if (error)
2481                          break;
2485
2486                      switch (optval) {
2487                      case IPV6_PORTRANGE_DEFAULT:
2488                          in6p->in6p_flags &= ~(IN6P_LOWPORT);
2489                          in6p->in6p_flags &= ~(IN6P_HIGHPORT);
2490                          break;
2491
2492                      case IPV6_PORTRANGE_HIGH:
2493                          in6p->in6p_flags &= ~(IN6P_LOWPORT);
2494                          in6p->in6p_flags |= IN6P_HIGHPORT;
2495                          break;
2496
2497                      case IPV6_PORTRANGE_LOW:
2498                          in6p->in6p_flags &= ~(IN6P_HIGHPORT);
2499                          in6p->in6p_flags |= IN6P_LOWPORT;
2500                          break;
2501
2502                      default:
2503                          error = EINVAL;
2504                          break;
2505                      }
2506                      break;
```
_____ip6_output.c

2476–2506 The `IPV6_PORTRANGE` option is specific to some BSD variants, which specifies the port range for a TCP or UDP socket with an unspecified (zero) port number. The code simply sets or clears some flag bits in the socket.

Listing 7-52
_____ip6_output.c
```
2652                  default:
2653                      error = ENOPROTOOPT;
2654                      break;
2655                  }
2660                  break;
```
_____ip6_output.c

2652–2655 An error of `ENOPROTOOPT` is returned if an unknown option type is encountered.

Get Operations

In this part, we show the getsockopt() operations for IPv6 socket options. Most options are handled within this function. Some others, especially the multicast-related options and options defined in [RFC3542], need additional subroutines.

Listing 7-53

```
_____ip6_output.c
2663                        case SOPT_GET:
2667                             switch (optname) {
2668
2669                             case IPV6_2292PKTOPTIONS:
2670    #ifdef IPV6_PKTOPTIONS
2671                             case IPV6_PKTOPTIONS:
2672    #endif
2674                                 if (in6p->in6p_inputopts &&
2675                                     in6p->in6p_inputopts->head) {
2676                                     struct mbuf *m;
2677                                     m = m_copym(in6p->in6p_inputopts->head,
2678                                         0, M_COPYALL, M_WAIT);
2679                                     error = soopt_mcopyout(sopt, m);
2680                                     if (error == 0)
2681                                             m_freem(m);
2682                                 } else
2683                                         sopt->sopt_valsize = 0;
2694                                 break;
_____ip6_output.c
```

2669–2694 The getsockopt() operation for the IPV6_PKTOPTIONS socket option retrieves option information, such as IPv6 extension headers that are stored in the socket. [RFC3542] deprecated this and the kernel no longer stores any information on the socket. The code simply provides backward compatibility to older applications by always returning empty data.

Listing 7-54

```
_____ip6_output.c
2696                        case IPV6_RECVHOPOPTS:
2697                        case IPV6_RECVDSTOPTS:
2698                        case IPV6_RECVRTHDRDSTOPTS:
2699                        case IPV6_UNICAST_HOPS:
2700                        case IPV6_RECVPKTINFO:
2701                        case IPV6_RECVHOPLIMIT:
2702                        case IPV6_RECVRTHDR:
2703                        case IPV6_RECVPATHMTU:
2704
2705                        case IPV6_FAITH:
2706                        case IPV6_V6ONLY:
2708                        case IPV6_PORTRANGE:
2710                        case IPV6_RECVTCLASS:
2711                        case IPV6_AUTOFLOWLABEL:
2712                             switch (optname) {
2713
2714                             case IPV6_RECVHOPOPTS:
2715                                 optval = OPTBIT(IN6P_HOPOPTS);
2716                                 break;
2717
2718                             case IPV6_RECVDSTOPTS:
2719                                 optval = OPTBIT(IN6P_DSTOPTS);
```

```
2720                                  break;
2721
2722                          case IPV6_RECVRTHDRDSTOPTS:
2723                                  optval = OPTBIT(IN6P_RTHDRDSTOPTS);
2724                                  break;
2725
2726                          case IPV6_UNICAST_HOPS:
2727                                  optval = in6p->in6p_hops;
2728                                  break;
2729
2730                          case IPV6_RECVPKTINFO:
2731                                  optval = OPTBIT(IN6P_PKTINFO);
2732                                  break;
2733
2734                          case IPV6_RECVHOPLIMIT:
2735                                  optval = OPTBIT(IN6P_HOPLIMIT);
2736                                  break;
2737
2738                          case IPV6_RECVRTHDR:
2739                                  optval = OPTBIT(IN6P_RTHDR);
2740                                  break;
2741
2742                          case IPV6_RECVPATHMTU:
2743                                  optval = OPTBIT(IN6P_MTU);
2744                                  break;
2745
2746                          case IPV6_FAITH:
2747                                  optval = OPTBIT(IN6P_FAITH);
2748                                  break;
2749
2750                          case IPV6_V6ONLY:
2752                                  optval = OPTBIT(IN6P_IPV6_V6ONLY);
2756                                  break;
2757
2759                          case IPV6_PORTRANGE:
2760                            {
2761                                  int flags;
2762                                  flags = in6p->in6p_flags;
2763                                  if (flags & IN6P_HIGHPORT)
2764                                          optval = IPV6_PORTRANGE_HIGH;
2765                                  else if (flags & IN6P_LOWPORT)
2766                                          optval = IPV6_PORTRANGE_LOW;
2767                                  else
2768                                          optval = 0;
2769                                  break;
2770                            }
2772                          case IPV6_RECVTCLASS:
2773                                  optval = OPTBIT(IN6P_TCLASS);
2774                                  break;
2775
2776                          case IPV6_AUTOFLOWLABEL:
2777                                  optval = OPTBIT(IN6P_AUTOFLOWLABEL);
2778                                  break;
2779
2783                          }
2784                          if (error)
2785                                  break;
2787                          error = sooptcopyout(sopt, &optval,
2788                                  sizeof optval);
2794                          break;
```

——— ip6_output.c

2696–2794 These `case` statements return an integer value to the application, which indicates whether a particular option is enabled or not. The `OPTBIT()` macro returns 1 if
the given option is enabled and the macro returns 0 otherwise. `IPV6_UNICAST_HOPS`
is an exception where the actual hop limit value is returned. The other exception

is IPV6_PORTRANGE, which returns the range identifier, that is, either
IPV6_PORTRANGE_HIGH or IPV6_PORTRANGE_LOW.

The sooptcopyout() function copies the option value into the application memory
space.

Listing 7-55

_____ip6_output.c
```
2796                    case IPV6_PATHMTU:
2797                    {
2798                            u_long pmtu = 0;
2799                            struct ip6_mtuinfoxo mtuinfo;
....
2801                            struct route *ro = &in6p->in6p_route;
....
2805
2806                            if (!(so->so_state & SS_ISCONNECTED))
2807                                    return (ENOTCONN);
2808                            /*
2809                             * XXX: we dot not consider the case of source
2810                             * routing, nor optional information to specify
2811                             * the outgoing interface.
2812                             */
2813                            error = ip6_getpmtu(ro, NULL, NULL,
2814                                &in6p->in6p_fsa, &pmtu, NULL);
2815                            if (error)
2816                                    break;
2817                            if (pmtu > IPV6_MAXPACKET)
2818                                    pmtu = IPV6_MAXPACKET;
2819
2820                            bzero(&mtuinfo, sizeof(mtuinfo));
2821                            mtuinfo.ip6m_mtu = (u_int32_t)pmtu;
2822                            optdata = (void *)&mtuinfo;
2823                            optdatalen = sizeof(mtuinfo);
2825                            error = sooptcopyout(sopt, optdata,
2826                                optdatalen);
2836                            break;
2837                    }
```
_____ip6_output.c

2796–2837 IPV6_PATHMTU is a read-only socket option that returns the path MTU value
obtained for the remote address of a given connected socket. An ENOTCONN error is
returned if the socket is not connected. The ip6_getpmtu() function stores the path
MTU value in variable pmtu (see Section 3.13.8). The code states that the path MTU value
may be inaccurate if the application uses source routing or if the application explicitly
specifies the outgoing interface. In such cases, the outgoing interface may differ from that
stored in the cached route ro, and the link MTU of the interface can be smaller than the
stored path MTU.

Listing 7-56

_____ip6_output.c
```
2839                    case IPV6_2292PKTINFO:
2840                    case IPV6_2292HOPLIMIT:
2841                    case IPV6_2292HOPOPTS:
2842                    case IPV6_2292RTHDR:
2843                    case IPV6_2292DSTOPTS:
2844                            if (optname == IPV6_2292HOPOPTS ||
2845                                optname == IPV6_2292DSTOPTS ||
2846                                !privileged)
2847                                    return (EPERM);
```

```
2848                                        switch (optname) {
2849                                        case IPV6_2292PKTINFO:
2850                                                optval = OPTBIT(IN6P_PKTINFO);
2851                                                break;
2852                                        case IPV6_2292HOPLIMIT:
2853                                                optval = OPTBIT(IN6P_HOPLIMIT);
2854                                                break;
2855                                        case IPV6_2292HOPOPTS:
2856                                                if (!privileged)
2857                                                        return (EPERM);
2858                                                optval = OPTBIT(IN6P_HOPOPTS);
2859                                                break;
2860                                        case IPV6_2292RTHDR:
2861                                                optval = OPTBIT(IN6P_RTHDR);
2862                                                break;
2863                                        case IPV6_2292DSTOPTS:
2864                                                if (!privileged)
2865                                                        return (EPERM);
2866                                                optval = OPTBIT(IN6P_DSTOPTS|
    IN6P_RTHDRDSTOPTS);
2867                                                break;
2868                                        }
2870                                        error = sooptcopyout(sopt, &optval,
2871                                            sizeof optval);
2877                                        break;
```
── ip6_output.c

— Line 2866 is broken here for layout reasons. However, it is a single line of code.

2839–2877 These cases are provided for backward compatibility to [RFC2292]. Each of the cases returns if the corresponding option is enabled on the socket. A superuser privilege is required for `IPV6_2292HOPOPTS` and `IPV6_2292DSTOPTS`, which is actually too restrictive. Since these operations just provide the fact if the corresponding bit is set, there is no reason to prohibit those. In fact, `getsockopt()` for similar options in [RFC3542] (such as `IPV6_RECVHOPLIMIT`) does not require the privilege.

Listing 7-57
── ip6_output.c
```
2878                        case IPV6_PKTINFO:
2879                        case IPV6_HOPOPTS:
2880                        case IPV6_RTHDR:
2881                        case IPV6_DSTOPTS:
2882                        case IPV6_RTHDRDSTOPTS:
2883                        case IPV6_NEXTHOP:
2884                        case IPV6_OTCLASS:
2885                        case IPV6_TCLASS:
2886                        case IPV6_DONTFRAG:
2887                        case IPV6_USE_MIN_MTU:
2888                        case IPV6_PREFER_TEMPADDR:
2890                                error = ip6_getpcbopt(in6p->in6p_outputopts,
2891                                    optname, sopt);
2896                                break;
```
── ip6_output.c

2878–2896 These options have either a large or variable length option value and are processed in `ip6_getpcbopt()`. `ip6_getpcbopt()` is described in Section 7.4.4.

Listing 7-58
── ip6_output.c
```
2898                        case IPV6_MULTICAST_IF:
2899                        case IPV6_MULTICAST_HOPS:
```

```
2900                             case IPV6_MULTICAST_LOOP:
2901                             case IPV6_JOIN_GROUP:
2902                             case IPV6_LEAVE_GROUP:
2904                                 {
2905                                     struct mbuf *m;
2906                                     error = ip6_getmoptions(sopt->sopt_name,
2907                                         in6p->in6p_moptions, &m);
2908                                     if (error == 0)
2909                                         error = sooptcopyout(sopt,
2910                                             mtod(m, char *), m->m_len);
2911                                     m_freem(m);
2912                                 }
2917                                 break;
                                                                        ip6_output.c
```

2898–2917 The `getsockopt()` operation for multicast-related options are handled in `ip6_getmoptions()`. For portability reasons, the function internally allocates a new mbuf and stores the option values to it. Since FreeBSD does not use an mbuf for `getsockopt()`, the `sooptcopyout()` function copies the stored value to the application space here, and frees the mbuf.

Listing 7-59

```
                                                                        ip6_output.c
3035                             default:
3036                                 error = ENOPROTOOPT;
3037                                 break;
3038                             }
3039                             break;
3040                         }
                                                                        ip6_output.c
```

3035–3038 An `ENOPROTOOPT` error is returned if an unknown option type is encountered.

Listing 7-60

```
                                                                        ip6_output.c
3041             } else {                  /* level != IPPROTO_IPV6 */
3042                 error = EINVAL;
3047             }
3048             return (error);
3049     }
                                                                        ip6_output.c
```

3041–3049 This `else` statement corresponds to the `if` clause at line 2019 (Listing 7-37), which means the option level is not IPv6. An `EINVAL` error is returned in this case.

7.4.4 Getting Socket Options—`ip6_getpcbopt()` Function

The `ip6_getpcbopt()` function, shown in Listing 7-61, is a subroutine of `ip6_ctloutput()`, which performs the actual socket option processing for the `getsockopt()` operation.

Listing 7-61

```
                                                                        ip6_output.c
3303     static int
3304     ip6_getpcbopt(pktopt, optname, sopt)
3305             struct ip6_pktopts *pktopt;
```

```
3306            struct sockopt *sopt;
3307            int optname;
3315    {
3316            void *optdata = NULL;
3317            int optdatalen = 0;
3318            struct ip6_ext *ip6e;
3319            int error = 0;
3320            struct in6_pktinfo null_pktinfo;
3321            int deftclass = 0, on;
3322            int defminmtu = IP6PO_MINMTU_MCASTONLY;
3323            int defpreftemp = IP6PO_TEMPADDR_SYSTEM;
3327
3328            switch (optname) {
3329            case IPV6_PKTINFO:
3330                    if (pktopt && pktopt->ip6po_pktinfo)
3331                            optdata = (void *)pktopt->ip6po_pktinfo;
3332                    else {
3333                            /* XXX: we don't have to do this every time... */
3334                            bzero(&null_pktinfo, sizeof(null_pktinfo));
3335                            optdata = (void *)&null_pktinfo;
3336                    }
3337                    optdatalen = sizeof(struct in6_pktinfo);
3338                    break;
3339            case IPV6_OTCLASS:
3340                    /* XXX */
3341                    return (EINVAL);
3342            case IPV6_TCLASS:
3343                    if (pktopt && pktopt->ip6po_tclass >= 0)
3344                            optdata = (void *)&pktopt->ip6po_tclass;
3345                    else
3346                            optdata = (void *)&deftclass;
3347                    optdatalen = sizeof(int);
3348                    break;
3349            case IPV6_HOPOPTS:
3350                    if (pktopt && pktopt->ip6po_hbh) {
3351                            optdata = (void *)pktopt->ip6po_hbh;
3352                            ip6e = (struct ip6_ext *)pktopt->ip6po_hbh;
3353                            optdatalen = (ip6e->ip6e_len + 1) << 3;
3354                    }
3355                    break;
3356            case IPV6_RTHDR:
3357                    if (pktopt && pktopt->ip6po_rthdr) {
3358                            optdata = (void *)pktopt->ip6po_rthdr;
3359                            ip6e = (struct ip6_ext *)pktopt->ip6po_rthdr;
3360                            optdatalen = (ip6e->ip6e_len + 1) << 3;
3361                    }
3362                    break;
3363            case IPV6_RTHDRDSTOPTS:
3364                    if (pktopt && pktopt->ip6po_dest1) {
3365                            optdata = (void *)pktopt->ip6po_dest1;
3366                            ip6e = (struct ip6_ext *)pktopt->ip6po_dest1;
3367                            optdatalen = (ip6e->ip6e_len + 1) << 3;
3368                    }
3369                    break;
3370            case IPV6_DSTOPTS:
3371                    if (pktopt && pktopt->ip6po_dest2) {
3372                            optdata = (void *)pktopt->ip6po_dest2;
3373                            ip6e = (struct ip6_ext *)pktopt->ip6po_dest2;
3374                            optdatalen = (ip6e->ip6e_len + 1) << 3;
3375                    }
3376                    break;
3377            case IPV6_NEXTHOP:
3378                    if (pktopt && pktopt->ip6po_nexthop) {
3379                            optdata = (void *)pktopt->ip6po_nexthop;
3380                            optdatalen = pktopt->ip6po_nexthop->sa_len;
3381                    }
3382                    break;
3383            case IPV6_USE_MIN_MTU:
```

```
3384                    if (pktopt)
3385                            optdata = (void *)&pktopt->ip6po_minmtu;
3386                    else
3387                            optdata = (void *)&defminmtu;
3388                    optdatalen = sizeof(int);
3389                    break;
3390            case IPV6_DONTFRAG:
3391                    if (pktopt && ((pktopt->ip6po_flags) & IP6PO_DONTFRAG))
3392                            on = 1;
3393                    else
3394                            on = 0;
3395                    optdata = (void *)&on;
3396                    optdatalen = sizeof(on);
3397                    break;
3398            case IPV6_PREFER_TEMPADDR:
3399                    if (pktopt)
3400                            optdata = (void *)&pktopt->ip6po_prefer_tempaddr;
3401                    else
3402                            optdata = (void *)&defpreftemp;
3403                    optdatalen = sizeof(int);
3404                    break;
3405            default:                /* should not happen */
3406                    printf("ip6_getpcbopt: unexpected option: %d\n", optname);
3407                    return (ENOPROTOOPT);
3408            }
3409
3411            error = sooptcopyout(sopt, optdata, optdatalen);
3422
3423            return (error);
3424    }
```
                                                                    ———————— ip6_output.c

3303–3323 The option values to be returned to the application will be copied to
`sopt.ptdata` and `optdatalen` specify the address of option value and its length,
respectively, which will be used at the end of this function as generic parameters.

3328–3404 The corresponding member in the `ip6_pktopts{}` structure is examined depending on the option name. If the option is present and succeeds validation, then `optdata`
is set to point to the option data, and `optdatalen` is set to the size of the option. Otherwise, either that particular option has been unset or no option has ever been set (in which
case `pktopt` is NULL), and `optdata` and `optdatalen` is set as specified in [RFC3542].
For example, if no option value has been set for the `IPV6_PKTINFO` option, `optdata`
points to `null_pktinfo`, a zero-cleared `in6_pktinfo{}` structure.

3405–3408 Since `ip6_ctloutput()` calls this function only when a supported option is specified, the default case should not occur. Otherwise, it means a bug in the kernel code and
an `ENOPROTOOPT` error is returned.

3411–3423 `sooptcopyout()` copies the identified data into `sopt`, and the return value of
that function, which is usually 0, will be returned to the application.

7.4.5 Setting Socket Options and Ancillary Data

In this subsection, we describe the processing of socket options and ancillary data objects for
outgoing packets. It covers the following four functions:

- `ip6_pcbopts()`
- `ip6_pcbopt()`

- `ip6_setpktoptions()`

- `ip6_setpktoption()`

The first two are for socket options and act as a subroutine of `ip6_ctloutput()`.
The last two are common routines for socket options and ancillary data objects. For the
latter usage, an upper layer output function calls `ip6_setpktoptions()`, which then calls
`ip6_setpktoption()`.

ip6_pcbopts() *Function*

The `ip6_pcbopts()` function is a dedicated processing function for handling the
`setsockopt()` operation on the `IPV6_PKTOPTIONS` socket option.

Listing 7-62
─── ip6_output.c

```
3193    /*
3194     * Set up IP6 options in pcb for insertion in output packets or
3195     * specifying behavior of outgoing packets.
3196     */
3197    static int
3199    ip6_pcbopts(pktopt, m, so, sopt)
3203            struct ip6_pktopts **pktopt;
3204            struct mbuf *m;
3205            struct socket *so;
3207            struct sockopt *sopt;
3209    {
3210            struct ip6_pktopts *opt = *pktopt;
3211            int error = 0;
3216            struct proc *p = sopt->sopt_p;
3223            int priv = 0;
3224
3225            /* turn off any old options. */
3226            if (opt) {
3227    #ifdef DIAGNOSTIC
3228                    if (opt->ip6po_pktinfo || opt->ip6po_nexthop ||
3229                        opt->ip6po_hbh || opt->ip6po_dest1 || opt->ip6po_dest2 ||
3230                        opt->ip6po_rhinfo.ip6po_rhi_rthdr)
3231                            printf("ip6_pcbopts: all specified options are cleared.\n");
3232    #endif
3233                    ip6_clearpktopts(opt, -1);
3234            } else
3235                    opt = malloc(sizeof(*opt), M_IP6OPT, M_WAITOK);
3236            *pktopt = NULL;
```
─── ip6_output.c

3225–3233 `opt` points to the `pktopt` variable containing the existing option structure if
`pktopt` is a valid pointer. Since `IPV6_PKTOPTIONS` controls all possible options in
a single operation, the side effect is that all of the options will be turned off at once. This
inconvenience is in fact one of the motivations for revising this API. The already allocated
space is reused for the new set of options.

3235 A new `ip6_pktopts{}` structure is allocated if there have been no options set for the
socket.

3236 The pointer stored in `pktopt` is cleared for possible error or clearing cases below.

Listing 7-63

_____ ip6_output.c
```
3238            if (!m || m->m_len == 0) {
3239                    /*
3240                     * Only turning off any previous options, regardless of
3241                     * whether the opt is just created or given.
3242                     */
3243                    free(opt, M_IP6OPT);
3244                    return (0);
3245            }
```
_____ ip6_output.c

3238–3245 The existing options are cleared if either no actual data is given or the given data
is empty.

Listing 7-64

_____ ip6_output.c
```
3247            /*  set options specified by user. */
3249            if (p && !suser(p))
3250                    priv = 1;
3255            if ((error = ip6_setpktoptions(m, opt, NULL, priv, 1,
3256                so->so_proto->pr_protocol)) != 0) {
3257                    ip6_clearpktopts(opt, -1); /* XXX: discard all options */
3258                    free(opt, M_IP6OPT);
3259                    return (error);
3260            }
```
_____ ip6_output.c

3249–3260 Function   `ip6_setpktoptions()`   performs   the   actual   operation.
`ip6_clearpktopts()` frees all intermediate structures if `ip6_setpktoptions()`
returns a failure code. In that case the option structure itself is also freed and the corresponding error code is returned.

Listing 7-65

_____ ip6_output.c
```
3261            *pktopt = opt;
3262            return (0);
3263    }
```
_____ ip6_output.c

3261–3262 The setsockopt operation succeeded. The new or updated option structure is stored
in the socket.

ip6_pcbopt() Function

`ip6_pcbopt()` is a wrapper function for `ip6_setpktoption()` that handles the set operations for [RFC3542] socket options. Only `ip6_ctloutput()` calls this function.

Listing 7-66

_____ ip6_output.c
```
3282    static int
3283    ip6_pcbopt(optname, buf, len, pktopt, priv, uproto)
3284            int optname, len, priv;
3285            u_char *buf;
```

```
3286              struct ip6_pktopts **pktopt;
3287              int uproto;
3288    {
3289              struct ip6_pktopts *opt;
3290
3291              if (*pktopt == NULL) {
3292                      *pktopt = malloc(sizeof(struct ip6_pktopts), M_IP6OPT,
3293                          M_WAITOK);
3294                      init_ip6pktopts(*pktopt);
3295                      (*pktopt)->needfree = 1;
3296              }
3297              opt = *pktopt;
3298
3299              return (ip6_setpktoption(optname, buf, len, opt, priv, 1, 0, uproto));
3300    }
```
── *ip6_output.c*

3282–3300 pktopt points to the address of the pointer to the socket options of a given socket. A new structure is allocated and is initialized if the socket options pointer is NULL. The needfree member is set to 1 to indicate that the structure is dynamically allocated and needs to be freed later in function ip6_clearpktopts(). After preparing pktopt, it is then passed to ip6_setpktoption() along with other parameters for processing.

ip6_setpktoptions() *Function*

The ip6_setpktoptions() function is called within two different code paths. The first code path comes from the ip6_pcbopts() function, which sets [RFC2292] style socket options. The other code path is from the transport layer output functions for configuring per-packet ancillary data object.

Listing 7-67
── *ip6_output.c*

```
4366    /*
4367     * Set IPv6 outgoing packet options based on advanced API.
4368     */
4369    int
4370    ip6_setpktoptions(control, opt, stickyopt, priv, needcopy, uproto)
4371              struct mbuf *control;
4372              struct ip6_pktopts *opt, *stickyopt;
4373              int priv, needcopy, uproto;
```
── *ip6_output.c*

4366–4373 A non-0 value of needcopy implies the first code path is taken. opt points to the option data structure to be configured, while stickyopt is the same structure that is already set on the socket as sticky options. The stickyopt variable is only necessary for the configuration of ancillary data. Variable control is an mbuf that stores user-supplied options.

Listing 7-68
── *ip6_output.c*

```
4374    {
4375              struct cmsghdr *cm = 0;
4376
4377              if (control == 0 || opt == 0)
4378                      return (EINVAL);
```
── *ip6_output.c*

4377–4378 In general, `control` contains the socket option requested by the application, and the result is returned in `opt`. Both varibles must be non-NULL.

Listing 7-69

```
                                                          ip6_output.c
4380            if (stickyopt) {
4381                    /*
4382                     * If stickyopt is provided, make a local copy of the options
4383                     * for this particular packet, then override them by ancillary
4384                     * objects.
4385                     * XXX: need to gain a reference for the cached route of the
4386                     * next hop in case of the overriding.
4387                     */
4388                    *opt = *stickyopt;
4389                    if (opt->ip6po_nextroute.ro_rt)
4390                            opt->ip6po_nextroute.ro_rt->rt_refcnt++;
4391            } else
4392                    init_ip6pktopts(opt);
4393            opt->needfree = needcopy;
4394
4395            /*
4396             * XXX: Currently, we assume all the optional information is stored
4397             * in a single mbuf.
4398             */
4399            if (control->m_next)
4400                    return (EINVAL);
4401
4402            for (; control->m_len; control->m_data += CMSG_ALIGN(cm->cmsg_len),
4403                control->m_len -= CMSG_ALIGN(cm->cmsg_len)) {
4404                    int error;
4405
4406                    if (control->m_len < CMSG_LEN(0))
4407                            return (EINVAL);
4408
4409                    cm = mtod(control, struct cmsghdr *);
4410                    if (cm->cmsg_len == 0 || cm->cmsg_len > control->m_len)
4411                            return (EINVAL);
4412                    if (cm->cmsg_level != IPPROTO_IPV6)
4413                            continue;
4414
4415                    error = ip6_setpktoption(cm->cmsg_type, CMSG_DATA(cm),
4416                        cm->cmsg_len - CMSG_LEN(0), opt, priv, needcopy, 1, uproto);
4417                    if (error)
4418                            return (error);
4419            }
4420
4421            return (0);
4422    }
                                                          ip6_output.c
```

4380–4392 A non-NULL `stickyopt` prompts the creation of a merged structure that contains both the existing sticky option and the per-packet objects. The content of `stickyopt` is copied into `opt`. If a route to a particular next hop is cached, the reference counter to the route is incremented, since the copy implicitly requests a new reference.

The `init_ip6pktopts()` function prepares a clean set of option structure if the sticky option is missing.

4393 The `needfree` member controls if the internal data of the `opt` structure should be dynamically allocated and freed.

4399–4400 As indicated by the comment, the current implementation requires all the option data to be stored in a single mbuf. This requirement is just for simplicity but is probably sufficient in practical usage.

4402–4422 The for loop iterates through all the options specified in the control variable. Each option must be at least CMSG_LEN(0) bytes to ensure the cmsg_len and the cmsg_level members can be safely referenced. cmsg_len must not be 0 or else it would cause an infinite loop. This routine is only interested in IPv6-related options, and thus options other than those at the IPPROTO_IPV6 level are ignored. Function ip6_setpktoption() processes one given option at a time. ip6_setpktoptions() terminates the process and returns the error if any invocation of ip6_setpktoption() indicates an error condition.

ip6_setpktoption() Function

The ip6_setpktoption() function processes a given socket option or ancillary data object, most of which are defined as advanced API options.

Listing 7-70
_____ ip6_output.c
```
4424    /*
4425     * Set a particular packet option, as a sticky option or an ancillary data
4426     * item.  "len" can be 0 only when it's a sticky option.
4427     * We have 4 cases of combination of "sticky" and "cmsg":
4428     * "sticky=0, cmsg=0": impossible
4429     * "sticky=0, cmsg=1": RFC2292 or rfc2292bis ancillary data
4430     * "sticky=1, cmsg=0": rfc2292bis socket option
4431     * "sticky=1, cmsg=1": RFC2292 socket option
4432     */
4433    static int
4434    ip6_setpktoption(optname, buf, len, opt, priv, sticky, cmsg, uproto)
4435            int optname, len, priv, sticky, cmsg, uproto;
4436            u_char *buf;
4437            struct ip6_pktopts *opt;
```
_____ ip6_output.c

4433–4437 Whether the function operates on a socket option or an ancillary data object depends on the values of sticky and cmsg. The semantics of each combination is summarized in Table 7-18.

TABLE 7-18

Sticky	Cmsg	Meaning
0	0	An impossible case
0	1	An ancillary data object (for [RFC2292] and [RFC3542])
1	0	An [RFC3542] socket option
1	1	An [RFC2292] socket option

Listing 7-71

```
4438    {
4439            int minmtupolicy, preftemp;
4440
4441            if (!sticky && !cmsg) {
4442    #ifdef DIAGNOSTIC
4443                    printf("ip6_setpktoption: impossible case\n");
4444    #endif
4445                    return (EINVAL);
4446            }
4447
4448            /*
4449             * IPV6_2292xxx is for backward compatibility to RFC2292, and should
4450             * not be specified in the context of rfc2292bis.  Conversely,
4451             * rfc2292bis types should not be specified in the context of RFC2292.
4452             *
4453             */
4454            if (!cmsg) {
4455                    switch (optname) {
4456                    case IPV6_2292PKTINFO:
4457                    case IPV6_2292HOPLIMIT:
4458                    case IPV6_2292NEXTHOP:
4459                    case IPV6_2292HOPOPTS:
4460                    case IPV6_2292DSTOPTS:
4461                    case IPV6_2292RTHDR:
4462                    case IPV6_2292PKTOPTIONS:
4463                            return (ENOPROTOOPT);
4464                    }
4465            }
4466            if (sticky && cmsg) {
4467                    switch (optname) {
4468                    case IPV6_PKTINFO:
4469                    case IPV6_HOPLIMIT:
4470                    case IPV6_NEXTHOP:
4471                    case IPV6_HOPOPTS:
4472                    case IPV6_DSTOPTS:
4473                    case IPV6_RTHDRDSTOPTS:
4474                    case IPV6_RTHDR:
4475                    case IPV6_REACHCONF:
4476                    case IPV6_USE_MIN_MTU:
4477                    case IPV6_DONTFRAG:
4478                    case IPV6_OTCLASS:
4479                    case IPV6_TCLASS:
4480                    case IPV6_PREFER_TEMPADDR: /* XXX: not an rfc2292bis option */
4481                            return (ENOPROTOOPT);
4482                    }
4483            }
```

4441–4446 The impossible combination of `sticky` and `cmsg` is explicitly rejected for safety.

4454–4462 The option must be an [RFC3542] socket option if `cmsg` is 0, and thus [RFC2292] option names are invalid.

4466–4483 The option must be an [RFC2292] socket option if both `sticky` and `cmsg` are true. In this case, option names that are only valid in the context of [RFC3542] are rejected. `IPV6_PREFER_TEMPADDR` is rejected here because it is an experimental option for source address selection and is not defined in either [RFC2292] or [RFC3542].

The following part of the function processes the given option identified by `optname`.

Set Packet Information

Listing 7-72

_____ip6_output.c

```
4484
4485              switch (optname) {
4486              case IPV6_2292PKTINFO:
4487              case IPV6_PKTINFO:
4488              {
4489                      struct ifnet *ifp = NULL;
4490                      struct in6_pktinfo *pktinfo;
4491
4492                      if (len != sizeof(struct in6_pktinfo))
4493                              return (EINVAL);
4494
4495                      pktinfo = (struct in6_pktinfo *)buf;
4496
4497                      /*
4498                       * An application can clear any sticky IPV6_PKTINFO option by
4499                       * doing a "regular" setsockopt with ipi6_addr being
4500                       * in6addr_any and ipi6_ifindex being zero.
4501                       * [rfc2292bis-02, Section 6]
4502                       */
4503                      if (optname == IPV6_PKTINFO && opt->ip6po_pktinfo) {
4504                              if (pktinfo->ipi6_ifindex == 0 &&
4505                                  IN6_IS_ADDR_UNSPECIFIED(&pktinfo->ipi6_addr)) {
4506                                      ip6_clearpktopts(opt, optname);
4507                                      break;
4508                              }
4509                      }
4510
4511                      if (uproto == IPPROTO_TCP && optname == IPV6_PKTINFO &&
4512                          sticky && !IN6_IS_ADDR_UNSPECIFIED(&pktinfo->ipi6_addr)) {
4513                              return (EINVAL);
4514                      }
4515
4516                      /* validate the interface index if specified. */
4517                      if (pktinfo->ipi6_ifindex > if_index ||
4518                          pktinfo->ipi6_ifindex < 0) {
4519                              return (ENXIO);
4520                      }
4521                      if (pktinfo->ipi6_ifindex) {
4523                              ifp = ifnet_byindex(pktinfo->ipi6_ifindex);
4527                              if (ifp == NULL)
4528                                      return (ENXIO);
4529                      }
4530
4531                      /*
4532                       * We store the address anyway, and let in6_selectsrc()
4533                       * validate the specified address.  This is because ipi6_addr
4534                       * may not have enough information about its scope zone, and
4535                       * we may need additional information (such as outgoing
4536                       * interface or the scope zone of a destination address) to
4537                       * disambiguate the scope.
4538                       * XXX: the delay of the validation may confuse the
4539                       * application when it is used as a sticky option.
4540                       */
4541                      if (sticky) {
4542                              if (opt->ip6po_pktinfo == NULL) {
4543                                      opt->ip6po_pktinfo = malloc(sizeof(*pktinfo),
4544                                          M_IP6OPT, M_WAITOK);
4545                              }
4546                              bcopy(pktinfo, opt->ip6po_pktinfo, sizeof(*pktinfo));
4547                      } else
4548                              opt->ip6po_pktinfo = pktinfo;
```

```
4549                    break;
4550            }
```

4486–4493 The `IPV6_PKTINFO` option can specify both the source address and the outgoing interface for packets transmitted over the given socket.

The option argument is a fixed size of the `in6_pktinfo{}` structure. An `EINVAL` error is returned if the given data size does not match the expected value.

4498–4509 In the context of [RFC3542], if the given `pktinfo` structure is empty and the `pktinfo` structure is already set for the socket, then the operation clears the previous `pktinfo` structure.

4511–4514 An `EINVAL` error is returned if a non-0 address is being set as an [RFC3542] socket option on a TCP socket. The reason is that the source address of a TCP connection cannot be changed dynamically once the connection is established. In fact, an application can specify the source address for a TCP socket using the `bind()` system call.

4516–4529 The interface index is checked against a valid range of interface indices if the outgoing interface is specified. This interface index must also correspond to a valid `ifnet{}` structure. The second condition is usually satisfied, but is not always the case if interfaces have been dynamically destroyed and re-created.

4531–4550 The given option is stored for either the socket or the packet. Although both [RFC2292] and [RFC3542] require that the specified address be a valid unicast address of the sending node, address validation is postponed because the address itself may not have sufficient information for scope zone validation (see Section 3.13.1). As the code comment indicates, this behavior may confuse the application when this is used as a socket option because an invalid address may not be detected until packet transmission occurs. An application should therefore `bind()` the address to a socket first if the application wants that address to be the source address for subsequent outgoing packets, rather than taking the `IPV6_PKTINFO` socket option approach.

Set Hop Limit

Listing 7-73

```
4552            case IPV6_2292HOPLIMIT:
4553            case IPV6_HOPLIMIT:
4554            {
4555                    int *hlimp;
4556
4557                    /*
4558                     * rfc2292bis-03 obsoleted the usage of sticky IPV6_HOPLIMIT
4559                     * to simplify the ordering among hoplimit options.
4560                     */
4561                    if (optname == IPV6_HOPLIMIT && sticky)
4562                            return (ENOPROTOOPT);
4563
4564                    if (len != sizeof(int))
4565                            return (EINVAL);
4566                    hlimp = (int *)buf;
```

```
4567                    if (*hlimp < -1 || *hlimp > 255)
4568                            return (EINVAL);
4569
4570                    opt->ip6po_hlim = *hlimp;
4571                    break;
4572            }
```
——————————————————————————————————————— ip6_output.c

4557–4562 Since the basic API defines options to manipulate the hop limit for both unicast and multicast packets, [RFC3542] deprecated the usage of IPV6_HOPLIMIT as a socket option.

4564–4570 This option has a fixed-length argument that specifies the hop limit value. If the length is correct and the value is within range, the hop limit value is set in the corresponding field of the option structure. A value of −1 has a special meaning that the system's default hop limit will be used.

Set Traffic Class (Old Style)

Listing 7-74
——— ip6_output.c
```
4574            case IPV6_OTCLASS:
4575                    if (len != sizeof(u_int8_t))
4576                            return (EINVAL);
4577
4578                    opt->ip6po_tclass = *(u_int8_t *)buf;
4579                    break;
```
——————————————————————————————————————— ip6_output.c

4574–4579 IPV6_OTCLASS is only provided for binary backward compatibility to an old specification of the Traffic Class API.

Listing 7-75
——— ip6_output.c
```
4581            case IPV6_TCLASS:
4582            {
4583                    int tclass;
4584
4585                    if (len != sizeof(int))
4586                            return (EINVAL);
4587                    tclass = *(int *)buf;
4588                    if (tclass < -1 || tclass > 255)
4589                            return (EINVAL);
4590
4591                    opt->ip6po_tclass = tclass;
4592                    break;
4593            }
```
——————————————————————————————————————— ip6_output.c

4581–4593 This option specifies the value for the Traffic Class field for outgoing packets. Since the field length is 8 bits, a non-negative option argument must be between 0 and 255. A value of −1 has a special meaning that the system's default value will be used.

Specify the Next Hop Address

Listing 7-76

─── ip6_output.c
```
4595                    case IPV6_2292NEXTHOP:
4596                    case IPV6_NEXTHOP:
4597                            if (!priv)
4598                                    return (EPERM);
4599
4600                            if (len == 0) {          /* just remove the option */
4601                                    ip6_clearpktopts(opt, IPV6_NEXTHOP);
4602                                    break;
4603                            }
4604
4605                            /* check if cmsg_len is large enough for sa_len */
4606                            if (len < sizeof(struct sockaddr) || len < *buf)
4607                                    return (EINVAL);
4608
4609                            switch (((struct sockaddr *)buf)->sa_family) {
4610                            case AF_INET6:
4611                            {
4612                                    struct sockaddr_in6 *sa6 = (struct sockaddr_in6 *)buf;
4613                                    int error;
4614
4615                                    if (sa6->sin6_len != sizeof(struct sockaddr_in6))
4616                                            return (EINVAL);
4617
4618                                    if (SA6_IS_ADDR_UNSPECIFIED(sa6) ||
4619                                        IN6_IS_ADDR_MULTICAST(&sa6->sin6_addr)) {
4620                                            return (EINVAL);
4621                                    }
4622                                    if ((error = scope6_check_id(sa6, ip6_use_defzone))
4623                                        != 0) {
4624                                            return (error);
4625                                    }
4627                                    sa6->sin6_scope_id = 0; /* XXX */
4628                                    break;
4629                            }
4630                            case AF_LINK:           /* should eventually be supported */
4631                            default:
4632                                    return (EAFNOSUPPORT);
4633                            }
4634
4635                            /* turn off the previous option, then set the new option. */
4636                            ip6_clearpktopts(opt, IPV6_NEXTHOP);
4637                            if (sticky) {
4638                                    opt->ip6po_nexthop = malloc(*buf, M_IP6OPT, M_WAITOK);
4639                                    bcopy(buf, opt->ip6po_nexthop, *buf);
4640                            } else
4641                                    opt->ip6po_nexthop = (struct sockaddr *)buf;
4642                            break;
```
─── ip6_output.c

4597–4598 [RFC2292] and [RFC3542] require the application to have the superuser privilege to specify the next hop.

4600–4603 The current next hop value is cleared if the application gives an empty argument.

4605–4607 The option argument must be at least as large as the generic socket address structure. Note that the first byte of a socket address structure on FreeBSD stores its length.

4609–4610 This implementation only supports IPv6 next hop addresses that are stored in `sockaddr_in6{}` structures. In fact, [RFC3542] clearly concentrates on the case of IPv6 next hop.

4618–4621 Semantically invalid next hop addresses are rejected here.

4622–4630 The `scope6_check_id()` function validates the address with respect to the scope zone ID stored in the `sockaddr_in6{}` structure. If the application does not specify a zone ID when the zone information is required and the system allows the use of the default zone ID, then the function sets the `sin6_scope_id` field to the default zone. Note, however, that line 4627 then clears the zone ID value. The reason is that the current kernel implementation does not honor the zone ID for routing unless an experimental kernel option is defined.

4636–4637 The `ip6_clearpktopts()` function once clears the previously specified next hop information if any.

4638–4642 If this is specified as a socket option, new memory space is allocated to store the address, and the socket address structure is copied to the allocated space. Otherwise, `ip6po_nexthop` simply points to the address structure.

Listing 7-77

_____ ip6_output.c
```
4645                case IPV6_2292HOPOPTS:
4646                case IPV6_HOPOPTS:
4647                {
4648                        struct ip6_hbh *hbh;
4649                        int hbhlen;
4650
4651                        /*
4652                         * XXX: We don't allow a non-privileged user to set ANY HbH
4653                         * options, since per-option restriction has too much
4654                         * overhead.
4655                         */
4656                        if (!priv)
4657                                return (EPERM);
4658
4659                        if (len == 0) {
4660                                ip6_clearpktopts(opt, IPV6_HOPOPTS);
4661                                break;          /* just remove the option */
4662                        }
4663
4664                        /* message length validation */
4665                        if (len < sizeof(struct ip6_hbh))
4666                                return (EINVAL);
4667                        hbh = (struct ip6_hbh *)buf;
4668                        hbhlen = (hbh->ip6h_len + 1) << 3;
4669                        if (len != hbhlen)
4670                                return (EINVAL);
4671
4672                        /* turn off the previous option, then set the new option. */
4673                        ip6_clearpktopts(opt, IPV6_HOPOPTS);
4674                        if (sticky) {
4675                                opt->ip6po_hbh = malloc(hbhlen, M_IP6OPT, M_WAITOK);
4676                                bcopy(hbh, opt->ip6po_hbh, hbhlen);
4677                        } else
4678                                opt->ip6po_hbh = hbh;
4679
4680                        break;
4681                }
```
_____ ip6_output.c

4651–4657 [RFC2292] and [RFC3542] conditionally require the application to have the superuser privilege in order to set a Hop-by-Hop options header. This current implementation only supports per-header control even though the RFCs describe per-option control. The reason is that parsing the options can incur performance penalty, especially when parsing ancillary data objects.

4659–4662 The option data that was set previously is cleared when presented with empty data.

4664–4670 The option argument must contain a valid Hop-by-Hop options header. The length validation against the size of the `ip6_hbh{}` structure ensures safe access to the length field in the header.

4672–4681 The code logic here is the same as that of `IPV6_NEXTHOP`: clear the previous option data, allocate new space if necessary, and copy the new data.

Specify Destination Options Headers

According to [RFC2460], a Destination options header can appear before and after the Routing header (see Section 3.3.1). In order to deal with the different positions, the code to specify the Destination options headers becomes a bit complicated.

Listing 7-78

```
                                                                  ip6_output.c
4683            case IPV6_2292DSTOPTS:
4684            case IPV6_DSTOPTS:
4685            case IPV6_RTHDRDSTOPTS:
4686            {
4687                    struct ip6_dest *dest, **newdest = NULL;
4688                    int destlen;
4689
4690                    if (!priv)       /* XXX: see the comment for IPV6_HOPOPTS */
4691                            return (EPERM);
4692
4693                    if (len == 0) {
4694                            ip6_clearpktopts(opt, optname);
4695                            break;          /* just remove the option */
4696                    }
4697
4698                    /* message length validation */
4699                    if (len < sizeof(struct ip6_dest))
4700                            return (EINVAL);
4701                    dest = (struct ip6_dest *)buf;
4702                    destlen = (dest->ip6d_len + 1) << 3;
4703                    if (len != destlen)
4704                            return (EINVAL);
4705
4706                    /*
4707                     * Determine the position that the destination options header
4708                     * should be inserted; before or after the routing header.
4709                     */
4710                    switch (optname) {
4711                    case IPV6_2292DSTOPTS:
4712                            /*
4713                             * The old advacned API is ambiguous on this point.
4714                             * Our approach is to determine the position based
4715                             * according to the existence of a routing header.
4716                             * Note, however, that this depends on the order of the
4717                             * extension headers in the ancillary data; the 1st
4718                             * part of the destination options header must appear
4719                             * before the routing header in the ancillary data,
4720                             * too.
4721                             * RFC2292bis solved the ambiguity by introducing
```

```
4722                             * separate ancillary data or option types.
4723                             */
4724                            if (opt->ip6po_rthdr == NULL)
4725                                    newdest = &opt->ip6po_dest1;
4726                            else
4727                                    newdest = &opt->ip6po_dest2;
4728                            break;
4729                    case IPV6_RTHDRDSTOPTS:
4730                            newdest = &opt->ip6po_dest1;
4731                            break;
4732                    case IPV6_DSTOPTS:
4733                            newdest = &opt->ip6po_dest2;
4734                            break;
4735                    }
4736
4737                    /* turn off the previous option, then set the new option. */
4738                    ip6_clearpktopts(opt, optname);
4739                    if (sticky) {
4740                            *newdest = malloc(destlen, M_IP6OPT, M_WAITOK);
4741                            bcopy(dest, *newdest, destlen);
4742                    } else
4743                            *newdest = dest;
4744
4745                    break;
4746            }
```
—— ip6_output.c

4683–4691 Similar to the requirement for setting the Hop-by-Hop options header, an application must have the superuser privilege in order to set the Destination options header.

4693–4704 The option data that was set previously is cleared when presented with empty data.

4711–4728 In [RFC2292], the location for the Destination options header can be specified ambignously, regardless of the presence of a Routing header. This behavior is confusing to say the least and thus has been revised in [RFC3542].

4728–4731 [RFC3542] introduces a separate option name, IPV6_RTHDRDSTOPTS, to specify the location before a Routing header. This position is used only when a Routing header is actually specified.

4732–4735 In [RFC3542], IPV6_DSTOPTS means the location after a Routing header. This position is used regardless of the existence of a Routing header.

4737–4745 The code logic here is the same as that of IPV6_NEXTHOP (Listing 7-76).

Specify Routing Header

Listing 7-79
—— ip6_output.c
```
4748            case IPV6_2292RTHDR:
4749            case IPV6_RTHDR:
4750            {
4751                    struct ip6_rthdr *rth;
4752                    int rthlen;
4753
4754                    if (len == 0) {
4755                            ip6_clearpktopts(opt, IPV6_RTHDR);
4756                            break;          /* just remove the option */
4757                    }
4758
```

```
4759                          /* message length validation */
4760                          if (len < sizeof(struct ip6_rthdr))
4761                                  return (EINVAL);
4762                          rth = (struct ip6_rthdr *)buf;
4763                          rthlen = (rth->ip6r_len + 1) << 3;
4764                          if (len != rthlen)
4765                                  return (EINVAL);
4766
4767                          switch (rth->ip6r_type) {
4768                          case IPV6_RTHDR_TYPE_0:
4769                                  if (rth->ip6r_len == 0)       /* must contain one addr */
4770                                          return (EINVAL);
4771                                  if (rth->ip6r_len % 2) /* length must be even */
4772                                          return (EINVAL);
4773                                  if (rth->ip6r_len / 2 != rth->ip6r_segleft)
4774                                          return (EINVAL);
4775                                  break;
4776                          default:
4777                                  return (EINVAL);             /* not supported */
4778                          }
4779
4780                          /* turn off the previous option */
4781                          ip6_clearpktopts(opt, IPV6_RTHDR);
4782                          if (sticky) {
4783                                  opt->ip6po_rthdr = malloc(rthlen, M_IP6OPT, M_WAITOK);
4784                                  bcopy(rth, opt->ip6po_rthdr, rthlen);
4785                          } else
4786                                  opt->ip6po_rthdr = rth;
4787
4788                          break;
4789                  }
```
—— ip6_output.c

4748–4757 The option data that was set previously is cleared when presented with empty data.

4759–4765 At a minimum the option must contain the fixed part of the Routing header (i.e., the size of the `ip6_rthdr{}` structure). The header length as specified by the `ip6r_len` field must be consistent with the data length.

4767–4778 The API implementation only supports the type 0 Routing header, that is, it does not consider the type 2 Routing header for Mobile IPv6. At least one intermediate address must be given for the type 0 header. `ip6r_len` must be an even integer as specified in [RFC2460], and must be consistent with the number of segments left that is given in the `ip6r_segleft` field.

4780–4788 The option data is stored in the socket at the completion of all the necessary validations.

Specify Reachability Confirmation

Listing 7-80
—— ip6_output.c

```
4790
4791          case IPV6_REACHCONF:
4792                  if (!cmsg)
4793                          return (ENOPROTOOPT);
4794
4795  #if 0
4796                  /*
4797                   * it looks dangerous to allow IPV6_REACHCONF to
4798                   * normal user.  it affects the ND state (system state)
```

```
4799                        * and can affect communication by others - jinmei
4800                        */
4801                       if (!priv)
4802                               return (EPERM);
4803   #else
4804                       /*
4805                        * we limit max # of subsequent userland reachability
4806                        * conformation by using ln->ln_byhint.
4807                        */
4808   #endif
4809                       if (len)
4810                               return (EINVAL);
4811                       opt->ip6po_flags |= IP6PO_REACHCONF;
4812                       break;
```
── ip6_output.c

4791–4812 The `IPV6_REACHCONF` option was introduced briefly in the revision of the
advanced API, but has finally been removed in [RFC3542] due to lack of practical usage
scenarios. This code is thus experimental and may not appear in future implementations
that conform to [RFC3542].

Specify Sending Packets with the Minimum MTU

Listing 7-81
── ip6_output.c

```
4814               case IPV6_USE_MIN_MTU:
4815                       if (len != sizeof(int))
4816                               return (EINVAL);
4817                       minmtupolicy = *(int *)buf;
4818                       if (minmtupolicy != IP6PO_MINMTU_MCASTONLY &&
4819                           minmtupolicy != IP6PO_MINMTU_DISABLE &&
4820                           minmtupolicy != IP6PO_MINMTU_ALL) {
4821                               return (EINVAL);
4822                       }
4823                       opt->ip6po_minmtu = minmtupolicy;
4824                       break;
```
── ip6_output.c

4814–4824 The `IPV6_USE_MIN_MTU` option takes an integer argument and its effect on path
MTU discovery and fragmentation is described in Table 7-10 (Section 7.3.6 and Listing
3-170). The option value is saved in the socket after successful validation.

Specify Sending Packets without Fragmentation

Listing 7-82
── ip6_output.c

```
4826               case IPV6_DONTFRAG:
4827                       if (len != sizeof(int))
4828                               return (EINVAL);
4829
4830                       if (uproto == IPPROTO_TCP || *(int *)buf == 0) {
4831                               /*
4832                                * we ignore this option for TCP sockets.
4833                                * (rfc2292bis leaves this case unspecified.)
4834                                */
4835                               opt->ip6po_flags &= ~IP6PO_DONTFRAG;
4836                       } else
```

```
4837                        opt->ip6po_flags |= IP6PO_DONTFRAG;
4838                    break;
```
————————————————————————————————————— ip6_output.c

4826—4838 The `IPV6_DONTFRAG` option instructs the kernel to avoid fragmentation even when packets do not fit in the path MTU. This option is usually set for debugging purposes. The option data is a Boolean value and must be an integer. [RFC3542] does not specify the expected behavior of this option when applied to a TCP socket. The KAME implementation ignores any attempts to set this option on TCP sockets.

Specify Preferring Temporary Addresses

Listing 7-83

————————————————————————————————————— ip6_output.c
```
4840        case IPV6_PREFER_TEMPADDR:
4841            if (len != sizeof(int))
4842                return (EINVAL);
4843            preftemp = *(int *)buf;
4844            if (preftemp != IP6PO_TEMPADDR_SYSTEM &&
4845                preftemp != IP6PO_TEMPADDR_NOTPREFER &&
4846                preftemp != IP6PO_TEMPADDR_PREFER) {
4847                return (EINVAL);
4848            }
4849            opt->ip6po_prefer_tempaddr = preftemp;
4850            break;
4851
4852        default:
4853            return (ENOPROTOOPT);
4854        } /* end of switch */
4855
4856        return (0);
4857    }
```
————————————————————————————————————— ip6_output.c

4840—4849 The `IPV6_PREFER_TEMPADDR` option specifies that IPv6 temporary addresses for privacy extension (Section 5.10.4) should be preferred as the source address of packets sent over the given socket (Section 3.13.1). This option is not defined in any standard documents and is experimental. The option data must be an integer that indicates the preference.

4852—4856 An `ENOPROTOOPT` error is returned if an unknown option type is encountered.

7.4.6 Cleaning Up—`ip6_freepcbopts()` Function

The `ip6_freepcbopts()` function, shown below, is called to free all sticky options when a socket is closed. Its behavior is trivial: releasing all interal resources by `ip6_clearpktopts()` and freeing the options structure.

Listing 7-84

————————————————————————————————————— ip6_output.c
```
3547    void
3548    ip6_freepcbopts(pktopt)
3549        struct ip6_pktopts *pktopt;
3550    {
```

```
3551            if (pktopt == NULL)
3552                    return;
3553
3554            ip6_clearpktopts(pktopt, -1);
3555
3556            free(pktopt, M_IP6OPT);
3557    }
```
—— ip6_output.c

7.4.7   IPv6 Multicast Socket Options

In this subsection, we describe the processing of multicast-related socket options. It covers three functions for setting, getting, and freeing these options.

ip6_setmoptions() Function

The ip6_setmoptions() function is a subroutine of ip6_ctloutput() that handles the multicast-related socket options for the setsockopt() system call.

These socket options are maintained in the in6p_moptions member of the corresponding PCB (see Section 6.6.1), which points to an ip6_moptions{} structure. We first examine this structure, shown in Listing 7-85.

Listing 7-85
—— ip6_var.h
```
111    struct  ip6_moptions {
112            struct          ifnet *im6o_multicast_ifp; /* ifp for outgoing multicasts */
113            u_char          im6o_multicast_hlim; /* hoplimit for outgoing multicasts */
114            u_char          im6o_multicast_loop; /* 1 >= hear sends if a member */
115            LIST_HEAD(, in6_multi_mship) im6o_memberships;
116    };
```
—— ip6_var.h

im6o_multicast_ifp holds a pointer to the outgoing interface for multicast packet transmission. im6o_multicast_hlim defines the hop limit value to be placed in the Hop Limit field of the IPv6 header of the outgoing multicast packets. im6o_multicast_loop specifies whether the transmitting node should receive its own transmissions if the node is a member of the destination multicast group on the outgoing interface. The im6o_memberships member is a list of membership information about multicast groups that the application joins on this socket. Each entry of the list is an in6_multi_mship{} structure, which was described in Figure 2-14.

Through the following listings, we see the details of ip6_setmoptions(). The calling function, ip6_ctloutput(), passes a pointer to the PCB's ip6_moptions{} structure and socket option parameters stored in an mbuf.

Listing 7-86
—— ip6_output.c
```
3559    /*
3560     * Set the IP6 multicast options in response to user setsockopt().
3561     */
3562    static int
3563    ip6_setmoptions(optname, im6op, m)
3564            int optname;
```

```
3565               struct ip6_moptions **im6op;
3566               struct mbuf *m;
3567      {
3568               int error = 0;
3569               u_int loop, ifindex;
3570               struct ipv6_mreq *mreq;
3571               struct ifnet *ifp;
3572               struct ip6_moptions *im6o = *im6op;
3573               struct sockaddr_in6 sa6_mc;
3575               struct route ro;
3579               struct in6_multi_mship *imm;
3585               struct proc *p = curproc;          /* XXX */
3596
3597               if (im6o == NULL) {
3598                       /*
3599                        * No multicast option buffer attached to the pcb;
3600                        * allocate one and initialize to default values.
3601                        */
3602                       im6o = (struct ip6_moptions *)
3603                               malloc(sizeof(*im6o), M_IPMOPTS, M_WAITOK);
3604                       *im6op = im6o;
3605                       im6o->im6o_multicast_ifp = NULL;
3606                       im6o->im6o_multicast_hlim = ip6_defmcasthlim;
3607                       im6o->im6o_multicast_loop = IPV6_DEFAULT_MULTICAST_LOOP;
3608                       LIST_INIT(&im6o->im6o_memberships);
3609               }
```
── ip6_output.c

3532–3585 im6op is a pointer to the address of the inp6_moptions member of a PCB. Its
value is NULL unless a multicast-related socket option has been set for that PCB. curproc is
a global variable that identifies the process that issued the socket option, which will be used
to determine whether the process has sufficient privilege to perform such socket operations.

3357–3608 If there has been no multicast socket option set for the socket (i.e., PCB),
inp6_moptions is NULL, and so is im6o. Then a new object is allocated and initialized
with the system's default values.

Listing 7-87
── ip6_output.c
```
3611               switch (optname) {
3612
3613               case IPV6_MULTICAST_IF:
3614                       /*
3615                        * Select the interface for outgoing multicast packets.
3616                        */
3617                       if (m == NULL || m->m_len != sizeof(u_int)) {
3618                               error = EINVAL;
3619                               break;
3620                       }
3621                       bcopy(mtod(m, u_int *), &ifindex, sizeof(ifindex));
3622                       if (ifindex < 0 || if_index < ifindex) {
3623                               error = ENXIO;          /* XXX EINVAL? */
3624                               break;
3625                       }
3629                       ifp = ifindex2ifnet[ifindex];
3631                       if (ifp == NULL || (ifp->if_flags & IFF_MULTICAST) == 0) {
3632                               error = EADDRNOTAVAIL;
3633                               break;
3634                       }
3635                       im6o->im6o_multicast_ifp = ifp;
3636                       break;
```
── ip6_output.c

3613–3620 The `IPV6_MULTICAST_IF` socket option takes an integer argument that is the interface index of the outgoing interface of multicast packets sent over the given socket. An `EINVAL` error is returned if an argument is missing or if the argument has an invalid length.

3621–3625 The argument value is copied to variable `ifindex`. An `ENXIO` error is returned if the value is outside the valid range.

3629–3634 An `EADDRNOTAVAIL` error is returned if either the specified interface has been dynamically detached or the interface does not have multicast capability. Note the error code is derived from the IPv4 multicast API, which identifies the interface by an IPv4 address. In fact, since the IPv6 API uses an interface index for identifying an interface (see Section 7.2.5), the error code is misleading in its name.

3635–3636 The specified interface is set in the `im6o_multicast_ifp` member at the completion of successful validation.

Listing 7-88

```
                                                                     ip6_output.c
3638            case IPV6_MULTICAST_HOPS:
3639                {
3640                    /*
3641                     * Set the IP6 hoplimit for outgoing multicast packets.
3642                     */
3643                    int optval;
3644                    if (m == NULL || m->m_len != sizeof(int)) {
3645                            error = EINVAL;
3646                            break;
3647                    }
3648                    bcopy(mtod(m, u_int *), &optval, sizeof(optval));
3649                    if (optval < -1 || optval >= 256)
3650                            error = EINVAL;
3651                    else if (optval == -1)
3652                            im6o->im6o_multicast_hlim = ip6_defmcasthlim;
3653                    else
3654                            im6o->im6o_multicast_hlim = optval;
3655                    break;
3656                }
                                                                     ip6_output.c
```

3638–3650 The `IPV6_MULTICAST_HOPS` option takes an integer value that is between −1 and 255 (inclusive) as an argument. An `EINVAL` error is returned if the argument is missing, has an invalid length, or is out of scope. Refer to Listing 3-155 in Section 3.13.3 to see how this value is used in the IPv6 output function.

3652–3655 The option value −1 implies reinitializing `im6o_multicast_hlim` with the system default value. Any other option value will be set as the Hop Limit for outgoing multicast packets.

Listing 7-89

```
                                                                     ip6_output.c
3658            case IPV6_MULTICAST_LOOP:
3659                    /*
3660                     * Set the loopback flag for outgoing multicast packets.
```

```
3661                      * Must be zero or one.
3662                      */
3663                     if (m == NULL || m->m_len != sizeof(u_int)) {
3664                             error = EINVAL;
3665                             break;
3666                     }
3667                     bcopy(mtod(m, u_int *), &loop, sizeof(loop));
3668                     if (loop > 1) {
3669                             error = EINVAL;
3670                             break;
3671                     }
3672                     im6o->im6o_multicast_loop = loop;
3673                     break;
```
―――――――――――――――――――――――――――――― ip6_output.c

3658–3673 `IPV6_MULTICAST_LOOP` takes an unsigned integer Boolean as an argument. A valid option value will be stored in `im6o_multicast_loop`. Refer to Listing 3-164 in Section 3.13.3 to see how this value is used in the IPv6 output function.

Listing 7-90
―――――――――――――――――――――――――――――― ip6_output.c
```
3675             case IPV6_JOIN_GROUP:
3676                     /*
3677                      * Add a multicast group membership.
3678                      * Group must be a valid IP6 multicast address.
3679                      */
3680                     if (m == NULL || m->m_len != sizeof(struct ipv6_mreq)) {
3681                             error = EINVAL;
3682                             break;
3683                     }
```
―――――――――――――――――――――――――――――― ip6_output.c

3675–3683 The argument to the `IPV6_JOIN_GROUP` option must be an `ipv6_mreq{}` structure. An `EINVAL` error is returned if the argument is not provided or has an invalid length.

Listing 7-91
―――――――――――――――――――――――――――――― ip6_output.c
```
3684                     mreq = mtod(m, struct ipv6_mreq *);
3685                     if (IN6_IS_ADDR_UNSPECIFIED(&mreq->ipv6mr_multiaddr)) {
3686                             /*
3687                              * We use the unspecified address to specify to accept
3688                              * all multicast addresses. Only super user is allowed
3689                              * to do this.
3690                              */
3692                             if (suser(p))
3696                             {
3697                                     error = EACCES;
3698                                     break;
3699                             }
3700                     } else if (!IN6_IS_ADDR_MULTICAST(&mreq->ipv6mr_multiaddr)) {
3701                             error = EINVAL;
3702                             break;
3703                     }
```
―――――――――――――――――――――――――――――― ip6_output.c

3684–3699 `ipv6mr_multiaddr` field must hold a valid IPv6 multicast address. The KAME implementation allows a privileged application to specify the IPv6 unspecified address. While the intention may be to allow the socket to accept packets from any multicast address, the system does not actually behave that way. First, the `IN6_LOOKUP_MULTI()` macro does not have a special matching rule for the unspecified address. Secondly, in order to accept any multicast addresses on an interface, it is necessary to specify the promiscuous mode for the interface's multicast filter, which will not actually be done in this case. Later versions of the KAME implementation removed this code and similar code that exists for `IPV6_LEAVE_GROUP`.

3700–3703 An `EINVAL` error is returned if the given address is neither the unspecified address nor a multicast address.

Listing 7-92

_____ip6_output.c
```
3705                    bzero(&sa6_mc, sizeof(sa6_mc));
3706                    sa6_mc.sin6_family = AF_INET6;
3707                    sa6_mc.sin6_len = sizeof(sa6_mc);
3708                    sa6_mc.sin6_addr = mreq->ipv6mr_multiaddr;
3709
3710                    /*
3711                     * If the interface is specified, validate it.
3712                     */
3713                    if (mreq->ipv6mr_interface < 0
3714                    || if_index < mreq->ipv6mr_interface) {
3715                            error = ENXIO;          /* XXX EINVAL? */
3716                            break;
3717                    }
3718                    /*
3719                     * If no interface was explicitly specified, choose an
3720                     * appropriate one according to the given multicast address.
3721                     */
3722                    if (mreq->ipv6mr_interface == 0) {
3723                            struct sockaddr_in6 *dst;
3724
3725                            /*
3726                             * Look up the routing table for the
3727                             * address, and choose the outgoing interface.
3728                             *   XXX: is it a good approach?
3729                             */
3730                            ro.ro_rt = NULL;
3731                            dst = (struct sockaddr_in6 *)&ro.ro_dst;
3732                            *dst = sa6_mc;
3733   #ifndef SCOPEDROUTING        /* XXX this is actually unnecessary here */
3734                            dst->sin6_scope_id = 0;
3735   #endif
3736                            rtalloc((struct route *)&ro);
3737                            if (ro.ro_rt == NULL) {
3738                                    error = EADDRNOTAVAIL;
3739                                    break;
3740                            }
3741                            ifp = ro.ro_rt->rt_ifp;
3742                            rtfree(ro.ro_rt);
3743                    } else {
3747                            ifp = ifindex2ifnet[mreq->ipv6mr_interface];
3749                    }
3750
3751                    /*
3752                     * See if we found an interface, and confirm that it
3753                     * supports multicast
3754                     */
3755                    if (ifp == NULL || (ifp->if_flags & IFF_MULTICAST) == 0) {
3756                            error = EADDRNOTAVAIL;
3757                            break;
3758                    }
```
_____ip6_output.c

3705–3708 Variable `sa6_mc` is a `sockaddr_in6{}` structure that is initialized for later use. The supplied multicast address is saved in the `sin6_addr` field.

3713–3717 An `EINVAL` error is returned if the given interface index is out of range. Note that index 0 is explicitly allowed.

3722–3743 The application sets `ipv6mr_interface` to 0 when the application wants the kernel to automatically choose an appropriate interface for transmission. The KAME implementation simply follows the traditional IPv4 implementation logic in this case (i.e., calling `rtalloc()` to search the routing table for the specified destination multicast address and use the interface returned in the route entry as the outgoing interface). Variable `ro` holds the returned route. An `EADDRNOTAVAIL` error is returned if `rtalloc()` fails. The route entry is detached because it is not used anymore. Note that if the node cuts through a scope zone boundary of a multicast address, the routing table lookup approach is not applicable because the destination multicast address is ambiguous without the corresponding interface. Such is usually the case for interface-local and link-local multicast addresses, and thus the application must explicitly specify the interface index.

3743–3747 `ifp` is set to point to the corresponding interface structure by calling `ifindex2ifnet()` if the application provides an interface index.

3755–3758 `ifp` can be NULL if the specified interface has been dynamically detached. Even if the interface is valid, it may not support multicast. In either case an `EADDRNOTAVAIL` error is returned.

Note: As discussed in the case of `IPV6_MULTICAST_IF` (Listing 7-87), this error code is not really appropriate for the IPv6 multicast API, which does not use an IP address to specify an interface.

Listing 7-93
———————————————————————————————————— ip6_output.c
```
3760                    /* Fill in the scope zone ID */
3761                    if (in6_addr2zoneid(ifp, &sa6_mc.sin6_addr,
3762                                        &sa6_mc.sin6_scope_id)) {
3763                            error = EADDRNOTAVAIL; /* XXX: should not happen */
3764                            break;
3765                    }
3766                    in6_embedscope(&sa6_mc.sin6_addr, &sa6_mc); /* XXX */
3767
3768                    /*
3769                     * See if the membership already exists.
3770                     */
3771                    for (imm = im6o->im6o_memberships.lh_first;
3772                         imm != NULL; imm = imm->i6mm_chain.le_next)
3773                            if (imm->i6mm_maddr->in6m_ifp == ifp &&
3774                                SA6_ARE_ADDR_EQUAL(&imm->i6mm_maddr->in6m_sa,
3775                                                   &sa6_mc))
3776                                    break;
3777                    if (imm != NULL) {
3778                            error = EADDRINUSE;
3779                            break;
3780                    }
3781                    /*
3782                     * Everything looks good; add a new record to the multicast
```

```
3783                    * address list for the given interface.
3784                    */
3789               imm = in6_joingroup(ifp, &sa6_mc, &error);
3790               if (imm == NULL)
3791                      break;
3796               LIST_INSERT_HEAD(&im6o->im6o_memberships, imm, i6mm_chain);
3797               break;
```
── ip6_output.c

3760–3766 `in6_addr2zoneid()` (Section 2.9.4) is called to set an appropriate multicast
scope zone identifier in the `sin6_scope_id` member of `sa6_mc` once the interface
is identified. This operation should not fail because both the address and the interface are
known to be valid, but the error cases are considered for safety. `in6_embedscope()`
then embeds the zone ID (if necessary) into the 128-bit `sin6_addr` field. In theory such
a step is unnecessary because `sa6_mc` has complete information to disambiguate the
address in terms of scopes. Unfortunately, however, the kernel code still needs to compare
the addresses only by the `sin6_addr` field. This is the reason that `in6_embedscope()`
must be called here.

3771–3780 An `EADDRINUSE` error is returned if the specified group address is already present
in the `im6o_memberships` over the given interface.

3781–3797 Finally, function `in6_joingroup()` completes the join process. On failure,
`in6_joingroup()` returns a NULL pointer and sets the appropriate error. On success,
`imm` points to a valid multicast group membership structure and then `imm` is inserted into
the `im6o_memberships` list. `in6_joingroup()` is described in Section 2.9.3.

Listing 7-94
── ip6_output.c

```
3799          case IPV6_LEAVE_GROUP:
3800               /*
3801                * Drop a multicast group membership.
3802                * Group must be a valid IP6 multicast address.
3803                */
3804               if (m == NULL || m->m_len != sizeof(struct ipv6_mreq)) {
3805                      error = EINVAL;
3806                      break;
3807               }
3808               mreq = mtod(m, struct ipv6_mreq *);
3809               if (IN6_IS_ADDR_UNSPECIFIED(&mreq->ipv6mr_multiaddr)) {
3811                      if (suser(p))
3815                      {
3816                             error = EACCES;
3817                             break;
3818                      }
3819               } else if (!IN6_IS_ADDR_MULTICAST(&mreq->ipv6mr_multiaddr)) {
3820                      error = EINVAL;
3821                      break;
3822               }
```
── ip6_output.c

3799–3807 Similar to `IPV6_JOIN_GROUP`, the `IPV6_LEAVE_GROUP` socket option takes an
`ipv6_mreq{}` structure as the option argument. An `EINVAL` error is returned if the
argument is not provided or if it has an invalid length.

3808–3822 Similarly, the `ipv6mr_multiaddr` field must be either the unspecified address or
a valid IPv6 multicast address.

Listing 7-95

ip6_output.c
```
3824                    bzero(&sa6_mc, sizeof(sa6_mc));
3825                    sa6_mc.sin6_family = AF_INET6;
3826                    sa6_mc.sin6_len = sizeof(sa6_mc);
3827                    sa6_mc.sin6_addr = mreq->ipv6mr_multiaddr;
3828
3829                    /*
3830                     * If an interface address was specified, get a pointer
3831                     * to its ifnet structure.
3832                     */
3833                    if (mreq->ipv6mr_interface < 0
3834                    || if_index < mreq->ipv6mr_interface) {
3835                            error = ENXIO;          /* XXX EINVAL? */
3836                            break;
3837                    }
3841                    ifp = ifindex2ifnet[mreq->ipv6mr_interface];
3843
3844                    /* Fill in the scope zone ID */
3845                    if (ifp) {
3846                            if (in6_addr2zoneid(ifp, &sa6_mc.sin6_addr,
3847                                &sa6_mc.sin6_scope_id)) {
3848                                    /* XXX: should not happen */
3849                                    error = EADDRNOTAVAIL;
3850                                    break;
3851                            }
3852                            in6_embedscope(&sa6_mc.sin6_addr, &sa6_mc); /* XXX */
3853                    } else {
3854                            /*
3855                             * The API spec says as follows:
3856                             *  If the interface index is specified as 0, the
3857                             *  system may choose a multicast group membership to
3858                             *  drop by matching the multicast address only.
3859                             * On the other hand, we cannot disambiguate the scope
3860                             * zone unless an interface is provided.  Thus, we
3861                             * check if there's ambiguity with the default scope
3862                             * zone as the last resort.
3863                             */
3864                            if ((error = scope6_check_id(&sa6_mc,
3865                                ip6_use_defzone)) != 0) {
3866                                    break;
3867                            }
3868                    }
```
ip6_output.c

3824–3827 `sa6_mc` is a `sockaddr_in6{}` structure containing the specified multicast address.

3829–3841 An `ENXIO` error is returned if the given interface index stored in `ipv6mr_interface` is out of range. Otherwise, `ifp` points to the corresponding `ifnet{}` structure. `ifp` may still be NULL if `ipv6mr_interface` is 0 or if the interface has been dynamically detached. The latter case should be caught separately and an appropriate error should be returned, but the current code ignores this condition, which is a bug but is effectively hidden (see below).

3845–3853 The corresponding scope zone identifier is set in the `sin6_scope_id` member of `sa6_mc` if `ifp` points to a valid `ifnet{}` structure. Similar to the implementation for `IPV6_JOIN_GROUP`, `in6_embedscope()` is called so that the `sin6_addr` member contains enough information to disambiguate the address.

3853–3858 As explained earlier, `ifp` is NULL if the application does not specify the interface index. The API specification allows the 0-valued interface index, but the given address may be ambiguous without the actual interface information, especially for interface-local and link-local addresses. As a last resort, the implementation tries to disambiguate the address using the default scope zone if the use of the default zone is permitted. Any failure will cause the process to be terminated, and the error from `scope6_check_id()` will be returned to the application.

In any event, applications should not rely on this feature; it must always specify the corresponding interface to avoid ambiguity (see also Listing 7-92).

Listing 7-96

```
                                                                   ip6_output.c
3870                    /*
3871                     * Find the membership in the membership list.
3872                     */
3873                    for (imm = im6o->im6o_memberships.lh_first;
3874                        imm != NULL; imm = imm->i6mm_chain.le_next) {
3875                            if ((ifp == NULL || imm->i6mm_maddr->in6m_ifp == ifp) &&
3876                                SA6_ARE_ADDR_EQUAL(&imm->i6mm_maddr->in6m_sa,
3877                                    &sa6_mc))
3878                                    break;
3879                    }
3880                    if (imm == NULL) {
3881                            /* Unable to resolve interface */
3882                            error = EADDRNOTAVAIL;
3883                            break;
3884                    }
3885                    /*
3886                     * Give up the multicast address record to which the
3887                     * membership points.
3888                     */
3889                    LIST_REMOVE(imm, i6mm_chain);
3890                    in6_leavegroup(imm);
3891                    break;
```

           (MLDv2 specific code, omitted)

```
4277            default:
4278                    error = EOPNOTSUPP;
4279                    break;
4280            }
                                                                   ip6_output.c
```

3870–3884 An `EADDRNOTAVAIL` error is returned if the given multicast address over the given interface is not found in the multicast membership list stored in `im6o_memberships`.

3885–3891 The multicast address is removed from the group membership list. Function `in6_leavegroup()` (Section 2.14.3) will complete the process by sending an MLD Done message if necessary and reset the interface accordingly.

4277–4280 An `EOPNOTSUPP` error would be returned if an unsupported option type were encountered. However, this error condition should not occur here because this function is called only for the supported options.

Listing 7-97

```
                                                                   ip6_output.c
4282                    /*
4283                     * If all options have default values, no need to keep the mbuf.
4284                     */
4285                    if (im6o->im6o_multicast_ifp == NULL &&
4286                        im6o->im6o_multicast_hlim == ip6_defmcasthlim &&
```

```
4287                      im6o->im6o_multicast_loop == IPV6_DEFAULT_MULTICAST_LOOP &&
4288                      im6o->im6o_memberships.lh_first == NULL) {
4289                      free(*im6op, M_IPMOPTS);
4290                      *im6op = NULL;
4291              }
4292
4293              return (error);
4294      }
```
── ip6_output.c

4282–4291 In some cases, `im6o` results in its default status after the process of the option. In
those cases, the allocated option structure is freed to save memory.

ip6_getmoptions() Function

The `ip6_getmoptions()` function handles the `getsockopt()` system call for three
IPv6   multicast   options: `IPV6_MULTICAST_IF`,   `IPV6_MULTICAST_HOPS`,   and
`IPV6_MULTICAST_LOOP`.   Like   `ip6_setmoptions()`,   it   is   a   subroutine   of
`ip6_ctloutput()` and takes the PCB's `ip6_moptions{}` structure.

Listing 7-98
── ip6_output.c
```
4296      /*
4297       * Return the IP6 multicast options in response to user getsockopt().
4298       */
4299      static int
4300      ip6_getmoptions(optname, im6o, mp)
4301              int optname;
4302              struct ip6_moptions *im6o;
4303              struct mbuf **mp;
4304      {
4305              u_int *hlim, *loop, *ifindex;
4306
4308              *mp = m_get(M_WAIT, MT_HEADER);                   /* XXX */
4312
4313              switch (optname) {
4314
4315              case IPV6_MULTICAST_IF:
4316                      ifindex = mtod(*mp, u_int *);
4317                      (*mp)->m_len = sizeof(u_int);
4318                      if (im6o == NULL || im6o->im6o_multicast_ifp == NULL)
4319                              *ifindex = 0;
4320                      else
4321                              *ifindex = im6o->im6o_multicast_ifp->if_index;
4322                      return (0);
4323
4324              case IPV6_MULTICAST_HOPS:
4325                      hlim = mtod(*mp, u_int *);
4326                      (*mp)->m_len = sizeof(u_int);
4327                      if (im6o == NULL)
4328                              *hlim = ip6_defmcasthlim;
4329                      else
4330                              *hlim = im6o->im6o_multicast_hlim;
4331                      return (0);
4332
4333              case IPV6_MULTICAST_LOOP:
4334                      loop = mtod(*mp, u_int *);
4335                      (*mp)->m_len = sizeof(u_int);
4336                      if (im6o == NULL)
4337                              *loop = ip6_defmcasthlim;
4338                      else
4339                              *loop = im6o->im6o_multicast_loop;
```

```
4340                     return (0);
4341
4342             default:
4343                     return (EOPNOTSUPP);
4344             }
4345     }
```
                                                                    ip6_output.c

4299–4308 m_get() tries to allocate a new mbuf to store the return value of the
getsockopt() call. Note that because the FreeBSD kernel has restructured socket option
framework to avoid the use of the intermediate mbuf, there is actually no need for an mbuf
to store the return value. However, the KAME implementation still uses an mbuf here for
portability with other BSD variants.

4313–4345 The appropriate option value is copied into the allocated mbuf based on the given
socket option name. The default value for an option is returned if that option has never
been set before. For the IPV6_MULTICAST_IF option, the index of the outgoing interface stored in im6o_multicast_ifp is returned. For the IPV6_MULTICAST_HOPS
option, the hop limit stored in im6o_multicast_hlim is returned. For the
IPV6_MULTICAST_LOOP option, the Boolean value stored in im6o_multicast_loop
that controls whether outgoing multicast packets should be looped back to local listeners is returned. An EOPNOTSUPP error is returned if unsupported option type is
encountered.

ip6_freemoptions() Function

The ip6_freemoptions() function releases all dynamically allocated multicast options of a
socket.

Listing 7-99
                                                                    ip6_output.c
```
4317     /*
4318      * Discard the IP6 multicast options.
4319      */
4320     void
4321     ip6_freemoptions(im6o)
4322             struct ip6_moptions *im6o;
4323     {
4324             struct in6_multi_mship *imm;
4325
4326             if (im6o == NULL)
4327                     return;
4328
4329             while ((imm = im6o->im6o_memberships.lh_first) != NULL) {
4330                     LIST_REMOVE(imm, i6mm_chain);
4331                     in6_leavegroup(imm);
4332             }
4333             free(im6o, M_IPMOPTS);
4334     }
```
                                                                    ip6_output.c

The function iterates through each entry of the im6o_memberships list, calling function
in6_leavegroup() to perform the necessary steps to leave a multicast group. Then the
memory for the option structure is released.

7.4.8 IPv6 Raw Socket Options—`ip6_raw_ctloutput()` Function

The `ip6_raw_ctloutput()` function is a dedicated processing function for handling the `IPV6_CHECKSUM` raw IPv6 socket option.

Listing 7-100

ip6_output.c

```
3055    int
3056    ip6_raw_ctloutput(so, sopt)
3057            struct socket *so;
3058            struct sockopt *sopt;
3067    {
3068            int error = 0, optval, optlen;
3069            const int icmp6off = offsetof(struct icmp6_hdr, icmp6_cksum);
3073            struct in6pcb *in6p = sotoin6pcb(so);
3076            int level, op, optname;
3080            struct proc *p;
```

ip6_output.c

3055–3080 `so` points to the socket and `sopt` contains information about the socket option. `icmp6off` is set to the offset length from the top of the `icmp6_hdr{}` structure to the checksum field, which is 2. Variable `p` is necessary for checking privilege of the caller but this variable is effectively unused here. The reason is `ip6_raw_ctloutput()` is always called within the context of a raw socket and the owner of a raw socket must already have the necessary privilege level in order to open the socket in the first place.

Listing 7-101

ip6_output.c

```
3087            if (sopt) {
3088                    level = sopt->sopt_level;
3089                    op = sopt->sopt_dir;
3090                    optname = sopt->sopt_name;
3091                    optlen = sopt->sopt_valsize;
3095                    p = sopt->sopt_p;
3097            } else {
3098                    panic("ip6_ctloutput: arg soopt is NULL");
3099            }
```

ip6_output.c

3087–3099 The socket option parameters are extracted. The function name in the panic message is inaccurate but was not fixed when this code was copied out of the `ip6_ctloutput()` function.

Listing 7-102

ip6_output.c

```
3104            if (level != IPPROTO_IPV6) {
3109                    return (EINVAL);
3110            }
```

ip6_output.c

3104–3110 The socket option level must be `IPPROTO_IPV6`. This check should have been done by the caller and thus is actually redundant here.

Listing 7-103

```
                                                            ip6_output.c
3112            switch (optname) {
3113            case IPV6_CHECKSUM:
3114                    /*
3115                     * For ICMPv6 sockets, no modification allowed for checksum
3116                     * offset, permit "no change" values to help existing apps.
3117                     *
3118                     * XXX 2292bis says: "An attempt to set IPV6_CHECKSUM
3119                     * for an ICMPv6 socket will fail."
3120                     * The current behavior does not meet 2292bis.
3121                     */
                                                            ip6_output.c
```

3112–3121 This function only supports the IPV6_CHECKSUM option. The code comment indicates that the implementation allows the set operation on this option for an ICMPv6 raw socket, which does not conform to the specification, but this behavior remains for supporting old applications that assume the allowance of the set capability.

Listing 7-104

```
                                                            ip6_output.c
3122                switch (op) {
3124                case SOPT_SET:
3128                        if (optlen != sizeof(int)) {
3129                                error = EINVAL;
3130                                break;
3131                        }
3133                        error = sooptcopyin(sopt, &optval, sizeof(optval),
3134                                            sizeof(optval));
3135                        if (error)
3136                                break;
                                                            ip6_output.c
```

3122–3136 The argument to this socket option must be an integer. The value is copied to the local variable optval if the length validation succeeds.

Listing 7-105

```
                                                            ip6_output.c
3140                if ((optval % 2) != 0) {
3141                        /* the API assumes even offset values */
3142                        error = EINVAL;
                                                            ip6_output.c
```

3140–3142 Odd integer values as an offset are rejected as required by [RFC3542].

Listing 7-106

```
                                                            ip6_output.c
3143                } else if (so->so_proto->pr_protocol ==
3144                    IPPROTO_ICMPV6) {
3145                        if (optval != icmp6off)
3146                                error = EINVAL;
                                                            ip6_output.c
```

3143–3146 The application must provide the standard offset to the checksum field for an ICMPv6 raw socket if the application were to specify an offset. This behavior is not fully compliant to [RFC3542] that disallows any set operation on ICMPv6 raw sockets.

Listing 7-107
                                                                                     ip6_output.c
```
3147                            } else
3148                                    in6p->in6p_cksum = optval;
3149                            break;
```
                                                                                     ip6_output.c

3147–3149 The offset value to the checksum field is stored in the PCB for later use (see Section 6.10.2).

Listing 7-108
                                                                                     ip6_output.c
```
3152                    case SOPT_GET:
3156                            if (so->so_proto->pr_protocol == IPPROTO_ICMPV6)
3157                                    optval = icmp6off;
3158                            else
3159                                    optval = in6p->in6p_cksum;
3160
3162                            error = sooptcopyout(sopt, &optval, sizeof(optval));
3168                            break;
```
                                                                                     ip6_output.c

3152–3168 The get operation retrieves the offset value to the checksum field from the PCB and returns it to the application. Note that the `in6p_cksum` member is initialized to −1, which means the kernel will perform any checksum operation on a raw socket for both inbound and outbound packets.

Listing 7-109
                                                                                     ip6_output.c
```
3170                default:
3171                        error = EINVAL;
3172                        break;
3173                }
```
                                                                                     ip6_output.c

3170–3173 An invalid operation will trigger an `EINVAL` error being returned, but this default case statement is actually redundant because the caller should have performed the necessary validation.

Listing 7-110
                                                                                     ip6_output.c
```
3174                    break;
3175
3176            default:
3177                    error = ENOPROTOOPT;
3178                    break;
```
                                                                                     ip6_output.c

3176–3178 An `ENOPROTOOPT` error is returned if an option other than `IPV6_CHECKSUM` is encountered.

Listing 7-111
—— ip6_output.c
```
3179                }
3185
3186            return (error);
3187    }
```
—— ip6_output.c

3179–3187 If everything is okay, the default error code, 0, is returned to indicate the success of this operation.

7.4.9   ICMPv6 Socket Options—`icmp6_ctloutput()` Function

The `icmp6_ctloutput()` function is called from `rip6_ctloutput()` to handle ICMPv6 specific socket options (see Figure 7-5). `ICMP6_FILTER` is the only option in this category that is defined in [RFC3542].

Listing 7-112
—— icmp6.c
```
3262    int
3264    icmp6_ctloutput(so, sopt)
3265            struct socket *so;
3266            struct sockopt *sopt;
3274    {
3275            int error = 0;
3276            int optlen;
3278            struct inpcb *inp = sotoinpcb(so);
3279            int level, op, optname;
3280
3281            if (sopt) {
3282                    level = sopt->sopt_level;
3283                    op = sopt->sopt_dir;
3284                    optname = sopt->sopt_name;
3285                    optlen = sopt->sopt_valsize;
3286            } else
3287                    level = op = optname = optlen = 0;
3294
3295            if (level != IPPROTO_ICMPV6) {
3300                    return EINVAL;
3301            }
3302
3303            switch (op) {
3304            case PRCO_SETOPT:
3305                    switch (optname) {
3306                    case ICMP6_FILTER:
3307                        {
3308                            struct icmp6_filter *p;
3309
3310                            if (optlen != sizeof(*p)) {
3311                                    error = EMSGSIZE;
3312                                    break;
3313                            }
3315                            if (inp->in6p_icmp6filt == NULL) {
3316                                    error = EINVAL;
3317                                    break;
3318                            }
```

```
3319                            error = sooptcopyin(sopt, inp->in6p_icmp6filt, optlen,
3320                                    optlen);
3331                            break;
3332                    }
3333
3334            default:
3335                    error = ENOPROTOOPT;
3336                    break;
3337            }
3342            break;
3343
3344    case PRCO_GETOPT:
3345            switch (optname) {
3346            case ICMP6_FILTER:
3347                    {
3349                            if (inp->in6p_icmp6filt == NULL) {
3350                                    error = EINVAL;
3351                                    break;
3352                            }
3353                            error = sooptcopyout(sopt, inp->in6p_icmp6filt,
3354                                    sizeof(struct icmp6_filter));
3369                            break;
3370                    }
3371
3372            default:
3373                    error = ENOPROTOOPT;
3374                    break;
3375            }
3376            break;
3377    }
3378
3379    return (error);
3380 }
```
_____ icmp6.c

3262–3300 Whereas the caller has already verified `sopt`, validation on `sopt` is performed
here again. The option parameters are then extracted from `sopt`. An `EINVAL` error is
returned if the socket level is not `IPPROTO_ICMPV6`.

3303–3313 The `ICMP6_FILTER` option takes a fixed length of an `icmp6_filter{}` structure
as the argument. An `EMSGSIZE` error is returned if the option length is invalid. Section 6.10.4
gives an example of the effect of `ICMP6_FILTER` in the ICMPv6 input processing routine.

Note: `EMSGSIZE` is not a very appropriate error code. `EINVAL` would be better here.

Note: From the API point of view, `icmp6_filter{}` is an opaque structure; applications
do not have to (or even should not) care about its actual implementation.

3315–3318 If the pointer to the filter specification were NULL, an `EINVAL` error would be
returned. Note that this should actually be impossible to happen, since the `rip6_attach()`
function allocates the memory for this member when it creates the PCB (see Listing 6-151).
Even though there is a bug in `rip6_attach()`, `icmp6_ctloutput()` can never be
called with `in6p_icmp6filt` being NULL.

3319–3332 `sooptcopyin()` transfers the given filter specification to the corresponding PCB.

3334–3342 An `ENOPROTOOPT` error is returned for all other option names.

3344–3370 For the get operation, an `EINVAL` error would be returned if `icmp6filt` is NULL (again, this should be impossible). Otherwise, `sooptcopyout()` transfers the stored specification to `sopt` for returning back to the application.

3372–3376 For option names other than `ICMP6_FILTER`, an error of `ENOPROTOOPT` will be returned.

3378–3380 Unless `sooptcopyin()` or `sooptcopyout()` fails, which is unlikely to happen, 0 will be returned indicating that the operation was successful.

7.4.10 Delivering Incoming Information—`ip6_savecontrol()` Function

The transport layer input routine calls `ip6_savecontrol()` when the application to which the incoming packets are destined has informed the kernel to notify the application either when certain types of information are present in the incoming packets, or of certain information for every packet to the application. For example, an application may request the kernel for notification when some IPv6 extension headers are present, or the application may request the kernel to always return the hop limit value back to the application. Listing 6-131 shows the case where the raw IPv6 input routine calls this function.

The information passed from the upper layer is stored in the `ip6_recvpktopts{}` structure shown in Listing 7-113.

Listing 7-113
                                                                                        ip6_var.h
```
202    struct ip6_recvpktopts {
203            struct mbuf *head;          /* mbuf chain of data passed to a user */
204
205    #ifdef SO_TIMESTAMP
206            struct mbuf *timestamp;     /* timestamp */
207    #endif
208            struct mbuf *hlim;          /* received hop limit */
209            struct mbuf *pktinfo;       /* packet information of rcv packet */
210            struct mbuf *hbh;           /* HbH options header of rcv packet */
211            struct mbuf *dest;          /* Dest opt header of rcv packet */
212            struct mbuf *rthdr;         /* Routing header of rcv packet */
213    };
```
                                                                                        ip6_var.h

202–213 The packet information is actually stored in a chain of mbuf blocks. The `head` member points to the head of the chain. Each of the remaining structure members point to a single mbuf if and only if the information requested by the application is present in the incorming packet.

> *Note*: The old advanced API defined in [RFC2292] required to remember the previous information for optimization, the behavior which was deprecated in [RFC3542]. This structure was introduced to keep the previous set of information. However, the code described in this book basically conforms to [RFC3542] and the optimization was removed, and so there is actually no need to keep the separate structure. In fact, this feature has been removed in later versions of the implementation for simplicity.

Listing 7-114

_____ ip6_input.c

```
1583    /*
1584     * Create the "control" list for this pcb.
1585     * The function will not modify mbuf chain at all.
1586     *
1587     * with KAME mbuf chain restriction:
1588     * The routine will be called from upper layer handlers like tcp6_input().
1589     * Thus the routine assumes that the caller (tcp6_input) have already
1590     * called IP6_EXTHDR_CHECK() and all the extension headers are located in the
1591     * very first mbuf on the mbuf chain.
1592     */
1593    void
1594    ip6_savecontrol(in6p, ip6, m, ctl)
1596            struct inpcb *in6p;
1600            struct ip6_hdr *ip6;
1601            struct mbuf *m;
1602            struct ip6_recvpktopts *ctl;
```
_____ ip6_input.c

1583–1602 `in6p` points to the PCB that corresponds to the receiving socket. `ip6` points to the IPv6 header of the incoming packet. Mbuf `m` holds the entire packet. The `ctl` member is a control structure containing the optional information from this function to the caller.

Listing 7-115

_____ ip6_input.c

```
1603    {
1604    #define IS2292(x, y)            ((in6p->in6p_flags & IN6P_RFC2292) ? (x) : (y))
1605            struct mbuf **mp;
1613            struct proc *p = curproc;        /* XXX */
1619            int privileged = 0;
```
_____ ip6_input.c

1604–1619 The `IS2292()` macro returns true if and only if the application requested the old [RFC2292] style option. The code has a bug: `curproc` is a meaningless pointer because this function runs in an interrupt context (see discussions below).

Listing 7-116

_____ ip6_input.c

```
1621            if (ctl == NULL)        /* validity check */
1622                    return;
1623            bzero(ctl, sizeof(*ctl)); /* XXX is it really OK? */
1624            mp = &ctl->head;
```
_____ ip6_input.c

1621–1624 This function assumes the caller passes a non-NULL control structure or else the function terminates immediately.

Listing 7-117

_____ ip6_input.c

```
1626
1631            if (p && !suser(p))
1632                    privileged++;
```
_____ ip6_input.c

1631–1632 The intention of the privilege check here is to determine whether the receiving process is run by a superuser. As explained above, however, referring to a process by means of p in the interrupt context is wrong. As we will soon see, the privilege check is to ensure that only privileged applications can receive Hop-by-Hop or Destination options headers. However, such privilege validation is not necessary because `ip6_ctloutput()` should have already verified the necessary privilege level at the time when the application set the corresponding socket options (see Listing 7-38).

Listing 7-118

```
                                                                      ip6_input.c
1643    #ifdef SO_TIMESTAMP
1644            if ((in6p->in6p_socket->so_options & SO_TIMESTAMP) != 0) {
1645                    struct timeval tv;
1646
1647                    microtime(&tv);
1648                    *mp = sbcreatecontrol((caddr_t) &tv, sizeof(tv),
1649                                    SCM_TIMESTAMP, SOL_SOCKET);
1650                    if (*mp) {
1651                            /* always set regradless of the previous value */
1652                            ctl->timestamp = *mp;
1653                            mp = &(*mp)->m_next;
1654                    }
1655            }
1656    #endif
                                                                      ip6_input.c
```

1643–1656 If the application requested the packet timestamp of each received packet, then the timeval{} structure tv is set to the current time maintained in the kernel. Function sbcreatecontrol() allocates a separate mbuf and copies the values in tv to the mbuf data buffer. The mbuf chain is adjusted.

Listing 7-119

```
                                                                      ip6_input.c
1658            /* RFC 2292 sec. 5 */
1659            if ((in6p->in6p_flags & IN6P_PKTINFO) != 0) {
1660                    struct in6_pktinfo pi6;
1661
1662                    bcopy(&ip6->ip6_dst, &pi6.ipi6_addr, sizeof(struct in6_addr));
1663                    in6_clearscope(&pi6.ipi6_addr);         /* XXX */
1664                    pi6.ipi6_ifindex = (m && m->m_pkthdr.rcvif)
1665                                    ? m->m_pkthdr.rcvif->if_index
1666                                    : 0;
1667
1668                    *mp = sbcreatecontrol((caddr_t) &pi6,
1669                                    sizeof(struct in6_pktinfo),
1670                                    IS2292(IPV6_2292PKTINFO, IPV6_PKTINFO),
1671                                    IPPROTO_IPV6);
1672                    if (*mp) {
1673                            ctl->pktinfo = *mp;
1674                            mp = &(*mp)->m_next;
1675                    }
1676            }
                                                                      ip6_input.c
```

1658–1676 If the application requested the packet information of each received packet, the
in6_pktinfo{} structure is filled with the destination address and the identifier of the
receiving interface.

The scope zone ID may be embedded in a nonglobal scope destination address,
which should not be visible to the application. Function ip6_clearscope() removes
the zone ID from the address.

Function sbcreatecontrol() prepares a new mbuf and stores the request packet
information. The new mbuf is linked into the mbuf chain.

Listing 7-120

ip6_input.c
```
1678                if ((in6p->in6p_flags & IN6P_HOPLIMIT) != 0) {
1679                        int hlim = ip6->ip6_hlim & 0xff;
1680
1681                        *mp = sbcreatecontrol((caddr_t) &hlim, sizeof(int),
1682                                               IS2292(IPV6_2292HOPLIMIT, IPV6_HOPLIMIT),
1683                                               IPPROTO_IPV6);
1684                        if (*mp) {
1685                                ctl->hlim = *mp;
1686                                mp = &(*mp)->m_next;
1687                        }
1688                }
```
ip6_input.c

1678–1688 If the application requested the hop limit value of each received packet, the Hop
Limit value is copied from the IPv6 header to a new mbuf and that mbuf is then linked to
the mbuf chain.

Listing 7-121

ip6_input.c
```
1690                if ((in6p->in6p_flags & IN6P_TCLASS) != 0) {
1691                        u_int32_t flowinfo;
1692                        int v;
1693
1694                        flowinfo = (u_int32_t)ntohl(ip6->ip6_flow & IPV6_FLOWINFO_MASK);
1695                        flowinfo >>= 20;
1696
1697                        v = flowinfo & 0xff;
1698                        *mp = sbcreatecontrol((caddr_t) &v, sizeof(v),
1699                                               IPV6_TCLASS, IPPROTO_IPV6);
1700                        if (*mp) {
1701                                ctl->hlim = *mp;
1702                                mp = &(*mp)->m_next;
1703                        }
1704                }
```
ip6_input.c

1690–1704 If the application requested the 8-bit Traffic Class value of each incoming packet,
that value is copied from the IPv6 header to a new mbuf. Since the Traffic Class field is
not aligned at a natural byte boundary (see Section 3.2), bitwise operations are necessary
for its extraction from the IPv6 header.

The `hlim` member is overridden at line 1701, and this is a bug. However, the overwrite is harmless because the use of the `hlim` member in the KAME implementation has been deprecated as part of the migration to [RFC3542].

Listing 7-122

ip6_input.c

```
1706                /*
1707                 * IPV6_HOPOPTS socket option. We require super-user privilege
1708                 * for the option, but it might be too strict, since there might
1709                 * be some hop-by-hop options which can be returned to normal user.
1710                 * See RFC 2292 section 6.
1711                 */
1712                if ((in6p->in6p_flags & IN6P_HOPOPTS) != 0 && privileged) {
```

ip6_input.c

1706–1712 If the application with the superuser privilege requested the Hop-by-Hop options header (when included) of each incoming packet, the following code will prepare the data for passing to the application. As code comments indicate, the superuser privilege requirement is too restrictive but is imposed by the implementation for performance reasons (see also Listing 7-38).

Listing 7-123

ip6_input.c

```
1713                    /*
1714                     * Check if a hop-by-hop options header is contatined in the
1715                     * received packet, and if so, store the options as ancillary
1716                     * data. Note that a hop-by-hop options header must be
1717                     * just after the IPv6 header, which fact is assured through
1718                     * the IPv6 input processing.
1719                     */
1720                    struct ip6_hdr *ip6 = mtod(m, struct ip6_hdr *);
1721                    if (ip6->ip6_nxt == IPPROTO_HOPOPTS) {
1722                            struct ip6_hbh *hbh;
1723                            int hbhlen = 0;
1727
1729                            hbh = (struct ip6_hbh *)(ip6 + 1);
1730                            hbhlen = (hbh->ip6h_len + 1) << 3;
1746
1747                            /*
1748                             * XXX: We copy the whole header even if a
1749                             * jumbo payload option is included, which
1750                             * option is to be removed before returning
1751                             * in the RFC 2292.
1752                             * Note: this constraint is removed in
1753                             * 2292bis.
1754                             */
1755                            *mp = sbcreatecontrol((caddr_t)hbh, hbhlen,
1756                                            IS2292(IPV6_2292HOPOPTS,
1757                                                IPV6_HOPOPTS),
1758                                            IPPROTO_IPV6);
1759                            if (*mp) {
1760                                    ctl->hbh = *mp;
1761                                    mp = &(*mp)->m_next;
1762                            }
1766                    }
1767            }
```

ip6_input.c

1720–1721 A Hop-by-Hop options header, if contained, can only appear just after the IPv6 header (Section 3.3.1). Thus, a check on the Next Header field of the IPv6 header suffices in determining whether the Hop-by-Hop options header is present.

Note: The current implementation does not always reject a Hop-by-Hop options header appearing after a header other than the IPv6 header (Listing 6-133). In any event, the implementation of this function is correct: It should not care about the invalid case and should not pass an ill-ordered Hop-by-Hop options header to the application.

1722–1767 The IPv6 input routine has ensured the entire Hop-by-Hop options header fit in the first mbuf. Therefore the start address and the length of the header is simply passed to the `sbcreatecontrol()` function to copy the header content to a separate mbuf. [RFC2292] required that some Hop-by-Hop options including the Jumbo Payload option be removed before passing the options header to the application. However, the KAME implementation intentionally skips that process due to possible overhead. [RFC3542] has removed that constraint; thus the implementation is compliant with the latest RFC.

Listing 7-124

ip6_input.c

```
1769            if ((in6p->in6p_flags & (IN6P_RTHDR | IN6P_DSTOPTS)) != 0) {
1770                    struct ip6_hdr *ip6 = mtod(m, struct ip6_hdr *);
1771                    int nxt = ip6->ip6_nxt, off = sizeof(struct ip6_hdr);
1772
1773                    /*
1774                     * Search for destination options headers or routing
1775                     * header(s) through the header chain, and stores each
1776                     * header as ancillary data.
1777                     * Note that the order of the headers remains in
1778                     * the chain of ancillary data.
1779                     */
1780                    while (1) {         /* is explicit loop prevention necessary? */
```

ip6_input.c

1769–1780 Destination options headers and the Routing headers can appear at any position and for any number of times in the received packet (see Section 3.3.1). Thus a necessary step is to go through the entire packet until a transport layer header is found in order to pass all these headers to the application as requested.

Variable `nxt` is set to the Next Header field of the IPv6 header, and the `while` loop iterates through all extension headers, updating `nxt`.

Listing 7-125

ip6_input.c

```
1781                        struct ip6_ext *ip6e = NULL;
1782                        int elen;
1786
1787                        /*
1788                         * if it is not an extension header, don't try to
1789                         * pull it from the chain.
1790                         */
```

```
1791                          switch (nxt) {
1792                          case IPPROTO_DSTOPTS:
1793                          case IPPROTO_ROUTING:
1794                          case IPPROTO_HOPOPTS:
1795                          case IPPROTO_AH: /* is it possible? */
1796                                  break;
1797                          default:
1798                                  goto loopend;
1799                          }
```
—— ip6_input.c

1791–1799 The headers of interest are the Destination options header, the Routing header, the Hop-by-Hop options header and the Authentication header (AH). Any other header types will terminate the while loop, which includes the Encapsulated Security Payload (ESP) header because information cannot be interpreted after the ESP header. The reassembly process would have removed the Fragment header if it were present in the packet. The same logic applies to the AH, but a sanity check is done for it.

Listing 7-126
—— ip6_input.c
```
1802                          if (off + sizeof(*ip6e) > m->m_len)
1803                                  goto loopend;
1804                          ip6e = (struct ip6_ext *)(mtod(m, caddr_t) + off);
```
—— ip6_input.c

1802–1804 The while loop will terminate if the first mbuf is too short to hold the common part of the extension headers. ip6e points to the extension header with respect to the current offset.

Listing 7-127
—— ip6_input.c
```
1805                          if (nxt == IPPROTO_AH)
1806                                  elen = (ip6e->ip6e_len + 2) << 2;
1807                          else
1808                                  elen = (ip6e->ip6e_len + 1) << 3;
1809                          if (off + elen > m->m_len)
1810                                  goto loopend;
```
—— ip6_input.c

1805–1810 nxt specifies the type of the extension header we are now looking at. The header length is calculated based on the semantics of the length field (note that the AH has a different definition of header length calculation). If the current mbuf does not store the entire header, the process is terminated. Again, this behavior should be reasonable, assuming the logic in the IPv6 input routine.

Listing 7-128
—— ip6_input.c
```
1829                          switch (nxt) {
1830                          case IPPROTO_DSTOPTS:
1831                          {
1832                                  if (!(in6p->in6p_flags & IN6P_DSTOPTS))
1833                                          break;
1834
1835                                  /*
```

```
1836                                        * We also require super-user privilege for
1837                                        * the option. See comments on IN6_HOPOPTS.
1838                                        */
1839                                       if (!privileged)
1840                                               break;
1841
1842                                       *mp = sbcreatecontrol((caddr_t)ip6e, elen,
1843                                                       IS2292(IPV6_2292DSTOPTS,
1844                                                               IPV6_DSTOPTS),
1845                                                       IPPROTO_IPV6);
1846                                       if (ctl->dest == NULL)
1847                                               ctl->dest = *mp;
1848                                       if (*mp)
1849                                               mp = &(*mp)->m_next;
1850                                       break;
1851                               }
```
                                                                            ip6_input.c

1829–1840 If this header is a Destination options header, the application wanted to see it, and
the application has the superuser privilege, then the following part will copy the header
data to pass it to the application. Again the privilege check is too strict, but this is based
on an implementation decision.

1842–1851 Function sbcreatecontrol() copies the Destination options header content
into a separate mbuf. The new mbuf is linked into the buffer chain. The appropriate field
in ip6_recvpktopts{} is initialized if this header is the first Destination options header
encountered.

Listing 7-129

                                                                            ip6_input.c
```
1852                               case IPPROTO_ROUTING:
1853                               {
1854                                       if (!in6p->in6p_flags & IN6P_RTHDR)
1855                                               break;
1856
1857                                       *mp = sbcreatecontrol((caddr_t)ip6e, elen,
1858                                                       IS2292(IPV6_2292RTHDR,
1859                                                               IPV6_RTHDR),
1860                                                       IPPROTO_IPV6);
1861                                       if (ctl->rthdr == NULL)
1862                                               ctl->rthdr = *mp;
1863                                       if (*mp)
1864                                               mp = &(*mp)->m_next;
1865                                       break;
1866                               }
```
                                                                            ip6_input.c

1852–1866 The similar process logic for retrieving the option header content applies to the
Routing header.

Listing 7-130

                                                                            ip6_input.c
```
1867                               case IPPROTO_HOPOPTS:
1868                               case IPPROTO_AH: /* is it possible? */
1869                                       break;
1870
```
                                                                            ip6_input.c

1867–1870 Other extension headers are skipped.

Listing 7-131

_____ip6_input.c
```
1871                          default:
1872                                  /*
1873                                   * other cases have been filtered in the above.
1874                                   * none will visit this case.  here we supply
1875                                   * the code just in case (nxt overwritten or
1876                                   * other cases).
1877                                   */
1881                                  goto loopend;
1882
1883                          }
```
_____ip6_input.c

1871–1883 The default case statement should not occur because these conditions have been
eliminated at the beginning of the `while` loop (recall Listing 7-125). These conditions
are explicitly considered here again for safety because the `while` loop is long and
unintentional error can happen.

Listing 7-132

_____ip6_input.c
```
1884
1885                          /* proceed with the next header. */
1886                          off += elen;
1887                          nxt = ip6e->ip6e_nxt;
1888                          ip6e = NULL;
1893                  }
1894          loopend:
1895                  ;
1896          }
1904  #undef IS2292
1905  }
```
_____ip6_input.c

1885–1905 The offset and the Next Header values are updated based on the current header,
and the loop continues to search for other possible headers to be passed to the application.

7.5 Socket Options and Ancillary Data Examples

This section describes the relationships among various structures that are required for IPv6
UDP packet transmission to illustrate how IPv6 socket options and ancillary data objects work
as defined in the advanced socket API specification.

7.5.1 Example of the Send Path

Assume an application has specified the following socket options for a UDP socket:

- Set the hop limit for outgoing multicast packets to 8 through the
  `IPV6_MULTICAST_HOPS` socket option.

- Set the Traffic Class for outgoing packets to 1 through the `IPV6_TCLASS` socket option.

- Set a Hop-by-Hop options header for outgoing packets through the `IPV6_HOPOPTS`
  socket option.

Now, the application sends UDP datagram to the socket with the following set of ancillary data:

- Set the Traffic Class value 8 using the `IPV6_TCLASS` ancillary data type.
- Set a Destination options header using the `IPV6_DSTOPTS` ancillary data type.

Figure 7-9 shows the contents of some relevant arguments to function `udp6_output()`. Section 6.9.2 describes function `udp6_output()` in detail.

Function `udp6_output()` calls `ip6_setpktoptions()` with its local variable `opt` in order to construct the packet options by merging the sticky options with the ancillary data objects (see Listing 6-82).

Figure 7-10 shows the data structures at the point of calling `ip6_output()` after merging the options and ancillary data. As the figure shows, `opt` contains the Hop-by-Hop options header that was specified as a socket option and the Destination options header that was specified in the ancillary data object. Note that the Traffic Class value stored in `opt` is the value that was specified in the ancillary data object rather than the value set via the socket option.

FIGURE 7-9

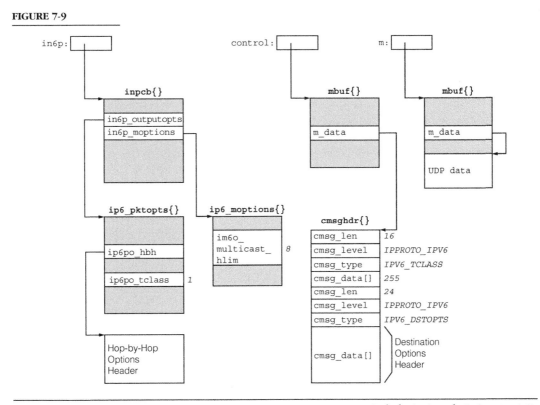

At the beginning of `udp6_output()`.

FIGURE 7-10

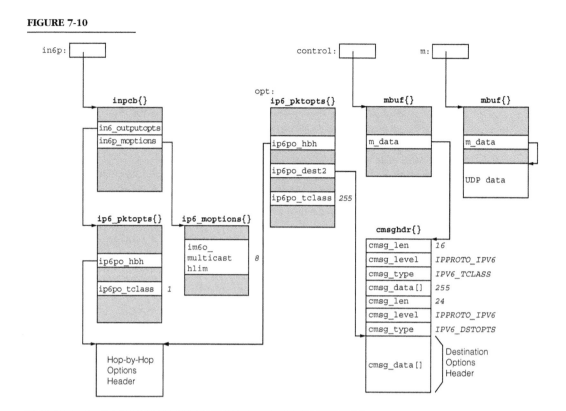

Before calling ip6_output () *from* udp6_output ().

The ip6_pktopts{} structure stored in opt and the ip6_moptions{} structure pointed from the PCB are passed to ip6_output () along with the UDP packet (see Listing 6-91).

Figure 7-11 shows the content of some relevant arguments to ip6_output () at the entrance of the function (Section 3.13.3). m0 points to the UDP packet with the IPv6 header, opt points to the ip6_pktopts{} structure, and im6o points to the ip6_moptions{} structure.

ip6_output () constructs a complete packet from these arguments. Since some extension headers are provided, the packet is split up at the boundary between the IPv6 and the UDP headers (see Section 3.13.5). The two extension headers are copied from the ip6_pktopts{} structure and are inserted between the IPv6 and UDP headers. The Traffic Class and Hop Limit fields of the IPv6 header are filled with values from the ip6_pktopts{} structure and the ip6_moptions{} structure, respectively (see Listings 3-154 and 3-155). Figure 7-12 shows the complete packet.

7.5.2   Example of the Receive Path

Our next example illustrates the construction of ancillary data objects from the received packet based on the socket options that were set in advance.

FIGURE 7-11

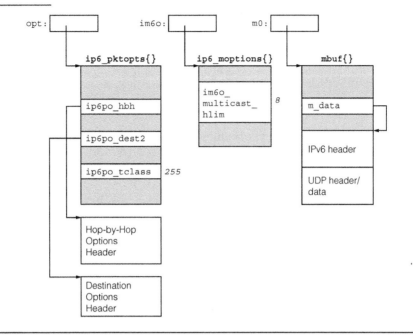

At the entrance of `ip6_output()`.

FIGURE 7-12

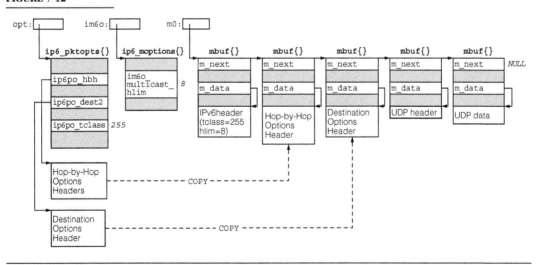

The complete outgoing packet with options.

Suppose an application has requested the following information on a UDP socket, if available, from each received UDP packet along with the packet data:

- The destination address and the receiving interface by means of the `IPV6_RECVPKTINFO` option
- The IPv6 Hop-by-Hop options header by means of the `IPV6_RECVHOPOPTS` option
- The IPv6 Routing headers by means of the `IPV6_RECVRTHDR` option

Now, assume an IPv6 UDP packet containing a Routing header arrives and `udp6_input()` calls `ip6_savecontrol()` to construct ancillary data objects based on the specified values. Figure 7-13 shows the contents of the various data structures after the ancillary data objects have been built.

`in6p` points to the PCB structure of the receiving socket. The flag bits in the `in6p_flags` member are set to mark the types of information requested by the application.

`m` is the mbuf structure containing the arriving packet. Note that in this figure the mbuf is depicted as if the base mbuf structure could contain the entire packet for simplicity. However, we would actually need an mbuf cluster, according to the length of the packet.

`ctl` is passed from `udp6_input()` to store the ancillary data objects, which will then be passed to the application via the receiving socket. Based on the content of the arriving packet and the flag bits in `in6p_flags`, two new mbufs are created to store ancillary data objects for `IPV6_PKTINFO` and `IPV6_RTHDR`.

FIGURE 7-13

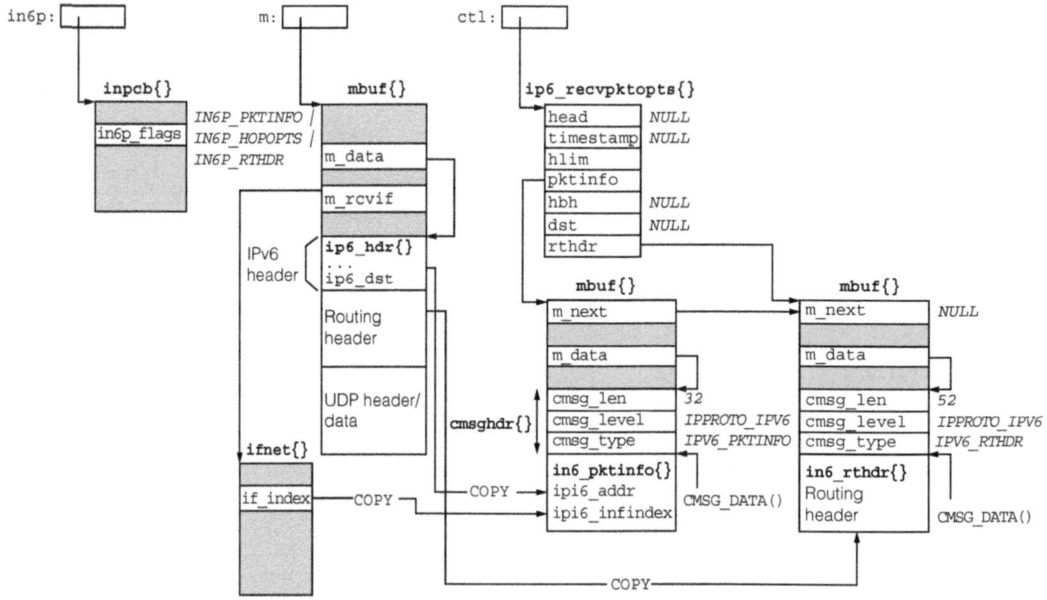

After constructing ancillary data objects in `ip6_savecontrol()`.

The IPv6 destination address and the receiving interface index are copied into `cmsg_data` of the first mbuf as the `in6_pktinfo{}` structure. Similarly, the content of the Routing header from the packet is copied into `cmsg_data` of the second mbuf. Notice that no mbuf for the `IN6P_HOPOPTS` flag is created since the arriving packet does not contain a Hop-by-Hop options header.

7.6 Implementation of Library Functions—`libinet6`

In this section, we will show the implementation of some basic API library functions with detailed explanation. Specifically, we will describe the following four functions:

- `inet_pton()`
- `inet_ntop()`
- `getaddrinfo()`
- `getnameinfo()`

These are conversion functions between host names or textual addresses and IPv6 addresses in binary forms. The reason we are concentrating on these is that they are complicated and interesting due to the variety of IPv6 address representation. This also means learning these functions will help understand IPv6 addresses per se.

Table 7-19 summarizes source code files described in this section.

TABLE 7-19

File	Description
`${KAME}/kame/kame/libinet6/getaddrinfo.c`	`getaddrinfo()` and `gai_strerror()` functions
`${KAME}/kame/kame/libinet6/getnameinfo.c`	`getnameinfo()` function
`${KAME}/kame/kame/libinet6/inet_pton.c`	`inet_pton()` function
`/usr/src/lib/libc/net/inet_ntop.c`	`inet_ntop()` function

7.6.1 `inet_pton()` and `inet_pton6()` Functions

The `inet_pton()` function is the simplest function to use to convert a textual representation of IP addresses into the binary form. Unlike its predecessors, such as `inet_aton()`, `inet_pton()` supports multiple address families, (i.e., it performs the address conversion according to the address family). Listing 7-133 shows the main part of the `inet_pton()` function.

Listing 7-133

```
                                                                    inet_pton.c
80   int
81   inet_pton(af, src, dst)
82         int af;
83         const char *src;
84         void *dst;
```

```
85      {
86              switch (af) {
87              case AF_INET:
88                      return (inet_pton4(src, dst));
90              case AF_INET6:
91                      return (inet_pton6(src, dst));
93              default:
94                      errno = EAFNOSUPPORT;
95                      return (-1);
96              }
97              /* NOTREACHED */
98      }
```
———inet_pton.c

The main part of inet_pton() is simple: It only contains a switch statement that invokes the appropriate subroutine based on the given address family. As shown in the source code, this function currently supports AF_INET and AF_INET6. For other address families, −1 will be returned and errno will be set to EAFNOSUPPORT.

Listing 7-134 shows function inet_pton6(), which handles the AF_INET6 address family and converts a textual representation of an IPv6 address into its binary form. Function inet_pton6() supports the various textual representations of addresses given in Section 2.3. In this function, the following macro constants will be used.

Name	Value	Description
NS_INADDRSZ	4	The size of an IPv4 address
NS_IN6ADDRSZ	16	The size of an IPv6 address
NS_INT16SZ	2	sizeof(u_int16_t)

Listing 7-134
———inet_pton.c

```
164     static int
165     inet_pton6(src, dst)
166             const char *src;
167             u_char *dst;
168     {
169             static const char xdigits_l[] = "0123456789abcdef",
170                               xdigits_u[] = "0123456789ABCDEF";
171             u_char tmp[NS_IN6ADDRSZ], *tp, *endp, *colonp;
172             const char *xdigits, *curtok;
173             int ch, saw_xdigit;
174             u_int val;
175
176             memset((tp = tmp), '\0', NS_IN6ADDRSZ);
177             endp = tp + NS_IN6ADDRSZ;
178             colonp = NULL;
179             /* Leading :: requires some special handling. */
180             if (*src == ':')
181                     if (*++src != ':')
182                             return (0);
183             curtok = src;
184             saw_xdigit = 0;
185             val = 0;
186             while ((ch = *src++) != '\0') {
187                     const char *pch;
188
189                     if ((pch = strchr((xdigits = xdigits_l), ch)) == NULL)
190                             pch = strchr((xdigits = xdigits_u), ch);
```

```
191                         if (pch != NULL) {
192                                 val <<= 4;
193                                 val |= (pch - xdigits);
194                                 if (val > 0xffff)
195                                         return (0);
196                                 saw_xdigit = 1;
197                                 continue;
198                         }
199                         if (ch == ':') {
200                                 curtok = src;
201                                 if (!saw_xdigit) {
202                                         if (colonp)
203                                                 return (0);
204                                         colonp = tp;
205                                         continue;
206                                 } else if (*src == '\0') {
207                                         return (0);
208                                 }
209                                 if (tp + NS_INT16SZ > endp)
210                                         return (0);
211                                 *tp++ = (u_char) (val >> 8) & 0xff;
212                                 *tp++ = (u_char) val & 0xff;
213                                 saw_xdigit = 0;
214                                 val = 0;
215                                 continue;
216                         }
217                         if (ch == '.' && ((tp + NS_INADDRSZ) <= endp) &&
218                             inet_pton4(curtok, tp) > 0) {
219                                 tp += NS_INADDRSZ;
220                                 saw_xdigit = 0;
221                                 break;          /* '\0' was seen by inet_pton4(). */
222                         }
223                         return (0);
224                 }
225         if (saw_xdigit) {
226                 if (tp + NS_INT16SZ > endp)
227                         return (0);
228                 *tp++ = (u_char) (val >> 8) & 0xff;
229                 *tp++ = (u_char) val & 0xff;
230         }
231         if (colonp != NULL) {
232                 /*
233                  * Since some memmove()'s erroneously fail to handle
234                  * overlapping regions, we'll do the shift by hand.
235                  */
236                 const int n = tp - colonp;
237                 int i;
238
239                 if (tp == endp)
240                         return (0);
241                 for (i = 1; i <= n; i++) {
242                         endp[- i] = colonp[n - i];
243                         colonp[n - i] = 0;
244                 }
245                 tp = endp;
246         }
247         if (tp != endp)
248                 return (0);
249         memcpy(dst, tmp, NS_IN6ADDRSZ);
250         return (1);
251 }
```
—— inet_pton.c

Initial setup

176–178 inet_ntop() uses a temporary work buffer buf to store intermediate conversion results. This buffer is zero-cleared and tp points to the head of this buffer while endp marks the end of this buffer to prevent buffer overrun. `colonp` will be non-NULL if and only if the input string contains a double colon (`::`), in which case `colonp` will specify the position in the output buffer where the expansion of the double colon should start.

180–182 A special case where the input starts with "`::`" is caught here in order to make the main parser simple. If the first character is a colon, then a valid input must start with "`::`". Otherwise, parsing the input fails here and 0 will be returned, indicating an error as described in Section 7.2.4.

183–185 During the parsing, `curtok` points to the location of the head of the last hexadecimal character that the parser has seen. It will eventually be used as an input to `inet_pton4()` in case the input contains a textual representation of an IPv4 address. `saw_xdigit` is a flag that indicates the parser has just recognized some hexadecimal string when non-0. `val` stores temporary results of a hexadecimal value in the input.

Handle hexadecimal string

186–198 The parser iterates through the entire input string character by character and assigns each character to `ch`. Inside the loop, the parser first checks whether the character is a hexadecimal number. If it is, `pch` has a non-NULL value pointing to the corresponding position in either the `xdigits_l` or the `xdigits_u` array. Then `val` is updated with the character just recognized. Note that `pch − xdigits` is the integer corresponding to the recognized character. The temporary variable must not exceed the maximum value of a 16-bit integer (0xffff) in a valid textual representation. Otherwise, parsing fails and 0 will be returned. `saw_xdigit` marks the fact that the parser just parsed a hexadecimal character.

Handle colon

199–205 If the parser encounters a colon, the parser saves the position immediately after the colon in `curtok`. If `saw_xdigit` is false, this means the parser is at the head of input which starts with "`::`" or else the parser has parsed another colon after a hexadecimal string. In the former case `colonp` must be NULL; otherwise, the input string contains two sets of "`::`", which is an invalid textual representation. The parser stores the colon position in the corresponding output buffer in `colonp`.

206–208 The parser is looking at the single colon that follows a hexadecimal string if `saw_xdigit` is true. Thus, this position must not be the end of input.

209–216 At this position the parser has a parsed hexadecimal value terminated by a colon, which should be a 16-bit integer. The input string is invalid if the temporary buffer does not have space to store the value. Otherwise, the value is stored in the next 16 bits of the output buffer and `tp` is incremented accordingly. `saw_xdigit` is reset to false. `val` is also cleared.

Handle an IPv4 address

217–223 If the parser is looking at a period "`.`" character, the parser has encountered the beginning of a textual representation of an IPv6 address embedding an IPv4 address (Section 2.3). In this case the output buffer must have the space to store the address whose length is `NS_INADDRSZ`. If enough space is given, `inet_pton4()` is called to parse the text. `saw_xdigit` is cleared on successful return of `inet_pton4()`. Note that the loop terminates because an IPv4 address can only appear at the end of the original IPv6 address string.

Process the last hexadecimal value

225–230 If `saw_xdigit` is true after exiting from the loop, there is still a hexadecimal value that is not yet stored in the output buffer. The remaining value is stored if there is enough space left in the buffer.

Fill zero for a double colon

231–246 The parser has encountered a double colon if `colonp` is non-NULL. Since parsing of the input string is complete, the parser can determine the length for which the double colon should be expanded.

236–237 This part calculates n, the length of the stored value in the output buffer that corresponds to the part of input after the double colon.

239–240 There is no available space left to expand the double colon if the end of the output buffer is reached. Note that `inet_pton()` without this check would allow input strings such as:

```
1111:2222:3333:4444::5555:6666:7777:8888
```

which is an invalid string as an IPv6 address.

241–245 The last n bytes of the output buffer are shifted to the end of the buffer. `tp` is set to `endp` to mark the end of the output buffer after expanding the double colon.

Post process

247–250 The input string is too short to be valid if the parser has not reached the end of the output buffer. Otherwise the conversion is successful and the converted value is copied from the temporary buffer into the buffer provided by the caller.

Note: Despite the careful coding, this code still has a controversial behavior. Since it accepts any hexadecimal string less than or equal to 0xffff, it does not impose a limitation on the length of the string. Thus, for example, it will accept 00000 (5 zeros) as a 16-bit integer. You may think this is a bug, but this is actually intentional. In fact, [RFC3513] only says each piece separated by colons is a 16-bit hexadecimal value. This ambiguity was then discussed in the IETF, and a new version of the address architecture document [RFC4291] clearly specifies that each 16-bit value is up to four hexadecimal digits. Newer implementations of `inet_pton()` were also updated so that it would not allow the above example.

inet_pton6() Example

We will illustrate the inner workings of `inet_pton6()` through an example to help gain solid understanding of the function. Suppose that this function is called with an input "2001:db8::1234". In lines 176–185, pointers and buffers are initialized as depicted in Figure 7-14.

After parsing the first colon, the first piece of 16-bit value, 0x2001, is copied to the output buffer (`tmp`). `src` and `tp` are incremented accordingly (Figure 7-15).

FIGURE 7-14

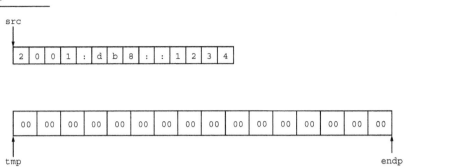

FIGURE 7-15

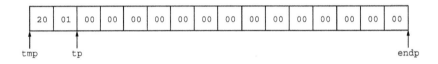

FIGURE 7-16

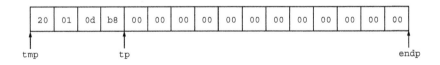

Similarly, after reading the second colon, the next piece of 16-bit value, 0x0db8, is copied (Figure 7-16). These processes correspond to lines 169–180 and 191–197 of Listing 7-134.

FIGURE 7-17

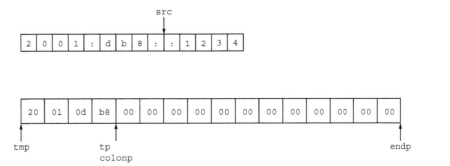

FIGURE 7-18

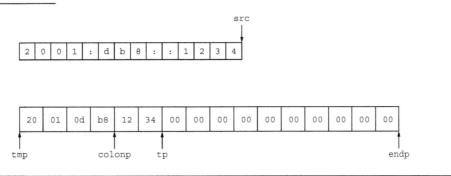

Then the parser encounters a double colon. `colonp` is set to the location where `tp` currently points, which corresponds to lines 183–186 (Figure 7-17).

Eventually, the parser completely parses the input and the 16-bit piece after the double colon is copied to the output buffer, which corresponds to lines 225–230 (Figure 7-18).

The parser must now expand the double colon in the output buffer. The length n of data that needs to be shifted toward the end of the buffer is `tp - colonp`, which equals to 2 bytes in this example. These 2 bytes are shifted toward the end of the output buffer and the original space is filled with zeros, which corresponds to lines 231–246 as in Figure 7-19.

7.6.2 `inet_ntop()` and `inet_ntop6()` Functions

The `inet_ntop()` function performs the reverse function of `inet_pton()`, which takes an IP address in the binary form and converts it to a printable string. `inet_ntop()` supports multiple address families.

`inet_ntop()` is not a product by the KAME's implementation. However, we explain the implementation merged in FreeBSD for reference.

FIGURE 7-19

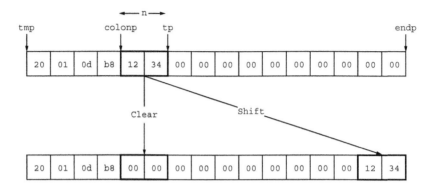

Listing 7-135

_____ inet_ntop.c

```
47    const char *
48    inet_ntop(af, src, dst, size)
49            int af;
50            const void *src;
51            char *dst;
52            size_t size;
53    {
54            switch (af) {
55            case AF_INET:
56                    return (inet_ntop4(src, dst, size));
57            case AF_INET6:
58                    return (inet_ntop6(src, dst, size));
59            default:
60                    errno = EAFNOSUPPORT;
61                    return (NULL);
62            }
63            /* NOTREACHED */
64    }
```

_____ inet_ntop.c

47–64 Similar to inet_pton(), the main body of inet_ntop() is a dispatcher that invokes the right subroutine according to the address family. If the given address family is not supported in this implementation, −1 is returned and global variable errno is set to EAFNOSUPPORT.

Listing 7-136 shows function inet_ntop6(), which handles the AF_INET6 address family.

Listing 7-136

_____ inet_ntop.c

```
99    static const char *
100   inet_ntop6(src, dst, size)
```

```
101             const u_char *src;
102             char *dst;
103             size_t size;
104     {
105             /*
106              * Note that int32_t and int16_t need only be "at least" large enough
107              * to contain a value of the specified size. On some systems, like
108              * Crays, there is no such thing as an integer variable with 16 bits.
109              * Keep this in mind if you think this function should have been coded
110              * to use pointer overlays. All the world's not a VAX.
111              */
112             char tmp[sizeof "ffff:ffff:ffff:ffff:ffff:ffff:255.255.255.255"], *tp;
113             struct { int base, len; } best, cur;
114             u_int words[NS_IN6ADDRSZ / NS_INT16SZ];
115             int i;
116
117             /*
118              * Preprocess:
119              *      Copy the input (bytewise) array into a wordwise array.
120              *      Find the longest run of 0x00's in src[] for :: shorthanding.
121              */
122             memset(words, '\0', sizeof words);
123             for (i = 0; i < NS_IN6ADDRSZ; i++)
124                     words[i / 2] |= (src[i] << ((1 - (i % 2)) << 3));
125             best.base = -1;
126             cur.base = -1;
127             for (i = 0; i < (NS_IN6ADDRSZ / NS_INT16SZ); i++) {
128                     if (words[i] == 0) {
129                             if (cur.base == -1)
130                                     cur.base = i, cur.len = 1;
131                             else
132                                     cur.len++;
133                     } else {
134                             if (cur.base != -1) {
135                                     if (best.base == -1 || cur.len > best.len)
136                                             best = cur;
137                                     cur.base = -1;
138                             }
139                     }
140             }
141             if (cur.base != -1) {
142                     if (best.base == -1 || cur.len > best.len)
143                             best = cur;
144             }
145             if (best.base != -1 && best.len < 2)
146                     best.base = -1;
147
148             /*
149              * Format the result.
150              */
151             tp = tmp;
152             for (i = 0; i < (NS_IN6ADDRSZ / NS_INT16SZ); i++) {
153                     /* Are we inside the best run of 0x00's? */
154                     if (best.base != -1 && i >= best.base &&
155                         i < (best.base + best.len)) {
156                             if (i == best.base)
157                                     *tp++ = ':';
158                             continue;
159                     }
160                     /* Are we following an initial run of 0x00s or any real hex? */
161                     if (i != 0)
162                             *tp++ = ':';
163                     /* Is this address an encapsulated IPv4? */
164                     if (i == 6 && best.base == 0 &&
165                         (best.len == 6 || (best.len == 5 && words[5] == 0xffff))) {
166                             if (!inet_ntop4(src+12, tp, sizeof tmp - (tp - tmp)))
167                                     return (NULL);
168                             tp += strlen(tp);
```

```
169                              break;
170                          }
171                          tp += sprintf(tp, "%x", words[i]);
172                      }
173                      /* Was it a trailing run of 0x00's? */
174                      if (best.base != -1 && (best.base + best.len) ==
175                          (NS_IN6ADDRSZ / NS_INT16SZ))
176                              *tp++ = ':';
177                      *tp++ = '\0';
178
179                      /*
180                       * Check for overflow, copy, and we're done.
181                       */
182                      if ((size_t)(tp - tmp) > size) {
183                              errno = ENOSPC;
184                              return (NULL);
185                      }
186                      strcpy(dst, tmp);
187                      return (dst);
188  }
```
_____ inet_ntop.c

Local variables

112–115 The `tmp` buffer is the output buffer that is large enough to hold any valid textual representation of an IPv6 address. `words` is an array of eight 16-bit integers for storing each 16-bit portion of the given IPv6 address in binary form.

Copy the address

122–124 The `words` buffer is initially zero-cleared. Then each 16-bit portion of the address, which is in the network byte order, is copied into the array.

Find the longest zeros

125–126 This segment of code tries to find the longest continuous zeros in the address so that these zeros can be compressed as the double colon "`::`". Two instances of a structure of two integers defined at line 113 are used to track and compare the longest continuous zero blocks: `best` is the longest zero block that has been seen while `cur` is the zero block currently under consideration. The `base` member of the structure specifies the starting location of the zero block in the words array, which has the −1 value as the initial state. The `len` member is the length of the zero block.

127–140 The `for` loop iterates through all the entries of the `words` buffer one at a time. If an array entry has the value of zero and the parser is not currently looking at zeros, then `cur.base` stores this array location and its `len` member is initialized to 1. If the entry value is zero and the parser is already processing zeros, the `len` member is simply incremented. If the parser encounters a non-0 array entry and `cur.base` contains a valid location, the current zero block is compared against the longest known zero block that is stored in `best`. `best` is updated with `cur` if either `best` has not been set or the current zero block is longer than what is stored in `best`, and then `cur` is re-initialized.

141–144 `cur.base` holds a valid location at the completion of the `for` loop if the address terminates with a sequence of zeros. `best` is replaced with `cur` if this sequence is the longest sequence in the address.

Check the need for compression

145–146 No compression can be done if the length of the zero sequence is less than 2. In this case best is cleared.

Convert the address

151–152 tp advances in the tmp buffer as the address is converted to textual representation. The for loop makes a single path to convert the address.

153–159 If best.base specifies a valid location and the for loop is at the start of the longest zero block, a colon is written out in the output buffer. There is no output written for the remaining bytes of the zero block.

160–162 The delimiter colon is written out, which may be the other colon for the double colon compressed form.

163–170 The given address may be an IPv4-compatible IPv6 address if there are 12 consecutive zero bytes from the start of the address. The given address may be an IPv4-mapped IPv6 address if there are 10 consecutive zero bytes from the start of the address followed by 0xFFFF. In either case the remaining 32 bits are passed to function inet_ntop4() to obtain the textual representation of the IPv4 address. tp is then updated to point to the end of the resulting string.

Note: The condition for the IPv4-compatible address is incomplete, which is missing the IPv4 addresses that begin with zeros, for example, 0.0.1.2, which will be converted to "::102" instead of "::0.0.1.2". However, such a case should not be a problem in practice because these types of addresses are rarely if at all used. In addition, the address space defined by the IPv4-compatible IPv6 addresses is inherently ambiguous because of the conflicting definition with the loopback address "::1". The loopback address would better be printed as "::1" instead of "::0.0.0.1".

173–177 If best.base specifies a valid zero block that terminates at the end of the address, only a single colon has been written out at line 157 in the for loop. The terminating colon is added here. The temporary buffer is terminated with the null character. Note that the output buffer is big enough to contain any textual representation of IPv6 addresses including the terminating character.

Copy the result

179–187 If the buffer given by the caller is too small to hold the resulting string, a NULL pointer is returned and global variable errno is set to ENOSPC. Otherwise, the content of the internal output buffer tmp is copied into the caller-supplied buffer.

7.6.3 getaddrinfo() Function

Function getaddrinfo() is a name to address conversion function used by the majority of dual stack applications. Specifically, it retrieves a list of "address information" for a given hostname and service name, whose elements are pairs of addresses and port numbers. In

addition to the definition given in [RFC3493], the KAME implementation of `getaddrinfo()`
supports extensions such as the preferred extended format for IPv6 scoped addresses specified in [RFC4007] (Section 2.4.3), and the destination address selection algorithm specified in
[RFC3484] (see Section 3.4.3).

In the description below, we generally assume `AF_INET` and `PF_INET` are identical and
so are `AF_INET6` and `PF_INET6` and so on, as indicated in [RFC3493]. In general, we will use
the `AF_xxx` notation with the exception that we will refer to `PF_xxx` when the corresponding
source code uses those definitions.

afd{} Structure

In the following discussion, a dedicated structure called `afd{}` (shown in Listing 7-137) will be
used several times. It contains a list of generic information for each supported address family.

Listing 7-137

── getaddrinfo.c

```
153    static const struct afd {
154            int a_af;
155            int a_addrlen;
156            int a_socklen;
157            int a_off;
158            const char *a_addrany;
159            const char *a_loopback;
160            int a_scoped;
161    } afdl [] = {
163            {PF_INET6, sizeof(struct in6_addr),
164             sizeof(struct sockaddr_in6),
165             offsetof(struct sockaddr_in6, sin6_addr),
166             in6_addrany, in6_loopback, 1},
168            {PF_INET, sizeof(struct in_addr),
169             sizeof(struct sockaddr_in),
170             offsetof(struct sockaddr_in, sin_addr),
171             in_addrany, in_loopback, 0},
172            {0, 0, 0, 0, NULL, NULL, 0},
173    };
```

── getaddrinfo.c

153–160 `a_addrlen` is the length of the address and `a_socklen` is the length of the socket
address structure for the corresponding address family. `a_off` is the offset from the start
of the socket address structure to the address field in the structure. `a_addrany` and
`a_loopback` are the addresses in the binary form that represent the all-zero and the
loopback addresses for the address family. The latter is expected to be the address for
the host named "localhost". `a_scoped` specifies whether the address family supports
the notion of scoped addresses. This field is actually intended to support IPv6 scoped
addresses in `explore_numeric_scope()` to be discussed in Listing 7-144.

161–173 A static array `afdl` contains the definitions for the `AF_INET6` and the `AF_INET`
address families. Figure 7-20 shows some of the values of these structures.

getaddrinfo() Overview

The `getaddrinfo()` function is a large function that invokes complex subroutines. We will
describe the overall function structure followed by a detailed description of each subroutine.
Listing 7-138 shows the overall structure of `getaddrinfo()`.

FIGURE 7-20

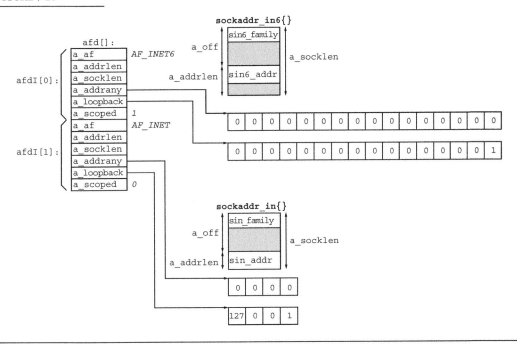

Predefined `afd{}` structures for AF_INET and AF_INET6.

Listing 7-138

```
420    int
421    getaddrinfo(hostname, servname, hints, res)
422            const char *hostname, *servname;
423            const struct addrinfo *hints;
424            struct addrinfo **res;
425    {
426            struct addrinfo sentinel;
427            struct addrinfo *cur;
428            int error = 0;
429            struct addrinfo ai, ai0, *afai;
430            struct addrinfo *pai;
431            const struct afd *afd;
432            const struct explore *ex;
433            struct addrinfo *afailist[sizeof(afdl)/sizeof(afdl[0])];
434            struct addrinfo *afai_unspec;
435            int pass, found;
436            int numeric = 0;
437
438            /* ensure we return NULL on errors */
439            *res = NULL;
440
441            memset(afailist, 0, sizeof(afailist));
442            afai_unspec = NULL;
443
444            memset(&sentinel, 0, sizeof(sentinel));
445            cur = &sentinel;
446            pai = &ai;
447            pai->ai_flags = 0;
448            pai->ai_family = PF_UNSPEC;
```

```
449                pai->ai_socktype = ANY;
450                pai->ai_protocol = ANY;
451                pai->ai_addrlen = 0;
452                pai->ai_canonname = NULL;
453                pai->ai_addr = NULL;
454                pai->ai_next = NULL;

        ---------------------------------------------------
/* validate argument */

/* handle NULL or numeric host name */

/* handle FQDN host name */

/* reorder results */
        ---------------------------------------------------

732    bad:
733                if (afai_unspec)
734                        freeaddrinfo(afai_unspec);
735                for (afd = afdl; afd->a_af; afd++) {
736                        if (afailist[afd - afdl])
737                                freeaddrinfo(afailist[afd - afdl]);
738                }
739                if (!*res)
740                        if (sentinel.ai_next)
741                                freeaddrinfo(sentinel.ai_next);
742                return error;
743    }
```
                                                                                    _getaddrinfo.c

Initialization

438–454 afailist is an array of pointers each of whose entries points to an addrinfo{}
structure of a supported address family. It has two entries in the KAME implementation,
one for AF_INET and one for AF_INET6. This array will be used to store the results for
a NULL or numeric hostname. afai_unspec will be used to store temporary results for
an FQDN hostname. sentinel will be used to reorder the results. pai will store hint
parameters that are given by the caller.

Post process

732–742 Temporary resources are freed. *res points to sentinel.ai_next if function
getaddrinfo() returns successfully. Otherwise a nonempty list referenced by
sentinel.ai_next is freed.

Parameters Validation

The first main section of getaddrinfo(), shown in Listing 7-139, validates the parameters
that are passed in from the caller.

Listing 7-139
                                                                                    _getaddrinfo.c
```
456                if (hostname == NULL && servname == NULL)
457                        return EAI_NONAME;
458                if (hints) {
459                        /* error check for hints */
460                        if (hints->ai_addrlen || hints->ai_canonname ||
461                           hints->ai_addr || hints->ai_next)
462                                ERR(EAI_BADHINTS); /* xxx */
463                        if (hints->ai_flags & ~AI_MASK)
```

```
464                            ERR(EAI_BADFLAGS);
465                switch (hints->ai_family) {
466                case PF_UNSPEC:
467                case PF_INET:
469                case PF_INET6:
471                        break;
472                default:
473                        ERR(EAI_FAMILY);
474                }
475                memcpy(pai, hints, sizeof(*pai));

477                /*
478                 * if both socktype/protocol are specified, check if they
479                 * are meaningful combination.
480                 */
481                if (pai->ai_socktype != ANY && pai->ai_protocol != ANY) {
482                        for (ex = explore; ex->e_af >= 0; ex++) {
483                                if (!MATCH_FAMILY(pai->ai_family, ex->e_af,
484                                    WILD_AF(ex)))
485                                        continue;
486                                if (!MATCH(pai->ai_socktype, ex->e_socktype,
487                                    WILD_SOCKTYPE(ex)))
488                                        continue;
489                                if (!MATCH(pai->ai_protocol, ex->e_protocol,
490                                    WILD_PROTOCOL(ex)))
491                                        continue;

493                                /* matched */
494                                break;
495                        }

497                        if (ex->e_af < 0) {
498                                ERR(EAI_BADHINTS);
499                        }
500                }
501        }

503    #if defined(AI_ALL) && defined(AI_V4MAPPED)
504            /*
505             * post-2553: AI_ALL and AI_V4MAPPED are effective only against
506             * AF_INET6 query. They need to be ignored if specified in other
507             * occassions.
508             */
509            switch (pai->ai_flags & (AI_ALL | AI_V4MAPPED)) {
510            case AI_V4MAPPED:
511            case AI_ALL | AI_V4MAPPED:
512                    if (pai->ai_family != AF_INET6)
513                            pai->ai_flags &= ~(AI_ALL | AI_V4MAPPED);
514                    break;
515            case AI_ALL:
517                    /* illegal */
518                    ERR(EAI_BADFLAGS);
522                    break;
523            }
524    #endif

526            /*
527             * check for special cases. (1) numeric servname is disallowed if
528             * socktype/protocol are left unspecified. (2) servname is disallowed
529             * for raw and other inet{,6} sockets.
530             */
531            if (MATCH_FAMILY(pai->ai_family, PF_INET, 1)
533             || MATCH_FAMILY(pai->ai_family, PF_INET6, 1)
535                ) {
536                    ai0 = *pai;             /* backup *pai */

538                    if (pai->ai_family == PF_UNSPEC) {
540                            pai->ai_family = PF_INET6;
```

```
544                            }
545                            error = get_portmatch(pai, servname);
546                            if (error)
547                                    ERR(error);
548
549                            *pai = ai0;
550                    }
551
552            ai0 = *pai;
```
                                                                    _getaddrinfo.c

456–457 According to [RFC3493], at least one of `hostname` and `servname` must be a non-NULL pointer. Otherwise, an error of `EAI_NONAME` will be returned.

458–462 [RFC3493] also requires that every member of the `hints` structure other than `ai_flags`, `ai_family`, `ai_socktype`, and `ai_protocol` be set to zero or a NULL pointer. Otherwise, an error of `EAI_BADHINTS` will be returned. Note that `EAI_BADHINTS` is not a standard error code and is specific to the KAME implementation (see Table 7-3).

463–464 `AI_MASK` combines all of the supported flags for `ai_flags`. At the time of this writing, the definition of `AI_MASK` is as follows:

```
#define AI_MASK \
(AI_PASSIVE | AI_CANONNAME | AI_NUMERICHOST | AI_ADDRCONFIG)
```

An `EAI_BADFLAGS` error is returned if an unsupported flag is specified in `ai_flags` of the `hints` structure. Note the implementation does not completely conform to [RFC3493], which also defines `AI_NUMERICSERV`, `AI_V4MAPPED`, and `AI_ALL`.

465–474 An `EAI_FAMILY` error is returned if `ai_family` has an unsupported address family value.

475 Validation completes and the `hints` structure is copied in `pai`.

481–500 If both the socket type `ai_socktype` and the protocol `ai_protocol` fields have values, the coherence of the combination against the `explore` array is checked. For example, the combination of `SOCK_STREAM` socket type and `IPPROTO_UDP` is illegal and is rejected here. In this case an `EAI_BADHINTS` error will be returned.
    The definition of the `explore{}` structure is given in Listing 7-140.

Listing 7-140
                                                                    _getaddrinfo.c

```
175    struct explore {
176            int e_af;
177            int e_socktype;
178            int e_protocol;
179            const char *e_protostr;
180            int e_wild;
181    #define WILD_AF(ex)              ((ex)->e_wild & 0x01)
182    #define WILD_SOCKTYPE(ex)        ((ex)->e_wild & 0x02)
183    #define WILD_PROTOCOL(ex)        ((ex)->e_wild & 0x04)
184    };
```
                                                                    _getaddrinfo.c

The supported combinations of socket type and protocol for each address family are given in Table 7-20. As shown in the table, this implementation takes SCTP into account.

TABLE 7-20

Address family	SocketType	Protocol	Wild flags
INET6	SOCK_DGRAM	UDP	AF|SOCK|PROTO
INET6	SOCK_STREAM	SCTP	AF|SOCK|PROTO
INET6	SOCK_STREAM	TCP	AF|SOCK|PROTO
INET6	SOCK_SEQPACKET	SCTP	AF|SOCK|PROTO
INET6	SOCK_RAW	ANY	AF|PROTO
INET	SOCK_DGRAM	UDP	AF|SOCK|PROTO
INET	SOCK_STREAM	SCTP	AF|SOCK|PROTO
INET	SOCK_STREAM	TCP	AF|SOCK|PROTO
INET	SOCK_SEQPACKET	SCTP	AF|SOCK|PROTO
INET	SOCK_RAW	ANY	AF|PROTO

SCTP is a new transport protocol defined in [RFC2960], and its technical details are beyond the scope of this book. For our discussion below, it is enough to understand that SCTP is a stream-based transport protocol like TCP.

The values for e_protostr are omitted because these values are not used in the source code. The "wild flags" column specifies which field of the address family, socket type, and protocol is allowed to have a wildcard ("any") value during matching. For example, the fifth row shows SOCK_RAW does not match if a wildcard is specified for the socket type.

We now turn back to Listing 7-139.

503–524 [RFC3493] clarifies that the AI_ALL and the AI_V4MAPPED flags are only meaningful for an AF_INET6 socket. Therefore these flags are cleared for an AF_INET socket. The code also regards the case where only AI_ALL is specified as an error. However, this treatment of AI_ALL does not conform to [RFC3493], which simply ignores the case.

531–552 If the specified address family is PF_INET, PF_INET6, or PF_UNSPEC, function get_portmatch() checks whether servname is a valid service name for the given protocol family. get_portmatch() will return an error code if there is a mismatch. For simplicity, the code assumes PF_INET6 when PF_UNSPEC is specified, but this behavior is incorrect because there is no guarantee that PF_INET and PF_INET6 have the same service name space.

Converting NULL or Numeric Host Name

The second main section of getaddrinfo() shown in Listing 7-141 handles either the NULL or numeric host names.

Listing 7-141

getaddrinfo.c

```
554          /*
555           * NULL hostname, or numeric hostname.
```

```
556                    * If numeric representation of AF1 can be interpreted as FQDN
557                    * representation of AF2, we need to think again about the code below.
558                    */
559                   found = 0;
560                   for (afd = afdl; afd->a_af; afd++) {
561                           *pai = ai0;
562
563                           if (!MATCH_FAMILY(pai->ai_family, afd->a_af, 1))
564                                   continue;
565
566                           if (pai->ai_family == PF_UNSPEC)
567                                   pai->ai_family = afd->a_af;
568
569                           if (hostname == NULL) {
570                                   /*
571                                    * filter out AFs that are not supported by the kernel
572                                    * XXX errno?
573                                    */
574                                   if (!addrconfig(pai->ai_family))
575                                           continue;
576                                   error = explore_null(pai, servname,
577                                       &afailist[afd - afdl]);
578                           } else
579                                   error = explore_numeric_scope(pai, hostname, servname,
580                                       &afailist[afd - afdl]);
581
582                           if (!error && afailist[afd - afdl])
583                                   found++;
584                   }
585                   if (found) {
586                           numeric = 1;
587                           goto globcopy;
588                   }
589
590                   if (hostname == NULL)
591                           ERR(EAI_NONAME);           /* used to be EAI_NODATA */
592                   if (pai->ai_flags & AI_NUMERICHOST)
593                           ERR(EAI_NONAME);
```
                                                                                    ————getaddrinfo.c

559–567 The `for` loop compares each supported address family against the address family given in the hints. If the given address family is unspecified, it will be set to the value in the `afd` entry that is based on the current loop index.

569–577 Function `addrconfig()` will check whether the current address family is available on the node if the caller does not specify a hostname. If the address family is available, function `explore_null()` is called to return either the "any" or the "loopback" address depending on the type of socket, that is, the socket being passive or active.

578–580 If the caller specifies a hostname, function `explore_numeric_scope()` is called to try to convert the hostname assuming the hostname is in the numeric format.

582–584 The `found` variable indicates whether a numeric address has been obtained. If so, the resolved address information has been stored in `afailist[afd - afdl]`.

585–588 The conversion process terminates if at least one address is found. Variable `numeric` is set to 1 to mark the fact that the case of FQDN hostnames has not been explored.

590–593 No attempts succeeded so far. If the caller did not provide a hostname or the `AI_NUMERICHOST` flag was specified, there is no need to explore the case of FQDN hostnames. An error of `EAI_NONAME` will simply be returned.

explore_null() *Function*

The explore_null() function returns either the "any address" or the address of "localhost,"
together with the port number for the given service name back to the caller.

Listing 7-142

```
                                                                              getaddrinfo.c
1235    /*
1236     * hostname == NULL.
1237     * passive socket -> anyaddr (0.0.0.0 or ::)
1238     * non-passive socket -> localhost (127.0.0.1 or ::1)
1239     */
1240    static int
1241    explore_null(pai, servname, res)
1242            const struct addrinfo *pai;
1243            const char *servname;
1244            struct addrinfo **res;
1245    {
1246            const struct afd *afd;
1247            struct addrinfo *cur;
1248            struct addrinfo sentinel;
1249            int error;
1250
1251            *res = NULL;
1252            sentinel.ai_next = NULL;
1253            cur = &sentinel;
1254
1255            /*
1256             * if the servname does not match socktype/protocol, ignore it.
1257             */
1258            if (get_portmatch(pai, servname) != 0)
1259                    return 0;
1260
1261            afd = find_afd(pai->ai_family);
1262            if (afd == NULL)
1263                    return 0;
1264
1265            if (pai->ai_flags & AI_PASSIVE) {
1266                    GET_AI(cur->ai_next, afd, afd->a_addrany);
1267                    /* xxx meaningless?
1268                     * GET_CANONNAME(cur->ai_next, "anyaddr");
1269                     */
1270                    GET_PORT(cur->ai_next, servname);
1271            } else {
1272                    GET_AI(cur->ai_next, afd, afd->a_loopback);
1273                    /* xxx meaningless?
1274                     * GET_CANONNAME(cur->ai_next, "localhost");
1275                     */
1276                    GET_PORT(cur->ai_next, servname);
1277            }
1278            cur = cur->ai_next;
1279
1280            *res = sentinel.ai_next;
1281            return 0;
1282
1283    free:
1284            if (sentinel.ai_next)
1285                    freeaddrinfo(sentinel.ai_next);
1286            return error;
1287    }
                                                                              getaddrinfo.c
```

1251–1253 *res is initialized to NULL in case of failure. sentinel.ai_next will have a
  pointer to a valid result. This function is actually simple enough that we could have
  written it without using the sentinel parameter.

1255–1259 get_portmatch() checks whether servname is a valid service name for the protocol family. The function fails and returns if the service name is invalid. The caller interprets the empty addrinfo chain as a failure.

1261–1263 find_afd() iterates through the afdl array to find an appropriate afd entry for the given address family.

1265–1270 The caller wants the "any address" if the AI_PASSIVE flag is set, which is suitable for binding with a listening socket. The GET_AI() macro allocates a new addrinfo{} structure and initializes it with information from the afd structure and its a_addrany member. Then the GET_PORT() macro converts servname to a 16-bit integer and sets that value into the port field of ai_next.ai_addr. The code jumps to the free label if either of GET_xxx() macros fails.

Note that when this code was first written, the specification was not clear on how the AI_CANONNAME flag should be processed for a NULL host name. Thus, the code is commented out for AI_CANONNAME. Then [RFC3493] clarifies that this flag is only meaningful for non-NULL hostnames.

1271–1277 The caller wants the address for "localhosts" if the AI_PASSIVE flag is not set. The process is identical to the previous case except that the a_loopback member is used instead.

1278–1287 On success, *res is set to point to the newly created addrinfo{} structure and 0 is returned to the caller.

1283–1287 Any allocated memory is freed when an error occurs and the appropriate error code is returned to the caller.

explore_numeric() Function

The explore_numeric() and explore_numeric_scope() functions try to convert a hostname assuming it is in a numeric form. The latter also supports the extension of the textual representation of IPv6 addresses for scoped addresses (Section 2.4.3). In fact, explore_numeric() acts as a backend function of explore_numeric_scope() in this implementation. We first explain the explore_numeric() function in Listing 7-143.

Listing 7-143

——getaddrinfo.c
```
1289    /*
1290     * numeric hostname
1291     */
1292    static int
1293    explore_numeric(pai, hostname, servname, res, ohostname)
1294            const struct addrinfo *pai;
1295            const char *hostname;
1296            const char *servname;
1297            struct addrinfo **res;
1298            const char *ohostname;
1299    {
1300            const struct afd *afd;
1301            struct addrinfo *cur;
1302            struct addrinfo sentinel;
1303            int error;
1304            char pton[PTON_MAX];
```

```
1305
1306              *res = NULL;
1307              sentinel.ai_next = NULL;
1308              cur = &sentinel;
1309
1310              afd = find_afd(pai->ai_family);
1311              if (afd == NULL)
1312                      return 0;
1313
1314              switch (afd->a_af) {
1315      #if 0 /*X/Open spec*/
1316              case AF_INET:
1317                      if (inet_aton(hostname, (struct in_addr *)pton) == 1) {
1318                              if (pai->ai_family == afd->a_af ||
1319                                  pai->ai_family == PF_UNSPEC /*?*/) {
1320                                      GET_AI(cur->ai_next, afd, pton);
1321                                      GET_PORT(cur->ai_next, servname);
1322                                      while (cur && cur->ai_next)
1323                                              cur = cur->ai_next;
1324                              } else
1325                                      ERR(EAI_FAMILY);            /*xxx*/
1326                      }
1327                      break;
1328      #endif
1329              default:
1330                      if (inet_pton(afd->a_af, hostname, pton) == 1) {
1331                              if (pai->ai_family == afd->a_af ||
1332                                  pai->ai_family == PF_UNSPEC /*?*/) {
1333                                      GET_AI(cur->ai_next, afd, pton);
1334                                      GET_PORT(cur->ai_next, servname);
1335                                      if ((pai->ai_flags & AI_CANONNAME)) {
1336                                              /*
1337                                               * Set the numeric address itself as
1338                                               * the canonical name, based on a
1339                                               * clarification in rfc2553bis-03.
1340                                               */
1341                                              GET_CANONNAME(cur->ai_next, ohostname);
1342                                      }
1343                                      while (cur && cur->ai_next)
1344                                              cur = cur->ai_next;
1345                              } else
1346                                      ERR(EAI_FAMILY);          /* XXX */
1347                      }
1348                      break;
1349              }
1350
1351              *res = sentinel.ai_next;
1352              return 0;
1353
1354      free:
1355      bad:
1356              if (sentinel.ai_next)
1357                      freeaddrinfo(sentinel.ai_next);
1358              return error;
1359      }
```

———getaddrinfo.c

1306–1312 The initialization of the variables is similar to explore_null(). As already explained, this implementation of this function could be simplified by eliminating sentinel. Additionally, the validation by find_afd() is redundant because the caller has already performed that validation.

1314–1328 [RFC3493] requires getaddrinfo() to accept the IPv4 numeric addresses that are in the class-based address form, for example, "10" for "10.0.0.0." This requirement means function inet_pton() cannot be used as the backend conversion function because `inet_pton()` does not accept class-based address by definition. Thus, `inet_aton()` should be used instead for the `AF_INET` address family. As shown in Listing 7-143, however, this segment of code is disabled. The reason is that at the time when that code was written, [RFC2553] was not clear on the treatment of class-based IPv4 addresses.

Similar to `explore_null()`, on the successful return of `inet_aton()`, `GET_AI()` allocates a new `addrinfo{}` entry to store the converted hostname followed by `GET_PORT()`, which sets an appropriate port number in the appropriate field of the `ai_addr` member.

The `while` loop starting at line 1322 is meaningless and can be ignored here because the `ai_next` member must never be non–NULL.

1330–1349 For all the address families other than `AF_INET`, function `inet_pton()` can simply be used for the conversion. (Note: In this particular code, `inet_pton()` is also used for `AF_INET` due to the preprocessor condition at line 1315.) On success, `GET_AI()` allocates a new `addrinfo{}` entry to store the converted hostname followed by `GET_PORT()` that sets an appropriate port number in the appropriate field of the `ai_addr` member. The same converted hostname is used as the "canonical" name (i.e., it is also copied into the `ai_canonname` field of the `addrinfo{}` structure when the `AI_CANONNAME` flag is set in the `hints{}` structure).

1351–1352 `*res` stores the conversion results, which can be NULL if either `inet_aton()` or `inet_pton()` failed.

1354–1356 The allocated `addrinfo{}` entry is freed on error and an appropriate error code is returned to the caller.

Now it is time to describe the `explore_numeric_scope()` function, shown in Listing 7-144.

Listing 7-144

──getaddrinfo.c

```
1361    /*
1362     * numeric hostname with scope
1363     */
1364    static int
1365    explore_numeric_scope(pai, hostname, servname, res)
1366            const struct addrinfo *pai;
1367            const char *hostname;
1368            const char *servname;
1369            struct addrinfo **res;
1370    {
1374            const struct afd *afd;
1375            struct addrinfo *cur;
1376            int error;
1377            char *cp, *hostname2 = NULL, *scope, *addr;
1378            struct sockaddr_in6 *sin6;
1379
1380            afd = find_afd(pai->ai_family);
1381            if (afd == NULL)
1382                    return 0;
1383
1384            if (!afd->a_scoped)
1385                    return explore_numeric(pai, hostname, servname, res, hostname);
1386
```

```
1387                cp = strchr(hostname, SCOPE_DELIMITER);
1388                if (cp == NULL)
1389                        return explore_numeric(pai, hostname, servname, res, hostname);
1390
1403                /*
1404                 * Handle special case of <scoped_address><delimiter><scope id>
1405                 */
1406                hostname2 = strdup(hostname);
1407                if (hostname2 == NULL)
1408                        return EAI_MEMORY;
1409                /* terminate at the delimiter */
1410                hostname2[cp - hostname] = '\0';
1411                addr = hostname2;
1412                scope = cp + 1;
1414
1415                error = explore_numeric(pai, addr, servname, res, hostname);
1416                if (error == 0) {
1417                        u_int32_t scopeid;
1418
1419                        for (cur = *res; cur; cur = cur->ai_next) {
1420                                if (cur->ai_family != AF_INET6)
1421                                        continue;
1422                                sin6 = (struct sockaddr_in6 *)(void *)cur->ai_addr;
1423                                if (ip6_str2scopeid(scope, sin6, &scopeid) == -1) {
1424                                        free(hostname2);
1425                                        freeaddrinfo(*res);
1426                                        *res = NULL;
1427                                        return(EAI_NONAME); /* XXX: is return OK? */
1428                                }
1429                                sin6->sin6_scope_id = scopeid;
1430                        }
1431                }
1432
1433                free(hostname2);
1434
1435                if (error && *res) {
1436                        freeaddrinfo(*res);
1437                        *res = NULL;
1438                }
1439                return error;
1441        }
```
—————————————————————————————————————— *getaddrinfo.c*

1380–1387 As in explore_null(), find_afd() provides the afd entry for the given address family. If this does not have scoped addresses, explore_numeric() does the job. In this implementation, explore_numeric() will simply be used for the AF_INET family. Then strchr() searches for the delimiter character in case hostname is formatted in the extended representation. As specified in [RFC4007], the delimiter is the percent character ("%"). If hostname does not contain the delimiter, it is enough to pass hostname to explore_numeric().

1406–1415 If hostname contains the delimiter character, a copy of hostname is made and stored in hostname2. hostname2 is then divided into two parts: the address and the scope zone ID. The address part is passed to explore_numeric() for conversion.

1416–1431 If explore_numeric() succeeds, the entire addrinfo{} entries are examined in the for loop. For each AF_INET6 entry function ip6_str2scopeid() (see Listing 7-145) is called to parse the scope zone ID. scopeid contains a 32-bit scope zone ID on successful return from ip6_str2scopeid(), which is then set into the sin6_scope_id field of the sockaddr_in6{} structure. An EAI_NONAME error is returned on failure after freeing the necessary resources.

1433–1441 Temporary resources are freed and an appropriate error code is returned.

ip6_str2scopeid() Function

Function `ip6_str2scopeid()` converts a textual representation of a given scope zone index into a 32-bit integer.

Listing 7-145

```
                                                                    getaddrinfo.c
1653    /* convert a string to a scope identifier. XXX: IPv6 specific */
1654    static int
1655    ip6_str2scopeid(scope, sin6, scopeid)
1656            char *scope;
1657            struct sockaddr_in6 *sin6;
1658            u_int32_t *scopeid;
1659    {
1660            u_long lscopeid;
1661            struct in6_addr *a6 = &sin6->sin6_addr;
1662            char *ep;
1663
1664            /* empty scopeid portion is invalid */
1665            if (*scope == '\0')
1666                    return -1;
1667
1668            if (IN6_IS_ADDR_LINKLOCAL(a6) || IN6_IS_ADDR_MC_LINKLOCAL(a6) ||
1669                IN6_IS_ADDR_MC_NODELOCAL(a6)) {
1670                    /*
1671                     * We currently assume a one-to-one mapping between links
1672                     * and interfaces, so we simply use interface indices for
1673                     * like-local scopes.
1674                     */
1675                    *scopeid = if_nametoindex(scope);
1676                    if (*scopeid == 0)
1677                            goto trynumeric;
1678                    return 0;
1679            }
1680
1681            /* still unclear about literal, allow numeric only - placeholder */
1682            if (IN6_IS_ADDR_SITELOCAL(a6) || IN6_IS_ADDR_MC_SITELOCAL(a6))
1683                    goto trynumeric;
1684            if (IN6_IS_ADDR_MC_ORGLOCAL(a6))
1685                    goto trynumeric;
1686            else
1687                    goto trynumeric;          /* global */
1688
1689            /* try to convert to a numeric id as a last resort */
1690    trynumeric:
1691            errno = 0;
1692            lscopeid = strtoul(scope, &ep, 10);
1693            *scopeid = (u_int32_t)(lscopeid & 0xffffffffUL);
1694            if (errno == 0 && ep && *ep == '\0' && *scopeid == lscopeid)
1695                    return 0;
1696            else
1697                    return -1;
1698    }
                                                                    getaddrinfo.c
```

1664–1666 The function terminates immediately on an empty string.

1668–1679 The implementation allows the interface names to be used as zone identifiers for link-local and interface-local addresses. From an architectural perspective, however, links can be larger in scope than interfaces (Section 2.4.1). Nevertheless, the implementation assumes one-to-one mapping between links and interfaces and thus it makes sense to use interface names under this assumption.

Note that macro `IN6_IS_ADDR_MC_NODELOCAL()` identifies the interface-local multicast addresses. The API standard follows an older version of the address architecture that has the notion of node-local but was replaced with interface-local (see the note for Table 7-4).

The interface index for the given interface name is simply used as the zone ID when interface names are used as zone IDs. Function `if_nametoindex()` does the conversion. Strictly speaking, this conversion is not sufficient because the specification requires encoding the scope type (e.g., a "link") into each zone ID to ensure uniqueness among all zone identifiers.

1681–1687 There are no valid strings except numeric IDs defined as scope zone IDs for scopes that are larger than the link scope.

1690–1698 [RFC4007] specifies that an implementation that supports the extended format must at least support numeric zone IDs. `strtoul()` attempts to convert the string to an integer. On success the result from `strtoul()` is returned along with a 0 error code. Otherwise, −1 is returned to indicate the failure.

Example—Convert an IPv6 Link-Local Address to the Extended Format

Figure 7-21 depicts how `getaddrinfo()` converts the string "`fe80::1234\%ne0`" to the corresponding `sockaddr_in6{}` structure. Figure 7-21 concentrates on the conversion process performed in `explore_numeric_scope()` and its backend functions.

FIGURE 7-21

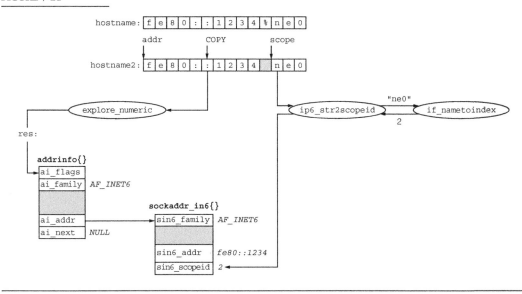

Convert `fe80::1234%ne0` *by* `getaddrinfo()`.

The hostname variable stores the string "fe80::1234\%ne0." Function explore_numeric_scope() first makes a copy of the string in hostname2 and then divides the string in hostname2 into the address part and the scope zone ID part.

The address part is passed to explore_numeric(), which returns an addrinfo{} chain in variable res that has a single entry. The ai_addr member of the addrinfo{} structure points to a sockaddr_in6{} structure whose sin6_addr member is fe80::1234 in the binary form.

The scope zone ID part, "ne0," is passed to function ip6_str2scopeid() and then to function if_nametoindex(), and is converted to the corresponding interface index as the link zone ID. We assume the interface identifier for the interface name "ne0" is 2 in this example.

The explore_numeric_scope() function finally sets the sin6_scope_id member of the sockaddr_in6{} structure pointed from the addrinfo{} structure to 2. The conversion process completes successfully and the addrinfo{} structure will be returned to the caller.

Converting FQDN Domain Names—*explore_fqdn()*

The third main section of getaddrinfo() shown in Listing 7-146 attempts to convert an alphabetical hostname to an IP address by means of DNS resolution.

Listing 7-146
                                                                    ___getaddrinfo.c
```
595              /*
596               * hostname as alphabetical name.
597               * first, try to query DNS for all possible address families.
598               */
600              /*
601               * the operating systems support PF_UNSPEC lookup in explore_fqdn().
602               */
603              *pai = ai0;
604              error = explore_fqdn(pai, hostname, servname, &afai_unspec);
```
                                                                    ___getaddrinfo.c

603–604 pai is reinitialized to ai0 in case pai has been modified. Function explore_fqdn() is called to perform the conversion procedure, which is shown in Listing 7-147.

Listing 7-147
                                                                    ___getaddrinfo.c
```
4130     /*
4131      * FQDN hostname, DNS lookup
4132      */
4133     static int
4134     explore_fqdn(pai, hostname, servname, res)
4135             const struct addrinfo *pai;
4136             const char *hostname;
4137             const char *servname;
4138             struct addrinfo **res;
4139     {
4140             struct addrinfo *result;
4141             struct addrinfo *cur;
4142             int error = 0, i;
4143
4144             result = NULL;
4145             *res = NULL;
4146
4147             /*
```

```
4148                 * if the servname does not match socktype/protocol, ignore it.
4149                 */
4150                if (get_portmatch(pai, servname) != 0)
4151                        return 0;
4152
4153                if (!_hostconf_init_done)
4154                        _hostconf_init();
4155
4156                for (i = 0; i < MAXHOSTCONF; i++) {
4157                        if (!_hostconf[i].byname)
4158                                continue;
4159                        error = (*_hostconf[i].byname)(pai, hostname, &result);
4160                        if (error != 0)
4161                                continue;
4162                        for (cur = result; cur; cur = cur->ai_next) {
4163                                GET_PORT(cur, servname);
4164                                /* canonname should already be filled. */
4165                        }
4166                        *res = result;
4167                        return 0;
4168                }
4169
4170    free:
4171                if (result)
4172                        freeaddrinfo(result);
4173                return error;
4174    }
```
——— getaddrinfo.c

4144–4151 get_portmatch() verifies whether the given servname is meaningful for the given socket type and protocol. This validation should not fail here because the check has already been done for AF_INET and AF_INET6 (Listing 7-148) and get_portmatch() unconditionally succeeds for other address families.

4153–4154 If this is the first time for the execution of getaddrinfo(), _hostconf_init() is called to parse the /etc/host.conf file and to construct the _hostconf array. This is an array of the _hostconf{} structure, each of which has a single member, byname, a method to convert a hostname to an IP address.

Note that _hostconf_init_done is a static variable in the source file, which is set to 1 in _hostconf_init(). Since this variable is not protected from simultaneous accesses by multiple threads, this implementation of getaddrinfo() is not thread safe, whereas [RFC3493] requires getaddrinfo() function to be so. This is the only part described in this chapter that breaks thread safeness. It is not so hard to fix this particular part, but backend resolver routines are not thread safe either and it is much harder to fix that part. We will discuss thread safeness of the backend routines in Chapter 3 of *IPv6 Advanced Protocols Implementation*.

The content of /etc/host.conf in the default installation of FreeBSD is as follows.

Listing 7-148
——— /etc/host.conf
```
# First try the /etc/hosts file
hosts
# Now try the nameserver next.
bind
# If you have YP/NIS configured, uncomment the next line
# nis
```
——— /etc/host.conf

Each line specifies a method for converting hostnames into addresses with decreasing preference. A line that begins with the pound sign is a comment line. As commented in the file, the static database stored in the host's /etc/hosts file is examined first, followed by DNS resolution. If the last line is uncommented, YP/NIS can also be available, although this function is not enabled in this getaddrinfo() implementation by default.

The supported name resolution method functions that are set in the _hostconf array are:

- hosts _files_getaddrinfo()
- bind _dns_getaddrinfo()
- nis _nis_getaddrinfo()

We will discuss _dns_getaddrinfo() in detail in Chapter 3 of the *Advanced Protocols* book.

4156–4168 Each iteration of the for loop invokes the byname method in the current _hostconf array entry with the given hostname until a method succeeds. The result variable will then point to a chain of addrinfo{} structures containing the conversion result. The GET_PORT() macro sets the port value for the given servname in the appropriate field of the ai_addr member of each addrinfo{} structure. Finally, *res is set to result and the conversion procedure terminates.

This organization of loop is important from the performance point of view. Suppose that the application specifies the AF_UNSPEC for the ai_family member of the hint structure, indicating that the application wants both IPv4 and IPv6 addresses for the given host name. With the default configuration of /etc/host.conf, we first try to find both IPv4 and IPv6 addresses in the /etc/hosts file. We will only try using the DNS method when we cannot find either IPv4 or IPv6 addresses. A previous version of getaddrinfo() did this by a per-address family loop, first trying all the methods for a single address family, say IPv4, and then trying the methods for the other address family. Thus, even if the answer we wanted could be found in the /etc/hosts file, we could have tried DNS at least once, causing unnecessary delay.

4170–4173 If all the methods fail or an error occurs in the GET_PORT() macro, the incomplete result in the result chain is freed (if any), and an appropriate error is returned. In the former case, the error code returned by the last method is remembered and returned to the caller.

Note: GET_PORT() should actually not fail, because get_portmatch() already checks the validity of servname.

Reorder the addrinfo Chain

The last main section of getaddrinfo() first constructs an addrinfo{} chain with the base information for all possible combinations of address family, socket type, and protocol. getaddrinfo() then rearranges the addrinfo{} chain based on the implementation-specific policy and, if applicable, the address selection algorithm per [RFC3484].

Listing 7-149

_____getaddrinfo.c

```
630    globcopy:
631            pass = 1;
632    copyagain:
633            for (ex = explore; ex->e_af >= 0; ex++) {
634                    *pai = ai0;
635
636                    if (pai->ai_family == PF_UNSPEC)
637                            pai->ai_family = ex->e_af;
638
639                    if (!MATCH_FAMILY(pai->ai_family, ex->e_af, WILD_AF(ex)))
640                            continue;
641                    if (!MATCH(pai->ai_socktype, ex->e_socktype, WILD_SOCKTYPE(ex)))
642                            continue;
643                    if (!MATCH(pai->ai_protocol, ex->e_protocol, WILD_PROTOCOL(ex)))
644                            continue;
645
646    #ifdef AI_ADDRCONFIG
647                    /*
648                     * If AI_ADDRCONFIG is specified, check if we are
649                     * expected to return the address family or not.
650                     */
651                    if ((pai->ai_flags & AI_ADDRCONFIG) != 0 &&
652                        !addrconfig(afd->a_af))
653                            continue;
654    #endif
655
656                    /*
657                     * XXX: Dirty hack.  Some passive applications only assume
658                     * a single entry returned and makes a socket for the head
659                     * entry.  In such a case, it would be safer to return
660                     * "traditional" socktypes (e.g. TCP/UDP) first.
661                     * We should, ideally, fix the applications rather than to
662                     * introduce the grotty workaround in the library, but we do
663                     * not want to break deployed apps just due to adding a new
664                     * protocol type.
665                     */
666                    if ((pai->ai_flags & AI_PASSIVE)) {
667                            if (pass == 1 && ex->e_protocol == IPPROTO_SCTP)
668                                    continue;
669                            if (pass == 2 && ex->e_protocol != IPPROTO_SCTP)
670                                    continue;
671                    }
672
673                    if (pai->ai_family == PF_UNSPEC)
674                            pai->ai_family = ex->e_af;
675                    if (pai->ai_socktype == ANY && ex->e_socktype != ANY)
676                            pai->ai_socktype = ex->e_socktype;
677                    if (pai->ai_protocol == ANY && ex->e_protocol != ANY)
678                            pai->ai_protocol = ex->e_protocol;
679
680                    /*
681                     * if the servname does not match socktype/protocol, ignore it.
682                     */
683                    if (get_portmatch(pai, servname) != 0)
684                            continue;
685
686                    if (afai_unspec)
687                            afai = afai_unspec;
688                    else {
689                            if ((afd = find_afd(pai->ai_family)) == NULL)
690                                    continue;
691                            /* XXX assumes that afd points inside afdl[] */
692                            afai = afailist[afd - afdl];
693                    }
694                    if (!afai)
695                            continue;
```

```
696
697                             error = explore_copy(pai, afai, &cur->ai_next);
698
699                         while (cur && cur->ai_next)
700                                 cur = cur->ai_next;
701             }
702         if ((pai->ai_flags & AI_PASSIVE) && ++pass <= 2)
703                 goto copyagain;
704
705         /* XXX inhibit errors if we have the result */
706         if (sentinel.ai_next)
707                 error = 0;
708
709         /*
710          * ensure we return either:
711          * - error == 0, non-NULL *res
712          * - error != 0, NULL *res
713          */
714         if (error == 0) {
715                 if (sentinel.ai_next) {
716                         /*
717                          * If the returned entry is for an active connection,
718                          * and the given name is not numeric, reorder the
719                          * list, so that the application would try the list
720                          * in the most efficient order.
721                          */
722                         if (hints == NULL || !(hints->ai_flags & AI_PASSIVE)) {
723                                 if (!numeric)
724                                         (void)reorder(&sentinel);
725                         }
726                         *res = sentinel.ai_next;
727                         error = 0;
728                 } else
729                         error = EAI_FAIL;
730         }
731
732     bad:
733         if (afai_unspec)
734                 freeaddrinfo(afai_unspec);
735         for (afd = afdl; afd->a_af; afd++) {
736                 if (afailist[afd - afdl])
737                         freeaddrinfo(afailist[afd - afdl]);
738         }
739         if (!*res)
740                 if (sentinel.ai_next)
741                         freeaddrinfo(sentinel.ai_next);
742         return error;
743     }
```
                                                                                    —————————getaddrinfo.c

630–644 The `for` loop examines all supported combinations of address family, socket type, and protocol. `pai` is re-initialized with `ai0`, a copy of the hint parameters. Unless `pai` matches the address family, the socket type, and the protocol, this combination is ignored (see Table 7-20, page 869).

646–654 A combination is ignored if the `AI_ADDRCONFIG` flag is specified but the node does not support the address family that is currently being examined.

656–670 If the `AI_PASSIVE` flag is specified in the hint, the loop considers non-SCTP protocols in the first pass. The loop is then repeated and only SCTP is considered in the second pass. The reason for this complicated process is that some legacy applications assume that the `AI_PASSIVE` flag will cause `getaddrinfo()` to return at most one `addrinfo{}` structure for a fixed combination of address family and socket type. If `getaddrinfo()`

happens to return an `addrinfo()` chain beginning with one for SCTP to such an application, then the application will try to open an SCTP socket only. This is probably not the result that the application wants and an undesirable side effect is likely to happen.

673–684 If some parameters are unspecified in the hint structure, specific values from the `explore{}` structure are substituted. Then `get_portmatch()` checks to see whether `servname` is a valid service name for the given socket type and protocol family.

686–695 If `hostname` has been successfully resolved as an alphabetical name (typically an FQDN), `afai_unspec` should be non-NULL and will be used in the following process. Otherwise, `find_afd()` identifies the corresponding `afd{}` structure and `afai` is set to point to the corresponding `addrinfo{}` structure in the `afailist` array that has been initialized in the second main section of `getaddrinfo()` (see Listing 7-141).

697–701 At this point, `afai` contains a chain of `addrinfo{}` structures in each of which the `ai_addr` member is the `sockaddr{}` structure corresponding to the given `hostname`. `explore_copy()` makes a copy of the chain for the socket type and protocol that is being examined by the current iteration of the `for` loop. Then the `while` loop resets the `cur` pointer to point to the last entry of the copied chain to ensure that `explore_copy()` concatenates each new copy at the end of intermediate results.

Note: The code here has a bug. If `explore_copy()` fails after several successes, the error will be cleared just after the loop because `sentinel.ai_next` is non-NULL (see below).

702–703 Another iteration of the loop is necessary if the `AI_PASSIVE` flag is specified (recall the discussion for lines 656 through 670).

705–706 An intermediate error is reset to 0 if there is a non-empty `addrinfo{}` chain.

714–727 `getaddrinfo()` finally tries to "optimize" the order of the `addrinfo{}` chain according to [RFC3484] when the following conditions are met:

- No error has been encountered thus far.

- A non-empty `addrinfo()` chain exists.

- The conversion is not for a passive socket.

- `hostname` is an alphabetical name not numeric.

A separate function `reorder()` performs the reordering of the `addrinfo{}` chain. `sentinel` will be modified accordingly. Then `*res` is set to point to the result chain.

728–730 The `addrinfo{}` chain may still be empty even when there is no explicit error because some functions called by `getaddrinfo()` can fail without indicating a particular error. Since [RFC3493] specifies that `getaddrinfo()` return a non-empty chain on success, an error of `EAI_FAIL` is assigned here.

733–743 This part is shared by both erroneous and successful cases. All of the temporary resources are freed. If no `addrinfo{}` chain is going to be returned but we have an intermediate non-empty result, it is also freed.

reorder() Function

The `reorder()` function shown in Listing 7-151, which is called from the body of `getaddrinfo()`, sorts the `addrinfo{}` chain in the preferred order according to both local policies and the address selection rules defined in [RFC3484].

Function `reorder()` uses a separate structure, `ai_order{}` shown in Listing 7-150 for performing the necessary sorting. Each `ai_order{}` structure corresponds to a single `addrinfo{}` entry.

Listing 7-150
```
                                                                      getaddrinfo.c
219    struct ai_order {
220           union {
221                   struct sockaddr_storage aiou_ss;
222                   struct sockaddr aiou_sa;
223           } aio_src_un;
224    #define aio_srcsa aio_src_un.aiou_sa
225           u_int32_t aio_srcflag;
226           int aio_srcscope;
227           int aio_dstscope;
228           struct policyqueue *aio_srcpolicy;
229           struct policyqueue *aio_dstpolicy;
230           struct addrinfo *aio_ai;
231           int aio_matchlen;
232    };
                                                                      getaddrinfo.c
```

219–231 The `aio_src_un` union stores the socket address structure of the source address that would be used for the corresponding `addrinfo{}` entry as the destination. This is a union of `sockaddr_storage{}` and `sockaddr{}` in order to support all possible address families. `aio_srcflag` holds flags representing properties of the source address. Currently, `AIO_SRCFLAG_DEPRECATED` flag is the only available flag, which indicates that the source address is an IPv6 deprecated address. `aio_srcscope` and `aio_dstscope` specify the address scope type of the source and destination addresses, respectively. These two fields are integers that map to the "scope" field of IPv6 multicast addresses (see Section 2.5.3). For example, value 2 refers to the link-local scope and value 8 refers to the organization-local (multicast) scope, and so forth. Notice that the notion of scopes also applies to IPv4 addresses as specified in [RFC3484]. `aio_srcpolicy` and `aio_dstpolicy` point to entries of the policy table as defined in [RFC3484], which are the most suitable policies for the source and destination addresses, respectively (see Section 3.4). `aio_ai` points to the corresponding `addrinfo{}` entry in the given chain. `aio_matchlen` is the bit length of the source address that matches the destination address. This value will be used as a "tie-breaker" in the comparison for sorting.

We now explain the `reorder()` function.

Listing 7-151
```
                                                                      getaddrinfo.c
745    static int
746    reorder(sentinel)
747           struct addrinfo *sentinel;
748    {
```

```
749              struct addrinfo *ai, **aip;
750              struct ai_order *aio;
751              int i, n;
752              struct policyhead policyhead;
753
754              /* count the number of addrinfo elements for sorting. */
755              for (n = 0, ai = sentinel->ai_next; ai != NULL; ai = ai->ai_next, n++)
756                      ;
757
758              /*
759               * If the number is small enough, we can skip the reordering process.
760               */
761              if (n <= 1)
762                      return(n);
763
764              /* allocate a temporary array for sort and initialization of it. */
765              if ((aio = malloc(sizeof(*aio) * n)) == NULL)
766                      return(n);           /* give up reordering */
767              memset(aio, 0, sizeof(*aio) * n);
768
769              /* retrieve address selection policy from the kernel */
770              TAILQ_INIT(&policyhead);
771              get_addrselectpolicy(&policyhead);
772
773              for (i = 0, ai = sentinel->ai_next; i < n; ai = ai->ai_next, i++) {
774                      aio[i].aio_ai = ai;
775                      aio[i].aio_dstscope = gai_addr2scopetype(ai->ai_addr);
776                      aio[i].aio_dstpolicy = match_addrselectpolicy(ai->ai_addr,
777                                                            &policyhead);
778              }
779
780              /* perform sorting. */
781              qsort(aio, n, sizeof(*aio), comp_dst);
782
783              /* reorder the addrinfo chain. */
784              for (i = 0, aip = &sentinel->ai_next; i < n; i++) {
785                      *aip = aio[i].aio_ai;
786                      aip = &aio[i].aio_ai->ai_next;
787              }
788              *aip = NULL;
789
790              /* cleanup and return */
791              free(aio);
792              free_addrselectpolicy(&policyhead);
793              return(n);
794      }
```
                                                                                 ———getaddrinfo.c

754–767 The number of addrinfo{} entries in the chain is first calculated, and then stored in n. If the chain consists of a single entry, the expensive sorting operations are omitted. Otherwise, memory is allocated for an array of n ai_order{} structures, which is initialized with zeros.

769–771 get_addrselectpolicy() retrieves the address selection policy table from the kernel and copies the table to policyhead as a list of entries.

773–777 For each addrinfo{} entry of the given chain, a separate ai_order{} structure is allocated, whose aio_ai member is set to the addrinfo{} entry. Destination-related parameters are also set. gai_addr2scopetype() returns the scope type of the destination address. match_addrselectpolicy() returns the most suitable policy table entry for the destination address.

Note: This version of the code has a serious bug. A separate function named set_source()
is expected to be called just after line 777 in order to fill in source-related fields of the
ai_order structure. Older versions of this code had invoked set_source(), but this
function call was removed by an accident. In examples shown below, however, we will
assume these parameters are set correctly.

780–781 The ai_order array is then sorted in the preferred order according to the given
parameters. comp_dst() compares the given two ai_order entries and returns the
preferred entry.

783–788 The addrinfo{} chain starting at ai_next of sentinel is then reordered as
sorted in the ai_order array.

790–794 Temporary resources are freed. This function finally returns the number of entries in
the chain.

Note: In earlier versions of this implementation, the return value is used for code that updates
the corresponding statistics purposes. In this version, n is unused.

comp_dst() *Function*

The comp_dst() function is the comparison method called via qsort(). Listing 7-152 shows
the function.

Listing 7-152

```
                                                                    getaddrinfo.c
1023    static int
1024    comp_dst(arg1, arg2)
1025            const void *arg1, *arg2;
1026    {
1027            const struct ai_order *dst1 = arg1, *dst2 = arg2;
1028
1029            /*
1030             * Rule 1: Avoid unusable destinations.
1031             * XXX: we currently do not consider if an appropriate route exists.
1032             */
1033            if (dst1->aio_srcsa.sa_family != AF_UNSPEC &&
1034                dst2->aio_srcsa.sa_family == AF_UNSPEC) {
1035                    return(-1);
1036            }
1037            if (dst1->aio_srcsa.sa_family == AF_UNSPEC &&
1038                dst2->aio_srcsa.sa_family != AF_UNSPEC) {
1039                    return(1);
1040            }
1041
1042            /* Rule 2: Prefer matching scope. */
1043            if (dst1->aio_dstscope == dst1->aio_srcscope &&
1044                dst2->aio_dstscope != dst2->aio_srcscope) {
1045                    return(-1);
1046            }
1047            if (dst1->aio_dstscope != dst1->aio_srcscope &&
1048                dst2->aio_dstscope == dst2->aio_srcscope) {
1049                    return(1);
1050            }
```

```
1051
1052                    /* Rule 3: Avoid deprecated addresses. */
1053            if (dst1->aio_srcsa.sa_family != AF_UNSPEC &&
1054                dst2->aio_srcsa.sa_family != AF_UNSPEC) {
1055                    if (!(dst1->aio_srcflag & AIO_SRCFLAG_DEPRECATED) &&
1056                        (dst2->aio_srcflag & AIO_SRCFLAG_DEPRECATED)) {
1057                            return(-1);
1058                    }
1059                    if ((dst1->aio_srcflag & AIO_SRCFLAG_DEPRECATED) &&
1060                        !(dst2->aio_srcflag & AIO_SRCFLAG_DEPRECATED)) {
1061                            return(1);
1062                    }
1063            }
1064
1065                    /* Rule 4: Prefer home addresses. */
1066                    /* XXX: not implemented yet */
1067
1068                    /* Rule 5: Prefer matching label. */
1070            if (dst1->aio_srcpolicy && dst1->aio_dstpolicy &&
1071                dst1->aio_srcpolicy->pc_policy.label ==
1072                dst1->aio_dstpolicy->pc_policy.label &&
1073                (dst2->aio_srcpolicy == NULL || dst2->aio_dstpolicy == NULL ||
1074                 dst2->aio_srcpolicy->pc_policy.label !=
1075                 dst2->aio_dstpolicy->pc_policy.label)) {
1076                    return(-1);
1077            }
1078            if (dst2->aio_srcpolicy && dst2->aio_dstpolicy &&
1079                dst2->aio_srcpolicy->pc_policy.label ==
1080                dst2->aio_dstpolicy->pc_policy.label &&
1081                (dst1->aio_srcpolicy == NULL || dst1->aio_dstpolicy == NULL ||
1082                 dst1->aio_srcpolicy->pc_policy.label !=
1083                 dst1->aio_dstpolicy->pc_policy.label)) {
1084                    return(1);
1085            }
1087
1088                    /* Rule 6: Prefer higher precedence. */
1090            if (dst1->aio_dstpolicy &&
1091                (dst2->aio_dstpolicy == NULL ||
1092                 dst1->aio_dstpolicy->pc_policy.preced >
1093                 dst2->aio_dstpolicy->pc_policy.preced)) {
1094                    return(-1);
1095            }
1096            if (dst2->aio_dstpolicy &&
1097                (dst1->aio_dstpolicy == NULL ||
1098                 dst2->aio_dstpolicy->pc_policy.preced >
1099                 dst1->aio_dstpolicy->pc_policy.preced)) {
1100                    return(1);
1101            }
1103
1104                    /* Rule 7: Prefer native transport. */
1105                    /* XXX: not implemented yet */
1106
1107                    /* Rule 8: Prefer smaller scope. */
1108            if (dst1->aio_dstscope >= 0 &&
1109                dst1->aio_dstscope < dst2->aio_dstscope) {
1110                    return(-1);
1111            }
1112            if (dst2->aio_dstscope >= 0 &&
1113                dst2->aio_dstscope < dst1->aio_dstscope) {
1114                    return(1);
1115            }
1116
1117                    /*
1118                     * Rule 9: Use longest matching prefix.
1119                     * We compare the match length in a same AF only.
1120                     */
1121            if (dst1->aio_ai->ai_addr->sa_family ==
1122                dst2->aio_ai->ai_addr->sa_family) {
```

```
1123                    if (dst1->aio_matchlen > dst2->aio_matchlen) {
1124                            return(-1);
1125                    }
1126                    if (dst1->aio_matchlen < dst2->aio_matchlen) {
1127                            return(1);
1128                    }
1129            }
1130
1131            /* Rule 10: Otherwise, leave the order unchanged. */
1132            return(-1);
1133    }
```
── getaddrinfo.c

This function basically just performs the pair-wise comparison of two `aio_ai` entries corresponding to two different `addrinfo{}` entries, as described in [RFC3484] (see Section 3.4.3). We just make comments where an explicit note is necessary.

[RFC3484] says in its Rule 1 that if one destination is known to be reachable while the other is known to be unreachable, the former should be preferred. However, it is generally difficult to know whether a particular destination is reachable or not, especially in a user space program. Thus, this implementation only checks to see if each destination has a source address in Rule 1.

A couple of rules are not yet supported in this implementation. One is Rule 4 that prefers destinations that would have Mobile IPv6 home addresses as the source address. The other one is Rule 7 that prefers destinations that are reached over native IPv6 networks, that is, nontunneling networks. It is generally difficult to detect if a particular destination is reached over a tunnel, and thus this rule is not implemented.

Other Subroutines for `getaddrinfo()`

`getaddrinfo()` depends on many subroutines that are not yet described. These functions are summarized in Table 7-21. The essential implementation of `getaddrinfo()` that we have described in detail should allow the reader to understand the details of these minor subroutines. All of the functions can be found in `getaddrinfo.c`.

7.6.4 Address Ordering Examples

We will examine some examples in order to describe the address ordering procedure together with how the `getaddrinfo()` implementation itself works. In the following examples, we will concentrate on address families and addresses, ignoring socket types, protocols, and ports.

Consider a network depicted in Figure 7-22 where two hosts, a client and a server, are connected via the IPv4/IPv6 Internet. Both hosts have IPv4 and IPv6 addresses as shown in the figure. We assume all of the server's addresses are stored in the DNS.

Note that the server has a 6to4 address(*) as well as "normal" IPv6 addresses (i.e., non-6to4 address). This example is not common because 6to4 addresses are not necessary when normal global IPv6 addresses and IPv6 connectivity are available. This configuration is created purely for illustration and explanation.

(*) 6to4 is a transition technology defined in [RFC3056], which is beyond the scope of this book. For the discussion here, it is enough to know that 6to4 addresses are identified by the prefix `2002::/16`.

TABLE 7-21

Function name	Function prototype and description
`get_ai()`	```static struct addrinfo *get_ai(const struct addrinfo *pai,``` ```const struct afd *afd, const char *addr);```
	Allocates a new addrinfo{} structure, and copies the parameters specified in `pai` and `afd` to the new structure. If memory allocation fails, returns a NULL pointer. This function allocates the entire memory for the addrinfo{} structure and the corresponding ai_addr space at once.
`get_canonname()`	```static int get_canonname(const struct addrinfo *pai,``` ```struct addrinfo *ai, const char *str);```
	If the `AI_CANONNAME` flag is specified in `pai`, duplicates the string specified by `str`, and sets it to the ai_canonname member of `ai`. Returns 0 on success or EAI_MEMORY if memory allocation for the copied string fails.
`get_port()`	```static int get_port(struct addrinfo *ai, const char *servname,``` ```int matchonly);```
	Converts the appropriate port value for servname and the protocol stored in `ai`, and sets the corresponding port field of the ai_addr member of `ai` (sin6_port for IPv6) to the port value. If matchonly is non-0, it just validates the parameters, and keeps `ai` intact. Returns 0 on success, or EAI_xxx error codes.
`get_portmatch()`	```static int get_portmatch(const struct addrinfo *ai,``` ```const char *servname);```
	This function is equivalent to get_port(ai, servname, 1).
`copy_ai()`	```static struct addrinfo *copy_ai(const struct addrinfo *pai);```
	Allocates a new addrinfo{} structure and copies all the parameters from `pai` to the new structure. Returns the pointer to the structure, or a NULL pointer.
`explore_copy()`	```static int explore_copy(const struct addrinfo *pai,``` ```const struct addrinfo *src0,``` ```struct addrinfo **res);```
	Copies the entire addrinfo{} chain stored in src0. Values for ai_socktype and ai_protocol are copied from pai. On success, sets *res to the head of the copied chain and returns 0. Otherwise, EAI_MEMORY will be returned.

(Continued)

TABLE 7-21 (*Continued*)

Function name	Function prototype and description
find_afd()	static const struct afd *find_afd(int af);
	This function iterates through the afdl array to find an appropriate afd entry for the given address family (see Section 7.6.3).
addrconfig()	static int addrconfig(int af);
	Returns 1 if the given address family (af) is available on the system, or returns 0. The current implementation simply checks if the system can open a SOCK_DGRAM socket for the address family, and is almost meaningless.
get_addrselectpolicy()	static void get_addrselectpolicy(struct policyhead *head);
	Issues the IPV6CTL_ADDRCTLPOLICY sysctl (see Section 3.13.1) to get the address selection policy, constructs a list of policy table entries, and sets head to the head of the list.
free_addrselectpolicy()	static void free_addrselectpolicy(struct policyhead *head);
	Frees all resources allocated for head.
match_addrselectpolicy()	static struct policyqueue *match_addrselectpolicy(struct sockaddr *addr, struct policyhead *head);
	Searches in the policy table from head for the entry that best matches addr. Returns the pointer to the best match entry. If nothing is found, returns NULL.
set_source()	static void set_source(struct ai_order *aio, struct policyhead *ph);
	Gets the source address for the destination address stored in aio by trying to connect to the destination and then getting the local socket address, and sets related parameters in aio, referring to ph when necessary.
gai_addr2scopetype()	static int gai_addr2scopetype(struct sockaddr *sa);
	Returns scope type number for the given socket address.

Often the get_xxx() functions are used through wrapper macros, GET_AI(), GET_CANONNAME(), and GET_PORT(). On failure, these macros stop the procedure immediately, going to label free. GET_AI() also sets variable error to EAI_NOMEMORY. A similar macro, ERR(), is often used, also. It takes an error code, sets the error variable to it, and goes to the bad label.

FIGURE 7-22

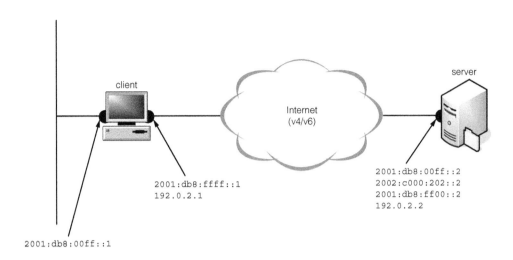

client

server

Internet
(v4/v6)

2001:db8:00ff::2
2002:c000:202::2
2001:db8:ff00::2
192.0.2.2

2001:db8:ffff::1
192.0.2.1

2001:db8:00ff::1

Example network topology with multiple candidates of address.

Let us assume an application program running on the client wants to communicate with the server either via IPv6 or via IPv4 and passes the server's hostname to getaddrinfo().

getaddrinfo() calls the explore_fqdn() function, which makes several DNS queries (through its backend functions) to resolve IPv4 and IPv6 addresses. The ordering of the addrinfo{} chain at this stage depends on the details of the backend function and the ordering of resource records provided by the DNS. In this example, we assume we have the chain as shown in Figure 7-23.

In the for loop of Listing 7-149, the addrinfo{} chain is copied to a separate chain beginning at sentinel.ai_next. Although the list could be reordered inside the for loop, the chain of this example does not change. In any event, the reordering at this stage does not matter because the reorder() function changes the list again regardless of the temporary result.

The reorder() function allocates an array of ai_order{}, filling in each entry with parameters to reorder the chain. Figure 7-24 shows the content of the array and the relationship between the array and the addrinfo{} chain before reordering.

Notice that the source address for the destination 2001:db8:00ff::2 should be 2001:db8:ffff::1, not 2001:db8:00ff::1 which is the longest match of bit-wise comparison. The reason is that the former is assigned on the outgoing interface to the Internet while the latter is on an internal interface (source address selection Rule 5).

In this example, we assume the default policy table as defined in [RFC3484]. We can review the content of the policy table installed in the kernel by the **ip6addrctl** command. The following is an example output of this command.

% ip6addrctl

```
Prefix                    Prec Label    Use
::1/128                     50     0      0
::/0                        40     1  38940
```

FIGURE 7-23

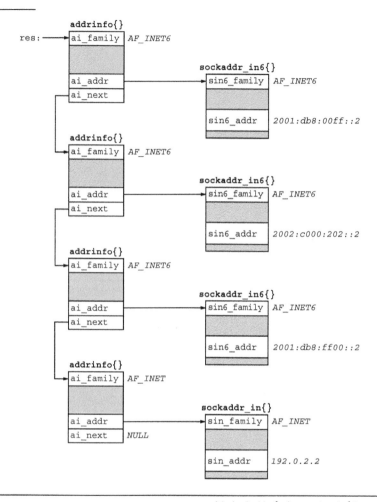

addrinfo{} chain constructed in `explore_fqdn()`.

```
2032::/16                    30      2        0
::/96                        20      3        0
::ffff:0.0.0.0/96            10      4        0
```

The left-hand 3 columns are the table entries, and the rightmost column shows statistics of how many times each entry is used, which is collected in the kernel.

In Figure 7-24, values for `aio_srcpolicy` and `aio_dstpolicy` should read like this: `::/0`(40, 1) means the key of the policy table entry for this address is `::/0`, and its precedence and matching label are 40 and 1, respectively. Also, the prefixes followed by values of `aio_matchlen` mean the longest prefix shared by the source and destination addresses, providing the match length value.

FIGURE 7-24

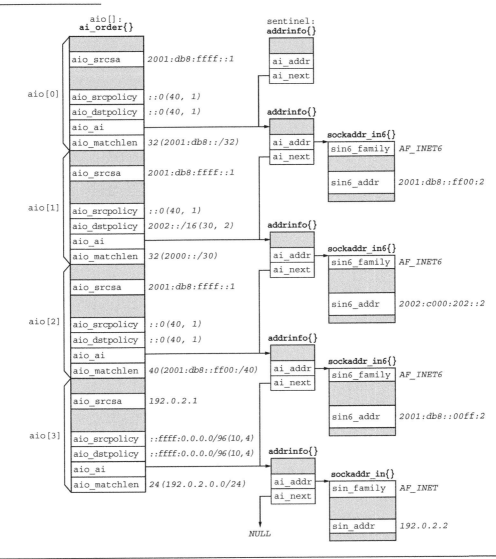

ai_order array before reordering.

Note that the prefix corresponding to the IPv4-mapped IPv6 address (`::ffff:0.0.0.0/96`) simply represents IPv4 addresses for comparison purposes only. This is irrelevant to the usage of this type of address described in [RFC3493].

Figure 7-25 shows the result of reordering in the `reorder()` function. The given `addrinfo{}` chain is also reordered accordingly. In Figure 7-25, we show the `ai_order` members that tie-break each pair-wise comparison by dotted lines labeled with the rule number: `2001:db8:ff00::2` is preferred to `2001:db8:00ff::2` because the former has the

FIGURE 7-25

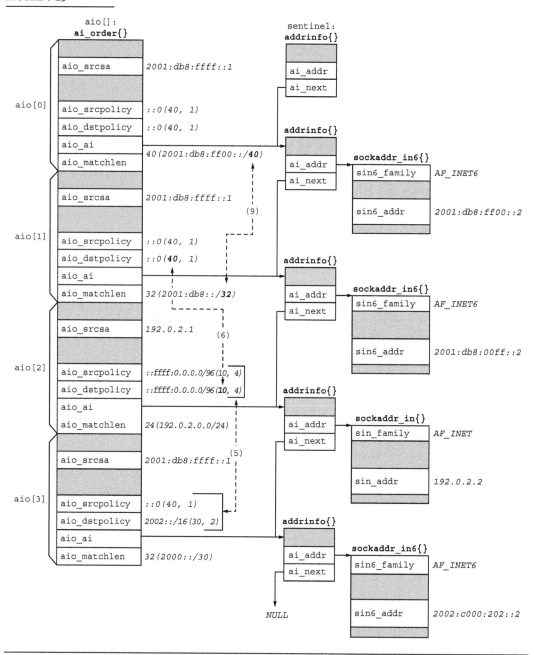

Result of address reordering.

longer matched source address (by Rule 9); `2001:db8:00ff::2` is preferred to `192.0.2.2` because the former has a higher precedence value (Rule 6); `192.0.2.2` is preferred to `2002:c000:202::2` because the former has the same precedence value for the source and destination while the latter does not (Rule 5).

If the application calling `getaddrinfo()` goes through the `addrinfo{}` chain, trying to connect to the address stored in each `addrinfo{}` entry until the attempt succeeds, which is the behavior of most of today's dual stack applications, then the application will try the addresses in the preferred order.

The default policy table shown on pages 891–892 prefers IPv6 communication over IPv4 communication. In some cases, however, an administrator might configure the host to prefer IPv4 communication instead, for example, when it is known that the quality of IPv6 connectivity is poorer than that of IPv4. This policy can be implemented by modifying the policy table. The administrator can create a new policy file with the following content:

```
::1/128                 50      0
::ffff:0.0.0.0/96       45      4
::/0                    40      1
2002::/16               30      2
::/96                   20      3
```

and then install the new policy file into the kernel using the **ip6addrctl** command:

```
# ip6addrctl install newpolicy
```

Note that installing a new policy table requires the superuser privilege.

Figure 7-26 is the reordering result for the previous network configuration with the new policy table. As shown in the figure, the pair of IPv4 addresses is most preferred.

7.6.5 `freeaddrinfo()` Function

The `freeaddrinfo()` function is the destructor of an `addrinfo{}` chain provided by `getaddrinfo()`.

Listing 7-153

———`getaddrinfo.c`
```
387   void
388   freeaddrinfo(ai)
389          struct addrinfo *ai;
390   {
391          struct addrinfo *next;
392
393          do {
394                  next = ai->ai_next;
395                  if (ai->ai_canonname)
396                          free(ai->ai_canonname);
397                  /* no need to free(ai->ai_addr) */
398                  free(ai);
399                  ai = next;
400          } while (ai);
401   }
```
———`getaddrinfo.c`

`freeaddrinfo()` iterates through the entire chain and frees resources for each `addrinfo{}` entry. Since the memory for `ai_addr` is allocated inside the `addrinfo{}` structure, freeing the `addrinfo{}` structure should be sufficient except for the memory pointed

FIGURE 7-26

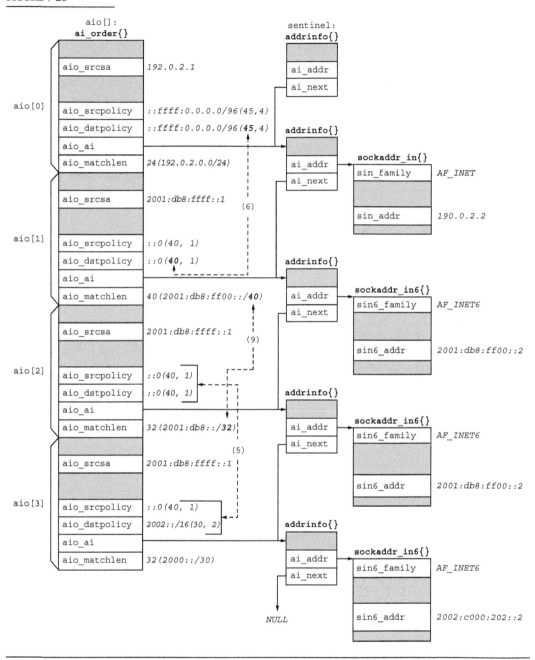

Reordering result preferring IPv4 communication.

by `ai_canonname`. Note that this implementation assumes the argument `ai` is non-NULL. [RFC3493] is silent on this point and it is the application's responsibility to ensure the assumption.

7.6.6 `gai_strerror()` Function

The `gai_strerror()` function converts an error code from `getaddrinfo()` to a readable string.

Listing 7-154
```
                                                                      getaddrinfo.c
300    static struct ai_errlist {
301            const char *str;
302            int code;
303    } ai_errlist[] = {
304            { "Success",                                    0, },
305    #ifdef EAI_ADDRFAMILY
306            { "Address family for hostname not supported",  EAI_ADDRFAMILY, },
307    #endif
308            { "Temporary failure in name resolution",       EAI_AGAIN, },
309            { "Invalid value for ai_flags",                 EAI_BADFLAGS, },
310            { "Non-recoverable failure in name resolution", EAI_FAIL, },
311            { "ai_family not supported",                    EAI_FAMILY, },
312            { "Memory allocation failure",                  EAI_MEMORY, },
313    #ifdef EAI_NODATA
314            { "No address associated with hostname",        EAI_NODATA, },
315    #endif
316            { "hostname nor servname provided, or not known", EAI_NONAME, },
317            { "servname not supported for ai_socktype",     EAI_SERVICE, },
318            { "ai_socktype not supported",                  EAI_SOCKTYPE, },
319            { "System error returned in errno",             EAI_SYSTEM, },
320            { "Invalid value for hints",                    EAI_BADHINTS, },
321            { "Resolved protocol is unknown",               EAI_PROTOCOL, },
322            /* backward compatibility with userland code prior to 2553bis-02 */
324            { "Address family for hostname not supported",  1, },
325            { "No address associated with hostname",        7, },
330            { NULL,                                         -1, },
331    };

374    char *
375    gai_strerror(ecode)
376            int ecode;
377    {
378            struct ai_errlist *p;
379
380            for (p = ai_errlist; p->str; p++) {
381                    if (p->code == ecode)
382                            return (char *)p->str;
383            }
384            return "Unknown error";
385    }
                                                                      getaddrinfo.c
```

330–331 `gai_strerror()` uses a separate local array, `ai_errlist`, as the database for the conversion, which is an array of structures of the same name. Each structure is simply an error code and the corresponding string. `EAI_ADDRFAMILY` and `EAI_NODATA` were deprecated by [RFC3493], and the corresponding definitions are disabled by default in this code. In order to provide binary backward compatibility, however, the old code values are kept at the end of this array. `EAI_BADHINTS` has never been defined in RFCs. This code is specific to this implementation. Such definition and usage are still acceptable because applications typically use the error codes as opaque values through the `gai_strerror()` function. Still, portable applications should not directly use the unofficial definition.

374–385 The `for` loop iterates through the entire `ai_errlist` array, looking for the entry that matches the given code. This function returns the corresponding error string if a match is found. Otherwise, the default string "Unknown error" will be returned.

7.6.7 `getnameinfo()` Function

In this section, we describe KAME's implementation of the `getnameinfo()` function. It implements the function specification as defined in [RFC3493], and it also supports the extended format for IPv6-scoped addresses specified in [RFC4007].

Similar to `getaddrinfo()`, `getnameinfo()` uses a supplemental structure named `afd{}` (see Listing 7-137). The `afd{}` structure for the `getnameinfo()` function is a subset of the same named structure for `getaddrinfo()`.

Another supplemental structure for `getnameinfo()` is the `sockinet{}` structure, which holds the common fields of the `sockaddr_in{}` and `sockaddr_in6{}` structures. The only purpose of this structure is to provide the offset to the port number field of these structures. These structures are shown in Listing 7-155.

Listing 7-155

```
_____getnameinfo.c
70    static const struct afd {
71            int a_af;
72            int a_addrlen;
73            int a_socklen;
74            int a_off;
75    } afdl [] = {
77            {PF_INET6, sizeof(struct in6_addr), sizeof(struct sockaddr_in6),
78                    offsetof(struct sockaddr_in6, sin6_addr)},
80            {PF_INET, sizeof(struct in_addr), sizeof(struct sockaddr_in),
81                    offsetof(struct sockaddr_in, sin_addr)},
82            {0, 0, 0},
83    };
84
85    struct sockinet {
87            u_char  si_len;
89            u_char  si_family;
90            u_short si_port;
91    };
_____getnameinfo.c
```

Through the following listings, we describe the details of the `getnameinfo()` function.

Initial Checks

Listing 7-156

```
_____getnameinfo.c
99     int
100    getnameinfo(sa, salen, host, hostlen, serv, servlen, flags)
101            const struct sockaddr *sa;
103            socklen_t salen;
107            char *host;
108            size_t hostlen;
109            char *serv;
```

```
110              size_t servlen;
111              int flags;
112     {
113              const struct afd *afd;
114              struct servent *sp;
115              struct hostent *hp;
116              u_short port;
117              int family, i;
118              const char *addr;
119              u_int32_t v4a;
120              int h_error;
121              char numserv[512];
122              char numaddr[512];
123
124              if (sa == NULL)
125                      return EAI_FAIL;
126
128              if (sa->sa_len != salen)
129                      return EAI_FAIL;
131
132          family = sa->sa_family;
133          for (i = 0; afdl[i].a_af; i++)
134                  if (afdl[i].a_af == family) {
135                          afd = &afdl[i];
136                          goto found;
137                  }
138          return EAI_FAMILY;
139
140     found:
141              if (salen != afd->a_socklen)
142                      return EAI_FAIL;
```

getnameinfo.c

124–129 An EAI_FAIL error is returned if the sockaddr{} structure is not provided or if the sa_len member of the structure is inconsistent with the given salen parameter.

132–138 The for loop searches for the appropriate afd{} structure for the given address family. An EAI_FAMILY error is returned if no entry is found.

140–142 An EAI_FAIL error is returned if the given salen value does not match the length of the corresponding afd{} structure.

Extract Port and Address

Listing 7-157

getnameinfo.c

```
144          /* network byte order */
145          port = ((const struct sockinet *)sa)->si_port;
146          addr = (const char *)sa + afd->a_off;
```

getnameinfo.c

144–146 The port number of the given sockaddr{} structure is extracted by casting sa to the generic sockinet{} structure. The address field is referred to from variable addr using the offset value from the head of the sockaddr{} structure provided by the corresponding afd{} structure. Note that the extracted number is expected to be passed to the getservbyport() function, where the port number is in the network byte order, and so ntohs() is not performed here.

Convert the Port Number

Listing 7-158

————————————————————————————————————getnameinfo.c
```
148            if (serv == NULL || servlen == 0) {
149                    /*
150                     * do nothing in this case.
151                     * in case you are wondering if "&&" is more correct than
152                     * "||" here: rfc2553bis-03 says that serv == NULL OR
153                     * servlen == 0 means that the caller does not want the result.
154                     */
```
————————————————————————————————————getnameinfo.c

148–154 If the buffer for the service name serv is a NULL pointer or if the length of the buffer is 0, then according to [RFC3493] the caller does not want a result for the service name.

Listing 7-159

————————————————————————————————————getnameinfo.c
```
155            } else {
156                    if (flags & NI_NUMERICSERV)
157                            sp = NULL;
158                    else {
159                            sp = getservbyport(port,
160                                    (flags & NI_DGRAM) ? "udp" : "tcp");
161                    }
162                    if (sp) {
163                            if (strlen(sp->s_name) + 1 > servlen)
164                                    return EAI_MEMORY;
165                            strlcpy(serv, sp->s_name, servlen);
166                    } else {
167                            snprintf(numserv, sizeof(numserv), "%u", ntohs(port));
168                            if (strlen(numserv) + 1 > servlen)
169                                    return EAI_MEMORY;
170                            strlcpy(serv, numserv, servlen);
171                    }
172            }
```
————————————————————————————————————getnameinfo.c

155–172 Unless the NI_NUMERICSERV flag is specified, getservbyport() is called to convert the port number to a servent{} structure, which contains a printable string for the number. If servent{} is found and the given buffer length is large enough to store the string with the terminating null character, the string is copied to the serv buffer. On failure in getting servent{}, the port number is converted to a digit string and is copied to the serv buffer if the buffer has enough space. In either case, the EAI_MEMORY error is returned if the given buffer is not big enough.

Note: EAI_MEMORY is not an appropriate error in such a case. EAI_OVERFLOW, which is newly defined in [RFC3493], would be better. The same note applies to the other code below.

Note: getservbyport() that is provided in FreeBSD targeted in this book is not thread safe. Consequently, getnameinfo() is not thread safe either.

Consideration for Special Addresses

The rest of this function tries to convert the address to a printable string. As part of the preprocess operation, some special addresses are explicitly considered to avoid meaningless operation such as issuing DNS queries for nonexistence records. This validation process is not documented in the API specification but is useful in terms of reducing resolution time and network traffic.

Listing 7-160
getnameinfo.c

```
174              switch (sa->sa_family) {
175              case AF_INET:
176                      v4a = (u_int32_t)
177                          ntohl(((const struct sockaddr_in *)sa)->sin_addr.s_addr);
178                      if (IN_MULTICAST(v4a) || IN_EXPERIMENTAL(v4a))
179                              flags |= NI_NUMERICHOST;
180                      v4a >>= IN_CLASSA_NSHIFT;
181                      if (v4a == 0)
182                              flags |= NI_NUMERICHOST;
183                      break;
185              case AF_INET6:
186                  {
187                      const struct sockaddr_in6 *sin6;
188                      sin6 = (const struct sockaddr_in6 *)sa;
189                      switch (sin6->sin6_addr.s6_addr[0]) {
190                      case 0x00:
191                              if (IN6_IS_ADDR_V4MAPPED(&sin6->sin6_addr))
192                                      ;
193                              else if (IN6_IS_ADDR_LOOPBACK(&sin6->sin6_addr))
194                                      ;
195                              else
196                                      flags |= NI_NUMERICHOST;
197                              break;
198                      default:
199                              if (IN6_IS_ADDR_LINKLOCAL(&sin6->sin6_addr)) {
200                                      flags |= NI_NUMERICHOST;
201                              }
202                              else if (IN6_IS_ADDR_MULTICAST(&sin6->sin6_addr))
203                                      flags |= NI_NUMERICHOST;
204                              break;
205                      }
206                  }
207                      break;
209              }
```
getnameinfo.c

174–209 For the following addresses, getnameinfo() will simply try to convert them to textual representation as numeric addresses. Additional processes for DNS-based conversion will be suppressed.

- IPv4 multicast addresses

- Class E IPv4 addresses (240.0.0.0 – 255.255.255.255)

- IPv4 addresses beginning with 0x00

- IPv6 addresses beginning with 0x00 except IPv4-mapped IPv6 addresses and the loopback address

- IPv6 link-local addresses

- IPv6 multicast addresses

The `NI_NUMERICHOST` flag is set for the above addresses as if the caller originally intended to retrieve only numeric results.

Convert the Address
Listing 7-161
_____getnameinfo.c
```
210             if (host == NULL || hostlen == 0) {
211                     /*
212                      * do nothing in this case.
213                      * in case you are wondering if "&&" is more correct than
214                      * "||" here: rfc2553bis-03 says that host == NULL or
215                      * hostlen == 0 means that the caller does not want the result.
216                      */
```
_____getnameinfo.c

210–216 If the buffer for the hostname `host` is a NULL pointer or if the length of the buffer is 0, then according to [RFC3493] the caller does not want a result for the hostname.

Listing 7-162
_____getnameinfo.c
```
217             } else if (flags & NI_NUMERICHOST) {
218                     int numaddrlen;
219
220                     /* NUMERICHOST and NAMEREQD conflicts with each other */
221                     if (flags & NI_NAMEREQD)
222                             return EAI_NONAME;
223
224                     switch(afd->a_af) {
226                     case AF_INET6:
227                     {
228                             int error;
229
230                             if ((error = ip6_parsenumeric(sa, addr, host,
231                                                     hostlen, flags)) != 0)
232                                     return(error);
233                             break;
234                     }
236                     default:
237                             if (inet_ntop(afd->a_af, addr, numaddr, sizeof(numaddr))
238                                 == NULL)
239                                     return EAI_SYSTEM;
240                             numaddrlen = strlen(numaddr);
241                             if (numaddrlen + 1 > hostlen) /* don't forget terminator */
242                                     return EAI_MEMORY;
243                             strlcpy(host, numaddr, hostlen);
244                             break;
245                     }
```
_____getnameinfo.c

217–222 As commented at line 220, the simultaneous use of both `NI_NUMERICHOST` and `NI_NAMEREQD` flags contradicts each other. This implementation throws an error of `EAI_NONAME` when both the flags are specified.

224–234 For an IPv6 address, a separate function `ip6_parsenumeric()` will convert the address into textual representation. `inet_ntop()` is not appropriate here because it cannot handle IPv6 scoped addresses well.

236–245 For addresses of other address families, `inet_ntop()` converts the name to a textual string in the local `numaddr` buffer. Since `inet_ntop()` does not need a temporary resource and we already know the address should be valid (Listing 7-156), `inet_ntop()` should not fail here. If it ever happens, an error of `EAI_SYSTEM` is returned, indicating the unexpected result. After the conversion, the result is copied to the `host` buffer with the terminating NULL character if the given buffer length is enough to store the entire result. Otherwise, the `EAI_MEMORY` error is returned.

Listing 7-163

getnameinfo.c

```
246              } else {
248                      hp = getipnodebyaddr(addr, afd->a_addrlen, afd->a_af, &h_error);
257
258                      if (hp) {
259   #if 0
260                              /*
261                               * commented out, since "for local host" is not
262                               * implemented here - see RFC2553 p30
263                               */
264                              if (flags & NI_NOFQDN) {
265                                      char *p;
266                                      p = strchr(hp->h_name, '.');
267                                      if (p)
268                                              *p = '\0';
269                              }
270   #endif
271                              if (strlen(hp->h_name) + 1 > hostlen) {
273                                      freehostent(hp);
275                                      return EAI_MEMORY;
276                              }
277                              strlcpy(host, hp->h_name, hostlen);
279                              freehostent(hp);
```

getnameinfo.c

246–248 `getipnodebyaddr()` tries to convert the address to an FQDN, often by DNS reverse lookups. Note that [RFC3493] obsoletes this function and is not expected to be called from applications. `getipnodebyaddr()` was once implemented and was used by `getnameinfo()` as a backend function. Note that `getipnodebyaddr()` is a thread-safe function and it is safe to use it as a backend without breaking the thread-safeness of the `getnameinfo()` implementation.

258–270 According to [RFC3493], the `NI_NOFQDN` flag means that only the node name portion of the FQDN should be returned for local hosts (see Table 7-2). However, this implementation intentionally disables this part; otherwise, the code would return the first label of the FQDN, that is, the part before the first period. The reason behind the current implementation is due to the fact that the meaning of "for local hosts" is vague. If an application only wants to get the first label, the application will have to truncate the result from `getnameinfo()`.

271–277 As was done before, the result hostname is copied to the `host` variable with the terminating NULL character. If the buffer is too short, an `EAI_MEMORY` error is returned.

Listing 7-164

getnameinfo.c

```
281              } else {
282                      if (flags & NI_NAMEREQD)
```

```
283                                        return EAI_NONAME;
284                            switch(afd->a_af) {
286                            case AF_INET6:
287                                {
288                                        int error;
289
290                                        if ((error = ip6_parsenumeric(sa, addr, host,
291                                                                      hostlen,
292                                                                      flags)) != 0)
293                                                return(error);
294                                        break;
295                                }
297                            default:
298                                        if (inet_ntop(afd->a_af, addr, host,
299                                            hostlen) == NULL)
300                                                return EAI_SYSTEM;
301                                        break;
302                                }
303                            }
304                    }
305            return(0);
306    }
```
—————————————————————————————— getnameinfo.c

281–303 At this point, getipnodebyaddr() has failed. An EAI_NONAME error is returned
if the NI_NAMEREQD flag is specified. Otherwise, either ip6_parsenumeric() or
inet_ntop() will try converting the address to textual representation similar to the
case where NI_NUMERICHOST is specified.

ip6_parsenumeric() *Function*

ip6_parsenumeric() is called by getnameinfo(), which converts an IPv6 address into
printable textual representation taking into consideration the address scopes.

Listing 7-165
—————————————————————————————— getnameinfo.c

```
309    static int
310    ip6_parsenumeric(sa, addr, host, hostlen, flags)
311            const struct sockaddr *sa;
312            const char *addr;
313            char *host;
314            size_t hostlen;
315            int flags;
316    {
317            int numaddrlen;
318            char numaddr[512];
319
320            if (inet_ntop(AF_INET6, addr, numaddr, sizeof(numaddr)) == NULL)
321                    return EAI_SYSTEM;
322
323            numaddrlen = strlen(numaddr);
324            if (numaddrlen + 1 > hostlen) /* don't forget terminator */
325                    return EAI_MEMORY;
326            strlcpy(host, numaddr, hostlen);
327
328            if (((const struct sockaddr_in6 *)sa)->sin6_scope_id) {
329                    char zonebuf[MAXHOSTNAMELEN];
330                    int zonelen;
331
332                    zonelen = ip6_sa2str(
```

```
333                             (const struct sockaddr_in6 *)(const void *)sa,
334                             zonebuf, sizeof(zonebuf), flags);
335                     if (zonelen < 0)
336                             return EAI_MEMORY;
337                     if (zonelen + 1 + numaddrlen + 1 > hostlen)
338                             return EAI_MEMORY;
339
340                     /* construct <numeric-addr><delim><zoneid> */
341                     memcpy(host + numaddrlen + 1, zonebuf,
342                         (size_t)zonelen);
343                     host[numaddrlen] = SCOPE_DELIMITER;
344                     host[numaddrlen + 1 + zonelen] = '\0';
345             }
346
347             return 0;
348     }
```
———getnameinfo.c

320–326 inet_ntop() converts the IPv6 address into textual representation and stores the result into the local buffer numaddr. inet_ntop() should succeed because all the input is known to be valid. The length of the converted string is set in numaddrlen, and strlcpy() copies the string to the host, ensuring it is terminated by a NULL character. (Using strlcpy() is actually redundant because inet_ntop() should have null-terminated the original string.)

328–345 If a non-0 value is specified in the sin6_scope_id field of the socket address structure, which should be a sockaddr_in6{} structure, ip6_sa2str() is called to convert the ID value to textual representation. The result is stored in a local buffer zonebuf. If the conversion succeeds and the buffer for the entire hostname has enough space to store the address with the ID string, then the delimiter character ("%") followed by the string is appended to the textual representation of the address. The EAI_MEMORY error is returned if something unexpected happens.

ip6_sa2str() *Function*

The ip6_sa2str() function, shown in Listing 7-166, is called by ip6_parsenumeric().

Listing 7-166
———getnameinfo.c
```
350     /* ARGSUSED */
351     static int
352     ip6_sa2str(sa6, buf, bufsiz, flags)
353             const struct sockaddr_in6 *sa6;
354             char *buf;
355             size_t bufsiz;
356             int flags;
357     {
358             unsigned int ifindex;
359             const struct in6_addr *a6;
360             int n;
361
362             ifindex = (unsigned int)sa6->sin6_scope_id;
363             a6 = &sa6->sin6_addr;
364
365     #ifdef NI_NUMERICSCOPE
366             if ((flags & NI_NUMERICSCOPE) != 0) {
```

```
367                        n = snprintf(buf, bufsiz, "%u", sa6->sin6_scope_id);
368                        if (n < 0 || n >= bufsiz)
369                                return -1;
370                        else
371                                return n;
372                }
373    #endif
374
375            /* if_indextoname() does not take buffer size.  not a good api... */
376            if ((IN6_IS_ADDR_LINKLOCAL(a6) || IN6_IS_ADDR_MC_LINKLOCAL(a6) ||
377                IN6_IS_ADDR_MC_NODELOCAL(a6)) && bufsiz >= IF_NAMESIZE) {
378                    char *p = if_indextoname(ifindex, buf);
379                    if (p) {
380                            return(strlen(p));
381                    }
382            }
383
384            /* last resort */
385            n = snprintf(buf, bufsiz, "%u", sa6->sin6_scope_id);
386            if (n < 0 || n >= bufsiz)
387                    return -1;
388            else
389                    return n;
390    }
```
———getnameinfo.c

365–373 If the NI_NUMERICSCOPE flag is defined and specified, the application wanted to convert the ID part into numeric representation. snprintf() does the conversion and returns the length of the string (excluding the terminating NULL character) on success. This function returns −1 if the conversion fails. Note that NI_NUMERICSCOPE is not officially defined in [RFC3493]. Applications should avoid using the flag.

375–382 The KAME implementation supports interface names such as "ne0" as scope zone indices for the interface-local scope (multicast only). Additionally, the implementation assumes a one-to-one mapping between links and interfaces and allows interface names as zone indices for this scope type (Section 2.9.1). In these cases, the sin6_scope_id value is assumed to be an interface index and is passed to if_indextoname() to convert the value to an interface name. If the conversion succeeds, the interface name will be used as a printable representation. The sin6_scope_id value is handled as an opaque value in that the process continues even if if_indextoname() fails.

384–389 For scope types other than interface-local and link-local, or in the case where if_indextoname() fails above, the sin6_scope_id value is converted to a digit string similar to the case where the NI_NUMERICSCOPE flag is specified.

7.6.8 Other Library Functions

As shown in Sections 7.2 and 7.3, the API specifications define several other library functions. KAME's implementation provides almost all of them, and we could describe those line-by-line. However, since the implementation is quite trivial and may not be very interesting, we simply give a list of files that implement these library functions.

When needed, the source code is available on the companion website. [Ste94] also provides implementation of if_xxx() functions explained in Section 7.2.2.

The additional library functions defined in [RFC3493] are listed in Table 7-22. All files are located under the ${KAME}/kame/kame/libinet6/ directory.

TABLE 7-22

Function	File
if_indextoname()	if_indextoname.c
if_nametoindex()	if_nametoindex.c
if_freenameindex()	if_nameindex.c
if_nameindex()	if_nameindex.c

The additional library functions defined in [RFC3542] are listed in Table 7-23. All files are located under the `${KAME}/kame/kame/libinet6/` directory.

TABLE 7-23

Function	File
inet6_rth_space()	rthdr.c
inet6_rth_init()	rthdr.c
inet6_rth_add()	rthdr.c
inet6_rth_reverse()	rthdr.c
inet6_rth_segments()	rthdr.c
inet6_rth_getaddr()	rthdr.c
inet6_opt_init()	ip6opt.c
inet6_opt_append()	ip6opt.c
inet6_opt_finish()	ip6opt.c
inet6_opt_set_val()	ip6opt.c
inet6_opt_next()	ip6opt.c
inet6_opt_find()	ip6opt.c
inet6_opt_get_val()	ip6opt.c
rresvport_af()	rresvport_af.c
rcmd_af()	rcmd.c
rexec_af()	(not implemented)

References

Most of the references for this book are RFCs. Some specifications are in the process of standardization or revision, for which Internet Drafts are referred to. Both types of documents are freely available from the IETF web page: http://www.ietf.org. Note, however, that an Internet Draft is a work-in-progress material, which may expire or may have become an RFC by the time this book is published. There are WWW or FTP sites on the Internet that provide a copy of old versions of Internet Drafts when necessary. At the time of this writing, the KAME project's FTP server provides this service, which is located at ftp://ftp.kame.net/pub/internet-drafts/.

The following list of references are categorized into three parts: The first part consists of non-IETF references; the second part is a list of RFC referred to or mentioned in this book; the last part is a reference list of Internet Drafts.

[Hag00]   J. Hagino, "Mbuf Issues in 4.4BSD IPv6 Support—Experiences from KAME IPv6/IPsec Implementation," in proceeding of 2000 USENIX Annual Technical Conference, June 2000.

[Jin99]   T. Jinmei, et. al., "An Overview of the KAME Network Software: Design and Implementation of the Advanced Internetworking Platform," in proceeding of INET '99, June 1999 (available at http://www.isoc.org/inet99/proceedings/4s/4s_2.htm).

[Ken87]   C. Kent and J. Mogul, "Fragmentation considered harmful," in proceeding of SIGCOMM '87 Vol. 17, No. 5, October 1987.

[Lem02]   J. Lemon, "Resisting SYN Flood DoS Attacks with a SYN Cache," in proceeding of BSDCON 2002, February 2002.

[Ste03]   W. Stevens, et al., "Unix Network Programming, Vol. 1: The Sockets Networking API, Third Edition," Addison-Wesley, 2003.

[Ste94]   W. Stevens and G. Wright, "TCP/IP Illustrated, Volume 2: The Implementation," Addison-Wesley, 1994.

[RFC792]   J. Postel, "Internet Control Message Protocol," RFC792, September 1981.

[RFC1035]   P. Mockapetris, "Domain names—implementation and specification," RFC1035, November 1987.

[RFC1191]   J. Mogul and S. Deering, "Path MTU discovery," RFC1191, November 1990.

[RFC1519]   V. Fuller, et al., "Classless Inter-Domain Routing (CIDR): an Address Assignment and Aggregation Strategy," RFC1519, September 1993.

[RFC1812]   F. Baker, "Requirements for IP Version 4 Routers," RFC1812, June 1995.

[RFC1858]   G. Ziemba, et al., "Security Considerations for IP Fragment Filtering," RFC1858, October 1995.

[RFC1883]   S. Deering and R. Hinden, "Internet Protocol, Version 6 (IPv6) Specification," RFC1883, December 1995.

[RFC1981]   J. McCann, et al., "Path MTU Discovery for IP version 6," RFC1981, August 1996.

[RFC2133]   R. Gilligan, et al., "Basic Socket Interface Extensions for IPv6," RFC2133, April 1997.

[RFC2292]   W. Stevens and M. Thomas, "Advanced Sockets API for IPv6," RFC2292, February 1998.

[RFC2373]   R. Hinden and S. Deering, "IP Version 6 Addressing Architecture," RFC2373, July 1998.

[RFC2375]   R. Hinden and S. Deering, "IPv6 Multicast Address Assignments," RFC2375, July 1998.

[RFC2460]   S. Deering and R. Hinden, "Internet Protocol, Version 6 (IPv6) Specification," RFC2460, December 1998.

[RFC2461]   T. Narten, et al., "Neighbor Discovery for IP Version 6 (IPv6)," RFC2461, December 1998.

[RFC2462]   S. Thomson and T. Narten, "IPv6 Stateless Address Autoconfiguration," RFC2462, December 1998.

[RFC2463]   A. Conta and S. Deering, "Internet Control Message Protocol (ICMPv6) for the Internet Protocol Version 6 (IPv6) Specification," RFC2463, December 1998.

[RFC2464]   M. Crawford, "Transmission of IPv6 Packets over Ethernet Networks," RFC2464, December 1998.

[RFC2465]   D. Haskin and S. Onishi, "Management Information Base for IP Version 6: Textual Conventions and General Group," RFC2465, December 1998.

[RFC2466]   D. Haskin and S. Onishi, "Management Information Base for IP Version 6: ICMPv6 Group," RFC2466, December 1998.

[RFC2474]   K. Nichols, et al., "Definition of the Differentiated Services Field (DS Field) in the IPv4 and IPv6 Headers," RFC2474, December 1998.

[RFC2497]   I. Souvatzis, "Transmission of IPv6 Packets over ARCnet Networks," RFC2497, January 1999.

[RFC2553]   R. Gilligan, et al., "Basic Socket Interface Extensions for IPv6," RFC2553, March 1999.

[RFC2675]   D. Borman, et al., "IPv6 Jumbograms," RFC2675, August 1999.

[RFC2710]   S. Deering, et al., "Multicast Listener Discovery (MLD) for IPv6," RFC2710, October 1999.

[RFC2711]   C. Partridge and A. Jackson, "IPv6 Router Alert Option," RFC2711, October 1999.

[RFC2730]   S. Hanna, et al., "Multicast Address Dynamic Client Allocation Protocol (MADCAP)," RFC2730, December 1999.

[RFC2734]   P. Johansson, "IPv4 over IEEE 1394," RFC2734, December 1999.

[RFC2740]   R. Coltun, et al., "OSPF for IPv6," RFC2740, December 1999.

[RFC2765]   E. Nordmark, "Stateless IP/ICMP Translation Algorithm (SIIT)," RFC2765, February 2000.

[RFC2893]   R. Gilligan and E. Nordmark, "Transition Mechanisms for IPv6 Hosts and Routers," RFC2893, August 2000.

[RFC2894]   M. Crawford, "Router Renumbering for IPv6," RFC2894, August 2000.

[RFC2960]   R. Stewart, et al., "Stream Control Transmission Protocol," RFC2960, October 2000.

[RFC3041]   T. Narten and R. Draves, "Privacy Extensions for Stateless Address Auto-configuration in IPv6," RFC3041, January 2001.

[RFC3056]   B. Carpenter and K. Moore, "Connection of IPv6 Domains via IPv4 Clouds," RFC3056, February 2001.

[RFC3122]   A. Conta, "Extensions to IPv6 Neighbor Discovery for Inverse Discovery Specification," RFC3122, June 2001.

[RFC3142]   J. Hagino and K. Yamamoto, "An IPv6-to-IPv4 Transport Relay Translator," RFC3142, June 2001.

[RFC3168]   K. Ramakrishnan, et al., "The Addition of Explicit Congestion Notification (ECN) to IP," RFC3168, September 2001.

[RFC3286]   L. Ong and J. Yoakum, "An Introduction to the Stream Control Transmission Protocol (SCTP)," RFC3286, May 2002.

[RFC3306]   B. Haberman and D. Thaler, "Unicast-Prefix-based IPv6 Multicast Addresses," RFC3306, August 2002.

[RFC3307]   B. Haberman, "Allocation Guidelines for IPv6 Multicast Addresses," RFC3307, August 2002.

[RFC3484]   R. Draves, "Default Address Selection for Internet Protocol version 6 (IPv6)," RFC3484, February 2003.

[RFC3493]   R. Gilligan, et al., "Basic Socket Interface Extensions for IPv6," RFC3493, February 2003.

[RFC3513]   R. Hinden and S. Deering, "Internet Protocol Version 6 (IPv6) Addressing Architecture," RFC3513, April 2003.

[RFC3542]   W. Stevens, et al., "Advanced Sockets Application Program Interface (API) for IPv6," RFC3542, May 2003.

[RFC3678]   D. Thaler, et al., "Socket Interface Extensions for Multicast Source Filters," RFC3678, January 2004.

[RFC3697]   J. Rajahalme, et al., "IPv6 Flow Label Specification," RFC3697, March 2004.

[RFC3736]   R. Droms, "Stateless Dynamic Host Configuration Protocol (DHCP) Service for IPv6," RFC3736, April 2004.

[RFC3775]   D. Johnson, et al., "Mobility Support in IPv6," RFC3775, June 2004.

[RFC3879]   C. Huitema and B. Carpenter, "Deprecating Site Local Addresses," RFC3879, September 2004.

[RFC3927]   S. Cheshire, et al., "Dynamic Configuration of IPv4 Link-Local Addresses," RFC3927, May 2005.

[RFC3956]   P. Savola and B. Haberman, "Embedding the Rendezvous Point (RP) Address in an IPv6 Multicast Address," RFC3956, November 2004.

[RFC3971]   J. Arkko, et al., "SEcure Neighbor Discovery (SEND)," RFC3971, March 2005.

[RFC4007]   S. Deering, et al., "IPv6 Scoped Address Architecture," RFC4007, March 2005.

[RFC4022]   R. Raghunarayan, "Management Information Base for the Transmission Control Protocol (TCP)," RFC4022, March 2005.

[RFC4034]   R. Arends, et al., "Resource Records for the DNS Security Extensions," RFC4034, March 2005.

[RFC4191]   R. Draves and D. Thaler, "Default Router Preferences and More-Specific Routes," RFC4191, November 2005.

[RFC4193]   R. Hinden and B. Haberman, "Unique Local IPv6 Unicast Addresses," RFC4193, October 2005.

[RFC4213]   E. Nordmark and R. Gilligan, "Basic Transition Mechanisms for IPv6 Hosts and Routers," RFC4213, October 2005.

[RFC4291]   R. Hinden and S. Deering, "IP Version 6 Addressing Architecture," RFC4291, February 2006.

[RFC4302]   S. Kent, "IP Authentication Header," RFC4302, December 2005.

[RFC4303]	S. Kent, "IP Encapsulating Security Payload (ESP)," RFC4303, December 2005.
[RFC4443]	A. Conta, et al., "Internet Control Message Protocol (ICMPv6) for the Internet Protocol Version 6 (IPv6) Specification," RFC4443, March 2006.
[RFC4489]	S. Park, et al., "A Method for Generating Link-Scoped IPv6 Multicast Addresses," RFC4489, April 2006.
[FRAG-HARMFUL]	J. Heffner, et al., "Fragmentation Considered Very Harmful," Internet Draft: draft-heffner-frag-harmful-02.txt, June 2006.
[NAME-LOOKUPS-10]	M. Crawford, "IPv6 Node Information Queries," Internet Draft: draft-ietf-ipngwg-icmp-name-lookups-10.txt, June 2003.
[NAME-LOOKUPS-12]	M. Crawford and B. Haberman (editor), "IPv6 Node Information Queries," Internet Draft: draft-ietf-ipngwg-icmp-name-lookups-12.txt, July 2005.
[NAME-LOOKUPS-13]	M. Crawford and B. Haberman (editor), "IPv6 Node Information Queries," Internet Draft: draft-ietf-ipngwg-icmp-name-lookups-13.txt, January 2006.
[NAME-LOOKUPS-15]	M. Crawford and B. Haberman (editor), "IPv6 Node Information Queries," Internet Draft: draft-ietf-ipngwg-icmp-name-lookups-15.txt, February 2006.
[PIM-SM-V2]	B. Fenner, et al., "Protocol Independent Multicast – Sparse Mode (PIM-SM): Protocol Specification (Revised)," Internet Draft: draft-ietf-pim-sm-v2-new-12.txt, September 2006.
[PRIVACY-ADDRS2]	T. Narten, et al., "Privacy Extensions for Stateless Address Autoconfiguration in IPv6," Internet Draft: draft-ietf-ipv6-privacy-addrs-v2-04.txt, May 2005.
[RFC2461BIS]	T. Narten, et al., "Neighbor Discovery for IP version 6 (IPv6)," Internet Draft: draft-ietf-ipv6-2461bis-07.txt, May 2006.
[RFC2462BIS]	S. Thomson, et al., "IPv6 Stateless Address Autoconfiguration," Internet Draft: draft-ietf-ipv6-rfc2462bis-08.txt, May 2005.
[TCP-TO-ANYCAST]	J. Itoh, "Disconnecting TCP connection toward IPv6 anycast address," Internet Draft: draft-itojun-ipv6-tcp-to-anycast-01.txt, July 2001.
[ULA-08]	R. Hinden and B. Haberman, "Unique Local IPv6 Unicast Addresses," Internet Draft: draft-ietf-ipv6-unique-local-addr-08.txt, November 2004.
[V4MAPPED]	C. Metz and J. Hagino, "IPv4-Mapped Address API Considered Harmful," Internet Draft: draft-cmetz-v6ops-v4mapped-api-harmful-01.txt, October 2003.
[V6-ACAST]	J. Abley, "Anycast Addressing in IPv6," Internet Draft: draft-jabley-v6-anycast-clarify-00.txt, March 2005.

Index

A

accept() system call, 678
accept TCP connections,
    tcp6_usr_accept()
    function, 678, 680
Address 1..N field, Routing
    headers, 138
address configuration, IPv6
    cleanup on error, 114
    configuration call graphs,
      74–75
    ifconfig command, 127–128
    in6_addmulti() function,
      116–118
    in6_control() function,
      95–101
    in6_delmulti() function,
      116–118
    in6_ifaddloop() function,
      120–122
    in6_ifinit() function,
      118–120
    in6_ifloop_request()
      function, 120–122
    in6_leavegroup()
      function, 115–116
    in6_purgeaddr() function,
      101, 123–124

in6_update_ifa()
    function, 101–114
  initial checks, 95–96
  inserting new addresses,
    105–109
  joining multicast groups,
    109–114, 115–116
  utility, 127–130
  validation, 97–98
addresses, IPv6, *see also*
    getaddrinfo() function
  add or update addresses,
    98–100
  address testing macros, 67,
    763–764
  : (colon) and :: (double colon)
    notation, 31
  anycast address, 30
  broadcast, 30
  comparison macros, 50–51
  configuration, *see* address
    configuration, IPv6
  conversion, getaddrinfo()
    function, 753–757,
    863–888
  converting, getnameinfo()
    function, 757–759, 853,
    898–906

conversion, inet_ntop()
    function, 752–753, 853,
    855, 859–863
conversion, inet_pton()
    function, 752–753,
    853–859, 873, 874
deleting, 100–101, 122–127
deprecated address, 66
deprecation of unicast
    site-local addresses,
    39–40
described, 30–31
duplicates, *see* DAD
format, 40–44
global, 33–34, 41–42
global ID, 40
interface address structures,
    64–70
interface identifier, 29, 41
interface identifier generation,
    42–43
interface-local multicast,
    33–34, 50
invalid address, 413–414
IPv4-compatible IPv6
    addresses, 32
IPv4-mapped IPv6 addresses,
    32, 169–170, 618,
    750–752, 760–764
link-local, 33–34, 41, 46, 50

loopback, 31–32, 50
loopback interface, 32
manipulation routines, 73–76
masking, macros and variables
    for, 49
multicast, 30
multicast address format, 44–46
node address requirements,
    46–47
node-local vs. interface-local,
    33, 50
on-link condition, 568–570
ordering examples, 888–895
predefined, 50
preferred address, 413–414
preferred lifetime, 66, 413–414
prefix structure, 70–73,
    434–436
resolution and ND protocol,
    390, 410–411
scope, *see* address scopes;
    scope zones
scoped, 33–40
% (percent) scoped address
    delimiter, 39
selection, 144–149
site-local, 33–34, 39–40, 41
6to4 addresses, 888
stateless, *see* Stateless Address
    Autoconfiguration
subnet prefix, 41
subnet-router anycast, 41
tentative address, 413–414
textual representation of, 31–32
textual representation of
    scoped, 38–39
ULAs, 40
undefined source, 148
unicast, 30, 33–34, 40
unspecified, 31–32, 50, 51, 169,
    207
valid lifetime, 66, 413–414
well-known multicast, 45
zone indices, 36–38
addressing architecture, IPv6
    enhancements, 29
Address Resolution Protocol,
    see ARP
address scopes
    ambiguity of scoped addresses,
        diagram of, 36
    default assignment of zone
        IDs, diagram of, 37
    deprecation of unicast
        site-local addresses,
        39–40

in6_addr2zoneid()
    function, 59–60
in6_addrscope() function,
    57–59, 60
in6_clearscope()
    function, 62–63
in6_embedscope()
    function, 60–61
in6_recoverscope()
    function, 61–62, 104
macros, 51
scope6_check_id()
    function, 63, 253, 632
scope zone architecture,
    diagram of, 56
scope zones, 34–36, 46, 52–53
textual representation of
    scoped addresses,
    38–39
types, described, 33–34
zone IDs, *see* zone IDs
zone indices, 36–38
address selection, *see* source
    address selection
address space management, 47
address structures, IPv6, 48
addrinfo{} chain, 880–883
AdvAutonomousFlag variable, 421
AdvCurHopLimit variable, 420
AdvDefaultLifetime variable, 420
AdvLinkMTU variable, 420
AdvManagedFlag variable, 419
AdvOnLinkFlag variable, 421
AdvOtherConfigFlag variable, 419
AdvPreferredLifetime variable, 421
AdvPrefixList variable, 421
AdvReachableTime variable, 420
AdvRetransTimer variable, 420
AdvSendAdvertisements variable,
    419, 420
AdvValidLifetime variable, 421
AF_INET6 socket, 55, 618, 622,
    634, 637–638, 651, 738, 740,
    741, 742, 760, 761–762, 796
    IPv4 communication over,
        750–752
    open for ICMPv6 transport, 767
AF_INET6 socket,
    communication over,
    750–752
AF_INET socket, 653, 738, 740,
    741, 742, 751
    implication in binding, 637–639
AfriNIC (African Network
    Information Center), 47
all-nodes multicast addresses,
    46, 50

all-routers multicast addresses, 46
ambiguity
    binding, 751
    scoped addresses, 36
    multicast, 751
ancillary data, 767, 768–770, 777,
    807–808
anycast addresses, IPv6
    described, 30
    subnet-router, 41
APIs, *see* kernel implementation of
    IPv6 APIs; RFC3493 (Basic
    Socket API); RFC3542
    (Advanced Socket API)
APNIC (Asia Pacific Network
    Information Center), 47
Apple Computer Mac OS, 6
Apple Computer Mac OS,
    diagram, 5
Application Layer Gateway, 2
ARIN (American Registry for
    Internet Numbers), 47
ARP (Address Resolution
    Protocol), 12, 90
    IPv4-based, 389, 441, 447, 448,
        471, 504, 607
arpa/inet.h, 752
Asynchronous Transfer Mode,
    Permanent Virtual Circuit
    (ATM-PVC), 81
ATM-PVC (Asynchronous Transfer
    Mode, Permanent Virtual
    Circuit), 81
attached addresses, 569
attached prefixes, 569–570
attach PCBs
    rip6_attach() function,
        730–732, 839
    tcp_attach() function,
        680–681
    udp6_attach() function,
        702–704

B

backup, system, 8
BaseReachableTime variable, 433,
    440, 517
BaseReachableTime variable, host
    operations, 424
Berkeley Software Distribution,
    see BSD
binding
    AF_INET socket, implication
        in, 637–639
    duplicate binding check,
        634–637

in6_pcbbind() function,
630–639
parameter validation, 631–634
port number allocation, 637
rip6_bind() function,
732–734
tcp6_usr_bind() function,
681–683
udp6_usr_bind() function,
704–705
UDP sockets, 738–740
binding ambiguity, 751
bind() system call, 627, 630,
637, 681, 683, 685, 704,
732, 738, 769, 796, 815
broadcast addresses, IPv4, 30
broadcasting, 29, 30
BSD (Berkeley Software
Distribution)
history of IPv6 and KAME, 3–5
releases used in this book, 6
releases used in this book,
diagram of, 5
__bsdi__ macro, 16
BSD network implementation,
11–14
extension headers, IPv6, 11,
134–135
Fine Grained Locking system, 13
imp and net interrupt levels, 13
socket queue/buffer, 14
system call, 12
BSD networking stack, diagram
of, 12
buffers
memory, *see* memory buffers
(mbufs)
MLD query, 776–777
build procedures, 7–11
backup, 8
build kernel and kernel
modules, 9–10
installing FreeBSD, 7–8
installing startup scripts, 11
preparing source tree, 9
user space programs, 10–11

C

cached route, 237–239
CE (Congestion Experienced)
code point, 197
chains, mbuf, 17, 18, 19, 26–27,
248–251
diagrams of, 20, 21
checksum
algorithm, 617

differences between IPv4 and
IPv6, 134, 617–618
ICMPv6 value in messages,
299, 396, 397, 401,
402, 404
in6_cksum() function, 347,
484, 510, 535, 668, 670,
691, 717
pseudo header for IPv6,
616–617
TCP, 616, 668
UDP, 616
Classless Inter-Domain Routing
assignment rule, 40
cloning
route, 173, 212, 441, 443
RTF_CLONING flag, 331,
441–443, 446
close() system call, 706, 735
cluster, mbuf, 17
cmsg and sticky combinations,
812–813
code portability, 759, 760–762
: (colon)
encountered by
inet_pton() parser,
856–857, 859
notation for IPv6 addresses, 31
companion website, xxv, 7,
14, 15
comparison macros, address,
50–51
comparison state variables, source
address selection, 224
comp_dst() function, 886–888
configuration, address, *see* address
configuration, IPv6
configuration file, kernel, 9
connect() system call, 222, 627,
630, 639, 683, 705, 734
control input
rip6_ctlinput() function,
159, 724–725
tcp6_ctlinput() function,
159, 664, 675–679
udp6_ctlinput() function,
699–702
control message signaling,
in6_pcbnotify()
function, 655–659
converting
FQDN, 878–880
getaddrinfo() function,
753–757, 863–888
getnameinfo() function,
757–762, 853, 898–906

in6_control() function,
96–97
inet_ntop() function,
752–753, 853, 855,
859–863
inet_pton() function,
752–753, 853–859,
873, 874
IPv6 link-local address to
extended format,
877–878
NULL or numeric host names,
869–870
port numbers, 900
copy_ai() function, 889
CurHopLimit variable, 425, 433
CurHopLimit variable, host
operations, 424

D

DAD (Duplicate Address
Detection)
described, 75–76
in6if_do_dad() function,
94–95
nd6_dad_duplicated()
function, 598–599
nd6_dad_find()
function, 590
nd6_dad_na_input()
function, 601–602
nd6_dad_ns_input()
function, 600–601
nd6_dad_ns_output()
function, 599–600
nd6_dad_start() function,
591–594
nd6_dad_starttimer()
function, 590
nd6_dad_stop()
function, 594
nd6_dad_stoptimer()
function, 590–591
nd6_dad_timer() function,
594–598
queue entry, dadq{}
structure, 437–438, 593,
599
Stateless Address
Autoconfiguration,
415–416
dadq{} structure, 437–438,
593, 599
default interface, 542
default routers

Default Router List, 393, 399,
        402, 410, 425, 426,
        433–434
defrouter_addifreq()
        function, 542–544, 548
defrouter_addreq()
        function, 540–541, 550
defrouter_delifreq()
        function, 544–545,
        548, 549
defrouter_delreq()
        function, 541–542,
        550, 552
defrouter_lookup()
        function, 468, 545–546
defrouter_select()
        function, 469, 470, 540,
        546–550, 552, 555
defrtrlist_del()
        function, 475, 550–552,
        553, 611
defrtrlist_update()
        function, 517, 546,
        553–555
    management functions,
        540–555
    nd_defrouter{} structure,
        433–434, 435, 516,
        549, 556
    nd_defrouter{} structure,
        diagram of, 551
    selection, 426
    selection diagram, 551
DELAY_FIRST_PROBE_TIME
        variable, 439, 453
deleting addresses, 100–101,
        122–127
    in6_ifremloop() function,
        124–125
    in6_purgeaddr() function,
        101, 123–124
    in6_unlink_ifa()
        function, 125–127
deprecated address, 66, 413–414
dest6.c
    code listings, 185–187
    file location and description,
        150
dest6_input() function,
        185–187
destination address selection,
        148–149
Destination Cache, 411, 438
Destination options header, 137
    ip6_dest{} structure,
        153–154
    manipulation of, 774

    processing, dest6_input()
        function, 185–187
    processing unknown option,
        ip6_unknown_opt()
        function, 184–185
    specifying, 819–820
Destination Unreachable message,
        ICMPv6, 288, 289–292,
        307, 768
detached prefixes, 569–570
detach PCBs
    in6_pcbdetach() function,
        653–655
    rip6_detach() function,
        735–736
    udp6_detach() function,
        706
DHCPv6
    host configuration, 391–392
    KAME distribution, 6, 7
diagnosing, mbuf chains, 26–27
DIAGNOSTIC macro, 16
differentiated services codepoint
        (DSCP), 256
directories, KAME source tree
        structure, 7
    diagram, 8
DNS Security Extensions, 298
:: (double colon)
    encountered by parser,
        856–857, 859, 862
    notation for IPv6 addresses, 31
drafts, *see* Internet Drafts
DSCP (differentiated services
        codepoint), 256
Duplicate Address Detection,
        see DAD
duplicated address state, 413–414

E

Echo Reply message, ICMPv6, 288,
        294–295, 317–318
Echo Request message, ICMPv6,
        288, 294, 316–317
    diagram, 333
ECN (Explicit Congestion
        Notification), 197–198,
        202, 256
ellipsis in source code, 15
Encapsulating Security Payload
        header, 134, 135, 766, 846
error codes, 308, 320, 759
    gai_strerror() function,
        897–898
    getnameinfo() function,
        759

error messages, *see also* ICMPv6
    containing error packet, 339
    creation of, diagram, 340
    notifications and callback
        functions, 679, 726
    notifying errors,
        icmp6_notify_error()
        function, 320–329
    rate limited, 296, 341–342
errors
    cleanup on address
        configuration error, 114
    icmp6_error() function,
        266, 333–340
    notifying,
        icmp6_notify_error()
        function, 320–329
    sending error,
        icmp6_error()
        function, 333–340
etc/host.conf file, 879
etc/rc.conf file, 11, 146
/etc/rc.d directory, 146
etc/rc.network6 file, 11
Ethernet
    addresses, 41, 45, 389, 406
    address scopes, 37–38
    assumed interface, 17
    introduction, 12–13, 20
EUI-64 identifier, 42–43, 91, 127
Explicit Congestion Notification
        (ECN), 202, 256, *see* FQDN
explore_copy() function, 889
explore_null() function,
        871–872
explore_numeric() function,
        872–876
explore_numeric_scope()
        function, 872–876
extension headers, IPv6
    building, 244–251
    described, 11, 134–135
    Destination options header,
        137
    Fragment headers, 134,
        140–142
    Hop-by-Hop options
        header, 136
    ip6_output() function,
        242, 276
    MAKE_EXTHDR() macro, 244
    make using
        ip6_copyexthdr(),
        276–277
    manipulation of, 773–778
    mbufs, 17
    options, 142–144

order of, 135–136
Routing headers, 137–140
split using
`ip6_splithdr()`, 277

F

filtering, ICMPv6 message,
719–721, 767, 839
`find_pfxlist_reachable_router()`
function, 568
Fine Grained Locking system, 13
fix remote address
`in6_pcbconnect()`
function, 639–641
`rip6_connect()` function,
734–735
`udp6_connect()` function,
705–706
Flags field, IPv4 headers, 134
Flow Label field, IPv6 headers, 48,
132–133
flush cached route,
`in6_rtchange()`
function, 659–660
forwarding
diagram of, 35
`ip6_forward()` function,
209–218, 528
`ip6_forwarding` variable,
492, 522
packets, if not ours, 177–178
packets using link-local
addresses, 213, 214
point-to-point interface,
215–216
FQDN (fully qualified domain
name)
converting, `explore_fqdn()`
function, 878–880,
891, 892
converting, `getnameinfo()`
function, 757–759, 853,
898–906
described, 753
`NI_NOFQDN` flag, 758, 903
`frag6.c`
code listings, 190–204
file location and description,
150
`frag6_input()` function,
190–204
fragmentation
fragmentable part, 141
of outgoing packets, 269–275
of outgoing packets, whether
to, 266–268

overlapping fragment
attack, 199
send packets without, 268–269
specify sending packets
without, 822–823
unfragmentable part, 141
Fragment headers, 134, 140–142
insertion process, diagram
of, 274
`ip6_frag{}` structure,
156–157
`ip6_insertfraghdr()`
function, 281–282
processing, `frag6_input()`
function, 190–204
reassembly, 142
Fragment Offset field, IPv4
header, 134
Fragment Offset field, Fragment
header, 140
fragment reassembly
`frag6_input()` function,
190–204
fragmented packets, 187–204
Fragment headers, 142
maximun number of
fragments, 193
maximun number of
packets, 194
`freeaddrinfo()` function, 755,
895–897
FreeBSD
history of IPv6 and KAME, 4–6
KAME distribution, overview,
6–7
versions requiring updates to
run example, 332
FreeBSD 4.8-RELEASE, 7–8, 14
FreeBSD 4.8-RELEASE, diagram, 5
FreeBSD 4.9-RELEASE, 7
`freebsd4` directory, 7
`__FreeBSD__` macro, 16
freebsd.org, 8
Fujitsu, 6
fully qualified domain name,
see FQDN

G

`gai_strerror()` function,
897–898
garbage collection process, 451,
468, 473, 474, 499, 545, 608
`GENERIC.KAME` file, 9
`getaddrinfo.c`
code listings, 864–879,
881–888, 895, 897

file location and description,
853
`getaddrinfo()` function,
753–757, 863–888
`addrconfig()` function, 889
address ordering examples,
888–895
`afd{}` structure, 864
code portability, 759
`comp_dst()` function,
886–888
converting FQDN,
`explore_fqdn()`
function, 878–880,
891, 892
converting IPv6 link-local
address to extended
format, 877–878
converting NULL or numeric
host names, 869–870
`copy_ai()` function, 889
`explore_copy()`
function, 889
`explore_null()` function,
871–872
`explore_numeric()`
function, 872–876
`find_afd()` function, 889
flags, described, 754
`free_addrselectpolicy()`
function, 889
`gai_addr2scopetype()`
function, 889
`get_addrselectpolicy()`
function, 889
`get_ai()` function, 889
`get_canonname()`
function, 889
`get_port()` function, 889
`get_portmatch()`
function, 889
initialization, 866
`ip6_str2scopeid()`
function, 876–877
`match_addrselectpolicy()`
function, 889
overview, 864–865
parameters validation, 866–869
post process, 866
reorder `addrinfo{}` chain,
880–883
`reorder()` function, 883,
884–886, 891, 893
`get_ai()` function, 889
`get_canonname()` function, 889
`get_hw_ifid()` function, 89–92
`get_ifid()` function, 87–89

getnameinfo.c
  code listings, 898–906
  file location and description,
    853
getnameinfo() function,
  757–762, 853, 898–906
  considerations for special
    addresses, 901
  code portability, 759
  converting addresses, 902–904
  converting port number, 900
  described, 757–759
  extract port address, 899
  ip6_parsenumeric()
    function, 904–905
  ip6_sa2str() function,
    905–906
  NI_DGRAM flag, 758
  NI_NAMEREQD flag, 758
  NI_NOFQDN flag, 758, 903
  NI_NUMERICHOST flag, 758
  NI_NUMERICSERV flag, 758
  obsolete flag,
    NI_WITHSCOPEID, 757
  supported flags, 758
getpeername() system call,
  660, 778
get_port() function, 889
get_portmatch() function, 889
get_rand_ifid() function,
  93–94
getsockname() system call, 662
getsockopt() function, 760,
  771, 779, 783, 784, 790,
  801–805, 833
getsockopt() system calls, 783,
  790, 791, 833
global addresses, 33–34, 41–42
global ID, 40
global routing prefix, 42

H

hash tables, 620, 637, 641, 645
Hdr Ext Len field, IPv6 headers,
  136, 137, 138
Header Checksum field, IPv4
  headers, 134
header files, 10
Header Length (IHL) field, IPv4
  headers, 133
headers, ICMPv6, 308
headers, IPv6
  Address 1..N field, 138
  compared to IPv4 headers,
    133–134
  continuity and mbufs, 24–26

Destination Address field, 133
extension headers, *see*
  extension headers, IPv6
Flow Label field, 48, 132–133
format, 132–133
Fragment Offset field, 140
Hdr Ext Len field, 136, 137,
  138
Hop Limit field, 133, 616,
  668–669
Identification field, 140
ip6_dest{} structure,
  153–154
ip6_ext{} structure, 153
ip6_frag{} structure,
  156–157
ip6_hbh{} structure, 153–154
ip6_hdr{} structure, 151–152
ip6_opt_jumbo{} structure,
  154–155
ip6_opt_router{}
  structure, 155
ip6protosw{} structure,
  157–160, 663, 664, 685,
  686, 709, 710
ip6_rthdr0{} structure, 156
ip6_rthdr{} structure, 156
M bit field, 140
minimum length, 616
Next Header field, 133, 136,
  137, 138
Option Data field, 143
Option Data Length field, 143
Options field, 136, 137
Option Type field, 142
Payload Length field, 133
pseudo header, 616–617
Reserved field, 138, 140
Res field, 140
Routing Type field, 138
Segments Left field, 138
Source Address field, 133
Traffic Class field, 132
Type specific data field, 138
Version Field, 132
headers, TCP, 21, 666
  initializing, 669–670
Hitachi, 6
Hop-by-Hop options header, 136
  inserting using MAKE_CHAIN()
    macro, 248–250
  ip6_hbh{} structure, 153–154
  manipulation of, 774
  processing each option,
    ip6_process_hopopts()
    function, 180–184,
    265–266

processing,
    ip6_hopopts_input()
    function, 179–180
  processing, ip6_input()
    function, 174–177
  processing unknown option,
    ip6_unknown_opt()
    function, 184–185
  Router Alert option, 777
hop limit
  Hop Limit field, IPv6 headers,
    133, 616, 668–669
  IPV6_HOPLIMIT ancillary
    data item, 771, 782, 798
  IPV6_MULTICAST_HOPS
    socket option, 711, 763,
    780, 848
host names, *see also* FQDN
  converting, explore_fqdn()
    function, 878–880,
    891, 892
  converting, getaddrinfo()
    function, 753–757, 853,
    863–888
  explore_null() function,
    871–872
  explore_numeric()
    function, 872–876
  inet_pton() function,
    752–753, 853–859,
    873, 874
  NULL or numeric host names,
    869–870
hosts
  default router selection, 426
  processing Router
    Advertisements,
    425–426
  sending Router Solicitations,
    423–425
  variables and constants for
    ND-related operations,
    423, 424, 433
HTTP connection
  actively open, 755–756
  passively open, 756–757
Huston, Geoff, 2

I

IANA (Internet Assigned Number
    Authority), 44, 45, 47, 145,
    155, 420, 424
iana.org, 47
icmp6.c
  code listings, 310–331,
    334–348, 367–387,

521–536, 721–724,
838–839
file location and description,
426
icmp6_ctloutput() function,
838–840
icmp6_error() function, 266,
333–340
ICMP6_FILTER socket option,
719–720, 767, 780
icmp6_filter{} structure,
719–721, 767, 839
icmp6.h
code listings, 308, 428–429,
719–721
file location and description,
426
icmp6_hdr{} structure, 308,
427, 835
icmp6_mtudisc_update()
function, 329–332
icmp6_notify_error()
function, 320–329
icmp6_ratelimit() function,
341–342
icmp6_redirect_input()
function, 462, 521–528
icmp6_redirect_output()
function, 216, 218, 528–536
icmp6_reflect() function,
342–348
complete and send message,
346–348
initialize buffer and headers,
343–344
source address selection,
344–346
icmp6_rip6_input() function,
719–724
ICMPv6 (Internet Control Message
Protocol for IPv6)
checksum value in messages,
299, 396, 397, 401,
402, 404
compared to ICMPv4, 11–12
creation of error message,
diagram, 340
Destination Unreachable
message, 288, 289–292,
307, 768
Echo Reply message, 288,
294–295, 317–318
Echo Request message, 288,
294
Echo Request message
diagram, 333

error message containing error
packet, 339
filter specifications, 720
header, 308
header type and code field
values, 309
input processing, *see* input
processing, ICMPv6
introduction, 287–288
ip6ctlparam{} structure,
327, 328, 677, 701
IPv4 Addresses query, 304
message filtering, 719–721
message processing rules,
295–296
messages, described, 288
NI Query, *see* NI (Node
Information) Query
Node Addresses query,
303–304
Node Information message
format, 299–300
node information operation,
387–388
Node Name query, 301–302
NOOP query, 300
Packet Too Big message, 288,
291–292
Parameter Problem message,
288, 293
PMTU discovery
implementation,
329–332
PMTU discovery mechanism,
140, 296–297
pseudo header, 616–617
rate limited error messages,
296, 341–342
statistics, 304–307
Supported Qtypes query, 301,
362–365, 388
Time Exceeded message,
288, 292
Identification field, IPv4
headers, 134
Identification field, Fragment
header, 140
identifying addresses, 96–97
IETF (Internet Engineering Task
Force), 2, 4, 7
ifaddr{} structure, 64–67
ifconfig command
interface initialization, 76
route creation call graph,
441–442
using, 127–128
if_loop.c, code listings, 26

if_loop.h, 26
ifmcstat command, 129
if_var.h
code listings, 64
file location and description, 47
IGMP (Internet Group
Management Protocol) in
IPv4, 12
IHL (Header Length) field, IPv4
headers, 133
IIJ (Internet Initiative Japan), 6
imp interrupt level, BSD
networking, 13
in6_addmulti() function,
116–118
in6_addr2zoneid() function,
59–60
IN6ADDR_ANY_INIT macro, 50
IN6ADDR_INTFACELOCAL_ALLNODES_INIT
macro, 50
IN6ADDR_LINKLOCAL_ALLNODES_INIT
macro, 50
IN6ADDR_LINKLOCAL_ALLROUTERS_INIT
macro, 50
IN6ADDR_LOOPBACK_INIT
macro, 50
IN6ADDR_NODELOCAL_ALLNODES_INIT
macro, 50
in6_addrscope() function,
57–59, 60
in6_addr{} structure, 48
in6_aliasreq{} structure,
67–68, 95, 585
IN6_ARE_ADDR_EQUAL
macro, 51
in6.c
code listings, 15, 76–77, 94–126
file location and description, 47
in6_cksum() function, 347, 484,
510, 535, 668, 670, 691, 717
in6_clearscope() function,
62–63
in6_control() function,
95–101
in6_delmulti() function,
116–118
in6_embedscope() function,
60–61
in6.h
code listings, 48
file location and description, 47
in6_ifadd() function, 580–584
in6_ifaddloop() function,
120–122
in6_ifaddr{} structure,
64–67, 438

`in6ifa_ifpforlinklocal()`
function, 80, 86, 489,
531, 581
`in6ifa_ifpwithaddr()`
function, 80, 97, 488, 497,
584, 587
`in6_ifattach.c`
code listings, 78–94
file location and description, 47
`in6_ifattach()` function,
78–81
`in6_ifattach_linklocal()`
function, 82–87
`in6_ifattach_loopback()`
function, 81–82
`in6if_do_dad()` function,
94–95
`in6_ifinit()` function,
118–120
`in6_ifloop_request()`
function, 120–122
`in6_ifremloop()` function,
124–125
`in6_ifreq{}` structure,
67–68, 95
`in6_ifstat{}` structure,
151, 152
`in6_if_up()` function, 76–77
IN6_IS_ADDR_LINKLOCAL
macro, 764
IN6_IS_ADDR_LOOPBACK
macro, 51
IN6_IS_ADDR_MC_GLOBAL
macro, 764
IN6_IS_ADDR_MC_LINKLOCAL
macro, 764
IN6_IS_ADDR_MC_NODELOCAL
macro, 50, 764, 877
IN6_IS_ADDR_MC_ORGLOCAL
macro, 764
IN6_IS_ADDR_MC_SITELOCAL
macro, 764
IN6_IS_ADDR_MULTICAST
macro, 764
IN6_IS_ADDR_SITELOCAL
macro, 764
IN6_IS_ADDR_UNSPECIFIED
macro, 51
IN6_IS_ADDR_V4COMPAT
macro, 51
IN6_IS_ADDR_V4MAPPED
macro, 51
`in6_joingroup()` function,
115–116
`in6_leavegroup()` function,
115–116
IN6MASKxxx macros, 49

`in6_multi_mship{}` structure,
68–70
`in6_multi{}` structure, 68–70
`in6_pcbbind()` function,
630–639
`in6_pcb.c`
code listings, 630–634,
636–647, 650–663
file location and description,
619
`in6_pcbconnect()` function,
639–641
`in6_pcb.h`
code listings, 619–620
file location and description,
619
`in6_pcbladdr()` function,
642–644
`in6_pcblookup_hash()`
function, 650–651
`in6_pcblookup_local()`
function, 644–647
`in6_pcbnotify()` function,
655–659
`in6_purgeaddr()` function,
101, 123–124
`in6_recoverscope()` function,
61–62, 104
`in6_rtchange()` function,
659–660, 702
`in6_selecthlim()` function,
668
`in6_setpeeraddr()` function,
660–661
`in6_setsockaddr()` function,
662–663
`in6_src.c`
code listings, 60–63, 220–233
file location and description,
47, 150
`in6_tmpifadd()` function,
584–588, 592
`in6_unlink_ifa()` function,
125–127
`in6_update_ifa()` function,
101–114
`in6_var.h`
code listings, 16, 64–70, 220
file location and description,
47, 150
incoming packet options, 781
INET6 kernel configuration
option, 9, 16
`inet_ntop()` and
`inet_ntop6()` functions,
752–753, 853, 859–863

checking need for
compression, 863
copying addresses, 862
copying results, 863
finding longest zeros, 862
local variables, 862
`inet_ntop.c`, 14
code listings, 860–862
file location and description,
853
`inet_pton()` and
`inet_pton6()` functions,
752–753, 853–859, 873, 874
example, 857–859
handle colon, 856
handle hexadecimal string, 856
handle IPv4 address, 856–857
initial setup, 855–856
post process, 857
process last hexadecimal
value, 857
`inet_pton.c`
code listings, 853–855
file location and description,
853
initialization
buffer and headers,
`icmp6_reflect()`
function, 343–344
`in6_ifattach()` function,
78–81
`in6_ifattach_linklocal()`
function, 82–87
`in6_ifattach_loopback()`
function, 81–82
`in6_if_up()` function, 76–77
`init_ip6pktopts()`
function, 788–789
interface, *see* interface
initialization
`ip6_clearpktopts()`
function, 789–790
`ip6_ctloutput()` function,
790–791
`nd6_ifattach()` function,
440–441
`nd6_init()` function,
439–440
of scope zones, 52–53
`tcp6_usr_connect()`
function, 683–684
`tcp6_usr_listen()`
function, 685
TCP headers,
`tcp_fillheaders()`
function, 669–670

init_ip6pktopts() function, 788–789
INP_ANONPORT flag, 621
in_pcballoc() function, 627–630
in_pcb.c, 14
  code listings, 629, 648
  file location and description, 619
in_pcb.h
  code listings, 619, 620, 623–627
  file location and description, 619
in_pcblookup_hash() function, 651–653
in_pcblookup_local() function, 647–649
inpcb{} structure, 238, 618–627
INP_HDRINCL flag, 622
INP_HIGHPORT flag, 621
INP_LOWPORT flag, 621
INP_RECVDSTADDR flag, 622
INP_RECVIF flag, 622
INP_RECVOPTS flag, 622
INP_RECVRETOPTS flag, 622
input processing, ICMPv6
  copying Echo Request packet, 316–317
  described, 308–310
  diagram of, 311
  icmp6_input() function, 308, 310–320
  notifying errors, icmp6_notify_error() function, 320–329
input processing, IPv6
  call upper layer routines, 178–179
  check and fix mbuf assumptions, 166–168
  described, 164–165
  determine if packet is ours, 171–174
  forward if not our packet, 177–178
  hop-by-hop option processing, 174–177
  ip6_input() function, 164–179
  packet input/output flow diagram, 151
  validate packets, 168–171
INRIA (Institut National de Recherche en Informatique et Automatique), 3
inserting new addresses, 105–109
INSTALL file, 7, 8

Institut National de Recherche en Informatique et Automatique (INRIA), 3
interface address configuration
  in6_addmulti() function, 116–118
  in6_control function, 95–101
  in6_delmulti() function, 116–118
  in6_ifaddloop() function, 120–122
  in6_ifinit() function, 118–120
  in6_ifloop_request() function, 120–122
  in6_joingroup() function, 115–116
  in6_leavegroup() function, 115–116
  in6_update_ifa() function, 101–114
interface address structures
  ifaddr{} structure, 64–67
  in6_aliasreq{} structure, 67–68, 95, 585
  in6_ifaddr{} structure, 64–67, 438
  in6_ifreq{} structure, 67–68, 95
  multicast address structures, 68–70
  multicast address structures diagram, 71
interface identification, API, 749–750
interface identifier
  described, 29, 41
  generation, 42–43
interface index, 52–53, 54
interface initialization
  get_hw_ifid() function, 89–92
  get_ifid() function, 87–89
  get_rand_ifid() function, 93–94
  ifconfig command, 76
  in6_ifattach() function, 78–81
  in6_ifattach_linklocal() function, 82–87
  in6_ifattach_loopback() function, 81–82
  in6if_do_dad() function, 94–95
  in6_if_up() function, 76–77

interface-local multicast addresses, 33–34, 50
interface-local vs. node-local addresses, 50
Internet Assigned Number Authority (IANA), 44, 45, 47, 145, 155, 420, 424
Internet Control Message Protocol for IPv6, *see* ICMPv6
Internet Drafts
  draft-cmetz-v6ops-v4mapped-api-harmful-01, 618, 751
  draft-heffner-frag-harmful-01, 141
  draft-ietf-ipngwg-icmp-name-lookups-10, 349
  draft-ietf-ipngwg-icmp-name-lookups-12, 299, 301
  draft-ietf-ipngwg-icmp-name-lookups-13, 298
  draft-ietf-ipngwg-icmp-name-lookups-15, 297
  draft-ietf-ipngwg-icmp-v3-07, 290
  draft-ietf-ipv6–2461bis-07, 501, 542
  draft-ietf-ipv6-rfc2462bis-08, 416, 519, 633, 674
  draft-ietf-ipv6-privacy-addrs-v2-04, 419, 565, 566, 586
  draft-ietf-ipv6-unique-local-addr-08, 48
  draft-ietf-pim-sm-v2-new-12, 618
  draft-itojun-ipv6-tcp-to-anycast-01, 671
  draft-jabley-v6-anycast-clarify-00, 30
Internet Engineering Task Force (IETF), 2, 4, 7
Internet Group Management Protocol (IGMP) in IPv4, 12
Internet Initiative Japan (IIJ), 6
Internet Protocol version 4, *see* IPv4 (Internet Protocol version 4); IPv4
Internet Protocol version 6, *see* IPv6 (Internet Protocol version 6)
invalid address, 413–414
Inverse Neighbor Discovery Protocol, 437
ip6addrctl_enable configuration variable, 146

ip6addrctl utility, 145, 146, 221, 891, 895
ip6asfrag{} structure, 187
ip6aux{} structure, 23
ip6_clearpktopts() function, 789–790
ip6_copyexthdr() function, 276–277
ip6_ctloutput() function, 282, 790–805
   get operations, 801–805
   initialization, 790–791
   set operations, 791–800
ip6ctlparam{} structure, 327, 328, 677, 710
ip6_dest{} structure, 153–154
IP6_EXTHDR_CHECK() macro, 25, 27, 168, 485
ip6_ext{} structure, 153
ip6_forward.c
   code listings, 209–218
   file location and description, 150
ip6_forward() function, 209–218, 528
ip6_forwarding variable, 492, 522
ip6_frag{} structure, 156–157
ip6_freepcbopts() function, 823–824
ip6_getdstifaddr() function, 162
ip6_getpcbopt() function, 805–807
ip6_getpktaddrs() function, 164
ip6_getpmtu() function, 264–265, 282–285
ip6.h
   code listings, 25, 151–157
   file location and description, 150
ip6_hbh{} structure, 153–154
ip6_hdr{} structure, 151–152
ip6_hopopts_input() function, 179–180
ip6_input.c
   code listings, 162–185, 841–848
   file location and description, 150
ip6_input() function, 164–179, 308. *see also* input processing, ICMPv6; input processing, Ipv6
ip6_insertfraghdr() function, 281–282

ip6_insert_jumboopt() function, 278–280
ip6_mloopback() function, 285–286
ip6_opt_jumbo{} structure, 154–155
ip6_opt_router{} structure, 155
ip6_output.c
   code listings, 179–180, 235–286, 788–838
   file location and description, 14, 150
ip6_output() function, 219–220
ip6_parsenumeric() function, 904–906
ip6_pcbopt() function, 796, 809–810
ip6_pcbopts() function, 808–809
ip6_pktopts{} structure, 219, 786–790
IP6PO_TEMPADDR_NOTPREFER flag, 231
IP6PO_TEMPADDR_PREFER flag, 231
IP6PO_TEMPADDR_SYSTEM flag, 231
ip6_process_hopopts() function, 180–184, 265–266
ip6protosw.h
   code listings, 157–158, 328
   file location and description, 150
ip6protosw{} structure, 157–160, 663, 664, 685, 709, 710
ip6q{} structure, 187–190, 194
ip6_raw_ctloutput() function, 835–838
ip6_rthdr0{} structure, 156
ip6_rthdr{} structure, 156
ip6_sa2str() function, 905–906
ip6_savecontrol() function, 840–848
ip6_selectroute() function, 234–242
ip6_setdstifaddr() function, 162
ip6_setpktaddrs() function, 163
ip6_setpktoptions() function, 810–812, 849
ip6s_exthdrtoolong variable, 27

ip6_splithdr() function, 277
ip6_unknown_opt() function, 184–185
ip6_var.h
   code listings, 187–188, 786–788, 824, 840
   file location and description, 150
IPng (Next Generation IP), 2
IPsec protocol, 134, 258, 559
IPv4 (Internet Protocol version 4), *see also* IPv4-mapped IPv6 addresses
   addressing architecture, compared to IPv6, 29
   address structures, 48–49
   BSD network implementation, 11–12, 24
   checksum algorithm, 617
   checksum differences between IPv6 and, 134, 617–618
   communication over AF_INET6 socket, 750–752
   headers, compared to IPv6, 133–134
   history of, 1–4
   ICMPv4, 11–12
   IPv4-compatible IPv6 addresses, 32
   TCP processing, 663
   TTL field, 616
IPv4 Addresses query, 304
IPv4-mapped IPv6 addresses
   binding UDP sockets, 738–740
   described, 32
   receive and demultiplex UDP packets, 741–742
   search for, in_pcblookup_local() function, 647–649
   security concerns, 32, 683, 751
   TCP-over-IPv6, 663
   transmitting UDP packets, 740–741
   usage, 618
IPv6 (Internet Protocol version 6), *see also* IPv4-mapped IPv6 addresses
   checksum algorithm, 617
   checksum differences between IPv4 and, 134, 617–618
   headers, *see* headers, IPv6
   input processing, *see* input processing, IPv6
   introduction, 131–132

output processing, *see* output processing, IPv6
statistics, 151, 152, 153
IPV6_ADDR_INTxxx macros, 49
IPV6_ADDR_SCOPE_xxx macros, 51, 57
IPV6_AUTOFLOWLABEL socket option, 622
IPV6_CHECKSUM raw socket option, 624, 767, 780
IPV6_DONTFRAG socket option, 267, 268, 779, 783, 823
IPV6_DSTOPTS socket option, 771, 782, 849
IPV6_HOPLIMIT ancillary data item, 771, 782, 798
IPV6_HOPOPTS socket option, 771, 782, 848
IPV6_MULTICAST_HOPS socket option, 711, 763, 780, 848
IPV6_MULTICAST_IF socket option, 236, 751, 763, 782
IPV6_MULTICAST_IF socket option, 751, 763, 780, 829
IPV6_MULTICAST_LOOP socket option, 763, 780
IPV6_NEXTHOP socket option, 771, 772, 782
IPV6_PATHMTU socket option, 268, 779, 783
IPV6_PKTINFO socket option, 235, 771, 772, 774, 781, 852
IPV6_PREFER_TEMPADDR socket option, 231, 782, 813, 823
IPV6_REACHCONF socket option, 264, 822
IPV6_RECVDSTOPTS socket options, 622, 772, 781
IPV6_RECVHOPLIMIT socket option, 622, 772, 781
IPV6_RECVHOPOPTS socket option, 662, 772, 781, 854
IPV6_RECVPATHMTU socket option, 622, 659, 779, 783, 796
IPV6_RECVPKTINFO socket option, 622, 722, 781, 854
IPV6_RECVRTHDRDSTOPTS socket option, 622, 781
IPV6_RECVRTHDR socket option, 622, 772, 781, 854
IPV6_RECVTCLASS socket option, 622, 772, 781
IPV6_RTHDR socket option, 771, 782, 852

IPV6_TCLASS socket option, 771, 782, 848, 849
IPV6_UNICAST_HOPS socket option, 668, 760, 771, 780, 793, 802
IPV6_USE_MIN_MTU socket option, 779, 783, 822
IPV6_V6ONLY socket option, 622, 757
ISC (Internet Systems Consortium), 6
IsRouter flag, 410, 430, 459, 460, 504

J

joining multicast groups
in6_joingroup() function, 115–116
in6_update_ifa() function, 109–114
Jumbo Payload option
ip6_insert_jumboopt() function, 278–280
ip6_opt_jumbo{} structure, 154–155
usage warning, 183, 269
Juniper Networks, 6

K

KAME
commercial success of, 6
history of IPv6 and, 1–6
project, 3
KAME distribution, 6–11
build procedure, 7–11
diagram of source tree structure, 8
snapshots used in this book, 6–7
snapshots used in this book, diagram of, 5
source tree structure, 7
${KAME} notation, 7
kernel
build procedure, 9–10
configuration file, 9
function call graphs, 784–786
options, 9
kernel implementation of IPv6 APIs
cleaning up, ip6_freepcbopts() function, 823–824
code introduction, 783–786

delivering incoming information, ip6_savecontrol() function, 840–848
getting socket options, ip6_getpcbopt() function, 805–807
icmp6_ctloutput() function, 838–840
init_ip6pktopts() function, 788–789
ip6_clearpktopts() function, 789–790
ip6_pktopts{} structure, 786–790
multicast socket options, 824–834
raw socket options, ip6_raw_ctloutput() function, 835–838
setting socket options and ancillary data, 807–823
socket option processing, ip6_ctloutput() function, 282, 790–805

L

label value, address selection, 145
LACNIC (Latin American and Caribbean IP address Regional Registry), 47
leaving multicast groups
in6_leavegroup() function, 115–116
IPV6_LEAVE_GROUP socket option, 762, 780
libinet6 library, 853
additional library functions, 906–907
licenses, software, 6
lifetime
preferred, 66, 413–414
of temporary addresses, 417–419
two-hour rule, 417
valid, 66, 413–414
Link-Layer Address options, 405–406
Source Link-Layer Address option, 397, 398, 401, 405–406, 410, 412, 427, 485, 510, 539
Target Link-Layer Address option, 403, 404, 405–406, 408, 427, 488, 490, 498, 504

link-local addresses, 33–34, 41, 46, 50
  diagram of forwarding, 35
  forwarding, 213, 214
LinkMTU variable, 424, 425, 433
listen() system call, 685
llinfo_nd6{} structure, Neighbor Cache, 429–432
loopback addresses, IPv6, 31–32, 50
loopback interface
  IN6ADDR_LOOPBACK_INIT macro, 50
  in6_ifaddloop() function, 120–122
  in6_ifattach_loopback() function, 81–82
  in6_ifloop_request() function, 120–122
  in6_ifremloop() function, 124–125
  IN6_IS_ADDR_LOOPBACK macro, 51
  loopback addresses, IPv6, 31–32, 50
  looutput() function, 25–26, 259, 611
  multicast loopback, ip6_mloopback() function, 285–286
looutput() function, 26, 259, 611

M

MAC-48 hardware interface address, 42–43
macros, assumed values in kernel, 16, *see also specific macros*
MADCAP protocol, 45
MAKE_CHAIN() macro, 248–250
Management Information Base objects, *see* MIB (Management Information Base) objects
manipulation routines, address, 73–76
masking addresses, macros and variables for, 49
MAX_ANYCAST_DELAY_TIME constant, 439, 504
MAX_FINAL_RTR_ADVERTISEMENTS constant, 421, 422
MAX_INITIAL_RTR_ADVERT_INTERVAL constant, 421, 422
MAX_INITIAL_RTR_ADVERTISEMENTS constant, 421, 422

MAX_MULTICAST_SOLICIT constant, 439, 453
MAX_NEIGHBOR_ADVERTISEMENT constant, 439, 504
MAX_RA_DELAY_TIME constant, 421, 423
MAX_RANDOM_FACTOR constant, 424, 439
MaxRtrAdvInterval constant, 419, 420, 422
MAX_RTR_SOLICITATION_DELAY constant, 424, 425, 596
MAX_RTR_SOLICITATIONS constant, 424
MAX_UNICAST_SOLICIT constant, 439, 454
mbuf.h
  code listings, 18–19, 21
  file location, 18
mbufs, *see* memory buffers (mbufs)
MCLGET macro, 22
m_data field, 19, 22
M_DONTWAIT value, 22
memory buffers (mbufs)
  adjustment macros, 22
  allocation macros, 22
  chains, 17, 19, 248–251
  check and fix mbuf assumptions, 166–168
  diagnosing chains, 26–27
  diagram of chains, 18, 20, 21
  diagram of TCP packets, 21
  diagram of UDP packets, 18, 20
  header continuity, 24–26
  ip6_getdstifaddr() function, 162
  ip6_getpktaddrs() function, 164
  ip6_setdstifaddr() function, 162
  mbuf cluster, 17
  mbuf.h, 18–19, 21
  packet address information in, 160–163
  release macros, 23
  requirement for IPv6, 24–26
  tagging, 20–24
  tags (mtags), 20
  TCP packets, 20
  UDP packets, 17, 19
M_EXT flag, 19, 22
M field, Fragment header, 140
m_flags field, 19, 20
m_freem() function, 23
MGETHDR macro, 22
MGET macro, 22

m_hdr structure, 19–20
MIB (Management Information Base) objects
  ICMPv6, 304–306
  IPv6, 151
Microsoft Windows XP, 4
MIN_DELAY_BETWEEN_RAS constant, 421, 423
MIN_RANDOM_FACTOR constant, 424, 439
MinRtrAdvInterval constant, 419, 422
MIP6_HOME_AGENT kernel configuration, 9, 16
MIP6 kernel option, 9, 16
MIP6_MOBILE_NODE kernel configuration, 9, 16
MLD (Multicast Listener Discovery), 12, 69–70, 76, 155, 305–307, 766
  query, 774, 776
m_len field, 19, 22
M_LOOP flag, 19
m_next field, 19, 23
Mobile IPv6, 6, 7, 9, 11
modifiable option type, IPv6 options, 143
m_pktdat field, 20
M_PKTHDR flag, 19, 22
M_PREPEND() macro, 22
m_pullup() function (IPv4), 24
m_pullup() macro, 22, 24
m_tag_len field, 23, 24
m_tag_link field, 22
m_tag{} structure, 21–22, 24, 160–164
  diagram, 23
MTU
  minimum, 78, 822
  TCP output, 665–666
  UDP output, 700
  values, ip6_ctloutput() function, 282, 790–805
MTU option, ND Protocol messages, 405, 407–408
multicast addresses, IPv6
  all-nodes, 46, 50
  all-routers, 46
  described, 30
  flags field, 44
  format, 44–46
  group ID, 44–45
  in6_multi{} and in6_multi_mship{}, 68–70
  interface-local, 33–34, 50

joining multicast groups,
    109–114, 115–116
network prefix field, 44
permanent, 45
plen field, 44
processing, multicast-specific,
    261–263
related structures, diagram
    of, 71
reserved field, 44
scope field, 44
solicited-node, 46, 401
multicast groups
    IPV6_MULTICAST_HOPS
        socket option, 711, 763,
        780, 848
    IPV6_MULTICAST_IF socket
        option, 751, 763, 780,
        829
    IPV6_MULTICAST_LOOP
        socket option, 763, 780
    joining, in6_joingroup()
        function, 115–116
    joining, in6_update_ifa()
        function, 109–114
    joining, IPV6_JOIN_GROUP
        socket option, 762
    joining when using
        IPv4-mapped IPv6
        addresses, 742
    leaving, in6_leavegroup()
        function, 115–116
    leaving, IPV6_LEAVE_GROUP
        socket option, 762, 780
Multicast Listener Discovery
    (MLD), 69–70, 76, 155,
    305–307, 766
    query, 774, 776
multicast loopback,
    ip6_mloopback()
    function, 285–286
multi-path routing, 545
M_WAIT value, 22

N

NAPT (Network Address and Port
    Translator), 2
NAT (Network Address
    Translator), 2
nd6.c
    code listings, 439–440,
        444–452, 454–457,
        461–478, 536–540, 546,
        588–589, 602–610,
        611–613

file location and description,
    426
nd6_cache_lladdr() function,
    452–463, 465, 492, 513,
    520, 527
nd6_dad_duplicated()
    function, 598–599
nd6_dad_find() function, 590
nd6_dad_na_input() function,
    601–602
nd6_dad_ns_input() function,
    491, 600–601
nd6_dad_ns_output()
    function, 599–600
nd6_dad_start() function,
    591–594
nd6_dad_starttimer()
    function, 590
nd6_dad_stop() function, 594
nd6_dad_stoptimer()
    function, 590–591
nd6_dad_timer() function,
    594–598
nd6_free() function, 467–470,
    473, 475, 545, 611
nd6.h
    code listings, 429, 432–437
    file location and description,
        426
nd6_init() function, 439–440
nd6_is_addr_neighbor()
    function, 602–604, 607
nd6log() function, 105, 320,
    490, 513, 524
nd6_lookup() function, 446,
    455, 456, 463–467, 498,
    533, 604, 607
nd6_na_input() function,
    493–504, 546, 611
    diagram, 443
nd6_na_output() function,
    492, 504–510
nd6_nbr.c
    code listings, 437–438,
        478–500, 503–510,
        590–602
    file location and description,
        426
nd6_ns_input() function,
    484–493
nd6_ns_output() function,
    474, 478–484, 602
nd6_option() function, 437,
    536–538, 539
nd6_option_init() function,
    487, 526, 536

nd6_options() function, 487,
    526, 538–540
nd6_output() function, 217,
    218, 447, 604–611
nd6_prefix_offlink()
    function, 578–580
nd6_prefix_onlink()
    function, 443, 575–578
nd6_prelist_add() function,
    443, 555–557
nd6_ra_input() function,
    513–521, 558, 562
nd6_rs_input() function,
    510–521
nd6_rtmsg() function, 612–613
nd6_rtr.c
    code listings, 510–521,
        540–545, 547–568,
        571–587, 591
    file location and description,
        426
nd6_rtrequest() function, 66,
    120, 121, 441–452, 578
nd6_timer() function, 470–478,
    557, 588, 610
nd_defrouter{} structure,
    433–434, 435, 516, 549, 556
    diagram, 551
nd_ifinfo{} structure, 432–433,
    440, 473, 475
nd_opt{} structure, 436–437
ndp command, 445, 515
    example, using, 128, 130
    -I option, 542, 582
    Neighbor Cache entries,
        432, 441
    setting flags using, 232
nd_prefixctl{} structure, 86,
    436, 519, 556
nd_prefix{} structure, 72,
    434–436, 555
NDPRF_DETACHED flag, 435
NDPRF_HOME flag, 435
NDPRF_ONLINK flag, 435
ND (Neighbor Discovery) protocol
    DAD queue entry, dadq{}
        structure, 437–438,
        593, 599
    default routers, *see* default
        routers
    Destination Cache, 411, 438
    example exchanges, 393–395
    file location and description,
        426
    icmp6_redirect_input()
        function, 462, 521–528

icmp6_redirect_output() function, 216, 218, 528–536
initialization functions, 439–441
IsRouter flag, 410, 430, 459, 460, 504
message definitions, 427–429
message options, nd_opt{} structure, 436–437
messages, described, 392–393
MTU option, 405, 407–408
nd6_ifattach() function, 440–441
nd6_init() function, 439–440
nd6_is_addr_neighbor() function, 602–604, 607
nd6_na_output() function, 492, 504–510
nd6_ns_input() function, 484–493
nd6_ns_output() function, 474, 478–484, 602
nd6_option() function, 437, 536–538, 539
nd6_option_init() function, 487, 526, 536
nd6_options() function, 487, 526, 538–540
nd6_output() function, 217, 447, 604–611
nd6_ra_input() function, 513–521, 558, 562
nd6_rs_input() function, 510–521
nd6_rtmsg() function, 612–613
Neighbor Advertisement messages, 392, 393, 402–403
Neighbor Cache entry, 410, 429–432
Neighbor Cache, llinfo_nd6{} structure, 429–432
Neighbor Solicitation messages, 392, 393, 401
next-hop determination and address resolution, 390, 410–411
NUD algorithm, 391, 411–412
on-link assumption for routing, 542, 547
operational variables, nd_ifinfo{} structure, 432–433, 440, 473, 475

operation constants, 438–439
options processing functions, 536–540
option types and formats, 405–410
overview, 390–391
packet types and formats, 395–404
prefix control, nd_prefixctl{} structure, 86, 436, 519, 556
Prefix Information option, 405, 406–407
Redirected Header option, 405, 407
Redirect messages, 392, 393, 403–404
Route Information option, 405, 408–410
Router Advertisement messages, 397–401
Router Solicitation messages, 392, 393, 396–397
rt6_flush() function, 552, 611–612
Source Link-Layer Address option, 405–406
target address validation, 488
Target Link-Layer Address option, 403, 404, 405–406, 408, 427, 488, 490, 498, 504
TLV format, 405
Neighbor Advertisement messages, 392, 393, 402–403
IsRouter flag, 410, 430, 459, 460, 504
nd6_na_input() function, 443, 493–504, 546, 611
nd6_na_output() function, 492, 504–510
Neighbor Cache state transition diagram, 502
Override flag, 404, 490, 492, 495, 501–502, 504–505
Solicited flag, 402, 492, 493, 501–502, 504, 505
Neighbor Cache entry, described, 410
llinfo_nd6{} structure, 429–432
state transition diagram, 502
Neighbor Cache management functions

nd6_cache_lladdr() function, 452–463, 465, 492, 513, 520, 527
nd6_free() function, 467–470, 473, 475, 545, 611
nd6_lookup() function, 446, 455, 456, 463–467, 498, 533, 604, 607
nd6_rtrequest() function, 66, 120, 121, 441–452, 578
nd6_timer() function, 470–478, 557, 588, 610
Neighbor Discovery protocol, *see* ND (Neighbor Discovery) protocol
Neighbor Solicitation messages, 392, 393, 401
nd6_ns_input() function, 484–493
nd6_ns_output() function, 474, 478–484, 602
NetBSD, KAME distribution, 6–7
__NetBSD__ macro, 16
netdb.h, 758
code listings, 753–755, 757
net/if.h
code listings, 749
file location and description, 68
netinet/in.h, 760, 764, 772
code listings, 762, 772–774
net interrupt level, BSD networking, 13
netstat command, 167, 450
-an option, 743, 744, 745
-Iifname-s option, 151, 153, 304, 307
-rn -f inet6, 543, 606
-rn -f inet6 option, 129, 130
-r option, 444
-s -p ip6 option, 27, 168, 233–234
statistics, ICMPv6, 304, 307
viewing IPv6 connections, 743–747
Network Address and Port Translator, *see* NAPT (Network Address and Port Translator)
Network Address and Port Translator (NAPT), 2
Network Address Translator, *see* NAT; NAT (Network Address Translator)

networking device and
architecture
assumptions, 17
Network Time Protocol (NTP)
servers, 45
NEW_STRUCT_ROUTE kernel
configuration option, 16
Next Header field, IPv6 headers,
133, 136, 137, 138
next hop
address, specifying, 817–819
determination and address
resolution, 390, 410–411
IPV6_NEXTHOP socket
option, 771, 772, 782
ni6_dnsmatch() function, 372,
376, 379
ni6_input() function, 367–375
ni6_nametodns() function,
372, 375, 376
ni6_store_addrs() function,
383–387
NI_DGRAM flag, 758
NI (Node Information) Group
Address, 298
calculate, nigroup()
function, 352–353
nigroup() function, 352–353
NI_NAMEREQD flag, 758
NI_NOFQDN flag, 758, 903
NI_NUMERICHOST flag, 758
NI_NUMERICSERV flag, 758
NI (Node Information) Query
calculate packet size for query,
pingerlen()
function, 353–354
calculating number of
addresses for reply,
381–383
create reply,
ni6_store_addrs()
function, 383–387
described, 297–299
Destination address, 369
IPv4 Addresses query, 304
message format, 299–300
Node Addresses query,
303–304
node information operation,
387–388
node name manipulation,
376–383
Node Name query, 301–302
NOOP query, 300
print node addresses, **ping6**
command, 365–366

print Supported Qtypes, **ping6**
command, 362–365
processing, types and variables,
348–350
query processing,
ni6_input()
function, 367–375
receive replies, **ping6**
command, 355–361
reply, ni6_store_addrs()
function, 383–387
send queries, **ping6**
command, 350–355
Supported Qtypes query,
301, 388
node addresses
printing, pr_nodeaddr()
function, 365–366
requirements, 46–47
Node Addresses query
described, 303–304
flags, 351
reply, calculating number of
addresses, 381–383
reply, ni6_store_addrs()
function, 383–387
sending, 350
Node Information Group Address,
see NI (Node Information)
Group Address
Node Information Query, *see* NI
(Node Information) Query
node-local vs. interface-local
addresses, 50
node name manipulation, 376–383
Node Name query, 301–302, 388
NOOP query, 300
Not-ECT (ECN-Capable Transport)
code point, 197
notification commands, 656, 658,
676, 678
notifications and callback
functions, 726
NRL (Naval Research
Laboratory), 3
NUD (Neighbor Unreachability
Detection) algorithm, 391,
411–412
NULL host names, converting,
869–870
numeric host names, converting,
869–870

O

off-link prefix, 578–580
on-link prefixes, 72, 406–407,
568–570

assumption, 542, 547
nd6_prefix_onlink()
function, 443, 575–578
pfxlist_onlink_check()
function, 469, 470,
571–575, 587
OpenBSD, KAME distribution, 6–7
__OpenBSD__ macro, 16
open source software, 6
Option Data field, IPv6
options, 143
Option Data Length field, IPv6
options, 143
Options field, IPv6 options,
136, 137
options, ND protocol
nd6_option() function, 437,
536–538, 539
nd6_option_init()
function, 487, 526, 536
nd6_options() function,
487, 526, 538–540
Option Type field, IPv6
options, 142
originating interface, 259, 263, 610
OUI (Organizationally Unique
Identifier), 42
outbound packet options, 781–782
outgoing interface pointer,
243, 263
output processing, ICMPv6
build and send errors, 338–340
complete and send message,
346–348
described, 332–333
error rate limitation,
icmp6_ratelimit()
function, 341–342
icmp6_reflect() function,
342–348
initialize buffer and headers,
343–344
output path, 333
output path diagram, 334
send errors, icmp6_error()
function, 266, 333–340
source address selection,
344–346
whether to generate errors,
336–338
output processing, IPv6
address selection policy
structure, 219–221
build extension headers,
244–251
cleanup, 275–276
clear scope zone IDs, 265

fill in IPv6 header and
determine route,
255–261

fragmentation,
`ip6_insertfraghdr()`
function, 281–282

fragment packets, 269–275

fragment packets, whether to,
266–268

insert Jumbo Payload option,
`ip6_insert_jumboopt()`
function, 278–280

`ip6_output()` function,
219–220

`ip6_pktopts{}` structure,
219

make extension headers,
`ip6_copyexthdr()`
function, 276–277

multicast loopback,
`ip6_mloopback()`
function, 285–286

multicast-specific, 261–263

packet input/output flow
diagram, 151

packet options, 219

Path MTU determination,
`ip6_getpmtu()`
function, 264–265,
282–285

process Hop-by-Hop options
header, 180–184,
265–266

reachability confirmation via
API, 263–264

route selection,
`ip6_selectroute()`
function, 234–242

routing header processing,
252–255

saving outgoing interface for
caller, 263

send packets without
fragmentation, 268–269

source address selection,
`in6_selectsrc()`
function, 219, 221–234,
508

split headers,
`ip6_splithdr()`
function, 277

unreachable destination, 226

overlapping fragment attack, 199

Override flag, 404, 490, 492, 495,
501–502, 504–505

P

packets, IPv6
address information in mbuf,
160–164
forwarding, `ip6_forward()`
function, 209–218
forwarding using link-local
addresses, 213, 214
forwarding using link-local
addresses, diagram
of, 35
fragmentable part, 141
incoming packet options, 781
input processing,
`ip6_input()`
function, 164–179
`ip6_getdstifaddr()`
function, 162
`ip6_getpktaddrs()`
function, 164
`ip6_setdstifaddr()`
function, 162
`ip6_setpktaddrs()`
function, 163
IPV6_DSTOPTS socket
option, 771, 782, 849
IPV6_HOPLIMIT ancillary
data item, 771, 782, 798
IPV6_HOPOPTS socket
option, 771, 782, 848
IPV6_NEXTHOP socket
option, 771, 772, 782
IPV6_PKTINFO socket
option, 235, 771, 772,
774,
781, 852
IPV6_RTHDR socket option,
771, 782, 852
IPV6_TCLASS socket option,
771, 782, 848, 849
`m_tag{}` structure, 21–22, 24,
160–164
`m_tag{}` structure diagram, 23
outbound packet options,
781–782
processing flow, 150–151
processing flow diagram, 151
reassembling, `ip6asfrag{}`
structure for, 187–190
reassembling, `ip6q{}`
structure for, 187–190,
194
receive information, 772–773

send information, 771–772
set packet information,
814–815
specify sending with minimum
MTU, 822
specify sending without
fragmentation, 822–823
sticky options, 771
TCP packets, 20
TCP packets, diagram of, 21
UDP packets, 17, 19
UDP packets, diagram of,
18, 20
PACKET_TAG_ESP identifier, 23
PACKET_TAG_INET6 identifier,
23, 166
Packet Too Big message, ICMPv6,
288, 291–292
parameter discovery, ND
protocol, 390
Parameter Problem message,
ICMPv6, 288, 293
parsing
`inet_pton()` function,
857–859
`ip6_parsenumeric()`
function, 904–906
ND options, 538–540
Path MTU (PMTU), 779, 783
APIs, 778, 779
Destination Cache entry, 438
determination,
`ip6_getpmtu()`
function, 264–265,
282–285
determining, 264–265
discovery, ICMPv6, 140,
296–297
discovery implementation,
ICMPv6, 329–332
example, using **ping6**
command, 332, 333
`icmp6_mtudisc_update()`
function, 329–332
IPV6_DONTFRAG socket
option, 267, 268, 779,
783, 823
IPV6_PATHMTU socket
option, 268, 783
IPV6_RECVPATHMTU socket
option, 622, 659, 779,
783, 796
IPV6_USE_MIN_MTU socket
option, 779, 783, 822
specify sending packets with
minimum MTU, 822

TCP output adjustments for, 666

ÚDP output, 700

PATH shell script variable, 11

Payload Length field, IPv6 headers, 133

PCBs (Protocol Control Blocks), 618–627

allocation, in_pcballoc() function, 627–630

attach, rip6_attach() function, 730–732, 839

attach, tcp_attach() function, 680–681

attach, udp_attach() function, 702–704

bind local addresses, in6_pcbbind() function, 630–639

chaining diagram, 621

control message signaling, in6_pcbnotify() function, 655–659

detach, in6_pcbdetach() function, 653–655

detach, rip6_detach() function, 735–736

detach, udp6_detach() function, 706

fix remote address, in6_pcbconnect() function, 639–641

flag macros, 622

flush cached route, in6_rtchange() function, 659–660

in6_pcbbind() function, 630–639

in6_pcbladdr() function, 642–644

in6_pcblookup_hash() function, 650–651

in6_pcblookup_local() function, 644–647

in6_pcbnotify() function, 655–659

in_pcballoc() function, 627–630

in_pcblookup_hash() function, 651–653

in_pcblookup_local() function, 647–649

retrieve local address, in6_setsockaddr() function, 662–663

retrieve peer address, in6_setpeeraddr() function, 660–661

search for entry, in6_pcblookup_hash() function, 650–651

search for entry, in6_pcblookup_local() function, 644–647

search for IPv4-mapped PCB, in_pcblookup_hash() function, 651–653

search for IPv4-mapped PCB, in_pcblookup_local() function, 647–649

pfxlist_onlink_check() function, 469, 470, 571–575, 587

pim6sd daemon, 774

ping6.c, code listings, 350–366

ping6 command
example, using, 332, 443
option flags, 350
print node addresses, 365–366
print Supported Qtypes, 362–365
receive replies, 355–361
send queries, 350–355

pingerlen() function, 353–354

pkthdr{} structure, 21

__P() macro, 16–17

PMTU (Path MTU), *see* Path MTU

policy table, address selection, 145, 219–221

port addresses, extracting, 899

port numbers, 627, 637
converting, 900

port theft, 635, 638

PRC (protocol independent control command), 308, 310

PRC_HOSTDEAD notification, 656, 679, 702, 726

PRC_IFDOWN notification, 679, 702, 726

PRC_IFUP notification, 679, 702, 726

PRC_MSGSIZE notification, 656, 679, 702, 726

PRC_PARAMPROB notification, 656, 679, 702, 726

PRC_REDIRECT_HOST notification, 656, 679, 702

PRC_TIMXCEED_INTRANS notification, 656

PRC_TIMXCEED_REASS notification, 656

PRC_UNREACH_HOST notification, 656, 679, 726

PRC_UNREACH_NET notification, 656, 679, 702, 726

PRC_UNREACH_PORT in6 notification, 726

PRC_UNREACH_PORT notification, 656, 679, 702

PRC_UNREACH_PROTOCOL notification, 656, 679, 702, 726

PRC_UNREACH_SRCFAIL notification, 656, 679, 702, 726

precedence value, address selection, 145

preference, router, 400–410, 408–412, 426

preference rules
destination address selection, 148–149
source address selection, 146–148

preferred address, 413–414

preferred lifetime, 66, 413–414

prefix(es)
attached/detached, 569–570
control, nd_prefixctl{} structure, 86, 436, 519, 556
discovery, ND protocol, 390
global routing prefix, 42
IPv6 prefix structure, 70–73
nd_prefix{} structure, 72, 434–436, 555
on-link condition, 72, 406–407, 568–570
subnet prefix, 41

Prefix Information option, 405, 406–407

prefix management functions
find_pfxlist_reachable_router() function, 568
nd6_prefix_offlink() function, 578–580
nd6_prefix_onlink() function, 443, 575–578
nd6_prelist_add() function, 443, 555–557
pfxlist_onlink_check() function, 469, 470, 571–575, 587
prelist_remove() function, 101, 126, 478, 557–558

`prelist_update()`
        function, 519, 558–567,
        584, 587
prefix structure, `nd_prefix{}`
        structure, 72, 434–436, 555
`prelist_remove()` function,
        101, 126, 478, 557–558
`prelist_update()` function,
        519, 558–567, 584, 587
preprocessed variables, 16–17
`pr_flags`, 158, 159
printable strings, coverting from
        addresses to, 752–753
printing Supported Qtypes,
        `pr_suptypes()` function,
        362–365
privacy extensions, 417–419
`pr_nodeaddr()` function,
        365–366
probably reachable routers, 547
Protocol Control Blocks, *see* PCBs
        (Protocol Control Blocks)
protocol independent control
        command (PRC), 308, 310
protocol switch table, 157–160
`pr_suptypes()` function,
        362–365
`pr_usrreqs{}` structure, 678,
        679, 702, 703, 730
`pseudo-device hif` kernel
        configuration option, 9
pseudo headers, 616–617
public addresses vs. temporary
        addresses, 147, 231
`PULLDOWN_TEST` kernel
        configuration option, 16

Q

Qtype field
        in NI message format, 299, 300
        values, 349
query, *see* NI (Node Information)
        Query

R

RA messages, *see* Router
        Advertisement (RA)
        messages
rate limited ICMPv6 error
        messages, 296, 341–342
`raw_ip6.c`
        code listings, 711–718, 725–737
        file location and description,
        619

`raw_ip6.h`
        code listings, 709
        file location and description,
        619
Raw IPv6
        attach PCBs, `rip6_attach()`
                function, 730–732, 839
        bind local addresses,
                `rip6_bind()`
                function, 732–734
        control input,
                `rip6_ctlinput()`
                function, 159, 724–725
        control output,
                `rip6_ctloutput()`
                function, 725–730
        detach PCBs,
                `rip6_detach()`
                function, 735–736
        fix remote address,
                `rip6_connect()`
                function, 734–735
        ICMPv6 message filtering,
                719–721
        input, `icmp6_rip6_input()`
                function, 719–724
        input, `rip6_input()`
                function, 159, 715–719
        instance of `ip6protosw{}`
                structure, 709, 710
        notification call flow
                diagram, 725
        notifications and callback
                functions, 726
        output, `rip6_output()`
                function, 710–715
        send packets, `rip6_send()`
                function, 736–737
        statistics, 709–710
        user requests, 730–737
`rc.mobileip6` script, 11
`rc.netwok6` script, 11
`rc` script, 11
reachability confirmation
        `IPV6_REACHCONF` option
                (ancillary data), 264, 822
        positive, 412, 453–454
        specifying, 821–822
        variables, 424
        via API, 263–264
ReachableTime variable, 425, 433,
        439, 517
ReachableTime variable, host
        operations, 424
reassembly, fragment, *see*
        fragment reassembly
reassembly queue

check logic diagram, 201
check logic of, 200
creating, 193–194, 197
`recvmsg()` system call, 767
Redirected Header option, ND
        Protocol messages, 405, 407
Redirect messages, 392, 393,
        403–404
        diagram of, 395
        `icmp6_redirect_input()`
                function, 462, 521–528
        `icmp6_redirect_output()`
                function, 216, 218,
                528–536
`regen_tmpaddr()` function,
        476, 584, 588–590
Regional Internet Registries
        (RIRs), 47
Rendezvous Point, 44
`reorder()` function, 883,
        884–886, 891, 893
replying to NI Node Addresses
        query, calculating number
        of addresses for, 381–383
Reseaux IP Européens Network
        Co-ordination Centre
        (RIPE-NCC), 47
Reserved field, Fragment
        header, 140
Reserved field, Routing header,
        138, 140
retransmission timing diagram, 610
RetransTimer variable, 425, 433,
        439, 517
RetransTimer variable, host
        operations, 424
retrieve local address,
        `in6_setsockaddr()`
                function, 662–663
retrieve peer address,
        `in6_setpeeraddr()`
                function, 660–661
RFC792, 287, 291
RFC1519, 40
RFC1883, 2
RFC2133, 54, 747
RFC2292, 205, 622, 623, 748, 775,
        791, 793, 794, 795, 796,
        798, 799, 804, 810, 812,
        813, 815, 817, 818, 819,
        820, 840, 841, 845
RFC2373, 33
RFC2375, 45, 764
RFC2460, 2–3, 78, 131, 134, 138,
        142, 188, 194, 195, 207, 247,
        264, 266, 269, 284, 295, 330,
        616, 694, 718, 819, 821

RFC2461, 3, 288, 392, 397, 398, 405, 419, 446, 447, 463, 481, 488, 489, 492, 493, 497, 501, 505, 534, 539, 542, 547, 603, 608, 609

RFC2462, 3, 228, 390, 392, 416, 562, 563, 564, 567, 581, 592, 594, 633, 673, 674

RFC2463, 215, 287, 288, 296, 304, 308, 318, 341, 345

RFC2464, 44

RFC2465, 151, 191

RFC2466, 304

RFC2529, 79

RFC2553, 55, 747, 758, 874, 903

RFC2675, 142, 154, 176, 191, 269

RFC2710, 766

RFC2711, 142, 155, 182

RFC2730, 45

RFC2734, 90

RFC2740, 616, 719

RFC2765, 32, 291

RFC2893, 32, 91, 92

RFC2894, 765

RFC2960, 869

RFC3041, 67, 100, 147, 369, 417, 418, 419, 587, 787

RFC3056, 79, 145, 149, 888

RFC3122, 437

RFC3142, 95, 650

RFC3168, 132, 197, 256

RFC3286, 158

RFC3306, 44

RFC3307, 45

RFC3452, 721

RFC3484, 131, 144, 145, 146, 147, 226, 231, 232, 345, 542, 864, 880, 883, 884, 888, 891

RFC3493 (Basic Socket API), 48, 50, 615, 618, 747, 796, 864, 868, 869, 872, 873, 879, 883, 893, 897, 898, 900, 902, 903, 906
    address and name conversion functions, 752–760
    address testing macros, 67, 763–764
    basic definitions, 748–749
    basic socket options, 760–764
    binding ambiguity, 751
    code portability, 759, 760–762
    error codes, 759
    getaddrinfo() function, 753–757, 863–888
    getnameinfo() function, 757–759, 898–906

inet_ntop() function, 752–753, 853, 855, 859–863, 903, 904, 905

inet_pton() function, 752–753, 853–854, 857, 873, 874

interface identification, 749–750

IPv4 communication over AF_INET6 socket, 750–752

IPV6_JOIN_GROUP socket option, 762

IPV6_LEAVE_GROUP socket option, 762

IPV6_MULTICAST_HOPS socket option, 711, 763, 848

IPV6_MULTICAST_IF socket option, 751, 763, 829

IPV6_MULTICAST_LOOP socket option, 763

IPV6_V6ONLY socket option, 757, 760–762

multicast ambiguity, 751

multicast socket options, 762–763

socket options handling, 751

unicast option, IPV6_UNICAST_HOPS, 760, 771

RFC3513, 30, 33, 41, 42, 44, 91, 210, 225, 403, 764, 766, 857, 859

RFC3542 (Advanced Socket API), 50, 153, 224, 226, 237, 268, 270, 427, 659, 718, 719, 720, 730, 747, 764, 791, 792, 793, 796, 797, 798, 799, 801, 804, 807, 809, 812, 813, 815, 816, 817, 818, 820, 822, 823, 836, 837, 838, 840, 844, 845, 907
    advanced definitions, 764–766
    ancillary data, 767, 768–770, 777, 807–808
    Destination options header manipulation, 774
    Hop-by-Hop options header manipulation, 774
    icmp6_filter{} structure, 719–721, 767, 839
    IPv6 raw sockets, 766–767
    IPV6_V6ONLY socket option and code portability, 757, 760–762

manipulation of IPv6 extension headers, 773–778

MLD queries, 774, 776–777

packet information, IPv6, 770–773

Path MTU options, 778, 779, 783

receive information, 772–773

Routing header manipulation, 773

socket extensions for "r" commands, 778

socket options summary, 780–783

transport layer considerations, 773

RFC3678, 763

RFC3697, 132

RFC3736, 392, 397

RFC3775, 400

RFC3878, 39

RFC3879, 764

RFC3927, 148

RFC3956, 44

RFC3971, 417

RFC4007, 33, 36, 37, 38, 39, 53, 58, 60, 208, 260, 864, 875, 877, 898

RFC4022, 669

RFC4034, 298

RFC4191, 9, 40, 398, 399, 401, 516, 517

RFC4193, 40, 764

RFC4213, 92

RFC4291, 30, 32, 43, 92, 857

RFC4302, 134

RFC4303, 134

RFC4443, 3, 24, 215, 287, 296

RFC4489, 57

rip6_attach() function, 730–732, 839

rip6_bind() function, 732–734

rip6_connect() function, 734–735

rip6_ctlinput() function, 159, 724–725

rip6_ctloutput() function, 725–730

rip6_input() function, 159, 715–719

rip6_output() function, 710–715

rip6_send() function, 736–737

RIPE-NCC (Reseaux IP Européens Network Co-ordination Centre), 47

RIRs (Regional Internet
    Registries), 47
rlogin command, 778
route6.c
    code listings, 204–208
    file location and description,
        150
route6_input() function,
        204–209
route command, 606
Route Information option, ND
    Protocol messages, 405,
        408–410
Router Advertisement messages
    described, 392–393, 397
    extensions to, 399–401
    format, 397–399
    nd6_ra_input() function,
        513–521, 558, 562
    processing, 416–417, 423
    processing, by hosts, 425–426
    sending unsolicited, 422
    two-hour rule, 417
Router Alert option
    Hop-by-Hop options
        header, 777
    ip6_opt_router{}
        structure, 155
router, IPv6
    configuration variables,
        419–421
    Default Router List, 393, 399,
        402, 410, 425, 426,
        433–434
    defrouter_addifreq()
        function, 542–544, 548
    defrouter_addreq()
        function, 540–541, 550
    defrouter_delifreq()
        function, 544–545,
        548, 549
    defrouter_delreq()
        function, 541–542,
        550, 552
    defrouter_lookup()
        function, 468, 545–546
    defrtrlist_del()
        function, 475, 550–552,
        553, 611
    defrtrlist_update()
        function, 517, 546,
        553–555
    discovery, ND protocol, 390
    forwarded packets,
        unfragmented, 140,
        214, 218

nd_defrouter{} structure,
    433–434, 435, 516,
    549, 556
nd_defrouter{} structure,
    diagram of, 551
node address requirements, 47
on-link assumption, 542, 547
preference, 400–401, 408–412,
    426
probably reachable, 547
processing Router
    Advertisements, 423
processing Router Solicitations,
    422–423
selection, 426
sending unsolicited Router
    Advertisements, 422
terminology, 390
Router Solicitation messages
    described, 392, 393
    format, 396–397
    nd6_rs_input() function,
        510–521
    processing, 422–423
    sending, by hosts, 423–425
routes
    cached, 237–239
    cloning, 173, 212, 441, 443
    determining, 255–261
    next hop, *see* next hop
    selecting,
        ip6_selectroute()
        function, 234–242
route segments, 137
Routing headers, 137–140
    ip6_rthdr0{} structure, 156
    manipulation of, 773
    multicast address in, 46
    output processing, IPv6,
        252–255
    processing,
        route6_input()
        function, 204–209
    specifying, 820–821
Routing headers, type 0
    described, 138
    diagram of, 139
    forwarding, 209
    ip6_rthdr0{} structure, 156
    multicast address exclusion,
        46, 138
    processing, ICMPv6, 323
    processing, IPv6, 252
    processing,
        route6_input()
        function, 205
routing, multi-path, 545

Routing Type field, IPv6
    headers, 138
rt6_flush() function, 552,
    611–612
rtadvd.c, 768
rtadvd program, 510, 744, 767
rtalloc1() function, 111–112,
    239, 331, 465, 525
rtentry{} structure, 430,
    432, 438
    diagram, 239, 431
RTF_CACHE flag, 466
RTF_CLONING flag, 331,
    441–443, 446
RTPREF kernel configuration
    option, 9, 16
RTR_SOLICITATION_INTERVAL
    constant, 424

S

s6_addr macro, 48
SA6_ARE_ADDR_EQUAL
    macro, 51
SA6_IS_ADDR_UNSPECIFIED
    macro, 51
scope6.c
    code listings, 57–60
    file location and description, 47
scope6_check_id() function,
    63, 253, 632
scope6_var.h
    code listings, 52
    file location and description, 47
% (percent) scoped address
    delimiter, 39
scoped addresses
    ambiguity of, diagram, 36
    described, 34
    textual representation of, 38–39
SCOPEDROUTING kernel
    configuration option, 16
scope zones, 34–36, 46
    implementation architecture,
        diagram of, 56
    in6_addr2zoneid()
        function, 59–60
    in6_addrscope() function,
        57–59, 60
    in6_clearscope()
        function, 62–63
    in6_embedscope()
        function, 60–61
    in6_recoverscope()
        function, 61–62, 104
    initialization of, 52–53

scope6_check_id() function, 63, 253, 632
zone IDs, *see* zone IDs
zone indices, 36–38
security
    concerns and IPv4-mapped IPv6 addresses, 32, 683, 751
    DNS Security Extensions, 298
    Encapsulating Security Payload header, 134, 135, 766, 846
    IPsec protocol, 134, 258, 559
    overlapping fragment attack, 199
    port theft, 635
    vulnerabilities, 323, 330, 542, 559
Segments Left field, Routing header, 138
sendmsg() system call, 707, 736, 767, 768
sendto() system call, 707
set packet information, 814–815
setsockopt() function, 760, 771, 783, 784, 791–800, 824
setsockopt() system call, 760, 824
set_source() function, 886, 890
set Traffic Class (old style), 816
singly linked list (SLIST_HEAD) macro, 21
site-border configuration, 34
    diagram of, 35
site-local addresses
    deprecation of unicast site-local addresses, 39–40
    described, 33–34
    format, 41
6to4 addresses, 888
SLIST_HEAD (singly linked list) macro, 21
sockaddr_in6{} structure, 48–49, 627
SOCK_DGRAM type, 158–159, 869
socket buffer, 14
socket options
    getsockopt() function, 760, 771, 779, 783, 784, 790, 801, 805, 833
    handling, 751
    ICMP6_FILTER socket option, 719–720, 767, 780

ip6_pcbopt() function, 796, 809–810
ip6_pcbopts() function, 808–809
ip6_setpktoptions() function, 810–812, 849
IPV6_AUTOFLOWLABEL socket option, 622
IPV6_CHECKSUM socket option, 624, 767, 780
IPV6_DSTOPTS socket option, 771, 782, 849
IPV6_HOPOPTS socket option, 771, 782, 848
IPV6_JOIN_GROUP socket option, 762, 780
IPV6_LEAVE_GROUP socket option, 762, 780
IPV6_MULTICAST_HOPS socket option, 711, 763, 780, 848
IPV6_MULTICAST_IF socket option, 751, 763, 780, 829
IPV6_MULTICAST_LOOP socket option, 763, 780
IPV6_NEXTHOP socket option, 771, 772, 782
IPV6_PKTINFO socket option, 235, 771, 772, 774, 781, 852
IPV6_PREFER_TEMPADDR socket option, 231, 782
IPV6_RTHDRDSTOPTS socket option, 771, 772, 782
IPV6_RTHDR option, 771, 782, 852
IPV6_TCLASS socket option, 771, 782, 848, 849
IPV6_V6ONLY socket option, 757, 760–762
multicast socket options, 762–763
processing, ip6_ctloutput() function, 790–805
receive path example, 850–853
send path example, 848–850
setsockopt() function, 760, 771, 783, 784, 791, 796, 824
setting, and ancillary data, 807–823
socket queue, 14

sockets, *see also* PCBs; RFC3493 (Basic Socket API); RFC3542 (Advanced Socket API)
    extensions for "r" commands, 778
    IPv6 raw sockets, 766–767
socket() system call, 627, 702, 730, 731, 754, 767
SOCK_RAW type, 158–159, 869
SOCK_SEQPACKET type, 869
sockstat command, 744
SOCK_STREAM type, 158–159, 869
Solicited flag, 402, 492, 493, 501–502, 504, 505
solicited-node multicast addresses, 46, 401
Source Address field, IPv6 headers, 133
source address selection
    comparison rules, 146–148
    comparison state variables, 224
    default address selection, 144–146
    destination address selection, 148–149
    first candidate, 234
    icmp6_reflect() function, 344–346
    in6_selectsrc() function, 219, 221–234, 508
    label value, 145
    policy structure, 219–221
    policy table, address preferences, 145
    precedence value, 145
    undefined addresses, 148
source code narrations, 14–17
    format of code and narrations, 15–16
    networking device and architecture assumptions, 17
    preprocessed variables, 16–17
    typographical conventions, 14–15
source code, on companion website, 7, 14, 15
Source Link-Layer Address option, 397, 398, 399, 401, 405–406, 408, 410, 412, 427, 485, 510, 539
Source Quench message, 218
source tree, KAME
    preparing, 9
    structure, 7
    structure diagram, 8

`splimp()` function, 13
`splnet()` function, 13
`splxxx()` functions, 13, 192
stack
 BSD networking, diagram of, 12
 TCP, 675–678
startup scripts, 11
stateful configuration/protocol,
 392
Stateless Address
 Autoconfiguration
 address formation and address
 states, 413–414
 DAD algorithm, 415–416.
 see also DAD (Duplicate
 Address Detection)
 deprecated address state,
 413–414
 duplicated address state,
 413–414
 `in6_ifadd()` function,
 580–584
 `in6_tmpifadd()` function,
 584–588, 592
 invalid address state, 413–414
 overview, 391–392, 412
 preferred address state,
 413–414
 preferred lifetime, 66, 413–414
 privacy extensions, 417–419
 processing Router
 Advertisement, 416–417
 `regen_tmpaddr()` function,
 476, 584, 588–590
 tentative address state, 413–414
 valid address state, 413–414
 valid lifetime, 66, 413–414
Stateless Address
 Autoconfiguration
 specification, RFC2462, 3
`sticky` and `cmsg` combinations,
 812–813
sticky options, 771
subnet ID, 42
subnet prefix, 41
subnet-router anycast address, 41
Supported Qtypes
 print, 362–365
 query, 301, 388
sysctl command, 341, 348, 471,
 475, 476, 515, 522, 582,
 592, 629, 630, 731
`sys/socket.h`, 748
 code listings, 748, 768–769
system call, 13

T

tagging, mbuf, 20–24
tags (mtags), 20
`tags` field, 21
target address,
 `in6ifa_ifpwithaddr()`
 function, 488
Target Link-Layer Address option,
 403, 404, 405–406, 408,
 427, 488, 490, 498, 504
TCP (Transmission Control
 Protocol)
 accept TCP connections,
 `tcp6_usr_accept()`
 function, 678, 680
 attach PCBs, `tcp_attach()`
 function, 680–681
 bind local addresses,
 `tcp6_usr_bind()`
 function, 681–683
 BSD network implementation,
 overview, 11–14
 checksum, 616, 668
 control input,
 `tcp6_ctlinput()`
 function, 159, 664,
 675–679
 headers, 21, 666, 669–670
 initializing headers,
 `tcp_fillheaders()`
 function, 669–670
 initiate active connection,
 `tcp6_usr_connect()`
 function, 683–684
 initiate passive connection,
 `tcp6_usr_listen()`
 function, 685
 input, `tcp6_input()`
 function, 159, 664,
 670–674
 input, `tcp_input()`
 function, 670–674
 instance of `ip6protosw{}`
 structure, 663, 664
 mbufs chains for packets, 20
 mbufs chains for packets,
 diagram of, 21
 notification call flow
 diagram, 675
 notifications and callback
 functions, 679
 output, 663–669
 over IPv6, 616
 pseudo header, 616–617
 stack, 675–678
 user requests, 678–685

`tcp6_ctlinput()` function,
 159, 664, 675–679
`tcp6_input()` function, 159,
 664, 670–674
`tcp6_usr_accept()` function,
 678, 680
`tcp6_usr_bind()` function,
 681–683
`tcp6_usr_connect()` function,
 683–684
`tcp6_usr_listen()` function,
 685
`tcp6_usrreqs` variable, 678
`tcp_attach()` function,
 680–681
`tcp_input.c`
 code listings, 670–674
 file location and description,
 619
`tcp_input()` function, 670–674
`tcp_output.c`
 code listings, 664–668
 file location and description,
 619
`tcp_subr.c`
 code listings, 669–670, 675–679
 file location and description,
 619
`tcp_usrreq.c`
 code listings, 680–685
 file location and description,
 619
telnet command, 761
temporary addresses
 `in6_tmpifadd()` function,
 584–588, 592
 `IP6PO_TEMPADDR_NOTPREFER`
 flag, 231
 `IP6PO_TEMPADDR_PREFER`
 flag, 231
 `IPV6_PREFER_TEMPADDR`
 socket option, 231, 782,
 813, 823
 lifetime of, 417–419
 privacy extensions, 417–419
 vs. public addresses, 145,
 147, 231
 `regen_tmpaddr()` function,
 476, 584, 588–590
tentative address, 413–414
Time Exceeded message, ICMPv6,
 288, 292
timer granularity, Neighbor
 Cache, 471
Time-To-Live (TTL) field, IPv4, 616
TLV (Type-Length-Value)
 format, 405

traceroute command, 232
Traffic Class field, IPv6
    headers, 132
    setting (old style), 816
Transmission Control Protocol,
    see TCP
transmitting UDP packets and
    IPv4-mapped IPv6
    addresses, 740–741
transport layer
    checksum differences between
        IPv4 and, 134, 617–618
    IPv4-mapped IPv6 addresses,
        32, 618
    PCBs, 618–627
    protocol selection
        considerations, 773
    pseudo header for IPv6,
        616–617
    TCP over IPv6, 616. *see also*
        TCP (Transmission
        Control Protocol)
    UDP over IPv6, 616. *see also*
        UDP (User Datagram
        Protocol)
TTL (Time-To-Live) field, IPv4, 616
turtle mascot, KAME, 3
two-hour rule for valid lifetime of
    Router Advertisement, 417
Type-Length-Value (TLV)
    format, 405
Type of Service field, IPv4
    headers, 134
Type specific data field, IPv6
    headers, 138
typographical conventions, in
    book, 14–15

U

UDP (User Datagram Protocol)
    attach PCBs, udp6_attach()
        function, 702–704
    binding sockets when using
        IPv4-mapped IPv6
        addresses, 738–740
    bind local addresses,
        udp6_usr_bind()
        function, 704–705
    BSD network implementation,
        overview, 11–14
    checksum, 616, 618
    control input,
        udp6_ctlinput()
        function, 699–702

detach PCBs,
    udp6_detach()
    function, 706
input, upd6_input() function,
    159, 692–698, 852
instance of ip6protosw{}
    structure, 685, 686
joining multicast groups when
    using IPv4-mapped
    addresses, 742
mbufs chains for packets, 17, 19
mbufs chains for packets,
    diagram of, 18, 20
notification call flow
    diagram, 699
notifications and callback
    functions, 702
output function,
    udp6_output()
    function, 17, 685–692
output, udp6_output()
    function, 709, 849
over IPv6, 616
pseudo header, 616–617
receive and demultiplex
    packets when using
    IPv4-mapped IPv6
    addresses, 741–742
send packets, udp6_send()
    function, 707–709, 741
socket options when using
    IPv4-mapped IPv6
    addresses, 742
transmitting packets when
    using IPv4-mapped
    IPv6 addresses, 740–741
user requests, 702–709
udp6_attach() function,
    702–704
udp6_connect() function,
    705–706
udp6_ctlinput() function,
    699–702
udp6_detach() function, 706
udp6_output.c
    code listings, 686–692
    file location and description,
        619
udp6_send() function, 707–709,
    741
udp6_usr_bind() function,
    704–705
udp6_usrreq.c
    code listings, 692–698, 700–709
    file location and description, 619
uipc_mbuf2.c, 23

ULAs (Unique Local IPv6 Unicast
    Addresses), 40
unassigned types, 33, 58
undefined source addresses, 148
unfragmentable part, packets, 141
unicast addresses, IPv6, 30
    address scopes, 33–34
    deprecation of site-local
        addresses, 39–40
    format, 40
unreachable destination, 226
unspecified addresses, IPv6,
    31–32, 50, 51, 169, 207
upd6_input() function, 159,
    692–698, 852
updating addresses, 98–100
User Datagram Protocol, *see* UDP
user space programs, 10–11
/usr/include directory, 8
/usr/local/v6/ directory,
    10, 11
/usr/sbin/config
    command, 9

V

valid address state, 413–414
validating
    addresses, 97–98
    packets, 168–171
valid lifetime, 66, 413–414
Version field, IPv6 headers, 132

W

well-known multicast
    addresses, 45
WIDE (Widely Integrated
    Distributed Environment)
    project, 3–5
wildcard addresses, 649, 738, 745,
    751, 761
Wind River Systems, 6

Z

zone IDs
    in address structures, 54–57
    clearing, 265
    conversion functions, 60
    default assignment of,
        diagram, 37
zones, *see* scope zones

Printed and bound by CPI Group (UK) Ltd, Croydon, CR0 4YY

03/10/2024

01040326-0018